Digital Marketplaces Unleashed

Claudia Linnhoff-Popien · Ralf Schneider · Michael Zaddach

Editors

Digital Marketplaces Unleashed

 Springer

Editors

Claudia Linnhoff-Popien
Institut für Informatik
LMU München
Munich, Germany

Michael Zaddach
Munich Airport
Munich, Germany

Ralf Schneider
Allianz SE
Munich, Germany

ISBN 978-3-662-49274-1
https://doi.org/10.1007/978-3-662-49275-8

ISBN 978-3-662-49275-8 (eBook)

Library of Congress Control Number: 2017953953

Printed on acid-free paper

This Springer imprint is published by Springer Nature
The registered company is Springer-Verlag GmbH Germany
The registered company address is: Heidelberger Platz 3, 14197 Berlin, Germany

Foreword

The technological change of the 21st century is decisively shaped by the digital upheaval: there is no future without digitalization.

The sale of products and services has left the classical point of sale and takes place via a variety of channels. Whether in the automotive industry, travel and traffic, in cities, or the financial industry – newly designed ecosystems are being created everywhere.

Data is being generated and analyzed in real time. Companies compete for mobile access channels to the customer in order gain knowledge about context and personal preferences. The customer has the facility to publish opinions, experience and knowledge as User Generated Content. He himself creates an impact on the market and is able to build or destroy trust. He turns into a brand ambassador in the network, furthermore, customer trust in his suppliers and protection of sensitive customer data is of utmost importance.

With such aspects our Innovation Center Mobile Internet is engaged with. It is supported from the Bavarian Ministry of economic affairs and media, energy and technology.

For the following book from a multiplicity of submissions in a two-step-review phase together with a Scientific Board we have chosen 81 chapters including the forewords. All together in more than 3200 e-mails and diverse face-to-face-meetings the following book was developed. We could obtain famous managers and experts from industry to share with us their view on special topics.

- Section I: Prefaces
- Section II: Introduction
- Section III: Digital Society
- Section IV: Individualized Digital Learning
- Section V: Disruptive Technologies & Entrepreneurship
- Section VI: Digital Business Outcomes
- Section VII: Cognitive Systems
- Section VIII: Fin- & Insuretech
- Section IX: Smart Traffic Hubs
- Section X: Mobility Services
- Section XI: Industry 4.0
- Section XII: Intelligent & Autonomous Enterprise

- Section XIII: Big Data and Analytics
- Section XIV: Cloud Technologies
- Section XV: Internet of Things
- Section XVI: Global Challenges – Local Solutions
- Section XVII: Active Cyber Defense

Enjoy the extensive observation of the Digital Marketplaces Unleashed from different perspectives!

Claudia Linnhoff-Popien, Ralf Schneider, Michael Zaddach

Acknowledgment

Scientific Board

We would like to sincerely thank the following people for reviewing the contributions:

- Marco Autili, University of L'Aquila, Italy
- Jan Bosch, Chalmers University of Technology, Sweden
- Antoine Bossard, Kanagawa University, Japan
- Hans-Bernd Brosius, Ludwig-Maximilians-Universität München, Germany
- Mehmet Celenk, Ohio University, USA
- Michal Choras, University of Science and Technology Bydgoszcz, Poland
- Vytautas Čyras, Vilnius University, Lithuania
- Rik Eshuis, Eindhoven University of Technology, Netherlands
- Stefan Fischer, Universität zu Lübeck, Germany
- José Manuel Fonseca, Uninova, Portugal
- Rossitza Ivanova Goleva, Technical University of Sofia, Bulgaria
- Bernd Heinrich, Universität Regensburg, Germany
- Thomas Hess, Ludwig-Maximilians-Universität München, Germany
- Dieter Hogrefe, Georg-August-Universität Göttingen, Germany
- George Kakarontzas, Technological Educational Institute of Thessaly, Greece
- Jun Kong, North Dakota University, USA
- Robert S. Laramee, Swansea University, UK
- Kun Chang Lee, Sungkyunkwan University, Republic of Korea
- Michael Meyen, Ludwig-Maximilians-Universität München, Germany
- Andrzej Niesler, Wroclaw University of Economics, Poland
- Óscar Mortágua Pereira, University of Aveiro, Portugal
- Jose Raul Romero, University of Cordoba, Spain
- Anthony Savidis, Institute of Computer Science, Greece
- Wieland Schwinger, Johannes Kepler University, Austria
- Qi Shi, Liverpool John Moores University, UK
- Javid Taheri, Karlstad University, Sweden

- Marten van Sinderen, University of Twente, Netherlands
- Giovanni Vincenti, University of Baltimore, USA
- Gianluigi Viscusi, École Polytechnique Fédérale de Lausanne, Switzerland
- Franz Wotawa, Graz University of Technology, Austria
- Mudasser F. Wyne, National University, USA
- Sherali Zeadally, University of Kentucky, USA
- Kamil Zyla, Lublin University of Technology, Poland

Editorial Team
For their assistance with the organization of this book we would like to sincerely thank:

- Sebastian Feld, Ludwig-Maximilians-Universität München
- Kerstin Fischer, Ludwig-Maximilians-Universität München
- Katja Grenner, Ludwig-Maximilians-Universität München
- Carsten Hahn, Ludwig-Maximilians-Universität München

List of Contributors

Editors

Claudia Linnhoff-Popien | LMU München
Prof. Dr. Claudia Linnhoff-Popien holds the chair „Mobile and Distributed Systems" at the Ludwig-Maximilians-Universität in Munich. She did postdoctoral research at the Washington University of St. Louis, Missouri, USA before she was appointed to a professorship at the LMU Munich in 1998. She is board member of the Institute for Informatics, member of the research committee „Münchner Kreis" and co-founder of the ALOQA GmbH. The latter had one million registered users when it was sold to Motorola Mobility in 2010 marking one of the biggest exits in the history of start-ups of German universities. Further, she is head of the lead project „Innovationszentrum Mobiles Internet" of the Zentrum Digitalisierung.Bayern (ZD.B) funded by the state of Bavaria. She is also scientific advisor of the VIRALITY GmbH.

Ralf Schneider | Allianz
Dr. Ralf Schneider has been Group CIO of the Allianz since October 2010. Before he was an additional Board Member for IT of Allianz Managed Operations Services SE (2010–2016) and CIO of Allianz Deutschland AG (2006–2010). As a graduate mathematician with a doctor's degree in computer science he joined Allianz 1995. For over 18 years he worked in several IT executive positions at Allianz and there he was always appointed as the youngest among his peers. He was the department head of Allianz Sales Information Systems, division head of

E-business and Project Controlling Germany and division head of Dresdner Bank Sales Information Systems. Additionally he holds various mandates in different Cyber Security related organizations such as Cyber Security Sharing Analytics e.V., Deutsche Cyber Sicherheitsorganisation and the Digital Society Institute.

Michael Zaddach | Flughafen München
Michael Zaddach is Senior Vice President and CIO at Flughafen München GmbH since 2000, which was awarded as Europe's best airport repeatedly - most recently in 2016. His area of responsibility covers system development, system operation, and the whole IT-infrastructure of Munich airport. After completing a university degree in communications engineering he worked at Siemens, AEG and debis Systemhaus in various capacities and several management functions, for example, in system development, Product-Line-Management, and Consulting. At debis Systemhaus he lead a business unit for IT consulting services. As a head of that unit he conducted several outsourcing projects of debis Systemhaus. He is also the chair of the ACI World Airport IT Standing Committee.

Authors of Prefaces

Gerald Hüther | Universität Göttingen
Prof. Dr. Gerald Hüther is one of the most well-known brain researchers in Germany. Practically he concerns himself in the context of various initiatives and projects with neurobiological prevention research. He writes nonfiction, gives lectures, organizes congresses, works as a consultant for politicians and entrepreneurs. As the co-publisher of scientific journals, co-founder of a network for education, frequent conversation guest on radio and television, he is imparting and implementing knowledge at the same time. First he studied and researched in Leipzig and Jena , then since 1979 at the Max Planck Institute for Experimental Medicine in Göttingen. He was a Heisenberg Fellow of the German Research Foundation and from 1994–2006 he headed a research department at the psychiatric clinic in Göttingen that he established.

Fredmund Malik |
Malik Institute St. Gallen
Fredmund Malik is internationally acclaimed scientist, advisor and educator for complexity management, governance and leadership as well as chairman and member of several governance and advisory boards in the business and in the public sector. He is author of over 15 books, among them several award-winning bestsellers. His classic Managing Performing Living was selected amongst the best 100 business books of all time. Malik is a pioneer of system-oriented holistic management and cybernetics of complex systems. He founded the Malik Institute in St. Gallen, Switzerland in 1984, which shaped generations of managers. With its international subsidiaries and global partnerships, Malik Institute is one of the leading knowledge organizations for systemic general management, cybernetic thinking and governance solutions. In the course of two science projects for the Swiss National Research Fund for fundamental research, he received his doctor's degree with his work on the Strategy of Managing Complex Systems. He taught at the universities St. Gallen, Innsbruck and Vienna. Malik is special and honorary professor at the Capital University of Economics and Business (CUEB) in Beijing, at IMAU and at the Jilin University in Changchun.

Florian Leibert | Mesosphere
San Francisco-based entrepreneur Florian Leibert serves as the founder and CEO of Mesosphere, Inc., a technology firm focused on simplifying the design and management processes of distributed systems websites. His responsibilities include writing software, recruiting members of his engineering and marketing teams, and maintaining business relationships with top-tier funding partners Vinod Khosla and Andreessen Horowitz. In his recent ventures, Florian Leibert has invested in the Boston-based software company Driftt. Prior to launching his products and services at Mesosphere, Inc., he developed software at Airbnb. Among other achievements, he created Chronos, which facilitates more efficient job scheduling. Florian Leibert received a bachelor's degree in computer science and business from the International University in Germany Bruchsal.

Section Board

Sabine Bendiek | Microsoft

Sabine Bendiek has been Chairwoman of the Management Board, Microsoft Germany since January 2016. She holds a Master of Science degree in Management Science from the Massachusetts Institute of Technology (MIT) in Cambridge (MSc) and a Bachelor of Arts degree in Economics from the University of Mannheim. At the beginning of her career, Bendiek worked for McKinsey, Booz Allen as well as Siemens Nixdorf Information Systems. Subsequently, she was responsible for Dell's Small and Medium Business in Germany, Switzerland and Austria. Prior to joining Microsoft Germany, Bendiek held the position of Vice President and General Manager for EMC Germany. Meanwhile, Bendiek looks back on more than 20 years of professional experience as an executive in the technology industry. She is also a member of the executive board of the industry trade association BITKOM.

Robert Blackburn | BASF

Prof. Dr. Robert Blackburn is President of Supply Chain Operations & Information Services of BASF Group located in Ludwigshafen, Germany. Additionally, he currently serves as a non-executive Director on several Boards and is a visiting lecturer at Massachusetts Institute of Technology and Karlsruhe Institute of Technology. Robert earned his PhD in Economics and Operations Research from the University of Würzburg. He joined BASF Group in 2007 as Senior Vice President Head of Global Supply Chain Operations, additionally leading the company's enterprise transformation program. Robert previously was Senior Vice President Head of Corporate Portfolio Development at Siemens AG and Vice President at IBM Corporation where he was responsible for several global HW, SW and Service businesses.

Yuval Diskin | Diskin Advanced Technologie

In 2016 Diskin co-founded with VW AG, Cymotive Technologies Ltd over which he serves as chairman, and Cymotive Gmbh. The companies offer Cyber security solutions and exclusive Cyber security managed services for the Connected car and in the future for the Self-driving car. In 2012 Diskin co-founded DAT a high-tech cyber security company over which he served as chairman. The company offers cyber defense against cyber-attacks and provides cyber security solutions. Between 2005 and 2011 he served as the Director of the Israeli Security Agency (aka Shin Bet). In 2003, he became special advisor to the Mossad Director. Between 2000 to 2003, as the Shin Bet Deputy Director, he implemented the use of advanced technological capabilities and new operational doctrines against suicide attacks and terror attacks. In 1997, Diskin was appointed commander of the Jerusalem District. Between 1974 to 1997 Diskin served in several operational and commanding positions in the Shin Bet and the IDF.

Sandro Gaycken | ESMT

Dr. Sandro Gaycken is a technology- and security-researcher, exploring the nexus of digital technology, economies and politics. Sandro's research focus is on cyberwarfare, cyber defense, cyber intelligence, and high security IT. He is a strong advocate of disruptive innovation and regulation in IT-security, proposing to solve the more high-end cyber problems through high security IT concepts from computer science, employing a range of industrial policies and economically beneficial market and investment strategies. Sandro has published more than 60 articles and books on his topics, regularly writes op-eds in leading news papers and has authored official government publications. He is a fellow of Oxford university's Martin College, in the working group on cyber defence and cyber intelligence and a director for strategic cyber defense projects in the NATO SPS Program.

Daniel Hartert | Bayer AG

Daniel Hartert took over as Chairman of the Executive Board of Bayer Business Services and CIO of Bayer AG in 2009. He studied computer science and business administration at the University of Kaiserslautern and began his career by joining Robert Bosch GmbH in Reutlingen. In 1992 Daniel Hartert joined Bertelsmann Music Group International in Munich. In 1995 he moved to New York to head up the group's global IT operations. In 1999 Daniel Hartert was appointed CIO of Bertelsmann AG in

Gütersloh. In 2002 Hartert was appointed Executive Vice President and CIO of Philips Electronics in Eindhoven. In August 2003 he was also made a member of the Philips Group Management Committee. From 2007 onwards Daniel Hartert had served as CEO and Executive Vice President of Imaging Systems at Philips Healthcare in Boston.

Gerhard Hastreiter | Allianz

Dr. Gerhard Hastreiter is Managing Partner at Allianz Consulting, Germany's biggest in-house consultancy. He holds a PhD in Theoretical Physics and has been working for over 20 years in different roles at Allianz. Amongst others he was in charge of sales-, web- and BI-applications at Allianz Germany, of Organizational Management in the German sales division, CEO of AllSecur, Allianz Germany's direct insurer, and Program Manager for a global "Greenfield" operations project before taking over responsibility for Allianz Group's global consultancy.

Markus Heyn | BOSCH

Dr. Markus Heyn has been a member of board of management of Robert Bosch GmbH since April 2015. He bears corporate responsibility for automotive original equipment sales and marketing and sales. Dr. Heyn is also responsible for the Automotive Aftermarket division as well as the subsidiaries Bosch Engineering GmbH and ETAS GmbH. After completion of his doctorate in mechanical engineering he joined Bosch in 1999 as a consultant in the corporate office for coordinating productivity and process optimization. In the further course Dr. Heyn held various management positions both nationally and internationally, among them he was responsible as Technical Plant Manager at the Jihlava plant in Czech Republic. Most recently he was in charge for Bosch's business sector Diesel Systems.

Wolfgang Hildesheim |
IBM Watson and AI Leader DACH

Wolfgang Hildesheim is a high energy physicist by education. He worked at CERN and DESY. After more than ten years in research and consulting he took the Executive Vice President role for Worldwide Sales and Marketing of a family owned company that focuses on Big Data and Communication Intelligence. Being a member of the board he significantly grew revenues and profits, in particular through individual custom solutions and strong client orientation. In 1997 Wolfgang Hildesheim joined IBM to lead the Automotive, Aerospace and High Tech Practice. Since 1999 he led IBM's Big Data Industry Solution Business in Europe helping client enterprises to become more data driven and create business value by using Advanced Analytics. Since 2012 Wolfgang Hildesheim is responsible for creating and growing IBM´s Watson Business in Europe with a major focus on Germany. Watson Solutions are IBM's answer to the current worldwide Cognitive Computing mega trend, offering unmatched intelligent services and competitive edge based on Artifical Intelligence. He is regularly presenting at several conferences and publications.

Martin Hofmann I Volkswagen

Dr. Martin Hofmann is since 2011 the Group CIO of the Volkswagen AG. Since he joined Volkswagen several years ago he holds multiple senior management positions. He holds in 2007 the position as Head of Organizational Development at VW. Since 2004 he leads the division for Process-and Information management. In 2001 he was the responsible manager for the Group Procurement Process and Information Management at Volkswagen. He started his career in 1995 at EDS Plano in USA as an Executive Director Digital Supply Chain. His university degrees include Harvard Business School AMP, a PhD in engineering from ETH Zürich and a Degree in business informatics and business administration from the University of Mannheim.

Kerstin Jeger I Montessori

Kerstin Jeger is a Montessorian, childhood education expert who has devoted her life to individualized learning and character development Kerstin became dean of the private Montessori specialized Secondary School Lauf Germany in 2013. A school which was founded in 2008. From 1992–2012 she hold different teaching positions at various trade schools in the Nuremburg area. In March 2008 she was promoted to senior teacher and in 2015 to Director of Studies. Kerstin was 5 years on parental leave to raise and educate her two children who joined a Montessorian elementary school. After finishing her undergraduate studies in business administration, Kerstin received a Masters Degree with a focus on computer science and psychology of learning at the Friedrich-Alexander-University Nuremberg in 1992.

Steve Lee Hee Kwang | Changi Airport

Steve is currently the Chief Information Officer and Senior Vice President, Technology at Changi Airport Group. His responsibilities includes: IT project management, operations and support, architecture and strategy for both airport operations, commercial and corporate systems. Prior to joining CAG, Steve was the CIO at Kuok (Singapore) Ltd, a company with businesses in trading, shipping, logistics and other businesses across the region. He spent his earlier years in the Ministry of Defence where he held the post of Deputy Director, MINDEF CIO Office before leaving to join the private sector. Steve is also currently the President of the ITMA, Singapore and on the Advisory Committees of the Temasek Polytechnic, Informatics IT School and Singapore Management University School of Information Systems. Steve is also the Chairman of ACI World Airport IT Standing Committee.

Goodarz Mahbobi | axxessio

Goodarz Mahbobi studied computer science at the Technical University of Vienna and at UC Berkeley in the United States of America. Due to the many years of experience as an independent operational IT-architect, strategic consultant and as a project and program manager, he has an extensive know-how especially in the areas of telecommunications and logistics and change processes (e.g. smart factory). In 2006, he and his partner Walter Brux founded the IT and Management consultancy axxessio GmbH. Moreover, Goodarz Mahbobi is a member of the board at IT FOR WORK – one of Germany's leading networks for small and medium-sized enterprises in the field of information and communication technologies - with particular focus on software development.

Hartmut Mai | Allianz

Hartmut Mai is responsible for the company's global Property, Financial Lines, Engineering, Liability, and Mid-Corporate underwriting as well as for its Risk Consulting unit since 2012. Mai began his insurance career in 1995 with AIG EUROPE, as a Directors and Officers liability underwriter. Since then he held various management positions for AIG's German operation such as Member of the Board of Management. In 2003 Mai relocated to London for AIG's Financial Lines operation and headed up the Commercial Management Liability team for the

UK/Ireland region. In 2006 he joined MARSH GmbH to head up their German FINPRO team. He joined AGCS as Global Head of Financial Lines in 2007. Mai has studied law at the University of Cologne and at Emory Law School in Atlanta, GA.

Rolf Schumann | SAP SE

As General Manager Platform and Innovation at SAP, Rolf Schumann (SVP) runs all go-to- market activities for the Business Unit SAP HANA Cloud Platform globally. In his role, he represents the customer and market perspective in SAP's Global Leadership Team. He is known as a leading Technology and Innovation Entrepreneur who brings more than twenty-five years of experience. Previously, he headed the platform and innovation business in EMEA as Chief Technology Officer at SAP. He received a degree in Master of Science Business Administration and Computer Science from the University of Mannheim (GER), a Master of IT Management from ZfU International Business School (CH) and possesses multiple IT certifications. He published the books "Simplify your IT" and "Update – why the data revolution affects all of us", which was honored with the GetAbstract International Book Award as the best business book in 2015.

Jan Zadak | HP Enterprise Services

Jan Zadak served as President HP Enterprise Services Europe, the Middle East and Africa (EMEA) till December 2016. Previously, Zadak was executive vice president for HP globally and senior vice president for Europe, the Middle East and Africa (EMEA) responsible for the management of top corporate and enterprise accounts. Zadak joined Compaq Computer in 1997 and held several senior management roles in EMEA's emerging markets, including Central and Eastern Europe, the Middle East and Africa. Before joining Compaq, Zadak spent five years with Olivetti Czech Republic. A native of the Czech Republic, Zadak graduated from the Czech Technical University of Prague, Faculty of Electrical Engineering in1988. He did a one year Ph.D. study program at Universität Erlangen-Nuernberg in Germany in 1991 and gained a Ph.D. from his alma mater, the Czech Technical University in 1992.

Contents

Part X   Mobility Services

Part XI   Industry 4.0

List of Authors

Josef Adersberger QAware GmbH, Munich, Germany

Robin Ahlers University of Applied Sciences South Westphalia, Iserlohn, Germany

Peter Altendorf Institut für Rundfunktechnik, Munich, Germany

Thomas Altenhain ALTENHAIN Unternehmensberatung GbR, Starnberg, Germany

Anders Andersen UiT The Arctic University of Norway, Tromsø, Norway

Lefteris Angelis Aristotle University of Thessaloniki and TEI of Thessaly, Thessaloniki, Larissa, Greece

Marcelo A. de Barros Federal University of Campina Grande, Campina Grande, Brazil

Michael Beck Ludwig-Maximilians-Universität München, Munich, Germany

Fernando Beltrán University of Auckland Business School, Auckland, New Zealand

Lenz Belzner Ludwig-Maximilians-Universität München, Munich, Germany

Sabine Bendiek Microsoft Deutschland GmbH, München Schwabing, Germany

Hendrik Berndt Universität Kassel, Kassel, Germany

Robert Blackburn BASF Group, Ludwigshafen, Germany

Thomas Bocek University of Zürich UZH, Zurich, Switzerland

Mahdi Bohlouli University of Siegen, Siegen, Germany

Andreas Braun Allianz SE, Munich, Germany

Ellena Brenner The Nunatak Group GmbH, Munich, Germany

Walter Brenner University of St. Gallen, St. Gallen, Switzerland

Falko Brinkmann KPMG AG, Hamburg, Germany

Martin Buske Buske Consulting GmbH, Sankt Augustin, Germany

Matteo Cagnazzo Institute for Internet-Security, Gelsenkirchen, Germany

Michael Cebulsky KPMG AG, Düsseldorf, Germany

Christina Czeschik Serapion Beratung & Fachredaktion, Essen, Germany

Klaus David Universität Kassel, Kassel, Germany

Yuval Diskin Cymotive Technologies Ltd., Herzlia, Germany

André Ebert Ludwig-Maximilians-Universität München, Munich, Germany

Tobias Emrich Ludwig-Maximilians-Universität München, Munich, Germany

Sebastian Feld Ludwig-Maximilians-Universität München, Munich, Germany

Rolf Felkel Fraport AG, Frankfurt on the Main, Germany

Frank Follert Fraport AG, Frankfurt on the Main, Germany

Florian Fuchs doo GmbH, Munich, Germany

Thomas Gabor Ludwig-Maximilians-Universität München, Munich, Germany

Gemma Garriga INRIA Research Center, Rocquencourt, France

Heidi Gautschi École Polytechnique Fédérale de Lausanne, Lausanne, Switzerland

Sandro Gaycken ESMT, Berlin, Germany

Jörg Günther KPMG AG, Frankfurt, Germany

Daniel Hartert Bayer AG, Leverkusen, Germany

Gerhard Hastreiter Allianz, Munich, Germany

Kiki Hatzistavrou Aristotle University of Thessaloniki and TEI of Thessaly, Thessaloniki, Larissa, Greece

Andreas Hausotter University of Applied Sciences and Arts in Hanover, Hanover, Germany

Peter Heidkamp KPMG AG, Cologne, Germany

Andreas Hein Technical University of Munich, Munich, Germany

Christoph Heinemann Christoph Heinemann Vermögensverwaltung GmbH, Munich, Germany

Andreas Herrmann University of St. Gallen, St. Gallen, Switzerland

Markus Hertlein XignSys GmbH, Gelsenkirchen, Germany

Markus Heyn BOSCH, Gerlingen, Germany

Alexander Hildenbrand Cross-Business-Architecture Lab, Bonn, Germany

Wolfgang Hildesheim IBM Deutschland GmbH, Düsseldorf, Germany

Martin Hofmann Volkswagen Group, Wolfsburg, Germany

Gerald Hüther Universität Göttingen, Göttingen, Germany

Robert Iberl Bayerische Forschungsallianz GmbH, Munich, Germany

Klaus Illgner-Fehns Institut für Rundfunktechnik, Munich, Germany

Robert Jacobi The Nunatak Group GmbH, Munich, Germany

Kerstin Jeger Montessori-Vereinigung Nürnberger Land e.V., Lauf/Pegnitz, Germany

Alexander W. Jonke KPMG AG, Munich, Germany

Gunnar Jöns biners – business information security, Bonn, Germany

Gregor Jossé Ludwig-Maximilians-Universität München, Munich, Germany

George Kakarontzas Aristotle University of Thessaloniki and TEI of Thessaly, Thessaloniki, Larissa, Greece

Randi Karlsen UiT The Arctic University of Norway, Tromsø, Norway

Madeleine Keltsch Institut für Rundfunktechnik, Munich, Germany

Marie Kiermeier Ludwig-Maximilians-Universität München, Munich, Germany

Joachim Kistner Sonus GmbH, Baden-Baden, Germany

Georg Klassen Rohde & Schwarz GmbH & Co. KG, Munich, Germany

Roxane Koitz Technische Universität Graz, Graz, Austria

Arne Koschel University of Applied Sciences and Arts in Hanover, Hanover, Germany

Andreas Kovar Kovar & Partners GmbH, Vienna, Austria

Britta Krahn Bonn-Rhein-Sieg University of Applied Sciences, Rheinbach, Germany

Andreas Kranabitl SPAR Business Services GmbH, Salzburg, Austria

Helmut Krcmar Technical University of Munich, Munich, Germany

Peer Kröger Ludwig-Maximilians-Universität München, Munich, Germany

Christian Kurze Denodo Technologies, Munich, Germany

Steve Lee Changi Airport Group, Singapore, Singapore

Florian Leibert Mesosphere Inc., San Francisco, USA

Michael Liebmann doo GmbH, Munich, Germany

Claudia Linnhoff-Popien Institut für Informatik, LMU München, Munich, Germany

Julian Lopez University of Alicante, Alicante, Spain

Goodarz Mahbobi axxessio GmbH, Bonn, Germany

Hartmut Mai Allianz Global Corporate & Specialty SE, Munich, Germany

Fredmund Malik Malik Institute, St. Gallen, Switzerland

Pascal Manaras XignSys GmbH, Gelsenkirchen, Germany

Chadly Marouane Virality GmbH, Munich, Germany

Andy Mattausch Ludwig-Maximilians-Universität München, Munich, Germany

Björn Matthies CoCoNo GmbH, Hamburg, Germany

Stefan Meinzer Volkswagen Data:Lab, Munich, Germany

J. Antão B. Moura Federal University of Campina Grande, Campina Grande, Brazil

Paul Moxon Denodo Technologies, Munich, Germany

Ruan P. Oliveira Federal University of Campina Grande, Campina Grande, Brazil

Luigi Orsenigo Scuola Universitaria Superiore IUSS, Pavia, Italy

Philipp Osl Institute of Information Management, St. Gallen, Switzerland

Hubert Österle Business Engineering Institute St. Gallen, St. Gallen, Switzerland

Bernhard Peischl Technische Universität Graz, Graz, Austria

Christoph Pflügler Technical University of Munich, Munich, Germany

Robert Pikart Pikart IT Advisory GmbH, Vienna, Austria

R. Radhakrishna Pillai IIM Kozhikode, Kerala, India

Norbert Pohlmann Institute for Internet-Security, Gelsenkirchen, Germany

Gordana Polanec-Kutija Institut für Rundfunktechnik, Munich, Germany

L. L. Ramachandran BPCL, Kochi, India

Aurora Ramírez University of Córdoba, Córdoba, Spain

Rauthgundis Reck Allianz Technology SE, Munich, Germany

Peter Reichl University of Vienna, Vienna, Austria

Florian Richter Ludwig-Maximilians-Universität München, Munich, Germany

Ralf Rieken Uniscon GmbH, Munich, Germany

Christian Rietz University of Cologne, Cologne, Germany

Maik Romberg Rohde & Schwarz GmbH & Co. KG, Munich, Germany

José Raúl Romero University of Córdoba, Córdoba, Spain

Hans Rösch Vattenfall GmbH, Berlin, Germany

Benno Rott Virality GmbH, Munich, Germany

Maxim Roubintchik rev, Munich, Germany

André Ruegenberg University of Applied Sciences South Westphalia, Iserlohn, Germany

Rubén Salado-Cid University of Córdoba, Córdoba, Spain

Ali Reza Samanpour University of Applied Sciences South Westphalia, Iserlohn, Germany

Lucas Sauberschwarz Venture Idea GmbH, Düsseldorf, Germany

Anthony Savidis University of Crete, Crete, Greece

Sebastian Saxe Hamburg Port Authority AöR, Hamburg, Germany

Rainer Schäfer Institut für Rundfunktechnik, Munich, Germany

Martin Schallbruch ESMT Berlin, Berlin, Germany

Lorenz Schauer Ludwig-Maximilians-Universität München, Munich, Germany

Helmut Scherzer Giesecke & Devrient, Munich, Germany

Rolf Schillinger Fachhochschule Würzburg Schweinfurt, Würzburg, Germany

Christian Schläger Giesecke & Devrient GmbH, Munich, Germany

Mark Schleicher University of St. Gallen, St. Gallen, Switzerland

Ralf Schneider Allianz SE, Munich, Germany

Michael Schopp Denodo Technologies, Munich, Germany

Maximilian Schreieck Technical University of Munich, Munich, Germany

Matthias Schubert Ludwig-Maximilians-Universität München, Munich, Germany

Katharina Schüller STAT-UP Statistical Consulting & Data Science GmbH, Munich, Germany

Stefan Schumacher VOICE – Bundesverband der IT-Anwender e.V., Berlin, Germany

Rolf Schumann SAP SE, Walldorf, Germany

Karsten Schweichhart Cross-Business-Architecture Lab, Bonn, Germany

M. P. Sebastian IIM Kozhikode, Kerala, India

Attul Sehgal RedOctopus Innovation, London, UK

Thomas Seidl Ludwig-Maximilians-Universität München, Munich, Germany

Haya Shulman Fraunhofer Institute for Secure Information Technology SIT, Darmstadt, Germany

Johannes Siedersleben QAware GmbH, Munich, Germany

Aleksandra Solda-Zaccaro TERRITORY Content to Results GmbH, Munich, Germany

David Soto Setzke Technical University of Munich, Munich, Germany

Dieter Steinmann Fraport AG, Frankfurt on the Main, Germany

Burkhard Stiller University of Zürich UZH, Zurich, Switzerland

Marco Streng Genesis Mining, Reykjavik, Iceland

Frank Thelen e42 GmbH, Bonn, Germany

Yannis Valsamakis Foundation for Research and Technology Hellas (FORTH), Crete, Greece

Ines Varela Stadtwerke Düsseldorf AG, Düsseldorf, Germany

Armando Vieira RedOctopus Innovation, London, UK

Gianluigi Viscusi École Polytechnique Fédérale de Lausanne, Lausanne, Switzerland

Aylin Vogl Institut für Rundfunktechnik, Munich, Germany

Jo Barbara Volkwein KPMG AG, Düsseldorf, Germany

Uwe Weber Detecon International GmbH, Munich, Germany

Patrick Wegner Institute for Internet-Security, Gelsenkirchen, Germany

Lysander Weiss Venture Idea GmbH, Düsseldorf, Germany

Martin Werner Ludwig-Maximilians-Universität München, Munich, Germany

Karsten Weronek Frankfurt University of Applied Sciences, Frankfurt on the Main, Germany

Manuel Wiesche Technical University of Munich, Munich, Germany

Nils Winkler CoCoNo GmbH, Hamburg, Germany

Franz Wotawa Technische Universität Graz, Graz, Austria

Christian Wrobel Fraport AG, Frankfurt on the Main, Germany

Jan Zadak Hewlett-Packard Enterprise, Vresova, Czech Republic

Michael Zaddach Munich Airport, Munich, Germany

Johannes Zenkert University of Siegen, Siegen, Germany

Malte Zuch University of Applied Sciences and Arts in Hanover, Hanover, Germany

Part I
Prefaces

Preface: Humans in Digital Marketplaces

Gerald Hüther

Considering the history of mankind, not much time has passed, since Friedrich Schiller captured the dilemma of his time in a nutshell in his famous Wallenstein trilogy: "The world is narrow, wide the mind of man". Today, in our digitalized and globalized world, Friedrich Schiller would describe the dilemma precisely in the opposite way: The world has become wide, but our brains are too narrow for the new world we live in.

The articles in this book underline the wide range of opportunities for innovative business enterprises offered by digital technology in our global and connected world. There is no doubt that this rapid development will not only continue, but even accelerate during the next years. The most important perspectives and directions of this process are clearly pointed out in this book.

Technological innovations do not only alter our previous means of production or change economic developments, they also offer completely new instruments to academic research. The use of digital media allows previously inconceivable insights into the structure and the organization of complex phenomena. This does not only concern classical natural sciences, such as astrophysics, but also and above all the so-called life sciences, the research of living systems from cellular and organic systems to the ecological and social systems.

The new opportunities of data collection and analysis are particularly suitable for the research of complex relationship patterns and their underlying laws. The so far prevailing analysis of isolated phenomena in laboratories will increasingly be replaced by the research of their interactions in natural conditions. Necessarily this will help to gain new insights. The last century's predominant deterministic idea concerning the structure of living systems through genetic programs is slowly being replaced by new findings on the

G. Hüther (✉)
Universität Göttingen
Göttingen, Germany
e-mail: ghuethe@gwdg.de

© Springer-Verlag GmbH Germany 2018
C. Linnhoff-Popien et al. (eds.), *Digital Marketplaces Unleashed*,
https://doi.org/10.1007/978-3-662-49275-8_1

increasingly visible and measurable skill of living systems for self-organization. A majority of findings and meta-analyses show that self-organizing relationship-patterns are responsible for further structure formation on all levels of development of living systems: during the development of embryos, the development of brains, the emergence of ecosystems or during the formation of social systems. In the 21st century, as a "side effect" of the introduction of technological innovations, "self-organization" has become a key term for the understanding of development and transformation processes of living beings. Also social development and transformation processes, like the cohabitation of human beings, are the expression of such self-organizing processes.

The so called Kontratieff-cycles describe how economic developments are placed on new foundations again and again through so called basic innovations. These can entail decades-long adaption processes in all areas of production, consumption or trade that manifest in phases of economic upturn. Examples for technological innovations that trigger respective economic growth are the steam engine (1st cycle), steel production and the invention of the railway (2nd cycle), the innovations in the area of electrical technology and chemistry (3rd cycle), the introduction of cars and petrol-chemistry (4th cycle) and finally, in the second half of the last century, the development of information technology (5th cycle).

However, these cycles have not only gone along with economic growth. They were always accompanied by noticeable changes to human life, especially to the cohabitation of humans. In particular these changes led to unavoidable, not intended (self-organized) adjustment processes affecting social relationships in the corresponding era.

Currently, with the globalization and the digitalization, we are experiencing a technological innovation which is not only of economic importance but also influences all areas of human cohabitation. This time even to a previously unknown extent.

The manner how humans will live together, work together and learn from each other in the future will probably change both fundamentally and permanently. To stay with the picture of Friedrich Schiller, the brain therefore has to significantly develop further.

The key to this development are offered by the most recent findings in the area of brain science: the human brain is more vivid than assumed. The brain is able to modify, add and expand neural networks even into the old age. For this reasons humans are capable to learn throughout their whole life. And: the human brain's structure is determined more than previously assumed by social experiences, the exchange of knowledge and skills and through collaborative design performances. It is therefore an organ that is formed by and optimized through social relationships. Whoever wants to further develop and "enlarge" his brain, or the brain of others, should to invest in social relationships, in mutual exchange and in the search of joint solutions.

In case it is true that every living system reorganizes the relationships of its members until the perpetuation of the regarded system is ensured with a minimal input of energy, it is possible to predict how the future coexistence of human beings, considering digitalization and globalization, will develop at the beginning of the 21st century. The former friction losses that were part of the traditional relationships, in other words, the enormous expenses of energy and resources that are used to maintain our current way of cohabitation, has to shrink. New digital communication technologies and learning programs can be considered helpful instruments in this regards. However, the key to the transformation of our present (energy intensive) relationship culture might be found elsewhere and is more of a fundamental nature: As long as humans treat each other like objects to achieve their own goals and objectives, those communities create too much friction loss and thereby hinder themselves to evolve their existing potentials.

As a result we infringe against a generally valid principle concerning the development of the universe that has been identified by atomic physicists. That this is about the progressive opening and development of opportunities. Gregory Bateson already reminded us that there is no opportunity to change the nature, except one comply with it. But in order to comply with human nature, we need to know how it works.

With their research neurobiologists made a huge contribution to answer this question. In a nutshell their discovery points out: humans do not exist as individual entity, just as much as the brain does not exist without the body. In order to mature as humans beings and to become the designers of our own lives, we need other humans, we need communities where their members consider each other as subjects instead of objects of their own expectations and valuations, objectives and intentions, measures and orders. This makes it clear, where digitalization might finally lead us to. What remains uncertain, is the question when the actors and designers of this digitalized World recognize that this world persist over time, if it offers a familiar and comfortable feeling to people. This can only be offered through the satisfaction of the deepest human need for solidarity and security on one side and autonomy and freedom on the other side. "Digital marketplaces unleashed" could help to transform the world into a global village. And Schiller would be right again. However, it would be better if the unleashed digitalization increases the diversity and richness of the world and its cultures into the unknown. In this case Schiller would need state: As long the world is widening, the brain can never be narrowing.

Fredmund Malik

2.1 Digital Society

2.1.1 From the Old World to a New World

Globally, economies and societies are going through the most fundamental change in history. We are experiencing the displacement of the Old World, as we have come to know it, by the New World, which is still largely unknown. It is the origin of a new order and a new societal functioning—a new kind of societal revolution. I called this process "Great Transformation21" in my book about "Governance" back in 1997. It will change almost everything: *What* we do, *how* we do it and *why* we do it—and, lastly, *who we are*. In just a few years almost everything will be new and different: How we manufacture, transport, finance and consume, how we educate, learn, do research and innovate; how we share information, communicate and cooperate; how we work and live. That will also change *who* we are.

A new dynamic order is forming, and—more importantly—so is a new mode of functioning of society and its organizations. Digitalization is one of the most powerful of several major driving forces. Its full potential will be exploited by an equally powerful force which is a new kind of management, governance and leadership. It is the *system-cybernetic kind of managing complex systems*. As I will later show, both have much in common since they had their birth at the same time and in same place.

The Great Transformation21 is the reason why ever more organizations—in the business as well as in the non-business sector—operate in a zone of excessive challenges. The origin of bureaucratic paralysis and ossification lies in the obsolete methods of con-

F. Malik (✉)
Malik Institute
St. Gallen, Switzerland
e-mail: info@malik-management.com

© Springer-Verlag GmbH Germany 2018
C. Linnhoff-Popien et al. (eds.), *Digital Marketplaces Unleashed*,
https://doi.org/10.1007/978-3-662-49275-8_2

ventional mechanistic management. Today's organizations prevent solutions and even contribute to the intensification of crises with their growing inability to master complexity. Digitalization on the one hand is aggravating the difficulties and on the other hand it will be one of the major solutions.

All the social mechanisms that make organizations function will change fundamentally and irreversibly—worldwide. Millions of organizations of every kind and size will have to adapt and be rebuilt, as they no longer meet the new standards. Across the generations, people will be required to rethink and relearn.

2.1.2 The Map of Growth, Uncertainty, and Creative Destruction

Change in itself—even big change—is not unusual. There is always improvement, adaptation, innovation and also disruption. Here, I am talking not about any kind of change but about a very specific kind of change, the kind that will replace the existing with something new according to a pattern. We are talking about *substitution*. The famous Austrian economist Joseph Schumpeter called this kind of change "creative destruction". With that, he put in words the basic law of change that also governs evolution in nature.

My paradigm of the Great Transformation21 is two overlapping s-curves (Fig. 2.1). My research into this pattern goes back to the late 1970s. In the graph, the red curve represents what I call the Old World. The green curve represents the New World and the foundations of tomorrow's world.

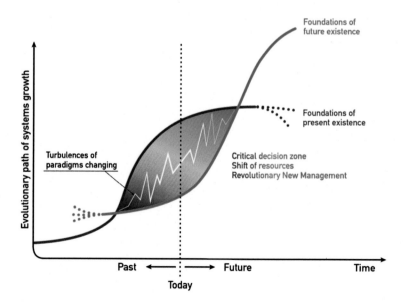

Fig. 2.1 The paradigm of the Great Transformation21

Between the curves, we see an area of increasing turbulences, as the old is replaced by the new. This is the critical decision zone; this is also where disruptions can take place; this is where the Old World starts dissolving and the New World begins to take shape.

This is the zone where the really difficult questions and risks of navigation and management occur. Previous key resources become increasingly meaningless; they have to be shifted or newly created.

In search of answers, we reflexively cling to old methods, although they are becoming increasingly useless. These old methods are what have caused the troubles in the first place.

Among other things, one key question is whether people in a "red" business will also be able to contribute to a "green" business, and all of a sudden it is doubtful as to whether you will have use for even your best people in the future. This zone of shifts is a black box—as it is named in the science of cybernetics, which is the basis for communication, control and navigation. It is a system which, due to its immense complexity, is incomprehensible, unpredictable and incomputable. However, with a new kind of management we are able to cope with it—just not with conventional methods.

2.1.3   Navigating into the Unknown by Systematically Misleading Signals

One basic rule of change is: *Whatever exists will be replaced.* Looking at it with hindsight, you know what the pattern looks like. You also know then what would have been the right decision at any given point. Standing in the here and now (Fig. 2.2), the existing

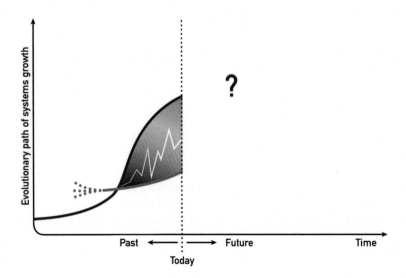

Fig. 2.2 Here and now: Navigating into the unknown with misleading signals?

information systems in our present organizations deliver systematically misleading signals as their output.

In today's world, the signals tell us to continue on the red curve. To the extent that—even if we notice the green curve at all and take it seriously—our old compass warns us not to pursue that route. Only when it is too late do our old systems sound the alarm. However, by knowing the entire pattern up to a certain degree, the risk of making wrong decisions can be circumvented.

2.1.4 Needed: Three Different Strategies and Systemic Leadership

There is yet another important challenge. We need three different strategies: The first strategy is to take advantage of the red curve as long as possible. We need a second strategy to build the green curve in time to have it when we need it. And we need a third strategy to make the transition from red to green.

At this point, it also becomes evident where we need real leadership and what it must entail. True leadership is needed for the start into an unknown future, when all visible signs seem to indicate that we should stay in the past. There are such organizations that have mastered change several times in the course of their existence, mainly by making it happen themselves. Examples include Siemens, Bosch and General Electric, but not Kodak. For instance, nothing could be more useless than having the world's best chemists in the photo industry when the substituting technology is digital. Virtually overnight Kodak's most valuable asset—the knowledge of its top people—had become worthless. What is worse, apart from having become "useless", these same people offered the strongest resistance to digitalization.

2.1.5 Being Ahead of Change

Just as there is a substitution pattern, there is also a strategic principle that successful companies and organizations adhere to: *Be ahead of change!* They actively make change happen instead of waiting for it to hit them. They take advantage of the forces of this relentless law of business—and not only business—to start into a new dimension of performance rather than fight it. They keep the initiative and determine the rules. Hence, change is not a must but a want to them. The organization itself determines what happens instead of drifting along. By outgrowing itself and its previous limits, it in effect substitutes itself. *If we don't do this, others will. It will happen one way or another*—that is their maxim.

2.2   Radical New Governance Thinking

2.2.1   From the Mechanistic to System-Cybernetic Management of Complexity

Information technology is one of the major drivers of the Great Transformation21. However, digitalization alone would soon freeze within the labyrinths of obsolete organizations and mechanistic management processes. Most probably it would just reinforce already existing bureaucracy. Successful digitalization needs system-cybernetic complexity management. Only together will they create the ability and willingness of people and organizations for fast change.

What does digitalization really mean? Properly managed it is the potential of rapidly growing interconnectedness of hitherto separated systems. And it also means doing things simultaneously which so far could only be done sequentially. As a consequence, this means an exponential increase in intelligence, adaptivity, speed and productivity. This is what challenges millions of organizations in our modern complexity society. Without functioning organizations a collapse of societal functioning looms.

The danger is real. Because the origin of most of today's organizations' morphology and principles of functioning reach far back into the last century. Therefore, they are ever less equipped to deal with the challenges of today's complexity and speed. They are too slow for the transformation, too stolid, neither efficient enough nor adaptable enough.

Decision-making processes seem paralyzed and block themselves. Collective intelligence, creativity, innovation and ability for change are lacking, as well as self-coordination, self-regulation and self-organization. If we were to stick to conventional ways of thinking and methods, a social disaster would be inevitable. On the other hand, a historically unique period of prosperity on a global scale could be reached if we rethink now. A new societal order—facilitating a *humane as well as functioning way of living together*—could thus be created, beyond the more than 200 year old and gridlocked political ideologies.

2.2.2   Digitalization and System-Cybernetic Complexity Management Have a Common Basis

Digitalization and the management of complex systems have the same hour and place of birth. The power of holistic, system-cybernetic management far surpasses the mechanistic linear management—many today call it "completely new". Its origin lies exactly in the time and place that also saw the development of today's computer technology. Partly the same pioneers were responsible who also build the fundament for modern computer technology and simultaneously for the proper management of societal organizations: They realized early on that the same principles apply to both areas.

One of them is mathematician Norbert Wiener, founder of modern cybernetics, with his book "Cybernetics: Control and Communication in the Animal and the Machine" (1948). Also the British neurophysiologist Ross W. Ashby with his revolutionary book "Design for a Brain. The origin of adaptive behavior" (1952). Add John von Neuman, the inventor of the modern computer, Claude Shannon's information theory and Heinz von Foerster's Causal Circularity.

With their early theories on information and communication, algorithms and heuristics and on the design and navigation of complex systems, they have created the prerequisites for today's real "cyberspace" as well as for the cybernetics of the management of complex systems. It was still too early for this new system-cybernetic management though. For decades, the industrialized society's mechanistic notion of management would continue to dominate, and it would be taught at thousands of universities and business schools—until today.

2.2.3 Organizations as Living Organism

The current challenge of the Great Transformation21 forces the renunciation of mechanistic management. The prevalent notion of the last decades that the company is a machine which can be steered with the linear principles of cause and effect blocked the necessary progress.

The more helpful notion is the organization as a living organism in its evolutionary environment. Management then is responsible for enabling organizations to self-organize and self-regulate wherever numerous and ever more people work together to reach common goals. Contrary to wide-spread fears this is exactly what allows people the freedom for the first time to unfold their intelligence and creativity in the digital world in a new and better way.

The new goal is the adaptive viability of a flexible organization that far surpasses the notion of sustainability. *What* needs to be done has been identified—and system-cybernetic management provides the *How* and *Whereby*. Hence, digital interconnectivity and system-cybernetic management of complexity will become the very societal functions that enable people to effectively exploit the new possibilities and opportunities.

Preface: New Computing in Digital Marketplaces Unleashed

3

Florian Leibert

We are at an inflection point where consumer technologies and innovation have forced their way into Global 2000 enterprises. People are asking themselves why enterprise software should be so much worse than someone's experience on an ecommerce travel site or searching for something on Google. And disruptive technologies such as new digital consumer devices and services have disrupted the datacenters at the heart of every large company in the world.

These advances in enterprise IT require new methods of computing, and a new breed of entrepreneur able to capitalize them. The unleashed digital market places are an exciting time that arguably began with the rise of the Worldwide Web just more than a decade ago, but really accelerated with the rise of social networks and mobile devices in the more-recent past.

Think about the shifts that have occurred since the 1990s, and have really picked up their pace in the past decade. One of the biggest is the proliferation of computing and the ability (or requirement) to reach consumers where they spend so much of their time—on their smartphones, tablets and laptops, or via connected devices that interface with those computers. A large enterprise application in 1995 might have involved thousands of client desktops connected to a single big-iron application server or database server. Now tens of thousands to millions of laptops, tablets, smartphones and other devices have to access a single application at any given time.

What happened was that giant web-scale companies such as Google, Facebook, Yahoo! and Twitter—all successful consumer web companies—grew so big, so fast that they had to invent distributed computing systems to prevent themselves from falling over or drowning in complexity. Because they were solving new classes of problems that legacy systems

F. Leibert (✉)
Mesosphere Inc.
San Francisco, USA
e-mail: flo@mesosphere.com

© Springer-Verlag GmbH Germany 2018
C. Linnhoff-Popien et al. (eds.), *Digital Marketplaces Unleashed*,
https://doi.org/10.1007/978-3-662-49275-8_3

could not manage, they typically invented new open source frameworks themselves or they jumped on nascent projects coming out of top computer science universities.

Without distributed computing on the backend systems, there is no way any application could handle that much traffic—much less store, process and serve, in any reasonable amount of time, all the user and log data that millions of users can generate. This is why from Apache Spark to Apache Mesos to Apache Cassandra, almost every new technology of any real utility (and popularity) over the past decade is a distributed system.

Distributed computing is so commonplace in some areas that a single Google search or Facebook update on your smartphone touches dozens of such systems at very large scale—each spanning the equivalent of thousands to hundreds of thousands of nodes—in order to process data, rank results, serve ads, tap the social graph or knowledge graph, and much more. In fact, companies such as Google, Facebook, Microsoft and Amazon are so adept at managing and automating entire datacenters full of computers that they don't even think about units as small as server racks anymore. They buy machines by the shipping container and compete for bragging rights over who has the most, biggest and best datacenters.

3.1 From the Fringes to the Mainstream

Today, the types large-scale distributed systems, real-time data processing and service-oriented architectures these web companies built are business imperatives in corporate digital transformations. Executives and boards around the world are demanding their companies deliver products that can compete with the likes of Google, or at least can mimic Google-like efficiencies and innovation within their own IT departments. This leaves CIOs looking for new IT allies that truly understand the technologies their enterprises will need in order to deliver on these mandates.

While few organizations will ever reach that level of scale, the techniques these companies have developed to manage their datacenter environments are very useful for small startups and large traditional enterprises, as well. That mundane startup news website or innovative mobile game you love, for example, is probably running on some combination of, say, MongoDB, Elasticsearch, Spark and Amazon S3. Traditional enterprises are getting increasingly hip to distributed systems, too, targeting data analytics with systems such as Hadoop and Spark, or faster application performance with a distributed database.

More and more enterprises are exploring Docker containers and want to deploy microservice applications—that is, packaging each component of an application (sometimes dozens of them) as connected, but loosely coupled and separately-managed services. Microservices are frequently more about improving developer agility and simplifying IT operations than they are about scalability, but containers themselves have proven remarkably useful for technology pioneers such as Google, Facebook and Twitter. But even established enterprises like Verizon, Disney, and GE are embracing big data and re-architecting their computing around microservices and a containerized infrastructure.

Example

They have seen the business-changing, if not world-changing, applications that are possible when we monitor data from mobile devices, park visitors and jet engines—along with just about everything else in our physical world. They have seen the multi-billion-dollar potential of building first-of-a-kind and user-friendly consumer experiences. And they know the technologies that can help them deliver on these goals.

3.2 Distributed Computing is Hard—Good News for Entrepreneurs

For these reasons, I believe the movement toward this new distributed computing stack is inevitable. But it is not without its challenges. This creates business opportunities for entrepreneurs.

Most new distributed systems technologies require deep technical expertise to use in their raw forms. Many are open source software, oftentimes developed at large web companies and now managed by the Apache Software Foundation. They're appealing because they're free and proven to work at large scale. But you need teams of very smart engineers—who are hard to find and expensive to hire—to make it all work.

I experienced this firsthand at Twitter and Airbnb, where technologies such as Apache Mesos and Apache Hadoop helped us dramatically improve our ability to manage an ever-increasing number of servers (and the applications running on them) and process big data. However, there is no way we could have achieved those end results without some of the smartest computer scientists in Silicon Valley adapting those open source technologies to fit our specific production environments.

Example

Truly capitalizing on the distributed computing movement will require new ideas about how applications are built and new technologies to make them possible. Mainstream businesses will require software that lets developers unleash their ideas by tapping into a platform composed of thousands of servers and complex data-processing systems—without having to understand everything that's happening below the surface. They'll need software that automates the day-to-day experience of operations staff, so they can kiss goodbye the late-night outage emergencies and confusing catalogs of which applications are running on which servers.

3.3 A New Class of Startups for a New World of Computing

This means there is a golden opportunity for a new class of enterprise IT startups that is born out this datacenter-scale world. These are companies that understand the technologies at play—their founders have often worked with or created them at large consumer web companies—and understand how to turn them into products that large enterprises will actually buy. From Day One, this new class of startups has operated with the knowledge that their success hinges on how well they can balance cutting-edge technology, real-world requirements, and an ecosystem of partners working on other pieces of the new distributed stack.

Open source software is a common, although not entirely necessary, component of the business model for many of these companies. The depth of a company's open source commitment is often tied to the technologies upon which its product is built, and to the level of software stack at which it plays. Popular infrastructure-level software, for example, is often open source today (for reasons that have more to do with innovation and lock-in than desire for *free* software), whereas application-level software is less frequently open source.

For startups, like Mesosphere, that sell products based on open source software, a lot of value lies in the community engagement and crowdsourced innovation that open source technologies facilitate. Smart enterprise IT startups understand that they don't know everything and it's impossible for them to stay current on all the latest technologies. There's a lot to be learned (and gained) from internalizing feedback from a diverse set of users, and from letting subject-matter experts bolster platform capabilities in areas in which your company is not an expert. This is a departure from many legacy IT practices, but also from the practices of web giants, who often build tools or distributions designed *specifically for their own environments* before releasing them to the world under an open source license.

Turning remarkably scalable, remarkably complex and remarkably valuable systems into easily consumable products is a huge challenge, requiring a remarkably different type of IT company. As you watch the current generation of enterprise IT startups continue to grow, to partner with one another and to innovate on the business side, you're actually watching the maturation of the next wave of IT giants in the unleased digital marketplaces—tomorrow's Microsoft, Oracle and SAP. Their technologies and their methods might seem foreign at times, but that's all part of coming of age in today's technology landscape. When it's all said, these are the companies that will dominate the era of data-center computing.

Part II
Introduction

Welcome to the Age of Spontaneous Business Models: Start Shaping or Be Shaped

4

Claudia Linnhoff-Popien, Ralf Schneider, and Michael Zaddach

Abstract

Digitization makes our lives faster and faster. Communication happens in real-time, products are being developed on demand. I do not occasionally visit a market place any longer, I am always right there – as a particle of an amorphous group that continuously adapts its structure. We present you some thoughts about the proliferation of markets and the emergence of spontaneous business models, on how to cope with the fear of failure, how important and how demanding it is to arouse your clients' curiosity, and about opportunities for exponential growth based on the real-time ability to decide whether an innovation will be successful or not.

4.1 Proliferation – Market Places Branching out

Markets are undergoing continuous diversification. They are becoming more and more individualized. Customization of offerings is a crucial factor for success. The old economy

C. Linnhoff-Popien (✉)
Institut für Informatik, LMU München
Munich, Germany
e-mail: linnhoff@ifi.lmu.de

R. Schneider
Allianz SE
Munich, Germany
e-mail: ralf.schneider@allianz.de

M. Zaddach
Munich Airport
Munich, Germany
e-mail: michael.zaddach@munich-airport.de

© Springer-Verlag GmbH Germany 2018
C. Linnhoff-Popien et al. (eds.), *Digital Marketplaces Unleashed*,
https://doi.org/10.1007/978-3-662-49275-8_4

knew standard products. If you were lucky enough, at least there used to be a small group of products to choose from. Both products and services were tailored for mass production and mass consumption. They maybe were aligned to target a specific group of customers. Today, however, clients are being addressed individually and receive highly personalized offers.

Proliferation takes place. Products and business models keep branching out more and more – just like a cauliflower. One has to look for those buds of critical mass capable of attracting millions of customers. These are the buds, i. e., products, worthwhile developing. It does not matter where these customers are physically located. The only thing that counts is their common interest in and need for the same product a vendor can develop and bring to market.

An airline cannot build an own airport for everyone eager to fly. But it can search for groups of travelers willing to take a flight from Munich. Munich Airport itself has highly individualized offerings. There are vegan restaurants and steak houses. Some visitors and passengers only want to go shopping, others seek the tranquility of a lounge.

4.2 Marketplaces Unleashed Becoming Ever Faster

Market places are developing rapidly. They are digital. Even when looking for a physical product, I will choose the provider based on how fast it is able to deliver. I can get everything I want within 24 h. Customers demand instant gratification. Upon being pointed to a specific product, a customer wants it be delivered right away and in highest quality. This concept let corporations like Amazon grow big. They are highly reliable. They know that also for customers, "time is money" holds true. Indeed, they are able to deliver within 24 h or less.

And this time span shall become even shorter. Amazon recently filed a patent for flying warehouses to further reduce physical distance to its customers. The Internet merchant plans to set up so called "Airborne Fulfillment Centers" (AFC), floating up in the sky like an airship. Dependent on customer needs, different goods can be provisioned. They will be brought to the customer by drones, which do not have to queue up in the congested streets of a metropolis, but offer way shorter delivery times by air. Amazon makes a promise – and they will deliver on it.

4.3 The Emergence of Spontaneous Business Models

Our time has become fast moving. Vendors often do not exactly know yet what they want to offer or what they will be able to do, but they are already looking for first feedback on early thoughts and ideas. If an idea is well received, a corresponding product will be developed. Sometimes an existing product only has to be upgraded with new features or an existing service optimized. In any case, however, resources will only be spent if an idea goes down well. Market analysis in the classical sense takes a step back and is conducted only concomitantly. New business models are given a try. They evolve spontaneously and will be extended if they are successful and scale. Only under these circumstances the growth rates required for a product to be worth developing are possible.

The market's complexity is unforeseeable. It cannot be reliably predicted which development comes next. Instead, one has to try an innovation in the wild. Public awareness and interest for a new product that customers are not used to yet have to be created. Even more, they have lived well without it until now. One has to succeed in putting it on the public agenda in order to gain publicity and acceptance.

4.4   That Said, Nothing Digital Without its Physical Counterpart

Pure software products are known to scale very well. However, as soon as there is a physical product involved, things get more complicated.

This leads to the following aspect, which is often neglected when discussing Digitization: Apart from software-only products, there exists nothing exclusively digital without an analog counterpart. A promise digitally made by a merchant must be delivered on in the physical world. A physical object has to be produced and must be physically brought to the customer, a promised service has to be executed in the real world. The digital promise made has to match its physical realization. Otherwise, the customer will be disappointed by the seller.

4.5   Market Places Unleashed Not Offering Final Products, but Testing Demand

During the old economy, different products were in store the customer could choose from. He/she was only able to decide which standard product he/she wanted to buy. Today, we experience a new economy with market places being unleashed.

The customer is market places' new focus point that everything centers on. Market places hence have become customer centric. This also created completely new interfaces between a customer and a market, where user experience became a dominating factor. Customers must be addressed and be inspired. They must feel a certain urge. This market does not sell a finished product any more, it makes its sales way earlier in a product's lifecycle. That market place sells enthusiasm for a product, creates new needs on the customer's side. If necessary, entire new products are developed based on the customers' desires and requirements.

4.6   Create Curiosity

The digital world is in a state of constant change. Structures dissolve and reassemble to new patterns. Novel devices, gadgets, concepts and applications are offered in high frequency.

People find themselves spellbound to their devices and different types of media. Distractions everywhere and at any time. In order to attract customers' attention, sellers have to create extremely strong curiosity.

Take "Bibi's Beauty Palace" as an example. The young German vlogger, born 1993 in Cologne, published her first video on YouTube on December 2nd, 2002. In 2015, she had 2.5 million followers and more than 450 million views of her videos focusing on the topics of beauty, lifestyle and fashion. She reaches to young girls mainly.

Literally without any financial investment, she gained unbelievable numbers in coverage and popularity, only by means of the Internet. It would take decades or even centuries for any naturally grown company to achieve the same. Coverage simply explodes here. Not long ago, such numbers used to be exclusively reachable by big media corporations sharing expensive cable or satellite bandwidth with each other. Today, everyone can become such a media station. Now that is "unleashed".

4.7   Customer Interfaces Are A-Changing

During the days of the old economy, the product itself used to be a company's contact point to the customer offered by a merchant. The client entered a store, had a look around and talked to the person at the counter about what he was about to buy. Today, that "guy behind the counter" usually is a computer system, with an analog system behind it. It simply cannot work without the latter.

However, during the buying process, only a digital interface supports the decision to buy or not to buy. This leads to a completely new sales process. Buying interest is triggered by digitally distributed media. If the online buying incentive fails, however, the purchase will not be made. So, the desire for high coverage is accompanied by the need to have several sales channels being functional and successful. High coverage of these channels will then boost sale numbers.

4.8   The Perfect Offer's Triad

There always is a triad that has to be taken care of for correctly positioning a product during sales and distribution. First, one has to succeed in creating needs. The customer should be brought to the following insight: "I did not even know this thing existed, but now I want it." This is a hard task, especially if a product is completely new. The potential buyer does not know it yet and is not used to its function or appearance. Also, until now he has done well without it. As an example, let us have a look at the InfoGates terminals at Munich Airport. Passengers see the video chat to the call center and wonder: "Is there a person sitting in that thing?" They press a button and get a video connection to a human being, and they just did not expect this to happen. Plus, until now, traveling used to work without such technology. People might have reservations and fear of contact. So the provider of such technology has to create acceptance. Second, the digital world is a rather complex one, so every new product must be convenient and easily operated. Customers should be able to understand and affect a new product right away. If rejected by the customers, the product cannot successfully be placed in the market. Finally, the new product's vendor needs to have a good estimation for the price tag put on it. Customers want to have the impression that they get something of adequate value in return for their money. This might be a small perception only, however this perception is crucial. The price must be considered fair, and at the end of day the customer does not want to pay more for a product that he would have paid somewhere else for a comparable piece.

The price might even vary in real-time. The right, individualized offer depending on the customer's current situation must be made. This situation and context must be analyzed in real-time. The correct target group for a certain product must be analyzed and brought together. One has to find out who belongs to that group, who has a need for the offered product, and who is able and willing to afford it. If you will, you need a flock of customers, as humans are herd animals. Customers hence seek and trust other customers' experiences in form of product reviews and buying recommendations.

4.9   If Something Performs, It Performs Well

Today, if a product is a success, it becomes a real big one. The speed of the Internet can lead to vast propagation in almost no time. In the optimal case, huge amounts of response and awareness are created, letting a (small) idea become a big deal.

As an example, have a look at Pokémon Go. Developed in Australia, the free-to-play mobile game hit the App Store on July 6th, 2016. It uses the player's location data and smartphone camera in order to enable real world interactions such as Pokémon fights as well as catching and trading of the popular virtual creatures. The game was officially presented in North America the next day. On July 13th, the game's German version was released, followed by Japanese, Spanish, French and Italian ones. The users' reaction was phenomenal, creating a massive hype. Millions of people started hunting virtual monsters, making the physical and virtual worlds fuse together. Such digital markets scale very well and supported by social media products spread quickly. The once struggling video game pioneer Nintendo dared entering the mobile platforms – and was back in the game immediately. The cliché of couch potato video gamers vanished and augmented reality put millions of people around the globe under its spell.

On the other side, however, the Internet's excessive supply also makes it hard to get attention. The app stores host millions of applications, and only a tiny number are actually being used on a regular basis. Customer attention is split between too many new ideas and business models, a majority of which hence must fail.

4.10   Locally or Globally – How to Roll out a Product?

Software products are easy to roll out. However, platform development is expensive, let alone bug fixing, patching, extending, testing, optimizing and customizing for different interfaces, operating systems and device types.

Yet platform development only pays off as soon as there is a big enough user base. Sales and distribution are hence a crucial factor. "I need users, users, users!" So, the following questions come up: "How to do the roll out for my new platform? How can I reach the market share I need?"

The more the merrier: The more a product receives global acceptance, the more people can be reached and the higher is the chance to get attention. However, customers behave differently in different regions, industries or business sectors. Asian markets have to be addressed quite differently from European or American markets.

Entering a market must be conducted in a context-dependent manner. The market place itself can be reached "anytime, anyplace and through any device". Yet there are local and global restrictions. There are different languages I have to use for successful communication. English for the English speaking countries only, French for the French speakers and Japanese for the Japanese. When addressing people using a language they do not understand, I will not be able to reach them. However, market places can be constructed to support such aspects, e. g., switching languages depending on who comes to the market. Likewise, products that are globally available must be localized. That is the only way to achieve economies of scale.

4.11   Real-Time Feedback

The Internet offers another huge advantage for providers: It has real-time response and feedback. So the provider is able to learn extremely fast what customers think of his product. When using a digital distribution channel reaching millions of people, one can see if a product will perform or not within a few hours. Success can be monitored immediately. Digitization enables real-time feedback and control loops. But the provider, his marketing and sales departments must be prepared for this and react fast. In earlier times, test runs were conducted over several months. Then the aftermath analysis was done, and one could see what is working or not. Valuable time was lost. Today, you know what works the same day. There might remain some hope that numbers improve, however the customer behavior is representative even from the very first day. So in the age of Digitization, reacting to customer feedback extremely fast is key.

4.12 Battling for the Best Start-Ups

Start-up projects are highly interesting, as no one knows where the journey leads. Future trends cannot be predicted. Nobody can estimate how much attention which thing will receive. The market cannot be foreseen, ideas have to be given a try.

Start-ups are free to try out new things. There is plenty of money in the market to do just that. An innovative idea might fail, but not being a grown brand a start-up company has no reputation to lose. They simply have no reputation at all, yet, instead they are trying to build one. This is why they can cope with the fear of failure more easily than existing companies. Quite honestly, what is at stake? What is the worst thing that can happen? The project does not grow, it fails. It might even crash. This however doesn't prevent another new idea to be developed. If a grown company fails, however, that is a real problem. Existing sectors and jobs might be affected. Nothing like that can happen to a start-up, so this makes them quite attractive.

Start-up projects thrive on establishing new business models. It's not in their responsibility to redesign and improve existing products without taking any risks and without making any mistakes. Their goal is to create completely new business models, and they hunger for success.

They can work under fewer restrictions and obligations. Injecting a new idea into a grown and rigid corporate structure takes much longer. And it is way more complex, as there are hundreds of obstacles to overcome. Executives and managers who have faith in the idea must be found. Preserving and protecting existing assets are essential parts of a grown corporate's creed and mindset. Also, a ready business case must be presented first. Introducing new models into an established corporate structure is a much slower process than doing the same in a young company. In a start-up, you simply start with a new topic. Things happen faster. The founders invest all their power and resources into the project.

For a large company, it is thus easier to try out a new idea within a start-up – or buy a successful one – than to build an innovative product far from their own core expertise themselves. With the potential benefit for a large company being so high, start-up success rate being so low, and so much money being out there, real competition for successful start-up business models can be observed.

4.13 Digitization Duality

Digitization changes our lives in two aspects. On the one hand, it offers complete automatization and efficiency. Digitization automates everything that can be automatized – including cognitive systems that automate our thinking.

On the other hand, automatization leads to previously unknown types of services, products and business models. This creates a battle for reaching customers on a specific sales channel. More and more providers are competing for one and the same customer. This will eventually lead to the situation that the customer concludes: "I do not want to see ten different merchants making me offers anymore, I want to have one personal assistant who knows about my preferences, behavior and interests and that uses this knowledge to choose what I really want. Pretty much like a travel agency agent, who takes care of my journey including flights, hotel, rental car, train-to-flight and lounge access as well as travel and cancellation insurances."

4.14   The Bottom Line: Deploy or Invent New Business Models

Start shaping or be shaped. The high velocity that our market places evolve with compels every entrepreneur to keep pace. Idleness means downfall. Only those able to reinvent themselves over and over again are able to compete. Every provider of goods or services is forced to launch new business models and innovations.

Digitization has made the world smaller. Everyone can communicate with everybody else. And compete with everybody else – this made everyone a potential competitor. But the world has also become more complex, so everyone needs everybody else as a partner. I can build my own channels to reach my customers or use my partners' channels. I am literally forced to join forces, as partnerships will let me grow. That is just how Uber or AirBnB did it: They created an ecosystem and shared it with everyone. In this business model, the partners earn money as you earn money. And it is so attractive that many partners lined up.

There is no more market place that I have to go to. An unleashed market place is everywhere. Any business can explode or be suffocated by others. Attracting customers to my own product is hard work and art at the same time.

Today, the market place with all its products comes to me as a customer. It is always there, at any day or night time. It pervades my routines and daily life. It is the Internet. As soon as I am online, I am at the market place right away. That market place is amorphous. It's moving. And I have to move with it.

Part III
Digital Society

Preface: So Far, so Bad – the Complexity-Fear Dilemma in Cybersecurity and Its Lesson for Digitalization at Large

5

Sandro Gaycken

The new waves of the ongoing digital revolution are certainly of high importance to everyone. New markets are created in a highly dynamic fashion, with the industrialized West and its backbone of technology manufacturers undergoing fundamental changes in the coming years, and new products flood our lives, whether directly as consumer goods or, a step before that, as baseline technologies, infrastructures, production machinery, new cars, new drug pumps, new reactors, parts of our formerly dumb and blind environment of "old tech". In sum, businesses and technologies in Germany and Europe are faced with enormous options for change – and their according sets of opportunities and threats.

Yet while everyone agrees that something great and, in a business sense, oceanic is under way, the question whether we will master this change and benefit from it, economically and individually, is somehow open. All commercial benefactors from industry captain to startup hipster agree, of course, that they do or will master this new surge in digitalization. And most of them, to be fair, try hard. But is it really enough? And do they try in the right way?

These questions are very hard to answer. Success is difficult to measure, at any rate, and many paradigms are young and technically inasmuch as commercially still in their infancy. However, we may be able to learn some lessons from other fields of IT with more history to them.

One such field is cybersecurity. The insecurity of computers is known for quite some time, and Germany has been part and parcel of the games surrounding the attempts to generate cybersecurity (or IT-security, as the old folks say). We have had our share of attackers, of technologies and policies, of responsibilities and laws, of small and medium IT-security companies, of research, and of larger government and large enterprise units

S. Gaycken (✉)
ESMT
Berlin, Germany
e-mail: Sandro.Gaycken@esmt.org

© Springer-Verlag GmbH Germany 2018
C. Linnhoff-Popien et al. (eds.), *Digital Marketplaces Unleashed*,
https://doi.org/10.1007/978-3-662-49275-8_5

concerned with this problem. We know of terrible risks, like mass surveillance, attacks prepared for nuclear weapons, or SAP-outages at outraging costs of 22 million US-Dollars per minute. We even have one of the oldest federal institutions in this field, the Bundesamt für Sicherheit in der Informationstechnik (BSI), devising and implementing laws for more than 20 years now.

A clear set of conditions, specifications, powerful actors, options, threats, opportunities. So did we secure our computers? Did we maybe even generate a market out of this huge opportunity? How did we fare?

The answer is: not so well. In very lengthy, tedious, slow and complicated procedures full of rivalries, politics and interests, we managed to come up with only tiny bits of progress on standards and laws, both still difficult to implement, and a few niche security products. And that's it. Years into what can be called an elevated state of this problem and its underlying market, we still don't have proper security. The technologies are piecemeal and patchwork with limited functionality, understanding is still very low, the market is not any more mature than ten years ago, research and development have grown, but are stuck to conservative paradigms and face difficulties when trying to become industrialized. And still there are only a very few (real) experts.

The situation may look different on glamorous reports and slidedecks. But by and large, measured by the distance to actual 99% security, it's failure. Neither the technical, nor the regulatory, industrial or managerial part has performed well. Despite the fact that there are technical, regulatory, industrial and managerial options to achieve 99% security. Disruptive options, to be sure. But isn't that the word of the day in any presentation or brochure on digitalization? So what happened? Why didn't we manage to disrupt cybersecurity? And could such a drama repeat itself in other areas of digitalization?

Among a larger set of particular issues, two closely entangled core problems appeared at the black heart of the cybermisery: complexity and fear. Complexity was and continues to be a fundamental obstacle to anything digital. Any product more complex than a dogfood app requires many different and very high levels of expertise. Decision-makers in industry and government usually don't have this kind of knowledge. Unfortunately, in cybersecurity, the field is so complex that even the best experts in the field hardly understand more than their own vertical and a few topics left and right. As an additional problem, experts in a highly complex field enjoy a lot of options to craft their opinion on both, the problem and the solution. In turn, the few experts capable to master larger pieces of the puzzle tend to disagree quickly on details. The end-result is a zoo of opinions, analyses and potential solutions, with no chance for the lay person to judge between different approaches. Independent, objective methods to measure problems and solutions comparatively are almost impossible to develop at present.

So how do we decide what to pursue and what not? At this point, fear comes to play. German Angst, one might say, which has developed its very own culture among German engineers, managers and regulators. That culture is one of success: Germans hate to fail, and failure is punished, explicitly and implicitly. As a result, technological design, managerial decision-making, the development of business models and the crafting of laws all are extremely cautious, consensual and highly incremental.

When confronted with a highly complex problem with no definite answer, this mentality drives perceptions and procedures. People in charge always gleam left and right what their peers are doing, to do the very same with a slightly different pitch to it. This way, they can easily disperse responsibility to "what everybody does". On more expensive topics, they call in dozens of assessments and evaluations, simply to compare them for overlap, in order to refer to "most experts". Or they delegate the problem away to a large company or a unit or agency in charge, even if that entity has no good track record itself. Hackers are so used to this mechanism, they invented their own description for this procedure. It's the "OGP"-, the "other guys problem"-strategy. In a variation of this OGP-strategy, disruptive ideas are being tosses around among each other until their executive level has forgotten about it, and it can be dropped safely to return to the old paths of maximum diffusion of responsibility.

The list of evasive maneuvers could be continued for a few more pages. Over time, these evasion create dangerous path dependencies, implicit tolerance and wrong sub-incentives, and bring forth a self-fulfilling prophecy. With a constant mentality to shun the unknown and shine the known, the least controversial solutions gain ever more "support", rendering them ever more "accepted" for the lay persons eye, followed by a lot of "told you so" from those generating this effect. But in truth, this is just the center of gravity of a defective decision-making process.

Now does this apply to digitalization at large? Most likely it does. Digitalization is complex, especially its new surge, risk and money are involved, and the people in charge are of the same kind and breed. Cheap, consensual, boring and incremental solutions will quite likely always have an upper hand in the coming years. And that will clearly put others in the lead of this revolution. We may be bound to lose this race.

A recommendation would be that executives, regulators, entrepreneurs, researchers will have to start their innovative process earlier and at a different place. Before disrupting technologies or markets, they have to disrupt the complexity-fear-dilemma. And they have to disrupt it in an invisible and somewhat intangible layer, they have to change their culture. This, of course, should be done with great care, only in solidly separated units and in phased models with room for trial and error. But setting up exotic enclaves, where "the rules" don't count and where incentives are upside-down, may have to be an important requirement for future growth and survival as a technology innovator.

The present book will hopefully support this process or, even better, provide smarter ideas than this one. At any rate, it must be seen as a guide to master a new field we shouldn't yet consider mastered, an important voice of criticism and encouragement, and, most importantly, a call to practice: to act, to do, to try, to fail and finally, to win.

Valuation, Recognition, and Signaling in the Digital Public Sphere: the TED Talk Ranking Ecosystem

6

Heidi Gautschi and Gianluigi Viscusi

Abstract

In the past few years a new actor, who is playing an increasingly important role in ranking ideas and the scholars who share them, has emerged: the TED organization. While debate has surrounded popular academic research output rankings such as, impact factor, h-index, Times Higher Education Ranking and Google Scholar, the TED Talk phenomenon does not seem to have garnered the same amount of interest. We argue that TED talks can be seen as a social form of ranking which specifically affects higher education and potentially research and innovation through decisions on what to invest in next. The TED organization then becomes a gatekeeper in the production and the cultural valuation of symbolic goods and social practices, especially with regard to research and innovation worth spreading. In this chapter we attempt to demonstrate how the TED ecosystem is a marketplace for ideas. By applying the concepts of recognition, valuation and signaling, we show how the TED ecosystem functions as both a means of gaining recognition for speakers and their ideas, but also provides a means of ranking those ideas and projects by signaling their importance by inclusion in the curated collection of talks accessible on the TED website.

H. Gautschi (✉) · G. Viscusi
École Polytechnique Fédérale de Lausanne
Lausanne, Switzerland
e-mail: heidi.gautschi@epfl.ch

G. Viscusi
e-mail: gianluigii.viscusi@epfl.ch

© Springer-Verlag GmbH Germany 2018
C. Linnhoff-Popien et al. (eds.), *Digital Marketplaces Unleashed*,
https://doi.org/10.1007/978-3-662-49275-8_6

6.1 Introduction

With the advent of the Internet and its potential for multidirectional, interactive communication, we have seen the emergence of a digital public sphere. Numerous websites these days are set up in such a way as to encourage Internet mediated participation in ongoing discussions.

In the past few years a new actor, who is playing an increasingly important role in ranking ideas and the scholars who share them, has emerged: the TED organization. While debate has surrounded popular academic research output rankings such as, impact factor, h-index, Times Higher Education Ranking and Google Scholar, the TED Talk phenomenon does not seem to have garnered the same amount of interest. We argue that TED talks can be seen as a social form of ranking which specifically affects higher education [1] and potentially research and innovation through decisions on what to invest in next. In this paper, we posit the following: TED talks can be considered to be a valuation device, in part because of their popularity. The TED organization then becomes a gatekeeper in the production and the cultural valuation of symbolic goods and social practices [2], especially with regard to research and innovation worth spreading. A valuation device is a process by which something, in our case ideas and innovations, is evaluated and ranked.

Valuation can be studied and observed in two different ways, either by looking at categorization and/or at legitimation [3]. As such, we argue that TED Talks form a ranking ecosystem encompassing both categorization (the multitude of ranking and ratings available internally and externally – which refer back to TED. These include number of views, popularity, inclusion in playlists etc.) and legitimation (recognition-based valuation). To this end, we use the concept of recognition [4] as an interpretative lens, specifically focusing on "achievement" as a form of recognition which may be gained by participating in a TED event. In short, giving a TED talk, especially one that has a large number of views, increases both the TED talker's recognition and the recognition of whatever discovery, or innovation it was about. And, this within both the digital public sphere made up of a diverse group of people and potentially the TED talker's professional community.

In addition to recognition, we also focus on a sociological interpretation of signaling theory [5] in order to make sense of the categorical aspects making up what we define to be the TED talk ranking ecosystem. Considering the integration of IBM Watson to "find nuanced answers to your big questions", it can be argued that TED is actually a digital infrastructure for selection and promotion of research in science and innovation. Furthermore, Gambetta (2005) raised important points regarding signaling which we believe are applicable to TED talks: "*under what conditions can a signal be rationally believed by the receiver, when the signaller has an interest in merely pretending that something is true, when he has in other words an interest in mimicking truthfulness in some way?*" Given this, it is important to study the role signaling plays in the TED talk ranking ecosystem and its relationship to recognition, providing insights on the challenges as well as the potential transformation drivers for academic institutions and R&D departments in private companies.

The Chapter is structured as follows. We first provide a discussion of our theoretical background, thus explaining in more detail certain concepts and terms we use to analyze the TED talk ecosystem. We then provide a brief history of the TED organization, which leads us to then further describe the structure and reach of the TED ecosystem. Finally, we open up a discussion about the relationship between signaling, recognition and valuation based on a conceptual model.

6.2   Theoretical Background

6.2.1   Public Sphere and Valuation

Public speaking acts serve four basic purposes: to *reaffirm cultural values*, to increase democratic participation, to bring about justice and to *promote social change* [6]. With the increasing presence of the media as a place where ideas are circulated and debated, increasing importance has been placed on the "art" of public speaking. The presence of the media means a larger, more diverse public, which will change the delivery and content of a speech. A timely example would be the popularity of the TED talk and the proliferation of affiliated events around the world. Public speech acts occur in public and as such can be considered to be part of the public sphere.

According to Habermas [7], the public sphere is both a physical and metaphorical space where public opinion is formed outside of the structure of the State and the private sphere represented by the family. It is an intermediary space. The public sphere can be conceived of as a network of people, physical places and media outlets that circulate ideas that are debated in a rational and critical manner. In short, the public sphere is a space where the focus is on public discourse not on the person speaking [8]. Habermas [9] retraces the evolution of the public sphere and reaches the conclusion that the original "bourgeois public sphere" has been distorted, thus public discussion has been turned into a commodity [10]. Furthermore, the advent of the Internet has further transmogrified the publicness of the public sphere into *publicity* [10] while increasing the public's ability to join in the discussion. It would appear that the TED ecosystem is an example of an Internet mediated public sphere, which we call the TED talk sphere.

Taking these issues into account, we further argue that TED talks can be considered to be a valuation device. According to Doganova et al. [11], the sociology of valuation looks at how "the value or values of something are established, assessed, negotiated, provoked, maintained, constructed and/or contested." Valuation can be studied and observed in two different ways, either by looking at categorization (classification systems, stabilization, institutionalization), or at legitimation (the mechanisms by which an object gains value, recognition of value by you and me) [3]. The TED organization thus becomes a gatekeeper in production and the cultural valuation of symbolic goods and social practices, determining social status and class [12].

6.2.2 Recognition

Recognition has been defined according to three main dimensions: equal respect awarded to all agents capable of autonomy; esteem due to one's achievements, emphasizing difference and the uniqueness of specific and cultural features; recognition of concrete individuality such as love and friendship [13]. In general, one of the key characteristics of recognition consists in the affirmation of *positive qualities* of single individuals or groups [14]. Further elaborating from the Hegelian argument that we gain self-consciousness only through a process of mutual recognition, Brandom [15] claims that this elementary form of recognition, on the one hand, allows for the creation and preservation of a subject's identity, granting others the status of an epistemic authority; on the other hand, it denotes a basic normative attitude and allows one to build a normative space of reasons, commitments and entitlements, enforcing the subject as being capable of responsibilities and exercising authority [13]. Taking these issues into account, it is worth noting that Honneth [14] points out distinct stages of recognition along which individuals gain self-confidence, self-respect and self-esteem, the latter related to personal "achievements".

How, TED Talks contribute to recognition as an institutional fabric of a person's identity, granting others the status of an epistemic authority is still little explored and worth investigating.

6.2.3 Signaling Theory

Signaling theory attempts to understand a two pronged communication problem that we have all encountered: How can the receiver (the person receiving information from a specific source) determine whether, or not the signaler (the person communicating the information) is telling the truth? How can the signaler persuade the receiver that he is telling the truth, regardless of the truthfulness of his communication [16]?

Much of what we want to know about someone is hidden from us. There is an information asymmetry. How then, do we discern the truthfulness of what is being communicated to us? Signaling theory, through analysis of a variety of situations, attempts to respond to this question.

One way of "signaling" who we are and what we stand for, what our beliefs are and our moral standards, occurs through what communication scholars call nonverbal communication. This form of communication encompasses body language, dress, smell, the environment within which the communication occurs, nervous tics ... In signaling theory, these elements are divided into signals and signs. "Signals are the stuff of *purposive* communication. Signals are any observable features of an agent which are intentionally displayed for the purpose of raising the probability the receiver assigns to a certain state of affairs (...) Signs are a different concept from signals. Signs can be just anything in the environment that is perceptible and by being perceived happens to modify our beliefs about something or someone. But signs are dormant potential signals. They are the raw material of signals. The basic form of the sign—signal transformation is that a signaler takes steps to display the sign [16]."

A sign can become a signal when the signaler purposefully displays the sign. For example, I happen to have a nasty scar on my arm that I normally keep covered up. However, in situations where I want to appear tough, I purposefully display the scar. Depending on how I received the scar (an accident, a knife wound during a fight) displaying the scar in specific situations could be an example of emitting a false signal—one that is strategically meant to misrepresent and mislead.

Another key element in signaling theory is the cost of emitting a signal depending on whether, or not the signaler is being truthful or not. Let us consider two types of signalers, someone who is truthfully emitting a signal and someone who is not. If only the truthful signaler can emit the signal, then we are in a state of "equilibrium". "In this equilibrium signals are unambiguous, and the receiver is perfectly informed [16]." In the opposite case, when both types of signalers can afford to signal the same thing, then the receiver is no better informed than before the signaling occurred [16]. In real life, we generally encounter situations that are somewhere in between these two extremes. We are "informed, but not perfectly [16]."

6.3   TED

The TED (technology, education, design) conference, cofounded by Richard Saul Wurman in 1984, was meant to be a one off conference which brought together influential people in the areas of technology, education and design. In 1990, the second TED conference was organized and from then on, the conference was held twice a year. Wurman curated TED until 2000 and then sold it to UK entrepreneur, Chris Anderson. Anderson coined TED's tagline, "ideas worth spreading" [17]. In 2006, the TED website was launched and it currently hosts a selection of over 2000 talks divided into categories like "jaw dropping" and "beautiful". Furthermore, according to Sugimoto et al. [18] the TED Talks website is the fourth most popular technology website in the world.

While the TED organization offers more than just talks, the talks are what they are best known for. A typical TED talk lasts 18 min. Close attention is paid to not just the content, but also the narrative structure and delivery. Speakers are provided coaches so as to deliver high impact talks. People present official TED talks at a limited number of venues, either at one of the two main conferences, or at the TED global conference. There is a selection process for choosing TED talkers and audience members so as to maintain quality and diversity [19] After conferences and other TED talk venues, the organization then carefully selects which talks to upload onto their website. "Most TED talks are edited, lightly but carefully." [20]. Viewers are able to stream the talks, or download them. And, like most sites on the social web, viewers are able to interact with the talk by liking it, commenting on it, sharing it and rating it [21]. Aside from the talks, the TED organization, however, is comprised of numerous ventures, such was TEDEd which provides playlists to use in the classroom, a TED-Watson collaboration, a weekly show on NPR and a start-up competition.

TED's flagship product is the talk, an 18-minute, carefully crafted speech performed in front of a live audience. The TED talk is offering a re-packaged public speaking format that uses identifiable and well known rhetorical devices that have been studied in public speaking classes and put into practice by public speakers [22]. A large part of the TED website is dedicated to providing access to a curated group of talks. Talks are also accessible through other media outlets, such as a dedicated youtube channel, iTunes, the TED talk app and a few digital television providers.

6.3.1 TED Ecosystem

In this section, we describe the various products and partnerships of the TED organization. We start by describing the events hosted, or affiliated with TED and then move on to the other types of initiatives the organization engages in. We conclude the section by briefly outlining the layers of publics the organization touches through its products and partnerships.

Official TED talks performed and recorded during a number of events, in front of a live audience. TED hosts an annual 5-day conference in Vancouver, British Columbia every year. 70 speakers are invited to give talks on the main stage in front of 1000 audience members, who have applied to attend the conference. However, during this annual event, additional people also give talks on smaller stages—selected TED fellows, the best of TED-Ed club members and selected TED residents. There is also an annual TEDGlobal conference, which is organized like the Vancouver event. The most recent TEDGlobal event was held in Geneva. It is now possible to subscribe to TEDLive, a livestream service that allows you to view the current conference, as well as past conferences, in their entirety.

TED also organizes three other special events which are open to the public: TEDSummit, TEDWomen and TEDYouth. TEDSummit is a 5-day event with 111 speakers (popular past speakers and new speakers), interactive workshops and community building events. TEDSummit is, according to the TED website, for the most engaged members of the TED community. TEDWomen is a 3-day annual conference about, well, women and issues that concern them. TEDYouth is an annual 1-day conference catering to secondary school students.

The best talks from these events appear online. There are numerous other TED-branded venues where people can give talks, such as TEDx events, TEDxsalon and corporate TEDx events. In actuality, however, the link between these events and the official ones is tenuous. Still, the best TEDx talks do appear on the official TED website in two different ways. The very best are integrated into the official TED talk list. Those relegated to the TEDx section of the website are less interactive for the viewer, thus it appears that the TED organization is setting the agenda in terms of what talks garner the most reactions in the

TED talk sphere consequently further influencing the flows of information and the internal hierarchy among talks.

A TEDx event can be organized by an individual, an organization, or a community. A standard TEDx event cannot exceed 100 audience members, must include screening of 2 official TED talks and the event can only take place during 1 day. TEDx events come in many flavors: University events, Youth events, Women events (these can only occur during the official TEDWomen event), Library events, TEDxLive (simulcast of a TED conference) Internal events and Business events. For communities in the developing world, TED has kindly put together TEDx in a box. There are also TEDxSalon events, smaller, more focused events, that must occur three times in a given year. TEDx events do not have to be limited to 100 audience members. An organizer, however, who wishes to organize a bigger event must attend an official TED conference. These are expensive events and range from $2495 for the 3-day TEDWomen event to $8500 for the 5-day events.

The TED talk has proven to be sufficiently popular (the top viewed talk has been watched 39 million times), that the organization has begun using the talk as a building block for developing additional products and services.

In keeping with its mission of spreading ideas, TED now has a dedicated TEDEd platform where teachers and university professors can develop lesson plans built around a TED talk, a youtube video, or a TEDEd original (an animated segment using educators' ideas and words). To date, 185,552 lesson plans have been created. TED has made using TED talks in the classroom easy, thus inciting educators to adopt them as teaching tools and consequently expanding the TED talk sphere to include students from around the world. TED has recently partnered with the publisher, Wiley, to produce subject specific instructor manuals built around a series of TED talks. In this case, the talks function as virtual guest lecturers.

TED has partnered with the publisher, Simon & Schuster, to produce short books based on the most popular talks in the collection. This is an interesting partnership in that the organization is partnering with a representative of a traditional medium for disseminating information. The end result, however, is a book with a twist. Recognizing that 18 min isn't enough time to delve deeply into a subject, TED Books provide speakers with the opportunity to develop the subject of their talk in a short book format. Indeed, the tagline for these books is "short enough to read in one sitting."

The American radio station, NPR (National Public Radio), also broadcasts a weekly one-hour radio show dedicated to a specific theme and built around TED talks. The radio show includes additional content, mainly interviews with the TED talkers included in that week's show. This radio show, however, is not a direct means to accessing TED talks and so, we consider it to be a partnership, as well as an example of TED's expanding reach. (NPR is known for its somewhat highbrow audience.)

With the ambient popularity of the TED talk and the organization's overarching mission, TED has also begun providing companies with internal TED-like conferences. The goal of these TEDInstitute conferences is to identify thought leaders amongst the employees and give them a platform where they can circulate their ideas. This service has a hefty price tag, $1.5 million [29]. In return, TED provides coaching and guidance in producing an internal event. As with other TED events, the best TEDInsitute talks appear in the online collection, with the company's approval.

TED has recently partnered with IBM Watson to provide a Watson powered platform that, after signing in with your Facebook or TED account, allows you to ask questions and receive answers in the form of short clips from a selection of TED talks. The TED-Watson platform also provides personalized playlists based on your social posts. Recently, TED has partnered with Wikipedia. TED will provide the open source encyclopedia with metadata from its collection of talks to increase the accuracy of Wikipedia's entries.

The TED studio produces content for companies in a TED-like style. TED also offers consulting services which bring together speakers who have given a TED talk and company employees in order to spur on human-centered collaboration.

TED's primary focus appears to be the ability of a well-crafted talk to increase the dissemination of information. As such, through a number of different initiatives, the organization also provides ways in which individuals can learn the necessary skills to produce a TED style talk. TED Ed clubs are a clear example of this type of initiative. Students in secondary schools around the world can apply to start such a club. In 13 sessions, club members learn how to write and deliver a powerful 4-minute speech. The club's final session is a TED Ed club event where members give their talks. Teachers can nominate the best students to perform at the annual TEDYouth event. Italy's minister of education has recently advocated that TED Ed clubs be created in all of Italy's secondary schools.

The TED organization also nominates 400 fellows per year and has recently launched the TEDResidents program that will host 28 people for 4 months. Fellows receive access to meet ups, workshops and public relations training for communicating their ideas effectively. The best talks are presented at one of the official TED events, but more importantly fellows become lifelong members of the TED community.

6.4 Discussion

Characteristics that are opaque indicators of research projects and individual researcher's quality can become, through TED, credible signals and screening criteria, thereby affecting their valuation (see [23] for a close argument on signaling and screening of new firms in emerging markets).

Fig. 6.1 shows the conceptual model for interpreting as well as empirically investigating the TED-related signaling environment and the role of recognition. The signaling timeline is adapted from [24]. It is worth noting that recognition as achievement has a role both before the signaling process starts and during the feedback phase at $t = 3$.

As pointed out by [25], TED has the features of an infrastructure for recognition in the form of achievements "worth" spreading, where individual speakers gain self-esteem and a new self-image, yet encoded in terms of marketing content, leading the achievement principle to 'marketize' itself. In actuality, the TED Infrastructure frames the *property* the

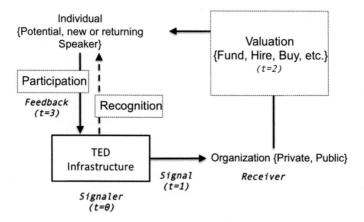

Fig. 6.1 Signaling environment and recognition (*t* time)

signaler (t = 0) wants to *signal* for a receiver at t = 1 (key elements for signaling pointed out by [16]); although generic, the *receiver* is in principle any organization (either private or public) capable of valuing the worth of each individual speaker's proposal. Thus, in a sense the TED Infrastructure is the co-signaler at t = 0. The TED Infrastructure signals recognition through inclusion of TED talks on the official website, in playlists etc. The individual speaker may, or may not be chosen by the receiver as worthy of funding, etc., depending on the outcome of the signal at t = 1. In case of actual valuation, the individual provides the received *feedback* to the TED Infrastructure (t = 3) in terms of news related to the outcome of the valuation after participation at a TED event either as i) a new TED presentation on the new project or ii) number of views of the previous TED presentation as a consequence of the new project(s). This increases the appeal of TED for other individuals looking for recognition of their achievements, thus creating a self-reinforcing mechanism of the TED Infrastructure itself. This mechanism makes the TED Infrastructure different from traditional conference systems, where recognition is limited to a certain domain or audience and is not a "public sphere". Furthermore, a TED talker already has to have a certain status in order to be chosen to be a TED talker, and among other ways this status is achieved in academic and practitioner conferences; thus academic and practitioners conferences are part of the background for the individual proposals' ideas "worth" spreading.

6.5 Conclusion

Cognitive-cultural economy or cognitive capitalism emphasizes the role of computers and digital technologies first in the valuation of cognitive tasks (the cognitive processing of information) as the core element of production systems. These tasks require specific intellectual skills and competences. Cognitive-cultural economy or cognitive capitalism also focuses on the contribution of digital technologies in the displacement of the cognitive tasks from the human jurisdiction [26]. Vercellone [27], makes reference to the Marxian notion of *general intellect*[1] and points out that the key dimension of this mutation concerns the hegemony of knowledge created by a diffuse intellectuality. This leads to the consequent supremacy of the *"knowledge of living labor over knowledge incorporated in fixed capital and in corporate organization"*. In turn, there is a move from *"the static management of resources to the dynamic management of knowledge"*. It is important to keep in mind that intellectuality does not refer primarily to expertise acquired through education or books, by scientists or engineers, but first and foremost to the simple faculty of thought, memory, and verbal communication, as these are the necessary elements of productive co-operation in a cognitive cultural economy. In this context, the communication industry is actually the *industry of the means of production* [28].

Taking these issues into account, in this chapter we have attempted to demonstrate how the TED ecosystem is a marketplace for ideas. By applying the concepts of recognition, valuation and signaling, we show how the TED ecosystem functions as both a means of gaining recognition for speakers and their ideas, but also provides a means of ranking those ideas and projects by signaling their importance by inclusion in the curated collection of talks accessible on the TED website. Furthermore, we argue that the TED infrastructure is also a new form of public sphere where public discourse, in the form of TED talks, is debated, ranked and rated by a broad audience. It remains to be seen how this new type of ranking mechanism impacts research funding and policies in the long term.

References

1. H. Shema, The Impact of TED Talks, Sci. Am., 2014.
2. P. Bourdieu, Les trois états du capital culturel, 30 Hrsg., Actes Rech. Sci. Soc., 1979, pp. 3–6.
3. M. Lamont, "Towards a Comparative Sociology of Valuation and Evaluation," in *Annu. rev. Sociol., Annual Reviews*, Bd. 38, 2012, pp. 201–221.
4. A. Honneth, The I in We: Studies in the Theory of Recognition, Polity, 2014.
5. D. Gambetta, "More Hedgehog than Fox – The common thread in the study of criminals, taxi drivers and suicide bombers," in *unpubl. Present. Nuff. Sociol. Semin. Oxford*, 2005.
6. J. Alberts, T. Nakayama und J. Martin, Human Communication in Society, 3 Hrsg., Pearson, 2014.
7. J. Habermas, The structural transformation of the public sphere: an inquiry into a category of bourgeois society, MIT Press, 1991.
8. J. Habermas, Public space and political public sphere – the biographical root of two motifs in my thought, Commem. Lect., 2004.
9. J. Habermas, Structural Transformation of the Public Sphere, Cambridge: Polity Press, 2003.
10. P. Scannell, Media and Communication, London: Sage, 2013.

---

[1] As pointed out by [28, p. 106] the general intellect includes "formal and informal knowledge, imagination, ethical propensities, mindsets, and *'linguistic games'*", becoming *"attribute of living labor when the activity of latter consists increasingly of linguistic services"*.

11. L. Doganova, M. Giraudeau, C.-F. Helgesson, H. Kjellberg, F. Lee, A. Mallard, A. Mennicken, F. Muniesa, E. Sjörgren et al., Valuation studies and the critique of valuation, Linköping University Electronic Press, 2014.
12. P. Bourdieu, La Distinction. Critique sociale du jugement, Paris: Les Éditions de Minuit, 1979.
13. M. Iser, "Recognition," Stanford Encycl. Philos. (Fall 2013 Ed., E. N. Zalta Ed.), [Online]. Available: http://plato.stanford.edu/archives/fall2013/entries/recognition/.
14. A. Honneth, The Struggle for Recognition: The Moral Grammar of Social Conflicts, Cambridge: MIT Press, 1996.
15. R. Brandom, Making it Explicit: Reasoning, Representing, and Discursive Commitment, Cambridge: Harvard University Press, 1994.
16. D. Gambetta, "Signalling," in Oxford Handb. Anal. Sociol., Oxford, UK, Oxford University Press, 2011.
17. N. Heller, "Listen and Learn," in New Yorker, New York, 2012.
18. C. Sugimoto, M. Thelwall, V. Larivière, A. Tsou, P. Mongeon und B. Macaluso, Scientists Popilarizing Science: Characteristics and Impact of TED Talk Presenters, Bd. 8, PLoS One, 2013.
19. TED, "Debunking TED myths I How TED works I Our Organization I About I TED," 2016. [Online]. Available: https://www.ted.com/about/our-organization/how-ted-works/debunking-ted-myths. [Accessed 08 01 2016].
20. TED, "TED Talks I Programs & Initiatives I About I TED," [Online]. Available: https://www.ted.com/about/programs-initiatives. [Accessed 08 01 2016].
21. C. Sugimoto und M. Thelwall, "Scholars on soap boxes: Science communication and dissemination in TED videos," in J. Am. Soc. Inf. Sci. Technol., Bd. 64, 2013, pp. 663–674.
22. L. Ford-Brown, DK Guide to Public Speaking, 2 Hrsg., Pearson, 2013.
23. W. Sanders und S. Boivie, "Sorting Things out: Valuation of New Firms in Uncertain Markets," in Strateg. Manag. J., Bd. 25, Wiley, 2004, pp. 167–186.
24. B. Connelly, S. Certo, R. Ireland und C. Reutzel, "Signaling Theory: A Review and Assessment," J. Manag., Bd. 37, pp. 39–67, 2011.
25. H. Gautschi und G. Viscusi, "Information-based recognition: TED talks and the institutional fabric of valuable innovation," in EGOS (European Gr. Organ. Stud. Colloq.), Nales, Italy, 2016.
26. F. Levy und R. Murnane, The New Division of Labor – How Computers Are Creating the Next Job Market, Princeton, New Jersey, USA: Princeton University Press, 2005.
27. C. Vercellone, From Formal Subsumption to General Intellect: Elements for a Maxist Reading of the Thesis of Cognitive Capitalism, Bd. 15, Hist. Mater., 2007, pp. 13–36.
28. P. Virno, A Grammar Of The Multitude – For an Analysis of Contemporary Forms of Life, Cambridge, MA, USA: MIT Press – Foreign Agents, 2004.
29. C. Winter, "The TEDification of Corporate America," Businessweek, New York, 2014.

Consumers' Digital Self-Determination: Everything Under Control?

7

Britta Krahn and Christian Rietz

Abstract

The analysis and use of steadily growing sets of data from business processes and consumer interactions and the intelligent linking of data provide tremendous development potential for the digital economy, but also involve risks that are widely discussed in association with data privacy. At the same time, of course, consumers also benefit from innovative and new products and services which are only made possible by intelligent data analysis. But when digital data becomes the raw material for value added on the one hand and appealing products for connected life and work on the other hand it appears that these principles alone do not suffice any longer. Not least because due to technical reasons alone the cross-linking of economy and society generates large amounts of new data that are often not even acknowledged by consumers and the creation of which they cannot prevent. Up until now, there has only been insufficient systematic assessment of the consumers' experience associated with their data sovereignty, digital self-determination respectively. However, the exercise of digital self-determination by the consumers themselves and a corresponding rise of awareness is a key prerequisite for acting confidently in the digital world of the Internet of Things and in digital business processes. The following study provides answers to the following questions related to consumers' digital self-determination: What is a coherent, plausible concept of 'digital self-determination'? How can we measure (dimensions

B. Krahn (✉)
Bonn-Rhein-Sieg University of Applied Sciences
Rheinbach, Germany
e-mail: britta.krahn@h-brs.de

C. Rietz
University of Cologne
Cologne, Germany
e-mail: christian.rietz@uni-koeln.de

© Springer-Verlag GmbH Germany 2018
C. Linnhoff-Popien et al. (eds.), *Digital Marketplaces Unleashed*,
https://doi.org/10.1007/978-3-662-49275-8_7

of) 'digital self-determination'? What degree/amount of 'digital self-determination' do customers/users of digital media want? Based on the empirical results the concept of "digital self-determination" is described and accentuated. On the one hand, it can thus be a foundation for a consumer-centered adaptation of manufacturing or business processes. On the other hand, it can also provide implications for policy-steering considerations.

7.1 Introduction

The analysis and usage of steadily increasing data sets from business processes and from consumer interactions and the intelligent data linking offer enormous development potential for the digital economy [1]. Collection and analysis of consumer data by companies with regard to competitive advantages as such is not new [2]. However, with smartphones playing an increasingly crucial role – used by 63% of the German consumers aged 14 and over in 2015 with a continued upward trend [3] – the comprehensive data, which are not only collected but now also generated and transmitted by the users themselves, are evolving from an attractive byproduct to the center of a digital economy [4].

Meanwhile, the value chains of the digital and the analog world are inextricably linked; partially, digital channels even replace brick-and-mortar offerings so that not only the exchange of products and services but also the communication between provider and consumer is changing fundamentally. The new "currency" and foundation of many current business models is personal information in the form of socio-demographic data, location and movement data and, in particular, data concerning current and prior preferences, behaviors, habits, life situations, and needs. The exchange of information and data has not only become faster, more diverse, more comprehensive and more direct but also more automated, more specific to situations and persons than in the time before mobile Internet technologies.

This can be viewed favorably, as a development towards a "desired state, where knowledge of customers leads to ultra-efficient communication to exactly the right target audiences about product/service offerings perfectly matching the needs and desires of those same groups" [5, 6]. Actually, the conveniences of an offer tailored to changing individual situations and individual needs and which is easily accessible, consumable independent of time and location, maybe even via "one click" (such as Amazon for example), is a welcome simplification of everyday purchasing methods and purchasing decisions for many consumers. At the same time, in many cases this leads consumers to "willingly, even eagerly, part with intimate details of their lives" [7]. In this context, a rather imbalanced ratio can often be observed between the high value of the data divulged voluntarily and/or involuntarily and the low value of the consideration received, for instance in the form of information on web pages or apps or minor price savings [8–11]. On the one hand, there are great opportunities in respect of partaking and accessing digital or digitally issued products and services for a larger, and due to the increasing dissemination of mobile communication technologies still growing, share of consumers. Fully-informed consumers become business partners on an equal footing and can use their freedom of choice in the competition of the various providers to their advantage. On the other hand there are risks, among others with regard to the right of informational or "digital" self-determination[1], often also discussed in respect of data security [12]. Often in this context, rather oversimplified attributions draw attention, contrasting the risks of non-transparent, purely growth-driven business models, on the one hand, and, on the other hand, citizens' basic mistrust in "the Internet" and the market players involved. In view of highly complex technologies and value chains that are difficult to comprehend such simplifications are understandable. However, they do not befit a more differentiated approach to permanently and fast changing market environments which is needed if the adjustments to existing regulations in partially entirely new fields of interaction in the digital space are meant to balance the interests of providers and consumers. So far, the general effort of collecting, processing or using no personal data or as little personal data as possible has been considered one of the most appropriate means of data protection (such data avoidance and data economy is required by section 3a of the German Federal Data Protection Act, BDSG[2]).

Article 8 of the Charter of Fundamental Rights of the European Union also specifies everyone's right to protection of personal data on him/her.[3]

When digital data become, on the one hand, the raw material for value added and attractive products for connected life and work, it appears on the other hand, that these principles do not suffice any longer and/or need to be addressed. Not least because due to technical reasons alone the cross-linking of economy and society generates large amounts of new data, often even without consumers' acknowledgment and the creation of which they cannot prevent. Further, a (re-)assessment has to consider both the balance between the value for the consumer and the individual costs (and, in the next stage, the social costs) as well as how these short- and long-term effects relate to each other.

A further complication lies in the fact that this assessment changes relatively quickly in the course of the development of technology itself, human-machine-interaction, and the subjective user experience [13]. Therefore, regulations with regard to protecting personal data based on consumer-oriented digital self-determination should be flexible enough to enable appropriate responses to these developments. Another problem is that data pro-

---

[1] The right to informational self-determination "grants the individual's general authority to decide for themselves on the disclosure of their personal data. The right to informational self-determination is part of the general right of personality, protected by Article 2 (1) in conjunction with Article 1 (1) of the German Constitution. Therefore, it has constitutional status and constitutes an essential characteristic of human dignity and of the general freedom of action" (cf. http://www.bmi.bund.de/DE/Themen/Gesellschaft-Verfassung/Datenschutz/Informationelle-Selbstbestimmung/informationelle-selbstbestimmung_node.html).

[2] cf. Bundesdatenschutzgesetz, BDSG, p. 6, see https://www.gesetze-im-internet.de/bundesrecht/bdsg_1990/gesamt.pdf.

[3] cf. Charter of Fundamental Rights of the European Union, see http://www.europarl.europa.eu/charter/pdf/text_en.pdf.

tection, data security, and data usage issues are often viewed from what is feasible from a technical or legal point of view, yet the majority of the existing principles and consumer protection provisions originate in the analog world.

However, a strictly consumer-oriented consideration of the opportunities and risks of digitization to consumers and deriving corresponding measures is also made difficult by the fact that with many issues and problems it is not that easy to determine what constitutes a desirable consumer-orientation in that context. Consumers' security concerns and/or actual vulnerabilities on the one hand and extensive disclosure of personal data on the other hand often go together. This phenomenon, known as "Privacy Paradox" [14], is not restricted to the digital world, but it has greater significance here because although opportunities and risks are often much higher, the consequences are hardly comprehensible and data, once disclosed, are hard to erase. Also, it is possible that there no longer exists a direct ownership which would allow an immediate, direct intervention.

In this context, more attention should be given to the consumers' subjective experience with regard to their own data sovereignty and thus their digital self-determination; empirical approaches in particular are suited to shed light on this topic. But the latter are still seldom to be found. The systematic collection of consumers' own perception of their digital self-determination could for instance make a useful contribution to target audience-orientated communication, information, and awareness-raising as key prerequisite for acting competently in the world of the Internet of Things and digital business processes.

Against this background, a study commissioned by Deutsche Telekom AG in 2016 and conducted by the Cologne Center for Ethics, Rights, Economics, and Social Sciences of Health (CERES) explored the digital self-determination from the consumer perspective [15]. The study provides answers to the following key questions related to consumers' digital self-determination:

- "What is a coherent, plausible concept of 'digital self-determination'?" (philosophical interest)
- "How can we measure (dimensions of) 'digital self-determination'? Which empirical phenomena/causalities are part of this theoretical construct?" (social science interest)

7.2 Components of Digital Self Determination

Mertz et al. [15] build a comprehensive, theoretically determined framework model which provides, first, a definition of digital self-determination and, second, also derives influencing factors and determinants.[4] Accordingly, digital self-determination consists of the following dimensions

---

[4] Determinants include autonomy and overall self-determination, but also factors from the technical, socio-cultural, and person-related areas.

- competency,
- level of information,
- values,
- voluntariness,
- will-formation,
- options,
- behavior.

This comprehensive and theoretically sound analysis and definition of digital self-determination allows an empirical analysis of how consumers perceive and act on this very digital self-determination.

7.3   Empirical Findings on Digital Self-Determination

Ultimately, one could spend a long time pondering the term digital self-determination from the various specialist perspectives and background experiences, proposing working hypotheses on how consumers assess themselves with regard to self-determination and how this assessment affects actual (consumer) behavior. Up until now, there were no empirically substantiated answers in this area and many approaches dealing with the topic of self-determination from both providers' and consumers' perspective are rather anecdotal in nature. Only the study by Mertz et al. [15], surveying a representative sample of N = 1056 German Internet users, now provides answers on how "normal Internet users" assess themselves with regard to digital self-determination and its components (for sample composition [15]). Specifically, the study explores the following questions from a consumer perspective:

1. How *competent* do consumers feel conducting digital transactions?
2. How *informed* are consumers about the "rules of the game" in the digital world?
3. Which concerns and *expectations* do consumers associate with digitization?
4. Just how *"voluntary"* is the participation in the digital world at present?
5. How important is the Internet for the freedom of expression and *will-formation*?
6. Are consumers at the Internet's mercy or do they experience certain *options*?
7. How do consumers *behave* in the web? (from their perspective)

7.3.1   Competency

With respect to competency it is shown that most Internet users have the feeling that they find information which is relevant for them. With respect to finding information only 23% of the respondents state that it is difficult to find desired information. Another question, which is highly relevant in view of digital consumption, referred to evaluating the transparency of online ordering processes. 74% of the users know which required fields need to be filled in and which optional entries are possible. Yet, when ordering online, 27% of the respondents are uncertain as to at which point an order is binding, which indicates a certain level of uncertainty.

All in all, digital transactions are considered comprehensible and also the acquisition of information (no longer) poses a hurdle.

7.3.2 Level of Information

91% of the Internet users believe that it is important to know which personal data on them are stored. On the other hand, there is a huge mistrust particularly concerning these data as 82% of the users are convinced that most companies also share these data with other companies. Apparently this is not only a question of trust but also of transparency since 85% of the Internet users also firmly believe that it is not possible to find out which private companies or government agencies store their customers' personal data. This concern not only applies to the use of paid offerings, 87% of the Internet users also believe this to apply to free applications. 78% of the Internet users assume that data once published, stored respectively on the web cannot be removed by the users themselves; this result shows a significant "loss of control" over one's own data. Fitting in with this result is the finding that 84% of the respondents assume it to be very cumbersome to get information about the data stored about them. In general, 88% of the respondents would like to have an influence on the sharing of data in the web.

Most Internet users assume that many of their data are stored. Apart from the fact that most consumers would like to have an influence on the sharing of data, most users are rather helpless with regard to the amount of data stored and the control of these data.

7.3.3 Expectations of Digitization

As can be expected, the attitude towards digitization is ambivalent: 80% attribute great opportunities to the increasing digitization, but 55% of the respondents view the increasing digitization of everyday life with concern.

It is of major importance for 94% of the respondents that programs and applications are easy (and transparent) to handle, which includes high usability [13].

Apart from the classic "skepticism towards technology", it is shown that the opportunities of digitization have been recognized by all parts of the population. Progressive digitization can be supported by an ever improving usability and transparency.

7.3.4   Voluntariness

86% of the Internet users in Germany still assume that in all areas it is their decision whether they want to use digital media. Then again, 95% of the respondents acknowledge that dependency on modern technology and digitization in society will increase significantly. 74% of the respondents state that already today – despite the voluntariness of use, one is excluded from some areas of life without the use of digital technology. The other way round, 63% of the respondents assume that people not using digital media are excluded from many areas of social life. This also ties in with the finding that already 30% of the users have the feeling to miss out on something when they are not online.

Digitization with its impact is accepted by the Internet users. Ultimately, these findings indicate that there are no major obstacles to a further digitization of all areas of life.

7.3.5   Will-Formation

93% of the Internet users associate the Internet with the opportunity to engage with topics that are relevant to them personally. 79% of those surveyed describe the Internet as platform for freedom of speech which shows the high significance of the Internet related to fundamental democratic rights. There are, however, limits to the freedom of speech from the users' perspective: A significant proportion of 83% of the respondents is in favor of censoring hate comments and insults on the Internet. Meanwhile, the Internet has become highly important when it comes to researching information and shaping opinions. However, the representative Internet users' attitude appears unclear towards the question of how far freedom of speech may go in the Internet.

7.3.6   Options

Even though nearly one third of the Internet users surveyed has the feeling to miss out on something when they are not online (see above), 90% of the Internet users surveyed nevertheless consider it important to be deliberately offline sometimes or to be able to be offline. Equally clear is the finding that 92% of the respondents consider it legitimate to not install programs that access personal data. Yet here too, this shows ambivalence to the effect that 91% of the respondents assume that many of the Internet offerings can access personal data unnoticed. These findings again illustrate just how important transparency related to data collection and transfer really is. Ultimately, the Internet users just want more control in this area.

7.3.7   Behavior on the Internet

How do the Internet users behave? For instance, 74% of the Internet users state that they do not read the general terms and conditions at all when carrying out transactions. 92% of the users claim to take simple precautions (e. g. not reading attachments in emails with unknown senders). Only 27% of the users claim to take further measures for safeguarding identities on the Internet (e. g. deliberate mispresentation, setting up temporary email addresses).

Generally, there is sensitivity to the issue of data protection, on the operational level however, it is obvious that actions exceeding simple precautions are (still) quite rare.

7.3.8   Digital Self-Determination and Digital Market Places: Conclusion

The study by Mertz et al. [15] is making an important contribution to understanding digital self-determination from a consumer perspective in two ways. For one, the identified dimensions of the construct of digital self-determination illustrate more clearly the various characterizing facets. In addition to more person-related facets, such as competence and level of information, there are expectations as well as characteristics of interaction with the facets of voluntariness, options, and will-formation. In the overall context, the behavioral information can be seen as a kind of calibration of the aforementioned information, since the above-mentioned discrepancy between experience, perception, and behavior also becomes evident here.

The security of personal data on the Internet is questioned by a large part of the respondents, the opportunities to get information on personal data stored appears unsatisfactory and the respondents want more influence on the storage and usage of personal data. There is ground to be made up with regard to a consumer-friendly, transparent display of information about consequences and framework of web activities. However, when looking at many business models and the documentation of processes and conditions, it appears that transparency and traceability are of limited desirability for many companies. Possibly, this has to do with not wakening "sleeping dogs" and reinforcing consumers' mistrust and thus maybe even deter them from using online offerings. But when looking at the findings it could also be assumed that digital applications have become a key part of everyday life anyway, widely used despite existing security concerns. Thus, committing to more transparency (expressly wanted) and consumer-orientation could be perceived positively and may well be appreciated in the competition.

It can be also observed that the importance and function of data protection, privacy, and informational self-determination with regard to the Internet are changing significantly, not least across generations. What was deemed private in the pre-Web 2.0 period, the smartphone era respectively, has today become normal or common in social networks, blogs, chats, and tutorials and considered part of the consumers' social analogue as well as digital identity and personality (on the use of social networks at the work place see [16]).

Against this background the question is whether privacy, data protection, and also digital self-determination need fundamental re-consideration [17]. In any event, the perception of the consumers, of the younger digital natives generations in particular [18], with its characteristics of experience, decision, and behavior, need to be taken into account in both regulatory policy decisions and responsible corporate actions.

With regard to the perception of risks related to personal data one explanation may be that consumers either do not understand the risks at all or make incorrect assumptions or lack the technical skills to take appropriate protective measures. However, the findings at hand give reason to confirm the above-mentioned "Privacy Paradox" insofar as there is awareness of (poor) data security and there are respective concerns, yet rather simple measures such as reading the terms and conditions are not taken (against better judgment).

Possibly, experience and behavior on the Internet are influenced by the same psychological effects that are at work in the analog world, such as present-orientedness, the focus on "short-term betterment" respectively [19], the illusion of control or over-optimism, a tendency towards over-estimation respectively. These are well known from psychological consumer research [19, 20] and it is only with difficulty that their impact can be reduced by means of information and education. For instance, the frequently encountered focus on the consent for transactions does not seem very useful against this background, since this consent is or should primarily be based on voluntariness and knowledge. While the respondents consider themselves quite competent in reaching their goals on the Internet, they also state deficits in understanding (partly background) processes and a desire for a better level of information. At the same time, and this is where the de facto relevance is, even a well-informed and cautious consumer apparently does not read text-heavy terms and conditions, as is clearly substantiated by the study results. It appears that conventional tools of data security and self-determination based on this, such as consent, opt-outs, and anonymization cannot really meet the requirements of the multi-facetted construct of digital self-determination and the consumers' ambivalence. Simple, supporting measures could be helpful here, that take into account the decision-making structure of consumers, which is based on complexity-reduction, habits, and cognitive "short-cuts" [19, 21].

A large majority also requested transparency in the application and ease-of-use. A corresponding reduction of complexity in this context should not be interpreted as patronizing but rather as a measure that does not palm off to the consumers the entire responsibility for processes and consequences, which cannot be overseen by them anyway. Simplicity in this context means the opportunity to having to make only few, ideally no, resource-binding decisions in a comprehensible decision space. If a proposed or preset alternative reliably is the secure one, this will not only reduce unexpected negative consequences, but will also help to increase trust in web interactions and transactions thereby reducing the frequently expressed mistrust in companies' data storage and data usage.

Also, access rights may be derived from the desire to know what happens to one's own data on the Internet and beyond. For this, however, the legal framework also needs to be reviewed and amended to motivate providers to offer the technologies and services necessary for making the routes and value of their data clear to consumers. Due to the severe competitive pressure among digital services providers those companies that could take a competitive advantage from a carefully interpreted privacy policy or provisions to safeguard digital self-determination might be encouraged to move towards the desired consumer-oriented direction [22].

Greater transparency, higher comprehensibility, and more control over their own data: Nothing more and nothing less is what consumers want. And that is how digital services providers can gain trust and secure a significant competitive advantage.

References

1. C. Linnhoff-Popien, M. Zaddach und A. Grahl, Marktplätze im Umbruch – Digitale Strategien für Services im Mobilen Internet, Heidelberg: Springer, 2015.
2. M. Culnan und P. Armstrong, Information Privacy Concerns, Procedural Fairness, and Impersonal Trust: An Empirical Investigation, 1 Hrsg., Organizational Science, 1999, pp. 104–115.
3. Bitkom, "44 Millionen Deutsche nutzen ein Smartphone," 2015. [Online]. Available: https://www.bitkom.org/Presse/Presseinformation/44-Millionen-Deutsche-nutzen-ein-Smartphone.html. [Accessed 15 08 2016].
4. B. Bloching, L. Luck und T. Ramge, Data user – Wie Kundendaten die Wirtschaft revolutionieren, München: Redline Verlag, 2012.
5. P. Norberg, D. Horne und D. Horne, "The Privacy Paradox: Personal Information Disclosure Intentions versus Behaviors," in *The Journal of Consumer Affairs*, 1 Hrsg., 2007, pp. 100–126.
6. Y. Moon, "Intimate Exchanges: Using Computers to Elicit Self-Disclosure from Consumers," in *Journal of Consumer Research*, 4 Hrsg., 2000, pp. 323–339.
7. R. O'Harrow, No Place to Hide, New York: Free Press, 2005.
8. J. Phelps, G. Nowak und E. Ferrell, "Privacy Concerns and Consumer Willingness to Provide Personal Information," in *Journal of Public Policy and Marketing*, 1 Hrsg., Bd. 19, 2000, pp. 27–41.
9. P. Han und A. Maclaurin, Do Consumers Really Care about Online Privacy?, 1 Hrsg., Marketing Management, 2002, pp. 35–38.
10. S. Sayre und D. Horne, Trading Secrets for Savings: How Concerned Are Consumers about Privacy Threat from Club Cards?, 1 Hrsg., Advances in Consumer Research, 2000, pp. 151–155.
11. S. Spiekermann, J. Grossklags und B. Berendt, "E-Privacy in 2nd Generation E-Commerce: Privacy Preferences vs. Actual Behavior," in *Proceedings of the 3rd ACM conference on Electronic Commernce*, 2001, pp. 38–47.
12. D. Hallinan, M. Friedewald und P. McCarthy, Citizens' perceptions of data protection and privacy in Europe, 28 Hrsg., Bd. 2, Computer Law & Security Review, 2012, pp. 263–272.
13. B. Krahn, User Experience: Konstruktdefinition und Entwicklung eines Erhebungsinstruments, Bonn: GUX, 2012.
14. S. Barnes, "A privacy paradox: Social networking in the United States, First Monday," 2006. [Online]. Available: http://firstmonday.org/ojs/index.php/fm/article/view/1394/1312. [Accessed 15 08 2016].
15. M. Mertz, M. Jannes, A. Schlomann, E. Manderscheid, C. Rietz und C. Woopen, Digitale Selbstbestimmung – Cologne Center for Ethics, Rights, Economics, and Social Sciences of Health (CERES), Cologne, 2016.

16. C. Rietz, A. Knieper und B. Krahn, Soziale Netzwerke am Arbeitsplatz: Eine Bestandaufnahme, 18 Hrsg., Bd. 1, Wirtschaftspsychologie, 2016, pp. 46–54.

17. M. Hotter, Privatsphäre – Der Wandel eines liberalen Rechts im Zeitalter des Internets, Frankfurt a. M.: Campus Verlag, 2011.

18. M. Prensky, Digital Natives, Digital Immigrants Part 1, On the Horizon, Bd. 5, 2007, pp. 1–6.

19. E. Kirchler, Wirtschaftspsychologie, Göttingen: Hogrefe, 2011.

20. R. Thaler und C. Sunstein, Nudge – Wie man kluge Entscheidungen anstößt, Berlin, 2015.

21. M. Grubb, "Overconfident Consumers in the Marketplace," in *Journal of Economic Perspectives*, 4 Hrsg., 2015, pp. 9–36.

22. G. Spindler und C. Thorun, "Eckkpunkte einer digitalen Ordnungspolitik," 2015. [Online]. Available: https://sriw.de/images/pdf/Spindler_Thorun-Eckpunkte_digitale_Ordnungspolitik_final.pdf. [Accessed 15 08 2016].

Digitally Mature? Ready for the Digital Transformation?

8

Maik Romberg

Abstract

Above all, in this article we would like to raise questions, which need to be addressed if we want to become mature citizens of a digital society – and to be successful in mastering this digital transformation, in Germany. The article also shows potential solutions to the deciding questions we have to answer in order to avoid becoming powerless marionettes attached to the strings of the digital revolution. It is also a question of bridging the gap between our private app behavior and the resulting implications for successful digital strategies in enterprises, society and politics. Oftentimes we are well aware of the successful digital solutions available, but are simply not able to identify the deciding success factors and to adapt them to entrepreneurial areas. In the consumer market place, major and minor global players are demonstrating how digital interactions can, and need to function in order to meet customer needs (see amazon, google, Facebook, Alibaba, airbnb, ebay, etc ...). Why is it then that it is so difficult for IT departments of large corporations to offer equally successful functional digital applications for their employees? What is the significance of UI and UX designs in the consumer market on the one hand, and the influence of company culture on the success of digital strategies on the other? Is there a correlation or can the two worlds – private and professional, consumer and enterprise markets – be viewed independent of each other? How can digital corporate strategies profit from our digital commonplace? In order to answer these questions we need to recognize our ways of dealing with digital media, and analyze which conscious or subconscious mechanisms we use to navigate through in an ever increasingly digital world.

M. Romberg (✉)
Rohde & Schwarz GmbH & Co. KG
Munich, Germany
e-mail: maik.romberg@rohde-schwarz.com

© Springer-Verlag GmbH Germany 2018
C. Linnhoff-Popien et al. (eds.), *Digital Marketplaces Unleashed*,
https://doi.org/10.1007/978-3-662-49275-8_8

8.1   What Does the Digital Transformation Do to Us?
What Do We Gain from the Digital Transformation?

Are we mature in handling digital media, and able to form our own opinion? What decides our action and our decisions in working with smart phones, tablets, apps and IoT? Accordingly, with which criteria do we click our way through an ever more digital world? Are we self-determining, and, if so, to what degree, or do we allow ourselves to be led by cleverly programmed algorithms through a world which we don't understand ourselves anymore? Can we really actively structure the digital change, or are we being overwhelmed by the digital revolution? And if we, the inhabitants of this digital modern time, do not want to accept this disruptive transformation as a force of nature, how can we have an influence on it?

8.1.1   Our Conscious and Unconscious Motives
Accepting Digital Achievements

In order to answer these questions I believe a differentiated view is necessary – a close look at our conscious and unconscious actions within the spreading digital development around us. It is a view at our true motives, either to accept digital achievements with enthusiasm or to reject them with a high degree of skepticism. A view at required political measures for a socially and humanely justifiable transition into the digital age 4.0. Along with this, we take a view at our changing working world. How will we work in future? How do we want to work in future? Does digital work 4.0 offer us the chance for individual fulfillment or does it mean an increase in external control and exploitation? In order to approach these questions we firstly have to clarify why, and to what extent, we interact with digital achievements today.

8.1.2   How Does Our Association with Digital Media Function?

It was Aristoteles, who put forward the thesis that happiness was the highest asset and ultimate goal of every action, in "Nicomachean Ethics". According to latest findings in brain research Aristoteles was not only right, but our decisions are made even before we realize it, in the orbitofrontal cortex. If no reward is recognized there is no positive decision. The reward principle describes the influence of positive reinforcement, according to psychology. This is one personality trait of the human, which also works in the digital world. If users receive an answer to a question, support or help in everyday life and the working world, it is felt as a reward – Aristoteles would have called this happiness. It is an important reason why only applications, which produce genuine added value for the user, can be successful: they reward the user. We immediately recognize the advantages of digital communication and collaboration, if they facilitate our analog daily life. We are rewarded by not having to go to supermarkets, not having to take our shirts to the laundry, and being able to book our tickets online.

8.1.3 Key Success Factors

We won't have to go to the travel agent anymore or to line up at a desk, admission tickets will not have to be printed anymore or to be picked up at the ticket agency, etc. ... the further development of these digitally organized services will escalate rapidly. In this development it will be exciting to see which innovations really ease our daily life, reward us by using them, and therefore soon become a part of the digital achievements which have an above average half-life value. An essential success factor of the generation of measurable digital added value will be the finesse of usability through which we are literally enticed to move from the well-worn analog trail to the new, alluring, and convenient digital path. Applications such as, for example, Airbnb, succeed in giving, with apparent ease to the user – whether it be guest or host, a responsive user interface so that one is positively seduced to join the Airbnb community by one click, s. Fig. 8.1.

There is nothing which hasn't already been considered by the makers and integrated into the UI design. This is not meant to sound deprecatory – quite the contrary. In this instance, it has been possible to successfully reproduce the real world and its complexity in a digital process. The interaction with other users turns into social collaboration. In spite of heterogeneous user structures a homogeneous entity is produced for those who participate, who receive their personal and individual advantages, who are rewarded and would like to continue.

Fig. 8.1 Number of guests staying with Airbnb hosts during the summer

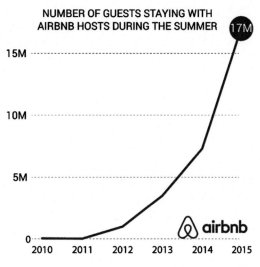

A successful application, such as Airbnb, attracts other services like a magnet. In the periphery surrounding the practical everyday function, which renting out private living space brings with it, a number of add-on services have been created or have smartly docked onto the success. These are, of course fully digitalized, cleaning and housekeeping services, car and bike sharing services, delivery services of different flavors, etc. ... This momentum is, on the one hand, stamped by economic interests, and, on the other hand, shows how important suitability of digital applications for everyday use has become. Practicable use is in the foreground. The user wants to be positively sanctioned for his digital action – at best, immediately and noticeably.

In this connection, the pragmatic use of new media technologies has become second nature to most people for quite some time. They are happy to use mobile devices and apps, especially in view of the fact that they not only become more attractive, but also more user-friendly with every innovation and new version. Besides the joy of gained time, new application areas, the esthetics of new media, and one's own gain of multimedia competency, the digital revolution also brings with it complex challenges to the inhabitants of modern digital life – mentally, socially and psychologically.

8.1.4 Typical Factors to Fail with an Application

If the users are overly challenged by the possibilities of an application, or if they feel overburdened by the mass of information, they will be irritated; the app will never be used again or de-installed immediately.

Applications, which push their way into the foreground, will be found to be troublesome by users. In the meantime, there are many smart phone users, who have moved away from Android, because this annoys them immensely: being constantly confronted by unasked and unwanted messages on their device, which bring no noticeable use or advantage. Here, the digital industry must understand that it is no longer dealing with undiscerning users, but increasingly with digital natives, who know exactly what they want and have a deep understanding of what is technically viable today.

8.1.5 Mature User

Users have become more demanding. The demands on mobile devices, smart phones, tablets and their apps have risen exponentially during the last few years. Not so long ago we were happy if we were able to surf and mail on our cell phones, but today we expect a fully-fledged computer, equipped with OS and apps, which organize and optimize our everyday life with one click, anytime and anywhere.

8.2   Work and Private Aspects

How do our behavior patterns vary in association with digital media, when we navigate through our private everyday life, or move through our working world? Are there any differences at all?

8.2.1   More Stakeholder, More Complex Demands

How does cooperation between employees happen today and how do digital technologies and media change future collaboration within a company? In this case, the situation is similar to the everyday and private aspects: about the direct and instantaneous added value of a new technology or mobile application, which decides success or failure. Only in this case, contrary to the private world, there is a far larger variety of stakeholders, usually with diverse interests, diverse duties, and diverse benchmarks for the qualification of added values.

Concretely, this means that the meaningful deployment of digital technologies in the enterprise environment places even more complex demands, than already exist in the consumer market. If it is only left to the IT departments to try to do justice to the digital transformation, with however much enthusiasm, boundless innovation and much know-how, efforts of this kind, nevertheless, are doomed to fail.

8.2.2   Strategy vs. Culture

Only if the corporation dares to admit that it doesn't know the perfect route itself – vertically and horizontally – and that it needs cooperation from all departments and employees, then it is able to move into the digital age 4.0. The underused networking potentials, which sound so enticing using the buzz word "Industry 4.0 and digital transformation", can only be identified and utilized by interdisciplinary working groups.

8.2.3   The Importance of Culture

In plain language, however, this also means that a revolutionary philosophy and culture change needs to take place within the company. Management Guru, Peter Drucker, once said "Culture eats strategy for breakfast" [1], s. Fig. 8.2.

This "old" realization suddenly becomes red-hot when we talk about the digital transformation in our working world and when senior staff wants to successfully drive the digital transformation within their department or the entire company. Company culture is certainly not the panacea for the sick and lame patient, but it can unleash cascading effects, which are necessary to excite the employees to take new digital paths.

Fig. 8.2 Culture eats strategy for breakfast

Company culture gives the initial impulse to embark on the path together in order to find and invent a new and suitable work place of the future together. In the implementation, however, there are a number of stumbling blocks. The enterprise not only has to take new paths technologically, but organizationally and process-oriented as well. There must be a collaboration of teams and communities, which are interested in a genuine and profitable digital transformation for all interested parties and the corporation. The immediate and direct involvement of workers' councils must not be neglected in this process.

8.2.4   Collaboration and Humanization of Work

Here, it is necessary to get across to the employees that it would be fatal to oppose or be skeptical towards digital transformation, simply because of the technical changes necessary. After all, ultimately a genuine digital collaboration, in combination with the associated company culture, is precisely what workers' council committees always demand – collegial cooperation and humanization of work.

8.2.5   Success or Failure

Ultimately, the success or failure of the "digital revolution" in a company, is decided by the end user (employee). If he or she sees reward (added value), if he or she utilizes the newly created digital features of the employer, not only will there be wide acceptance, but excitement in the way the potentials of industry and work 4.0 can unfold in the entire corporation. That means Aristoteles continues to be right in the enterprise environment, as well. The reward principle determines our actions, whether we want to or not: faster results, less annoying and unpopular work, simpler communication and collaboration, more agreeable working environment, better working conditions (analog or digital, real or virtual, offline or online) or more (free) time, is all true "bait" for our actions.

Fig. 8.3 Henry Ford (1863–1947). An American industrialist and the founder of the Ford Motor Company

> *„If I had asked my customers what they wanted, they would have said faster horses."*
>
> - Henry Ford -

8.2.6   Real Added Values for the User

In order to produce a positive balance of resonance it is, however, not enough to simply give the employees digital tools. Besides the digital spaces, for example enterprise social media, new analog spaces must be created. The new collaboration tool alone does not produce appreciable added value for the employees unless it is embedded sensibly in a total work 4.0 concept: a total concept which doesn't only drive digital aspects, but which cleverly networks these with working place economy, innovative room architecture, working time models, conferencing systems, work-life-balance concepts, and the new design of production facilities and office space. The employee has to be at the center of this – the person as an individual with her or his individual world. Digital applications need analog partners in the real working and private world so that they can be an experience with real added value for the user, s. Fig. 8.3.

8.2.7   Digital Germany

Regarding the digital transformation in Germany, the EU Digital Commissioner, Günter Oettinger indicated: "We have lost the connection". Is this true? Has Germany already missed the digital transformation bus?

"75 years ago Konrad Zuse presented the first functional computer in Berlin: the Z3. The pioneering country of the past has turned into a follower. We are suffering from the symptom of neophobia – the fear of the new" [2].

I consider these views to be exaggerated and, ultimately, they only mirror a part of the truth. Germany also boasts successful start-ups and companies which have actively devised digital change, recognizing the potential of these new technologies (e. g. Scout24, KaufDa, Jimdo, reBuy, daWanda, QYPE, Sport1, SoundCloud, etc. ...) However, there could be far more companies, IT departments and organizations, which could follow the digital transformation in a smart, fast and safe fashion, if they were only courageous enough to more precisely analyze, adapt, and implement the already tested recipes for success. Nobody has to reinvent the wheel – neither the analog nor the digital one.

Aristoteles 4.0!

Perhaps another quote from Aristoteles may gain significance for enterprises and entrepreneurs if they do not want to miss the boat with the ever-increasing velocity of the digital transformation: "The beginning is half of the whole".

References

1. C. Keese, Silicon Germany, Wie wir die digitale Transformation schaffen, München: Albrecht Knaus Verlag, 2016.
2. P. Drucker, *Culture eats strategy for breakfast.*

Blockchain – the Case for Market Adoption of the Distributed Ledger

9

Marco Streng

Abstract

The effort to verify identity and authenticity has influenced much of human history. It is so central to civil society that it has been the subject of plays [1], great literature, famous laws, and is more relevant in the age of computers and passwords than ever before. But more tediously, authenticity has been an obstacle that has slowed the advance of humanity for centuries. The inability to quickly and absolutely verify an individual's identity or know with certainty the value or existence of a thing remains one of the great obstacles to progress in our day. But that problem could have a technological solution [2]. The technology is called Blockchain and there is an intense, ongoing debate over whether it is capable of progressing authentication practices beyond the clunky system of signatures, notaries, and records that we use today. In this paper, we will consider arguments for and against the widespread adoption of Blockchain. I will seek to make the case for greater reliance on Blockchain technology as a means of modernizing identity management and value transactions. To do so, we necessarily must consider its biggest use case to-date: Bitcoin. But we will look further, into emerging efforts to apply the technology to real world problems and how it is changing the world.

9.1 Introduction

History is marked by great technological leaps. Inventions change the world and the way we live in it. The wheel revolutionized travel; the telescope placed us in the galaxy; the airfoil let us fly. But the casual observer of history will miss some of the most formative

M. Streng (✉)
Genesis Mining
Reykjavik, Iceland
e-mail: marco.streng@genesis-mining.com

© Springer-Verlag GmbH Germany 2018
C. Linnhoff-Popien et al. (eds.), *Digital Marketplaces Unleashed*,
https://doi.org/10.1007/978-3-662-49275-8_9

discoveries and inventions of the last 10,000 years because they are not so tangible as an engine or a medicine. And yet a handful of discoveries have been foundational to human progress. High on the list of overlooked historical turning points is money: where it comes from, how it has evolved, and how it has shaped the world. It is important that we trace the history of money because its story is the story of value and how we establish what it is and how we transfer value from one individual to another. If we follow the story of money, we arrive at Blockchain.

9.2 A History of Money

It is a mind-boggling idea to think of a world before money, but there was one. Simple trade was the only means of exchanging goods and services. But here we see the origin of the idea of money because two individuals trading items that are not exactly the same must decide how to determine what they are worth. At the core of money is the idea of mutually determined worth. Whatever civilization first decided to assign value to an abstract object or substance in order to better facilitate trade truly changed the world.

Money has experienced numerous iterations over the last several millennia. Historians have discovered societies that decided finely polished stones would be their currency and others that used furs and skins. Camels and sheep were assigned a particular value in some tribes and could be used as a form of currency [3]. Money began to assume the form and function that is most familiar in today's economy when central governments began to issue currency. These early currencies were stamped coins made of different metals, commonly gold or silver [4].

Currency opened the door for banking because a banking institution could keep a ledger of how much currency an individual had deposited. Banking opened the door for credit, credit facilitated enormous capital investments, and economies began to grow on a massive scale.

9.2.1 Currency Today

In the year 2016, currency has been obfuscated. The common man touches real currency far less frequently than even ten years ago. And the currency itself means something different than it did a hundred years ago when the U.S. Dollar was backed by gold. Today, the entire world is functionally operating on a highly sophisticated system of IOUs. When an individual swipes their bank card to make a purchase at a grocery, the only change is the exchange between computer servers of some data that says money has been transferred from on person's account into another's [5]. But in real terms, those digits reflect paper currency somewhere, and that paper is meaningless unless everyone agrees to its value. Its value actually fluctuates as a result of a thousand influences, including inflation, interest rates, speculation, the performance of other currencies, and more.

The arbitrary nature of currency and the compounding effect of modern, computerized banking has so radically changed the common man's understanding of what money is that monetary disasters have occurred. One does not have to look far to find a fiat currency that is defunct, its money worth less than the paper it is printed on. How does such an event occur? Centralized institutions that distribute fiat currency can and do lose sight of the central tenant of money: mutually determined value. When they print money without restraint to meet their own financial needs, it undermines that premise. Repeated failures on the part of governments to respect that relationship has given rise to a new era of money.

9.3 Cryptocurrency

Currency's most modern iteration is cryptocurrency. This form of money is not fiat money, meaning it is not issued by a central government. It also is not physical – not made of a rare earth substance or printed and distributed in any form. Cryptocurrency is digital, residing on servers all over the world. The most prominent one is called Bitcoin, and the hundreds of others are collectively referred to as Altcoins. While the subject of this paper is not about any of those currencies, we have taken this discussion to this point because it establishes the foundation for the technology that powers crypto currencies. That technology is called blockchain.

9.4 Blockchain

Blockchain at its core is a decentralized authenticity mechanism. When a legal contract is signed today, perhaps for an asset like a building or a car, that transaction is authenticated by witnesses who sign their names and are legally responsible for verifying the transaction took place. In an abstract sense, they are attesting to what reality is or is not. Blockchain is capable of accomplishing the same ends, that is proving what is real and what is not, but in a technologically advanced, decentralized fashion.

9.4.1 Blockchain Technology

When Blockchain is described as being decentralized, a number of attributes are being considered. To begin with, Blockchain is a public ledger, meaning that it is a framework that logs and publicly displays every transaction it processes [6]. Of course, it does so in an encrypted and anonymous way, but when anything is encoded into the Blockchain, it can be verified in the public ledger. As such, the authentication element is decentralized, empowering everyone who sees or uses a particular Blockchain to be witnesses to a thing or transaction.

Additionally, the technology relies on a diaspora of servers to store information. There is not single server containing the keys to all of the information stored on the Blockchain, making the intelligence of the public ledger decentralized in a physical sense as well. This in itself is an important piece of the security that makes the technology nearly unbreakable. Its encryption and decentralization make it as secure as any method that currently exists for storing and transacting information.

Blockchain's encryption technology is inherently a one-way street, meaning data is locked away and can only be accessed by keys which users generate. Bitcoin has had great success with this security apparatus in which users transfer Bitcoin by verifying keys to confirm exchanges. The public ledger is an added verification mechanism for ensuring the global security of the currency.

9.5 Market Use Cases

The conversation about Blockchain is happening at a moment in modern history that is uniquely volatile. Technology is not only globally connecting people, it is making those connections more tenuous than ever before. Friction points are materializing in areas as obvious as immigration and as remote as health records and voting in civil elections. In all of those cases, there is a conflicting demand for privacy and transparency, a balance that is poorly managed by most of the systems currently operating today.

9.5.1 Voting

This year may well see one of the most controversial not just in U.S. history, but because of its far-reaching implications, world history as well. Whoever is elected to lead the world's largest economy, there is no doubt that cries of voter fraud will be heard in key states and voting districts, just like there have been in every election in recent memory. These recurring doubts about the legitimacy of the electoral process undermine the democratic process and leave the door open for subversive control of outcomes. Blockchain is a viable solution to the problem of voter fraud. The public ledger would allow anyone to see and count the votes. Furthermore, because each vote would require the authentication of the vote caster, voter fraud could be solved at the same time.

9.5.2 Personal Records

The number and importance of the records we keep is growing. Any given individual in a first world economy is likely to have extensive medical records, identification documents, tax documents, legal papers, and more. These all must be kept in their original form and transferring them is a laborious process that leaves the owner vulnerable to identity theft or worse. It is puzzling that in a world that is almost completely digital, the core of the global economy and people's most important records are still kept on printed paper. Blockchain facilitates a completely secure transfer to an entirely digital world in which records are encrypted and secured by user-generated keys, yet also easily transferable without risking their security. It is not utopian thinking to suggest that the entire segment of the global economy dedicated to issuing and verifying records could be replaced by various applications of Blockchain technology.

9.5.3   Currency

It is a misconception to think that Bitcoin and other Altcoins are the only currency application of Blockchain. By contrast, Blockchain technology has the potential to integrate with traditional fiat currency in numerous ways. In fact, this area is already being explored by numerous major banks, which are looking for ways to improve their processes and compete with increasingly popular cryptocurrencies. Financial applications of Blockchain technology are likely to be the use cases that achieve the most success in the coming years and pave the way for broader adoption.

9.6   Global Impacts of Blockchain

The globalization of the world has improved the conditions of the world's poor, advanced the rate and significance of our scientific discoveries, and by certain metrics, improved global stability. But this progress comes with inherent complications and risks. More than ever, the world's problems share a common theme: authenticity and information security. It is foreseeable that without modern solutions to these issues, much of the last century's progress could be lost. The argument for Blockchain is not just that it is a good business proposition and one that would make many aspects of daily life more convenient. The argument is that there are legitimate areas where current systems are showing signs of stress and may fail in the near term, the consequences of which could be disastrous.

By the same token, there is reason to be optimistic that the solution has been discovered at the right moment. The success of Bitcoin in a relatively short period of time and against so many formidable obstacles is one such proof. As this paper has outlined, it is possible that there may soon be others.

References

1. Appearances and Reality. (n.d.). Retrieved August 12, 2016, from http://www.bbc.co.uk/education/guides/zcpfvcw/revision/4.
2. Yurcan, B. (2016, April 8). How Blockchain Fits into the Future of Digital Identity. Retrieved August 15, 2016, from http://www.americanbanker.com/news/bank-technology/how-blockchain-fits-into-the-future-of-digital-identity-1080345-1.html.
3. Glyn, D. (2015). History of money. Place of publication not identified: Univ Of Wales Press.
4. Fiat paper money: the history and evolution of our currency, Ralph Foster - Paul Myslin - Ralph T. Foster - 2008
5. The New Yorker Mark Gimein - http://www.newyorker.com/business/currency/why-digital-money-hasnt-killed-cash
6. The age of cryptocurrency: how bitcoin and digital money are challenging the global economic order, Paul Vigna - Michael Casey.

'Local' Is an Asset, Response Time Is Key: Lessons Learned from the Amiona St. Gallen Local Digital Marketplace

10

Mark Schleicher, Philipp Osl, and Hubert Österle

Abstract

The Amiona digital marketplace allows citizens of St. Gallen, a city of 75,000 people in eastern Switzerland, to make appointments 24/7 with quality-assured, trustworthy local service providers, as well as to provide informal support to neighbours and coordinate local events. The lessons learned reveal the benefits of a local service marketplace for both consumer and provider, highlight the criticality of response time for user acceptance and ensure additional improvements. Iterative enhancements of the platform based on these learnings from daily operation have already resulted in a ready-to-use standard software solution for digital marketplaces that addresses the varying needs of users with highly diverse levels of digitisation, in particular by supporting three different processes for appointment coordination – also allowing those with paper-based agendas to participate – in combination with a variety of notification channels to shorten response time.

M. Schleicher (✉)
University of St. Gallen
St. Gallen, Switzerland
e-mail: mark.schleicher@amiona.com

P. Osl
Institute of Information Management
St. Gallen, Switzerland
e-mail: philipp.osl@amiona.com

H. Österle
Business Engineering Institute St. Gallen
St. Gallen, Switzerland
e-mail: hubert.oesterle@unisg.ch

© Springer-Verlag GmbH Germany 2018
C. Linnhoff-Popien et al. (eds.), *Digital Marketplaces Unleashed*,
https://doi.org/10.1007/978-3-662-49275-8_10

10.1 Motivation and Challenges

The Amiona St. Gallen digital marketplace was supported by the Gebert Rüf Foundation within the framework of "The Viral Digital Village – Services for Citizens", a project that aimed to provide access to local service providers, social services organisations and informal services in the neighbourhood more easily than by phone, and bring people together using a user-friendly organisational and enrolment tool for local events.

When the platform was launched in October 2014, finding businesses from the user perspective was already very easy thanks to search engines and online directories, such as yellowpages.com or local.ch; however, when it came to making use of specific services, a phone was still required as most directories did not provide an additional function to connect the user to the provider. Such media breaks are an inconvenience, especially as providers also often only have specified calling hours when calls are answered. Although an e-mail address is sometimes provided, stating services, dates, personnel and any other preferences can be quite tedious, especially on mobile devices, and the entire process has to be repeated for every new appointment.

In contrast to the search engines and online directories missing the function, there were also a range of vertical direct booking platforms that offered convenient access to specific services, such as Treatwell.ch or Quap.ch for hairdressers, and Eat.ch or Foodarena.ch for food delivery; yet none covered the bandwidth of everyday needs. Access to services via these platforms is quite handy, as the user can view the available dates and book accordingly, alike the functionality of provider-specific booking software such as Appointmind or Shore. However, it means that consumers have to use several platforms or systems to access the services they require. In addition, some smaller-scale providers might not be available on these platforms as direct booking requires a minimum level of digitisation in the form of an electronic calendar, and currently there is no competing system pursuing a similar approach.

What was missing from the user perspective was therefore a combination of the two types of solution described above: the Amiona St. Gallen local digital marketplace[1], an online platform that provides easy-to-use 24/7 appointment coordination processes and a single point of contact for all kinds of services, including anything from driving services by social services organisations and food and drink delivery services by local bicycle couriers from local bakeries and breweries, to physiotherapist, dentist or car repair appointments and tailored shirt and dry cleaning services.

As we discovered that new users might be confused by the wide scope of the service portfolio, we adjusted the design of the landing page in an aim to target users in different demand situations, such as the need for a hairdresser, a craving for ice cream or seasonal offers like occasional personal city tours for charity. As can be seen in Fig. 10.1, the landing page focuses on the idea of making appointments with service providers in St. Gallen by showing examples and providing a familiar search field for immediate access to

---

[1] To discover the platform visit sg.amiona.ch.

Fig. 10.1 Landing page of the Amiona St. Gallen local digital marketplace

the comprehensive portfolio below. Scrolling down further leads the user to a catalogue of categories for browsing services and an information section at the bottom of the page. The entire platform uses responsive web design for optimised use on mobile devices, which were observed as a frequent point of access.

In order to simplify everyday life we had to master the following challenges: create an open marketplace that allows all providers and consumers to participate; assure the required quality standards; overcome the low level of digitisation at many smaller-scale providers; bring about a change in consumer service searching and booking behaviour; and improve the consumer and provider experience through quick response times and efficient end-to-end processes for confirmed appointments. The following chapters describe our technical and organisational solutions in addressing these challenges. In combination with a range of marketing measures, we were able to accumulate over 600 registered service offerings and record increasing levels of usage among the citizens of St. Gallen.

10.2 Addressing the Challenges of Local Service Marketplaces

10.2.1 The Open Marketplace and Required Quality Standards

In order to make the marketplace available to as many users as possible, it had to have low entry barriers whilst still fulfilling vital quality standards. Both consumers as well as service providers had to be able to register by themselves. Identification by e-mail address and confirmation link, as well as a business phone number made sure that only real service companies and private offerors could register. In the case of uncertainties, we contacted the provider in question personally and double-checked the provided information. As we also encountered varying requirements from other regions with regard to the platform's "degree of openness", we decided to make self-registration for providers an optional tool to be opted for or declined at every new marketplace.

However, many customers and service providers do not want to register when using a platform for the first time and registration is therefore not required to request a listed service. Instead, we created a new temporary user account for every request without registration. If the user later decides to register, they can easily activate their account by clicking on the "benefit from all advantages of Amiona St. Gallen by registration" button that is in all e-mails that are sent, e. g. for appointment confirmations.

In addition, we also introduced the option for users to send requests to non-registered providers, such as their favourite small business next door, by simply entering the phone number or e-mail address of the provider to enable viral seeding, e. g. like the seeding of WhatsApp. In this scenario, a temporary provider account is created and can again be activated and completed later by the new provider.

10.2.2 Critical Mass

Despite the above-mentioned measures to allow for viral growth and keep entry barriers as low as possible, we were unable to overcome the critical mass problem in double-sided markets, where a broad range of consumers and providers is required for a growing and interesting user experience. We therefore had to implement additional measures to extend the number and scope of providers listed in the marketplace. The best way to achieve this was to also integrate all service providers in St. Gallen listed in Google Places (i. e. almost everyone) in addition to the acquisition campaign. Additionally using the Google Places API offered the advantage of allowing us to detect which providers were of particular interest to our users, so that we could commence talks with the companies in question with the bonus of immediately gaining new customers.

In order to provide an adequate degree of transparency, we wanted a slightly different design for the external search results that would not confuse users who are indifferent to the source of the provider and simply want to send an appointment request as easily as possible. We therefore used two different colours, one for the registered providers and one for the additional results supplied by the integrated Google Places search, and decided to display the external results below the registered providers (thereby also complying with the Google regulations that prohibit the manipulation of listings from their Places API).

As can be seen in Fig. 10.2: Different search results for car repair shops, the yellow search results from Google's API only display the name of the provider (car repair shops

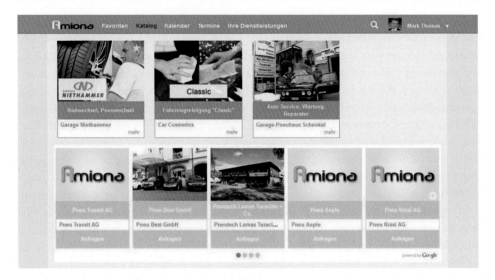

Fig. 10.2 Different search results for car repair shops

in this example) and an image, if available (otherwise the default Amiona image is displayed). Unlike the green search results for the registered providers above them, they do not list any specific services, such as tyre fitting or car cleaning. By doing so we ensure that providers still have an excellent reason to register on the platform, as it will allow them to serve their customers more directly with their specific offerings. The functionality for requesting an appointment does not differ for registered and non-registered providers, thereby serving the user with a similar process and consumer experience.

We received very positive feedback for the additional Google Places API listings in terms of general user acceptance ("Oh, it's cool that you extended your portfolio by also making this information available") and provider reactions to the request. The influence on viral seeding was however not as high as we had hoped for. A possible explanation could be the missing information on specific services offered by the provider, including pricing, which may cause a high level of uncertainty for the user before requesting.

10.2.3   Low Level of Provider Digitisation

When talking to and registering some of the smaller-scale businesses in St. Gallen we encountered many providers who used paper-based agendas for scheduling appointments, checked their e-mail only once a day or even less, and sometimes possessed only very elementary computer literacy. Providing sufficient information on how to use basic functions, e. g. on how to respond to appointment requests or change a service's pricing information, was therefore crucial. We also ensured help for new providers with the first requests that they received and offered phone-based support during business hours.

Due to the large number of paper-based agendas, providing a direct booking function that integrated with providers' calendars was not an option at the start. Instead, we first developed a request-answer-based coordination system that had to be designed as flexibly and conveniently as possible, whilst still assuring confirmed appointments through structured processes. As we had to set up a structure for service providers with paper-based agendas, electronic calendars and mixtures of both systems we finally came up with three different process scenarios that a user could choose from when sending a request. The first, basic scenario was to *ask the provider for some available and bookable dates* that consumers could then choose from. In order to improve the success rate of this type of request, there was also a hint to add the preferred dates and times to the request by using the comments field below. As it is sometimes very important to have an appointment on a very specific date, the second scenario was to *request a preferred date* right away. In this case the provider would only have to click an accept button if the date was available or, if it was unavailable, reply with alternative dates by selecting them from a calendar view for the user to choose from as in the first scenario. The third, most convenient solution, at least for consumers, is to select an appointment from *a list of directly bookable dates*. In order to also allow providers with paper-based agendas to offer this third option, the directly bookable dates are entered by the service provider manually and supported by the option to import external calendars or export the Amiona calendar to other calendar systems via ICS feed. By offering these three different options to request appointments, it is possible to cover all types of service provider, calendar system and service type. The result is haircut requests are mainly sent for a preferred date; gardener requests are mostly without a date with effort and time restrictions in the comments field; and Sunday morning bakery deliveries are best done by direct booking. In the long run we expect direct booking to be the standard for nearly all providers, particularly as soon as big players like Google or WhatsApp would implement local marketplace and booking system interfaces.

10.2.4 Change in Consumer Behaviour and Marketing Measures

Whereas the digitisation of many consumers is already advanced and smartphones make up an integral part of everyday life for many people in Switzerland, this is certainly not true for everyone. Furthermore, while using smartphones or computers for online shopping, food delivery or train tickets is broadly accepted and frequently used, the idea of "shopping" for services using appointment coordination systems is still quite novel and certain services are even exclusive to the platform (e. g. a service for hiking with goats in the Appenzell Alps). We therefore had to provide easily accessible support for users via a free of charge telephone hotline and real-time chat service using ClickDesk software.

It was also very important and useful to have a Facebook page for communicating with the citizens of St. Gallen, as it allowed us to inform them on new services on the platform and upcoming events, like the personal charity city tours, or to set up targeted and smaller-scale advertising campaigns. We also launched several promotional campaigns, such a competition where we collected wishes for new providers by raffling a tablet computer, or service specials with a local or seasonal focus, e. g. winning tickets to the OLMA Agriculture and Food Fair, the biggest in St. Gallen, or a special Valentine's Day package delivered by the bakery. We also used the page to attract attention by promoting time-limited coupons for certain businesses.

In order to reach consumers directly on the web pages where they search for service providers and appointments, we also ran Google AdWords campaigns and introduced an "Amiona request button" to be added to the service provider websites (see Fig. 10.3). The button links to all of the provider's services listed on the Amiona St. Gallen marketplace.

We also created a visual presence at the shops of registered service providers by producing QR code stickers and applying them to the shop doors. Scanning the QR code displays a list of the provider's services on Amiona and offers consumers the option to also request appointments outside business hours. In addition, we printed flyers for every new provider with a readable short URL and corresponding QR code, both linking to the provider's services available at the Amiona marketplace. We sometimes also included temporary coupons in cooperation with the provider to encourage consumers to use the new appointment requesting method.

Finally, we posted printed promotional material with online coupon codes for special discounts on the platform into letter boxes and distributed coupon booklets among the almost 1500 new students at the University of St. Gallen during "freshers' week". As the majority of these students are quite price-conscious and most of them are new to the city without provider contacts for hairdressers and the like, the two freshers' week coupon booklets became our most successful printed marketing measure, with over a hundred transactions resulting from every booklet. In total we distributed over 50,000 individual coupons with a value of over CHF 1.5 million financed by local service providers in St. Gallen.

Despite all these measures, altering consumer behaviour continues to require time and patience is called for until online searches for service appointments become the normal

Fig. 10.3 Amiona request button on a provider's website

behaviour of St. Gallen's average consumer, always bearing in mind the amount of time that has been needed to make electronic banking a service accepted by about 50% of the population in Switzerland.

10.2.5   Response Time and Efficient End-to-End Processes

Given the described lack of digitisation and need for assistance from our customer support, it came as no great surprise that we occasionally encountered very long response times for requests or comments from both consumers and providers.

When we first launched the platform, we pushed all sorts of notifications via e-mail (e. g. appointment booked, request for a specific date or request without dates to send suggestions) to the providers. This meant that they had to check their e-mail on a regular basis in order to answer consumer requests within an adequate time frame. This worked very well for about half of the providers; however, unfortunately, the other half checked their e-mail less than once a day, which meant we had to find other solutions to ensure successful appointment coordination via the digital marketplace without impatient consumers making an additional phone call. We also discovered that the consumers' response time to e-mail notifications, e. g. rescheduling or available date suggestions, often also left a lot to be desired. These delays can be quite troublesome for the other party and result in complications, such as double bookings if another consumer requests a specific date, via Amiona or phone, which has already been suggested to someone else.

We therefore decided to opt for a more direct channel at the end of the first year and started pushing notifications to users via SMS. This required us to make entering the mobile phone number mandatory when requesting a service (previously only the name and e-mail were mandatory). We also made it a mandatory field for new providers to complete and added SMS numbers for the existing registered providers. The SMS message lists the most important information, i. e. what was requested by whom, what has been agreed or must be done next, and also includes a tiny URL that takes the user to the appointment view for the request (without login), where they can accept, reschedule or reject it, and add any comments where applicable. The addition of SMS notifications turned out to be an enormous improvement. Some providers now confirm requests within a minute and the consumers' response time using their mobile phones has also greatly improved.

However, you never stop learning and we noticed that the requests to certain providers were still remaining unanswered for a long time. It turned out that these businesses (most of them with three or more employees) had strict "no phones at work" policies and did not want to have even a single phone lying around as they were worried it might cause too much of a distraction. Based on the coloured LED signals on smartphones, we therefore came up with the idea of a simple button on the main desk displaying new requests, new comments and "everything OK" in three different colours: blue means new message, red means action required and green means OK. The button only requires a USB connection to the main computer and also offers an additional feature: When it is pushed, it launches the browser, goes to Amiona.ch, logs into the user's account and opens the messages view. The button therefore offers another convenient option to make users aware of new requests with a quick and easy response solution. This additional notification channel allowed us to resolve complications with businesses that did not want to receive any SMS notifications.

10.3   Lessons Learned

While the digital appointment coordination and functions of the platform were based on our scientific research (cf [1–3]). , we also learned some anticipated and less anticipated lessons when the platform went "live" and we were presented with the users' actual behaviour.

The findings led to many improvements, which were already implemented during the iterative development process, and also confirmed the potential benefit of a local service marketplace for both consumers and service providers.

10.3.1   Consumers Use the Option to Coordinate Services Outside Business Hours

As we assumed that the opportunity to request services outside business hours would offer a great benefit to employed consumers in particular, we were very interested to see how this would actually develop. We did indeed witness a large proportion of requests being submitted during the evening hours or on weekends from the very beginning; however, until now, this has not translated into a large number of repeat requests, as we were unable to ensure adequate response times before the introduction of the SMS notifications, and even less so outside business hours.

10.3.2   Service Providers Benefit from an Easy-to-Use Digital Consumer Channel and Less Interruptions from Phone Calls During Their Daily Business

While most appointment requests are still submitted by phone, service providers were delighted by the simplification of their workday as a result of the online requests submitted via Amiona. Small business owners in particular, who like most service providers in St. Gallen, do not have an employee dedicated to answering the phone, offered positive feedback with regard to improvements to their processes and, consequently, greater customer satisfaction, as there were less interruptions by phone calls while serving customers. As the owner of a small barber shop put it: "I would appreciate it if all of my customers used Amiona, as it makes my life that much easier. I really enjoy using the platform and it is of great value to me and the customers I serve". In addition, it helps providers to attract new customers, as the owner of a beauty salon pointed out: "Visitors to my website really like the easy and convenient appointment request service provided by the Amiona button and I was able to gain many new clients through it as well".

10.3.3 The Provided Infrastructure Motivates Providers to Offer New Services

The possibility to easily communicate new services online and handle requests efficiently via Amiona has also motivated local providers to introduce new services. A local bakery, for example, restarted its Sunday morning bread delivery service that had been discontinued a couple of years ago due to the high administrative effort.

10.3.4 Service Providers Appreciate Local Initiatives

Many of the service providers that we had addressed prior to and after the launch of the platform immediately saw the benefit of being part of the local marketplace and we were able to convince many of those who were reluctant by highlighting the local approach of the marketplace in St. Gallen. This local approach turned out to be a valuable unique selling proposition in comparison to other appointment coordination service providers and industry-specific booking platforms. Apparently, many service providers feel responsible for their towns or cities to a certain extent and do not wish to jeopardise local initiatives.

10.3.5 Local Digital Marketplaces Must Provide the Means to Include Providers Who Only Have Paper-Based Agendas

Whereas digitisation is the general trend being implemented on a large scale in the financial or manufacturing industries, we learned that it is quite the opposite in the case of smaller-scale service providers. This offered us the opportunity to step in and provide easy-to-understand, structured digital processes; however, often only to a certain limit. As described above, Amiona's functions include direct booking and integration with other calendars via ICS feed; however, as we learned, most smaller-scale businesses only use paper-based agendas and are not yet willing to change. This represents a very important issue and the reason why we implemented three different appointment coordination processes. We remain convinced that for now and the foreseeable future, all local digital marketplaces must offer these three options to include the majority of businesses and provide users with an interesting range of services.

10.3.6   Provider and Consumer Response Time Is the Most Critical Factor in Successful Appointment Coordination

The support of differently structured processes in appointment coordination to address the differing levels of digitisation, however, did not yet lead to an entirely satisfactory approach. As already described above, inadequate response times resulted in many impatient (and probably irritated) users calling the provider to get a response and it is quite apparent that a digital marketplace has no added value in comparison to a simple online directory if the user still has to call the provider to arrange an appointment. Request-answer-based appointment coordination therefore has to be accompanied by different push channels to notify users of new requests or status changes that require their action. This conclusion and the complications, in the form of double- and overbookings that result from missing and delayed consumer responses (e. g. when another consumer requests a specific date that has been suggested to a non-responsive consumer), quickly made improving response time our main priority.

Fortunately, the introduction of SMS notifications and the desk button massively improved the user experience and increased the satisfaction ratings of both consumers and providers. This was confirmed both by the feedback we received and the subsequent increase in transactions among returning users.

As new requests are still overlooked from time to time, we still track transactions in our quality management system and use phone calls as a last resort to notify users of unanswered messages after a specified time frame. Fortunately, this is required far less often than in the beginning when we only operated with e-mail notifications and is therefore further proof of the success of the measures we have since introduced to improve response time.

10.4   Exploitation and Outlook

The feedback we received from providers and consumers in both St. Gallen and other regions was very positive and resulted in a number of social services organisations, real estate companies and larger-scale employers expressing an interest in marketplaces for citizens, tenants and employees. We therefore pushed development further to offer a ready-to-use and easily adaptable standard software solution for local service marketplaces. This solution has since been implemented in various forms, such as a local marketplace for professional and informal services in Weil der Stadt, a platform for neighbourly help in Hamburg, or a platform for the residents of an independent living facility in eastern Switzerland. The concept of coordinating local services has now also been adapted by the major IT corporations. It is therefore vital that future implementations and software developments focus on very specific scopes and usage scenarios.

The lessons learned, insights gained and user feedback received generated many new ideas for technical improvements and development, of which not all could be implemented immediately.

Certain users expressed the wish to have a first come first served policy for requests to multiple personally selected providers. This would be beneficial among others to care-givers in retirement homes, e. g. when they need to organise social driving services on a specific date for one of their residents. In such cases they could send the request to all of the collaborating driving services and the first to answer would get the order as the request would be closed to the others. Similar requirements were also requested by people in need of time-critical appointments, e. g. with a doctor. Such users would also greatly benefit from the first come first serve policy for their requests, as they would no longer have to make a dozen phone calls to schedule a single appointment.

In order to access more external providers and continue to improve response times, we are additionally considering the use of automated phone call systems as an easy-to-use and very "pushy" request-notification channel. The integration of existing vertical direct booking platforms, e. g. for cleaning services, might also be an option in the near future. The expansion of the service portfolio and directly bookable dates would be similar to what has already happened on hotel reservation and flight booking platforms. Finally, we hope to extend the coordination processes in the not too distant future to facilitate "naturally speaking" requests through text mining and artificial intelligence to enhance the consumer experience, including with adjusted services for the handicapped.

References

1. P. Osl, Dienstleistungen für Independent Living: Kundenanforderungen, Potenzialbewertung und Handlungsempfehlungen, Berlin: Logos Verlag, 2010.
2. E. Sassen, Elektronische Dienstvermittlung für Independent Living: Geschäftsmodelle und Gestaltungsempfehlungen, St. Gallen, 2012.
3. P. Schenkel, Elektronische Dienstleistungsmarktplätze – Prozessmodell, IT-Architektur und Demonstration, St. Gallen, 2015.

How Large Corporations Survive Digitalization 11

Robert Jacobi and Ellena Brenner

Abstract

The transformation brought about by digital marketplaces will be the key challenge for any industry in the coming years. The media, IT and telecommunications sectors have struggled to adjust to a changing business environment for almost two decades. Now, companies from the financial services, transportation or even engineering sectors are ripe for disruption caused by technology and new business models. The only way to survive this process is by thoroughly preparing the entire organization for a transformation of unprecedented scope.

Providing strong leadership and vision or turning over the corporate culture is just a first step. In addition, cross-functional teams should become the norm, as well as incentive systems that reward risk-taking and agile development processes on the technical side. Taking cues from scientific literature, the authors' personal experience as digital transformation consultants and interviews with top executives, this article delivers a set of recipes for C-level management on how to transform their organizations for digital success.

11.1 Large Corporations in the Context of Digital Transformation

The extent to which the digital transformation disrupts large corporations is unprecedented. Technological advances make product life cycles shorter. Consumers expect in-

R. Jacobi (✉) · E. Brenner
The Nunatak Group GmbH
Munich, Germany
e-mail: robert.jacobi@nunatak.com

E. Brenner
e-mail: ellena.brenner@nunatak.com

© Springer-Verlag GmbH Germany 2018
C. Linnhoff-Popien et al. (eds.), *Digital Marketplaces Unleashed*,
https://doi.org/10.1007/978-3-662-49275-8_11

creasingly personalized services. Hardware becomes a commodity, and it is the seamless user experience that creates value and revenue. Chances actually are that not winning the race implies not surviving at all [1].

Since the turn of the century, over half of the companies on the Fortune 500 list have been replaced by faster-growing peers. Alongside industry-specific reasons, such as low oil prices in recent years, digital transformation is the main cause. Not only players from traditional industries are affected. Companies that were considered cutting-edge innovators some ten or fifteen years ago have not been able to keep up with technological change. Take Finnish handheld-maker Nokia, which stopped continuously reinventing itself at some point and was taken over by Microsoft as a consequence. The same is true for Blackberry Ltd.: Its revenues plummeted from 19.9 billion USD in 2011 to 2.2 billion USD in 2016, while the market for smartphones exploded worldwide.

So, who are the newcomers? They are companies such as Netflix, which started with delivering DVDs to doorsteps in a subscription model in the U.S. in 1997. It is now the world's largest online video-on-demand service with 86 million subscribers [2]. Salesforce, the cloud computing company that was founded in 1999 and employs some 19,000 people, is another example. The company that was leading the pack of Fortune 500 newcomers in 2016 is PayPal, the payment service built by the digital disruptors Elon Musk and Peter Thiel, among others. After the spin-off from Ebay, it is independent yet again, offering free peer-to-peer payment services while collecting revenue from big merchants.

It is not even necessary to reinvent the wheel in order to run a successful business in a digital world. Across developed economies, home-order services stopped printing their catalogs and went out of business. At the same time, online retailers such as Amazon or Zalando, the Germany-based fashion powerhouse, watched their turnover skyrocket. Not because they invented a new business model, but because they anticipated technological developments and changing customer expectations. This was made possible by constantly evolving internal structures and by strong beliefs centered around innovation, speed and agility – as well as a focus on building up a great product and a loyal customer base first, then thinking about profitability.

So what about the Citibanks, Comcasts and Chryslers of the world? Is there a chance for them to survive digital transformation against dynamic, well-financed newcomers that attract the best management and engineering talent in the world? Or will all of them succumb to the innovator's dilemma, which states that incumbents doing everything right in their present environment might still lose out to new market entrants who manage to anticipate future customer needs? Yes, there is a chance, and the older giants must find the courage for open-heart surgery in order to keep our economic system balanced and prosperous. Let's look at some strategies for survival and how to implement them in a large, bureaucratic organization.

11.2   Key Dimensions for Successful Organizational Change

Corporate managers have access to an extensive body of literature on organizational change, with theories and approaches that are sometimes useful, but often too academic by nature [3]. Many change process models have been developed in the tradition of Kurt Lewin's work [4]. Lewin's three-step model for social change, from unfreeze to move to refreeze was developed back in the 1940's and much quoted ever since. It assumes that driving forces must always outweigh resisting forces if change is to happen [5]. The change process aims to introduce temporary instability and is driven from the top [4].

According to the work of Lewin, Bullock and Batten, 'planned change' (1985) consists of four stages: exploration, planning, action and integration [6]. Beckhard and Harris suggest that organizations change when there is a current dissatisfaction combined with a desirable vision. In sum, the product of desire and vision must be larger than the resistance to change [7]. Also, 'change' should not be looked upon as an episode but an ongoing process [8].

While it always helps to reflect on cultural and structural change, the specific requirements of digitalization have not yet been amplified in scientific literature. The pressure from digitalization is so strong that simple change is insufficient and deep transformation needed. In a relatively short time span, businesses have to fundamentally alter entire strategies and cultures. That's where theory ends and a mindset of change has to be established not as an exception, but as a corporate norm. To do so, it is advisable to start at the top with a bold digital leadership, then begin changing the corporate culture and bring outside knowledge in, before adjusting corporate processes and structures to a new world. Fig. 11.1 provides an overview of key success factors for digital transformation.

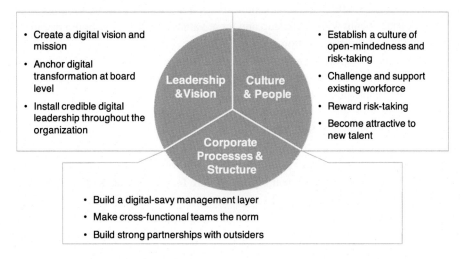

Fig. 11.1 Key success factors for digital transformation

11.2.1   Leadership & Vision

In the last century, selling airplane seats at a high margin and providing planes to move people from London to New York or to the Maldives was a prosperous business model. Today, successful carriers price some of their tickets below cost while making money with high-margin added services. Even further, an online travel service has never met its clients in person, but knows much more about their travel preferences than their favorite airline and is savvy enough to monetize accordingly. It's about selling travel time and experience, not transportation itself.

Nonetheless, in a 2016 board meeting of one of the world's leading airlines, the discussion about how to adjust to a digital marketplace was lacking some real sense of urgency. "Why should we fear Google?", a seasoned board member asked. "They don't even own planes." True, but nowadays, it is absolutely possible to run an airline without taking on the risk of buying a single plane. You simply lease the hardware and build a premium customer experience on top.

Even today, you will need mechanical engineers for maintenance, but without data scientists knowing what customers will want next, every airline is doomed to failure. "I see Ryanair as a digital travel leader that happens to have an airline attached to it," its chief technology officer, John Hurley, said. To reach its goal of becoming the Amazon of air travel, the company invested 36,000 developer hours, which is equivalent to 18 business years, in building a new mobile platform [9].

As the previous example shows, the lack of awareness of digital change among executives can be frightening. They tend to overestimate the traditional infrastructure's edge over aspiring, digitally-minded competitors. However, executives need to be ahead of the curve to make positive transformation happen. Horst Kayser, who leads transformation efforts as the Chief Strategy Officer at engineering giant Siemens, acknowledges that "all company changes begin with leadership and these values and attitudes should inspire and motivate the rest of the organization."

Leadership in the digital age requires a deep knowledge of digital business models, the courage to transform structures and processes against corporate inertia, and, last but not least, an unmistakable public commitment.

Create a Digital Vision and Strategy

The example of the airline board member is anything but unique. In a 2015 McKinsey study, only 17% of top executives said that their boards were sponsoring digital initiatives [10]. C-level executives of traditional big players are feeling outmatched by the ferocity of changing technology, emerging risks and new competitors. Only a few boards are able to reflect and reorient concerning their strategic goals and would subscribe to a recent statement by outgoing General Electric CEO, Jeff Immelt: "The digital pivot is the most important thing I've ever worked on and I'm totally juiced about the changes" [11].

The vision needs to be integrated into a digital strategy that focuses not only on external measures such as investing in start-ups, hiring agencies to build mobile apps or setting up an e-commerce channel. The strategy needs to address all elements of the core value chain and shouldn't spare support functions such as legal, human resources or finance. "At some point soon, it should even become the overall corporate strategy," the digital transformation officer of a leading services company said.

So, what are other key ingredients for a digital strategy? It needs to set clear, measurable goals with regards to (a) future digital revenue shares, (b) investments and expenditures in technology and (c) training hours for management and lower-level employees as well. Priorities need to be defined and actions coordinated. The strategy has to be credibly backed up by fast action and a roadmap for implementation. It's equally important to communicate the vision and strategy in a unified voice both internally and externally to customers, investors and other stakeholders in order to make it binding for all parts of the company.

Anchor Digital Transformation at Board Level

The awareness of the relevance of digital methods and technologies is greatly lagging among many of today's C-level executives. They were trained in business schools or finance or engineering departments of leading universities in the '80s or '90s, when digital business was a footnote in booming Western economies.

A Capgemini study showed that when CEOs communicate a clear digital vision, 93% of the employees agree that transforming the company is the right thing to do [12]. So, the vision is important, but only credible if it is backed up by knowledge and actions. "Our executives make headlines with how digital change affects us, but this only helps if we build a true momentum for change across the company," a senior manager of an international financial conglomerate said.

Digital transformation can only succeed as a company-wide initiative when CEOs, along with their boards, are its advocates and evangelists. They need to facilitate and effectively coordinate digital initiatives across the whole organization to develop a holistic digital corporate identity. Simply traveling to Silicon Valley is not sufficient to create a credible digital image.

In order to increase awareness for digitalization within the board, implementing a Chief Digital Officer (CDO) is one of the methods of choice among many large corporations (s. Fig. 11.2). Even if this is a first good step, it comes with several risks. First, integrating a CDO, often hired from a big digital player such as Google, into a traditional corporate culture is a major challenge. The person might behave somewhat undiplomatic, thereby creating a backlash against transformation among longer-standing management, and in return becoming frustrated very soon. This is particularly true when the CDO has little or no profit & loss responsibility.

Second, the implementation of a CDO creates the risk that other board members feel relieved from the pressure of thinking more digitally themselves. They perpetuate their long-standing offline business principles, even though digitalization should be the guiding principle for each and every decision taken at board level. The impact of digital trans-

Number of Chief Digital Officers (CDOs)
Worldwide, 2011-2015

- CDOs coordinate digital initiatives enterprise-wide
- CDOs indicate that "someone is taking care of digitalization". Having a CDO is an internal and external signal and might help in recruiting digital talent
- CDOs need to be assertive, experienced, achievement-oriented to cut through bureaucracy, take initiative and test limits
- CDOs need to be provided with authorization, decision-making power power and sufficient digital budgets

Fig. 11.2 The role of CDOs worldwide. (eMarketer [13])

formation must be fully recognized by every single board member as they ideally form a digital committee in order to shape the digital future for the whole corporation.

> **CASE: How has Siemens AG Changed its Organizational Setup in the Context of Digital Transformation?**
> Siemens decided not to hire a Chief Digital Officer, but to include digital competencies deeply into every division. Horst Kayser, Chief Strategy Officer at Siemens AG, explains why:
> *"The fundamental organizational question we faced when we began this transformation was whether to centralize our digital capabilities into one separate organization or to embed them into our existing market-sector-focused divisions. We chose the latter approach, because we felt that for a true business transformation to occur we had to be more digital everywhere rather than completely digital all in one place.*
> *Some companies create separate digital units, however, they face the issue of acceptance by the traditional businesses and the continued silo mentality which digitalization needs to break down. That said, we have implemented a centralized corporate digitalization strategy and some technology and governance functions to coordinate and measure the implementation of digital initiatives across all divisions."*

Install Credible Digital Leadership Throughout the Organization

Leadership with a vision is important at the top level but doesn't help if it doesn't trickle down into the organization, particularly to the second and third management level. "That's where the most conservative layer sits, full of managers reluctant to make changes that threaten their kingdoms," the head of digital strategy of a leading automotive company said. 60% of managers assess their own digital competency as high to very high. On the contrary, only 26% of their respective subordinates say so about their managers [14].

"These people are very busy producing presentations and planning budgets, but are neither incentivized nor inclined by nature to promote real change."

In 2013, Bertelsmann, the German-based media conglomerate, introduced a format called "Digital Bootcamp" produced by Bertelsmann University and The Nunatak Group. From the CEO level downwards, the top 300 managers of all divisions were asked to participate in a two-day immersive format where they experimented with mobile games, 3D printing or social media advertising and discussed potential impacts on their lines of business. Those who were most skeptical at the beginning turned out to become the strongest internal promoters of the program, even years after, when it was turned into a regular coaching format offered to all management levels.

In addition, 'reverse mentoring' provides an opportunity for the older employees to learn from their younger, digitally-skilled counterparts unlike traditional mentoring where learning is dispensed hierarchically from an older mentor to a younger protégé. Thus, reverse mentoring is an inverted type of mentoring relationship [15]. Sylvain Newton, Global Head of Talent Sourcing and Development at Allianz SE, has successfully supported the implementation of the initiative and participated himself as a reverse mentee both at GE as well as at Allianz. He highlights the possibility to leverage the mutual expertise of digital natives and digital immigrants by being perceptive of their different needs, value systems, and work demands.

11.2.2 Culture & People

When you meet employees in an industrial-style open-space office, wearing shorts and making coffee with an Italian espresso machine, their fixed-gear bicycles parked inside the door and office walls covered with slogans such as "Distinguish sense from nonsense" or "Accept change is inevitable", you might assume you're visiting a cutting-edge start-up in Berlin.

The truth is that you are in one of four innovation labs opened worldwide by the reinsurance company Munich Re, founded in 1890 and one of the most traditional DAX 30 companies. Engineers, mathematicians and marketers jointly work on new insurance models and sales channels while listening to Spotify playlists and discussing the latest episode of "Games of Thrones".

Compared to similar efforts, the innovation labs are not some distant satellites but deal with issues relevant to the core business of Munich Re. "Yes, I'm personally afraid because our business model is severely threatened," a board member answered when asked about his perspective on Fintech companies and disruptive insurance start-ups [16]. Nonetheless, if the people working at the innovation lab attended a meeting at the corporate headquarters in Schwabing, a mere 15-minute ride by subway, without changing their attire, they would stand out from their colleagues working in the business culture of a reinsurer.

At some stage of the transformation process, entertaining different cultures at the same time is the right way to go. However, one should begin with the end in mind and with an answer to how these cultures will merge into a new corporate DNA down the road. The bigger challenge is not to motivate young employees to work in innovation labs but to induce their more conservative peers to break out of silo thinking and orientation on short-term benefits. In addition, innovators must be encouraged to remain creative and continue to think outside the box, instead of adjusting to the legacy corporate culture.

Establish a Culture of Open-Mindedness and Risk-Taking

Organizational structures of large corporations are characterized by lengthy approval processes instead of trial and error and hierarchical decision-making instead of en-trepreneurial leeway. To keep up with the higher speed and shorter product life cycles of small, agile start-ups, large corporations need a massive cultural shift towards open-mind-edness and risk-taking. Siemens' Chief Strategy Officer, Horst Kayser, agrees: "Speed is a critical success factor and whilst large global companies like Siemens may have the advantage of size and scale, the slower speed of decision-making and execution is sometimes a hindrance, especially given the pace of change within software industries."

So, how can large corporations win this game? More than ever, fostering creativity and innovation is key in order to keep up with fast-changing customer needs. Giving employees the opportunity to contribute to idea contests or similar programs is no news to many corporations. However, in order to implement thinking outside of the box permanently, it is important to create a culture of openness and exchange. Here, design-thinking approaches help. Building upon the work of scientists Herbert A. Simon and Robert McKim from the late 1960s, it was introduced to the business world by David M. Kelley, the founder of design-thinking agency IDEO. In design thinking, teams are built across functions and divisions, meet in creative environments and follow an overall goal and vision, instead of trying to solve a very specific issue. In a recent study, the Hasso-Plattner-Institut confirms that the approach is not only helpful when building new products, but also contributes to changing patterns of problem-solving and collaboration [17].

For a limited period, a parallel culture, as in the Munich Re example above, is one way to go. It creates an innovative, agile playing ground for digital initiatives while also keeping up the old wallpaper for traditional business relationships. That's also how many IT departments in large corporations try to reinvent themselves: In a bimodal structure (as conceptually introduced by Gartner in 2014 [18]), agile and flexible units are used for the development of innovative software, while legacy technology continues to be maintained through traditional processes. Obviously, someone – in this case, the original IT depart-ment – must maintain and update the accounting software or manage user accounts on corporate computers.

Regarding risk-taking, corporations have a harder time than young, venture-backed companies that have to try new things in order to find a path to success. However, this doesn't mean you have to constantly reward those who don't take any risks but just im-prove their current business bottom line. "In fact, we should tell our shareholders that we will invest all our earnings of the next two years in digital projects," the interviewee from a large automotive company said. "This doesn't mean that we stop taking care of our daily business, but it would help us to remain competitive with the tech giants a few years down the road."

Challenge and Support Existing Workforce

Today's workplace is a highly demanding, complex environment that requires flexible minds and the willingness to learn and adopt new digital technologies. Digital expertise needs to be profoundly integrated into the mindset of workers to develop successful platforms and products. This doesn't create any hurdles for recent university graduates who have grown up using several mobile devices at the same time. However, no large company would be able to exchange its seasoned workforce with newcomers instantaneously, and would be ill-advised to do so.

So, how to combine the two worlds? The newcomers will make their way naturally, if they're open to learning some of the corporate lingo and understanding corporate processes. Overcoming the fears of more experienced employees is the bigger challenge. In their famous book "Reengineering the Corporation", Hammer and Champy state that the whole idea of change always brings deeper instincts such as fear to the surface [19]. The productivity of employees feeling left behind suffers greatly.

When guided with appreciation, provided with access to digital expertise and steered by ambitious yet reachable digital goals, employees are willing to join the transformational path. Thus, refocusing existing education programs around digital topics is obvious but by far not sufficient. "My social media training was not really helpful. It lacked practical elements and a trainer with online journalism experience," a spokesman from a major financial company complains. Integrating external experts and providing hands-on training in educational programs for employees are methods of choice.

Setting the right incentives is another important step. Goal-setting with a focus on longer-term success instead of short-term profits represents a cornerstone for digital transformation. Only if goals such as the number of client touchpoints on digital platforms or successful digitalization of internal processes make up a sufficient portion of the overall bonus, managers and their teams will be incentivized to change behavior substantially. "At the beginning, our top management strictly opposed including goals dependent on the results of neighboring departments," a chief human resources officer of an international services company remembers. "A year later, this was fully accepted and made collaboration much more commonplace in our company."

Similarly, a large manufacturer introduced so-called "stretch goals" that are impossible to reach by one single employee, such as introducing a certain number of new business models or opening up new sales channels. It required individuals to pull together throughout divisions and hierarchy levels. Silo mentality was reduced and collaboration enhanced, which is a key ingredient for digital success [20]. Setting such ambitious goals typically brings about another benefit: They help spread a sense of ownership and shared responsibility for entrepreneurial success.

Become Attractive to New Talent

Large corporations tend to entertain pin boards for internal openings in some common area. An international consumer goods company is no exception here: Just outside the headquarters' cafeteria, dozens of positions are offered on letter-size pages. It is worth taking a closer look: Almost two-thirds bear headlines such as "Data Scientist", "Data Engineer" or "User Interface Designer". It is hard to fill such newly created positions with current employees but not much easier to attract external talent with fresh degrees into a corporate position.

The attractiveness to digital talent is dependent on the employer's reputation and branding as well as individual working models. Particularly when hiring graduates for jobs in data analytics or software development, it is hard to compete with attractive digital giants such as Google or with start-ups that provide sweat equity. To get it done nonetheless, (a) employer branding needs to be enhanced, (b) screening of candidates must be improved using data-based methods and (c) hiring processes have to provide lessons and lasting experiences even for those who don't make the threshold.

In times when employers are rated on platforms such as Glassdoor or Kununu, it is equally important to make sure that companies keep promises made during the recruiting process. Offering a flexible working environment, like at media and investment conglomerate Virgin, with self-determined weekly working hours and number of holidays, is only part of the story [21]. Most importantly, corporations need to offer a working environment that leaves enough freedom of decision to staff on all levels.

Online retailer Zalando sets an example with its management method of radical agility. After an internal analysis showed high employee turnover and low productivity growth, traditional hierarchy levels were abolished and developers got more decision power, e. g. which programming languages to use. As a result, job applications for tech profiles more than quadrupled since 2014 and departures dropped by 35% [22].

11.2.3   Corporate Processes & Structure

When an international industrial company introduced an entirely new and powerful data management structure across all units, protests were immense. Some departments had invested millions to keep legacy systems running and wanted to keep them. Others didn't see the need for such a system in the first place. In the short run, streamlining processes made things more cumbersome as many units had to adapt their internal processes. The benefits of integrated data storage and accessibility would only become visible at a later stage.

So, when is the right time to introduce such a far-reaching change in technology, and how do you go about it? How do you make sure all relevant stakeholders are taken on board for the journey? Implementing a digital strategy is only possible if corporate processes and structures are reformed. How can corporations align numerous digital initiatives into a holistic transformation process?

Determine Your Digital Maturity and Act Accordingly

As mentioned previously, an important stepping stone is the definition of an organizational setup that allows maintaining traditional business models as long as they are profitable while getting future ready at the same time. Becoming an integrated digital company should be the goal for all, regardless of whether it is a B2C or B2B company. Typically, the latter ones show lower levels of digital maturity, with some digital initiatives in place but little coordination and a lack of consideration at the holding level. Our framework (Fig. 11.3) helps corporations to determine the level of digital maturity already reached and to act accordingly.

Many traditional companies are now at a stage where some early flagship initiatives have been started and some digital business models have been tried out. Here, it is important to collect and assess them, measure their success, continue the ones performing well and discontinue others. At the same time, digital knowledge and experience gained through these projects should be collected at a corporate level.

To enter the second stage, it is helpful to install a digital unit within the strategy or business development department. This unit should be staffed by a mix of resources from the outside – people who've worked in online-only businesses, or at least in digitally more advanced B2C corporations – and some insiders who know the processes, can guide the newcomers through the corporate jungle and are able to build alliances for them. Such a digital unit will play a key role in developing guidelines for successful digital products and preparing a digital strategy and vision for the board. This is also the time when bi-modal structures might still be beneficial, such as innovation labs that spill over culturally to the main company.

"Our job is temporary," said a digital unit head of a large mobility company. "We're here to help the entire organization reinvent itself, and if we're successful, we're making ourselves obsolete." Typically, at the beginning of the journey, dependence on external agencies for implementation is rather high. For the next level, it is important to build up relevant internal structures, particularly in IT, in order to provide a steep learning curve to employees and keep the knowledge and experience gained within the corporation itself.

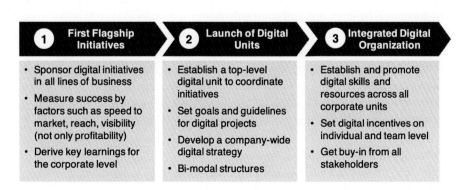

Fig. 11.3 Structural steps in a digital transformation process

At a later stage of digital development – some consumer-facing companies are about to reach this level already – digital resources have to be evenly distributed across all relevant units. For example, product development teams will then develop digital-first products only, rather than adjusting existing offline products to online business models. Marketing departments will develop digital channels first, with offline channels being phased out gradually, as target groups move completely online. At that stage, digital thinking has become an integrated part of the corporate DNA and the company is fully transformed and even able to disrupt its competitors.

Make Cross-Functional Teams the Norm

For decades, one of the key trends in business was to build separate profit centers for each line of business. In large corporate holdings, this might be without alternative. However, even there, and in somewhat smaller companies as well, digital transformation requires thinking and acting across units instead of thinking in silos and short-term individual gains [23]. In the medium term, this will deliver a positive contribution to everyone's bottom line.

Integrated knowledge tools, information streams and communication processes will speed up product development and help businesses keep up with shorter product life cycles. Integrating teams is also a necessity when it comes to distributing digital talent across the corporation. For example, having a user experience specialist on every product development team will help with seizing opportunities and implementing tools for its exploitation right away.

Take the example of a consumer-products company which realized during a workshop about the internet of things that some of its business was massively threatened by new competitors. They tore down the traditional horizontal structure that was built along value and organized the company around vertical spaces such as the home, the car and the office, allocating support functions to all of these individual divisions. This move helped them to innovate faster and to create interconnected products with a higher use for customers [24].

Agile project management methods, such as rapid prototyping or daily collaboration, are key for digital success, not only in IT departments, but across all units. An agile team is cross-functional by definition and constantly readjusts to meet the needs of the marketplace, not the corporation. The "Agile Manifesto", published in 2001 by a group of leaders in the discipline, contains twelve key rules for agile software development. It states that responding to change is more important than following a plan, and a working product is more important than comprehensive documentation: "Simplicity – the art of maximizing the amount of work not done – is essential." Some of these notions are difficult to entertain in a corporate context, but starting today, not tomorrow, is a good idea [25].

Build Strong Partnerships

At a time when it takes just a few months for a new technology to become mainstream, it is important to join forces and learn from each other, particularly in complex environments where vertical integration is too costly. Partnerships can take on several forms. Companies can jointly fund expensive research and development efforts. They can build joint ventures that represent an entire value chain for a certain line of product. Another model is joining forces in using digital technology and data-oriented customer data to jointly promote and distribute non-competing products and services. Similarly, cooperating with innovative start-ups might be an attractive alternative to a risky acquisition.

As an example, in September 2016, corporate technology giants Amazon, Google, Facebook, IBM and Microsoft announced an Artificial Intelligence alliance. Primarily, the partnership aims at clarifying ethical values of new technologies by exchanging best practices and publishing the obtained results. The cooperation indicates that even the largest and most innovative, cutting-edge corporations are aware that large benefits can be reaped from knowledge exchange with peers [26].

Just a few months earlier, IBM and SAP announced a large program to drive the modernization of clients' systems and processes and "accelerate them into the digital economy". The alliance focuses on providing efficient cloud-computing services and real-time maintenance and support of enterprise solutions. "We're formalizing a complementary set of capabilities to simplify and speed outcomes for clients," an IBM senior manager explained [18].

So, how do you know if a digital partnership is successful? The exchange of knowledge should spill over into the individual companies themselves. Motivation of the workforce should increase by opening up to the outside world. New markets are accessed. And, most importantly, products and services will be delivered to the customers faster and more closely to their needs.

11.3 Summary and Outlook: Key Success Factors for Surviving the Digital Transformation

The previous chapters introduced a variety of measures for corporations to assure the successful digital transformation of their organizations. It is important to keep in mind that the three dimensions of leadership & vision, culture & people, as well as corporate processes & structure are highly interdependent. Successful change in one area doesn't mean that the job is done across the entire corporation.

All things considered, what can we conclude about traditional corporations' chances of survival in a digitalized world? A study from the John M. Olin School of Business at Washington University estimated that 40% of today's Fortune 500 companies will no longer exist in ten years due to digitalization [27]. Similarly, John Chambers, the CEO of Cisco, one of the leading network providers worldwide, explains that 40% of Cisco's business customers will not exist anymore in ten years [28]. This is the paradox of transformation. Urgency is high, yet it might take time to reap the benefits: Every decision-maker is aware that building a new factory entails substantial investments and time to break even, while new digital projects are expected to return positive cash flows right away. It is important to think in longer cycles instead of short-term gains in order to survive digital transformation.

However, this does not mean that there's still some time left to start the process. Companies that want to be in the driver's seat of the transformation vehicle must start to radically alter their organizations on all levels now. The alternative, waiting for the burning platform phenomenon, is worse: Initiating radical cuts when the threat to existence is no longer deniable will be too late.

Even from a shareholders' perspective, adjusting to a digital world is the right step. Tech companies enjoy high valuations primarily because of their future potential, while more traditional peers are valued by their current performance. Why not change this rule? Any car maker, airline or engineering company will be able to improve its valuation by laying out a concise digital strategy for the next five to ten years and delivering examples of success sooner rather than later.

On the flip side, corporations must resist the temptation of using digital transformation as a scapegoat. In the next economic downturn, a corporate tendency to cut costs on behalf of digital transformation will most likely emerge. Robotics and automatization will definitely decrease the headcount needed in some areas. However, building up a digital-savvy workforce in other areas will have to outweigh this reduction. Simply reducing costs and increasing efficiency in a legacy business will not make any organization more digital after all.

Maximilian Hoffmann, The Nunatak Group, contributed to this article.

References

1. Handelsblatt, "Die deutsche Karte," 26 August 2016.
2. CNN, 21 October 2016. [Online]. Available: http://money.cnn.com/2016/10/17/technology/ netflix-earnings-subscribers/.
3. R. Todnem By, Organisational change management: A critical review, Bd. 5, Journal of change management, 2005, pp. 369–380.
4. S. Woodward und C. Hendry, Leading and coping with change, Bd. 4.2, 2004, pp. 155–183.
5. E. Cameron und M. Green, Making sense of change management: a complete guide to the models, tools and techniques of organizational change, Kogan Page Publishers, 2015.
6. P. Bullock und D. Batten, It's just a phase we're going through: a review and synthesis of OD phase analysis, Bd. 10.4, 1985, pp. 383–412.
7. McAllen Williams Consulting, 28 August 2016. [Online]. Available: http://www. mcallenwilliams.com/wpcontent/uploads/2016/02/Change-Management-2nd-Edition.pdf.
8. C. Deuringer, Organisation und Change Management: Ein ganzheitlicher Strukturansatz zur Förderung organisatorischer Flexibilität, Springer Verlag, 2000.
9. J. Kennedy, 31 August 2016. [Online]. Available: https://www.siliconrepublic.com/enterprise/ ryanair-digital-disruption-myryanair.
10. McKinsey, 30 August 2016. [Online]. Available: http://www.mckinsey.com/business-functions/ business-technology/ourinsights/adapting-your-board-to-the-digital-age.

11. The Telegraph, 31 August 2016. [Online]. Available: http://www.telegraph.co.uk/finance/newsbysector/industry/11909721/Thevisionary-rebuilding-GE-from-scratch-to-become-a-digital-powerhouse.html.

12. Capgemini, 30 August 2016. [Online]. Available: https://www.capgemini-consulting.com/resource-fileaccess/resource/pdf/embracing_digital_technology_a_new_strategic_imperative.pdf.

13. eMarketer, 30 August 2016. [Online]. Available: http://www.emarketer.com/Article/Chief-Digital-Officers-Continue-Global-Explosion/1012489.

14. Wirtschaftswoche, 28 August 2016. [Online]. Available: http://blog.wiwo.de/look-at-it/2015/10/01/digital-loser-statt-leader-nur-jeder-12-manager-in-deutschland-fit-fur-digitale-transformation/.

15. S. Chaudhuri und G. Rajashi, Reverse mentoring a social exchange tool for keeping the boomers engaged and millennials committed, Bd. 11.1, 2012, pp. 55–76.

16. A. Kaspar, 31 August 2016. [Online]. Available: http://versicherungswirtschaft-heute.de/koepfe/munich-re-vorstand-siehtgeschaftsmodell-gefahrdet/.

17. Hasse Plattner Institut, 09 September 2016. [Online]. Available: http://hpi.de/pressemitteilungen/2015/design-thinking-erste-grosse-studie-weisterfolg-in-unternehmen-nach.html.

18. Gartner, Inc., [Online]. Available: https://www.gartner.com/doc/2798217/bimodal-it-digitally-agile-making. [Accessed 26 October 2016].

19. M. Hammer und J. Champy, Reengineering the Corporation: Manifesto for Business Revolution, Zondervan, 2009.

20. McKinsey, 12 September 2016. [Online]. Available: http://www.mckinsey.com/businessfunctions/organization/our-insights/making-collaboration-across-functions-areality.

21. Co.Exist, 05 September 2016. [Online]. Available: https://www.fastcoexist.com/3043269/vacation-policies-youll-envy-fromcompanies-you-dont-work-for.

22. T3N, 31 August 2016. [Online]. Available: http://t3n.de/news/zalando-modekonzern-739646/.

23. Accenture, 29 August 2016. [Online]. Available: https://www.accenture.com/_acnmedia/Accenture/Conversion-Assets/DotCom/Documents/Global/PDF/Digital_2/Accenture-Digital-Transformation-In-The-Age-Of-The-Customer.pdf.

24. McKinsey, 30 August 2016. [Online]. Available: http://www.mckinsey.com/business-functions/business-technology/ourinsights/adapting-your-board-to-the-digital-age.

25. M. Fowler und J. Highsmith, The agile manifesto, Software Development, 20101, pp. 28–35.

26. The Guardian, 24 October 2016. [Online]. Available: https://www.theguardian.com/technology/2016/sep/28/google-facebook-amazon-ibm-microsoft-partnership-on-ai-tech-firms.

27. Deloitte Digital, 12 September 2016. [Online]. Available: http://www.deloittedigital.com/us/blog/find-your-disruptive-advantage.

28. U. Schäfer und M. Beise, Deutschland Digital, Frankfurt: Campus, 2016, p. 91.

Further Reading

29. Strategy+Business, 12 September 2016. [Online]. Available: http://www.strategybusiness.com/article/Siemens-CEO-Joe-Kaeser-on-the-Next-Industrial-Revolution?gko=efd41.

30. IBM, 12 September 2016. [Online]. Available: http://www-03.ibm.com/press/us/en/pressrelease/49458.wss.

31. Fortune, 06 September 2016. [Online]. Available: http://fortune.com/2015/06/04/fortune-500-facts/.

Part IV
Individualized Digital Learning

Preface: Individualized Digital Learning

12

Kerstin Jeger

> What purpose would education serve in our days unless it helped humans to a knowledge of the environment to which they have to adapt themselves? (Maria Montessori)

If one would conduct a historic review of educational systems one observes a coevolution of society and education. In the agricultural period education was characterized by an apprenticeship model which reflected the needs of the prevailing family and community settings. The current educational model was formed by the industrial revolution ("first machine age") and is often referred to as the factory model. Today's world, however, is characterized by the automation of cognitive tasks designed to substitute human activities with software based machines, the so called "second machine age". This is triggering a new era of complexity with large scale social changes. While the concrete implications of that shift are still unclear, certain patterns with implications for an adjusted educational model can be detected. The digital champions of today are no longer relying primarily on an efficiency and cost savings focus, on hierarchical structures, and on placing the shareholder value at center stage. Thus, the hierarchical build factory model for education, which focuses on rote learning and standardized testing, with an emphasis to efficiently produce graduates, is put into question as well. A knowledge based, creative and innovation economy, which is less-hierarchical and is focusing on customer value, requires a different set of skills. In a nutshell, I argue that it requires the ability to maintain a life-long lasting curiosity and to be collaborative. Only a curious mindset, inquisitive and open to new situations, can transform complex problems into manageable situations. Collaboration is thereby the imperative for acting in complex settings. Our educational system has not yet adapted to the new requirements of the digitalized world. Rather than producing mines of information, educational institutions should foster curiosity and collaboration.

K. Jeger (✉)
Montessori-Vereinigung Nürnberger Land e.V.
Lauf/Pegnitz, Germany
e-mail: Kerstin.Jeger@gmail.com

© Springer-Verlag GmbH Germany 2018
C. Linnhoff-Popien et al. (eds.), *Digital Marketplaces Unleashed*,
https://doi.org/10.1007/978-3-662-49275-8_12

Curiosity or the "inner flame" is innate. Humans are born with an inherent urge to learn, to grow and to understand. The "inner flame" determines our learning potential which equals our human potential in many ways. If you stop learning you metaphorically "die". Our current educational system based on the standardized transfer of knowledge is further extinguishing this flame. The "one size fits all" standardized education threatens our curiosity. To maintain our curiosity students need to be provided with an individualized learning environment that offers the opportunity to follow their own interests and foster their curiosity. Having spent my live in education, I believe that the framework of the Montessori method is an effective example or may even constitute a blueprint for a new educational model which values individual learning.

At the beginning of the 20th century, the Montessori Method was developed by Maria Montessori, an Italian physician and educator. The method considers teachers as facilitators of children, who are helped "to help themselves" rather than to be taught and instructed. Key features of the Montessori method are mixed-age classrooms, student choice of activity, uninterrupted work time and a constructivist "discovery" model in which students learn concepts from working with materials rather than by direct instruction. The individualization of education is thereby strengthening curiosity and the desire for lifelong learning. Living in complex systems, solution to problems need to be found in an exploration not a pure analytical manner. Maintaining curiosity and, linked to this, the desire for lifelong learning is a prerequisite to get along well in today's world.

Equally important to the Montessori approach is Collaboration. The open learning environment, the free movement and the multi-age classrooms is designed to facilitates collaborative learning. For me, there is nothing more satisfying than seeing an eight year old child explaining what it just learned to a five year old. Imitative learning and peer tutoring offers students daily opportunities to teach, to share information and to collaborate all around. This collaborative environment is of immanent relevance as it demonstrates how respectful relationships can be established. In fact, the mutual relationships based on freedom of movement and the recognition of capabilities and interests help children to develop respect for themselves, others and the environment. This process is of particular importance in times where virtual worlds and a shield of anonymity provide new opportunities to engage in disrespectful and even inhuman behaviors.

Digital learning is complementary to individualized learning by further individualizing the learning experience through adaption and customization of the content for a certain group or person. The opportunities to implement Montessori's idea of "thinking through doing" are manifold and teachers should consciously introduce digital media to the classroom. Cloud solutions, for example, give students the possibility to access information on demand, on their terms and from everywhere and thereby remove physical and social barriers to education. Social media enables them to interactively exchange information, share knowledge and build valuable connections. The application of multimedia devices and tangible interfaces facilitates the multisensory learning of abstract concepts such as "area", "space", "number" or even geometrical shapes. Technology offers completely new possibilities of multisensory learning by coordinating auditory, visual and kinesthetic education. Many programs designed for struggling readers, for example, use auditory elements in order to stimulate multiple senses. Simulation tools interact with every respective student and provide instant feedback guiding it through the customized virtual learning environment. Consistent with the Montessori philosophy, this as well helps to take away the fear of failure, which is then replaced by a sense of safety that encourages learning through trial and error. History classes can be enriched by educational games that retell historic events in an interactive way, with implemented rules and objectives, enhancing the learning experience. Finally, applied data measurement and analysis can further contribute to the individualization of learning fostering curiosity and collaboration. As a result, digital technologies allow students to explore the world safely on their terms in a collaborative way. The use of technology in an educational framework offers many advantages. However, it can only support, but never replace the interaction between a teacher and a student, since deep inter-personal relationships have the biggest impact on the development of students. This fundamental role of personal relationships will never change even with an increasing deployment of digital technologies in classrooms.

The Montessori education has spawned a long list of overachievers, such as management guru Peter Drucker, Gabriel Garcia Marquez, Taylor Swift, George Clooney or Jacqueline Kennedy Onassis. But especially when it comes to unleashed digital marketplaces it seems that it is particularly suited if one considers its alumni, such as the Google founders Larry Page and Sergei Brin, the Amazon founder Jeff Bezos, Wikipedia's Jimmy Wales, AOL's Steve Case and the creator of SimCity, Will Wright. In the case of Google, Montessori does not only effected the mindset of the two founders, but also the company's DNA. In fact, Google did not start as a big idea, but was built trough experimentation out of a small digital library project at Stanford University. Page and Brin discovered their business model while solving upcoming problems with a sense of stipulating curiosity. Today, the Montessori methodology is spread throughout the company. In fact, Marissa Mayer, former Vice President at Google, explained that "you can't understand Google unless you know that both Larry and Sergey were Montessori kids. In a Montessori school, you go paint because you have something to express or you just want to do it that afternoon, not because the teacher said so. This is baked in how Larry and Sergey approach problems. They're always asking, 'Why should it be like that?' It's the way their brains were programmed early on." Similarly, Jeff Bezos of Amazon, is crediting his Montessori education for experimenting even if it may lead to failure or as he puts it: "I like going down blind alleys".

To gain such an innovative, explorative mindset I believe the following aspects need to be taken into consideration. On a generic level, Montessori encourages students to ask questions, to experiment and to discover new things, relationships and possibilities. Reflecting on today's world, the problem is not that we don't have the right answers, but that we are often not generating the right questions. The fast pace of change causes many answers to be outdated or irrelevant quickly. It is clear that asking questions is an highly creative act as it requires considerations beyond the as-is. Eric Schmidt, executive chairman of Alphabet Inc., outlined the importance of questions to his organization when he said that "we run this business on questions, not answers." Google's strategies always find their origin within questions, as questions stimulate conversations and conversations drive innovation. To install a setting or culture in which asking questions is trained and welcomed is therefore of equal importance in both the educational setting as well as the corporate environment.

However, more concretely, there are also many striking similarities if one compares popular innovation frameworks, such as agile development or the lean startup methodology with the Montessori method. Montessori and agile projects are planned very similarly. In both cases there are no teachers, but only guides and mentors, that facilitate discussions on important events and to dos. Mixed-age learning groups are equaling cross function teams. Task are voluntarily picked up – within a predefined range – by the preference of the student, just as developers would do it according to the Scrum method. Uninterrupted working blocks correspond sprints or epics. With regard to the discovery model, agile IT concepts such as continuous integration or test automation have built in control of error, which is an important part of the Montessori environments as well. Children can check their own work frequently and instantly without the help of their teachers. Instant feedback cycles guide the students through a process of exploration and trial and error. In this regard, even the hacker mentality ("fail fast, fail forward") demonstrates certain similarities with the Montessori method. Just as within a Montessori classroom, agile startups often designed their office spaces as a heterogeneous, controlled environment which allows for free movement and spontaneous gatherings in order to trigger knowledge sharing, collaboration, well-being and creativity instead of productivity. We are currently witnessing one of the most profound changes in human history and therefore have to significantly adjust the way we teach and learn. The whole educational system has to transform itself to adapt to the new requirements of the second machine age. The Montessori educational approach may hereby constitute a heuristic that enables us to comfortably navigate through this demanding, complex world. The spirit of Montessori shall therefore not only flourish in niches, but should find widespread application in our educational systems. For that we ensure that our education enables us to see the world as it is, to explore it with a curious mind and helps us to adopt to the given environment.

Corporate Learning in Upheaval

13

Rauthgundis Reck and Gunnar Jöns

Abstract

Digitalization and innovation pressure are changing the world of corporate learning, new rules of learning are emerging. Today competent learners seize the initiative and form great networks. They quickly get learning contents out of the internet, learn in online courses with high quality videos, visit virtual conferences, give webinars and finally exchange information in expert networks with people of their own academic level. Colleagues help one another with podcasts and short video clips. They get to know new approaches and methods of work through agile and digital collaboration. Today learning in technology-oriented business units is increasingly informal, individual an independent of intermediary educational institutions and services (HR, trainingsprovider). The progress leading from just learning to individual learning is particularly emphasized by 'learning analytics'. Several promising examples show how structured learning contexts lead to a more individual and efficient learning of facts. More general models of individual learning are conceivable if learners own, use and analyze their personal data. If the possibilities of digitalization are combined with concepts of pedagogy and learning psychology, every learner could take another advantage. The change of corporate learning in the future will be diverse.

R. Reck (✉)
Allianz Technology SE
Munich, Germany
e-mail: gundi.reck@web.de

G. Jöns
biners – business information security
Bonn, Germany
e-mail: gunnar.joens@biners.eu

© Springer-Verlag GmbH Germany 2018
C. Linnhoff-Popien et al. (eds.), *Digital Marketplaces Unleashed*,
https://doi.org/10.1007/978-3-662-49275-8_13

13.1   How Digital Transformation Influences the World of Learning

A new era of customer communication has started as a consequence of the rapid spread of mobile social media. Companies now can serve their customers' needs more specifically. It is for this reason that experiences, empathy, enthusiasm and passion matter to customers interests. In a similar manner, digital learning focuses on individuals and their interests and needs. The main focus therefore is not the applied technology but the aim to provide personalized education to many.

The digital working world is characterized by quickly changing processes as well as by knowledge intensive, creative and networked services. Work gets reorganized through mobile communication and collaboration platforms. Highly specialized professionals work together directly and globally in interdisciplinary teams. The availability of knowledge and information explodes, especially technical knowledge increases exponentially whereas its half-life declines. That's why we constantly learn something new in shorter and shorter periods of time. This development requires to rapidly acquire knowledge in a direct, adaptive, concrete and flexible way.

Disruptive innovations lead to new demands of human expertise. The digitalization and automatization proceed with 'internet of things' and 'cognitive computing solutions'. The automatization of knowledge work and cognitive processes result in the acquisition of decision and management processes by machines in many areas. Humans will work together with machines. Hence, their skills will mostly be required in areas where machines have not yet overtaken human work completely [1].

This development strongly influences corporate learning. The previous digital approaches such as e-learning and mobile learning could not achieve significant learning improvements within the company. Pretty often conventional learning concepts are simply digitalized instead of improved. If one wants to support sustainable and operative learning the consideration of impact factors is essential. For this purpose we examine the three core issues of effective learning – cognition, creativity and skills. Thereafter we name examples of these issues showing improvements of learning concerning the chances of digitalization.

13.2   The Learner – Many Variables Influence Successful Learning

Cognitive science and neuroscience describe human learning as a highly individual process that is based on unique, intellectual structures of the brain which are constantly reorganized. Today learning is considered as an active and constructive process. Learning contents need to be integrated in the individual and unique cognitive-emotional structures. Therefore learning processes need to be mainly self-controlled. Human learning depends on several factors and frameworks that vary a lot between individuals. For example prior knowledge favors the acquisition of new knowledge as well as motivation and emotions underlining sense and significance to the learner. Study speed and strategies differ individually since everyone learns in a different way. We have to keep in mind that knowledge cannot be transformed, but has to be acquired actively. So even though people have the great opportunity to easily access 'the world of knowledge' they still need to work for it themselves. To conclude, we just get smart through highly individual and active cross-linking of our own level of knowledge [2]. Therefore the dogma 'you don't have to know it yourself but only where you can find it' is not far-reaching.

13.3 The Human Spirit – Source of Creativity and Innovation

Learning is the interaction of remembrance and oblivion. What we perceive as individuality of humans is directly connected to its memory (commemoration, feelings, dreams, experiences). In this process the people themselves change and especially they do in times when they forgot most details. These consciously unavailable memory contents can be considered the treasure of the human spirit since they deliver our fantasy, creativity and imagination. Non-cognitive shares of the human spirit enable creative and witty ideas, the creation of new knowledge and conceptual or experimental innovation. Creative ideas can be understood as the artefacts of the vague state of the human mind. Rambling thoughts, daydreams, stories, images or metaphors draw of these unconscious memory contents and can lead to creative solutions. One of the reasons that we as humans are superior towards cognitive machines are our diverse 'spectra of spirit' [3]. Humans being in their creative mode see connections and potential correlations whereas the sharp mind does not notice them at all. Original thinking gains more and more importance. Everything that requires a new knowledge base and new skills can increase the imagination and innovation [4]. No one knows what the future will look like but it seems likely that creativity is going to play an unimaginably big role in the future.

13.4 From Learning-Sportsperson to an Expert – Practical Experience and Feedback

Knowledge cannot be equalized with ability and skills. It is decisive what humans are able to do independently from their knowledge. Many studies have shown that knowledge, gained over a period of several years, barely can be transformed into practical skills. It shows that there is more required than just learning facts in order to get from knowledge to ability. Leaving the comfort zone and using deliberate practices new skills can be trained and step by step turned into expertise. To gain and improve skills the learner has to manage challenges that are beyond the present level of performance. This procedure has to be repeated several times especially through practical experience in order to expand one's personal limits [5]. Learning is motivating in case we succeed in managing challenging tasks or solving problems. Suitable to this statement start-up-experts say 'one has to learn and to show ability and push the envelope at the same time'.[1] Passion, vision and purpose empower each individual to achieve expertise and even overtop lack of knowledge [6].

In order to structurally learn and teach one has to take into consideration activating elements, including practical experience, possibilities of interaction and direct feedback. These methods, providing everyone with the best possible individual training to enhance demanded skills, are now directly available on digital platforms. Digital learning concepts have their main focus on collaboration, cooperation and networking. Since individual learning is social learning at the same time these concepts significantly increase the quality of teaching and learning. MOOC's (Massive Open Online Courses) are a prime example representing the connection of cognitive and non-cognitive learning processes. Formal study matter is combined with informal learning arrangements in forms of virtual, social communities.[2]

13.5 Systematic Promotion of Individual Learning with Support of Learning Analytics

Even though the characteristics of the digital transformation can be constantly optimized, the human learning procedure can barely be accelerated. The learning process needs time. But with the help of learning analytics we are at least able to improve inefficient standardized processes. In this way it is possible to avoid boredom, over- and under challenging situations and, in general, a waste of time.

Learning analytics help to create personalized learning environments. Therefore content, chronological order and processing time of modules are matched with former individual experiences and expertise. During the learning process a further amount of data is saved which is used to generate additional academic offers. Special tools facilitate the perfect program by providing adequate tasks and exercises on a difficult and demanding level, but giving people motivating lifts as well. Learning bots notice the individual strengths and weaknesses of learners. This allows them to concentrate on each person and to adapt the exercises to everyone's individual needs [7]. Therefore each participant is able to learn in the best possible way – including even to offer actual human support. Learning analytics has already shown remarkable results in curricular structured learning arrangements with didactic content [8]. Further fields of application of self-regulated learning are imaginable. There are huge possibilities, if people build up reliable networks that enable access, use and analysis of their learning and communication data.[3] A more detailed self-

---

[1] Quotation: Co-Founder of Celonis Process Mining (Start-up) Alexander Rinke, Frankfurter Allgemeine, 2016.
[2] A recent example for a connective MOOC is the "Corporate Learning 2025 MOOCathon" (e.g. with components such as public Working Out Loud Circles, various informal learning groups, an Hackathon in between and a Learning Camp to the end).
[3] Decentralized data collection is not far developed yet. For experimental projects view www.coss.ethz.ch/ or mesinfos.fing.org.

observation can end up in an improved self-regulation of learning. Personal information systems analyze optimal individual learning conditions such as time, content, and duration. In addition these systems can give advises whether to rather learn alone or in a group or whether to continue the learning progress or to get an evaluation on the previous work [9].

This personal information system offers a lot more opportunities for a self-regulated learning than the former metaphors of learning styles or types.

13.6 Awaken the Spirit of Discovery – Learn Failure and Improvisation

Despite the above mentioned numerous advantages of individualization on the basis of big-data-analysis we must not forget: "When everything is optimized, we do not learn anymore."[4] Apart from algorithms, coincidences, surprises, disorder and instinct play a major role to create something new for our world.

The key element of disruptive innovation is to find new ways and to sometimes even fail. Solving challenges without mistakes is not required until the end of the process. Hence, failure is an essential part of the educational journey. New insights can only be developed after several failures. Then we try and experiment and we fail – the sooner the better. This way we can experience how faith in others, belief in ourselves and the courage to try something new influence our skills and expertise (creative confidence).[5]

Many people are afraid of the unknown, of the judgement of strangers, of mistakes or they are simply afraid to lose control. This is the reason why we need to promote the spirit of discovery and effective strategies to deal with these fears. Especially in games or in situations of improvisation (e. g. theaters) we can cultivate the desire of the unknown, spontaneity and surprises. Improvisation acts help us to gain a healthy attitude towards failure. Games enhance our willingness and skills to react spontaneously and in accordance with the situation without following a plan. We learn to open up to new uncontrollable situations we haven't experienced beforehand. The presence to mobilize our resources to create an innovative, unique story designs the games creatively.

If the rule-based work in scientific sectors is done by algorithms we need – whenever there come up unforeseeable problems or any unwanted surprises – human skills that can manage and succeed the situation with individuality, critical reflection and creativity. As you can see, the main focus for individual learning should be to gain improvisation skills and creativity which means to practice decisions without the right knowledge, form judgements, train to recognize and change patterns and structures rather than to convey or reproduce 'prefabricated' knowledge.

---

[4] Cf. C. Ratti/D. Helbing, 2016.
[5] Cf. T. Kelly/P. Kelly, 2012.

13.7   Connected and Agile – How IT Professionals Are Learning Today

The best way to get an idea on how learning in organizations is adapting to the new rules of digitalization is by looking at IT professionals. They learn with the internet, from the internet and in the internet. Highly valuable content – for self-instruction or for exchange with experts in personal networks – is available for nearly every topic. Professionals learn in online courses, they read online journals or contributions from peers, they listen to expert talks and watch presentations and videos, e. g. TED Talks and DLD (Digital Life Design), they visit virtual tech-conferences, bar-camps or learning expeditions, they learn with the help of expert blogs, instructional videos, podcasts, slides, they give webinars and collaborate in social networks. These professionals are networked very well and, according to the requirements of the digital working environment, they learn in an "agile" or "incremental" way.[6] Small fractions of information are exchanged in well-known online forums, blog wikis and communities. Knowledge circulates there and can be found and used when needed. New knowledge is discussed critically and further deepened at conferences, hackathons or other kind of meetings. In case of problems, questions can be asked directly to the well-organized communities, networked colleagues help each other with screencasts and video tutorials. Colleagues first interview each other in small podcasts and then pass the unplugged audio files on to their network. Different forms of dialogue contribute to constant knowledge sharing, during pair-programming professionals alternate in learning and teaching. Competent professionals learn autonomously and socially connected by using digital and social media. [7]

13.8   Corporate Learning Today and in the Future –
Individuals and Connected Learning

Corporations today have highly standardized learning contents at their disposal, which they make available in accordance with the principles of economies-of-scale. Modern media and innovative networks support the whole organization in satisfying educational needs. From the perspective of the organization there is a mix between formal and informal learning. Experts in education are ready to provide support in developing and implementing comprehensive learning approaches if needed. Education-controlling has a strong focus on the organization and usually measures input-oriented parameter of formal learning.

   In the future, corporate learning will increasingly emphasize individual learning and therefore even better satisfy the educational need of organizations and learners. The key is to put the learner at the heart of the thinking and the process. It's a shift toward employee-

---

[6] The meaning of workplace learning is emphasized particularly by Jane Hart.

[7] The prevailing assumption of incompetence regarding learners is being reversed by an increasing competence assumption concerning participants in networks. M. Serres describes this with regard to the connected generation.

centric learning design and it means "bringing learning to where employees are".[8] Formal and informal learning is going to be more and more integrated and implemented on every available channel, whether digital or analogue. Continuous support and social interaction will be available at the touch of a button. In order to overcome human obstacles to change and permanent learning, this system actively fosters inquisitive and creative minds. Learning content from the catalogue will be reduced in favor of small learning elements that are integrated into the day-to-day working routine. The diversity regarding available media and content ensures that the learner can access and incorporate motivating learning contents from everywhere and in an individual way. Furthermore, knowledge that has been gained in an informal way is generally accepted more and more. All business divisions are going to use all necessary media and formats, even tools that allow self-production of digital content. Learning analytics will replace education-controlling. New parameter will emerge that rather focus on the output of learning, on the use of informal learning paths, on innovation and, finally, on the applicability to the business. This development will be based on constant big-data analyses, which, in a continuous improvement process, provide insights concerning optimization of individual learning.

References

1. E. Brynjolfsson and A. McAfee, The second machine age. Wie die nächste digitale Revolution unser aller Leben verändern wird, 2015.
2. D. Wahl, Lernumgebungen erfolgreich gestalten. Vom trägen Wissen zum kompetenten Handeln, 2013.
3. D. Gelernter, "Gezeiten des Geistes. Die Vermessung unseres Bewusstseins," 2016, pp. 222–254.
4. A. Grant, How Non-Conformists Move the World, 2016.
5. K. A. Ericsson and R. Pool, Peak: Success from the New Science of Expertise, 2016.
6. D. Pink, The surprising truth about what motivates us, Drive, 2010.
7. V. Mayer-Schönberger and K. Cukier, Lernen mit Big Data. Die Zukunft der Bildung, 2014.
8. J. Dräger and R. Müller-Eiselt, "Die digitale Bildungsrevolution. Der radikale Wandel des Lernens und wie wir ihn gestalten können," 2015, pp. 61–73.
9. F. Breithaupt, "The talking method. The future of learning in the Digital World, speech at the exhibition," 2016. [Online]. Available: http://blog.zukunft-personal.de/en/2016/09/13/further-training-bots-the-digital-teacher-will-now-be-our-constant-companion/.

Further Reading
10. J. Bersin, "The Disruption of Digital Learning: Ten Things we have learned," 28 March 2017. [Online]. Available: https://www.linkedin.com/pulse/disruption-digital-learning-ten-things-we-have-learned-josh-bersin
11. Corporate Learning Community, CL2025 MOOCathon "Learning and Development in the Digital Age," 2017. [Online]. Available: https://colearn.de/

---

[8] Cf. Nick Shakelton-Jones, 2017 and cf. Josh Bersin, 2017.

12. N. Shackleton-Jones, "How to design your learning organisation around the learners," 7 March 2017. [Online]. Available: https://www.linkedin.com/pulse/how-design-your-learning-organisation-around-learners-nick
13. "Moderne Mineure," *Frankfurter Allgemeine,* 2016.
14. M. Ford, The rise of the robots: technology and the threat of a jobless future, 2015.
15. J. Hart, 2016. [Online]. Available: http://modernworkplacelearning.com/ and http://c4lpt.co.uk/.
16. D. Helbing and C. Ratti, "MarketWatch: Opinion," 19 August 2016. [Online]. Available: http://www.coss.ethz.ch/news/news/2016/08/marketwatch-opinion---big-data-is-making-us-more-boring-and-less-innovative.html.
17. T. Kelly, "Reclaim Your Creative Confidence," December 2012. [Online]. Available: https://hbr.org/2012/12/reclaim-your-creative-confidence.
18. C. Ratti, "MIT SENSEable City Lab," 2016 January 2016. [Online]. Available: www.dld-conference.com/events/data-drives-business.
19. G. Roth, Aus Sicht des Gehirns, 2009.
20. M. Serres, Erfindet euch neu! Eine Liebeserklärung an die vernetzte Gemeinde, 2012.

Digitalization in Schools – Organization, Collaboration and Communication

14

Benno Rott and Chadly Marouane

Abstract

Digitalization drives information and workflows to new possibilities. The exchange of necessary information is a critical process in every organization to deliver best results. This is truth for private organizations like companies as well as public organizations like schools. State-owned institutions are in particular affected of privacy protection and judicial conditions. Thus, digitalization is the key to success and needs to fulfill diverse requirements – legal regulations, social restrictions and at least technical restrictions. Examples are the diversity of the target groups inside a school – parents, teachers, scholars with different backgrounds as well as technical skills or the diversity of existing software and data sources inside the school. In addition, the use of digital tools for communication in schools needs and teaches specific media literacy and is integrated in a system for education. At least, communication channels must be secure to keep private or personal information as a secret inside the school family. In this chapter, the authors provide an overview over possibilities and requirements of digital collaboration, communication and organization in schools with the experience of a self-developed and provided software for German schools, called "DieSchulApp".

14.1 Introduction

Every type of association, organization, club or society is a complex combination of individuals, workflows, appointments, meetings and management of people and objects. The

B. Rott (✉) · C. Marouane
Virality GmbH
Munich, Germany
e-mail: rott@virality.de

C. Marouane
e-mail: marouane@virality.de

© Springer-Verlag GmbH Germany 2018
C. Linnhoff-Popien et al. (eds.), *Digital Marketplaces Unleashed*,
https://doi.org/10.1007/978-3-662-49275-8_14

objective should always be a smooth mode without distraction on important or needless tasks in the operative work. The aim of school is to teach pupils – both with deep professional experience and with necessary soft-skills for their future lives. All tools and improvements in processes and staff should focus this target.

One effective way to reach this goal is digitalization. We live in a world that is characterized with information, knowledge-management and a rapid change of technology. Individuals as well as organizations are forced to deal with these issues and especially the ones who actively integrate new possibilities for improvement of their work approaches can design their own future. Everyone who ignores the change of digitalization will be forced to it.

If we like to talk about digitalization as a possibility for fundamental improvement in school, we have to consider the relevant target group and stakeholders: The *headmaster* is the managing director of a school. He or she is responsible for an unobstructed flow in the whole organization. One or more *secretaries* support him in the daily work. The secretariat is the first contact person for every concern of the *parents* and *pupils*. A specialty of the target group *pupil* is the age: in most cases they are underage. The main staff of a school is the group of *teachers*.

Digitalization in schools can have different aspects – teaching aspects, digital literacy, and organizational improvements. Many articles consider digitalization in schools with a digital classroom: Digital learning material, whiteboards and tablets should be the answer on digitalization demand. But the transformation goes deeper into the organization: It includes internal workflows, speeds up communication between different stakeholders and gives new possibilities for collaboration. This article shows the current state of digitalization in German schools. Therefore the following paragraphs focus on requirements and restrictions for digital transformation in schools. The next part of this article describes current solutions with their constraints and possibilities. The article concludes with a description of relevant concepts for a scalable digitalization platform for schools with an example implementation called "DieSchulApp".

14.2 Requirements and Restrictions for Digitalization in Schools

Schools in general are a special context for digitalization – there are special legal circumstances, social restrictions and technical requirements. They all have to be considered by the introduction of new digital tools in schools.

Need for digitalization in school is often discovered from the inside of the school family. Teachers realize a problem and try to search for a solution. Especially teachers for information systems, math and physics are firm to generate software with technologies like Excel, Access or basic programming knowledge with languages like VisualBasic, PHP or Java. Some also motivate pupils to develop a solution for an occurring problem. On the one hand this is a very good way to teach pupils software development and informatics with a real world problem. On the other hand it often results in amateurish software caused by the missing professional experience. In this case the alignment between business and IT is really high but can be improved with a better implementation and specialized knowledge on the side of IT.

The following paragraphs give an overview on the most critical parts and show the difficulty and various aspects of digital innovation in the environment of schools.

14.2.1   Legal Regulations

As an organization with a public mandate, schools are under special governmental control. The integration of software and autonomous, digital data handling is mostly related to privacy aspects and private data – but this is a complex situation for schools: Next to the German Data Protection Act (BDSG), there exists several local Data Protection Acts in Germany. As an example, a Bavarian school is bind to nine different laws and legal ordinances [1].

The complexity of different laws and by-laws is a relevant showstopper for digital innovations and should be considered on all levels of school management while introducing new digital interaction possibilities.

14.2.2   Social Restrictions

Business transformation and especially digital transformation is a change process in every organization. It means to abandon old habits and acquire new ones. This is a necessary challenge for the headmaster to get in touch with the person concerned and integrate new tools and processes at the right time. Wrong timing or bad training of relevant key players can destroy the whole new plan.

One challenge in schools is the broad range of different subgroups: The group of teachers can be separated in digital/open-minded and analog/closed-minded people. While some teachers are very open to digital or new procedures, other employees don't see the positives aspects and don't want to change their habits. A broad range is inside the group of parents and families too: If a school wants to include pupils and parents into a digital process, they need a digital device like a personal computer or smartphone. While some families are very wealthy and a modern smartphone is not a problem, other families are not. Therefore it is necessary that digital tools in school don't require e. g. the newest smartphone-feature and -versions.

Digitalization, which affects the pupils of a school, has a direct impact on the media- and digital literacy of the children. As one example, if a school introduces an internal smartphone app for communication and collaboration, the app will be an important example of a reasonable way to use a smartphone. The students can learn that their phones are not only a game console but also a tool to interact with others with a meaningful topic and a professional matter. This process can be pushed in subjects like information technology as well as in interdisciplinary courses and improved with discussions about data privacy, the need for strong authentication methods and necessary content in such an app.

Every school employs a data protection officer, who has to ensure lawful processes and systems inside the organization. He also must clear software with data privacy aspects together with the headmaster. In most situations, a teacher takes this task additionally to his regular function. Though there exists advanced training and exchange between different data protection officers, the person is not deeply specialized to the different regularizations and possibilities. The resulting uncertainty can also block the intro of digital innovations, because new system will not be cleared.

The sum of such an opaque system with different laws and mostly not specialized staff for digital data privacy in schools is a big problem and should be considered as a special management task while introducing a new digital system in schools. In all cases, it is a crucial point for the headmaster to ensure an innovative spirit and to communicate the need for improvement and digital tools in the right way.

14.2.3 Technical Requirements

Digital tools in schools have to ensure different technical requirements, based on the systems purpose. One overall relevant and non-function requirement is the focus on security. If the software deals with privacy data, it must be ensured that only authorized users have access to critical data – both in case of read- and write-transactions. An example is software that manages grades and school certificates. It is the worst scenario that pupils can improve their grades without the knowledge of the teachers or a student is reported as absence in case he is truant or even worse kidnapped. Therefore, all systems should be bound behind a strong authorization process.

In most cases, users of software in schools are not deeply technical experienced. Thus, the user interface should be clear, easy and useable. Complex forms, distracting colors or the use of complex authentication-methods will end in dissatisfaction and in the worst case in no use of the newly introduced software. This is a challenge for modern software development, because it has to be considered that today's users like to decide on their own, which device they like to use. Some years ago, the most common system in schools was a personal computer with the operating system called Windows. Today's technical map is more diversified: Beside of Windows as the standard system there exists several other systems like macOS, Android or iOS. All systems are connected through the Internet and teachers as employees or pupils and parents as customers of a school like to bring their own device (BYOD) for school matters. In contrast to companies there is no possibility to dictate the use of a special device to pupils or parents. Having this in mind, development for school-wide digitalization innovations is more complex than ever.

Usually, software should be developed as a multi user systems, which is available from different workstations. Every user should be able to interact with the software from his own device with his own credentials. This enables distributed work, e. g. to cover sickness of one employee. It also guarantees that no passwords are shared between the employees, so it is possible to protocol the access to private data. Thus, concrete authentications of every single user as well as the access from different workplaces are critical technical requirements for digitalization in schools.

Particular in the modern world with the need of interactions between different software it is mandatory that software provide full import- and export-possibilities. "API management is an enabler for process automation and digital workflows" [2]. This could be done in different ways (e. g. file-exchange, XML/SOAP, REST) but it has to be documented and open for other developers to maximize the positive effects of digitalization inside the organization.

Another important part is the strategy for the operations and maintenance of the software: The whole database has to be stored against loss or technical defects in a backup. Like in all other cases, the backup has to implement the requirements of security: It has to be stored in a protected space and should also be encrypted if some gets through the barriers. Additionally it is recommended that the backup is done automatically on a regular basis and that the system supports the restoring-process. Another topic for operations is to keep the software up-to-date: The system should be updated regularly along with the operating systems or other changing general requirements.

Summarized, it is to say that the development of digitalization software for schools is a challenging business and should be done with professional experience.

14.3 Digital Tools in Schools

The previous chapter shows the difficulties for digital business in schools and gives an insight in legal, social and technical restrictions and requirements. The following paragraphs show different examples for successful integration of digital tools in administrative workflows in schools. The list is not exhaustive but widely used in Germany. Most software is useable for only one special purpose:

14.3.1 Timetable Planning Software

The generation of a complete timetable for all classes in a school is a complex task: Every pupil/class and every teacher can only be at one place each time. The room planning management must ensure that the resources are available and the personal planning management must consider some special planning like part-time workers or a longer illness. There also exist some special conditions – e. g. personal preferences of some teachers or concentration experiences of different classes. In addition, every class and age group has another number of courses of the same school subject. Table 14.1 shows two examples of such a software.

Table 14.1 Overview on different timetable planning software

Name	Website	Pricing model
Timefinder	timefinder.sourceforge.net	Open source and free
Untis Express	www.school-timetabling.com	309–441 € excl. Updates

Table 14.2 Overview on different absence management software

Name	Website	Pricing model
MGSD	www.mgsd.de	280 € incl. Updates
Absenzen!	www.absenzen.de	Open source and free
Absenzen Manager 2	www.absenzen-manager.de	250 €

14.3.2 Absence Management

A school has a special responsibility for their (underage) pupils: If one child doesn't come to school in the morning, the secretary has to do research about his location and well-being. Mostly, schools expect the parents to call the secretariat in the morning. They have to inform the school actively about the absence of the pupil on this day. A problem of this procedure are that the phone calls came all at the same time: If the school starts at 8 am, the parents call the school between 07:30 and 08:30 – in an average school with 700 pupils this can explode up to 80 phone calls in this time. Additionally, the secretary has to keep the overview on handwritten and signed absence excuses: The phone call is only for quick information, but for ensuring the illness is confirmed from the parents, a handwritten signed excuse is standard in schools. There is a huge demand for digital improvement in this scenario:

- Automated statistics and warnings if a student is absence periodically
- Digital sick notes with digital signed sender
- Immediate notification of relevant teachers after an incoming of a sick note

Nonetheless, some software already exists to support this process (see Table 14.2).

14.3.3 Substitution and Cover Planning

The timetable for pupils and teachers cover the standard and plan for the whole school year. It is very common that there are variations in the daily business: Regularly, teachers need to do a further training for their subject or their personal development. They can also be ill or with different reasons absent. In this case, another teacher has to undertake the working hours of the absent colleague. Only in exceptional cases, the lesson is changed to free time for the student. In both cases, the students and the supply teacher has to be informed as quick as possible.

Table 14.3 Overview on different substitution software

Name	Website	Pricing
Webuntis	untis.de/untis/webuntis/	658–3288 € [3]
VPM 8	www.dklinger.de/html	450 €

Table 14.4 Overview on different data for pupils

Name	Address	Birthday	Actual class
Religion	Birth country	Date of joining school	Date of exit
List of parents	Class history	Reasons for retry class	Censures

Mostly, substitution plans are analog paperwork and are only visible at the same day in the morning. A first way of digitalization is the integration of TV screens to integrate multiple views on the display (e. g. the mensa menu card). In same cases, there already exists a possibility to export the supply lessons to websites or even smartphone-apps. Table 14.3 shows a selection of such software.

14.3.4   Central Pupil Management

Every school has to manage their pupils with all relevant information. There exists diverse information for each student. Table 14.4 only shows a part of available and necessary data.

The software for central pupil management is crucial for the daily work of the secretariat and to plan classes, teachers and rooms. If the government centralizes such software, it can also be used to predict the future demand of such resources – even to predict the demand for new schools. For this reason, Bavarian schools are forced to use such a comprehensive solution, called *Allgemeine Schüler Verwaltung* (ASV) [4].

14.3.5   Grade Management

Software for grade management is a big challenge for system-provider: It needs strong requirements for security, because it is relevant aim for hacking students to improve their own grades. Nonetheless, such software should be open enough that every teacher can add new grades directly – independently from which place or system he works. Particular teachers are not directed to one place for marking the exams: They can do it at school, at home or even while traveling. Wherever they work, they have to have the ability to safe the results directly into the grade management software. In most cases, software uses a combination from username and password as protection. Thus, the security of the platform depends on the complexity of the password and therefore on the user. Additional security through 2nd factor authentication with systems like Authy [5] or KeyPocket [6] is recommended.

One example for software for grade management is "Notenmanager" [7] in Germany.

14.3.6   Events/Calendar

Like in every other organization, school is regularly the host of different kind of events. The following list provides an overview on different kind of dated activities in schools:

- Events for pupils like field days or examinations
- Events for teachers like attended training courses or teacher's conferences
- Events for parents like parent's evening
- Global events like holidays.

A school has to synchronize all activities on a central platform and have to inform all related guests. For this task, many secretariats organize their calendar with a software like open exchange. Many schools also synchronize their parents calendar via export on the website. This has big disadvantages regarding security and data privacy and should not be recommended without an authentication method.

14.3.7   Parent Information Systems

Due to the age of pupils, communication to parents is a central task for the school. The standard of the analog age were letters to parents. They were printed and delivered by the pupils to the parents. In some cases, a return with an answer or a signature was necessary and again, the pupils acted as couriers. This procedure has several disadvantages: Every letter to the parents needs minimum a day since he reaches his destination. Sometimes, a letter does not reach the parents, because their child has forgotten to hand it over. Last but not least, a printed letter is expensive and harmful to the environment. There exist several approaches to digitalize this process: A software called "Eltern Portal" [8] provides a password-protected website. Parents can pull information like event dates, messages or substitutions via their Internet browser, but are not notified actively. A similar system is provided by Untis [9]: A website provides information with calendar events, the current time table and substitutions. A smartphone app is connected to a service called WebUntis and shares information about the substitutions. The website and the smartphone app is protected with a password. Some schools provide important messages via SMS directly on the mobile phones of the parents. This is very expensive and complex to handle for the secretariat but notifies parents within minutes. A system called "ESIS" [10] sends out a newsletter on the technical standard of E-Mail. This is a common way to send messages, but it is not a secure way: Every E-Mail is sent unencrypted through the Internet.

In summary, there exist some systems and providers to inform parents about news from school but they all have some disadvantages.

14.4   DieSchulApp

The previous presented software solutions are all designed to fulfill only one purpose. But digitalization takes it full prospects especially in consequent linking and connecting different systems to one workflow. Therefore the authors introduce one more digital system for schools called DieSchulApp [11]. The solution provides open programming interfaces to connect different tools, but remains on very high security-standards. For this, identity- and rights management is a central part of the software. Furthermore, the system is designed to safe diverse objects – e. g. messages, calendar events, substitutions or sick notes. All entities of the platform can be accessed via a defined and structured REST-API. This *API-first-design* makes it possible to interact with nearly every external system. Legal factors and the identity management, that grants different rights to different users, regulate the possibilities for import- and export – but it is not technically limited. This solution makes it possible to interact with different users and from different devices – such as Internet browsers or – based on smartphones and tablets – Android-Apps or iOS-Apps.

14.4.1   Identity- and Right Management

Software should diverse the content and rights for different users. It is necessary to be sure, that a user of the software is really the one who he impersonates his self. For this, DieSchulApp uses a combination of the secure activation protocol Vis-a-Vis [12] and a self-service registration form. The activation of a smartphone app via optical transmission and one-time-passwords ensures that no one else can use the activation credentials. Combined with a registration form the workload to set up the user accounts is shifted and evenly distributed from the secretariat to the end-users. With a signed and detailed form for the data privacy aspects, the system works within judicial specifications in schools.

DieSchulApp also adds information about family relationships and courses of the student to the data set. With these data, the system generates a set of groups for every user automatically. Every group is associated with specific rights on a filter-mechanism called *channels* and different types of *objects* and *services*. A rule engine checks permissions on every request and allows only write- or read-access if the current user is in a privileged group for the inquired resource.

This extensive right management is the key point to ensure data privacy and the correctness of the saved information.

14.4.2   Functionality

The main function of DieSchulApp is the immediately information of different target group via smartphones. Thus, the software consists of different components:

- A flexible backend server with strong authentication methods
- A defined REST-Interface for external software communication
- A web-interface for the secretary to manage content, users and messages of the system
- An Android- and iOS-Client for -endusers like pupils, parents or teachers

Schools are able to send diverse information to every subgroup inside the school: Teachers, classes, and attendees of additional courses, parents or even unique students. The information can be a text notification, calendar events, homework or the current substitution plan. Grounded on the identity management it is also possible for parents to report sickness of their children to school over a highly secure channel. This is a big advantage and optimizes the work for the secretariat.

All information can be actively pushed to the clients. Especially the users of smartphones are used to push notifications that tell them that there are news inside the app. For reasons of data privacy, no private information is sent to push servers of Apple or Google.

14.4.3   Open-API and Integration

"The API economy is an enabler for turning a business or organization into a platform" [3]. With a defined REST-API, DieSchulApp automatically communicates with other services and software components. The most used feature is the combination with substitution management software, which can be totally proprietary: A small middleware reads the substitution file and changes nearly every format in structured data. The middleware authenticates with an API-token to DieSchulApp and adds new substitutions to the system in real-time. The backend service is responsible for identity management and storage of the substitution events. Diverse clients can then requests actual substitutions – the smartphone-apps for iOS and Android as well as the website or a big TV screen that shows cancellations at the auditorium. With the same structure, diverse information resources can be integrated into DieSchulApp – e. g. RSS-Feeds, calendar events or absences. Particular in automated handling of information, all aspects of data privacy should be considered.

14.4.4   Software as a Service

Operating and support of software is a necessary task for every digital system. The circumstances and technologies are changing in a very fast way and software is in current modification to ensure security, functionality and usability with new devices. DieSchulApp runs as a centralized service in a professional data center with highest standards. This is especially necessary for privacy concerns of such a software: The control on physical access control and the data medium can only guaranteed in a highly specialized environment. Additionally the software has to run with high encryption of the data transport to eliminate attacks like man-in-the-middle. With the use of trusted certificates and encryption on transport, no other than the receiver can read or change the content of a data package. This requires certain knowledge of server administration and is a key point to offer such software as a service without technical administration or further knowledge inside of the school and with the legal requirements for data privacy and data protection.

14.5   Summary

Digital innovation and the introduction of new software at schools is a challenging task for every stakeholder – the headmaster, new user of the systems as well as for the provider of the systems. In school sector, some special laws and by-laws exist – especially the field of data privacy is very relevant for present and future implementations. Caused by the diversification of the stakeholders, there are complex social restrictions that impede an innovative technical spirit. To ensure the non-functional requirements like security, encryption as well as user orientated suggestions like usability it is necessary to observe special technical aspects in the implementation of such a solution. There already exist several digital tools and software in schools – examples are parent information systems, substitution management, pupil administration tools or absence statistics. The different tools are built for different platforms, developed with different programming skills and with heterogeneous data-sets. This shows the need for a central surface with open programming interfaces that is able to unify and harmonize the different tools in an extensible, privacy-affine and secure way.

The demand on open APIs for school software will increase in future. The combination of administrative tools and educational software will be fluent if eBooks and other systems with digital right management will find their way into classrooms. This is a challenge for providers of software as well as for the government to ensure a legal and transparent way of data transmission in these systems.

References

1. Bayerisches Staatsministerium für Unterricht und Kultus, "MEBIS," 09 04 2013. [Online]. Available: https://www.mebis.bayern.de/wp-content/uploads/sites/2/2015/04/handreichung_dsb_version_3_inkl_anlagen.pdf. [Accessed 11 09 2016].
2. A. Sandeen, P. Manfredi und K. Chinnagangannagari, 19 04 2016. [Online]. Available: http://www.cioinsight.com/it-management/expert-voices/the-need-for-a-platform-approach.html#sthash.gxaMPLNl.dpuf. [Accessed 11 09 2016].
3. Untis Preisliste. (2015). [Online]. Available: http://untis-baden-wuerttemberg.de/archiv/Preisliste_Stand_01.03.2015.pdf. [Accessed 01 08 2017].
4. ASV Bayern, [Online]. Available: https://www.asv.bayern.de/asv/basisinformationen.html. [Accessed 11 09 2016].
5. "Twilio," 09 11 2016. [Online]. Available: https://twilio.com/authy.
6. C. Marouane und B. Rott, "Mobile Authentisierung im Unternehmensalltag," *Informatik Spektrum*, Bd. 39, Nr. 2, pp. 112–130, 2016.
7. "Notenmanager," 09 11 2016. [Online]. Available: http://www.notenmanager.net/.

8. Arts Soft and More GmbH, [Online]. Available: http://www.artsoftandmore.com/. [Accessed 11 09 2016].
9. "Untis Manual," 2015. [Online]. Available: http://www.grupet.at/Downloads/Manuals/de/WebUntis.pdf.
10. "ESIS," 2016. [Online]. Available: http://www.esis.de/.
11. "DieSchulApp," 2016. [Online]. Available: http://www.dieschulapp.de/.
12. M. Maier, C. Marouane, C. Linnhoff-Popien, B. Rott und S. A. W. Verclas, "Vis-a-Vis Verification: Social Network Identity Management Through Real World Interactions," *3rd International Conference on Social Eco-Informatics,* 2013.

The Unsung Power of Horizontal Grassroots

15

Aleksandra Solda-Zaccaro

Abstract

Technology corporations such as Google and Facebook are investing billions of dollars to provide internet access for people in remote areas on the African continent via WLAN drones. But even in Western society there are blank spots on the network map. The respective countries and economies should do something about this. This essay researches how digital media use influences the lives of marginalized groups in Germany and other countries. The focus is on media use of elderly people. Various projects and models are introduced which are used by government agencies and private initiatives in order to measure and improve the digital competence of this population section. By analyzing online user data and reviewing various other studies, the goal is to define how elderly users utilize digital media and what kind of benefits they derive from it. Further, it should be analyzed if the communication space deserves the stamp of being "barrier free". Is there sufficient accessibility and clarity that even marginalized groups like seniors can fully use the opportunities that new media offers?

15.1 Introduction

A picture tells more than a thousand words and there is more in one meme than in many books. There are innumerable videos in the net with the tag "Elders react to ..." [1]. In these videos, pensioners show their surprise at Twitter, the video games StarCraft and Dubstep, new technologies and modern dance music. The viewers of these videos, which sometimes have many million views, are usually not interested in the opinions of test

A. Solda-Zaccaro (✉)
TERRITORY Content to Results GmbH
Munich, Germany
e-mail: asoldazaccaro@gmail.com

© Springer-Verlag GmbH Germany 2018
C. Linnhoff-Popien et al. (eds.), *Digital Marketplaces Unleashed*,
https://doi.org/10.1007/978-3-662-49275-8_15

persons with life experience, but expect astonishment, lack of understanding and comical curses. Instead of active users, elders are depicted as a symbol of the incompetence and backwardness of the mainstream. In spring 2016, the technology magazine WIRED then published a video with the title "Elders react to self-driving Cars" [2]. While, according to the study done by the American Automobile Association, 75% of Americans are "afraid of" a trip in a computer-operated automobile [3], elders had fewer reservations. "If my son takes my car away from me at some stage, I will get something like that", an elderly lady said. Another user merely said: "Simply practical".

Perhaps we should start a video series with the title "Elders interact with …" After all, elderly people are not all culturally pessimistic enemies of progress, but are curious, adventurous users, who are particularly able to profit from the new technologies and connections. "Elders are 'late but fast adopters'", says Dagmar Hirche, who manages the club "Ways out of loneliness" [4] and who has initiated the action "We will silver-plate the net" in Hamburg. The executive consultant teaches older users "what a browser is, how the train-app functions, and how to reach their grandchildren via WhatsApp". Above all, easy gadgets, such as tablets and smartphones, make sure that elders use Internet communication and e-commerce to a larger degree. Dagmar Hirche says: "Once the initial timidness has been overcome and our participants notice that, firstly, it is not witchcraft, and secondly, they are able to improve their mobility and autonomy, they soon send partners and friends to our courses".

Digital competency "must be seen as a set of knowledge, attitude and abilities, which are required to act as a partner of the digital environment and to enjoy the advantages of technology in daily life", write Minocha, McNulty and Evans in a report from the British Open University, and emphasize that it is "not so much a customary educational attainment, but rather a continuous learning project" [5].

All the more important is the requirement that groups within the population, which are not automatically in contact with new media through their place of employment or their education, are included in the process. In Germany there are mainly private initiatives, such as the Hirches association, besides adult education classes, which handle the topic. In England the organization "Age UK" offers appropriate courses nationwide [6]. The initiative of the Philippine megacity Quezon-City, which offers free IT lessons for all elders and persons with physical disabilities [7], must be seen as downright visionary under these considerations.

When talking about the Internet as a tool for empowerment, it is usually about grassroots movements, that is, about digitally organized groups, which connect "the many" at "the base", in order to push through their interests at a higher level. The evaluation of the effectiveness of these initiatives remains rooted in empiricism: how many signatures are collected for an online petition? How many million dollars will be collected on Kickstarter.com for the development of a revolutionary entertainment system? But grassroots don't only grow from bottom to top, but also to the side, a fact that every hobby gardener will confirm. There were visions, which predicted an enlightened, democratic and more just society through digital tools. Instead, it turned out to be one-dimensional and a little naïve.

Therefore, the individual effect of communicative mobility and the experience of interaction, which elders can enjoy, cannot be overrated. The grassroots may not grow into the sky, but they form a barely visible network, which connects people with each other and through which new techno-social possibilities are discovered.

In this essay we aim to examine how older users utilize digital media – and what uses they get from them. On the other hand, we aim to analyze whether communication spaces deserve the rating "barrier-free": Are accessibility (infrastructure etc.) and comprehensibility (design of interface etc.) present to an extent, so that marginalized groups such as elders, can use these new possibilities? And, if not, what is to be done?

15.2   Development of Media Usage Among Seniors

Even if elders are often presumed to lack acceptance for new media, it seems that the educational campaigns by adult education centers as well as courses there, and the permanent help from their own children are having an effect (see Fig. 15.1). In the year 2015 exactly half [8] of all interviewed elders over 60 said that they used the Internet, at least occasionally. In the year 2000 only 4.4% [9] of all elders occasionally looked at the net – only 20% of over 65's use a smartphone [10].

According to this finding, Germany is only in the upper center in a comparison with the EU-average – in 2014, 38% of all 65–74 year olds indicated using the Internet occasionally [11]. Specifically in the Benelux states and the Scandinavian countries the digital media has a higher penetration in this age-group, for example in Luxemburg (79%), Denmark and Sweden (76%) or the Netherlands (70%) [12]. In the USA, on the other hand, the spread is a moderate 58% [13]. Similar to Germany, however, there is an above-average

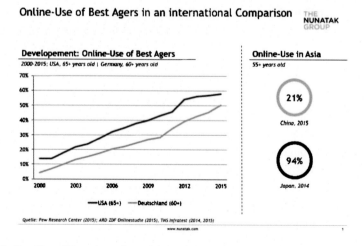

Fig. 15.1 Online-Use of Best Agers in an international Comparison

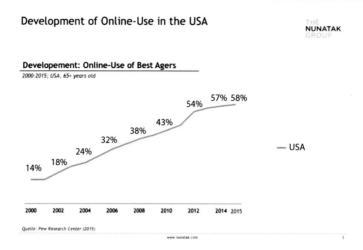

Fig. 15.2 Development of Online-Use in the USA

high rise in the usage rate among older people. See Fig. 15.2. In 2004 in the EU merely seven percent of the people interviewed indicated using the Internet once a week [14].

If one looks, not only at the quantity but also the quality of usage, one can see that elders use the entire range of offers on the Internet. See Fig. 15.3. Right at the top is the use of emails: almost three quarters of active users over 60 use that communication service at least once a week [15]. Information research is also high on the list (59%) and current events (36%). Videos and online shopping appear with 25 and 10% respectively. Online banking is used by just under a quarter. It is, however, noticeable that Internet services, which serve interpersonal communication, are at the bottom of the list of favorites. Social networks, such as Facebook, are used by only eleven percent of older Internet users, and even fewer use web, 2.0 offers such as Instagram or blogs (three percent), two percent are active regularly in Internet forums [16]. To a large extent this user profile matches that of other EU countries [17].

It can also be noticed that elders indeed use the net for self-realization, but that there is room for increase in the social component of the medium. That matches with the view of the Internet that older people have. More than a quarter of the interviewees over 60 agree with the following statement: "I have found the sites, which interest me on the Internet and hardly look for additional offers". A personal identification with the medium, as it is widespread among younger social environments, hardly takes place. The lowest agreement find statements such as: "I always like to be stimulated by new sites and offers on the Internet" or "The Internet is especially important for me, since I can present myself with a personal profile" – only 7% of the interviewees recognized their own usage behavior here [18]. All of this, report Frees and Koch in their evaluation of the ARD/ZDF online study 2015, indicates a "pragmatic usage of the net by the older generation". But, because of the "natural evolution" of media-competent generations, this functional spread will soon

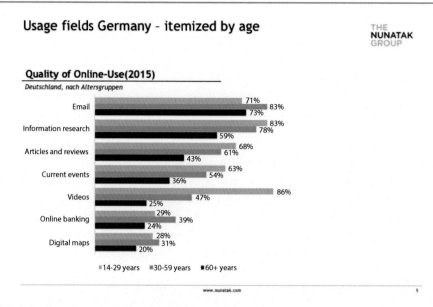

Fig. 15.3 Usage fields Germany – itemized by age

change and the activities of older people will increase, even "in the case of applications which are currently still in the domain of the youthful" [19]. Thus, it is only a question of time before elders look at the Internet not just as a communication tool, but realize that it is a natural part of life. But why wait?

15.3   Positive Potential of Digital Media Usage

The anecdotes, which Dagmar Hirche tells from her daily work, almost sound like DSL flatrate and smartphone commercials – too good to be true. There was the Hamburg pensioner who, with the help of a user-generated wheelmap.org map [20] on which barrier-free restaurants and shops were indicated, organized his daily life around these entries. Then there was the elderly lady, who "really perked up since she understood the Whats-App group of her sports club". There are innumerable grandmothers and grandfathers, who communicate with their grandchildren and family via Facetime, Line, Skype, WhatsApp and other channels. "We are living in a mobile age", says Hirche, "People move to other continents, or relocate debates which used to take place at regulars' tables, to WhatsApp groups. We have to take older people with us – it's in everybody's interest"

There are numerous studies, which are dedicated to the (harmful) effects of digital media on the attention span, IQ and empathy ability of (young) people. The impacts of digital media on the condition, health, as well as economic or social integration respectively, of older people have been researched to a much lesser degree. It would exceed the scope of this essay to give a systematic analysis of the current state of research. Nevertheless, the following positive potentials are worth mentioning:

- **Subjective contentedness**: In the year 2000, psychologists from the Carnegie Mellon University found that people "became more depressive the more they used the Internet" [21]. Kraut and Burke based this effect on the idea that "the Internet at that time consisted mainly of academic aspects; one didn't talk to friends, but rather with strangers and colleagues". In a comparative study from the year 2015, Kraut and Burke asserted that the ramifications on the frame of mind depends on the usage of the medium: "The more people communicate with good friends, write comments or posts, the more the contentedness rises" [22]. Especially older citizens, who often live isolated in apartments or establishments for elders, profit from the new contact possibilities with friends and family. And in contrast to other important factors which influence contentment in life, such as income, religion or health, digital competency can be "influenced comparatively easily" [23].
- **Health**: The social capital of people has a direct influence on their health. Yvonne Michael, an epidemiologist at the Drexel University School of Public Health, found this out from an extensive referendum. Social activities not only have a positive effect on factors such as cognitive capability, but they also increase the likelihood that one will look after one's own health and, for example, regularly go to preventive medical checkups [24]. In a time when the medical insurances are suffering from a demographic change, this factor cannot be underestimated.
- **Economy**: The age group of over 55-year-olds does not count as an important economic factor. The Golden Age Index 2016 [25] of the Management Consultancy PwC, however, asserts that countries such as Great Britain or Germany [26], in which less that 60% of over 55-year-olds work, could raise their GNP by up to five percent, if it reached "Swedish conditions": 68% of this age group there works.

15.4   Who Benefits from the Internet and Who Does Not

In July 2016, free access to the Internet was officially declared to be a human right by the General Assembly of the United Nations [27]. Yet, the world is still far from implementing this right. Rough estimates indicated in 2015 that approximately 3.2 billion people are online, thus, not even half of the total population. Mary Meeker, market researcher, investment banker, and author of Internet Trend Report, renowned for more than 20 years, in her current edition, identifies four main factors, which make access to the Internet difficult [28]. Among these are: inadequate infrastructure, low income and affordable access, as well as the lack of personal competency of the users and incentives to use the net.

Therefore, it is a case of extrinsic as well as intrinsic and technical as well as socioeconomic factors. It may be surprising that especially the first two factors are comparably easy to eliminate. More than three quarters of all people worldwide are within the physical reach of a mobile Internet signal, according to the "State of Connectivity 2015" report, which Facebook issues annually [29]. In addition, the percentage of people who are able to afford a base monthly rate of 500 megabyte per month, is rising considerably: within the last two years by about 500 million people.

Much more serious, however, are the education and motivation factors. Anyone who can neither read nor write is hardly able to fully use the Internet. Sufficient linguistic skills are fundamental for complete usage of the Internet. More than 80% of all websites worldwide are constructed in one of only ten languages (English, French, Spanish and Chinese, among others) [30]. Anyone who is not skilled in these languages will find that the Internet suddenly becomes a much smaller system. From that, the last factor becomes apparent: Whoever does not understand what the Internet is, and what possibility it offers, will not find a reason to be connected. According to the Facebook study, approximately two thirds of all non-connected people in developing countries belong to this group.

It is, therefore, not surprising when the management consultancy McKinsey, write in their report "Offline and Falling Behind: Barriers to Internet Adoption," [31] that approximately 75% of all people not connected to the net indicate very similar characteristics: they come from one of 20 developing countries, live predominantly in rural areas, have a relatively low income, can neither read nor write, and are female.

More surprising, however, is the fact that hindrances in developed countries are apparently very similar. The Digital-Think-Tank D21, situated in Berlin, identifies six different user classes in Germany in its Digital-Index 2015 [32]. The least connected archetype, named "Outside skeptic" is of advanced age, has a low available income and a low formal education, lives in a rural area – and is female. It is necessary to "promote user types according to their requirements" and "overcome structural handicaps" [33], according to the conclusions of the D-21 study. As long as this does not take place there is a cycle. Marginalized groups stay offline because they are marginalized – and they stay marginalized because they are offline.

15.5   Digital Media and the Ability for Empathy

When Dr. Sonya Kim visits a senior citizens' home she brings new perspectives. The American doctor is founder of the organization One Caring Team [34], whose concept so far has consisted of connecting volunteers with elderly people in institutions, typically via telephone. The young people call, listen, ask questions and so give the inhabitants the feeling of still being anchored in the world. Recently, Kim has been experimenting additionally with Virtual-Reality-Glasses [35], a program with the appropriate name "Aloha VR" which relocates the elders to a virtual beach on Hawaii. According to Kim, the artificially produced world is meant to let them forget their "chronic pains, their fears and the fact that they are alone" [36]. There are already several independent studies, which document that the new technology can achieve this.

However, virtual reality (VR) is not only supposed to amuse elderly people [37], but also to help people worldwide find togetherness and to understand each other. Virtual reality is the "ultimate empathy machine", as moviemaker Chris Milk said in 2015 during a presentation at the idea-conference, TED [38]. With his production company With.in, Milk has produced so-called 360° movies which depict one of the currently most popular virtual reality applications. These movies give the viewer the feeling of being in another place right in the midst of what is happening – the technical term is "Telepresence". When you put on the VR glasses every head movement of the viewer becomes a camera movement. Thus, there is an immediateness, so far unknown. "It is a machine, but on the inside it feels like real life, if it is true – one becomes part of that world" as Milk endeavors to describe why his films touch the viewers to such an extent [39].

Therefore, it is only consistent that Milk showed his first documentation in the beginning of 2015, named "Clouds Over Sidra", at the World Economic Forum in Davos [40]. The film, which is eight-and-a-half minutes long, documents the life of Syrian refugees. The viewer sees, no, he finds himself in a Jordanian refugee camp, a veritable city with about 80,000 inhabitants. If he looks down on himself he sees children running around, going to school, playing football, going hungry – and he is in the midst of it. Boys crowd in front of a few archaic computers, on the screens: "Ego-Shooter games." "After all that has happened they still want to fight", comments the narrator [41].

"There is no possibility of understanding how intense and convincing Virtual Reality works, if you haven't tried it yourself", according to people who have worked with the medium for years [42]. Therefore, it is no wonder that people who have tried the new medium for the first time, report that the directness brought them to tears [43].

In the meantime, VR and especially 360° films, are used by renowned media companies such as the New York Times [44] or the Süddeutsche Zeitung [45], to show scenes and fates in a manner which was never possible before: Refugee fates, reports from slums and the epicenters of local and global catastrophes. The media start-up Ryot, sent one of its VR film teams to the ruins of the capital city Kathmandu, after the earthquake in Nepal in the spring of 2015, a further setting: the destroyed Aleppo. Once the smartphone is in front of your eyes, you suddenly find yourself in the streets of the Syrian city, no person in sight, only rubble and chaos. Then again, the film team has set up the camera on a rooftop: smashed facades everywhere, satellite dishes pointing aimlessly at the sky [46].

They are powerful pictures, which are being played directly before your own eyes. It is no wonder that the United Nations wanted to use the 360° films in order to collect donations. Firstly, non-representative calculations show that the engagement of the users, after consuming such a video, really rises [47] – a technology of the future as a tool for the poor and the weak?

New media enable their users to have more participation in current world events [48]. The Internet itself has simplified the sending and receiving of messages from the most remote regions of the world. But viewing the pictures on the computer screen – no matter how urgent they were – was just a more or less passive experience. VR could change that; the viewer would find himself in the midst of the happening. And one could well imagine what uses these "empathy-machines", could have for people whose social contacts and mobility is inhibited: a VR meeting with the granddaughter seems more emotional and more genuine than a telephone call and the exchange of letters.

Technology will spread further and change rapidly. Some things, which still seem like science fiction today, will be part of everyday life tomorrow. In his efforts to "connect the whole world", Facebook CEO Mark Zuckerberg, for example, wants to start so-called Aquila drones, which can reach and connect areas, where there are neither fiber optics nor mobile communication technology – the remote areas of Central Africa, for example [49]. But one should not forget that there are still "dark continents" in the western, apparently highly technological states which are waiting for a connection to the present time and society. Thus, the grassroots may proliferate in all directions.

And, of course, there is a video in the net with the title "Elders React to Oculus Rift", the VR glasses of the Facebook enterprise. After the test persons in the video, which is over 7 min long, initially react with reservations to the foreign object ("it looks like a tool to control my thoughts"), they still decide to put on the black, clumsy glasses, and, while they are taking a virtual walk through a villa in Tuscany, their attitude and statements change: "Is that George Clooney's house?" says one elderly lady. Another one says: "It looks artificial and feels genuine". A gray-haired gentleman says: "That is really damn cool".

15.6   Conclusion

The analysis of user data and social debate shows that elderly people are increasingly using digital media and that they are absolutely open to some of the newest technologies such as virtual reality. Citizens and researchers are both noticing during studies and educational projects that the use of digital media shows a lot of positive potential. Marginalized groups such as seniors are benefiting especially if it means that they regain access to social and economic structures through social media. The analysis of existing educational programs shows that the program is neither universally introduced nor strategically managed. Especially in times of rampant technological change it is even more important that all human beings gain access to media and the inherent possibilities. This is a challenge for the country, the economy and our society as a whole.

References

1. "Youtube," [Online]. Available: https://www.youtube.com/channel/UC0v-tlzsn0QZwJnkiaUSJVQ. [Accessed 30 August 2016].
2. "WIRED.com," 30 08 2016. [Online]. Available: https://www.wired.com/video/2016/05/seniors-react-to-driverless-cars. [Accessed 30 August 2016].

3. "Newsroom.aaa.com," 30 August 2016. [Online]. Available: http://newsroom.aaa.com/2016/
   03/three-quarters-of-americans-afraid-to-ride-in-a-self-driving-vehicle/. [Accessed 30 August 2016].
4. "Wege aus der Einsamkeit," [Online]. Available: http://www.wegeausdereinsamkeit.de. [Ac-
   cessed 30 August 2016].
5. S. Minocha, Imparting digital skills to people aged 55 years and over in the UK, S. M. C. a. E.
   S. Minocha, Ed., Milton Keynes: The Open University, 2015.
6. "ageuk," [Online]. Available: http://www.ageuk.org.uk/work-and-learning/technology-and-
   internet/computer-training-courses/. [Accessed 30 August 2016].
7. "http://digitalinclusionnewslog.itu.int/2016/07/27/persons-with-disabilities-youth-and-senior-
   citizens-from-quezon-city-will-receive-free-digital-literacy-training/," [Online].
8. "http://www.ard-zdf-onlinestudie.de/index.php?id=533," [Online].
9. "ibid.," [Online]. Available: http://www.ard-zdf-onlinestudie.de/index.php?id=533. [Accessed
   30 August 2016].
10. "heise.de/ix/meldung/Bitkom-Studie-Gut-ein-Viertel-aller-deutschen-Senioren-nutzt-
    Smartphones-3198087.html," [Online]. Available: http://www.heise.de/ix/meldung/Bitkom-
    Studie-Gut-ein-Viertel-aller-deutschen-Senioren-nutzt-Smartphones-3198087.html.
    [Accessed 30 August 2016].
11. "http://ec.europa.eu/eurostat/statistics-explained/index.php/People_in_the_EU_%E2%80%93_
    statistics_on_an_ageing_society#Senior_citizens_online_.E2.80.94_silver_surfers," [Online].
12. "ibid," [Online]. Available: ibid. [Accessed 30 August 2016].
13. "pewinternet.or," [Online]. Available: http://www.pewinternet.org/2015/06/26/americans-
    internet-access-2000-2015/. [Accessed 30 August 2016].
14. "ec.europa.eu/eurostat/statistics-ex-plained/," [Online]. Available: http://ec.europa.eu/eurostat/
    statistics-ex-plained/index.php/People_in_the_EU_%E2%80%93_statistics_on_an_ageing_
    society#Senior_citizens_online_.E2.80.94_silver_surfers. [Accessed 30 August 2016].
15. "ard-zdf-onlinestudie," [Online]. Available: http://www.ard-zdf-onlinestudie.de/index.php?
    id=533. [Accessed 30 August 2016].
16. "ibid.," [Online]. [Accessed 30 August 2016].
17. "ec.europa.eu/eurostat/statistics-ex-plained," [Online]. Available: http://ec.europa.eu/eurostat/
    statistics-ex-plained/index.php/People_in_the_EU_%E2%80%93_statistics_on_an_ageing_
    society#Senior_citizens_online_.E2.80.94_silver_surfers. [Accessed 30 August 2016].
18. "ard-zdf-onlinestudie.de," [Online]. Available: http://www.ard-zdf-onlinestudie.de/fileadmin/
    Onlinestudie_2015/0915_Frees_Koch.pdf. [Accessed 30 August 2016].
19. "ibid," [Online]. Available: ibid. [Accessed 30 August 2016].
20. "wheelmap.org," [Online]. Available: http://wheelmap.org/map#/?zoom=14; (Berlin-Mitte).
    [Accessed 30 August 2016].
21. R. a. B. M. Kraut, Internet use and psychological well-being: Effects of activity and audience.
    Communications of the ACM, vol. 12, New York, NY, USA: Carnegie Mellon University, Pitts-
    burgh, PA, December 2015, pp. p. 94–100.
22. "/research.facebook.co," [Online]. Available: https://research.facebook.com/blog/online-or-
    offline-connecting-with-close-friends-improves-well-being. [Accessed 30 August 2016].
23. "www.cbs.gov.i," [Online]. Available: http://www.cbs.gov.il/www/skarim/social_surv/internet.
    pdf. [Accessed 30 August 2016].
24. "greatergood.berkeley.edu," [Online]. Available: http://greatergood.berkeley.edu/article/item/
    how_social_connections_keep_seniors_healthy. [Accessed 30 August 2016].
25. ".pwc.co.uk," [Online]. Available: http://www.pwc.co.uk/services/economics-policy/insights/
    golden-age-index.html. [Accessed 30 August 2016].

26. "statistik.arbeitsagentur.de,"   [Online].   Available: https://statistik.arbeitsagentur.de/
    Statischer-Content/Arbeitsmarktberichte/Personengruppen/generische-Publikationen/Aeltere-
    amArbeitsmarkt-2014.pdf. [Accessed 30 August 2016].
27. "https://www.article19.org/data/files/Internet_Statement_Adopted.pdf," [Online].
28. "http://www.kpcb.com/blog/2016-internet-trends-report p. 14," [Online].
29. "http://newsroom.fb.com/news/2016/02/state-of-connectivity-2015-a-report-on-global-
    internet-access/," [Online].
30. "http://labs.theguardian.com/digital-language-divide/," [Online].
31. "http://www.mckinsey.com/industries/high-tech/our-insights/offline-and-falling-behind-
    barriers-to-internet-adoption," [Online].
32. "http://www.initiatived21.de/portfolio/d21-digital-index-2015/," [Online].
33. "ebd.," [Online].
34. "https://onecaringteam.com/," [Online].
35. "http://www.npr.org/sections/health-shots/2016/06/29/483790504/virtual-reality-aimed-at-the-
    elderly-finds-new-fans," [Online].
36. "ebd.," [Online].
37. "http://www.fastcompany.com/3051672/tech-forecast/how-the-united-nations-is-using-
    virtual-reality-to-tackle-real-world-problems," [Online].
38. "https://www.ted.com/talks/chris_milk_how_virtual_reality_can_create_the_ultimate_
    empathy_machine?language=en," [Online].
39. "ebd.," [Online].
40. "https://techcrunch.com/2015/01/23/un-launches-powerful-oculus-virtual-reality-film-
    following-syrian-refugee-girl/," [Online].
41. "http://with.in/watch/clouds-over-sidra/," [Online].
42. "http://nypost.com/2015/04/12/virtual-reality-enahnces-the-big-screen-at-tribeca-film-
    festival/," [Online].
43. "http://www.cnet.com/news/the-day-virtual-reality-made-me-cry/," [Online].
44. "http://www.nytimes.com/marketing/nytvr/," [Online].
45. "http://www.sueddeutsche.de/kultur/virtual-reality-im-schatten-der-spiele-1.3098851,"
    [Online].
46. "http://ryot.huffingtonpost.com/," [Online].
47. "http://www.unicefstories.org/2015/10/13/how-the-united-nations-is-using-virtual-reality-to-
    tackle-real-world-problems/," [Online].
48. "http://www.theverge.com/a/mark-zuckerberg-future-of-facebook#part3," [Online].
49. "http://thepenguinpress.com/book/reclaiming-conversation-the-power-of-talk-in-a-digital-
    age/," [Online].

The COMALAT Approach to Individualized E-Learning in Job-Specific Language Competences

16

Lefteris Angelis, Mahdi Bohlouli, Kiki Hatzistavrou, George Kakarontzas, Julian Lopez, and Johannes Zenkert

Abstract

COMALAT (Competence Oriented Multilingual Adaptive Language Assessment and Training) project aims to strengthen the mobility of young workers across Europe, by improving job-specific language competence tailored individually to particular needs. In this work we will concentrate on the COMALAT learning management system (LMS), which is a language learning system for Vocational Education and Training (VET). COMALAT LMS aims at providing learning material as an Open Educational Resource (OER) and is capable of self-adapting to the needs of different learners. Each learner is treated individually in acquiring new language skills related to job-specific

L. Angelis (✉) · K. Hatzistavrou · G. Kakarontzas
Aristotle University of Thessaloniki and TEI of Thessaly
Thessaloniki, Larissa, Greece
e-mail: lef@csd.auth.gr

K. Hatzistavrou
e-mail: kikihatzistavrou@gmail.com

G. Kakarontzas
e-mail: gkakaron@teilar.gr

M. Bohlouli · J. Zenkert
University of Siegen
Siegen, Germany
e-mail: mahdi.bohlouli@uni-siegen.de

J. Zenkert
e-mail: johannes.zenkert@uni-siegen.de

J. Lopez
University of Alicante
Alicante, Spain
e-mail: jlopez@csidiomas.ua.es

© Springer-Verlag GmbH Germany 2018
C. Linnhoff-Popien et al. (eds.), *Digital Marketplaces Unleashed*,
https://doi.org/10.1007/978-3-662-49275-8_16

competences. In addition, it is specifically tailored towards addressing competence areas, and therefore it is not a generic language learning platform. We discuss some technical details of the COMALAT platform and present the various aspects of system adaptability which tries to imitate the help provided by an instructor by observing the users' strengths, weaknesses and progress in general, during the learning process. Also we discuss the digital e-learning materials in COMALAT.

16.1 Introduction

Language competences are essential in order to find and keep a job and manage everyday life [1]. In [1] it is stated that "Internationalization should become an everyday feature in vocational training. Qualification should include foreign languages and international cooperation between institutions should encourage new approaches to teaching and learning". So, the challenge is the language proficiency needed for better employability and mobility of people in EU and new, better and more flexible training approaches to support it.

The COMALAT project[1] addresses the problem of language hurdles which greatly limits employability and mobility across EU. In this regard, we propose a competence oriented multilingual adaptive language training platform. In our past work we have also used competencies for Human Resources Management in enterprises [2]. This project is important for proper assessment and targeted improvement of the multilingual competencies of youth, adults and (low-)skilled workers in the European Union (EU) in order to boost their mobility in EU, increase their employability chances and facilitate their cultural adaptation. The current drawbacks of the available language training portals and the previously granted EU projects are: (a) they are not or cannot be considered as OERs (Open Educational Resources), (b) they are not adaptable to the needs and goals of individuals, (c) they cannot be used offline from e. g. disconnected smartphones, (d) they are either targeting the general aspects of the language skills or are very specifically designed for particular groups of people not being flexible in both of these aspects simultaneously, and (e) the software supporting these platforms is not provided with a permissive license and it cannot support a digital marketplace for foreign language e-learning.

The intellectual outputs of COMALAT have the advantage of being available to all as OER. The platform is competence-oriented and adaptable to the needs and goals of users. The system will support both online and offline learning, through synchronized apps, on different devices. It is designed so that it can handle different training materials including general language courses as well as specifically designed courses targeting special interests. We also plan to disseminate the source code of the platform under a commercial-friendly open source license (e. g. Apache License 2.0). This ensures that anyone can build

---

[1] http://www.comalat.eu.

free and commercial services around the product effectively creating a digital marketplace in language e-learning.

In the rest of this chapter in Sect. 16.2 we review related works. Then in Sect. 16.3 we provide some technical details of the COMALAT platform. Particularly, in Sect. 16.3.3 we discuss adaptability and statistical evaluation of learners. In Sect. 16.4 we discuss the learning materials for the COMALAT platform. Finally, in Sect. 16.5 we provide some future steps and conclude this chapter.

16.2   Related Work

A large theme of the work in COMALAT is related to adaptability. According to [3] adaptability in e-learning environments can be related to interaction, course delivery, content discovery and assembly as well as collaboration support. COMALAT will focus its adaptability efforts in adaptive course delivery as well as adaptive collaboration support. Adaptive learning environments require detailed descriptions of learners and learning objects, trying to adapt the learning objects to the needs of the learners. LOM [4] and LIP [5] are two standards that can be used for describing learning objects and learners, respectively. In COMALAT we focus in providing metadata for the learning material, that allow the platform to infer automatically if and what additional content is required for a specific learner. Also learners' characteristics include, among others, characteristics related to language learning (e. g. desired level can be Beginner or Intermediate), to the reason why someone wants to learn a second language (e. g. the specific purpose) etc.

Descriptions of learning objects and learners are used by appropriate mechanisms that take advantage of this knowledge to adapt the learning activity and facilitate learning [3]. Some approaches that have been proposed towards this direction include [6] in which AI planning is used for course generation but not subsequent adaptation and [7] in which Key Performance Indicators (KPIs) at various levels in business environments as well as ontologies are used for the generation of customized exams as well as learning syllabus. COMALAT's focus, on the other hand, is course adaptability for language e-learning.

Also popular e-learning environments, such as Moodle[2] and Sakai[3], support all the standard features (learning, collaboration etc.), but lack adaptability features. On the other hand, less known Adaptive Learning Environments, such as Alfanet, Interbook etc., support adaptability features but lack standard e-learning features [8]. In the COMALAT project a popular platform, supporting all standard features, has been selected and was enriched with adaptability features.

For the recommendation of suitable lessons for learners and the prediction of the effort that is needed in order to reach a specific level, we plan to use in COLAMAT Association Rules Mining (see Sect. 16.3.3 for more details).

---

[2] https://moodle.org/.
[3] https://sakaiproject.org/.

Regarding data mining in general in educational environments some indicative works are the following. In [9] the author used web mining techniques to build an agent that could recommend on-line learning activities and in [10] two technologies were developed in order to construct a personalized learning recommender system; a multi-attribute evaluation method and a fuzzy matching method to find suitable learning materials. In [11] the researchers focus on the discovery of interesting contrast rules and in identifying attributes characterizing patterns of performance disparity between various groups of students. In [12] evolutionary algorithms as data mining method are used to discover interesting relationships from student's usage information in order to provide feedback for course content effectiveness. Data mining techniques (association rules and symbolic data analysis) are used in [13] to gain further insight on the students' learning and improve teaching. The aim of [14] was to guide the search for best fitting transfer model of student learning by using association rules, and the researchers in [15] proposed a framework for personalizing e-learning based on aggregate usage profiles and a domain ontology. Finally, in [16] Web Usage Mining approach was combined with the basic Association Rules, Apriori Algorithm to optimize the content of an e-learning portal.

Regarding language materials (Sect. 16.4), there has been some research on the effectiveness of Language Learning Software, Platforms and Apps, in some cases requested by governments making outstanding investments in Language Training. Analysis and assessment of Rosetta Stone™ [17] in 2008 by the Centre of Advanced Study of Language at the University of Maryland outlined some of the main problems (consistently confirmed by research later on [18, 19]) facing independent or self-access language learning to the present: high levels of attrition, lack of motivation, limited improvement in productive skills, lack of interaction and sense of community, and language learner autonomy issues. Recent related works insist on similar parameters [20], with the addition of the new importance social technologies and media will have in Language Learning environments and, particularly, in learner's autonomy developments [21].

16.3 The COMALAT Platform

In the frame of the COMALAT project available open source e-learning software platforms with potential language training capabilities have been investigated. While most of the currently available LMS and CMS are not directly advertised at the market as language training environments, they may provide basic functionality for language e-learning and assessment. The aim of the e-learning systems study was to investigate existing features of each platform and compare their suitability for extension towards the language training and assessment platform which is developed in the COMALAT project. We evaluated Moodle, Chamilo, ILIAS, eFront, Sakai, .LRN, Claroline and ATutor. The details of this investigation are beyond the scope of this chapter. However, the final evaluation given several criteria relevant to language learning are given in Table 16.1.

Table 16.1 Overall platform evaluation

	Moodle	Chamilo	ILIAS	eFront	Sakai	.LRN	Claroline	ATutor
Evaluation (in %)	66.85	55.88	55.46	55.73	54.19	50.65	53.07	54.10

This evaluation was only supportive for the purpose of the COMALAT project, and finally Sakai was selected. First, there was a constraint that the platform selected should have a permissive Open-Source License which would allow its commercial use. This indicated Sakai as a possible candidate. Nevertheless, we wanted to know the advantages and disadvantages of Sakai in relation to other platforms and this is why the detailed evaluation and comparison was carried out. Furthermore, Sakai was quite high in the list in our comparison of LMS's, although not the first choice, without any serious shortcomings for language e-learning. At a technical level Sakai's functionality is provided by mostly independent *tools*. Tools use the Sakai framework which provides common functionality shared by all tools. Examples of tools are the Grade Book tool, the Syllabus tool, the Samigo (aka Tests and Quizzes) tool and many others. For the purposes of the COMA-LAT project we have chosen to provide two additional tools which are shortly described next.

16.3.1   COMALAT Guide Tool

This tool is responsible for providing guidance during users' interaction with the system. It provides a learning path comprising of lessons and quizzes. Based on results, the tool provides additional content to learners according to their needs. This is one aspect of the adaptability of the learning content to the users. In addition, users get instructions in their chosen instruction language (English, Spanish, German) and specify their job-specific preference (Health, Tourism & Hospitality, Science & Technology and Business & Professional Language). This information is provided in the user's profile using the Guide tool profile page (see Fig. 16.1).

The provided guiding functionality by this tool, makes it possible to combine and include other tools, like the Test & Quizzes tool. As a result, sequences of learning materials, like the implementation of a learning path for language training can be realized inside Sakai. Technically, the Guide tool uses the "Group" concept of Sakai to filter the suitable content for users. Users are registered to and are unregistered from specific groups depending on their achievements in specific activities. As a final result, the content is made visible to the learner at the right time and is delivered step-by-step using the Guide tool.

Fig. 16.1 COMALAT Guide
profile page

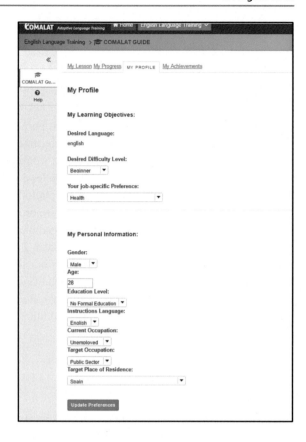

16.3.2 COMALAT Authoring Tool

This tool is used by the teachers who upload content to the system. It allows them to provide specific metadata for this content, as can be seen in Fig. 16.2.

Fig. 16.2 COMALAT Authoring Tool

Provided metadata can be in relation to isolated activities spread throughout the lessons in a learning path as well as metadata for final tests. Furthermore, the system is extensible in the sense that it allows teachers to define further metadata tags than the ones already defined. For example, an activity within a lesson can be characterized by the path as normal or extra, with extra activities being presented to learners as additional content when they fail to complete successfully the normally provided activities.

16.3.3   Adaptability and Statistical Evaluation of Learners

The increased competition in online training platforms, requires that the platforms should be more adaptive and "intelligent". This is achieved by providing to learners, fair and innovative evaluation methods, motivation for studying and suitable lessons for each learner individually. All these facilities, aim to boost the learning process.

In COMALAT platform we have selected to use fuzzy grading [22] for learners' evaluation. The reason for this is that (a) The evaluation method can be more flexible about who will "pass" or "fail" a quiz and partially compensate for the absence of a human evaluator who could decide, for example, if a learner with a score close to the baseline – but below it – should pass taking into account the overall performance of the learner, (b) The system can determine automatically the difficulty of the quizzes based on all the other learners' performances in a quiz. Fuzziness could be used to make a quiz quite easier (or quite harder) for a learner to pass it, depending on the difficulty characterization of a quiz based on all learners' performance, without changing dramatically the overall learners' performance scores.

Another important point that has to be addressed is the assignment of the "right" lessons to the learners depending on various characteristics of the learner. The main concern is the assignment of inappropriate lessons, which do not reflect learners' overall interest or their needs; this may create serious problems such as poor commitment and underachievement. The output of association rules are logical expressions of the "if-then" form and are very useful in uncovering the systematic effects of learners' demographics (e. g. mother tongue, age, education, occupation etc.) on their performance on specific lessons. The correct interpretation of the extracted association rules leads to efficient decisions that improve not only the learners but also the entire educational environment, which is another aspect of intelligence. The ultimate goal of such a system should be the recommendation of the most suitable lessons for learners and the prediction of the effort that is needed in order to reach a specific level. The application of Association Rules, however, requires a large amount of data, which means a long-term collection of information from participating learners. At the time of authoring the book chapter, while the platform is under development, such data are not available.

16.4   Digital E-Learning Materials in COMALAT

From the introduction of CALL (Computer Assisted Language Learning) concept in the 60's, the pendulum moving from enthusiasm to skepticism in the language teaching community has not stopped swinging, despite the normalization process of the ever-increasing-reborn technologies and the arrival of a new generation of teachers, researchers and, of course, language learners. The author of the concept of normalization, Stephen Bax, talks, in a later revision, about poles of "awe" and "fear" towards technology, and admits some excesses of optimism as to the positive-only effects of technology in education [23]. It seems unnecessary to review again the many benefits CALL or TELL (Technology Enhanced Language Learning, in Walker and White terms [20]) bring to both language learners and public institutions in the search for intercultural and multilingual citizenship, but to enter into the discussion of how methodological issues in creating materials for CO-MALAT have been addressed, we must briefly mention a few of the limitations of CALL, particularly when dealing with self-access, self-study materials.

First of all, it is necessary to recall the need for an adequate methodological stand, since technology, as Bax warned us, cannot be the "single agent" [24] of change, nor, as Blake pointed out, it does constitute a methodology [25] for Language Learning in itself, as it has been sometimes misunderstood. Massive drop-outs in self access courses, apps, and platforms make it obvious that their availability, cost-effectiveness and practicality are not compelling or motivating enough for continued study, as the reports and analysis of different platforms by the Centre of Advanced Study of Language at the University of Maryland have proved [18, 19]. Proper curriculum design and adequate planning of the activities/materials will always be the key element, if we are really to live in the "constructivist phase" of "Integrative CALL", according to the well-known chronology proposed by Warschauer [26], or in the normalized, integrated CALL approach according to Bax's terms. Otherwise, we will be using "new" technology only to insist on "traditional" learning materials. To accept some of the autonomous, self-access learning limitations and to avoid promising what cannot be achieved we decided to strive for attainable goals within the scope of the COMALAT project: (a) a focus on adaptability and a search for consistency in development of language materials and their proper sequence of contents, (b) moderate ambition to include, together with the usual grammar and vocabulary settings, as much multimodal work/presentations, culture, discourse and strategic information/practice as possible, and (c) an attempt to face partially the major problem of how to include some interaction, meaningful communication and cooperative learning in a self-study open-source platform.

Second language Acquisition (SLA) research and most methodological standpoints would agree on the importance of strategic competence, meaningful communication and feedback in Language Learning [27, 28]. In fact, learning languages in the digital era has not (yet) become as easy and widespread as one would expect partly due to MOOCs, platforms, apps, online courses, etc. falling short on these aspects of Language Learning, even in the case of "blended" learning, and much more so in the case of independent learning, self-study, autonomous learning, etc. (different terms have been employed – for a review, see Morrison [29]). How did the COMALAT project address those limitations? Here we will briefly explain the solutions proposed and attempted within the limited scope of a project such as COMALAT.

16.4.1   Strategies and Skills

As far as Strategic Competence is concerned, cues, presentations and activities in COMA-LAT try to not just deploy strategies but to stimulate reflection and explicit knowledge. Even today, experts are not sure about the effectiveness of Strategy Based Instruction or, more specifically, about how to assess scientifically that effectiveness, how to demonstrate, as stated by Macaro, that "strategic behavior is the key independent variable in bringing about higher proficiency" but there is certain consensus about the connection between strategy use and motivation and its relevance in language learners' achievement [30]. In developing materials for Sakai, and due to the restrictions regarding individualized feedback, most strategic work has been included in presentations and activities, mainly in receptive skills (reading and listening). However, from the intermediate level on, a great deal of work has been done in including strategy-based material in writing activities, and some peer assessment of strategies in the social module of the platform. A combination of top-down and bottom-up strategies has been sought in reading and listening materials, and of course, despite skill-specific work and sections, a good deal of the course tries to integrate different skills in tasks, exercises and activities in the same way they would be integrated in real life situations and contexts. Thus, five sections were created for assessment, statistical analysis and adaptability purposes (Functions/Grammar, Listening/Speaking, Reading/Writing, Vocabulary and Language for Specific Purposes, this last one only being present in the Intermediate level) but the student moves naturally from one to the other depending on the content, not on the internal course /assessment structure. Each section includes three subsections, allowing for different contents and strategies to be focused on in a unit and for recurrence of both lexical and functional items to be considered. The learning path is, then, thoroughly designed, but adapted to a learners' profile and performance after completion of each subsection, when the learner receives feedback and further practice on the specific contents he/she had more difficulties with, since one major characteristic in the materials to face the limitations is adaptability: COMA-LAT provides the student with a certain degree of fine-grain feedback and opportunities for content-specific extra practice and self-monitoring that can foster his/her autonomy, tracking his/her progress, identifying weaknesses and establishing a basis and an impetus for further learning. Extra practice, when completion is not satisfactory, does not mean here repeating the same exercises/sentences again but in a different order, as is the case in some self-study apps or courses, trying to avoid discouragement and attrition issues and looking for "stickiness" [31], commitment and motivation. In productive skills, particularly from the Intermediate level on, some activities encourage peer-correction and allow to partially compensate for the lack of corrective feedback an actual teacher would provide.

16.4.2 Meaningful Communication and Cooperative Work

There has been a move in research trends from the role of interaction and negotiation of meaning as an addition to comprehensible input to its evolution/inclusion in task-based approaches [32]. Although there are open issues as to their weight in SLA, their being a panacea for all levels of proficiency, learning contexts and languages, their relationship to formal explicit knowledge, etc., hardly anyone would question the importance of meaningful communication, open-ended activities and tasks, interaction and cooperative learning [33]. For this reason, these elements represent the biggest challenge for any self-study material, and there is actually little evidence of this type of work taking place out of teacher-driven courses. In COMALAT, we addressed this problem and the inevitable limitations of self-study platforms mainly in two ways: (a) having meaning in mind as much as possible in grammar presentations and activities, reading/listening work, etc. trying to create the conditions, awareness and reflection to prepare for communication (and to keep the will and motivation to do so), and (b) including, from the intermediate level on, a social tool/chat available for learners. The social module allows a Student A to contact and communicate with a student B, native or highly proficient speaker of Student A's target language and in turn learning Student A's mother tongue. Participation in the social module of the platform is highly encouraged by part of the activities and materials, although cannot be assessed by the system, and some open-ended activities are designed to be carried out cooperatively or with the help and peer correction of another learner. Finally, some chat/forum materials have been devised, to include community development and thus allow for some of the possibilities for Independent Language Learning that have been pointed out for the future, in environments, developments and directions we cannot/should not really envision or control [21]. In any case, we depart from a "multicompetence" point of view, and even if we assume some learners will not develop all skills to the same level, we would still be achieving interesting results in creating multicompetent plurilingual citizens, with different degrees or competence in different languages (including their mother tongue) for different purposes in different situations.

16.5 Conclusions and Future Work

COMALAT is a project that targets the acquisition of language skills from learners mainly wishing to pursue a career in another country. We discussed the platform under development for this purpose and we explained the rationale for selecting a specific platform that could be used as a base for the COMALAT project. We also discussed the digital e-learning materials and their design philosophy. Since COMALAT has the goal of language learning for the European workforce it is highly relevant to enterprises in Europe because workforce mobility is a prominent goal of the EU. Furthermore, the materials will be provided as Open Educational Resources to allow the usage by interested parties at no cost. The platform itself will be provided with a permissive Open Source license which may allow the creation of a digital marketplace around COMALAT with related business and services that will be offered in the future by other parties.

References

1. European Commission, "The Bruges Communiqué on enhanced European Cooperation in Vocational Education and Training for the period 2011–2020," European Commission, 2010.
2. N. Mittas, G. Kakarontzas, M. Bohlouli, L. Angelis, I. Stamelos and M. Fathi, "ComProFITS: A web-based platform for human resources competence assessment," in *6th International Conference on Information, Intelligence, Systems and Applications (IISA)*, Corfu, 2015.
3. A. Paramythis and S. Loidl-Reisinger, "Adaptive Learning Environments and eLearning Standards," *Electronic Journal of E-Learning*, vol. 2, pp. 181–194, 2004.
4. IEEE, "Learning Object Metadata standard," IEEE, 2002.
5. IMS Global Learning Consortium, "IMS Learner Information Packaging Information Model Specification," 2001.
6. Kontopoulos, E. et al., "An ontology-based planning system for e-course generation," *Expert Systems with Applications*, vol. 35, p. 398–406, July-August 2008.
7. Jia, Haiyang et al., "Design of a performance-oriented workplace e-learning system using ontology," *Expert Systems with Applications*, vol. 38, p. 3372–3382, April 2011.
8. D. Hauger and M. Köck, "State of the Art of Adaptivity in E-Learning Platforms," *15th Workshop on Adaptivity and User Modeling in Interactive Systems*, pp. 355–360, 2007.
9. O. Zaiane, "Building a Recommender Agent for e-Learning Systems," in *International Conference in Education*, 2002.
10. J. Lu, "Personalized e-learning material recommender system," in *International Conference on Information Technology for Application*, 2004.
11. Minaei-Bidgoli, B. et al., "Mining interesting contrast rules for a web-based educational system," in *International Conference on Machine Learning Applications*, 2004.
12. Romero, C. et al., "Knowledge discovery with genetic programming for providing feedback to courseware author," *User Modeling and User-Adapted Interaction: The Journal of Personalization Research*, vol. 14, no. 5, p. 425–464, 2004.
13. A. Merceron and K. Yacef, "Mining student data captured from a web-based tutoring tool," *Journal of Interactive Learning Research*, vol. 15, no. 4, p. 319–346, 2004.
14. Freyberger, J. et al., "Using association rules to guide a search for best fitting transfer models of student learning," in *Workshop on Analyzing Student-Tutor Interactions Logs to Improve Educational Outcomes at ITS Conference*, 2004.
15. Markellou, P. et al., "Using semantic web mining technologies for personalized e-learning experiences," in *Web-based education*, 2005.
16. A. Ramli, "Web usage mining using apriori algorithm: UUM learning care portal case," in *International. Conference on Knowledge Management*, 20005.
17. K. Doughty and C. Nielson, "Rosetta Stone™ Evaluation Executive Report.Final Technical Report E.3.1," University of Maryland, College Park, MD, 2008.
18. K. B. Nielson, "Self-study with language learning software in the workplace: What happens?," *Language Learning & Technology*, vol. 3, no. 15, pp. 110–129, 2011.

19. Nielson, K. et al., "Learning foreign languages at a distance: Characteristics of effective online courses (TTO 32131).," 2009.
20. A. Walker and G. White, Technology Enhanced Language Learning: Connecting Theory and Practice, Oxford: Oxford University Press, 2013.
21. H. Reinders and C. White, "20 years of autonomy and technology: how far have we come and where to next?," *Language Learning & Technology,* vol. 20, no. 2, pp. 143–155, June 2016.
22. C. Law, "Using fuzzy numbers in educational grading system," *Fuzzy Sets and Systems,* vol. 83, pp. 311–323, 1996.
23. S. Bax, "Normalisation Revisited: The Effective Use of Technology in Language Education," *International Journal of Computer-Assisted Language Learning and Teaching,* vol. 2, no. 1, April-June 2011.
24. S. Bax, "CALL past, present and future," *System,* vol. 1, no. 31, pp. 13–28, 2003.
25. R. J. Blake, Brave New Digital Classroom, Washington, DC: Georgetown University Press, 2013.
26. M. Warschauer, "Computer Assisted Language Learning: an Introduction," in *Multimedia language teaching*, Tokyo, Logos International, 1996, pp. 3–20.
27. R. Ellis, The Study of Second Language Acquisition., Oxford University Press, 2008.
28. M. Celce-Murcia, Teaching English as a Second or Foreign Language, Boston: Heinle and Heinle, 2001.
29. B. Morisson, Independent Language Learning, Hong Kong University Press, 2011.
30. E. Macaro, "Developments in Language Learner Strategies," in *Comtemporary Applied Linguistics vol. 1*, London, Continuum, 2009, pp. 10–36.
31. Clark M. et al., "Stickiness and Online Language Learning Pedagogical Suggestions for Engaging Learners in Languagenation.," University of Maryland Center for Advanced Study of Language, 2014.
32. D. Nunan, Task-based language teaching, Cambridge: Cambridge University Press, 2004.
33. P. Robinson, Task-based language learning, Malden,MA: Blackwell, 2011.

Part V
Disruptive Technologies & Entrepreneurship

Preface: Reprogramming Your Corporate Immune System

Gerhard Hastreiter

17.1 The Billion Dollar Questions

A number of automotive managers attended the recent SingularityU Summit in Berlin. They face serious disruptive changes. As Volkswagen CIO Martin Hofmann put it: "As soon as the customer no longer touches the steering wheel, the emotional bond to his car gets lost and we enter a completely different game". Later, one of the managers present asked Salim Ismail, author of the book "Exponential Organizations", how a big corporation can manage disruptive innovation from the inside. Ismail's answer was disillusioning. Better you move it to the fringes of your company and run it in absolute stealth mode, he recommended, otherwise the "corporate immune system" will strike back and devour both, the innovation and the innovators.

Quite a dire outlook. These are the billion Dollar questions indeed: How can a big incumbent corporation manage disruption? How can it re-invent its own business model from the inside instead of falling victim to disruption from outside entrepreneurs? Can it after all or are the odds so much in favor of start-ups or spin-offs that the best it can do is deferring demise by incremental improvement?

History doesn't provide much reason for optimism for the big fishes. Only very few companies of reasonable size succeeded in "re-inventing" themselves. Looking for examples, we have to start looking back to the time when the pony-express rose and fell (Amex and Western Union), few of them pass the test of time (Nokia) and hardly any are to be found in the recent past. On the other hand, examples of start-ups eating into traditional companies' businesses or inventing completely new ones abound.

G. Hastreiter (✉)
Allianz
Munich, Germany
e-mail: gerhard.hastreiter@allianz.de

© Springer-Verlag GmbH Germany 2018
C. Linnhoff-Popien et al. (eds.), *Digital Marketplaces Unleashed*,
https://doi.org/10.1007/978-3-662-49275-8_17

Thus, is the answer relinquishing to the corporate immune system, making do with incremental progress, leveraging new technology in order to continuously improve but not going for the quantum leap?

If we believe it is true that as Lucas Sauberschwarz and Lysander Weiss argue in this book that it is almost impossible to replace a company's profit pool through disruptive innovation from the fringes, if we trust Salim Ismail's assessment that the corporate immune system is the force that thwarts innovation from the inside and if we finally believe that some kind of disruptive innovation is crucial for success or even survival of corporate incumbents, the only way out is *reprogramming this corporate immune system.*

As any immune system, this one has more than but one way of defense and attack. In order to understand what needs to be changed and how we may possibly achieve this reconditioning, we have to delve a little deeper onto these ways.

17.2   Death by a Thousand Cuts

"Death by a thousand cuts" is one of the most common strategies of our companies' immune system. Assume, you have a setup that would have the potential to earn its constituents fortunes at the likes of WhatsApp or Airbnb. A dozen of gifted people, having the right idea at the right point in time, working hard and passionately to give birth to and grow this project. Then, put this into your regular corporate context.

Immediately, all the team's capacity will be drawn away from getting the thing done, bringing it to the marketplace, experimenting, re-working, re-trying and finally succeeding (or at least failing fast) towards dealing with dozens of issues that emerge from the inside: "Doesn't that cannibalize our existing business?", "Shouldn't we better leverage our excellent supply chain?", "Have you considered offshoring the service to our new center?", "Why don't you use our standard IT architecture?" . . .

A sub-strategy of "death by a thousand cuts" is "death by committee". "Do you have approval by the Finance Committee?", "Please report to the steering committee on a bi-weekly basis", "Please update your project charter" . . .

The core of the problem (and our immune system's strategy) is not that these questions would be wrong or irrelevant. Neither is it that these questions couldn't be answered properly. Actually, the team will put all its effort into answering them. The true problem is simply their number. Not even the strongest team can stand against that tide for a sustained period of time and will inevitably be absorbed by activities that are directed towards the inside instead of delivering to the customer.

So what can be done against these workings of the corporate immune system that – by the way – are in most cases not reflections of ill will but themselves an effect of the pure arithmetic of size?

Again, some will argue that the death-by-a-thousand-cuts dynamic is close to a law of nature and the only way to avoid it is running your disruptive projects in skunk- or stealth-mode. But, again, that is basically a bet on replacing your business by a completely new one you are starting up in this mode; -and the odds of succeeding this way aren't very promising.

So we need to sandbox these endeavors *inside* the company. They need light touch. They need strong gatekeeping and senior managements' deliberate protection against interference. On the other hand, this protection has to rest on actual *delivery*, not plans or aspirations. The deal is: as long as you deliver (to the customer), we will grant you protection and discuss results only.

17.3 Death by Desiccation

Though sandboxing may be the first life support to the (potentially) disruptive initiative, the corporate immune system may leverage just that lifeline in order to suffocate this initiative. Rather sooner than later the project needs access to the company's operations. Otherwise it can neither gain relevance nor can it live up to its promise of delivery that is the basis for the protection it gets from death by a thousand cuts.

The ways of denying access to the real world are many and varied. "We love the idea but ... our project pipeline is already full", " ... your solution can hardly be integrated", " ... your team is too small to support a large scale operation", " ... these are the approval processes you have to go through" ...

A sub-category of "death by desiccation" is "death by division". As division of labor has been the paradigm of the pre-digital era, the company's organization may show a tendency towards driving wedges into our team of innovators and entrepreneurs, (re-)claiming resources and thus depriving it of the power to deliver.

Both ways, the initiative gets stuck. It doesn't get beyond the stage of presentations, prototypes, mock-ups and focus groups. It doesn't reach the final proof: the customer. It becomes just another piece of conceptual work.

Once again, this reaction has to be countered by force. The path towards implementation has to be paved from the beginning. Even more: (partial) failure has to be part of the calculation from the beginning, allowing for either re-work or discontinuation of the effort; – without loss of face.

17.4 Death by Mediocracy

Corporate immune systems tend to favor mediocracy. They tend to punish failure as well as outstanding success. This strategy is more subtle and sustainable than the ones described previously. It goes to the heart of the company's culture.

It works on both ends. Whilst there is common agreement today that taking risks and potential failure are essential prerequisites for success, careers may still be spun in a less than neutral direction by the corporate immune system in case of outright and "proven" failure (as a result of taking significant risks, again).

Strangely enough though, the system may react similarly on the side of exceptional success. Assume our team of entrepreneurs (or "intrapreneurs") manages to avoid death by a thousand cuts, actually delivers to the customer, recovers again and again from setbacks, re-works, improves, scales up; – makes its innovation an outstanding success. What is going to happen?

Most probably there will be some recognition and rewards. Surely, some will go to the team. But about as likely as not, success will acquire many more parents; – well beyond the core team. The corporate (immune) system will also ensure that recognition and rewards stay moderate as they must "fit into the broader picture". In the worst case, it will even take care that the success itself is watered down, dissolved into the wider corporate ocean.

The effects are subtle. Failure isn't punished outright and achievement is actually rewarded. But the system offers another, safer and less arduous path towards success: play it safe, stand by and jump on the bandwagon (only) as soon as it has gained significant momentum. This way, you hedge your downside risk and the upside potential is almost as good. This though is close to the opposite of entrepreneurship.

Dealing with this reaction of our corporate immune system proves to being complex. On the one side, incentive systems have to be changed towards rewarding risk taking as such and taking these risks has to come along with opportunities to earn significant rewards. On the other side, repeated failure must not be rewarded and the prospect of reaping huge benefits comes with the risk of abuse and short-sightedness.

17.5 Reprogramming the Immune System

Death by a thousand cuts, death by desiccation and death by mediocracy as well as their siblings may not be the only strategies the immune systems have devised to maintain disruption and entrepreneurship at a level that is bearable for the corporate organism. But quite possibly, our corporate organisms can bear much more today than our immune systems have been used to.

Thus, if we believe in disruption, re-invention and entrepreneurship from the inside, we have to re-program that systems. The paragraphs above indicate the direction. But reprogramming the system is far from an easy task. It needs fine tuning but it needs speed and some force at the same time.

Finally, the immune system will apply the very strategies it has developed against those who want to reprogram it. If the alternative is a demise into irrelevance though, reprogramming it should be worth the risk and effort.

How Corporations Can Win the Race Against Disruptive Startups

18

Lucas Sauberschwarz and Lysander Weiss

Abstract

Following the rise of digital technologies, more and more large corporations and entire industries are disrupted by technology startups. In the past it was Airbnb disrupting the hospitality industry with more beds around the world than any hotel chain. Now it's Tesla who is disrupting automotive companies by selling more premium vehicles then BMW or Porsche, and in the future it might be new P2P-insurances or bitcoin-based payment apps that disrupt the financial industry. These are just a few examples of disruptive digital startups that are winning against powerful corporations and traditional industries. Looking at the big picture, it increasingly seems that even abundant with money and resources, large, complex corporations still cannot find a way to compete against agile startups that are able to exploit disruptive technologies much faster.

Built on secondary research and experiences with more than 50 innovation projects, the authors aim to shed light on the disruption paradox for large corporations and offer an efficient innovation framework including the 5C-Process as a novel managerial solution to it. This should sensitize decision makers in established companies in regards to their innovation challenges and any digital disruption threats, and provide them with new tools to act and win the race against disruptive startups.

L. Sauberschwarz (✉) · L. Weiss
Venture Idea GmbH
Düsseldorf, Germany
e-mail: lucas.sauberschwarz@venture-idea.com

L. Weiss
e-mail: Lysander.weiss@venture-idea.com

© Springer-Verlag GmbH Germany 2018
C. Linnhoff-Popien et al. (eds.), *Digital Marketplaces Unleashed*,
https://doi.org/10.1007/978-3-662-49275-8_18

18.1   Introduction: The Rise of Disruption

> The Americans may have need of the telephone, but we do not. We have plenty of messenger boys.

This quote, published in 1876 in the "Economist" from Sir William Preece, chief engineer of the British General Post Office shows that the danger of ignoring potentially disruptive technologies is nothing new [1]. However, disruptive forces seem to accelerate exponentially with the rise of digital technologies like broadband internet, 3D-printing, wearable sensors, internet of things or virtual and augmented reality. The threat of disruption has become the "new normal" [2] for established companies since Christensen defined the term in 1995 [3]. In a recent study, 65% of global CEOs fear "new disruptive entrants in the market" [4]. This is no coincidence, with famous startups from the likes of Uber, Airbnb, Tesla, or previously Facebook and Google driving disruptive innovations and leaving large corporations behind [5]. Thus, these incumbents seem to have only one choice: "Disrupt or be disrupted" [6]. Consequently, they take part in the race and try to win against disruptive startups by playing the same game: Disruption is set as a goal in many innovation efforts, and company-owned incubators, accelerators or startup-hubs are set up to develop disruptive technology startups for the company [5].

But what does "disruption" actually mean? Is it really the new normal? Do large corporations always need to be disruptive? And how can they win the race against disruptive startups?

18.2   The Disruption Paradox of Large Corporations

18.2.1   Disruption Challenges of Large Corporations

"Disruption" has become a buzzword for every innovation effort [7]. The *Frankfurter Allgemeine Zeitung* named "disruption" the "business term of the year 2015," and authors are voting to "retire Silicon Valley's emptiest buzzword" [8]. With all this buzzing, the actual definition and theory seem to be lost.

In 1995, Clay Christensen's originally named the term "disruptive technologies". The theory was built on technology cases like the disk drive industry and minicomputers. Here, successful companies first ignored emerging "relatively simple, convenient, low-cost technology" until they suddenly couldn't compete with it anymore [9]. These disruptive technologies are contrasting "sustaining technologies" which are normally produced by successful established companies. They focus on improving their existing products and service offerings – also known as incremental innovation [3] (s. Fig. 18.1).

In following books and articles, Christensen and other scholars continued to enhance the theory by also including *business models* (such as low-cost airlines, discount-stores, or online-education) [1] and novel technology that *creates new markets* (such as mobile

Fig. 18.1 Sustaining and disruptive innovation. (Adapted from Christensen [7])

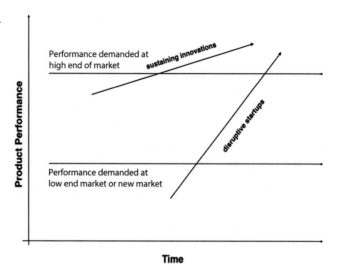

phones disrupting landline phones) [1, 7, 10]. Consequently he changed the term "disruptive technologies" into *"disruptive innovation"*, setting the stage for the term to become ubiquitous [11, 12].

The subtitle of Christensen's book "the innovation dilemma: When new technologies cause great firms to fail" [9] already foreshadows who tends to lose the "disruption" race. In contrast to startups, large corporations already have a successful core business with demanding customers, established structures and optimized processes, high worth patents, brands and specialized and skilled employees [12]. Their main goal is to continue the currently successful path with certain revenue and profit goals. Thus, they consequently ignore new startups with "disruptive" business models and technologies, as they do not match these goals [13]. When the disruptive startups are eventually successful, their disruptive innovation cannot be adapted quickly due to the high, change-resistant complexity of the incumbent [14, 15]. This describes the "dualism problem" or *disruption paradox* for the incumbents [16]: They always have a tradeoff between the successful existing and the disruptive new business; by trying to win the one, they risk to lose the other [17]. In contrast, startups without any customers, employees and processes actually need to act as risky and disruptive as possible to have a chance to win against the established players.

18.2.2 Current Managerial Solutions for the Disruption Challenges

Following the mantra "disrupt or be disrupted" without any pre-existing customers, many large companies take on the goal to be disruptive and put it on top of their innovation agenda, as they fear to otherwise miss the "digital disruption" [18, 19]. To fulfill the goal of being disruptive, managers build on the strategies Christensen deducts from his cases in "The innovator's dilemma" and "The innovator's solution" [9, 10]: Here, case studies show that incumbents could build *separate units* to develop disruptive innovations. These units do not follow the business goals of the core business, they try different business models and research emerging technologies – essentially, they copy the startup model [5, 9]. The hope is, that these separate units discover disruptive innovations or can adapt them before entirely new entrants win the market. Nowadays, many large corporations are building "company accelerators, incubators or innovation labs" as separate units to develop digital disruptive innovations. They are based in Silicon Valley, Berlin, London and Tel Aviv, often far away from the mother company and try to attract tech-talent or whole startups to find the "next big thing" [16].

This strategy sounds great, it might even be successful in some cases and calm investors because the disruption threat is addressed [20] – but unfortunately it will not close the innovation gap and solve the disruption paradox in the long term as several problems are ignored:

- The *goal to be disruptive* can be dangerous in itself, as it actually describes the elimination of the current company or market as the desirable outcome. Thus it needs to be driven by business goals such as new profit or revenue. Take the Kodak-Case for example: It is widely used as *the* classic case for digital disruption, in which a company missed a new disruptive technology. However, Kodak actually developed and patented the first digital camera. Kodak invested millions in research & development to disrupt the market with digital cameras and printing kiosks, it even bought a photo-sharing website before Facebook even existed. It just failed to look for a business model based on cheap cameras and online-sharing instead of printing that would work with their core business. Kodak had great success in disrupting itself and the photo industry, it just failed to bring it in their core business on the way [21].
- The *use of separate units* to develop disruptive digital innovations circumvent the goal of *integrating these emerging technologies in the core company.* Iansiti, McFarlan, and Westermann [22] report that "spinoffs often enable faster action early on but later have difficulty achieving true staying power in the market. Even worse, by launching a spinoff, a company often creates conditions that make future integration very difficult". Furthermore, the separate units do not leverage the existing capabilities of the large corporation that would be an advantage against other startups. Therefore, ability of these separate units to actually *influence the core business* with innovations seems limited, leaving the company with the existing innovation gap behind [5, 23, 24].
- The *probability of success* for company-owned startups or separate units to develop significant digital disruptive innovations is very low, as most new startups usually fail. The probability of these company startups to actually develop innovations with a revenue and profit high enough to *substitute the core business* in case of its disruption (which must be the goal of disruptive separate units) is 1:117,000, according to a re-

cent Brain study.[1] Imagine a fin-tech startup from a bank accelerator that substitutes the revenue of the entire private wealth management business with a mobile banking app or a startup in an energy company tech incubator that makes more profit by selling smart-home services then the core business of selling energy as a quasi-monopolist. Hard to imagine? Still, for many companies out there these are the biggest hopes against the digital disruption they have today.

To actually close the innovation gap between startups and incumbents and solve the disruption paradox for the latter, a different managerial solution is necessary. To address the weaknesses of Christensen's proposed separate units, a new innovation method should a) leverage the capabilities of large companies as an advantage against new entrants, b) work in the core business and restrictions of a company to actually influence it instead of ignoring it and c) lead to new business to bring the company forward.

18.3 Efficient Innovation: Solving the Disruption Paradox

The proposed new managerial solution aims to solve the disruption paradox for companies that want or need to participate in disruptive market changes as an opportunity, but have an existing successful profit model [17][2]. These corporations can participate in the digital disruption race; they even have the best capabilities to win it – but they need to play the game differently than startups [17]. As long as they only act as startups with separate units or transformation approaches, they remain pale copies, while the existing core business "drags them down". Dualism and the ambidextrous organization theory describe the problem as *functioning efficiently today while innovating effectively for tomorrow* [13, 16]. Here, scholars call for a managerial solution that keeps the innovation *as close as possible to the core business*. Thus, the goal for corporations should be to integrate disruptive innovations into the core assets [5] and leverage the company capabilities for new uses and new users [6, 24]. That way, they can manage the interplay between disruptive technologies and stay ahead of every new entrant due to their existing customers, capabilities, and resources [14]. These companies have operational needs and drivers that are more important than just hunting for the next big thing or a new disruptive technology [16].

Consequently, to successfully "disrupt the disruptors with their own strengths" [17], the incumbents must develop innovations, which are as *close to the core as possible* and – in contrast to sustaining innovations – *as disruptive as necessary*. With these "*efficient inno-*

---

[1] Zook 2016, When large companies are better at Entrepreneurship than Startups, HBR, https://hbr.org/2016/12/when-large-companies-are-better-at-entrepreneurship-than-startups.
[2] For some companies or situations, ignoring a disruption or a complete transformation may be gainful. However, this will not be discussed here further [2].

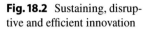 **Fig. 18.2** Sustaining, disruptive and efficient innovation

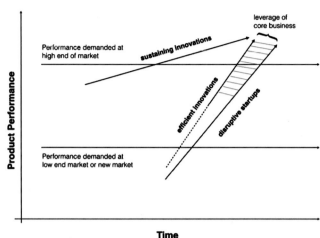

vations", incumbents can maximize the impact of the core business and defend themselves against disruptive startups (s. Fig. 18.2).[3]

Efficient innovations have the following characteristics: They

- bring a *new technology* to the existing business model or a *new business model* to the existing business or *combine* a new technology with a new business model
- match specific *business goals/KPIs* in terms of revenue/profit/costs/time/etc.
- fit into the *restrictions* of the core company to leverage its capabilities

These characteristics are deducted from the theory mentioned above, but can actually be seen in many cases as well. To name two examples:

- The *Apple Appstore* disrupted the smartphone and software *market (= as disruptive as necessary)* with a new business model (platform) and new technology (mobile apps). However it still builds on the preexisting iPhone hardware *(= as close to the core business as possible)*. Soon realizing that the apps would become more important than the phone itself, apps would only run on the iPhone within this controlled ecosystem. Thus users were limited to using iPhones, preventing Apple from disrupting itself in the existing market. Today, it is the largest appstore and Apple is the most profitable smartphone seller worldwide.
- The *Daimler Car2Go carsharing* disrupted the automotive market with a new business model *(= as disruptive as necessary),* but uses the existing Smart car model from Daimler *(= as close to the core business as possible)*. Thus, Daimler can prevent itself from being disrupted as a car manufacturer, as their existing products are used to gain new market shares (additionally, potential car owners have the chance to experience

---

[3] Sauberschwarz & Weiss, 2017: Das Comeback der Konzerne, Vahlen Verlag.

a Smart car). Today, Car2Go is the world's largest carsharing service and the Smart car model is selling better than ever before [25].

These cases show that large companies have every means they need to "disrupt" better than any startup – but need to leverage them more "efficiently" [26]. But how can the companies develop these *efficient innovations*?

18.4 Efficient Innovation with the 5C-Process

The theory mentioned above and the experience of more than 50 innovation projects in 20 different industries for large corporations in Germany provide the groundwork for the "5C-process for efficient innovation"[4]. During six years of research, the authors combined findings from management, psychology and neuroscience literature with hands on project experience to develop an innovation method that suits the described challenges of large corporations. As a result, the systematic innovation process allows to develop efficient innovations in five steps. In contrast to other innovation processes (s. Fig. 18.3), the 5C-process is designed to work on any restricted "brownfield" instead of starting blank on a greenfield: By starting with the goals and restrictions of the company instead of the customer need or technology opportunity, new ideas and innovations are developed within a specified "innovation space"[5]. The problem: People are not used to developing "disruptive" new ideas in a restricted innovation space, thus creativity techniques alone do not work here. Instead, a systematic process is necessary, which is a lot lengthier and more complex than simple brainstorming – but in return guarantees implementable, *efficient innovations* (s. Fig. 18.4). An overview of the different process steps is given in the following paragraph, and in more detail in the following subchapters.

Fig. 18.3 Model of innovation. (Adapted from Meyers and Marquis in [16])

---

[4] Sauberschwarz & Weiss, 2017: Das Comeback der Konzerne, Vahlen Verlag.
[5] Even when a promising new technology is already identified, goals and criteria need to be defined before any ideation and development starts.

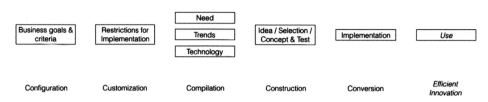

Fig. 18.4 Model of 5C-process

18.4.1 Configuration: Defining the Innovation Setup

Configuration is the first step in the 5C-Process. Like an archaeologist who needs to first specify what he is looking for and why, the starting point here is to specify goals, criteria and the core business of the company [18].

1. *Which business goals do we want to reach? (revenue growth, market share, profit growth, better company image, higher employee satisfaction, etc.)*
2. *Which criteria do we need to match? (timeframe, scalability, budget, etc.)*
3. *What business are we in today? (the job to be done)*

The answers to these questions do not need to be concrete in terms of numbers, but they give a first direction to specify the innovation project and its desired outcome. These questions and answers make sure that the right innovation field is chosen and resources are not wasted on innovation efforts aiming for "the next big thing" or follow the non-concrete goals of "disruption" or "transformation" [18]. An accompanying workshop format the relevant project owners helps to further define the relevant goals, criteria and innovation fields.

18.4.2 Customization: Setting the Innovation Space

Customization is the second step in the 5C-process. Continuing the metaphor of the archaeologist, he would now need to define where he wants to search for artifacts, depending on his rights, tools, and search goals. Similar, customization defines the concrete innovation space in which new innovations can emerge. It is based on specific KPIs (e. g. ROI, potential market size, NPS, costs) and criteria for implementation (e. g. physical and human resources, patents, processes, regulations) together with their degree of changeability. These are not only restrictions, but also advantages: As Scott Anthony [21] states, large companies have "many capabilities that entrants are racing to replicate, such as access to markets, technologies, and healthy balance sheets". All these capabilities must be clear from the beginning in order to leverage these in the following steps.

To make sure that all relevant KPIs and criteria are taken into account, information from every important stakeholder must be included, e. g. through interviews, documents or workshops. The whole checklist essentially works like a "functional specification" to make sure that the future innovations are implementable and *as close to the core as possible*. This step is significantly longer than the usual "project kick-off" – but drastically simplifies the implementation in the end [14].

18.4.3   Compilation: Scanning the Outside World

Compilation describes the third step of the 5C-process. Here, the archaeologist would divide his whole search space into different search fields and collect as much information as possible to increase his chance of success. In the innovation process, the innovation space can be divided into different search fields. In these specific fields, intelligence for customer needs, trends and technology can be collected. Due to the restricted search fields, it becomes possible to "dig" deeper instead of working rather broadly on a greenfield [16]. This step includes

- *Insights* of existing and potentially new customers and their needs e. g. through focus groups, visits and observations [12]. The key insights should then be used to define concrete *search fields* along a customer journey that answers the question, where innovation will have the biggest impact for the customer within the innovation space. Secondary research through studies and reports can further validate these insights.
- *Research of trends and innovation best practices* in the market and especially in analogue markets to see how other companies and startups solve the customer needs. This research should be based on the previously customer-defined search fields within the innovation space.
- Specific *technology research* through patent research, startup reviews, mapping and similar techniques [12]. Additionally, potentially disruptive new technologies and startups can be reviewed here to consider in future innovations or as investment and acquisition targets [27].

The visualized results of the compilation will be used in the next step as inspirations to develop matching innovation concepts (see Sect. 18.4.4). Additionally, it can serve to focus the innovation efforts on the most promising search fields within the innovation space before even developing ideas and concepts. The identification of all relevant trends and technologies based on the needs of the customer make sure that the innovations will be *as disruptive as necessary*.

18.4.4   Construction: Multidimensional Systematic Ideation

Construction is the fourth step of the 5C-process and the heart of the front end of the innovation process. For the archaeologist, this step would describe the actual search for valuable artifacts with special techniques and tools. In the 5C-process, ideas are generated through a multidimensional ideation and conceptualization as described below. Hereby, the goal is to integrate new/disruptive technologies or mechanisms as efficiently as possible into the core business of the company with the following steps:

1. *Define ideation tasks* based on the defined search fields and overall innovation field. As each search field lies inside the innovation space and is based on customer insights, it is assured that ideas are *as sustainable as possible.* Although it might seem harder at first to find novel ideas in the very restricted spaces, experience shows that the possibilities are always infinite. In other words: The possibilities between 0 and 1 are as numerous as between 0 and ∞.
2. Use *inspiration from the compilation* (see Sect. 18.4.1) in each search field to think about new applications for existing technology, new adaptions from best practices or new ways of integrating trends in the business [12]. This way, all relevant external factors are taken into account to make sure that ideas are *as disruptive as necessary.*
3. *Ideate* to find a diverse set of new ideas and solutions for each task by taking different perspectives into account (e. g. different target groups, value propositions, profit models, product characteristics, and various triggers like roleplaying, doodling, group discussions, building, immersion, lateral thinking, etc.).
4. *Review & select* all possible solutions based on their quality and fulfillment of criteria (as defined in the *customization*). During the review, promising ideas should be enhanced to evolve into concrete solutions.
5. *Conceptualize* selected ideas into innovation concepts. They need to contain the solution and include a viable business model, defined KPIs, an implementation plan and other documents based on the specific project needs (e. g. marketing plan, communication concepts, potential partners, etc.). Furthermore, each concept should be checked for *feasibility* with experts (e. g. lawyers, engineers, agencies) and be *validated* by customers with focus groups and/or surveys. By doing this, each final concept can be implemented easily as it fulfills all goals and criteria (as defined in the *configuration* and *customization*) as well as being feasible and viable [16].
6. *Visualize* the final concepts e. g. through images, video sketches, mockups, or prototypes allowing an instant understanding of each solution. Based on this, the decision board can select the best concepts for further testing and implementation.

The ideation and conceptualization within the specific search fields in combination with the inspiration from external sources and the use of different perspectives and triggers helps to develop efficient solutions, that are simultaneously *as close as possible to the core business* and *as disruptive as necessary to the outside world.*

18.4.5 Conversion: Lean Implementation

Conversion is the fifth step in the 5C-process and describes the translation of selected innovation concepts into actual innovations. In this step, the archaeologist would try to make sense of his artifacts to eventually be able to put them in a museum. In terms of the innovation process, the concrete procedures in this step are highly dependent on the type of organization and type of innovation project. Thus, this step needs to be planned more individually than the previous steps. In any case, the following factors should be considered:

- A *knowledge transfer* from the ideation team to the implementation team is necessary, if these differ from one another. Besides just handing over the concepts, this knowledge transfer should include detailed discussions, accompanying documents, and regular meetings to exchange problems and solutions during the implementation process.
- An *ownership transfer* from the ideation team to the implementation team is also necessary. As people tend to be more passionate about their own ideas, additional brainstorming sessions can kick off the *conversion* in which the concept can be enhanced with additional ideas by the implementation team.
- *Viability testing* of the concepts should be done as fast as possible. Following the lean startup process a minimum viable product that can be tested inside the company and with potential customers is advisable [5, 16].

With concepts that already take all capabilities, structures, resources and processes into account, the implementation phase carries significantly lower risks than with other innovation projects, but still offers opportunity for innovations to be as disruptive as necessary. This way, *efficient innovations* can be developed in a systematic process that can solve the disruption paradox for large corporations and help them to win the race against disruptive startups.

As the 5C-process partly uses proven concepts from management science, psychology and neuroscience, but combines them in a new way, each project step has it's scientific right to exist. Even though a detailed dive into the different sources is not suitable in this context, a few examples can show the breadth of inspiration: The "configuration" is inspired by business planning and the business model canvas, the "customization" resembles a technical spec sheet from IT project management, and the "compilation" partly uses proven trend research, design thinking and market research methods. The "construction" combines various concepts such as lateral thinking, flow-theory, and creativity techniques with system theory, neuroscience, finance, philosophy and other disciplines, and the "conversion" is partly based on psychological concepts (for idea ownership) and (lean) startup management methods.

18.5 Outlook: Large Corporations Can Lead the Race Against Disruptive Startups!

Large corporations have all advantages at hand to win the race against disruptive startups. The efficient innovation approach aims to help these companies to use and further develop their advantages in the core business instead of ignoring them. Their capabilities, structures, processes and resources make them strong and build a barrier that is hard to overcome for startups, if used properly. This way, instead of being disrupted or disrupting itself, incumbents can disrupt the disruptors.

The digital wave changes marketplaces and brings an ever-increasing complexity into the business world. This complexity is difficult to tackle for small startups, but can be navigated by large corporations. By focusing their innovation efforts in the right direction with *efficient innovations*, they can lead the next wave of innovation.

References

1. G. Cosier und P. Hughes, The problem with disruption, 4 Hrsg., Bd. 19, BT Technology Journal, 2001, p. 9 ff.
2. "Huffingtonpost," [Online]. Available: http://www.huffingtonpost.de/adam-tinworth/disruption-ist-der-neue-n_b_4671895.html. [Accessed 07 08 2016].
3. J. Bower und C. Christensen, Disruptive technologies: catching the wave, Harvard Business Review, 1995.
4. KPMG, "2016 Globald CEO Outlook," 2016. [Online]. Available: https://home.kpmg.com/content/dam/kpmg/pdf/2016/06/2016-global-ceo-outlook.pdf. [Accessed 15 08 2016].
5. Reis, The lean startup, New York: Crown Business, 2011.
6. N.D., Disruptive innovation in mature industries, INSEAD Articles, 2015.
7. C. Christensen, What is disruptive innovation?, Harvard Business Review, 2015, pp. 44–53.
8. The Guardian, "Why its time to retire 'disruption'," 11 01 2016. [Online]. Available: https://www.theguardian.com/technology/2016/jan/11/disruption-silicon-valleys-buzzword. [Accessed 15 08 2016].
9. C. Christensen, The innovator's dilemma: when new technologies cause great firms to fail, Harvard Business School Press, 1997.
10. C. Christensen, The innovator's solution: Creating and sustaining successful growth, Harvard Business Review Press, 2013.
11. Markides, Disruptive innovation, In need of a better theory, 1 Hrsg., Bd. 23, Journal of Product Innovation Management, 2006, pp. 19–25.
12. Y. Dan und C. Hang, "A reflexive review of disruptive innovation theory," *Journal of Management Reviews,* Bd. 4, pp. 435–452, 2010.
13. C. Markides, Business Model Innovation: What can the ambidexterity literature teach us?, 4 Hrsg., Bd. 27, The Academy of Management Perspectives, 2013, pp. 313–323.
14. G. Berglund, M. Magnusson und C. Sandström, Symmetric assumptions in the theory of disruptive innovation, 4 Hrsg., Bd. 23, Creativity and Innovation Management, 2014, pp. 472–483.
15. M. Assink, "Inhibitors of disruptive innovation capability: A conceptual model," *European Journal of Innovation Management,* Bd. 2, pp. 215–233.

16. J. Paap und R. Katz, Anticipating disruptive innovation, 5 Hrsg., Bd. 47, Research-Technology Management, 2004, pp. 13–22.
17. C. Charitou und C. Markides, Responses to disruptive stategic innovation, 2 Hrsg., Bd. 44, Massachusetts: MIT Sloan Management Review, 2002, pp. 55–64.
18. J. Gans, Keep calm and manage disruption, 3 Hrsg., Bd. 53, MIT Sloan management Review, 2016, p. 83 ff.
19. "The Atlantic," 10 2014. [Online]. Available: http://www.theatlantic.com/magazine/archive/2014/10/the-disruption-myth/379348/. [Accessed 08 08 2016].
20. "Handelsblatt, the electric Audi challenge," [Online]. Available: https://global.handelsblatt.com/edition/378/ressort/companies-markets/article/audi-gets-digital. [Accessed 16 08 2016].
21. S. Anthony, "Kodak's downfall wasn't about technology," 07 2016. [Online]. Available: https://hbr.org/2016/07/kodaks-downfall-wasnt-about-technology. [Accessed 15 08 2016].
22. M. Iansiti, F. McFarlan und G. Westerman, Leveraging the incumbent's advantage, 4 Hrsg., Bd. 44, MIT Sloan Management Review, 2003, pp. 58–65.
23. T. Kohler, Corporate Accelerators: Building bridges between corporations and startups, 3 Hrsg., Bd. 59, Business Horizons, 2016, pp. 347–357.
24. King und B. Baatartogtokh, How useful is the theory of disruptive innovation?, 1 Hrsg., Bd. 57, MIT Sloan Management Review, 2015, p. 77.
25. N-TV, "Dickes Absatzplus: Neuer Smart schiebt Daimler an," [Online]. Available: http://www.n-tv.de/wirtschaft/Neuer-Smart-schiebt-Daimler-an-article14466976.html. [Accessed 18 08 2016].
26. Wall Street Journal, "Can big companies be truly innovative?," 17 08 2012. [Online]. Available: http://blogs.wsj.com/atwork/2012/08/17/can-big-companies-be-truly-innovative. [Accessed 08 08 2016].
27. "Future Matters," [Online]. Available: http://future-matters.com/innovation-und-zukunftsforschung/. [Accessed 18 08 2016].

Further Reading

28. Ignatius, The disruption conversation, Harvard Business Review, 2015, p. 14.
29. J. Gans, The other disruption, 3 Hrsg., Bd. 94, Harvard Business Review, 2016, p. 17 ff.
30. Markides, Business Model Innovation: What can the ambidexterity literature teach us?, 4 Hrsg., Bd. 27, The Academy of Management Perspectives, 2013, pp. 313–323.
31. Disruptive innovation – but is it?, 6 Hrsg., Bd. 25, Strategic Direction.
32. The New Yorker, "The disruption machine," 23 06 2014. [Online]. Available: http://www.newyorker.com/magazine/2014/06/23/the-disruption-machine. [Zugriff am 08 08 2016].

Smart Contracts – Blockchains in the Wings

19

Thomas Bocek and Burkhard Stiller

Abstract

In recent years, electronic contracts have gained attention, especially in the context of the blockchain technology. While public blockchains are considered secure, legally binding under certain circumstances, and without any centralized control, they are applicable to a wide range of application domains, such as public registries, registry of deeds, or virtual organizations. As one of the most prominent blockchain examples, the Bitcoin system has reached large public, financial industry-related, and research interest. Another prominent block-chain example, Ethereum, which is considered a general approach for smart contracts, has taken off too. Nevertheless, various different set of functions, applications, and stakeholders are involved in this smart contract arena. These are highlighted and put into interrelated technical, economic, and legal perspectives.

19.1 Introduction

Technology has progressed in the past decades. However, the role of disruptive technology may have become even more prominent with "Blockchains" or "Distributed Ledgers". They pave the path for trustworthy, decentralized applications, and new stakeholder's relations. As such they have the potential to revolutionize public administration, commercial interactions, *and* scattered data – all secured, tamper-proof, and effectively useable with

T. Bocek (✉) · B. Stiller
University of Zürich UZH
Zurich, Switzerland
e-mail: bocek@ifi.uzh.ch

B. Stiller
e-mail: stiller@ifi.uzh.ch

© Springer-Verlag GmbH Germany 2018
C. Linnhoff-Popien et al. (eds.), *Digital Marketplaces Unleashed*,
https://doi.org/10.1007/978-3-662-49275-8_19

easy to set-up and fully integrated smart contracts. A **smart contract** was first introduced in 1994 [1], which is considered an influential work for blockchain-based **cryptographic currencies**.

▶ *A smart contract is a computerized transaction protocol that executes the terms of a contract. The general objectives of [a] smart contract design are to satisfy common contractual conditions (such as payment terms, liens, confidentiality, and even enforcement), minimize exceptions both malicious and accidental, and minimize the need for trusted intermediaries. Related economic goals include lowering fraud loss, arbitrations and enforcement costs, and other transaction costs [1].*

However, a smart contract alone is not "smart" as it needs an infrastructure that can run, execute, and verify the respective contract's transaction data. In combination with such an infrastructure and its interaction with the real world, the smart contract becomes "smart". Recently, smart contracts have gained dedicated attention in the context of blockchains that provide a fully decentralized infrastructure to run, execute, and verify such smart contracts.

Smart contracts can be used for financial transactions and crypto currencies. The first and currently most popular blockchain to address a crypto currency is the **Bitcoin blockchain** [2], which was publically introduced in the beginning of 2009 by Satoshi Nakamoto, a pseudonym leaving room for speculations about the true identity, still unknown to this date. Although the Bitcoin system uses a scripting language, it is not Turing-complete, e. g., it does not support loops. However, for smart financial transactions these scripts can create different kinds of financial contracts, such as escrow contracts, multi-signature contracts, or refund contracts.

Ethereum [3], another current blockchain approach, offers a Turing-complete scripting language, independent of any dedicated application field. The smart contract in Ethereum runs in a sandboxed Ethereum Virtual Machine (EVM) and every operation executed in the EVM has to be paid for to prevent Denial-of-Service (DoS) attacks. Without such a payment, a script with a loop could run forever and, in turn, can overload the EVM so that other scripts cannot be executed. With a general purpose blockchain, new types of contracts compared to the Bitcoin blockchain can be created, e. g., a fully distributed digital organization, such as the DAO (Decentralized Autonomous Organization) [4].

In general, smart contracts need to run on a blockchain to ensure (a) its permanent storage and (b) extremely high obstacles to manipulate the contract's content. A node participating in the blockchain runs a smart contract by executing its script, validating the result of the script, and storing the contract and its result in a block. A block stores multiple smart contracts and is typically created at a constant time interval. For instance, Bitcoin had chosen to create a block every 10 min [2], while Ethereum blocks are created every 14 s [5]. A block has always a reference to the previous block, forming a chain of blocks, hence the term blockchain (cf. Fig. 19.1). In general, a block contains an increasing block number, a hash, a reference to the previous block, a crypto puzzle's solution in case

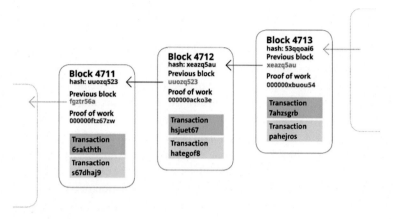

Fig. 19.1 Blockchain Example

of Proof-of-Work (PoW), and one or several transaction-related content information with encoded smart contracts.

Therefore, blockchains show the following main characteristics: full decentralization, traceability and transparency of transactions, proof of transaction viability, prohibitively high cost to attempt to alter transaction history, i. e. 51% attacks, an automated form of resolution, e. g., avoiding double spending, incentives required to participate, and trust enabling among non-trusted peers. The key advantages of blockchains are that stakeholders do not have to share a common trust basis, blockchains decentralized data storage, typically in a peer-to-peer-based network structure and replicated to all interested peers, making data loss impossible, besides act-of-god situations. Note that the terms blockchain, distributed ledger, and shared ledger are often used interchangeably [6].

The remainder of this chapter is structured as follows. Sect. 19.2 discusses Bitcoin and Ethereum, followed by current blockchain developments and limitations in Sect. 19.3. While Sect. 19.4 classifies blockchains and reviews other blockchains besides Ethereum and Bitcoin, Sect. 19.5 outlines insights into new types of applications and uses cases for the blockchain approach and highlights benefits using a blockchain. Additionally, Sect. 19.6 enlightens economic and legal challenges as well as related pitfalls. Finally, Sect. 19.7 draws conclusions.

19.2   Bitcoin and Ethereum

Once *transactions* are stored in a block they are considered secure after other blocks have been added to the blockchain. *E. g.*, Bitcoin suggests to wait for 3 to 6 blocks [7], Ethereum suggests to wait for 10 to 12 blocks [8]. Since blocks are created in a distributed manner, two or more blocks can be created at the same time with potentially conflicting transactions. Accepting a conflicting transaction in those blocks created at the same time could result in "double-spending", that means the user could spend "coins" in another transaction, leaving the other user with an invalid transaction. Thus, a resolution or consensus protocol is required to discard conflicting blocks. Waiting for a certain amount of blocks practically eliminates this double-spending possibility.

The *creation of a block* requires the use of a scarce resource. Currently in Bitcoin and Ethereum this is processing power and electricity. This means that creating a block requires time and energy. To incentivize the creation of blocks, a reward is given to those who created a block. The reward in the Bitcoin system is currently 12.5 bitcoins for creating a block, which has at the time of writing a value of approximately 8125 €, in Ethereum it is 5 ethers with a value of 50 € for every block created. The creation of a block requires the solving of a crypto puzzle, in case of Bitcoin it is the solution of partial SHA256 hash collisions, thus, requiring to invest in processing power and energy. Those who create these blocks are termed miners, as they generate "coins", which is an analogy to the extraction of valuable minerals. Miners compete with each other to solve respective crypto puzzles, leading in the case of Bitcoin to a specialization and recently to a centralization of miners [9]. As one of the key ideas of Bitcoin is its decentralization, the centralization of miners is considered an unfavorable development. Thus, Ethereum has taken countermeasures in order to keep its system fully decentralized. One of these measures is the change of the crypto puzzle to a Proof-of-Stake (PoS) in the near future, making any hardware investment difficult to amortize, since PoS does not need a lot of processing power or electricity.

Fig. 19.2 shows the big picture, how the blockchain is used by users, miners, and exchanges – the three key stakeholders in such an approach. When a user sends coins to other users, it creates a smart contract, encodes the contract in a transaction, and broadcasts the

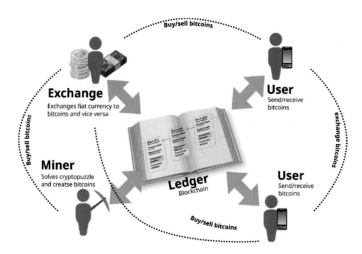

Fig. 19.2 The Big Picture of Blockchain Stakeholders with Miners, Users, Blockchain, and Exchanges

transaction. The recipient user may see the transaction broadcasted within seconds, but as this transaction is not yet in the blockchain, double spending is still possible. The miner also will receive the transaction broadcasted and will start to solve the crypto puzzle. Once a puzzle is solved by a miner, the block will be broadcasted to all peers and other miners will know that they have to restart their process and start solving another crypto puzzle.

Every block that contains a solved crypto puzzle will be added to the blockchain by each node in the system by applying the consensus mechanism in case of needs. The miner that solved the crypto puzzle gets rewarded and can use these coins or exchange them to a government-issued currency at an exchange site. This is often required as electricity bills are typically paid with "fiat" currency. Any user receiving bitcoins can also exchange these to fiat currency. Exchange sites, such as Bitstamp, the first EU-licensed Bitcoin trading site [10], require the user to register and conform to regulations such as Know Your Customer (KYC) [11]. Such regulations are not required when transferring bitcoins, however, as soon as bitcoins are exchanged to a government-issued currency (e. g., US$ or €), a user can be identified. For Bitcoin and Ethereum Table 19.1 overviews the key technical and design features as well as current statistics as of September 2016.

Table 19.1 Bitcoin and Ethereum Key Technical and Design Features

Bitcoin [2]	Ethereum [12]
A maximum of 21 million bitcoins supply, halving newly generated supply every 4 years	Unlimited ethers supply
10 min block creation time	14 s block creating time
Crypto puzzle via partial SHA256 hash collision, requiring CPU time and minimal RAM; dedicated hardware, application-specific integrated circuit (ASIC) used [9]	Crypto puzzle is variation of Dagger-Hashimoto [13], which requires besides CPU time also RAM; GPU cards currently used
Limited scripting language, not Turing complete	General-purpose scripting language, Turing complete
Started in 2009, creator unknown (pseudonym used: Satoshi Nakamoto)	Started in 2015, initiator Vitalik Buterin
Balance based on unspent transaction outputs	Balance is account-based
Transaction costs driven by transaction size	Transaction costs driven by operations in the smart contract
Max throughput: 3–7 transactions per second	Max throughput: 23–25 transaction per second
Transactions created by users	Transactions created by users or smart contracts
Market capitalization: 9.9 billion USD [14]	Market capitalization: 1 billion USD [14]
Bitcoin created: 15.8 million BTC [14]	Ethers created: 83 million ETH [14]

19.3   Current Blockchain Developments and Limitations

In general and as of today, blockchains, especially for Bitcoin or Ethereum, *do not scale*. The ever increasing number of transactions makes the blockchain grow. Currently, Bitcoin transactions stored in the Bitcoin blockchain show a size of 75 GByte. The Ethereum blockchain, while still much younger than the Bitcoin blockchain, observes the same issue and has as of today a size of 24 GByte. While scalability is being discussed between many researchers and companies in the world and solutions are being proposed, the specific scalability solutions differ greatly for Bitcoin or Ethereum. The latter uses a general purpose blockchain, while the former is based on a specialized blockchain. This specialized blockchain offers mechanisms – typically specified to meet application demands and to make the approach scalable –, while the general purpose blockchain is much more difficult to scale for a general application.

Specifically, Bitcoin is introducing a mechanism termed "segregated witnesses" [15], which removes besides transaction malleability also signatures in the transaction resulting in smaller transactions. As of today and in the long term other solutions are discussed, such as snapshots or pruning of spent transactions. For Ethereum, "sharding" has been proposed, where an Ethereum node stores only parts of the blockchain, while other nodes host other parts. However, as of today sharding exists only in theory and shows other unresolved issues, such as rogue validators, communication across multiple shards, and reaching global consensus, while working on partial data only. The key future challenge is to design and build scalability mechanisms for general purpose blockchains, without trading their inherent advantages discussed above.

Currently the debate in the Bitcoin system either to increase the block size or to make the protocol more efficient with segregated witnesses will not solve scalability in the long term. Also with segregated witnesses, which is planned to be integrated soon, the Blockchain is only growing slower by a constant factor. Scaling to the volume to VISA credit card transaction numbers, which show around Christmas 57,000 transactions per second, is not feasible anytime soon, as the Bitcoin system currently allows for only 3–7 transaction per second. Ethereum has a similar low number of 25 transactions per second and adopting Ethereum- or Bitcoin-based products may suffer from increased transaction fees when the limit is reached. It is expected that Ethereum reaches a much higher transaction per second rate, once the switch from PoW to PoS has been performed.

Smart contracts execute based on their input and contract code. If the smart contract was not properly designed, e. g., allowing to withdraw funds from an unauthorized address, such a withdrawal may be unintentional, although the smart contract executed correctly. To reflect the intention of the smart contract creator, a language is used to specify the contract. Ethereum offers the language Solidity, a typed JavaScript dialect. However, Solidity it is not concise and easy to use as seen with the DAO disaster [4], although the DAO smart contract code was written by Ethereum experts. Yet, a security problem allowed to withdraw funds. Current best practices recommend to keep the contract as simple as possible, which may not be doable in all situations, since some contracts are complex by design. Ethereum runs smart contracts in the EVM. To produce respective code, a language needs to compile Solidity-based smart contracts written to EVM byte code. Future language research may reveal better alternatives, such as using a functional language for the EVM or adding functional elements to improve Solidity.

Lastly, while many factors affecting a blockchain's security, either permissionless or permissioned (cf. Sect. 19.4 below), such as block size, network size, or end-to-end delay, have been evaluated in the recent past, a comprehensive approach to a blockchain *security and performance evaluation* is still missing. Thus, the need for (a) a comprehensive threat model, (b) an impact model of the infrastructure (either the public network, separate clouds, or cross cloud-based alternatives), (c) a Service Level Agreement for a blockchain's performance, and (s) a suitable testing as well as management framework has emerged.

19.4 Classification, Related Work, and Key Characteristics

As of today major observations on smart contracts in general and blockchains specifically are summarized here to establish a basis for future application evaluations and to benefit investigations with respect to technology, economics, and regulation/law. Thus, blockchains can be classified using the following dimensions: (a) accessibility, (b) consensus mechanisms, and (c) its crypto currency.

The first dimension determines how the blockchain can be accessed (*accessibility*), whether it is publically available or if it requires permission to access it. The two main categories in the accessibility dimension cover: public blockchains (permissionless) and private or private group-based (consortium [3], permissioned) blockchains as shown in Table 19.2.

The second classification dimension is the *consensus mechanism*. A consensus mechanism is one of the key features in a distributed system in order that all nodes will reach eventually the same state. Distributed systems can use Byzantine Agreement Protocols such as Paxos [16] or Raft [17] as a consensus mechanism, however, Sybil attacks [18] can

Table 19.2 Accessibility

Public Blockchain (PUB)	Private or Private Group-based (Consortium) Blockchain (PRIV)
A public blockchain can be accessed and used by anyone following the respective protocol. E. g., in Bitcoin, there is one reference implementation and several independent libraries that can participate in the Bitcoin network written in Go, Java, JavaScript, C, C++, Python, or Objective-C	A private blockchain is controlled by (a) a single organization that manages the permission or (b) a consortium with known members. The access is controllable and permissioned. Any open source blockchain could be used as a private blockchain with small modifications, however, there exist specialized blockchains for running a private blockchain

render those consensus mechanisms useless. Thus, consensus mechanisms for blockchain need to by Sybil-proof. For public blockchains this is typically a PoW or PoS approach, for private or consortium blockchains it is PoS or a Trusted Entity (TE) acting as a gatekeeper and may be used in combination with the Byzantine Fault Tolerant protocol. Sidechains may leverage the consensus mechanism of its parent chain [19]. provides an overview on consensus protocols in blockchains. Table 19.3 summarizes the key three categories.

The third dimension distinguishes, whether the blockchain uses a **crypto currency** or not. This currency can be either mined or pre-created/burned (cf. Table 19.4). In the following existing blockchains are reviewed and categorized according to these dimensions. Many of those blockchains listed are a Proof-of-Concept (PoC) and it is yet to be seen how reliable they will work in the future. Since over 600 crypto currencies with a market capitalization exist [14], the focus here is laid on the most important, influential ones, while many specifically Bitcoin-based altcoins are omitted.

Bitcoin has the largest market capitalization and uses a PoW consensus mechanism. All blocks are created, as shown above, every 10 min and the reward is currently at 12.5 bitcoins, halving every 4 years. Bitcoin is a public blockchain with many clients and libraries available. Many variations of Bitcoin exist, the most popular with respect to market capitalization is *Litecoin*, which is based on the Bitcoin source code, but has a different PoW mechanism that makes it hard to use dedicated hardware for mining. Litecoin shows a block creation time of 2.5 min.

Ethereum also uses PoW, however, Ethereum plans to switch from PoW to PoS soon, especially to relax from the strong power and energy dependency of crypto puzzle usage. As such it is planned to lower costs of mining and increase the scalability. While some

Table 19.3 Consensus Mechanisms

Proof-of-Work (PoW)	Proof-of-Stake (PoS)	Trusted Entity (TE)
PoW is the consensus mechanism used in Bitcoin and Ethereum. A difficult crypto puzzle ensures that possible double spending attempts are expensive	PoS defines a consensus mechanism, where owners of a crypto currency have to prove ownership (proof for their stake). A user with 1% of the crypto currency can create 1% of the blocks	Trusting entities defines another form of consensus, where multiple trusted entities can vote (and/or apply a Byzantine Fault Tolerant protocol) or a single trusted entity can decide for or against adding a block to become part of the blockchain
The main drawback is the huge amount of energy used to solve these crypto puzzles	The main concern with PoS is "nothing at stake", with several mechanisms proposed to solve it [19]	Similar to PoS, TE is resource-friendly
PoW can run with dedicated hardware (ASIC) or with a memory and bandwidth-hard crypto puzzle (MEM-HARD)	A mix between PoS and PoW is termed Proof-of-Activity (PoA) PoS is considered resource-friendly Several schemes exist with voting delegates (DELEG) or prepaying crypto currency (PRE)	Many private blockchains use TE, however, there are also public blockchains, where trusted entities can vote or trusted entities can be chosen

Table 19.4 Crypto Currencies

Mining Crypto Currency (CRY-M)	Pre-creating Crypto Currency with Distribution (CRY-P)	No Use of Crypto Currency (NCRY)
The result of mining is a block with a reward in the form of crypto currency. Bitcoin and Ethereum reward with bitcoins and ethers, respectively. Some blockchains allow to define various other crypto currencies or assets besides its native crypto currency	Instead of mining crypto currency, the currency can be pre-created and distributed in an Initial Coin Offering (ICO). The incentive to mine a block is to collect transaction fees. Other variations include "Proof-of-Burn" (PoB) or "Proof-of-Possession" (PoP) using another crypto currency	Some blockchains do not need any kind of native crypto currency, but allow for overlay assets. Especially private blockchains do not use a native currency

elements may require PoW initially, it is planned to switch entirely to PoS. The status is a PoC that was released in March 2016 [20]. Ethereum can also be used as a private blockchain, as the source code is open and accessible.

BlockApps is such a provider for a private Ethereum blockchain. Eris Industries with their *eris:db*, which also uses Ethereum as a basis, is already using PoS, however, not in a public blockchain. Eris:db is a business-focused blockchain, where the Tendermint Consensus protocol is used for PoS. Although this protocol follows an interesting concept, if many validators sign each block, storage and network limitations may become an important issue for scalability. *Chain Core* is another company offering a blockchain for business. They provide a private blockchain with a controlled access. Further scalability improvements are planned for Ethereum with the Casper/Serenity release, such as sharding [20], which is the concept of horizontal partitioning of a database. In the case of Ethereum it is to split the space of possible accounts. Each shard gets its own validators with the idea that those validators only validate transactions within a shard and a special handling for inter-shard communication, where transactions from different accounts in different shards need to be consistently validated.

Monero is an anonymous crypto currency. It achieves this goal by using ring signatures with one real signature and several decoy signatures. Furthermore, a mixing of inputs is enforced in the network. Stealth addresses are used, making it difficult to trace the sender and recipient. Monero uses its own network, based on CryptoNote, and it uses a memory-hard PoW. Future plans consist of including the I2P protocol, an anonymization protocol to hide the real Internet Protocol (IP) address in use. Monero recently gained traction due to media coverage and the integration by darknet marketplaces, where privacy is a big concern.

Lisk is a public blockchain written from scratch. Lisk enables the development of "Dapps" (Distributed Applications), which are decentralized applications in an autonomous operation in terms of a peer-to-peer management. It uses a PoS mechanism using delegates and voting. However, a node can become a delegate only, if it owns many Lisk coins. Lisk uses smart contracts to determine procedures and constraints, which formulate rule-based, automatically operated processes.

Another blockchain written from Scratch is *IOTA*. The goal of IOTA is to become the backbone of IoT by supporting real-time transactions without fees. As it does not store the complete history, nodes going offline may take offline important history data. IOTA does not support mining; tokens will be distributed in an Initial Coin Offering (ICO) phase. Tokens are accessed using passwords rather than public/private key pairs.

Hyper Ledger an Open Source Linux Foundation project since January 2016, is a blockchain project creating a modular blockchain, specifically as an open standard for the basis blockchain technology of the Distributed Ledger Technology. The aim is to bring the blockchain technology a step forward to mainstream commercial adoption. They offer a modular architecture so that they can use any kind of consensus mechanism, such as PoW, PoS, or TE.

Nxt uses PoS as well and similar to IOTA is uses passwords to access crypto assets rather than public/private key pairs. Another business-oriented blockchain is *R3 Corda*. R3 Corda is a distributed ledger for recording and managing financial agreements. Unlike other blockchains, R3 Corda does not share transactions with other nodes. Only those parties involved in that transaction can access the data. Also validation is done by those parties involved and not by a random node. *Openchain* is a private blockchain for organizations that can be configured as a Bitcoin side chain. It supports smart contracts. It uses a trust-based consensus mechanism and uses a client/server architecture.

Stratis is built on top of the Bitcoin blockchain and allows to create private sidechains. Another business-oriented blockchain is *Multichain*, where private blockchains can be built. It is compatible to the Bitcoin API, however, allows many configuration options, such as block size, types of transactions, who can access it, and its assets. Any type of assets can be used and created on Multichain, allowing to trade shares, bonds, or commodities. In terms of scalability, *BigchainDB* claims to allow 1 million writes per second and petabytes of capacity. It is a private blockchain connecting to a RethinkDB cluster to achieve that speed. *Rootstock* (RSK) is a Bitcoin sidechain, which offers smart contracts with a Turing-complete language. RSK is compatible with the Ethereum VM and can run its smart contracts. Its currency Rootcoins can be exchanged to Bitcoins and vice versa. Similar to Rootstock is *Counterparty* that allows Ethereum smart contract to run on the Bitcoin platform. Counterparty uses a native currency, but allows to create any kind of assets. Another company working on sidechains is Blockstream, also providing an im-

Table 19.5 Classification

Approach	Accessibility	Consensus	Crypto Currency
Bitcoin	Public	PoW/ASIC	CRY-M/Bitcoins
Ethereum	Public	PoW/MEM-HARD	CRY-M/Ethers
Ethereum Casper/Serenity	Public	PoS/PoA	CRY-M/Ethers
Litecoin	Public	PoW/MEM-HARD	CRY-M/Litecoin
Monera	Public	PoW/MEM-HARD	CRY-M/XMR
Lisk	Public	PoS/Del	CRY-M/Lisk
R3 Corda	Private	TE	NRCY
Openchain	Private/sidechain	TE	NRCY/various
IOTA	Public	PoW	CRY-P/IOTA tokens
Eris:DB	Private	PoS	CRY-M/Ethers
Chain Core	Private	TE	NRCY/various
Hyper Ledger	Private	TE/PoW/PoS	NRCY
Nxt	Public	PoS	CRY-P/various
Stratis	Private/sidechain	PoW (PoS in future)	CRY-M/STRAT token
Multichain	Private	PoW	NRCY/various
BigchainDB	Private	TE	NRCY/various
Rootstock	Public/sidechain	PoW (Bitcoin)	CRY-M/Bitcoin-Root-coin
Counterparty	Public	PoW (embedded Bitcoin consensus)/PoB	CRY-P/various
Ripple	Public	TE	CRY-P/Ripple/various
Stellar	Public	TE/PoP	CRY-P/Lumen/various

plementation of the *Lightning* network, which allows micro transaction on the Bitcoin blockchain.

Ripple is different since it uses trust to find consensus and nodes not behaving well are blacklisted. Ripple can send any currency and can automatically exchange currencies, while each transaction is verified in seconds. *Stellar* is based on Ripple, but uses its own consensus mechanism. Table 19.5 classifies these blockchains.

19.5   New Applications

Blockchains allow for new distributed applications. The main interest in the financial sector is to digitalize processes with other stakeholders and to eventually save money. In this chapter new types of distributed applications besides those financial ones, such as remittance, crowdfunding, or money transfer, are discussed. An example of such an application is *CargoChain*, which is a Proof-of-Concept (PoC) created at a hackathon to show how to reduce paperwork, such as purchase orders, invoices, bills of lading, customs documentation, and certificates of authenticity.

Other popular non-financial areas with active blockchain projects are (a) fraud detection with *Everledger, Blockverify, Verisart, Ascribe, Provenance,* and *Chronicled,* (b) global rights databases with *Mediachain, Monegraph,* and *Ujo Music,* (c) identity management with *Blockstack, UniquID, ShoCard,* and *SolidX,* (d) ridesharing with *La-Zooz* and *Arcade City,* and (e) document verification with *Tierion* and *Factom.* Many other types and applications in smaller application areas for the blockchain exist, such as *Augur* aiming at the prediction of markets with crowd intelligence. *Swarm* is a distributed storage platform and content distribution service. Dispute resolution systems based on blockchains or *Enigma,* a decentralized cloud platform with guaranteed privacy. *ChromaWay* has a first pilot carried out with a private blockchain for land registry. The *Blockchain Voting Machine* is a digital voting solution using its own VoteUnit blockchain. Temperature monitoring is performed by *modum.io* to enable cost savings in the pharmaceutical cold chain by combining sensor devices with blockchain technology.

[6] argues that many public, governmental applications can be implemented in form of a permissioned ledger, in which the party of the transaction needs to proof access via a dedicated credential. Transaction parties may be authorized governmental or public offices, for which each beneficiary may access his rights from a centralized authority, controlling the distributed ledger system's access. Obviously, only to trusted parties and beneficiaries such credentials will be granted. Upon such an approach, participants may – driven by the system-inherent proof of a transaction – interact reliably and trustworthy without any third party.

Finally, any application, which requires a trusted third party as a mediator between at least two stakeholders being involved in the process to conclude a contractual relationship, potentially can benefit from a blockchain. Besides the roles of banks and their mediation role for financial transactions, notaries as mediators for, e. g., property sellers and buyers – including respective enforcement options on the basis of related smart contracts – and escrow agents with a fulfillment mandate serve as an excellent application domain, largely unexploited as of today.

19.6 Legal and Economic Challenges

Blockchains are termed the "Blockchain revolution" [21] and adoption in domains requiring a very clear, stable, and secured state for all transactions is increasing as outlined above. Although the example of Bitcoins shows that crypto currencies on the basis of blockchains have reached a much wider adoption than any other electronic and fully digital payment system of the past, Bitcoin payments have been made possible by complementing other payment channels, such as restaurant payments [22], governmental transaction fee payments [23], and person-to-person payments [24]. Bitcoin has been regulated by national banking authorities, such as the Swiss Financial Market Supervisory Authority

(FINMA) [25], and different exchanges for bitcoins are possible into any regularly tradable fiat currency. Thus, a legally acceptable, however not uniform situation has been reached besides from a technical perspective of trading bitcoins and paying with bitcoins.

Therefore, it could be concluded that blockchains – the key underlying distributed technology – have been blooded, since they have been applied in the financial market sector. However, that needs to be considered as a short-handed argument, since other examples of a blockchain use in the financial markets have shown errors as in The DAO [4], malfunction as with Mt Gox [26], or get-quick-rich schemes [27]. Thus, in general it is too early to determine principle legal problems with blockchains, however, as [28] states, "how self-regulation has failed" and "how Bitcoin has not matched the expectations of some proponents. Various crashes and wave after wave of scandals and allegations of fraud have decidedly dented the perception that Bitcoin is the currency of the future." Nevertheless, legal frameworks and governmental regulation (for a very recent per-country regulation on Bitcoin see [29]) may need to adapt to take blockchain developments into account, while assuring at the same time data privacy, security, and other key facets of data handling, maintenance, and storage, many of which are determined and regulated already for other ICT-related applications and technologies. Thus, the perception of blockchains in society, with governments, and their possibly new reach in respective law and jurisdictions cannot be foreseen, however, the technical potential to offer trusted communications and persisted storage without any central element of control or operations offers opportunities, where especially human-based counseling of contact negotiations may not be required anymore.

Besides these views, it has to be stated that the economic perspective of blockchains is often broken down to an optimized performance and operation view, especially in comparison to today's technology in operation. Still, this has to be proven in a larger scale, since those approaches, which need to solve crypto puzzles do need a significant amount of electrical energy to perform the computations, determining a very clear factor for operational costs (OPEX). Thus, the PoW approach shows drawbacks compared to the PoS approach and others. It is estimated that mining actions require approximately 370 MW of energy for 2015 [30], the capacity of a smaller nuclear power plant.

As this determines a large amount of energy, optimizations in that dimension are essential. However, a future prediction of the energy consumption of Bitcoin miners in 2020 is difficult as relevant factors for a viable prediction will include at least: (a) the value of 1 Bitcoin in 2020, (b) the development of new hardware to solve crypto puzzles, (c) the reaction of miners to the halving of mining rewards, (d) the costs of energy applicable to which parts of the world, (e) the role will the Bitcoin blockchain may have in 2020, (f) the possibility to reach a practically infeasible blockchain length by or before 2020, (g) the effects of "side-chains" being developed these days, and (h) if Bitcoin is still using PoW and not, e. g., PoS.

19.7 Summary and Conclusions

A blockchain is a distributed database maintaining securely a continuously growing list of transactional data, which are hardened against tampering and forgery. The discussion of main characteristics as well technical features of blockchains or distributed ledgers above reveals that such technology is in the wings to simplify administrative and transactional procedures and many applications in the future. While the simplification mainly relates to the decentralization and distribution of the data (at the same time assuring a lossless storage), the security and access control of those data is maintained efficiently, though, performance-wise not fully optimized yet. A unique proof of a transaction – including payments, access right grants, contracts operations, or data entry updates for commercial parties, citizens, companies, and governmental organizations – can be reached today. However, the cost-benefit ratio of blockchains cannot easily be quantified. Although, costs for, e. g., hardware, virtual machines, the network, and setups, are known, the benefits of less centralized infrastructure including soft factors, such as less trust and more transparency, are difficult to assess.

Specifically in the context of formal procedures, say for (a) commercial orders between a customer and a supplier or for (b) administrative acts between a citizen and a governmental organization, all participating parties will have the chance to check the status of such a procedure, since all parties do have access to all related data in a distributed manner, independent of their current location. Cross-organizational procedures, such as approvals, clearances, and permits, can relate to the same blockchain maintained for them to ensure an optimized handling. Note that only key information may become part of the blockchain itself, such that related electronic documents can be related via dedicated cryptographic hash values in time to the respective party. Signed time stamps can potentially speed up processes, maximizing the customer-supplier or citizen-governmental organization relationships. A public and legal acceptance of such procedures needs to be seen.

Blockchains are considered the "blueprint for a new economy" [31], which suggests that new technology can improve efficiently the existing status-quo of many application fields for distributed and reliable storage of secured transactions between customers and suppliers as well as citizens and governments. As discussed above, besides these new application domains digital market transactions, the financial industry, and governmental or private smart contracts in a decentralized form can be embedded into today's IT landscape. And due to the multitude of applications discussed many start-ups follow the blockchain path today, since an emerging potential and economic benefit is commonly considered to be in place. The survival rate of those start-ups and the success rate of the blockchain technology in the private and public application domain will tell, if all or only parts of those technically available characteristics and advantages can be practically exploited.

Acknowledgements
This work was partially funded by the FLAMINGO Network-of-Excellence (NoE) within the EU FP7 Program under Contract No. FP7-2012-ICT-318488.

References

1. N. Szabo, "Smart Contracts," 1994. [Online]. Available: http://szabo.best.vwh.net/smart. contracts.html. [Accessed 6 August 2016].
2. S. Nakamoto, "Bitcoin: A Peer-to-Peer Electronic Cash System," 2008.
3. V. Buterin, "On Public and Private Blockchains," Ethereum.org, 7 August 2015. [Online]. Available: https://blog.ethereum.org/2015/08/07/on-public-and-private-blockchains/. [Accessed 6 August 2016].
4. "The DAO," [Online]. Available: https://daohub.org/. [Accessed 6 August 2016].
5. "Ethereum Average BlockTime Chart," Etherscan – The Ethereum Block Explorer, [Online]. Available: https://etherscan.io/charts/blocktime. [Accessed 6 August 2016].
6. "Distributed Ledger Technology: Beyond Block Chain," UK Government Chief Scientific Advisor, 19 January 2016. [Online]. Available: https://www.gov.uk/government/publications/ distributed-ledger-technology-blackett-review. [Accessed 29 August 2016].
7. "Confirmation," bitcoin wiki, 14 June 2016. [Online]. Available: https://en.bitcoin.it/wiki/ Confirmation. [Accessed 29 August 2016].
8. V. Buterin, "On Slow and Fast Block Times," 14 September 2015. [Online]. Available: https:// blog.ethereum.org/2015/09/14/on-slow-and-fast-block-times/. [Accessed 29 Augest 2016].
9. J. Tuwiner, "Bitcoin Mining Centralization," bitcoinmining.com, [Online]. Available: https:// www.bitcoinmining.com/bitcoin-mining-centralization/. [Accessed 8 August 2016].
10. "Bitstamp to Become the First Nationally Licensed Bitcoin Exchange and Launches BTC/EUR Trading," Bitstamp, [Online]. Available: https://www.bitstamp.net/article/bitstamp-first-nationally-licensed-btc-exchange/. [Accessed 8 Augusst 2016].
11. "Europen Union: Directive 2005/60/EC of the European Parliament and of the Council on the Prevention of the Use of the Financial System for the Purpose of Money Laundering and Terrorist Financing," 25 October 2005. [Online]. Available: http://eur-lex.europa.eu/legal-content/ EN/TXT/?uri=CELEX%3A32005L0060.
12. G. Wood, "Ethereum: A Secure Decentralized Generalized Transaction Ledger," 2015. [Online]. Available: http://gavwood.com/paper.pdf. [Accessed 29 August 2016].
13. "ethereum/wiki," September 2015. [Online]. Available: https://github.com/ethereum/wiki/blob/ master/Dagger-Hashimoto.md. [Accessed 29 August 2016].
14. "Crypto-Currency Market Capitalizations," [Online]. Available: https://coinmarketcap.com/all/ views/all/. [Accessed 29 Augest 2016].
15. "Segregated Witness Benefits," Bitcoin Core, 26 January 2016. [Online]. Available: https:// bitcoincore.org/en/2016/01/26/segwit-benefits/. [Accessed 29 August 2016].
16. L. Lamport, "Generalized Consensus and Paxos," Microsoft, March 2005. [Online]. Available: https://www.microsoft.com/en-us/research/publication/generalized-consensus-and-paxos/. [Accessed 29 August 2016].
17. D. Ongaro and J. Ousterhout, "In Search of an Understandable Consensus Algorithm," in *2014 USENIX Annual Technical Conference (USENIX ATC 14)*, Philadelphia, PA, USA, 2014.
18. J. Douceur, "The Sybil Attack," in *Revised Papers from the First International Workshop on Peer-to-Peer Systems (IPTPS 2001)*, London, UK, 2002.
19. M. Swan, "Blockchain Consensus Protocols," Bitcoin Meetup, 6 May 2015. [Online]. Available: http://www.slideshare.net/lablogga/blockchain-consensus-protocols. [Accessed 29 August 2016].
20. V. Buterin, "Serenity PoC2," 5 March 2016. [Online]. Available: https://blog.ethereum.org/2016/ 03/05/serenity-poc2/. [Accessed 29 August 2016].
21. D. Tapscott and A. Tapscott, How the Technology Behind Bitcoin is Changing Money, Business, and the World, New York, USA: Penguin Random House LLC, 2016.

22. "What Can You Buy with Bitcoin?," CoinDesk, 19 October 2015. [Online]. Available: http://www.coindesk.com/information/what-can-you-buy-with-bitcoins/. [Accessed 29 August 2016].

23. E. Aschwanden, "Stadt Zug wird weltweit zum Bitcoin-Pionier," 10 May 2016. [Online]. Available: http://www.nzz.ch/schweiz/crypto-valley-zukunftsmodell-oder-marketing-gag-ld.22911. [Accessed 29 August 2016].

24. "Coinblesk," [Online]. Available: https://bitcoin.csg.uzh.ch/. [Accessed 29 August 2016].

25. "Swiss Financial Market Supervisory Authority FINMA," [Online]. Available: https://www.finma.ch/. [Accessed 29 August 2016].

26. Y. B. Perez, "Mt Gox CEO Mark Karpeles Charged With Embezzlement," CoinDesk, 11 September 2015. [Online]. Available: http://www.coindesk.com/mt-gox-ceo-mark-karpeles-embezzlement/. [Accessed 29 August 2016].

27. "Bitcoin Nachahmer: Riskante virtuelle Währungen," 8 August 2016. [Online]. Available: https://www.test.de/Bitcoin-Nachahmer-Riskante-virtuelle-Waehrungen-5057128-5057138/. [Accessed 29 August 2016].

28. A. Guadamuz and C. Marsden, "Blockchains and Bitcoin: Regulatory Responses to Cryptocurrencies," *First Monday,* vol. 20, no. 12, 7 December 2015.

29. "Legality of bitcoin by country," [Online]. Available: https://en.wikipedia.org/wiki/Legality_of_bitcoin_by_country. [Accessed 29 August 2016].

30. V. Tombez, "Le bitcoin a consommé en 2015 autant d'énergie que 620'000 ménages," RTS Info, 26 April 2016. [Online]. Available: http://www.rts.ch/info/sciences-tech/7674767-le-bitcoin-a-consomme-en-2015-autant-d-energie-que-620-000-menages.html. [Accessed 29 August 2016].

31. M. Swan, Blueprint for a New Economy, Sebastopol, California, USA: O'Reilly Media, 2015.

The Last Step Remains Analogue...

20

Joachim Kistner

Abstract

Despite the continuous increase of digital exposure, the human senses remain analogous recipients. Therefore, creators and operators of visionary marketplaces need to put high emphasis on a multi-sensory customer approach at the Point of Sale (POS). Although the sense of hearing plays, next to the eye, an essential role in the processing of information, the impact of sound is often underestimated in this context. Sound can work as element of communication to emotionally charge brands, products and services while improving the atmosphere of retail locations.

20.1 What Is the Status Quo of Multimedia in Open Spaces?

The availability of networks with great data volumes and the increasing usage of smart devices for information and communication offer new possibilities to approach customers. They can be reached through personalized hardware (mobile phone, tablet) or public devices (digital-signage displays).

Hence, it is possible to selectively target people or certain groups in public spaces. Until now this form of communication is mainly done through purely visual content. Personalized messages can't be distributed acoustically in public spaces without harming ones privacy. Therefor, the possibility to approach people acoustically within the boundaries of their privacy zone is not yet given.

J. Kistner (✉)
Sonus GmbH
Baden-Baden, Germany
e-mail: kistner@sonus.de

© Springer-Verlag GmbH Germany 2018
C. Linnhoff-Popien et al. (eds.), *Digital Marketplaces Unleashed*,
https://doi.org/10.1007/978-3-662-49275-8_20

The deliberate application of sound and acoustic communication is a promising addition in the dialogue of brands. Nevertheless, it has mostly been neglected due to the missing expertise regarding acoustics in public spaces.

In certain cases efforts have been made to change this situation. Brand rooms of automotive companies (Audi) and fashion stores (Abercrombie and Fitch) already apply sound in a consequent and active manner at the Point of Sale, in order to emotionally charge their brands [1] and to improve the atmosphere of the store. Steering and usage of these applications is currently limited to local systems.

The increasing availability of networks with great data volumes allows for new applications like "ambient-sensitive" installations. The Internet of Things constitutes the prerequisite to collect data through sensors, which measure location specific parameters like climate, temperature and sounds of the environment. These sensors are able to collect information as BIGDATA through the Internet and analyze them. If needed the generated data can be used for dynamic real time steering of atmospheric conditions in the room, including acoustic elements for advisory, communication and retail spaces.

The implementation of these sensors demands, besides networks and data processing know how, also a specific expertise regarding the acoustic layout of rooms and the principles of the impact of sounds on humans.

20.2   How Do We Hear?

The ear is never asleep and is always ready to analyze offered contents and translate them into immediate reactions. All acoustic events are on the one hand perceived through hearing and but also the body. In this context our ear works as sensor. Mainly the dynamics of air pressure in the low and high frequency areas are perceived. Evolutionary determined, the ear has the greatest sensitivity for frequencies of human speech, as this is the most dominant communication channel. But also the human body is able to feel acoustic events with very low frequencies but high intensities as waves and vibrancies. Consequently we can hear through sensoric and tactile perceptions.

20.3   How Do We Process Acoustic Events?

At first, collected information is neutrally forwarded to two different brain areas. The process of differentiating happens through the absolute volume of the sound varying between the perception threshold and the pain threshold, and the dynamic of the sound (the difference in volume between the experienced sound relative the loudness of the environment).

The brain stem, responsible for essential life functions and instincts, evaluates acoustic impressions immediately according to the sound dynamics (difference in sound volume). This (archaic) component is responsible for the direct, not reflected, unanalyzed reaction and leads to the release of hormones like noradrenalin and endorphin. The process happens instantly and can't be humanly influenced. In a way, our body is powerless regarding the reaction on acoustic events. We can't quit the hormonal reaction or deliberately influence it. Our brain gets information about acoustic events through the limbic system. It recognizes, analyses and processes the structure, as well as the content of the acoustic signal.

Recognition effects, associations and impressions emerge, which lead to differing emotional states. This process only takes a couple of milliseconds and after the successful analyses and resulting findings a "controlled" reaction of our organism happens.

The consequences of these two differing processes can be displayed through the following examples of the drippy water-tap at night and the burst of a balloon:

Regarding their perception, both acoustic events have something in common: an immediate, impulsive and intensive change in the loudness of the environment. This leads, despite the completely different volume of the sound, to an uncontrollable startling condition due to the spontaneous initiated release of hormones as archaic relict of our brain. In this case a warning parameter for the immediate escape (escape, protection) …

The reaction to steady and uniform acoustic events with only slight changes does occur in a completely different manner. The human hearing sense reacts in this case with slow, diminishing sensitivity. This process resembles a protection function of our body through a gradually familiarization to avoid damages of our hearing sense.

Sound events with language contents are again processed differently. Even in cases of foreign or unclear language fragments the brain tries to convert and establish a sense full context, without a deliberate order. Compared to "looking away", "not listening" is almost impossible. Trying to ignore sounds demands high concentration efforts. Therefor, irrelevant information in the surrounding of communication spaces (office, retail, advisory) is experienced as highly annoying and disturbing.

Nevertheless, unpleasant sound and speaking can be covered by nice, monotonous acoustic events. Through these "Markers" not only discretion, but also an improvement of the atmosphere of the room can be achieved.

From these findings, the basic rules for acoustic design of rooms with good conditions for communication – and selling-processes – can be derived.

20.4   Room Acoustics

Insufficient acoustic conditions in advisory – and sales situations in the surrounding of valuable products and services are experienced as huge annoyance, from the personnel and customers. Research of Dr. Meis, Hörzentrum Oldenburg and Dr. Schlittmeier [2, 3] from the year 2010, shows a correlation of the experienced disturbance intensity through different sources and inappropriate acoustics conditions of the room.

A pleasant acoustic surrounding does not imply, that the optimal value for background noises should be zero. This accounts analogous for the conditions of light, temperature and humidity. For communication, retails and advisory spaces the following qualitative room conditions should be pursued:

- Assurances of adjusted room acoustics to room size, geometry, division and furnishing with acoustic appropriate materials of the room limiting space
- Assurance of sufficient discretion between the specific relevant areas
- Avoidance of the "waiting room" effect

20.5   Acoustic Irradiation

The application of background acoustics is an established practice for the further improvement of the atmosphere of the room. Usually, target group specific music is played in the entire space. Although this might be an effective practice for a young target group in case of a minimum quality level, for the segment of high value services, products and advisory situations it is controversially discussed and can be counterproductive.

The ability of association, often leads to an immediate connection of the played music program to a certain experience in life, which can result in an entirely different emotional evaluations of the customers. While one might start to dance to the played music and is enthusiastic to buy a product, another associates the same music with a very sad event and leaves the store. Neither represents a good foundation for a concentrated and intensive advisory conversation with the employees of the store.

Therefore, the usage of recognizable music titles and artists needs to be seen with great cautions. An alternative measure, to positively influence the acoustical quality of rooms has already been established in the 1950's: "functional music". Adjusted to the hour of the day, suitable rhythms are used, which in spectral inconspicuous, unrecognizable compositions establish a homogenous sound landscape. This is a measure, which is still applied in many department stores and office buildings.

Still, many suppliers and users unfortunately work with the easiest technologies and low quality contents, which lead to a generally negative evaluation of acoustic measures and actions by employees and customers [4]. "Departmentstore radio" and "elevator music" are the generally known synonyms, which describe a bad atmospheric quality.

Today, due to the available products for room- and electroacoustic and the knowledge about the applicability and relevance, acoustic applications of high quality are possible. They increasingly become an important element in the creation of high quality rooms for information and retail.

20.6   What Do We Want to Hear, What Are We Supposed to Hear?

Besides the usage of state of the art technologies, new approaches regarding the sound content have been established in order to create acoustically active rooms.

For leading companies "Sound Design" is an essential tool of brand communication. Sound is increasingly becoming an element of multi sensoric brand communication. The creation of content has become a crucial component in the process improving the atmospheric quality of brand rooms not only through the profane play of music, but also to integrate further functions in the played contents, which lead to an improvement of the room atmosphere, acoustic discretion and help to convey brand values [1, 5]. Influencing and guiding the customer journey is one of the added values, which a high quality sound installation can provide.

Since many years, audio designer and composer create sounds together for different applications and investigate the reactions of these measures on their customers. The composed contents can be played through loudspeaker technologies, which can be integrated in the room almost invisibly.

Today, highly efficient loudspeaker technologies can be integrated into walls and ceiling to work optically and acoustically inconspicuously. Sounds can be distributed broad and evenly or highly focused. Therefor, even in very small rooms, different acoustic information can be played at the same time without disturbing each other.

The Internet of Things allows for new possibilities for the distribution and control of acoustic contents for sales- and advisory rooms. The connection of IT and Content-Distribution enables the application of "ambience sensitive" room creation through the coupling of local sensors and BIGDATA information for the dynamic adjustment of contents in real time.

The following case studies describe, from an acoustical point of view, three different solution approaches. For different rooms sizes and customer needs, holistic solutions have been realized and reached the following results:

- Improvement of the atmosphere of the room through customized room acoustics and usage of active background sounds
- Creation of situation specific incentives through passive media consumption or interactive influencing of available digital contents
- Active support of marketing initiatives through the dynamic adjustment of room conditions

Case 1 (Medium Sized Room with Interactive Sound Irradiation)
Location: The customer information center of an internationally operating specialty chemicals producer in Frankfurt-Hoechst (Fig. 20.1). In 2013, the first application of an interactive installation of this kind was realized. The usage scenario of 30m2 demanded the implementation of the following functions: Up to 4 single person or a small groups should be able to interactively use and consume digital contents, which are available through a touch wall, while images, graphs and videos are played simultaneously with corresponding sound. Further they should not disturb each other.

The necessary sound installation was invisibly integrated in the room context, which is also responsible for the room's acoustic conditioning. Through the combination of an appropriate room condition, integration of suitable acoustic products and an actively steered controlling technique, the desired scenario has been realized: the simultaneous interactive usage of digital contents in a small room without reciprocal disturbance.

Fig. 20.1 Frankfurt Hoechst, Consumer Information Center

Case 2: Personal Media Solution

Due to the availability of mobile communication devices and digital services, the supply of personalized, individual media contents in public spaces is possible at any time. Nevertheless, the "acoustically added value" of digital information demands the usage of earplugs, to consume personal contents discreetly without the disturbance of others. This application unfortunately leads to an acoustic isolation of the consumer. The response or perception of other acoustic signals is almost impossible. The demand for personalized information and discrete communication without personal isolation can be satisfied through the following solution:

A piece of furniture, which has the ability to play visual and acoustic contents discretely and focused. Via permanently installed or BYOD devices (tablet or smartphone) the visual content is offered and an integrated "acoustic shower" is responsible for the

Fig. 20.2 Application of sound showers in a museum – www.soundbuoy.com

acoustic component (Fig. 20.2). The connection of the consumer to the environment remains. Brand messages or information can be communicated individually and focused without disturbing the surrounding environment.

20.7   A Future Scenario

The retail space of a telecommunication products producer is located in premium positions of city centers. Next to services, also products are sold. The store is equipped with multi functional elements on walls and on the ceiling. These elements are invisible for the eye and stocked with several technologies: sensors, which record room data like lightness, temperature, noise of the environment and number of person in the store, and send this data to a data analytics service provider through an intelligent router.

Acoustics and sound technology, but also ambient light, are equally integrated into the room elements and get their steering orders through the same router. Next to the local sensoric data, central or local influences like weather, temperature and time are also taken in consideration as further parameters and used to steer the ambient situation of the retail space dynamically and almost in real time.

The customer enters the room and is greeted with a specific "sound logo" of the company. This sound logo is only hearable in the entrance space and does not represent a disturbance for other people in the room. The room is divided in one or more function spaces, which are supported by a steady play of the brands sound landscape (brand sound). These brand sounds are differentiated for the different zones of the room though content and volume.

Sound landscapes are developed and composed by sound designers for the communication of brand values and aim to induce associations by the employees and customers, which correspond to the targets of the brand communication as well as the acoustic brand recognition. In connection with comfortable sound, adjusted room acoustics allow for a high quality atmosphere and can increase the length of stay of the customer.

Additionally integrated language covering contents lead to an improvement of the discretion in the advisory – and sales situation between employee and client and further allows for more intensive conversations. Product displays inform and entertain clients with targeted contents regarding the product features through focused sound techniques (sound shower/audio focus) in the immediate surrounding of the product, without acoustically disturbing other areas.

Through local steering systems this scenario can be adjusted automatically, according to the current surrounding environment. Simultaneously, the corporate headquarter also has the ability to control the contents in the store or in specific parts of it. Changes of the local or central environmental situation are used for a change in the room entertainment.

Example: A change in the weather condition around the store. It begins to rain.

The ambience system technique in the store will adjust several of the functions in the room to this change of the outdoor environment. From content with "sunshine offers and events" a change to "rain weather appropriate" sound landscapes happens. The ambient music changes from the "Sunshine" Playlist to "Rainy Days". Through this dynamic change, employees and customer experience a harmonic adjustment of the atmosphere of the store to the outside environment. The quality of the room enables a fast concentration on the products, immediately when entering the store. While exiting the store, the impression of the room remains in the customer head for a longer time and the length of remembering the company and its products increases. Long-term relationship building of the company with its customer is facilitated.

The possibility of automated application diversity has emerged, which reaches the room through digital networks but the consumers' senses in an analogues way.

20.8   Conclusion

The last step remains analogue. Despite the acceleration of digital networks in many areas of our daily lives, the human senses still remain analogues recipients and constitute an essential component in companies' customer approach. The thorough creation of room acoustics and the usage of appropriate stimuli display a further channel for the communication with customers. The achieved improvement and the ambience of the room allow for a sustainable, improved sales results and supports a positive attitude towards the brand.

References

1. K. Bronner and R. Hirt, Audio-Branding. Entwicklung, Anwendung, Wirkung akustischer Identitäten in Werbung, Medien und Gesellschaft, Reinhard Fischer, 2007.
2. M. Klatte, T. Lachmann, S. Schlittmeister and H. J., "The irrelevant sound effect in short-term memory: Is there developmental change?," in *European Journal of Cognitive Psychology, 22(8), doi:10.1080/09541440903378250*, 2010, pp. 1168–1191.
3. S. J. Schlittmeier and H. J., Background music as noise, 2009.
4. D. Davis and C. Davis, If bad sound were fatal, audio would be a leading cause of death, Author-House, 2004.
5. H. G. Häusel, Emotional Boosting – Die hohe Kunst des Kaufverführung, Haufe-Lexwa-re, 2009.

Marketplace-Driven, Game-Changing IT Games to Address Complex, Costly Community Problems

21

J. Antão B. Moura, Marcelo A. de Barros, and Ruan P. Oliveira

Abstract

This chapter illustrates how digital marketplaces may be allied to gamified IT applications/systems to support solutions for complex, costly community challenges in a sustainable manner. A generic modular architectural design for these marketplace-based games is proposed and instantiated to public health and water management problem scenarios so that the resulting games support expected solutions. Preliminary validation studies of the games' usefulness as a solution-support and business-promotion tool have been carried out for the cases of a game to combat disease-carrying mosquitoes and of a water conservation game. These games have then been applied to real-case scenarios pilot tests. The chapter reports on validation results and the contribution the embedded marketplaces may bring to these games and their sustainability.

21.1 Introduction

Government attempts to solve complex, costly community problems usually have a greater chance of success with the engagement of the population. For instance, one cannot reasonably expect to reduce water pollution without a properly educated and vigilant population about rubbish disposal. Engaging the population to contribute to the solution to such prob-

J. A. B. Moura (✉) · M. A. de Barros · R. P. Oliveira
Federal University of Campina Grande
Campina Grande, Brazil
e-mail: antao@dsc.ufcg.edu.br

M. A. de Barros
e-mail: mbarros@dsc.ufcg.edu.br

R. P. Oliveira
e-mail: ruanp@copin.ufcg.edu.br

© Springer-Verlag GmbH Germany 2018
C. Linnhoff-Popien et al. (eds.), *Digital Marketplaces Unleashed*,
https://doi.org/10.1007/978-3-662-49275-8_21

lems is often difficult because one may not envisage incentives (to overcome the inertia) to change behavior. As a result, governments end up investing resources without achieving desired changes in problematic scenarios. For instance, despite mounting billionaire government spendings to fight Aedes aegypti – the mosquito that transmits zika, chikungunya, dengue and yellow fever – it has proven difficult to control worldwide. In fact, it has spread to many countries, putting millions of persons at risk of being infected, including pregnant women whose babies may have micro encephalitis and other defects [1]. As another illustration, despite worldwide efforts to clean the environment, half of the world's hospital beds are filled with people suffering from a water-related disease [2]. Turning affliction into opportunity for (economic) gain by businesses and by the population may provide important incentives to change the game in these cases.

Digital games (or even *gamified* software applications or information systems – IS) embed incentives to attract and maintain the interest of players [3]; games are also popular education vehicles [4]. *Gamification* is thus an important strategy for training and solving problems, but so far, it has *mainly* been applied to situations where players are not very numerous – as in a company or in experiments to elicit user experiences with web resources offered by a company [5] –, for the size of the public presents challenges of its own. Economically incentivized games for large crowds to help solve complex and costly problems are rare. Digital marketplaces may offer the means for such incentivizing. The bibliography however, is modest in what concerns the integration of digital marketplaces into games to support and enhance (economic) incentives to help solve costly, chronic problems that afflict an entire population.

This chapter discusses the use of *marketplace*-driven games to engage large crowds in solving, in a *game-changing* way, complex, costly community problems. Here, one such game is called *match* for short. A *match* is a gamified app or information system (IS) or a game proper that is part of the solution for or serves as decision support in a given community problem. It offers both intrinsic and extrinsic incentives [5] to attract and maintain players from the crowd – i.e., a *match* is a crowdsourced game. Other gamified IS that seek to resolve community complaints – e.g., SeeClickFix [6] and TrashOut [7] that allow users to report and notify authorities about annoying problems such as a cracked sidewalk or a burnt street lamp and to denounce illegal dumps, respectively – do exist but seem to lack the economic incentives typical of a marketplace which are integrated into a *match*.

The integration of a marketplace allows for short term economic rewards thus favoring sustainability, cost-effective deployment and running of a *match* by its "owner" (e. g., government), and for lucrative usage by its players and sponsors. (Humanity tends to solve problems when there is economic compensation for doing so.)

After briefly reviewing related work, this chapter proposes an architectural design for *matches* in general and presents results of preliminary validation studies of their usefulness as a solution-support and business-promotion tool for the cases of an Aedes aegypti-fighting and a water conservation gamified mobile app and IS in real-case scenarios.

21.2   Related Work

A crowdsourcing system "enlists a crowd of humans to help solve a problem defined by the system owners" [6]. A *match* is a gamified crowdsourcing IT system that attracts human resources to act as amateur agents in the solution of a community problem – e. g., prevention of child obesity, mosquito-borne diseases or water waste (the last two being case studies here). As such, the present chapter adds a new class of crowdsourcing system research from a human resources management perspective to the classification in the comprehensive review [7]: that of marketplace-incentivized human resources working in alternate reality (virtual/internet and physical/real world) for the good of a population at large (as opposed to a specific organization). Also, considering the references in [7] that report on combinations of CS and marketplace, *matches* appear to innovate with the proposition that the combination serve the common good (as opposed to pure corporate financial profits). Further, m*atches* in the case studies, namely *AedesBusters* (*AB*) and *AquaGuardians* (*AG*), can easily accommodate changes through their modular structure and may thus, be used to experiment with two critical aspects of (digital) marketplace integration into crowdsourced gamified apps/IS/games: incentive design and trust modeling.

Incentive design is one of the most studied topics in economics in recent years [8]. Of particular interest is determining uncontaminated cause-effect relationships between an employee's impact on firm objectives and his/her attributed individual rewards in a corporate setting. Studies on eliciting such relationships in a large population (crowdsourcing) setting, such as that of a *match*, are less frequent. Some recent, notable exceptions are the work: in [3] that considers internet gaming with the main purpose of studying addiction rather than economics; in [9] that models and simulates incentive policies to maintain member presence in a community network; [5] that focus on idea sharing for crowdsourced innovation rather than on public problem solving through gamified apps/games; and in [10] for human and hybrid human-machine computing. Both *AB* and *AG* offer the possibility to experiment with intrinsic, extrinsic, tangible, intangible incentive trade-off and timing to (dynamically) set attributes of a digital marketplace in a gaming strategy of a solution for a given public problem. Experiments may be used to complement arguments and models in [11] where distinct behavioral scenarios are considered.

Trust modeling is used in a *match* to reduce fraud (claiming rewards for bogus accomplishments). Some of the already mentioned work treats trust in passing (e. g [11]); others do it more extensively from a crowdsourcing perspective [12–14]: trust in an actor is modelled as a top level weighed sum [13] or a probabilistic function [14] of confidence and reputation variables. Little is said on lower level details that lead to values for these weights or variables or probability distributions which are determined by simulation. Again, *AB* and *AG* may serve to validate simulators and to experiment with trust assessment in crowds engaged in solutions for mosquito-borne diseases and to water conservation problems respectively. (Proposed IT solutions for these problems, as in [15] and; [16], are mostly informative or educational Web sites with no business drive. The gaming features aligned to marketplace facilities in *AB* and *AG* make them more proactive.)

21.3 Match System Proposal

Particulars of a *match* depend on problem specifics and on the objectives of its solution – e. g., sustainability, preventive actions. These details are to be elicited as requirements from the *match owners* – sanitary or health authorities for the case of *AedesBusters* (*AB*), for instance. *Matches* however, present common characteristics that may be represented in a generic architecture – e. g., most population-wide problems are facilitated by georeferenced notifications of incidents (e. g., a water leakage). We first present a generic *match* architecture and then, instantiate it to *AB* and *AquaGuardians* (*AG*) cases.

21.3.1 Methodology

The proposed generic *match* architecture was extracted from generalizations of the *AB*, *AG* specifications/implementations which were produced using an agile methodology [17] with project clients being potential players and professional agents associated with environment/epidemiology agencies (VA/VE) and the National Agency for Water (ANA) in Brazil, respectively. These agents defined success indicators for *match* results and participated in every step of the methodology to validate and steer the development of both *AB* and *AG*.

The methodology covers eight main steps: 1) Field research to understand the problem owners' business processes (BPs); 2) Semi-structured interviews with owners' agents to identify bottlenecks in BPs; 3) Interviews with users of incident notification channels that feed BPs; 4) Success indicators identification; 5) Architecture definition and validation by owners and players; 6) Prototype implementation to define roadmap of features and functionalities; 7) Test and validation of modules in *match* first deployable version (V1); and, 8) Generalization of requirements and characteristics for the generic *match* architecture.

Steps 5 to 7 are of an iterative nature, where critical decisions are made by owners, sponsors and players. Rigorously, step 7 output would feed back into step 1 input, for new cycles of adjustments in the *match* itself, in owners' BPs and additional validation studies – which may even impact the result of step 8. The R&D efforts reported in the present chapter are recent, having gone through the first cycle of the methodology for initial versions of *AB* and *AG* only.

21.3.2 Generic Match Architecture

A *match* is a set of IT tools to intermediate interactions between a crowd and owners' agents towards implementing a solution to a community problem. The architecture of a *match* consists of 3 major components (Fig. 21.1): a *Web Georeferenced Information System* (GIS), a *Gamified Mobile App* and a *Marketplace*.

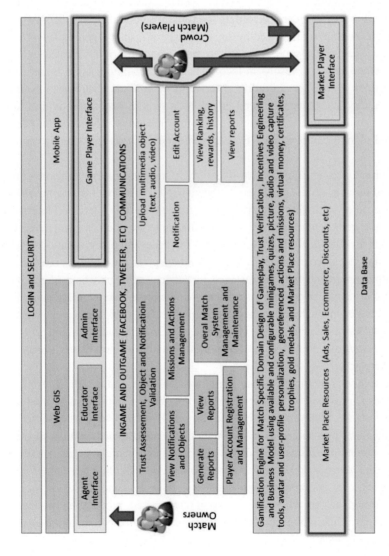

Fig. 21.1 Proposed architecture for a generic match

The Web GIS main modules support decisions by owners' agents, validating (by assessing trust) and storing (in the database) information related to the success indicators and results of players' actions, including missions they execute by assignment and under supervision of agents or their proxies (e. g., teachers, community leaders, trusted players) and granting rewards. The types of information, results, rewards and missions depend on the logic of the target problem-solution (in fighting the Aedes aegypti mosquito, players notify georeferenced mosquito hatcheries and closed properties; missions could include learning about the mosquito lifecycle or "opening up" a property for inspection). Validated results lead to rewards according to the adopted incentive policy in the form of marketplace goods and services or reputation enhancement of players amongst their peers. The Web component also handles management reports on the success indicators and other metrics of interest. For efficiency and according to problem-solution logic, groups of players are led by agents who in turn, are led by supervisors. For instance, some players in a location may be organized to serve as volunteer field-agents for a given agent who gives them missions and validates results in loco or using the communication facilities. One professional in the owners' organization(s) serves as system administrator to oversee all operations, security and players' related information such as account activities, logs of achievements and marketplace activities. Like communications, other features permeate both Web and mobile components – e. g., trust assessment may be done by accredited players.

Players normally come from the crowd and notify incidents (as per the problem-solution logic) and mission results according to the gameplay (with built-in incentives) using the multimedia object georeferenced upload facilities in their map interface. (Internet may be bypassed with georeferenced data from the online map provided whenever possible.)

The modular architecture in Fig. 21.1 allows for replacement of a given module insides without affecting the *match* overall functional operation, given the module's interface (i. e., input and output) are maintained. For instance, incentive weights may be configurable (for the sake of experiments, say); trust assessment may be done automatically by an implemented algorithm or manually by an agent. *Match* execution performance may change in these cases, but not its functionality. The architecture also includes link-up with social networks for *match* dissemination, player recruiting and even non-player access to the *match*'s marketplace.

The *marketplace* is the pivotal, trans-component module of a *match*: it levels stakeholders' interests, provides for economic exchanges and for innovations in the problem solution. For instance, a player with an Aedes aegypti biological trap may use *AB*'s marketplace as a natural first choice of sales channel. The marketplace modules of different *matches* have common features and functionality since they share the common objective of supporting the *match* stakeholders' business goals. As such, the marketplace is likely the main motivator for continuing player interest in the *match* and for its long-term sustainability – through ads, merchandising, sales of (customized) products and services, and sales commissions. Thus, amongst research questions (RQs) that pertain to the success indicators of a specific *match*, a RQ of particular interest to be answered here is: "Is a *match* marketplace a significant business channel?" Respondents should include members of the population at large, owners' representatives and potential business partners.

21.4   Case Studies: AedesBusters and AquaGuardians

Initial versions for *AB* and *AG* were implemented based on the generic architecture in Fig. 21.1 and with assistance from VA/VE and ANA agents, respectively. Part of any screen in either *match* will be used for ads, e-commerce access or shortcuts to other marketplace functions/facilities for players to exchange points for goods, services or discounts at partner virtual or brick stores or for a player-entrepreneur to place ads or create (offerings in) a virtual store.

21.4.1   AedesBusters

Analysis of existing VA/VE notification channels and interviewed VA/VE agents in Northeastern Brazil, elicited the success indicators in fighting Aedes aegypti: i) number of notifications; ii) number of uninspected closed properties; iii) VA/VE response time to action (from the notification instant); iv) level of integration and synchronization between the VA and VE agencies; and v) resources allocated to fighting the mosquito. If AB is to contribute to the fight against Aedes aegypti, one expects it to produce higher numbers for indicators i), iv) and v) and lower values for the others, when compared to existing notification channels (or equivalently, *AB* is used more often to notify mosquito infestations, fewer properties are left "closed" due to accomplishment of "property opening missions" and authorities become more efficient in their operations).

The mobile app (Fig. 21.2) has a map with icons for georeferenced actions by the player (notify mosquito hatcheries; destroy hatchery; report zika, chikungunya or dengue patients, make an appointment to open a property). On the middle screen, the player may examine her/his conquest history, *ranking*, points and rewards. The screen on the right shows a game level change and accumulated points. The bottom of this screen brings a link to an *AB*'s partner business. Access to the marketplace is possible from any page through a specific hot button. V1 of *AB*'s mobile component was implemented for Android, with Google maps native GPS.

V1 for AB's Web component was implemented as a *Restful* Web Service using JAX-RS. Further implementation details may be found in [17, 18]. According to granted permissions by the sys admin, VA/VE agents or high level players (who have made important conquests which were endorsed by the associated supervisor and can thus act as volunteer agents) use *AB*'s Web component basic screen map (Fig. 21.2) to: as "regular agents" view data on notifications (location, time and player), mission results, etc.; as "supervisor", to edit such data (e. g. validate an uploaded object), invite or endorse volunteer agents, attribute missions; or, as "sys admin", manage the database, the problem-solution

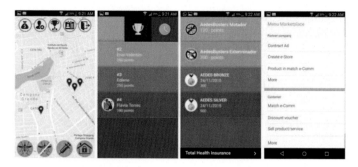

Fig. 21.2 Some screens for AedesBusters

logic (e. g., changing incentives), produce reports for decision support and manage the marketplace.

21.4.2 AquaGuardians

Interviews with ANA professionals, expert university professors, local water management agents, educators and business people conducted in the first semester of 2016 in the state of Paraíba, Brazil, led to the following success indicators for *AG*: a) student awareness of water conservation and b) number of community actions towards saving, preservation and monitoring of water. Indicator a) is to be evaluated by the (increase) of photographic, artistic, theatrical, reading, writing, video and other works by students on the general theme of water. *AG* V1 Web GIS was implemented using MySQL; the mobile App used Unity (Fig. 21.3).

Fig. 21.3 Some screens for AquaGuardians

AG screens bear close functional similarity to *AB*'s and details may be found in [19]. Children and teenagers play AG by doing georeferenced missions for caring for available water resources and producing (and uploading proof of) their works; local school teachers play by creating, coaching and assessing these missions in the virtual and real worlds; water agents play to validate the other players' actions and by making strategic decisions for water management. Any business person or consumers – not only players – may participate by offering or buying products and services in the marketplace. Differently from *AB*, *AG* offers a physical *gameboard* (possibly sold separately) for playing with the mobile app.

21.5   Validation Studies

Preliminary validation studies were carried out to check whether V1 for *AB* and *AG* would impact the success indicators favorably and whether the associated marketplace would be attractive to the *match* stakeholders as a business channel – i. e., to answer the Research Question (RQ) at the end of Sect. 21.3. Please note that, since fully validated feedbacks in the iterative methodology (Sect. 21.3.1) may take months, years even to be completed (i. e., to ensure claims that solutions are sound and encompassing), one may only argue for face validity [18] for now.

21.5.1   AedesBusters

AB V1 interface and functionality were first evaluated by 24 VA/VE staff who unanimously found the *match* features "likely to improve success indicators i) to iv)". A field trial was conducted in the week of July 13–17, 2015 in a suburb of the city of Campina Grande, Brazil, whose *Quick Mapping for Aedes aegypti Infestation Index* ("LIRAa" in Portuguese) had reached 11.5% then (Brazilian health authorities consider LIRAa $< 1\%$ to be satisfactory; between 1 and 3.9%, state of alert; and $\geq 4\%$ to be in "risk of surge"). Thirty volunteers (students, housewives, teachers, police and sales people) participated in the field trial, 53.33–46.66% male-female, 20–36 years old; all trained in *AB* gameplay; 10 VA/VE agents acted as supervisors, validating notifications for intangible incentives only. During the week, *AB* increased notifications by 520% (compared to previous week averages) and reduced VA/VE average response time (from notification to decision to act) from 15 h to 5 min (supervisors monitored notifications on the map and sent messages with action missions to players acting as field agents). At the end, all 30 volunteer players and 10 staff were interviewed, in addition to 150 residents in the trial suburb. Ninety percent of players and residents agreed they would recommend that friends and relatives play *AB*; 90% of the agents said "*AB* would much facilitate combating the mosquito and integrating actions between the environment and epidemiology agencies". These results establish "face validity" for *AB* as a useful tool for checking the spread of Aedes aegypti.

21.5.2 AquaGuardians

In July 2016, thirty-three users – 20 students, 6 teachers and 7 water agents 54.54–45.46% male-female, 16 to 41 years old; all trained in *AG* gameplay mechanics – were questioned about their level of motivation to play *AG* V1: 26.1% responded they felt very motivated by the *match*'s features; 65.2% felt motivated; and, just 8.7% felt neutral. When asked about the utility of AG features to support educational tasks ("missions"), 41.2% answered they were "very useful"; 44.1% said "useful"; and, 14.7% remained neutral. Water agents, when asked whether *AG* would increase success indicator b) in their city, responded: very much, 43.5%; yes, 47.8%; and, only 8.7% remained neutral. These favorable percentages establish *AG* face validity for its features concerning success indicators a) and b).

21.5.3 Marketplace

Since marketplace features are common to *AB* and *AG*, answers to the RQ in subsection 21.3.2 for both *matches* are discussed together in this subsection. All 33 *AG* users in 21.5.1 graded the importance of the marketplace for the *match* attractiveness in a five-point scale from 1 (not important at all) to 5 (very important): the agents' grades averaged 4.74; the teachers', 4.80; and, the students', 4.91.

As for *AB*, 26 UFCG students played *AB* as volunteers in early 2016. They had no tangible intrinsic incentives – e. g., no marketplace features: they just played to "do good". When asked whether the AB *match* would motivate their engagement as "volunteer agents" only 24% said yes (62% were in doubt and 14% answered "no"). The introduction of a marketplace however, would make 92% answer "yes", thus providing for an affirmative answer to the RQ and implying face validity of a marketplace match to fight Aedes aegypti. Further evidence of the interest by entrepreneurs and business leaders on *AB* was collected through a survey in the city of Iguatú, Ceará state, Brazil, in late 2015. Eleven interviewees from the education, radio, franchise, furniture and appliance retail, office supplies, cosmetics, photography, party and event promotion, male fashion and beverage industries, unanimously said they would use *AB*'s marketplace to advertise and to offer discounts to outstanding players, paying commission on sales. Since Iguatú had LIRAa < 1% then, the surveyed subjects' position may be projected more favorably to cities where LIRAa > 1%, adding credence on the validity of *AB*'s marketplace significance for business and consequently, interest on *matches*.

21.6 Conclusion

This chapter discussed an IT system whose intersection to digital marketplaces supports educational and operational efforts to address complex, costly community challenges in a cost-effective manner for governments, in a lucrative way for users, and with sustainability for the system itself. The system incorporates concepts and facilities from alternate reality games, crowdsourcing, incentive engineering, georeferenced information systems, trust systems, computer-based education, mobile computing, knowledge management, marketplaces and entrepreneurship. The proposed system is seen as a marketplace-driven, game-changing game, or *match* for short. A generic *match* modular architecture was proposed, implemented and applied to two real problem cases for preliminary validation experiments in the public health and water conservation areas.

This chapter offered preliminary evidence that (digital) marketplaces contribute to attract and retain players to *matches*. As such, the chapter contributed to the on-going discussion on the role and impact of IT and digital marketplaces to the economy and well-being of society in general. Work in this theme is just beginning, however. Applications of *matches* to other areas and more extensive validation may yield more encompassing, statistically significant evidence.

Acknowledgments
The comments of anonymous referees helped improve the contents of this chapter. Their time is much appreciated. The authors also thank Valéria Andrade, Irivaldo Oliveira, Hugo Morais, Gabriel Cintra, Francisco Edeverson, Rafaela Araújo from Atelier de Computação of the Federal University of Campina Grande (UFCG), Brazil for implementing AB and AG and helping with the validation experiments. The authors are grateful for the financial support received from the National Agency for Water – ANA, from the Coordination for the Improvement of Higher Education Personnel – CAPES, Foundation for Research Support of Paraíba State – FAPESQ-PB, and the Ministry of Communications of Brazil for the development of AedesBusters and AquaGuardians within the ClipCult project.

References

1. World Health Organization WHO Mosquito control: can it stop Zika at source? |Update 17 February 2016. http://www.who.int/emergencies/zika-virus/articles/mosquito-control/en/ Available at. Accessed Oct 22, 2016.
2. UNEP / UN-Habitat "Sick water? The central role of wastewater management in sustainable development". Available at http://www.grida.no/publications/rr/sickwater/. Acessed 22 Oct 2016.
3. D. J. Kuss, Internet gaming addiction: current perspectives, Psychology *Research* and Behavior Management, 2013; 6: 125–137. DovePress. Published online 2013 Nov 14. DOI: 10.2147/PRBM.S39476
4. Muntean, C. I. (2011). Raising engagement in e-learning through gamification. In The 6th International Conference on Virtual Learning ICVL 2012 (pp. 323–329)
5. M. Kosonen et al., "User motivations and knowledge sharing in idea crowdsourcing." International Journal of Innovation Management, 2014; v18, n5: 6-18.
6. Seeclickfix. Seeclickfix: Better Communication, Stronger Communities. Available at http://en.seeclickfix.com/ Acessed 22 Oct 2016, 2016, New Haven.
7. Trashout. Trashout: localization of illegal dumps. Available at https://www.trashout.ngo//? ref=trashout.me. Accessed 22 Oct 2016. 2016. Prague

8. Gibbs, M., Designing Incentive Plans: New Insight from Academic Research, World at Work Journal, Fourth Quarter 2012, 29-47.
9. K. Song et al., Game Theoretical Analysis on Cooperation Stability and Incentive Effectiveness in Community Networks. 11(2): e0148688., 2016.
10. J. Chandler et al., Risks and Rewards of Crowdsourcing Marketplaces, February 4, 2014, Handbook of Human Computation, pp. 377-392, Springer, New York, USA.
11. U. Gneezy et al., When and Why Incentives (Don't) Work to Modify Behavior, JEP, Fall 2011, V 25, N 4; 191–210.
12. H. Yu, "Building Robust Crowdsourcing Systems with Reputation-aware Decision Support Techniques," Available at https://arxiv.org/ftp/arxiv/papers/1502/1502.02106.pdf., Acessed 22 Oct 2016.
13. M. H. Nguyen and D. Q. Tran, A Trust-based Mechanism for Avoiding Liars in Referring of Reputation in Multiagent System, International Journal of Advanced Research in Artificial Intelligence, 2015 Vol.4, No.2; 28-36.
14. W.T. Luke Teacy et al., An efficient and versatile approach to trust and reputation using hierarchical Bayesian modelling, 2012, Artificial Intelligence 193; 149–185.
15. J. Y. Geronimo, Crowdsourcing dengue alert. Available at www.rappler.com/nation/31760-nationwide-dengue-vector-surveillance. Accessed 14 11 2016. 2016.
16. IBM, Sistema Agua Viva. Available at http://agua-viva.org. Accessed 17 Oct 2016. New York. 2016.
17. Larman, Craig. Agile and Iterative Development: A Manager's Guide. Addison-Wesley. p. 27. ISBN 978-0-13-111155-4. 2004. New York.
18. M. Litwin, How to Measure Survey Reliability and Validity, Sage Publications, 96 pp. 1995. Los Angeles.
19. Federal University of Campina Grande. CompCult - Atelier de Computação e Cultura da UFCG, Available at www.compcult.net. Accessed at 22 Oct 2016. 2016. Campina Grande.

Further Reading

20. G. Coulouris, J. Dollimore and T. Kindberg, "Distributed Systems – Concepts and Design," Amsterdam: Addison-Wesley Longman, 2005.
21. R. Buettner, "A Systematic Literature Review of Crowdsourcing Research from a Human Resource Management Perspective.," *Proceedings of HICSS-48.,* Bd. DOI: 10.13140/2.1.2061.1845., Nr. DOI: 10.13140/2.1.2061.1845., p. DOI: 10.13140/2.1.2061.1845., January 2015.
22. A. Doan et al., "Crowdsourcing Systems on the World-Wide Web," *CACM,* Bd. 54, Nr. 4, pp. 86–96, 2011.

Industrial Evolution and Disruptive Innovation: Theories, Evidence and Perspectives

Luigi Orsenigo

Abstract

The notion of disruptive technologies has become in recent years a prominent concept in industrial dynamics and strategy. Yet, we still know too little about the frequency, intensity and modalities of this crucial phenomenon, let alone about the implications for strategy and policy making. There are indeed various meanings and interpretations of this concept, in the literature and in practice, but they often lack generality and in most instances theories rely on a quite narrow set of specific cases of particular firms, products and industries. This paper will not review the details of this debate. Rather, some more basic issues are discussed about the intensity and forms of disruptive innovation and the strategies and reactions of incumbents to the threats presented by new technologies. The paper presents and discusses the various meanings and forms of this concept as well as the conflicting evidence coming from different sources and methodologies in order to clarify its relevance and the differentiated ways in which it appears (or it doesn't appear), thus providing very preliminary and basic indications for analysis and action. The paper concludes that in the aggregate and over time what we observe is a puzzling co-existence and turbulence and stability in industrial dynamics, which appears to be driven by the complex interplay of differentiated processes of market selection and – above all – learning within firms. The specific characteristics of the relevant technologies, markets and firms are fundamental determinants of the patterns of competition and industrial change and they have to be considered carefully in the development of theories, strategies and policies.

L. Orsenigo (✉)
Scuola Universitaria Superiore IUSS
Pavia, Italy
e-mail: luigi.orsenigo@iusspavia.it

© Springer-Verlag GmbH Germany 2018
C. Linnhoff-Popien et al. (eds.), *Digital Marketplaces Unleashed*,
https://doi.org/10.1007/978-3-662-49275-8_22

22.1 Introduction: From Creative Destruction to Disruptive Innovation

The idea of disruptive innovation has at the same time a very long and a very short history. Yet, we still know too little about the frequency, intensity and modalities of this crucial phenomenon, let alone about the implications for strategy and policy making. There are indeed various meanings and interpretations of this concept, in the literature and in practice, but they often lack generality and in most instances theories rely on a quite narrow set of specific cases of particular firms, products and industries. This paper will not review the details of this debate. Rather, some more basic issues are discussed about the intensity and forms of disruptive innovation and the strategies and reactions of incumbents to the threats presented by new technologies. Thus, this paper aims at locating the concept of disruptive innovation into a broader context in order to clarify its relevance and the differentiated ways in which it appears (or it doesn't appear), thus providing very preliminary and basic indications for analysis and action.

The long part of the story can be traced back to the Classical economists. The notion that markets and market leadership are constantly changing through the appearance and introduction of new technologies and more generally innovations was forcefully advanced by Marx, who wrote almost poetic pages describing the hectic and irresistible pace of capitalism driven by continuous technological change: *"All that is solid melts into the air"* [1].

Yet, the idea that innovation was the hallmark of economic competition and growth was only systematically introduced in 1911 by Josef A. Schumpeter [2]. He advanced the concept that new firms – the heroic entrepreneur – would continuously threaten and then substitute old incumbents by introducing new processes, new products, new markets and new "combinations of factors". Yet, 30 years later he partly changed his mind. In "Capitalism, Socialism and Democracy" [3], while still maintaining that *"the process of creative destruction is the essential fact about capitalism"*, (p. 83), he also suggested that entrepreneurial innovation was being replaced by the routinized activity of R&D labs within large corporations enjoying long lasting monopoly power: in his view, these developments were doomed to bring capitalism to an end.

The shorter part of the story begins in the last three decades of the XX century, when economists began to study innovation in earnest, realizing that technological progress was the single most important source of growth. The advent of the information and communication technologies (ICT) revolution and the emergence of the Silicon Valley prompted an enormous amount of empirical and theoretical research on innovation and entrepreneurship, which became important autonomous fields in economics and management. In the eyes of the larger public, innovation became the "new industrial religion" (as the title of an issue of "The Economist" declared in 1999) and the new mantra for strategy and organization studies in business schools as well as in public policies.

This body of studies produced invaluable knowledge into the sources, patterns and consequences of innovation. Of course, it is impossible to review these findings here (For a recent survey, see [4]). However, a few main broad results can be emphasized here at the very beginning to set the stage for the following discussion.

First, there is little question that technological innovation is the single major engine of economic growth and of industrial change. Major episodes of industrial transformation, with dramatic reshuffling of dominant positions, are typically associated to the appearance of new technologies. The introduction of new technologies brings about the emergence of new products, processes, markets, firms, organizational forms and business models, etc. Some of these technological innovations are so pervasive and revolutionary – sometimes called General Purpose Technologies or Techno-Economic Paradigms – to produce structural transformations in the economy, in the institutions and in the society at large: steam power, electricity, information technologies, etc. [5, 6].

Second, the development and diffusion of new technologies takes time and requires a multitude of incremental and cumulative innovations. But these processes are not smooth: turbulence and ultimately disruption occurs by impulses, which are typically industry-specific [7].

Third, however, that there is no such thing as "technological innovation", but diverse and variegated forms of innovation in different industries according to the specific nature and characteristics of the relevant technologies and markets.

Thus, it should come as no surprise that many representations of the innovative process have been proposed, sometimes complementary to and sometimes conflicting with each other. Against this background, the concept of disruptive innovation was introduced by Clayton Christensen in 1995 [8] and received quickly an enormous popularity. This idea adds significant nuances and try at the same time to generalize older insights about "creative destruction". A widely used and workable definition can be found in Wikipedia: an innovation that creates a new market and value network and eventually disrupts an existing market and value/support network, displacing established market leaders and alliances. This definition highlights the main substantial features of the concept. First, the adjective "disruptive" is applied to innovations rather than to technologies, because few technologies are intrinsically disruptive (or sustaining); rather, the disruptive character of the innovation is linked to the business model that the new technology enables. Second, emphasis is attributed to the disruption of the value/support network of a company or an industry, that is to say to the set of relationships with customers and suppliers, rather than to the ability of extant market leaders to absorb and master the new required technological capabilities. Thus, "..., *disruptive innovations were technologically straightforward, consisting of off-the-shelf components put together in a product architecture that was often simpler than prior approaches. They offered less of what customers in established markets wanted and so could rarely be initially employed there. They offered a different package of attributes valued only in emerging markets remote from, and unimportant to, the mainstream.*" (Christensen 1997, p. 15). In particular, disruption is more likely to occur starting from market niches where customers do not need the full performance valued by customers at the high end of the market and/or in new markets previously unserved by the products supplied by existing incumbents Hence, third, disruptive innovations tend to be introduced by outsiders and entrepreneurs, because market leaders downplay the potential threat of these innovations, considering them less profitable than current products and absorbing resources from the current businesses.

Unsurprisingly, the notion of disruptive innovation triggered controversies and debates. Some criticism claims that there is nothing inherently new in the concept or that it is only a refinement or a particular case of broader processes of creative destruction. Others have pointed that the evidence on which the theory is based is actually made out of a few, debatable case studies (For reviews, see [9] and [10–13]).

In what follows, this article will not review the details of this debate. Rather, some more basic issues are discussed about the intensity and forms of and the strategies and reactions of incumbents to the threats presented by new technologies. Different explanations are available but they often lack generality and in most instances theories rely on a quite narrow set of specific cases of particular firms, products and industries.

In effect, our knowledge of how creative destruction/disruptive innovation[1] occurs is still limited: it is possible to cite many examples of disruption, where industry leaders were actually swiped away by new competitors (Kodak in digital photography, Nokia for a while in cellular phones, etc.) as well as many cases where industry leaders were able to maintain or even increase their dominance (Fuji in digital photography, big pharma companies vs. new biotechnology firms, etc.). Sweeping generalizations are hard to make in this context, much depending on the industry as well as on the specific characteristics of individual firms. To be sure, the destruction of dominant positions – especially by new entrants – is a much less frequent and in any case a much more nuanced phenomenon than is often assumed.

Indeed, some very basic questions remain open and difficult to resolve, due both to limitations in the data and sometimes in less than robust conceptual clarity about the specific phenomena that are analyzed.

For example:

(i)   How frequent and how strong is actually "creative destruction", and how long does it take? How often do we observe dramatic changes in industry leadership? Is disruption a continuous, systematic process? Or is it a punctuation over the history of any one industry or product?

(ii)   Where does creative destruction come from and where does it occur? Are always (or most of the time) new firms that introduce disruptive innovations?

(iii)   How does disruption occur? Through direct competition and head-on attack on the products of industry leaders or indirectly, via the introduction of products, processes or business models in different market segments that progressively weaken dominant positions?

---

[1] In this article, the terms "creative destruction" and "disruptive innovation" will be used – somewhat in an undisciplined way – almost interchangeably.

(iv) When and how industry leaders able to maintain their leadership despite the appearance of potentially disruptive innovations?

22.2   The Aggregate Background

To begin with, it might be useful to recall a few important and robust aggregate results that have been emerging from empirical studies made possible from the growing availability of data at the firm level for sufficiently long periods of time. These results help in providing a broader perspective to the analysis of creative destruction/disruptive innovation (see [14] for a survey).

First, relatively high rates of entry of new firms are seen in virtually all industries, even those marked by high capital intensity and other apparent barriers to entry. Further, and contrary to what standard economic textbooks would suggest, rates of entry do not appear to be particularly sensitive to the average rate of profit in an industry. And in most industries there is considerable exit as well as entry. Indeed, exit and entry rates tend to be strongly correlated. Both entry and exit tend to be significantly higher in new industries, and to decline somewhat as the industry matures. However, even relatively mature industries often are marked by continuing entry and exit.

Second, the vast majority of entrants are small firms, and most of them exit the industry within a few years: 20–40% of entrants die in the first two years and only 40–50% survive beyond the seventh year in a given cohort. Survivors grow faster but more erratically than incumbents and they reach average levels of productivity only gradually and slowly over time (around a decade). Only a few outliers in an entry cohort are able to attain superior performances, but, especially in the presence of significant technological and market discontinuities, they sometimes displace the incumbents and become the new industry leaders. Even in relatively mature industries one often observes persistent turbulence and churning in the profile of industrial evolution, due not only to continuous entry and exit flows but also to changes in the incumbents' market shares.

Third, even in mature industries there tends to be persistent heterogeneity among firms regarding any available measure of firms' traits and performance: size, age, productivity, profitability, innovativeness, etc. (For an overview, see [15]). The distributions of these variables tend to be highly asymmetric, and often display fat tails in their rates of change. What is even more interesting though, is that heterogeneity is persistent: more efficient firms at time t have a high probability to be highly efficient also at time t+T, and the same applies for size, profitability, and (more controversially) innovation. The degree of persistence tends to decline the longer the time span considered. However, this tendency is weak and thus heterogeneity decays slowly and it is still present in the limit.

Fourth, positive relationships are typically found among these variables: more efficient firms tend to be also more innovative and profitable and to gain market shares as time goes by. The magnitude of these relationships, however, is extremely variable across samples and across industries. Thus, most studies find only weak or no relationship at all between productivity and profitability on the one hand, and growth on the other. Firms' expansion appears to be independent from size, possibly with smaller companies exhibiting higher but more variable growth rates. And in general, firms' growth remains very hard to explain. While some studies describe it as driven by small, idiosyncratic, and independently distributed shocks – and therefore as essentially erratic – others find highly complex underlying structures. If anything, the evidence would seem to suggest that firms grow and decline by relatively lumpy jumps which cannot be accounted by the accumulation of small, "atom-less", independent shocks. Rather "big" episodes of expansion and contraction are relatively frequent. (For an overview, see [14].)

Sixth, further important results are offered by studies which decompose aggregate (sectoral or economy-wide) productivity growth, separating (i) idiosyncratic changes in firm/plant productivity levels – the so called within component – that broadly captures improvements occurring within incumbent firms; (ii) changes in average productivity due to reallocation of output or employment shares across firms – the between component – that imperfectly measures the impact of market selection in shifting resources to the more efficient firms; and (iii) the contribution thereof due to entry into and exit from the market. Summarizing heroically, most studies do indeed find further evidence of a steady process of creative destruction involving significant rates of input and output reallocation even within 4-digit industries. Again these studies confirm that the process is accompanied by a good deal of "churning" with relatively high flows of entry and exit. However, the most interesting finding is that the largest contribution to productivity growth comes by far from the within component, that is to say from the learning processes of existing firms. The role of the between component – market selection – is much smaller and in some cases it has even a negative sign. Last, as already mentioned above, the contribution of net entry is highly variable, possibly with exit rather than entry showing a larger impact.

These findings suggest that heterogeneous processes of learning and selection drive industry dynamics, generating a puzzling coexistence of remarkable stability and drastic change. Moreover, continuous change and turbulence and permanent differences among firms coexist with the emergence of remarkably stable structures at higher levels of aggregation. However, the strength, speed and directions of these processes vary significantly across sectors and countries.

22.3   Sectoral Patterns of Innovation and Industrial Dynamics

Indeed, while some of these aggregate properties of the processes of industrial evolution are common to most industries, still fundamental differences appear across sectors. Thus, for example, [16] found that while innovative firms are likely to be rather small in industrial machinery, big companies prevail in chemicals, metal working, aerospace and electrical equipment, and many "science-based" sectors (such as electronics and pharmaceuticals) tend to display a bimodal distribution with high rates of innovativeness associated to small and very large firms.

Analyses have increasingly emphasized the relevance of various factors that impact the patterns of innovation and industrial dynamics. To begin with, it is now acknowledged that technology often develops according to its own internal logic, following trajectories that are only partially responsive to market signals [17]. Moreover, there is no such thing as "technology in general" but rather an array of different technologies, with different properties and characteristics, yielding different patterns of technological advance [18]. Technologies differ in terms of opportunities for innovation, and in terms of the degree of appropriability of its benefits. Including measures of these variables in the analysis (either statistical or qualitative) almost always improves results. Typically technological change proceeds cumulatively: creative accumulation rather than creative destruction is the norm in many industries and over relatively long periods of time. Yet, in some technologies and industries – pharmaceuticals being a clear example – it is harder to use cumulated knowledge to develop new products and processes. This difference has implications for the evolution of industry structure. In some industries, largely public or semi-public organizations produce much of the relevant knowledge base on which innovation depends, which is in principle available to everybody who has the requisite scientific and technological absorptive capabilities. In other cases, technological advances do not rely much on publicly available knowledge, but on private and firm-specific know-how and expertise. Clearly, innovation can arise in and impact on very different industry structures.

The well-known taxonomy by Keith Pavitt [18] was a first and still invaluable attempt at mapping 'industry types' and industry dynamics. Pavitt taxonomy comprises four groups of sectors, namely:

(i) 'supplier dominated', sectors whose innovative opportunities mostly come through the acquisition of new pieces of machinery and new intermediate inputs (textile, clothing, metal products belong to this category);
(ii) 'specialized suppliers', including producers of industrial machinery and equipment;
(iii) 'scale intensive' sectors, wherein the sheer scale of production influence the ability to exploit innovative opportunities partly endogenously generated and partly stemming from science based inputs;
(iv) 'science based' industries, whose innovative opportunities co-evolve, especially in the early stage of their life with advances in pure and applied sciences (microelectronics, informatics, drugs and bioengineering are good examples).

Other, rather complementary, taxonomic exercises have focused primarily on some characteristics of the innovation process, distinguishing between a 'Schumpeter Mark I' and a 'Schumpeter Mark II' regime, dramatizing the difference between the views of innovative activities from Schumpeter (1911) and Schumpeter (1942): see [19–21].

As mentioned previously, Schumpeter himself distinguished two (extreme) patterns of innovation. In the first one, as theorized in *The Theory of Economic Development* (1911) and often labeled as Schumpeter Mark I [22], innovation is created by the bold efforts of new entrepreneurs, who are able and lucky enough to displace incumbents, only to be challenged themselves by imitative entrants. At the other extreme, as described in *Capitalism, Socialism and Democracy* (1942) and often referred to as Schumpeter Mark II, the main sources of innovation are instead large corporations, which accumulate difficult-to-imitate knowledge in specific domains, and are therefore able to gain long-lasting and self-reproducing technological advantages (and economic leadership). Following this intuition, the notion has been developed that innovation and market structure evolve according to different technological regimes [23]. distinguished between science-based vs. cumulative regimes [24]. Further developed this concept by modeling the different evolution of industries under an "entrepreneurial" as opposed to a "routinized" regime [25] and [20]. provided further empirical evidence concerning the relationships between the properties of technologies, the patterns of innovation, and market structure.

More specifically, a technological regime may be defined by the combination of some fundamental properties of the relevant technology, namely the degree of opportunities for innovating; the degree of appropriability, i. e. the ease and the instruments by which innovators are able to appropriate the economic benefits stemming from innovation; the degree of cumulativeness of innovation, i. e. the extent to which innovators today enjoy cognitive and/or economic advantages vis-a-vis competitors that make it more likely to innovate again the future.

Thus, the Mark I regime is characterized by high opportunities, low appropriability conditions and low cumulativeness: innovations are therefore carried out to a good extent by innovative entrants who continuously challenge incumbents. Market structure is highly unstable, with leadership changing frequently. Examples might be biotechnology, mechanical engineering, furniture, etc.. Conversely, at the other extreme, under the Mark II regime innovative activities are much more cumulative and imitation is difficult. Innovation is therefore undertaken to a greater extent by a few incumbents which turn out to be 'serial innovators': chemical engineering, semiconductors, aerospace, etc..

The structure of the demand side of the market – the demand regime – plays also an important role in shaping the patterns of industrial dynamics. In particular, when the aggregate market is actually composed by a large number of (actual and potential) almost independent niches, it is more difficult for any one firm to build a dominant and persistent leadership in the aggregate market: pharmaceuticals is a classic example (see [21]).

Different technological regimes are also supported by distinct institutions governing public research and training and, at the market end, the interactions among producers. Such institutions, together with the corporate actors involved contribute to define distinct sectoral systems of innovation and production: see [26] and [27].

22.4 Innovation, Dominance and the Reasons for Disruption at the Firm Level

The aggregate and sectoral evidence provides precious insights into the broad patterns of creative destruction/disruption. Innovation, industrial change and turbulence are systematic features of industrial dynamics. The timing and the specific features of these processes vary substantially over time and across technologies and industries. Creative destruction and disruptive innovations are more likely to occur – but not exclusively – in Schumpeter Mark I sectors or in the early stages of the life cycle of a new industry. Yet, evidence shows at the same time aspects of remarkable stability, with incremental, path-dependent innovation and persistence of firms' traits and performances.

At the level of individual firms the picture remains however much less clear, to say the least.

This observation should not be surprising. It is intuitive and should be almost common sense (although not always recognized in standard economic textbooks and literature) that firms simply differ widely from each other. The empirical evidence cited previously confirm that heterogeneity in firms' characteristics, behavior and performances is strikingly high. There are obviously good reasons for this observations. Indeed, a large stream of literature in management (more than in economics) has emphasized that firms are to be conceived as bundles of idiosyncratic resources and capabilities, which are built over time, are highly contextual and difficult to change quickly. In this view, the competitive advantages of any one company derive precisely from the specific combination of resources that are uniquely controlled by the firm and even more importantly for the competences and capabilities that have been acquired over time through processes of technological and organizational learning. Such learning processes are typically cumulative and path-dependent: what a firm is and does now is the outcome of its past history and such history heavily constrains what it will possible to do in the future. Moreover, facing an uncertain future, companies place different bets on the perceived opportunities and threats: diversity is therefore a systematic aspect of economic life, even in extremely narrowly defined business lines [28, 29].

Thus, individual firm would typically react differently to the threats coming from new technologies and innovations. Indeed, coming back to the broad questions raised in Sect. 22.1, it is not clear at all that incumbents are always doomed to fail when confronted with disruptive innovation, nor that new firms are always the winners. Even more difficult it is to identify robust regularities about the strategies which lead to success or failure.

An immense literature – mainly based on case studies – provides however a few important suggestions.

First, disruption in almost by definition hard to predict and it is to a large extent an ex-post phenomenon. When new technologies appear, uncertainty is the name of the game and firms – both incumbents and new entrants – experiment with different visions and approaches. As mentioned previously, most of them will fail and turn out as dead ends. Prediction is almost impossible, unless perhaps is too late, and often nothing more than an educated guess.

Second, disruption does not always come from new firms, but also from existing organizations diversifying into new business lines and products: IBM from punching cards to mainframe computers is only a prominent example among many others. Similarly, disruption seldom occurs through head-on, direct confrontation with extant products and industry leaders. Much more often, it happens through the development of initially small and unprofitable market niches at the flanks of the main product. An iconic example is personal computers (PC), which created a new mass market for computers whereas previously expensive mainframe computers were sold only to large organizations. Another example is given by mini-mills vs. integrated steel mills. Mini-mills used scrap to make cheap, low quality steel of it and the integrated steel companies were not interested at all in this low margin business. However, slowly but steadily, the quality of the mini-mills steel improved and gained systematically new market segments.

The attack to dominant positions comes from multiple directions and potential competitors, who encircle and put under siege the current leader, often for prolonged periods of time. In this respect, the popular representation of disruption as a cruel frontal battle could be better understood – if it ever happens – as the final episode of a longer war, in which it is not clear who the enemy is – a heterogeneous and constantly changing army of autonomous tribes – and where the battlefield is actually located and how it looks like.

But when and why dominant positions are severely challenged or even destroyed?

There are entirely rational reasons why an incumbent may decide not to invest in innovation threatening to displace them or to delay such investment (e. g. cannibalization of current products), but the managerial literature does not seem to attribute a fundamental role to them. When clear incentives motivations are absent, the literature remains underdeveloped [30].

A first natural candidate for explanation is that new technologies may turn out to be "competence destroying" [31]: that is to say, they overturn and render obsolete existing competencies, skills and know-how (e. g. transistors and vacuum tubes, quartz and mechanical watches, etc.). In this respect, the very factors that made a firm dominant – the core capabilities – may become "core rigidities" in a new, different technological environment [32].

In more recent interpretations, however, the main cause of "competence destruction" is not the inability to master the new technology as such, but rather the difficulty established firms encounter in responding to shifts in the market place [33], the challenges that innovation poses to their value and support network [34] and in the larger institutional and social regime [35]: again, the PC was directed to groups of customers (individuals) which had never been the focus of mainframe producers.

It has to be stressed that competence destruction in this wider interpretation does not simply or mainly depends on mistakes in decision making at the most senior levels. Certainly, senior teams are likely to be captured by their largest, most profitable customers, making it difficult to allocate resources to initiatives that serve new customers at (initially) lower margins. But such emphasis might be too simplistic or potentially misleading. Recent studies suggest that organizational competences, in the sense of the embedded organizational routines of established companies, may be much more central to established firm failure in the face of disruptive innovation than is generally acknowledged [36]. Organizational capabilities are almost inherently inertial as they based on and expressed by routines which have been learned and developed over time. They are robust and provide stability to the organization and become deeply embedded cognitive models, shared systems of understanding and of incentives that reinforce, and are in turn reinforced by, the local experience of the firm [37]. Thus, they are path-dependent and rigid. Exploring a new, possibly disruptive, market thus requires major and difficult changes in patterns of behavior and search that may look unprofitable in the face of deep uncertainty or, even more so, may be not even conceived given the current organizational architecture.

A further important interpretation recently provided by [30], suggests that incumbents failure reflect diseconomies of scope rooted in assets that are necessarily shared across both businesses. Specifically, they show that both Microsoft and IBM were initially very successful in creating free standing business units that could compete with entrants on their own terms, but that as the new businesses grew, the need to share key firm level assets imposed significant costs on both businesses and created severe organizational conflict. In IBM and Microsoft's case this conflict eventually led to control over the new business being given to the old and that in both cases effectively crippled the new business.

22.5 Survival and Persistent Leadership

Defeat of the incumbent and victory for the attacker, however, is not the only or even more frequent outcome. In many occasions, dominant firms retreat and diversify into related but different lucrative business. Once again IBM provides an example: it succeeded in entering the new market for personal computers, obtaining a good, but not dominant position. When profit margins fell into that segment, IBM left the PC market and transformed itself into an immensely successful organization selling services and consultancy. In this respect, it remains also to clarify what exactly is destroyed, when disruption occurs: firms, products, business models?

In many other instances, current leaders are able to win, let alone survive. So, what are the capabilities and strategies that allow for maintaining persistent leadership in markets undergoing technological change and potential disruption?

First, it has been long recognized that technological change as such needs not to be destructive for market leaders. In these cases, technological change is defined as "competence enhancing", meaning that the new technology strengthens rather than weaken the core competences and capabilities of incumbents. The ability of (some) companies to innovate cumulatively and systematically is actually a fundamental source of sustained leadership. But, more than this, in many instances, major – and not simply incremental – innovations, new products and markets have been created by established firms: chemicals, pharmaceuticals, oil, important segments of the "information technology" industry.

Second, incumbents are able to defend their leadership by relying on their big pockets, by imposing their standards, by forging alliances with new firms and maintaining the control of crucial complementary assets, i. e. the upstream and downstream assets necessary to successfully commercialize an invention, like marketing, sales forces, experience and influence with regulatory issues [38]: pharmaceuticals and biotechnology are a textbook example.

More generally, some basic concepts have been proposed as essential strategic and organizational components for sustained leadership in environments characterized by continuous and sometimes disruptive technological change.

Absorptive capacities, i. e. a firm's "ability to recognize the value of new information, assimilate it, and apply it to commercial ends" is the first on the list [39] and [40]. Absorptive capacities are strongly cumulative, as they are built on previous knowledge and continuous research and development (R&D) investment aiming not only at discovering and developing innovations but, even more importantly to create the competences needed to perceive potential threats and opportunities, to effectively absorb the new relevant knowledge and to put it into use within the organization.

More generally, the notion of dynamic capabilities [38] provides an important framework for devising sustaining strategies. Dynamic capabilities are defined as "the firm's ability to integrate, build, and reconfigure internal and external competences to address rapidly changing environments." They are actually composed by a combination of multiple capabilities: "the capacity (1) to sense and shape opportunities and threats, (2) to seize opportunities, and (3) to maintain competitiveness through enhancing, combining, protecting, and, when necessary, reconfiguring the business enterprise's intangible and tangible assets." The dynamic capabilities theory provides an important intellectual structure for businesspeople to start thinking systematically about why companies succeed—or fail. It is not a recipe, however: it must be made operational case by case considering the specific attributes of the company, of the technology and of the competitive context.

22.6   Conclusion and Ways Forward

Clearly, much more research – both at the empirical and at the theoretical level – is needed in order to grasp some better understanding of the pace and properties of creative destruction and of disruptive innovation. Better and deeper knowledge of these phenomena must be gained by looking at the same time at different but complementary levels: the broad aggregate properties of the patterns of industrial dynamics, the diversity across sectors, the specificities of individual firms.

Here, only a couple of remarks may be proposed in the view of suggesting avenues of future research. First, almost all of the available research relates to threats to existing products/business models of a company. Much less is known about the behavior and performance of industry leaders when the threat is not directly to their core product(s), but to the business models and products of its customers and suppliers, thereby forcing upstream and downstream incumbents to adapt to those changes. Examples might be the oil industry facing the advent of electric cars or insurance companies having to devise new strategies, products and organizational changes in the light of the diffusion of autonomous driving, robotics or next generation genomics. Analysis of industrial change in interdependent industries is notoriously difficult: it implies the study of complex dynamics and co-evolutionary processes that may entail a variety of direct and indirect feedbacks as well as unintended consequences. Some work in this direction has been developed but a lot remains to be done [41]. Yet, this is a crucial source of challenges for both incumbents and potential competitors.

A second important area of research concerns the role of regulation and standards in the processes of creative destruction and innovative competition. They clearly play a major role in shaping the evolution of the industries and the fate of the companies involved. The case of the Internet is an excellent example and recent studies show how important and complex are the processes that lead to the development of those rules, standards and laws [42]. Here again, much remains to be understood.

References

1. K. Marx and F. Engels, The Manifesto of the Communist Party, 1848.
2. J. A. Schumpeter, The Theory of Economic Development: An Inquriy into Profits, Capital, Credit, Interest and the Business Cycle, Transaction Publishers, 1934.
3. J. A. Schumpeter, Captialism, Socialism and Democracy, New York: Harper & Row, 1942.
4. G. Dosi and R. R. Nelson, "Technical change and industrial dynamics as evolutionary processes," in *Handbook of the economics of innovation, Volume 1*, Burlington, Academic Press, 2010, pp. 51–128.
5. C. Freeman and C. Perez, "Structural crisis of adjustment, business cycles and investment behaviour," in *Technical Change and Economic Theory*, London, Frances Pinter, 1988, pp. 38–66.
6. T. Bresnahan, "General Purpose Technologies," in *Handbook of the Economics of Innovation, Volume 2*, Amsterdam, Elsevier, 2010, pp. 761–791.
7. F. Louçã and S. Mendonça, "Steady change: the 200 largest US manufacturing firms throughout the 20th century," *Industrial and Corporate Change, 11 (4)*, pp. 817–845.
8. J. L. Bower and C. M. Christensen, "Disruptive Technologies: Catching the Wave," in *Harvard Business Review 73, no 1*, 1995, pp. 43–53.
9. E. Danneels, "From the Guest Editor: Dialogue on The Effects of Disruptive Technology on Firms and Industries," *Journal of Product Innovation Management, 23 (1)*, pp. 2–4.
10. e. Danneels, "Disruptive Technology Reconsidered: A Critique and Research Agenda," *Journal of Product Innovation Management. 21 (4)*, pp. 246–258.
11. J. Lepore, "The Disruption Machine. What the gospel of innovation gets wrong," *The New Yorker, Annals of Enterprise*, 23 June 2014.
12. A. A. King and B. Baatartogtokh, "How Useful Is the Theory of Disruptive Innovation?," *MIT Sloan Management Review*, September 2015.
13. M. Weeks, "Is disruption theory waring new clothes or just naked? Analyzing recent critiques of disruptive innovation theory," *Innovation: Management, Policy & Practice, 17:4*, pp. 417–428, 2015.
14. G. Dosi, "Statistical regularities in the evolution of industries. A guide thorugh some evidence and challenges for the theory," in *Perspectives on innovation*, Cambridge/New York, Cambridge University Press, 2007.
15. N. Bloom and J. Van Reenen, "Why Do Management Practices Differ across Firms and Countries?," in *Journal of Economic Perspectives 24 (1)*, 2010, pp. 203–24.

16. K. Pavitt, M. Robson and J. Townsend, "The Size Distribution of Innovating Firms in the UK," *The Journal of Industrial Economics, Vol. 35, No. 3*, pp. 297–316, 1987.
17. G. Dosi, "Technological paradigms and technological trajectories. A suggested interpretation of the determinats and directions of technical change," in *Research Policy, 11 (3)*, 1982, pp. 147–162.
18. K. Pavitt, "Sectoral Patterns of Technical Change: Towards a Taxonomy and a Theory," *Research Policy, 13*, pp. 343–373.
19. G. Dosi, O. Marsili, L. Orsenigo and R. Salvatore, "Learning, market selection and the evolution of industrial structures," in *Small Business Economics, 7*, 1995, pp. 411–436.
20. S. Breschi, F. Malerba and L. Orsenigo, "Technological regimes and SChumpeterian patterns of innovation," in *Economic Journal, 110 (463)*, 2000, pp. 388–410.
21. F. Malerba, R. Nelson, L. Orsenigo and S. Winter, Innovation and the Evolution of Industries. History Friendly Models, Cambridge: Cambridge University Press, 2016.
22. C. Freeman, J. Clark and L. Soete, Unemployment and Technical Innovation, London: Pinter Publishers, 1982.
23. R. R. Nelson and S. G. Winter, An evolutionary theory of economic change, Cambridge Mass: Harvard University Press, 1982.
24. S. G. Winter, "Schumpeterian competition in alternative technological regimes," *Journal of Economic Behavior & Organization, Vol. 5(3–4)*, pp. 287–320, 1984.
25. F. Malerba and L. Orsenigo, "Technological regimes and sectoral patterns of innovative activitives," *Industrial and Corporate Change, 6(1)*, pp. 83–117.
26. F. Malerba, "Sectoral systems of innovation and production," *Research Policy 31*, pp. 247–264, 2002.
27. F. Malerba, Sectoral Systems of Innovation: Concepts, Issues and Analyses of Six Major Sectors in Europe, Cambridge: Cambridge University Press, 2004.
28. R. Rumelt, "How much dies industry matter?," *Strategic Management Journal, 12(3)*, pp. 167–185, 1991.
29. R. R. Nelson, "Why do Firms Differ, and How Does it Matter?," *Strategic Management Journal 12(S2)*, pp. 61–74.
30. T. Bresnahan, S. M. Greenstein and R. M. Henderson, "Schumpeterian Competition and Diseconomies of Scope; Illustrations from the Histories of Microsoft and IBM," in *The Rate and Direction of Inventive Activity Revisited*, Chicago, University of Chicago Press, 2012, pp. 203–271.
31. M. Tushman and P. Anderson, "Technological Discontinuities and Organizational Environments," *Administrative Science Quarterly, 31(3)*, pp. 439–465, 1986.
32. D. Leonard-Barton, "Core Capabilities and Core Rigidities: A Paradox in Managing New Product Development," *Strategic Management Journal 13(2)*, pp. 111–126.
33. W. J. Abernathy and K. B. Clark, "Innovation: Mapping the Winds of Creative Destruction," in *Research Policy 14(1)*, 1985, pp. 3–22.
34. C. Christensen and R. S. Rosenbloom, "Explaining the attacker's advantage: technological paradigms, organizational dynamics, and the value network," in *Research Policy 24*, 1995, pp. 233–257.
35. H. Chesbrough, "Assembling the Elephant: A Review of Empirical Studies on the Impact of Technical Change upon Incumbent Firms," in *The Netherlands: Research on Technological Innovatioin, Management and Policy*, 2001, pp. 1–36.
36. R. Henderson, "The Innovator's Dilemma as a Problem of Organizational Competence," *The Journal of Product Innovation Management, 23*, pp. 5–11, 2006.
37. D. Levinthal, "Adaptation on Rugged Landscapes," *Management Science 43(7)*, pp. 934–950.

38. D. Teece, G. Pisano and A. Shuen, "Dynamic Capabilities and Strategic Management," *Strategic Management Journal, 18(7),* pp. 509–533, 1997.
39. Cohen and Levinthal, "Innovation and learning: The two faces of R&D," in *The Economic Journal, Volume 99,* September, pp. 569–596.
40. Cohen and Levinthal, "Absorptive capacity: A new perspectiveon learning and innovation," in *Administrative Science Quarterly, Volume 35, Issue 1,* 1990, pp. 128–152.
41. F. Malerba, R. Nelson and L. W. S. Orsenigo, "Vertical integration and disintegration of computer firms: a history-friendly model of the coevolution of the computer and semiconductor industries," *Industrial and Corporate Change, 17(2),* pp. 197–231, 2008.
42. S. Greenstein, How the Internet Became Commercial: Innovation, Privatization, and the Birth of a New Network, Princeton: Princeton University Press, 2015.

Further Reading

43. R. Adner, "When Are Technologies Disruptive: A Demand Based View of the Emergence of Competition," in *Strategic Management Journal 24(10),* 2002, pp. 1011–1027.
44. C. M. Christensen, The innovator's dilemma: when new technologies cause great firms to fail, Boston, Massachusetts, USA: Harvard Business School Press, 1997.
45. R. M. Henderson and K. B. Clark, "Architectural Innovation: The Reconfiguration of Existing Product Technologies and the Failure of Established Firms," *Administrative Science Quarterly 35(1),* pp. 9–30.
46. F. Malerba and L. Orsenigo, "Technological Regimes and Firm Behavior," *Industrial and Corporate Change, 2,* pp. 45–74, 1993.
47. D. Teece, "Profiting from technological innovation: Implications for integration, collaboration, licensing and public policy," *Research Policy, 15(6),* pp. 285–305, 1986.

Part VI
Digital Business Outcomes

Preface: Digital Business Outcomes

23

Jan Zadak

The *Global world* is transforming at an unprecedented speed offering unique opportunities to new market players yet representing sometimes unique challenges to established companies. Whilst many aspects of a typical company operations have been digitized over the past decades, we are currently experiencing true *Digital* disruption in every industry.

Fundamentally *New Business Models* on the one hand and *Digital Transformation* of the established business architectures on the other are offering both newcomers as well as established firms a unique possibility to challenge the status quo and impose disruptive market movements.

Over the past decades, the IT industry has often played an enablement role: ranging from ERP systems, transactional CRM system, supply-chain systems, manufacturing execution systems, data archiving and records management systems, etc. IT has mostly been positioned as the "to have" cost item on the company strategy charts and investment priorities.

Yet the *Global Digital World* has changed the competitive landscape once and forever. Achieving business agility and market reach, creating brand awareness and product preference, driving ongoing compliance and market leadership through differentiated capabilities and unique customer experience is mostly impossible without IT taking on a central role within the company strategy, unleashing hidden internal company resources and assets while opening potential new external market opportunities.

Yet the central questions for most of the established players are *"How do I approach my company Digital Transformation?"*, *"Where do I start?"*, and *"How do I fund it?"*.

Many leaders have found inspiration in the *value disciplines strategy framework* originally developed by Michael Treacy and Fred Wiersema well outlined in their book *"The*

J. Zadak (✉)
Hewlett-Packard Enterprise
Vresova, Czech Republic
e-mail: jan.zadak@hpe.com

© Springer-Verlag GmbH Germany 2018
C. Linnhoff-Popien et al. (eds.), *Digital Marketplaces Unleashed*,
https://doi.org/10.1007/978-3-662-49275-8_23

Discipline of Market Leaders"1 [1] and centered around three value disciplines: *operational excellence, product leadership,* and *customer intimacy.*

In his very inspirational book *"Digital Disciplines"2.* Joe Weinman introduces four *Digital Disciplines*: *information excellence, solution leadership, collective intimacy,* and *accelerated innovation* [2].

"Playing To Win"3, [3] is one of the best business books ever published on this subject providing pragmatic and practical playbook on how to makes strategic choices and implement winning strategy in practice.

The author firmly believes that *Business strategy* and *Business architecture* should and must be the starting points when building *Digital strategy.* Answering questions about "How will the company differentiate and compete in the marketplace? How will it win? How will it create value?" are at the core of the matter. Those answers help articulate essential points of view of "What is core" and "What is non-core" in terms of company portfolio, go-to-market strategy, company value proposition and innovation as well as company core assets and investment focus areas.

Underlying company *Business processes* then reflect the above strategy and the way company intends to execute and define its *Management system.*

Digital architectures offer a myriad of opportunities to leveraging external marketplace for sourcing, delivery and executing those business processes, tasks and activities that are non-core to company value creation, value proposition and business architecture. As an example Software as a Service (*SaaS*) offerings, Business Process as a Service (BPaaS) capabilities, etc. offer consumption based models to deploy target business architecture, at highly competitive cost. Their effective and efficient integration with the retain organization and the delivery operating model are one of the major cornerstones to drive true *Business Outcomes from Digital transformation.*

Over the past 20 years, Global corporations have been deploying *global shared services* architectures mostly aimed at reducing costs. Different *maturity models* have been applied to achieve synergies and drive evolution of the global shared services models. The underlying benefit comes from the fact that those models in general forced corporations to think hard about their organization efficiency, effectiveness and value creation. The time is ripe to take full benefit from Digital Transformation in the broadest sense. Whilst global shared services organizations have been mostly focused on the efficiency to be gained in the back-end part of the company, digital transformation can be deployed across the entire value-creation chain. Creating *Digital transformation maturity model* helps drive the right discussion yet it is important that *Business Outcomes* "lenses" are extensively used to prioritize and sequence the digital transformation programs.

Strategy – technology – people – processes underpinned by a major management of change. This is a typical framework for digital transformation.

Starting with the *business model and strategy* angle, the business model innovation anchored on digital technologies has firmly established itself as a major market disruptor. More than $77 trillion global economy offers vast playing field – essentially unlimited opportunities exit to replace and disrupt existing market players by serving existing customer needs through new digitally-enabled means. This includes many well-known examples from the travel & transportation industry (Uber) and hospitality industries (Airbnb). Retail digital disruption is firing on all cylinders as well. Several major established industry conglomerates are either entering the digital arena through their own "4.0" products and capabilities (e. g. GE, Bosch IoT Cloud) or are transforming their internal digital capabilities.

On the *technology* side *Hybrid cloud, IaaS, PaaS, BPaaS, master-data management, security and risk management, business outcome service SLA's, big data and information management, DevOps, automation, robotics, IoT* are some equally typical cornerstones of Digital Transformations. These can define whether a corporation will prosper in the new Digital world or whether it is going to disappear from the list of meaningful industry players.

The *People* aspect of the digital transformation is in the authors' experience vastly underestimated, vastly underleveraged and in many transformations grossly neglected. It is essential to map out the talent, skills, experience and capabilities needed to succeed in the transformation as well as to land the new business model.

Let's go back to one of the central questions for any company Digital Transformation *"How do I fund it?"*. Most of the established corporations rely on highly customized operations. This highly customized business architecture is often underpinned by expensive, monolithic applications enabling the company to execute on the exiting business model yet imposing high costs, low flexibility and a lack of agility. Any change in company direction aiming at increasing market relevance and competiveness is cumbersome, expensive with poor time-to-results.

Most companies can unlock short-term and mid-term value by improving the IT delivery model on their global infrastructure through appropriate deployment of the hybrid cloud in direct combination with IT operations automation. This approach can free-up capital and execution bandwidth to start deploying agile development method or directly DevOps methodology to exponentially increase company IT agility, responsiveness and ability to build digital assets. When well executed both steps also typically yield better operational stability and IT services availability.

Mid- and long-term funding opportunities exist in unlocking value from non-core yet highly customized parts of the operations. This is the more complex Digital Transformation part yet the one offering typically sustainable roadmap to creating meaningful business outcomes. Whilst IT can help connect the dots, creating customer and shareholder value, market leadership and sustainable competitive differentiation won't happen without the top company leaders leading along the way.

This part of the Digital transformation is highly complex and offers multiple different approaches. Segmenting such transformation into smaller transformational programs offers a way to de-risk the transformation and also to prioritize the execution of the individual transformation modules based on business outcomes (= value) vs. risk assessment.

It is important to note that any such transformation is making the traditional perimeter-based security approach obsolete. New *cyber-defense* strategy and deployment is needed to assure appropriate security and safeguarding of the company assets.

Innovation is the more intriguing and often highly unpredictable aspect of the Digital Transformation. Creating meaningful business outcomes through *digital (business model) innovation* often requires a whole new set of topics to be addressed: where do you focus your innovation, how do you enable it, how do you encourage it, how do you take benefit of it? Establishing Innovation labs and Digital Innovation centers of excellence is key to enabling the employees to focus on innovation, stimulating fast prototyping and fast learning accelerating the idea-to-concept-to-solution cycles and ultimately maximizing the company business outcomes in the shortest timeframe.

In summary, the global world is going through one of its largest transformations ever fueled by Digital technologies. Global economy is being fundamentally reshaped. New and established players are taking advantage of the new digital business models, digital innovations and underpinning technologies. Established players do not need to be necessarily on the losers' side. They can benefit from their established brands, scale and market credibility yet need to embark on an end-to-end digital transformation of their business models, management systems, IT and operations to remain relevant. Meaningful business outcomes can be derived from such transformation if well planned and executed with total endorsement of the company leadership.

References

1. Treacy, M., & Wiersema, F. (1995). *The Discipline of Market Leaders.* Addison-Wesley.
2. Weinman, J. (2015). Digital Disciplines. Hoboken, New Jersey: John Wiley & Sons.
3. Lafley, A., & Martin, R. L. (2013). *Playing To Win.* Boston: Havard Business Review Press.

Software Industrialisation – How to Industrialise Knowledge Work?

24

Josef Adersberger and Johannes Siedersleben

Abstract

Industrial production has been paramount for survival on competitive markets. But what does this mean for software development? Will occidental programmers be supplanted by computers churning out software? Or by hordes of low paid programmers in India as clothing manufacturers have been by sewers in Bangladesh? Industrialisation is usually measured in terms of production capacity (how much can you produce per day?) and production price (at what unit costs?). This raises two questions: (1) What is a suitable unit of software quantity? And (2) how do you calculate the unit price? The answer to (1) should depend on the value a piece of software really affords the user, which leads to the notion of a *feature* with measurable benefit. A rash answer to (2) would be "required time multiplied by labour costs" but this neglects quality debts caused by flaws such as unclean code, careless testing, lacking functions, breached architecture, poor performance or insufficient data security. Software debts tend to go unnoticed for a while but lead to a dead end in the long run: time and money is squandered on imperative repairs while new features grow more and more expensive, with the project being finally brought to a grinding halt. This article explains what software industrialisation really means and how it is achieved. And, most importantly, it tells how to keep quality debts close to zero.

J. Adersberger (✉) · J. Siedersleben
QAware GmbH
Munich, Germany
e-mail: josef.adersberger@qaware.de

J. Siedersleben
e-mail: johannes.siedersleben@qaware.de

© Springer-Verlag GmbH Germany 2018
C. Linnhoff-Popien et al. (eds.), *Digital Marketplaces Unleashed*,
https://doi.org/10.1007/978-3-662-49275-8_24

24.1   What is Software Industrialisation?

This paper is based on our experience with small to large scale industrial applications in areas such as automotive and telecommunication. We believe our observations valid for knowledge work in general, and by no means confined to any particular type of software such as cloud applications or embedded systems. In every area there are specific tricks of the trade, but any type software production is knowledge work performed by humans and quite different from industrial production on assembly lines, with analogies being rare and often misleading.

The world needs more software than it is able to produce. But programs can be written all over the world, well-trained programmers in many countries are globally available. We therefore should be able to

- Increase the software production capacity,
- Decrease the unit costs.

Industrialisation simply boils down to increasing capacity at decreasing unit costs. Industrialisation is well defined for conventional manufacturing processes but not so for knowledge work. This raises two questions:

1. What is a suitable unit of software quantity?
   This should depend on the value a piece of software really affords the user. We therefore suggest measuring the quantity of software produced by the accumulated *business value* of all implemented *features*.
2. What is the cost of a software unit?
   A rash answer would be "required time multiplied by labour costs" but this formula neglects quality debts caused by flaws such as unclean code, careless testing, lacking functions, breached architecture, poor performance or insufficient data security. Software debts tend to go unnoticed for a while but lead to a dead end in the long run: time and money is squandered on imperative repairs while new features grow more and more expensive, with the project being finally brought to a grinding halt. This undesirable state is sometimes called software bankruptcy. The difference between costs of a software change in a normal state and those in a degenerated state is called quality debts, aka technical debts (see Fig. 24.1).

Modifying degenerated software is expensive because in excess of the proper change there is a lot of work to do:

- The spots affected are hard to find,
- The change itself is hard to design,
- Side effects are hard to predict and even harder to eliminate if they arise.

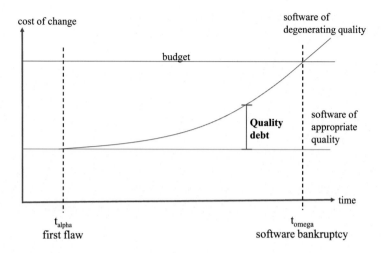

Fig. 24.1 Quality Debts

This extra work gets more expensive as software degenerates. We therefore urge to put all quality debts on the TCO bill. This paragraph can be summarised by two simple equations:

a) Production capacity = accumulated business value of all implemented features divided by required time.
b) Unit costs = required time × labour cost + quality debt

24.2   How Software Industrialisation Doesn't Work: Offshore

We are talking about the well-known approach having software developed offshore, by hordes of low paid programmers. The idea is simply to

1. Increase capacity by large teams and to
2. Decrease unit costs by low wages

This might have worked in special cases but cannot be considered a sound recipe in the long run. There are at least two objections:

1. Team size can only be increased to a hard upper bound [1]. Tom DeMarco's rule defines it as the square root of the total project effort in man months [2]. Teams larger than that are hard to manage and find their productivity decreased.
2. Unit labour costs tend to increase because good developers have always been rare, regardless of global availability. The cheap price of average developers is more than compensated by the quality debts they induce.

24.3 How Software Industrialisation Does Work: Increase of Productivity and Quality

We are suggesting a different approach, suitable for highly industrialised countries like Germany.

1. Increase productivity at constant team size, that is: reduce the time per unit of business value generated, meaning simply to accelerate processes and to concentrate on the most highly valued features. This increases productivity and decreases unit costs at the same time.
2. Keep quality high and quality debts close to zero. Measure quality debts continuously and eradicate them as they sprout. This again decreases unit costs and increases productivity.

The following paragraphs explain by examples how to increase productivity and quality simultaneously.

24.3.1 Productivity by Flow

Whoever has written a program, a book, or done handicrafts knows what flow is: a state of concentration, dedication to a task, undisturbed by the outside, feeling the progress and being imbued with ideas [3]. People are productive when in flow, so we would like them to get there and to stay as long as possible.

Uninterrupted Working
It has been show that interruptions of only a few seconds can reduce concentration and divert from flow for as long as 20 min [4]. This is illustrated by the saw tooth effect: productivity is increasing for a while and then plummeting on the next interruption. Getting back into flow is a painful battle, soon frustrated by another interruption. Minimising interruptions can be achieved by obvious means:

- Small offices tend to be quieter than open-plan ones. There are fewer phone calls, fewer chats.
- Quiet hours are guarded time slots with no phone calls and no conversations allowed. Even emails must wait.
- Rules for interruptions define accessibility. This can be a closed door, a signal light on the desk or any other sign.
- Opportunities for retreat: particular offices or the home office as a quiet place to retire to.
- Tools protecting against distraction: several tools (editors and others) provide a *Distraction Free Mode*, inhibiting whatever could get you out of flow.

Perfect Working Environment

It has not always been recognised that flow requires a perfect working environment. People won't get into flow unless they feel happy and are provided with the best tools available. This means in particular:

- The offices should be friendly and welcoming, with plenty of light and space.
- User friendly tools on efficient hardware are a must. Programmers need two or three large screens of the highest available quality.

24.3.2   Productivity by Automation

Tedious, repetitive tasks cut into the programmer's flow as much as unwelcome interruptions. We therefore must automate the development process as much as possible, and really, there is a lot one can do, after several errors and dead ends in the past such as model-driven software development. The first thing to note is that there are two completely different jobs: *invention* and *production*. It is *invention* that adds the value, and it is *production* that makes it available to users of all kinds, from seasoned testers to unskilled end users. Software developers continuously invent new solutions, casting requirements into code. They therefore need freedom to invent and tools to pin down, try and fix their inventions. Once the software is finished it is passed over to the *Build Pipeline* [5] which integrates the artefacts of many developers into new software versions delivered to test, training or production. It automatically processes software through stages such as unit test, quality-check, integration, deployment and distribution.

24.3.3   Productivity by Low Vertical Integration

Minimizing vertical integration means just maximising reuse, and that in three regards: reuse of *software*, of *infrastructure* and of *knowledge*.

Reuse whatever *software* has been programmed by others, what is available in reusable form and useful to your project. Software development today involves much software OEM (original equipment manufacturing) and comparatively little original programming. A plethora of powerful and well-tried open source components are available at no royalties. Evaluation and integration are not free, of course, but it would be foolish not to benefit from this treasure. Samples on real, large scale projects have shown vertical integration rates of only 1 to 7% (i. e. share of original code). But quality debts are ever looming large: open source components must be thoroughly evaluated, scrutinized and integrated. Obvious criteria include licence issues, security, side effects, and hidden dependencies. GitHub affords a simple, fool proof access to whatever open source products you can dream of.

Reusing *infrastructure* is achieved by getting it from professional providers through simple plug-in mechanisms. The build pipeline, repositories and many more tools run like any other mission critical production software on a professionally managed infrastructure. Processes are automated using tools like Jenkins for continuous integration and delivery. Private servers running unmanaged under the desk and crashing at inappropriate times are long gone. This is a beautiful example of self-reference: the rules applicable to the development environment are identical to the ones the developed software is subjected to.

Reusing *knowledge* is achieved by visiting websites like Google Search, stackoverflow and many others. The world's knowledge is never more than few clicks away. Gone are long shelves of unreadable and outdated manuals. But searching the internet is an art to be taught: how to tell reliable information, which site is useful for what question?

24.3.4 Productivity by Focusing on Real Benefit

Software development has often been regarded as a process casting requirement into code: requirements in, code out. But this simple model falls short of taking into account the requirement's real benefit. Questions to ask include obviously the following:

- What is the real benefit of a requirement? Can it be measured?
- What if it is dropped?
- Are there cheaper alternatives? There might be a completely different approach.
- Are there any tools around able to do the job?

The overall objective function of software development is the accumulated benefit of all implemented features, not their sheer number. Focusing on the right features (doing the right things) can increase productivity vastly more than just optimizing the development process (doing things right).

24.3.5 Productivity by Quality

Software quality is holistic. The standard ISO/IEC 9126 defines a comprehensive set of quality indicators but even lousy software sometimes complies with it. Software quality is much more than working functions and few crashes. It includes properties such as

- Security, data protection, non-hackability
- Performance, reliability, resilience, scalability
- Maintainability, portability
- Usability, freedom from barriers

All of these properties must be continuously measured, recorded, analysed and published by tools integrated into the build pipeline. This guarantees immediate detection of quality debts and induces within the team the feeling of a crack unit as long as the debts

Fig. 24.2 The Essence of
Quality Debts

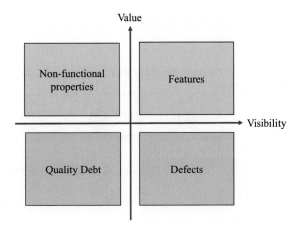

are close to zero. And if they are higher than expected, the management knows at least where the problems are. Let us dwell on this point a bit longer.

Quality debts have the undesirable property to turn up late, when things have really gone wrong. The problem is this (see Fig. 24.2): functions and defects are visible for all users. But compliance to quality measures and the amount of quality debts is often invisible and assessed if at all in selective reviews only.

We therefore suggest proceeding in three steps:

Step 1: Defining Measures
We identify measurable properties suitable as quality indicators, including static features laying in the source code and dynamic ones measurable only when the software is running. Fig. 24.3 shows samples of both types.

Step 2: Defining a Quality Contract
For each selected quality indicator we define lower and/or upper bounds, we define what values are desirable, barely acceptable or to be refused to pass the build pipeline. The set

Static Analysis	**Dynamic Analysis**
• Code anomalies	• Runtime anomalies
• Code metrics	• Runtime metrics
• Code conventions	• Test coverage
• Dependency structures	• Time and resource behaviour
(e.g. cycles)	• Errors and exceptions
• Duplications	• User behaviour
• Architecture violations	• Possible attack vectors
• …	• Accessibility problems
	• …

Fig. 24.3 Static and Dynamic Analysis

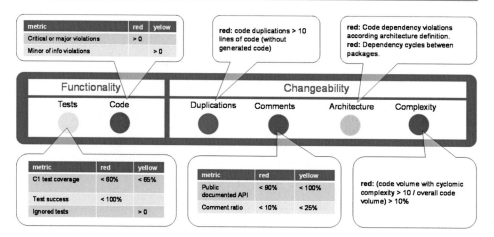

Fig. 24.4 Our Quality Contract

of these rules is called the *quality contract*, see Fig. 24.4. The example shown is the one we are using daily.

Step 3: Visualising Deviations

Like any contract the quality contract must be supervised, deviations detected and reacted upon. We are obviously not suggesting a pillory for the culprits, but software debts must be made visible, analysed and repaired.

We use an information radiator (see Fig. 24.5) for this purpose. This is a large screen, conspicuously placed in the coffee corner, showing the software quality or the lack thereof.

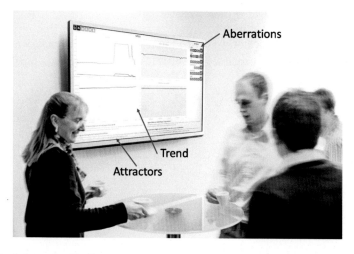

Fig. 24.5 An Information Radiator

Reported quality puts everybody in a good mood, beginning decay can be thwarted early. Gimmicks (or attractors) such as news or comics can increase the attention allocated to the radiator.

24.4   Conclusion

Software development can be industrialised by improving productivity and quality at the same time. We have presented some well-tried recipes, with offshore deliberately excluded, focusing on increasing each individual's productivity, the degree of automation, the reuse of software, infrastructure and knowledge. Implementing the right things in the right order is often the most important clue to productivity. High quality increases productivity if suitably managed. It is hence one of the few free lunches in this world.

This is how software development will be fit for international competition, even in a high-wage country like Germany.

References

1. F. Brooks, The mythical man-month, Addison-Wesley, 1975.
2. T. DeMarco, T. R. Lister and D. House, Peopleware: productive projects and teams, Pearson Education, 2013.
3. M. Csikszentmihalyi, Flow: The psychology of optimal experience, HarperPerennial, 1991.
4. L. Seiwert, Das neue 1x1 des Zeitmanagements, Gabler, 2006.
5. J. Humble and D. Farley, Continuous delivery: reliable software releases through build, test, and deplyoment automation, 2010.

From Digital Retail to Real-Time Retail

Andreas Kranabitl and Robert Pikart

Abstract

The chapter is about how customer behavior in the digital world challenges retailers to reinvent its current enterprise setup and IT approach and shift to a Digital Division Enterprise.

While in the past, retailers tried to create customer categories out of statistical, historical data, today we have to satisfy the customer's here-and-now mentality with dynamic information related exactly on the customer's here-and-now perception.

That is why we have to connect the customer over different technologies, over different touch points with digital data and digital knowledge. Touch points to reach the customer are currently digital signage environments, ibeacons and the customer's smartphone.

The key point is a digital platform, acting as interface between the customer touch points and the multiple frontend and backend systems, which are the owners of all data and information. In fact, we need to know the customer needs and desires just in the moment he is touching the touch point.

A. Kranabitl (✉)
SPAR Business Services GmbH
Salzburg, Austria
e-mail: Andreas.Kranabitl@spar-ics.com

R. Pikart
Pikart IT Advisory GmbH
Vienna, Austria
e-mail: Robert.pikart@a1.net

© Springer-Verlag GmbH Germany 2018
C. Linnhoff-Popien et al. (eds.), *Digital Marketplaces Unleashed*,
https://doi.org/10.1007/978-3-662-49275-8_25

25.1   The Digital Retail Tsunami – Retail 4.0

The retail business area is changing due to the fact that customers are more and more using online, realtime applications to gather information on what's interesting, helpful and attractive. Consequently, the traditional way of how to inform and prepare customers about buying opportunities gets less relevant. Customers are pulling information when they want. Here and Now.

On the other hand, huge customer behavior related data-volume creates the opportunity for retailers to learn and understand customer needs and desire on individual level. Using these data leads/helps to generate holistic customer's insights, predict customer's shopping activities and find out which model of online stimulation motivates and supports the customer best. This means to establish a process, which is permanently monitoring customer's activities, analyzing reactions, creating stimulation and connect to retailer's strategies and business models – in real-time!

Future retail is not only online and mobile. It's necessary and business relevant to connect online/mobile with physical store shopping experience. This will be one of the key-success-factors for the near future. Providing a seamless platform that takes perfect care of its customers by having a tight and ongoing connection to retailer's guidance and services either through digital channels or directly at the retailer's store.

We have to achieve customer insights by analyzing and assembling different data in real time. This completely new approach, how to serve, guide, manage and attract customers has a significant impact on the retailer's strategies and priorities, overall on the internal organization.

While in the past of retail sales was supported by marketing and IT was a technology supporting department, internal positions and responsibilities are now changing. Sales is moving to a more operational level while Marketing takes over the extensive communication with customers. Marketing is strongly using the power of social media and communication. With the support out of the growing market of social services and analytics providers, they are in the perfect position to drive, influence and lead the business strategy. Because more and more activities of retail are becoming customer focused, marketing is starting to act as the strategic dispatcher between business and customer. This means, that most of customer related activities have to pass marketing processes and organization. Many of these activities are based on digital, online and mobile services.

This development, moving the strategic focus of retail on digital areas, changes the role of IT organization inside the retail companies and this change moves IT in a strong strategic position very close to the marketing division. This, too, leads to the fact that the collaboration between Marketing and IT becomes much more important and relevant. Both organizations are forced to establish appropriate processes, methodologies, teams and processes to follow the new business requirements. A key success factor in this phase is to align speed of reaction and speed of delivery to the expectations of this dynamic here-and-now business approach.

IT is now strongly challenged by the transformations that drive IT to a historical change of directions and focus areas. This means significant adjustments for IT in the areas of business-focus, application-portfolio, job-models, project- and delivery processes and IT organization. This is **RETAIL 4.0**

25.2 The IT Challenge

The evolution of retail business over the last two years forces IT divisions to rethink their mission and strategy to achieve a digital retail readiness. Why – because retailers can follow the developments in the business described above only if they have a powerful IT platform in place, which is able to deliver the right solutions for these business requirements.

The main challenge for IT divisions is to establish a digital strategy, a digital organization and a digital architecture. A historic opportunity for IT divisions in this scenario is to take over the leadership in digital retail innovation.

25.3 The Digital Division-How to

The entire development in the retail business, moving into a digital real-time retail era and the fact that digital is a domain of IT divisions, shifts IT from a supporting to a strategic business entity.

For a successful journey to the digital division it's essential to focus on the entire future digital ecosystem and develop along the following streams:

1. Explain the Digital Impact and Opportunities
2. Transform the IT Organization Digital Ready
3. Develop a Digital Innovation Network
4. Establish the Digital Platform
5. Take over the Digital Strategy
6. Become the Digital Division

25.3.1 Explain the Digital Impact and Opportunities

To achieve understanding of how digital will influence the retail business IT must be the incubator for translating digital into the language of retailers and show, how and why technology is the key success factor in the near future.

Examples from other business areas like automotive could help to understand the effect of creating customer value by using technology and real-time customer focused business models.

TRADITIONAL DEVELOPMENT AREAS   DIGITAL BUSINESS DEVELOPMENT AREAS

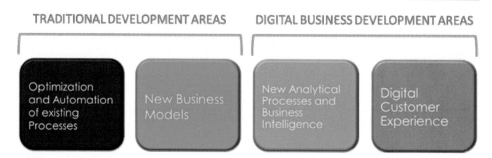

Fig. 25.1 Development Areas

Already existing digital solutions as benchmarks and best practice must be shown to support common understanding of what digital means on business level.

A specific digital readiness assessment is an effective exercise to show areas of strengths and weaknesses and provides a starting point for strategic development. From experience the outcome motivates the business to change mindset and strategic priorities.

IT divisions and CIO proactively must start initiatives in PRESENTING, STRATE-GIZING, MEDIATING and DIRECTING.

To support a rethinking of traditional retail business a model must be introduced, where the traditional, more inside oriented retail processes are detached from the future, outside oriented. The future strategic business areas in retail are potentially Digital Customer Experience and New Analytical Processes by Business Intelligence.

Strategic areas for digital business development are shown in Fig. 25.1.

25.3.2 Transform the IT Organization Digital Ready

Until now, IT organizations followed more or less the PLAN – BUILD – RUN model, which is the baseline for structure, processes, strategy and the mindset. For future challenges of IT, this model has to be extended and adjusted to the new strategic requirements, priorities and opportunities.

To enable the IT division to drive digital inside the enterprise, a culture of entrepreneurship, digital leadership and digital commitment has to be driven by the IT management. Focal area is the people area where new job opportunities and personal requirements for the digital environment must be shown and offered.

The organizational structure has to be extended by a strong architecture entity and a strategic innovation team. Both new parts of the IT organization have to be connected very close to the CIO to guarantee a strong strategic focus and make them able to overcome traditional conditions.

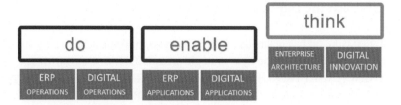

Fig. 25.2 DO-ENABLE-THINK Model

The traditional RUN and BUILD areas have to be split each into a ERP and a DIGITAL part to enforce digital ecosystems. Essential for a winning development is, to discover and utilize the right people for the new assignments.

The model DO – ENABLE – THINK, as shown in Fig. 25.2, offers the right setting to combine the traditional (ERP) and the new digital IT workforce and enable IT to drive and support the entire business.

In the THINK area, the future of the business is the focal perspective. Plan and establish the right IT architecture is essential to support innovative projects. Having the right architecture in place when needed is a prerequisite for short-time-to-market projects.

The digital innovation team is widely self-contained and must be driven in a disruptive mindset and working methodology.

25.3.3 Develop a Digital Innovation Network

To drive the digital evolution inside the enterprise, IT can act as an incubator to motivate and enable business to understand and execute digital opportunities.

Precisely because IT divisions are familiar with development, project execution and experimental environment, IT can offer methodologies and experience to the business to support, drive and lead digital innovation initiatives. An innovation team out of selected open-minded people with the right spirit and ability to execute like a start-up is the key success factor for this approach.

Sustainable senior management support, to connect this storming team with enterprise strategy and resources enables the team to influence the business by showing realistic and disruptive opportunities.

Beyond internal engagements, an open collaboration with business partners, who are supporting common innovation projects, will open completely new opportunities by connecting knowledge and ideas from different business levels. A perfect teamwork between retailers and technology driven companies can lead to outstanding business solutions, which are only achievable out of this framework.

25.3.4 Establish the Digital Platform

After the digital tsunami has reached retailer's business, priorities are step by step chang-ing and activities are started in the new strategic areas DIGITAL CUSTOMER EXPERI-ENCE and NEW ANALYTICAL PROCESSES BY BUSINESS INTELLIGENCE. How-ever, existing platforms representing the traditional ERP architecture cannot fulfill the business expectations.

The challenge in this area is to setup a future-proof architecture for new solutions, integrate the legacy environment and establish a strategy to plan and execute. Due to the fact that the number of Applications (APPS) is growing fast and wild, the new architecture must deliver a centralized, high-flexible, digital backbone of business-functionality which acts as service-provider for all the business APPS. This digital backbone is connected to the legacy application environment and this is the one and only way, how digital APPS can access the ERP environment.

25.3.5 Take over the Digital Strategy

From experience, companies do not focus on the digital wave. They are either driven by external influencers or they react on digital conditions step by step as they appear. The IT division is in most cases effected first by digital requirements. Out of this situation, IT is the more probable candidate to initiate the strategic preparation of the digital era on enterprise level. After showing what digital means, a proper and high-level picture must be provided together with a raw strategic orientation of activities to move from theory into practice.

IT has to act very proactive in this role and should offer methodology and structure to create a digital enterprise roadmap. In this scenario, a holistic picture considering also the legacy stuff is important to guarantee the right strategic balance.

25.3.6 Become the Digital Division

Summarizing all the activities, IT is able to execute a movement from the business sup-porting into a strategic enterprise entity. Main objectives of this new role is to be the first reference for digital affairs inside the enterprise as well as for external partners.

This means a significant change for IT divisions because beyond digital competences and strategies, IT has to improve the way to communicate and behavior that is more fo-cused on business strategy and digital innovation driver.

From a retailer's perspective, IT has to join the strategic circle of sales and marketing.

25.4　Unleashed Real Time Retail

After the IT organization and the IT platforms are digital ready it's time to deploy business functionality and show the retail business how the future will work.

Reflecting the digital platform, a highly flexible, time-to-market focused infrastructure has to be in place. This means technology like in-memory databases, cloud solutions and new dimension of customer relationship management (CRM) environments.

Fig. 25.3 shows the combinations that will be described in the next paragraphs.

25.4.1　The Basic Steps

In our specific case, we extended our long-term architecture approach. In a first step, we set up an in-memory infrastructure of a strategic software partner to have this in-memory technology in place. Furthermore, be ready to use business solutions for real time retail, which are consequently only available on this future oriented technology.

Next step is to implement a customer-experience-engine for a 360° customer experience service to fulfill a complete customer journey online, store and mobile. The platform is highly connected to all business and customer relevant systems and is acting as business-intelligence and customer-experience-provider.

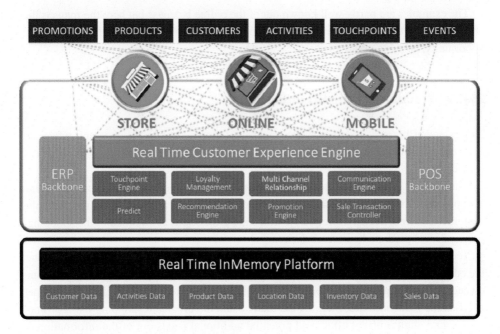

Fig. 25.3　Real Time Customer Experience Platform

Beyond the functional improvements, this architecture will possibly solve historical lacks and issues in the existing architecture because it's an opportunity to hide historical complexity for new requirements and systems and act as an accelerator to simplify technology and provide speed and flexibility.

A powerful platform allows storing all relevant data along the customer journey and a real-time communication with the customer whenever he touches our retail business.

25.4.2   Digital Customer Experience Solutions

Cool technology is of course the enabler for digital customer experience, furthermore impressing digital touch points are ultimate success-factors to generate competitive advantages and benefits. These digital touch points must support and inspire the customers and push them, to appreciate our services and our offerings. For all solutions in this area it's a must to think and design from the customer's perspective and celebrate a strict outside-in-approach.

A very tight collaboration between sales, marketing and IT in a corresponding environment with innovative processes and methodologies is the baseline and a winning approach.

The following solutions should show prototypes for innovative retailers to support them to understand the capabilities they could have in hand with a digital ready IT division and real-time technology.

The examples are partly well known out of the online business but here the focus is the physical store. It should demonstrate that also in physical environment digital steps are an opportunity, possible and realistic.

25.4.3   Solution #1 – the Extended Brain

The extended brain is a customer experience solution where in the moment, when the customer is touching a shopping-touch-point, a custom-made real-time shopping list is provided.

The content of this shopping list is assembled out of the customer's manual online shopping list, shopping-proposals out of historical purchases and sequences matching the customer's current needs. Moreover, just-in-time promotions are aligned to the shopping-proposals and predicted customer desires.

Technology: Via mobile app, beacon technology and the customer-experience-engine, the customer is identified when he enters a store. In real-time, historical purchases are analyzed to discover patterns in products and sequences and predict the articles the customer needs at the moment. After merging the manual and the predicted shopping list, a promotion engine aligns current offers and potential additional needs out of the information of the shopping list. In the last step, the availability of the proposed articles in the specific store is checked and in case of not-in-stock substitutes can be proposed. The maximum of value generation in shopping stimulation.

Assuming the proposal fits the customer's expectations on high-level, a customer experience like the support of a living, personal shopping assistant, who is reading the customer desires from his eyes, is in place.

25.4.4   Solution #2 – the Virtual Physical Store

Retailers and especially food retailers are facing two developments in the market. First, more and more different and specific products enter the market and the frequency of change is becoming faster than in in the past. Secondly, customers focus on specific brands, types and quality of food and health conditions are influencing the customer's shopping expectations.

These developments are stressing retailers and customers. Retailers are investing much to find the right presentation and the best location for the specific article out of several factors of influence. The customer on the other side is suffering to find his preferred type of articles in the store out of thousands. Here, a digital, mobile solution could simplify our life.

In a mobile App, customers can create their specific world of articles using various selection options – for example vegan, sugar free or specific brands – and get a mobile shopping layout out of articles in the selection area which are right-now available. They get a virtual store layout where they could check their current location in the store and see "their" articles only. Additionally, the customer gets support via a mobile in-store navigation to make him very easy to find his preferred products.

Technology: Again, the customer-experience-engine delivers the customers product-world. It assembles out of the real-time stock-information and the store/product shows the virtual assortment and virtual store layout.

25.5   Summary

In RETAIL 4.0 IT is facing the main challenge to establish a digital strategy, a digital organization and a digital architecture. This chapter showed a roadmap with six steps on how to develop an IT digital division to ensure real-time data availability and a unique digital customer experience.

In order to pro-actively support customer decisions and to identify customer needs before they even have identified it by themselves, it is highly recommended to connect the customer "live" to business processes. Moreover, depending on the business strategy of a retailer, and again especially in the food sector, a personal communication with the customer could be a key-success-factor to create an exciting shopping experience.

Having a look on the possibilities in Solution #1 and #2, retailers can apply this digital knowledge for direct and personal communication. Customer related information can be provided real-time when the customer enters the store on a mobile device of the shop-assistant. The shop-assistant then knows the specific expectations and regulations of the customer, the current shopping list and of course he gets relevant promotions based on real-time customer data. A perfect setting to positively attract the customer and show a perfect, individual service.

When being digital ready in the described way, having technology, knowledge and first-of-all the right digital team in place, then the possibilities to improve retail have no limits.

With a mindset to follow digital opportunities and with the ability to understand the interaction of physical and online business, retailers could be able to deploy an inspiring customer experience and improve business results.

Privacy Preserving Personalization in Complex Ecosystems

26

Anders Andersen and Randi Karlsen

Abstract

Personalization can be used to improve the quality of a service for a user. From the providers' perspective personalization can be used to better target its users. Personalization is achieved by creating and maintaining a user profile that describes the user, her interest and her current context. A major concern with creating, maintaining and using user profiles is user privacy and trust. In this chapter we will discuss the process of creating and maintaining user profiles with a privacy preserving focus.

26.1 Introduction

A typical user access and consumes products and services from a wide range of providers through many different channels. In a given example, music is streamed from a streaming service through a mobile network using a smart phone application distributed through the App Store of the smart phone platform. The discovery of the played music might be based on music reviews, news articles, friend's recommendation, search services, different forms of (internet) radio and TV, and automatic recommender systems. Even in this simple example it is difficult to get a complete overview of all the potential participants (companies, people, software) involved. Many of these participants might collect and provide data relevant for the user. Such data are both valuable and sensitive. From the provider's perspective such data can be used to create a product or a service that better targets the

A. Andersen (✉) · R. Karlsen
UiT The Arctic University of Norway
Tromsø, Norway
e-mail: Anders.Andersen@uit.no

R. Karlsen
e-mail: Randi.Karlsen@uit.no

© Springer-Verlag GmbH Germany 2018   247
C. Linnhoff-Popien et al. (eds.), *Digital Marketplaces Unleashed*,
https://doi.org/10.1007/978-3-662-49275-8_26

users. From the user's perspective such data can be used to improve the quality of received product or service. This is personalization.

Personalization is achieved by creating and maintaining a user profile. It includes user provided data, aggregated data from the user history, the current context, and integration of other data of relevance for the user (e. g. friend's data and data of users with similar behavior). The data involved in creating and maintaining the user profile might disclose a lot of information about the user. The privacy concerns should therefore be of great importance in such systems.

In this chapter, the process of creating and maintaining user profiles in a complex ecosystem with a wide range of participants is discussed. A major concern is user privacy and trust. This should include the ability of the user to influence what information about her that is shared and used. She should also herself decide when trust is established and what kind of trust that is established. The discussion includes the collection of input data to the process and approaches to process the data. The role of cryptography is also discussed.

26.2 Personalization and User Profile

Personalization is described as the ability to provide tailored content and services to individuals based on knowledge about their preferences and behavior [1]. With the huge amount of information and services available on the Internet, personalization has become a valuable tool for assisting users in searching, filtering and selecting items of interest. Examples of application areas include personalized search and recommendation, decision-making, and social and collaboration networks.

Personalization is well known in online stores and web based information systems, and is used in a wide range of applications and services including digital libraries, e-commerce, e-learning, search engines and for personalized recommendations of movies, music, books and news. Also, health-care, in particular in combination with Internet of Things (IoT), has a great potential of improving by applying personalization [2]. Techniques used for such personalization include demographic filtering [3], content-based filtering [4], collaborative filtering [5], social networks tagging [6], query and click-through history [7], collective search trails [8], implicit relevance feedback [9, 10], and hybrid approaches [11]. Personalization generates significant revenue for the advertising industry, and is used by businesses of various types to offer tailored goods and services to their customers.

26.2.1 User Profile

Existing personalization strategies require construction of *user profiles* that identify interests, behavior and other characteristics of individual users. A user profile can be described through a number of dimensions, including personal data (such as gender, age, nationality and preferred language), cognitive style (the way in which the user process information), device information (that may be used to personalize presentation of information or to deliver information or services to the right device), context (that describes the physical environment when the user process information), history (the user's past interactions), behavior (the user's behavior pattern), interests (topics the user is interested in), intention (goals or purposes of the user), interaction experience (the user's competence on interacting with the system) and domain knowledge (the user's knowledge of a particular topic) [12].

To construct a user profile, information can be collected *explicitly*, through direct user participation, or *implicitly*, through automatic monitoring of user activities [13, 14].

Implicit gathering of user information traditionally includes systems that automatically infer user interests or behavior by keeping track of the user's search history in terms of submitted queries, clicked results, dwell time on clicked documents, processing of stored documents, and harvesting of information from the user's interaction with social applications [13]. Other types of user information can be obtained implicit from interaction with sensors or through use of short range communication (such as NFC, BLE or LTE) on a mobile device. For example, when a user touches an NFC tag to pay for a coffee in a restaurant or obtain a description of some tourist attraction, information about this activity (including location and time) can be intercepted and included in a user profile [15]. Wearable sensors can provide health-related information about a user, such as heart rate, blood pressure or activity monitoring (for example walking or sleeping pattern), while sensors monitoring the physical environment (such as temperature, noise and air pollution measurements) provide information about the surrounding of the user.

In explicit information gathering, the users themselves provide information through for example specification of interests, and positive or negative feedback to retrieved documents [13]. Implicit collection of profile information is a continuous process, where the current interests and behavior is constantly mined. The user profile can thus change over time and periodically be changed to reflect long lasting, short term and new user interests.

A user profile can be represented by different structures. Well known representations are *keyword vectors* and *semantic networks* [13, 14]. Using a vector, the user interests are maintained as a set (vector) of weighted terms, while semantic networks represent user interests as nodes and associated nodes that capture terms and their semantically related or co-occurring terms respectively [13]. Weights can also be assigned to nodes. The terms used in these models are either directly mined from the captured user information or some conceptual terms that are drawn from some knowledge source (based on the user information).

Vector-based user models may consist of one or multiple vectors. One vector can for example represent *short-term user interests* while a second vector represents the *long-term interests* [13]. One may also consider using different vectors for different purposes, such as different user contexts or applications.

A user activity always happens in some *context*, and can thus be linked to for example location, time, task, project or event. To make the personalization context relevant, one should distinguish between different user contexts, and manage the user profile so that relevant parts of the profile can relate to the different contexts. This will support *adaptive context-aware personalization.*

26.2.2 Personalization and Privacy

There is often a dichotomy between personalization and privacy. A user profile can contain highly sensitive information, and should, on one hand, be kept as a secret to guard the privacy of the user. On the other hand, a profile contains very useful information for personalizing applications and services to improve convenience, accuracy and efficiency for the user. To allow others to personalize a service for you, it is required that you give up some private and potentially sensitive information. This might take the form of shopping or movement patters, or even health related information.

Most people are happy to give up personal information as long as their perceived benefit of the services outweighs the perceived cost of giving up said information. However, it is unclear if this pragmatic approach will be possible in the general case. An empirical study [16] shows that users exhibit a preference for personalization in their search results, but are unwilling to give out private information to achieve personalization when searching for topics they deem sensitive. From a societal perspective it is preferable if people make an informed decision about the amount and type of information they are sharing. Thus, encouraging people to give up as little information as possible, thereby ensuring that privacy is not breached and peoples' integrity is maintained. From the perspective of a serious business, it is preferable to acquire as much information as possible, and still protect the customers' privacy.

Due to the dynamic interests of individual users and different privacy attitudes and expectations, privacy concerns when doing information retrieval or service selection are different for different users in different contexts [17]. The goal must be to achieve the appropriate level of privacy of all user data in context-based personalized services, including user profiles, context data and other user related information. Also, there is a need for new approaches to client-side personalization; balancing the personalization requirements from the service providers with privacy protection requirements of the users.

26.3 Data Collection

Data collection is essential in the process of creating and maintaining adaptive user profiles. This involves many participants with different interests and roles. The quality (precision) and amount of data (number of data providers and frequency) will affect the quality of the outcome of the processing. We will discuss the different sources of relevant data and how the interests and roles of the different participants might influence the collection process. Examples of such data are user selection, user activities, user context, user interaction, current user devices, and a wide range of sensor data. Included in this we will present usage of Near Field Communication (NFC), Bluetooth Low Energy (BLE) beacons, and LTE Direct.

26.3.1   Server-Side Data Collection

Usage information can be obtained both from the server-side and the client-side of a system [13]. Examples of systems where user interactions are maintained and processed on the server-side include Facebook, Amazon, and search engines like Google, Yahoo and Bing.

The server-side is a much used approach for collecting application specific information about users. This could be any kind of data, including user location (if the user has approved to share this information), performed search queries, when and how often the service is used, user transactions, and much more. Since the server-side is controlled by the service provider, there is no limit on what the service provider can collect on the server-side. But for the user to use the service, a form of trust has to be established between the user and the service provider. The combination of the value of the service (how important is the service for me), the cost (including the risk of sharing usage data), and the trust (how is my usage data used and protected) is used to determine if the condition to use the service is acceptable. Fig. 26.1 illustrates the user profile (UP) in the server side approach.

However, the actual participants involved in accessing a web based service is much more complex. Most advertisement funded services are connected to large advertisement networks that collect and combine usage data from a huge number of such services. The

Fig. 26.1 Server side user profiles (*UP*)

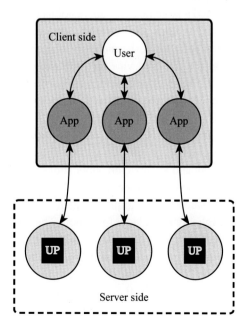

user experiences this, when searching for one thing at one service provider, then shortly after is presented an advertisement for this or similar products at the web page of another service provider.

The main concern with the server-side approach is the privacy concerns that come with the automatic collection and storing of user information outside the control of the user.

26.3.2 Client-Side Data Collection

Client-side user profiling and personalization has been proposed as a means for protecting the privacy of users. With client-side user profiling, usage information is stored and processed on the user's own device. This approach also allows for the collection and combination of usage information from a number of applications accessed by the user [13].

A user normally has a number of different devices available, and client-side user profiling will thus imply mining of user activities over multiple user-devices. Profile information from different devices must be combined and distributed, so that each device holds a user profile reflecting relevant user interests and preferences that support client-side personalization. Client-side data collection should support storage of user profiles on the edge devices and provide privacy-preserving distribution of profile information.

The smart phone is a central device in many people's lives, and is therefore a device of specific interest with respect to user profiling. It follows the user everywhere and is used for a whole range of activities, such as connecting with others, searching and sharing information, getting directions and recommendations, gaming, streaming videos/radio/music, buying products online, social network interaction, and much more. Recently, this has also included a large range of applications based on short range communication such as Near Field Communication (NFC), Bluetooth Low Energy (BLE) beacons, and LTE Direct. The importance of the mobile phone and the variety of mobile user activities makes the phone the central device for client-side data collection and a natural basis for client-side user profiling and subsequent client-side personalization.

In [15], we describe how a variety of NFC applications, accessed through a single personal device (i. e. a smart phone), collectively may provide useful information concerning user activity and interests. NFC is used in mobile applications to provide easy and convenient access to information and services. Examples of NFC-based applications include payment and loyalty card applications, access keys, ticketing, and various forms of information services. We believe that NFC-based services are well suited for user profiling as information can be implicitly gathered, while they also inhibit some of the preciseness of explicitly provided information. The touch of an NFC tag represents an explicit action including an implicit statement of interest.

An NFC interaction can provide information about user activity, interest (through for example the information tags we choose to touch), physical location and date/time of activity. Identity of the user is known, as it is assumed to be the owner of the mobile device. The environment (context) of the user can be determined through the physical location, and possibly combined with sensor data in the vicinity to determine for example weather and/or pollution conditions. User context can also be described through nearby points of interest and who we interact with (through peer-to-peer NFC interaction).

BLE provides another mobile phone type of interaction that could become of importance for personalization. A beacon is a small (battery powered) BLE device that could be used to detect the proximity of a mobile phone. A typical example of usage is to detect when the user (with her phone) is at or close to a store, a bus stop, or another point-of-interest. A service (application) on the phone can automatically present personalized offers or news related to this store when the user is close enough to the BLE beacon. BLE enabled data, such as physical location, time spent in a location (for example a specific store) and user interaction with offered services, can also be collected, analyzed and used in a user profile. BLE can also provide information of the user context in terms of available nearby services.

LTE Direct is a combination of direct communication between LTE Direct enabled mobile phones (without using cell towers) and proximity detection. This technology is still at an early stage, but the combination of communication between devices and proximity detection gives room for the realization of a large range of applications and services. The common example is to detect and communicate with people with a common interest that are close by. With LTE Direct, only the mobile devices are involved and no server-side is necessary. Data on LTE Direct proximity detection and communication could be of great interest in creating user profiles for personalization.

26.3.3 Application-Independent User Profiling

A user profile can either be obtained within a single application or be application-independent. The difference is illustrated in Fig. 26.2. With application-independent user profiling, user profile information is collected from a variety of applications that collectively describe user interests and activities. The resulting user profile will in this case be made available as a basis for personalization within multiple applications.

In vertically partitioned datasets, different types of data of each user are distributed over a number of nodes. In horizontally partitioned datasets, one type of data about users is distributed over a number of nodes. For each user we have one complete user profile, typically stored on a user device (on the mobile phone in a single security domain). Other users have separate complete user profiles accessible on their devices. These complete user profiles located at each user's secure domain are part of a horizontal partitioned data set. The other partitions in the data set are located at other users' secure domains. Up till now, the predominant approach has been to track user interaction within a single application in order to support personalization within the same application. Each application has a partial user-profile stored in separate security domains. Such an approach is a form of vertical partitioning of user related data sets. To best capture a comprehensive user profile that reflects the variety of user activities and interests, we believe that a cross-application

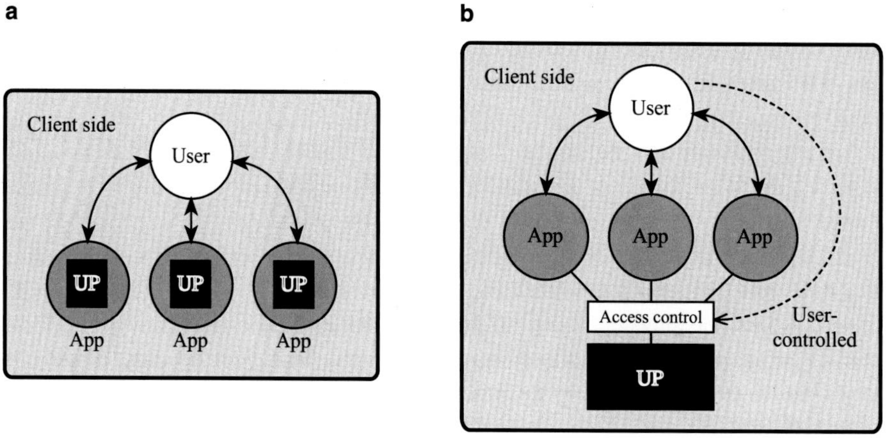

Fig. 26.2 Application-dependent user profiles (**a**) and application-independent user profiles with client side data collection (**b**)

user profiling approach is beneficial. The consequence is that user profile data will be horizontal partitioned data sets.

To achieve application-independent user profiling, the involved application providers have to agree that the increased access to user profile data adds a significant value to their application, and the cost and risk of sharing this data with the other providers are reasonable.

26.3.4   User Profiling and Privacy

Despite the obvious conflict of interest, we believe that personalization can be combined with user privacy guarantees. This can be achieved through a privacy preserving framework handling generation, storing and controlled access to client-side user profiles. Such a framework must manage a user's profile so that the user is put in charge of her own private information. It should provide privacy guarantees through use of privacy preserving techniques, including cryptography, while at the same time allowing personalization and controlled sharing of personal information. In Fig. 26.2 we have illustrated this for the client side user profile management with the user controlled *access control*, where the user can decide what user profile data a given application can access in the current context.

Both with server side managed user profiles and during the process of creating and updating user profiles, user profile data might have to be shared among user devices and with servers. Such data has to be protected by encryption, but at the same time it has to be available for participating processes. In the Ensafer project [18], the focus has been efficient and user friendly secure storing and sharing of data. By combining end-to-end symmetric and public key encryption, smart encryption key management, cloud storage, and user controlled sharing, the user is put in charge of her own private information. The Ensafer approach can be used to provide fine-grained user-controlled access to user-profile data. The user can enforce explicit control to what user-profile data that should be available for a given service. In principle, this means that a copy of a subset of a user's user-profile is encrypted with the use of the service provider's public key. This copy can only be accessed by this service provider and is used to personalize the service for the user.

26.4   Privacy Preserving Processing

Processing and mining of user data creates and updates the user profiles. User privacy concerns influence how and where this processing is performed, and can be performed on server side, at user devices, and/or in a distributed fashion.

In a personalization system, user profiles are important since they identify interests, behavior and other characteristics of individual users. Data processing in a personalization system involves analysis of user profiles, content models (which models the content that users may be interested in) and also social or community-based information describing preferences for groups of users.

For personalization systems, we can distinguish between individualized, community-based and aggregate-level personalization [12, 13]. In *individualized personalization*, tailoring of content is based on information about each individual user as it is found in the user profile, and perform content filtering by comparing user profile to content models. In *community-based personalization*, the relevance of a certain item is determined based on information of preferences among groups of similar users. Collaborative filtering is an example of this approach. In *aggregate-level personalization*, tailoring of content is based on collective usage data and not on an individual user profile. This provides a general recommendation, based on for example the most popular films or books, and not a recommendation that is explicitly tailored to specific interests of the user.

There are many approaches to reduce privacy risks in personalization systems. A number of them are surveyed in [19, 20]. We will in the following present some privacy preserving techniques, and describe their relevance to data processing performed in user profiling and personalization systems.

26.4.1   Client-Side Processing

Client-side personalization [21], is assumed to give the user better control over their personal data, since data is collected and stored on a client-side device. The user can then determine how and when to use this data for personalization. This is closely related to *scrutability*, that emphasizes the user's ability to understand and control what is included in the user profile, and what is made available to different personalization systems [19, 22].

Fig. 26.3 Client side user
profile management

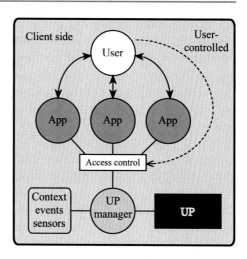

Another advantage of the client-side approach is the ability to collect, on a single device, a wide range of user interest and behavior data form multiple applications. Client-side personalization will, on the other hand, complicate community-based personalization, such as collaborative filtering, since usage data from a group of users is more difficult to obtain.

Applications on a client device, like a mobile phone, are typically executed in separate security domains or sandboxed. To achieve application independent user profiling with client-side only processing, a way to share data between applications has to be available [15]. This might also include applications and data in secure elements on the device [23]. What applications or service (background process) performing the maintenance of the user profile is also of interest. Is each application responsible for maintaining its sub (but potentially overlapping) parts of the user profile in a shared database, or is a service running in the background collecting data from all registered applications? Access to a shared resource has to be controlled even on a personal mobile device. A user might install applications and services that she prefers to use but only share a limited or no user profile data with.

Updating the client-side user profile is based on application requests to access and update user profile data, and the context. Context is a collection of information that describes a given situation. It can include sensor data (e. g. temperature, GPS location, and proximity), calendar data, registered events, and so on. As illustrated in Fig. 26.3, on the client a process maintaining the user profile, called the UP manager, collects and analyze all this data to create and update the user profile. The UP manager *can* participate in a distributed computation involving other devices or servers to perform its task.

26.4.2   Obfuscation and Anonymization

Anonymization or pseudonyms is a privacy preserving technique that shields the true identity of the user. A system can for example track a pseudonym across different sessions, and provide personalization without knowing the user identity. A system providing user anonymization, typically use some de-identification solution, such as replacing the user identity with some random number.

Differential privacy is a method for preserving privacy, which ensures that the removal or addition of a data item does not (substantially) affect the outcome of any analysis [24]. It is a statistical approach to learn as much as possible about a group without exposing individual users. Differential privacy typically uses *perturbation*, where user data are systematically altered or randomized. A commonly used approach to differential privacy is through use of the Laplace mechanism, where noise sampled from the Laplace distribution is added to a computation [20].

Non-perturbative techniques are also used. In contrast to perturbative techniques, non-perturbative techniques do not modify the data. They reduce the details by generalization and suppression of data. For example by replacing numerical values with intervals.

All these obfuscation and anonymization techniques should be used with care. If not, the risk of exposing sensible information about individuals could be high. Examples include, combining several anonymized data-sets to de-anonymize the data, and gaining access to individual data when differential privacy is used by repeating the same data request (question).

When analyzing and maintaining user profile data a combination of these techniques are used. The obfuscation and anonymization techniques described should be considered a part of the toolbox available when performing privacy aware (distributed) processing of user-sensitive data.

26.4.3   Privacy Preserving Algorithms

Secure Multi-Party Computation (SMC) is an algorithmic approach to protect privacy, which allows to gain new knowledge based on user data in a distributed computation, while keeping user data confidential. In principle, an SMC algorithm performs a distributed computation where each node involved access its local data as part of the overall computation, but does not expose any of its local data to the other nodes. In practice, this means that the local data at each node can be involved in and contribute to the computation without being exposed.

In [25], the usage of SMC to process sensitive health data is discussed. The same approach can be used to process data for personalization. Correlation between two types of data in a distributed data set is a typical example of what we can compute using SMC.

Detecting correlation between parameters in a data set, is a common approach to improve and personalize a user application or service. For a horizontal partitioned data an SMC algorithm can be used to calculate the Pearson product-moment correlation coefficient (Pearson's r). Pearson's r is used to measure the correlation (linear dependence) between n samples of two variables x and y, where $\bar{x}$ and $\bar{y}$ are the mean value of x and y, respectively:

$$r = \frac{\sum_{i=1}^{n} (x_i - \bar{x})(y_i - \bar{y})}{\sqrt{\sum_{i=1}^{n} (x_i - \bar{x})^2 \sum_{i=1}^{n} (y_i - \bar{y})^2}}$$

In the case of m user profiles with s_j samples of x_{ji} and y_{ji} at each user, r can be rewritten like this:

$$r = \frac{\sum_{j=1}^{m} \sum_{i=1}^{s_j} (x_{ji} - \bar{x})(y_{ji} - \bar{y})}{\sqrt{\sum_{j=1}^{m} \sum_{i=1}^{s_j} (x_{ji} - \bar{x})^2 \sum_{j=1}^{m} \sum_{i=1}^{s_j} (y_{ji} - \bar{y})^2}}$$

For each user j the following three intermediate results have to be calculated:

$$u_j = \sum_{i=1}^{s_j} (x_{ji} - \bar{x})(y_{ji} - \bar{y})$$

$$v_j = \sum_{i=1}^{s_j} (x_{ji} - \bar{x})^2$$

$$w_j = \sum_{i=1}^{s_j} (y_{ji} - \bar{y})^2$$

When all intermediate values are calculated at each user (node) and collected, Pearson's r can be calculated:

$$r = \frac{\sum_{j=1}^{m} u_j}{\sqrt{\sum_{j=1}^{m} v_j \sum_{j=1}^{m} w_j}}$$

The mean values $\bar{x}$ and $\bar{y}$ can be securely calculated using another SMC algorithm. We assume that all messages between the nodes are protected by encryption. The trick to make this calculation secure is how we calculate the three sums in the equation above. A coordinator generates three large random unique values u_0, v_0, w_0. These values are the initial sum values and they are kept secret at the coordinator. The initial sum values are sent to the first node, who adds its values u_1, v_1, and w_1 to the sums. The first node sends the partial sums to the next node who performs the same calculations. The algorithm continues until the last node performs its calculations and forwards the sums to the coordinator. The coordinator subtracts the initial sum values from the sum to get the real sum values. And these values are used to finally calculate Pearson's r. Fig. 26.4 illustrates the messages and

Fig. 26.4 Three nodes and a coordinator C calculating Pearson's r

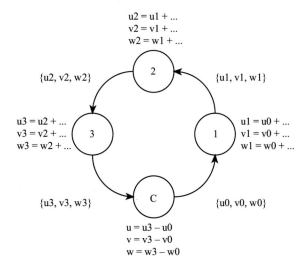

$$u2 = u1 + ...$$
$$v2 = v1 + ...$$
$$w2 = w1 + ...$$

{u2, v2, w2}

$$u3 = u2 + ...$$
$$v3 = v2 + ...$$
$$w3 = w2 + ...$$

{u3, v3, w3}

{u1, v1, w1}

$$u1 = u0 + ...$$
$$v1 = v0 + ...$$
$$w1 = w0 + ...$$

{u0, v0, w0}

$$u = u3 - u0$$
$$v = v3 - v0$$
$$w = w3 - w0$$

node calculations when calculating Pearson's r with three nodes and a coordinator C. The final calculation performed at the coordinator C is the following:

$$r = \frac{u}{\sqrt{vw}}$$

A more complete description of this approach applied to processing of health data is found in [25].

Homomorphic encryption [26] allows us to perform computation on encrypted data. In principle, this could be a good match for personalization where privacy is a major concern. However, currently such computation is inefficient and does not scale very well.

26.5   Conclusion

The creation and maintenance of user profiles involves private and potential sensitive user data. We have in this chapter discussed how to protect this data when providing personalized services. We have also illustrated how Secure Multiparty Computation (SMC) can be used to process user profile data from a number of users without compromising their privacy.

References

1. M. Gao, K. Liu and Z. Wu, "Personalisation in web computing and informatics: Theories, techniques, applications, and future research," *Information Systems Frontiers,* vol. 12, no. 5, pp. 607–629, 2010.

2. M. Wiesner and D. Pfeifer, "Health recommender systems: concepts, requirements, technical basics and challenges," *International journal of environmental research and public health,* vol. 11, no. 3, pp. 2580–2607, 2014.

3. B. Krulwich, "Lifestyle finder: Intelligent user profiling using large-scale demographic data," *AI magazine,* vol. 18, no. 2, p. 37, 1997.

4. S.-H. Min and I. Han, "Detection of the customer time-variant pattern for improving recommender systems," *Expert Systems with Applications,* vol. 28, no. 2, pp. 189–199, 2005.

5. A. S. Das, M. Datar, A. Garg and S. Rajaram, "Google news personalization: scalable online collaborative filtering," in *Proceedings of the 16th international conference on World Wide Web,* Banff, AB, Canada, 2007.

6. I. Guy, N. Zwerdling, I. Ronen, D. Carmel and E. Uziel, "Social media recommendation based on people and tags," in *Proceedings of the 33rd international ACM SIGIR conference on Research and development in information retrieval,* Geneva, Switzerland, 2010.

7. R. W. White, P. Bailey and L. Chen, "Predicting user interests from contextual information," in *Proceedings of the 32nd international ACM SIGIR conference on Research and development in information retrieval,* Boston, MA, USA, 2009.

8. R. W. White and J. Huang, "Assessing the scenic route: measuring the value of search trails in web logs," in *Proceedings of the 33rd international ACM SIGIR conference on Research and development in information retrieval,* Geneva, Switzerland, 2010.

9. M. Harvey, F. Crestani and M. J. Carman, "Building user profiles from topic models for personalised search," in *Proceedings of the 22nd ACM international conference on Conference on information & knowledge management,* San Francisco, CA, USA, 2013.

10. P. N. Bennett, R. W. White, W. Chu, S. T. Dumais, P. Bailey, F. Borisyuk and X. Cui, "Modeling the Impact of Short- and Long-term Behavior on Search Personalization," in *Proceedings of the 35th International ACM SIGIR Conference on Research and Development in Information Retrieval,* Portland, Oregon, USA, 2012.

11. M. Balabanovic and Y. Shoham, "Fab: content-based, collaborative recommendation," *Communications of the ACM,* vol. 40, no. 3, pp. 66–72, 1997.

12. M. Gao, K. Liu and Z. Wu, "Personalisation in web computing and informatics: Theories, techniques, applications, and future research," *Information Systems Frontiers,* vol. 12, no. 5, pp. 607–629, 2010.

13. M. R. Ghorab, D. Zhou, A. O'Connor and V. Wade, "Personalised information retrieval: survey and classification," *User Modeling and User-Adapted Interaction,* vol. 23, no. 4, pp. 381–443, 2013.

14. S. Gauch, M. Speretta, A. Chandramouli and A. Micarelli, "User profiles for personalized information access," in *The adaptive web,* P. Brusilovsky, A. Kobsa and W. Nejdl, Eds., Berlin Heidelberg New York, Springer, 2007, pp. 54–89.

15. A. Andersen and R. Karlsen, "User profiling through NFC interactions: Mining NFC-based user information from mobile devices and back-end systems," in *Proceedings of the 14th International Symposium on Mobility Management and Wireless Access,* Malta, 2016.

16. S. Panjwani, N. Shrivastava, S. Shukla and S. Jaiswal, "Understanding the privacy-personalization dilemma for web search: a user perspective," in *Proceedings of the SIGCHI Conference on Human Factors in Computing Systems,* Paris, France, 2013.

17. M. Alaggan, S. Gambs and A.-M. Kermarrec, "Heterogeneous differential privacy," *arXiv preprint arXiv:1504.06998,* 2015.

18. A. Andersen, T. Hardersen and N. Schirmer, "Privacy for Cloud Storage," in *ISSE 2014 Securing Electronic Business Processes: Highlights of the Information Security Solutions Europe 2014 Conference,* Springer, 2014.

19. E. Toch, Y. Wang and L. F. Cranor, "Personalization and privacy: a survey of privacy risks and remedies in personalization-based systems," *User Modeling and User-Adapted Interaction,* vol. 22, no. 1–2, pp. 203–220, 2012.
20. A. Friedman, B. P. Knijnenburg, K. Vanhecke, L. Martens and S. Berkovsky, "Privacy aspects of recommender systems," in *Recommender Systems Handbook*, Springer, 2015, pp. 649–688.
21. L. Cassel and U. Wolz, "Client Side Personalization," in *Proceedings of the joint DELOS-NSF workshop on personalization and recommender systems in digital libraries*, Dublin, 2001.
22. M. Asif and J. Krogstie, "Mobile client-side personalization," in *Proceedings of the 2013 International Conference on Privacy and Security in Mobile Systems (PRISMS)*, 2013.
23. A. Munch-Ellingsen, A. Andersen, S. Akselsen and R. Karlsen, "Customer managed security domain on mobile network operators' SIM cards: Opportunities to enable new business models," in *Marktplätze im Umbruch: Digitale Strategien und das Zusammenwachsen von Shop, Online-Business sowie Services im Mobilen Internet*, Springer, 2015.
24. C. Dwork, "Differential privacy: A survey of results," in *Proceedings of the International Conference on Theory and Applications of Models of Computation*, 2008.
25. A. Andersen, K. Y. Yigzaw and R. Karlsen, "Privacy preserving health data processing," in *Proceedings of the 16th International Conference on e-Health Networking, Applications and Services (Healthcom)*, 2014.
26. C. Gentry, A fully homomorphic encryption scheme, Stanford University, 2009.

Further Reading

27. M. K. L. Z. W. Gao, "Personalisation in web computing and informatics: Theories, techniques, applications, and future research," *Information Systems Frontiers,* vol. 12, no. 5, pp. 607–629, 2010.

Part VII
Cognitive Systems

Cognitive Computing – the new Paradigm of the Digital World

27

Wolfgang Hildesheim

27.1 Cognitive Computing – the new Paradigm of the Digital World

27.1.1 A Brief History of Eras

Cognitive systems like IBM Watson understand at scale, reason with a purpose, learn with each new interaction, and interact naturally with humans, augmenting human intelligence – but before discerning the significance of cognitive computing, it is firstly important to place it within historical context. To date, there have been three distinct eras of computing: 1) The Tabulating Era which helped revolutionize the way in which we were able to manage large volumes of structured data like the census; 2) The Programmatic Era which ushered in the computer revolution allowing us to apply rules and logic revolutionizing the ways in which large and complex transactions were automated (e. g. financial systems, travel systems, etc.); and 3) The Cognitive Era which is extending our ability to work with information of all types, structured and unstructured (e. g. text, pictures, video), with natural conversational interaction, exploration not simple search, decision optimization based on evidence and confidence, all in a time frame that allows us to achieve better results.

The Tabulating Era, from the early 20th Century to the 1940s, was the birth of computing, consisting of single-purpose mechanical systems that used punch cards to tabulate. World War ll moved us from tabulators to electronic systems and marked the beginning of the Programmatic Era. Subsequent to the war the age of 'digital computers' evolved, moving into businesses and governments. They performed logical operations from a set of structured instructions (i. e. rules). This is very much what we have known of computing since the 1950's, and while the languages we use to program have evolved the basic premise of computing is the same.

W. Hildesheim (✉)
IBM Deutschland GmbH
Düsseldorf, Germany
e-mail: hildeshe@de.ibm.com

© Springer-Verlag GmbH Germany 2018
C. Linnhoff-Popien et al. (eds.), *Digital Marketplaces Unleashed*,
https://doi.org/10.1007/978-3-662-49275-8_27

Now we have entered the Cognitive Computing Era, developing systems that can use natural language processing to extract meaning from large volumes of unstructured data and learn as they do so. Cognitive systems such as IBM Watson make sense and give purpose to a world awash in an overwhelming deluge of data. Cognitive computing uses technologies like machine learning to find meaning by discovering previously unseen patterns, drawing new inferences and identifying new relationships from vast amounts of data, and helping humans make confidence weighted, evidence based, decisions more rapidly. Existing computers – let alone humans – simply cannot handle the volume and diversity of data being generated everywhere, by everyone, every day. We are not just trying to improve productivity with cognitive – doing things faster and more efficiently; we are trying to augment human decision-making; we are trying to use these computers to digest data and come up with better outcomes. Unlike existing computers that must be programmed, cognitive computing understands the world in the way that humans do: through senses, learning, and experience. What "search" is to literal data retrieval (i. e. key word match), "cognitive" is to better, more informed and more timely discovery and decision making.

27.1.2 What is Cognitive Computing's Relationship with Artificial Intelligence (AI)?

Cognitive computing brings together technologies associated with artificial intelligence (AI) with deep subject matter expertise and relevant content. It offers the ability to boost productivity and nurture new discoveries across a broad range of industries. Based upon AI technologies such as machine and deep learning; language, speech and vision capabilities; high-performance cloud computing; and new computing physical devices (e. g. smartphones, robots, etc.), cognitive computing is changing the way we work with technology. Guided by the view of "augmented intelligence" rather than "artificial intelligence" cognitive systems enhance and scale human expertise, side-by-side with humans to accelerate and improve our ability to act with confidence and authority. Focused on developing practical applications that assist people with specific challenges and tasks, cognitive computing exposes a wide range of specific artificial intelligence services that support a range of applications to help augment human intelligence. The power of cognitive systems is today helping mankind better understand our world and make more informed decisions about how we live in it. We believe that in the future, every critical decision will be informed by systems like Watson.

27.1.3 How Cognitive Moves Beyond Narrow Aspects of Artificial Intelligence

Unlike other areas of computer science that align to a single discipline, cognitive computing combines a variety of academic fields, from machine learning and algorithmic strategy, to neural networks and natural language processing, to industry knowledge and beyond. We see, in our everyday lives, examples of narrowly focused, purpose-built aspects of artificial specific intelligence (ASI) such as data discovery in genomics and facial recognition for physical device access, each applying select cognitive computing capability. In contrast, however, cognitive solutions bring together all the abilities to understand in context (i. e. comprehend), reason (deductive, inductive, abductive and adaptive), learn, and interact naturally with humans (natural language processing, natural language generation).

Cognitive systems take advantage of a plethora of data to create a more human-like interaction with people, based on the method, type and the preference of each person. Because the volume of data being generated in today's world is so large and happening so quickly, Watson can do what humans – and today's programmable computers – simply can't: ingest incredible amounts of data in every form imaginable to help support better decision-making. Collating information such as geolocation, medical records and images, and transactional data with other details that have been traditionally difficult to access and understand: sentiment, emotions, personality – allowing cognitive systems to adapt to the individual. Continuously learning from these engagements, cognitive systems deliver increased value and are emotionally astute.

Secondly, cognitive systems are designed to help organizations augment and scale expertise in order to enhance the performance of their employees. With the pace of an industry's and profession's knowledge increasing at an untold rate, cognitive systems are able to master a domain's language and terminology enabling professionals to become experts more efficiently. Cognitive computing represents a necessary next step in our ability to harness technology in the pursuit of knowledge – which goes beyond improving productivity and efficiency, to actually augmenting human decision-making. Taught by leading experts in the field, systems like Watson learn at scale, reason with purpose and interact with humans naturally.

Business processes are also changing with the introduction of cognitive computing, transforming how a company operates. Incorporating internal and external data sources, cognitive systems enable organizations a greater awareness of processes, industry contexts and business environments – feeding a process of continuous improvement and operational excellence. Further amplified by the Internet of Things (IoT) which with the help of cognitive capabilities can sense, reason and learn about their users and the world.

Finally, cognitive systems equip businesses with perhaps their most powerful tool – a better vision, exploration and discovery of their future. From health research to product innovation, cognitive computing is allowing businesses to spot patterns, trends and opportunities that would be almost impossible for traditional programmatic systems to identify. To foster this level of innovation systems like Watson are built on an open platform, cloud accessible, allowing everyone access to the technology. This affords third parties the ability to build out services, products and solutions unencumbered by restrictions and benefiting from the ongoing investments made in R&D. In the case of Watson the user's IP remains with the user as well as their data rights. This is a fundamental departure from what has been a growing trend for organizations to aggregate and take ownership of others' content.

27.1.4 Stretching the Boundaries of Cognitive Computing

Cognitive computing has come a long way since Watson first appeared on the gameshow Jeopardy in 2011. The game playing Watson in that case was limited to understanding a single corpus of data and responding to a single questions. Today Watson can see images, helping radiologist make sense of MRIs and CAT scans, analyze audio and help music producers develop award winning songs, discover hidden patterns in geological patterns, navigate financial regulations, help optimize legal decisions, and more. In just five years, we have evolved from Watson at play to Watson at work, helping doctors, lawyers, accountants, and engineers, to name a few, address the growing challenges of their respective vocations and tackling some of societies greatest problems.

Cognitive computing is not a single thing but a compendium of capabilities, technologies, resources, services, and the like. By delivering a broad and robust set of individual APIs, systems like Watson spark creativity and business innovations. For example, in a short amount of time, we've seen Watson technology applied to everything from cutting edge cancer research and better understanding how diabetes works to oil exploration, educational toys and the world's most complex financial systems. Watson's industry domain knowledge continues to expand across industries and Watson has learned the idiosyncrasies and colloquialisms in languages like Arabic, Spanish, Brazilian Portuguese, Korean and Japanese, to name a few. We have witnessed the growth and adoption of cognitive technologies among industry leaders like Apple, Johnson & Johnson, Medtronic, Memorial Sloan-Kettering, Thomson Reuters, Swiss Re, and many others. To scale systems like Watson globally, we have witnessed important partnerships with organizations such as SoftBank in Japan, SK Holdings C&C in Korea, Mubadala in the Middle East and Africa, and GBM in Latin America – all accelerating the availability of this new era of computing in their respective geographies.

In order to achieve all of this, and more, our approach to advancing Watson is to focus on three core tenets: science, simplicity and scale.

Science Over the past two years, IBM has taught Watson new languages; increased its core knowledge of key industry domains; made it available via new form factors (tablets, smartphones, robotics and smart watches); and enhanced it with technology allowing it to "see", understand tone and emotion, and more.

Simplicity Our ongoing commitment to research, upwards of $6 billion a year is allowing us to make Watson easier to teach, easier to use, and easier to connect to existing technologies, systems, and data sets. As well as making it easier for developers to build Watson into their applications.

Scale IBM is committed to scaling Watson by creating a repeatable, robust and secure platform that is flexible enough to use across a wide variety of domains and industries.

27.1.5   The Partnership on Artificial Intelligence

We have seen tremendous advances since 2014 in the deployment of cognitive technologies across industries and professions to address some of the world's most complex challenges. In order to advance the public understanding and use of these technologies, IBM, Amazon, Google, Facebook and Microsoft have created a non-profit organization, named the Partnership on Artificial Intelligence to Benefit People and Society. Together, the organization's members will conduct research, recommend best practices, and publish research under an open license in areas such as ethics, fairness and inclusivity; transparency, privacy, and interoperability; collaboration between people and AI systems; and the trustworthiness, reliability and robustness of the technology.

AI has touched many parts of today's world and cognitive computing is augmenting humans' ability to understand – and act upon – the complex volumes of data being generated across society. Providing consumers of cognitive systems a critical voice in the development of this great technology – through rigorous research, the development of best practices, and an open and transparent dialogue – the founding members of the Partnership on AI hope to maximize this potential further and ensure it benefits as many people as possible.

27.2   The Implications of Cognitive Computing on Business

27.2.1   Without Cognitive You Cannot Achieve Digital Intelligence

Cognitive computing is a broad and flexible platform that can be applied to every company, industry and profession. Watson is helping inspire innovation and transformation. In a world where every business is digital, what is the differentiator? With data as an enabler those organizations that can infuse digital intelligence into the mix will be able to learn more, adapt faster, and provide a more personalized and relevant engagement with all stakeholders. Digital business is a recipe for growth, not a destination. Where data goes cognition follows, and can be embedded in everything we do – it will touch billions of people forever changing the world we live in.

27.2.2   Market Penetration

Healthcare & Life Sciences
Today, the healthcare industry is coping with a significant upheaval due to unprecedented disruption from economic, societal and industry influences. It's an industry that is undergoing tremendous change with more than $8 trillion spent annually worldwide. In the U.S. it represents over 17% of the national GDP and is growing at an unsustainable rate. Health leaders are facing new and increasingly complex challenges; from rapid digitalization and

rising consumer expectations to rising costs and shortages of skilled resources. As a result, it is critical that healthcare providers are smart in how they approach data in order to unlock its full potential and conquer the disruptive forces within the industry. Cognitive solutions provide new capabilities to health organizations and have the potential to transform disruption into focus.

In 2015, IBM launched Watson Health and the Watson Health Cloud platform. Since then, we have invested more than $4 billion dollars in acquisitions and partnerships to build up our capabilities. The key to success in this new space is access to large, diverse and meaningful data sets around health and health-related activities. In just one year, we have amassed one of the world's largest and most essential sets of health-related data, including information on more than 300 million patients "lives" and more than 30 billion medical images. The Watson Health Cloud allows this information to be de-identified, shared and combined with a dynamic and constantly growing aggregated view of clinical, research and social health data.

Watson Health will help improve the ability of doctors, researchers and insurers to innovate by surfacing insights from the massive amount of personal health data being created and shared daily. Cognitive systems can help increase consumer engagement, discover new trends in big data at an accelerated pace, and finally, augment intelligence to the optimize decision-making processes. Oncologists across the world are leveraging cognitive computing as an assistant, trained by experts in the domain, to evaluate specific details of each patient against clinical evidence. Watson neither diagnoses nor prescribes. Rather, it analyzes massive amounts of medical data – ranging from EMRs to scientific papers to images – to provide doctors and care providers with the best information needed to make quick and informed decisions that support patient well-being. We applied Watson to healthcare first because it is the most complex industry and contains the biggest data set imaginable.

With the power of cognitive computing, health organizations have a new resource to help address consumer and patient concerns quickly and comprehensively. These systems have the ability to provide timely, evidence-based support to clinicians, patients and consumers; providing individuals access to an expert assistant twenty-four hours a day, seven days a week. With the ability to read millions of pages of text in a matter of seconds, cognitive systems are enabling health organizations to discover insights in their data that could potentially be missed with traditional methods; thus overcoming the restrictions faced today. What's exciting to the medical community is Watson's ability to help doctors keep up with the incredible volume of data and knowledge that is being generated, over 8000 new reports daily. Watson augments a doctor's capability by bringing together all of the best available information and knowledge that humans have created. Watson looks at that data and brings forth the best of what we know.

Accurate, evidence-based decision-making is vital in the health industry as, very often, patient lives can depend on this. With the exponential growth in health related data, organizations must ensure they leverage insights for all their data to optimize decisions relating to spending, strategy and diagnoses whilst adhering to complex regulatory pressures. Watson works with doctors to assist them in their day-to-day routines, but ultimately it's the doctors and patients that will make the final decisions on the course of action.

Financial Services

As banks struggle to balance fiscal responsibility, with operational complexity and regulatory mandates, cognitive computing is changing the way financial service organizations address these challenges through a data driven, human centric approach to decision-making. Allowing personalized communication capabilities on a scalable platform, cognitive systems are drastically improving the way organizations approach areas like customer engagement in order to provide a better experience whilst simultaneously reducing inefficiency and poor experiences. For example, banks today are applying cognitive capabilities to provide personalized wealth management advice to assist the bank's relationship managers in analyzing vast amounts of data including research reports, product information and customer profiles; identifying connections between customers' needs and the growing corpus of investment knowledge, and weighing various financial options available to customers.

Furthermore, cognitive capabilities can help banks extract meaningful patterns from data about markets, customers, partners and employees – and use information to better anticipate change and shape the future. At the Royal Bank of Scotland they are using Watson to help customers who are contacting their call center. By developing a Watson powered Chatbot, they are able to offer their customers a personal, ever present and powerful route of contact with the bank. Watson services are continuing to break boundaries in the core areas of speech and language to ensure chatbots are truly effective for the future. Financial service organizations are embracing cognitive computing to transform internal operations and the way they interact with customers to produce a data driven approach to decision-making and a tailored approach to customer engagement.

Industrial

Eighty-three percent $(83\%)^1$ of oil and gas executives believe that cognitive technologies will play a critical role within their industry as a response to significant disruption in energy prices, reserve replenishment, high resource development costs and constantly changing health and safety regulations. Amid this disruption, oil and gas companies need to focus on their capabilities on discovering key insights to decide the best actions to take at a rapid rate. Cognitive computing is tackling these challenges, transforming the discovery and decision making, enhancing the way business is done. Cognitive systems will help bridge the information gap and avoid leakage of valuable data insights.

Heightening the ability of finding new data insights cognitive systems are learning from the best engineers to uncover new ground and unearth new insights and connections from the information spread across an Oil & Gas organization. For example, Woodside, based

---

[1] http://www-01.ibm.com/common/ssi/cgi-bin/ssialias?subtype=XB&infotype=PM& htmlfid=GBE03747USEN&attachment=GBE03747USEN.PDF.

in Australia, is integrating cognitive technologies across their enterprise for a variety of functions such as to scale an engineer's knowledge and analyze large volumes of data to rapidly help produce better informed, timed and expert decisions in one of the world's harshest working environments.

Retail, Travel & Hospitality

Continuing to advance what Watson can do, cognitive capabilities have been embedded into new form factors and interfaces, changing the way businesses interact with their customer, most notably in retail, travel and hospitality. Today's self-service options in retail environments are typically tablets or kiosks, limiting the scope of how truly interactive and intuitive a customer experience can be. With an avatar based interaction of robotic assistant, users can have a more natural conversation in which their words, and even their gestures and expressions, are understood. Robots for example offer a multi-dimensional experience between human and machines, expanding beyond the traditional two-dimensional interfaces that have existed for over the last 60 years. Watson-enabled robots can understand, reason, and learn as well as express and read emotional cues. They combine the intricate ability to understand the nuances of natural language, including intent and intonation, with physical achievements, such as gesturing through body language and eye movement, to reinforce an understanding of what's being expressed.

Japan's SoftBank Robotics are leveraging cognitive capabilities in their Pepper robots to allow systems to make sense of the hidden meaning in data that traditional computers cannot comprehend – including social media, video, images and text. SoftBank is using Pepper as a shopping assistant and concierge, among other applications. Various hotels are piloting robots with Watson to serve as a concierge. Imagine having a conversation with an AI in order to get answers about the hotel (e. g. where is the pool? when does breakfast start?), dining recommendations, directions, and information about local attractions. With the combination of Watson technologies and WayBlazer's extensive travel domain knowledge, they are delivering an on-line personalized experience more emblematic of the interaction one would have with a travel agent.

Communications

Cognitive systems are shifting the way Communication Service Providers (CSPs) interact with their customers through the use of interactive, intelligent, augmented service support. CSP customers have increasingly high expectations relating to access, service, quality and experience, driving the need for providers to change the way they work. Leveraging insights from cognitive systems can help organizations put the customer at the center of their service and operations, aide market forecasts and help determine next best actions, in order to address these growing trends.

With the swell in mobile traffic, CSPs are being pushed to invest heavily in new generation mobile and data networks, whilst, at the same time, mobile revenue growth is expected to slow. Advances in cognitive computing can help bridge the gap between data quantity and data insight, helping locate the proverbial needle in a haystack, identifying new patterns and insights and significantly transforming the way in which customers interact with their providers at every touch point.

Public Sector

The public sector faces significant challenges of meeting the ever increasing demand of services, living up to citizen expectations and defending their systems and infrastructure from constant security threats. These challenges are exacerbated by budgetary pressures and the constraints of resources. The digital age has helped the public sector move forward their data driven approach to decision-making, yet government organizations struggle to unlock the full potential of this data and keep up as it grows rapidly in volume, variety and complexity.

Cognitive computing is transforming the way Government and Public Sector organizations operate by discovering insights from healthcare, to public intelligence to education. Over 80% of government officials, familiar with cognitive computing, believe it will have critical impact on the future of their organization with a further 87%[2] believing it will play a disruptive role in their organization. In one case, career advisers are getting help from cognitive systems to discover the root cause of a chronically unemployed citizen's struggle to find a job. At the other end of the spectrum, in California, USA, organizations like OmniEarth are leveraging Watson's advanced processing, learning and visual recognition capabilities to quickly make sense of an extensive collection of aerial images allowing them to analyze drought-stricken lots, looking for specific areas where water usage could be scaled back. Elsewhere, cognitive systems are enabling intelligence agencies to identify patterns and trends currently invisible to traditional systems. Cognitive can be embedded into every process, every application and every organization.

Education

Data-driven cognitive technologies will enable personalized education and help improve outcomes for students, educators and administrators. Traditional classrooms contain students of ranging abilities and favored learning styles, making it an inherently difficult task for anyone to target curriculum towards such a diverse ability-set. Cognitive systems are able to extend the capabilities of educators by providing deep domain insights and expert assistance through the provisioning of information in a timely, natural and personal way. IBM are teaming with organizations like Sesame Street to transform early childhood learning. Research shows that a significant extent of brain development occurs in the first five years of a child's life, making this window critical for learning and development[3]. Sesame Street has over 45 years of deep expertise gained through research and more than 1000 studies on how young children learn best. Watson's ability to absorb, correlate and

---

[2] http://www-01.ibm.com/common/ssi/cgi-bin/ssialias?subtype=XB&infotype=PM&htmlfid=GBE03714USEN&attachment=GBE03714USEN.PDF.
[3] Shonkoff, J. P., Phillips, D. A., & National Research Council (U.S.). (2000). From neurons to neighborhoods: The science of early child development. Washington, D.C: National Academy Press.

learn from huge amounts of unstructured data and then deliver very personalized educational experiences will help transform the way in which kids learn and teachers teach.

Sesame Workshop and IBM are collaborating on a wide variety of interactive platforms and interfaces for use in homes and schools. The two companies are working with leaders in the education and technology community to allow continued refinement based on feedback and domain expertise. Watson's natural language processing, pattern recognition, and other cognitive computing technologies will enable highly personalized learning experiences which are intended to complement the roles that parents and teachers play in early development. Watson will work to continuously hone and improve educational activities by studying and adapting to the aggregate experiences of anonymized groups of students. Cognitive systems, capable of driving adaptive learning, are already being welcomed by the teaching profession, with the notion of having prescriptive diagnostic programs, allowing teachers to better understand individual students.

27.3 Conclusion

27.3.1 Cognitive Is Changing the World We Live in

Cognitive systems can understand, reason and learn to interact more naturally with human beings than traditional systems. Augmenting and scaling expertise, cognitive computing is here – and this transformative technology is becoming ubiquitous in the day-to-day working of the business world, fundamentally changing how we perform our jobs, engage and interact with others, and learn and make decisions. Organizations across all industries and in every continent are already leveraging cognitive capabilities to uncover significant business value, transform the fundamentals of their organization and help solve some of society's greatest challenges.

From Tweet to Chatbot – Content Management as a Core Competency for the Digital Evolution

28

Alexander W. Jonke and Jo Barbara Volkwein

Abstract

This article examines the development of content management in digital marketplaces and illustrates why it will remain a core competency for e-commerce brands in the future. The article explores the journey of digital, leading e-commerce brands becoming publishers and subsequently investing in technology, people and processes accordingly to address topics such as segmenting content into owned, earned and paid media, and change of human capital in a differentiated world of online communication. With a view to content management systems and tools, the article details how technology can contribute to this change, but also demonstrates the challenges faced by organizations while considering the role of content creation, publishing and monitoring processes and the requirements for content management for each of these processes. Presenting 'chat bots' as a future scenario of digital communication, the article argues which of the stated requirements might change or remain necessary for organizations to compete in the digital market place.

A. W. Jonke (✉)
KPMG AG
Munich, Germany
e-mail: contact@alexwjonke.com

J. B. Volkwein
KPMG AG
Düsseldorf, Germany
e-mail: jovolkwein@yahoo.de

© Springer-Verlag GmbH Germany 2018
C. Linnhoff-Popien et al. (eds.), *Digital Marketplaces Unleashed*,
https://doi.org/10.1007/978-3-662-49275-8_28

28.1 Digital Evolution Changing the Business World

The past decades have been a time of digital evolution. The term describes the continuous transformation and adaptation of businesses to the opportunities of digital technologies [1], or the adaption of digital transformation to the next stages. In this process, companies try to continuously optimize their workflow and maximize customer satisfaction in order to generate higher profits. Thus, businesses need to keep up with the latest technologies. Table 28.1 provides selected examples of changes in the business world over the past years due to the digital evolution.

These examples demonstrate that technology as well as people and processes are affected and influenced by the digital transformation, referred to as 'digital evolution'. The digital evolution is an ongoing phenomenon, which includes continuously evolving technology [technology], increasing digitalization of processes [processes] and shifting labor skill sets towards digital jobs [people]. As a consequence, technology has started to evolve quite fast, requiring a rearrangement of processes and finally a cultural adaption of the people in between.

28.2 Content Management from a Current Perspective

From a current perspective (2017), 'content' includes all forms of information presented in the form of text, images, graphs and sounds, which are published on a website [2]. Content management in turn describes the systematic preparation and processing of information. The distinction between content and layout is an integral part of content management [3]. Content Management Systems (CMS) such as WordPress, TYPO3 and Drupal are envisaged to easily manage digital data and offer a variety of solutions, depending on the needs of users. The success of content management can be measured for example by how accurate the published information is and how easily users can find a website on the World Wide Web [4].

Table 28.1 Examples of changes in the business world due to the digital evolution

From	To
Demand analysis	Push & pull innovation
Rigid development	Agile development based on feedback
Strict division of tasks	Culture of change and initiative
Steep hierarchies	Open communication
Delegation of narrow tasks	Innovative leadership
Focus on implementation	Giving directions
Focus on business scenarios	Diversified portfolios
Development of existing business segments	Simultaneous vertical and horizontal development

Reading about content management frequently raises the issue of 'owned', 'paid' and 'earned' media, which hereafter is important to further investigate the role of content management in the digital evolution. *Owned* media describes content that is published on the brand's 'owned' channels (e. g. website, mobile site, social media, or blogs). The brand manager has complete control, but it is difficult to acquire new users with it. *Paid* content is used to illustrate information about the brand, including advertisements and higher rankings in search engines. It is useful to raise awareness, but the information is not always trusted by readers. *Earned media* embodies all the information that users publish about you such as mentions, likes, shares, reposts, tweets and feedback through your own, or third party websites.

28.2.1 Content Management and E-Commerce: How Products Become Content and Content Becomes a Product

Since the beginning of e-commerce, the internal and external communication of brands has shown steep increases in mostly all forms of digital media. Nowadays, it is not sufficient to solely use one digital marketing instrument in order to reach the target, but different channels such as display advertising, social media, e-mail marketing, have to be taken into consideration, to name but a few. The precise orchestration of all instruments used, including owned, paid and earned media, in an efficient manner is the solution to digital success.

One way to reach the target is arranging an e-commerce shop in an influential context by using the instrument 'content management'. With content management, a brand can tell its story and connect it to its products – in short: is practicing 'content marketing'. Some brands might not even know that they have already implemented content marketing which can be realized through upsell or cross-sell opportunities such as writing an article or a blog post about an important topic and suggesting the related products on the page or giving more information to the customer on the product page by putting links to related blog posts and indirectly linking more products [5].

In Germany, several best practice e-commerce brands such as Zalando and Saturn (e. g.) demonstrate how to use and implement purposeful content marketing: 'Turn on' is Saturn's online magazine giving illustrative information without too much technical detail in easily understandable language. Even though 'Turn on' might not be the best form of storytelling, it follows an exemplary content strategy: Saturn has clearly identified its target group as well as their interests and tailors content accordingly. On doing so, Saturn positions itself as an expert of entertainment equipment in the long run. Fashion magazines are a dime a dozen. But fashion magazines which are connected to sales as a marketing instrument are rare. Zalando's 'Zalando Lounge' is one of those magazines where website visitors can buy even fashion at a cheaper price or in special sales during "unique sales campaigns" from time to time [6]; to mention but a few examples.

The reason for content management is perfectly plain: content can drive conversions of e-commerce websites, which means that content can drive sales by making a website more appealing for search engines (SEO) as well as easier to find and more valuable for internet searchers who might be (potential) consumers [7]. It is just as important to remember that increasing traffic, in the end, does not automatically mean better conversion rates. According to HubSpot, only companies with a plan focused on conversion are twice as likely to see a large increase in sales [8]. With this in mind, besides SEO content, marketing can

- raise brand, product and service awareness
- push customers further down the purchase funnel by giving help and advice
- build audiences and communities
- bring traffic that ideally leads to conversion and thus to sales
- give brands something else to post on social media and thus improve their social reach [9].

The foregoing makes it obvious that e-commerce brands face a lot of challenges and have to fulfil many requirements to perfectly realize content marketing. Those challenges and requirements affect people, processes and technology, and some of them are shown in the next chapter.

28.2.2 Challenges and Requirements for E-Commerce Brands Becoming Publishers

According to a current study, the investment in content marketing in Europe will reach 2.12 billion euros by 2020 [10]. This corresponds to a growth rate of about 330% in Germany. Nevertheless, spending the whole budget on media would not be sustainable because one of the biggest challenges of brands is to reach "operational excellence" [11] and the ability to compete with other market participants.

Besides, brands are forced to acquire new systems and tools to manage the content assets, define new processes with new or adapted methodologies such as style guidelines and editorial procedures [12] and recruit employees with an appropriate skill set, such as for example writers or brand journalists.

Owned, paid and earned media should interact to reach the aforementioned goals and the best possible effectiveness of a brand's digital marketing strategy [13]. Using all three dimensions together is a tough challenge for many marketers. How should the process of directing publishing to the most effective content type at the right time be orchestrated? The most successful companies in content marketing generate a high impact because of their mature content management processes.

These processes can be divided into the three different stages – sourcing, publishing and monitoring content – and present many *challenges* and certain *requirements*, which have to be fulfilled to achieve successful online publishing. In the initial phase (content sourcing), a brand is focused on gathering information. Afterwards it has to be translated into meaningful content. What is 'meaningful' content? As mentioned before, publishing content to sell products is not led by a certain quantity but more so by the quality of content. It is still common to equate scaling content with simply producing *more* content, regardless of its quality. But that approach is flawed, as it becomes increasingly difficult to achieve more visibility when content is not that great [8]. The fact is that 73% of consumers get frustrated by irrelevant web content [14]. As a result, search rankings go down. However, brands that publish quality content such as helpful information, reviews, videos, blogs and pictures, can engage customers, satisfy their needs, and keep them coming back for more. Further quality content can help put an e-commerce business on the map for other businesses or publications in the industry and potentially turn it into a well-known name and trusted resource as well [7].

Table 28.2 Examples of requirements for the content management process

	Sourcing	Publishing	Monitoring
People's knowledge involved	Protection of copyrights, as the importance of 'unique' content has grown (especially since the Google Panda Update)	Protection of know-how and data to prevent the unwanted access to company-related data and content	Definition of internal company guidelines that define communication using digital channels and rules for meeting commitments defined therein
Process implications	Implementation of controls in CMS to prevent loss of intellectual property on internal/external platforms and networks, as well as regular proof of edited content to avoid plagiarism for example	Implementation of controls in CMS to ensure dual control and to regulate the release process, resulting in equal treatment of market participants	Implementation of controls in CMS to clearly define effective processes in case of a crisis such as a 'shitstorm' that ensures consistent exchange of information between digital communication platforms and a physical department ('social disconnect')
Technological requirements	Choice of IT systems that offer the right combination of costs and guarantee for right of use with due consideration of meeting rules and commitments Monitoring of license agreements and access rights for research portals, picture data bases and more	Definition of authority concept and regular inventory of users in communication systems Compliance check of tools used (especially freeware) and regulatory requirements (especially hosting)	Obligations to archive and preserve business records: How and at what intervals is public communication archived? What are the considerations for designing obligations, for example pursuant to commercial law or Securities and Exchange Commission (SEC) rules?

The second phase covers the publishing of content. While trying to integrate e-commerce and content management, brands are confronted with the limits of technology. Content such as information on the product, and user-generated content such as feedback, rates and questions, should ideally be found in the same location as the actual buying options, so both can be mixed manually or automatically and be easily customized as well [5]. Many e-commerce solutions have become more complex over the years, but almost none combine all needed shop and content management features so far. Thus, a common approach to combining CMS and e-commerce is to either use one product with simple additional features to cover the other requirements or to take two products and integrate them via different technical temporary solutions such as subdomains [5]. Managing products and content together becomes very important, and making this happen through tightly integrated CMS and e-commerce systems seamlessly even more important. Thus, synchronizing a CMS with other systems such as the Customer Relationship Management (CRM) system or the Enterprise Resource Planning (ERP) system should be a regular feature of the development of any web solution that has a business objective, but is also a very dynamic process consisting of different sub-processes.

In a last step, it is essential to monitor the impact of publications in order to continuously improve the scope of content, to adapt the content strategy when needed and to make sure that guidelines and regulations have been obeyed and will be kept in future by changing them or implementing new ones when necessary.

Table 28.2 gives examples of specific requirements for the content management process. It further demonstrates that insufficient content management – meaning content management that does not take into consideration different requirements – can involve risks to the organization in all three categories of digitalization: people, processes and technology. It also shows the importance of analyzing technological conditions, processes, data and regulatory requirements, because analysis – as a buzzword – will play an increasingly important role in the future of content management.

28.2.3 Content Management of the Future Putting the Customer First

From a current perspective, content management can be seen as a core competency of the digital evolution as its success is dependent on regularly changing technology, processes that have to be adapted in line with regulations and guidelines, and the involvement of people who have to be taught both of the above. As a core competency, it does not only leverage but also harm the progress of digitalization of e-commerce brands.

What does tomorrow's content look like and how will it be managed? Communication, sourcing of information and entertainment have become more interpersonal and individual already. This change has to be transferred to a company's interaction with its customers as well as other business. Hence, customer service has changed and companies have to improve their CRM with due consideration of content management. Besides a neat product data base and real-time inventory management, e-commerce brands have to offer their customers diverse touchpoints such as owned, earned and paid media for example, as well as interactive communication with a focus on quality and meaningful content [15].

As demonstrated, content management is going to consider organizational and regulatory processes and technologies that allow extensive **analytics**. It is even imaginable that the term 'content management' will change into 'experience management', 'customer engagement' or similar terms that put customer satisfaction first. A direct customer approach will be one of the key competencies of CRM and content management in the future and companies will have to offer more direct, easier and more attractive ways for customers to get in touch with a brand – ideally automatically, as marketing **automation** is another key word for the content management of the future. That is why intelligent assistants such as chat bots could serve as a major interface between companies and users in future, as an interested party turns into a potential buyer or customer just because of an interesting conversation [15].

28.3   Chat Bots: Content Management System for the Digital Evolution

Chat bots – digital real time channels that are further defined as speech-driven or virtual communication assistants [16] – analyze the context of the users' messages and react to them. They usually consist of an input and output form which enables the dialogue with an underlying system or database. Hence, these systems and databases are being filled with knowledge and answers based on 'typical' communication and often follow pre-defined patterns [17] and thus meet the requirements of the buzzword 'conversational commerce'. Bots constantly learn the users' needs by adding structure and fast and cheap information to the users' lives (e. g. answering questions or giving updates automatically). As a result, user satisfaction is not the only benefit, as other brands can save money and time in their marketing operations as well [18].

Intelligent assistants get to know a brand's customers better and better by exploiting smart data from conversations. Data such as for example gender, favorite colors and travel destinations are full of value for e-commerce brands as they can be used to create individualized offers in the form of content for their target group based on a clear picture about them and their needs and wishes [15]. Bots are already able to automatically spread content such as news or brochures for a brand matching the information given by users [17].

Usage of applications that integrate chat bots such as WeChat is becoming ever more popular. The instant messenger has been developed much further than any usual messenger and has become its own ecosystem. For example, users can place orders, pay bills, book appointments and much more [19]. Briefly summarized, WeChat directly aims at peoples' daily routines and satisfies their need for less complexity. Nevertheless, WeChat records lower user numbers than WhatsApp and Facebook Messenger. But, an increase of almost 40% has been observed in the number of monthly active users between Q1 15 and Q1 16 from 549 million to 762 million, which is pointing to the way ahead [20].

Still, in the context of the digital evolution, chat bots have to be developed further to keep user satisfaction high. Currently, human intelligence is still strongly involved in the activity patterns of bots, as they either have to be taught by a developer or at least have to learn from conversations and interactions with humans. When it comes to situations that exceed clearly defined processes or simple structures, bots still regularly fail. Nevertheless, bots are expected to address even more (potential) customers in future and fulfill their wishes while working even more automatically and being able to learn and develop themselves further. They might be integrated into the operating systems of smartphones or tablets and thus be able to complete all tasks of a user on their own. Customer service will then reach a new technical level [15].

28.4 Conclusion: Digital Governance Framework for Content Management

Our conclusion is that, from a current and future perspective, content management can and must be seen as one of the core competencies of the digital evolution, as it provides the basis of any information shared with the (digital) public, which increasingly becomes important for digital marketplaces.

By segmenting the digital evolution into the three categories people, technology and processes, and by defining content management as three main processes (sourcing and editing, publishing and monitoring), we set a clear, however incomplete scope for our arguments within this theoretical article.

Within this scope, we illustrate the comprehensive impact content management has on corporate digital marketing instruments and on their economic objectives. We provide recent examples of German e-commerce brands, relating to investments in all three categories of the digital evolution. On the other hand, we claim that insufficient content management can trigger risks and harm corporations. We show examples of requirements that need to be fulfilled for the different content management processes and the respective categories of evolution.

Chat bots as a scenario for future content management have great potential, but are not a remedy to fulfill the aforementioned requirements. Quite the opposite is expected: for increasing automation of the spread of content all three categories of the digital evolution, namely technology, processes and people, have to be equipped with profound know-how. Enough resources have to be provided, and commitments, guidelines and regulations for content management have to be met and their compliance be monitored.

One basic element that focuses adherence to these rules is the development of a 'digital governance framework' for content management systems that defines clearly structured processes, addressing stakeholders both internally and externally. Such a framework contains the objectives of a brand's digital communication as well as risks of content management, the programs used, structural and procedural organization and processes to guide monitoring and reporting operations in a particular direction. At the same time,

Fig. 28.1 Elements of a digital governance framework considering three areas of the digital evolution. (KPMG 2016)

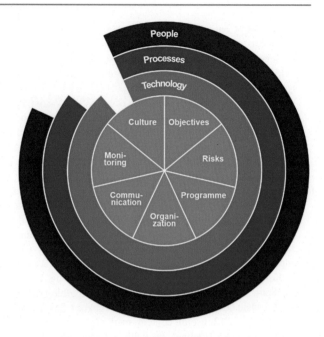

this framework contains practicable guidelines for a company's communication in general and enables decision makers to develop and live programs for the promotion of a digital culture. Fig. 28.1 provides as an example an overview of all the aforementioned elements.

The example of chat bots makes it clear that technology is going to develop further and will improve continuously and fast. From an ethical and economical point of view the question arises as to how big and uncontrolled the gap between technology and its users will grow. Accepting content management as a core competency for digital transformation will not be sufficient to fill this gap in the long term. An active, well considered implementation of a governance framework for content management and thus adaption of existing governance instruments would be suitable to meet modern responsibilities in this area and would provide an adequate basis for the future of a brand's digital communication.

As stated above, we have only looked at selected examples to examine content management as a core competency for the digital evolution. In order to support the argument with sustainable data, we suggest to further examine this area in a scientific manner, e. g. through comparisons of investments within the three areas of evolution with key performance indicators (KPIs) or a mature existing content management with requirements of a given governance framework.

References

1. i-scoop, "Digital transformation: online guide to digital business transformation," i-scoop, [Online]. Available: http://www.i-scoop.eu/digital-transformation/. [Accessed 13 07 2016].

2. "Stichwort: Content Management," Gabler Wirtschaftslexikon, [Online]. Available: http://wirtschaftslexikon.gabler.de/Definition/content-management-v9.html. [Accessed 06 07 2016].
3. ecommerce Magazin, "Content-Management-Systeme (CMS)," ecommerce magazin, 22 12 2015. [Online]. Available: http://www.e-commerce-magazin.de/themen/content-management-systeme-cms. [Accessed 06 07 2016].
4. Vasont Systems, "What is the value of a CMS?," Vasont Systems, [Online]. Available: https://www.vasont.com/resources/what-is-the-value-of-a-cms.html. [Accessed 07 07 2016].
5. I. Lukač, "The importance of integrating e-commerce and content management on a deeper level (let's tango)," eZ, 26 10 2015. [Online]. Available: https://ez.no/Blog/The-importance-of-integrating-e-commerce-and-content-management-on-a-deeper-level-Let-s-Tango. [Accessed 29 08 2016].
6. G. Grunert, "5 Beispiele für exzellentes Content Marketing im E-Commerce," Crispy Content, 28 01 2016. [Online]. Available: http://blog.crispycontent.de/5-beispiele-fuer-exzellentes-content-marketing-im-e-commerce. [Accessed 29 08 2016].
7. J. Pavelka, "The Importance of Quality Content in eCommerce Sites," Clarity Ventures, Inc., 31 12 2014. [Online]. Available: https://www.clarity-ventures.com/articles/article/1596/the-importance-of-quality-content-in-ecommerce-sites. [Accessed 29 08 2016].
8. L. Kolowich, "4 Mistakes to Avoid When Scaling Your Content Marketing [Infographic]," HubSpot, 31 05 2016. [Online]. Available: http://blog.hubspot.com/marketing/scaling-content-mistakes#sm.000mfdcdd1old5s10bd25btkfwua4. [Accessed 29 08 2016].
9. G. Charlton, "12 useful content marketing examples from ecommerce brands," Econsultancy, 12 05 2015. [Online]. Available: https://econsultancy.com/blog/66432-12-useful-content-marketing-examples-from-ecommerce-brands/. [Accessed 29 08 2016].
10. eMarketer, "Advertising & Marketing: Site Visits, Social Shares Measure Content Marketing Success in Europe," eMarketer, 18 03 2016. [Online]. Available: http://www.emarketer.com/Article/Site-Visits-Social-Shares-Measure-Content-Marketing-Success-Europe/1013970. [Accessed 29 08 2016].
11. G. Satell, "Marketing: Content Marketers Need to Act Like Publishers," Harvard Business Review, 21 03 2016. [Online]. Available: https://hbr.org/2016/03/content-marketers-need-to-act-like-publishers. [Accessed 29 08 2016].
12. J. Lee, "Editorial Strategy and Planning/Operations, Teams and Process: A Step-by-Step Guide to Becoming a Brand Publisher," Content Marketing Institute, 22 03 2015. [Online]. Available: http://contentmarketinginstitute.com/2015/03/guide-brand-publisher/. [Accessed 29 08 2016].
13. E. Machin, "What is earned, owned & paid media? The difference explained.," Titan SEO, [Online]. Available: https://www.titan-seo.com/newsarticles/trifecta.html. [Accessed 06 07 2016].
14. S. Johnson, "13 Spooky Stats to Scare Your Boss Into Better Marketing [SlideShare]," HubSpot, 31 10 2013. [Online]. Available: http://blog.hubspot.com/marketing/13-spooky-stats-to-scare-your-boss-into-better-marketing. [Accessed 29 08 2016].
15. TWT Digital Group GmbH, "The Next Big Thing im eCommerce: Verkaufen per Chatbot," 01 07 2016. [Online]. Available: https://www.twt.de/news/detail/the-next-big-thing-im-ecommerce-verkaufen-per-chatbot.html. [Accessed 31 07 2016].
16. TWT Digital Group GmbH, "Chatbots: Umsatz dank neuem Kommunikations-Assistenten," 05 25 2016. [Online]. Available: https://www.twt.de/news/detail/chatbots-umsatz-dank-neuem-kommunikations-assistenten.html. [Accessed 31 07 2016].
17. C. Erxleben, "Wie Bots Marketing und E-Commerce verändern," INTERNET WORLD Business, 22 06 2016. [Online]. Available: http://www.internetworld.de/technik/bots/bots-marketing-e-commerce-veraendern-1109221.html. [Accessed 31 07 2016].

18. TWT Digital Group GmbH, "Chatbots: Umsatz dank neuem Kommunikations-Assistenten," 25 05 2016. [Online]. Available: https://www.twt.de/news/detail/chatbots-umsatz-dank-neuem-kommunikations-assistenten.html. [Accessed 31 07 2016].

19. J. Kaczmarek, "Das Phänomen WeChat," DK Online-Medien UG, 09 03 2016. [Online]. Available: https://web.archive.org/web/20160310160456/http://www.digitalkompakt.de/uebersicht/wechat-messenger/. [Accessed 31 97 2017].

20. Tencent, "Tencent announces 2016 firt quarter results," 18 05 2016. [Online]. Available: http://www.tencent.com/en-us/content/ir/news/2016/attachments/20160518.pdf. [Accessed 31 07 2016].

Further Reading

21. G. Coulouris, J. Dollimore and T. Kindberg, Distributed Systems – Concepts and Design, Amsterdam: Addison-Wesley Longman, 2005.

22. Wikipedia, [Online]. Available: http://de.wikipedia.org/wiki/Remote_Method_Invocation. [Accessed 26 05 2011].

23. 7 Connections, "http://www.7connections.com," [Online]. Available: http://www.7connections.com/blog/how-marketing-channels-have-changed. [Accessed 14 07 2016].

24. Pardot, "http://www.pardot.com," [Online]. Available: http://www.pardot.com/what-is-marketing-automation/. [Accessed 13 07 2016].

25. Hasecke, "http://www.hasecke.com," [Online]. Available: http://www.hasecke.com/plone-benutzerhandbuch/4.0/cms/cms.html. [Accessed 06 07 2016].

26. Socialmediaführerschein, "http://socialmediafuehrerschein.de," 05 04 2011. [Online]. Available: http://socialmediafuehrerschein.de/2011/04/05/was-ist-earned-owned-und-paid-media/. [Accessed 06 07 2016].

27. Gründerszene, "http://www.gruenderszene.de/," [Online]. Available: http://www.gruenderszene.de/lexikon/begriffe/earned-media. [Accessed 06 07 2016].

28. C. Messina, "Tweet: how do you feel about using # (pound) for groups. As in #barcamp [msg]?," 23 08 2007. [Online]. Available: https://twitter.com/chrismessina/status/223115412. [Accessed 31 07 2016].

29. C. Messina, "2016 will be the year of conversational commerce," Medium, 19 01 2016. [Online]. Available: https://medium.com/chris-messina/2016-will-be-the-year-of-conversational-commerce-1586e85e3991#.yapmq2x7t. [Accessed 31 07 2016].

30. TWT Digital Group GmbH, "Wie Chatbots lernen und den Umsatz steigern," 23 06 2016. [Online]. Available: https://www.twt.de/news/detail/wie-chatbots-lernen-und-den-umsatz-steigern.html. [Accessed 31 07 2016].

31. F. Schmiechen, "Hallo Bot: Das Ende der Apps, wie wir sie kennen," 05 07 2016. [Online]. Available: http://www.gruenderszene.de/allgemein/ende-der-apps?utm_source=feedly&utm_medium=rss&utm_campaign=rss&utm_source=rss&utm_medium=rss&utm_campaign=ende-der-apps&_lrsc=9760a935-96f4-4097-aeab-b989a72e9fee&utm_source=twitter&utm_medium=social&utm_campaign=Ele. [Accessed 31 07 2016].

32. W3Techs, "Usage Statistics and Market Share of Content Management Systems for Websites, July 2016," Q-Success, 31 07 2016. [Online]. Available: https://w3techs.com/technologies/overview/content_management/all. [Accessed 31 07 2016].

The European Network and Information Security Directive – a Cornerstone of the Digital Single Market

29

Martin Schallbruch

Abstract

Digital markets strongly depend on a sufficient level of network and information security. As the digitization of all business processes leads to a complex landscape of digital networks, systems, and services, overarching security standards become crucial for the economic development. Thus, state actors worldwide aim to build regulatory frameworks to somehow guarantee network and information security. Right now, with regard to the digital economy, Europe is not at the forefront of the global economic regions. By passing a new regulation on network and information security, the Union aims to present a modern regulatory approach to a key issue of the digital economy. The EU directive, set into force in August 2016, is a major step to a stable regulatory environment, that might be a raw model for regulators worldwide. However, from a technology perspective, the legislation will predominantly lead to compliance efforts of market operators, not to technological innovations. To some extent, this can be bridged by the development of market standards under the regulation. Nevertheless, further regulatory action is suggested.

29.1 Network and Information Security for Digital Markets

Not a big surprise: The digitization of the economy is essential for growth and prosperity in Europe. Comparing the global economic regions, the EU is not at the forefront of digitization. According to studies by the European Commission, 41% of European companies are not digital, only 2% take full advantage of digital opportunities [1]. Few European

M. Schallbruch (✉)
ESMT Berlin
Berlin, Germany
e-mail: martin.schallbruch@esmt.org

© Springer-Verlag GmbH Germany 2018
C. Linnhoff-Popien et al. (eds.), *Digital Marketplaces Unleashed*,
https://doi.org/10.1007/978-3-662-49275-8_29

companies are amongst the world's ICT leaders. The long term investment level in digital networks in Europe is below the US and Asia [2]. At the same time, it is estimated that a further digitization of the European economy can create up to 1.5 million new jobs [3]. The completion of a Digital Single Market in Europe is therefore one of the Junker Commission's key policy objectives. With the Digital Single Market Strategy of 2015, the EU Commission presented its program for achieving this goal [1].

A high level of cybersecurity is a crucial prerequisite for Europe's digital growth. Cybersecurity of digital infrastructures and digital services plays an important and ever growing role for the functioning of the internal market. Different levels of cybersecurity among the Member States are hindering transnational electronic services. Economic theory holds that an appropriate level of cybersecurity cannot be achieved by market actors alone. Government action is required [4].

With the adoption of the EU Directive on Network and Information Security (NIS) in the summer of 2016, Europe has established requirements and management structures for network and information security. This article examines the role of the new EU legislation in the development of digital technology and digital business models. It looks into the legislation from a technology perspective, asking whether technological development to reduce cyber risks is stimulated by the regulation.

29.2   Regulatory Approaches to Cybersecurity

For a long time, the only international cybersecurity regulation was the *Council of Europe Cybercrime Convention* of 2001 (Budapest convention), set into force in 2004 [5]. Up to now, 49 countries worldwide have ratified the convention [6]. The aim of the convention is mainly a common criminal policy on cybercrime, i. e. the classification of criminal offences. It is not the objective of the Budapest Convention to, at some extent, stimulate technological or organisational means to enhance cybersecurity. The starting point for a broader discussion about cybersecurity regulation can be placed in 2003, when the *G 8 principles for protecting critical infrastructures* were adopted. This international document was one of the first to call for legislative cybersecurity measures by nation states. Subsequent recommendations by the UN, OECD, and ITU intensified the international pressure on states to act for the rising issue of cybersecurity [7].

The core element of the first regulatory discussion was ensuring the security of critical infrastructures. Critical infrastructures such as energy and water supply, health systems, transport, finance, and public administration, are crucially important for the functioning of modern societies. At the same time, these infrastructures are highly dependent on reliable information technology. Critical infrastructure protection is therefore a key issue of almost all national cyber security strategies worldwide [8]. Although in general privately owned, most critical infrastructures are already regulated to implement public requirements such as the safety of energy supply.

Therefore, initial regulatory approaches to protect the IT of critical infrastructures had a strong reference to prevailing models of safety regulation of infrastructures. However, the regulation models differ from country to country. In particular, rule-based approaches and risk-based approaches confront each other. In rule-based approaches, the state poses specific requirements to the operators of critical infrastructures; fulfilment of the requirements have to be demonstrated or certified. Under risk-based legislation operators have to build up their own risk management system. Defining the appropriate means to meet the risks is up to them [9]. The complex nature of risks in cyberspace, the low level of particular technical knowledge of the regulatory bodies, and the high technical development speed makes a purely rule-based approach too complicated. A classic top down regulation by the state is not possible [4].

Often Public Private Partnerships are considered suitable means for solving this problem. Also at European level, a corresponding PPP, the European Public Private Partnership for Resilience (EP3R), was established in 2009 [4]. However, the idea of ensuring cyber security solely through PPP has proved difficult to implement. Robust empirical evidence of the success of a pure PPP approach still does not exist. The interests of the parties are too divergent. The commitment of the private side in the PPP often follows regulatory threats coming about [4]. Nonetheless, PPP elements can make a contribution to increasing cyber security of critical infrastructures. The technical expertise of the private side helps to compensate for a lack of sector specific technical understanding on the side of the rule-setting regulator.

There is broad consensus in the literature that so called mixed regulatory responses are the best choice for the legislation of cybersecurity of critical infrastructures [4, 9]. Rule setting, elements of self-regulation and stimulating market mechanisms are regarded to be most successful in combination. Regulators, on the one hand, get an instrument to check compliance of companies (with respect to the set of rules). Private sector actors, on the other hand, get the chance to define levels and measures of security improvement on their own, meanwhile they have to comply with basic government rules. Technological solutions for cybersecurity are stimulated by giving the market actor the freedom to ask for innovation to fulfil their own, majorly risk based interest in appropriate cybersecurity.

The advantages of a mixed approach are especially obvious with regard to the different security maturity of market operators. While small and medium enterprises have to comply with the minimum security requirements posed by the regulator, bigger and more security mature companies easily meet the regulators' demand. For them, a risk-based innovation of their security preparedness can be stimulated by regulation [9].

An important reference to the European discussion were the US policy plans for cybersecurity and critical infrastructure protection. With a Presidential Executive Order, adopted in 2013, together with a Presidential Policy Directive (so called PPD-21), the US government set out the strategy and action points for cybersecurity of critical infrastructures. As several bills on cybersecurity failed in congress, the president's initiative follows a completely voluntary approach for private companies. On the basis of PPD-21, the US National Institute of Standards and Technology (NIST) issued a Cybersecurity

Framework, a set of risk-based cybersecurity standards that had been developed in close collaboration with industry [7]. In fact, as a result of long-term disputes in congress, the Cybersecurity Act of 2015 has recently been passed. However, it doesn't change the voluntary character of the technical and organizational standards issued by NIST. The US has decided to move forward with the soft-law approach to cybersecurity standards.

29.2.1   EU Directive on Network and Information Security

European Institutions started to work on network and information security in 2001. One of the first steps was the implementation of a *European Network and Information Security Agency* (ENISA), based in Heraklion, Greece. Over the years, ENISA gained influence on the development of cybersecurity structures in the member states (see Table 29.1), assisting in building up Computer Incident Response Teams (CIRTs) and advising European Commission and Member States. Following this, European Commission and EU Council adopted various communications on critical information infrastructures and network and information security. In 2012, the European Commission started an impact assessment to cover policy options to improve the network and information security. The assessment involved many stakeholders in Europe, such as Member States, academics, private companies and the general public. The results were presented in 2013 [10]. Grounded on the findings of the impact assessment and framed by the strategic objectives of the simultaneously developed *Cybersecurity Strategy of the European Union* [11], the European Commission decided for regulatory action.

Based on the EU competence in harmonisation of the internal market pursuant to Art. 114 TFEU, the Commission submitted a proposal, which contained, on the one hand, obligations for Member States, and on the other, requirements for market participants. While Member States should strengthen their preparedness and cooperation, the market participants were required to improve the information security of their systems and to report cyber incidents to relevant authorities [7]. From the beginning, the Commission's proposal overarched the field of critical infrastructures ("operators of critical infrastructures", later renamed to "operator of essential services") and also took into account the

Table 29.1 Importance of sectors for NIS regulation. (European Commission [10])

Sector	No. of respondents who see the need to ensure NIS in this sector (in %)
Banking and finance	91.1
Energy	89.4
Health	89.4
Internet services	89.1
Public administrations	87.5
Transport	81.7

providers of digital services, which were initially called "provider of information society services." This was somehow a result of the impact assessment. Internet services were seen as one of the most important sectors for security of network and information systems.

As a result of a three-year legislative procedure between the European Parliament, EU Council, and European Commission, an agreement was reached on a *Directive Concerning Measures for a High Common Level of Security of Network and Information Systems Across the Union* at the end of 2015 [12]. It contains three pillars. The first pillar obliges the EU Member States to step up their own structures for cybersecurity. The adoption of a national cybersecurity strategy (art. 7), the designation of one or more competent authorities (art. 8) and the establishment of a *Computer Security Incident Response Team* (CIRT) are mandatory. The second pillar is the establishment of a cooperation mechanism at EU level. EU and national measures to cybersecurity will be strategically coordinated in a permanent *Cooperation Group*, composed of representatives from Member States, European Commission, and the ENISA (art. 11). The more practical exchange about risks, incidents, and best practices will take place in a newly founded European *CSIRTs Network* (art. 12).

The third pillar of the EU Directive concerns the market operators. The EU requires Member States to impose cybersecurity requirements on operators of critical infrastructures and providers of digital services. Here, the EU chooses a mixed regulatory approach, however, with slight differences between the two kinds of companies: Operators of essential services have to take technical and organisational measures to manage the risks posed to the security of their network and information systems. Here, the operator's measures must be appropriate to the specific risks. The directive does not specify which concrete measures are to be taken. However, Member States have to carefully identify the operators of essential services and ensure compliance with the obligations, for example by conducting security audits or inspecting results of independent audits. Therefore, it is up to the Member States to more specifically define what technical and organizational measures meet compliance requirements. Penalties for the infringements of the security provisions have to be laid down under national law (art. 21).

The regulation of digital services is less rule based. The inclusion of digital services was one of the focal points of the political debate. In particular, US based over-the-top providers massively rejected specific security regulations for their services. Following lengthy discussions in the legislative process EU institutions agreed to include a part of the digital services in the regulation, but those which are especially relevant for the digital economy. These are online marketplaces (including app stores), online search engines, and cloud computing services. Beyond that, the concept of cloud services is interpreted very broadly ("a digital service that enables access to a scalable and elastic pool of shareable computing resources," Art. 4, No. 19).

For the provider of such digital services the Directive presents much more specific requirements on the technical and organizational means to protect their services (see Art. 16 NIS directive). However, for digital services, Member States are not required to identify companies governed by these regulations or to check their compliance with the obligations. Both groups, operators of essential services and digital service providers must report

Table 29.2 Policy instruments used in the EU directive. (Source: Own adaption, based on Irion [4])

Policy Instruments	Positive Incentives	Negative Incentives
Legal and regulatory measures	Public ICT security trustmark	*National legislation/regulation of information security*
	Setting-up national CERT functionality	Mandating best practices to enhance information security
		Liabilities in case of failure to meet required standards
		Security breach information duties
		Compulsory memberships in professional organizations/PPP
Economic measures	Tax credits and privileges for certain initiatives	*Financial penalties for violation of legal/regulatory provisions (compensatory, punitive)*
	Public subsidies for certain investments in information security	Payments for access to valuable information
		Insurance markets
Technical measures	*Technical guidance*	*Information security standards*
	Offering technical assistance	*Mandating security testing, audits or peer-evaluation*
	Education and training relevant to ICT security	Mandating participation in security exercises
Informational measures	*National and international information sharing in information security*	*Publication of individual operator's ICT security breach notifications*

security incidents to the appropriate authorities. If there were a public interest in knowing about the incident, the competent authority should inform the public.

With the mixed approach regulation and the extension of minimum security standards to digital service providers, the EU is taking a major step in regulating the security of cyberspace. The italic fields in Table 29.2 show the negative and positive incentives that the EU directive takes to enhance cybersecurity. The table is based on a scheme developed by Kristina Irion out of the variety of policy instruments for cybersecurity found in literature. It shows that European regulators take up a majority of respective policy instruments. By May 2018, the Directive must be implemented by the Member States to their national law. It goes into effect for market operators after that implementation.

29.3 EU Directive and Technology Development – A Critical View

A major objective of the EU's cybersecurity strategy is to enhance cybersecurity in technology development and digital business innovation. Companies are requested to use advanced cybersecurity technology and to take cyber risks into account when digital business models are further developed. In this respect, the Directive could be characterised as a first attempt to incentivize more secure technology and services. The regulation of cyber risks is still in its infancy. Worldwide it is based on a weak empirical basis. Also, the EU proposal was based on an extremely limited number of well-evaluated cyber incidents [13]. Risk assessment and risk regulation of cyber risks are not yet appropriately developed, i. e. compared to the banking and finance sector, where regulation followed much more substantial risk models [13].

With the mixed regulation approach, the EU has chosen the regulation method with the best prospects of success [7]. It combines a "check box approach," i. e. the need for market operators to meet compliance requirements, with an obligation to set-up or improve a particular risk management system. The central requirement for private companies to "take appropriate and proportionate technical and organizational measures to manage the risks posed to the security of network and information systems" (art. 14, similar in art. 16) is open for a sector or company specific choice of measures. Therefore, "the EU approach has the potential to set an example to the rest of the world regarding the interests and values to be preserved through legislation in this field" [7].

What is astounding is the almost total abandonment of self-regulation elements in the Directive. In particular, a cooperative element could help to improve the technical measures to be taken [4]. An example of such an instrument can be found in the German IT security law of 2015, adopted before the passing of the Directive. There, critical infrastructure operators are entitled to define industry standards as minimum security standards. After approval by the competent authority, these standards are obligatory for the relevant industry [14]. The EU Directive leaves it open to Member States' implementation for incorporating such participatory elements – at least for the essential services. However, in the design of technical standards in the context of such self-regulation, European or internationally accepted market standards must be taken into account (art. 19). Regarding the sector of digital services, the consideration of participatory elements is not possible as the Member States have very little implementation flexibility. The European Commission is entitled to adopt implementing acts to specify the standards digital service providers have to comply with. An involvement of the private sector in the development of these standards is not provided. The cooperation group, composed of European Commission, ENISA, and Member States, will only discuss standards with representatives from the relevant European standardisation organisations (art. 11).

Internationally ground-breaking is the specification of security requirements of digital services [7]. By regulating not only the critical infrastructure, but also the most important digital services (especially the cloud services), the Directive will immediately influence the technology development of digitization. Here, Europe goes far beyond the approach of the United States, which is solely targeting critical infrastructure. In Europe, the "internet giants [are] involved in the goal of achieving critical infrastructure protection" [7].

More could have been done by the EU to stimulate the development of security technology. After all, the "mismatch between functional ICT developments and an appropriate level of cybersecurity to those developments" [15] is one of the biggest challenges for cybersecurity, so far barely seen by regulators. Only Germany and Japan have addressed this issue in their cybersecurity strategies. Japan particularly addresses the cybersecurity challenge from a more technological viewpoint, taking into account the need for technical agility to address the dynamic cyber threats [15].

In this regard, the issue of stronger liability of ICT producers for vulnerabilities in their products had been discussed in the legislation process. One of the most important reasons for security incidents is the exploitation of vulnerabilities in immature software products. Unfortunately, the Directive could not bring about a system which increases the liability. To tackle the root of many cybersecurity problems, an increased liability of ICT producers cannot be avoided. The existing liability regimes have not led software manufacturers to bring mature products to the market, even if those products are intended for use in essential services.

For now, the EU Directive at least offers an initial starting point to come to greater responsibility of manufacturers. By requiring "state-of-the-art" security technology for appropriate cybersecurity, the EU Directive stimulates the development of industry-specific and cross-industry market standards. First manufacturer organisations have developed state-of-the-art handbooks to assist market operators in choosing the best technology (for example [16] in Germany). For the operators of essential services, Member States may take up the European regulation further; for the digital service providers, it is up to the European Commission to enhance technological cybersecurity by adopting demanding implementing acts.

References

1. European Commission, "A Digital Single Market Strategy for Europe {COM(2015) 192 final}," 2015.
2. OECD, "OECD Communications Outlook 2013," 2013. [Online]. Available: http://www.oecd.org/sti/broadband/oecd-communications-outlook-19991460.htm. [Accessed 26 08 2016].
3. S. Muylle und E. Vijverman, "Online Jobs Boosting Europe's Competitiveness," 2013. [Online]. Available: http://www.vlerick.com/en/research-and-faculty/knowledge-items/knowledge/online-jobs-boost-europes-competitiveness. [Accessed 25 08 2016].
4. K. Irion, "The Governance of Network and Information Security in the European Union: The European Public-Private Partnership for Resilience (EP3R)," in *27th European Communications Policy Research Conference (EUROCPR)*, 2012.
5. Council of Europe, "Convention of Cybercrime," *European Treaty Series,* Nr. 185, 23 11 2001.
6. Council of Europe, "Chart of signatures and ratifications of Treaty 185 (Convention of Cybercrime)," 2016. [Online]. Available: https://www.coe.int/en/web/conventions/full-list/-/conventions/treaty/185/signatures?p_auth=JhfeP2x7. [Accessed 25 8 2016].
7. A. Segura Serrano, "Cybersecurity: towards a global standard in the protection of critical information infrastructures," *European Journal of Law and Technology,* Nr. 3, pp. 1–24, 2015.
8. S. J. Shackelford und A. Kastelic, "Toward a State-Centric Cyber Peace: Analyzing the Role of National Cybersecurity Strategies in Enhancing Global Cybersecurity," *New York University Journal of Legislation and Public Policy,* Nr. 4, pp. 895–984, 2015.

9. F. Massacci, R. Ruprai, M. Collinson und J. Williams, "Economic Impacts of Rules- versus Risk-Based Cybersecurity Regulations for Critical Infrastructure Providers," *IEEE Security & Privacy,* Bd. 14, Nr. 3, pp. 52–60, 2016.

10. European Commission, "Impact Assessment – accompanying the document "Proposal for a Directive of the European Parliament and of the Council concerning measures to ensure a high level of network and information security across the Union" {COM (2013) 48 final}," 2013.

11. European Commission; High Representative of the European Union for Foreign Affairs and Security Policy, *Cybersecurity Strategy of the European Union: An Open, Safe and Secure Cyberspace {JOIN(2013) 1 final},* 2013, pp. 1–20.

12. European Parliament and Council of the European Union, "Directive (EU) 2016/1148 of the European Parliament and of the Council of 6 July 2016 concerning measures for a high common level of security of network and information systems across the Union," *Official Journal of the European Union,* Nr. L194, 19 7 2016.

13. E. Fahey, "The EU's Cybercrime and Cyber-Security Rulemaking: Mapping the Internal and External Dimensions of EU Security," *European Journal of Risk Regulation,* Bd. 5, Nr. 1, pp. 46–60, 2014.

14. A. Könen, "IT-Sicherheit gesetzlich geregelt," *Datenschutz und Datensicherung,* Nr. 1, pp. 12–16, 2016.

15. E. Luiijf, K. Besseling und P. de Graaf, "Nineteen national cyber security strategies," *Int. J. Critical Infrastructures,* Bd. 9, Nr. 1/2, pp. 3–31, 2013.

16. TeleTrusT e. V., "Handreichung zum "Stand der Technik" im Sinne des IT-Sicherheitsgesetzes (German)," 2016. [Online]. Available: https://www.teletrust.de/fileadmin/docs/fachgruppen/ag-stand-der-technik/TeleTrusT-Handreichung_Stand_der_Technik.pdf. [Accessed 26 08 2016].

Further Reading
17. E. G. Baud, P. Bru, L. de Muyter, E. Fortunet, J. Little und S. Macchi di Cellere, "Europe proposes new laws and regulations on cybersecurity," 2 1 2014. [Online]. Available: http://www.lexology.com/library/detail.aspx?g=1f872876-3d23-44e7-a8f1-92a9be8d080b. [Accessed 25 8 2016].

The Future of Machine Learning and Predictive Analytics

30

Ali Reza Samanpour, André Ruegenberg, and Robin Ahlers

Abstract

The history of artificial intelligence shows us that there has been a gradual and evolutionary development within the special aspects of computational sciences that underlie the technologies prevalent in machine learning. Most of the technologies consist of methods defined by so-called computational intelligence, including neural networks, evolutionary algorithms and fuzzy systems. Data mining topics have also become more significant, due to the rapid growth in the quantities of data now available (Big Data), combined with having to face the same challenges encountered in the IoT (Internet of Things). The question now is: How can computers be made to do what needs to be done without anyone prescribing how it should be done? Nowadays, a whole range of providers offers frameworks for machine learning. Some of them allow us to use machine learning tools in the cloud. This option is mainly provided by the big players like Microsoft Azure ML, Amazon Machine Learning, IBM Bluemix and Google Prediction API, to name but a few.

Machine learning algorithms extract high-level, complex abstractions as data representations by means of a hierarchical learning process. Complex abstractions are learnt at a given level based on relatively simple abstractions formulated in the preceding level in the hierarchy. Deep learning is a subarea of machine learning, and could even be described as a further development of this. While traditional machine learning al-

A. R. Samanpour (✉) · A. Ruegenberg · R. Ahlers
University of Applied Sciences South Westphalia
Iserlohn, Germany
e-mail: samanpour.ali-reza@fh-swf.de

A. Ruegenberg
e-mail: ruegenberg.andre@fh-swf.de

R. Ahlers
e-mail: ahlers.robin@fh-swf.de

© Springer-Verlag GmbH Germany 2018
C. Linnhoff-Popien et al. (eds.), *Digital Marketplaces Unleashed*,
https://doi.org/10.1007/978-3-662-49275-8_30

gorithms rely on solid model groups for recognition and classification, deep learning algorithms develop and create their own new model levels within the neural networks independently. New models do not need to be repeatedly developed and implemented manually for each new set of data based on different structures, as would be the case for classic machine learning algorithms. The advantage of deep learning is the analysis and learning of massive amounts of unsupervised data, making it a valuable tool for Big Data Analytics where raw data is largely unlabeled and uncategorized.

30.1   Introduction

The World Wide Web offers a multitude of opportunities for anyone who wants to share their views with a wide audience or comment on products, movies etc., in particular through social media platforms like Twitter and Facebook.

Assuming that all profit-seeking companies aspire to maximize their share of the market – if not to become market leader – they depend on a high degree of customer satisfaction and will therefore strive to fulfill as many customer wishes as possible.

Companies are extremely keen to make good use of any information they can garner from social media in order to achieve this goal. Reviews and opinions that consumers share voluntarily on the Internet can be collated and analyzed to draw conclusions about customer preferences and identify potential product improvements. Thanks to information systems like sentiment analysis the wealth of information available can be translated effectively into useable knowledge. The challenge lies in obtaining sufficiently accurate data and applying efficient analysis methods [1].

This article aims to provide an insight into the enigma of artificial intelligence – no longer limited to science fiction – and to illustrate some useful applications for companies with a strong consumer focus, as well as a brief look ahead to the future of machine learning.

30.2   Categorization – Machine Learning and Data Mining

As Fig. 30.1 shows, in addition to machine learning and data mining there are several other terms which should be defined here. *Data mining* refers to a process of pattern recognition in existing, structured data. This process may be carried out automatically with the help of machine learning or semi-automatically by applying statistical methods [2].

Whereas data mining draws from structured data stored in databases, the huge quantities of data we want to analyze from the web are largely unstructured. According [31] to more than 80% of this data is in text form, which is where *text mining* comes in, i. e. the extraction of useable information from input text. Text mining tasks include linguistic analysis and statistical pre-processing [4]. Text mining starts with document or information retrieval, followed by document preparation. First of all, text is tokenized, in other

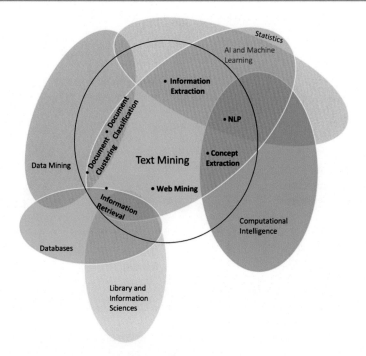

Fig. 30.1 Venn diagram – Categorization. (WinfWiki [3])

words broken up into segments, usually individual words, and the punctuation removed. Stop words (non-content words), such as articles and conjunctions are usually discarded. The next step is part-of-speech tagging, which involves marking each token with a word category. Many tokens can be further reduced to their root form by lemmatizing and stemming. Tokenization thus converts a text into a format that lends itself to more effective analysis. These final steps of document preparation are followed by document transformation.

Transformation often involves weighting the relevance of words in a text using tf-idf (term frequency – inverse document frequency). The tf-idf value reflects the significance of a word in a document, increasing, for example, in proportion with a word's frequency.

This refined data is then stored in a structured form that allows data mining and the application of analysis algorithms, including document classification (Sect. 30.3.2), cluster analyses and association analyses [4].

Fig. 30.2 illustrates the steps involved in the data mining and text mining process.

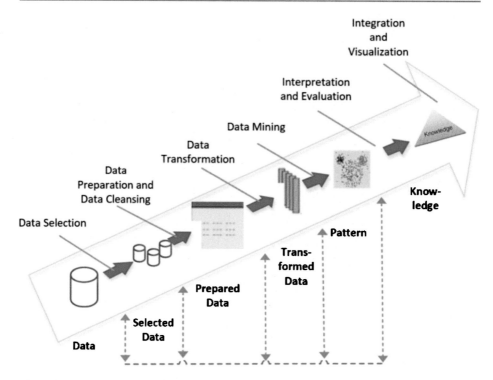

Fig. 30.2 Steps of data mining and text mining. (Sharafi [4])

30.3 Sentiment Analysis in Practice

To better organize the overwhelming quantities of available online content for accurate analysis, it makes sense to classify texts according to *sentiment*. Sentiment analysis, or sentiment detection, serves a number of purposes, including text summarization, the moderation of online forums and monitoring the acceptance levels of a product or brand by following blog discussions [5]. Sentiment analysis is considerably more complex than traditional subject-based classification. For example, although the sentence "How can anyone sit through this movie?" does not contain any obviously negative words, it nevertheless hints at a strongly negative sentiment [6].

Companies from all industry sectors can benefit from sentiment analysis in many different ways, most notably through the increasingly widespread use of customer feedback and review sites for rating films, cars, books, travel, in fact an infinite number of products and services [5].

Sentiment analysis is applied to social media platforms and online retailers for a range of purposes, such as competitor analysis, trend and market analysis, campaign monitoring, event detection, issues and crisis management, to name but a few.

Media-savvy company managers are increasingly recognizing the value of social networking websites as an incredibly rich source of information to identify market opportunities, improve product placement or keep an eye on their competitors. In other words, it allows them to analyze the entire structure of the market.

Most studies classify sentiment by polarity as either positive, negative or neutral [5–7], usually by applying one of two common approaches: dictionary-based and machine learning.

30.3.1   Lexicon-Based Approaches

One method of the dictionary-based approach is *word spotting*. This technique identifies words or phrases and either compares them with a dictionary database, or uses algorithms to determine their sentiment. To begin with, a sentence is segmented and a part of speech is assigned to each word (*POS tagging*). Then every word that is considered relevant to the sentiment of the text is categorized by polarity using a dictionary for reference. This procedure is called the *dictionary-based approach* [5].

Words can be analyzed in isolation or in context, by taking *valence shifters* into consideration. These include negations, intensifiers and diminishers that can reverse, augment or lessen the meaning and thus the polarity value of a sentiment word. If a *valence shifter* is found in the vicinity of a sentiment word the weighting of this is multiplied with the original value of the word [5].

The SO-A approach (*semantic orientation from association*) allows an automated prediction of polarity based on statistical allocation to a collection of negative and positive sample words [5]. The SO-A of a word or a sentence is calculated from the difference between its strength of association with a positive set and its strength of association with a negative set [8]. The polarity of the text as a whole is then determined by calculating the average SO-A value of all the sentences that make up the text. A document is classified by counting the positive or negative words in a text. If the majority of sentiment words in a text are classified as positive, the text as a whole will be regarded as positive. The same applies for negative words. The advantage of *word counting* as opposed to *machine learning* approaches is that this method does not require any machine training and can also be applied when no training data is available.

However, the sheer quantities of information available from different domains render an automated approach to sentiment analysis almost indispensable [5].

30.3.2   Machine Learning

What exactly is meant by *machine learning*? Machine learning has become an intrinsic part of our daily lives. For example, when a customer makes an online purchase, they will then be presented with a range of similar or complementary products. Machine learning is defined as the process of generating models to learn from available data so as to be able to make predictions about future data.

Microsoft's cloud-based Azure Machine Learning Studio, for example, allows the user to create workflows intuitively for machine learning, and there is a wide range of machine learning libraries available for developing prediction solutions. Users can also extend these solutions with their own R or Python scripts [9].

One of the most frequently used methods of machine learning for classification in the context of data and text mining are *naive Bayes, support vector machines* and *maximum entropy classification* [1, 6].

Naive Bayes

Naive Bayes is a simple learning algorithm that applies the Bayes rule in combination with the assumption that the features are independent for a given class. Although the independence assumption does not always apply in practice, naive Bayes nevertheless suffices in many situations as a reliable method of classification. Naive Bayes uses the information from a random sample – the training set – to estimate the underlying probability that a document belongs to a class [10].

The advantages of this approach are that it is more robust for non-relevant features than other, more complex learning methods. Furthermore, it is a very quick classification technique that requires only a small amount of storage capacity [11].

Support Vector Machines (SVM)

Support vector machines are a type of linear algorithm used for classification. In the simplest form of binary classification SVM finds a hyperplane that separates the two classes of the dataset with as wide a gap as possible [12]. The number of separating hyperplanes is infinite in linearly separable training sets. All hyperplanes separate the training set accurately into two classes, but with a variety of results. The optimum separation shows a clear gap between the categories. In other words, the *margin* between the groups of data points should be as wide as possible.

The hyperplane which separates the classes from one another can be pinpointed from a small number of data points that lie on the margin. These are referred to as *support vectors*. First these *support vectors* are identified, then the margin is maximized and the separating hyperplane determined [11]. In practice, however, many problems in data analysis are described with non-linear dependencies. The SVM technique can still be applied in such cases by simply adding kernel functions. The advantages of the SVM method lie in its high accuracy, flexibility, robustness and efficiency [12].

Maximum Entropy Classification

The *entropy* of a word is a quantitative measurement of its information content. For example, the word "beautiful" has a higher weighting than the word "nice". In contrast to the naive Bayes classifier, maximum entropy classification uses weighted properties. It is assumed that properties with a higher weighting also classify the training set most accurately. However, relationships between words are disregarded entirely [13]. From a set of models that are consistent with the observation values the classifier seeks to find an optimum that maximizes the entropy. A higher entropy indicates a higher uncertainty in the probability distribution. The theory behind this is that every other model whose entropy value is not maximum assumes values that have not been considered [14].

30.4   Machine Learning – Inspired by Biology

Computers, or rather classical computer programs, have to know everything. Bits and bytes are being processed, stored and retrieved every millisecond. The results can be reproduced at any time and traced logically. The computer strictly follows its instructions to the end. Although we have come a long way in the last 60 years with this type of programming, we are now beginning to encounter problems and issues that demonstrate that this classical type of information acquisition can be unmanageable, and might even become antiquated and useless.

The time has come for new concepts: software that writes software, algorithms that adapt, optimize themselves and can even predict future results. On the face of it machines do just what we tell them to do. But many problems nowadays are too complex, and cannot be described with exact instructions. We are familiar with a multitude of survival strategies from the natural world. Nature constantly offers us new ways of confronting and mastering difficult situations. The question is therefore: How can machines be created that do exactly what is needed without having to be instructed [15]?

This takes us into the field of artificial intelligence or, more precisely "computational intelligence". Inspired by biology, this field comprises three areas of information processing. These technologies offer mechanisms of biological problem-solving strategies for mathematical or engineering problems, so that these can be made useful. The challenge is to derive a general rule from a quantity of data without explicitly instructing the system what rules to apply for the classification. Using large quantities of data a software construction trains computers to accurately interpret other data quantities autonomously. Although they are trained to learn predictable behavior, the system does not allow any insights into the learned approaches. This is where the analogy to the biological example becomes clear.

Computational intelligence is based on algorithms of fuzzy logic [16], neural networks [17] and evolutionary algorithms [18]. These specialist fields often overlap. Evolutionary algorithms, for example, are used for the design of neural networks or fuzzy systems, or even neuro fuzzy systems [19], which on the one hand are visualized in the more comprehensible fuzzy form and on the other hand use the efficient learning behavior of neural networks.

30.4.1 The Origins of Machine Learning

The Dartmouth Summer Research Conference on Artificial Intelligence in Hanover, New Hampshire, is widely acknowledged as the birthplace of artificial intelligence research. It was in the summer of 1956 that John McCarthy organized a 10-person, two-month workshop to study neural networks, automata theory and intelligence in general. Although the workshop itself did not present any new findings, the participants were able to agree on a name for their new field of research. Besides McCarthy the attendees included Marvin Minsky and Claude Shannon who, over the next 20 years, came to dominate the field of *artificial intelligence* [20].

John McCarthy's core idea was "that every aspect of learning or any other feature of intelligence can in principle be so precisely described that a machine can be made to simulate it." Following the Dartmounth Conference the newly established AI community set to work with great optimism and developed the first approaches to solving puzzles, logical reasoning and games like chess [20–22].

Groundbreaking theoretical preliminary work had been carried out several years earlier, however, by Alan Turing. According to Turing we speak of "artificial intelligence" when an algorithm successfully solves a problem using human-like responses, so that an evaluator is unable to distinguish whether the answer comes from a human or a machine [23].

30.4.2 The 60s and 70s

The 1960s saw the first programs to demonstrate intelligent behavior. In computer games like chess or draughts these programs were already following strategies that enabled them to beat human opponents. Research had brought computers to a level where they were able to develop their own solutions to a problem. Soon after, pattern recognition procedures were being explored for image and speech processing, with systems learning to process simple commands of natural speech and recognize patterns in images. These developments then flowed into industrial robot control. In spite of the huge expectations, AI research made slow progress, which eventually led to several major sponsors withdrawing their support. This period came to be known among the AI community as the first "AI winter" [20, 24].

30.4.3 to the Present Day

From 1980 onwards, however, AI research enjoyed fresh impetus – both financially and conceptionally. Greater emphasis on mathematization, neural networks, which had been somewhat neglected in the last 20 years, and multi-agent systems – also referred to as *distributed AI* – shaped the next phase of research. Expert systems had by this time reached a level that made them attractive for industrial applications [20].

Based on the findings of the last few years, where a system "only" had to respond to problems, these approaches were now applied to robots which, equipped with a body of their own, came to be perceived as autonomous beings. The obvious progression was to add rudimentary actions such as autonomous movement and facial expressions. A well-known example was the Mars robot, Sojourner, which landed on Mars in 1997 and explored its surroundings on wheels. Since then, scientists and other tech-savvy hobbyists have organized competitions to show off their skills. One of the most famous competitions is the RoboCup, organized by the Federation of International Robot-soccer Association and first held in South Korea in 1996 (FIRA), where soccer-playing robots compete against one another in different categories [25].

Even if it at first seems like trivial amusement, Marvin Minsky once described the problems of AI research quite aptly:

> *AI researchers have worked to solve those problems we humans find difficult, such as chess, but they didn't make any progress on the problems that humans find easy* [20].

30.5   Learning Methods

Machine learning therefore offers automated and precise predictions from dense, disordered information and converts this into a format that is useful to humans. Depending on the purpose of a machine learning system or algorithm, these models recommend future actions based on so called empirical values or probabilities. However, the learning process is crucial for a system to be able to make predictions. This process always follows the following sequence:

To begin with, the model is trained using sample data. It calculates a task, and the result is compared with the desired result. The target vs. actual difference is then returned to the model and recalculated according to a suitable procedure (e. g. the gradient descent of the back propagation algorithm) in order to reduce the error to a pre-defined minimum.

By continually adding data and empirical knowledge a machine learning system can be trained to visualize the predictions for a specific use case even more accurately [26].

30.6   Implementation Options

There are many different options for implementing machine learning. Besides the various methods – which can also be applied in combination – the question arises: Which is the most suitable programming language, which frameworks or tools lend themselves to the task?

In the science sector, script and standard languages have prevailed. Instead of the classical C/C++ programming, prototypical developments in Matlab, Python, Julia or R are often deployed. For this reason the larger frameworks offer interfaces to further programming languages, so that the methods of these machine learning libraries can be used in combination with the user's own preferred programming languages. The largest overlap can be achieved with the GPL script language Python, which works very well in different environments and can be extended with the preferred programming languages (C/C++, Java, C#, etc.).

In this context there are various prefabricated frameworks. These can be implemented in many different ways. Thanks to documentation and numerous user boards, among other things, pre-fabricated frameworks are relatively easy to get started with, compared with single-handed implementation [27].

Acceleration/Parallelization

To meet the growing demand for more and more processing power, huge advances have been made in the development of high-performance computer systems, along with faster and more reliable communication networks. At present these systems work at rates of several gigahertz and communicate with one another through transmission networks at several gigabits per second. But existing technology may eventually no longer be able meet our demand for data. Physical constraints like the speed of light mean that researchers will have to start looking for alternatives. The parallelization of data offers one solution.

30.7   The Current Situation and Trends

Current trends point to an increased outsourcing of IT structures to the cloud. The cloud, or cloud computing, offers a variety of service models: from complete infrastructures with virtual computers that can communicate with one another in virtual networks to the more basic software-as-a-service (e. g. Microsoft Office 365). Furthermore, clouds offer an enormous computing capacity, since they are not constrained by the limitations of a local server or network. Instead, cloud computing offers every network-compatible device access to an almost unlimited pool of processing and storage resources.

Beyond advancing performance, researchers are exploring the development of new models for practical applications.

One major area of application for machine learning is *predictive maintenance* in the context of Industry 4.0 and the *smart factory*. ThyssenKrupp, CGI and Microsoft, for example, have together developed thousands of sensors and systems to network elevators directly to the cloud. Data from the elevators is fed into dynamic prediction models, giving Microsoft Azure ML uninterrupted access to current datasets. The data are then transferred to a dashboard, where continuously updated KPIs (**K**ey **P**erformance **I**ndicator) [4] can be identified live on computers and mobile devices. This allows ThyssenKrupp to monitor things like elevator speed and door operation around the clock with minimal effort and expenditure [28].

In current research, scientists are reporting on the support of automated production planning and control systems. As the latest findings allow planners to put their ideas into practice, the focus continually moves to new challenges. For example, the planning of a new production facility involves the manual design of several alternative models, which are then tested and optimized using virtual simulation – a time-consuming and costly procedure [29].

A common problem encountered by many pattern recognition processes is incomplete or missing data. The ability to process incomplete data is a fundamental prerequisite for pattern classification, since the omission of certain values for relevant data attributes can seriously compromise the accuracy of the classification results [30].

30.8   Conclusion and Outlook

When looking at developments in machine learning over the last few decades, it is evident that the terminology and methods in this context have evolved on both technological as well as algorithmic and functional levels. If we consider that the complex issues of machine learning and predictive analytics are supported by highly parametric, multi-variant mathematical functions, which can be trained or applied to new problems using sophisticated methods such as neural networks or deep learning, it becomes clear that the rapid growth of all recent developments is, on the one hand, thanks to the major developments in hardware and, on the other, to the high scalability made possible by cloud solutions.

Although this may make us think that developments could go on growing in this direction forever, we should always be aware that technology faces physical limitations as well.

So it could be that the next era of machine learning is not ushered in by taking another step towards more technological development, like we have seen with In-Memory-Computing or Microsoft Azure ML in recent years. Instead the next step might be something more revolutionary, such as new insights into genetics and evolution and a deeper understanding of the human brain above and beyond classic neural networks/deep learning, which can then be transferred to deal with technological challenges. These new prospects for research will require adaptations to existing algorithms and, much more than that, the creation of new ones.

References

1. Y. D. W. &. C. Q. Yu, The impact of social and conventional media on firm equity value: A sentiment analysis approach, Decision Support Systems, 55.
2. I. Witten, E. Frank and M. Hall, Data Mining: Practical Machine Learning Tools and Techniques, Burlington: Morgan Kaufmann Publishers, 2011.

3. WinfWiki, "Analyse Text Mining mit R," 2014. [Online]. Available: http://winfwiki.wi-fom. de/images/5/5d/A_Venn_Diagram_of_the_Intersection_of_text_mining.PNG. [Accessed 14 08 2016].

4. A. Sharafi, Knowledge Discovery in Databases. Eine Analyse des Änderungsmanagements in der Produktentwicklung, Wiesbaden: Springer Gabler, 2012.

5. F. Pimenta, D. Obradovic, R. Schirru and S. &. D. A. Baumann, Automatic Sentiment, 2010.

6. B. Pang and L. &. V. S. Lee, "Thumbs up? Sentiment classification using machine learning techniques," in *Proceedings of the 2002 Conference on Empirical Methods in Natural Language Processing (EMNLP)*, 2002.

7. F. Nielsen and M. &. H. L. Etter, Real-time monitoring of sentiment in business related Wikipedia articles, 2013.

8. P. &. L. M. Turney, "Measuring praise and criticism: Inference of semantic orientation from association," in *ACM Transactions on Information Systems*, 2003.

9. C. Manzei, L. Schleupner and R. Heinze, Industrie 4.0 im internationalen Kontext. Kernkonzepte, Ergebnisse, Trends, Berlin: VDE VERLAG GMBH, 2016.

10. G. Webb, "Naive Bayes," in *Encyclopedia of Machine Learning*, Springer Verlag, 2010, p. 713.

11. C. R. P. &. S. H. Manning, Introduction to Information Retrieval, Cambridge University Press, 2008.

12. X. Zhang, "Support Vector Machines," in *Encyclopedia of Machine Learning*, Springer Verlag, 2010, pp. 941–946.

13. D. Jansen, Sentiment Classification, Duisburg: Universität Duisburg-Essen, 2008.

14. A. Ratnaparkhi, "Maximum Entropy Models," in *Encyclopedia of Machine Learning*, Springer Verlag, 2010, pp. 647–651.

15. M. Schoenherr, "Ohne Verstand ans Ziel," 2016. [Online]. Available: http://www. deutschlandfunk.de/maschinelles-lernen-ohne-verstand-ans-ziel.740.de.html?dram:article_id=349980. [Accessed 08 01 2016].

16. L. A. Zadeh, Fuzzy Sets, Information and Control, Elsevier Inc., 1965.

17. R. Rojas, Therorie der Neuronalen Netze, Springer-Lehrbuch, 1993.

18. J. R. Koza, Genetic Programming, MIT Press, 1992.

19. R. Kruse, C. Borgelt, F. Klawonn et al., Computational Intelligence. Eine methodische Einführung in Künstliche Neuronale Netze, Evolutionäre Algorithmen, Fuzzy-Systeme und Bayes-Netze, Wiesbaden: Vieweg + Teubner Verlag, 2011.

20. Lomu.net, "50 Jahre Künstliche-Intelligenz-Forschung," 2016. [Online]. Available: http://www. lomu.net/lomu7_KI-ueberblick.html. [Accessed 28 07 2016].

21. P. McCorduck, Machines who Think: A Personal Inquiry Into the History and Prospects of Artificial Intelligence, San Francisco: W. H. Freeman, 1979.

22. P. Koenig, "Künstliche Intelligenz," 2007. [Online]. Available: http://www.heise.de/-280227. [Accessed 09 08 2016].

23. A. Turing, Computing Machinery and Intelligence, 236 Hrsg., Bd. 59, 1950, pp. 433–460.

24. P. Ford, "Unsere letzte Erfindung?," 2016. [Online]. Available: http://www.heise.de/tr/artikel/ Unsere-letzte-Erfindung-3152050.html. [Accessed 09 08 2016].

25. Wikipedia, "RoboCup," 2016. [Online]. Available: https://en.wikipedia.org/wiki/RoboCup. [Accessed 08 01 2016].

26. E. Chin, "The Future of Fraud Fighting," Sift science, 2015. [Online]. Available: http://start. siftscience.com/the-future-of-fraud-fighting-ebook?_ga=1.55925928.267213647.1472580662. [Accessed 08 01 2016].

27. S. Bahrampour, N. Ramakrishnan, L. Schott and M. Shah, Comparative Study of Deep Learning Software Frameworks, 2015.

28. Microsoft, "Internet der Dinge," Azure IoT Suite, 2016. [Online]. Available: https://www.microsoft.com/de-de/server-cloud/customer-stories/thyssen-krupp-elevator.aspx. [Accessed 24 08 2016].
29. S. Fernández Arregui, S. Jiménez Celorrio and T. de la Rosa Turbides, "Improving Automated Planning with Machine Learning," in *Handbook of Research on Machine Learning Applications and Trends: Algorithms, Methods, and Techniques*, New York, IGI Global, 2010.
30. P. Garica Laencina, J. Morales-Sanches, R. Verdu-Monedero and et al., "Classification with Incomplete Data," in *Handbook of Research on Machine Learning Applications and Trends: Algorithms, Methods, and Techniques*, New York, IGI Global, 2010.
31. Herschel, R.T. and Jones, N.E., "Knowledge management and business intelligence: the importance of integration", Journal of Knowledge Management, Vol. 9 No. 4, pp. 45-55, 2005.

How Banks Can Better Serve Their Customers Through Artificial Techniques

Armando Vieira and Attul Sehgal

Abstract

Thanks to the big data revolution and advanced computational capabilities, companies have never had such a deep access to customer data. This is allowing organizations to interpret, understand, and forecast customer behaviors as never before. Artificial Intelligence (AI) algorithms will play a pivotal role in transforming business intelligence into a fully predictive probabilistic framework. AI will be able to radically transform or automate numerous functions within companies, from pricing, budget allocation, fraud detection and security. This chapter will present some approaches on advanced analytics and provide some examples from the financial sector on how AI is helping institutions refine small business credit scoring, understand online behavior and improve customer service. Further, we will also explore how integration with traditional business processes can work and how organizations can then take advantage of the data driven approach.

31.1 The Impact of Big Data in Banks

Data generated from online bank transactions, digital sensors and mobile devices is being produced and recorded at an astonish rate. Every day 2.5 quintillion bytes of data are created and it is predicted that about 90% of all data processed was produced in the past two years [1].

A. Vieira (✉) · A. Sehgal
RedOctopus Innovation
London, UK
e-mail: Armando@redoctopusinnovation.com

A. Sehgal
e-mail: Attul@redoctopusinnovation.com

© Springer-Verlag GmbH Germany 2018
C. Linnhoff-Popien et al. (eds.), *Digital Marketplaces Unleashed*,
https://doi.org/10.1007/978-3-662-49275-8_31

The amount of data needed to be stored in servers is ever expanding, and for banks the opportunity to have a 360° perspective of the customer life has never been so high. These developments provide a huge business opportunity for banks, not only by improving their core business – risk assessment and investment – but also by creating new marketing opportunities and reducing costs. The challenge is how to extract the intelligence effectively [2].

Traditionally, banks have tried to extract information from a sample of its internal data and produced periodic reports to improve decision making. Nowadays, with the availability of vast amounts of structured and unstructured data from both internal and external sources, there is increased pressure and focus on obtaining an enterprise view of the customer in real-time, on a self-service basis and in a more systematic way.

By integrating predictive analytics with automatic decision making, a bank can better understand the preferences of its customers, identify customers with high potential to spend, be able to promote the right products to the right customers, improve customer experience, and drive revenue. However there are several challenges: i) **engineering** (how to store, organize and create views over the unstructured data in a cost-effective way); ii) **analytics** (how to process real-time analytics within an ever changing environment); and **business** (how to apply these insights to transform the business processes and translate into competitive advantages).

Advanced data storage for structured and unstructured data based on technologies like Hadoop and Spark – in the form of the so called "data lakes" – is becoming a standard. On the analytics side, Deep Learning based machine learning is making a tremendous progresses in extracting powerful insights from vast quantities of structured (transactional data), semi-structured (social networks activity) and mostly unstructured data (images, video or text) [3–5] (see Fig. 31.1).

With online banking, credit card and mobile payment systems, banks have access to a large amount of customer information. Furthermore, social media data can shed light on brand sentiment and brand loyalty. However, most traditional customer behavior analytics techniques only focus on hard information and disregard soft and unstructured information.

Traditional customer behavior analytics have four dimensions: customer identification, customer attraction, customer retention, and customer development. Among them,

Fig. 31.1 Deep Learning algorithms have a higher learning capacity

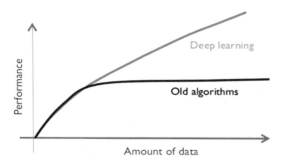

customer identification is the most fundamental and widely implemented in the banking industry. Customer identification includes customer segmentation and targeting.

Each component of customer behavior analytics is linked to some standard data mining techniques. In customer identification, classification and clustering methods are usually used to target a specific customer group based on the business objective. In addition, regression techniques are applied to predict new potential customers. Almost all frequently used data mining techniques can be applied to better understand customer loyalty, including classification, clustering, sequence discovery, association, and regression.

Association techniques are often used in customer development in affinity analysis to find the relationship between different products that are bought by a given customer over his or her lifetime. Numerous solutions have been developed and studies done on traditional customer behavior analytics. For example, a framework for analyzing customer value and segmenting customers based on their value was proposed in [6].

31.2 Addressing the Opportunity

With the deriving of new customer insight through advanced analytics marketeers need to organize themselves internally to take full advantage of the available information. Here are some suggestions:

1. **Build a Robust 360 degree Customer View** – banks need to think beyond 'one-size-fits-all' as relationship pricing and product bundling become ever more important. Banks should look at products and pricing based on CLTV – the value that customers bring to the bank across the spectrum of rates, fees, features and services. Despite the challenges in integrating data from multiple systems and data sharing impediments due to opt-out policy and regulatory requirements, it is crucial to have a 360 degree view of customer to improve customer satisfaction and maximize lifetime value.
2. **Adopt Advanced Customer segmentation** – this is key to cater to individualized needs and should be based on standard banking metrics – tenure with the bank, number of accounts, balances of accounts and loans, frequency of interaction, behavioral (usage rate, price sensitivity, brand loyalty) and demographic variables (occupation, income, and family-status). Traditional segmentation is dead -each customer is a segment.
3. **Formulate Intelligent Real time cross–selling/up–selling Campaigns** – banks can use real-time events and customer insight to offer cross-channel marketing campaigns where relevant events are acted on as a way to deepen customer relationships.
4. **Design Innovative Reward Models** – banks need to move beyond a "one-size-fits-all" reward model and design a system where valuable customers enjoy premium benefits and redeem rewards points easily and in various ways.
5. **Enable Automated Customer care Systems** – In the digital era, customers demand more self-service options, any-time and anywhere. So expanding customer self-ser-

vice, case management, dispute management and event-based decision-making can be perceived as better customer care, while lowering operational costs and increasing effectiveness.

6. **Enable Prediction through Big Data** – Big data is the new disruptive technology. Big data technologies provides banks the ability to understand their clients at a more granular level and more quickly deliver targeted personalized offers. Being able to anticipate customer needs and resolve them before they become problems, allows banks to deliver timely, concise and actionable insight to contact center agents. This can also lead to increased sales, improved customer satisfaction and a reduction in operating costs. Fighting fraud, financial crimes and security breaches, in all forms, is among the most costly challenges facing the finance industry. Big data benefits include: Reduced costs of fraud screening and monitoring fewer false positives, reduced cost of fraud investigations, reduced payment fraud losses, real time fraud detection and mitigation, optimized offers and cross-sell.

7. **Improve Multi-Channel Experience** – banks should seek to attract and retain customers with a compelling multi-channel experience across all touch-points (branches, online, mortgage and investment advisors, etc.) Virtual channels are becoming more relevant, with the increasing penetration of high-speed Internet connectivity and Web-enabled mobile devices allowing consumers to spend more time online. Online banking and call centers already account for 55% of transactions [7].

Compared with traditional customer behavior analytics methods most used in banking, there are two major challenges in the big data era. The first involves how to handle the massive amount of complex data in a cost-effective and efficient way. The availability of data has grown in magnitude, speed, and dimensionality. Second challenge is in new data analytical models required to capture the value behind the increasing amount of unstructured, soft information [8].

Traditionally, solutions to manage the large amount of data are unable to provide reasonable response times in handling expanding data volumes, leaving few options-either to run the analytics models in batch mode or perform piecemeal transactions for a more reasonable response time. Therefore, a bank needs to ensure the real-time response which requires new expertise in the data management and the latest systems management methods [9].

31.3   What Is Artificial Intelligence?

Asking whether a computer can think is a bit like asking whether submarines can swim (Edger Dijkstra).

In its simplest form, Artificial Intelligence (AI), consists of a set of algorithms that can perform complex cognitive tasks, some deem – up to now – being exclusive to humans, and makes them amenable to machines. AI is today one of the most exciting research fields with plenty of practical applications, from autonomous vehicles to drug discovery, robotics, language translation and games [5]. Challenges that seemed insurmountable just a decade ago have been solved and are now present in products and ubiquitous applications, like voice recognition, navigation systems, facial emotion detection and even in art creation – like music and painting.

Inspired by the depth structure of the brain, deep learning architectures have revolutionized the approach to data analysis [3–5]. Deep Learning networks have won a paramount number of hard machine learning contests, from voice recognition, image classification, Natural Language Processing (NLP), to time-series prediction – sometimes by a large margin [3]. Traditionally AI relied on heavily handcrafted features, for instance, to have decent results in image classification, several pre-processing techniques have to be applied, like filters, edge detection, etc. The beauty of DL is that most, if not all, features can be learned automatically from the data – provide enough (sometimes millions) training data examples are available.

31.3.1   Deep Neural Networks

Deep models have feature detector units at each layer (level) that gradually extract more sophisticated and invariant features from the original raw input signals. Lower layers aim at extracting simple features that are then clamped into higher layers, which in turn detect more complex features. In contrast, shallow models (two-layers neural network or support vector machine) present very few layers that map the original input features into a problem-specific feature space. See [3, 4] and for a review and [5] for a business oriented perspective.

Being essentially non-supervised machines, deep neural architectures can be exponentially more efficient than shallow ones. Since each element of the architecture is learned using examples, the number of computational elements one can afford is only limited by the number of training samples – which can be of the order of billions. Deep models can be trained with hundreds of millions of weights and therefore tend to outperform shallow models such as Support Vector Machines. Moreover, theoretical results suggest that deep architectures are fundamental to learn the kind of complex functions that represent high-level abstractions [4] (e. g. vision, language, semantics), characterized by many factors of variation that interact in non-linear ways, making the learning process difficult.

There are many DL architectures, but most of the DNNs can be classified into five major categories (see Fig. 31.2).

1. Networks for unsupervised learning, designed to capture high-order correlation of data by capturing jointly statistical distributions with the associated classes – when available. Bayes rule can later be used to create a discriminative learning machine.

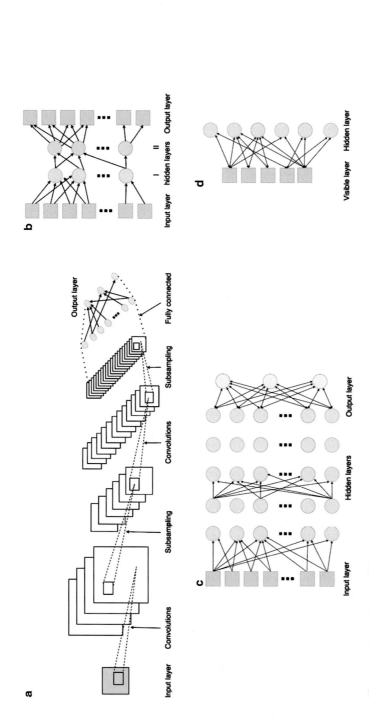

Fig. 31.2 Several types of deep neural networks. **a** Convolutional neural network (*CNN*) has several levels of convolutional and subsampling layers optionally followed by fully connected layers with deep architecture. **b** Stacked autoencoder consisting of multiple sparse autoencoders (**c**). Deep Belief Network (*DBN*) (**d**). Restricted Boltzmann Machine (*RBM*) architecture includes one visible layer and one layer of hidden units

2. Networks for supervised learning. These networks are designed to provide maximum discriminative power in classification problem are trained only with labeled data – all the outputs should be tagged.
3. Hybrid or semi-supervised networks, where the objective is to classify data using the outputs of a generative (unsupervised) model. Normally, data is used to pre-train the network weights to speed up the learning process prior to the supervision stage.
4. Reinforcement learning – the agent interact and changes the environment and receives feedback only after a set of actions are completed. This type of learning is normally used in the field of robotics and games.
5. Generative Neural Networks – Deep generative models are a powerful approach to unsupervised and semi-supervised learning where the goal is to discover the hidden structure within data without relying on labels. Since they are generative, such models can form a rich imagery the world in which they are used: an imagination that can harnessed to explore variations in data, to reason about the structure and behavior of the world, and ultimately, for decision-making – an example is the variational auto-encoder.

DNN have been successfully applied to several problems, ranging from natural language processing, time-series prediction and image annotation. In the context of banking, and customer care, the most relevant applications are in customer segmentation, recommendation algorithm, fraud detection and credit scoring.

The main characteristics that make DNN unique can be summarized in the following points:

1. High learning capacity: they don't saturate easily – the more data you have the more they learn.
2. No feature engineering required: learning can be performed end-to-end.
3. High generative capability: DNN can generate unseen – but plausible – data based on latent representations.
4. Knowledge transfer: we can teach a machine in one large set of data and transfer the learning to a similar problem where less data is known.
5. Excellent unsupervised capabilities – DNN can learn hidden statistical representations without any labels required.
6. Multimodal learning – DNN can integrate seamlessly disparate sources of high-dimensional data, like text, images, video and audio to generate conditional probability distributions.

31.3.2 Why Deep Neural Networks is a Game Changer?

To demonstrate why DNN are so effective, let's consider the case of weather forecasting. It's a very complex problem that takes as inputs many measurements of previous conditions in a space-time mesh. Current predictions models are based on huge grid based finite-element method calculations and large sets of fluid dynamics differential equations are solved iteratively so that the results are used as initial conditions for the next step. This is computationally extremely expensive and the predictive accuracy limited as errors multiply for each predictive time step.

However, recently, using a combination of 3D Convolutional Neural Networks with neural networks with Long-Short Term Memory (LSTMs) cells, it was possible to build an accurate model, using up to 100 million parameters, trainable end-to-end, to predict in less than 0.1 s on a laptop, the weather up to two days ahead achieving a better accuracy than models that need several hours of computations on a supercomputer [10].

Deep Learning was also applied to other very challenging problems, like image annotation, voice recognition and control, sometimes with super-human accuracy – for instance in the ImageNet competition [6].

31.4 Deploying Artificial Intelligence in Banks

In 2015, technology companies spent $8.5 billion on deals and investments in artificial intelligence, four times more than in 2010. In 2016, Deutsche Bank announced a "crowd-storming" ideas initiative on how artificial intelligence can be used in the financial services industry, by inviting people to submit their concepts for the chance to develop them at the German giant's innovation labs and win cash prizes [11]. With the likes of Google, Facebook and IBM among those pouring resources into AI, Deutsche Bank is hoping to be at the forefront of the technology's application in financial services and arrest some of the AI talent away from the big technology firms. What is driving this change?

The goal of customer analytics is to create a deeper understanding of customers and their behavior to maximize their lifetime value to the company. Customer analytics can be applied to many applications, like customer marketing, credit scoring and approval, profitable credit card customer identification, high-risk loan applicant identification, payment default prediction, fraud detection, money laundering detection, etc. Banks are using these techniques to reduce costs and simplify customer interactions. Some early examples can be seen through recent activities in RBS and Barclays.

After falling £2 billion in the red in 2016, RBS, a UK Bank, announced it will replace staff who offer investment tips with so-called 'robo-advisers' in order to reduce costs. Robo-advisers have been around for a while in the US. A report from Cerulli Associates in August 2016 said that robo-advice platforms are expected to reach $489 billion (£323 billion) in assets under management by 2020, up from $18.7 billion today. Current robo-advisers are essentially online wealth management services which use algorithms to suggest automated investment portfolios based on customers' goals and attitude to risk. The RBS deployment will provide an automated system to offer customers advice based on their responses to a series of questions. At the same time RBS will reduce internal headcount by over 550 staff [7].

With the aim to boost its multi-channel delivery and understand customer behavior, Barclays' South African subsidiary, Absa, announced a trial of chatbots, using artificial intelligence to answer simple customer queries posted over popular smart messaging apps. The goal of the bank is to connect with customers through their conversational channels of choice rather than by traditional, and more limited options such as SMS or email. The use of two-way messaging is expected to create a feedback loop to help the bank better understand the most pressing issues for improving customer service [12].

31.4.1   Customer Segmentation and Preference Analysis

By deploying fine-grained customer segmentations in which customers share similar preference for different sub-branches or market regions, banks can get deeper insights in their customer characteristics and preferences. This allows improved customer satisfaction and improved precision marketing by personalizing banking products and services, as well as marketing messages.

31.4.2   Recommendation Algorithms for Marketing

Recommendation algorithms are ubiquitous in almost any ecommerce site. A Recommender System (RS) is an algorithm that suggest items to a user that he may be interested. It uses as input information on past preferences of users (transactional data) over a set of finite items, either explicitly (ratings) or implicitly (monitoring users behavior, such as songs heard, applications downloaded, web sites visited) and information about the users or the items themselves.

Deep Learning can address this problem through an hierarchical Bayesian approach. Collaborative Deep Learning (CDL) [13] can jointly learns deep representations from the content of items/users while also considering the ratings matrix with significant better results in a self-consistent way. It relies on a method using tightly coupled schemes that allow two-way interaction between rating matrix and content: the rating information guides the learning of features and, on the other hand, the extracted features can improve the predictive power of the CF models.

31.4.3   Credit Scoring

Credit risk analysis is a very important and actual topic. Neves and Vieira [14] pioneered the use of Deep Artificial Neural Networks for the distress prediction of SME companies. They showed that these types of ANNs substantially outperform traditional methods based on Logistic Regression or Support Vector Machines. Recently, Lopes and Ribeiro [24] also applied a model based on deep belief networks (DBN) for bankruptcy prediction. Despite being a small dataset, they showed that DBN can achieve better accuracy than SVM or Restricted Boltzmann Machines (RBM).

31.4.4 Churn Management

Churn is a classical, but important, problem for banks. It cost five times more to acquire a new customer than to retain an existing one. To prevent such attrition (churn) it is critical to be able to identify the early warning signs of churn. Artificial Intelligence has been applied with success in this problem through the selection of features that work as proxies for early indicators of churn using a semi-supervised approach. This can be done using either a more conventional transactional data perspective or analyzing the network activity – relationships between customers, their degrees of connectivity and influence.

The Churn Score, that assigns a probability to each customer indicating the predicted likelihood that the particular subscriber will churn within a predefined period of time, is constructed based on different models, the most useful are Random Forest (or an upgraded version of gradient boosting trees) or more advanced Convolutional Neural Networks. Depending on the quality of data and business activity, accuracies of up to 90% are common.

31.4.5 Customer Identification

This problem consists of identification of potential high-revenue or loyal customers who are likely to become profitable to the bank but are not on the books. These methods rely on template matching (target new customers based on past behavior) and allow banks to get a more complete and accurate target customer list for high-value customers, which can improve marketing efficiency and bring huge profits.

Other technique is customer network analysis. It consist of understanding customer and product affinity through analysis of social media networks and their relations through exploration of graph connectivity analysis. Customer network analysis can improve customer retention, cross-sell, and up-sell.

Market potential analysis: Using economic, demographic and geographic data, we can generate the spatial distribution for both existing customers and potential customers. With the market potential distribution map, banks can have a clear overview of the target customers' locations, and identify the customer concentrating/lacking areas for investing/divesting, which will support the banks' customer marketing and exploration [15].

Channel allocation and operation optimization: Based on the banks' strategy and spatial distribution of customer resource, this module optimizes the configuration (i. e., location, type) and operations of service channels – i. e., retail branch or automated teller machine [16].

31.4.6   Conversational Bots (Chatbots) for Customer Service

Probably the largest, and most immediate, impact of AI anywhere, supported by DNN, will not be in self-driving cars or robotics but in customer service. Services like sending a specific email, a mobile push, or a customer pass for a specific shop or event; predictive analytics to help support decisions and call centers. Contact centers deal with very mundane interactions that soon will be serviced through automated messaging like chat bots and personal assistants. AI can help suggest how to deliver a conversation; user interests and product. It can even use the data for secondary purposes, like risk assessment based on previous interactions.

Chabots have gone a long way since Eliza, the first conversational machine invented in the 60's. Trained in large corpus of data, they are capable of answering almost any type of question. The technology behind chatbots is based on recurrent neural networks (RNN) for text generation that can be trained end-to-end [17]. In recent years, the demand for Chatbots has changed from answering simple questions (almost as a toy) to performing smooth in open-domain conversations – like real humans. The challenge is to model conversation within a given domain. By introducing trainable gates to recall the global domain memory, deep learning models can incorporate background knowledge to enhance the sequence semantic modeling ability of LSTMs.

Banks channel users to customer-service representatives—generally via a call or live chat, but chatbots are a new medium for communication that are fastly making inroads at other financial institutions. Some examples already implemented based on chatbots:

- DBS in Singapore recently launched Mykai, a conversational bot (created by the startup Kasisto) to help customers perform routine operations, like payments and checking. In the future the plan is to integrate it in messaging platforms, like telegram or WhatsApp [18].
- Digibank, recently launched in India, allows to open an account with a bank that's only accessible via mobile devices. It's based on chatbots intelligent enough to answer thousands of questions submitted via chats [19].
- Penny is a conversational personal financial assistant [20]
- Bank of America allows customers to interact with a bot on Facebook's Messenger platform [21].

31.4.7   Fighting Financial Crime and Money Laundering

IT companies are working with banks to create tools to increase robustness in the transaction monitoring process and the detection of unusual financial activity. These systems are based on standard typologies of money laundering such as spikes in value or volume of transactions, monitoring high risk jurisdictions, identifying rapid movement of funds, screening against sanctioned individuals and politically exposed persons (PEPs) and monitoring enlisted terrorist organizations. Challenges today are in setting up the correct threshold levels and parameters, Identifying 'false positives' quickly and accurately, streamlining operations to minimize costs, accurate data sources and accurate and timely reporting. The future lies in seeing how the intrinsic benefits of DL can play a role. For example, if the IT system could learn from previous cycles and identify false positives before an alert was generated, it would be a 'game-changing' factor in transaction monitoring, speeding up and increasing the accuracy of identifying the truly suspicious activity.

We are seeing increasing examples of machine learning in many areas of technology and financial institutions should grasp the opportunity to use it for repetitive analysis. There are also alerts that are generated which carry a relatively low money laundering risk, e. g. an alert based on a counterparty moving funds between their own accounts (possibly held in different jurisdictions or in different banks). False positives are, however, still very common for most algorithms. If the system could perform a simplified up-front analysis to exclude these types of alerts, or move them to a specially quarantined area, then allied with self-learning, the alert landscape becomes cleaner and only the truly suspicious transactions require costly human intervention.

31.5   Challenges to Artificial Intelligence Deployment

From the industrial revolution to the emergence of the Internet age there have always been challengers to the deployment promoting fear of a change in traditional roles and jobs being lost. AI adoption is very much in the eye of the storm with its perceived ability to provide reliable results from large data sets and to carry out cognitive and creative tasks more competently than humans.

31.5.1   Consumer Data Protection and Privacy Challenges

The use of big data raises a number of privacy and data protection concerns, including transparency (what data are being used and where did it originate) and customer consent (was permission provided for its use and possibilities of access/redress, can the consumer see their own data and request that errors be corrected). While these issues may be addressed for the data in credit bureaus – which originate with banks and other formal lenders and service providers – the same protections do not typically extend to big data that are amassed from a combination of private commercial transactions, government sources and publicly available information such as social media posts. Developing a practical approach to consumer protection for big data, which balances privacy and consumer protection with commercial applications that can facilitate commerce and even access to credit, is a challenge that remains to be met.

31.5.2 Automation of White Collar Jobs

AI is having an impact not just on routine and repetitive tasks but also on cognitive, and even creative tasks, as well – see for example [22] where authors used Generative Adversarial Networks to generate faces and bedrooms. A tipping point seems to have been reached, at which AI-based automation threatens to supplant the brain-power of large swathes of middle-income bank employees. The example raised earlier of RBS of releasing 550 staff, to be replaced with 'robot-advisers', is evidence that AI will have a tremendous impact in workforce by rendering many jobs obsolete [7].

Not only is AI software much cheaper than mechanical automation to install and operate, there is a far greater incentive to adopt it—given the significantly higher cost of knowledge workers compared with their blue-collar brothers and sisters in the workshop, on the production line, at the check-out and in the field. The impact is real as far few new white-collar jobs are expected to be created to replace those at risk of being lost—despite the hopes many place in technology, innovation and better education.

What constitutes work today—the notion of a full-time job—will have to change dramatically. The things that make people human—the ability to imagine, feel, create, adapt, improvise, have intuition or act spontaneously—may remain comparative advantages with respect to machines, but even those are not guaranteed as the processes where these competencies emerge can themselves be described by algorithms [1]. The most recent advanced in AI proved powerful enough to beat the best human players in the challenging game of GO [23] – something regarded as impossible a few years ago as it requires the machine to learn high level strategy – though to be an human exclusive capability.

There is another flipside of AI. The fact that Deep Learning algorithms are probabilistic cognitive machines controlled by million of parameters, makes them almost impossible to be understood. This is particularly restrictive for banks as, for instance the scoring algorithms, have to be white boxes, due to regulation requirements. Furthermore, other risks may emerge as a consequence of relying on "black box" algorithms: how can we be sure they less biased than humans? How will they cope with novelty or non-stationary data? How can we be sure they are reliable?

We should be prepared for smarter than human systems acting in reality that may encounter situations beyond both the experience and the imagination of the programmers – see [1] for further exploration of these possibilities.

31.6 Conclusions and Recommendations

Despite the technological threats, Deep Learning powered AI is transforming businesses at an accelerating speed. According to IDC, by 2020, the market for machine learning applications will reach $40 billion. In 2015, only 1% of software include AI, in 2020 this number will be above 50%. In the future, AI will fundamentally change and automate innumerous functions within companies: from pricing, budget allocation, fraud detection and security to marketing optimization if organizations implement it in the right way.

Machine Learning will make everything in the organization programmatic, from advertising to customer experience. This allows companies to create products that interact naturally with humans and will force reorganize several departments in financial institutions.

Deep Learning is well suited for activities that are heavily data intensive, like advertising and click-through information. Most of the data will be collected by the mobile phones and a myriad of devices delivering real time geo-referenced information. Multimodal learning will allow the integration of text, images, video and sound within a unified representation.

Banks need to exploit the opportunity of digitalization and advanced algorithms capable to radically change their business. Banks have deployed online servicing, capacity-management software, interactive voice response systems but they're not using them widely and still dragged by inertia. They also need to avoid the trap of deploying AI purely for cost saving initiatives and build forums that could potentially stifle innovation. Banks need to take positive lessons from the large IT firms open up their APIs and adopt a more customer centric approach allowing the real innovators to innovate with more freedom to enable the rapid turnaround of exciting applications.

Too often, banks manage the progress of their digital transformations by tracking activity metrics, such as the number of app downloads and log-in rates. Such metrics are, however, inadequate proxies for business value. Banks must set clear aspirations for value outcomes, looking at productivity, servicing-unit costs, and lead-conversion rates, and link these explicitly to digital investments. Additionally, deeper awareness of the technical capabilities available and how they can affect processes will be a prerequisite to effectively manage in this new world.

We are on the verge of the biggest revolution of all times. Banks can take huge opportunities in assuming digitization will change the traditional retail-banking business model, in some cases radically. The good news is that there is plenty of upside awaiting those European banks willing to embrace it. The bad news is that change is coming whether or not banks are ready.

This disruptive technology do not come without risks. The relentless data stream that no one can cope but the inscrutable algorithms that process it, can have consequences that no individual can plan, control or comprehend. Maybe that no one really needs to understand as long as it increase the profitability and loyalty of customers. Users, however, will be more preoccupied by the lack of privacy, The risk of data-processing system becomes all-knowing and all-powerful, so connecting to the system becomes the source of all meaning. This concentration of cognitive computing in a handful of players will create a threat to banks.

References

1. Y. N. Harari, Homos Deus, Harvill Secker, 2016.
2. B. Agarwal, S. Ambrose, S. Chomsisengphet und C. Liu, The role of soft information in a dynamic contract setting: Evidence from the home equity credit market, Bd. 43, J. Money Credit Banking, 2011, p. 633.
3. J. Schmidhuber, "Deep learning in neural networks: An overview," in *Neural Networks*, Bd. 61, 2015, pp. 85–117.
4. I. Goodfellow, Y. Bengio und A. Courville, "Deep Learning," MIT Press, 2016. [Online]. Available: http://www.deeplearningbook.org.
5. A. Vieira, Deep Neural Networks: review and business applications, Apress (in preperation).
6. A. Krizhevsky, I. Sutskever und G. Hinton, "Imagenet classification with deep convolutional neural networks," in *Advances in Neural Information Processing Systems*, Bd. 25, Curran Associates, 2012, pp. 1106–1114.
7. The Guardian, "RBS to cut 550 jobs as part of plan to automate investment advice," 03 2016. [Online]. Available: https://www.theguardian.com/business/2016/mar/13/rbs-royal-bank-scotland-cut-550-jobs-automating-investment-advice.
8. M. Lin, N. Prabhala und S. Viswanathan, Judging borrowers by the company they keep: Friendship networks and information asymmetry in online peer-to-peer lending, Bd. 59, Manag. Sci., 2013, pp. 17–35.
9. S. Agarwal, S. Chomsisengphet, C. Liu und N. Souleles, "Benefits of relationship banking: Evidence from consumer credit markets," J. Social Sci. Res. Netw., Rochester, NY, USA, 05 2009. [Online]. Available: http://papers.ssrn.com/sol3/papers.cfm?abstract_id=1647019.
10. Convolutional LSTM Network, "A Machine Learning Approach for Precipitation Nowcasting," 2015. [Online]. Available: http://arxiv.org/pdf/1506.04214v2.pdf.
11. Finextra, "Deutsche Bank crowdstorms AI ideas," 05 2016. [Online]. Available: https://www.finextra.com/newsarticle/28855/deutsche-bank-crowdstorms-ai-ideas.
12. Finextra, "Absa to trial AI-driven chatbots to answer customer queries," 04 2016. [Online]. Available: https://www.finextra.com/newsarticle/28794/absa-to-trial-ai-driven-chatbots-to-answer-customer-queries.
13. McKinsey Global Inst., Big Data, The Next Frontier for Innovation, Competition, Productivity, New York, NY, USA, 2011.
14. J. Neves und A. Vieira, Improving bankruptcy prediction with hidden layer learning vevtor quantization, Bd. 15, European Accounting Review, 2006, pp. 253–271.
15. A. Kracklauer, D. Mills und D. Seifert, Customer management as the origin of collaborative customer relationship management, C. C. R. M. T. C. t. t. N. Level, Hrsg., Berlin, Germany: Springer-Verlag, 2004.
16. E. Ngai, L. Xiu und D. Chau, Application of data mining techniques in customer relationship management: A literature review and classification, Bd. 36, Exp. Syst. Appl., 2009, pp. 2592–2602.
17. O. Vinyals und Q. Le, "A Neural Conversational Model," 2015. [Online]. Available: https://arxiv.org/pdf/1506.05869.pdf.
18. Kasisto.com, "ai-driven-virtual-assistant-from-kasisto-powers-indias-first-mobile-only-bank," 04 2016. [Online]. Available: http://www.kasisto.com.
19. *Indian mobile-only bank handles customer service with chatbots*, 2016. http://www.forwardlook.com/indian-mobile-only-bank-handles-customer-service-with-chatbots/
20. techncrunch.com, *penny-is-a-chat-based-personal-finance-coach*, 2015.
21. *do-your-banking-with-a-chatbot*, Massachusetts: MIT Technology Review, 2016.

22. A. Radford, L. Metz und S. Chintala, "Unsupervised Representation Learning with Deep Convolutional Generative Adversarial Networks," corr/RadfordMC15, 2015. [Online]. Available: https://arxiv.org/abs/1511.06434.
23. nature.com, 2016. [Online]. Available: http://www.nature.com/news/google-ai-algorithm-masters-ancient-game-of-go-1.19234.
24. B. Ribeiro und N. Lopes, "Deep belief networks for financial prediction," in *International Conference on Neural Information Processing*, 2011.

Part VIII
Fin- & Insuretech

Preface: Fin- & Insuretech

32

Hartmut Mai

Abstract

FinTech and InsurTech provide technologies that can make financial services more efficient, but also have the potential to disrupt the marketplace. They have assumed an increasingly high profile in the past five years, with investment and research in the InsurTech sector accelerating dramatically since the beginning of 2015. In this article I focus on the current position from the point of view of the non-retail insurer, a space which InsurTech has not yet disrupted, but which it has already begun to make more efficient and innovative. I look briefly at the FinTech and InsurTech landscape, before analyzing possible insurer responses and strategies. I cover the various stages of the customer journey, from initial contact to claims payment.

32.1 The Landscape

32.1.1 There Is Nothing New About Technology

Technology and finance have gone hand in hand for decades, if not centuries. The insurance underwriter who has been abreast with the new trends was usually the underwriter who made the largest profit. That knowledge was based mainly on having the best contacts and the best technology.

When communications improved dramatically in the 19th century, insurers did not launch their own telegraph companies. They knew that this was something that other com-

H. Mai (✉)
Allianz Global Corporate & Specialty SE
Munich, Germany
e-mail: hartmut.mai@allianz.com

© Springer-Verlag GmbH Germany 2018
C. Linnhoff-Popien et al. (eds.), *Digital Marketplaces Unleashed*,
https://doi.org/10.1007/978-3-662-49275-8_32

panies could do best. However, astute insurers realized that speedier communications and more efficient technologies would have a profound impact on their business.

All parts of the insurance value chain can become more efficient by understanding the potential of new technology, and exploiting it. You don't need to know precisely how a car works, but it helps if you know how to drive one. The same applies to InsurTech today. Insurers and their staff do not necessarily have to understand the technical details of a new process, but they do need to know how to exploit it to its utmost potential.

32.1.2   The FinTech Investment Universe

According to US-based Route 66 Ventures [1] (see Fig. 32.1), the FinTech sector – including InsurTech – is being serviced by three types of companies: the existing financial services groups, the FinTech service and product providers, and the Fintech disruptors. Those three types of companies are all working on back-end, middleware and front-end services.

In turn, these operate in the business to business, the business to consumer and the so-called B2B2C spaces. And bridging and linking these spaces and companies, within this we have a distinct dimension of its own: the highly important "protocol" dimension.

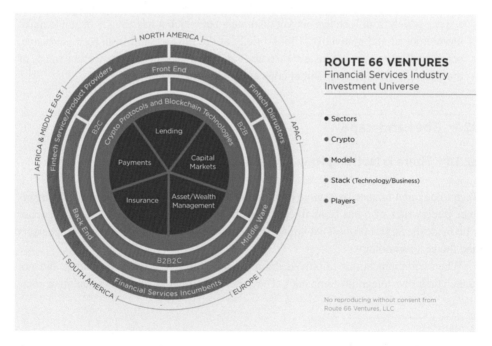

Fig. 32.1 US-based Route 66 Ventures. (Accenture [1])

Blockchain is the highest profile example of this area of FinTech, which increasingly extends both outside, and deeply within, every part of the sector.

Finally within the sector, we have the five FinTech core business sectors, namely Lending, Payments, Capital Markets, Asset/Wealth Management and Insurance, It is these in which the incumbents, the service providers and the disruptors are looking to operate.

32.1.3   FinTech: A Short but Exciting History

The mass infiltration of technology that we know of as "FinTech" – and its insurance subset, "InsurTech" is about five years old. It did not suddenly appear out of nowhere. Extraneous events – the financial crisis of 2008/09 and the subsequent collapse in interest rates – served as catalysts. The banking crisis showed that things could not go on as they had before, and the plummeting of interest rates forced insurers to face the fact that there was a "new normal".

Global investment in FinTech grew from \$930 m in 2008 to more than \$12 bn in 2014 [1] and to \$19.1 bn in 2015 [2].

Because banking suffered a bigger capital crisis than did insurance, banks had to respond faster. Accenture's report on "The Future of FinTech and Banking" [3] identified three key responses necessary for a financial operation to survive and thrive, to turn threat into opportunity.

They were:

1) Engage in a transparent way with technology solutions providers, permitting an interchange of intellectual property and data with chosen outside innovators;
2) Collaborate with partners beyond the financial services industry, partners who can provide a new perspective and who would not tend to travel the obvious path;
3) Invest, using venture investment to source new technology, to the benefit of the insurer.

This does not mean that each part of the value chain in insurance needs to employ all three strategies, but it does mean that insurers, if they are to fully exploit the potential of InsurTech, must devise strategies that will work in the short-, medium- and long term.

32.1.4   FinTech Today – As at September 2016

FinTech is continuing to branch outward beyond the traditional payments and lending space, possibly because the "obvious" FinTech areas are now rather crowded with startups. InsurTech, Asset Management (Robo-Advisory) and Capital Markets offerings have become increasingly popular in the past 18 months. "RegTech" companies have been offering companies automated systems to ensure that they are in compliance with regulations in various jurisdictions. InsurTech is just one of eight key verticals – among them wealth management, payments, blockchain, mobile banking or financial data – listed in the KPMG report on the Pulse of FinTech [4].

We have already seen significant disruption in the traditional banking processes, with PayPal now processing more than 11 million transactions a day, while Apple Pay is likely to be a major force in cutting banks out of the small wealth transfer process. On the lending side, Kickstarter and other crowdfunding investment operations currently tend to offer options for businesses locked out of traditional markets. But there is no reason why they should not enter the traditional market space as well.

Also on the lending side we have, among many others, Lending Club in the US, CreditEase in China, Zopa in the UK. They serve to provide borrowers with new sources of cash and lenders with more attractive, albeit less liquid and less secure, forms of investment.

Competing with financial institutions are retailers, and not just Amazon. Starbucks is exploring a mobile payment strategy, while OpenTable is another high-profile player; device makers (Samsung); tech companies (Apple, Microsoft) and online companies (Alphabet, parent of Google). What the companies have in common is a direct link to the consumer – one that could bypass a financial institution if a separate wealth transfer infrastructure was in place.

The largest deals of Q2 2016 according to the KPMG "Pulse of Fintech" were with Lu. com ($1216 bn), the largest online P2P marketplace in China, and JD Finance ($1.01 bn), the consumer finance subsidiary of Chinese e-commerce company JD.com – both of them in Asia. Three more: Oscar Health Insurance; Welab Holdings, and Betterment, were for more than $100 m. Two of these were in the US. Of the 25 largest FinTech deals in Q1 2016, only one – Spotcap – was in Europe.

JD Finance provides a number of online financial services to consumers, startups, and companies in China. As with Lu.com, one of its operations – JD-ZestFinance Gaia – appears to be trying to bring into the investment and borrowing space the millions of Chinese who, until only recently, would have had only a tangential link with this sector. It aims to offer new microloan options to Chinese consumers, particularly those who not have credit history and other credentials traditionally required to land a credit card or other finance options.

New York City-based **Betterment** is a leader in the robo-advisor sector. The US company is a disruptor to traditional asset-management businesses providing a combination of goal-based tools and low management fees, particularly for accounts over $100,000; those accounts pay just 0.15% of assets managed. Like other robo-advisors, Betterment uses exchange-traded funds (ETFs), and clients pay no commissions or transaction fees. It claims more than $3.9 bn in assets under management, and more customers than all of the competition combined. **WePay**, based in San Francisco, processes credit card payments online, focusing on crowdfunding platforms such as GoFundMe. It is a low-cost option both deploying FinTech and being used by other FinTech operations.

Two US operations – **Affirm** and **Kabbage** – take an old-fashioned offline operation in short-term loans at relatively high interest rates, and transfer it to a lower-cost online space.

The above all fit into the "disruptor" space, but there are many companies in the service provision space. One is Reykjavik-based **Meniga,** has developed money-management software which it is licensing to banks, on a subscription basis. It has signed a deal with Santander, one of the largest banks in Europe, as well as 24 other banks.

These are but a few examples out of many. FinTech business models range from subscriptions to commissions to (less commonly) sales. Some are units of larger e-commerce operations; some are independent. Some see the retail customer as their target market; some see other online operations as their potential customers, while many are looking to sell to the traditional financial sector, helping them transition to the new world.

32.1.5   InsurTech – the Current State of Play

In 2015 there remained a disconnect between banking FinTech and InsurTech. Accenture observed that FinTech investment in the Asia-Pacific region increased four-fold in 2015, to \$4.3 bn. China attracted 45% of that investment, while India received 38%. However, 78% of FinTech deals targeted banking. Only 1% targeted the insurance sector.

Indeed, the United States currently dominates InsurTech investment. In the first quarter of 2016 there were 45 InsurTech deals concluded, and most went to US firms (compared with FinTech as a whole, where the big money tends to be in Asia and, particularly, China).

CB Insights [5] believes that this temporary skewing towards the US is likely to lessen as InsurTech matures, with funding likely to follow the geographical pattern seen in retail banking and payments processing.

Meanwhile, analyst firm Gartner has predicted that there will be 20.8 bn "things" connected to the internet by 2020 – about six devices for every person on the planet [6]. Jean-Francois Gasc, managing director of Accenture's strategy for insurance in Europe, Africa and Latin America, said in a 2016 blog post that "our research shows that 45% of insurers believe this trend will be a major driver of revenue in the next three years". Not only will product providers be seeking more liability cover, but the "Internet of Things" will provide insurers with a great deal more data on customer habits. This in turn will offer the opportunity to provide new products, based on data that had not previously been available to actuaries [7].

Greater levels of individualized rating are already available via wearables, connected cars, connected homes, and data gleaned from smartphone apps. The concept of risk assessment before a premium is calculated could be changed into real-time risk assessment.

The concept of "always on" insurance could become outdated. The ability for the customer to turn cover on and off as and when required – with a corresponding increase in unit premiums but a potential decrease in premiums per year – will change radically the actuarial approach to risk management.

New entrants will have sophisticated data modelling tools to hand, exploiting technique such as those used in high-frequency trading. Insurers will need to choose the right partners when exploiting new techniques. New companies have appeared providing customized insurance solutions in response to changing customer demands.

The ultimate disruption threat would be where deployers of InsurTech tried to render the existing insurance stack irrelevant, creating an entirely new marketplace concept.

32.2 Threats to Insurers

Within the insurance sector described above there are four distinct divisions and three "spaces" between those divisions. There is the customer, the broker, the insurer and the reinsurer as "divisions" and B2B, B2C, and B2B2C as "spaces".

InsurTech can serve as a cooperator in those sectors or as an aid in bridging the spaces between those sectors helping traditional insurers to create more customer value. However, InsurTech companies could attempt to disrupt the status quo by using their more efficient technology to "invade the space" providing more customized responses to customer needs.

There are IT and tech players, whose names one would not automatically associate with the insurance business, that are investing heavily in advanced data analytics. At the moment these companies are not attacking the insurance business – preferring instead to collaborate with established partners – but this is mainly because they know that the hurdles of regulation are high. If the regulatory hurdle were not there, there is nothing to stop them underwriting their own insurance products.

At the time of writing, most of the InsurTech companies are looking into the B2C retail business space, for example motor insurance, but we see already the first companies looking into the B2B commercial space. It will probably start with SMEs, but will then creep up the ladder, serving larger companies.

Insurance is about much more than the sale of a policy. Pricing and conditions must be correct (risk assessment); potential loss levels for the insurer need to be controlled (risk management); claims need to be verified (loss adjustment) and payments in both directions need to be efficiently processed.

The entire insurance cycle needs to be as smooth as possible. Although InsurTech can be used to help established insurers and brokers make the insurance cycle more efficient and user-friendly, there is also the threat that new companies will invade spaces that up until now had been the preserve of established brokers or insurers.

The higher one climbs the insurance ladder, from retail to commercial, the harder it becomes to manage the customer experience in an efficient fashion. For the large corporates and multi-national accounts that remains a challenge today. Customers' expectations also shift as they move from retail, through SME, to large corporate segments.

What InsurTech can do in the large corporate space is expedite speedier, more efficient and accurate risk assessment, pricing, risk management, loss assessment. and payment.

Although this will cause evolution and, indeed, some disruption, it does not fundamentally alter the insurer/customer relationship.

However, that does not mean it will never do so.

No-one knows yet what will be the Uber in the insurance segment, but there are many parts of the insurance space where it might appear. Insurers needs a coherent digital strategy that will make it ready if and when a major disruptive threat takes hold.

32.3   A Digital Strategy Response

Traditional insurers – in parallel with incumbent companies from more industrial sectors – have evolved a number of response strategies to position themselves most effectively in the future insurance eco-system (see Fig. 32.2).

32.3.1   Pillar 1: Investor Approach/Strategic Partnerships

The traditional insurance sector can participate in the wider digital ecosystem through the establishment of digital partnerships – leveraging the scale and scope of the established insurer to complement the innovations of InsurTech businesses.

PricewaterhouseCoopers (PwC) observed recently that "the majority of InsurTech startups are focused on activities that will help incumbent insurers to do a better job, rather than to steal their business". In terms of the earlier roadmap, this means they would lean towards the "provider" sector rather than the "disruptor" sector.

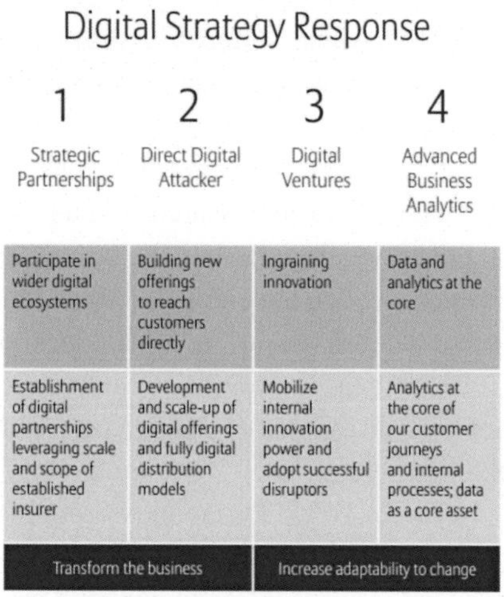

Fig. 32.2 Digital strategy responses by traditional insurers

Digital Strategy Response

1	2	3	4
Strategic Partnerships	Direct Digital Attacker	Digital Ventures	Advanced Business Analytics
Participate in wider digital ecosystems	Building new offerings to reach customers directly	Ingraining innovation	Data and analytics at the core
Establishment of digital partnerships leveraging scale and scope of established insurer	Development and scale-up of digital offerings and fully digital distribution models	Mobilize internal innovation power and adopt successful disruptors	Analytics at the core of our customer journeys and internal processes; data as a core asset
Transform the business		Increase adaptability to change	

Many insurers see InsurTech's potential for transforming the back office, noting for example the opportunity for innovation in data and analytics, plus new approaches to underwriting risk and loss prediction.

Allianz entered a cooperation and investment partnership with Berlin-based simplesurance, an e-commerce provider which now distributes Allianz insurance products in 28 European countries via customer portals such as Schutzklick.de, as well as some 1500 online shops. Allianz took a minority stake in the InsurTech company. Established in 2012, simplesurance has developed software that enables customers to buy products online and purchase corresponding insurance coverage in a few completely paperless steps.

Munich Re has invested in several "Internet of Things" startups. These include Helium, Waygum, and Augury through its corporate venture arm, Munich Re/HSB Ventures. Munich Re's subsidiary American Modern helped underwrite venture-capital-backed pet insurer Embrace Pet Insurance. It has partnered with drone start-startup PrecisionHawk and with disease outbreak risk analytics firm Metabiota.

32.3.2 Pillar 2: Direct Digital Attacker

A second strategy, which can blur into the first, is for an insurer itself to offer digital products and channels. These can include the development of customer apps or in-house client portals as product and service platforms.

A client portal such as myAGCS.com requires registered commercial users to log in to manage their policies and global programs or access risk reports from one online touchpoint. Other large insurers have also developed client portals. These include myAviva, RSA Travel Insurance and partnerportal from HDI.

"AGA (Allianz Global Assistance) Mobil" is a smart travel cover application offering a range of travel insurance services on the customer's mobile phone. These not only include policy details, but also useful local telephone numbers, an international drug directory to make obtaining the right medication as easy as possible, first-aid terms, an international hospital search, and a hotline to assistance experts.

Offering tailored solutions through digital channels in a fast and convenient way can be enabled through the employment of white-label technologies such as Blockchain, adapted to suit the purposes of individual insurance companies or contractual scenarios.

Blockchain is one of the most interesting FinTech and InsurTech areas. It will be the next big disruptor for the banking and insurance industries, both from an internal and external perspective.

A recent World Economic Forum report said that distributed ledger technology (DLT) has "great potential to drive simplicity and efficiency through the establishment of new financial services infrastructure and processes".

In June 2016 Allianz Risk Transfer, the alternative risks transfer specialist of Allianz, worked with Nephila Capital to pilot the use of blockchain smart contract technology. The "proof of concept" put forward by ART and Nephila transacted a natural catastrophe swap. In the case of a financial cat swap, the insurer pays a third party to assume the financial risk of a defined catastrophe event, such as a Florida hurricane, in exchange for a payment or series of payments. If the event occurs and meets the pre-defined trigger criteria, the third party is responsible for the pre-agreed financial risk. This was a transfer from A to B. However, the process could also be used for catastrophe bonds, where a number of parties assume the catastrophe exposure through a securitized financial instrument.

The neatness of blockchain is that each validated contract contains data and self-executable codes inherent to that contract. When a triggering event occurs which meets the agreed conditions, the blockchain smart contract picks up the predefined data sources of all participants, and then automatically activates and determines payouts to or from contract parties. Blockchain acts as a distributed ledger, enabling transactional history, contracts and integrity to be maintained and stored. Any party in the transaction can access these details. Further, "smart contracts" could see the contracts, and the securities underlying them, to be created in a single blockchain. Compare that with the process which currently takes place with catastrophe bonds and the increased efficiencies and speed are plain to see.

The potential use cases in both retail and corporate insurance are pretty apparent: any kind of contract we have in paper or pdf today could be translated into a smart contract on the blockchain. You could close such contracts online and it would be immediately available to all the participants. The contract would be immutable, and could even have program code embedded that executes automatically based on events or a certain point in time. There are a lot of contracts and transactions in insurance and other industries and these could be modeled, transacted and stored on a blockchain – providing more transparency, speed and convenience to all.

32.3.3   Pillar 3: Digital Ventures Accelerator Programs

Several major insurers have developed their own "accelerator" programs in response to the flourishing InsurTech startup environment, although how they define the word can vary. In some cases it is an internal division, while in others they are closed-end programs, seeking applications from external startups to benefit from an established insurer's mentoring and contacts.

Whatever the precise structure of the accelerator, in all cases opportunistic minds within the insurance sector encourage new "big ideas" – with the hope of being at the head of the queue should an individual idea prove successful.

One of the most high-profile InsurTech moves in 2016 was **Swiss Re's** insurance accelerator program in Bangalore, India, running from mid-July to mid-October. The reinsurer actively sought out companies that might be threats. Swiss Re's program mentored and helped curate startups aimed at disrupting insurance practices. Startups engaged with Swiss Re executives and were given access to Swiss Re's expertise.

In September 2016 **Munich Re** established MundiLab which is divided into two phases: A five-week program starting in February 2017 will take 10 selected teams in diverse industries to the next level, opening opportunities to them within the insurance market (cash and equity free for participants). Within this phase startups will take part in workshops to improve their entrepreneurial toolkit, and gain links to the network of Munich Re partners and clients.

Munich Re will then select the best-performing companies with the highest potential to disrupt the insurance industry. The startups will be offered an opportunity to work on a pilot program with Munich Re, an opportunity to pitch their ideas at Munich Re demo day and access to key investors from European top VCs. Entrepreneurs will also be given access to key decision-makers at Munich Re to learn how corporates think and take sourcing and partnership decisions.

Allianz X is the company builder of the Allianz Group, identifying, building and globally scaling new business models in the InsurTech space. A more open-ended operation than the Swiss Re or Munich Re programs, Allianz X offers "a unique working environment and a world-class team to launch new ventures in less than six months from idea to market entry".

Allianz X has backed Fairfleet, which provides a platform for a community of amateur drone pilots. In the past, if there were a natural catastrophe, it would often be several days, weeks or even months, before loss adjustors could enter safely an area where the loss had occurred. Fairfleet aims to solve that problem, amongst others by creating a 'drone on demand' marketplace.

For example, a certified drone pilot can apply on that platform to be part of a global community. This enables the community member to combine a hobby with revenue. As soon as Allianz has a relevant risk- or disaster assessment, it places the job into the platform, and that job is available to the pilots close to the area. They then fly their drone over that area in a pre-determined way to produce pictures, for which they get paid.

32.3.4 Pillar 4: Advanced Business Analytics

Analytics are at the core of customer journeys and internal processes. Data is a core asset. Since the turn of the century advances in technology and an incredible expansion in new digital data sources have expanded and reinvented the core disciplines of insurers. Actuarial science is becoming not only about more data, but also real-time data.

In future, efficient sourcing of data and innovative analytics methods will be much greater sources of competitive advantage in insurance than the traditional combination of scale of exposures and underwriting expertise.

Data monitoring on its own can influence customer behavior. New data sources, and new tools for underwriting risk, will all be major factors for the insurer of tomorrow.

With better access to publicly available third-party data from a wide variety of sources – the so-called "data exhaust" from social media, smartphone apps, connected cars and connected homes – insurers will learn to ask new questions that will help them understand better their existing exposures, and also to create new products for exposures that were previously uninsurable because of a lack of data.

Erwann Michel-Kerjan, Executive Director at Wharton Risk Center see data analytics to be at the core of rejuvenation of insurance [8]: "We are now seeing more companies spending a fair amount of time and money upgrading their risk selection processes, from improving their understanding of their maximum exposure to extreme events around the world (direct, business interruption, contingent business interruption), to extracting information from decades of claims data and combining those with other sources of knowledge."

The Supply Chain Stack

An Allianz Global Corporate & Specialty (AGCS) project demonstrates how data analytics can improve supply chain risks assessment for a corporate insurer: Any kind of multinational has a first-tier supply chain – the direct suppliers they need to have operating in order to keep production running. But these suppliers also have suppliers, the tier-two supply chain. So if one of these tier two players falls down, then the tier one supplier has a problem, which means that the insured has a problem. This can be extended to tier-three, tier-four and tier-five supply chains.

An insurer's risk manager needs to go through the slow process of checking the various levels of the supply chain and the back-ups in place. What the insurer needs is to know more about the client, and the client's suppliers down through the various tiers, without having to ask any questions of that client.

AGCS has developed a linguistic algorithm that can read all of the publicly available information on the client and its suppliers. This information is visualized and helps making complex supply chains more transparent and identifying bottleneck suppliers.

Praedicat: "The Next Big Thing" in Liability

Los Angeles-based Praedicat is another example of innovative data analysis. The company focuses on "improving the underwriting and management of liability catastrophe risk" using big data analytics.

Praedicat sets out a methodology that uses big data to improve insurers' understanding of liability risk. The new technology mines data from scientific research associated with potential liability risks, generating a probability of a consensus being reached that exposure to a substance or product causes a particular form of injury.

The key factor here is that this consensus is seen as the critical threshold at which lawsuits become more likely to succeed. This information is overlaid on an insurer's portfolio to identify potential accumulations of liability risk. The analysis can be used to develop quantitative estimates of mass litigation, allowing a liability catastrophe model to be built from the bottom up.

32.4 A Company Is Its People

Digitalization is not only about embracing and integrating new technology. It is also about a major cultural change; agility, trial and error, less hierarchy in decision making, fewer silos, more cross-functional collaboration.

It is also about new capabilities.

Insurers must spot and exploit opportunities sooner rather than later, creating a vision for the fully digital customer journey.

Although companies such as Google, Amazon and Facebook have accumulated huge amounts of data, insurers not only have a considerable amount of data in store, they have also been accumulating it for a long time and, most significantly, they know what to do with it.

For InsurTech the challenge is correlating that unstructured data with the risk. At the moment the major data collectors do not have the knowledge of risk that an insurance company has.

Within AGCS there is a division called AZT (Allianz Zentrum für Technik) that analyzes the root causes of 8000 losses a year, correlating this engineering information with policy pricing.

Companies such as Microsoft have developed engines to analyze unstructured data, but it is still necessary to teach the engines what to do. Currently the established insurers are well-positioned to do that, much more so than the pure data engines out there. But tomorrow's world might be totally different, because the opposition is learning fast.

An example of how insurers can use unstructured data in innovative and inductive ways was a small pilot AGCS ran which looked for correlations between data and fire exposure. It was nothing big. It was young talents, without much money or investment, who were told to "go off and do something". What they discovered was the data gleaned from online reviews about any lack of cleanliness of hotels had a positive correlation with a higher likelihood of a fire claim.

The new staff insurers are employing today need to be different from the people they employed when they themselves were youngsters in the early 1990s. The job of the underwriter will change dramatically over the next few years. It will still be there, but the underwriter in five or 10 years' time will be a data scientist. He or she will have the ability to understand data from a completely different angle; to be able to express data into algorithms.

It is vital that insurers support their long-serving staff on that journey, through internal or possibly external programs.

32.5 Conclusion

The progress of InsurTech in insurance can be a partnership rather than a battle. We do not need to blow everything up and start again from scratch.

But there is without doubt a possibility of disruption from outsiders. Real disruption so far has always come from the customer acquisition angle. These companies want to disrupt the current placement process. It will not be like the current insurance industry placement process with a bit of technology attached to it. It will be something completely re-imagined.

InsurTech will have wide-ranging implications for the industry, both short-term and long-term. It will cover the entire customer process, from customer acquisition through to claims payment, and will influence the entire insurance "stack", from customer to reinsurer, via internal and external processes. Insurers need to react nimbly to ensure that the opportunities offered by InsurTech are used to the advantage of the industry rather than exploited by non-insurers to negatively impact what is a sound, reputationally strong and robust macro-model.

Traditional market leaders need to make the most of the opportunities presented by the digital age being amongst those spearheading change and taking an active role in shaping its course, instead of letting the change drive them. Many organizations in the financial services sector are undergoing a process of fundamental transformation to incorporate disruptive technologies. What will emerge are organizations that are close to their customers, better at responding to their wishes and demands and capable of creating closer emotional ties between the customer and the company.

References

1. Route 66 Ventures LLC, Alexandria, VA 22314: Graphic "Financial Services Industry Investment Universe"
2. Accenture: "The Boom In Global Fintech Investment"
3. Accenture: "The Future of Fin5Tech and Banking". https://www.weforum.org/agenda/2016/08/the-rejuvenation-of-insurance-this-is-why-it-matters/
4. http://www.FinTechinnovationlablondon.co.uk/media/730274/Accenture-The-Future-of-FinTech-and-Banking-digitallydisrupted-or-reima-.pdf.
5. KPMG & CB Insights, "The Pulse of FinTech", March/August 2016.The eight verticals listed were Lending Tech; PaymentsTech; Wealth Management/Personal Finance; Money Transfers; Blockchain; Institutional/Capital Markets Tech; Equity Crowdfunding; InsurTech. https://assets.kpmg.com/content/dam/kpmg/pdf/2016/05/the-pulse-of-fintech.pdf
6. https://www.cbinsights.com/blog/insurance-tech-startup-funding-2015/.
7. www.gartner.com/newsroom/id/3165317
8. insuranceblog.accenture.com/author/jean-francois-gasc

Fintech Hypes, but Wealthy Internet Savvy Investors Prefer to Stay Hybrid

33

Thomas Altenhain and Christoph Heinemann

Abstract

Digitalization has changed the way customers interact with their banks and financial advisors. Fintech companies restructure the value chain, re-bundle offerings and create new services that are to be presented and processed digitally – perhaps completely. Nevertheless, recent research with wealthy internet savvy investment customers in Germany shows that this attractive segment can be regarded as hybrid in respect of their demand for digital as well as personal asset management services and products. On the one hand wealthy internet savvy investors indicate a high level of satisfaction with advice and products from their traditional financial services partners. On the other hand they continue to search for better investment opportunities, thus showing significant demand for innovative digital banking/brokerage/advice products. Ultimately, research gives strong evidence for a high need for personal advice and human guidance. This is particularly valid when answering the question which (traditional vs. innovative) partner to choose as the future (exclusive or additional) bank, broker or financial advisor.

This paper outlines the world of Fintech start-up companies, presents key findings regarding the attractive and large segment of wealthy internet savvy investors and also explores how the new Fintech conquerors as well as established banks and advisors might embrace this new business environment.

T. Altenhain (✉)
ALTENHAIN Unternehmensberatung GbR
Starnberg, Germany
e-mail: altenhain@gmx.net

C. Heinemann
Christoph Heinemann Vermögensverwaltung GmbH
Munich, Germany
e-mail: heinemann@investagent.de

© Springer-Verlag GmbH Germany 2018
C. Linnhoff-Popien et al. (eds.), *Digital Marketplaces Unleashed*,
https://doi.org/10.1007/978-3-662-49275-8_33

33.1   Fintech Hypes, Particularly in the Past Two Years

Selling financial services products by using technical equipment as well as electronic media reaches back a couple of decades. Back then players in retail banking and asset management used technology that offered the ability to secure unlimited operational readiness and to make advice and sales independent from branch locations: ATMs and statement printers had been on the rise since the early 1980s, electronic cash POS-systems as well as home banking with videotext had been broadly offered since the late 1980s, and the 1990s saw the emergence of online banking & direct brokerage.

In the past two decades the continually spreading use of the internet, the prevalence of mobile technology as well as digital innovation have lead to new and revolutionary technologies that serve as impulse generators for deep changes to the ecosystem of financial institutions: The brick-and-mortar-centered financial industry has embarked on separating customer liaison, customer advice, information gathering, product sales and product servicing from long-established human interaction in branches. Thus, the value chain is constantly being restructured, offerings are getting re-bundled, information gathering and treatment are redefined and new services are created that are presented and processed digitally.

Today banking and brokerage by telephone, internet, and mobile/app have fundamentally changed the way retail as well as corporate and institutional customers interact with their banks and financial advisors. As a consequence, long-established players like high street banks and traditional brokers are confronted with new entries, so called *Fintech* companies, that apply 'technology to conduct the fundamental functions provided by financial services, impacting how consumers store, save, borrow, invest, move, pay, and protect money' [1][1]. The following statistics illustrate the growing importance of Fintech start-up-companies and might potentially point up the 'hype':

The current number of Fintech companies in the world is estimated anywhere between 5000 to 6000 with some recent sources also quoting an amount of 12,000 – although there even might be a high underestimation as startup companies that have not used external funding might not to be recorded in any database [1, 2, 3, 4, p. 354 f.].

Fintechs are new ventures founded in the last ten years: According to joint research by KPMG and H2Ventures published in December 2015, only 18% of the global top-50 Fintech-companies are older than eight years, 28% are between six and eight years old and the remaining 54% were set-up in 2011 or later [5].[2]

---

[1] "Unless mentioned otherwise Fintech in this paper encompass technology solutions for retail customers (b-to-c and/or c-to-c). If used in a broader sense, Fintech also include solutions for small and medium sized businesses as well as big corporates and institutional customers of banks/financial institutions (b-to-b); or, in the widest sense, also for the insurance sector ('Insurtech').

[2] The quoted list of top 50 established Fintech companies produced by KPMG and H2Ventures is based on four groups of factors (total capital raised, rate of capital raising, location, degree of sub-industry disruption) and an adjustment by a judging panel's subjective rating of the degree of

Fintech companies have been set up all over the world, although some regional clusters can be identified: An indication for the regional distribution may be that out of the top 50 Fintechs, 40% are headquartered in North America, 20% in Europe, 14% in China, 10% in South America and 12% in the rest of the world [5].

Globally, already 29 Fintech start-up companies founded after the year 2000, can be regarded as '*unicorns*' with a market valuation of more than USD one billion [6].[3] Another about 50 firms qualify as '*narwhals*' or '*semi-unicorns*', each with an estimated value of at least USD 500 million. In total, all these 'animals' together are valued at about USD 120 billion. In comparison, the banking group with the highest market capitalization in the world and going back to the 1850s, Wells Fargo Group, was at the same time valued at about USD 300 billion; the next biggest banking conglomerate and also from the early 1800s, J.P. Morgan Chase, as well as Industrial & Commercial Bank of China (at least over 30 years old) were worth USD 260 billion each [10]. The 20 biggest European banks have a market capitalization between USD 30 and 160 billion, but most of them, if not all, look back on a history of more than 100 years [11].

Their big number as well as the high valuations of Fintechs also indicate that they have very successfully attracted investors: During the last seven years, global investments into financial technology have increased from slightly above USD one billion to nearly USD 20 billion in 2015 [1, 12, p. 46]. Funding is geared towards regional clusters with fluctuations in its distribution: In the year 2015, venture-capital backed Fintechs received USD 14.5 billion in equity investments overall, an amount of USD 4.9 billion was invested in the first quarter of 2016 alone. Out of this, North America received 56% (in brackets: Q1/2016: 37%), Asia 32% (53%), Europe 10% (6%) and the rest of the world 2% (4%) [13].

Interest has not only increased amongst financial investors, e. g. business angels, venture capitalists, mutual/private equity/hedge funds. Also public interest as measured by Google searches for the keyword 'Fintech' has rocketed in the past seven years: Average popularity of searches in comparison to all other searches in Google was stable for the first five years, in 2014 it approximately doubled and in 2015 it again went up five to six times [14]. Average relative popularity of keywords as 'internet, mobile, e-commerce, online banking, retail banking' in the same seven years remained or rather declined slightly.

Fintechs span their offering of products and services as well as their customer reach over all segments of financial services: 88% of the already mentioned top 50 Fintechs focus on banking and only 12% on insurance products and services [5]. With 32%, the majority of the banking-related top 50 Fintechs focus on lending to retail as well as SME clients; wealth management and trading services are offered by 23%, payment services by 14%; other products and services account for the remaining 31% [5].

---

product, service, customer experience and business model innovation; the definition of Fintech also includes Insurtech and solutions for corporate/institutional customers.

[3] Numbers on Fintechs in this paragraph include direct services to clients and software suppliers founded since 2000, valued at USD 500 million or more, also exits, public companies, real estate plays and not pure-play Fintech but with substantial operations in that vertical; also see [5, 7–9].

A slightly different view on the product and customer orientation is given by recent McKinsey research on more than 350 mainly smaller banking-related Fintechs: With a share of 43% the main product area is payments, followed by 24% for lending, 19% for asset management/sales & trading/securities services ('financial assets and capital markets'), and the remainder for account management [1]. 62% of the companies registered in this database focus on the retail customer segment, 28% on small and medium-size enterprises, the remainder on large corporates, public entities and nonbanking financial institutions [1].[4]

25 to 30% of established top players in the banking field are also active outside their home market; at the moment, none of the insurance Fintechs has a multi-country or even global reach (yet) [5].

33.2 Wealthy Internet Savvy Investors Between High Acceptance of Fintechs' Offerings and Uncertainty of Their Choices

Fintech companies intend to fundamentally disrupt the traditional way of banking, brokerage and financial advice: Long established personal relationships between clients and their bankers/brokers disconnect and move to a digital environment. Thereby Fintechs' offerings serve as strong impulse generators for deep changes in the industry particularly as the traditional value chain of attraction, information, advice, sales, servicing and processing is broken up, re-designed and re-bundled.

This provides big opportunities for new entrants, but also for established players that are either able to cement historic relationships to their customers 'forever' or to use the new technologies to also play the digital game. This chapter will point at the customers' view. Although probably all customers of the financial services industry will be affected in some form by digitalization of the industry, this paper exemplifies the effect on wealthy and at the same time internet savvy investors.[5]

---

[4] Different to [1], the top 50 banking-related Fintechs illustrate a slightly different view: between 45 to 50% focus on retail solutions, approx. 40% on SMEs and the rest on bigger corporates and platform/enabling technologies [5].

[5] Based on research commissioned by the authors of this paper, executed in November 2015 by Norstat Deutschland GmbH (Kaflerstr. 8, D-81241 Munich), in the form of an online panel with 1048 participants from Germany; in the research internet savvy individuals are defined and pre-screened as willing to participate in an online panel and indicate to use internet/mobile for banking and/or brokerage [15].

33.2.1 Wealthy Internet Savvy Investors as an Attractive Showcase Segment

Wealthy internet savvy investors can be characterized by two dimensions: On the one hand they are open for innovative technology and apply modern communication, thus belonging to the about 75% of all EU citizens that form the community of internet users.[6] And they are also part of those 60% who use internet or mobile for banking and/or brokerage [18].

On the other hand these digital natives have money to invest, either in cash or in any form of securities, like stocks, bonds or mutual funds (*'liquid monetary assets'*; with investments in real estate, alternative investments, commodities etc. as well as pension entitlements not being considered). Wealthy internet savvy investors work with banks, brokers, financial advisors and financial sales organizations to fulfill their financial requirements. But they do not only belong to the small group of high net worth-/ultra high net worth- or affluent-/mass affluent-individuals at the top of the wealth pyramid[7]. Instead they form the mass market of individuals who have to invest (at least some) money and want to increase their fortune. Taking Germany as an example, they represent about 15% of the country's population above the age of 18 years and own liquid monetary assets of EUR 600 to 700 billion.[8]

Quantity and magnitude of their accumulated wealth make this broad sector of the population an attractive customer segment for the financial services industry and a focus area for Fintech entrants as well. An extrapolation of the German figures to EU-level should give a range of assets of between €3500 to 4000 billion held by the respective between 70 and 80 million individuals in Europe. Applying a gross revenue margin for asset management of 1%, European wealthy internet savvy investors offer a gross revenue pool of about €35 to 40 billion for the financial services industry.[9]

This estimate of gross revenue might be too conservative and a doubling of the presented range for the near future should be considered: On the one hand the researched group in Germany as well as the extrapolated population in Europe does not include people 65+ years, which make up approx. 20% of the German and 18% of EU population. This group is also a target group of banks and brokers and therefore should be in the focus

---

[6] Data from Eurostat with EU28 average [16]; minimum internet usage once a week, but less than daily; daily usage by ca. 60% of citizens [17, p. 9]. report that 83% of households have access to the internet at home and 43% through mobile phone.

[7] Approaches to segmentation in wealth management are offered by [19, p. 5 f., 20, p. 3 f.]; an example for segmentation using asset and income situation is delivered by [21, p. 328 f.]; an empirical analysis of a specific investor segment can be found at [22, p. 194 f.].

[8] Research in Germany: aged 25 to 65 years; individuals with net household income < €3000 excluded unless possession of liquid monetary assets > €30,000.

[9] Extrapolation is based on population data only as average possession of liquid assets per capita in Germany is about Euro zone level [23, 24, pp. 6–12]; population in Germany ca. 16% of EU28 with about similar share of age group 18–65 on total age structure in EU28 countries; extrapolation factor of six applied based on German share of EU population; no consideration of different internet/mobile usage in Europe vs. Germany.

of Fintechs as well: It has to be regarded as above-average moneyed. But it shows a lower than average propensity to deal with digital media and equipment, thus it might be less straightforward to be targeted and reached by digital offerings.

On the other hand digitalization is not static. In the near future, the general public will get more and more comfortable to follow the digital natives interviewed and make use of digital media and equipment for their banking and brokerage needs: On average as opposed to the researched wealthy internet savvy individuals, only 51% of the Germans use the internet for banking/brokerage. The European average is 46%. However, some countries show a much higher usage already today that can be regarded as a benchmark for the near future: France and the UK 58%, the BeNeLux countries between 62 and 85%, Scandinavia between 85 and 90% [18].[10]

33.2.2   The Grass Is Always Greener on the Other Side of the Fence

Looking at the researched wealthy internet savvy investors aged 25 to 65, about 65% of them show special interest in all aspects of managing money.[11] This interest is far greater than in other financial services products as e. g. payment services and credit cards with 33%, insurance products with 30%, real estate financing with 27% and financing a new car with 18%.

The special interest slumps with age but it increases with net household income and liquid assets. As an example, 84% of individuals worth €100,000+ express special interest in money matters.

30% of the respondents say that that they use only one bank for the investment/management/custody of their liquid assets.

But 70% keep (at least) a second relationship with another financial services provider where they deposit cash, hold securities or trade stocks, etc.[12] A relationship with another financial player has to be regarded as an act of reduced loyalty, looking through the eyes of the management of a bank that provides asset management services to their customers (and wants to keep or even increase this business) [25, p. 361].

Yet, opening a second relationship does not need to result in a complete relocation of the former liaison; it might only lead to some cherry-picking outside the original connection: Customers are attracted e. g. by slightly better interest rates, more valuable investments tips, a friendlier personal advisors in the branch or a more modern, attractive digital offering from one of the new Fintech entries. The checking account and the mortgage might stay with the 'old player', but liquid assets will be transferred or new monies from a gratuity or the sale of real estate will directly find a new home.

---

[10] A more general view on variations among countries in Europe with respect of being digitized economies is presented by [17, p. 27 f.].

[11] All subsequent research data on wealthy internet savvy investors is taken from [15].

[12] Includes all traditional branch based banks as well as online banks and online brokers, operating in Germany, irrespective whether the providers offer digital and/or brick & mortar services.

Table 33.1 Satisfaction levels of wealthy internet savvy investors (top 2 grades of 6, in %)

		Liquid assets (EUR)			
		Up to 50,000 (in %)	50 to 100,000 (in %)	More than 100,000 (in %)	Average (in %)
Main bank relationship	'Get (very) good advice'	72	77	72	73
	'I think that investment opportunities on offer are (very) satisfactory'	59	59	59	59
Secondary bank relationship	'I get (very) good advice'	58	58	61	58
	'I think that investment opportunities on offer are (very) satisfactory'	60	61	55	59
'I am looking for better investment alternatives for my assets'		43	61	67	49

The high proportion of multi-bank usage leads to the question of satisfaction of the wealthy internet savvy investors with their current banking partners. The above Table indicates that on average 73% claim to get good or even very good advice from their main bank, and 58% from their secondary banking relationship as well (see Table 33.1).

It is also remarkable that the investment opportunities on offer are also regarded as (very) satisfactory, more or less irrespectively whether main or secondary providers are used and also independent from the magnitude of the liquid assets owned by the respondents.

However, on average half of the wealthy internet savvy investors state that they are looking for better investment alternatives for their assets. This is particularly true for the wealthier segments with more than EUR 50,000 or even more than EUR 100,000 to invest.[13,14] The observed high level of satisfaction with advice and investment opportunities offered by the current institution(s) is contradictory to the claim that customers are looking for better investment alternatives for their assets.

Obviously better investment alternatives can either be expected to be offered by the existing banking/brokerage partner(s). Otherwise, better investment alternatives are searched for and originate from a new relationship. Therefore, it was researched whether wealthy internet savvy investors agree with the claim *the grass is always greener on the other side of the fence*. This means that those who agree undertake the burden to change banks, at least

---

[13] Average liquid assets of the participants in the underlying research are about €60,000 which is ca. 150% of German average; participants in the middle column of the table own approx. €71,000, right-hand column on average €267,000 [15, p. 218 f.]; the European average of liquid assets is estimated by the authors at approx. €50,000.

[14] Additional research shows that those who move banks or at least open new accounts have a higher income and are younger than average, can rather be found amongst real estate owners and more often have a secondary bank relationship [15, pp. 225–227].

open a new relationship, and voluntarily undergo the necessary bureaucratic hurdles imposed by *know-your-customer* and *anti-money-laundering* regulation. As a consequence, the revenue pool of the incumbent bank will diminish:

- 25% of the wealthy internet savvy investors do not envisage shipping their liquid assets from their traditional banking and brokerage partners to (new) specialized institutions for deposits, asset management or brokerage. For answering this question, respondents were informed that these specialized firms would offer tailor-made investment opportunities as well as independent advice, present reputable products with appropriate risk-return-profile, and would have the same guarantee level as their current bank(s).
- However, 38% might envisage working with those specialized institutions – although on average 70% already have a secondary relationship for managing their liquid assets.
- The consensus that the grass is greener on the other side of the fence is even higher amongst those internet savvy investors owning more than €50,000 (43%) or more than €100,000 (48%).
- In addition, investors in the highest monthly net income bracket of €6000+ agree with 51%; real estate owners concur with 43%.
- Only 26% of internet savvy investors aged 60 years+ might envisage shipping their liquid assets; the highest consent of 50% is found in the age range from 30 to 40 years.

These numbers indicate that wealthy internet savvy investors '*hang on but keep digging*', particularly if they are younger, earn an above average salary, own a (paid-off) house and have accumulated a bigger then average fortune.

33.2.3 No Clear Preference for Digital vs. Analog – But Personal Investment Advice Appreciated

Wealthy internet savvy investors offer opportunities and threats for all players in the financial industry. The winners can be traditional and established firms that are able to convince new customers with e. g. proven quality or sound reputation. But winners might also be the new Fintech entries on the marketplace with innovative products, seamless digital processes or an attractive pricing. Fig. 33.1 answers the question what service is expected by those who go for a new/additional financial partner for deposits, asset management or brokerage – online, mobile, phone, social media or personal. As there is no clear preference for one service channel, wealthy internet savvy investors may be regarded as being *hybrid* – somewhere between being attracted by digital offerings and capabilities, but also sticking to human interaction.

Slightly above 60% want to be serviced online through the providers' websites. Slightly below 60% of the wealthy internet savvy investors name personal advice as their primary required form of service delivery. Both channels claim about the same level of importance.

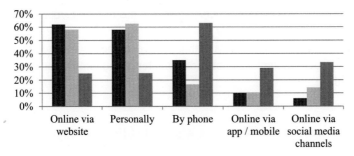

■ How should the specialist present its services?

▨ Which channel is most important?

■ Which channel is second in importance?

Fig. 33.1 Required service channels of (new/additional) specialized institutions for deposits, asset management, brokerage (German wealthy internet savvy investors, aged 25 to 65; multiple selections possible). (Altenhain [15, p. 233])

Advice by phone is asked for much less than both preferred service channels, but is looked upon as the most preferred fall-back offer.

Although the researched customers belong to a tech-friendly and internet savvy segment, they do not expect their partners for deposits, asset management or brokerage to offer mobile or social media services. This might be explained by mobile and social media being used predominantly for information gathering and information sharing; it looks like the media (at least today) are not in focus of wealthy internet savvy investors when looking for advice, opening an account, shipping money, making a transaction, etc.

An even deeper insight in customers' (hybrid) needs is gained when asking the wealthy internet savvy investors whether they appreciate human support when looking for new/additional financial partners:[15]

- 51% deem personal advice by human experts as (very) important when trying to find the best specialized institution for deposits, asset management or brokerage.[16]
- And 70% of those who go for personal advice might consider working with the proposed new/additional financial partner – which is about double the amount of the above reported average of 38% of all respondents.

---

[15] Face-to-face conversation or by phone; following questions asked to sub-group looking for better investment alternatives for assets, according to above Table.

[16] Corresponds to top two out of six possible entries. It should be also reported that just about 27% (bottom three out of six possible entries) do not regard personal advice as important; two thirds of those inform themselves online, 64% quote that they suspect advisors to 'only sell' a product, and 52% imply that advice is never objective.

As a consequence, availability of personal advice has to be regarded as the key driver for answering the question of whether to add a new banking/brokerage relationship, with whom to liaise and how much business to transfer over to the new partner. Personal advice seems to be the underpinning for stepping over the fence and finding out whether the grass is greener out there.

33.3 Opportunities for New but Also Established Players

According to the research findings reported in this paper, wealthy internet savvy investors can be regarded as an attractive customer segment:

- They like to deal with money matters and more than two thirds of them already work with more than one dedicated bank or broker.
- They are highly satisfied with the advice they are getting from their financial partners as well as the products and services.
- However, every other investor is looking for better investment alternatives for their liquid assets. This is even more applicable for the richer and younger individuals.
- Consequently, almost half of the respondents, depending on wealth, age and income level, might open up additional relationships with financial services providers dedicated to servicing, managing and brokering liquid assets.

This new orientation of the investors provides a significant opportunity for those institutions that can capture the business, be it the incumbents of the industry or the new Fintech players: Wealthy internet savvy investors are identified as an attractive market segment for the financial services industry worth billions of EUR in gross revenue.

Does this mean that the Fintech companies as digital newcomers will take it all, thus kicking the traditional players out of the market? The research presented in this paper does not support this threat to the incumbents, as a significant portion of the wealthy internet savvy investors has to be regarded as a hybrid consumer segment – positioned between being highly responsive for modern technology and similarly distinctively prefer human interaction.

Responsiveness for modern technology ...
The respondents are digital citizens who are use modern innovative technology to perform their digital needs, to communicate and search for information digitally, to shop on digital marketplaces and to achieve their banking and brokerage needs digitally.

All this explains the high affinity to players that present themselves as digital. As a consequence, they might source their banking and brokerage needs from the new Fintech players. The successful development of this fairly new cluster of industry players is described in the first chapter of this paper.

However, wealthy internet savvy investors might also rely on the established incumbents that they have been working with for a long time – obviously only with those that have understood the investors' digital demands and have geared up their digital offerings and capabilities to meet the digital natives' financial needs. An example for traditional players '*reverse-disrupting*' the Fintechs and tying in their established customer base can be found with the so called robo-advisors in the United States.

Robo-advisors are automated software platforms for financial advice, usually targeted to smaller portfolios and promising lower fees, but in general applying a standardized, algorithm-driven investment management approach. The biggest robo-advisors are *Betterment* (USD 4 billion under management) and *Wealthfront* (USD 3 billion); both companies are Fintech '*semi-unicorns*' valued at approx. USD 700 million [26].

In early 2015, the major US online broker *Charles Schwab* and the worlds' biggest asset manager *Vanguard* launched their own rob-services. Meanwhile, they have surpassed the new players in terms of assets under management (Charles Schwab USD 5+ billion; Vanguard 12 USD billion). The main reason for this volume buildup was the ability to convince existing customers to shift their assets from other (potentially endangered) product areas to the new robo-services, thus protecting these assets [27–29]. Similar developments might happen in Europe as well, with banks like Barclays Bank, Deutsche Bank, Lloyds Bank, Royal Bank of Scotland, Santander Group and UBS Group recently having announced to launch, buy or partner with robo-services.

... as well as preference for human interaction

The broad demand of the wealthy internet savvy investors for digital financial products and services is obvious. But this does not mean that all members of the analyzed customer segment will completely shift their demand from traditional person-to-person banking to the internet/mobile world. A large percentage shows an equally high preference for personal/analog delivery. In addition, half of the digitally educated individuals prefer personal advice on their choices – they ask for human guidance and answers to questions which financial partner to choose, be it new vs. traditional, but also digital vs. analog offerings. The following sections discuss some hypotheses on three typical, generic customer profiles and outline opportunities for new, but also established players [30, p. 242 f.].

(a) *Self-directed investors*: Within the attractive but hybrid consumer segment of wealthy internet-savvy people, there are self-directed individuals who do not want to or do not have to rely on personal advice. For more than two decades they have had the opportunity to work with online banks and direct brokers; they are able and willing to inform themselves about their choices, take the necessary decisions and perform the bureaucratic activities needed to manage their liquid assets. They might find the following new Fintech offerings attractive (in brackets: examples for companies):
  - search engines dedicated to financial products (*voola*),
  - services that comb through social media for investment trends (*stockpulse*),
  - platforms for investment portfolios from non-professional managers (*wikifolio*),
  - new banks to deposit cash (*number26*).

(b) *Convenience-driven investors*: Wealthy internet savvy investors also include people who want to delegate as many money matters as possible to their partners from the financial industry: On the one hand they are highly attracted by the capabilities of modern digital technologies in many areas of interest, e. g. when it comes to using social media apps for communicating with friends or colleagues or booking holiday trips and shopping online etc. But on the other hand, when it comes to money matters they do not particularly want to deal with or devote time to all necessary aspects.

These customers might use discretionary investment management services offered by robo-advisors – given the growing number of players in Europe, this paper can only draw a short and incomplete list of incumbents, e. g. *MoneyFarm* from Italy, *Nutmeg* from the UK, *Ginmon, Scalable* and *Vaamo* from Germany, *Indexacapital* from Spain, *Yomoni* from France. As the above mentioned examples from the USA show, also European convenience-driven but also technology-affine investors might alternatively stick to the newly introduced robo-solutions offered by their above mentioned traditional wealth managers, e. g. brokers, asset managers and private banks [31, 32].

(c) *Hybrid, advice-seeking investors*: Finally, there are hybrid investors who on the one hand want digital services to e. g. receive up to date information on the performance of invested assets, to secure transparent and lean administration and to receive modern portfolio allocation enabled by artificial intelligence. But on the other hand they also expect personal communication and advice up to regular face-to-face meetings with their account manager.

These investors might be served by 'hybrid-robos'. An example for this approach integrating technology-enabled investment management and the availability of a tied force of agents is the US-based company *Personalcapital*. It offers digital investment management solutions like the 'traditional' clean-play robo-advisors, but also gives access to their team of financial advisors – this ranges from a digital, video-based offering for smaller portfolios to personal visits of advisors to major clients. In addition, it provides a suite of self-service financial calculation and reporting tools that even might be interesting for the above mentioned self-directed investors.[17]

Integrated, hybrid robo-approaches have not been developed for Europe yet. But partnerships of clean-play robo-advisors with independent financial advisors or acquisitions by banks have recently been announced (e. g. cooperation of *Scalable* with KSW, acquisition of *easyfolio* by bank Hauck & Aufhäuser in Germany). Depending on the underlying financial services license (e. g. portfolio management under § 33 of KWG/German Banking Act), smaller portfolios with a discretionary mandate can be handled in a more stan-

---

[17] With assets under management of USD 2+ billion, *Personalcapital* is ranked number three by assets under management in the United States, after clean-play robo-advisors *Betterment* and *Wealthfront; Personalcapital's* valuation is not disclosed [26].

dardized and cost-effective way, while wealthier clients receive the opportunity to access personal advice.

A similar approach might be developed by the administrators of broker pools. Today, they support their member IFAs[18] and provide access to product suppliers for investment funds and ETFs, offer operational as well as sales support and organize mutual liability protection. In addition to these traditional services, the pools might partner with Fintech companies or themselves build a standardized algorithm-driven portfolio management comparable to robo-advisors. If they offer a suite of self-service financial calculation and reporting tools in addition, their member IFAs will be able to combine their today's personal sales approach with more sophisticated consulting and portfolio management skills, as a consequence approaching the hybrid advice-demanding investors.

In the end, the question remains how wealthy internet-savvy investors will find their way through the broad spectrum of digital, analog and even hybrid offerings of banks, brokers, advisors, robots, etc., irrespective of their (generic) customer profile.

One answer might be the creation of a new type of player, comparable to an 'investor's agent': To begin with, it can help the investor to analyze and understand his/her needs, e. g. define long term targets, become clear on risk/return expectations, but also sort out own skills and willingness to manage the investments themselves or outsource it to a financial partner. Like a portal, the investor's agent might also provide access to self-service financial tools for those who deserve so, and propose e. g. potential brokers, banks, custodians as well as IFAs and robo-advisors to self-directed or convenience-driven investors. Those wealthy internet savvy investors who demand a more tailored or an even personal advice can be serviced accordingly: The investor's agent will offer a human interface (e. g. video conferencing, IP-telephone, instant messaging, screen sharing, or even a visit at home or in the office). In addition, the agent might change role from a more neutral gateway to financial services to a long term investment advisor – in the latter case, the services offered may span from pure funds/ETF sales to discretionary management to family office type of full-service.

Another answer might be that due to their high affinity to technology and digital services wealthy, internet savvy investors themselves will move toward the most appropriate solutions for their liquid assets. Those solutions are then (still) sourced from traditional players that have understood the digital needs of the investors and either come up with own digital offerings or invest in/partner with Fintech players. Alternatively, the solutions to manage the huge amount of funds of this attractive customer segment may be provided by new Fintechs that are able to position themselves as 'best-in-class', thus capturing a significant part of the wealth management industry's gross revenues.

---

[18] Independent financial advisors, operating e. g. in Germany under a license according to § 34 GewO/trade law ('Finanzanlagenvermittler').

References

1. M. Dietz, S. Khanna, T. Olanrewaju and K. Rajgopal, "Cutting through the noise around financial technology," [Online]. Available: http://www.mckinsey.com/industries/financial-services/our-insights/cutting-through-the-noise-around-financial-technology. [Accessed 21 6 2016].
2. F. Desai, "Fintech Startups Face Difficult Market Ahead," 2016. [Online]. Available: http://www.forbes.com/sites/falgunidesai/2016/01/04/fintech-startups-face-difficult-market-ahead/#7831fc9a3145. [Accessed 21 6 2016].
3. F. Desai, "The Fintech Boom And Bank Innovation," 2016. [Online]. Available: http://www.forbes.com/sites/falgunidesai/2015/12/14/the-fintech-revolution/#7327008336da. [Accessed 21 6 2016].
4. S. Kirmße, "Die Herausforderungen für die etablierten Finanzintermediäre durch die Digitalisierung," in *Management in Kreditinstituten und Unternehmen – ein Querschnitt aktueller Entwicklungen; Festschrift für Henner Schierenbeck*, M. Lister, B. Rolfes and S. Kirmße, Eds., Frankfurt/Main, 2016, pp. 347–358.
5. KPMG and H2Ventures, "FINTECH 100 – Leading Global FinTech Innovators Report 2015," [Online]. Available: http://www.fintechinnovators.com/. [Accessed 22 6 2016].
6. J. Bruene, "Fintech Unicorn List Q2 2015: An Estimated 46 Have Arrived + 38 On Their Tails," 22 6 2015. [Online]. Available: http://finovate.com/fintech-unicorn-list-q2-2015-46-arrived-37-closing-in/. [Accessed 21 6 2016].
7. Fortune.com, "The Unicorn List 2016," [Online]. Available: http://fortune.com/unicorns/. [Accessed 21 6 2016].
8. CBInsights, "The Unicorn List: Current Private Companies Valued At $1B And Above," [Online]. Available: https://www.cbinsights.com/research-unicorn-companies. [Accessed 21 6 2016].
9. GP_Bullhound, "European Unicorns 2016, suvival of the fittest," [Online]. Available: http://www.gpbullhound.com/wp-content/uploads/2016/06/GP-Bullhound-Research-European-Unicorns-2016-Survival-of-the-fittest.pdf. [Accessed 27 6 2016].
10. E. Glazer, "Wells Fargo & Co. is the Earth's Most Valuable Bank," 22 7 2016. [Online]. Available: http://www.wsj.com/articles/wells-fargo-co-is-the-earths-most-valuable-bank-1437538216. [Accessed 27 6 2016].
11. Banksdaily.com, "The 20 largest banks in Europe by market capitalization (as of March 24, 2015)," [Online]. Available: http://banksdaily.com/topbanks/Europe/market-cap-2015.html. [Accessed 22 6 2016].
12. U. Rohner, "Why partnerships are appealing," *McKinsey Quarterly,* vol. 2, pp. 45–49, 2016.
13. KPMG and CBInsights, "The Pulse of Fintech, Q1 2015," [Online]. Available: https://home.kpmg.com/xx/en/home/insights/2016/03/the-pulse-of-fintech-q1-2016.html. [Accessed 22 6 2016].
14. GoogleTrends, "Search for Keywords," [Online]. Available: https://www.google.com/trends/explore#q=fintech&date=1%2F2009%2084m&cmpt=q&tz=Etc%2FGMT-2. [Accessed 22 6 2016].
15. T. Altenhain, "Der digital-aktive Anlagekunde – Erkenntnisse aus einer empirischen Studie," in *Management in Kreditinstituten und Unternehmen – ein Querschnitt aktueller Entwicklungen; Festschrift für Henner Schierenbeck*, M. Lister, B. Rolfes and S. Kirmße, Eds., Frankfurt/Main, 2016, pp. 215–239.
16. Eurostat, "Frequency of internet use, 2014 (% of individuals aged 16 to 74)," [Online]. Available: http://ec.europa.eu/eurostat/statistics-explained/index.php/File:Frequency_of_internet_use,_2014_(%25_of_individuals_aged_16_to_74)_YB15-de.png. [Accessed 24 6 2016].

17. J. Bughin, E. Hazan, E. Labaye, J. Manyika, P. Dahlström, S. Ramaswamy and C. Cochin de Billy, "Digital Europe: Pushing the Frontier, capturing the Benefits," [Online]. Available: http://www.mckinsey.com/business-functions/digital-mcKinsey/our-insights/digital-europe-realizing-the-continents-potential?cid=other-cml-alt-mip-mgi-oth-1606. [Accessed 1 7 2016].

18. EUROSTAT, "Individuals using the internet for internet banking, % of individuals aged 16 to 74," [Online]. Available: http://ec.europa.eu/eurostat/tgm/table.do;jsessionid=Hv-Cqj47pmm_bCiGiZAajUo1LaJ2dmJNEhxao6G3HYYpz5JlW1sj!-1610507484?tab=table&plugin=1&language=en&pcode=tin00099. [Accessed 24 6 2016].

19. H. Schierenbeck, "Private Banking: die Herausforderung für den Finanzplatz Schweiz," in *Tagungsband zum 5. Basler Bankentag 20. November 1997*, Bern et. al., 1998, pp. 3–51.

20. C. E. Riegler, Kunden- und ertragsorientierte Ansätze der Preisgestalung für Beratungsleistungen im Private Banking, Bamber, 2005.

21. H. Echterbeck and C. v. Villiez, "Vertriebssteuerung," in *Herausforderung Bankmanagement, Entwicklungslinien und Steuerungsansätze, Festschrift zum 60. Geburtstag von Henner Schierenbeck*, Frankfurt/Main, 2006, pp. 325–340.

22. E. Stumpfegger, Social Identity and Financial Investment Decisions, Empirical Insights on German-Turks, Cham, 2015.

23. P. Plickert, "Deutsche kaum reicher als Euro-Durchschnitt," 20 10 2015. [Online]. Available: http://www.faz.net/aktuell/wirtschaft/deutsche-sind-laut-ezb-studie-kaum-reicher-als-der-euro-durchschnitt-13867082.html. [Accessed 24 6 2016].

24. R. Ruttmann and D. Bellas, "Portrait of European Household Wealth," 2014. [Online]. Available: https://www.juliusbaer.com/files/user_upload/your-private-bank/investment-excellence/research/european-wealth-report/documents/Wealth_Report_Europe.pdf. [Accessed 24 6 2016].

25. T. Altenhain, K. Ess and A. Sehgal, "Nur Bares ist Wahres" – Kundenbindung in Zeiten der Digitalisierung des Retail-Bankgeschäfts, C. Linnhoff-Popien et al., Ed., Berlin Heidelberg, 2015, pp. 359–368.

26. J. Verhage, "Robo-Adviser Betterment Sees $700 Million Valuation After New Round of Funding," 29 3 2016. [Online]. Available: http://www.bloomberg.com/news/articles/2016-03-29/robo-adviser-betterment-sees-700-million-valuation-after-new-round-of-funding. [Accessed 2 7 2016].

27. H. Maccracken, "How Charles Schwab Fought Back Against The Robo-Adviser Startup Invasion," 11 5 2016. [Online]. Available: http://www.fastcompany.com/3059565/how-charles-schwab-fought-back-against-the-robo-adviser-startups. [Accessed 3 7 2016].

28. M. Collins, "The Vanguard Cyborg Takeover - The No. 1 mutual fund company wants to own cheap advice," 24 3 2016. [Online]. Available: http://www.bloomberg.com/news/articles/2016-03-24/the-vanguard-cyborg-takeover. [Accessed 3 7 2016].

29. finews.ch, "Das sind die grössten Robo-Advisor," 29 2 2016. [Online]. Available: http://www.finews.ch/news/banken/22148-fintech-robo-advisor-vanguard-ubs-true-wealth. [Accessed 3 7 2016].

30. H. Echterbeck, "Provisionen im Publikumsfondsvertrieb unter MIFID II," in *Management in Kreditinstituten und Unternehmen – ein Querschnitt aktueller Entwicklungen; Festschrift für Henner Schierenbeck*, M. Lister, B. Rolfes and S. Kirmße, Eds., Frankfurt/Main, 2016, pp. 241–253.

31. T. Laukötter, "Hauck & Aufhäuser übernimmt easyfolio," 3 5 2016. [Online]. Available: http://www.wallstreet-online.de/nachricht/8568364-hauck-aufhaeuser-uebernimmt-easyfolio. [Accessed 3 7 2016].

32. Deutsche_Bank, "Deutsche Bank launches maxblue robo-advisor," 7 12 2015. [Online]. Available: https://www.db.com/newsroom_news/2015/medien/deutsche-bank-launches-maxblue-robo-advisor-en-11366.htm. [Accessed 3 7 2016].

The Digital Insurance – Facing Customer Expectation in a Rapidly Changing World

Michael Cebulsky, Jörg Günther, Peter Heidkamp, and Falko Brinkmann

Abstract

Internal and external factors are driving change in the insurance market – at a pace not yet seen before. The focus of the insurance industry has shifted from managing the insurance sector itself to managing an agile cross-linked environment. Insurers are now part of a complex ecosystem consisting of companies from various industries that either are or want to be part of the end-to-end customer journey. Furthermore, customer demands like 'mobility' require a joined customer journey of traditional insurers, Fin-Techs and technology manufacturers. This article provides an in-depth insight into both the customer journey and ecosystem of insurers. It identifies common trends that require a fundamental realignment of the corporate culture and gives various examples of insurance companies that go new ways. By suggesting a 10-point roadmap, it proposes

M. Cebulsky (✉)
KPMG AG
Düsseldorf, Germany
e-mail: MCebulsky@kpmg.com

J. Günther
KPMG AG
Frankfurt, Germany
e-mail: JoergGuenther@kpmg.com

P. Heidkamp
KPMG AG
Cologne, Germany
e-mail: PHeidkamp@kpmg.com

F. Brinkmann
KPMG AG
Hamburg, Germany
e-mail: FBrinkemann@kpmg.com

© Springer-Verlag GmbH Germany 2018
C. Linnhoff-Popien et al. (eds.), *Digital Marketplaces Unleashed*,
https://doi.org/10.1007/978-3-662-49275-8_34

a guideline of how insurance companies can respond to the challenges of digitalization and what actions they should take to do so.

34.1 A Rapidly Changing World

The announcement by two companies that they will in future make common cause provoked a furore in the summer of 2016: Allianz, an insurance group with a history dating back almost 130 years and a stock market value of around 60 billion euros, will in future exchange staff and expertise with Rocket Internet, the start-up studio that is barely ten years old and that is valued on the stock market at around 3 billion euros. How extensive the co-operation will be remains uncertain, but the intention of Allianz's chief executive officer Oliver Bäte is clear: he wants to force the organisation of his company to become more agile so that it can meet the challenges of the future [1].

Quicker workflows, lower costs, more cross-selling, greater proximity to the customer – is there an insurer who is not pursuing these goals? For example, according to the KPMG study 'The Insurance Innovation Imperative', 60 per cent of insurers see process optimisation and the use of technology as offering the greatest potential in the next two years. The journey to that destination traverses an extensive realignment of the business model, the break-up of data silos in the company and the comprehensive digitalisation of processes. Only in this way will it be possible to recognise customer needs swiftly and to develop and market bespoke products for specific target groups.

Anyone facing a decision to make a major purchase or enter into a contract will generally visit company websites to inform themselves of the terms and conditions or browse comparison sites. The importance of these sites is growing enormously. Take Germany as an example: on YouGov's BrandIndex, which checks and monitors the perception and recognition of 60 major online brands, the leading German brand, behind international players such as Google, Facebook and Wikipedia, is Check24. Established in 1999, the portal presents the tariffs and rates of the most varied of companies – from energy suppliers to insurers – and earns money on each contract entered into between the users and the service providers [2].

It is not just consumers who are gaining greater insights into what is on offer. Service providers, too, are acquiring ever more information about customers – current as well as future customers. The traces that consumers leave behind on the Internet allow user profiles to be created, likes and dislikes to be identified, patterns of behaviour to be forecast. Companies such as Google, Amazon and Facebook are pioneers in this field and transform this information into revenues that run into the billions. Their business models have changed fundamentally the way in which products (and advertising) are sold and turned on its head the balance of power in whole industries (retailing, media).

Successful digital business models score points with their transparency, speed and proximity to the customer. This is also true in the financial services sector, which has lagged several years behind, but is now being seized by digitalisation: direct banks are winning market share at the expense of classic financial institutions thanks to their favourable cost structures (and competitive offers). Fintech companies such as Wealthfront, Betterment (both USA) and Nutmeg (Great Britain) have recently introduced automation into the investment business.

So what about the insurance industry? Is the revolution in full swing here, too?

- Price comparison sites such as Check24 in Germany and The Zebra in the US attract customers with comprehensive overviews of rates and prices on their web pages and are in the process of revolutionising the brokerage business.
- Peer-to-peer providers such as Friendsurance (Germany), Guevara (Great Britain) and Lemonade (US), are redefining the collective, as they bring together policyholders in small networks that provide mutual support in the event of a loss – which lowers the premium.
- Health insurers are using technical innovations such as health wristbands to track the behaviour of policyholders and to generate new products and premium models with the help of the findings they provide.

The speed at which new digital products are coming onto the market has accelerated enormously. Processes and structures that have taken years to build are increasingly giving way to agile models where the time from conception to market launch sometimes takes just a few weeks.

For insurance companies, this development offers a massive opportunity. It is not only that costs can be significantly reduced through automation. Beyond that, the wealth of information in their won systems offers the possibility of recognising the needs, likes and life choices of their target groups – and quickly proposing to customers' attractive personalised offers. With the help of needs-based processes and structures, these treasure troves of data can be tapped and sustainable business models can be established.

34.2   Re-Invention of the Insurance Business

Disruptive innovations are shattering business models and even entire markets: Amazon has reinvented the retail trade, even though the company does not operate any brick and mortar stores. AirBnB has risen to become the most important service provider in the hotel industry, even though the company does not own a single hotel room. And Uber ranks among the largest taxi companies in the world, even though it only brokers journeys. The lesson: it is no longer about selling one's own goods and services, but about negotiating between the producer and the consumer.

This is also the starting point for important aggressors in the insurance business. Comparison sites do not offer any policies of their own. They earn money exclusively by connecting customers with insurance companies. Peer-to-peer service providers do not (at the moment) take on the risks in their own books, but see themselves as agents for the insurance policies registered with the customer. The direct link to the customer is at risk of being lost – with unforeseeable consequences for the business model. It is important here to take resolute countermeasures and to strengthen the customer's loyalty.

Even well into the 1980s, the 'customer journey' in the insurance industry was simple and unassailable: the customer needed a policy, the local agent made an offer, the customer signed the policy. If an adjustment was required, the agent put forward a new proposal. In the event of a loss, the agent took care of the processing. Home visits, telephone calls, letters – no other communication channels were envisaged (see Fig. 34.1).

Today, it is essential for companies to use social networks and blogs in order to filter customer habits and propose suitable individualized offers. It has long been possible, using the location of a customer, to send a suitable product proposal to their smartphone, which they can immediately accept by pressing a button. Detailed questions about the policy can be clarified by video chat. Telematic applications continually deliver data from the customer to the insurer, which is then evaluated and incorporated in the calculation of the premium. The insurer has to move to where the customer is: in a digital world. This is how the insurer manages to become a constant companion.

These external factors increase the necessity to act. Those who want to survive on the market will have to organise their processes more efficiently and more cost-effectively. The resources that are freed up should be used to accelerate the conversion to a business model that accommodates the increased demands of customers. Customers who expect fairness and appreciation, high service quality and appropriate value for money. They want personalised, tailored offers. They expect short response times to communications, regardless of time, place, sales channel or device.

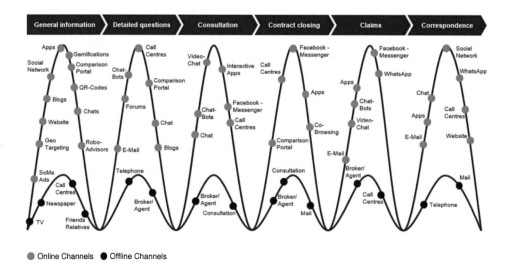

Fig. 34.1 The customer journey – online versus offline touchpoints

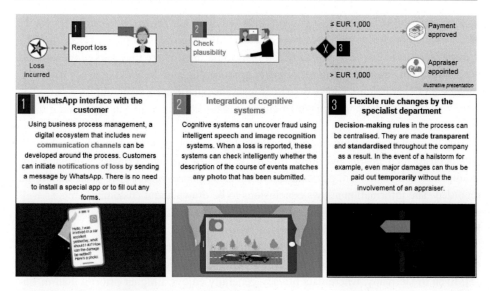

Fig. 34.2 Claims processing using cognitive systems

Digitalisation also brings perceptible customer benefits in the settlement of claims. It will be possible in future to initiate a notification of claim for example by sending a message through WhatsApp. There will be no need to fill in a form any more. Intelligent speech and image recognition will for example enable the plausibility of a rear-end collision to be checked using the description of the course of events and photos of the damaged car (see Fig. 34.2). In particular, minor damages could be settled with more automation in more individual cases than is the case today.

Successful innovations always follow the same motto: keep it simple! The customer is more likely to decide to take out a policy the easier it is made for them. Anyone who does not have to fill out pages and pages of forms, but simply press a 'buy' button in their app will be more prepared to take out travel health insurance or an accident policy. The opening of communication channels such as Facebook Messenger, which is offered by Axa for its Switch insurance offer in France for example [3], makes it easier to contact younger target groups.

A lot of customers want less 'full service' from their insurer and instead more 'bite-sized' offers that are tailored to their individual needs. For example, the service provider Trov has recently started selling on-demand policies for individual items such as laptops, snowboards and headphones in Australia. Using a virtual slider bar on their smartphone, the customer can decide for themselves how much the deductible – and thus the premium – will be [4].

When a customer buys a product online, the German start-up Simplesurance, which Allianz recently got on board with, immediately offers an insurance policy to match [5].

Metromile in the US offers a pay-per-mile policy to car drivers who only very rarely take their cars out for a spin. The driver can take advantage of additional services through a smartphone app. For example, they can mark on a map where they parked the car and get a warning if street cleaning services are approaching and the parking space has to be vacated. In Great Britain, Cuvva offers car insurance that can be taken out for a period of just a few hours or days. The customer enters into the contract using an app – and it takes just ten minutes [6].

Health insurers grant privileges if policyholders adopt patterns of behaviour that are beneficial to their health and allow this to be tracked through a fitness wristband, for example, which enables all physical activities, sleep phases and resting pulse data to be recorded. The information allows conclusions to be drawn about customer habits as well as a personalised training programme to be developed for the insured. The progress made by the customer can be rewarded through a bonus system.

The US insurer Oscar furnishes its customers with free wristbands and additionally even offers an app that enables policyholders to talk with a doctor or to get prescriptions [7]. Even in Germany, where data privacy generally enjoys a higher priority than in English-speaking countries, the Allgemeine Ortskrankenkasse (AOK), the statutory health insurer, and the Deutsche Angestellten Krankenkasse (DAK), the private health insurer, now subsidise the purchase of these devices [8].

The examples of the telematics tariffs and health wristbands show that customers are definitely ready to divulge data about themselves if the insurer can credibly prove that it will handle the data with care and they can derive a direct benefit. A positive selection is supported, as long as it is associated with lower rates or other benefits.

Nevertheless, the insurance companies are going to have to prepare for a discussion about the continued existence of the principle of collectivity. For example, consumer protection groups in Germany have for some time now criticised the fact that the increasing segmentation for example in occupational disability insurance is actually excluding many craftspeople from this type of insurance because of the prohibitively high premiums [9]. Something similar is happening in the area of professional liability, where midwives, for example, are finding it almost impossible to continue financing the premiums [10]. Not everything that is possible by imputation with the help of digitalisation will be feasible on the market.

The penetration of new products on the insurance market will not be without consequences for their sale. The classic sale of policies through insurance agents will be increasingly squeezed out by transactions conducted via digital channels. Direct insurers have already dispensed with a cost-intensive network of brokers and agents today. The market shares of the direct insurers are growing especially in the area of standard policies, such as third-party liability, motor and home insurance, which require little consultancy [11]. At the same time, classic brokers are coming under increasing pressure from price comparison website and peer-to-peer service providers, which connect customer directly to the insurance companies in return for commission.

The faster digitalisation progresses, the more intensively people, machines and other objects will be able to communicate with each other. The transmission of information and data in real time opens up the possibility for totally new products – also in the insurance industry. For example, Beam Technologies, a US start-up, offers dental insurance together with a toothbrush that records data about the brushing behaviour of the owner by Bluetooth and sends it via their smartphone to the company. Someone who regularly and thoroughly looks after their tooth runs less risk of developing caries and therefore pays lower premiums [12].

The example above illustrates the fact that classic insurers on their own have little chance of exploiting the possibilities of digitalisation to the full. This will depend more than ever on teaming up with other companies – from the insurance sector or from other industries – and developing new ecosystems that enable additional points of contract with (potential) customers. 54 per cent of insurers say that their motivation for collaboration and alliances is to promote ideas and talent, while 24 per cent say it is to promote a literal speed to market.

This crossing of borders has already been taking place in similar areas for several years: numerous car manufacturers offer their models in combination with motor insurance. A car insurer – Huk Coburg, Germany's industry leader – has recently started selling cars as well. The company had already entered into co-operation projects with partner garages, where Huk customers can enjoy benefits related to inspections, tyre services and general and exhaust emissions testing, and customer retention is now to be expanded to used car buyers [13]. It will be important to develop this way of thinking, which goes beyond traditional industry borders, and to transfer it into the digital sphere.

34.3   Fitting into the New Ecosystem

The new insurance world breaks with customs that have been handed down. Protectionist individualism, where information is partitioned to one's own advantage, will be replaced by an ecosystem in which the partners work together for their mutual benefit. Companies that want to survive will have no other choice but to engage in co-operative projects of this kind. The speed with which new technologies are coming onto the market and consumers are changing their preferences continues to increase. Companies will have to equally quick in adjusting to change. Sealed off from developments in other companies and industries, this will be almost impossible.

The change sounds more revolutionary than it is. Trying new things does not mean burning all your bridges behind you. Nor does it mean focusing exclusively on digital channels. 'Old' channels will remain important and will have to be maintained both for internal workflows and in the relationship with the customer. The customer may like to take out an insurance policy at the click of a mouse. Later, however, they may want advice and an agent to call on them at home. An app may be suitable as a sales channel for car insurance, but a complex occupational disability policy will always require more consulting time and effort. The key to success lies in correctly interpreting consumer behaviour and finding the right balance between analogue and digital possibilities for exchanging information.

Particular care is demanded in the handling of customer data here. Business models in which losses are supposed to be prevented by the 'positive' behaviour of the insured assign a new role to the customer – as a partner who is prepared to divulge extensive information about themselves. Unlawful use of personal data, for example the misuse of data to select risks, may bring with it not only fines for the insurer, but also significant reputational damage.

Customers have to be sure that the data that they provide is used in their best interests and not in order to discriminate against them or to force them from the market. The discussion on the employment of new technologies thus has an important ethical component. An important instrument in active data protection is clear communication between the company and the customer. What data is collected? What is it used for? Only someone who acts openly will encourage the acceptance of digital innovations and increase customer satisfaction – and will be able to take advantage of a positive image to implement better prices. Yet how can all these changes be put into practice in the day-to-day business operations? And in such a way that changes in the market can be reacted to quickly, without putting functioning work processes at risk?

Existing IT systems are not suitable for many of the requirements of the digital world. They allow customers to be addressed in equal measure across all relevant channels (omnichannel capability) and digital ecosystems to be developed only to an unsatisfactory extent. On the other hand, new systems are expensive and launching them is time-consuming and risky. The establishment of two-speed IT allows existing systems to be continued and new, agile processes to be saddled up. Digital technologies can be quickly adapted, the stability of conventional processes is retained (see Fig. 34.3).

Old and new systems are uncoupled in this process: the digital IT as the 'agility layer' lies on top of the mature IT as the 'stability layer'. Various user interfaces can be integrated through the agility layer. Existing specialist functions and the primary data storage remain in the old systems.

The newly designed processes will be integrated through an integration layer, in which process and control logics are separated. This structure allows adjustments to be made quickly and cost-effectively without any need to interfere with the old systems. Workflows can thus be swiftly developed and put into executable practice. This integration layer also offers the possibility of incorporating external service providers quickly and flexibly within a digital ecosystem.

The majority of management boards of insurance companies have understood the need to act. For example, Dr Thomas Blunk of Munich Re for example says: "We cannot wait for the structural changes to occur before we start moving; we need to address these changes now if we hope to offer the business new growth opportunities over the next 5 years."[14] Measures such as formal channels for generating new ideas or the co-operation with external stakeholders are regarded by the vast majority of executives as important or very important for the successful implementation of innovations. According to KPMG's

CEO Outlook, disruptive technologies are already employed in more than half of the companies surveyed, primarily in the interaction with customers [14].

34.4   Manoeuvring Change

The business model of insurance companies is undergoing a radical change:

- The customer is better informed and more demanding than ever. They expect transparent information at all times wherever they are and demand customised products that meet their individual needs. Depending on the requirement, they select digital or analogue channels to get in contact with the insurer.
- New technology-driven companies increase the pressure to act on both the product and the sales side. Newcomers are especially agile, because they come to the market without the baggage of mature data and IT systems.
- It is clear to see that old borders between industries are fading away. Companies must be prepared (and able) to co-operate across industries in order jointly to develop new and attractive products.

These trends require a fundamental realignment of the corporate culture: traditionally more risk-averse insurance companies will have to learn to embrace experimentation – without escalating the financial risks. KPMG's global study 'The insurance innovation

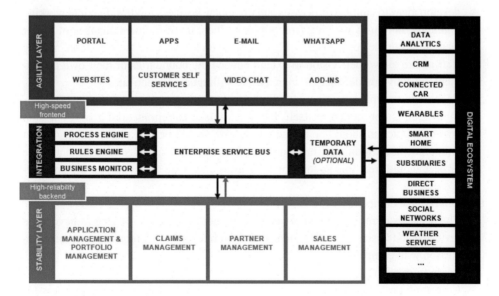

Fig. 34.3 Two-speed IT

imperative' describes a ten-point roadmap that insurance companies can use as a guide before and during this realignment:

1. Drive change
   The change that insurers are facing is massive. The size of the task and pride in one's own traditions frequently lead to a failure to take the necessary steps. A fatal error. Companies should analyse in detail how technological advances influence their own organisation – and draft a dedicated action plan in which digitalisation and innovation are given a prominent role.

2. Apply agile and dedicated leadership
   New mindsets can take root in a company only when the top management lead by example. Innovation is a leadership issue. The appointment of a chief digital officer who initiates processes and provides the resources required for the implementation is an important step here. The company should additionally train its staff and provide incentives to develop new ideas and put them into practice in the organisation. This includes questioning approaches that have been practised for decades.

3. Adapt structures
   For many insurers, the introduction of innovation management means a break with their culture. Organisational structures must be made more transparent, slimmed down and co-ordinated more closely with each other in order to pave the way for new products and business models that serve the customer's interests.

4. Develop talent
   Innovation takes place in the staff's heads. It is important to identify talent that can develop ideas to simplify processes and drive new business models. Flexible working hours, the option of working from a home office, more frequent changes of job or team are examples of measures that can be taken to anchor a 'new mindset' among staff and to allow their vision to extend beyond the boundaries of their own department. Inventive models help to increase the willingness to innovate.

5. Encourage entrepreneurship
   Innovation is not an end in itself, but must pursue entrepreneurial goals. The success of any action should be measured, the risk should be spread over time. A strict entrepreneurial attitude is important: anyone who wins a budget for an innovative project should treat this as their own business and share financially in the any successes.

6. Observe the competition
   The decision to restructure an organisation is not a single act. Strategies have to be reviewed and business models adapted at fixed intervals. This requires constant comparison with competitors.

7. Learn from others
   Co-operation – also with companies outside the industry – is the key to success for insurers in a digital world. This is a new experience especially for large organisations.

But it is unavoidable if new products with major customer benefits that will play a part in deepening value added are to be given a swift kick-start.

8. Leverage new technologies into the current business

Flexible IT systems make it easier to introduce new technologies and to link up with external partners. The streamlining of routine processes such as administrative tasks or claims processing frees up resources for developing new business models and adapting additional user interfaces. Information for staff and customers can be made available on demand using cloud computing, something that facilitates the scalability of processes and reduces fixed costs. Insurers are accorded a special role in publicly advocating for this technology to be meaningfully employed.

9. Create transparency

The increasing analysis and processing of customer data that accompany digitalisation requires a high degree of openness when communicating with the insured. Companies must make clear to customers what the benefits of evaluating personal information are – very much in the sense of customer centricity. The insurance industry is called on to conduct this discussion in public in order to be perceived as a credible partner. The goal must be to create maximum transparency without losing the benefits of asymmetrical information.

10. Question business models

Size alone does not help a company survive on the market. The players who will benefit most from the change in the insurance industry will be those who are able early on to combine developments, identify trends and throw out old business models. Developing and maintaining this innovative capability will in future make up the true strength of a company.

References

1. FAZ, [Online]. Available: http://www.faz.net/aktuell/wirtschaft/interview-mit-oliver-baete-und-oliver-samwer-14364672.html. [Accessed 06 08 2016].
2. WIWO, [Online]. Available: http://www.wiwo.de/unternehmen/dienstleister/brandindex-check24-verivox-und-co-die-vergleichsportale-im-vergleich/13915928.html. [Accessed 06 08 2016].
3. AXA, [Online]. Available: https://www.axa.com/en/newsroom/news/axa-adopts-facebook-messenger. [Accessed 06 08 2016].
4. news.com, [Online]. Available: http://www.news.com.au/finance/business/technology/trov-launches-tinderstyle-ondemand-insurance-for-individual-items/news-story/cba3d140809d5d850c8cecd5f5bb90d2. [Accessed 06 08 2016].
5. Heise, [Online]. Available: http://www.heise.de/newsticker/meldung/Allianz-steigt-bei-Startup-Simplesurance-ein-3241426.html. [Accessed 06 08 2016].
6. microinsurancenetwork.org, [Online]. Available: http://www.microinsurancenetwork.org/community/blog/insights-and-perspectives/microinsurance-insurtech-and-there-more-come. [Accessed 06 08 2016].

7. microinsurancenetwork.org, 06 08 2016. [Online]. Available: http://www.
    microinsurancenetwork.org/community/blog/insights-and-perspectives/microinsurance-
    insurtech-and-there-more-come.
8. P. Heidkamp und D. J. Günther, Digitale Interaktionsmethoden eröffnen Versicherern neue
    Geschäftspotenziale im Health Business, Versicherungswirtschaft, 2015, pp. 14–16.
9. versicherungsbote.de, [Online]. Available: http://www.versicherungsbote.de/id/4843014/
    Berufsunfaehigkeit-Schutz-fuer-jedermann-BdV-Verbraucherzentrale/. [Accessed 06 08 2016].
10. Stern, [Online]. Available: http://www.stern.de/gesundheit/hebamme-berufshaftpflicht-kosten-
    geburt-6926310.html. [Accessed 06 08 2016].
11. statista.com, [Online]. Available: http://de.statista.com/statistik/daten/studie/287180/umfrage/
    abschluss-von-versicherungen-ueber-das-internet/. [Accessed 06 08 2016].
12. fortune.com, [Online]. Available: http://fortune.com/2015/06/26/connected-toothbrush-
    insurance/. [Accessed 06 08 2016].
13. suttgarter-nachrichten.de, [Online]. Available: http://www.stuttgarter-nachrichten.de/inhalt.
    gebrauchtwagen-huk-steigt-in-den-markt-fuer-gebrauchte-ein.c664b8f9-b713-4f84-a1e7-
    a8637df85af8.html. [Accessed 06 08 2016].
14. KPMG, [Online]. Available: https://home.kpmg.com/content/dam/kpmg/pdf/2016/06/2016-
    global-ceo-outlook.pdf. [Accessed 06 08 2016].

FinTech and Blockchain – Keep Bubbling? Or Better Get Real?

35

Nils Winkler and Björn Matthies

Abstract

"If I had asked people what they wanted, they would have said faster horses", is a well-known quote of Henry Ford, the inventor of automobile mass production. And, it is a commonly used opening phrase for tech start-up investor presentations. Being "disruptive" and "innovative" are key ingredients for such pitch decks and are inflationary buzzwords in today's venture scene. What's often left out is being visionary and having the goal to create something substantial, something that generates a positive cash flow, building a lasting and leading business. Buzz has replaced reason in so many cases and cause has been replaced with reach, which is the usually the aim of businesses, rather than creating value.

When we take a look under the hood of FinTech, we can try to see whether it is actually something – or perhaps just a way of categorizing start-ups of a specific industry. And, as FinTech is very often associated with the omnipresent discussion about crypto currencies and blockchain, we'll take a look at that too. In discussions and in keynotes the word blockchain is also used as a buzzword. Everyone else seems to hop on the same train, leaving it pretty unclear what it actually means or does – what blockchain is. Hype bears the risk of blindness for the risks and limitations there might be. It appears as if everything in IT could be replaced by blockchain these days, yet it is reasonable to believe that might not be the case at all.

To start off, we will take a look at how trends have developed in digital business in recent times.

N. Winkler (✉) · B. Matthies
CoCoNo GmbH
Hamburg, Germany
e-mail: nils@winkler-online.org

B. Matthies
e-mail: bjoern@matthies-online.org

© Springer-Verlag GmbH Germany 2018
C. Linnhoff-Popien et al. (eds.), *Digital Marketplaces Unleashed*,
https://doi.org/10.1007/978-3-662-49275-8_35

35.1 FinTech – the Emperor's New Clothes?

FinTech stands for Financial Technology. It is an economic industry composed of companies that use technology to make financial services more efficient. Financial technology companies are generally startups trying to disrupt incumbent financial systems and challenge traditional corporations that are less reliant on software [1]. The segment is significantly clustered and a lot of buzz-words float in the discussion. Helpful to grasp the magnitude is a mind-map created by fintech.info. See Fig. 35.1.

FinTech is a trend – no one will deny that. But how is it different from other trends in the "startup business"? We have seen waves of excitement and euphoria over things that passed or became "normal" – unreasonable bubbles, which have propelled industries or industry sectors to become a new hype.

Who does not remember the times of AOL buying Time Warner and everyone believing that the "new economy" would take over the world? At least this is a concrete example of an unheard-of business transformation of a traditional, dinosaur publishing company and a traditional, dinosaur Internet access company – both being threatened by the Internet itself. But does MySpace ring a bell? Or Biotech? Or Marketplaces? Or Messengers? Or Photo sharing platforms? Or social platforms? Any and all of these trends have in common that there has been one player standing out, coming up with a new idea in a space that was overlooked by the venture investors. Money needs a place to go and it tends to flow toward the direction of a success. Or at least it tries to. So, when venture capital investors see that something works and that they have not seen it yet (where there is little or no competition), they will pump it up with cash. Old measures like a quick return on investment are no

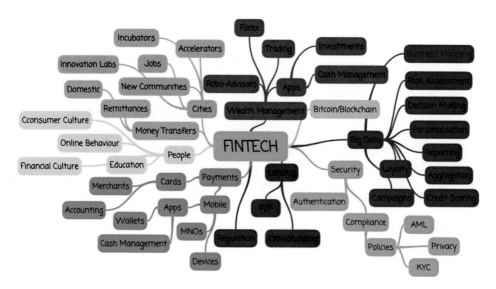

Fig. 35.1 Mind-Map showing the complexity of todays FinTech eco-system. (Source: www. FinTech.info)

longer relevant. Size matters. Ease matters. Scaling the business and taking as much space as possible. Because, what happens next is that other investors will see that they missed something and push a "me-too-product" – a copycat. And there you go – you have your hype. I admit this is a simplified view but nevertheless a view that can be validated by a simple Google search.

One major trend is that big corporations add "disruptive elements" to their portfolio by purchasing start-ups that have proven a point in something. Pharmaceutical companies buy biotech start-ups with promising new drugs in their portfolio (saving their own R&D cost by spending money on something they can already validate). Forbes asked in February 2015: "Are M&A replacing R&D in Pharma" [2]? – an interesting aspect stated is this: "The spike in mergers and acquisitions in Pharma is beginning to make the industry look more like a pyramid where more companies develop drug molecules at the bottom than they commercialize drug products at the top. This shift has many in the space wondering what exactly is happening and how it will affect health care in the short and long term."

Google, Facebook and the others do it the same way. While some exciting huge and visionary projects are kept in-house, like for instance the idea of bringing Internet to remote areas on the planet with balloons in the stratosphere in the case of Google – they are surrounded by a large number of start-ups that build product enhancements. For instance, things that work with Google or Apps for Facebook –work only in those environments. Or Apps that enhance mobile operating systems, like navigation apps did before navigation became an integral part of the maps solutions of the mobile operating systems. The benefit of the big internet players is that they can see whether something is successful and works for large audiences without spending a single cent, and then incorporate it in their environment when they see the value. Google is "building a start-up ecosystem" around itself, as the CEO and Founder of TraitPerception, Juan Cartagena, puts it [3]. This tendency sometimes, as we all know, is not even driven by an immediate urge to build revenue – but by the urge to make their footprint bigger and get access to additional audiences or data. Take the acquisition of the extremely popular WhatsApp by Facebook, followed by Facebook making it free of charge for everyone.

The same applies for Trends in FinTech, which is not so much "tech" after all when you look at it. In so many cases it is really just the Emperors new clothes. Most of the things FinTech startups do were possible before, but even more in this (partly) regulated environment than in overall "tech startups," it is evident that the old way of interacting between a solution provider (which might be a bank) and its customer has been somewhat clumsy (even though we were happy campers and used to it), and can be made so much more convenient. In an industry in which trust, history and reliability are strong values for consumers, convenience may not be the number one factor though. In Germany, a study by VuMA [4] shows that over 66% of the consumers in the country prefer to have their personal bank accounts with savings banks or cooperative (mutual) banks, which have a big network of outlets and interactions with real human beings.

If we take a look at the top topics in the FinTech area over the past years we can see that the focus has shifted from B2C to B2B and also that to a large part nothing revolutionary has happened at all – but the attempt was to make existing processes cheaper or more convenient. An indicator for that is the list of topics for the past years Finnovate Conferences, in which FinTech startups pitched their ideas to interested audiences. While in 2011 and 2012 the hot topics were ranging between Social Media integration, robo advice (for consumer investment products) and personal wealth management, this shifted to gamification (did not fly for banking, needless to say) and mobile solutions in 2013 and 2014, followed by more substantial topics like Bitcoin/crypto currencies, digital banking solutions and data mining in 2015 – and biometrics in 2016 [5]. Looking closer this shows that product enhancements in the digital field – solutions tailored to improve business processes that are sold to businesses rather than consumers – are leading the field now. B2C is much less attractive for FinTech these days, it seems, with many ePayment- and wallet-companies such as Powa in the UK disappearing or even CurrentC or respectively MCX, the "Merchant Consumer Exchange" with which Wal-Mart and many other merchants in the US meant to compete with PayPal. They de-activated all consumer accounts in early 2016 and announced, according to the website "Consumerist.com": "(We) will concentrate more heavily in the immediate term on other aspects of the business including working with financial institutions, like Chase, to enable and scale mobile payment solutions" [6]. This quite simply means: The merchants lost. The banks won. The same applies for Germany, where we as the authors of this chapter had some own experiences with the alternative payment scheme Yapital, which was driven as a merchant based solution – and now no longer exists. The German banks are trying to compete with PayPal with their co-operation "PayDirekt". This initiative again does not seem to be a very promising undertaking. PayDirekt, in its second year after launch, does not share any statistics about adoption or usage. They probably know why. There are many ways FinTech companies interact or interfere with traditional banks – which are nicely illustrated by José Antonio Gallego Vázquez: see Fig. 35.2.

To find out why this shift occurs and why this perhaps was bound to happen, it's worth a summary of the Finch market form it's beginning. Basically, it started when incumbents shifted some costly and labor-intensive processes (mainly in terms of time savings and the savings in personnel costs) to their existing contractors (both retail and business customers). Offering new applications and the partial opening of their APIs did this. Long before the invention of the term FinTech, but using new technology. An example of this is the introduction of self-service terminals and online banking to initiate transfer orders, retrieving account and deposit information, or to print and save account statements. This goes without saying for today's banking customers but around the turn of the millennium, however, this was a revolution. In the field of business partners (for example with car dealers) banks shifted in the lending business the input of all data necessary for a credit contract to the merchants. The so-called credit factories were born. The same was done in the area of securities trading. The banks not favored business with retail investors was left to the investment and contract intermediaries. However, only the time and cost intensive advisory business was shifted and in return they paid a little more commission. The deposits of course remained, partly because of regulatory requirements, in the hands of the banks.

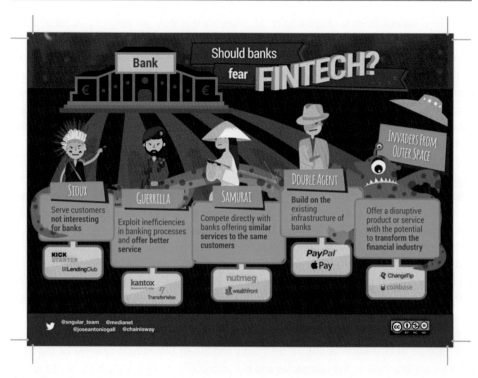

Fig. 35.2 A visualization impact of FinTech on traditional banks. (Source: José Antonio Gallego Vázquez)

Let's check out the "real" Finch topics of recent years in more details in this context. Have the developing approaches been truly revolutionary? Can this really be the downfall of the banks? Has the gatekeeper issue been solved? What about the technical possibilities, the regulatory requirements and for sure the revenue side?

Robo advice (a class of financial adviser that provides financial advice or *portfolio management online* with minimal human intervention [7].) and personal wealth management seems to be revolutionary, but is it really? To understand the backbone of this kind of applications we need to take a look under the hood of the used models and theories. An example is the use of Harry Markowitz model (developed in 1952) [8], which concept of efficiency was undoubtedly one of the essentials to the development of the capital asset pricing models. It's still used in many robo advisory tools to mitigate the risk of unwanted correlations and allocating given assets towards a portfolio that will give the highest expected return for its given level of risk. The fundamental problems of all different portfolio models and theories are not solved by robo advisory. The technical solutions can only process the amount of data provided. Everything is based on historical values (even when talking about swarm intelligence). They do not consider the transaction costs and do not consider sufficiently the automatic allocation shift by price changes in the market. The solutions offered suggest to retail investors that they are now in control of their investments themselves, but in the end all securities transactions are still carried out only through banks and stock exchanges. By the way, an old fashion stop-loss order is still faster to perform as a push notification from an app that only informs you that a threshold has been reached. Robo advisory therefore is not really revolutionary but it offers specialized investment advisors the opportunity to remodel the portfolios of their clients, based on the data provided to the system, to maximize their inventory and transaction commission, all with the painting of modern technologies and scientific evidence.

Is there anything revolutionary in the payment area? Technically, none of a single Fin-Tech Company has managed to disengage from the payment systems of the banks or the other current players (credit card schemes, payment service providers, network operators or terminal operators). The margin of a single payment transaction in this area are very low, because the competition between the existing players is very high and in some cases (e. g. Europe's regulation on interchange fees) are additionally fueled by the local legislation. Add to that the necessity to cooperate with the existing gatekeepers to use their existing infrastructure and carrier technology for the processing of transactions. It logically runs down to that it is only worth to be active in the payment area, when you can scale very quickly. Claiming that the required mass in transactions as well as the access to end customers may success without the goodwill of the banks is illusory. The disposable income of customers is still in the banks and not in blockchain systems or the like. Salaries are still paid in fiat currencies and not in crypto currencies like bitcoin. As stated by Jean-Pierre Buntinx on his article "Lack of innovation could turn FinTech into another buzzword": Not even popular solutions such as Apple Pay are innovative or revolutionary, but simply the old hiding under the cloak of the new, as it is essentially only the same credit card payment people have been making for years. The only difference is a fancy user interface accessible from a mobile device [9]. Who will pay the additional costs of the transactions, if it is not to make the customer? The merchants? Probably not, because they are experienced n negotiating their transaction costs with new vendors or with their existing payment service providers. In the final result, FinTech investors need to bear the cost of such experiments and therefore change the business model to B2B to get paid by the existing players for new fancy interfaces rather than taking up the fight with Goliath for B2C.

The only successful example, using the open interfaces and support technology of banks without paying the banks for it, is Klarna with its direct payment solution via online banking (part of Klarna's portfolio by acquiring Sofort AG). But this is more a European phenomenon rather than replicable to other markets such as North America or Asia. Real development potential therefore only is in under banked areas and countries where there is no such sophisticated regulation, as in Europe or North America.

The area of data mining and biometrics should also be evaluated in particular from a cost perspective. For sure banks have been forced and will be forced in the future to open up their interfaces for third party but that this is sufficient enough that new FinTech companies can offer their services to end customers cost-covering is more than a daring theory. Free service does not exist. Only the equivalent does not always exist in real money. Nowadays, the user pays rather with his transaction data for a fancy interface and slightly more convenience. Therefore, in the future the question will arise as to how much data security and sovereignty a consumer is willing to give up to obtain a few improved interfaces without real value. Is that something revolutionary? Of course not. Not even the area of social media and advertising needs to be used for this evidence. All established market players, such as MasterCard, Visa and Amex practice data mining and evaluation of transaction data or several decades continuously and highly professional. The results of their studies they then sell to their principal members, partners and whoever is willing to pay the asked price. Big data or data mining on the basis of transactions is therefore also no innovation but only somewhat pimped with some other data sources. Needless to say, using a B2B rather than a B2C business model in this area is more appropriate.

The winners in FinTech seem to be the traditional players – which is probably because of their customer reach and financial power, but also because they offer more than a product enhancement or an easier way to close a loan with a mobile app. They offer stability, reliability, and scale. They are partners which consumers may not like so much – but they trust them. They do it like the Pharmaceutical companies and wait for the start-ups to fail or succeed; picking the cherries that fit their overall strategy instead of taking the risk to develop solutions in-house. That in itself is a chance for the FinTech start-ups, but it also means that the hype we see is more a bubble than substance.

Yes, the industry needs more simplicity, especially for how consumers interact with their banks or lenders or other financial vendors. But it is still a numbers game and cost cannot and should not be ignored, nor can the cost of business easily be earned back with low user adoption instead of having one of their own.

Let's assume banks and traditional players in the financial sector are not the natural innovators and will probably never be – the most interesting aspect of starting up a business in this industry therefore seems to be one that fills a gap and provides additional value for the relationship between the traditional players and their end customers.

This assumption would also speak against the theory that FinTech means the death of personal service provided to consumers. In fact, it could mean that after a long time of suffering service could again become more personalized and individual, based on smart tools allowing exactly that. Markus Hill, an independent financial services consultant, writes about FinTech in funds-investment that "FinTech work with passive, low budget funds solutions. The standard topic active versus passive gets a constructive boost" because traditional players "need to find better arguments and explain better what the benefits of active funds management are" [10]. So in essence: competition helps the business – and the consumers.

In essence we can state that the trends in FinTech are not much different than the trends in general for the start-up industry. FinTech to a large degree provide solutions to fill gaps in the offering of traditional players – which could mean gaps in the sense of actual products or gaps in service and convenience. But, as Jens Munch of Hottopics.ht is writing, "FinTech has only just got started. The rise of FinTech has opened up a world of possibilities. Businesses can offer more services than ever and for a fraction of the price of what it would have cost before" [11]. While one might weigh in the necessity to consolidate to get to a relevant scale (in case there are too many FinTech companies doing the same thing there might be too little business for each) and question the cost, based on what scaling IT costs in a regulated environment, the direction is clear.

Of course, and for the sake of completeness, there are ground-breaking new things which are clearly FinTech and make such a difference – and at the forefront of that I would like to mention crowd funding, with vendors such as Kickstarter or Indiegogo enabling founders to attract money from a large number of individual contributors, who pretty much buy pre-production products and "back" the start-ups they support – so it's not a loan and it's not an investment but it helps to speed up innovation by reducing the burden for start-ups to get through the seed phase of their business. The phase that often takes a massive personal toll from the founders and is at the same time the phase in which they ideally focus on their products and inventions the most (and rather not spend time for investor road shows and venture capital pitches). So this is truly brilliant.

And then there is another big thing, crypto currencies like Bitcoin and the underlying new technology of a blockchain. Again: is this hype, a bubble or is there something to it? Being aware that there are more than 700 virtual currencies, divided into mineable and not mineable, closed and open systems. The ten most capital-based currencies stand for a turnover of about $92 million per day ... [12]

35.2   Blockchain, What Art Thou?

What is missing at times in the current discussion is a definition what we are actually talking about. It seems like blockchain technology is the perfect recipe for about everything and anything in IT and while "legacy technology" is outdated and cannot compete, blockchain is shining. I believe that a proper discussion, and more importantly business decisions should be based on a good understanding and reason. That is why the hype around blockchain raises concern for me, as reason and understanding do not seem to be a major ingredient to it.

So what is blockchain, the technology behind Bitcoins. Investopedia has a brief but abstract definition [13]. "A blockchain is a public ledger of all Bitcoin transactions that have ever been executed. It is constantly growing as 'completed' blocks are added to it with a new set of recordings. The blocks are added to the blockchain in a linear, chronological order. Each node (computer connected to the Bitcoin network using a client that performs the task of validating and relaying transactions) gets a copy of the blockchain, which gets downloaded automatically upon joining the Bitcoin network. The blockchain has complete information about the addresses and their balances right from the genesis block to the most recently completed block."

So in essence, the blockchain is getting bigger (or rather longer) with each transaction. While in the traditional way, the structure is to have an account structure for an account holder in which then the transactions and the balance of each account holder are stored, in a crypto currency using blockchain technology snippets of this information are distributed across many computers as some sort of swarm intelligence and added to one big ledger instead of many. And the value of a block is attached to an address, so it is possible to identify who owns (or owned) what and when.

That means a blockchain is getting bigger with every transaction. Bitcoin has far fewer transactions as the traditional transaction banking back-ends though. Currently it is only processing some 200K transactions a day according to blockchain. see Fig. 35.3.

Even though the transaction volume is low, the time to process has increased with time and volume and led to transaction delays, which fueled a new discussion about blockchain in early 2016. David Gilbert of Ibtimes.com writes: "Bitcoin is facing a major problem as the time it takes transactions to be processed has increased dramatically leading businesses to stop accepting the crypto currency and others to issue warnings that the problems might be terminal" [14]. He continues that the issue is not something that came out of the blue, but that researchers had pointed "to this looming issue for some time": "The problem relates to how transactions are processed in a blockchain, the decentralized, distributed ledger technology that underpins Bitcoin".

Too bad, because there is a lot appealing with blockchain technology, mainly that it is very democratic. In a blockchain, no institution or individual controls it, instead whoever participates controls a part of it. The theory is that also it becomes more resistant to all kind of attacks with the growing number of participants, making it harder to get the full picture and an entry point for malicious activities. There has not been a democracy invented which not someone tried to undermine and so it is with blockchain too. That happens when people pool their computing power in the blockchain – giving control of their power to a central wallet.

So, wait a moment – a de-centralized system that lives from no central control is being centralized somehow? Yes. And if the pools control more than 50% of the blockchain they control it completely. There is even a name for it, the "Greater than 50% attack". According to Bitcoin.info, in May 2016 there were four major pools controlling 58% of all Bitcoin transactions [15]. If these individuals would work together, they could essentially take over and re-write the whole blockchain.

According to Mike Hearn, an industry expert, it is even worse with two pools controlling over 50% of Bitcoin – and both coming from Mainland China [16]. His article "The resolution of the Bitcoin experiment" is eye opening and scary.

Nowadays, blockchain technology is much more powerful than in its beginning, when it was designed to only perform a small set of simple transactions like currency-like tokens. Today's blockchains are ready to perform more complex operations. Moreover, while not solving the essential problems of the first blockchain designs but starting licensing of bitcoin exchanges by applying existing regulatory and legislative frameworks, the next buzzword within the blockchain context already got off the starting blocks to take this bubble to the next level; smart contracts – with all its foreseeable legal uncertainty as well as growing detachment from existing legal structures and jurisdiction.

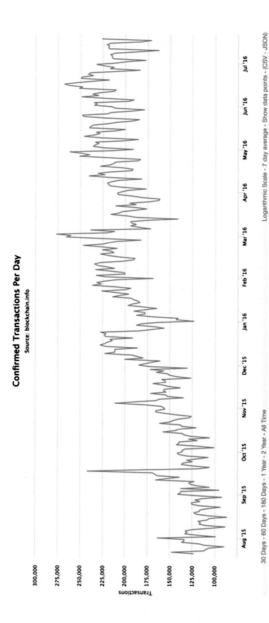

Fig. 35.3 The number of transactions executed in the BitCoin network is too low to be really relevant. (Source: www.blockchain.info)

We will not bother you with a description or contest between competing terminology of smart contracts as "autonomous machines", "contracts between parties tired on a blockchain" or "any computation that takes place on a blockchain" but refer to the pragmatic and straight forward classification as used by Josh Stark in his article "Making sense of blockchain smart contracts" [17]. For a specific technology – code that is stored, verified and executed on a blockchain we will use the definition "smart contract code". A specific application of that technology: as a complement, or substitute, for legal contracts we will use the definition "smart legal contracts". Now we will have a look at the different layers included and focus on the overall question, whether blockchain technology is ready for big business in the financial industry.

So things are not quite as they appear – neither is a blockchain necessarily superior in performance in scalability nor is it as democratic and secure as one might think. Which is probably what makes the leaders of big US banks less optimistic about blockchain, as heard at the Davos World Economic Forum 2016. Citi's chief economist Willem Buiter referred to "the number one law in programming software: that anything that can be programmed can be hacked". "It's not going to change everyone's life tomorrow", said the Chairman and CEO of Morgan Stanley, James Gorman. Garry Lyons, MasterCard's Chief Information Officer summarized: "It's not just the industry that's excited about blockchain, it's the world, everyone. Even at Davos, every single tech panel I have gone to mentions blockchain. But while we think it's very interesting, we don't want to, and no one wants to, be blindsided by rushing into it" [18].

The decentralization of the system is blessing and a curse. Especially in the financial industry trust and reliability are fundamental pillars. To use a new system like blockchain it is essential to be able to trust the program code and to ensure that necessary, practical extensions cannot be blocked; this for the protection and benefit of all participants. It therefore requires a certain institutionalization of the system, which is not given yet. In addition, as in any normal processing of transactions, sometimes there is a need for adjustment or even roll back. Current blockchain technology used for virtual currencies and smart contracts don't provide this function but are unidirectional updates that cannot be reversed. One of the recent examples from the current times, why can cause real big problems, is the hack at the DAO, the Distributed Autonomous Organization that lives on the Ethereum blockchain and that was supposed to take money from investors and invest it in projects voted on by the investors and administered through smart contracts. It is also a perfect example to have closer look on the different layers of this technology and the challenges to line up intention, implementation and results. First there is the intention of a contract and its expected results (set by the smart legal contract), followed by the smart contract code, stored, verified and executed on a blockchain, and at its end the real results which may differ from the initial expectations. In case of DAO the intention was to take money from investors and put it in projects voted on by the investors, administered through smart contracts. After coding the intentions and definitions didn't matter any longer but the code did and ended up in the loss of $60 million for the investors. Some may say that this has been a hack others may say it wasn't. The difference between the hack of Mt.Gox (valued \$500 million) or Bitfinex (valued \$70 million) where bitcoins were stolen from a system by unauthorized access is that at DAO the code of the smart contract was used to transfer the money. As a result, DAO was not hacked but the attacker executed the recursive splitting function, which was implemented, in the smart contract, just not for this kind of transaction and intention. In the regulated environment of banks and financial institutions customers would be safeguarded by regulatory frameworks against losing all their money and would have the possibility to sue the hacked company. Within the blockchain sector this is not the case.

This directly leads to a conclusion that blockchain, as a decentralized and open source technology is not ready for big business yet. Blockchain sector is not imbedded into the existing regulatory frameworks and legislature. As the intense legal risk attached to this kind of technology is just the expression of not existing trust and reliability there will be much more development necessary before the buzzwords will turn into real solutions and business cases. Maybe this is one of the reasons why Bitcoin and Blockchain as attempt to break through and skip the existing, traditional intermediary role of banks is not expected until 2027 by the Global Agenda Council of the Future of Software & Society's Technological Tipping Points and Social Impact survey 2015 [19].

35.3   So Where Does All this Lead Us to?

Let's go back and see what happened with the Pharmaceutical industry after it has been shaken up – and I refrain from using the word "disrupted" – by the biotech hype. Tremendous money was attracted by more or less obscure start-ups claiming nothing less than a cure for cancer and the likes. But there were also solid, legitimate companies in the field doing serious work with a professional approach. The hype is long gone and the industry adjusted to a new model, in which a lot of the R&D is done by startups attracting venture capital for meaningful research. And when the case is proven, the big corporations acquire the products or the companies and apply their power and financial means to bring it to market. Similar things happen in the Internet industry around the big Internet players in the US. Ecosystems for innovation are created and the industry changes its approach to innovation. The financial sector, being especially careful and conservative, has taken a little longer and became a target for hungry, well-funded start-ups. My prediction would be, and many examples can be seen already [20], that the traditional players embrace the FinTech sector and nurture the developments and innovation, then incorporating it when the case is proven. This will be a benefit for everyone – including the consumer.

References

1. [Online]. Available: https://en.wikipedia.org/wiki/Financial_technology. [Accessed 20 07 2016].

2. [Online]. Available: http://www.forbes.com/sites/nicolefisher/2015/04/22/are-ma-replacing-rd-in-pharma/#35e69441cb57. [Accessed 22 04 2015].
3. [Online]. Available: http://seedcamp.com/creating-a-startup-ecosystem/b. [Accessed 20 07 2016].
4. [Online]. Available: http://de.statista.com/statistik/daten/studie/171479/umfrage/geldinstitute-bei-denen-gehalts--bzw-girokonto-gefuehrt-wird/. [Accessed 20 07 2016].
5. [Online]. Available: http://finovate.com/.
6. [Online]. Available: https://consumerist.com/2016/06/07/currentc-ends-beta-tests-will-deactivate-accounts-later-this-month/. [Accessed 07 06 2016].
7. [Online]. Available: https://en.wikipedia.org/wiki/Robo-advisor. [Accessed 19 09 2016].
8. [Online]. Available: https://en.wikipedia.org/wiki/Harry_Markowitz. [Accessed 12 10 2016].
9. [Online]. Available: http://FinTechist.com/lack-of-innovation-could-turn-FinTech-into-another-buzzword/. [Accessed 03 10 2016].
10. [Online]. Available: http://de.e-fundresearch.com/markets/artikel/28271-FinTech-hype-versus-tod-der-persoenlichen-beratung-. [Accessed 19 07 2016].
11. [Online]. Available: https://www.hottopics.ht/stories/finance/what-is-FinTech-and-why-it-matters/. [Accessed 19 07 2016].
12. [Online]. Available: www.coinmarketcap.com. [Accessed 13 08 2016].
13. [Online]. Available: http://www.investopedia.com/terms/b/blockchain.asp. [Accessed 19 07 2016].
14. [Online]. Available: http://www.ibtimes.com/bitcoins-big-problem-transaction-delays-renew-blockchain-debate-2330143. [Accessed 04 03 2016].
15. [Online]. Available: https://blockchain.info/pools. [Accessed constantly updated].
16. [Online]. Available: https://medium.com/@octskyward/the-resolution-of-the-bitcoin-experiment-dabb30201f7#.73c2ty6p9. [Accessed 14 01 2016].
17. [Online]. Available: http://www.coindesk.com/making-sense-smart-contracts/. [Accessed 17 10 2016].
18. [Online]. Available: https://www.cryptocoinsnews.com/davos-elites-talk-bitcoin/. [Accessed 22 01 2016].
19. [Online]. Available: http://www3.weforum.org/docs/WEF_GAC15_Technological_Tipping_Points_report_2015.pdf#page=24. [Accessed 13 08 2016].
20. [Online]. Available: http://www.cnbc.com/2016/04/11/big-banks-shift-a-strategy.html. [Accessed 11 04 2016].

On the Quest to the Ultimate Digital Money

Helmut Scherzer

Abstract

Digital money in contrast to payment schemes has not received much attention through the last years. Although BitCoin (a digital currency) is unacceptable as digital money, its appearance pointed out the versatility of the digital money idea. The business models for digital money are not as apparent as compared to payment schemes. However, the most critical path for digital money is the technical implementation that has long-term security, e. g. the value of digital money shall not be breakable even after 40 years of evolutionary security analysis.

In our research, we wanted to know, which features a user would expect from an 'ultimate digital money' solution. We created a set of 'ultimate claims' of which we were prepared to be so hard, that no existing system would pass the entire set. As an example ... one claim demands that the ultimate digital money should allow the owner to create as many copies/backups as s(he) desires. Our plan was that by reducing our ultimate filter by some selected claims, we could expect to find the next best candidates to be as close to 'ultimate' as possible. After we created the 'impossible to pass' set of ultimate claims, to our surprise we found one system, that did pass all our claims without having to downsize our filter. The present article describes our 'ultimate filter' and presents the digital money system which we found to satisfy all our conditions.

H. Scherzer (✉)
Giesecke & Devrient
Munich, Germany
e-mail: helmut@hscherzer.de

© Springer-Verlag GmbH Germany 2018
C. Linnhoff-Popien et al. (eds.), *Digital Marketplaces Unleashed*,
https://doi.org/10.1007/978-3-662-49275-8_36

36.1 The Definition of Digital Money

Money from the first day it was invented around 2500 years ago – had always been a 'touchable thing' which represented a value. From the early trade of goods exchange (e. g. a chicken for a cluster of wood) humanity discovered the brilliance of a 'represented value' through shells, gem stones, pearls, silver, gold and whatever could represent a value.

Creating a gold coin is difficult since gold is a rare resource. It requires a large effort to find gold to finally create a gold coin – more effort than growing a cow. It is that major effort which generates the intrinsic value of the gold coin and that 'proof of work' it is the reason that farmers would rather grow cattle than trying to find gold.

Today the concept of a "Proof-of-Work" has come to the attention of civilization through the upcome of the BitCoin currency. Banknotes do no more keep their intrinsic value from its material (like gold). The "Proof-Of-Work" here comes from the extreme difficulty to create a valid banknote.

Information Technology – for the first time in history – allows an immaterial representation of money which breaks with the classical forms of money representation. Information can be copied, which is absolutely forbidden for a material representation. So how can we define "digital money" in contrast to "materialized money".

Money is the acknowledged representation of a recognizable value through a transferable carrier.

Digital money is the acknowledged and transferable off-line representation of a recognizable value through information.

Bank accounts do not qualify as "digital money" according to the above definition. Electronic payment does not actually transfer money but it commands a bank to send money from the sender's account to the receiver's account. Electronic payment transfers the right to claim money – it does not transfer money. Electronic payment with "Digital Money" implies sending data from the receiver to the sender which actually represents a value. The receiver can trade this data anonymously to any bank in exchange for bills, coins or other money representations – of course s(he) can also credit the data(!) to his/her bank account.

Like coins and bills, "Digital Money" changes between persons without the requirement of any bank account. This idea makes digital money highly attractive, but it also implies a high technical challenge to realize.

36.2 The Criteria to Ultimate Digital Money

On our quest for high end solutions we scrutinized the question of the "ultimate digital money" and our results will not answer this question forever, neither do we claim its universal acceptance. Yet the results have been found very helpful to distinguish between the existing solutions.

- Anonymous
- No Account
- Stability
- Currency bound
- Central bank option
- Free off-line Peer-2-Peer transfer
- Infinite hops
- Off-line-Exchange
- Online and off-line operations possible
- No forgery possible
- No double spending possible
- No risk to the issuer bank
- Not using cryptography
- Additional services
- Backing up money
- Instant invalidation
- Limited bad press

36.2.1   Anonymous

Quality No 1 of (digital) money is still the fact that the user can spend/earn it anonymously. People do not like to be tracked by their business operations – while this is an aspect that associates to criminal activities it is actually the very normal user who doesn't want to be read by any institution or individual. Business behavior is considered as a rather intimate property regardless from the content of the transaction.

36.2.2   No Account Required

The ultimate digital money shall not be account based. While the association of an account is already contradicting our definition of digital money, this does not require further consideration. It shall, however, be understood that any system providing account based transactions will not qualify as 'digital money' at all. This does not criticize account based systems which are very practical for other purposes than digital money and they are suitable for uni-directional payments (e. g. customer to merchant).

36.2.3 Currency Bound

The great inflation (Germany 1923) exchanged about 4.2×109 (4.2 Bio.) "Reichsmark" for one dollar. People did no more use any money since its value could change by a factor of 2 to 10 within a few days.

For digital money this has a consequence:

Digital money shall represent an existing currency
No matter what the currency is, the stability of digital money will consequently follow the stability of a currency that is managed by banks and finally the world bank.

Trust in digital money will only establish if it is backed by an official currency. Trying to invent a new currency (e. g. BitCoin) triggers consequences of changing value (BitCoin: from 20–200\$ within several months) that will hardly be honestly taken by any business except for those who are speculating on the stock exchange anyway. Hence digital money should represent an existing currency (\$, Yen, Euro, ...) and at best, it has the feature of a 'face value' i. e. the user can recognize the value of a digital bill by its intrinsic parameters.

36.2.4 Central Bank Option

A central bank, reserve bank, or monetary authority is an institution that manages a state's currency, money supply, and interest rates [1]. Part of this mission is to control the traded money flow. If digital money is simply bought as another representation of an actual currency (see above) then the central bank does not need to be worried about the actual money volume in a country. Nevertheless digital money should have the option to be controlled by the central bank. As with bank notes, this option does not mandate to trade in the quality of anonymity.

36.2.5 Free Off-line Peer-2-Peer Transfer

Off-line peer-2-peer transfer shall easily be possible between holders of digital money. As with bank notes, users want to be able to exchange money without having to consult an account, a network or any third party.

This quality also is an important aspect to prove anonymous transactions. Of course users do not want to pay for such transfer – like with bank notes. As a consequence such off-line-transfer shall be free of cost. And in addition, if the same amount was exchanged between two parties, the actual representation of money shall not change i. e. no traces of the exchange are attached to the money.

36.2.6   Infinite Hops

The basic definition of the ultimate digital money shall allow an infinite (practically a large) number of hops between peers. The size of the ultimate digital money token shall not change, neither shall it add signatures or traceable information when changing its holder. This does not exclude the option of a controllable number of hops. The popularity of block-cipher based approaches cannot stand this criteria because it is the nature of a block-cipher to accumulate signatures on every hop.

36.2.7   Off-line "Change"

A major quality of the ultimate digital money would be its ability to be off-line-splittable. This is a difficult claim that most available solutions do not satisfy. Off-line split associates the idea that a digital coin/bill can be split into the "exact change" and the remainder. The "exact change" can be spent whereas the remainder will stay with the payee. The typical problem on most digital money implementations is, that the split amounts need to be re-signed whereas the signing key is of course not allowed to stay on the user's side.

The ultimate digital money shall allow unrestricted off-line splits up to the granularity of the smallest represented value (for the $ or Euro this would be 1 cent).

36.2.8   Online and Off-line Operations Possible

Despite the fact that the ultimate digital money shall be off-line capable, it shall also be online-compatible. Money draft through a Smart Phone shall be possible and also any other banking operations (money transfer). In particular the ultimate digital money shall allow the exchange of digital money with paper based money (ATM draft) and vice versa.

36.2.9   No Forgery Possible

The ultimate digital money shall not be forgeable. This is a basic claim yet it is important to be named since the ultimate digital money shall also be allowed to be copied!

36.2.10   No Double Spending Possible

A copy, however, shall not be able to be used to pay twice with the same bill – this would turn a copy into forgery. The ultimate digital money shall solve this paradox.

36.2.11   No Risk to the Issuer Bank

The ultimate digital money will be risk-free for the issuing bank. This idea comprises that any duplication, forgery or theft will not lead to any financial damage of the issuer of the digital money. Although this claim may appear to be irritating, this is already partly fulfilled by the present paper based money (= bank notes/coins). Of course managing fake bank notes will not be entirely cost-free for the central bank, however, faking a banknote does not paralyze or kill an entire currency. In particular a fake bank note does not harm the issuing (central) bank nor any private or bank association.

The ultimate digital money would even improve the situation such that any duplication or (attempt of) generation will intrinsically give neither trouble nor cost to the issuing bank or instance and also cannot harm the digital money system itself.

36.2.12   Shall Not Use Cryptography

One of the hardest claims to the ultimate digital money is, that its representation is not depending on cryptology. While cryptology will be vital to many aspects of handling digital money (storage, transfer, exchange, online etc.). the actual representation of a digital money value shall be free from cryptography and hence not being attackable by cryptology.

The background of this claim is the idea that even if galactical numbers of security are used (e. g. 78,400 bit RSA) it will be hard to convince an issuing instance or central bank that there is no risk to the bank. This is given through the long-term existence of money (can be traded after 30 years) and the unpredictability of possible attacks through unforeseeable technology (e. g. Quantum Cryptography).

A central bank will still have a hard time to issue 100 Bio. units of digital money if they risk a security breach which today is still out of imagination. As the possible catastrophe is too large, even the security level of nuclear plants will not be convincing to central banks. So the ultimate solution to the ultimate digital money is not to use cryptography at all for the representation of digital money.

As secure cryptography is … there will be enough press out that puts it in question nevertheless. For instance a recent revelation regarding the NSA claims that the old work horses, AES, RSA, etc. have been compromised [2]. Such article does not prove the claim of broken cryptography, however, it can be sufficiently scaring to a decision maker with a potential victim as heavy as a digital money.

36.2.13   Additional Services

If money gets digital, the ultimate digital money shall allow to attach information to allow additional services. This can be qualities for privileges, spending limits, closed group application or purpose of spending – the range shall not be restricted, yet the representation of the ultimate digital money shall allow to attach attributes and these attributes shall be as secure as the digital money itself.

36.2.14 Backing Up Money

One of the qualities of digital money shall be that it can be copied by its legitimate owner, in particular for the purpose of backup. It shall even be possible that the legitimate owner of digital amount shall keep the same "bill" in different devices (backup or duplication) and s(he) would still be able to spent even parts of the "bill", from any device without having to communicate from one to the other.

The backup idea will be attractive to many users because for the first time in the history of money you would be able to backup money and if the "purse" (= Smart Phone /PC) gets broken, then the money does still exist and can be spent without any administrative interventions.

Account based systems provide this idea of course, but the challenge to the ultimate digital money is to solve this problem without any association to an account.

36.2.15 Instant Invalidation

Directly associated to the backup idea is the instant invalidation. A user would want to invalidate money that s(he) has stored on a device that gets stolen. By returning the backup copy of the stolen money to a financial institution, the user would expect to receive the same amount of fresh money whereas the money in the stolen device is invalidated without having access to the device.

At best, this shall be possible even without having to call an emergency number or the intervention of authorities.

36.2.16 Limited Bad Press

A killer of a digital money system can be a bad reputation which comes from bad press which comes from flaws in the system. The ultimate digital money shall survive successful attacks without raising attraction to bad press. This can be achieved by limiting the maximum possible damage. If for instance a person is robbed today and his/her purse is stolen, there will not be bad press about the systems of bank notes because such a thing cannot be avoided and is not something expected to be solved by the money system. The same shall be possible if the ultimate digital money as being attacked by hacking or typical system attacks. Bad press will not develop if the damage compares to the rather small damage of a stolen purse. Finally the "loss of confidence" will not occur if the attack cannot lead to disastrous results.

36.3   The Evolution of Digital Money

A view on the history of digital money is necessary to understand the basic principles of today's money systems. Digital money became public around 1990 and about 23 years later it has seen a high public attention through the availability of systems that could be implemented on the growing number of Smart Phones.

36.3.1   DigiCash

One cannot think of the history of digital money without mentioning DigiCash in the first row. DigiCash Inc. was an electronic money corporation founded by David Chaum in 1990. DigiCash transactions were unique in that they were anonymous due to a number of cryptographic protocols developed by its founder. The company failed, but not because of technical reasons.

Digicash is a payment scheme relying entirely on software, i. e. no hardware token is necessary. In addition, one of its most important goals is anonymity.

The so-called "blind-signature" scheme guarantees the anonymity. The bank signs coins without knowing their serial number and assigns them to an owner.

A payment between a spender and a receiver involves the bank as a third party: The coins the spender is willing to pay are transferred to the bank. The bank maintains a database of already spent coins. In this way, double-spending is prevented: The bank will refuse the payment if it realizes that any of the coins in the current transaction is already stored in the database. In spite of that, anonymity is granted, because the bank does not know to whom the coin has been issued at the beginning. In fact, the anonymity is complete, which also means that a thief can steal a coin and spend it without problems.

This implies that each coin can be spent only once. The receiver cannot use it anymore; it must be reimbursed to him by the bank (usually, in the form of conventional money).

This shows the characteristics of the payment scheme: It is anonymous, only software is needed – no secure token, but it involves the bank as a third party for each transaction (which has to maintain a database for digital coins).

Therefore the absence of an online connection cannot be fulfilled: Either the receiver of the payment must have the payment verified immediately (which definitely requires an online connection to the bank), or he must do it off-line after the transaction, in which case he would possibly realize a fraud too late. Thus, "peer-to-peer" payments are not possible or insecure.

36.3.2   Mondex

Mondex was founded in 1990 as an electronic purse with money directly stored in a smart card (and not a background system), with the possibility of a direct transfer of money between purses [3].

The security model for the MONDEX system was confidential. MONDEX didn't succeed in the long run because of concerns of the banks against purse-to-purse transactions. In particular MONDEX required a SmartCard and a small secure device, the "MONDEX wallet" to execute peer-2-peer payments between two persons.

The attraction of MONDEX was made by its ability of off-line transactions, its major acceptance flaw in the user acceptance came from the fact that people did not want to carry separate electronic devices. Today the Smart Phone is such a device, but its versatility is way beyond that of the MONDEX wallet.

Hence the transport in electronic devices is back and now possible, however, the security level of MONDEX cannot be expected a priori from today's Smart Phones. The current technology discussed the Trusted Execution Environment which is a step further into the direction of secure Smart Phones.

36.3.3   FairCASH

FairCash is a payment scheme based on digital coins and hardware-based electronic wallets (so-called "CASTORs", Cask for Storage and Transport of access restricted secrets). By using "P2P-Teleportation", electronic value is transferred from the spender to the receiver (i. e. the spender's wallet to the receiver's wallet).

FairCASH fulfills the principles of anonymity, peer-to-peer and transferability, but it has principally the same drawback as "Token money": It relies on the security of the "CASTOR", a secure element where the coins are stored. If an attacker manages to create copies of the coins inside his wallet, there is no way to stop or detect him.

The design presented in [4] is sophisticated, but it doesn't estimate the consequences on the payment scheme as a whole if an attack would nevertheless succeed. If these consequences are unknown, it is also impossible to estimate the ratio of benefit to effort for breaking the system, which is the crucial factor for determining the risk of a successful attack.

36.3.4   Google Wallet and Others

Although no digital cash in the strict sense of the definition, payment schemes offered by strong market players like Google, PayPal and others deserve some attention. Google Wallet [5] is a means for contactless payment, which is currently tied to certain technologies (NFC-capable mobile phones and Google's operating system Android). In addition, the user needs a Master card issued by the Citibank or a prepaid card from Google. Therefore, the focus of the concept is rather on the convenient contactless payment procedure than on the advantages of digital cash. Besides, privacy concerns arise because Google could (and will) relatively easily collect data about the consumer's behavior. Data about the purchased goods are not readily available, but the person and the place and date of payment are.

Facebook Credits [6] (deprecated in 2012) are a similar example for a scheme which does not put privacy at the top of the priority list. It can be expected that other big players will enter the market soon, however the concepts they offer despite a huge advertisement power and the availability of a lot of potential customers cannot compensate the fact that the offered systems are way apart from the idea of ultimate digital money.

The characteristics of "pure" digital cash, for example the possibility to pass cash from one end user to another one, are not in the focus of these schemes.

36.3.5 BitCoin

Satoshi Nakamoto proposed a payment scheme called Bitcoin [7] which is "peer-to-peer", thus fulfilling the requirement of "transferability". BitCoin is completely independent of an issuing authority like a bank, which makes it attractive to numerous users, but also raises legal and even political issues. In this sense, it is also a reaction to recent financial crashes, inflations and other considerations how to be independent from official banking and state economy. The basis for the Bitcoin concept is the so-called "b-money". A digital coin is designed as a chain of digital signatures. The owner of a coin can be recognized by the owner's public key contained in the coin. The transfer of a coin from A to B is achieved by adding B's public key to the coin and signing it with A's private key. Double-spending is prevented by storing all previous transactions in the network of peers. Before each transaction get closed the coin's validity will be checked. The potential trust in the validity of a received BitCoin depends on the number of confirmations collected in a 10-minute (or longer = better) confirmation cycle minutes which makes BitCoin unusable for the purpose of a typical purchase scenario by digital money (seconds).

Some disadvantages of this payment scheme are documented in [8] and [9]. The major drawback, however, for the serious user who is not considering money as an object of speculation is the idea that Bitcoin does not represent a currency but pretends to be a currency on its own.

Fig. 36.1 shows the Bitcoin exchange rate from January 2013 (Black graph). → http://www.coindesk.com/. Although the value was growing from below $20 to a peak of $220 in April, only users who like to gamble on the stock anyway would be enthusiastic about such a rapid change. But what about those who bought in April 2013? They already lost $60 on average until today which is more than 30% of the selling price. And in November the peak raised to 1300 USD falling by 600 USD within about 4 weeks.

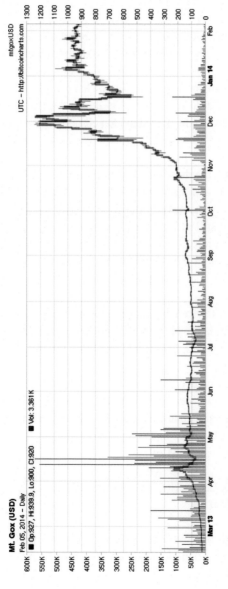

Fig. 36.1 Bitcoin Exchange rate 2013–2014

Some people pray Bitcoin for being revolutionary, however, they could pray for any other object of speculation except for the fact that Bitcoins are much easier to transfer than papers from the stock exchange.

As common digital money, Bitcoin has never had a chance to exist – it does not get even any close to the idea of ultimate digital money yet it might still have a standing as an electronic token that can be used for speculative actions.

36.4   Finding the Ultimate Digital Money

During our research we scanned many digital money schemes, first we dropped all the account based systems since by definition they would not qualify for a versatile global use.

In Africa it is known that many people do not have bank accounts (a native friend of mine confirmed this and told me that this is due to lack of trust to banks while in households there are the most sophisticated hidden corners where (older) people hide their valuables).

The next powerful filter was the off-line-option claim. Many suggested schemes did not pass and when we added the third and very hard claim of off-line-exchange capability we had already reduced the candidates down to less than five.

It was quite easy to apply the next hurdle which was the demand for a copyable implementation which should still prevent double-spending. As we had already planned to weaken our claims for the ultimate digital money we were prepared that final stroke of demanding the representation of the ultimate digital money without cryptography filtered out everything.

Everything ... but one.

As a matter of fact the last system was not created in a small Gallic village in the North West of France but a candidate who started to become more and more fascinating and finally showed up as the only idea that actually qualified for any of our claims on the way to the ultimate digital money.

It did even have features which exceeded our claims and at the same time it was so simple that at a first glance we were even a bit disappointed that a.) it had not been our idea and b.) that our hard claims could be answered with a system that was simpler that we could have imagined. But maybe that is the idea of geniality.

The name of the system was **BitMint.**

36.5   How BitMint Works

BitMint was invented by Professor Gideon Samid, PhD (mailto:Gideon@BitMint.com) leading academic research on digital currency in the department of Electrical Engineering and Computer Science at Case Western Reserve University. Prof. Samid also advises graduate students performing research on the topic of digital money – currently acquiring PhD candidates (gideon.samid@Case.edu).

The BitMint novelty is based on the idea that any bit string that represents contents is a bit string that reflects a pattern of some sort. That pattern may be deeply hidden (well encrypted), and may be masked with random bits, but it cannot be eliminated. If the pattern represents value (e. g. "I am 1000 USD") then it will be target of attack (e. g. changing it to "am 5000 USD").

That is where BitMint is different: the Bitmint-Bill bill is totally pattern-less, purely randomized. Since it carries no pattern, there is no pattern to discover, no credible way to fake or steal the money. A pattern-less string of data, however, cannot store information a-priori so how does the BitMint string convey information and remain pattern-less? In general the BitMint money string conveys its monetary value through a selected function of its cardinal number, or, say its size.

Indeed, the only attributes of a string that are not expressed by the identity of its bits are functions of the string size. It is this very principle that allows the BitMint money string to be immunized against future mathematical insight, or future technology.

Unlike any other of our scrutinized digital money systems BitMint withstands the coming onslaught of quantum computing. And that principle underlies the claim that the issuing bank of the BitMint currency does not take cryptographic risks, and is not subjecting its users to the horrific catastrophe of a total financial meltdown.

We will see later that cryptography is not shunned, but heavily used, albeit by traders and users who wish to store and move the money securely. Much as cash can be lost or stolen without undermining the mint, so it is with digital currency, it can withstand cryptographic risk to safeguard against retail fraud, while avoiding any cryptographic risk for the issuing bank, the mint, the total wealth, digitally expressed.

If you buy a Bitmint-Bill of value 100 $, than you buy a freshly generated random number which from the moment of your purchase is created in the BitMint factory. The random number does not have any cryptological signature nor encryption, it exists in plain text and (!) it is registered in the BitMint factory, as depicted in Fig. 36.2.

The perfect randomization of the Bitmint-Bill, undermines the efficacy of brute force crypto analysis, that requires a deterministic target. Of course the idea of a random number is well known as a one-time password. For the transmission, of course, cryptology is in place, yet it is not part of the representation of the currency but only required for its secure transport.

The random number may be digitally used to pay and purchase trade until finally the digital coin it is returned to the BitMint factory. On return the BitMint factory will pay the cash back – with the exact face value as returned by a Bitmint-Bill. As the idea is to keep the face value with no deductions (transaction fee) the question of the associated business model rises.

After pay-out of the cash the BitMint factory will delete the coin (or relevant parts of it) from its server. Hence any other return will not be successful. At this point the BitMint factory does not care whether the first return was coming from a fraudulent source

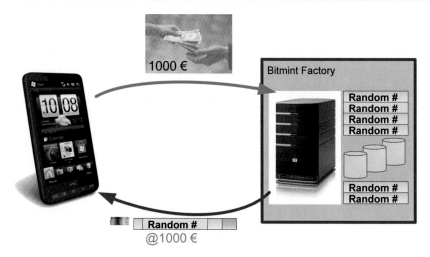

Fig. 36.2 BitMint trade cycle

or a legitimate one. The risk is not on the bank's side but on the user. This is a major advantage over any other digital cash system and very relevant for the acceptance of banks. It also solves the claim of "Limited bad press" as the maximum fraud (except for hacking the BitMint factory) hits one purse which compares to all the unlucky events happening in the criminal scene every day.

The BitMint factory keeps exactly the amount of cash that a client has bought. If a client buys $100, then the BitMint factory saves his $100. Since the client can only reclaim these $100, the BitMint factory is not exposed to any market risk. If the value of the $ falls drastically, the BitMint factory is untouched since they keep exactly those $100 of the customer. No risk, no speculation.

36.5.1 Online Verification

As the risk is on the user's side, the user might want to have a method to minimize this risk. So any user receiving a BitMint payment may online-verify the received Bitmint-Bill by a simple verification exchange with the BitMint server. The server will not credit cash, but it will return a new, fresh Bitmint-Bill random number in exchange. The returned Bitmint-Bill will be deleted and made unusable for any other imposter. If the random number is not found valid, the verifying user will be informed and can object the trade s(he) is planning to do. If the exchange was successful, the receiver may be 100% sure that s(he) has a fresh valid Bitmint-Bill that is free from any risk of fraud. This will promise a high confidence to the user.

36.5.2   BitMint Online World

The refresh example only works in the BitMint online world, i. e. an online connection shall be available on demand. There is also a BitMint off-line world which will be discussed later.

In the BitMint online world (Fig. 36.3) a transaction requires an Online verification if the receiver of a payment does not trust the payee. The advantage of online based transactions is, that they do not need any secure element or other security on the side of the user. Of course a user will be able to make clones of Bitmint-Bills. But since we are in online-world, he can spent such a Bitmint-Bill only once. The receiver of a clone will always verify the Bitmint-Bill and deny the trade, if the Bitmint-Bill did not qualify.

Clones become unusable with online verification. Online-Bitmint-Bills can be carried in unsecured devices, e. g. in mobile devices/phones that do not provide a secure element for the off-line variant.

Reasons to use the BitMint off-line world are the limited availability of networks or the associated roaming cost which can exceed the actual amount to pay.

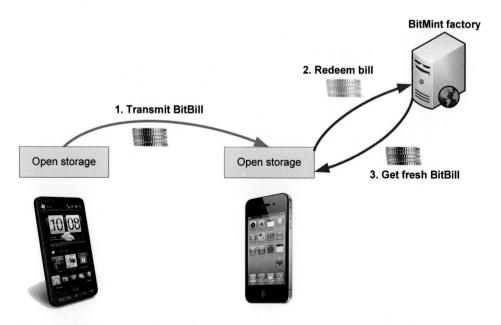

Fig. 36.3 BitMint Online Payment

36.5.3   BitMint Off-line World

Using Bitmint-Bills off-line makes BitMint more flexible. Off-line use, however shall avoid cloning of Bitmint-Bills although there is no risk to the bank, user's would not want to be rejected after they received a cloned Bitmint-Bill. As a consequence the Bitmint-Bills need to be kept in secure hardware and its security depends on the security level of this hardware. Again there is no risk to the bank who does not care about online or off-line world.

For the discussion of the off-line world we need to make an assumption that the secure hardware can be considered secure. In this case a Bitmint-Bill will be securely deleted in the sender's secure element after it was confirmed to be received by the receiver.

The attractive multi-device storage and backup facility of digital money is not solvable as easy as in the BitMint online world, however, as the online flavor can always be converted to an off-line money the user may determine a certain amount only that s(he) requires for the particular case of off-line payments ® 36.5.4 "Moving from world to another".

Bitmint-Bill will only go from one secure element to another secure element (Fig. 36.4). Since both secure elements will provide a mutual secure session, today's cryptology may well generate the associated security.

The advantage of the BitMint off-line world is the independence from networks. Online connection may also imply charges that exceed the actual amount of the transaction.

The disadvantage of the off-line world is the mandatory use of secure hardware. That, however, is only a relative disadvantage, any other digital money system mandates this claim nevertheless. BitMint still makes a difference because on breaking the security of secure hardware, the bank does not have any risk as argued above. The device containing the secure hardware shall be kept like a classical purse, once being stolen there is an exposure to the amount of off-line-stored Bitmint-Bills.

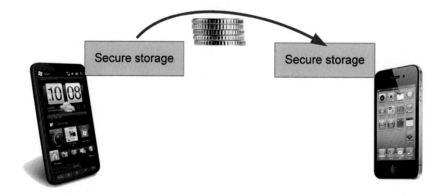

Fig. 36.4 BitMint Off-line payment

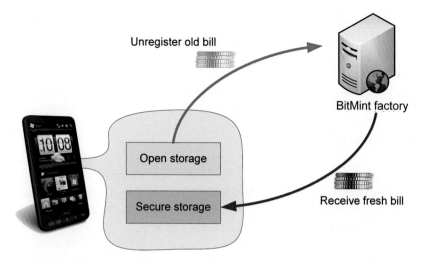

Fig. 36.5 BitMint Online Payment

36.5.4   Moving Between On-/Off-line World

A Bitmint-Bill may be imported and exported to/from the secure element that represents the off-line world. Export is uncritical – the secure element shall simply tag the Bitmint-Bill "unpayable" or even delete it after it has achieved confidence, that the Bitmint-Bill was exported properly.

The import of a Bitmint-Bill into the secure storage demands a mandatory online verification before made available in the secure element. The secure element will itself establish a secure session with the BitMint factory and replace the online Bitmint-Bill by a unique and fresh off-line Bitmint-Bill (Fig. 36.5).

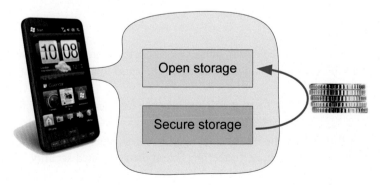

Fig. 36.6 Moving money to Online-Storage

Hence further attempts to recharge the same or another secure element with the same (old) online Bitmint-Bill will only result in bad verification and again the online-clone would be useless. To move a Bitmint-Bill from the secure storage (off-line) into the online-world, there is no server connection necessary because the Bitmint-Bill can be trusted as it comes from the secure storage featuring uniqueness and integrity (Fig. 36.6).

36.5.5   Off-line or Online?

The off-line mode is the preferred mode through its better flexibility in situations where online-verification is too expensive (data roaming) or simply not possible. Off-line is always available and independent from the local reception quality. Online mode is suggested in association with extended features like backing up Bitmint bills. For instance, a user may have cloned his/her entire purse, which can only be done in the off-secure element variant = online world.

At the time, the user needs to make an off-line payment, s(he) shall pick the desired Bitmint-Bills and import them to the off-line-world. Of course an online verification is inevitable for the transfer.

Which world to be used

- is up to the user and determined by the risk a user is able to take as a consequence of his (non-/secure) environment.
- depends on the environment and context a user wants to work in

The move between these worlds might be supported by applications. Unexperienced users might not even need to understand these ideas but may pay as just as usual and easy without having to care.

36.5.6   Giving a Change

As long as the idea of digital coins and bills exists, there is the problem of correct change. In particular in the off-line situation, a bill with the exact required amount cannot be ordered.

BitMint allows to split any Bitmint-Bill into accurate fragments to be used for a correct change.

If a Bitmint-Bill is split into a correct sub-part and a change remainder, both parts are independent Bitmint-Bills with no further impact on the associated security. This can be achieved off-line. The broken parts will contain the hash value of the original Bitmint-Bill which allows the verification system to recognize from which original Bitmint-Bill the split was made.

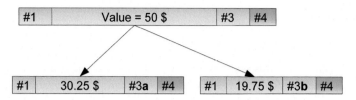

Fig. 36.7 Splitting a BitMint-Bill

Together with a position information

"I am a fragment of the original Bitmint-Bill (Hash: xxxx) at <Position Index>"

all information is available to resolve the fragment securely. The hash value does not provide further security. It is used to find the original bill in the database whenever a later verification is launched.

Fig. 36.7 shows a Bitmint-Bill being split for a change. The value can be split whereas the position information will be different for the fragments to indicate their position in the original bill.

36.5.7   Money Draft

Money draft from ATMs has always been subject to sometimes sensitive charges. Very often money draft is only possible with an ATM of the user's home bank.

Bitmint-Bills draft is possible wherever a network is available. This compares to a universal ATM system independent from home banks and cash issues.

Money draft means to access money on your own account. This is not a business transaction but indeed a service of most sensitive nature. Any attacker who is able to open such a transaction to your account could be thought of drafting Bitmint-Bills.

36.5.8   Using Special Features of Digital Money

Through the system of anonymously registered Bitmint-Bills it is possible to attach attributes to a Bitmint-Bill. These attributes may control the scope of the Bitmint-Bill and provide attractive use cases i. e. binding the money to a particular purpose (only organic food for the student) or person (cannot be traded/used by other than an "attached" assignee).

36.6 Summary

In our quest for the ultimate digital money we did not expect any system to survive our hard claims. Finally there was one candidate to overperform our filter and we identified BitMint as the only candidate qualifying as a universal digital representation of worldwide currencies. This led us to further investigation about BitMint's nature and features. The short perspective on BitMint made in this article cannot cover the versatile aspects that can be achieved by that system. Further information can be found on the inventor's website www.bitmint.com or optionally contacting the author helmut@hscherzer.de.

The worldwide spread of SmartPhones and the availability of the required security technology these device are most suitable as tomorrow's secure wallet. The elegance of digital money can unfold with the current attention on mobile payment – in particular if the ultimate criteria described in this article will be made available for the consumer.

References

1. [Online]. Available: http://en.wikipedia.org/wiki/Central_bank.
2. [Online]. Available: http://www.nytimes.com/2013/09/06/us/nsa-foils-much-internet-encryption.html?pagewanted=1&_r=0.
3. [Online]. Available: http://mondex.org/main_page.html.
4. H. Kreft, fairCASH based on Loss resistant Teleportation, Kiel: Dissertation, 2010.
5. [Online]. Available: https://www.google.com/wallet/.
6. [Online]. Available: https://en.wikipedia.org/wiki/Facebook_Credits.
7. [Online]. Available: https://en.wikipedia.org/wiki/Bitcoin.
8. [Online]. Available: https://en.bitcoin.it/wiki/Weaknesses.
9. [Online]. Available: http://networkcultures.org/moneylab/2015/11/30/10-bitcoin-myths/.

Part IX
Smart Traffic Hubs

Preface: Smart Traffic Hubs

Steve Lee

Abstract

An airport is an example of a traffic hub. In fact, a large airport like Changi Airport in Singapore is like a small city with its own hospitality, retail, logistics, transport and much more. With the growth of air traffic, alongside increasing competition and market challenges, and the need to cater for travellers' rapidly evolving expectations, airports need to expand and enhance their appeal to customers. In addition to infrastructure investments, Changi Airport has also been investing in technology to improve the customers' experience and enhance operations efficiency. Examples of these are data analytics and cloud solutions, robotics, autonomous vehicles, artificial intelligence, internet of things and many more. However, the deployment of new technologies alone will not be sufficient to keep Changi ahead, as IT systems and applications become more readily available and commoditised. Increasingly, the "smartness" of an airport will hinge on the strategic capability to collect data and on how intelligently the data can be exploited. To build data as a capability, Changi Airport adopts a Smart Airport Framework. **SMART** stands for **S**ervice, **S**afety & **S**ecurity **M**anagement through **A**nalytics and **R**esource **T**ransformation. The article uses examples to explain the core elements of the framework. The Smart Airport Framework has helped to focus clearly on the key outcomes and ensures that Changi continues to invest in the enablers needed to support Smart outcomes. Just as Singapore is pursuing Smart Nation initiatives to improve the lives of the citizens, Changi Airport has been and will continue to pursue Smart Airport ideas to improve the experience of the customers and to enhance operational efficiency at the airport.

S. Lee (✉)
Changi Airport Group
Singapore, Singapore
e-mail: steve.lee@changiairport.com

© Springer-Verlag GmbH Germany 2018
C. Linnhoff-Popien et al. (eds.), *Digital Marketplaces Unleashed*,
https://doi.org/10.1007/978-3-662-49275-8_37

37.1 About Changi Airport

An airport is an example of a traffic hub. In fact, a large airport like Changi Airport in Singapore is like a small city with its own hospitality, retail, logistics, transport and much more. In 2016, Changi Airport served a record of 58.7 million passengers. About 100 airlines flying to 300 cities in more than 70 countries and territories worldwide take off from the airport where a flight takes off or lands every 90 s. Despite the sheer volume of traffic, service standards are very high. The airport has won more than 525 awards since its opening in 1981. It has won the UK Business Traveller's "Best Airport in the World" Award for the past 27 years, and has also been conferred the Skytrax "Airport of the World" award 7 times including 2013 to 2016.

While the existing three terminals have an annual handling capacity of 66 million passengers, the growth of air traffic alongside increasing competition and market challenges will result in tighter capacity utilisation, especially during peak hours. The global airports landscape and travellers' expectations are also evolving rapidly. Airports today are no longer interchanges. Air hubs around the world are expanding and enhancing their appeal in order to increase their share of air travel and tourism. In this highly competitive environment, Changi Airport needs to continuously expand and innovate to strengthen its attractiveness to travellers. This is the reason for Changi's investment into new infrastructural projects such as Terminal 4 (which is planned to open in 2017) and in Changi East, a major initiative that will ensure that Changi Airport continues to have capacity for an adequate growth into the future.

37.2 What Makes a Hub Smart?

In addition to infrastructure investments, Changi Airport has also been investing in technology to improve the customers' experience and enhance operations efficiency. In connection with the sustained effort to become a Smart Airport Hub, Changi Airport has explored a range of technologies, some of which are mature and readily available, like data analytics and cloud solutions, while others are emerging, like robotics, autonomous vehicles, artificial intelligence, internet of things and many more.

However, the deployment of new technologies alone will not be sufficient to keep Changi ahead, as IT systems and applications become more readily available and commoditised. Increasingly, the "smartness" of an airport will hinge on the strategic capability to collect data and on how intelligently the data can be exploited.

Changi's Smart Airport initiative mirrors Singapore's Smart Nation Vision that defines *Smart* as the "harnessing of technology to the fullest with the aim of improving the lives of citizens, creating more opportunities, and building stronger communities", and states that a Smart Nation is "built upon the collection of data and the ability to make sense of information".

37.3   Why the Need for Smart Data Capability?

Data analytics will be a key driver in enabling the identification of patterns and the optimal deployment of resources to capitalise on the following opportunities. The following challenges are addressed:

Meeting the Expectations of Tech-Savvy Customers
Many travellers today live largely in the virtual world they create and curate for themselves via the social media and online services on their mobile devices. In order to gain mindshare, we must be able to deliver personalised value to individual customers. Customers' interactions and transactions with the airport provide an opportunity to collect data about their individual behaviours and needs, and to use that data to enhance their experience at the airport, or even to deliver new services.

Improving Partners' Performance and Productivity
A hub will need to develop a sound plan and invest into infrastructure to reduce manpower requirements and improve productivity and service, not only for the airport operator, but also for the airport tenants and partners. Hubs will increasingly have to innovate on how data exchange around airport wide processes can help each stakeholder with their own productivity.

Excelling in Spite of Increasing Business Complexity
With high traffic growth in many hubs, there is a need to optimise existing physical capacity through deeper collaboration and information exchange among all airport partners. Airport Collaboration Decision Making (A-CDM) is an example where airports have exploited greater accuracy of flight arrival times and their corresponding passenger loads, to better manage airport traffic levels and schedule scarce ground resources. Deep collaboration has also enabled more robust and integrated responses to crises and disruptions.

Maintaining Safety & Security
Safety and security of hubs are important aspects of hub operations. The deployment of sensors and sense-making technology will allow operators to quickly filter through "noise" and zoom in on incidents and exceptions to enhance safety and security. With the immense data being collected and processed and the response time needed for these incidents and situations, a smart way is needed to respond effectively.

Ensuring Cyber Security and Information Assurance
Even when exploiting the use of data analytics to transform the way resources are used, one needs to Ensure to invest adequately in information assurance and cyber security in order to ensure an effective and safe operation. Cyber Security Operations Centre (CSOC) is an important smart way to collect and analyse data on cyber attack attempts, allowing to understand patterns, to identify weaknesses, and to strengthen cyber defences.

37.4   What Benefits Has Smart Data Capability Achieved so Far?

Some examples of Changi's smart capability achieved so far include:

- Fuse airport operations information on maps and graphical charts, like for example the movements of planes or vehicles, or measures of on/off block timings. With this ability, the coordination and management of operations is highly improved.
- Digitise the position of aircraft and airside vehicles, status of key resources (for example, aircraft parking stands, runways), and other ground sensors (for example, perimeter security sensors) on an interactive airport map. This provides ground staff with the situational awareness of the airport to better manage operations.
- Help ground staff to quickly comprehend the situation on the ground such as upcoming flights and passenger volume through graphical charts of operations information. This helps operations staff to proactively prepare for possible surges in flight or passenger traffic.
- Exploit big data analytics. With 58.7 million passengers travelling through the airport last year, every transaction, whether at check-in, retail or boarding, gives Changi Airport tremendous insights into how it can serve customers better. For example, the airport electronically received instant feedback from the customers at the rate of 1.8 million per month. The repair and service recovery actions that had been performed provide another large data set to understand how an airport can innovate and improve. Aircraft movements are tracked and statistics and performance measures are also collated for touch points to measure service standards; as is the large data set in terms of retail transactions. Such data sets are being used to gain deep insights so as to help to better plan resource allocation for check-in and aircraft gates and other resources.

An example of a smart project is called SWIFT (Service Workforce Instant Feedback Transformation). The project is explained below.

37.5   Service Workforce Instant Feedback Transformation (SWIFT)

SWIFT was implemented in September 2010 to improve feedback management and raise performance standards of service personnel across all three terminals. It comprises two components – the instant feedback system (IFS) and e-Inspection as shown in Fig. 37.1.

e-Inspection enables timely responses to facility faults across all terminals through real-time inspections by service teams. The system also raises productivity levels of frontline staff such as washroom attendants, facilities management officers and other service personnel, with more streamlined workflows and processes. A total of 750 SWIFT instant feedback devices have been installed at nine key customer touch points. Each month, about 1.8 million instant feedback is collected from customers.

Fig. 37.1 Instant Feedback System (IFS) and e-Inspection

Achieving Operational Anticipation & Reaction

In the toilet cleanliness context, while anticipated passenger loads allow to deploy cleaners proactively, it would be too costly to deploy an army of cleaners to ensure that toilets meet cleanliness standards at all hours. By collecting instant feedback from passengers and putting in place the technology and processes to alert the cleaning crew so that they can act on specific feedback promptly, it is possible to greatly reduce the cleaning and maintenance resources required, while keeping cleanliness and maintenance standards high.

Achieving Data-Enabled Resource Planning

Over time, the data collected in SWIFT guides the allocation of resources as the patterns and correlation between flights and toilet cleanliness are being appreciated. The charts below (Fig. 37.2) are examples of the data analytics that is possible. It shows examples of analysis that can be performed to understand time of day effects on demand and top reasons of service feedback. This empowers the management teams to deep dive using data into areas for improvement.

Achieving Data-Driven Collaboration & Problem Solving

The SWIFT platform serves as a platform to share feedback data and patterns directly with partners, but the foundational technology platform itself is insufficient to drive collaboration. The data captured has helped Changi Airport to drive service enhancement

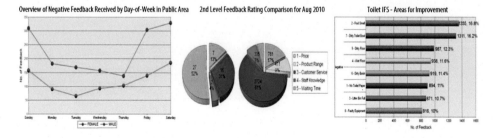

Fig. 37.2 Example analyses of the data collected in SWIFT

conversations with partners, and while the initial collaboration seen in SWIFT is encouraging, the project is still young to create a truly collaborative problem-solving culture.

37.6 SMART Framework

With the proliferation of technologies and ideas it is imperative to have a frame to think about smart projects. The smart data capability is premised on the SMART framework as shown in Fig. 37.3, which aptly stands for "**S**ervice, **S**afety & **S**ecurity **M**anagement through **A**nalytics and **R**esource **T**ransformation".

37.6.1 Smart Outcomes

The described smart data capability is more than a technology tool and involves the airport community coming together to share data and solve problems. There are three key outcomes envisioned:

1. **Operational Anticipation and Reaction**. Using information to anticipate and take pre-emptive measures if possible; furthermore respond promptly to operational issues across the airport, especially when situations change suddenly. With such data it will be possible to describe many of the situations that expert "intuitively" know. With

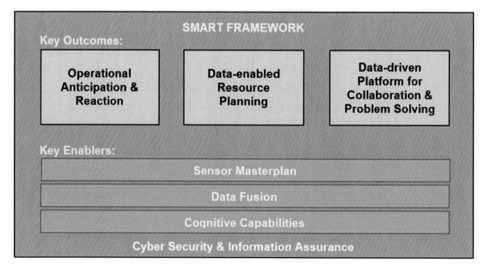

Fig. 37.3 SMART (**S**ervice, **S**afety & **S**ecurity **M**anagement through **A**nalytics and **R**esource **T**ransformation) Framework

increasing operational complexity, intuition without a Smart data capability may not be good enough.

2. **Data-enabled Resource Planning**. Allocating resources efficiently based on effective collection and analysis of data. There is often a gap between the design capacity and the actual operable capacity, and a data-enabled resource planning approach will help planners for resources like infrastructure or even manpower planning see trends over time; that cannot be solved or even justified without such a basis.

3. **Data-driven Platform for Collaboration & Problem Solving**. Building platforms for data sharing between airport partners that not only enable each other's outcomes, but also foster a data-driven approach to find airport-wide improvements, and institutionalise a culture of collaborative problem-solving for the benefit of the air hub. The A-CDM (Airport Collaborative Decision Making) platform mentioned earlier is an excellent example of such a platform.

37.6.2   Smart Enablers

Three key enablers underpin these Smart data capability outcomes. The ability to collect the right data and to make sense of the information will be central to the development of Changi's Smart Data Capability. To that end, Changi Airport will continue to invest in sensors and data fusion, as well as to begin investing in the rapidly-maturing machine cognitive capabilities.

1. **Sensor Masterplan**. Deploy sensors, collecting data via digital touchpoints, and even through travellers' mobile devices. This is Changi's own "Internet of Things". The sensors are used to help tracking the demand and supply of resources, tracking airside movements and status, and monitoring queues. Changi will continue to invest in 'eyes' on the ground to obtain real-time operations information for proactive and even predictive response, as well as longitudinal analysis. The Sensor Masterplan goes beyond data collection and includes data analytics and business intelligence that quantify performance and identify areas for improvement. Underpinning the sensor projects in the Masterplan is an investment in enabling IT infrastructure which provides connectivity for the sensors in Changi's "Internet of Things".

2. **Data Fusion**. Merge collected data into a coherent view, giving planners and operators Changi's "Comprehensive Awareness". For example, with the establishment of the Airport Operations Centre (AOC) in 2010, Changi Airport also implemented an AOC System that provided "comprehensive awareness" for everything needed to know to help coordinate and collaborate across the wider airport community, both airside and landside; Direct contractors and staff and partners like ground handlers and government agencies were also involved.

Another example is the fusion of customer data into insights into the needs of customers and passengers in both, online and offline channels, to help serve customers better.

3. **Cognitive Capabilities**. Use Smart data capability to move from predictive decisions to artificial intelligence (AI)-enabled prescriptive actions. Machine learning and artificial intelligence are quickly becoming accessible and available through applications (e. g. virtual assistants and chat bots) and more sophisticated predictive models for resource allocation and modelling. These cognitive capabilities have the potential to enhance sense-making abilities, and are still relatively new. Changi Airport is exploring use cases for such capabilities and will invest in proofs-of-concepts.

To illustrate the Smart Framework, the A-CDM implementation will be used as a case study. Changi Airport was fully operationalised A-CDM in Nov 2016, after more than 2 years of testing and pilots to ensure a smooth rollout.

37.7 Airport Collaborative Decision Making (A-CDM) as an Example of Smart Initiative

Changi's A-CDM program is a prime example of the Smart data capability and illustrates the SMART Framework well. In 2014, Changi Airport partnered with Air Traffic Control (ATC) on the A-CDM capacity enhancement programme whose objective is to improve operational efficiency, predictability and punctuality for the air traffic management (ATM) network and airport stakeholders. A-CDM shifts the concept of operations from "First Come First Serve" to "Best Planned Best Served", where flights would be sequenced for departure in a planned manner that would ultimately benefit the entire system with reduced variability.

A-CDM Operational Anticipation & Reaction
With A-CDM, ground handling agents (GHAs) and airlines work towards a common Target Off-Block Time (TOBT) for each flight. ATC uses the TOBT to set the best Target Start-up Approval Time (TSAT) and clear aircraft for departure, significantly optimising the usage of taxiways and runways.

A-CDM Data-Enabled Resource Planning
With tactical planning information such as TOBT and TSAT available in advance, airlines, GHAs, ATC, and Changi's airport operations planners are then capable of optimising the available resources to meet both the above-wing and below-wing operational needs.

A-CDM Data-Driven Platform for Collaboration & Problem Solving
By aligning airport partners (ATC, Airport Operations, airlines and GHAs) to a common operations framework, A-CDM becomes a data-driven collaboration platform for:

- Improving the operational efficiency of all airport partners by reducing delays;
- Increasing the predictability of events of a flight (turnaround; pre-departure plans; etc.);
- Maximising the utilisation of resources (manpower, airport fixed resources like gates, stands, airspace, etc.); and
- Paving the way for further benefits in baggage performance and passenger experience.

Changi's investment in airside initiatives like A-CDM is paying off in an average of 2 min taxi-out time savings per departure, and a 10% improvement in daily departure slots punctuality. The A-CDM framework has also enabled the airport community to recover effectively when runway capacity was disrupted.

To enable these A-CDM outcomes, Changi Airport invested systematically in:

- Sensors, as part of the wider **Sensor Masterplan**. To provide the awareness of aircraft position, docking status and other relevant useful information, several projects to link all the aircraft docking & guidance systems were completed, as well as sensor information from ATC and other sources. In addition to supporting A-CDM, Changi is leveraging these same sensors in various other service and security related applications.
- **Data Fusion** and Analytics. For A-CDM, data from various sources have been collected and fused into useful data sets for operational planning and anticipation. Sources include flight data from airlines' operational systems, arrival passenger load data, and airport gate allocation data. Changi Airport is currently integrating new air traffic information to better predict aircraft on-block time up to 20 min before arrival.
- **Cognitive capabilities**. Changi Airport is only starting to invest in this emerging area. The use of artificial intelligence and analytics to predict arrival times better are explored. Also, the arrival passenger loads for various arrival touch points such as immigration, arrival trolleys and taxi queues are anticipated. The ability to exploit cognitive capabilities is dependent and builds on the availability of large datasets that are now becoming available to Changi from internal and external sources.

37.8 Conclusion

Changi's progress on the Smart Airport initiative has been made possible largely by strong teamwork at all levels within the airport as well as the close collaboration with partners, airlines, government, and tenants. Changi Airport will continue to innovate with the best in the industry to develop the best possible data-driven collaborative problem-solving capability that enriches the passengers' experience, improves productivity for airport partners, and addresses complexities wrought by capacity constraints, while keeping Changi safe and secure in a sustainable manner.

The Smart Airport Framework that has been described has helped to focus clearly on the key outcomes and ensures that Changi continues to invest in the enablers needed to support Smart outcomes.

Just as Singapore is pursuing Smart Nation initiatives to improve the lives of the citizens, Changi Airport has been and will continue to pursue Smart Airport ideas to improve the experience of the customers and to enhance operational efficiency at the airport.

SmartPORT Traffic Hub – The Prospects for an Intermodal Port of the Future

38

Sebastian Saxe

Abstract

Due to the political geography of the Free and Hanseatic City of Hamburg, the physical limits of the area covered by the Port of Hamburg present special challenges. On the one hand, handling capacities will have to be increased substantially on an area that is virtually impossible to enlarge. On the other hand, for the future the port needs to develop in terms of quality from being merely a handling base to a hub for innovative industrial and service companies and for universities and non-academic research facilities. An important task for Hamburg as a commercial base will also be to develop new, data-driven business models.

By launching the smartPORT initiative, Hamburg Port Authority (HPA) is creating the conditions for boosting the efficiency of the port from an economic and ecological perspective by providing intelligent, digital solutions for the flow of traffic and goods.

In the future, the Port Traffic Center will integrate the traffic information from all water-, rail- and road-bound carriers and control all forms of transportation in order to guarantee optimum traffic flows in the port.

Regarding the infrastructure, digital, sensor-based solutions will make maintenance on and management of port railway facilities, bridges and locks, more efficient and cost-effective.

The following chapter outlines the status quo of traffic- and infrastructure-management at the Port of Hamburg and gives an insight into the HPA's strategic planning.

S. Saxe (✉)
Hamburg Port Authority AöR
Hamburg, Germany
e-mail: BueroSaxe@hpa.hamburg.de

© Springer-Verlag GmbH Germany 2018
C. Linnhoff-Popien et al. (eds.), *Digital Marketplaces Unleashed*,
https://doi.org/10.1007/978-3-662-49275-8_38

38.1 The Situation and the Challenge Entailed: The Port of Hamburg vis à vis International Competition

The Port of Hamburg is growing, albeit not as fast as predicted just a few years ago. According to an up-to-date handling potential analysis by the Institute of Shipping Economics and Logistics (ISL) [1], at the Port of Hamburg growth in container handling is set to jump from 8.9 million TEU (Twenty Foot Equivalent Units = standard container) in 2015 to about 18 million TEU by 2030. In terms of competition, particularly with the ports of Rotterdam and Antwerp, the port planners are faced with a complex problem. Hamburg is both a federal state and a city. As a result, the space available to extend the port is restricted to the south, in other words to the left of the river Elbe by the federal state of Lower Saxony and by Hamburg residential developments on the hillside in the north. Therefore, any growth in capacity has to be achieved from within the existing space.

Two factors come into play. On the one hand the use of the terminals and the traffic infrastructure are to become more efficient.

This is achieved by boosting the capacities of the gantry cranes which load and unload the container ships for example. However, on the other hand, digitisation plays the most crucial role in enhancing the efficiency of the Port of Hamburg as a whole.

How is digital technology used now and what is its potential in the future to improve the efficiency of the Port of Hamburg via smart, digital solutions for intermodal flows of traffic and goods?

Intelligent and increasingly interconnected systems are to be used to monitor, control and consequently improve merchandise logistics and flows of waterborne, road and rail traffic. In the mid-term autonomous vehicles will also play a role. At the same time, the operation and maintenance of the port infrastructure (roads, rails, bridges, traffic management systems, lighting, locks, dikes etc.) are to become more cost efficient, effective and safer via constant monitoring of all parts of the infrastructure. Monitoring is based on two systems: firstly, a network of sensors which report the current maintenance status to a central control centre of all components fitted with the sensors and secondly, drones which operate both above and below water and transmit photos, videos and measurement results. Finally, the level of sediment deposits in the fairway can be measured and the condition of dikes easily inspected at regular intervals.

38.2 The Digitisation of the Port of Hamburg – A Cornerstone of Strategic Planning

By launching the smartPORT [2] initiative, Hamburg Port Authority (HPA), together with all the other players at the Port of Hamburg, is creating the conditions for improving the efficiency of the port from a commercial and ecological perspective by providing intelligent, digital solutions for the flow of traffic and goods.

38.2.1   Traffic Management

Port traffic on the water, road and rail is already managed and monitored digitally. However, integration of management, monitoring and optimisation procedures to reflect the impact of each of the carriers on one another has not yet taken place; but it is a strategic planning objective.

Status Quo

Water shipping in the Port of Hamburg is monitored and coordinated in the Vessel Traffic Service Center which was inaugurated in 2014. Data is collated from existing systems and displayed with the help of the Port Monitor control centre software on one large high resolution monitor that can be viewed from all workspaces. The information provided includes nautical details such as charts, current shipping positions and berths, water level data, the heights and widths of bridges, but also dynamic data such as construction sites or scheduled dives. The technical architecture of the Port Monitor allows for mapping of rail and road traffic at a later developmental stage and for supporting monitoring of the port infrastructure, in other words of bridges, locks, tracks, signal boxes etc.

Rails the port railway has over 300 km of track. Some 200 trains per day leave the port for areas outside Hamburg, which also include eastern, south-eastern and southern Europe. In other words, 14% of all Germany's rail freight transport stems from or going towards the Port of Hamburg. This proportion will probably increase substantially because trains will play a significant role in the transportation of tomorrow. The assumption is that if the amount of traffic as a whole doubles, rail traffic will triple.

Currently, trains in the port are connected semi-automatically. Wagons are pushed by shunting locomotives onto humps and from this point their own weight propels them on to the target track. The points are switched and the speed and very precise braking of the wagons are controlled automatically. The sequence of the wagons and allocation of the right track on the shunting yards in the port are based on loading lists and specified by planners.

Road the purpose of the EVE system (Effektive Verkehrslageermittlung – effective traffic situation identification) is to control and optimise road traffic. Based on video images of the traffic junctions and data from inductive loops and Bluetooth detectors, it provides an overview of the volume of traffic. The idea behind the Smart Area Parking project already in production is to manage parking space in the port efficiently. It records the number of parking spaces occupied in real time and reports the results to truck drivers and terminal operators.

The overview of the traffic and parking space situation is used in the Port Road Management Center to give road users, terminal operators and the authorities up-to-date information on the traffic in the port. The DIVA system (Dynamische Information über das

Verkehrsaufkommen – dynamic information on volume of traffic) transmits the information via info panels located in the port area, on the access roads and motorways to the port and via a smartphone app. These options allow drivers to find out and decide for themselves which are the best routes to their destinations, whether it is worth waiting for a traffic jam to subside, or whether it is advisable to choose an alternative route instead.

Port Traffic Center to Control Waterborne, Rail- and Road-Bound Traffic

The technical architecture of the Port Monitor control system has already been primed so that in future all the information on movement and identity of all carriers can be incorporated into one integrated system, in other words rail- and road-bound traffic in the port. The goal is to achieve full traffic management in the Port Traffic Center (PTC) in which movable infrastructure is also to be included in order to guarantee ideal traffic flows in the port.

The PTC will therefore act as a traffic control centre for the whole port. All ships, road- and rail-bound vehicles, points and locks, as well as lift bridges and bascule bridges, will then be displayed on a high resolution monitor which shows the entire port. The current positions of all ships, complemented by information about their destinations and realistic speed estimations, enable very reliable forecasts of imminent traffic conditions. Floating car data, in other words movement data of trucks will play an important role. An increasing number of these will be fitted with Bluetooth detectors so that they can be measured at measurement points; when they drive by two measurement points the speed is recorded and the speed data of several vehicles indicates the volume of traffic. The rise in the amount of information from the PTC also increases the quality of the information given to the drivers.

Planning Traffic Capacities Based on Information About Goods from an Import Messaging Platform

Logistics companies and authorities involved in export and import already communicate today via the central data centre belonging to Dakosy, the IT company owned by Hamburger Seehafen-Verkehrswirtschaft. One of the things Dakosy provides is an import message platform (IMP) [3] which is used by forwarders and transportation companies, shipping firms, railway companies and feeders, but also by customs, the port police, fire brigade and other authorities, as well as production companies and enterprises in the port itself. The IMP is the result of a project group set up by Dakosy in 2004 whose work is subsidised as part of the ISETEC (Innovative Seehafentechnologien) II [4] research programme, initiated by the German Federal Ministry for Economic Affairs as part of the Lean Port Management project.

The IMP consists of a central data pool which collects and provides information about flows of goods into the port and forwarding of these goods from the port. As early as the planning stage, an individual logical data pool with a unique registration number for each import procedure is created, where all the data regarding the planned transportation is stored. Importers and other logistics companies report scheduled transports, what these transports include and their current status. Transatlantic carriers file their customs declarations on the IMP which can then be retrieved by customs and where the appropriate assessments and information on their statuses can be filed.

In this way, the port container terminals are told which containers have which customs status, when they will arrive and what type of onward transportation needs to be planned. Trucks, trains and feeder shipping which are loaded or unloaded at the container terminals receive their transportation orders based on this data.

The level of detailed data on the IMP will increase vastly in the future because a rising number of containers are being fitted with wireless tags. These allow identification of the position of individual containers in the port at any time, regardless of whether they are still located on the ships, on the terminal, or have already been loaded onto trucks or trains. In conjunction with information on destinations this will allow much more accurate traffic planning and faster responses. The limited road space available could therefore be used much more efficiently than in the past and energy efficiency of port traffic will rise too.

Smart Area Parking in the Port, to Relieve Pressure on Existing Road Space
Some of the Smart Area Parking project is already up and running. Its goal is to capture available capacities of four important truck parking spaces in the port and to inform parking space users and the terminal operators accordingly. The purpose is to make the offering of parking areas for trucks at the Port of Hamburg much more effective and environmentally friendly. Traffic resulting from drivers seeking parking spaces and the resulting disruptions on the road network is to be minimised and logistical processes made more efficient as a result.

Incoming and outgoing truck traffic is captured in the smart areas via inductive loop detectors. The vehicles are allocated unique fingerprints so that they can be identified when they depart; data protection considerations mean this is accomplished without linking information to vehicle number plates. The summary of incoming and outgoing vehicles according to quantity and vehicle type reveals the number of parking spaces available.

Furthermore, in the future, statistical data on the analysis of the length of time a vehicle is parked will be captured. This will enable forecasts on how the situation regarding parking spaces will develop in comparable situations. Information on parking spaces is published by the Port Road Management Center. Similarly to traffic updates, it will displayed on the road network on DIVA display panels and sent directly to road users via online information systems.

Pre-Port Hubs: Goods Handling Outside the Port to Cut Down on In-Port Traffic
In the long term, the purpose of pre-port hubs is to boost the benefits of Smart Area Parking as regards traffic in the port. These hubs are container transfer points outside the port site which still need to be constructed and which will also act as smart parking spaces where vehicles wait. Incoming traffic will be grouped into separate lanes for each target terminal and wait until loading capacities there are available. Waiting times at the terminal itself

will then be passé. At the same time, transporter shuttles will pass between the terminals and the hubs to hand over their loads there. The objective is to reduce the need for traffic areas and the emission of harmful substances. Overarching terminal handling planning will also shorten the times for handling and forwarding the goods and will therefore benefit the forwarders and their customers.

In the long term, driverless trailers are to be used for shuttle transport of containers between pre-port hubs and container terminals in order to make disruption-free handling easier.

38.2.2 Infrastructure Management and Operation

The infrastructure which the HPA is responsible for managing and operating includes all non-moveable and moveable technical equipment, but also environmental factors such as the Elbe's fairway. Monitoring operations, maintenance and repair currently entails huge manpower costs and other expenses. By using digital technology, the efficiency and quality of infrastructure maintenance is to be increased significantly in the future; experience is being gained at the moment in two pilot projects.

Status Quo

Smart Switch Pilot Project: Intelligent Points

The port railway has 880 points which need to be checked regularly to ascertain whether repairs or maintenance are necessitated. Despite all the effort required, on-site inspection teams cannot constantly inspect all points and take action if these prove to be hard to move.

For a while now, 11 points have been converted to smart switches; these include sensors which, based on the electricity consumption and also physical power each time a point is moved, measure whether a point is harder to move than normal and what the air and material temperatures are. Ice, blockages or other mechanical restrictions can therefore be identified immediately. Gradual, minimal increases in electricity consumption over a long period of time also suggest that maintenance on a point will soon be needed. In both cases, Port Monitor is informed accordingly via a network interface.

In this way, operational management of the port railway has an up-to-date overview of the condition of the points and can take action before malfunctions occur. Fewer preventative inspections have to be performed at the same time. The number of on-site staff deployments drops accordingly and fewer malfunctions occur when operating the railway.

Smart Tag Pilot Project: Intelligent Construction Site Beacons

Capture of the situation on daytime construction sites is currently being piloted. Smart Tags are used for this purpose and are integrated into construction site beacons. The tags are a combination of a mobile communications system, Global Positioning System (GPS) sensors and other sensors. The position of the beacon and the working order of its flashing light, the temperature and CO_2 levels in the air are recorded. An angle sensor also establishes whether the beacon is still standing or has fallen over. All data is sent to the Port Road Management Center and saved in a traffic data base in real time.

The digital beacon has an impact in two ways. The information collected helps to regulate traffic flow in the port. And the frequency of inspection trips to the construction sites falls drastically.

The intention of the pilot project is to try out a mobile multi-purpose sensor which in the future can be applied to indispensable objects, such as floating cranes or shunting locomotives in order to obtain environmental data, movement profiles and other information.

Central Infrastructure Control Centre

Intelligent points and intelligent construction site beacons are the first elements in a future sensor-based network that is to monitor and optimise the operation and maintenance of all the infrastructure in the port. Static bridges, bascule bridges, lift bridges, locks and barrages, track and railway systems with points, street lighting, traffic lights, electronic display boards and construction site equipment are some of the items that will be fitted with sophisticated sensors. Also included will be quays and dikes with components above and below the water.

Based on sensor data and other information supplied by autonomous surveillance vehicles, it will be possible to read all current load and maintenance conditions, as well as environmental information, at a central infrastructure control centre at any time. This will allow more efficient, forward planning of maintenance and repair work with a much lower impact on the logistical processes in the port. If for example work on a railway bridge and points in the same area of the port occurs at the same time, entailing a negative impact on road- and rail-bound traffic, the control centre will indicate this immediately. The work can then be planned in such a way that the bridge and points are repaired at the same time and minimises disruption to road traffic.

Autonomous Digital Technology for Monitoring and Predictive Maintenance

In addition to the sensor network, in the long term autonomous underwater and overwater vehicles are to be used. These drones can prevent time-consuming, complex and sometimes dangerous dives because they measure and capture sediment deposits on bridges and locks. They check the condition of quay walls and embankments under water, or capture flow data in the fairway and notify the infrastructure control centre accordingly. This is possible much more frequently than in the past with round-the-clock autonomous digital technology. Consequently, information on the condition of the infrastructure is much more up to date, more reliable and better quality.

The widespread use of sensor networks and drones will also enable what has in principle already been achieved with intelligent points. In other words, predictive maintenance which allows maintenance and repair to be tailored to current conditions and requirements.

Reliability is no longer based on safety margins, but on precise, up-to-date knowledge of how long a part of the infrastructure could still carry on working reliably.

Maintenance and Planning with the Aid of Augmented Reality

Augmented reality (AR) technology will take on a special role for two reasons. The HPA has collaborated with the University of Hamburg to develop an AR app. A smartphone's camera is held over a map of the port to show the location and functions of sensors and the IT systems they are connected with. In this case, the app is a type of meta information instrument regarding the systems and tools whose purpose is to enhance the infrastructure. Other applications for the app are conceivable. For example, underground pipes and lines, or networks of all types could be shown in detail on a map of the port.

Furthermore, in the mid-term AR will support mechanics carrying out special work on the infrastructure and under water. The technicians will have display devices which superimpose and complement the real image with additional information, for example the detailed design plan of a lock, where otherwise only a surface covered in sediment would be seen. What is more, the exact demonstration of work by video also serves as instructions for almost all repairs. Local manpower could then carry out this work immediately instead of possibly having to wait for specialists for a long time.

AR will play a third role in construction projects. Scheduled construction and infrastructure can be visualised at the design stage already in the context of real infrastructure. In fact, when planning a new cruise terminal, three-dimensional views have already been projected into an image of the real environment, including the access roads, in order to assess traffic management alternatives.

38.3 The Importance of Simulations and Big Data to the Port

38.3.1 Optimising Logistics and Traffic Flows

Thanks to satellite and positioning technology, traffic operations in the port, in particular container transports, are becoming increasingly more efficient, faster and less prone to disruptions. But the need for further, advanced measures is still enormous. Because port business is continuing to grow unabated, one question will continue to be relevant: how can containers be directed optimally through the port and what is the best way to design intermodal interfaces between the water-borne, rail- and road-bound traffic?

In the future, this issue will increasingly rely on big data to provide the answers. On the one hand it is a question of the vast and inexorable growth in data which is gained from logistical procedures and the operation and management of the infrastructure with the aid of sensors and traffic and infrastructure control rooms. A large proportion of this information will be movement data which is supplied by Smart Tags on containers and vehicles. On the other hand, it will also be necessary to use complex sensors to work out how to enhance the intermodal interaction of shipping, rail- and road-bound traffic from commercial and ecological standpoints.

38.3.2   Sediment Management

Big data analyses and simulations are also applied to sediment management, in other words preventing, controlling and removing deposits in the fairway. Due to larger and larger shipping with deeper and deeper draughts, this task is strategically important for the development of the Port of Hamburg.

In partnership with the Federal Waterways and Shipping Administration, the HPA is already analysing a variety of effects in the tidal Elbe to understand how sediment deposits occur. In future, the data will be much more comprehensive and detailed. Underwater drones will constantly measure the fairway and record parameters such as speeds of currents and the water temperature. These measurement results can be compared with other information, such as meteorological data, to detect interdependencies which would not have been uncovered with conventional analysis methods, but which play a pivotal role in sediment management.

38.3.3   Developing Data-Driven Business Models

The digitisation of traffic, logistics and infrastructure at the Port of Hamburg creates the cornerstones for developing data-driven business models. The data collated from all processes in the port contain values which need to be developed to the benefit of people and businesses.

Consequently, as part of the smartPORT initiative, the port industries and the HPA are collaborating with partners from the IT industry to set up a virtual market place to interconnect the port. The idea is that in the future software applications, services, apps and data are to be offered here. Apps with information on available parking spaces in the area surrounding the port, repair workshops for trucks, or an ordering service for supplies on inland waterway vessels are conceivable.

38.4   Outlook – Development of the Port into a Business and Science Hub

With these types of data-driven business models, the Port of Hamburg also has the opportunity to evolve from a handling hub to a research, development and production site and therefore a digital market place. It is not suitable for industries requiring vast amounts of space, but does offer excellent opportunities for research-focused and technology-centric companies. Ideal traffic conditions, a very powerful network infrastructure with gigabit transmission rates, as well as research facilities of international repute, such as HafenCity University Hamburg and the Kühne Logistics University, create the conditions for innovative companies, start-ups and established businesses to thrive – and not just on digital market places.

References

1. ISL, [Online]. Available: http://www.hamburg-port-authority.de/de/presse/studien-und-berichte/Documents/Endbericht_Potenzialprognose_Mai2015_5.pdf. [Accessed 29 08 2016].
2. Hamburg Port Authority, [Online]. Available: https://www.iaph2015.org/downloads//smartPORT-Brosch%C3%BCren/broschuere_smartportlogistics_web.pdf. [Accessed 27 07 2016].
3. Dakosy, [Online]. Available: https://www.dakosy.de/en/solutions/port-community-system/import-message-platform. [Accessed 27 07 2016].
4. BMWI, [Online]. Available: http://www.bmwi.de/BMWi/Redaktion/PDF/I/innovative-seehafentechnologien. [Accessed 27 07 2016].

An Overview of Technology, Benefits and Impact of Automated and Autonomous Driving on the Automotive Industry

Walter Brenner and Andreas Herrmann

Abstract

Autonomous driving is becoming a central moving force towards the change in vehicles and therefore among others the automobile and mobility business, as well as numerous other industries, which today still believe that they do not have a relationship to digitalized autonomous vehicles. The changes in different industries, which can be initiated by autonomous vehicles, are a good example of changes, which can be initiated by digitalization on market places. This article is based on the hypothesis that the development of automated and later autonomous vehicles are an unstoppable development, which will be of great use to the economy and society. Against this background, the article illustrates what is to be understood by the concepts of automated and autonomous driving, and what useful effects can be expected for a number of stakeholders. In addition to this, the article explains the technical fundamentals of automated vehicles and the changes in the traffic-related industry. In the last part, the article elaborates the impact on the automobile and traffic industry.

39.1 Introduction

Automated and autonomous driving has become a topic, which has gained broad attention in the public during the last few years. The handling of the update for automated driving, which has been available for the Tesla S for approximately one year, demonstrates the

W. Brenner (✉) · A. Herrmann
University of St. Gallen
St. Gallen, Switzerland
e-mail: walter.brenner@unisg.ch

A. Herrmann
e-mail: andreas.herrmann@unisg.ch

© Springer-Verlag GmbH Germany 2018
C. Linnhoff-Popien et al. (eds.), *Digital Marketplaces Unleashed*,
https://doi.org/10.1007/978-3-662-49275-8_39

intensity and emotionality of the public discussion. Immediately after the availability of this functionality euphoric reporting started. Autonomous driving with the Tesla S and the download of the software to the vehicle overnight was hailed by the press and by many potential customers as a masterpiece of innovation [1]. Tesla was incorrectly named as the pioneer of autonomous driving. Vehicles built by Audi, BMW or Daimler are more advanced in development and covered large distances completely autonomously or with speeds up to 240 km/h on closed racing circuits at a much earlier time [2]. However, Tesla and Google's small cars with panda faces dominate the discussion about autonomous driving [3]. From the start, it was predictable that automated and autonomous driving would lead to serious accidents, just the same as traditional driving. Very quickly, videos of the Tesla S appeared on YouTube, where it showed it being driven completely driverless, against the provisions of Tesla [4]. When "expectedly" information about a fatal accident with a Tesla S, which was travelling autonomously, appeared in June 2016, reporting tipped in the other direction [5]. The previously positive reporting changed to negative almost overnight. The fact that the driver of the Tesla S used the vehicle contrary to the provisions of Tesla played merely a subordinated role in the public discussion. Only a fact-based and unemotional discussion can indicate the uses and dangers of automated and autonomous driving, and establish a base for future-oriented decisions. This article seeks to make a contribution to this discussion. It is based on the fundamental statement that the uses of autonomous vehicles exceed the risks, and that autonomous driving as part of the digitalization of vehicles is an unstoppable development. The competitiveness of the European automobile industry will be determined decisively by the way digitalization is handled. In view of the dominance of American companies, especially the so-called internet giants such as Amazon, Apple, Google and Facebook, the discussion about automated and autonomous driving is a central one for the industrial location Europe.

Against this backdrop this article deals with the different aspects of automated and autonomous driving. In the first section we define automated and autonomous driving. The second part of our article is concerned with the uses of automated and autonomous vehicles. The third part shows changes in the vehicle, the traffic-related aspects and changes in the IT infrastructure. The last section handles changes in the automobile industry, and future developments in the mobility sector.

The article is based on discussions with experts and extensive literature analysis on the topic "Automated Driving", which was carried out in cooperation with Audi AG between July 2015 and August 2016.

39.2 Automated & Autonomous Driving

The current development of vehicles, which are primarily steered by drivers to autonomous vehicles, i.e. completely self-driving vehicles, can be divided into several developmental steps. The Society of Auto Engineers [6] and the respective department in Germany [7] has provided a structuring for those development steps. However, the model of the National Highway Traffic Administration (NHTSA), the civil regulating authority of the USA, has established itself as a "de-facto standard" worldwide [8]:

- *No-Automation (Level 0):* *The driver is in complete and sole control of the primary vehicle controls – brake, steering, throttle, and motive power – at all times.*
- *Function-specific Automation (Level 1):* *Automation at this level involves one or more specific control functions. Examples include electronic stability control or pre-charged brakes, where the vehicle automatically assists with braking to enable the driver to regain control of the vehicle or stop faster than possible by acting alone.*
- *Combined Function Automation (Level 2):* *This level involves automation of at least two primary control functions designed to work in unison to relieve the driver of control of those functions. An example of combined functions enabling a Level 2 system is adaptive cruise control in combination with lane centering.*
- *Limited Self-Driving Automation (Level 3):* *Vehicles at this level of automation enable the driver to cede full control of all safety-critical functions under certain traffic or environmental conditions and in those conditions to rely heavily on the vehicle to monitor for changes in those conditions requiring transition back to driver control. The driver is expected to be available for occasional control, but with sufficiently comfortable transition time. The Google car is an example of limited self-driving automation.*
- *Full Self-Driving Automation (Level 4):* *The vehicle is designed to perform all safety-critical driving functions and monitor roadway conditions for an entire trip. Such a design anticipates that the driver will provide destination or navigation input, but is not expected to be available for control at any time during the trip. This includes both occupied and unoccupied vehicles.*

Computer-assisted driving at level 1 and 2 is described as automated driving, while driving at level 3 is designated to be highly automated driving. The term autonomous driving is reserved for driving at level 4.

Automated and autonomous driving at the experimental stage is already reality today. Numerous vehicles already have relatively extensive packages of assisting systems, which correspond to level 1 or level 2. Examples of these assisting systems are emergency braking systems, lane or park assistant systems, and automatic vehicle interval control, sometimes called "adaptive cruise control".

Automated driving at level 3 will probably be feasible in the next few years, for example with the highway assistant, which will probably be on the market in 2017 or 2018, for instance with the Audi A 8. Autonomous driving is currently taking place at low speeds on closed off sections or testing grounds, or with special permissions in public transport. Google is testing autonomous vehicles in the vicinity of Mountain View. A vehicle made by Audi drove autonomously from San Francisco to Las Vegas [9]. A further vehicle developed by the automotive component supplier Delphi drove from the west coast to the east coast [10].

Even optimistic estimates go on the assumption that autonomous vehicles will, at the earliest, go into production between 2025 and 2030 [11, p. 8]. Against this background, many statements and reports on the chances and dangers of autonomous driving are to be viewed as speculation rather than based on facts and research. Major leaps in development are not to be expected. The Apple iPhone and the ensuing development it created, for example the app worlds, among them being Apple and Google, who initiated an app explosion, prove that unexpected disruptive developments are possible. Like these developments, app worlds have developed disruptively along new technical possibilities in the last ten years, automated and autonomous driving will steadily continue to develop over the next years.

There could possibly be resistance against new technologies. The past has proven that organized societal resistance can lead to the end of a technology, in spite of expert opinions, as can be seen from the example of nuclear energy, to name just one. The philosopher Nida-Rümelin demands, against this backdrop, an open discussion about the chances and dangers of automated and autonomous driving [12, 13]. Also against this background, the Tesla competitors should participate in the discussion about accidents through automated driving in a factual and businesslike manner. The discussion about the so-called dilemma situation should also be conducted at a broad societal level. When talking about dilemma situations we mean situations in which a robot must decide between two or more catastrophic situations. A classical question is, for example: "Will an autonomous vehicle, when faced with the situation of an unavoidable driving maneuver, run over a pedestrian or will it collide with an obstacle thus endangering the driver". Ultimately, these decisions are based on philosophical discussions, which have been conducted for years, on the so-called "Trolley Problem". From today's view, it remains a thought experiment as to how an autonomous vehicle must and will react to a dilemma situation. Nevertheless, the automobile industry will have to face this discussion and forward its assessment and possible solutions at a broad societal level. The discussion as to the feasibility and future of automated and autonomous driving in the US senate [14] and many parliaments worldwide and round-table discussions [15] in Germany all offer constructive contributions to these discourses.

Automated and autonomous driving does not only concern vehicles carrying persons, although these are currently often at the center of discussion. The starting point of the development of autonomous vehicles were two competitions run by DARPA, part of the American Ministry of Defense, in a desert-like area in the years 2004 and 2005, and a challenge in an urban area in the year 2007 (Urban Challenge [16]) The military continues to be an important driver in the development of automated and autonomous driving. Moreover, there is intensive work being done worldwide on automated and autonomous trucks [17–19], trucks for farming [20] and special vehicles, for example for mining [21].

39.3 Benefits of Automated & Autonomous Vehicles

The most important benefits of automated and autonomous vehicles is the reduction of the risk of accidents. Every year more than 1.2 million people die as a result of traffic accidents: In Germany approx. 3500 people die in traffic every year and more than 300,000 are injured, many of them seriously. According to coinciding estimates approx. 90% of these accidents were caused by human error [22]. Automated and autonomous vehicles, i.e. robots, work without error as long as they are programmed correctly. Robots are always attentive, never tire and carry out the programmed maneuver under all circumstances. In view of this, it can be assumed that the number of accidents will decrease with an increasing degree of automation. The higher the level of development of these robots, the more complex the traffic situations they can recognize, compute and master. Already currently the figures issued by insurances indicate that, for example, the automatic emergency brake assistant reduces rear-end collisions by 38%, the lane keeping assistant reduces accidents by 4.4% and the lane changing assistant by 1.7%. Whoever is driving on the highway using the adaptive cruise control knows how comforting it is when the robot "thinks in advance" and initiates a braking maneuver if another vehicle surprisingly pushes in ahead of you.

A further benefit of highly automated and autonomous vehicles in future, is the fact that the driver can better utilize the time spent in the vehicle. Initial tests show that the time can be used for entertainment, for example in the form of movies, work, and also resting up. Rupert Stadler, Audi CEO, speaks in this context of about 25 h, which customers can gain through the use of highly automated and autonomous driving [23]. A study by Horvath and partner, which was conducted in cooperation with the Fraunhofer Institute for Industrial Science, showed that the additionally gained time in the vehicle could lead to a billion Euro market [24].

Autonomous driving will make a contribution to increasing social justice. Older citizens, sick and physically challenged people are partially excluded from automobile individual mobility today. They cannot or are not permitted to drive vehicles themselves. Autonomous vehicles enable them to use this form of individual mobility, since a robot is the driver. In a video on user behavior in the case of autonomous vehicles from Google, shows a blind elderly man, as a representative of this group of people, who is quite obviously enjoying the trip [25].

Further benefits are expected from the influence on inner city traffic and city planning, once autonomous vehicles have become reality. Public space can most probably be utilized differently and more advantageously. It can already be seen that automated parking, which will be offered in vehicles in the near future, will improve the usage of parking space in park garages by approximately 30%. New traffic and city development concepts will be possible. In the context of the Audi Urban Future Initiative [26] the city of Somerville, a suburb of Boston, demonstrates what a suburb with autonomous vehicles could look like. It is planned to realize this concept in the near future [27].

The benefits mentioned are difficult to quantify. Nevertheless, there are first attempts. A study by Morgan Stanley estimates the benefits of automated and autonomous vehicles in a pessimistic scenario 0.7, an optimistic scenario 2.2 and in a realistic scenario 1.3 quadrillion USD [11, p. 8]. The 1.3 quadrillion are made up of mainly 488 trillion through savings by avoiding accidents, 507 trillion through productivity gains through better utilization of the time spent in the vehicle, 158 trillion through fuel savings and 138 trillion through the avoidance of traffic jams. A study by the Rand Corporation [28] goes on the assumption that autonomous driving reduces accidents, makes a contribution to social justice, avoids traffic jams, reduces land usage and reduces environmental damage, among others.

39.4 Automated & Autonomous Vehicles and Their Infrastructure

Automated vehicles can be seen as so-called cyber physical systems, i. e. a combination of physical product and associated computer supported information processing. Cyber physical systems address the close connection of embedded systems for the control and steering of physical processes using sensors and actuators via communications connections with the global digital net (cyberspace). The higher the proportion of information- and communication technology, i. e. the degree of automation in the vehicle, the larger and therefore more central will be the proportion of computer supported information processing in adding value and in the development of a vehicle.

Automated and autonomous driving can be described by the structure "Entry – processing – output", well-known from information processing. The input of the data, which the vehicle requires for automated driving, occurs via sensors. The sensor technology required for automated driving, is illustrated in Fig. 39.1 as an example on an Audi RS 7

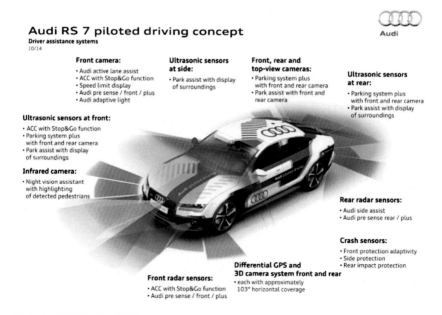

Fig. 39.1 Audi RS 7 piloted driving concept

[29]. This vehicle is able to drive automatically at speeds of up to 240 km/h on a closed racetrack. The cars available from other manufacturers currently possess – although there are manufacturer-specific differences – basically a sensor technology, which is comparable to that of the Audi RS 7. Not every model of car, however, has all of the sensors built into the Audi RS 7.

The sensor technology of the RS 7 consists of GPS, ultrasonic sensors, radar- and camera systems. Each of these sensors captures different aspects of the environment on the basis of specific features. Therefore, ultrasonic sensors, for example, are efficient only in the nearby area and are used for parking assistants. Radar systems are effective for greater distances and are used for automatic vehicle interval control (in Audi terminology: ACC Adaptive Cruise Control). Infrared sensors are used predominantly at night. Camera systems capture and identify objects, such as other vehicles, for example, and other motorists or pedestrians and follow these. The GPS system is a further part of the sensor technology, which recognizes the location and movements of a vehicle. Differential GPS is based on the well-known and commonly used GPS, but it is more precise. The Lidar (Light Detection and Ranging), a sensor technology based on laser technology, which is related to radar technology, will, in future, enhance the sensor technology of automated and autonomous vehicles in the near future and will increase the precision and range of environmental detection. Additionally, the entry of the destination takes place via the user interface of the navigation system. The development of the sensor systems and the software to recognize objects, identify them, track them and, in a best case scenario to predict their behavior is a focus of research and development for automated and autonomous vehicles. In the area of object recognition, identification and tracking, a jump in development is expected through the increased utilization of machine learning, or deep learning [30].

The perceptions of the individual sensors are compiled during processing to show an image of the environment. The processing system knows the destination from the entry into the GPS system and the route to this via the maps. On this basis how the vehicle should move is calculated in real time. Processing of the entries into driving commands is a computing process, which has to take place in real time. It places high demands on the computing process. The processors, which are responsible for this, will in future constitute a central component of vehicles. Individual experts are of the opinion that this central unit will equal the engine in significance for the vehicle. The issuing of the driving commands is effected by so-called actuators to the electronic accelerator, the electronic brakes and the electronic steering. In the automated vehicle, these power units are addressed via the network, i. e. "by wire" and moved by electric motors. The movement of a vehicle exclusively "by wire" is a jump in development, which is a deep encroachment into the development and operation of vehicles.

The actual process of automated and autonomous driving will be completed by further entry, processing and output functionalities. Above all, the interface to the driver, the so-called user interface, is of great significance. A central aspect in automated and autonomous vehicles is the process by which the driver wants to, or has to, because of a dangerous situation, return to taking control while the vehicle is travelling in automated mode. Problems, which have to be solved for this process are, for example, how the driver will be informed that he or she needs to take control, or how he or she receives the information that he or she can safely control the vehicle. Already today there are different interfaces to the driver in automated vehicles, for example warning lights, which are projected into the windscreen, acoustic signals or vibration of the steering wheel with or without automatic steering correction if the vehicle begins to leave the designated lane. A further aspect which will play a major role in future is the interface of highly automated and later autonomous vehicles with the environment, for example pedestrians.

When vehicles travel for longer periods of time in highly automated or later autonomous mode, it will be possible to construct and use the interiors of vehicles differently. In this context, one speaks of a change from driver-orientation to benefit-orientation. The benefit-creating usage of time in the vehicle is in the foreground. The steering wheel, for example, is reduced in significance in a highly automated vehicle. The Mercedes F015, a prototype of an autonomous vehicle, has only a rudimentary steering wheel. Autonomous vehicles will not have a steering wheel anymore. The Mercedes prototype and the Google vehicles illustrate that highly automated and autonomous vehicles enable innovative design of the interior. What these vehicles will eventually look like will be decided by the customer, or how they will imagine spending their time when the vehicle is travelling autonomously.

In future, not only the interior but also the external appearance, or the concept of the vehicle will most probably change [31]. The Google prototypes are built for low speeds and short distances, the so-called "last-mile". Their area of operation is the autonomous short-distance traffic, for example home from the railway station. Road trains, a type of bus with a capacity of up to 20 people, represent a mixture of classic bus and taxi. They serve the more individual transport of several people over short or medium distances. Contrary to these automatically travelling special vehicles will be the highly automated and later autonomous universal vehicles. They are similar to today's vehicles, but enable highly automated and autonomous driving.

Independent of the development of automated and autonomous driving, today's vehicles have already been connected over the last few years, mostly via the mobile network. Currently this interconnectedness is largely used for local communication, for text messages, and for entertainment. The interconnection of vehicles (Car2Car.communication) with the infrastructure (Car2Infrastructure-communication) and with cloud services will play a large role in highly automated and autonomous driving. Car2car-communication, for example, will enable the process where cars will transmit information about speed, directional change or danger situations directly to all other vehicles in the vicinity. Car2Infrastructure, for example, connects a vehicle with traffic signs or traffic lights. Of special significance for highly automated and autonomous driving is the interconnection of the vehicle with cloud services. Highly precise maps are of central significance for highly automated and autonomous driving. Through interconnection with, for example, highly precise maps available from the cloud, the steering of the vehicle can be improved in extension with the environmental images received in the vehicle by the sensors. Information about temperature, weather, roadworks or danger situations can be made available to the highly automated and autonomous vehicles. At a price of 2.4 billion euro Audi, BMW and Daimler have bought HERE, the map division of Nokia against this background [32]. The aim is to make available to highly automated and autonomous vehicles digital services, for example in the form of maps or route information, in the sense of a digital ecosystem together with other partners, based on the highly precise map material from HERE [33]. During the CeBIT 2016 in Hannover, Huawei presented a first prototype for 5G networks. This technology will be of great significance when large amounts of data are exchanged between vehicles, with the infrastructure or with cloud services [34, 35].

39.5 Automated & Autonomous Vehicles and Their Infrastructure

Highly automated and later autonomous vehicles will change the automobile industry. In a structure-changing manner, as we know it from, for example, electronic commerce, we will see the corresponding changes from a market penetration exceeding approximately 10%. The proportion of online purchases expressed as a percentage of total purchases in Germany in 2015 amounted to approximately 11.5% [36]. The repercussions on the retail trade are considerable. It is to be expected that the automobile industry will soon feel the effects of highly automated and autonomous driving and that this will cause structural changes shortly after 2020. These disruptive effects of automated and autonomous driving in the automobile industry will further be exacerbated by additional megatrends:

- The development towards electric vehicles is a trend change for the established automobile industry, whose consequences are currently not foreseeable. Tesla has proven that many customers in the high price bracket are willing to purchase electric vehicles, regardless of the fact that electric vehicles are afflicted with many uncertainties.
- A further megatrend, which can alter the changes in the automobile industry, results from the so-called "share-economy". Enterprises such as, for example, AirBnb or Uber have shown that the so-called share-economy was able to shake the lodging and taxi industries in its foundations. The trend of many young people to see themselves as participants of the so-called share-economy will have an effect on the mobility sector. Offerings such as Drive-Now and Moovel by Daimler or Mobility in Switzerland show that the share-economy is also moving into individual traffic.
- The growing environmental consciousness and, concretely, the aim of more and more people to reduce their carbon footprints, increases the speed of the change.

These three megatrends will intensify the structurally changing effects, which occur through the development towards autonomous vehicles.

39.5.1 The Growing Impact of Information Technology

Automated and autonomous vehicles can, as already indicated, be seen as so-called cyber physical systems. The proportion of information and communication technology to the added-value and the functionality of the vehicle is a deciding factor in automated and autonomous vehicles. In a study by the Fraunhofer Institute for Industrial Engineering and Organization, which was conducted by mandate of the Federal Ministry for Economy and Energy, it is estimated that the market volume of systems for highly automated driving will grow from 4.38 billion euro in 2014 to 17.3 billion euro in 2020 [37]. The valued percentages in this market are spread as follows: 36% for sensor technology, 19% for control units, 18% for software development, 17% for validation and testing (incl. sales margin) and 10% for user interface, maps and back-end services as well as systems integration [37].

The automobile industry has to establish expertise in the information and communications technology at the same high level as in the classic competencies, which it built up in over 100 years. Different automobile manufacturers and suppliers, which are affected by precisely these changes, are making great efforts to master this challenge. The absolute figure as well as the relative number of people working on information and communications competencies, above all software development, is rising. Continental, one of the large component suppliers, has already employed more than 10,000 software developers since 2012 [38]. Numerous automobile manufacturers, such as VW, BMW or Daimler and also suppliers such as Bosch or Michelin have established labs in Silicon Valley in order to be closer to the development of information and communication technology. The VW lab is integrated into the campus of Stanford University [39]. Many prototypes of automated and autonomous vehicles were developed in this laboratory in cooperation with the Engineering Department of Stanford University. General Motors works together with Carnegie Mellon University, one of the other hot spots of automated and autonomous driving [40]. Toyota invests a billion dollars in machine learning in universities on the west and east coats of the USA [41]. All of these efforts indicate that the traditional automobile industry and its suppliers have started with the so-called digital transformation. This transformation process is proving to be very difficult when talking to leading personalities from the automobile industry. The further development of vehicles to cyber physical systems is not undisputed with many experienced employees of the automobile industry. The cultural change of companies, which, in the past, produced mechanical products with a few electronics, to move to products for which, in future, software is the deciding component and the metrics of Silicon Valley apply, is a difficult step for traditionally thinking and classically trained engineers. A further reason for resistance is the development from driver to benefit orientation, which is being initiated by autonomous driving. For many traditionally thinking proponents of the automobile industry it is simply not feasible that, in future, not the sporting driver, but a programmed robot has control over the vehicle. The change in the sector is visible: In his speech at the Consumer Electronics Show 2014, Rupert Stadler made clear that digitalization in the automobile industry has top priority

[42]. Numerous CEO's of the automobile industry have followed his example. Today the CES is not only one of the most important fairs for consumer electronics, but also one of the most important automobile fairs.

39.5.2 New Competitors & New Suppliers

The digital transformation of the automobile industry opens, just like every technological change, chances for new suppliers. Above all, the combination of electro-mobility and digitalization motivates people from outside of the industry and start-ups to invest in mobility. Tesla is a well-known example, Faraday [43] is a further automobile manufacturer, which is developing in Silicon Valley. Mobileye, an Israeli high-tech company, which develops camera systems and the corresponding software, among others, delivers central components for automatic and autonomous driving to many traditional automobile manufacturers.

In the vicinity of Stanford University in Silicon Valley not only labs of the traditional automobile industry have been established, but also new players have been created. The most well-known example is Google, which is engaged in autonomous mobility. Google has enticed away numerous people, who worked on autonomous vehicles at Stanford or Carnegie Mellon University, for example Chris Urmson [44]. The next internet giant, which could become active on the automobile market is Apple. There have been rumors to this effect for some time. For these internet giants the development to autonomous driving, or the digitalization of vehicles is an ideal starting point. With their competency in information and communication technology, above all the ability to master complex problems with algorithms, and to utilize new technologies, such as machine learning in any given area, the internet giants are opening up the automobile market from the software side. One cannot say in the year 2016 whether these strategies will ultimately be successful, but they will definitely accelerate the digitalization process and contribute to the structural change in the automobile industry.

39.5.3 New Locations

Silicon Valley has been distinguishing itself for the last few years as the center for the future in the automobile and mobility industry. When talking to insiders of Silicon Valley one has been hearing now for several years "The valley loves mobility". Numerous companies and entrepreneurs are convinced that the increasing digitalization of vehicles, together with mobility platforms on the internet, such as Uber, offers the hard- and software industry in Silicon Valley the chance to penetrate the vehicle and mobility market. The unique mixture of innovation power, entrepreneurship and currently almost unlimited financial means in Silicon Valley, presents a good foundation for penetrating new markets. The simple motto of these new suppliers is "The more software, the more Silicon Valley".

When talking to politicians in Detroit, Munich and Stuttgart, one indeed gets the impression that these traditional locations for the automobile industry are in direct competition with Silicon Valley. For the automobile industry, on the other hand, there are no alternatives to a certain degree to the establishment of at least research and development centers on the west coast. Whether, in future, hundreds or thousands of software developers will program software for automated and autonomous driving for traditional automobile manufacturers in Silicon Valley cannot be predicted at the moment. It is, however, at least a realistic option.

A central aspect in the development of new future-oriented locations for the automobile industry is legislation. Automated and, in any case, autonomous driving requires changes in existing laws. A real competition among legislators can be observed. In the USA, the states California, Nevada, Michigan and Florida have taken the initiative [45]. In Germany, a draft legal bill for autonomous driving was tabled in summer 2016 [46].

39.5.4   From Car Produce to Mobility Provider

For a few years now the mobility landscape has been changing. Car-sharing for example, has been spread for example by Daimler's Car2Go, BMW's Drive-Now, or Audi's Unite [47] and also by vendors such as Mobility in Switzerland. Uber and Lyft, being so-called mobility platforms, are very successful in attacking established taxi companies. Additionally, they are building large customer bases, which can be analyzed for the mobility requirements of these customers. Railway companies such as the German Federal Railway or the Swiss National Railway collect extensive data on the mobility requirements of their customers on their websites (bahnd.de and sbb.ch). Automobile manufacturers are beginning to get increasingly involved in this market. Daimler has consolidated its mobility platform in Moovel [48] and plans to buy up taxi companies across Europe [49]. Daimler already participates in Mytaxi. Moreover, there are cooperations with German Federal Railways [50]. General Motors holds interests in Lyft [51]. According to press reports, Uber is negotiating with Daimler as to the purchase of a large number of S class models, which are suitable for autonomous driving [52]. Railway companies are busy in the sense of strategic early recognition with the effects of autonomous driving. There are indications that mobility platforms will play the central role in reaching so-called "Seamless mobility", i. e. optimal connection of different means of transportation. Autonomous automobile mobility will be an important contribution to the "Transportation chain". In view of this background, tests with the previously mentioned road-trains or the so-called "Last-mile-vehicles", which are similar to the Google vehicles, must be seen as a contribution to future mobility. In this view, automobile manufacturers should rethink their position in the transportation chain. Examples from other sectors, such as retail trade or the travel industry show that the companies, or platforms, who have customer contacts and customer data will ultimately determine which vendors under which conditions will be used in future, and who are able to set up digital ecosystems. In any case, it is becoming apparent that the requirements of the young generation, the so-called digital natives, will change the understanding of mobility.

39.6 Outlook: the First Steps on a Long Journey

Automated and autonomous vehicles are cyber physical systems, i.e. the mechanical components are enhanced by extensive information and communication technology. This means that in research and development, and also in the maintenance of the vehicles in future extensive competencies in information and communication technology will be required.

In view of this, the automobile industry and the entire mobility sector are facing a major upheaval. Software, whether it be in the car itself, or as a mobility platform, will become a, perhaps even the deciding, factor in competition. For the traditional manufacturers and component vendors, this represents a major challenge against this background of digital transformation.

The further development of vehicles primarily controlled by humans to automated and ultimately autonomous vehicles is unstoppable and offers numerous opportunities for economy and society. The inherent dangers must be extensively and openly discussed in political and social arenas.

At present, we still cannot predict how quickly or when autonomous vehicles will be available on the market, reach greater market penetration and start the disruptive process of change in the mobility sector. There are currently already automated vehicles on the market. The structure change has already started. Mobility vendors, which are unable to develop their core competencies will face great, perhaps existential problems. It seems clear today that stakeholders in the ecosystem "Mobility" will have to concern themselves with the digital transformation, in the sense of the Chinese philosopher Confucius, who said: "Every journey starts with the first step".

References

1. ZEIT Online, [Online]. Available: http://www.zeit.de/mobilitaet/2016-04/automobilindustrie-digitalisierung-elektromobilitaet-autonomes-fahren-tesla-wandel. [Accessed 17 08 2016].
2. YouTube, Audi AG, [Online]. Available: https://www.youtube.com/watch?v=eOYsI1cqUrw. [Accessed 16 08 2016].
3. Google Inc., [Online]. Available: https://www.google.com/selfdrivingcar/. [Accessed 17 08 2016].
4. YouTube, [Online]. Available: https://www.youtube.com/watch?v=UgNhYGAgmZo. [Accessed 17 08 2016].
5. FAZ, [Online]. Available: http://www.faz.net/aktuell/finanzen/aktien/teslas-gescheiterter-versuch-des-autonomen-fahrens-14344126.html. [Accessed 17 08 2016].
6. Societe of Auto Engineers, [Online]. Available: http://www.sae.org/misc/pdfs/automated_driving.pdf. [Accessed 22 08 2016].

7. Bundesministerium für Verkehr und digitale Infrastruktur, [Online]. Available: http://www.bmvi.de/DE/VerkehrUndMobilitaet/DigitalUndMobil/AutomatisiertesFahren/automatisiertes-fahren_node.html. [Accessed 22 08 2016].
8. NHTSA, [Online]. Available: http://www.nhtsa.gov/About+NHTSA/Press+Releases/U.S.+Department+of+Transportation+Releases+Policy+on+Automated+Vehicle+Development. [Accessed 17 08 2016].
9. Audi USA, [Online]. Available: https://www.audiusa.com/newsroom/news/press-releases/2015/01/550-mile-piloted-drive-from-silicon-valley-to-las-vegas. [Accessed 17 08 2016].
10. Newatlas, [Online]. Available: http://newatlas.com/delphi-drive-completed/36859/. [Accessed 17 08 2016].
11. M. S. Research, "Autonomous Cars – Self-Driving the New Auto Industry Paradigm," 2013. [Online]. Available: http://orfe.princeton.edu/~alaink/SmartDrivingCars/PDFs/Nov2013MORGAN-STANLEY-BLUE-PAPER-AUTONOMOUS-CARS%EF%BC%9A-SELF-DRIVING-THE-NEW-AUTO-INDUSTRY-PARADIGM.pdf. [Accessed 17 08 2016].
12. FAZ, [Online]. Available: http://www.faz.net/aktuell/wirtschaft/julian-nida-ruemelin-im-interview-ueber-kuenstliche-intelligenz-14084351-p2.html. [Accessed 17 08 2016].
13. ZDF, [Online]. Available: https://www.facebook.com/aspekte.kultur/videos/vb.117455221614291/1332960416730426/?type=2&theater. [Accessed 17 08 2016].
14. U.S. Senate Comitee, [Online]. Available: http://www.commerce.senate.gov/public/index.cfm/2016/3/hands-off-the-future-of-self-driving-cars. [Accessed 17 08 2016].
15. Bundesministerium für Verkehr und digitale Infrastruktur, [Online]. Available: http://www.bmvi.de/DE/VerkehrUndMobilitaet/DigitalUndMobil/AutomatisiertesFahren/automatisiertes-fahren_node.html. [Accessed 17 08 2016].
16. DARPA, [Online]. Available: http://archive.darpa.mil/grandchallenge/. [Accessed 17 08 2016].
17. FAZ, [Online]. Available: http://www.faz.net/aktuell/gesellschaft/who-statistik-1-2-millionen-verkehrstote-weltweit-12114595.html. [Accessed 17 08 2016].
18. Volkswagen AG, [Online]. Available: http://www.volkswagenag.com/content/vwcorp/info_center/de/themes/2016/04/Guetertransport_der_Zukunft.html. [Accessed 17 08 2016].
19. Daimler, [Online]. Available: https://www.daimler.com/innovation/autonomes-fahren/mercedes-benz-future-truck.html. [Accessed 17 08 2016].
20. The Washington Post, [Online]. Available: www.washingtonpost.com/news/the-switch/wp/2015/06/22/google-didnt-lead-the-self-driving-vehicle-revolution-john-deere-did/. [Accessed 16 08 2016].
21. ABC, [Online]. Available: http://www.abc.net.au/news/2015-10-18/rio-tinto-opens-worlds-first-automated-mine/6863814. [Accessed 17 08 2016].
22. Versicherungsjournal, [Online]. Available: http://www.versicherungsjournal.de/versicherungen-und-finanzen/die-haeufigsten-ursachen-von-schweren-verkehrsunfaellen-126342.php. [Accessed 17 08 2016].
23. Handelszeitung, [Online]. Available: http://www.handelszeitung.ch/unternehmen/rupert-stadler-wir-muessen-audi-neu-erfinden-1014060. [Accessed 17 08 2016].
24. Frauenhofer-Institut, [Online]. Available: https://blog.iao.fraunhofer.de/images/blog/studie-value_of_time.pdf. [Accessed 17 08 2016].
25. YouTube, [Online]. Available: https://www.youtube.com/watch?v=CqSDWoAhvLU. [Accessed 17 08 2016].
26. Audi AG, [Online]. Available: http://audi-urban-future-initiative.com/. [Accessed 17 08 2016].
27. The Boston Globe, [Online]. Available: http://www.betaboston.com/news/2015/11/24/this-car-will-park-itself-somerville-audi-prepare-to-test-self-driving-tech/. [Accessed 17 08 2016].
28. J. M. N. K. S. K. D. S. P. S. C. O. O. A. Anderson, Autonomous Vehicle Technology – A Guide for Policymakers 2014, Rand Corporation, 2014.

29. Audi AG.
30. nVIDIA, [Online]. Available: http://www.nvidia.com/object/drive-px.html. [Accessed 17 08 2016].
31. Roland Berger, [Online]. Available: https://www.rolandberger.com/de/Publications/pub_ autonomous_driving.html. [Accessed 17 08 2016].
32. Heise, [Online]. Available: http://www.heise.de/newsticker/meldung/Audi-BMW-und-Daimler-besitzen-nun-offiziell-Nokias-Kartensparte-Here-3032337.html. [Accessed 17 08 2016].
33. Handelsblatt, [Online]. Available: http://www.handelsblatt.com/unternehmen/industrie/ daimler-bmw-und-audi-krempeln-here-um-die-route-wird-neu-berechnet/12814486.html. [Accessed 17 08 2016].
34. Huawei, [Online]. Available: http://www.huawei.com/minisite/5g/img/GSA_the_Road_to_5G. pdf. [Accessed 17 08 2016].
35. CeBIT, [Online]. Available: http://www.cebit.de/en/news-trends/trends/big-data/articles/the-datamobile.xhtml. [Accessed 17 08 2016].
36. statista, [Online]. Available: http://de.statista.com/statistik/daten/studie/201859/umfrage/anteil-des-e-commerce-am-einzelhandelsumsatz/. [Accessed 17 08 2016].
37. Frauenhofer-Institut, [Online]. Available: http://www.bmwi.de/BMWi/Redaktion/PDF/H/ hochautomatisiertes-fahren-auf-autobahnen,property=pdf,bereich=bmwi2012,sprache=de, rwb=true.pdfS. 358. [Accessed 17 08 2016].
38. Continental, [Online]. Available: http://www.continental-corporation.com/www/presseportal_ com_de/themen/pressemitteilungen/3_automotive_group/interior/press_releases/pr_2012_03_ 15_software_de.html. [Accessed 17 08 2016].
39. Stanford University, [Online]. Available: http://web.stanford.edu/group/vail/. [Accessed 17 08 2016].
40. General Motors, [Online]. Available: http://gm.web.cmu.edu/. [Accessed 17 08 2016].
41. Digital Trends, [Online]. Available: http://www.digitaltrends.com/cars/toyota-invests-in-ai-robotics-research/. [Accessed 17 08 2016].
42. YouTube, Audi AG, [Online]. Available: https://www.youtube.com/watch?v=1YEWyZCqJNI. [Accessed 17 08 2016].
43. Faraday Future, [Online]. Available: http://www.ff.com/. [Accessed 17 08 2016].
44. TED Inc., [Online]. Available: https://www.ted.com/talks/chris_urmson_how_a_driverless_ car_sees_the_road?language=d. [Accessed 17 08 2016].
45. Stanford University, [Online]. Available: http://cyberlaw.stanford.edu/wiki/index.php/ Automated_Driving:_Legislative_and_Regulatory_Action. [Accessed 17 08 2016].
46. ZEIT Online, [Online]. Available: http://www.zeit.de/mobilitaet/2016-04/autonomes-fahren-gesetzentwurf-verkehrsrecht-alexander-dobrindt. [Accessed 17 08 2016].
47. Audi AG, [Online]. Available: https://www.audiunite.com/se/service/en_unite.html. [Accessed 17 08 2016].
48. Moovel, [Online]. Available: https://www.moovel.com/en/DE. [Accessed 17 08 2016].
49. Manager Magazin, [Online]. Available: http://www.manager-magazin.de/unternehmen/ autoindustrie/daimlers-mytaxi-fusioniert-mit-taxivermittler-hailo-a-1104802.html. [Accessed 17 08 2016].
50. Flinkster, [Online]. Available: https://www.flinkster.de/. [Accessed 17 08 2016].
51. Manager Magazin, [Online]. Available: http://www.manager-magazin.de/unternehmen/ autoindustrie/zukunftsmobilitaet-gm-steigt-bei-uber-konkurrent-lyft-ein-a-1070431.html. [Accessed 17 08 2016].
52. walstreet online, [Online]. Available: www.wallstreet-online.de/nachricht/8447306-s-klasse-autonom-milliardenauftrag-daimler-uber-forciert-autonomes-fahren. [Accessed 17 08 2016].

Further Reading

53. BMW AG, [Online]. Available: http://www.bmwi.de/BMWi/Redaktion/PDF/H/
    hochautomatisiertes-fahren-auf-autobahnen,property=pdf,bereich=bmwi2012,sprache=de,
    rwb=true.pdfS. S. 358. [Accessed 17 08 2016].

Hub Airport 4.0 – How Frankfurt Airport Uses Predictive Analytics to Enhance Customer Experience and Drive Operational Excellence

40

Rolf Felkel, Dieter Steinmann, and Frank Follert

Abstract

In this article, an overview is given of several recent projects at Frankfurt airport that broke new ground by using predictive analytics and adopting innovative approaches to tackle commercial and hub specific operational challenges with big data analytics. The first exemplary project focused on the design and implementation of a comprehensive passenger flow management solution, which resulted in reduced waiting times leading to significantly increased customer satisfaction. Furthermore, the Smart Data Lab concept is presented, an agile approach to investigate business opportunities with predictive analytics which has been successfully applied to various topics such as recognizing trends in retail revenues.

40.1 Introduction

With more than 61 mi. passengers in 2015, Frankfurt Airport is Germany's largest airport and a leading international traffic hub in the heart of Europe. At Frankfurt Airport, passenger demand has been growing incessantly over the past decades, pushing the capacity utilization of the airport infrastructure, such as security checkpoints and passport control, towards design limits. Currently, a major expansion program is in progress, including the

R. Felkel (✉) · D. Steinmann · F. Follert
Fraport AG
Frankfurt on the Main, Germany
e-mail: r.felkel@fraport.de

D. Steinmann
e-mail: d.steinmann@fraport.de

F. Follert
e-mail: f.follert@fraport.de

© Springer-Verlag GmbH Germany 2018
C. Linnhoff-Popien et al. (eds.), *Digital Marketplaces Unleashed*,
https://doi.org/10.1007/978-3-662-49275-8_40

construction of a new terminal. In parallel, latest advancements in technology are being implemented to support airport operations and to provide the passengers with a great travel experience.

In this context, Big Data technologies, and most notably predictive analytics, are a key success factor to enable Fraport, owner and operator of Frankfurt Airport,

- to continuously improve operational processes,
- to obtain a sound basis for business decisions, and
- to increase customer satisfaction.

Based on its integrated business model, Fraport is in the unique position to correlate and integrate data from various business domains such as flight data, ground handling data, and retail data and passenger data. This exclusive source is subsequently used to obtain new insights that serve as a basis for deriving consequential and adequate action strategies.

40.2 Passenger Flow Analysis

Smallest possible waiting times, e. g. at security checkpoints, are a critical factor for passenger satisfaction. In order to minimize waiting times, Fraport developed an integral strategy for advanced passenger flow management. It is based on the fact that the waiting time at a specific process point (such as security checkpoints or border control) is predominantly determined by the capacity, in terms of throughput, of the process point as well as the number of passengers appearing at the process point in a specific time frame. Core strategy of the selected approach is to continuously balance the effective throughput capacity and current passenger demand. Implementation of this procedural method is realized by either adapting the capacity to the expected demand or by redirecting the demand to process points with capacity available. This presupposes to permanently obtain an overview of the current passenger situation in the terminals as well as to predict its future development over the next hours – especially in terms of the demand at the various process points. From a conceptual point of view, Fraport's approach to passenger flow management comprises three consecutive steps:

The first step is to measure the passenger flow through the terminal at multiple process points. For this purpose, data is collected by means of various sensor technologies including video based solutions and boarding pass bar code scanners.

In a second step, forecasts of the future demand at different process points are calculated. This process uses sophisticated models to predict the number of passengers on each individual flight as well as the transfer relations between all flights. These are used to compute quantitatively corroborated passenger flow prognostications between different gates, gate areas, concourses and terminals. Finally, advanced technologies such as agent-based behavior simulation are applied to calculate the expected movement of the

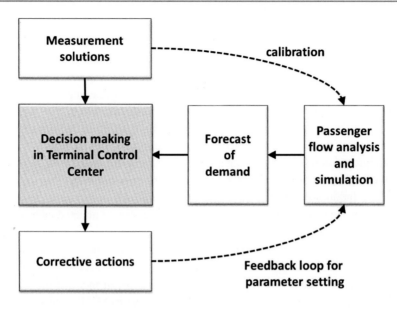

Fig. 40.1 Interaction of Disciplines

passengers through the terminal, allowing conclusions on the future demand at individual process points.

In the third step, the resulting data from the measurement and forecasting functions are taken as a basis for decision making processes, either affecting the staffing of the process points or passenger guidance via dynamic signage for wayfinding in the terminal. Each of the individual steps is described in further detail in the following sections.

For an adequate calculation of the future demand in step two an interaction between the three disciplines measuring, forecasting, and controlling the passenger flow is compulsory, as shown in Fig. 40.1. A more detailed insight in the whole passenger flow management is given in [1].

40.2.1   Measurement of the Passenger Flow

Fraport has been exploring various technologies to measure the actual passenger flow through the terminal building over the last decade, thereby gathering significant expertise in this challenging discipline. While some of the technical solutions that were implemented, tested and evaluated proved to be promising or adequate, others were removed after a few years, since technical developments or changing conditions inside the terminal negatively influenced the results with the technology. Fraport decided to make the experience gained in implementing and utilizing various passenger flow measurement technologies available for airports worldwide by coauthoring a paper on Best Practice on Automated Passenger Flow Measurement Solutions (version 1.1) [2] issued by ACI World[1]. Please see [3] for further information. Finally, two solutions have proven to deliver sufficient quality and reliability for permanent operational use at Frankfurt Airport: the boarding pass scan and a camera based passenger counting solution.

Passengers proceeding through a boarding pass checkpoint scan their 2D barcodes on the boarding passes they are carrying in digital form on their smartphones, or as print-outs. After the validity of the boarding pass was successfully checked, an anonymized excerpt of the data is transferred for further processing. Nevertheless, the majority of passenger flow related information is gathered with a video detection technology. It can provide data on the amount of passengers in a queuing area or at the checkpoint in close to real time. The specific solution used at Frankfurt Airport does not deliver video streams over the local IP network, but provides the results of a counting process conducted internally in the cameras.

The raw data delivered by the boarding pass scanners and the passenger flow measurement cameras are used to calculate several performance indicators, such as waiting times, throughput, arrival profiles[2], or area occupancy. Most of the measured and all of the calculated data is stored in the central data warehouse BIAF (Business Intelligence Architecture Framework) for further processing and analysis. This powerful BI platform supports all operational processes managed by Fraport at Frankfurt Airport and contains detailed historical data from the last decades as well as up to date process information from all relevant processes including ground handling. Consequently, the second step of the integral passenger flow management, calculation of forecasts on the future demand, is also implemented on the BIAF platform.

40.2.2   Forecast of the Passenger Demand at Process Points

The function calculating the passenger demand forecast is the core of the entire passenger flow management solution. It consists of four modules: the data preparation, the forecast of the passenger numbers on board of a flight and the number of transfer passengers between flights, the simulation of the passenger flow inside the terminal building, and finally the visualization of the results on a sophisticated HMI[3].

The data preparation module selects and prepares the historical data for calculating the subsequent forecast. Significant attention to this process step is necessary to achieve high data quality, which is automatically and manually double checked. This process requires diligent quality assurance measures, as inaccuracies at this stage would potentially render the final result inaccurate or incorrect.

---

[1] Airports Council International World.
[2] The arrival profile shows how many passengers typically show up at a process point in a predefined time pattern.
[3] Human Machine Interface.

The forecast module predicts two important variables: the number of passengers on board a future flight, represented by its flight number, as well as the transfer relations between inbound and outbound flights, in terms of how many passengers from an inbound flight A will transfer to an outbound flight B. This is a complex and comprehensive task, given the between 1200 and 1500 passenger flights operated in Frankfurt per day. The forecast takes into account various external influencing factors such as school holidays, public holidays, seasonal effects, and fairs. The transfer relations are of major importance since more than 50% of all passengers in Frankfurt are changing flights in Frankfurt and continue to their final destination. An unprecedented level of forecast precision was achieved by combining multiple statistical methods, including decision-trees, linear regression and multiple imputation.

In order to calculate future passenger demand at specific process points, a powerful simulation platform was erected. It operates on a detailed model of the terminal buildings, including security checkpoints, boarding pass control points, boarding gates as well as the corridors, stairs, elevators and terminal areas connecting them. By combining state-of-the-art simulation technologies, i. e. discrete event processing and agent-based behavior simulation, Fraport was able to achieve an adequate quality of the simulation results required for the subsequent process steps. The event discrete simulation is used to model process points (e. g. security checks). The future capacity of the process points is required as input data for the modelling process and is obtained from the relevant staff planning and scheduling systems. The agent-based simulation models the movement of passengers

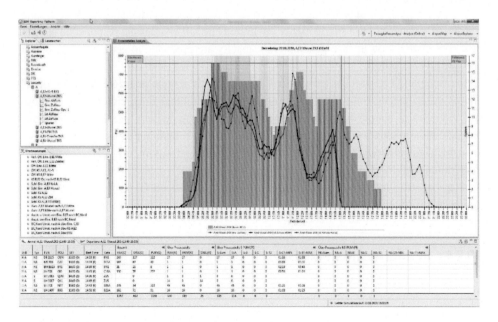

Fig. 40.2 Passenger Flow Analysis (PFA) HMI

through the terminals between the successional process points. For this purpose, probabilities for different connecting paths are assessed in order to represent the complex topology of the terminals, especially in Terminal 1. The processing time needed to simulate the entire airport for one day of operation was gradually reduced to less than two minutes by using an optimized behavior model for the agent-based part of the simulation platform. An integrated feedback loop analyzing discrepancies between the forecast and the subsequently measured passenger flow, is used to continuously improve the parameters used in the highly sophisticated simulation approach. The simulation phase results in detailed predictions on the number of passengers expected to reach a specific process point at a certain point in time in the future. This corresponds to the expected demand at the process points.

Fraport's IT department and experts from the Terminal Control Center (TCC) have jointly specified and developed a powerful HMI on the BIAF platform (see Fig. 40.2 Passenger Flow Analysis (PFA)), depicting the predicted demand and the measured passenger flow information at a process point. The HMI provides decision makers in the TCC with all information they need to efficiently manage the complex passenger flow at Frankfurt Airport, including the number of connecting passengers between flights and the corresponding connection times.

40.2.3   Managing the Passenger Flow

As depicted in Fig. 40.2, the decision makers in the TCC have access to all relevant information, the measured passenger flows, process point specific demand predictions, and transfer information, via a single highly integrated HMI. It enables the responsible staff to take corrective action in case demand and capacity are predicted to get out of balance at specific process points.

In principle, TCC staff has two options to tackle imminent imbalances. First, personnel can be instructed to move from one process point to another or to either open or close specific lanes at checkpoints. Second, passengers can be actively guided to alternative but functionally identical process points with sufficient remaining capacity immediately available. This process is implemented via 102 pre-defined wayfinding scenarios through the terminal buildings available to the TCC staff. Whenever a specific scenario is selected, in excess of 100 dynamic signage displays in more than 40 locations provide unambiguous guidance information to passengers.

40.2.4   Results and Next Steps

The innovative passenger flow management solution implemented at Frankfurt Airport has been leading to significant service improvements. Moreover, the data generated in the flow management process can be used on various communication channels to inform passengers as well as so called 'meeters and greeters' on the current situation in the terminals. Users of the Fraport Mobile Passenger App (FRA App) [4, 5] have for instance access to up to date measured queue times at security checkpoints. The same information is presented to passengers inside the terminal via displays. In the future, passenger flow management information and individual guidance instructions may also be integrated with way-finding and indoor navigation solutions in the FRA App.

40.3   Smart Data Lab

Fraport has recently started a new and innovative initiative for investigating new ideas for applying Big Data and predictive analytics to business problems (commercial as well as operational): the Smart Data Lab. In this environment, interdisciplinary teams of data analysts, mathematicians, business process experts, and IT specialists successfully work on clearly delimited business challenges with high relevance in a predefined time frame of several weeks. The most promising results achieved during a Smart Data Lab period will be turned into regular implementation projects in order to thoroughly prepare a sustainable utilization of the findings in daily operations or business.

The following elements were identified as key success factors for the Smart Data Lab:

- it is a mandatory prerequisite to provide the interdisciplinary working groups with unlimited access to all data the company possesses,
- the teams need to be composed adequately,
- the lab has to constitute a protected environment that accepts initial failure as progress towards the best possible solution, and
- a powerful analytic toolset is needed as well as agile working methods.

With regard to the first success factor "unlimited access to all data", Fraport has established two comprehensive centralized BI data repositories (the Business Intelligence Architecture Framework BIAF for operational data and SAP Business Warehouse for administrative/commercial data), which have been collecting relevant business data for many years and keep them available for detailed analysis through various channels and tools. Based on its integrated business model, Fraport owns data from various areas of the airport business' value added chain, including flight data, ground handling data, passenger flow data, retail data etc. It is essential that the Smart Data Lab team has access to all data across business units, as this allows for the identification and investigation of interrelations between different data sets and the related business processes.

The second key success factor is related to the best possible composition of the interdisciplinary teams. Besides experts in data analytics, the team needs to comprise representatives with detailed knowledge of the business processes related to the operational problem under investigation, such as business analysts and process experts. Moreover, the ICT department provides technical and methodical assistance – especially concerning the data repositories and the available tools.

Thirdly, it is important that the team is able to operate in a protected and non-constraining environment. This allows for the formulation of new hypotheses unpersuaded by typical limiting factors such as the previously established approach or political influences. Nothing is stigmatized as off-limits and the teams can use the available data to evaluate any correlation that appears constructive. Moreover, it is very important that failure is an accepted outcome of the investigation phase. The earlier an approach fails, the better, since it is then more likely that the team is able to find a better approach towards the right answer in the remaining available time.

In addition, the industry-leading BIAF platform provides a powerful toolset for customized analysis and reporting. One of the modules is a visual analytics tool that enables the user to display and explore georeferenced data as shown in Fig. 40.3. A typical exemplary application based on these capabilities is a visual analysis of the distribution of retail sales in different terminal areas. With the help of this tool set, data analysts can drill down into data sets in close to real time in order to identify superordinate patterns and trends.

Finally, the working methods in the Smart Data Lab follow agile principles, e. g. by using a Kanban board to illustrate tasks and progress and by holding short daily (standup) meetings to facilitate team communication and to scrutinize progress. Fraport has been making repeated use of the Smart Data Lab and achieved remarkable results. Some examples are presented in the following subsections.

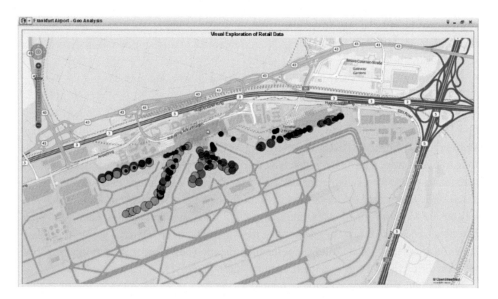

Fig. 40.3 Visual Analytics

40.3.1   Recognizing Trends in Retail

Today, non-aviation revenues contribute significantly to the overall financial success of an airport. An important source of non-aviation revenue is retail, where airport operators typically earn a share of the retail revenues of the stores in the terminal buildings as a concession fee.

Against this background, the Smart Data Lab was tasked to derive a method to forecast retail revenues and to identify deviations from earlier predictions. Based on a statistical analysis of historical data, it was found that the overall retail revenue can be predicted with high confidence based on only two parameters: number of passengers and time.

In order to detect deviations from the predicted trend, a control chart was developed which illustrates the deviation of the predicted retail revenue from the actual revenue over time. It includes lower and upper boundaries for the deviations which trigger a warning whenever they are crossed. These warnings subsequently lead to a root cause analysis of the deviation and enable the airport management to take corresponding actions.

40.3.2   Optimization of Aircraft Positioning

The Smart Data Lab recently investigated the impact of aircraft stand allocation on retail revenue. Previous analysis had exposed that different passenger groups, e. g. passengers to certain destinations, have different shopping preferences and behaviors. The resultant challenge for the Smart Data Lab was then to analyze how the planned allocation of aircraft to stands on the aprons – which in turn, at least to a large extent, determines the path of the passengers through the terminals – can influence retail revenue.

As a first step, a rather simple model only relying on gate information was considered, but this model had limited explanatory power only. Consequently, as a second step, a multivariate model taking into account gate, airline, destination, waiting time, dwelling time and other parameters was implemented and led to significant results. Based on these insights, a prototype was developed which allows to simulate effect on retail revenues of holistic positioning plans. Furthermore, the prototype is able to calculate the opportunity cost of suboptimal positioning plans and to suggest 'retail-optimized' positions for connecting flights.

40.3.3   Improvement of Estimated In-Block Time

Efficient planning of the ground handling activities at an airport requires precise estimations of the arrival times for incoming aircraft. An aircraft arriving at the parking position before the ground handing crew arrives on site may lead to fines to be paid by the ground handling department to the aircraft operator. On the other hand, if the aircraft arrives on stand a long time after the ground handling crew, they will be idle for some time, leading to inefficient resource allocation.

Currently, the time stamp "Ten Minutes Out" (TMO), i. e. the aircraft is expected to land (touch down) in ten minutes, is used as a major triggering milestone for ground handling operations. By definition, TMO does not take into account the taxi-in process of the aircraft from vacating the landing runway to the parking position. In the past, the taxi-in time was taken from a fixed tabulation providing standard taxi times based on the planned runway and the parking position only.

A Smart Data Lab project team analyzed the current situation and discovered that the majority of asynchronous arrivals of aircraft and ground handling crews at parking positions was due to unexpected high variations of the actual taxi-in times from the standard taxi time. The main causes of this effect are comprehensible with common sense: the traffic at Frankfurt Airport has been growing significantly over the last decade and the complexity in surface traffic management has been increasing simultaneously and especially since the new runway 25 R/07 L opened in 2011 leading to converging traffic flows on the airport surface. However, the majority of changes in the taxi route leading to unexpected taxi-in times is caused by runway changes during final approach, i. e. after TMO. The actual landing runway has a significant effect on the expected taxi time as the distances from the different landing runways to the allocated parking position may be very different.

An alternative and promising time stamp in the aircraft arrival process is the "Estimated In-Block Time" (EIBT) – the estimated time an arriving aircraft reaches its aircraft type specific stopping point on the parking position – including the taxi-in process. A high quality EIBT available 15 or 20 min prior to the real in-blocks event would be very helpful, since it would provide the ground handling crews with unprecedented planning reliability. Hence, the Smart Data Lab accepted the challenge to improve the EIBT calculation in a time range of approx. 15 min in advance of the actual event. As a first step, the team introduced a new time stamp called '15 min before On Block'(EIBT-15). In order to establish and to calibrate an adequate calculation model delivering the new time stamp in sufficiently high quality, the interdisciplinary working group used historical aircraft surveillance data of the final approach and the taxi-in phase.

Finally, the Smart Data Lab project team was also able to quantify the gain in accuracy of the new EIBT-15 time stamp compared to the currently used TMO plus fixed taxi-in time. Based on this information, the business case of a system wide change from TMO to EIBT-15 can be calculated: while the estimated gain in efficiency and reduction of penalties are the profits, CAPEX[4] and OPEX[5] for the change of various IT systems and procedures constitute the costs.

---

[4] Capital Expenditure.
[5] Operational Expenditure.

This example reflects the rationale behind the Smart Data Lab: the lab itself can demonstrate a possible improvement based on statistical information. Nevertheless, the decision to use this improvement in daily business can only be made based on a positive business case for Fraport AG as a whole, taking into account all cost and benefits.

40.4   Summary

The example of the Passenger Flow Analysis shows the potentials of predictive analytics for the operational, and indirectly also the commercial, further improvement of Frankfurt Airport. Based on this insight, Fraport AG has developed the organizational and methodical approach of the Smart Data Lab. It aims at exploring comparable potentials systematically all across the Fraport business units. The examples dealing with airport retail revenue trends and improvements by optimal aircraft positioning, and also the improved ground handling efficiency due to the implementation of EIBT-15, show how flexibly predictive analytics can be applied to various business scenarios – always assuming that a sound basis of historical data is available and powerful tools exist to explore them.

Fraport AG will reiterate the Smart Data Lab initiative annually and with the clear objective to improve the business step by step making Frankfurt Airport a Hub Airport 4.0.

References

1. R. Felkel and D. Klann, "Comprehensive passenger flow management at Frankfirt Airport," *Journal of Airport Management,* vol. 6, no. 2, pp. 107–124, 2012.
2. ACI World Airport IT Standing Committee, "Best Practice on Automated Passenger Flow Measurement Solutions," 27 August 2015. [Online]. Available: http://www.aci.aero/media/2c9abef1-ae58-40ed-9d33-4bdd925aee89/NGQA3Q/About%20ACI/Priorities/Facilitation/Best-Practice-on-Automated-Passenger-Flow-Measurement-Solutions.pdf.
3. C. Mayer, R. Felkel and K. Peterson, "Best practice on automated passenger flow measurement solutions," *Journal of Airport Management,* vol. 9, no. 2, pp. 144–153, Winter 2014–15.
4. "Google Play – FRA App," Goolge, [Online]. Available: https://play.google.com/store/apps/details?id=com.infsoft.android.fraapp&hl=de. [Accessed 09 08 2016].
5. "iTunes AppStore – FRA App," Apple, [Online]. Available: https://itunes.apple.com/de/app/frankfurt-airport-fra-airport/id453191399?mt=8. [Accessed 09 08 2016].

Part X
Mobility Services

Preface: Beyond the Hood: the Development of Mobility Services in the Mobile Internet

Markus Heyn

Abstract

It won't only be the engine that changes the mobility of tomorrow. Where in the past, the focus of attention in automotive development was on the technology under the hood, today it is much more on road traffic as a whole. Traffic that is regulated by odd and even numbered days both in Paris and in Beijing. Traffic that moves at a speed of 19 kilometers per hour in London and five in Mumbai. Yet not only is the volume of traffic rising. Higher mobility costs and an increasing shortage of parking space, particularly in urban areas, have resulted in a change in values away from car ownership and towards convenient use when needed. Young people are growing ever less interested in having their own car; the option of having access to one is enough. The motto is: Mobility without restrictions. An ever larger range of mobility services is available to this target group today. Besides standard car-sharing services, it is possible to rent bicycles in large cities, ride-sharing services are becoming ever more appealing, and the public transportation network is increasingly being supplemented by other modes of transport. For instance, China aims to build an expected 170 new local transportation systems such as subways and suburban trains by 2030. In addition, connectivity and the mobile internet have a decisive influence on mobility. Today, people have a high affinity with the use of web-based services. They take their smartphone with them everywhere and the next item of information is just a finger tap away. But not only information can be obtained on mobile devices: whether for search, bookings, payments, or reviews – today, a simple tap of an index finger on a smartphone display is enough to operate and manage end-to-end processes and functionalities.

All this shows that automotive manufacturers and suppliers must rethink mobility in big cities and beyond. Bosch sees the electrification of the powertrain and the au-

M. Heyn (✉)
BOSCH
Gerlingen, Germany

© Springer-Verlag GmbH Germany 2018
C. Linnhoff-Popien et al. (eds.), *Digital Marketplaces Unleashed*,
https://doi.org/10.1007/978-3-662-49275-8_41

tomation and connectivity of driving as the greatest challenges and transformations in the development of the mobility solutions of tomorrow. These three development paths make individual mobility resource-conserving and appealing. What's more, they complement each other: it makes driving more relaxing to know that you can go online to find and book not only the nearest free parking space but also the nearest free charge spot. And automated driving is even safer if vehicles warn each other of blind junctions or the tail end of a traffic jam. Through the development of the internet and mobile applications, connectivity opens up numerous new possibilities. Today, control unit data and driving profiles are recorded and transmitted to digital platforms. Terms such as fleet management and mobility portals are used in everyday language. The internet is already in cars, and cars are on the internet. New mobility services are being created as independent ecosystems on digital platforms. They bring together those offering mobility and those seeking it in a kind of marketplace, combining data from both sides to form innovative value-added services through new mobile access options. This means that on the one hand mobility services offer new products that go beyond the car, while on the other they attract new customers – since in the future these might be all road users. The future aim is therefore not only to make the technology under the hood more efficient, convenient, and safe but to organize traffic as a whole so that it is individual, connected, and intermodal.

41.1 Parking Spaces are Going Online

Typically, any trip in a car ends up at a parking space. Of course, the driver has to find one first. In downtown areas, the search for parking spaces is responsible for roughly one-third of traffic. Pressure on parking is growing, and curbside spaces are especially rare. Searching for an empty parking space is inconvenient, and usually time-consuming and stressful. No wonder that looking for a parking space ranks in tenth place of the greatest worries of German car drivers[1] and that, according to the online portal Statista, 87 % of drivers are interested in solutions that make it easier to find parking. That is why web-based parking services have gained considerably in importance in recent years. With what is referred to as "cellphone parking," drivers get a parking ticket from a machine when they drive into the parking lot but without paying. When they leave the parking lot, they send a text message with the parking number shown on their parking ticket to a number also shown on the ticket. The parking charges are then either deducted from their prepaid card or debited from their cellphone bill.

But even when cellphone parking, driver still have to find a parking space. On average people take ten minutes and cover around 4.5 km when looking for somewhere to park,

---

[1] GfK Verein (2014): Sorgen der Autofahrer in Deutschland im Jahr 2014, http://de.statista.com/statistik/daten/studie/431413/umfrage/sorgen-der-autofahrer-in-deutschland/.

resulting in vehicle costs of 1.35 € per search and CO_2 emissions of 1.3 kg per km^2. Connectivity now makes it possible for vehicles themselves to find a free curbside parking space. With community-based parking, the car becomes a driving parking sensor in the Internet of Things (IoT). It detects parking spaces on the side of the road with the sensors of its parking assistant. In Germany, the most common assistance systems in modern cars are parking assistants. According to a Bosch evaluation of the 2014 vehicle registration statistics, of the nearly three million cars that were registered that year, half of them (52 %) feature just such a system. The picture is fairly similar in other countries: in Belgium and the Netherlands, half of all new cars in 2014 (50 %) come equipped with a parking assistant. In the U.K., the figure is 19 %. Vehicles fitted with a parking assistant can recognize curbside spaces between parked cars as they drive past. The information is sent to the respective vehicle manufacturer by means of a communication interface and then forwarded in anonymized form to a cloud. Here, an intelligent process pools the data from all participating vehicles independently from thein brands to generate a digital parking map that is delivered back to the vehicle manufacturers. They in turn can share the map with all of their cars that are connected to the internet, for example via the navigation system. Drivers can then navigate straight to an available parking space. The search for a parking space could conceivably also be made less stressful by means of a mobile app. But the fact that not every curbside gap a car detects and reports automatically qualifies as a valid parking spot makes preparing the data a challenge. The gap could just as easily be a driveway, a bus stop, or a no-parking zone. Data mining methods can be used to identify gaps next to the curb unequivocally as parking spaces. Should several vehicles repeatedly report a curbside gap as unoccupied, it is most likely not a valid parking space. Accordingly, these gaps are then not labeled as parking spaces on the digital parking map. The more vehicles that participate in community-based parking, the more accurate and more comprehensive the service is. Once a certain number of users are participating, the digital finder for parking spaces can even provide information on a space's length and width. This makes it possible to search for spaces that fit a specific vehicle, for instance a motorhome or compact car, in addition to the general benefit of considerably shortening the overall search for a parking space and lessening its environmental impact in cities. To be able to offer the service throughout Germany, it is necessary to work with multiple automakers. That is why community-based parking was set up to be an open service platform in which multiple vehicle manufacturers can participate at the same time. The platform brings together a large number of participants and combines an offline parking offering with an innovative online service.

Another way of ending what is at times a nerve-wracking search for an empty parking space, especially in city centers, is an active parking lot management. This involves an intelligent technology detecting and reporting how many and which parking spaces are empty in a city center. These solutions are based on micromechanical components that are web-enabled and installed in special occupancy sensors, which are subsequently discreetly

---

[2] APCOA PARKING Deutschland (2013): APCOA PARKING Study 2013.

placed in parking areas. The occupancy sensors are barely larger than a CD in terms of circumference and measure around three centimeters in height. They are installed in parking garages and on-street parking spaces, either on or in the asphalt, as desired. Since they are battery-powered and communicate using radio, there is no complicated laying of cables. The sensors check at regular intervals whether a parking space is occupied or not. Using an internet connection, they relay the securely encrypted information to a cloud. There, a real-time parking map of all free and occupied spaces is created that can be accessed with the app or on the internet. Meta-information on each parking space is available as well, including whether it is a space reserved for families, women, or the disabled, what the parking time costs, and if a charge spot for electric vehicles is available. Drivers can have themselves guided straight to the parking space by a smartphone app. More comprehensive services are also possible, such as a payment function by app. Yet active parking lot management has further advantages for parking lot operators, particularly as it can further improve the occupancy rate of heavily used parking spaces. The key to this is intelligent data evaluation. A web portal provides parking lot operators with a clear overview of which parking spaces were occupied by how many vehicles and when. During peak times, this information can direct drivers to spaces that are less frequently occupied, for example. In the Stuttgart region, Bosch is conducting further development work on active parking lot management in a pilot project with the Verband Region Stuttgart. The main idea behind it is that if drivers know they can find a free park-and-ride space, they will be more willing to use the city trains. Sensors fitted in 15 park-and-ride facilities along two city train lines will detect whether parking spaces are available or occupied. They will report this up-to-the-minute information in real time to the Stuttgart transportation authority, VVS, which will make it available through its app and website. Eleven towns and municipalities in the northeast of the Stuttgart region have declared their willingness to support the pilot project. They will provide internet access and power connections for what are mostly municipal park-and-ride facilities. The Verband Region Stuttgart is supporting this project with a grant from the "Sustainable Model Region Stuttgart" state program.

41.2 Intermodality Made Easy: Connected Mobility is the Better Mobility

Many people, particularly in big cities, use more than one modes of transportation to get from A to B. They use buses, trams, trains, and car-sharing – depending on whatever is suitable for their current need for mobility, what times these run, and what the current traffic situation is like. At times it has to be fast, at times comfortable, and at times particularly affordable. This is where integrated and digital mobility platforms come into play. Users can first obtain information on door-to-door mobility chains, then reserve or book them and also pay for them. Examples include a Daimler subsidiary's moovel and Deutsche Bahn's Qixxit. These apps see themselves as intermodal travel planners and intermediaries between providers and users of mobility services. Users enter the starting point and destination into the apps, then select the combination they personally prefer from a list of suitable means of transport. Separate contracts are concluded between the user and the providers of the relevant services. "Smile – einfach mobil" is an integrated mobility platform that promises a broader, more strongly integrated and more flexible range. It was developed in a joint project between the Austrian Federal Railways, Wiener Stadtwerken, and further participants. Smile intends to provide users with a comprehensive mobility range that they can use to conveniently combine mobility with public transportation services. A special focus is placed on integrating electro mobility services, such as electro car-sharing, and using public charging infrastructure for electric vehicles used by their owners[3]. A new mobility assistant in the greater Stuttgart area is also acting on the idea of the innovative, intermodal connectivity of individual methods of transportation. It enables drivers to navigate routes using different modes of transportation, including bikes, trams and trains, buses, and sharing offers. It takes just one app to plan, book, and pay for a journey involving different modes of transportation. The mobility assistant for Stuttgart is supplied with real-time data from a big data platform. It accompanies road users live via an app and takes account of any disturbances or obstacles, for example traffic jams or train delays. In such cases, it suggests better ways of reaching the destination more quickly and conveniently. Drivers can also use the assistant to book parking spaces. No matter the modes of transportation, at the end of the month the user receives one easy-to-read bill that covers all the mobility services used. In addition, the system has an interface and provides support to the Stuttgart region's traffic management authority. For example, the assistant can be fed route recommendations that help manage traffic effectively and thus improve the traffic situation in the Stuttgart metropolitan area. Led by Bosch, the mobility assistant project is being implemented together with other urban mobility companies. Bosch is creating the central service platform, the intermodal navigation system, and the smartphone app used to operate the mobility assistant.

For individual mobility to become intermodal mobility, the relevant solutions have to be simple to use. The aim must be to keep barriers to registration, use, and billing as low as possible. In this regard, there is room for future improvements, for instance to simplify mobile access to digital mobility services. In Germany alone, the constantly growing sharing economy currently comprises around 150 services, covering everything from cars to bikes and scooters. New services are being added every year, such as Coup, the eScooter sharing service that Bosch first put on the market in Berlin. But at present, every sharing provider has its own registration procedure, some of them quite complicated. Often, a user's driving license has to be physically validated for each service. This is yet another area where new digital services can help: by considerably simplifying registration processes and thus access to sharing services. The idea is to implement simple, fast, and transparent central registration as a digital "master key" for the world of mobility. This

---

[3] Adam, S. und Meyer M. (2015): Integration der Kundenperspektive als Basis für Bedarfsorientierung und Weiterentwicklung integrierter Mobilitätsplattformen, In: C. Linnhoff-Popien et al. (editors): Marktplätze im Umbruch, p. 589–601.

would make the filling in of various forms and the multiple validation of the required documents a thing of the past. Once registered, users would have access to a whole range of sharing offers, including ones that they might not have heard of before. One look at a central app would suffice: it would take just one click to book any of the vehicles, bikes, and scooters available. Not only users but mobility services, too, stand to benefit from this service. Central registration lowers their individual registration process costs; the new service would allow them to attract new customers without themselves conducting complex registration and validation processes. This digital service clearly shows that users and their mobility needs and desires must be the focus of attention in the development of new mobility services. Users' smartphones serve as a universal medium. This is why issues of ergonomics in use, the flexibility of the offers, and the dovetailing of different modes of transportation with efficient data platforms plays a major role in helping intermodal mobility to enrich people's lives. This is why the term "mobile first" is becoming ever more important. In the future, this will no longer stand only for web pages being optimized first and foremost for mobile devices. Instead, it will mean developing digital strategies for services in the internet that primarily use mobile access to customers to create data-based additional value for them.

41.3 Digital Services for the Mobility of Tomorrow

Beyond the topics of parking, sharing offers and intermodal traffic solutions, there are more eco-systems in which a digital offering meets a connected customer in inner-city and suburban locations. Examples of this include smart apps for the charging of electric vehicles, connectivity solutions for trucks and the digitization of workshop appointments.

It is often a problem for drivers of electric vehicles to find a free charge spot. Anyone using an all-electric vehicle knows what it is like to look for one, and the frustration felt when the charge spot chosen is unavailable or first involves going through a complicated procedure to register for the different booking and payment systems. Innovative charging apps that help users to immediately find charge spots and pay with just one click are the solution. Here, too, smartphones are the key: charging apps on the phone allow drivers of electric cars to quickly find available charging stations in their area and then use them simply and conveniently. Working together with various automakers including smart, Mercedes-Benz, and Renault, Bosch offers charging apps along with the backend infrastructure. A major advantage of the Bosch solution is its scope: by 2016 it covered around 3700 – or around 80 % – of the web-enabled, public charge spots in Germany, and additional European countries will later follow. This means that app users can conveniently use the displayed charging stations without the need for cash, and without having to resolve complex technical and contractual issues themselves before doing so. Instead, all they need is a PayPal account and to have completed a one-time registration. Even the payment process is completed from within the app in a convenient and secure fashion. This digital service lays the foundation for bringing together various players such as automakers, charge spot operators, energy providers, retailers, and electric car drivers on a single software platform. Meanwhile, the charging app again places the customer at the center of the digital solution. It is intended to help make electro mobility a little more practical for everyday use throughout Germany: because aside from attractive vehicle offerings, a straightforward recharging procedure plays a critical role in the continued advancement of electro mobility.

Mobility services must not stop at the city limits. Connectivity is thus also a way of making commercial vehicles even more useful and of developing new digital business models both for truck drivers and for fleet operators. Connectivity makes trucks even smarter and connects them with the internet. The hardware this requires is a connectivity control unit – a box that connects the automotive electronics with a cloud. This enables freight forwarding companies to monitor the wear and tear of truck fleets via control units and the internet to assist with planning maintenance and repairs in advance. It is also suitable for the logistics sector. Furthermore, connectivity via the internet can ensure that transported goods are safe, for instance through an eCall solution or trailer monitoring with satellite positioning. Rest areas for truckers along freeways are often hopelessly overfilled – especially at night. That is also when the risk of theft increases. Bosch offers a new solution for this as well: the online reservation of secure truck parking spaces at rest areas along the freeway via a smartphone app. Whenever truck drivers are looking to park, their truck sends its location data and a parking request to the system. This finds a nearby parking space and sends the details directly to the truck's navigation system. These premium parking spaces can be video monitored, too, using camera systems and security control centers that track video footage.

A third example of new mobile services is the appointment at the workshop. How helpful would it be if the vehicle itself knew when it had to go the workshop and the spare parts needed were already in stock when it arrived? There are also digital solutions that generate, analyze, and correlate data to offer customers added value based on their mobile access. Since 2012, customers have been able to register with the Drivelog online portal and use a host of services for their own vehicle. In 2015, the new additional Drivelog Connect module expanded the car driver and workshop portal to include real-time information. A Bluetooth adapter transfers data from the vehicle's OBD interface to the Drivelog mobile app on the driver's smartphone. This gives the driver information on vehicle data, route, fuel economy, mileage, and time, with the details entered into a log book for every journey. A car check function shows the state of the vehicle and any fault signals. If necessary, the driver can then book a service appointment directly and, if desired, automatically transfer the data to the workshop, so that information on the vehicle, fault codes, and the necessary maintenance requirements is immediately available. Furthermore, the program provides feedback on driving style and tips for fuel-efficient driving. Digital communication and data transfer are playing an ever greater role at workshops. The workshop of the future can thus continually monitor the status of customers' vehicles and, if necessary, recommend a repair before a vehicle component stops working. Moreover, the workshop can order spare parts and organize employees' working hours much more effectively. If a customer arrives at the workshop on the agreed date, the fault memory is automatically read and the battery, tire pressure, and chassis geometry checked. But things could be even more convenient in the future: hardly any customers like taking their vehicle to the workshop appointment and either picking it up again in the afternoon or waiting until the repairs are completed. But this is yet another opportunity to put an app at the center of a digitalized business process. First, customers book their appointment via the app, regardless of whether this is for servicing, diagnosis, a repair, or a breakdown service. They state when a driver can collect the vehicle and where, for example from the customer's own home or place of work. If a customer wishes to stay mobile during the workshop appointment, a replacement vehicle is provided. Every step of the work in the workshop is then made transparent via the app. Customers are informed via their smartphone of the work performed, service results, and costs. Once all the work has been completed, a driver takes the vehicle back to the place stated by the customer. This makes the workshop appointment of the future transparent and convenient.

41.4   Technical Requirements for Mobility Services

The digital transformation of business models and increasing connectivity is an opportunity to redesign the mobility of the future and make it customer-centered. This requires software and IT skills on the one hand and expertise in sensor technology for connectivity on the other. New services are being created on the basis of these key technologies. Scalability is a key factor for the success of connected solutions. Scalable infrastructure is thus essential, especially for digital business models. It must be able to be flexibly designed, and it must analyze, evaluate, and correlate corporate, customer, and market data in real time and send the results back to the customer. Like other technology companies in the connected devices arena Bosch has launched its own cloud network for the Internet of Things, the Bosch IoT Cloud. The first cloud is located in Germany in Bosch's own computing center near Stuttgart. The software core of the Bosch IoT Cloud is the company's own IoT Suite. It identifies any objects that are web-enabled, orchestrates the exchange of data, and enables a multitude of services and business models. Big data management allows enormous amounts of data to be analyzed. Rules for automatic decisions can be stored in the Bosch IoT Suite – such as when patterns of wear and tear should be reported and preventive action taken to service machinery.

However, technology alone cannot guarantee the success of digital business models. Security is also an important precondition for customer and user confidence. Functional safety ensures that applications function reliably and that systems are safely deactivated if a fault occurs in one of the components. Data security, meanwhile, is about protecting against unauthorized external access. It is essential to ensure that data is protected against unauthorized use by third parties and that misuse is not possible. Here, Bosch for example relies on a multi-tier approach to both hardware and software so that it can maintain the high level of security it offers today in a future of increasingly connected applications. In the future, secure over-the-air updates will enable increasingly sophisticated functions, for example, but they will also entail potential security risks for which technological protection is required. Finally, data protection is a legal consideration that is defined by laws and regulations. If a mobility service uses the Bosch IoT Cloud, the fundamental legal framework for this is German or European data protection law. Customers and users thus have full transparency and decide for themselves how their data will be used. After all, a significant precondition for the introduction of new services is the sensitive and consistently secure handling of the data mobility services generate.

41.5   The Future Vision of Mobility Services

Vehicle connectivity and mobility services development have only just begun – and that includes for example work on connecting the car with the smart home. For instance, the car's navigation system can instruct the home's heating system to warm up the living room for when the driver gets back. In the future, then, it will not be enough for Bosch as a supplier of technology and services to merely bring greater efficiency, convenience, and safety to components and systems under the hood. Instead, the company is very much looking beyond the hood to solutions for road traffic as a whole. This is where Bosch is finding customers with a wide range of mobility requirements, is deriving ideas and measures for the future, and is developing new technologies and services for a world of changing mobility. The foundation for this is a strategy with defined priorities extending from connected, electrified, and automated mobility through to new mobility services on which all divisions are jointly working on a cross-company basis. However, people's mobility requirements will continue to change in the future; infrastructure, transportation routes, and mobility users will increasingly connect. Consequently, it will also be necessary to develop new mobility services that enable the safe, convenient, and economic transportation of people and goods on land, in the air, and on water. If these digital services and business models are also simple to use and thrill automotive manufacturers, mobility providers, and users, then they will rightly be seen as technology that is invented for life.

Analyzing the Digital Society by Tracking Mobile Customer Devices

42

Lorenz Schauer

Abstract

Nowadays, most people use smartphones or tablets for personal or commercial purposes in their daily life. Such mobile devices are electronic all-rounders equipped with several sensors and communication interfaces, e. g., Wi-Fi and Bluetooth. Both communication systems leak information to the surroundings during operation which can be used for monitoring customers and analyzing their behavior in an area of interest. This article shortly describes techniques for tracking mobile customer devices and identifies potentials and limitations for analyzing the digital society based on mobile tracking data. Both scientific papers and commercial projects are investigated focusing on trends for the digitalization of the retail industry. Furthermore, different start-ups currently working in the field of retail analytics are presented and compared in terms of their unique selling point (usp) and future oriented projects. Overall, this book chapter presents a compact overview of state-of-the art techniques and future works for analyzing the digital society by tracking mobile customer devices.

42.1 Introduction

The ongoing digitalization is not only changing business and marketplaces, it is also changing our complete society. One of the most evident observation of this trend can be made in our life every day, e. g. when we go to work, when we meet friends, or even when we have dinner: people use their smartphones or other modern mobile devices for making business, chatting with friends, buying new products, or reading the newspapers

L. Schauer (✉)
Ludwig-Maximilians-Universität München
Munich, Germany
e-mail: lorenz.schauer@ifi.lmu.de

© Springer-Verlag GmbH Germany 2018
C. Linnhoff-Popien et al. (eds.), *Digital Marketplaces Unleashed*,
https://doi.org/10.1007/978-3-662-49275-8_42

on their way. Hence, the increasing usage of these electronic all-rounders in nearly all situations of today's life is an obvious characteristic of our digital society. Technically, the permanent and ubiquitous connection to data networks plays a key role in this process rendering digital mobile applications and services very powerful. Overall, without Internet, most services are not able to provide full functionality.

Therefore, together with the immense diffusion of smartphones and tablets, the usage of Wi-Fi as state-of-the-art wireless communication standard, has increased dramatically. Wi-Fi infrastructures have been installed in many public spaces and buildings providing Internet access and local services to mobile clients. Both facts lead to a high percentage of Wi-Fi enabled mobile devices which can be used to analyze our digital society by tracking mobile customer devices and without the users' consent or even awareness. The extracted information from such tracking data might be very valuable and helpful for different kind of use cases, such as retail analytics, crowd control, emergency situations, or just commercial purposes. On the other hand, tracking mobile customer devices without asking for users' compliance represents a privacy attack.

This book chapter firstly describes the technical background of tracking mobile devices using Wi-Fi signals which are automatically sent out by any Wi-Fi enabled smartphone, or tablet. Secondly, both scientific and commercial projects are presented and compared using such tracking data for different purposes. Overall, we discover potentials, risks, and limitations of this analyzation technique and focus on trends for the digitalization of the retail industry. In this context, some start-ups are presented and evaluated in terms of their unique selling point (usp) and future oriented projects. The aim of this article is to give a compact overview of state-of-the-art methods nowadays, and how Wi-Fi tracking can be used in the near future, when even more people use more than one device and MAC-Address randomization is integrated in common phones.

42.2 Technical Background

As already mentioned, we firstly give a short description of why and how Wi-Fi tracking can be realized technically. Wireless local area networks, commonly known as Wi-Fi, are standardized in IEEE 802.11 [1]. The communication range varies from about 35 m for indoor to over 100 m for outdoor scenarios. The standard defines three individual frame types:

- Control frames, to support the delivery process of data frames and to manage the medium access
- Data frames, to transport user data for higher layers
- Management frames, to exchange management information for connection establishment and maintenance

For Wi-Fi tracking, only management frames are of interest being involved in the 802.11 network discovery and association process as shown in Fig. 42.1.

From the view of a mobile device, the discovery process can be either passive by just listening on beacon frames which are periodically transmitted by the access point (1) or it can be active by sending out probe request frames (2). The latter is preferred in mobile context, due to lower energy-consumption and shorter discovery time of access points which could come into reach while moving [2].

Hence, Wi-Fi enabled mobile devices periodically perform an IEEE 802.11 active scan, in order to discover available access points in their surroundings more quickly. The scanning interval depends on the used chipset and the Wi-Fi driver, but not on the association status. Our own investigations show that an active scan is performed at least once within two minutes on average for Android and iOS devices. Furthermore, we also found a maximum idle time of less than 5 min where no probe requests were sent out during a 10 h test phase, despite the case that the test device was associated to an access point or not.

Generally, a device starts an active scan by sending out probe requests and listens for probe responses (3). This is done for each channel iteratively. Each probe request frame contains the device specific MAC address of sender and receiver, supported rates, the destination's network name (SSID) and other management information. If the SSID field is left empty, then the probe request addresses all access points in range which is seen as broadcast. If the SSID field is filled with a specific network name, only the corresponding access point with the same SSID will answer with a probe response frame when it's within range. These directed active probe requests are the consequence of hidden networks, broadcasting beacons with an empty SSID field which makes a directed probe necessary. In practice, various mobile devices broadcast directed probes for each SSID, which is saved in the preferred network list (PNL). In combination with other information from periodical active probes, such as the device MAC address, this can be a serious privacy issue [3].

Fig. 42.1 IEEE 802.11 Network Discovery and Association Process

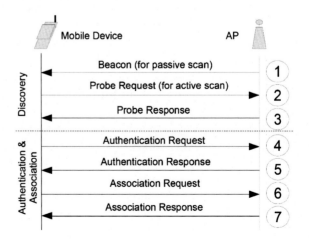

All of the mentioned Wi-Fi management frames can be easily captured by any Wi-Fi card within range which is set into a special monitor mode. Hence, it is very simple to implement this technique on almost any stationary device containing a Wi-Fi interface, e. g., access points, laptops, pcs, etc. The aggregation and analyzation of captured packets in an area of interest is also quite simple, due to the fact that management frames contain the essential information in plain-text, without any encryption. With the usage of advance algorithms in data analytics, one is able to gather useful information from the digital society in a very efficient and easy way. This information can be of high interest for different kind of purposes. Some of these will be presented in the sequel, where we describe scientific and commercial investigations based on captured Wi-Fi data from the digital crowd.

42.3 Wi-Fi Tracking as Emerging Research Field

Due to the increasing percentage of Wi-Fi enabled devices in our digital society, the topic of Wi-Fi tracking has gathered high interest in the scientific world since recent years. Some of the most relevant papers are presented in the following subsections, clustered by the kind of extracted information.

42.3.1 Crowd Data and Social Information

As already mentioned, probe request frames transport different types of management data which can be used to gather some general information about mobile users passing by a Wi-Fi monitor.

For instance, on the basis of the first three Bytes of a captured MAC-address, Barbera et al. [4] determine the manufacturer ID of the sender by performing an OUI – organizationally unique identifier – lookup. One observation of this investigation is the remarkable dominance of Apple devices, which was also detected by our tests at a major German airport [5]. However, these results have to be treated carefully, due to the fact, that Apple devices perform active scans more often, and thus, they might be detected more frequently than other devices.

Beside this, Barbera et al. focus on social relationships in their work and use captured Wi-Fi probes to uncover the social structure of the set of people in the crowd. They determine the similarity of users' context by comparing the SSIDs in the probes and performed a thorough social analysis in terms of social links, user languages, and vendor adoptions in different real-world scenarios.

Cunche et al. [6] also investigate social links based on captured Wi-Fi probes by comparing SSIDs fingerprints using different similarity metrics. On the basis of two large datasets, partly collected with the help of volunteers, the authors conclude that the detection of relationships by analyzing captured Wi-Fi probes is very easy and also a huge privacy risk.

Ruiz-Ruiz et al. [7] present several analysis methods for extracting knowledge from Wi-Fi tracking data. They perform a huge real-world study in a hospital and calculate various features, such as vendor adoptions, arrival and stay times, frequented places, densities, flows, and so on. The authors conclude that they could extract realistic information reflecting real behavior of people in such a complex environment.

42.3.2   Density and Pedestrian Flow Information

The current user density is quite easy to determine by the amount of captured unique devices being within a Wi-Fi monitor's coverage range for a certain time interval. Flow information can then be extracted out of the density information from more than one monitor node supervising an area of interest, as it is schematically illustrated in Fig. 42.2. The pedestrian flow is computed as the amount of people moving one way through this area which can be determined by comparing captured MAC-addresses at all of the installed monitor nodes [5].

Schauer et al. [8] used this procedure and deployed two monitor nodes in the public and security area of an airport divided by a single security check-in counter. With the access to corresponding boarding pass scans, they were able to compare their density and flow estimations with ground truth data. Overall, they determined a strong correlation of 0.75 between the Wi-Fi estimations and the real amount of people passing through the security check.

Fukuzaki et al. [9] claim that pedestrian flow sensing using Wi-Fi monitors is one of the most promising technique for smart cities. They conducted a two-month experiment with 20 Wi-Fi monitors deployed in a shopping mall and determined a coefficient to estimate the number of people. An error rate of 260 persons for weekdays has been achieved.

Li et al. [10] presented a system called *SenseFlow* for monitoring people density and flows based on Wi-Fi tracking data. The system was evaluated in four different application scenarios focusing on various parameters which may have an influence on the tracking accuracy e. g., the device type, the device's operational mode, or the underlying human walking behavior. Overall, the system showed an accuracy of up to 93% in case of Android and 80% for Apple devices in best case.

Fig. 42.2 Density and Pedestrian Flow in an Area of Interest

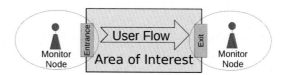

42.3.3 Location and Trajectory Information

One of the most interesting but also very challenging topic in the field of Wi-Fi tracking is the detection and determination of users' current locations and their trajectories. Due to arbitrary probe transmissions form moving mobile devices and significant fluctuations in the Wi-Fi based received signal strengths indicator (RSSI), simple positioning methods are not sufficient for achieving accurate localization results. Bonné et al. [11] confirm this statement claiming that several empirical tests have indicated that the RSSI value is not feasible in crowded environments for tracking the device's location. The authors conducted two large real-world experiments at their university campus and at a music festival.

A more sophisticated solution for tracking complete trajectories of unmodified smartphones is presented by Musa and Eriksson [12]. They used a probabilistic method based on Hidden Markov Model and Viterbi's algorithm and performed real-word experiments on a road network. Their Wi-Fi based trajectory estimations are compared to ground truth data provided by GPS resulting in a mean estimation error of under 70 m.

Chon et al. [13] performed a complete urban mobility monitoring project based on Wi-Fi tracking. They used the well-adopted fingerprinting technique and distinguished between stationary and moving users, in order to detect logical and revisited places. Their experiment was conducted with 25 students over a seven week period in Seoul.

Wi-Fi based trajectory estimations for indoor scenarios were also performed by Schauer et al. [14]. They investigated several probabilistic methods and introduced a modification to a common particle filter implementation in order to improve the tracking accuracy and its performance. Overall, a mean error of 11.65 meters for complete trajectories have been achieved indicating that highly accurate localizations of users based on Wi-Fi tracking data remain challenging.

42.3.4 Other Context Information

Beside the mentioned types of extracted information, there is still a lot of research inferring other context information from Wi-Fi tracking data.

For instance, Wang et al. [15] proposed a method for measuring human queues using a single Wi-Fi monitor. Such queues can be found in different business scenarios, such as retail stores, or at state departments. The authors infer typical and significant time spans, e. g., waiting in the queue, being attended, or leaving the queue, just by Wi-Fi signal readings form mobile devices. Their approach was tested within several experiments at different places, such as coffee shops, laboratory, or at an airport, reaching an estimation error of about 5 s for short and normal service times and under 10 s for longer service times.

Another interesting work is introduced by Maier et al. [16] who use Wi-Fi management frames for a privacy-preserving proximity detection for mobile users. The authors use a variation of the well-adopted cosine similarity to measure the degree of spatial closeness of mobile targets listening on probe requests from their environment. The idea behind is, that the collections of Wi-Fi probes in the surrounding of a mobile user depends on both spatial and temporal criteria. If two users capture a similar amount of probes, they can be seen in a spatial closeness at this moment. The results derived from conducted experiments at different scenarios yield to the conclusion, that a short-range and privacy preserving proximity detection is possible when using Wi-Fi tracking data.

Based on the presented scientific works, we conclude that Wi-Fi tracking involves high potentials for analyzing our digital society without requiring any active user participation nor any device or hardware modification. We have shown different aspects of extracting essential information from the crowd which can be very valuable for various use and business cases. Considering the ongoing digitalization with the increasing usage of Wi-Fi enabled devices, this technique becomes even more promising for innovative business cases in the near future.

42.4   Wi-Fi Tracking as Innovative Business Model

We have just demonstrated the potentials of Wi-Fi tracking and the kind of investigations which are performed in an experimental and scientific context. In this section, however, we highlight the business context and show how Wi-Fi tracking can be used economically.

Due to the increased attention of this technique, a lot of smaller and bigger companies exists offering products and special business services based on Wi-Fi tracking. Most customers of such products are retail shop managers who search for adequate analytic tools in order to analyze the behavior of their customers, like it is well-established in online shops. Hence, they require valuable insights about locations, interests, and all interactions of customers inside their shops. In the sequel, we present and compare some of the companies trying to solve this problem by Wi-Fi tracking:

42reports[1] is a Berlin Start-up focusing on Wi-Fi tracking to monitor customers in retail stores. It was founded in December 2012 and bought by DILAX Intelcom GmbH in April 2016. Beside Wi-Fi, they use other sensors, such as cameras and Bluetooth Beacons, and offer both the infrastructure and tools for retail analytics. Their services are divided into three packages and can be used to access different levels of information about customers' behavior and the shop's situation. Hence, shop managers get the possibility to see how their marketing performs and can make data-driven decisions. Some important features from the provided services are listed below:

- Detection and recognition of customers (new and old)
- Counting, frequency and success rates
- Forecasts

---

[1] https://42reports.com.

- Return of investment (ROI) analyzations
- Dwell times, density and flow information
- Visualization tools for different platforms in responsive design

Another important topic for 42reports is the protection of users' privacy. The start-up claim to be one of the leaders in security and protection of data privacy. Therefore, they perform 256-bit SSL encryption and a MAC-address anonymization for their retail analytic tools. Hence, third parties and shop owners don't get access to real MAC-addresses which belong to personal information (like IP-addresses).

sensalytics[2] provides similar services for retail shops, events and public buildings. Again, they offer different sensors, such as infrared, Wi-Fi, 3D-cameras, and a particular revenue sensor. Their basic concept is to measure all kind of customer and user interactions, in order to provide thorough analyzation possibilities for manager to make operational and strategic decisions. Based on Wi-Fi tracking, sensalytics extract similar information as 42reports, such as dwell times, detection and recognition of visitors, etc. On their website, they specify the counting accuracy between 40 and 70%. Note here, that other Wi-Fi tracking companies do not publish any data about accuracies and precisions of their services. Beside in-store analytics, sensalytics also focus on fairs and events, and offers a solution for human queue analysis which is, unlike to Wang et al. [15], based on 3D-camera sensors. Overall, with the fusion of the named sensors and the proposed software, they give retailers and event managers some of the possibilities which are quite common and well-adopted in e-commerce: the analyzation of customers. In this context, other German business rivals have to be mentioned, such as Infsoft[3], Crosscan[4], or RetailReports[5], providing similar analytic tools and services for retail shops.

Within the European market, walkbase[6] is one of the most famous retail analytics providers. Some of their key partners are IBM, Samsung, or Cisco. Beside the services we already mentioned above, walkbase also provides marketing optimization tools, queue management, passenger flow optimization, and location based services. They claim that "Wi-Fi is the most versatile technology for modern retail analytics". Using Wi-Fi and Bluetooth enabled devices, they even provide indoor positioning for opt-in passengers at travel hubs.

Euclid Analytics[7] is another company from the US using Wi-Fi probes from mobile devices for customer analytics. They offer "three distinct products to meet the needs of retailers, restaurants and malls". Their services include among others: visitor counts, evaluation of marketing campaigns, identifying visitor patterns, analyzation of visitor behavior, and understanding entire customer buying journeys. Like walkbase, Euclid was

---

[2] https://sensalytics.net/de.
[3] https://www.infsoft.de.
[4] http://crosscan.com/de.
[5] https://www.retailreports.de.
[6] http://www.walkbase.com.
[7] http://euclidanalytics.com.

founded in 2010 and states that it is nowadays "monitoring hundreds of millions of events daily".

Based on the introduced examples of companies and start-ups from above, one can get an adequate overview of the potentials of Wi-Fi tracking for innovative business models in our digital world where mobile devices are more and more popular. Hence, on the one hand, this technique renders digital analytic tools possible for retailers and offline marketplaces. On the other hand, we have to look carefully on social restrictions, such as users' privacy, and consider technical changes in the near future which may degrade these potentials and cause negative impacts. Thus, we will discuss these points in the following section.

42.5   Social and Technical Consequences of Wi-Fi Tracking

As we have demonstrated, Wi-Fi tracking combined with big data algorithms creates the ability to track and analyze mobile users without their consent or even awareness. No complex hard- or software is required, and thus, it is very easy for companies or even malicious persons to use this technique for their intents. Hence, anyone who carries a Wi-Fi enabled mobile device risks to be tracked all the time involuntarily. This fact is a major issue for users' privacy and their implicit rights on personal data.

So what are the consequences for our more and more digitalized society where a stable and fast connection to the Internet is treated as a valuable asset? Sure, the easiest and most effective way is just to disable Wi-Fi interfaces and use more mobile data connections. However, inside huge buildings, e. g., shopping malls, or airports, only Wi-Fi may provide a stable connection. Furthermore, we suppose that only a few people are willing to enable or disable the Wi-Fi adapter several times per day.

Stricter laws and penalties which prohibit passive Wi-Fi sniffing in public spaces would be a political way trying to reduce the risk of being involuntarily analyzed. However, this would probably not prevent malicious persons from sniffing Wi-Fi traffic, and would definitively destroy all the innovative business models we mentioned in the previous section.

Users could also actively remove network names from their PNL which are not going to be used anymore. This would at least decrease the number of SSIDs sent out by probe requests and thus, social profiling becomes more difficult and inaccurate. However, most users never delete their saved networks and furthermore, this method does not protect users from being analyzed by Wi-Fi sniffers.

A more sophisticated and technical method to protect users against efficient Wi-Fi tracking is provided by Apple's current mobile operating System (iOS 9). Since iOS 8, a mechanism for automatic MAC-address randomization is integrated in the OS which fakes the real hardware identifier of the device. Hence, continuous tracing or recognizing an iOS device by distributed Wi-Fi sniffers becomes more difficult. When Apple introduced this feature in 2014, it was hardly criticized as impractical, due to the fact that the new randomization process only worked for devices which entered into full sleep mode which was only in case of both disabled cellular data connection and disabled location services [17]. Hence, most users didn't really had MAC-randomization activated in their daily life. Thus, Apple recently improved and extended the mechanism to location and auto-join scans, meaning that MAC randomization is now available also for active devices and during IEEE 802.11 active scans [18]. Note, that the randomization process is not activated for associated devices.

So for the first time, Apple as one of the leading providers for mobile devices, has established an automatic method for protecting users' privacy against Wi-Fi sniffing which is directly integrated in the operating system. However, MAC-randomization makes Wi-Fi based analyzations more complicate, but it doesn't fulfill a complete privacy protection, as it is stated in [19]. Furthermore, Pang et al. [20] have already demonstrated in 2007 that so-called implicit identifiers and certain characteristics of 802.11 traffic can be used to identify many users with high accuracy and without knowing the device specific MAC-address. Hence, Apple's mechanism is just a first but also important step to react on the needs for complete privacy protection in our digital society. Overall, it has to be observed in the near future, how companies and people deal with this topic and how retail analytics can be performed when Wi-Fi tracking becomes inaccurate due to more sophisticated privacy-preserving mechanisms. Probably, the fairest and best way would always be to ask people for compliance before tracking them.

42.6 Conclusion and Future Impacts

In this book chapter, we have demonstrated the possibilities, risks and limitations of tracking mobile customer devices in our more and more digitalized world. Technical backgrounds to standard IEEE 802.11 Wi-Fi tracking have been described. Furthermore, both scientific and commercial works have been presented focusing on the type of crowd information which can be extracted from Wi-Fi tracking data. It was seen that this technique has gathered a high interest also for innovative business models and shows great potentials for the near future, due to an increasing amount of Wi-Fi capable mobile devices. On the other hand, the technique includes serious risks for users' privacy and people should be aware of the fact, that their phone is sending data without their awareness.

We have also demonstrated, that new privacy-preserving mechanisms are developed and partially integrated in current mobile operating systems. However, they still do not guarantee a complete protection against being tracked in public spaces, due to implicit identifiers. Hence, if users want to be sure they just have to switch off the Wi-Fi interface of their device.

For the near future, we assume that Wi-Fi tracking will even spread in public spaces, due to low cost, more mobile devices, and more sophisticated data mining algorithms. Especially retailers who require similar analytic tools as in online-shops will install such a technique in their business. The highest uncertainty for our prediction will be the prospective user acceptance and the development of more advanced privacy-preserving mechanism. Overall, voluntary tracking of mobile users will always be possible, which is the fairest way in our opinion.

References

1. IEEE Computer Society, "IEEE Std 802.11: Wireless LAN Medium Access Control (MAC) and Physical Layer (PHY) Specifications," 3 Park Avenue, NY 10016-5997, USA, June 2007.
2. S. Lee, M. Kim, S. Kang, K. Lee and I. Jung, "Smart scanning for mobile devices in wlans," *IEEE International Conference on Communications (ICC)*, pp. 4960–4964, 2012.
3. J. Lindqvist, T. Aura, G. Danezis, T. Koponen, A. Myllyniemi, j. Mäki and M. Roe, "Privacy-Preserving 802.11 access-point discovery," *Second ACM Conference on Wireless Networks Security*, pp. 123–130, 2009.
4. M. V. Barbera, A. Epasto, A. Mei, V. Perta and J. Stefa, "Signals from the crowd: uncovering social relationships through smartphone probes," in *Proceedings of the 2013 conference on Internet measurement conference*, ACM, 2013, pp. 265–276.
5. L. Schauer and M. Werner, "Analyzing Pedestrian Flows Based on Wi-Fi and Bluetooth Captures," in *EAI Endorsed Transactions on Ubiquitous Environments*, ICTS, 2015.
6. M. Cunche, M. A. Kaafar and R. Boreli, "I know who you will meet this evening! linking wireless devices using wi-fi probe requests," in *World of Wireless, Mobile and Multimedia Networks (WoWMoM), 2012 IEEE International Symposium on a*, IEEE, 2012, pp. 1–9.
7. A. Ruiz-Ruiz, H. Blunck, T. Prentow, A. Stisen and M. Kjaergaard, "Analysis methods for extracting knowledge from large-scale WiFi monitoring to inform building facility planning," in *Pervasive Computing and Communications (PerCom), 2014 IEEE International Conference on*, IEEE, 2014, pp. 130–138.
8. L. Schauer, M. Werner and P. Marcus, "Estimating crowd densities and pedestrian flows using wi-fi and bluetooth," in *Proceedings of the 11th International Conference on Mobile and Ubiquitous Systems: Computing, Networking and Services*, ICST, 2014, pp. 171–177.
9. Y. Fukuzaki, M. Mochizuki, K. Murao and N. Nishio, "Statistical analysis of actual number of pedestrians for Wi-Fi packet-based pedestrian flow sensing," in *Adjunct Proceedings of the 2015 ACM International Joint Conference on Pervasive and Ubiquitous Computing and Proceedings of the 2015 ACM International Symposium on Wearable Computers*, ACM, 2015, pp. 1519–1526.
10. K. Li, C. Yuen, S. Kanhere, K. Hu, W. Zhang, F. Jiang and X. Liu, "SenseFlow: An Experimental Study for Tracking People," arXiv, 2016.
11. B. Bonné, A. Barzan, P. Quax and W. Lamotte, "WiFiPi: Involuntary tracking of visitors at mass events," in *World of Wireless, Mobile and Multimedia Networks (WoWMoM), 2013 IEEE 14th International Symposium and Workshops on a*, IEEE, 2013, pp. 1–6.
12. A. Musa and J. Eriksson, "Tracking unmodified smartphones using wi-fi monitors," in *Proceedings of the 10th ACM conference on embedded network sensor systems*, ACM, 2012, pp. 281–294.
13. Y. Chon, S. Kim, S. Lee, D. Kim, Y. Kim and H. Cha, "Sensing WiFi packets in the air: practicality and implications in urban mobility monitoring," in *Proceedings of the 2014 ACM International Joint Conference on Pervasive and Ubiquitous Computing*, ACM, 2014, pp. 189–200.

14. L. Schauer, P. Marcus and C. Linnhoff-Popien, "Towards Feasible Wi-Fi based Indoor Tracking Systems Using Probabilistic Methods," in *Indoor Positioning and Indoor Navigation (IPIN), 2016 International Conference on*, IEEE, 2016.

15. Y. Wang, J. Yang, Y. Chen, H. Liu, M. Gruteser and R. Martin, "Tracking human queues using single-point signal monitoring," in *Proceedings of the 12th annual international conference on Mobile systems, applications, and services*, ACM, 2014, pp. 42–54.

16. M. Maier, L. Schauer and F. Dorfmeister, "ProbeTags: Privacy-preserving proximity detection using Wi-Fi management frames," in *Wireless and Mobile Computing, Networking and Communications (WiMob), 2015 IEEE 11th International Conference on*, IEEE, 2015, pp. 756–763.

17. M. Beasley, "More details on how iOS 8's MAC address randomization feature works (and when it doesn't)," 9to5mac.com, 26 09 2014. [Online]. Available: http://9to5mac.com/2014/09/26/more-details-on-how-ios-8s-mac-address-randomization-feature-works-and-when-it-doesnt/. [Accessed 29 07 2016].

18. K. Skinner and J. Novak, "Privacy and your app," in *Apple Worldwide Dev. Conf. (WWDC)*, 2015.

19. M. Vanhoef, C. Matte, M. Cunche, L. Cardoso and F. Piessens, "Why MAC Address Randomization is not Enough: An Analysis of Wi-Fi Network Discovery Mechanisms," in *Proceedings of the 11th ACM on Asia Conference on Computer and Communications Security*, ACM, 2016, pp. 413–424.

20. J. Pang, B. Greenstein, R. Gummadi, S. Seshan and D. Wetherall, "802.11 user fingerprinting," in *Proceedings of the 13th annual ACM international conference on Mobile computing and networking*, ACM, 2007, pp. 99–110.

Improving Urban Transportation: an Open Plat-Form for Digital Mobility Services

43

Maximilian Schreieck, Christoph Pflügler, David Soto Setzke, Manuel Wiesche, and Helmut Krcmar

Abstract

Due to the ubiquity of smartphones, the impact of digital mobility services on individual traffic behavior within cities has increased significantly over the last years. Companies, as for example Google, and city administrations or parastatal municipal transport providers issue digital mobility services. As a result, a heterogeneous landscape of digital mobility services has emerged. While the services serve different needs, they are based on similar service modules and data sources. By analyzing 59 digital mobility services available as smartphone applications or web services, we show that an integration of service modules and data sources can increase the value of digital mobility services. Based on this analysis, we propose a concept for the architecture of an open platform for digital mobility services that enables co-creation of value by making data sources and service modules available for developers. The concept developed for the platform architecture consists of the following elements: data sources, layers of modular services, an integration layer and solutions. We illustrated the concept by describing

M. Schreieck (✉) · C. Pflügler · D. Soto Setzke · M. Wiesche · H. Krcmar
Technical University of Munich
Munich, Germany
e-mail: maximilian.schreieck@in.tum.de

C. Pflügler
e-mail: christoph.pfluegler@in.tum.de

D. Soto Setzke
e-mail: setzke@in.tum.de

M. Wiesche
e-mail: wiesche@in.tum.de

H. Krcmar
e-mail: krcmar@in.tum.de

© Springer-Verlag GmbH Germany 2018
C. Linnhoff-Popien et al. (eds.), *Digital Marketplaces Unleashed*,
https://doi.org/10.1007/978-3-662-49275-8_43

possible modular services and how they could be used to improve urban transportation. Our work supports practitioners from industry and public administration in identifying potential for innovative services and foster co-creation and innovation within existing systems for urban transportation.

43.1 Introduction[1,2]

Today, the traffic situation in many cities is challenging. Due to an increasing degree of urbanization and traffic complexity people lose more and more time in traffic jams and during the search for parking spots. It is estimated that European cities lose between 2.69 and 4.63% of their Gross Domestic Product (GDP) because of traffic congestions [1]. Additionally, the increase in congestion leads to an aggravation of air pollution and greenhouse gas emissions in cities all around the globe [2].

Recently, IT has emerged as one of the key influencing factors on traffic [3]. City administrators operate intelligent transportation systems (ITS) that use IT to improve the safety, efficiency, and convenience of surface transportation [4] and it has been shown that ITS have a greater impact on energy and environmental benefits than construction-phase measures [5]. In the last few years, mobility and location-based services emerged on smartphones as well as within cars. As a result, mobile services have become an important influencing factor on individual mobility in addition to existing ITS [6]. The variety of services that is used by end users include journey planning, ride-sharing matching, maps, navigation etc. and use a variety of data sources.

Many of these solutions are dependent on accurate data, e. g. the location of the users, time-schedule of public transportation or information on the current traffic or parking situation. However, it is difficult for developers of mobility solutions to gather this data, because there are only a few platforms, such as Google Maps or Bing Maps, that offer mobility data and services through standardized interfaces. Service providers only offer isolated services with a specific focus; access to their data and services is often limited and restricted. Furthermore, existing services are not yet integrated and the landscape of digital solutions is vast and unstructured. On the other hand, smart cities generate extensive mobility data such as floating car data of individual vehicles but this data is not offered to external providers nor is it standardized. Making this data accessible and offering standardized modular services that aggregate and analyze the available mobility data would

---

[1] This chapter is based on the following two publications: Schreieck, M.; Wiesche, M.; Krcmar, H. (2016). Modularization of Digital Services for Urban Transportation. Twenty-second Americas Conference on Information Systems (AMCIS), San Diego and Pflügler C.; Schreieck, M.; Hernandez, G.; Wiesche, M. and Krcmar, H. (2016). A concept for the architecture of an open platform for modular mobility services in the smart city. International Scientific Conference on Mobility and Transport (mobil.TUM), Munich.

[2] We thank the German Federal Ministry for Economic Affairs and Energy for funding this research as part of the project 01MD15001D (ExCELL).

ease the effort for solution providers and foster further development of innovative mobility services. Especially in the case of small and middle-sized enterprises, this could lead to an increased use of mobility data since in these companies there often is a lack of highly specialized knowledge which would be required to analyze and make use of unstructured mobility data produced by smart cities [7]. However, until now it remains unclear what the concept for the architecture of an open and modular digital mobility services platform should look like.

In order to develop the requirements for a solution, we have conducted an analysis of already existing services [8]. We have identified distinct service modules and data sources that are used across these existing services in order to show that an integration of these can increase the value of digital mobility services. Based on our findings from the analysis, which will be presented in the next chapter, we developed a proposition of an architectural concept for an open digital mobility services platform, which we will present and discuss in the subsequent chapters. Our concept contributes to theory by giving guidance for future research on service platforms, especially in the context of mobility services. It also contributes to practice by showing how currently available mobility-related data can be made accessible for developers of digital mobility solutions.

43.2 Analysis of Existing Digital Mobility Services

For our analysis, we applied a methodology framework by Dörbecker and Böhmann [9] for the design of modular service systems. Based on service systems engineering theory, it helps with analyzing, designing, implementing and monitoring service modules as parts of a modular service system architecture. While previous research on modularity has focused mainly on products, recent studies have applied these concepts in the design of services [10]. Dörbecker and Böhmann [11] identified and analyzed 12 methods for designing modular service systems and, as a result, proposed their own iterative design framework. It addresses several limitations and weaknesses of the analyzed methods such as missing generalizability and introduces new aspects such as an iterative design approach across several distinct phases. Böhmann et al. [12] call for future research on service systems engineering in information systems and mention sustainable mobility as an area where services can generate significant benefits. With our analysis, we apply the second step of modularization within the mentioned framework, which comprises the identification and analysis of the service system's modules.

In order to provide an overview of existing mobility services for urban transportation, we conducted a broad search within app stores of mobile devices and tech blogs. All together, we identified 59 mobility services that we analyzed in more detail.

These services were first grouped into six categories, following a taxonomy development process described by Nickerson et al. [13]: Trip planners, ride and car sharing services, navigation services, smart logistics services, location-based services and parking services. A summary along with a description and example services is presented in Ta-

Table 43.1 Categories of Digital Mobility Services

Category	Description	Example service
Trip planners	Provide information for planning trips	moovel
Ride/Car sharing	Share cars and rides	flinc/drivy
Navigation	Follow a route by giving directions	Google Maps
Smart logistics	Facilitate the movement of goods	foodora
Location-based information	Provide location-relevant information	Services for radar controls
Parking	Provide information on parking lots	Parknav

ble 43.1. In a second step, we analyzed modules and data sources of all services. We will now further describe the results of our analysis.

Table 43.2 presents an overview of the modules that we identified. They can be structured according to the origin of their value proposition. One group of modules provides information, while a second group contributes analytics to enhance existing information. The modules map view, POIs, location sharing, traffic information and parking information provide the user with information he or she needs in a specific context. The modules routing and matching are based on analytic capabilities and combine existing information to derive new information.

An analysis of which service modules are included in which digital mobility service is shown in Fig. 43.1. Some service modules are integrated in most of the services. The map view, for example, is the most basic module and therefore integrated in almost all mobility services. Another important module is the routing module, which is integrated in navigation services and trip planners.

Some service modules are not yet integrated in many services although they might offer an additional benefit. The module that enables location sharing, for example, is mostly used in smart logistics services and car and ride sharing services. However, also trip planners or parking services could benefit from location sharing as it might be useful for users to know when a public transport vehicle is arriving or when a parking spot is left by another user. The matching module, as another example, is specific to services that match

Table 43.2 Modules of Digital Mobility Services

Module	Description	Example service
Map view	Show current location and surroundings, relevant information and directions	DriveNow
Routing	Provide suggestions on how to travel to a destination	Google Maps
POIs (Points of interest)	Provide information about relevant points of interest	ChargeNOW
Location sharing	Share location with other users	myTaxi
Traffic information	Provide information on the current traffic situation	Intrix Traffic
Parking information	Provide information on parking lots	Parknav
Matching	Match demand and supply	BlaBlaCar

Category	Service modules						
	Map view	Routing	POIs	Location Sharing	Traffic information	Parking information	Matching
Navigation	●	●	●	◔	◑	○	○
Trip planner	◕	●	◑	○	○	○	○
Smart logistics	◕	◔	○	◑	○	○	◑
Parking service	●	●	●	○	○	◕	◔
Car/ride sharing	●	◑	◑	◔	○	○	◑
Location-based info.	●	◑	◑	○	◕	○	○

Used in more than ● 80%, ◕ 60%, ◑ 40%, ◔ 20% of the services.

Fig. 43.1 Service modules of digital mobility services

supply and demand and is therefore mainly integrated in car and ride sharing services or smart logistics services that match free capacities with delivery requests.

Table 43.3 presents an overview of the data sources that we identified. Most services are based on more than one data source. Especially navigation services and trip planners integrate data from private and public sources and enhance the data via sensor and crowd-sourced data. Data from public transportation providers and from public administration is not yet integrated throughout the categories of digital mobility services. An analysis of which service modules are included in which digital mobility service is shown in Fig. 43.2.

Our analysis provides an overview of existing mobility services showing that there is a large number of different services that need to be combined by the users in order to fulfill their individual needs. Users need to switch between apps and providers since most of the services are not integrated.

However, in this chapter we have shown that services can be structured based on their modules and data sources. We have also shown that a lot of distinct services use similar modules and data sources which suggests that there is a lot of potential for reusing certain components. This serves as further motivation and guidance for the development of

Table 43.3 Data Sources of Digital Mobility Services

Data source	Provided data
Google	Map, routing and traffic information
Device sensors	User location
Crowdsourced data	Data aggregated across users
Other private providers	Solution-specific data
Public transportation providers	Time tables, information on delays and incidents
Public administration	E. g. traffic situation, usage of public parking decks

	Data sources					
Category	Google	Device sensors	Crowdsourced	Other private provider	Public transp. provider	Public administration
Navigation	◑	●	◑	◔	◑	◑
Trip planner	◕	●	◔	◕	●	◔
Smart logistics	◕	●	◑	◑	○	○
Parking service	◕	●	●	●	○	●
Car/ride sharing	●	●	◑	◑	○	○
Location-based info.	●	●	◕	◔	○	◑

Data source used in more than ● 80%, ◕ 60%, ◑ 40%, ◔ 20% of the services.

Fig. 43.2 Data sources of digital mobility services

an open platform for digital mobility services which facilitates the development of new services by providing reusable modules and services and pre-structured data. In the next chapter, we will outline our architectural concept for such a platform.

43.3 Architectural Concept of an Open Platform for Digital Mobility Services

We will first further define the requirements for our platform based on the findings of our analysis in the preceding chapter. The platform should offer several modular mobility services with different levels of granularity. These services should access different data sources and refine their information. All services should be hosted in a secure and safe environment. As many of these mobility services are quite computation intensive, the platform needs to be able to handle sufficient parallel service calls. Additionally, each user should be identifiable by the platform. Furthermore, the platform should support developers that contribute services to the platform's ecosystem by providing access to raw or analyzed data, analysis tools and specifications on how to develop the services according to the platforms standards. The resources on the platform should be standardized so that similar datasets from different sources can be presented and interpreted in a similar way. The platform should provide a web-based interface which allows browsing through the different resources by providing user credentials. The proposed platform should furthermore support cooperation between the public and the private sector. They can create consortia or public-private partnerships and define who will operate the platform.

Fig. 43.3 shows the concept for the architecture of an open platform for digital mobility services. It consists of the following elements and layers which we will now explain in further detail.

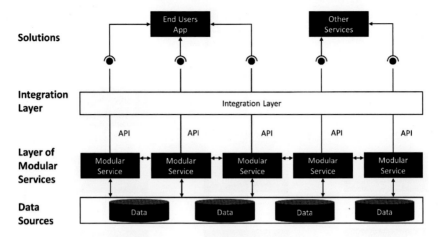

Fig. 43.3 Concept for the architecture of an open platform for digital mobility services

Data Sources The platform is based on several different data sets, for example floating car data or parking lot data. This data could be gathered through on board units within cars or through sensors in parking garages or on the streets. Additionally, data from public transportation providers and taxi corporations such as time tables or the positions of currently available cars could also be an important addition to the set of data sources.

Layers of Modular Services Modular services represent the core of the platform. They can be structured into several layers where the level of granularity increases from the top to the bottom. Services at the bottom focus on analyzing and refining the data sources, whereas services on higher levels reuse the services from lower levels and integrate them using their results. Services that will be used by end users can be found on the highest level. Fig. 43.4 illustrates these different levels and shows several example services which we will now explain in further detail.

- **Parking situation** The parking situation service shows the current availability of parking spaces. It is based on data provided by the parking garages, sensors, or the crowd.
- **Prediction of parking situation** This service predicts the parking situation for a certain point of time in the future. It is based on the parking situation service and the traffic information service. This service processes the provided data with machine learning algorithms. Additionally, it is possible that this service also accesses other information such as weather data.
- **Traffic situation** The traffic information service collects the traffic data from different sources like floating car data, road sensors and road alerts. Then, it combines this data and estimates the current traffic situation.
- **Prediction of traffic situation** This service predicts the traffic situation for a certain point of time in the future. It is based on the traffic situation service and on other data

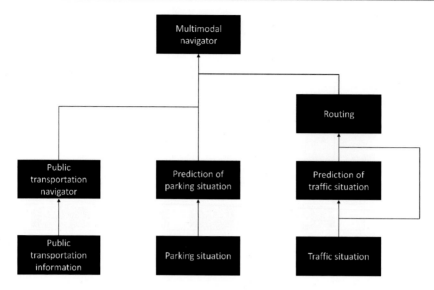

Fig. 43.4 Layer of modular services with example services

sources such as weather data. This service processes the data with machine learning algorithms.

- **Routing** The routing service calculates the best route between two points. The user can specify whether the current traffic situation or the predicted traffic situation for a certain point of time in the future should be considered.
- **Public transportation information** This service shows current and future time tables of trains, subways and buses. It also provides information about any failures or unforeseen situations.
- **Public transportation navigator** The public transportation navigator service suggests the best public transportation route between two points for a certain point of time. It is based on the public transportation information service.
- **Multimodal navigator** This service offers the optimal route within the city for car drivers. It considers the traffic situation for selecting the optimal route, but also checks where it is possible to find a parking space at the destination. Additionally, it checks whether it is better to park the car near a bus station and to use public transportation. This service is supposed to be used by end-users and is based on the previously described modular services.

Integration Layer The integration layer creates a secure and safe environment. Services can only be accessed through the integration layer which buffers service calls and acts as a load balancer. User management and access control also reside in this layer. Since all service calls have to pass this layer, it can also be used for analyzing service calls.

Solutions Developers who are using the platform can use the service to create new mobility solutions. These solutions could be solutions targeted to end-users or they could be integrated into services outside of the platform. An example for a possible solution is a scheduling and routing service for small and medium-sized businesses with multiple appointments within one or several cities. By considering the routes between the appointments and the predicted traffic situation at that point in time, appointment scheduling can be optimized. For example, a nursing service could optimize its daily schedule using this solution and save driving time that could be dedicated to the patient care instead.

43.4   Discussion

Our architectural concept for an open platform for digital mobility services can be used to make data of smart cities available, such as data on public transportation, parking spaces and traffic situation. Such a platform creates a mobility ecosystem and fosters the development of innovative mobility solutions based on the provided modular services. Without it, each developer has to gather data on his own, which is difficult if at all possible.

In this context, another challenge arises: Due to the highly dynamic nature of the platform, caused by the different stakeholders and participants, extensive control, also known as platform governance is required as a precondition for further success of the platform [14]. For example, the data that is aggregated from different sources and then made public by our platform could be used by other developers to strengthen their own competitive position vis-à-vis the platform owner [15]. The platform's standards and interfaces should be carefully examined in order to control the data flow and to avoid misuse. Although effective governance is crucial for the success of a platform, many operators still struggle with designing and implementing a suitable governance concept. The work of Hein et al. [16] and Manner et al. [17] analyses different governance mechanisms and proposes core principles for the governance of mobile platforms. Their findings can give guidance for the design and implementation of a governance concept for our proposed platform.

The example services in the previous section demonstrate and clarify different layers of services. Each service can be offered to the end-user individually, but it is also possible for external developers to combine them to offer new services.

Data related to mobility is of a highly sensitive nature and requires special mechanism for preserving privacy [18]. Methods for preserving privacy while storing and managing mobility-related data are presented as an alternative to a trusted authority by Sucasas et al. [19]. Based on these findings, we suggest to give users as much control as possible by providing standardized processes for setting privacy requirements in order to ensure privacy and transparency in the provided services. For example, tracking data is anonymized and assigned to a regularly changing identifier. Data set owners can then see and track the use of their data.

Our proposed concept is subject to a few limitations. As of now, the architecture of the service platform has not been evaluated. Additionally, only a few exemplary services have been presented. For mobility solution providers, a comprehensive list of services would be more useful. In future research, the remaining steps of the methodology framework by Dörbecker and Böhmann [9], such as implementation and validation, could be applied to our findings. The architectural concept and a concrete implementation could be evaluated by using qualitative and quantitative approaches such as expert interviews and surveys.

Our findings contribute to both theory and practice. As for theoretical implications, our results give guidance on potential future research on service platforms, especially in the context of mobility-related applications. Additionally, they show how the framework of Dörbecker and Böhmann [9] can be applied for the modularization of service systems as presented in our analysis on existing mobility services.

As for practical implications, our concept presents a way of making already existing mobility-related data available for mobility solution developers by fulfilling several requirements related to safety, privacy and governance mechanisms. The proposed platform can be used for the creation of integrated and innovative services and identifying further potential among data source providers for collaboration and synergies. Furthermore, existing systems for urban transportation can benefit from the platform by using offered services to enhance their own solutions and in turn provide new data to the platform, thus further fostering co-creation and innovation.

43.5   Conclusion

Individual mobility is heavily impacted by digital mobility services. Therefore, research on digital mobility services can contribute to the efforts of companies and policy makers to make transportation more sustainable. We analyzed existing mobility services with regard to their modules and data sources. We showed that some modules and data sources are integrated throughout almost all categories while others are only available in highly specialized solutions. Our analysis shows that there is a large number of different services that need to be combined by the users in order to fulfill their individual needs.

In order to ease development of new, integrated mobility solutions, we designed an architectural concept for an open and modular digital mobility services platform. The platform supports the development of solutions by providing mobility data and services through open and standardized interfaces. A broad variety of services at different levels of complexity is offered by the platform which encourages reuse of existing service. Developers can find and pick the services that best fit their needs and goals.

References

1. C. Willoughby, "Managing Motorization," 2000.
2. statista, "Städte mit der größten Luftverschmutzung (PM10) weltweit," 2016. [Online]. Available: http://de.statista.com/statistik/daten/studie/202366/umfrage/staedte-mit-der-groessten-luftverschmutzung-weltweit/. [Accessed 26 Februar 2016].

3. S. Wolter, "Smart Mobility – Intelligente Vernetzung der Verkehrsangebote in Großstädten," in *Zukünftige Entwicklungen in der Mobilität*, Springer Gabler, 2012, pp. 527–548.
4. R. J. Weiland and L. B. Purser, "Intelligent Transportation Systems," *Committee on Intelligent Transportation Systems*, 2000.
5. L. L. Tupper, M. A. Chowdhury, L. Klotz and R. N. Fries, "Measuring Sustainability: How Traffic Incident Management through Intelligent Transportation Systems has Greater Energy and Environmental Benefits than Common Construction-Phase Strategies for "Green" Roadways," *International Journal of Sustainable Transportation*, vol. 6, no. 5, pp. 282–297, 2012.
6. Forrester, "North American Techngraphics. Online Benchmark Survey (Part 1)," 2013. [Online]. Available: http://techcrunch.com/2013/08/01/despite-googles-gains-iphone-still-edges-out-android-devices-in-app-and-overall-smartphone-usage-says-forrester/.   [Accessed   21   Mai 2016].
7. V. Fries, C. Pfluegler, M. Wiesche and H. Krcmar, "The Hateful Six – Factors Hindering Adoption of Innovation at Small and Medium Sized Enterprises," in *Twenty-second Americas Conference on Information Systems*, San Diego, 2016.
8. M. Schreieck, M. Wiesche and H. Krcmar, "Modularization of Digital Services for Urban Transportation," in *Twenty-second Americas Conference on Information Systems*, San Diego, 2016.
9. R. Dörbecker and T. Böhmann, "FAMouS – Framework for Architecting," in *Thirty Sixth International Conference on Information Systems*, 2015.
10. R. Dörbecker and T. Böhmann, "The Concept and Effects of Service Modularity – A Literature Review," in *46th Hawaii International Conference on System Sciences (HICSS)*, 2013.
11. R. Dörbecker and T. Böhmann, "Systematic Design of Modular Service Architectures for Complex Service Systems," *Available at SSRN 2655945*, 2015.
12. T. Böhmann, J. M. Leimeister and K. Möslein, "Service Systems Engineering," *Business & Information Systems Engineering*, vol. 6, no. 2, pp. 73–79, 2014.
13. R. C. Nickerson, U. Varshney and J. Muntermann, "A method for taxonomy development and its application in information systems," *European Journal of Information Systems*, vol. 22, no. 3, pp. 336–359, 2012.
14. J. Manner, "Steuerung plattformbasierter Servicemarktplätze," 2014.
15. M. Schreieck, M. Wiesche and H. Krcmar, "Design and Governance of Platform Ecosystems – Key Concepts and Issues for Future Research," in *Twenty-Fourth European Conference on Information Systems (ECIS)*, Istanbul, 2016.
16. A. Hein, M. Schreieck, M. Wiesche and H. Krcmar, "Multiple-Case Analysis on Governance Mechanisms of Multi-Sided Platforms," in *Multikonferenz Wirtschaftsinformatik (MKWI)*, 2016.
17. J. Manner, D. Nienaber, M. Schermann and H. Krcmar, "Six Principles for Governing Mobile Platforms," in *Wirtschaftsinformatik Proceedings 2013*, 2013.
18. D. Christin, "Privacy in mobile participatory sensing: Current trends and future challenges," *Journal of Systems and Software*, vol. 116, pp. 57–68, 2016.
19. V. Sucasas, G. Mantas, F. B. Saghezchi, A. Radwan and J. Rodriguez, "An autonomous privacy-preserving authentication scheme for intelligent transportation systems," *Computers & Security*, pp. 193–205, 2016.

Safety Belt for Pedestrians

44

Klaus David and Hendrik Berndt

Abstract

The paper outlines an innovative and efficient pedestrian protection system. It is mobile phone based and easy to implement. It detects and evaluates context and surroundings of vulnerable road users to reduce their number of accidents, injuries and fatalities. Involved stakeholders and potential business scenarios are identified.

44.1 Heads Up

"Heads up! Cross the street and then update Facebook" that's how new street signs, installed to protect, seek pedestrians' attention in Hayward, CA, USA. According to [1] distractions from mobile phones divert attention from traffic similar as for a person with 0.8 per mill blood alcohol. Obviously this fact might just be seen as a minor influence on the number of traffic fatalities in total. Latest numbers from 2/2016 give an overview on road safety evolution in the European Union. According to CARE (the EU road accidents database) 25,900 people were killed [2] in 2014 within the EU. Pedestrians and other unprotected road users are vulnerable and highest in number amongst most severe injured persons. Worldwide 22% of all fatalities are pedestrians [3]. Something more has to be done to protect them.

Today's vulnerable road user (VRU) protection systems are mainly based on cameras, radar, infrared-systems, microwaves or combination thereof. They are predominantly

K. David (✉) · H. Berndt
Universität Kassel
Kassel, Germany
e-mail: klaus.david@comtec.eecs.uni-kassel.de

H. Berndt
e-mail: hendrik.berndt@comtec.eecs.uni-kassel.de

© Springer-Verlag GmbH Germany 2018   491
C. Linnhoff-Popien et al. (eds.), *Digital Marketplaces Unleashed*,
https://doi.org/10.1007/978-3-662-49275-8_44

placed in vehicles and request a line of sight to pedestrians to be faultlessly recognized. This line of sight however is often not available.

Moreover, a dangerous situation has to be detected as early as possible to start accident avoidance measures. For that it would be desirable to have more information such as position, direction, velocity of movement from both pedestrians and cars involved, available or projected. There can even more relevant information to be exploited, such as closeness of the pedestrian to the curb, or his/her step onto the street level and even personalized information about the height of the person (child or grown up) the age (young or elderly both with different movement patterns at one's disposal).

The presented solution allows for the pedestrian to play a decisive role in the prevention of accidents.

44.2 Communication Infrastructure

Our Pedestrian protection system assumes a mobile phone is available for the service user. Through optimal use of the phone's full capabilities it becomes part of a communication infrastructure, which as an overall solution will provide alerts and protection to participants. Communications between pedestrians and affected cars is using existing technologies and does not necessarily request a specific infrastructure or standard. Several possibilities are at disposal, such as WLAN, cellular or device-to-device communications. Unquestionably latency has to be low enough to allow for several message exchanges dur-

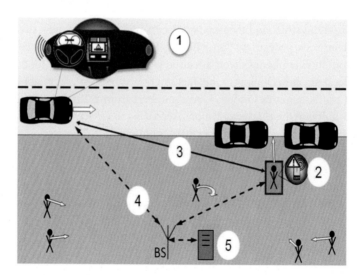

Fig. 44.1 ComTec 2016 – Communication infrastructure building blocks – *1* On Board Unit Inside Car, *2* Smartphone of pedestrian, *3* Ad-hoc WLAN communications, *4* Cellular communications (UMTS/HPSA/LTE/...), *5* Potential server for scenario calculation (can also be done on Smartphone and On Board Unit only)

ing an average accident avoidance response time, available typically at 2 s, as analyzed in [4]. LTE with its ± 50 ms round-trip delay is providing a time cushion that allows for several message exchanges, and next mobile generation, 5G, is targeting even single digit millisecond delays.

Fig. 44.1 below depicts a potential communications infrastructure for the pedestrian's safety belt.

Amongst the different options for a communication infrastructure the smartphone based WiFiHonk system, introduced in [5] is noted. It uses WiFi Beacon Stuffing, a method to exchange information between WiFi devices, without establishing a connection, through the SSID or BSSID in the WiFi beacon header of a Wifi network. Wifi Beacon Stuffing can be used to propagate the latitude and longitude, the speed, and the direction of both VRUs and vehicles. These data can be transmitted every 100 ms and thus also be seemly as infrastructure unit of a pedestrian protection system. [6] introduces another communication infrastructure unit for cooperative applications between vehicle and pedestrians based on DSRC modules.

44.3 Context Filter

At the core of our protection system is an architectural building block called context filter. It interprets and transforms sensor data, gathered through the pedestrian's mobile phone sensors into activity detection. Additionally it filters, fuses and evaluates available information from the pedestrian's surrounding context. To protect privacy of pedestrians all information gathered would be anonymized trough a specific component inside the context filter, the anonymizer. (Legal groundwork for data protection has been elaborated on in [7]).

Our context filter consists out of the modules, depicted in Fig. 44.2.

Fig. 44.2 ComTec 2016 –
Context filtering and collision
estimation

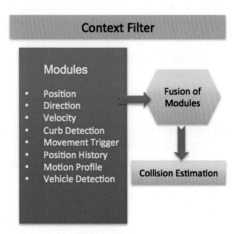

Once information is fused, filtered and evaluated a collision likelihood based on the situation is estimated and further actions are triggered if seen necessary. There are different possibilities to perform collision estimation e. g. at a central server, the onboard unit of the vehicle or the pedestrian's mobile phone, as depicted in Fig. 44.1.

Each context filter module follows its own mission as exemplified by the following instances:

Position Module

Positioning is based on a global navigation system such as Global Positioning System (GPS). GPS modules in Smartphones today however with a precision about 5 to 8 m and a sampling frequency of 1 Hz do not fulfill the necessary requirements for a safe pedestrian protection system. Our solution combines GPS with information from acceleration sensor and gyroscope for better precision and faster recognition of a position change. For the motion recognition, the data of the acceleration sensor and the gyroscope in the x-, y- and z-axis are captured with a sample rate of 40 Hz. Motion recognition is combined with walking speed estimation to develop a dead reckoning algorithm for pedestrians that takes their current movement state into account. Details about the algorithm can be found in [8].

Direction Module

This module gathers the movement of a pedestrian relative to the street utilizing the built-in magnetometer sensor of a smartphone. Results are important for verifying the likelihood of a collision with a vehicle. All pedestrians moving away from the street are not endangered; others have to be further observed, taking the information about the position, direction, speed and acceleration of the respective cars -provided by the vehicle detection module – into account. Attainable direction accuracy of the digital compass has been described through experiments in [9] and assessed as being suitable. However special attention shall be given to the impact of magnetic diversions since they influence the accuracy of the magnetometer (e. g. through parking cars). Our algorithm developed allows for necessary corrections and to compensate for any magnetic deviation, simply by subtracting the assessed deviation from the magnetometer sensor data in order to achieve a more precise movement direction detection of pedestrians.

Curb Detection Module

Our method developed for curb detection has shown, that with smartphone sensor data from accelerometer and gyroscope and combined with an appropriate classifier, it is possible for the system to recognize when the pedestrian steps down onto the street level. This stepping on the road detection is one of the most relevant indications for higher collision likelihood. Due to the short duration of "curb crossing", only 0.56 s on average, sliding window parameters are chosen to support its detection. In [10] a large number of experiments have been conducted to evaluate achievable results for stepping down from the curb recognition, taking into account several parameters such as different curb heights and different walking speeds. The context filter fuses this information about "curb crossing" into the situation assessment as a specific trigger for collision risk evaluation.

Complimentary approaches to solve the street crossing detections for pedestrians exist. In [11] street crossing detection relies only on GPS data. The street crossing algorithm checks if the path of a pedestrian will cross the street by extrapolating the user's path from its position using the bearing values from the GPS data over a fixed distance. In the evaluation it was found that the algorithm was able to detect 85% of all street crossings in a suburban and 78% in an urban environment at a maximum of 5 s after the person actually stepped on the street. The authors of [11] conclude that GPS only "does not serve well the fine-grained positioning needs of pedestrian safety applications in dense urban environments".

Motion Profile Module

The context filter offers to create a pedestrian specific motion profile. It provides important information that concern movement behavior patterns, maximum speed capabilities, age and height and additional personalized information about the pedestrian involved to be utilized for an even more efficient protection procedure. Of course under strict observance of privacy and data protection. Guidelines and first approaches have been published in [12].

Finally – after combining and filtering data available from all context filter modules – a collision estimation module computes the likelihood of an accident and if appropriate starts preset warning procedures, which can be acoustic, optic or haptic or any combi-

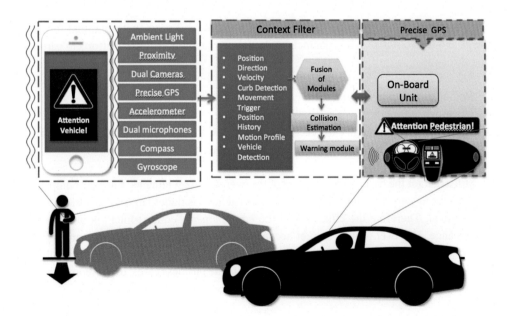

Fig. 44.3 ComTec 2016 – Safety Belt for pedestrian overall solution

nation thereof for user alerts, as depicted in Fig. 44.3. Within the collision avoidance scenarios "missed alarms" and "false alarms" are important performance indicators, they have been sampled for each of the context filter's modules and have to be continuously evaluated for improving the overall accuracy of collision estimation results.

44.4 Business Case Scenarios

The proposed "safety belt for pedestrian" solution provides a compelling approach to reduce an ever-increasing number of traffic casualties from vulnerable road users. Its market potential builds upon the high acceptance of communities and the society as a whole to overcome traffic fatalities and to reduce the related expenses. With that in mind it is envisioned that many stakeholders, from health insurance companies to elderly care centers, from safe community activists to OEM manufacturer will participate in a valuable set of business cases. The safety belt for pedestrian thus can foster business liaisons for all interested parties and establish a sustainable business organization for market coverage and growth.

A first use case could be based on low monthly fee for participants, who use the service. Other use cases foresee free services from e. g. infrastructure provider or apply a "pay per use", where service is only charged for if a warning has been issued to the pedestrian.

44.5 Conclusion

The paper presents a protection system for vulnerable road users, with minimal investments and high efficiency. It is distinct from existing road user protection efforts in particular through:

- No line of site as a prerequisite for pedestrian's detection
- The proposed solution works weather independent
- Time advantage, through early recognition of a developing dangerous situation, which will allow for earlier triggering of alerts and actions.

Still a risk for the best possible impact of the overall system remains, since the complexity for filtering and analyzing the situational data at hand is rather large and naturally very time-critical. Therefore the efficiency of the core element "context-filter" is of outmost significance. However a huge market acceptance for the proposed pedestrian protection system can be expected since it will interest many different players and all of the in public health care involved parties to participate in sustainable business cases, to overcome traffic fatalities and to considerably reduce related expenses.

References

1. S. Huber, "Kopf hoch, bitte!," *ADAC Motoerwelt Magazin,* pp. 34–35, 07 2015.
2. [Online]. Available: http://ec.europa.eu/transport/road_safety/pdf/observatory/historical_evol. pdf. [Accessed 31 08 2016].
3. World Health Organization, Global status report on road safety 2015: supporting a decade of action, Geneva, Switzerland: WHO, 2015.
4. A. Flach und K. David, "A Physical Analysis of an Accident Scenario vetween Cars and Pedestrians," in *IEEE 70th Vehicular Technology Conference (VTC 2009-Fall)*, Anchorage, AK, USA, 2009.
5. K. Dhondge, S. Song, B.-Y. Choi und H. Park, "WiFiHonk: Smartphone-Based Beacon Sutffed WiFe Car2X-Communication System for Vulnerable Road User Safety," in *IEEE Vehicular Technology Conference (VTC 2014-Spring)*, Seoul, South Korea, 2014.
6. A. Tahmasbi-Sarvestani, H. Kazemi, Y. Fallah, M. Naserian und A. Lewis, "System Architecture for Cooperative Vehicle-Pedestrian Safety Applications Using DSRC Communication," in *SAE 2015 World Congress & Exhibition*, Detroit, MI, USA, 2015.
7. T. Schulz, A. Roßnagel und K. David, Datenschutz bei kommunizierenden Assistenzsystemen, Bd. 11, Für Datenschutz ZD, 2012, pp. 510–515.
8. S. Engel, K. David, D. Warkow und M. Holzknecht, "Car2Pedestrian Positioning: Methods for Improving GPS Positioning in Radio-Base VRU Protection Systems," in *6. Tagung Fahrerassistenzsysteme*, Munich, Germany, 2013.
9. A. Memon, S. Lau und K. David, "Investigation and Compensation of the Magnetic Deviation on a Magnetometer of a Smartphone Caused by a Vehicle," in *IEEE 78th Vehicular Technology Conference (VTC 2013-Fall)*, Las Vegas, NV, USA, 2013.
10. A. Jahn, K. David und S. Engel, "5G/LTE based protection of vulnerable road users: Detection of crossing a curb," in *IEEE 82nd Vehicular Technology Conf. (VTC2015-Fall)*, Boston, MA, USA, 2015.
11. S. Jain, C. Borgiattino, Y. Ren, M. Gruteser und Y. Chen, "On the limits of position-based pedestrian risk awareness," in *Proc. Workshop Mobile Augmented Reality and Robitiy Technology-based Systems (MARS-2014)*, Bretton Woods, NH, USA, 2014.
12. O. Coutland, S. Lau und K. David, "Determining the behavior of mobile location-aware services based on user action history," in *GIITG KuVS Fachgespr. Selbstorganisierende Adapt. Kontextsensitive Verteilte Syst. SAKS*, Kassel, Germany, 2006.

Further Reading
13. K. David und A. Flach, "CAR-2-X and Pedestrian Safety: Innovative Collision Avoidance System," in *IEEE Veh. Technol. Mag.*, 2010.

The Impact of Indoor Navigation Systems for Public Malls – a Comprehensive Overview –

45

Karsten Weronek

Abstract

This paper introduces the most favored technologies for Indoor Positioning Systems and the features of Indoor Navigation Systems for malls. These systems guide the customer through a building on his way to a desired place. On the other hand it makes possible to analyze the customer's journey. Combined with retail business apps on the customers' smartphones promises to generate revenue and customer loyalty. An intellectual stakeholder analysis reveals the potential benefits and issues for the future. However, the technology is not mature yet, business integration is complex and the implementation and operation of such a system has to mitigate various risks to be able to reach its return of investment.

45.1 Introduction

Large e-tailers are disrupting the established shop retail business. Therefor these shops try to compensate their decreasing revenue by extending into online business [1]. Even so, shopping centers and malls have increased their market share recently and seem to play a distinct role [2]. To gain this momentum the upcoming possibilities of indoor positioning and indoor navigation may be a preferential way for mall managers (MM) to add value to customers and retailers within the mall.

The permissions by Fraport and infSOFT GmbH, SBB and Faveno GmbH to publish the screenshots are greatfully acknowledged.

K. Weronek (✉)
Frankfurt University of Applied Sciences
Frankfurt on the Main, Germany
e-mail: KWeronek@FB2.FRA-UAS.de

© Springer-Verlag GmbH Germany 2018
C. Linnhoff-Popien et al. (eds.), *Digital Marketplaces Unleashed*,
https://doi.org/10.1007/978-3-662-49275-8_45

This paper gives a comprehensive overview of Indoor Positioning Systems (IPS) and Indoor Navigation Systems (INS) in large malls or similar places (large railway stations, airport terminals, etc.). Starting with an overview of the actual possible technologies the conceptual layer is illustrated by some examples. On the business layer the impact of an INS will be discussed, especially owing to an expected conflict of the stakeholders in a mall. The primary goal for implementing indoor navigation is to generate revenue by guiding the customer and providing shopping information using a smart-phone app and optimizing this by acquiring customer behavior.

The second section after this introduction explains briefly the latest most promising technologies to detect the current position of the customer in a mall. The section thereafter shows the possibilities to use the IPS as basis for INS and some options for the user interface. The fourth section will identify the stakeholders of IPS and INS. An intellectual stakeholder analysis reveals the different interests and possible benefits of the stakeholders from such an infrastructure. It identifies similar but also competing aims and interests of the stakeholders. It also shows the outstanding role of the manager of a mall. In this paper the MM is synonym for the executive person of the operative mall management to act in the interest of the mall's owner. He is responsible for providing the technical infrastructure (TI) and thus the data owner of the position data. Due to lack of space, legal and contractual issues like data privacy as well as issues regarding business intelligence systems are not discussed in this paper.

The last section is about the different risks of implementing and operating an IPS/INS and how to mitigate them. At the end a conclusion will summarize the results and give a short outlook for the future.

45.2   Indoor Positioning Systems as Technology Enabler

Outdoor positioning systems rely on Global Navigation Satellite Systems and are mature using e. g. the Geographical Positioning System (GPS). They are a commodity and are used not only in cars and ships but also by byciclists, joggers and hikers. When approaching semi-outdoor or indoor environments the GPS-satellite signals become unreliable or unavailable due to reflection and/or absorption by the building. Thinking about large buildings like (sport-)stadiums, airports, railway stations, shopping malls or campuses with multiple buildings (fairs, universities, museums, etc.) there exists a desire to extend the outdoor navigation to indoor seamlessly. Gartner positions IPS in his technology hype cycle as "climbing of the slope of enlightening" and to reach "the platform of productivity" within the next two years [3]. Since smartphones are becoming more and more ubiquitous they are the perfect end user device (UD).

The aim of IPS is to determine the whereabouts of a pedestrian in a mall by using sensors of the UD and a terrestrial, inertial TI that is suitable to be installed in a mall. Most modern smartphones have the following sensors integrated by default: camera, microphone, accelerometer, gyroscope, WLAN, Bluetooth, GPS, GSM and a 3D-magnetic sensor. There are many publications about using all these sensors and the related physics for indoor positioning (light, radio waves, sound waves, magnetic fields and mechanical parameters) [4, 5]. However at the moment there are two sensors to favor for immediate practical use in malls namely WLAN and Bluetooth. Both of the technologies are also implemented in the UD as a transmitter which enables forward and reverse signal detection. Beacons are small transmitters of Bluetooth signals that frequently send a customable ID with a defined period and a defined power. Beacons use the Bluetooth Low Energy Protocol (released in 2009) that is an extension of Bluetooth. Since WLAN and Bluetooth work in the same frequency band they might interfere. Due to the frequency multiplex technology the interference can be minimized by skilled selection of the WLAN channels. The beacons may be installed as stand alone. Some types are manageable by beacon controllers or by using them as a mesh net. Controllers are still expensive and need LAN-connection and power-connection which leads to significant additional costs compared to the beacons themselves. The mesh net approach has often been the disadvantage of a reduced feature set and leads to addition power consumption. Since most of the beacons use batteries that have to be changed after a time (life-time depends on radio power and transmission rate and the battery size and ranges between a couple of weeks and few years). The management facility also allows to set all parameters, to update the firmware and to detect defective or lost beacons or identify weak battery status for replacement demand.

Since the position and the physics of the TI is well known there are different possibilities to determine the unknown position of the UD. There are mainly two dimensions of the IPS issue. The first one distinguishes if the UD is the transmitter and the TI determines absolute or relative physical parameters or if the TI is the transmitter and the UD has to measure the physical parameters. The second dimension is the mathematical way of how to calculate the UD's position. There are mainly three possibilities. First is the *trilateration* that needs at least three distances that are determined either by the signal amplitude and a simple propagation model of the radio waves or by using the time of arrival or time difference of arrival. The second possibility is the *triangulation* that measures the angle of arrival by using amplitude or phase differences of antenna arrays. The third possibility is to model the radio topology. This can be done by empirical investigation of the signal strength by grid measurements and/or by using a parametrical radio wave propagation model. By having the radio map and the indoor map joined it is possible to compare a received signal strength (RSS) by the UD with the offline determined radio map of the related area in real time [6]. The relative RSS will then be correlated with the most probable and reasonable position of the UD. This method is called *fingerprinting* or *received signal strength identification* [7]. When changing the TI or the building the radio map needs to be updated which is an additional effort. Whereas parametrical models do not need the cost to establish the empirical radio map, since they are not as accurate. On the other hand using an empirical radio map leads to better spatial accuracy but needs much more storage and computing time on the UD and increases the power consumption. For further reading about IPS see [5] and references therein.

45.2.1 Wireless LAN for Indoor Positioning

Wireless LAN seems to be a good possibility to implement IPS since WLAN is often already installed. However it has some weaknesses to be mentioned. Apple's iOS does not allow to detect the amplitude of the received WLAN. So the use of UD as the receiver is not suitable. The use of the UD as sender is suitable and commercial solutions of different vendors are available in the market. However this solution is cost intensive since you need to have many access points. For accurate position at any point in time the receiver should have at least 4 conventional access points. Furthermore WLAN-IPS is only possible for connected UD. The standard period of the access-point-request by the UD is about 2 min in the case that the UDs are not connected to the WLAN. In this case it is only possible to determine the position every 2 min which is inappropriate.

However practical experience shows that WLAN-IPS have good accuracy (see e. g. [8]). They are suitable for semi-indoor environments and large halls like terminals where few access points may cover a large area.

45.2.2 Beacons for Indoor Positioning

Recently more and more malls have started to implement beacon-based indoor-positioning-infrastructure. A thorough planning of the position of the beacons is necessary depending on the requirements. When only push notifications are required it is easy to implement single beacons at the required points of interest (POI) and to use a simple app to receive notifications or to display a website. Sometimes it is necessary to detect the transition between areas (geo-fencing) e. g. to detect if the customer is in front of or already in the shop. In this case the number of necessary beacons doubles. The change of floors by escalators seems to be very difficult due to the metal and the interference of beacons located in different floors. For indoor navigation a dense distribution of beacons is necessary to get the required accuracy of the position to be able to navigate the customer through the building. In this case the number of beacons increases dramatically. The issue is that in many cases it is not easy to put beacons in place due to optical or mechanical issues. The large height of a hall is also disadvantageous. As a rule of thumb the distance between beacons should be double the spatial resolution requirements. However depending on the topological circumstances this varies strongly. Best practice is to start with a standard distribution and to generate an empirical "heat map" that shows the special resolution and to add more beacons where necessary.

45.2.3 Improving Indoor Positioning by Sensor Fusion

Empirical measurements show that the radio level of beacons fluctuates significantly. This can be due to moving people or objects, or modifications of buildings. The RSS also depends on the specific UD and the spatial orientation of the device because of the anisotropy of the receiving antenna. The relative position of the user and the UD influences the RSS as well. These fluctuations and uncertainties can be reduced by mathematical methods. The most prominent and efficient ones are Bayesian statistical analysis and Kalman filtering.

In practice it turns out that due to the topology of the mall the different technologies differ in implementation costs as well as in accuracy of the error of the detected position of the device. To improve accuracy one possibility is to combine the detected position of two different IPS (mostly WLAN and Beacon-based). Different holistic algorithms exist to join the position results of different IPS to decrease the deviation error of the position. This is called Indoor Positioning by Sensor Fusion (IPSF). The factors of the conjunction metrics may depend on topology, time, possible error factors (like moving people or trolleys etc.), the device type or signal-to-noise ratio. The use of IPSF is not trivial because it may lead to a jitter of the position. This is not caused by the IPS but by artefacts of the IPSF algorithm, so intense testing is required. However if the coverage of WLAN and/or beacons' signals are not comprehensive and the user maybe switched off either Bluetooth or WLAN on the UD, IPSF is the only chance to achieve a comprehensive IPS/INS over the complete area. IPSF is also necessary when seamless navigation between outdoor semi-indoor and indoor navigation is required.

45.3   Indoor Navigation Systems as Business Enabler

This chapter introduces the "conceptual layer" based on an IPS as "infrastructure layer" to implement an INS. An INS gives the possibility to guide the customer dynamically through the building which adds the first value to the customer. Second it enables the integration of business applications to provide location-based services and to navigate the customer to required locations and enables business opportunities.

Assuming an IPS-System is providing an accurate and precise estimate of the actual position of the customer, it is possible to assign this position to distinct areas or to form routes and trajectories. Trajectories are directed graphs that contain digitized positions parameterized by time. By forming conceptual trajectories (ways and stops) and attaching geographical content and annotating semantic information it is possible to compute a semantic behavior of the consumer [9]. By aggregation of the trajectories of multiple customers, it is possible to learn about customer behavior and to group them into so called personas. This enables marketing, offerings and business opportunities.

45.3.1   Geo-Fencing Using Indoor Positioning Systems

A *geo-fence* is a virtual perimeter for a real-world geographic area. The use of a geo-fence is called geo-fencing. One example of usage involves a location-aware device of a user entering or exiting a geo-fence. This activity could trigger a push message to the device's user as well as a message to the geo-fence operator [10].

Geo-fencing in INS is to locate the customer in a specific area e. g. a specific shop or a waiting area or service area etc. If the exact position is not a requirement geo-fencing is easier than to determine the exact point of position, e. g. in airports it may be sufficient to detect if a flights passengers are already waiting in the waiting area of the flight gate. This can easily be solved by implementing a single beacon with a simple geo-fencing algorithm at each gate. To provide simple location based services this solution is also suitable. This may be a good cost effective starting point for implementing an IPS-infrastructure even if it does not allow to guide the customer through the mall.

45.3.2   Navigating by Indicating the Direction

One of the biggest issues of the customer is to find a POI in a large building environment. By calculating a route to the requested POI, it is possible to display the direction to walk on an indoor map (Fig. 45.1 right). The indoor map is needed as pictures in different sizes and resolutions as well as in a parametrized way to allocate the position onto the picture before displaying it on the UD. However you have two main issues with this approach. The customer expects to have the map in the direction of his front view. Therefor the UD needs to know the direction of the cardinal points. In buildings there are numbers of disturbances of the geomagnetic field so that this can't be detected by the UD's magnetic sensor in a constant reliable manner. The other issue is that the route has taken the non-trivial geographical topology into account. However since the assumption of the accurate and precise estimate of the position is still in dispute, this way of INS needs to be evaluated and tested properly at the moment.

45.3.3   Navigating by Following Virtual Walkways

A possibility to overcome the issues of the navigation by indicating the direction is to create virtual walkways like airways. The position of the IPS is then projected onto a position of the next walkway (Screenshots of different examples of Indoor-Navigation apps: Fig. 45.1). The routing is then along the walkway. The overall route is easy to calculate by having a repository of the routes in the mall and by using the Dijkstra Algorithm [11] to find the best route. This is a proven technology and also used in car navigation systems although the streets are real there. This solution therefor is expected to have a high user acceptance.

Using this approach you may get trouble with the calculation of the route. In many cases it is not likely to indicate the shortest and/or fastest way to the customer. Either you have issues in your mall like construction areas, moving stairways out of order or you have decided to take the elevators or stairways. If you have dynamic routing of customers (e. g.

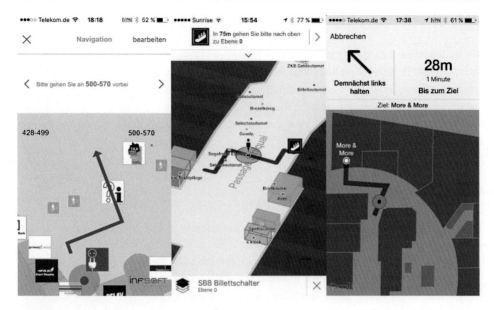

Fig. 45.1 *Left* Frankfurt Airport app, the starting point was detected using WLAN-IPS, *middle* SBB (Suisse Railway) Zurich railroad station using iBeacon IPS, *right* Prototype of INS using i-Beacon IPS, map oriented in viewing direction

in airports) the routing of your INS needs to have an interface to that system to dynamically change the routing accordingly. Otherwise the customer gets different directions from the static signs, from the dynamic signature and from the mobile app. In this case the customer will become confused and may de-install the app. Dynamic routing is also useful for marketing or revenue reasons.

45.3.4   Guiding by Description

Routing by following virtual walkways may not be accepted by people who have trouble with spatial imagination and abstraction. It may also lack of usability for certain consumer profiles (e. g. elder people). For these cases it may be better to visualize the route by one or more overview maps and to provide dynamically textual information about the route like: "follow the hallway for 30 m", "now, when you pass the service office on the right side, turn left", "walk 20 m straight" "use the escalator up . . ." (Fig. 45.1 left, middle). This leads to the necessity of having a repository of route segments in place, their routing messages, together with (changing) POIs and an engine to dynamically compile routes together with route-descriptions. By using route descriptions it is also possible to use text to speech software to enable blind people to navigate [12]. The best solution is to combine the virtual walkways with semantic annotations. Systems using virtual reality are under way but still not regarded as a solution.

45.4 How to Add Value to the Stakeholders

In a mall you have at least 3 stakeholders. These are consumers, shops (and chain stores) and the MM. In railway stations and airports you may have the so-called "meeters and greeters". These "customers" are summarized by consumers since they are potential consumers in most cases. In this section the aims and requirements for an INS by the stakeholder from the business point of view are summarized. It reveals that some requirements are similar but some of them are conflicting.

45.4.1 Consumer

The word consumer will summarize people independently if they intend to use a service or buy a product or not or have or haven't done it already. The indicator of a consumer is the presence in the area of the INS despite his intention to be there.

Most of the consumers try to get information of the location or are curious to use a new service like an INS-app. Some just want to be entertained. Some like hunting coupons. After having installed the app the consumer may look for opportunities like free services (complementary transportation, free WLAN, access to lounges, etc.). Other consumers have the intention to find services or products to satisfy an actual demand (e. g. a coffee, gifts, or to buy s.th. for immediate use etc.). When the customer wants to buy a distinct product or product group, he may want to find and compare similar products and their prices. After having identified the distinct facility (e. g. a certain shop), it is mostly required to get there comfortably. Often this is not feasible using static signatures since the number of possible destinations are too high. This is the point where the INS-app has its largest leverage for customer satisfaction. The consumer gets a personalized route and get a pleasurable feeling of being understood and being guided by the "hosting landlord". However it also has the largest risk to lose the customer as a buyer when the INS does not work reliably or lacks in usability.

After having reached the final destination, a feature to enable home delivery is really appreciated by the consumer. When buying clothes, different colors that are not available in the shop but in a central store are also required.

45.4.2 Retailer or Chain Store

The retailers are eager to make consumers to buyers or even to patrons. They aim to increase the number of potential consumers in their shop or in their online-shop. They try to have a big conversion rate from potential customers to buyers. They try to increase the visit frequency of patrons and to increase the check (revenue per buy) by up-selling or cross-selling. Therefor they also like customers possessing purchasing power.

In other words, retailers aim for everything that increases their revenue. However an INS-app facilitates to get information about the customer. In most cases a registration is necessary in which the customer has to at least release his e-mail address. He also has to commit the terms and conditions for the use of the system that includes the commitment of the Data Privacy Statement. This enables the retailer to perform marketing campaigns to get customer retention and loyalty. Marketing campaigns may be issuing newsletters, sending special offers or coupons. The retailer can also send messages to the consumer when he is approaching the shop to get him into the shop. These messages are most effective when personalized. However this form of real-time marketing is only in its infancy.

45.4.3   Mall Manager

The MM plays a special role. He is the only one who is able to integrate an IPS and to provide the position data to retailers or consumers. The business generation model of the MM is either to provide good services to attract consumers to increase their number to attract retailers that pay high rents for shops in the attractive mall. MMs often apply a retail-revenue dependent part of the rent. In these cases the MMs are also interested in increasing the overall revenue of all shops within his mall. He additionally aims to attract solvent buyers to his mall.

However the MM has to avoid that retailers cannibalize their shop revenue by moving transactions to their online store or lose the costumer to online shops of the external e-tailers. In this case the achievable rent for the mall manager decreases.

Mall managers also try to manage their shop portfolio to make the mall attractive to customers. They also try to position the different shops to optimize the revenue. By collecting customer movements and dwell and waiting times, the MM is the only one who is able to analyze customer behavior in his overall mall. He is then able to optimize the mall and can also advise the retailers to optimize their portfolio or their shop set-up. He also may sell consumer data or consumer positions (IPS-data) or behavior to refinance his infrastructure investment. But he needs to mind personal-data-security-compliance. He also need to orchestrate the requirements of the different shops regarding pop-ups of special offers. He also has to govern digital marketing campaigns. Otherwise sending too many messages annoys the customer and may led him to de-install the app. At the end of the day the MM is the hub of the spoke and has to be the "highlander" to run and to develop the overall system in a multi-win manner, which is a real challenge.

45.4.4   Possible Measures

Malls are usually equipped with a WLAN infrastructure. This needs to be optimized regarding indoor navigation (completeness of illumination and spatial distribution). Then a mobile-app needs to be developed accompanied by a marketing campaign to get the app onto potential customers' UDs. Afterwards a beacon-based IPS-solution needs to be implemented. The app needs to be extended accordingly. In parallel a stakeholder community needs to be established to understand the requirements of the shop-owners and to communicate the benefits of an INS. Additionally online-shops of the retailers may be already in place. Afterwards the MM may decide to implement either an app of app solution or to implement a "mall-shop-solution" and to implement interfaces to the other systems (the vision is "virtual mall solution"). Since most of the malls don't have an IT-department or in cases where they have one(e. g. big airports) but not having the expertise in IPS/INS, malls need to mandate and to partner with a professional IT-Integrator. Additionally a solution for operating and maintaining the systems as well as for the further development needs to be established.

However, the implementation of an IPS/INS-solution for malls that will generate a significant business benefit is extremely complex. It needs an extensive financial investment upfront and permanent management attention. The implementation and the operation need a cooperation on all levels (management, process, people and technology) as well as an excellent communication between all involved parties and participants. The risks of such a venture are crucial. Therefor the risk mitigation is mandatory and will be discussed in the next section.

45.5   Implementation Risks and Mitigation Thereof

When the first shop owner in a mall starts about or even thinks about introducing beacons in his shop, it is time to start thinking about the implementation of mall-wide IPS/INS. Only the MM is able to implement a mall-wide INS infrastructure. Unfortunately it is also necessary to provide an app which runs on different smartphones. Both need a significant up-front investment by the mall. This can be refunded by usage contracts or by increasing the rent after tenant changes. This risk is not mitigable because it is an entrepreneurial decision by the MM.

The technology still isn't a commodity. Therefor an integrator needs to be mandated who has already proved his expertise by reference projects and that his offered solution is able to fulfil the requirements. It needs to be decided if a prime contractor is applied or if the disciplines of indoor positioning and integrating the multichannel part (implementation and integration of app, website, online-shop) should be split into two specialized providers. The IPS is very technical whereas the INS is very end-user related, especial the front-end app.

The vertical integration starting from the physics of radio waves over mathematical methods and technology interfaces up to the GUIs for the end-user, combined with the retail and marketing processes in the back-office of the vendors is very complex. Therefor an "Enterprise Architect" is mandatory to oversee the overall architecture to assure that all components fit together seamlessly. Otherwise the solution does not work properly and won't be accepted by the customer and make the investment void.

The user acceptance of the solution is very critical. Only if numerous potential consumers use the solution and generate new revenue the ROI will be achieved. To gain customer satisfaction a continuous improvement process needs to be implemented that involves the customers. Requirements of the customers need to be discussed between managers, IT-personnel, as well as IT architects and vendors to consequently improve the solution. Additionally the vendor market and the activities of the competitors need to be traced to be able to react timely on market developments in this field in an appropriate manner.

Another risk is that the actual WLAN/beacon technology may be disrupted by other upcoming technologies. This risk is not mitigable because it is unforeseeable. Another sensor or positioning technology may have such a progress to be able to provide a better or cheaper solution than the actual one. It may also be a risk that large smartphone vendors introduce new possibilities or standards for their product or prevent using the sensors for IPS. This may induce a rapid depreciation of the investment for the already implemented solution.

Another risk is the hitchhiking of the IPS-infrastructure by other online retailers. Since the IDs of beacons and WLANs are often detectable the retailer who has an app with the detecting and transmitting features is able to detect that the customer is in a mall or in a certain shop. Doing so he is able to push an offer to the customer to prevent him buying in the shop but initiate to buy in his online shop. To prevent this hitchhiking an encryption and a frequent change of the IDs are required.

As already mentioned in the preceding section, the aims of the vendors may lead to conflicts since the consumer can only be in one shop at a time. So one vendor aims to get the consumer in his shop whereas the other vendor tries to keep the consumer in his shop as long as possible. This coopetition of the different shops may lead to a confusing situation for the consumer e. g. by receiving too many push notifications containing offers or coupons. The MM has to be the mediator by managing the app and the marketing campaigns in cooperation with all shops. In the future it may be that shop owners become shareholders of their mall for this reason. The other possibility is to form informal committees or formal subsidiaries to manage this complex issue. This is somehow comparable with the Prisoner's Dilemma [13]. At the end it is better to work together instead of aiming towards individual victory and in the end lose more than initially gained.

45.6   Conclusion

This paper has shown, that implementing Indoor Position Systems is still a technological challenge due to the necessity to combine different technologies. The indoor positioning-technology is on the slope to becoming mature. The horizontal and vertical business and technology integration is extremely complex and needs excellent multidisciplinary teams. However the increasing number of already implemented systems by early adopters proved the concept regardless of a bunch of areas for improvements.

There are different possibilities to develop an indoor navigation system based on an indoor positioning system to give the customer the possibility to find his way to his gate. Depending on the target user group you need to decide carefully how the user interface should be designed. Sole indoor navigation does not have a direct payback but is an excellent customer service. To achieve revenue it is necessary to combine it with business systems offerings e. g. an online-shop, couponing, loyalty programs etc. Be aware the following subjects are more or less still in an "experimental phase": Digital Market Malls, Customer Journey Analytics, Real-Time Marketing, Bluetooth Beacons and Multichannel Markets and need enormous investments with unforeseeable Return-of-Invest. Definitely it is crucial to cope continuously from the very beginning with stakeholders' competing interests.

Anyway, mall managers need to approach the outlined subjects to be able to consult their shareholder regarding their investments, risks and opportunities. At the end of the day it is not the question if, but when and how to start, not to be withdrawn by the competitive online retail market.

References

1. KPMG, "Trends in Retail 2020," EHI Retail Institute, 18 04 2012. [Online]. Available: https://www.kpmg.com/DE/de/Documents/trends-retail-2020-executive-summary-2013-kpmg.pdf. [Accessed 04 09 2016].
2. Handelszeitung, "Handelszeitung," [accessed on 02/09/16]. [Online]. Available: http://www.handelszeitung.at/handelszeitung/shopping-malls-erhoehen-marktanteil-129908. [Accessed 03 09 2016].
3. G. Inc, "Hype-Cycle-Mobile-Device-Technologies," 2016. [Online]. Available: https://www.gartner.com/doc/3374017/hype-cycle-mobile-device-technologies. [Accessed 04 09 2016].
4. Vittorio M. N. Passaro (. e. al., "Sensors | Free Full-Text | Sensors for Indoor Mapping and Navigation," MDPI, 5 2016. [Online]. Available: http://www.mdpi.com/1424-8220/16/5/655. [Accessed 04 09 2016].
5. a. S. Z. Kourosh Koshelham, "Sensors for Indoor Mapping an Navigation, an references therin," *Sensors,* vol. 16, no. 655, 2016.
6. Lohan, E-S., Talvitie, J., Figueiredo e Silva, P., Nurminen, H., Ali-Löytty, S., & Piche, R., "Received Signal Strength models for WLAN and BLE-based indoor positioning in multi-floor buildings".
7. Ph. Müller, M. Raitoharju, S. Ali-Löytty, L. Wirola, R. Piché, "A Survey of Parametric Fingerprint-Position Methods," *Gyroscopy and Navigation,* vol. Vol 7, no. Mo. 2, pp. pp. 107-127, 2016.
8. Gints Jekabsons, Vadim Kairish, Vadim Zuravlyov, "An Analysis of Wi-Fi Based Indoor Positioning," *Scientific Journal of Riga Technical University, Computer Science. Applied Computer Systems,* no. 47, p. 131, 2011.
9. Zhixian Yan, Dipanjan Chakraborty, Semantics in Mobile Sensing (Synthesis Lectures on the Semantic Web: Theory and Technology), San Rafael, CA, USA: Morgan & Claypool Publishers (May 1, 2014), 2014.
10. Wikipedia, [Online]. Available: http://en.wikipedia.org/wiki/geo-fence. [Accessed 04 09 2016].

11. E. W. Dijkstra, "A Note on Two Problems in Connexion with Graphs; Numerische Mathematlk 1, 269–27I," (1959). [Online]. Available: http://www-m3.ma.tum.de/foswiki/pub/MN0506/WebHome/dijkstra.pdf. [Accessed 04 09 2016].
12. S. F. Airport, "LowViz Guide – Indoor Navigation For The Visually Impaired," [Online]. Available: https://itunes.apple.com/us/app/lowviz-guide-indoor-navigation/id987917857?mt=8. [Accessed 04 09 2016].
13. Robert Axelrod; William D. Hamilton, "The Evolution of Cooperation," American Association for the Advancement of Science, [Online]. Available: http://www-personal.umich.edu/~axe/research/Axelrod%20and%20Hamilton%20EC%201981.pdf. [Accessed 04 09 2016].

Part XI
Industry 4.0

Preface: Industry 4.0

46

Robert Blackburn

Abstract

As President at BASF, the world's leading chemicals and specialty products company, I look after a 5.4 € bn. budget being responsible for BASF's vast global supply chain operations, including the global customer services team, IT operations and related shared services. Having kicked off BASF's digitalization in 2011, My team is composed of approximately 14,000 employees with operations in 140+ countries. Having joined BASF Group 10 years ago, I else led BASF's Global Enterprise Transformation program.

Prior BASF, after starting my career at Deloitte LLP, the global strategy and accountancy firm, I held several senior executive roles at leading hardware and software P&L businesses at IBM. Additionally, I serve on several boards as Chairman or as Non-Executive Director and I am a visiting lecturer at both Massachusetts Institute of Technology and Karlsruhe Institute of Technology.

46.1 Introduction

The economy is at the beginning of the next major industrial revolution, and technology is the driver, this time as the heart of both the production of many different products and as a core intelligent component of the things we use every day. Digitization has long since moved into factories, and is now enabling operations in which humans work side by side with intelligent machines.

R. Blackburn (✉)
BASF Group
Ludwigshafen, Germany
e-mail: robert.blackburn@alumni.uni-heidelberg.de

515

"Industry 4.0" is the catchphrase widely used to describe digital networking in the manufacturing industry. Industry 4.0 is the fourth industrial revolution after the mechanization of production in the 18th century, the electrification of production and the introduction of assembly lines in the late 19th century, and, finally, the automation of production beginning in the 1970 s and continuing ever since. This fourth revolution is set to raise automation to a new level, marked by the unstoppable march of information technology through all areas of industry, also known as the Internet of Things. Now businesses are gearing up to invest almost a trillion dollars a year in the digitization of production according to a global study by PricewaterhouseCoopers based on answers from managers of more than 2000 companies in nine areas of industry.

Over the last two to three years, many companies across all industries, including the world's leading chemical company – BASF –, have made major strides in this transformation process. Innovative developments in fields of artificial intelligence, virtual reality or smart factories, to name only a few, are already showing great promise in execution. It is clear that Industry 4.0 is and will remain a major business and societal topic for the foreseeable future, and not only in the chemicals industry. In my experience from leading both Boards of Directors as well as performing senior executive roles in leading high tech businesses, and now at BASF, I have seen how digital technologies have become part and parcel of serving customers around the world, optimizing a vast global supply chain, logistics operations and information services operations. Even though these technologies are often behind the scenes, they impact our lives every day and are blazing a trail for Industry 4.0. We recognize the potential of digital technologies to advance every part of a company, especially in areas such as logistics, engineering, production, procurement, supply chain, marketing and sales.

That is why, I will give examples in this article of how digitization is already changing how we work in the process industry, as well as share insights about both the opportunities and challenges for the future.

46.2 Industry 4.0 Shaping Our World

The intelligent merging of virtual and physical worlds is not only the basis of the smart factory of tomorrow, it is already becoming a part of our everyday lives. Autonomous cars, exercise clothing with sensors that analyze the wearer's posture, refrigerators which sound the alarm when a food item needs replenishing, as I have in my home already – these are just a few examples of how the Internet of Things raises the real world to a virtual level. Connected and mobile everyday items are becoming smart devices and creating a world we used to only imagine. Besides being able to drive itself, the car of the future will be able to find a parking spot, entertain us and do mandate tasks like scheduling appointments. Sensors inside the car can already track eye and head movements of the person behind the wheel and send a warning if the driver seems distracted. The passenger in the car will be able to reserve a hotel room by eye contact, simply by gazing at the hotel as they pass by and giving a voice command.

And that's just the start. In this attractive mass market, creativity in terms of the Internet of Things knows almost no bounds. According to Andrew McAfee and Erik Brynjolfsson, economists at the Massachusetts Institute of Technology (MIT) in Cambridge, Massachusetts, USA, the digital revolution is only just beginning. Their 2014 bestseller, "The Second Machine Age," took Silicon Valley by storm and spread like wildfire from there. The message: The second machine age will transform the world equaled only by the Industrial Revolution before it.

The reason is Moore's Law, attributed to visionary Gordon Moore, an Intel co-founder. He predicted already in 1965 that microchip performance would double every year until 1975. Amazingly, this law still applies to this day – except that the doubling now takes about 18 months rather than twelve, more than 40 years after 1975. What's more, Moore's Law applies in many areas of digital technology, not just microprocessors, where I have spent a large part of my early career: storage capacity, data transmission speeds, supercomputer energy efficiency – all these areas show more or less exponential growth.

In the smart factory of tomorrow everyone and everything communicates with each other. Consider the possibility that every part in a production factory, and entire factories can be interconnected. Measurement, monitoring, control and data processing units, which are fundamental elements of industrial control systems, connect via the Internet and interact creating an enormous network of valuable information. What experts call, "cyberphysical systems", or systems which combine both physical and virtual worlds, are transforming industry.

Connected production does not end in the smart factory. The entire value chain across different organizational structures – from ordering to product delivery – can be digitized. A digital interconnected supply chain furthermore involves harmonizing all internal decision taking structures and rules, processes before and after production, as well as integrating suppliers, logistics service providers and customers in the company's own value-adding processes. As I argued in my PhD, indeed this expedited information flow is the key to competitive supply networks – Industry 4.0 will only take it to hyper speed!

This way, digital connectedness enables highly efficient and highly flexible production. Real-time integration of customers' preferences allows a wide variety of product versions to be created. Industrial manufacture and information technology grow ever closer together. Better connectivity with customers, business partners and service providers is an increasingly important part of that process, which supports being a reliable supplier for customers. For instance, Hoffmann Group, a world leading system partner for quality tools, is working on the implementation of these strong and partner-like relationships to its customers and partners to provide agile and customized solutions in real-time. Already about six years ago, Hoffmann Group presented its so-called 360° Tooling Platform which lies at the heart of its Industry 4.0 strategy. This comprehensive service platform includes Tool Concept, a service providing CAD data of tools and helping customers to detect the best treatment for their components online. Another example is the Hoffmann eScanner, which empowers customers to automatically order a product at their production site. Through scanning a barcode on a tool, repeat orders are translated automatically into the order management system, which makes the order process for customers faster and very user friendly.

Machine manufacturers can already monitor their machines digitally in the future across national borders and continents. Parts heading for breakdown due to wear and tear or damage will be replaced before downtime occurs. The machine manufacturer simply sends digital product information to a local factory, which manufactures the spare part with 3D printing or has informed a supplier that a critical tool must arrive before the machine breaks.

Through various industry, expectations are very high all over the world and when it comes down to it, the possibilities are endless. Entirely new vistas – and certainly completely new business models – open up when everything in production is linked together in one huge network: An agricultural machinery manufacturer equips farm machinery, such as combine harvesters and tractors, with sensors that record data about the field as well as the machine's current position and fill level. This data is transmitted automatically to a control panel, which helps facilitating more efficient planning of how to use the specific machine. A precision toolmaker has developed a system to warn users of possible problems, for example if a drill is nearing breaking point. The information helps to pinpoint when the tool needs to be replaced. Airplane turbines are equipped with sensors which collect extensive data during every flight. The information provides a much better basis for evaluating turbine performance and doing maintenance when the airplane really needs it instead of the normal scheduled maintenance. Another benefit: existing turbines can be optimized to save fuel. The data is also used to further improve the performance and efficiency of the next turbine generation. In the end, customers benefit from longer machine lifetimes, fuel savings and reduced maintenance costs.

German manufacturing companies plan to invest an annual €40 billion in digital applications up to 2020 in order to increase their production efficiency, which recent studies expect to surge by up to 18 % in five years. This will clearly be transferred to BASF and the need to be prepared for higher automatized, efficient and customer centric solutions – system and organizational wise – will be a result. Regarding agile digitization, across all sectors, the automotive industry has made the most headway. Hoffmann Group, also being a leading supplier for the automotive industry offering a benchmark delivery reliability of 99 % today, is for instance already paving the way for a better connected and digitized automotive industry. This will be driven by a high level of real-time data transparency, automated warehouses and through an efficient network collaboration by integrating customers, partners and service providers. The capability to reliably commit to customers, strongly benefits the just-in-time production in the automotive sector. Companies like Hoffmann with these capabilities allow digitization in the automotive industry to be brought to the next level. The latest automotive market studies show the new challenges that digitization poses for carmakers in the coming years. The number of cars connected to the internet is predicted to rise more than six-fold from 23 million now to 152 million by 2020. The automotive industry also expects the number of machine-to-machine internet connections in the sector to reach 1.8 billion by 2022. That leads me to the point that not only the chemical industry or BASF, as the biggest automotive supplier in our industry, must be well equipped with new technologies and solutions to react to these kind of changing market trends.

Besides introducing new opportunities and business models, digitization is also changing the way we do business. In the Harvard Business Review, economist Michael S. Porter and CEO of Parametric Technology Corporation James E. Heppelmann predicted that digitization will revolutionize job roles and corporate structures. Jim and I discussed, that this means rethinking basically everything we do – starting with strategy. Porter and Heppelmann believe in the emergence of restructured departments and organization forms involving new collaborations, where IT and research and development divisions are integrated and cooperation is much higher. IT departments, traditionally focused on the company's internal IT structure and management of utilized software tools, has to play a more central role in future, as it does at BASF. Porter and Heppelmann expect that IT hardware and software will be designed and built into the actual products as well as the entire information technology architecture. My first experiences with this were at IBM in the early 2000s, when we were already doing exactly that in the business, I was leading.

According to a study undertaken by the German Fraunhofer Institute of Labor Economics and Organization (IAO) and the German professional IT association Bitkom, networking of product development, production, logistics, and customers in the chemical industry between 2013 and 2025 could boost its value creation by 30 %, which is quite a sum when you consider an annual turnover of around 190 billion euros. It is therefore hardly surprising that more and more chemical companies or other industry player are striving to harvest the potential "fruits" of Industry 4.0. One of the most important areas is the avoidance of unplanned production stoppages. Networked sensors in machines and equipment, systematic evaluation of machine data with special software, and utilization of mathematical models provide information, for example about the potential failure of a process pump, way before it will actually happen. However, utilization of data has so much more to offer than just improved predictive maintenance processes. If it proves possible to transfer existing production data into mathematical models of the process, companies could seize new competitive advantages: Products could be manufactured exactly to customers' specifications, using precisely the stipulated amounts of raw materials and energy.

There is another driving force for digitization in chemical factories: The current trend towards high-value specialty chemicals is lowering production volumes and requiring frequent product changes. This means flexible planning and production is needed, which in turn demands highly networked, adaptive, and self-configuring production processes, which follow a joint decision and customer centric approach aligned with all internal organizational parts.

46.3 The Digital Transformation of BASF

As the world's leading chemical company, the opportunities Industry 4.0 offers to boost BASF's competitiveness are enormous. As its digital journey has progressed, it's no longer only about optimizing the company's existing internal IT architecture to increase efficiency. The ability to respond and connect with customers and partners more reliably, much faster and more flexibly is increasing at a tremendous rate. Overall, we see that technological progress is changing the role IT and its experts play at BASF. It hasn't been simply about IT tools for over 5 years, it involves close collaboration across all divisions of our business including logistics, engineering, production, procurement, supply chain, marketing and sales. Networked production and distribution creates more transparency in our value chains, production processes and about our customer requirements, which is crucial to leverage the competitive benefits available now and for the future. Diverse examples show as to how BASF has been able to put Industry 4.0 into practice so far.

Digitization reached the warehouse long ago. BASF warehouses in both France and Poland were early adopters on the digital automation front. In the French facility high-bay forklifts, robots, cranes and conveyer belts for boxes and pallets work together in perfect harmony. In the high-bay warehouse in Poland, forklifts and pallets steer themselves to their destination, and goods are automatically wrapped, labeled and put in storage. These automated warehouses are the prelude to the smart factory of the future.

At BASF, we have been driving supply chain digitization forward since 2008 by developing and implementing business processes and digital solutions to improve production planning at our factories all over the world. More precise and flexible production planning and processes enable a more rapid response to fluctuating customer requirements. They also give central visibility into production planning and make fine planning processes more transparent.

46.3.1 Smart Supply Chain

The "smart supply chain" is another big topic here. It is about digital solutions that forge closer automated ties between BASF, its customers, 3rd party providers and suppliers – in essence the competitive supply network, I described in my PhD dissertation, referred to the above. The idea is called horizontal integration, which defines the integration of automated planning based on customer demand across BASF's businesses as well as with external customers and suppliers. A cloud planning platform allows BASF to exchange key data in near real-time with the customer. Where a customer chooses to share procure and production plans, this information can be used to automatically compute and plan replenishment. The planning should be fully automatized and without human intervention, except in cases for exception management and monitoring of the models. Demand and supply plans are shared with upstream partners and customers in real-time allowing us orchestrate the end-to-end value chain. This increases reliability and service levels, thereby improving customer satisfaction and loyalty which in turn can position BASF to become the customer's supplier of choice. Horizontal integration is an opportunity for supply networks to not only contribute to cost reduction due to improved inventory management, but more importantly to a shorter cash-to-cash cycle and improved effectiveness for the customer, thereby leading to an increased EBIT impact.

Digitization has also reached the global world of shipping containers. A sensor in a container records factors such as temperature, fluctuations and humidity and transmits the information in real-time leveraging mobile networks. The information is then passed to control centers which can act in real time as required. Performance features go beyond those of conventional track & trace systems because the new system reports details of what goes on during transportation and provides a basis for analysis and action. A customer receives the data before the container even arrives. This lets the customer know about anything that happened on route or during loading or unloading – for example, heavy impacts – and indicates the condition of the load in the container. The sensor also helps us show that the content of the container was maintained at proper temperatures without variation, which is critical for example, in temperature-sensitive pharmaceutical goods. BASF could provide guarantees to its customers, giving us a competitive edge.

Digitization also involves new digital business models. They arise when the technological opportunities of a digital world are used to harness new business potential. A BASF example from agriculture is called Maglis™. Maglis connects data, people and technology in a smarter way. It is linking information like local weather, soil conditions and crop growth stage predictions as a basis for generating crop protection recommendations. With the aid of apps linked to a database and available on mobile devices, users – farmers in this instance – have insights at their fingertips telling them when to use which crop protection product, what to use it for and how to use it. This promotes efficient, sustainable application of the products, helps farmers to understand their operation better and thus increases productivity. Farmers can also view information on all the BASF products that are relevant to their needs, which in an ideal scenario would help to build business and leverage BASF's portfolio. Additionally, BASF aims to increase efficiency in consulting and sales, expands its expertise and offers holistic solutions to their customers. The same principle can be applied in other business areas and for other customers, including the automotive industry, construction chemicals and food ingredients.

46.3.2   IT, the Great Enabler, Repackaged in Digital Approaches

Digitization has many opportunities to offer, none of which would be possible without smart IT solutions. For example, BASF's Supply Chain Early Warning System uses big data analysis for enterprise resource planning. We could predict future sales volumes more accurately and accelerate the logistics response to any changes. Thanks to innovative IT solutions like this, BASF is more agile and can, in the end, more reliably commit to customers. Through being better capable to fulfill customer's needs, customer satisfaction and loyalty will be increased, with all the benefits that follow. Additionally, a customer centric steering across different businesses is key.

Gathering information from value-added processes and chains and the ubiquitous real-time availability of that information allows companies to become faster, customer centric and – hence – more cost-effective. In the smart factory, parts and products have their own identity. Production processes self-improve on a permanent basis through continuous synchronization with factories. This only works if a suitably designed system delivers the necessary data across different businesses' value chains. A highly flexible but standardized application architecture is needed to support such automation, besides finding a common steering unit, which gathers these data in order to better predict, plan, commit and deliver reliably to customers.

To achieve this goal clear standards as well as consistent and joint decision processes across different businesses are needed. At BASF, a major step toward standardizing corporate processes in supply chain, procurement and finance was the migration of several different ERP systems to one BASF system in 2013. It was an essential prerequisite for BASF's digital future. On the basis of a consistent technological infrastructure, we were able to launch new processes for vertical- (in factory) and horizontal integration, as well as new tools supporting more effective collaboration in the company. The consolidation of data (structured and unstructured) provided the basis for assessment of large volumes of data throughout the organization and for big data analysis. But encountering horizontal integration only from a tool perspective is not enough to cater to the requested speed, agility and cost efficiency within all industries.

Digital technologies offer huge potential in accelerating the transformation of research outcomes into competitive innovations. In product development, big data analysis provides new opportunities to get to market faster and move closer to the customer. A BASF research division subsumes all topics coming from material sciences and systems technology. Its experts focus on developing new materials and improving material properties for research growth areas as diverse as lightweight design for the automotive industry, thermal management solutions for buildings, functional crop care, water treatment and coatings of all kinds.

To make sure customers get exactly the materials the market demands, extensive test scries are a standard procedure, followed by real-life application trials. Testing continues until a material with the ideal manufacturing properties has been found. This complex process generates huge volumes of information, which are stored in different systems. Part of these data are stored in an electronic lab journal, which at this time does not offer computer-based analysis of the unstructured data or enable design of experiments.

What if all research workers shared their experiments, analyses and test results and everybody could access the accumulated data? As part of an innovation project, we have started to develop a prototype – called Virtual Experiments Platform – involving four research projects. The platform analyzes lab data using a digital data model and supports researchers during the actual work process. The newly developed modeling program can calculate multiple parameters simultaneously and model highly complex improvements.

The platform cut the number of experiments in the second test series of one project by up to 90 % – and led straight to the desired outcome. Thus, the customer was presented with a valid result in a much shorter time.

We have shown that data modeling and optimization by computer can significantly accelerate research, which enables us to bring innovations to market much faster. What's more, digital data management secures know-how and provides access to the knowledge pool for every researcher who works with the system. The more people that actively use the platform, the more efficient the system actually becomes.

46.4   Success Factors for the Digital Transformation

46.4.1   Capturing the Potential of Big Data

Data is undeniably the currency of the 21st century, but to derive its true benefit, the right conclusions from the available information need to be drawn. Because of this, BASF has focused on data analytics and has been developing innovative, data-driven solutions to support BASF's businesses in decision-making.

Mathematical methods to evaluate large amounts of data for substantially more accurate prediction of future developments are a key element in these efforts. The ability to manage large volumes of data is also the basis for future-oriented methods like machine learning, examples of which include deep learning and cognitive computing that use models to approximate or mimic the functioning of the human brain. With cognitive computing, machines can learn, for example by cross-linking and analyzing source input – and by recognizing patterns. Machine learning is an area of major interest to BASF. It changes the way we use mathematical methods and enables to develop smart, self-learning solutions.

One example is a new solution called "Data Driven Sales," which gives the sales force access to the complete data set about their customer in real-time. With the aid of predictive algorithms, diverse information can be visualized such as the number of previously purchased product units or customer-specific product recommendations. The tool enables sales workers to respond faster to customer queries – anytime, anywhere.

46.4.2   Smart Manufacturing

BASF leverages potential applications for big data based tools in operations. "Smart manufacturing" is the key term here. It covers the production environment and engineering maintenance. An example would be the use of digital data analysis for predictive maintenance of factories and systems. "Smart manufacturing" shows how data analysis can be used for predictive maintenance in production operations in order to reduce or – ideally – completely eliminate unplanned downtime. For example, the steam cracker, which is one of BASF's key factories, is equipped with leading-edge measurement and control technology. The steam cracker has thousands of sensors monitoring process data, such as pressures and temperatures, so that the factory can be run from the control room and the condition of it can be monitored. Our experts have developed mathematical models with colleagues working in the factories to identify performance losses and abnormalities that would have gone unnoticed before. In the future, a dashboard will show if a particular column or factory component malfunction might occur. That information helps to manage the factory in a more targeted way and initiate counteractive measures. Gradual problems that develop over time can also be identified earlier. Moreover, the algorithms help to indicate the optimal time to choose for maintenance.

46.5 Challenges of Digital Evolution

The examples described in this article are just a taste of the opportunities tapped into so far as we transform BASF into a digital organization. The future holds many more, even though there are also challenges on the horizon where smart solutions are needed. The digitization and connection of everything makes businesses increasingly vulnerable to cyberattacks, a major challenge, which is increasing in both incidence and sophistication. To keep pace with these developments, businesses are raising their investment in IT security and joining forces to combat cybercrime. Only then can the potential of digitization be leveraged while companies also protect themselves effectively against cyberattacks.

The 2014 hack of Sony Pictures Entertainment and the 2015 infiltration of the German parliament's computer system shows that cyberattacks can strike anytime, anywhere. Cybercrime has grave implications and costs the global economy about \$450 billion a year, experts say. Intellectual property theft can delay technical progress and skew competitiveness. Moreover, falling victim to sabotage and hacktivism can significantly damage an organization's reputation. Security strategies and IT architecture need to meet ever-increasing demands to protect IT systems. Consequently, investment in cybersecurity is rising. A study by the National Initiative for Information and Internet Safety says more than one-third of surveyed German businesses expect spending on IT security and data protection to double by 2020. It is no surprise that Cybersecurity Ventures, a market research firm, expects the cybersecurity market to grow from \$75 billion in 2015 to \$170 billion in 2020.

Cybersecurity is also a top priority for all industry players. We have invested in extensive cybersecurity measures as part of a continuous drive to improve security. A comprehensive program has three main targets to improve resilience against cyber-attacks: raise security awareness among employees and implement robust security processes and organizational set-up, protect highly critical systems and information, such as research data, and improve overall security for systems throughout the organization.

BASF established a cyber defense organization to prevent cyberattacks more effectively and to minimize the impacts of potential attacks on business. The cross-functional organization is composed of IT experts with a variety of specialist areas including cyber security operations, security strategy and architecture, security analytics as well as risk management, who work hand in hand to recognize and respond to attacks on BASF's IT architecture as quickly as possible. Rapid response is key in the struggle against cybercrime. The longer an attack goes undiscovered, the more difficult it is to establish which systems are impacted and the more time the attacker has to harm the organization.

Modern security techniques analyze and monitor the IT network to counter known threats and predict new ones. BASF's team uses a threat intelligence platform, consisting of a monitoring and early warning system. The platform consolidates data from different sources and analyzes irregularities to enable early recognition and assessment of attack patterns as well as a timely and appropriate response. The intelligence obtained from data analysis helps to identify and pre-empt future cyberattacks before they have a chance to wreak havoc.

46.5.1   Strategic Alliances

Apart from close internal collaboration and bundling cyberattack defense resources, BASF, as announced in the press, leverages strategic alliances with other companies and organizations. In 2014, seven DAX 30 companies – including BASF – set up the Cyber Security Sharing and Analytics Association (CSSA) for this purpose. The objective of the association is to share information and intelligence across industries, build up more expertise, as well as improve defense techniques and counterstrategies for a faster and more effective collective response to cybersecurity challenges.

BASF also teamed up with DAX companies Allianz, Bayer and Volkswagen in 2015 to set up a dedicated cybersecurity service provider: the German Cybersecurity Organization (DCSO). The hope is that close collaboration between industry and government experts will contribute to meaningful improvement of corporate security architectures. The organization bundles expertise, offers security audits, as well as provides new services and corporate security technologies that are not commercially available today in that form. DCSO collaborates closely with the appropriate agencies in Germany. Apart from enabling the participating companies desire to better protect themselves, the collaboration via DCSO allows them to share access to IT infrastructures.

BASF collaborates with other industry leaders on the research end as well. An organization called the Digital Society Institute was set up with the support of BASF, Allianz and consultancy Ernst & Young (EY) at the European School of Management and Technology in Berlin in 2016 to deliver information as well as develop analyses and strategies for the digital future. This scientifically autonomous research institute investigates issues to do with digitization, including cybersecurity, and promotes dialogue with stakeholders in business, industry, politics and society at large.

46.5.2   Conclusion – Opportunities of Industry 4.0
for the Chemical Industry

While addressing cybersecurity concerns and preparing for continuously increasing and inevitable risks, the Industry 4.0 transformation offers huge opportunities – for all industry segments. For one, we are a process industry and already have relatively high levels of automation. Digitization promises a major efficiency boost for production operations and maintenance as well as opens up new opportunities for the automated manufacture of flexible, highly differentiated product offerings. Moreover, research and development will benefit too. For example in areas including new material modelling simulation and analyzing research data as it has been done for many years in the high tech industry.

Secondly, the chemical industry is part of a highly interconnected value chain. The interlinking and analysis of unimaginably large volumes of data, created not just within a company itself but within every step from raw material sourcing to end product usage in a customer's product, raises transparency and drives monetary value to be realized. The need for a holistic horizontal integration of all involved partners along the value chain is simply the next consequential step in the Industry 4.0 journey for supply networks to become ever more competitive. The newly emergent data, processes and insights optimally coming from joint customer centric interfaces, which moreover should rely on joint decision making processes, will also give rise to new business models. That makes us transform into a know-how hub in the industry.

Thirdly, digitization forges deeper relationships between industry partners and our customers in many ways and offers huge opportunities for higher customer value and higher reliability towards ever changing customer needs. Digitization has already transformed many areas, and this is only the beginning.

The entire marketplace stands to benefit from perhaps the most important of all perspectives: digitalization will allow us all to benefit from more effective and sustainable approaches to consuming planet earth's precious resources!

The Challenge of Governing Digital Platform Ecosystems

Maximilian Schreieck, Andreas Hein, Manuel Wiesche, and Helmut Krcmar

Abstract

Multi-sided platforms (MSPs) continue to disrupt long-established industries. Therefore, there is a growing popularity to scientifically examine how and why those platforms become more and more economically important. The centerpiece to orchestrate the interaction between the involved parties is the platform governance. While past studies concentrated on describing and identifying those mechanisms, this article aims to provide more detailed knowledge of the practical implications of implementing platform mechanisms differently. With this goal in mind, the article conducted a literature review to identify important platform governance mechanisms. Building on that, a multiple case analysis was carried out examining seven successful MSPs and how they governed their platform. The results indicate that platform governance mechanisms are incorporated in different shapes and characteristics. The governance structure, for example, ranged from a very centralistic and autocratic organization to a more split approach with empowerment on the user side. Also, the accessibility varies from a high degree of openness to detailed background checks users need to pass in order to participate in the platform. Out of these findings, different tradeoffs can be derived. A high

M. Schreieck (✉) · A. Hein · M. Wiesche · H. Krcmar
Technical University of Munich
Munich, Germany
e-mail: maximilian.schreieck@in.tum.de

A. Hein
e-mail: andreas.hein@in.tum.de

M. Wiesche
e-mail: wiesche@in.tum.de

H. Krcmar
e-mail: krcmar@in.tum.de

© Springer-Verlag GmbH Germany 2018
C. Linnhoff-Popien et al. (eds.), *Digital Marketplaces Unleashed*,
https://doi.org/10.1007/978-3-662-49275-8_47

degree of openness, for example, goes along with a greater quantity of products or services, but lacks in quality and indicates a higher perceived risk. Overall this article shows the practical implications and characteristics of different platform governance characteristics and helps practitioners and scientists to learn from successful MSPs.

47.1   Multi-sided Platforms[1,2]

Digital marketplaces such as multi-sided platforms (MSPs) are continuing to grow in importance [1]. Prominent representatives are start-ups like Airbnb or Uber who are challenging traditional business models in the taxi or gastronomy industry. These digital companies extend the classical point of sale by providing a platform where everyone can offer services or products to the corresponding market. Also, traditional industries like the equipment manufacturer Trumpf engage and invest in MSPs [2]. On the contrary, there are also companies who got market power but failed to establish a digital business model. Garmin, for instance, dominated the navigation market and was overran by Apple and Google offering various navigation applications [3]. The economic importance of MSPs can be highlighted by Alibaba initial public offering (IPO), which holds the title of the largest IPO in history [4].

The foundation of each MSP is the underlying platform which orchestrates the interactions between the different sides [3]. Within this platform, the interplay of actions is controlled and managed by various platform governance mechanisms [5, 6]. In order to understand why platforms are disrupting long-established industries, it is crucial to look closer on how those mechanisms work.

Even though platform governance mechanisms are theoretically well researched [5, 6], the practical implementation lacks examination. The degree of openness, for example, can be on the hand too low resulting in an insufficient growth or on the other hand too high, losing control over the platform [7, 8]. This article aims to improve the theoretical understanding by showing tradeoffs resulting from a different implementation of platform governance. Also, practitioners gain valuable insights on how to set up their platform governance strategy and which tradeoffs they need to take into consideration.

47.2   Multi-sided Platform Governance Mechanisms

In order to get a better understanding of a platforms governance, a literature research was conducted to identify important mechanisms according to science [7]. The results are

[1] This chapter is based on a publication at Multikonferenz Wirtschaftsinformatik 2016: Hein, A.; Schreieck, M.; Wiesche, M.; Krcmar, H. (2016). Multiple-Case Analysis on Governance Mechanisms of Multi-Sided Platforms. Multikonferenz Wirtschaftsinformatik (MKWI), Ilmenau.
[2] We thank the German Federal Ministry for Economic Affairs and Energy for funding this research as part of the project 01MD15001D (ExCELL).

displayed in Table 47.1 and range from dimensions like *Governance Structure* to *External Relationships.*

Governance structure, for example, contains decision rights and the ownership status of the company. An MSP can be organized centrally or diffused. There might also be an imbalance in power between the different parties in terms of authority and responsibility.

Platform transparency and usage of platform boundary resources are covered in the dimension *resources & documentation.* They describe the use of application programming interfaces (APIs) or helpful tools like software development kits (SDKs) as well as having a documentation in place.

Accessibility & control combines the mechanisms of output control & monitoring, input control and securing, as well as platform accessibility, openness and process control. They describe how the output of a developer is evaluated, penalized or rewarded, what is allowed to be on the platform, who is allowed to collaborate and which procedures are in place to regulate the platform.

Table 47.1 Platform governance mechanisms. (Own representation based on literature review)

Dimensions	Mechanisms	Description
Governance structure	Governance structure Decision rights Ownership status	Is the set-up centralized or diffused? How are authority and responsibility divided between the platform owner and module developers? Is the platform proprietary to a single firm or is it shared by multiple owners?
Resources & documentation	Platform transparency Platform boundary resources	Does the documentation ensure an easy understanding and usability of the platform? Are governance decisions concerning the platform's marketplace easy to follow and understandable? Are Application programming interfaces (APIs) used to cultivate the platform ecosystems through third-party development?
Accessibility & control	Output control & monitoring	How are outputs evaluated, penalized, or rewarded?
	Input control Securing	What mechanisms are in place to control which products or services are allowed? How to assess the quality of services or products?
	Platform accessibility Process control Platform openness	Who has access to the platform and are there any restrictions on participation? Who controls the process and is in charge for setting up regulations? Is the platform open or closed?
Trust & perceived risk	Strengthen trust Reduce perceived risk	Does the platform enhance trust? How can the perceived risk of platform participants be minimized?
Pricing	Pricing subsidy Revenue	Who is setting the price? Who decides on participation, who is paying and who values?
External Relationships	External relationship management	How are inter-firm dependencies managed? What is the architecture of participation? Does the platform allow technical interoperability between other systems?

Trust & perceived risk are forming the next dimension, which relates to the nature of a platform ecosystem to foster trust on the user or developer side.

The seventh section topic is *pricing* and clarifies which party is setting the price, who decides on participating on the platform, who is paying and which side profits. The last dimension is represented by managing *external relationships* and describes how inter-firm dependencies are governed. Apart from these dimensions, also the underlying business model might have an impact on how the implementation of governance mechanisms is shaped. Therefore, we complemented this dimension in the following multiple case study analysis.

47.3 Governance Mechanisms in Practice

After identifying important platform governance mechanisms, we wanted to analyze if and how successful MSP providers apply those aspects. Therefore, we selected seven MSP companies with four different underlying business models, each of them successful in terms of market capitalization or market shares. On the basis of these companies we identified several cases for each of them and conducted a multiple case study analysis [9]. Table 47.2 summarizes the final results and practical implications.

It can be shown that each of the previously defined platform governance mechanisms can be incorporated in a different way. The g*overnance structure* ranges from a very centralistic and autocratic organization to a more split approach with empowerment on the user side. In terms of *resources & documentation,* it can be shown that six out of seven companies used APIs to engage third-party application developers. *Accessibility and control* vary from having no restrictions to requiring users to pass a detailed background check if they want to enter the platform. The same applies to the *input control.* Measurements can be applying very basic community standards or reviewing each input manually. The *output control* describes how other users evaluate the user-generated output. A noticeable feature is that every analyzed MSP uses a rating or review system. If there are two distinct sides participating in the platform, the use of two-sided or asynchronous ranking systems was representative. In order to establish *trust* and decrease the *perceived risk,* all companies used techniques and tools. They include very basic forms of individualized privacy settings and account verifications, to more sophisticated solutions like offering extra services, insurances or requiring background checks. *Pricing* shows models like advertising, getting sales margins or one-time fees. The last mechanism deals with *external relationships* and indicates that all seven MSPs use forms of partnerships. Most common are strategic partnerships and partnerships through acquisition. As mentioned before each analyzed MSP can be categorized into a different *business model.* Facebook and WeChat, for example, fit in the category of social networks, Alibaba corresponds to the merchant model, Airbnb and Uber are service platforms and the App and Play-Store are application platforms.

Table 47.2 Result of the multiple case study analysis

Business Model	External relationships	Pricing	Trust & perceived risk	Accessibility & control			Resources & documentation	Governance structure	
				Output	Input	Control			
Social network	Strategic partnerships	Advertising, marketing, applications	Privacy settings/Privacy issues	Rating, "Likes", comments, Advertising dashboard	Community standards	No restrictions besides terms and conditions	API, Software Development Kit (SDK), documentation	Autocratic and centralized, self-organizing platform	Facebook
	Strategic partnerships, service extension	Advertising, marketing, applications	Account verification, limited number of messages	Follower, broadcast interfaces	Strict rules for platform curation	No restrictions for users, strict restrictions for businesses	API, SDK, help center, guides	Autocratic and centralized, high degree of control	WeChat
Merchant	Partnerships through acquisition	Sales margins, payment and service fees	Several services to strengthen trust (e.g. Trust pass)	Reviews, ratings, feedback profile, statistics	Optional inspection service	No restrictions	API, SDK, learning, and training center	Central, self-organizing	Alibaba

Table 47.2 (Continued)

Business Model	External relationships	Pricing	Trust & perceived risk	Accessibility & control			Resources & documentation	Governance structure	
				Output	Input	Control			
Service Platform	Localities and local communities	Service and conversion fee	Insurance, verification and rating system	Asynchronous ranking, reviews, statistics, comments	Identity verification	Host is in control, identity verification	Help center	Split, host has decision rights	**Airbnb**
	Strategic partnerships, service extension	Dynamic pricing, Service fee	Background check, pricing surging, insurance, privacy issues	Two-sided ranking, suspension on ranking, comments	Background check. Car requirements	Background check, Uber controls pricing	Help center, API, documentation	Split, Uber controls pricing, passenger controls through rating	**Uber**
Application Platform	Many partnerships	30% of sales, One-time registration fee	Malware, rating, diversity of systems	Ratings, comments, number of downloads	No manual App reviews	Google developer account needed	SDK, API, documentation, checklist	Centric, from loose to tight control	**Play-Store**
	Selective, strategic partnerships	30% of sales, Annual fee	Rating, feedback mechanism, less fraud, and malware	Ratings, comments, number of downloads	Manual reviews, censorship, protected system	Apple developer account needed	SDK, API, toolkits, documentation, guides	Centric, tight control	**App-Store**

After providing an overview of the different characteristics of implementing platform governance mechanisms, we will continue explaining their practical use and accompanied tradeoffs in detail.

47.4   Characteristics and Tradeoffs of Governance Implementation

This section discusses the characteristics and tradeoffs of a different platform governance mechanism implementation.

Governance Structure   This mechanism deals with centralistic and decentralistic structures, decision rights and the degree of ownership status. Different characteristics and implementations result in a high or low degree of platform monetization in exchange for user growth. A good example to show the implications of a low vs. a high degree of decision rights or ownership status can be found in the Google Play-Store. Fig. 47.1 illustrates the shift from a free to use open source version with a decentralistic governance (1) to a tighter led model in an inverted u shape. The decentral and open approach led to a rapid growth in terms of the user base in comparison to the App-Store but also brought tensions due to the lack of control and problems to commercialize the platform [10]. Therefore, the tradeoff of having a more closed and centralized governance with platform control and regulation abilities is a reduced user growth and problems with commercialization.

Across all cases, we could identify tradeoffs in implementing the platform governance structure in different ways. A more centralized governance model with moderate decision rights and ownership status offers a high degree of platform control and commercialization. On the other side, a more decentralistic approach allows benefitting from self-organizational effects by reducing administrative work when implementing for example rating systems to determine the product or service quality. In summary, low ownership causes a loss of control, while a too high degree of ownership restricts user interaction.

Fig. 47.1 Visualization of the tradeoff ownership status. (Own research)

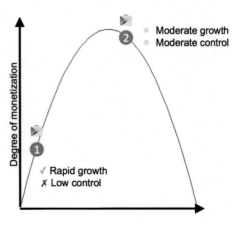

Resources & Documentation The two different characteristics of this dimension are if a platform provides additional resources like APIs or SDKs coupled with documentation or not. Providing insights and interfaces can open up new business opportunities while losing information superiority. Uber and Facebook for example both provide an API to open up new business markets [11]. In particular Uber expanded its platform by integrating the service of taxi reservations into hotel booking systems [12]. Facebook utilized the API to create the sub-market of applications, which is now a million dollar market with over 150 million users every month [13]. By providing an API, both companies allowed developers to create new out of the box applications. It needs to be mentioned, that even in the presence of APIs companies can still regulate how much access they want to provide. Nevertheless, they open up the platform and provide insights and information.

One example of not having an API is Airbnb. However, there is a sub-community hosted by Airbnb called "nerds.airbnb.com" illustrating concepts like deep linking to overcome the fact of not having an API. Furthermore, unofficial platforms like "airbnbapi.org" appeared, providing unofficial endpoints and a documentation on how to use it. The result of not having an API is that there are no interfaces available to get, analyze or validate the data, which leads to a high degree of information control. On the opposite, business opportunities are dismissed in order to keep information superiority.

The conclusion is that having an API, SDK and proper documentation offers companies to open up new business markets, increase interconnectivity and effectiveness of distribution, supply and customer channels. There are also arguments for not having an API. One might be information superiority by having a closed architecture, in return dismissing business opportunities and opening the field for third party platforms publishing platform data.

Platform Accessibility This dimension deals with making the platform accessible to everyone and having restrictions. While restrictions and control mechanisms might improve the quality and increase transparency, it also comes at the expense of quantity of provided applications and services and potential user growth. An example for accessibility or openness is Facebook, struggling with negative feedback and abuse but granting users anonymity [13, 14]. The platform started with a restriction that only allowed universities to join and opened in 2006 for the public, gaining massive user growth [15]. On the other hand, WeChat requires verification in order to open business accounts, increasing the entry barriers by creating transparency [16]. The blue graph in Fig. 47.2b illustrates the tradeoff between the degree of openness and a potential increase in user growth in exchange for anonymity vs. transparency.

After analyzing all companies and cases, we could identify that a high degree of openness went with a potential higher user base, a less secure platform due to anonymity and increased perceived risk. Having restrictions in place showed in the case of the App- and the Play-Store that the quality of products and services can improve if the process control is retained. The tradeoff is a lack of transparency and negative feedback limiting user freedom.

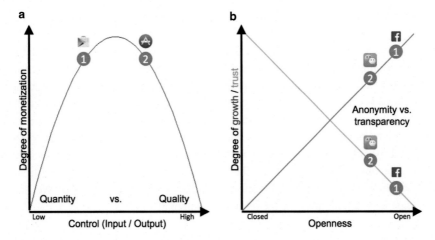

Fig. 47.2 Visualization of the tradeoff platform input & output control (**a**) and platform openness (**b**). (Own research)

Input Control and Securing The tradeoffs for this mechanism is strongly related to the previously discussed *Platform accessibility*. A vivid comparison of input control can be derived from the cases of the Google Play-Store and the Apple App-Store. Where the App-Store follows strict censorship and manual application review processes, Google's Play-Store is less strict and executes only automated reviews. The result is that Apple has less security or quality issues, where Android has a broader variety of applications [17, 18]. This comparison shows that no or laissez-faire input control causes a greater variety of input but entails a decreased quality.

Output Control and Monitoring The multiple case study showed, that all MSPs use an output control mechanism to check the quality of products or services. Facebook, for example, uses "Likes", comments and ratings to indicate the popularity of user-generated content. Especially likes are giving a quick hint on how popular the content is, which is an important part of Facebook's infecting success. Google and Apple implemented a one-way ranking system to check the quality of applications [18, 19], where Alibaba, Uber and Airbnb use a two-way-ranking system, where the demand and supply rank each other [20, 21]. Both mechanisms shift quality assurance to the respective parties and therefore reduce administrative work for the platform owner in a tradeoff for a decreased control [20].

In general Fig. 47.2a shows that control over *input and output* correlates in a non-linear relationship to the degree of monetization. If there is no control, users can create whatever they like, quality decreases and malware increases. Having on the other hand, full control narrows the created content and therefore decreases the reach of a wider audience.

Trust & Perceived Risk This mechanism describes how users and developers see the platform in terms of security and risks. Security measures lower the perceived risk in exchange for platform openness. WeChat for example, provides several services such as the business verification process or a security deposit for using the API to increase trust for the platform. Therefore users are likely to use the platform due to the protective mechanisms [16]. Facebook is offering privacy settings to reduce perceived risk but is not successfully overcoming those problems. The resulting tradeoff is that users have the chance to use Facebook anonymously without social consequences which can lead to a higher degree of perceived risk as the result of cyber mobbing or crimes [15], where WeChat's services decrease anonymity but increase trust. This correlation can be seen in the red graph in Fig. 47.2b, showing that a security measure like the verification process of WeChat reduces the perceived risk, in exchange for a less open platform.

Pricing Measures in this dimension address different price policies. There are indications that higher registration fees increase the quality for the sake of quantity. The case study review shows that all underlying price models are related to the associated business models (see Table 47.2). Therefore, a comparison between different business models does not seem to be constructive. Similar business models like the Play-Store and the App-Store show that high registration fees for the developer can be used as a quality gate trading quantity over quality [17]. The case of Uber shows that a lack of transparency on price setting can cause issues regardless of the business model.

External Relationships Establishing business relationships and strategic partnerships might help to grow the user base, but also giving up control over the platform. The example of the Google Play-Store and the Open Handset Alliance with 34 founding members aiming for an open standard for mobile phones illustrates the rise of the Play-Store's underlying operating system Android which even exceeded Apples' iOS growth [17]. As Google wanted to maintain the control of Android and the Play-Store to protect it from patent issues, the tradeoff was limiting the platform's openness and partnerships [10].

Business Model In order to reflect the fact that each of the selected business models has an impact on the setup of platform governance mechanisms, we included this dimension as well. Nevertheless, even similar business models like Airbnb and Uber, delivering services and described as shared economy, are different in terms of services like accommodations and transportations. This is also true for WeChat and Facebook. While WeChat concentrates on the digital market of mobile Social Networks, Facebook tries to cover the classical online- and the mobile market. In order to draw correct conclusions, we recommend comparing not only similar business models but also similar products and services like the App-Store and the Play-Store.

In general, all dimensions show tradeoffs if implemented differently. Especially interesting are the conclusions illustrated in Fig. 47.2. Nevertheless, it is important to stress that the figures and graphs are only a first conclusion of the multiple case study analysis.

In order to reach significance, it is crucial to gather more concrete facts supporting our claims.

47.5   Conclusion

Multi-sided platforms are continuing to disrupt long-established markets. Therefore, it is crucial to get a deeper understanding of how they work and which factors are of importance. The centerpiece of each MSP is the platform governance, which orchestrates the interaction between the different parties. They describe for example if the overall structure is organized centrally or decentrally, which resources like APIs or SDKs are used or what restrictions are in place to control the openness and the products and services offered on the platform. While the literature offered already theoretical insights about those mechanisms [1, 6, 22, 23], the practical application and tradeoffs were not examined in closer detail. Therefore, we conducted a multiple case analysis including seven different MSPs. All results were analyzed due to theoretically known platform governance mechanisms. The resulting table highlights for example that both, centrally and decentrally organized platforms exist. There are also different degrees of openness or in- and output-control. Influence factors might be the underlying business model or the current state of maturity of the MSP. Based on these results we observed different tradeoffs of implementing platform governance mechanisms differently. One hypothesis deriving from the case study is that the degree of platform control correlates in a non-linear relationship with the platform monetization. No control provides too much power to users or third-party developers, while too much control leads to a narrower range of products and services. Therefore, this article helps to understand how platform governance mechanisms are implemented by currently successful MSPs and which tradeoffs different implementation causes. Moreover, practitioners may learn from already established digital marketplaces and can transfer this knowledge to other industries.

References

1. J. Manner, D. Nienaber, M. Schermann and H. Krcmar, "Governance for mobile service platforms: A literature review and research agenda," *GOVERNANCE,* vol. 1, 2012.
2. F. Weigmann, "AXOOM is developing into a sought-after business platform for the manufacturing industry," AXOOM GmbH;, 2016. [Online]. Available: http://www.trumpf.com. [Accessed 19. 4. 2016].
3. K. J. Boudreau and A. Hagiu, "Platform rules: Multi-sided platforms as regulators," in *SSRN 1269966,* 2008.
4. Forbes, "Alibaba Claims Title For Largest Global IPO Ever With Extra Share Sales," [Online]. Available: http://www.forbes.com/sites/ryanmac/2014/09/22/alibaba-claims-title-for-largest-global-ipo-ever-with-extra-share-sales/. [Accessed 1. 7. 2015].
5. D. S. Evans, "Governing bad behavior by users of multi-sided platforms," *Berkeley Technology Law Journal,* vol. 2, no. 27, 2012.

6. A. Tiwana, B. Konsynski and A. A. Bush, "Research commentary-Platform evolution: Coevolution of platform architecture, governance, and environmental dynamics," *Information Systems Research,* vol. 21, no. 4, pp. 675–687, 2010.
7. A. Hein, M. Schreieck, M. Wiesche and H. Krcmar, "Multiple-Case Analysis on Governance Mechanisms of Multi-Sided Platforms," in *Multikonferenz Wirtschaftsinformatik,* 2016.
8. v. M. Alstyne, G. Parker and P. S. Choudary, "6 Reasons Platforms Fail," 2016. [Online]. Available: https://hbr.org/2016/03/6-reasons-platforms-fail. [Accessed 1. 8. 2016].
9. R. K. Yin, Case study research: Design and methods, Sage publications, 2013.
10. V. Fautrero and G. Gueguen, "The Dual Dominance of The Android Business Ecosystem," *Understanding Business Ecosystems,* 2013.
11. M. B. Goodman and S. H. Dekay, "How large companies react to negative Facebook comments," *Corporate Communications: An International Journal,* vol. 17, no. 3, pp. 289–299, 2012.
12. M. Grant, "Uber Now Integrates With United And Hyatt Apps," 2014. [Online]. Available: http://www.forbes.com/sites/grantmartin/2014/08/22/uber-now-integrates-with-united-and-hyatt-apps/. [Accessed 1. 7. 2015].
13. Facebook, "Facebook homepage," [Online]. Available: https://www.facebook.com. [Accessed 1. 7. 2015].
14. V. Champoux, J. Durgee and L. McGlynn, "Corporate Facebook pages: when 'fans' attack," *Journal of Business Strategy,* vol. 33, no. 2, pp. 22–30, 2012.
15. F. Stutzman, R. Gross and A. Acquisti, "Silent listeners: The evolution of privacy and disclosure on facebook," *Journal of privacy and confidentiality,* vol. 4, no. 2, 2013.
16. K. S. Staykova and J. Damsgaard, "Platform Expansion Design as Strategic Choice: The Case of Wechat and Kakaotalk".
17. D. Tilson, C. Sørensen and K. Lyytinen, "Change and control paradoxes in mobile infrastructure innovation: the Android and iOS mobile operating systems cases," in *45th Hawaii International Conference on System Science (HICSS),* 2012.
18. B. Pon, T. Seppälä and M. Kenney, "Android and the demise of operating system-based power: Firm strategy and platform control in the post-PC world," *Telecommunications Policy,* vol. 38, no. 11, pp. 979–991, 2014.
19. D. Pagano and W. Maalej, "User feedback in the appstore: An empirical study," in *21st IEEE International Requirements Engineering Conference,* 2013.
20. B. Tan, S. L. Pan, X. Lu and L. Huang, "The Role of IS Capabilities in the Development of Multi-Sided Platforms: The Digital Ecosystem Strategy of Alibaba. com," *Journal of the Association for Information Systems,* vol. 16, no. 4, pp. 248–280, 2015.
21. E. Isaac, "Disruptive Innovation: Risk-Shifting and Precarity in the Age of Uber," 2014.
22. M. Schreieck, M. Wiesche and H. Krcmar, "Design and Governance of Platform Ecosystems – Key Concepts and Issues for Future Research".
23. J. Manner, D. Nienaber, M. Schermann and H. Krcmar, "Six Principles for Governing Mobile Platforms," in *Wirtschaftsinformatik,* 2013.

Further Reading
24. A. Hagiu and J. Wright, "Multi-sided platforms," *International Journal of Industrial Organization,* 2015.

Transformation Not Completed – Identify Additional Business Opportunities by Digital Navigation

48

Karsten Schweichhart, Uwe Weber, and Alexander Hildenbrand

Abstract

Digital Transformation does have an immense impact on businesses and their processes. There are a lot of companies that already started to transform their processes, organization or even their business model. Often the transformation focuses on a certain aspect that might be helpful to the company. A framework is needed that helps to identify various aspects for transformation. The Digital Navigator provides a digital capability map that can be used to identify further digital possibilities for optimization of processes or creating new business models. This article provides a short description of the Digital Navigator and an example how to use it.

48.1 Digital Navigator

When Jack Welch says, "Willingness to change is a strength, even if it means plunging part of the company into total confusion for a while" this is especially valid for the Digital Transformation. When starting planning and transforming your business into a digital one this time frame of confusion should be as short as possible, because businesses today

K. Schweichhart (✉) · A. Hildenbrand
Cross-Business-Architecture Lab
Bonn, Germany
e-mail: schweichhart@cba-lab.de

A. Hildenbrand
e-mail: hildenbrand@cba-lab.de

U. Weber
Detecon International GmbH
Munich, Germany
e-mail: uwe.weber@detecon.com

© Springer-Verlag GmbH Germany 2018
C. Linnhoff-Popien et al. (eds.), *Digital Marketplaces Unleashed*,
https://doi.org/10.1007/978-3-662-49275-8_48

are faced with fast changing market conditions. From our experience with companies of different size and industry over the last years the adapted approach of "concurrent planning" from engineering will help to reduce the time from understanding demands and strategy definition until the products are available on the market.

People involved in a concurrent planning process moved from hierarchical organization structure into a project organization and collaborate based on a common language to overcome misunderstanding across different expertise. Capabilities in terms of a functional decomposition of relevant tasks within a specific enterprise can provide such a common language. The description of a capability comprises three dimensions:

- What are the processes and information that are needed for the capability?
- What are the skills and competencies people provide to work in these processes?
- And what is the technology that supports or drives the work within this capability?

Here is an example how to apply this approach in a manufacturing company and why this helps to avoid confusion about what Digital Transformation means. Let us have a look at the capability "Production Management" and one level deeper at capability "Worker Guidance". Customers expect individual products today even when they are produced at an assembly line. Guidance of workers at the assembly line about what is the next part and in which tray it can be picked up will change due to digitalization. Probably today, workers are supported with parts lists and configuration drawings for the product they have to assembly next (technology dimension). Tomorrow, workers are guided by a pick-up-by-voice solution, where the workers wear headphones and the information about parts and their location will be brought to the worker by a computer voice. The information provided is the same as before, but the provisioning is now digital to support an optimized process. There will also be a change in the worker's competencies. This example shows how powerful a capability-based planning approach as used in concurrent planning will lead to a lean and effective digital strategy and transformation project portfolio without any confusion.

Bringing this small example on a higher level, we asked ourselves, what is the difference in terms of capabilities we need for digitalization? How much change is necessary to become sustainable successful in a digital business world? Is it possible to share experience about patterns that worked at different companies? With the strong will to find the answers, some leading companies from Telecommunication, Automotive, Process Industry and High Tech as well as a consultancy company found together at Cross-Business-Architecture Lab to develop the Digital Navigator.

The six digital capabilities represented in the Digital Navigator (s. Fig. 48.1) close the gap between business and technical capabilities as the central structure to align strategy demands and solution supply.

Here is another example. Imagine your business strategy written in natural language and available in a more detailed form over the intranet. Are you sure that everyone in your company knows exactly how to decide about transformation programs according the

Fig. 48.1 Digital Navigator. (Cross-Business-Architecture [1])

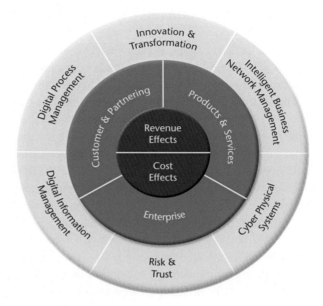

strategy? To make strategy explicit you can detail it using a driver tree. Map leafs of this tree expresses strategic demands onto to capability maps. More precisely, map the business demands onto the business capabilities, ask yourself what digital capabilities you need to enable the business and then think about the technical capabilities, which comprises also the real fancy staff like glasses for virtual reality. With this structured and consolidated view on demands, it is easier to find the right architecture and solutions. You can also start on the opposite site analyzing the relevance of a specific solution for a future scenario.

But what do these Digital Capabilities look like?

The top-level view on Digital Navigator comprises three circles. The grey one describes six digital capabilities that have been developed and proven by the partners within the Cross-Business-Architecture. More than that, the results of an empirical study [2] underline the relevance and completeness of these digital capabilities as well as the maturity across industries within the German-speaking countries at the time the study was conducted. The first blue circle expresses the so-called digital dimensions. Digital Transformation should always consider the complete value chain in order to provide best possible customer experiences. But the three dimensions "Customer and Partnering", "Products and Services" and "Enterprise" may be managed with different sub goals what means different patterns of digital capabilities. At the end, all transformation programs should lead to more revenue or less costs. That's why the three circles can be turned against each other in order to find different patterns for different goals that lead to more revenue or a reduction of costs. To develop this is an ongoing process and Life-Cycle-Management is managed by Cross-Business-Architecture and Detecon International.

48.2   Start Transformation: Use Your Data

To explain the usage of the Digital Navigator in more detail we introduce a scenario of a producer of home appliances that has been successfully transformed in a certain area. This is one of several possible approaches to apply this framework.

The regarded company produces washing machines among other things. From time to time, a service call from a customer requires sending a technician on site to fix a problem. If the problem is caused by a broken component, the technician has to order a spare part and come on site once again. In the meantime, the washing machine cannot be used.

The optimization of this scenario was based on the following idea: how can the number of visits at the customer site be reduced to one at most times. This would increase customer convenience and reduce costs. In context to the Digital Navigator, this use case addresses the cost effects in the products and services area for improvement.

To get closer to a solution, they focused on the information that they have from the customer and information they already have from calls of other customers up to now. To describe the transformation let's have a look at the process so far (s. Fig. 48.2 – left side).

A customer talks or sends a message to the service center and describes the failure of his washing machine. In general, the customer does not know the root cause of this failure. So he has to describe what happened and what can be seen from outside. At the service desk, the information is collected and described in a structured incident request by a service agent. This information will be sent to a technician who will be scheduled for a customer visit. The technician examines the failure on site and fixes the failure if possible. If a component is broken and no spare part is available by accident, he has to

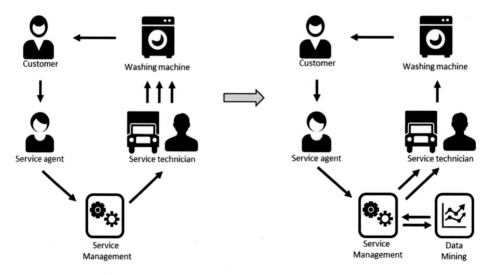

Fig. 48.2 Service process transformation

order it and arranges a new appointment. So the described process could cause multiple visits and increases service cost.

The approach that the company already implemented to improve this process is based on the information they have from other service calls or incidents. If it is possible to match a new incident with an existing and already fixed one, some activities can be done before the technician will be sent out to the customer.

For that purpose, they implemented a data mining system for analyzing the details of the current incident and comparing with similar requests of the past. If there is a match, the corresponding spare parts are send back to the Service Management System. If there are no corresponding spare parts, this could be an indication that there is no broken component. A rule framework in the Service Management System then determines based on specific rules whether a spare part should be ordered and when a visit could be scheduled.

Because of the probability that a certain component is required, the ordering can be done automatically. It is also possible that the time schedule of the technician can be updated and the van be loaded automatically.

Based on this extended software landscape the former process has been transformed to the following (see Fig. 48.2 – right side):

The customer calls the service desk and describes the failure. The service agent collects all provided information in a structured incident. In the next step, the incident is sent to the data mining system to be analyzed and compared with older incidents. If there is a match to an existing incident, the information about how the failure was fixed will be sent back including a description of the spare parts that were needed. Based on the specific rules in the Service Management, the system decides if spare parts are needed and then automatically orders them. According to the availability of the spare part and the service technician, a time schedule for the next visit to the customer is planned. The van of the assigned technician will also be loaded automatically. Most of these steps now can be done automatically.

Although the changes in the process steps seems to be rather minor, the impact of these changes through automation is huge: cost savings and improvement of customer convenience by

- reduced service time: automatic spare parts ordering, van loading and visit scheduling
- increased first implementation rate
- same day appointments, if there is no spare part needed
- decision support: decision makers can concentrate on complex repair cases

Looking at the Digital Navigator, the transformation has been conducted in the area of Digital Information Management (s. Fig. 48.3), especially in the context of Information Sourcing, Value Assessment, Analytics and Processing.

In Information Sourcing relevant data sources, in this case the already existing service calls, are identified and checked by significance and relevance through the digital capability Value Assessment.

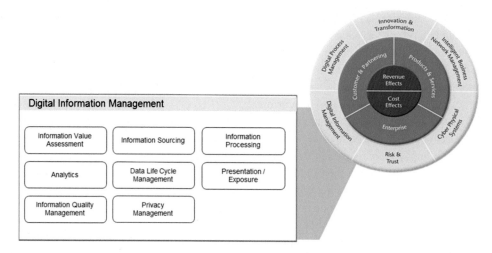

Fig. 48.3 Digital Information Management

Through Analytics a mapping is done to check, if the root cause of the current call can be solved in the same manner as an existing one. After collecting and analyzing the data, the call can be processed and the technician does have a lot more information about the scheduled customer visit.

48.3 Transformation Completion – New Horizons of Data

The situation is clear: the service use case described in the former section is completed. Really? How to check, if the ambition level has been as high as appropriate? Let's take the Digital Navigator from section one to double check the use case, finding out higher ambitions.

If we identify the functional capabilities addressed in the use case and map them to the digital navigator, the result is surprisingly, but clear. We identify mainly capabilities out of the digital information management domain:

- Data Life Cycle Management: Basic to decide, what data and structures should be used and to care on changes on them and their environment
- Information Processing: applying and processing the data for the purpose of the use case
- Information Quality Management to ensure, that the applied data are relevant and in sufficient quality
- Privacy Management, mission critical to ensure the distinguished use and integrity of the data

- Analytics, to create the best combination of service parts using the historical data in an intelligent way
- Presentation Exposure to offer the helpful results to all intended users, may be cross different devices

Great. Good coverage – of the information management domain only, to be precise. The opportunities of the information management domain are very well explored and applied. But, what about the other domains of digitization capabilities?

Remember – the story of digitization is about using data to create value. Of course, the first steps are about all the data, which are already available. Often, this is already a lot. Many companies are wondering, what to do with all the data, they collect and store into their databases. This companies should apply data strategies and business model strategies on their data as shown in our use case so far.

Anyway, in digitization this vision is not big enough. You have to care as well on a kind of data, which is not yet available. The Digital Navigator helps to find out. As an example we apply the functional domain Cyber Physical Systems (CPS) (s. Fig. 48.4). What is a cyber-physical system within the context of our service use case? Or: What asset could become a cyber-physical system, if it becomes connected? The basic idea in the phase of ideation is: Every asset coming along with the use case could become a cyber-physical one. This includes:

- the washing machine itself
- the storage
- the *spare part*
- the service technician
- the service car

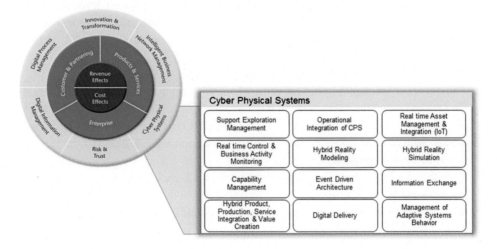

Fig. 48.4 Cyber Physical Systems

Creating a cyber-physical system out of them means, give them and their functions a kind of IT frame, which means represent their functions and data in IT structures – and connect them by an appropriate network. This includes fix line options as well as mobile networks including Bluetooth, WLAN, GSM, LTE or in the near future 5 G. At least they need an API as interface, so they can get a network connection and an appropriate IT integration.

The functional capabilities of the "Cyber Physical Systems" domain of the Digital Navigator give an overview, what is necessary to drive cyber physical systems. Some examples:

- Operational Integration of CPS: core to make it run
- Real time Asset Management and ...
- ... Real time Control and business monitoring: Both may be most important, because real time transparency is one of the core value driver
- Event Driven Architecture: to make most use out of real time information, the IT Landscape need areas able to handle events in a valuable manner
- Information Exchange, a difficult, but mission critical capabilities regarding different "languages" and standards in the communication between different assets

Most of these capabilities to use CPS today are pre-integrated to Internet-of-Things (IoT) – Platforms, often flexible and secure offered by a cloud provider. The Digital Navigator helps to check, whether all needed capabilities are available in the IoT-Platform of choice.

Applied to the use case, a lot of further opportunities are created immediately:

1. The washing machine gets a kind of self-awareness, knowing about its condition and sharing this condition online with the service center. Transparency occurs on the concrete problems and therefore on the needed spare parts. In a next level, applying intelligence to the condition monitoring, the machine is able on self-diagnoses in advance, prediction maintenance becomes possible, a new business model occurs: guarantee of the availability of the machine by the producer, a value which might be paid by users, especially professional ones (see Figs. 48.1, 48.2, 48.3 and 48.4)
2. The storage offers transparency on parts, which are available or which are not, where they are and when the next charge of missing parts will arrive. Linked to the messages of machine problems and linked to service orders it could become a self-organized storage with close to 100% guarantee, that needed parts are available and the storage size is as small as possible.
3. Even the spare part itself could contribute to transparency and service, especially the bigger ones. Are they in an appropriate condition? Are they available at the expected place and time in the required type or version? What is the amount of parts on the desired service car?

4. The service car itself is the most interesting asset unused within this use case. It moves around and transport the required parts. Therefore, it could know in advance, if all required and expected parts are (still) on board to avoid customer visits because of missing spare parts. Moreover, it's positon is known every time. Combining this with customer addresses and real-time (!) traffic information, estimated times of arrival could be offered to customers very precisely, even online by a customer app or a web portal. A new service level of very small time windows could be offered to the customers. And more: Knowing every time the location of each service car and it's available parts, it can be redirected by customer calls every time. A new kind of service can be offered: a same day service, in cities may be a same hour premium service.

An example deep dive into the service process shows, that a connected and self-aware washing machine already changes a lot (s. Fig. 48.5). First, the machine user is neither surprised nor disturbed by an unexpected defect, if the predictive analytics detects the problem in advance. Second, the machine will not call a call center agent, it informs directly the service dispatcher. You can even imagine, the machine informs directly the service car closest to the location, because it knows, that the needed spare parts are on board. Customer's will learn to be happy about the service technician knocking on the door, friendly announcing to care on the risky machine. In a near future, customers will expect it like this, never have to call again.

In consequence, Digital Transformation obviously was not completed only using the already available data. Applying the Digital Navigator, it was pointed out clearly, that

Fig. 48.5 CPS transformed process

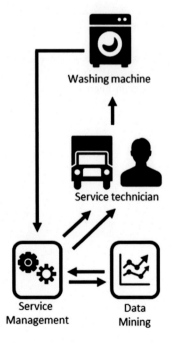

Washing machine

Service technician

Service Management

Data Mining

there were a lot of further opportunities out there, which means at the end: business opportunities. In our example this included

- a new business model on guarantee of availability,
- a second new business model on express service,
- an optimization of storage
- a decrease of double customer visits increasing the one touch repair rate

Not too bad for applying only one more domain of the Digital Navigator. Valuating the results from the perspective of the current business model, taking into account, that the business model could be changed, a strategic roadmap could be constructed, where the opportunities are taken into reality step by step. Real data driven value is created using existing data, and, may be even more important, further data, which can be created by new IT capabilities and new connections on so far unconnected assets. Valuable transparency occurs immediately, driven to much higher value by using real-time data and intelligence in analytics.

Embedding the roadmap into an overall digitization strategy of your company, all of the other domains of Digital Navigator help to identify, which current business functions have to change, or, what new ones should be established. Risk management for example gets an additional perspective. It becomes obvious, that a Digital Transformation Strategy touches wide areas of the company.

This is real digitization – initiated by the Digital Navigator

References

1. Cross-Business-Architecture, "Digital Navigator," [Online]. Available: http://www.cba-lab.de. [Accessed 2016].
2. Detecon International GmbH, "Studie Digital Navigator," Detecon, [Online]. Available: http://www.detecon.com/de/Publikationen/digital-navigator. [Accessed 01 09 2016].

The Data Science Lab at LMU Munich: Leveraging Knowledge Transfer, Implementing Collaborative Projects, and Promoting Future Data Science Talents

Thomas Seidl, Peer Kröger, Tobias Emrich, Matthias Schubert, Gregor Jossé, and Florian Richter

Abstract

In this paper, we describe the newly established Data Science Lab at the Ludwig-Max-imilians-Universität Munich (DSL@LMU) and its particular role as an interface between academia and industry. Initially co-funded by the Siemens AG, the DSL@DBS is open for innovative corporate partners and offers a platform for various joint activities between academia and industry. The DSL@LMU provides the following advantages to its corporate partners: Partners gain access to cutting-edge know how in analyzing data. Furthermore, the DSL@LMU provides connections to a worldwide academic network of top researchers in the area of Data Science. Collaborating with DSL@LMU offers a strong visibility among academia and industry. To bring the most recent research into practical use, joint research projects allow to develop specific solution for the use cases of the corporate partners of the DSL@LMU. Finally, the DSL@LMU

T. Seidl (✉) · P. Kröger · T. Emrich · M. Schubert · G. Jossé · F. Richter
Ludwig-Maximilians-Universität München
Munich, Germany
e-mail: seidl@dbs.ifi.lmu.de

P. Kröger
e-mail: kroeger@dbs.ifi.lmu.de

T. Emrich
e-mail: emrich@dbs.ifi.lmu.de

M. Schubert
e-mail: schubert@dbs.ifi.lmu.de

G. Jossé
e-mail: josse@dbs.ifi.lmu.de

F. Richter
e-mail: richter@dbs.ifi.lmu.de

© Springer-Verlag GmbH Germany 2018
C. Linnhoff-Popien et al. (eds.), *Digital Marketplaces Unleashed*,
https://doi.org/10.1007/978-3-662-49275-8_49

serves to connect companies to the highly talented students from the new elite master's program "Master of Data Science" at the LMU Munich. To illustrate the collaboration between the DSL@LMU with industrial partners, we describe the results of recent research projects at DSL@LMU that were conducted in collaboration with partners from industry. These projects exemplarily show how academia and industry can team up to transform cutting-edge research into innovative products.

49.1   Introduction

The digitalization of the world is an ongoing process, influencing all parts of everyday life. The search for valuable information in growing amounts of data is undoubtedly one of the major challenges in the upcoming decades to gain the full potentials out of this development. The key to transferring data to knowledge is Data science, an interdisciplinary field that deals with algorithms and systems to automatically detect patterns that allows to derive knowledge from data in various forms. It brings together statistics, machine learning, data mining, and data management, extending the well-established field Knowledge Discovery in Databases (KDD) by a more holistic approach.

Even though there is a high demand in know-how for companies, thorough expertise and talents are still rare to find. For example, the well-known report by McKinsey & Company projects a global excess demand of 1.5 million new data scientists. However, at least in Germany, there are only rare internationally visible research groups at universities and, thus, only few Master Programs with a strong and solid focus on Data Science are currently offered.

The Data Science Lab of the Ludwig-Maximilians University Munich (DSL@LMU) is an institution for research, development and education around the field of Data Science. It is attached to the Database Systems group of LMU that has a long standing tradition in research in the fields of Databases and Data Mining and is constantly among the top-10 leading research institutions world-wide in these fields. In addition, the DSL@LMU has tight connections to the Institute of Statistics at LMU and other Informatics groups such as the group for Mobile Computing. As a consequence, the DSL@LMU provides the expertise of leading scientists in the key research fields of Data Science.

The key idea of the DSL@LMU is to link this scientific know-how to Industry and Data Science students (see Fig. 49.1). The focus of the Lab is to bridge the gap from academia to industry and allow students and researchers to work on real-world Data Science challenges while giving their industry partners a substantial leap forward. Besides, the Data Science Lab offers a wide variety of activities for small, medium to large-scale companies that include professional training, trend flashes, summer schools, lecture series from international luminaries, workshops, guest lectures from industry, and many more. Thus, the top talents are linked to their potential future employers. A dedicated lab room gives the students the opportunity to work on the newest hard- and software products and at the same time offers an inspiring environment to discuss and elaborate new Data Sci-

Fig. 49.1 The DSL@LMU
aims at bringing together the
three groups including industry, students and academia in
the field of Data Science

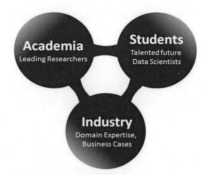

ence challenges. This room is also used for hands-on professional training in Data Science related courses.

The Lab also fosters strong ties to the new elite program "Master of Data Science" (see below). Even though LMU Master students that have a focus on Data Analysis lectures are already excellently educated and are currently highly respected as Data Scientists, the new Master program will generate a pool of more interdisciplinary oriented and qualified graduates.

The Data Science Lab has been founded in 2015 in cooperation with the Siemens AG, however, it is open to all prospective partners from industry that share the same visions on Data Science.

49.2   Supporting and Promoting Future Talents in Data Science

A major challenge in facilitating the full potential of Data Science in the corporate as well as in the scientific sector is the availability of young talents which poses the necessary skills to solve practical problems with cutting-edge data analytics methods.

To understand, apply and develop data-driven solutions, a profound knowledge in statistics is necessary in order to ensure the correctness of the derived knowledge. Aspects like the quality of available data and the significance of the computed patterns and predictions are mandatory to the usefulness of any data science process.

On the other hand, modern information technology like GPU computing and cloud based systems are key technologies to apply novel prediction techniques and analysis tools. Without the ongoing development in the area of informatics, the recent success stories in machine learning, data analytics and artificial intelligence would not have been possible. These rapid developments allowed for collecting, accessing and integrating data in new dimensions. Furthermore, new technologies to enable new hardware architectures were developed to store distribute and manage data. Finally, new data analytics methods improved the quality of predictions and patterns which are infeasible without massive amounts of data and large scale computational infrastructure.

To provide a training program teaching the key skills from statistics and informatics, the LMU started the new elite program "Master Data Science" in winter 2016. The program is funded by the Bavarian Elite Network and accepts highly skilled international talents having a background in both disciplines. The training program provides the necessary theoretical background, integrates recent technologies and puts a strong emphasize on the practical application of the acquired skills. Thus, the curriculum includes a practical data science project where the participants solve practical problems of corporate partners. Furthermore, there are summer schools and scientific talks from invited researchers and practitioners on recent developments. The pure analytical skills being acquired during the program are complemented with modules on data ethics, human computation and data security. The program concludes with a master thesis giving the students the opportunity to extend the state of the start when examining their own research project in the area of data science.

The DSL@LMU provides an interface for its industry partners to the students of this elite program. For example, it leverages joint projects between industry and students such as Master theses, seminars, use-cases, etc. supervised by a scholar from the DSL@LMU.

49.3 Sample Projects and Case Studies

The DSL@LMU aims at transferring knowledge in the form of latest scientific achievements to industry. This is typically implemented through joint research projects and/or case studies. In these cases, the DSL@LMU serves as an organizational umbrella for such projects (but is not involved in technical details as an entity in order to prevent IP issues which are negotiated with each project partner, separately). In the following, we sketch three sample projects that have been recently conducted under this umbrella.

49.3.1 Shared E-Fleet – Efficiently Using Fleets of Electric Vehicles

Mobility is the backbone of modern society. The economic and ecological challenges it bears arc enormous. Ambitious climate goals compete with ever-growing passenger and freight transport demands. Mastering these challenges without sacrificing driving convenience and efficiency, is the ultimate goal of modern mobility.

Recent studies reveal hints on how to cope with mobility requirements. The geo-data enterprise NAVTEQ has shown that drivers using navigation devices increase fuel efficiency by 12%. The McKinsey institute estimates around EUR 550 billion in annual consumer surplus from using personal location data. The biggest share coming from saving fuel and improving efficiency due to navigation systems relying on telematics. The great white hope is new technology, new data. The abundance of sensor data collected in traffic, summarized under the term (vehicle) telematics, is expected to optimize traffic, to reduce congestion and to improve logistic efficiency while at the same time increasing usability and convenience for drivers.

The Database Systems Group at LMU Munich has recognized this trend and its research opportunities early on. First publications in the field of traffic networks came as a natural extension to the field of spatial and temporal databases, the core topic of the group for which it has gained international renown. Shortly thereafter, members of the DSL@LMU helped to realize a large research project centered on electric mobility which was kicked-off in 2012. Funded by the German ministry of economics BMWi, the project united research partners with industry partners such as Siemens Corporate Technology, Carano Software Solutions and car technology manufacturer Marquardt GmbH. The project, named Shared E-Fleet, aimed at creating a comprehensive cloud-based solution for the efficient use of fleets of electric vehicles (EVs).

While electric mobility is not uncontroversial, its potential is certainly great. Electric infrastructure exists in all developed countries, electricity is relatively cheap and less prone to fluctuations of the market than oil and its CO_2 footprint is believed to be ecologically justifiable. In reality, however, electric mobility faces very basic limitations. The first limitation is the range, which varies between 100 to 150 kilometers. The second limitation are rather long recharging times. While refueling a car takes minutes, a full recharge can take several hours. Both limitations become particularly evident when one vehicle is shared among multiple drivers.

Over the course of the project, the Database Systems Group streamlined research and development and devised a spatial and temporal query system to counter these drawbacks. Based on real-time telematics and historic sensor data, the query system supports drivers and fleet managers alike. The system, for instance, informs the fleet manager preventively about critical situations such as expected belated returns or expected exceeded range limits. In addition, the system provides directions to the driver, for instance by computing the most efficient path to the nearest charging station or by visualizing reachable destinations within the given range limit.

Combined with the hardware and software components provided by the other partners, the query system was brought into action in pilot projects. From June 2014 until September 2015 seven BMW i3 were made available to employees of technology parks in four different German cities. During the test phase, the initial concepts were refined in close cooperation with the partners. The advancements fueled research findings and vice versa, leading to several publications in the international research community. While the query system tackled modern mobility requirements from a practical angle in a real-world project, the published research addressed them from a theoretic perspective.

An example: Modern traffic networks are usually modeled as graphs, i. e., defined by sets of nodes and edges. In conventional graphs, the edges are assigned numerical weights, typically reflecting cost criteria like distance or travel time. In so-called multicriteria networks, the edges reflect multiple, possibly dynamically changing cost criteria. While these networks allow for diverse queries and meaningful insight, query processing usually is significantly more complex. Novel means to keep query processing efficient were developed and published over the course of the project.

Another example: Modern cars use ultrasonic sensors or cameras to detect parking spaces. By exploring this problem probabilistically, a novel model for the abstract problem of consumable and reoccurring resources in road networks was devised. Based on this model, a stochastic routing algorithm was developed which maximizes the probability of finding the desired resource while minimizing travel time. Besides the original application of parking spaces, the model may for instance be applied to vacant or occupied charging stations for EVs. Inspired by the practical use of sensors, a ubiquitous traffic problem was formalized with the help of probability theory and solved with algorithmic insight.

It is this fruitful combination of theory and practice which helps understand and solve some of the problems of modern mobility. Where research papers lay the groundwork, demonstrations extend the theory and real-world projects test the reliability under authentic conditions. Thus, as demonstrated by the project Shared E-Fleet, cooperation between industry and research yields valuable results for both scopes.

49.3.2 VISEYE – A New Approach for Mobile Payment

In a collaboration with a small and medium-sized company (KMU) from the mobile payment sector, a new system for image mapping and classification on mobile devices was explored at DSL@LMU. As an alternative to existing technology such as QR codes, the main challenge was, that the system needs to be robust against frauds.

As a result, the system implemented a sequence of seven different algorithmic steps (from image processing through feature extraction to classification) in a distributed client/server setting. In this architecture, it turn out that several parameters are crucial for the efficiency of the process, and thus, decisive for a high consumer acceptance. Depending on the quality of the network and the status of the battery, it is generally favorable to do as many steps of the mobile device as possible. To formalize the allocation of steps of the overall process to the different parties (client: mobile device versus central server), a cost model was developed that decides this allocation of jobs ad hoc, given several parameters such as those mentioned above (battery status, network quality) as well as further potentially influencing parameters such as location and previously learned user preferences.

This project was also a prototype for a successful collaboration between industry and academia that leverages the transformation of cutting edge research into an innovative product. The commercial use case developed by the KMU lead to novel fundamental research questions, e. g. the development of the cost model and the integration of geo-coordinates or user preferences were, that had to be solved in theory first. The implementation of these theoretical results in turn tested their accuracy and reliability real-world scenarios.

49.3.3   Process Mining – Leveraging Automation and Logistics

Mid- and large scale businesses offer much possibility to collect lots of data during daily operations. While logging the business actions is rather easy and straight forward, the information is only revealed by analyzing it appropriately. Only transforming business data from simple log files to meaningful models creates valuable assets.

The emerging field of process mining aims at this problem by combining the research areas of data mining and business process modelling. The great focus is to develop tools to answer the arising questions of today's managers and decision makers: What happened? Why? What can be expected in the future? And what is the best choice I can take?

To answer these questions, the raw business logs, which offer timestamped event data, are taken into consideration to infer structural fitting workflow graphs to model the real world.

For a better imagination we illustrate this in a public transport service scenario (see Fig. 49.2). The sensors to log most data is already present nowadays as nearly everybody carries a smartphone and uses the mobile applications of their local transportation service provider. The collected events contain waiting times, vehicle entries and exits. A simple analysis can certainly identify choke points or idle spots for some routes. But process mining offers even better and more intelligent methods to analyze connections between parts of the processes. These dependencies are common, but not always obvious for humans to identify in complex networks.

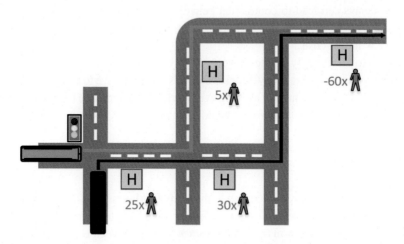

Fig. 49.2 Two buses operate in the same area. The blue bus has a high probability to stop at the traffic light controlled junction. That causes the red bus to overtake the other one most of the time. The red bus arrives first at the common bus stop. It will pass a second crowded stop before driving to the final bus stop. The blue bus, being the late vehicle, will be almost empty on this route. Analyzing the log files will show the reason why many people gave negative feedback in this area regarding overcrowded buses

A bus, which has a long stop time at a traffic light, might cause an even longer customer waiting time at the next bus stop. The people there will react, choosing maybe another bus line. Another line will be overcrowded, causing delays on other lines and so on. Most of these occurrences will weaken through the network, but in certain cases, a small influence in one part can cause a jam of the network in a distant part. Process mining assists in detecting those unobvious dependencies and finding solutions to prevent issues.

So analysis of historical data is used to reveal dependencies in graphs like workflow nets, which give insights on causal connections of different actions in the process. Using this knowledge can augment the decision making in future process instances. In our particular example, bus frequencies can be reduced or increased, or lines can be rerouted to circumvent difficult spots.

At DSL@LMU, we strongly consider changing temporal dependencies in processes. Drifts in service times or increasing production cycle times are often an important indicator for a necessary intervention of a supervisor. Many tools start working slower until they break completely. In hazardous environments, the critical parts should be replaced beforehand to save people. To achieve this goal, we analyze process events, extract temporal information and analyze shifts to identify and categorize the type of changes. Our next step involves the analysis of dependencies between delays in complex business workflow nets. For example can a problem in action A cause a delay in action B, although both actions seem to be rather independent? If A is only a minor action in the whole process, but B is rather significant, the benefit of this knowledge would be tremendous. A small delay of a secondary resource, which has been overseen, might cause production delays. These total delays can lead to contractual penalties everybody wants to avoid. Identifying the source of the problem, we could fix the problem at a point that allows a simple interference with low costs.

In addition to these timely problems we are highly interested in event streams as process logs grow larger and larger recently. Process analysis methods have to be time and memory performant to deal with frequently arriving events on the one hand and being able to return results within shorter reaction times on the other hand.

49.4 Conclusions

The newly established Data Science Lab at the Ludwig-Maximilians-Universität Munich (DSL@LMU) is an interface between academia and industry open for innovative corporate partners. It offers a platform for various joint activities between academia and industry providing access to cutting-edge know how in analyzing data, strong visibility among academia and industry, as well as a link to the highly talented Data Science students from LMU including those from the new elite Master program "Master of Data Science" at the LMU Munich.

Contact: http://dsl.ifi.lmu.de/data-science-lab

Diagnosis as a Service

50

Franz Wotawa, Bernhard Peischl, and Roxane Koitz

Abstract

One objective of Industry 4.0 is to further enhance automation and data exchange in manufacturing among the whole value chain in order to provide new services and to decrease the use of resources. Industry 4.0 relies on communicating systems aiming at decentralized decisions for manufacturing requested products and services comprising humans and machines. The availability of systems and their data, e. g., manufacturing or monitoring data, online is an enabler of new applications and services including diagnosis. In this article we focus on the diagnosis aspect and provide insights into a methodology that allows for bringing in diagnosis of interconnected systems as a service. The methodology is based on system models and monitoring observations and thus is highly adaptable to changes in the system. In addition, to the methodology we give examples from applications of diagnosis for wind turbines and other engineered systems.

50.1 Introduction

One aim of Industry 4.0 is to further automatize production as a whole via enhancing data exchange and flexibility in manufacturing in order to reduce costs and to allow a stronger

F. Wotawa (✉) · B. Peischl · R. Koitz
Technische Universität Graz
Graz, Austria
e-mail: wotawa@ist.tugraz.at

B. Peischl
e-mail: bpeischl@ist.tugraz.at

R. Koitz
e-mail: rkoitz@ist.tugraz.at

© Springer-Verlag GmbH Germany 2018
C. Linnhoff-Popien et al. (eds.), *Digital Marketplaces Unleashed*,
https://doi.org/10.1007/978-3-662-49275-8_50

customization of products accordingly to the users' needs. In order to increase flexibility of production for mass customization there is a strong need for optimization, configuration and diagnosis of all systems involved in manufacturing (see [1]).

A production facility has to react on different strongly customized orders coming in at real time. In case of faults occurring during manufacturing, the underlying cause has to be identified and the whole production process has to be reconfigured. In addition, production should be optimized during operation to allow fast delivery of products using lesser resources.

In this chapter we focus on diagnosis for Industry 4.0. In particular, we discuss the underlying requirements and afterwards present a methodology that serves this purpose. Diagnosis itself is the activity or task dealing with the identification of the underlying reason for a certain observed deviation from expected behavior of a system. Such a deviation is usually referred to as a symptom and diagnosis is for localizing the underlying root cause, which is later used for applying treatments in order to bring a system back into its desired ordinary state. For example, in medicine humans can be seen as systems. If a patient comes to a medical doctor with certain symptoms such as fever and headache, the doctor comes up with more or less hypotheses about the underlying disease. Via obtaining more information about the health state of the patient, those hypotheses are further reduced and finally in an ideal world there is a root cause, which serves as bases for further medical treatments. This described situation is the same for technical systems where diagnosis is one of the tasks of system maintenance.

Is diagnosis in the context of Industry 4.0 different from ordinary system diagnosis? The answer here is yes. Due to the required flexibility of manufacturing leading to systems that adapt themselves accordingly to certain demands, the structure of the system changes over time. For example, in one production step a certain work piece passing a drilling machine might be fed directly to a paint shop, whereas another work piece might go to further mechanical treatment before. Hence, when quality criteria of a work piece are not met, we have to know the responsible structure of the system and the behavior of the involved machine tools. Therefore, there is the requirement of having a diagnosis method that can adapt itself on structural changes without human intervention.

In addition, to this general requirement there is a need for having such a general diagnosis method easily accessible ideally without requiring a deep understanding of the underlying foundations. One idea in this direction is the concept of providing software as a service to the general public [2]. The Software as a Service (SaaS) concept has been intended for providing the software's functionality to customers without requiring them to think about deployment and maintenance. In SaaS the ownership of the software remains on side of the developer and only its use is granted to the customer. During the past years SaaS has moved in the direction of Everything as a Service (XaaS) [3] extending this idea to any potential services that can be provided using hardware and software.

SaaS and XaaS have gained more and more importance. Besides classical and popular cloud services for providing computing power or storage capacity, there is a growing interest in services for editing documents among others. Google documents is an example for this development and there are many more. For bringing diagnosis into practice and also increasing accessibility to diagnosis functionality, providing diagnosis services over the Internet would be required.

Unfortunately, this is not easy because diagnosis requires the knowledge about the system, for example, its structure and behavior, or other types of knowledge facilitating diagnosis. This is similar to a text editor, which requires documents comprising the textual information. For diagnosis, we need the documents describing diagnosis knowledge in a machine-readable form.

In the rest of this chapter we elaborate on the idea of providing diagnosis functionality as a service accessible over the Internet. We provide an overview about necessary prerequisites, discuss the functionality to be delivered, and introduce model-based diagnosis as a foundational method for implementing diagnosis as a service (ΔaaS).

50.2 Prerequisites

Let us start first with all prerequisites we need for diagnosis. First of all, we require knowledge about the system we want to diagnose. This knowledge has to include rules to allow reasoning from causes to potential effects. The causes themselves have to be formulated in an explicit way, i. e., via introducing a hypothesis for each cause. For example, a switch might be on or off. These two states of the switch have to be represented as hypotheses, e. g., switch_on, switch_off, in a knowledge base. In addition, we need observations of the system, i. e., the symptoms. Based on the knowledge base for diagnosis and the observations we further need a reasoning engine that returns potential causes for the given observations. A potential cause in this terminology would be a hypothesis or a set of hypotheses that have to be true in order to explain the given symptoms. We will discuss the reasoning aspect in more detail in Sect. 50.3.

In summary, a diagnosis service needs the following information to compute diagnoses:

- A diagnosis knowledge base comprising knowledge about the system to be diagnosed, where the knowledge should allow reasoning from causes to effects and explicitly introduce hypotheses, and
- A set of observations, i. e., the symptoms, to be explained.

Of course the necessary knowledge has to be available in a form that can be utilized by the underlying diagnosis reasoning-engine. For the reasoning engine, we require efficient computation and also independence from the diagnosis problem itself due to the fact that systems in case of Industry 4.0 change their structure and thus their underlying behavior over time. Independence from the underlying diagnosis problem means to be general applicable regardless of the given diagnosis knowledge and observations.

A concrete ΔaaS implementation should take the information relevant for diagnosis, i. e., the knowledge base and the observation, as input, and deliver certain hypotheses ex-

Fig. 50.1 ΔaaS architecture

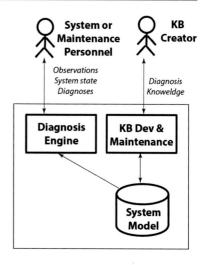

plaining the observations as an output. This view, however, is rather limited because it only considers the diagnosis part of ΔaaS but not how to develop and maintain the knowledge base. Hence, a ΔaaS implementation should deal with both aspects. Note that the two tasks, i. e., (1) developing and maintaining the knowledge base and (2) using diagnosis, are usually performed by different persons having different skills. Task (1) requires knowledge about how to formulate the required knowledge, whereas (2) only needs information about observations (and the current state of the system). In addition, and especially in the context of Industry 4.0, task (2) may be automatically performed. Therefore, the interfaces to ΔaaS may be closely adapted for the different tasks.

In Fig. 50.1 we show the architecture of a concrete ΔaaS implementation and the underlying diagnosis method including the interactions with users, which can be by either humans or other systems. We distinguish the users of the diagnosis engine (System or Maintenance Personnel) and the ones responsible for providing the diagnosis knowledge (KB Creator), which is stored in a system model. The diagnosis engine takes the system model together with the observations and the system state, and returns explanations, i. e., the diagnoses.

In the next section we discuss a diagnosis method that fits ideally the requirements of a ΔaaS as described before.

50.3 Diagnosis Methods and Techniques

A ΔaaS needs to be general enough to serve many purposes. Hence, we need an underlying diagnosis methodology that is as general as possible. In the early days of Artificial Intelligence (AI) rule-based expert systems [4] have been used for diagnosis (see for example [1]). A rule can be seen as an if-then construct, where the condition is a question to be answered by the user and a consequent the next possible state or a diagnosis results. Classical rule-based systems implement the reasoning in the direction from symptoms to responsible causes. A main drawback of these kinds of system for diagnosis is that the rule-base has to be always changed in case the system structure changes leading to high maintenance costs. Therefore, classical rule-based systems can hardly be used in the given setting of ΔaaS. In order to avoid the mentioned problem, the concept of model-based diagnosis has been suggested. We distinguish two types of model-based diagnosis: (1) consistency-based diagnosis (see [5] and [6]), and (2) abductive diagnosis [7]. In (1) only the correct behavior of a system based on the structure of the system and a formalization of the behavior of its parts has to be provided. In abductive diagnosis, rules that represent cause-effect reasoning are used. Both types of model-based diagnosis are very much appropriate in the context of ΔaaS because diagnosis only relies on the underlying models, i. e., a model of the system, and is thus generally applicable. It is also well known that both types have a strong relationship (see [8] for more information).

In this chapter, we suggest the use of abductive diagnosis and outline its underlying idea and concepts. The reason is that the necessary diagnosis knowledge can be easily obtained from system documentation available. For more information about the use of abductive diagnosis in industrial applications we refer the interested reader to [9].

In order to show the principles of abductive diagnosis and the required information, we make use of the following small example:

Example

Let us assume to come at home during the night. After unlocking the door and entering our home, we try to switch on the light at the entrance but there is no light. Maybe the bulb is broken. However, we first go to the nearby living room trying to switch on the light but again without success. We now have at least two potential causes. One states that the bulb at the entrance and the one in the living room are both broken. Another alternative explanation would be that the fuse responsible for the lights at the first floor is in state off or broken. The latter only requires one hypothesis to explain two symptoms. Hence, we would try to fix the problem using the smallest diagnosis first.

In this example, we use some implicit knowledge about the structure of the electrical system at home and about the behavior of involved parts, e. g., that a bulb has to submit light in case of being switch on, and that there are fuses for different electrical cables in order to prevent damage (mainly due to fire caused by too much electricity going through a cable). For automating diagnosis, we need a formal representation of the knowledge about the system.

Fig. 50.2 shows the structure of an electrical system we assume to correspond with our diagnosis example. In the schematics we see that we have one main fuse (F1) and two sub circuits with fuses F2 and F3 respectively. In the first sub circuit we have two switches connected (S1 and S2) turning on or off two bulbs (B1 and B2 respectively). In the second

Fig. 50.2 Simplified schematics of an electrical system for a domestic home

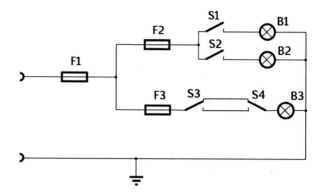

sub circuit we have two changeover switches S3 and S4 used to turn on and off bulb B3. From this schematic we are able to derive consequences, i. e., symptoms, of hypotheses. For example, when assuming that bulb B1 is broken, we know that B1 cannot emit any light. If fuse F2 is broken, we know that bulb B1 and B2 cannot be turned on anymore using switch S1 and S2 respectively. Similarly, we are able to derive what happens if both fuses F1 and F2 are not broken and S1 is set to on, then the bulb B1 should be on and thus transmit light.

Using this information we are able to construct a table where we have on one side the hypotheses and on the other their effects. Table 50.1 shows the entries only for the case of broken fuses or bulbs. For simplicity we do not consider the position of switches and the cases where a bulb is lighting.

The semantics behind the table is the following. In each row we have one cause-effect pair. The cause is a hypothesis mentioned in a row, while the corresponding effects are given in the second column. If there is more than one effect, the effects are put together using local operators like *AND* or *OR*. In the second line we see that a broken fuse F1 influences all the bulbs. In case of an *OR* at least one of the effects must hold. It is worth noting that there might also be more than one hypothesis given in a row. For example, in case two or more hypotheses are necessary for deriving the mentioned effects.

In abductive diagnosis accordingly to the definitions from [7] a diagnosis is a set of hypotheses that allows deriving all given symptoms. In addition, we do not allow hypotheses

Table 50.1 The cause-effect table for the electrical circuit for a domestic home

Hypotheses	Effects
Broken(F1)	No_light(B1) AND No_light(B2) AND No_light(B3)
Broken(F2)	No_light(B1) AND No_light(B2)
Broken(F3)	No_light(B3)
Broken(B1)	No_light(B1)
Broken(B2)	No_light(B2)
Broken(B3)	No_light(B3)

in a diagnosis to be contradictory, e. g., a diagnosis that would state that a fuse is broken and not broken at the same time is not a diagnosis. A diagnosis is said to be parsimonious if none of its subsets are themselves diagnoses. In practice, we are mainly interested in parsimonious, i. e., minimal, diagnoses.

Let us come back to our initial example. When entering our home we see that there is no light at the entrance, i. e., the observed symptom is *No_light(B1)*. From Table 50.1 we know that *Broken(F1)*, *Broken(F2)* or *Broken(B1)* are all valid diagnoses because they have *No_light(B1)* as effect and thus allow to derive the given symptom. When turning on the next light, i. e., B2, we obtain two symptoms *No_light(B1) AND No_light(B2)*. Hence, we have two single hypothesis explanations, i. e. *Broken(F1)* as well as *Broken(F2)*. Another larger explanations is *Broken(B1) AND Broken(B2)*. When preferring smaller explanation, we would first have a look at the fuses.

The abductive diagnosis approach as described can be extended to handle probabilities for diagnosis and also to support the user during the process of localizing the root cause. For example, the probability that a bulb is broken is often much higher than the probability of a broken fuse. This information can be utilized to rank diagnoses according to their likelihood. The diagnosis process itself includes adding new observations or measurements, i. e., symptoms, to further reduce the number of diagnoses, or to make appropriate repair actions.

50.4 Diagnosis

Continuous growth in magnitude and complexity of technical systems requires automatic diagnosis procedures to determine failure inducing system parts effectively. Particularly, in domains where maintenance costs constitute a significant portion of the life-cycle costs accurately deducing the root cause of an anomaly is essential. The industrial wind turbine domain is an application area experiencing a cost-intensive maintenance process. In this section we focus on improving fault diagnosis in real applications such as wind turbines by employing abductive model-based diagnosis to compute causes for measurable system anomalies.

The main hindering factor influencing the dissemination of model-based diagnosis in practice is the initial effort associated with the creation of a suitable system model. We devised a process that aims at integrating abductive diagnosis in real-world applications by automating the development of system models. By reusing knowledge frequently available, such as Failure Mode Effect Analysis (FMEA), the model creation time as well as cost necessary is decreased. Fig. 50.3 depicts the process that is divided into three main stages, i. e., (1) model development, (2) fault detection and (3) fault identification [9].

As the knowledge necessary for abductive reasoning describes the connection between causes, i. e. hypotheses, and their effects, i. e. symptoms, failure assessments such as FMEA provide appropriate information for abductive diagnosis, as they capture knowl-

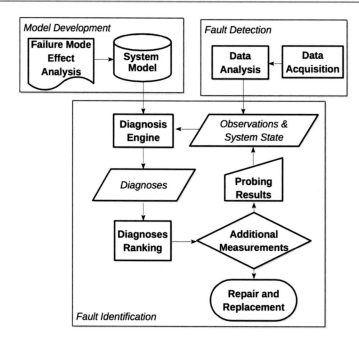

Fig. 50.3 Process for incorporating abductive model-based diagnosis into an industrial setting [9]

edge on causal relations between components based fault modes and their effects on system variables.

Table 50.2 shows a simplified FMEA taken from the industrial wind turbine domain. As can be seen there are three columns describing the relation between components, their fault modes as well as their effects on the system. Consider the first entry. This states that in case the pins of the fan are experiencing corrosion, an unexpected decrease in the generated power (*Power(Turbine,low)*) and an increase in the cabinet temperature (*Temperature(Cabinet,high)*) are observable.

There are two essential characteristics of the FMEA which we have to consider when mapping it to a cause-effect table. First, each fault mode is associated with a specific component. Thus, the hypotheses we are considering for our cause-effect table are a combination of a component and its fault mode. For example, the hypothesis inferred from the

Table 50.2 Exemplary FMEA of the converter of an industrial wind turbine

Component	Fault Mode	Effects
Fan – Pin	Corrosion	Power(Turbine,low), Temperature(Cabinet,high)
IGBT – Wire Bonding	High-cycle fatigue (HCF)	Power(Turbine,low), Temperature(Inverter_Cabinet,high), Temperature(Nacelle,high)

Table 50.3 The cause-effect table for the converter example

Hypotheses	Effects
Corrosion(Fan–Pin)	Power(Turbine,low) AND Temperature(Cabinet,high)
HCF(IGBT – Wire Bonding)	Power(Turbine,low) AND Temperature(Inverter_Cabinet,high) AND Temperature(Nacelle,high)

first entry would be *Corrosion(Fan–Pin)* implying that the pins of the fan are corroded. Further, all effects have to be connected by an *AND* as in case the fault is present all symptoms have to be existent. Table 50.3 depicts the cause-effect table created on basis of the FMEA in Table 50.2.

Once the system model has been created offline, the online portion of the process takes place. Diagnosis is always triggered by the observation of a symptom. Therefore, some mechanism must be present to determine a deviation from the expected to the current system behavior, i. e. a fault detection method. In the wind turbine domain a condition monitoring system provides information on anomalies among the system variables.

After a symptom has been observed, the diagnosis reasoning engine can be started. The engine takes as input on the one hand the system model generated offline and on the other hand the results of the fault detection, which are fed into the engine as observations about the current system state. The diagnosis engine then determines the hypotheses explaining the observations. Information such as probabilities can be used to refine the diagnosis and

Table 50.4 Experiment results on various FMEAs [9]

System	Model Size		Runtime [in ms]				#Diagnoses				
	#Hyp	#Eff	MIN	MAX	AVG	MED	MAX	AVG	S	D	T
Electrical Circuit	32	17	<1	994	48.0	2	792	191.6	11	22	44
Ford Connector System	17	17	<1	204	2.1	1	18	3.1	6	18	18
HIFI-FPU	17	11	<1	214	5.2	1	189	8.2	7	21	27
MiTS1	17	21	<1	307	7.6	1	12	5.4	3	3	6
MiTS2	22	15	<1	191	6.6	2	288	37.4	8	24	24
PCB	10	11	<1	140	1.3	<1	2	1.6	2	2	2
ACD	13	16	<1	210	4.5	1	15	2.4	5	8	15
Inverter	29	38	<1	4830	34.8	10	1280	33.0	19	57	76
Rectifier	20	17	<1	53	3.8	3	160	10.8	15	40	64
Transformer	4	8	<1	70	0.7	<1	4	1.2	4	2	2
Backup Components	25	30	<1	856	14.8	5	864	25.1	9	42	210
Main Bearing	3	5	<1	191	1.7	<1	3	2.4	3	0	0

additional measurements aid in reducing the number of solutions and confirming diagnoses.

We conducted several experiments on the diagnosis computation time for various FMEAs publicly available and project internal. The FMEAs analyze electrical circuits, a connector system by Ford, the Focal Plane Unit (FPU) of the Heterodyne Instrument for the Far Infrared (HIFI), printed circuit boards (PCB), the Anticoincidence Detector (ACD) of the Fermi Gamma-ray Space Telescope, the Maritim ITStandard (MiTS), as well as rectifier, inverter, transformer, main bearing, and backup components of an industrial wind turbine. Table 50.4 depicts information about the size of the model, i. e., *#Hyp* and *#Eff* determine the number of hypotheses and effects. The runtime results show the minimal, maximal, average and median runtime in milliseconds. The last five columns display the maximum and average number of diagnoses as well as the number of single hypothesis (*S*), double hypotheses (*D*) and triple hypotheses (*T*) diagnoses.

As the results show while there are maximum computation times of around five seconds, the median of the distributions is located around and below ten milliseconds. Further, on average we can record runtimes of fewer than half a second. These runtime results as well as the automated modeling argue in favor of our approach as a feasible method for diagnosis in practical applications.

50.5 Conclusion

In this chapter we introduced the concept of Diagnosis As A Service where we argued for the necessity of the availability of diagnosis functionality especially in case of Industry 4.0 comprising interconnected manufacturing plants and devices to be flexible enough for being adapted accordingly to specific customers' requirements. These underlying system requirements, i. e., distributed manufacturing and increased flexibility, demand a flexible diagnosis infrastructure. To serve this purpose we discussed the general diagnosis methodology abductive diagnosis where cause-effect knowledge is used for identifying root causes for given symptoms. Such cause-effect knowledge is often available in practice for engineered systems thus making the approach interesting for practical applications.

Besides discussing the basic principles of abductive diagnosis in this chapter, we also introduce requirements for implementing diagnosis as a service and present its underlying architecture. In addition, we recall the use of abductive diagnosis in an industrial context in order to show its feasibility for fault localization for several systems used in practice. In all cases except one the implemented diagnosis approach required less than one second for computing diagnosis candidates. Based on the diagnosis candidates the abductive diagnosis approach also allows for supporting the user in identifying the real root cause via asking questions about new symptoms. In order to come up with a diagnosis service the underlying cause-effect knowledge has to be formalized, which can be done using a table as described in this chapter.

Acknowledgements

The work presented in this paper has been supported by the FFG project Applied Model Based Reasoning (AMOR) under grant 842407 and the SFG project EXPERT.

References

1. Wikipedia, "Industry 4.0," 17 06 2016. [Online]. Available: https://en.wikipedia.org/wiki/Industry_4.0.
2. R. Reiter, A theory of diagnosis from first principles, 1 ed., Artificial Intelligence, 1987, pp. 38–44.
3. J. De Kleer and B. Williams, Diagnosing multiple faults, 32 ed., vol. 1, Artificial Intelligence, 1987, pp. 97–130.
4. G. Friedrich, G. Gottlob and W. Nejdl, "Hypothesis classification abductive diagnosis and therapy," in *Proceedings of the International Workshop on Expert Systems in Engineering*, vol. 462, Vienna, Springer Verlag, 1990.
5. L. Console, T. Dupré and P. Torasso, "On the relationship between abduction and deduction," *Journal of Logic and Computation*, vol. 1, no. 5, pp. 661–690, 1991.
6. R. Koitz and F. Wotawa, "From Theory to Practice: Model-Based Diagnosis in Industrial Applications," in *Proceedings of the Annual conference of the PHM Society (PHM-2015)*, San Diego, CA, USA, 2015, pp. 197–205.
7. Y. Duan, G. Fu, N. Zhou, X. Sun, N. C. Narendra and B. Hu, "Everything as a Service (XaaS) on the Cloud: Origins, Current and Future Trends," in *Proceedings of the IEEE 8th International Conference on Cloud Computing*, IEEE Press, 2015.
8. B. Buchanan and E. Shortliffe, Rule Based Expert Systems: The MYCIN Experiments of the Standord Heuristic Programming Project, Addison-Wesley, 1984.
9. P. Jackson, Introduction To Expert Systems, Addison Wesley, 1998.

Further Reading
10. M. Turner, D. Budgen and P. Brereton, Turning software into a service, 10 ed., vol. 36, IEEE Computer, 2003, pp. 38–44.

Part XII
Intelligent & Autonomous Enterprise

Preface: Intelligent & Autonomous Enterprise

Martin Hofmann and Stefan Meinzer

Abstract

The era of digitalization, that is already present, will significantly influence and change the today's enterprise in various ways. The way humans interact with their environment, the services that customers expect, the increasing speed of new competitive products and technologies that will emerge, or the changing product portfolio a customer perceives as comfortable are just some examples that illustrate the influence of digitalization. Customers will expect connected services combined with the existing tangible products to increase the perceived convenience. The expectations from the environment towards existing businesses will continuously change faster than ever before that forces companies for rapid actions, continuous adaptations and fast new product releases to remain competitive. The fundamental consequence is, that the business environment, the service industries in particular, must strive towards intelligent and autonomous enterprises in order to fulfill these requirements. New technologies, such as artificial intelligence, robotics, quantum computing or autonomous agents, will be the distinguishing features to survive in the future. A business that is most affected by this disruptive change is the automotive industry. This preface will illustrate the current situation for the automotive industry, the business areas that are most affected by digitalization, the new technologies that are required, the new orientation of the traditional business units and the benefits that will result from this disruptive change.

M. Hofmann (✉)
Volkswagen Group
Wolfsburg, Germany
e-mail: martin.hofmann@volkswagen.de

S. Meinzer
Volkswagen Data:Lab
Munich, Germany
e-mail: stefan.meinzer@volkswagen.de

51.1 Introduction

The automotive industry is in the midst of a disruptive change. While the car itself was in focus of the customer and the manufacturer so far, digital customer services around customers' mobility will be the future core value. The car must fit into the customer' digital ecosystem providing maximum convenience and safety.

The exponential growth of computing power, as illustrated by Fig. 51.1, leads to unforeseen possibilities in the automotive industry. Intelligent and autonomous cars; new mobility services due to artificial intelligence; cross-industrial knowledge transfer from other business areas like the health care [1] to provide the best safety features are three examples for the disruptive change. Therefore, new technologies, the corresponding skills and new IT models must be implemented. The automotive industry is following this path already [2]. In order to remain competitive, the companies must satisfy customers' expectations within these areas. Maximizing customer satisfaction by services is one core competence of the automotive industry [3]. While the goal to secure highest satisfaction remains the same, the services themselves will change towards data driven services.

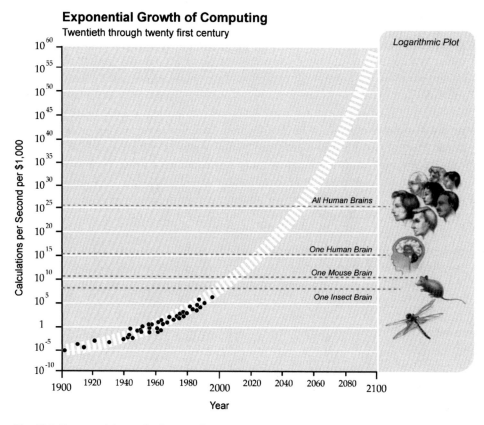

Fig. 51.1 Exponential growth of computing power. (Kurzweil [4])

According to Moore's Law, the possibilities of digital applications will be far reaching due to the almost exponential increase of calculations per second achieved by high end computer systems [5]. In future, the automotive industry will be one of the largest data generators and data provider within the service industries [6]. Latest car models are already creating more than 25 Gigabytes of data every hour. In the era of autonomous driving, 1 Terabyte is estimated to be produced every hour by sensors and services of the cars [7]. This estimation ends up in 2 Petabytes of data per car per year that need to be analyzed in real-time in order to create customized services. With the growing importance of battery cars, sensor fusion will be one central area in order to apply machine learning algorithms or artificial intelligence [8]. Internal sensor data from cars must be combined with external data sources from various digital ecosystems in order to secure maximum mobility of pure electric cars.

The traditional automotive industry has to overcome various challenges in the era of disruptive change. The most important areas that are touched by the fast growth of technological development are presented in the following section.

51.2   The Disruptive Change of the Automotive Industry

The change within the automotive industry due to new connected technologies is already proceeding [28]. In general, the disruption describes the move from cars towards mobility. The first step of the change is the development of connected cars, as illustrated by Fig. 51.2. The path reaches from connected car via the connected customer and the con-

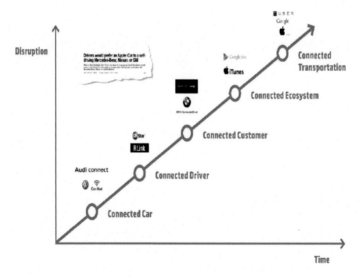

Fig. 51.2 Path of disruption of the automotive industry. (Seiberth [9])

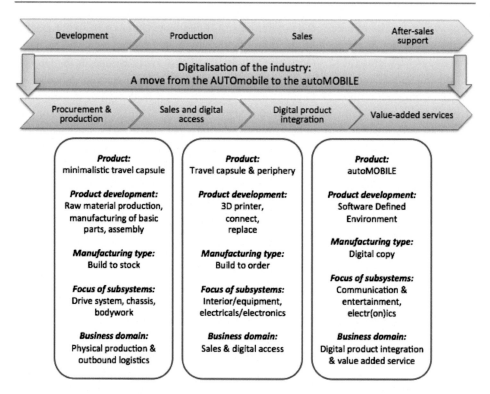

Fig. 51.3 Overview on business areas of the automotive industry affected by the change of the digitalization. (Wedeniwski [10])

nected ecosystem towards connected transportation [9]. Remarkably, new competitors of the traditional automotive industry already entered the market, such as Uber, Google or OnStar. Consequently, the existing manufactures must strengthen their core competences – producing cars and services around the cars and customers – enhanced by latest available technologies.

The change due to digitalization affects the complete supply and value chain of the automotive industry [10], as illustrated by Fig. 51.3. In the following, the focus is set on the most important business areas.

51.2.1 Autonomous Driving

The total number of cars is estimated to be more than 100 mio. worldwide [11]. A huge challenge and opportunity. In order to predict traffic or provide high safety standards, sensor based functionalities are already implemented that transfer signals for instance from radar or cameras. Machine learning models are implemented for features like traffic sign recognition or lane assists [11]. However, it is mandatory to enhance these functionalities to reach the goal of selling self-learning cars. This is fundamental to be able to provide customer services, such as the mobility on roads or at a time with low traffic. One vision of the future, related to autonomous cars, is the elimination of traffic jam. Based on car-to-car communication, vehicles will be intelligent enough to navigate in the most effective way. As the navigation of these cars will be based on applications related to artificial intelligence, the safety and the efficiency of driving will continuously increase.

From a customers' perspective, the value of autonomous driving is individuality. Services while driving and the driving behavior itself will be personalized. For the automotive industry it means Petabytes of data that need to be analyzed in real-time. Latest technologies, such as quantum computing, will be needed to handle these optimization problems from an analytics perspective. To realize such new capabilities, companies need to change their existing structures, especially the IT, and develop new skills [2]. Companies, such as Volkswagen, are already pioneering these new technologies for example using quantum computers for traffic flow optimisation [26].

51.2.2   Smart Cities

The urbanization yields to new concepts of living. Smart homes and smart cities are the two main pillars coming together with the urbanization and the digital ecosystem. The competitive advantage of companies offering digital services will be the degree of integration of these services into the connected ecosystem of the customer [9]. The automotive industry will play a significant role in designing smart cities. Intelligent parking systems, battery charging on demand or driving home functionalities in autonomous driving cars are just three representative examples [12]. Finally, the goal of smart cities is to increase the humans' quality of life. Taking the technological perspective, this goal can only be reached by integrating and combining the countless amount of transferred data [13]. Consequently, sensor fusion will be one of the most challenging and important capabilities to remain competitive and to enter this market. The city of Barcelona, as an example, is already changing their whole infrastructure towards a smart city concept. Today, more than 320 millions of sensor signals received from more than 1,800 different kinds of sensors produce more than 8 Gigabytes of compressed data each day [13]. The significance for the automotive industry shows the critical topic of parking. In mega-cities, such as Barcelona or Singapore, every third driver is searching for a parking spot for around 8 min [12, 14]. In order to increase quality of life as mentioned earlier, smart parking will be a core digitalized service for the automotive industry. Therefore, internal sensor data from the cars, infrastructure signals from the cities, geo-data, individual customer preferences and many more signals must be fused in order to offer the driver the best spot at the best location at the right time at the best price. Such scenarios are game-changer for traditionally acting manufacturers, technologically as well as from a structural-process perspective. While the analysis and storage of the internal data is already a core discipline, the analysis of merged internal and external data requires modern machine learning methods and state of the art computing technologies. In order to provide real-time services in smart cities, technologies like scalable cloud computing must be a standard element of the future IT environment.

51.2.3 After-Sales

The After-Sales business is the most important, established core business of the automotive industry. The margin and profit that is generated within After-Sales is already significantly higher than within sales [15]. An estimated revenue of 6–8 billion dollars is annually generated by After-Sales services only in the US [16]. As the importance of the product car itself will shift towards the importance of digital customer services around mobility, the significance of the After-Sales business will be even higher [17, 18]. Various applications based on machine learning techniques in order to improve the After-Sales business are already established, such as the prediction of churning customers, the modeling of customer satisfaction or the rule-based recommender systems [19–21]. However, following the trend of connected cars, autonomous driving and the integration of the mobility in customers' digital ecosystem, new and individualized customer services will form the future After-Sales business [27]. The classification of potentially dissatisfied customers before the customer-service interaction ends, is one representative example [27]. Predictive maintenance is one representative example. Generally, the goal of the After-Sales business will be mobility maximization, downtime reduction, and individualized service packages while the customer visits a dealer [22]. The big advantage of the After-Sales sector and thus the traditional automotive manufacturer, compared to the above mentioned new areas and competitors, is the fact that the fundamental basis for these new services is the already existing data. Years of service information, repair campaigns, etc. identify a vast amount of information [23] the automotive industry must make maximum value out of it. Therefore, new business approaches based on latest technologies are necessary to generate this value. Autonomous marketing campaigns, pricing, finance or controlling are exemplary areas where artificial intelligence needs to be applied to realize these new business potentials.

51.2.4 Production

The manufacturing process of the automotive industry is an area that produces a vast amount of data. It is an area that is changing rapidly towards an automated and autonomous industrial sector [2]. Due to the fast development of research in robotics and in particular human-robotics cooperation [24], this field will require special technological attention in the era of Industry 4.0. The evolution of robotics research yields to faster production processes with lower probability for quality failures. Additionally, from an economic perspective costs might become reduced significantly [25].

The integration of high automated manufacturing processes brings additional requirements for existing manufacturers. The importance of predictive maintenance, as already introduced as a customer service, will be fundamentally important in the field of robotics. With visionary applications, such as integrated factory optimization, new potentials arise [27]. Predicting potential downtimes, quality failures or missing parts for production are examples where the application of machine learning techniques is the basis. In order to cope with the increasing variety and complexity of car configurations, methods related to artificial intelligence will be needed in order to speed up the manufacturing process and increase the output quality.

51.3   Intelligent & Autonomous Enterprises to Remain Competitive

To remain competitive in the future, fundamental key requirements need to be fulfilled: Invest in new products, such as autonomous driving and electric cars; integrate the mobility and thus the car itself in customer' digital ecosystem; offer digital customer services to maximize the mobility, minimize downtimes and offer individualized predictive maintenance; automate the manufacturing process to make it more efficient. Three representative examples to improve established processes fundamentally within an autonomous enterprise are the following.

First, the planning of sales activities is a big potential of autonomous enterprises [27]. Based on sold cars, future customer preferences can be predicted. Even more, the configuration of cars that have the highest probability to be sold can be determined. Calculating similarity matrices, future trends can be predicted. Adapting anomaly detection methods, shifts in model selections or configuration choices can be identified even earlier than humans could do it today. The potential of an autonomous sales planning is the time saving compared to the expert knowledge that is needed today. The model portfolio can be suited to country and customer groups as soon as switching customer preferences are detected [27].

Second, financial controlling functions are significantly based on manual processes, such as the receiving process of invoices and forwarding them to the corresponding business units. Especially in traditional service industries, this is manual paperwork in order to read them but more important to check and proof the validity of these invoices. Adapting natural language processing, this whole process can be automated. By combining existing master data and finance systems, a classification of contents can be done based on cluster analysis for example. Using a semi-automated solution in a first step, these clusters need to be interpreted in order to assign the related business. Implementing machine learning algorithms, this assignment can be trained and thus in short term be done autonomously. Compared to solutions today, this system would be also tolerant to missing parameters in invoices as the system would know from historical data which parameters have the highest probability to be added in order to fully complete the invoice. This would reduce delays and contractual penalties to a minimum. However, the question will remain if this area won't be digitalized anyways as supplier will be forced to digitalize their financial outputs, as Amazon proofs. They established this as an assumption for suppliers on their platform.

Autonomous pricing is a third area of potential of autonomous enterprises. Today, prices, for instance of spare parts, are based on expert knowledge and are heterogeneously and decentralized defined in each country. The main problem is that a central market transparency is not present. Analyzing unstructured content, for instance from online platforms, would increase this transparency and will give a central idea about competitive pricing. The challenge is to find 100% matches between web content and internal parts distribution data. Machine learning methods, such as picture recognition, natural language processing or time series analysis [29], allow this matching procedure. Based on this information applications can be designed that define optimal prices in real-time, multiple times a day. Humans won't be able to do this independent to their degree of expertise. This scenario is a core business model for online platforms already and will be indispensable to survive in the future competition.

Summarizing, the big challenge is to bridge the gap between developing a new product portfolio and being more cost efficient.

To overcome these challenges, the importance of new technologies, such as machine learning, high speed computing or cloud services has never been higher. The potentials for the automotive industry by investing in these areas are significant:

- The amount of data will rapidly grow to amounts that overcome most of todays' architectures,
- The capabilities to analyze this amount of data will require machine learning and artificial intelligence techniques to generate the value that exists in this information,
- The internal, heterogeneous data sources must be homogenized in order to develop services that go beyond today's business models,
- Internal data must be merged with external data in order to provide services fitting to the concepts of smart cities and the customers' ecosystem,
- Sensor fusion will be a key requirement to establish smart production and predictive maintenance,
- Cost efficient business models will require autonomous enterprises.

To remain competitive, current business models need to change according to newly available technologies. Established processes will change towards data driven business models, e. g. the After-Sales sector in particular. More precisely, current processes will get autonomous. Taking Amazon as an example, autonomous pricing models are needed in order to be competitive in sales, in real-time. Such platforms are validating and optimizing their portfolio million times each day to increase market share. Automation of business processes have been in the focus and perfected by software companies. In the near future, business processes and functions, such as financially planning and controlling, will be run by machine learning algorithms – autonomously – without human intervention. This will be a completely new level of automation at the highest possible accuracy and quality level. Even decision making, in certain processes will be handled by the machine.

The automotive industry, together with their underlying potential of existing and continuously growing data, has the potential to gather the market leadership. The automation of already existing processes is mandatory to be cost efficient in order to develop the above mentioned capabilities and to follow the disruptive change that requires a new product and service portfolio. Without intelligent and autonomous business models, this will not be possible.

References

1. Meinzer, S., et al., *Translating satisfaction determination from health care to the automotive industry.* Service Business, 2016. **10**(4): p. 1-35.
2. Gehrke, L., D. Hajizadeh, C. Kreibich, S. Meinzer, S. Augustine, and J. S. Geffers, *Innovation Labs und Aktivitäten der Volkswagen Konzern IT im Zuge der Digitalisierung und Industrie 4.0*, in *Einführung und Umsetzung von Industrie 4.0: Grundlagen, Vorgehensmodell und Use Cases aus der Praxis*, A. Roth, Editor. 2016, Springer: Berlin, Germany. p. 231-246.
3. Hünecke, P. and M. Gunkel, *The influence of After-Sales service determinants on brand loyalty within the premium automotive industry: an empirical comparison of three countries.* Service Science, 2012. **4**(4): p. 365-381.
4. Singularity. *Exponential Growth of Computing.* 2016; Available from: http://www.singularity. com/charts/page70.html.
5. Kurzweil, R., *How to Create a Mind: The Secret of Human Thought Revealed.* 2012, London, England: Viking Adult.
6. IBM. *IBM big data for the automotive industry: Take advantage of new sources of data to reduce costs and increase competitive advantage.* 2013 09/10/2016]; Available from: http:// www.oesa.org/Doc-Vault/Knowledge-Center/Operational-Performance-Content/IBM-Big-Data-for-Auto-Industry.pdf.
7. Mearian, L., *Self-driving cars could create 1GB of data a second*, in *Computerworld.* 2013, Computerworld.
8. Rodgers, L., S. Zoepf, and J. Prenninger. *Analysing the energy consumption of the BMW ActiveE field trial vehicles with application to distance to empty algorithms.* in *Transportation Research Procedia.* 2014.
9. Seiberth, G., *Wie verändern digitale Plattformen die Automobilwirtschaft?*, in *Praxis – Industrie 4.0: Wie digitale Plattformen unsere Wirtschaft verändert - und wie die Politik gestalten kann*, Ansgar Baums | Martin Schössler | Ben Scott (Hg.): Editor. 2015, Kompendium Digitale Standortpolitik: Berlin, Germany. p. 28-41.
10. Wedeniwski, S., *The Mobility Revolution in the Automotive Industry: How not to miss the digital turnpike.* 2015, Berlin, Germany: Springer.
11. Tummala, R., et al. *New era in automotive electronics, a co-development by Georgia tech and its automotive partners.* in *2016 Pan Pacific Microelectronics Symposium (Pan Pacific).* 2016. IEEE.

12. Niculescu, A.I., et al., *Designing IDA - An Intelligent Driver Assistant for Smart City Parking in Singapore*, in *Human-Computer Interaction – INTERACT 2015: 15th IFIP TC 13 International Conference, Bamberg, Germany, September 14-18, 2015, Proceedings, Part IV*, J. Abascal, et al., Editors. 2015, Springer International Publishing: Cham. p. 510-513.

13. Sinaeepourfard, A., et al. *Estimating Smart City sensors data generation: Current and Future Data in the City of Barcelona*. in *2016 Mediterranean Ad Hoc Networking Workshop (Med-Hoc-Net)*. 2016.

14. Geng, Y. and C.G. Cassandras, *A new "Smart Parking" System Infrastructure and Implementation*. Procedia - Social and Behavioral Sciences, 2012. **54**: p. 1278-1287.

15. ADL, *Automotive After Sales 2015: Are you ready for the battle?*, in *Arthur D. Little - Automotive INSIGHT*. 2015, Arthur D. Little, Germany. p. 1-6.

16. Gaiardelli, P., N. Saccani, and L. Songini, *Performance measurement of the after-sales service network - evidence from the automotive industry*. Computers in Industry, 2007. **58**(7): p. 698-708.

17. Philipp Grosse Kleimann, Dorit Posdorf, Alexander Brenner, Swen Beyer, Dr. Ralf Kiene, Torsten Hunstock. *Customizing aftersales: Delivering the service that customers really want*. 2013 08/28/2016]; Available from: https://de.scribd.com/document/254676885/Roland-Berger-Customizing-Aftersales-20131120.

18. Singh, S. *Future Of Automotive Aftermarket And Car Servicing: Consumers Will Have More Channels To Shop Around*. 2015 08/30/2016]; Available from: http://www.forbes.com/sites/sarwantsingh/2015/06/02/future-of-automotive-aftermarket-and-car-servicing-consumers-will-have-more-channels-to-shop-around/#35235c0a4359.

19. Bandaru, S., et al., *Development, analysis and applications of a quantitative methodology for assessing customer satisfaction using evolutionary optimization*. Applied Soft Computing, 2015. **30**: p. 265-278.

20. Chougule, R., V.R. Khare, and K. Pattada, *A fuzzy logic based approach for modeling quality and reliability related customer satisfaction in the automotive domain*. Expert Systems with Applications, 2013. **40**(2): p. 800-810.

21. Mavridou, E., et al., *Mining affective needs of automotive industry customers for building a mass-customization recommender system*. Journal of Intelligent Manufacturing, 2013. **24**(2): p. 251-265.

22. Mikusz, M., C. Jud, and T. Schäfer, *Business Model Patterns for the Connected Car and the Example of Data Orchestrator*, in *Software Business: 6th International Conference, ICSOB 2015, Braga, Portugal, June 10-12, 2015, Proceedings*, M.J. Fernandes, J.R. Machado, and K. Wnuk, Editors. 2015, Springer International Publishing: Cham. p. 167-173.

23. Kohl, J., et al., *Using multivariate split analysis for an improved maintenance of automotive diagnosis functions*, in *15th European Conference on Software Maintenance and Reengineering (CSMR)*, T. Mens, Y. Kanellopoulos, and A. Winter, Editors. 2011, IEEE Computer Society: Oldenburg, Germany. p. 305–308.

24. Garcia, E., et al., *The evolution of robotics research*. IEEE Robotics & Automation Magazine, 2007. **14**(1): p. 90-103.

25. Scholer, M., M. Vette, and M. Rainer, *A lightweight robot system designed for the optimisation of an automotive end-off line process station*. Industrial Robot: An International Journal, 2015. **42**(4): p. 296-305.

26. DWave, Digital pioneering work: *Volkswagen uses quantum computers*, 2017. [Online]. Available: https://www.dwavesys.com/press-releases/digital-pioneering-work-volkswagen-uses-quantum-computers.

27. Meinzer, Stefan; Jensen, Ulf; Thamm, Alexander; Hornegger, Joachim; Eskofier, Björn M., *Can machine learning techniques predict customer dissatisfaction? A feasibility study for the automotive industry, Artificial Intelligence Research*, 2017, Vol. **6** (1), pp. 80-90.
28. Hofmann, Martin; Neukart, Florian; Bäck, Thomas, *Artificial Intelligence and Data Science in the Automotive Industry,* 2017. [Online]. Available: https://data-science-blog.com/blog/2017/05/06/artificial-intelligence-and-data-science-in-the-automotive-industry/.
29. Neukart, Florian: *Reverse Engineering the Mind: Consciously Acting Machines and Accelerated Evolution,* AutoUni – Schriftenreihe, 1st edition, Wolfsburg, Germany, 2017.

Successful Data Science Is a Communication Challenge

52

Martin Werner and Sebastian Feld

Abstract

Currently, we experience a growing number of highly sophisticated digital services in virtually every domain of our lives. Tightly coupled to this observation is the appearance of Big Data and consequently the need for Data Science. When trying to transform data into value, communication is key. However, communication can easily get ambiguous and may threat success by misunderstandings. Thus, this article reviews the (communication) model of Data Science and maps the ten V's of Big Data to this model. Finally, we propose four top skills that each and every data science group needs to have to operate successfully.

52.1 Introduction

In the last decades, digital marketplaces have seen a deep transformation from providing classical services over a digital channel to providing digital services. Examples for classical services over a digital channel are email service provider like Gmail as an alternative to fax and mail, Internet-based retailer like Amazon as an alternative to stores, and online trading companies as an alternative to equity traders. Examples for modern digital services are recommendation platforms like TripAdvisor for travel-related content, communication tools like TeamViewer, online social networks like LinkedIn, or media streaming services

M. Werner · S. Feld (✉)
Ludwig-Maximilians-Universität München
Munich, Germany
e-mail: martin.werner@ifi.lmu.de

S. Feld
e-mail: sebastian.feld@ifi.lmu.de

© Springer-Verlag GmbH Germany 2018
C. Linnhoff-Popien et al. (eds.), *Digital Marketplaces Unleashed*,
https://doi.org/10.1007/978-3-662-49275-8_52

583

like Spotify or Netflix. The most important change in this transformation is represented by the incorporation of added-value from user data.

This change has led to a situation in which companies are able to collect large amounts of data describing their customers, their behavior, and interaction with the products. Spotify, for example, one of the major music, podcast, and video streaming services, deals with the huge challenge of personalizing their music catalog of over 30 million songs for their more than 60 million active users [1] generating many terabytes of data every day [2]. Netflix, a media production and streaming company, processes more than one billion events per day while petabytes of data are persisted and made available to queries on Amazon's S3, a web storage service [3]. These examples are located at the core of business intelligence, business analytics, and Big Data. However, a large fraction of this data is unexplored due to corporations not following a sufficient digital strategy, i. e. a company's sustainable change to digital processes.

An integral part of a digital strategy is a data science strategy – that is the establishment and integration of strategic data science groups in corporations. In this article, we want to discuss what a data scientist is supposed to do and how one can create impact and value from data.

Therefore, we discuss the widely known model defining Data Science as an intersection of mathematics and statistics, computer science, and domain knowledge. We align these three characters with the following four skills to show that a successful data science group must have all of these skills: (1) handling Big Data as a programming challenge, (2) detecting limitations as a statistics and mathematics challenge, (3) awareness and management as a domain expert challenge, and finally (4) usefulness and understanding as an overall challenge.

52.2 The Ten V's of Big Data

On February 6th, 2001, Doug Laney published a report on data management [4]. In this report, Laney aligns the main challenges for data management into a 3D cube with dimensions Volume, Velocity, and Variety. These three dimensions stand for individual challenges, which are, however, not independent in practice. Usually, a data management problem can be projected into this 3D space giving attributes to the problem helping in identifying challenges, tools, and solutions.

This simple model proved expressive, powerful, and useful for a long time and was often used as one of the "definitions" of the term Big Data. In a recent blog post by Kirk D. Borne [5], this model gets very well commented, also together with an example: the Large Synoptic Survey Telescope (LSST) generates 30 terabytes of imagery every night and has been doing so for the last 10 years. While this clearly is a large volume summing up to 100–200 petabyte over a ten year survey, data velocity is a larger concern: there is one 6 gigabyte image every 20 s. Within 60 s, this image needs to be processed inside the project goals and will generate lots of alerts to be processed further. This is high velocity data. Furthermore, all of this data is processed into a dataset containing 50 billion astronomical objects each with 200,000 attributes. This is high variety. More information on this can be found from the references of the blog article [5].

This list of three V's has shaped the field of Big Data for a long time and even today, they seem to be the most important aspects of Big Data. However, data scientists are confronted with a lot of different problems in the field, some with overlap to the initial 3 V model, some without. In the mentioned blog post, big data influencer Kirk D. Bone presents a list of the 10 V's of Big Data, which actually covers lot of data science aspects. The viewpoint is widened to include knowledge extraction into the V's instead of focusing on processing, handling, and organization.

These 10 V's are given in this section to discuss them later with respect to communication challenges in data science groups. The interesting observation about those 10 V's is that they are clearly problems, but that different subdomains of Data Science will have different definitions or meanings for the terms. The 10 V's of Big Data as proposed by Kirk D. Borne are introduced as follows:

The first V is **Volume** – problems associated with large amounts of data collected in modern big data infrastructures. The second V on his list is **Variety**, that is, the problems related to very different aspects being realized in large data sets, especially in those coming from observations. The third V stands for **Velocity**, that is, the amount of data per time unit that needs to be processed, stored, analyzed, and visualized in a big data project. So far, this list resembles the original list of Big Data's 3 V's. However, the next V on the list is **Veracity**. This stands for the prerequisite that a dataset must contain enough knowledge (ground truth, number of samples, etc.) about effects to be mined in order to get reliable and statistically sound results out of it. Furthermore, one V for **Validity** is added to the set of V's summarizing the quality of the data, the metadata, and the acquisition process. One of the additional V's is **Value**. This covers all aspects of business insights from data and is very challenging. A lot of data science projects reach success rates of more than 95% measured during training, but actually remain useless in practice. This happens often, when the root cause of effects is not correctly identified. For example, when controlling the quality of an electric vehicle, one can count the number of times that a battery has been replaced for a specific model. By intuition, we could believe that an increase in the battery replacement rate means a decrease in battery quality. However, it can also be the case that the battery has been replaced by guessing a problem with the battery though there is one with the charging subsystem. While a data scientist might correctly detect an anomalous amount of battery replacements, this might have nothing to do with the battery. The next V on the list is **Variability.** This covers aspects of current research including non-stationary effects in spatiotemporal time series, from seasonal data, and from autocorrelation. Often, there is no useful summary statistic such as the mean value for a Gaussian distribution, therefore, analysis is unable to compress the data and lots of the large volume proceeds to the analytics layer. A more practical V on the list stands for **Venue**. Much data is generated in distributed, heterogeneous systems. This is true for a technical perspective, e. g. vendor lock-in and similar effects, but also for a global system with different, possibly contradicting rules for managing, exchanging, and communicating data across borders. Possibly the most important V for this article is then presented as **Vocabulary**. It is the problem that many data scientists use different vocabularies. Furthermore, structured data comes with data schemata which are usually tailored to one application but hindering another one. For example, temporal databases are often organized by rows identifying events and columns identifying properties or information associated with events. When running an analytics algorithm on such a property, however, the data needs to be reorganized into a column-oriented access pattern. Additionally, vocabulary problems start with definitions of very simple terms like "big" by different data scientists. While for a statistician, a megabyte of values might be big (depending on the algorithm to be used), a computer scientist tends to think that "big" starts when the main memory of a single computer does not suffice any-more. However, from a business perspective, "big" might start when the cloud hosting cost increases faster than the return on invest, completely independent of the amount of work actually being done. Finally, the list of 10 V's of Big Data is completed by **Vagueness**, which stands for the uncertainty about the meaning of specific data. Usually, this comes from bad structured or even lacking metadata. For example, a dataset with location read-ings can be very accurate (in the case of laser scanning or precise point positioning from GNSS) or only very rough (e. g., when created from cellular network information). How-ever, it is seldom the case that actual characteristics of the recordings are collected together with the data. Often, only very rough information like "smartphone GPS" is available, if any.

These 10 V's of Big Data go far beyond the 3 V's of Big Data incorporating many aspects. The interesting thing to note about the seven additional V's is the fact that they are less technical and focus on organizational or communication issues.

In fact, **Veracity, Validity, Value, Variability, Venue, Vocabulary** and **Vagueness** are not to be answered by a smart algorithm or infrastructure. Instead, they are related to the risk of wasting time in analyzing useless data or creating misinterpretation including wrong conclusions. Hence, we spot the central topic of this article in these 10 V's: success-ful Data Science is a communication challenge. Seven out of ten V's can't have a technical solution and for the other classical 3 V **Volume, Variety**, and **Velocity**, a single technical solution does not exist either.

Before diving into these aspects in more detail, the following section will focus on the field of Data Science and explains how it differs from various different approaches to data management.

52.3   Data Science Communication Model

Fig. 52.1 depicts three disciplines from which Data Science is often defined as some sort of intersection. Definitely, mathematics and statistics are a fundamental building block of Data Science in which statistical models need to be created and analyzed. The field of mathematics classically contributes two aspects: correctness of results and scalability. For

Fig. 52.1 Data Science (DS) as an intersection of three disciplines

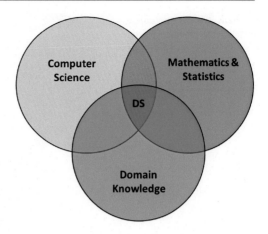

example, recent advances in calculating singular value decompositions of large matrices are clearly created by mathematicians as a contribution to their field, but find wide applications in Data Science due to the power of dimensionality reduction of, for example, singular value decomposition. However, mathematics and statistics alone do not represent Data Science. One reason is that mathematicians are usually fully happy when something is possible or exists. Additionally, they are not actually trained for developing large-scale systems beyond demonstration capabilities. Hence, the insights from mathematics and statistics must undergo a transformation into high quality software and tools. This is why the field of computer science plays a vital role in Data Science. Programming, software engineering, test-driven development, operational aspects, and distributed systems are some key ingredients to successful data science projects, which are usually available from the field of computer science. Still, all collected data originates from a world having rich semantic with meaning behind each and every piece of information. However, this meaning is still largely unavailable to computer systems. Therefore, there is a third aspect in every successful data science project which is based on domain knowledge. Asking the right question against a dataset, understanding unexpected issues with algorithms quickly, and – in general – having a well-working intuition in the domain is desperately needed for guiding the power and tools of Data Science towards valuable insights.

There might be the need for a fourth and fifth or even more additional disciplines for creating a successful data science team. One such aspect could be business development knowledge, or intimate knowledge of law. However, the three depicted domains are vital for Data Science. This becomes clear when discussing what would happen, if one of the fields is not well-represented in a data science project or data science team (see Fig. 52.2).

If we leave out mathematics and statistics, we are left with a team consisting of software developers and domain experts. This leads to very successful projects, but due to the missing awareness of mathematical limitations, this might as well diverge into a set of software tools and a set of claims, which are simply wrong. This is the reason for writing the word "risky" for the connection of these two fields. A team of that shape is able to

Fig. 52.2 Underrepresented fields lead to machine learning, traditional research and potentially risky projects

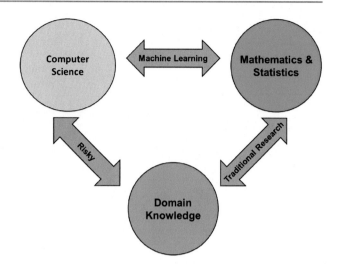

create something good, however, it does not know whether it actually is good and it does not proof basic assumptions about the result.

If we leave out computer science, we are left with mathematics, statistics, and domain knowledge. This creates very well working results along the line of classical research: a dataset is selected, extensive preprocessing and modeling is done, a heavy dose of self-criticism protects from over-claiming or over-interpreting results. However, the results don't get transformed into agile tools; they will usually be unavailable in real time, on demand, and, most importantly, the amount of data that can be handled by these two disciplines is limited. There will always be a point, where computer science skills are needed to scale out a successful statistical analysis to the big data space.

If we hold out domain knowledge from the data science triangle, we are left with computer scientists, mathematicians, and statisticians. This is an extremely powerful combination with respect to the ability of problem solving. However, as these groups might not understand the problem, they are likely to solve something less useful than a data science group under guidance of domain experts. To put in other words: The team will generate results, but they may not be able to interpret or utilize them.

This discussion makes clear that Data Science is an aggregate of sciences reaching higher levels of maturity by synthesis and composition of individual skills.

There might be the affect to try to find data scientists that can cover all these aspects. As such data scientists are rare, this simple intersection is often called "the unicorn of Data Science". It is much more important to form diverse teams and set specific emphasis on the various aspects of the data science triangle.

52.4   The Ten V's of Data Science

When reconsidering the ten V's of Big Data in the context of Data Science, we come up with a clear mapping of the challenges onto the communication diagram as depicted in Fig. 52.3. The 3 V **Volume, Velocity,** and **Variety** are clearly a challenge for an interdisciplinary discussion between mathematics, statistics and computer science. Approximation algorithms, smart index structures, randomization, and modern hashing architectures are computer science contributions to these three challenges. Local models, local analytics, treatment of missing data, and smart aggregation approaches with error bounds are contributions from mathematics and statistics.

Veracity and **Validity** are to be discussed between domain knowledge, mathematics, and statistics. While mathematics and statistics might find surprising insights from the dataset, these insights can actually be random effects or sampling errors. To the contrary, some assumptions about the data (such as error distributions, independence assumptions, and similar) often made by applying specific statistical tools can turn out to be false. The point of discussion at this intersection is between expectation and results: are data science results realistic? Do they resemble knowledge? How well do they generalize?

Variability and **Venue** are to be discussed between domain knowledge and computer science. Highly variable datasets pose challenges towards distributed computing and data organization. Knowing the exact patterns of data access can be a great deal here and the venue has to be chosen according to the domain expert's needs.

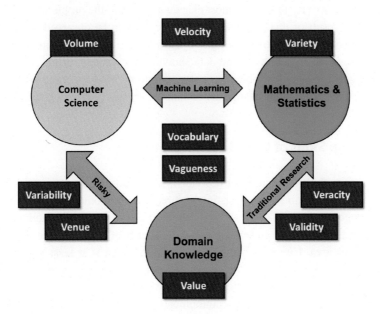

Fig. 52.3   Mapping of 10 V to Data Science Communication Diagram

The central V of **Value** is clearly a domain knowledge question: Given a statistically approved, well-scaling data science result with an error probability of 1%, how can the whole system be monetarized? How can the errors be treated and how do the errors harm from a business perspective? How much value can be generated by reducing this expected error even further?

The remaining two V's **Vocabulary** and **Vagueness** are to be discussed in the center of a data science group. It is difficult to find a working language across those three disciplines in order to facilitate talking about the same things.

For example, "Big Data" will mean something completely different for the three domains: For computer science, Big Data is usually linked to needing a distributed cloud infrastructure instead of a single cluster of computing devices and all methodologies needed for launching such distributed architectures. For statistics, Big Data starts when the usual algorithms and calculations take too long and less fail-safe approaches have to be put in place. So, Big Data is given when the road which is under perfect control of modern statistics has to be left. For mathematics, Big Data starts when lower bounds are being used. That is, when the data is compressed in a lossy way and we need to infer results (at least in a probabilistic way) about the outcome of an infeasible computation which has been replaced by some approximation algorithm. When assembling a data science team from experts on these three perspectives on Big Data, it is very difficult for a domain expert to talk to them about the real world and their real problems. The computer scientists will always tend to tell the expert that more data could be useful in the future, the statisticians try to help the expert selecting useful things out of the huge dataset available, and the mathematician will try to find the most elegant solution to the problem.

The expected result of this imaginary situation can often be observed in reality: first of all, all data is collected into a data lake – just to have it. Then, beautiful reports are generated using small fragments of the data showing microscopic results. Additionally, visionary projects for specific problems are started, but often do not come to a successful completion as the surroundings change faster than the project goals can be reached.

52.5 Four Top Skills of Data Science Groups

In order to cope with the situation just described, we propose to let data scientist groups organize around four main skills consisting of three specific domain challenges and one overall challenge, see Fig. 52.4. These skills should be read into two directions: First of all, the person or subgroup representing a specific aspect of Data Science must aim for excellence in this area. However, being excellent in this area is at least as important as being able to communicate a working knowledge of this area to the rest of the team. When we are able to reach a situation in which we have individual people or groups standing for the three aspects of the communication diagram and a group that is able to generate a common working knowledge of each of these expert areas, we have made

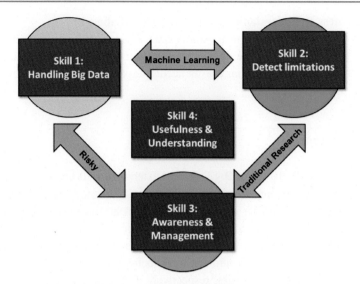

Fig. 52.4 Four main skills for successful data science groups

a large progress towards a successful and powerful data science group ready to deliver business value from data.

We align these three characters with the following skills of Big Data to show that a successful data science group must have all of these characters.

Skill 1: Handling Big Data (as a Computer Science Challenge)
The amount of data is so large that neither statisticians nor domain experts can extract knowledge directly with their most common tools. High performance computing, distributed systems, cloud computing, and GPU computing is needed.

Skill 2: Detect Limitations (as a Mathematics/Statistics Challenge)
The fact that a computer system makes perfect predictions on given datasets does not generalize. Actually, the most important challenge of artificial intelligence is the avoidance of overfitting and the question of how to get a system to learn the right concepts instead of the random sampling error.

Skill 3: Awareness & Management (as a Domain Expert Challenge)
Assuming we own skills one and two – we are able to cope with the amount of data and we are able to extract useful knowledge. How do we get this into a company? How can we communicate with the decision makers? How can we integrate domain knowledge? There is the need of a sustainable, well incorporated data science strategy that is actively supported by the management.

Skill 4: Usefulness & Understanding (as an Overall Challenge)
After transforming the data into insights via Data Science and after transforming the insights into business value by the domain experts, can we build a general uniform understanding such that the indirections are not needed anymore and data science results are recognized by decision makers?

52.6 Conclusion

This article discussed the 10 V's of Big Data that extend the well-known 3 V model consisting of Volume, Variety, and Velocity. Furthermore, the data science communication model has been reviewed together with the effects when omitting one domain. The 10 V's of Big Data have then been mapped to the data science communication diagram revealing that the original 3 V's of Big Data perfectly adapt to computer science, mathematics, and statistics, while the other seven V's align uniquely between domain knowledge and computer science or mathematics/statistics, respectively. Based on this distribution we have identified four top skills that a successful data science group needs to have.

References

1. M. B. Kinshuk Mishra, Personalization at Spotify using Cassandra, https://labs.spotify.com/2015/01/09/personalization-at-spotify-using-cassandra/: Spotify Labs, 2015.
2. D. Whiting, Data Processing with Apache Crunch at Spotify, https://labs.spotify.com/2014/11/27/crunch/: Spotify Labs, 2014.
3. C. S. Jeff Magnusson, *Talk "Watching Pigs Fly with the Netflix Hadoop Toolkit" at Hadoop Summit (June 27, 2013)*, 2013.
4. D. Laney, 3D Data Management: Controlling Data Volume, Velocity, and Variety, http://blogs.gartner.com/doug-laney/files/2012/01/ad949-3D-Data-Management-Controlling-Data-Volume-Velocity-and-Variety.pdf: META Group, 2001.
5. K. D. Borne, Top 10 Big Data Challenges – A Serious Look at 10 Big Data V's, https://www.mapr.com/blog/top-10-big-data-challenges-serious-look-10-big-data-vs, 2014.

The Future of Currency in the Direct Markets of Tomorrow – or: a Blueprint for a World Without Money

53

Maxim Roubintchik

Abstract

Our concepts of value are being challenged by new social/technological models like the share economy & the Bitcoin (Blockchain technology). This, however, is just the tip of the iceberg: There are bigger things to come that will shake up the very core of our value system: Our concept of money.

One of these models – the direct market – shall be the topic of this article. It's based on a combination of different intelligent algorithms and the basic premise that like-minded people think alike. It's a heuristic approach to the way we distribute goods in our society.

53.1 The Basics

53.1.1 Introduction

There are certain things in this world that we cannot close our eyes to. One of these things is the creeping digitalization that touches every part of our daily lives. We digitalize the way we listen to our music, how we select our partnerships, our social life, our transportation and many, many more things. Some people like to call this shift the "Digital Transformation". We don't need to discuss this, because of what it is: A fact. It is happening and most people are aware of it.

We are aware that our perception is constantly changing. People who grew up in the analog age are baffled by today's teenagers: Snapchatting, tweeting, whatsapping, tinder-

M. Roubintchik (✉)
rev
Munich, Germany
e-mail: mr@rev.digital

© Springer-Verlag GmbH Germany 2018
C. Linnhoff-Popien et al. (eds.), *Digital Marketplaces Unleashed*,
https://doi.org/10.1007/978-3-662-49275-8_53

ing and all of the other things they are doing. The former generations just used to go outside and play fetch with the dog. Often there is little understanding of these behavioral patterns. But, this is what the digitalization is all about: Change. A change in every aspect of our lives. It started with our communication and then went on to replace our social life. It has changed the way we consume goods, our perception of importance and value. And some day, it will change our concept of money into something most people have trouble imagining right now. And the markets will have to follow.

The digital markets of tomorrow won't be bound by any of our current limits. They will be able to break the monetary barrier by introducing a direct exchange of goods. Something we used to be able to do until we invented the money – at a point where we were still able to cope with the complexity of exchanging the things that we have. It might sound hard to imagine in a world that is bound to increasing complexity and is a hostage to the laws of entropy. But our world is actually becoming easier to understand – at least for us humans. Not because the complexity decreases but rather because of the tools that we have at our disposal. One of the major changes the "Digital Transformation" is introducing is the dawn of the Artificial Intelligence. Something that will change our world probably more than any other thing we will ever invent.

It will take quite some time until we create a real general level Artificial Intelligence – meaning a computer that is able to think about general problems the same way we humans do. But this is not what this topic is about: What we have today is very narrow level of Artificial Intelligence – also called an ANI (Artificial Narrow Intelligence). In most cases, this means that you have an algorithm that is, more or less, self-thought and can do a very specific thing. Like driving a car, selecting your music, connecting potential partners, flying a plane, organizing your meetings or predict your shopping behavior. This is where it gets interesting.

Our world is drifting in a direction that is the exact opposite of "easy to understand". The complexity of our interconnected and intertwined world has reached a point where we are hopelessly lost. We just didn't recognize it yet because denial is one of the best human tactics when it comes to coping with cognitive overload: The selection of products and services is way too big, the means of buying things are way too many and our essential mechanisms for evaluation of goods are corrupted by a permanent exposure to advertisement unlike anything any generation before has ever experienced. There are literally whole squadrons of market analysts, marketers, researchers and psychologists trying to predict our shopping behaviors, create a certain craving for things and thus force us to buy certain things. Everything resulting in more cognitive overload, mistrust and resistance. Even worse: Wrong decisions: We don't buy what we need or what is good for us – what be buy is a complex combination of advertising, social influence & many other things. That's the reason we end up with lots of stuff that we never use.

One of the possible solutions is a system that skips this whole vicious circle and reduces the cognitive overload by outsourcing a part of our thought process into an algorithm. If that sounds like science fiction to you, you should probably stop using amazons shopping predictions, Netflix' movie selections, Google's search results or Spotify's playlists, because all of these things are generated by intelligent algorithms that are trying to understand your needs and match these with possible offers. This is something we can already do – at least to some extent.

A system that is able to recognize my exact needs and match these, is going to revolutionize the markets of tomorrow. Not only by finding the right products and services to fit our intrinsic needs. The main difference is the way we evaluate things and create value – especially when it comes to digital objects and services. The current trend for share economy gives us an outlook into the world of tomorrow. A world with sparse resources, where it's no longer important to own things but to be able to use these, whenever and wherever we need them.

Why this is important and how such a system might work, shall be the topic of this article. The implications of such a system are way bigger, then you might imagine. It taps into the very foundation of our society and can thus change its very essence. I try to break it down as far as possible, to be able to understand why this is not just wishful thinking but rather a logical consequence of our current technological progress.

53.1.2   The Prerequisites

Coping with Cognitive Overload

We live complex world – one that is bound to exponential growth. This means that the complexity in our world is increasing faster the faster is increases. Like a vicious circle. It started of slowly and is gaining speed with every passing day. Here is an example: In the year 2010 Googles CEO, Eric Schmidt, told the world that we generate more data every two days than the whole mankind combined up to the year 2003. Some people were shocked by that statement – imagine all of the information we generated since the dawn of the mankind – being simple swamped by random data we generate by searching for cat pictures [1].

By the year 2014, an EY study concluded that we generate the same amount of data that the Google-CEO was speaking about in 2010 in about 10 min. So every 10 min we create more data than the whole mankind has created until 2003 – or let's rather say we did create. Because by now, the same kind of thing takes us only a few seconds.

The result of this overwhelming amount of data is mental overload. Things that used to be simple in the past are now immensely complicated – there is so much we know, so much information at our fingertips – literally. We are simply dwarfed by the complexity of our surroundings. Our brain is from a time where we had to fight bears for our survival, follow animal tracks and find edible things without being killed. So it's only logical that we are not prepared for coping with cognitive overload. There are some tactics we apply whenever we are faced with this kind of situation. The dominant being: Ignorance. We reduce the complexity of the situation to a simple fact, we understand, and make our decision based on that [2]. This is the reason why applications like tinder are so immensely successful: There are so many things you need to consider in order to find the correct partner – why not ignore all of these and focus on the looks. It taps directly into our brains thought patterns and our most basic limbic reasoning.

The reason why I bring up this topic is the same that drives the digitalization: We want to be able to cope with our surroundings. The way we go about it is: Minimizing our surrounding complexity to a degree we can handle. This means relying on tools to help us with our lives. Communication is just an example – partnerships is a different one. The digitalization is creeping its way into our lives – slowly and steadily. And its gaining momentum with every single day.

About Algorithms and Their Importance for Our Lives

Complex algorithms allow us to understand patterns and find sense in the data that surrounds us. Things we, as humans, might not be able to do ourselves. So the digitalization is a mere logical consequence of our technological progress. A way for us to use tools in order to be able to understand our world.

This "Digital Transformation" is going to hit us hard and fast. Because the tools we have, are becoming exponentially better. Computational power is quickly becoming one of the most abundant resources we have. It's actually cheaper to calculate something on a computer with a bad algorithm than to use a human to do the same kind of task [3]. The algorithms however are also bound to exponential growth and increase their effectiveness with every second spend improving them.

There is a basic thing you should understand about such algorithms: They don't need to understand you as a person in order to predict what you like. Most people tend to think that their desires are a very complicated miracle and unique. But in fact they aren't. What you want is a very complex combination of everything you experience. And most people experience similar ads, commercials, news and peer groups. So most of us crave the same things. We just react differently to them – based on our personality. Also: They do not look for a yes/now answer but rather for a probability – finding a pattern that covers the most cases. It does not need to solve 100% of the situations – just to come as close to it as possible.

The algorithms are already an important part of our daily life and their performance is going to exponentially increase in the near future – the more powerful they get. We, as humans, want to spend our lives as relaxed as possible: Example? If there would be an app to search your home for real objects like your car keys – trust me, we would download and use it – even if it means installing cameras everywhere and uploading our personal life into the cloud for everyone to see. We would use it, because there would be one less thing for us to worry about – a reduction in cognitive overload. Mental power that we can spend however we desire.

The question to every solution we find to reduce our cognitive overload is not – if?: Are we going to have it? The question is rather: When ... ?

Global Interconnectivity & Different Mindsets

One of the biggest impacts in the last few years happened in an area, that you'd probably wouldn't expect: Accessibility. By providing internet access to the many outback regions of the world, the web almost doubled its population – or is going to. Adding about five billion new internet users to the mix. Facebook (Internet.org—drones + satellites) [4], Google (Project Loon) [5], and Qualcomm and Virgin (OneWeb – satellites) [6] are just some examples of the efforts some companies are currently taking towards the goal of global connectivity. The final frontier is to get every person on this planet online. So the internet population grows steadily – adding new resources, but also new perspectives and problems to the mix.

We tend to think about applications and markets from our point of view – that of an already interconnected, first-world country. Other people have completely different problems though. There is a reason why mobile payment is dominant in Africa and has trouble taking hold even in the most technologically advanced countries: It all about the need & the set of requirements.

People from third world countries are probably not going to shop for things on amazon – they can't afford such a luxury. They have access to the web though and are going to look for some form of interaction that is suitable for their needs. Something where money is not involved – more on that later.

Please just bear in mind, that there is almost no way we can exclude and cocoon ourselves in a global and interconnected world. We have to understand that there are people with other needs out there. These need will influence us one way or another.

53.2   The System

53.2.1   The Algorithm that Knows You Better than You Know Yourself

This one is the basic requirement for the later: Imagine that you'd have an expert system that knows who you are. I mean who you are as a person. What you like, what you crave and what suits your needs. This system is based on an intelligent algorithm that collects data about your person. Afterwards it can match this data with that of other people. Cross-referencing it to find patterns in the data.

If you find such a system hard to believe, I have to disappoint you. Many things that you are using today are based on a very basic type of such a system. Examples? How about the Netflix' [7] or Spotify's [8] suggestions – or those on Amazon [9] and the Google's search results [10]. It's all about creating a detailed profile of a person and cross-referencing it with that of other people. The premise is always the same: Likeminded people like the same things.

If you spin this further and give the technology a few more years, we will eventually reach the point where we can exactly predict what people are like. What they want, when they want it and how happy they'll be with it. Whatever this "it" might be.

Some companies are currently working on more advanced adaptations of personalization technology. Systems that are fed with every piece of data you generate. Systems that can predict your mood just based on the data from the gyro-sensors of your smart phone for example (the sensors that detect rotations & relative movement). The goal is to create a suitable personality profiles that allow marketing & ad companies to target you even better. Help companies to build products based on the desires of the individual. Ways to shorten the development process of a new product trough data. And essentially ways to make more money.

On the other hand, there are virtual personal assistants: Siri, Alexa, Cortana and all the others. All of them strive to be helpful and to understand who you are in order to be more helpful.

One of this trends will lead us to the point where such an expert system will be unavoidable. Probably it will be a combination of both and some other factors we do not even realize yet. Long story short: We are already in the act of creating such a system.

53.2.2 The Selection Process from an AI Perspective

There is a major difference in the way we humans make our decisions compared to an AI algorithm [11, 12]. I already mentioned that we tend to apply a reductionist approach whenever we are faced with overwhelming complexity. As this might be a very abstract statement, let's rather look at an example:

Let's say I'm looking for a new smartphone. First of, most people don't even know which type of smart phone they need to get. Should it be the cheapest? Remember the cognitive overload and the ridiculous reduction we tend to apply when there are too many variables to consider? Most people will look for a new smartphone based on one or two variables: The price for example or the looks, the brand, the social status, color or any other thing there might be. To do a full on research based on all of the available variables and then take your personal resources (like your money, pocket size of your jeans, your available USB connectors, software compatibilities, battery usage, or simply time, ...) into account seems like an impossible task.

You could literally spend months doing research and calculations to solve this problem properly – or you'll do the same thing most other people do: Reduce the variables and ignore the rest. And then there is also no way of knowing if this smartphone is going to fit your personal needs and is more than just a mere shiny little toy.

Which type of algorithm to do you apply when selecting a new smartphone? Whichever it is: I promise you that it's going to be worse than the algorithm of a AI system that's sole purpose is to connect your personality profile with different selection criteria based on multidimensional variables.

The selection process is the second step to building the system. A way to filter the incredible amount of possibilities based on your personal profile. The system has to be able to scan the available resources and take all of the possible variables into account while doing so.

53.2.3   Predicting the User Reaction & Applying Heuristics

If you are familiar with the first two steps, this one should be very obvious: Imagine a meta system that is able to interconnect personal desires and needs in a way that is unprecedented in the history of the mankind. This is where the basic premise comes into play: Likeminded people are alike.

"People that bought this, also bought …"– is a very simple example of this type of heuristic (Amazon in this case) [9]. Netflix or Spotify are also famous examples of this type of algorithm. The basic thought is: People that buy/use the same kind of things tend to buy/use the same type of things again – because they seem to make similar decisions. Such types of algorithms are probably the most valuable in our current society, because they help us to classify customers into certain clusters. The state of the art is still very simple – from a complexity point of view – but yet very useful.

A more advanced version of such a clustering algorithm will be at the core of the suggested system. This version will take more variables into account and have access to almost unlimited amounts of data from the personality profile. So the prediction is going to be on point – at least most of the time. And if it's not – it will learn and improve.

Such a system is able to predict my reaction to certain objects or experiences because it can compare my data to that of likeminded people. People who already used this specific item or experienced what I'm about to. If they didn't then the algorithm is looking for the next best thing.

Why? The algorithm isn't looking for a binary yes/no answer but rather for a probability. The final decision is going to be still be up to you – the user.

Which brings us to the next step.

53.2.4   The Interconnection of Goods & Services in the Digital Age

So the system is aware of my desires and likings. It can predict my reactions to certain objects. Because such a system would have more than one user it will be aware of the current resources every person has – every user of the system (this can be done through regular 3D scans of your apartment [13] or more advanced IOT implementations [14] and interconnected items – just to name a few examples). So whenever I know what I'm looking for it will be able to find someone who has this specific item – or has something that comes close to what I crave.

So we are talking about a system that knows what I have and what I need and is able to match those needs with something another person has and needs. A direct exchange of goods and services – an intelligent and efficient distribution of those.

Because this is very abstract, let's rather get back to the example of me looking for a new smart phone.

Let's assume that the first steps delivered a desired result. Being: Me knowing what to look for. Now let's say there is a person owning two or three smartphones which he or she does not really use. This person however is in desperate need of a new microwave. I happen to have a spare microwave but need the smartphone. An expert system would be able to recognize such opportunities and interconnect us – so I give my microwave to the other person and receive my smartphone in exchange.

If this example sounds a little oversimplified and ridiculous this might be because it is: Depending on the user base there may be such opportunities from time to time. More realistically however would be a situation where you are going to have a three-way-exchange. Let's see what I mean by looking at one more example: I still have the microwave but the person with the smartphone actually needs a sofa in exchange. Luckily there is a third person who has a sofa a needs a microwave. So I give him my microwave, he gives me his sofa and I exchange it with the second person for the smartphone.

Please bear in mind that these examples are overly simplified and do not take the value of items into account. I'm going to cover this topic next, please just make a personal note for now.

Three-way-exchange is something that revolutionized the organ donations and saved many lives by doing so. Just a few years ago we were lacking the computational power and algorithms to calculate this kind of exchanges. Today we can. Imagine what we could achieve with an expert system that is not only able to calculate three-way but also four- or five-way-exchanges.

Let's go even further: Image that such a system would not only be able to exchange goods but also services. Example? Let's say I'm good at playing the piano and need a new wall in my house: I could find a mason that is able to do the deed in exchange for piano lessons for his daughter – or I just give him my smartphone instead. Whatever seals the deal – I don't have to worry about such things, because the systems takes care of those details for me.

Please reflect a little about the possibilities of such a system before you continue to the next part – which is what this whole topic is actually all about:

53.2.5 The Value Equation & the Shift in Perspective

Our value system is an essential core of our personality. We are living in a world where we constantly have to adapt our values in order to maintain our personality. So our values are drastically changing, the faster the change in our environment occurs. What do I mean by that? As we digitalize our life even further, there will be a drastic shift in our value perception. You can already see this kind of changes today: People who pay real money for virtual items in video games. They don't do this kind of thing because they are stupid. They do it because these items hold value for them. Some people find value in racing go carts around the race track and pay money for the activity – others buys expensive caviar because they like the taste. The more digital our live is, the more value digital items and activities will hold for us. Share economy is another great example for a value shift: Younger generations no longer care about owning things – they care about using them. Who can blame them in a world where all the goods are already spread among those who came before us and resources are and will be very limited.

There is a huge difference in the value of things that depends on a very subjective evaluation of these things. Meaning: Every person has its own value for every item or service. A system for direct exchange of goods should take this variable into consideration: The personal value for a certain thing. It should be able to balance the individual values and find deals that are suitable for all involved parties.

This is where it gets really interesting. Such a system does not rely on money in order to work. Even worse: Money is something that hinders such a system because it creates an additional and very abstract value. It complicates things in a world with direct exchange of goods.

You might shake your head in disbelieve because you think that there is no way in the world we might forfeit our monetary system someday. But we might. Money is a concept the mankind invented to balance the exchange of goods – when our world got too complicated for the direct exchange [15]: How many chicken is this cow worth? Three, maybe four or five? What about adding a quarter pig. The correct answer to that question would be: Whatever it is worth for me.

Money is a simplification – our current monetary system on the other hand is anything but simple. Benefiting only those who control it. In an interconnected, global and educated world – it will hit its limits. Resulting in either a revolution or a new and better system – just as monarchy was replaced by democracy. This is a part of the progress.

So one of the results we get from using such a system will be a formula to calculate individual value and an answer to an age old question: What is value actually about and what should hold value for us.

53.2.6   Privacy & Other Technicalities

While being a generally utopic and positive system, there are also some dangers involved in building it. Privacy and the protection of personal information is the major topic: Uploading every piece of your life to the cloud seems like a bad idea, coming from our current status quo. Unhappy ex-employees, hackers, corrupt governments and companies and many, many more are looking for ways to get their hands on our personal data.

There are certain approaches to solving this issue without giving up the comfort of this system: A very interesting solution would be an advanced application of the Blockchain technology – combined with a system that gives me (the user) full control over my data and whoever has access to it. Such a privacy control mechanism would allow the system to access my personal data, without actually knowing who I am [16]. And I, on the other hand, would be able to control who is able to see what parts of my personal data.

Apart from that – in order to build it: It's essential to isolate the organization that runs the system, because it would be very prone to every type of manipulation. It needs to stand on neutral ground and behave as a neutral entity. The organization itself should not be driven by financial goals because this would nip the whole concept in the bud and produce a clash of interests. Resulting in the premature death of the system. There are also many sociological consequences worth considering from using such a system on a global scale.

53.2.7 The System – Concluded

Let's conclude what we have so far: We are talking about a system that is able to recognize who I am as a person. Based on data I provide to it through various sources. It is able to select items and services based on a holistic approach considering more criteria than I could possibly imagine. It knows what I want and can predict how I'm going to react to it, based on data it cross-referenced from other "likeminded" people and their experience. It knows what I have and what other people, connected to the system, have. It can then create direct, three- or even four- or five-way-connections between users of the system, that allows each to get the item or experience that the person is looking for. Which in turn would feed more data into the system and help the algorithm to improve even further. Everything resulting in a positive exponential development of the system itself.

We can solve the biggest privacy issues by using a modified Blockchain algorithm that will allow the users to maintain control of their personal data and use the benefits of the personalization while staying anonymous.

Final thought: Such a direct exchange system would make us question our own values and essentially remove the need for money: Or rather replace it with a different, more advanced, concept – more suitable for our modern society. A way to focus on the real value of things and balance our consumption.

53.3 Excursus: About Change and the Law of Accelerating Returns

You can skip this passage, if you are only interested in the system itself. This is just background information that might help you to understand the accelerating rate of progress.

I'd like to conclude with an underlying principle that drives the kind of change, discussed in this article. This topic might seem far-fetched, when it comes to digital markets of tomorrow, but there is a certain reason I bring it up. The reason being: There are certain principles underlying everything in this universe. One of these is the exponential growth or decay of … well, basically everything there is. Because this is such an abstract topic, I'd like to explain it with a thought experiment.

Imagine that you'd have a time machine and use it to go 200 years back in time – to the beginning of the 19th century. Now imagine grabbing a person from that time, pulling him into your time machine and taking him back to our current time. What do you think would happen when he sees cars, plains, computers, the internet, smartphones, skyscrapers, hover trains and all of those things we crated in the last 200 years? I guess he will be so overwhelmed by these changes, that he will instantly drop dead.

Good thing we have great medical care nowadays and can actually revive the dead person from the 19th. century. Now imagine you excuse yourself and lend him your time machine to play the same prank to some stranger from back in his past. What he then does is: Going back to the 16. century, grabbing a random person and taking this person to the 18th century. The time delta is the same – 200 years. Now imagine what would happen next. Do you think the person from the 16th century will drop dead after seeing the 18th century progress? Faster carriages, new political structures, a little taller buildings and new fashion.

He actually won't drop dead, because the changes are not big enough to trigger such a kind of reaction. In order to achieve the same kind of relative effect the person from the 18th century would need to go back all the way to 10,000 BC. The visitor from the long gone past, would then be baffled by the buildings, ships, carriages or simply all those people living in one place and ... you guessed it drop dead.

You might already see a pattern here, but try imagining this thought experiment one step further. Imagine you'd want the person from 10,000 BC to play the same kind of prank on someone from his past. Going back 10,000 years to 20,000 BC would not do the trick. He would need to go back even further to, let's say, hunter-gatherer times – about 100,000 years BC. The huntsman would then again be baffled by the agriculture, settlements, language and many other things we consider as basic.

This is what the law of accelerating returns is all about [17]. The term has initially been coined by Ray Kurzweil, a futurist and now head of the tech department at Google. If you break it down even further, you can calculate the rate of the drop dead effect and get to the point where the changes in the next 20 years are going to be greater than everything we experienced in the past 200. So whenever you see someone with a time machine, he might not be coming from the year 4000 AD but maybe rather 2090.

The further we get within our rate of progress, the faster the progress will become, enabling us to progress even faster.

This is a very important thing because it concerns everything that surrounds us. From our political systems, to our relationships and most certainly our technology and the possibilities we have. All of these things are simply a product of our current progress. Whenever it comes to exponential growth, most people have trouble coping with this concept. This is a result of certain biological limitations of the human brain and our ability, or rather lack thereof, of abstract reasoning – or simply put: We tend to think linear. We interpolate the current position or tend to create predictions for the future based on the past. We can't be blamed for that – that's just the way we think and the data we have to evaluate our predictions.

Before I close this topic, try imagining yourself as being a horse carriage tycoon at the end of the 19th century. The time where the first automobiles started to appear. There is almost no way you could predict, that the automobile will, some day, play a major role in our society. The usual way of going about this kind of problem would be to look back at the past: The horse & carriage used to be a part of the society for thousands of years and there is no way around it. "So don't care about this whole automobile-hype ". This kind of reaction is based on data from the past.

If you would be a clever tycoon, you'd devote a part of your resources to this automobile thing, because … who knows, there might be something about it – it might sale to some rich people looking for fun – last year about a thousand of them sold, so why not. This kind of reaction and prediction is based on current facts and figures and is a simple interpolation of those. You'd be more correct in your prediction than the first tycoon but still far from the actual truth because you didn't take the exponential growth into account.

It's easy for us today to look back at such examples with a grin and shake our heads in disbelieve. But please remember that we make the same kind of mistake every day when we try to predict the future. Apart from that, there is a lot more prediction happening today than used to take place when the automobile was first introduced because of … you guessed it: The exponential growth. [MR]

References

1. Techncrunch, [Online]. Available: https://techcrunch.com/2010/08/04/schmidt-data/. [Accessed 09 11 2016].
2. B. Loasby, Choice, Complexity and Ignorance: An Enquiry Into Economic Theory and the Practice of Decision-Making, Cambridge: Cambridge UniversityPress, 1976.
3. ourworldindata.org, "Our World in Data," [Online]. Available: https://ourworldindata.org/technological-progress/. [Accessed 09 11 2016].
4. Reuters, [Online]. Available: http://www.reuters.com/article/us-facebook-internet-idUSBREA2Q27420140327. [Accessed 09 11 2016].
5. Solvefor X, Google X, "Solvefor X," [Online]. Available: https://www.solveforx.com/loon/. [Accessed 09 11 2016].
6. Oneweb, "Oneweb," [Online]. Available: http://oneweb.world. [Accessed 09 11 2016].
7. Netflix, "Netflix Techblog," [Online]. Available: http://techblog.netflix.com/2016/10/netflix-at-recsys-2016-recap.html. [Accessed 09 11 2016].
8. Github, [Online]. Available: https://benanne.github.io/2014/08/05/spotify-cnns. [Accessed 09 11 2016].
9. Fortune Magazine, [Online]. Available: http://fortune.com/2012/07/30/amazons-recommendation-secret/. [Accessed 09 11 2016].
10. H. Cheng, L. Koc, J. Harmsen, T. Shaked, T. Chandra, H. Aradhye und R. Anil, "Wide & Deep Learning for Recommender Systems," *Proceedings of the 1st Workshop on Deep Learning for Recommender Systems,* pp. 7–10, 2016.
11. H. Simon, Theories of decision-making in economics and behavioral sciencee, 3 Hrsg., Bd. 49, The American economic review, 1959, pp. 253–283.

12. G. Phillips-Wren und N. Ichalkaranje, Intelligent decision making: an AI-based approach, Bd. 97, Springer Science & Business Media, 2008.
13. K. Kolev, P. Tanskanen, P. Speciale und M. Pollefeys, "Turning mobile phones into 3D scanners," *2014 IEEE Conference on Computer Vision and Pattern Recognition,* pp. 3946–3953, 2014.
14. B. Shao, Fully printed chipless RFID tags towards item-level tracking applications, 2014.
15. M. Crawford, "Money and exchange in the Roman world," *Journal of Roman studies,* pp. 40–48, 1970.
16. G. &. N. O. Zynskind, "Decentralizing privacy: Using block-chain to protect personal data," *Security and Privacy Workshops (SPW),* pp. 180–184, 2015.
17. R. Kurzweil, "The Law of accelerating returns," in *Life and Legacy of a Great Thinker,* Heidelberg, Springer Berlin Heidelberg, 2004, pp. 381–416.

Further Reading
18. A. Andal-Ancion, P. Cartwright und G. Yip, The Digital Transformatioin of Traditional Business, 4 Hrsg., Bd. 44, Massachusetts: Massachusetts Institute of Technology Sloan Management Review, 2003.
19. S. Kotsiantis, "Supervised Machine Learning: A review of Classification Techniques," *Frontiers in Artificial Intelligence and Applications,* Nr. 226, pp. 3–24, 2007.

Digital Business Outcomes: Digital Innovation and Its Contribution to Corporate Development

54

Hans Rösch and Stefan Schumacher

Abstract

Nowadays, IT is an important component of a company's value chain. However, it has to face the latent suspicion of being 'too expensive anyway' as the management is constantly demanding cost savings. Furthermore, the modern role of IT also requires the implementation of innovative tasks to maintain sustainability for companies. From this, one can derive IT's task to translate its services and its technical and legal framework conditions into business language. The purpose of this article is to show the broad scope of IT in the value chain of today's companies. With this, we are moving away from a purely financial perspective and explicitly include organizational and process-related improvements. By the example of the relatively advanced implementation of IT strategy at Vattenfall, VOICE shows with a flagship project the versatility of IT's value contribution.

H. Rösch (✉)
Vattenfall GmbH
Berlin, Germany
e-mail: hans.roesch@vattenfall.de

S. Schumacher
VOICE – Bundesverband der IT-Anwender e.V.
Berlin, Germany
e-mail: stefan.schumacher@voice-ev.org

© Springer-Verlag GmbH Germany 2018
C. Linnhoff-Popien et al. (eds.), *Digital Marketplaces Unleashed*,
https://doi.org/10.1007/978-3-662-49275-8_54

607

54.1 The Organizations Involved

In the following sections the organizations contributing to this chapter will be introduced.

54.1.1 VOICE e. V.[1]

With approximately 400 members, VOICE is the largest representation of IT users in the DACH region. Its members represent a cross section of DAX-, MDAX,- and medium-sized companies. The association's network brings together decision makers in the IT and digital businesses from leading companies of different sizes and from different branches – in formats such as roundtables and business workshops, but also virtually on an exclusive online platform. VOICE offers a competent, attractive, and dynamic exchange platform for the interests of its members of which both them and their company IT and digitization projects can benefit. Trade information and best practice experiences are being discussed by decision makers across all levels. The economic power of our members corresponds with approximately 50% of German GDP. The primary goal of VOICE is to increase the competitiveness of its member companies further by using digital technologies – and a targeted exchange about the key topics of digitization by safeguarding the interests of the user companies [1].

54.1.2 Vattenfall

At Vattenfall we exist to help our customers power their lives in ever climate smarter ways and free from fossil fuel within one generation. Our climate and sustainability objectives are the basis of our strategy and our strategic targets. Our goal to be climate-neutral by 2050 – and by 2030 in the Nordic countries – entails a stepwise phase-out of fossil fuels. Vattenfall is phasing out fossil production and invests in renewables, mainly wind and increasingly in solar. Across all its markets, Vattenfall has approximately 6.2 million electricity customers, 3.3 million electricity network customers and 2.2 million gas customers. The Group is one of Europe's largest producers of electricity and heat. Electricity generation and sales of heat amounted to 119.0 and 20.3 TWh, respectively, in 2016. Vattenfall's main markets are Denmark, Finland, Germany, the Netherlands (operating under the Nuon brand), Sweden and the UK. The Group has approximately 19,900 employees and annual revenues of 15.6 billion EUR. The parent company, Vattenfall AB, is 100%-owned by the Swedish state, and its headquarters are located in Solna, Sweden. Vattenfall was founded in 1909, while some of its German business originated as early as 1884 [2].

---

[1] "e. V.": a registered association under German law with full legal personality.

54.2   Glossary of Terms

Within an economic environment, IT has always had two major goals: supporting the company in competition and effectively and efficiently implement business operations. It is too shortsighted to regard IT as a mere cost factor. On the opposite, flat budget cuts by the management or the demand for cost savings might be contra productive if, as a result, IT merely implements projects with evident monetary success. The modern role of IT also requires the implementation of innovative tasks in order to keep the company future-oriented. From this, one can derive the job of IT, to translate its services as well as its technical and legal framework into business language [3].

54.2.1   Value Contribution

In this article, we define the term value contribution very broadly and show how the ever increasing scope of IT supports the value chain of a modern company. With this, we move away from a purely financial perspective and explicitly include organizational and procedural improvements [4].

We identified at least the following business departments as examples for where companies can benefit from IT [5]. Some specific examples will be presented in the next section.

Communication
IT enables modern ways of using communication channels and shorten communication intervals. The market provides for an increasing number of communication tools and solutions such as Wikis, blogs, enterprise social media networks, or unified communication and collaboration.

Controlling & Finance
IT is constantly under the pressure of appropriate IT profitability. IT can install reporting tools throughout the company or check and implement suitable sourcing models.

Infrastructure & Operations
Provided IT services require appropriate hard- and software. This includes not only traditional IT components but nowadays also communication networks and new technologies such as Social Media, Analytics (to create value from "Big Data"), Mobile and Cloud.

Innovations
Today, dealing with innovation is regarded as an essential factor of long-lasting success. However, renewing processes are complex and resource consuming. IT can make a crucial contribution to innovation management.

Employees & Organization

Employees are one of the most important resources. All processes in connection with Human Resources (HR) can be supported with IT: recruiting, management, qualification, and retention of staff.

Projects

One of the structuring features of corporate activity is project and portfolio management. With the introduction of sets of rules (such as PRINCE2 – **Pr**ojects **In C**ontrolled **E**nvironments, version 2), IT can provide support and improve project controlling via tools.

Risk & Security

Security requirements have high priority. Incidents have a negative impact on the business result or even the entire company. IT is responsible for the introduction of a security management system and has to consider aspects such as business continuity, data governance, and data privacy.

IT Services

The constant improvement of IT services such as hosting or development provides for a Continual Service Improvement (CSI) system. Consequently, it is recommendable to introduce an IT service management system (ITSM).

54.2.2 Adaptability and Flexibility of IT

Companies are exposed to a large variety of external influences. Nowadays, competitiveness includes a high level of responsiveness. Responsiveness in turn means adapting to new challenges in a quick and flexible way. Therefore, IT has to be set up in a versatile and adaptable way. Flexibility takes different shapes in connection with technical terms and different departments. It can refer to "agile software development" or "agile company organization". Flexibility for IT services can also mean to create suitable, scalable offerings – e. g. computing power in the scope of growing or shrinking capacities [5]. The demand for high flexibility is a huge challenge because adaptability should be implemented in a resource-friendly way. Generous buffers with regard to staff, finances, and technology would unduly affect the value contribution of IT. In order to show how this strategic dilemma can be resolved, we are providing successful practical examples for the value contribution of IT in the next section.

54.2.3   Value Contribution and Role of IT According to Vattenfall

Vattenfall IT supports the transformation of the business, which needs to adapt to a new market environment. Business requirements on IT are getting more diverse in the race for more optimization and flexible adaptation to customer needs. They leverage technologies such as social media, mobile, analytics, and cloud (sometimes briefly referred to as "SMAC") as well as the convergence between commercial information technology and operational technology used in generation and distribution. To become more efficient and concentrate its own staff on the most value-adding projects and services, the IT department is managing a growing share of sourced services [6, 7].

Vattenfall aims to bring its IT up-to-date by adapting to the new business environment and taking on the challenges. The IT organization is committed to be

- at the forefront of digital transformation at the company
- an agile service provider – focused on problem solving and speed
- on top of business needs, propose and challenge the business with smart IT solutions
- open to utilize and manage market potentials and buy services when beneficial
- truly customer centric

Overview of Digital Use Cases
The following use cases (see Table 54.1) from Vattenfall demonstrate in how many ways modern IT solutions can contribute to the success of an enterprise.

In column 2 below, a description of the initial situation is given, column 3 lists the challenges facing the IT department, while the last column summarizes what was implemented and achieved.

The fourth column of the table shows practical applications. These provide valuable contributions to the company's success. The following section outlines the IT organization is being positioned to continue to drive value from digital technologies.

54.3   Implementation of IT Strategy

One of the key elements for the implementation of an effective IT landscape is a well thought out concept that is aligned with and sponsored by the business. This section highlights key facets of Vattenfall's digital transformation journey and how these led towards the recent redefinition of its IT strategy.

First Steps into Digitization
Vattenfall started its first digital business activities during the dotcom boom of the late 1990's by creating a digital channel to sell electricity, broadband, telecommunications, and insurance services. Moreover, a first attempt was made to sell intelligent home services. The latter venture failed and made it very hard to get management support for other

Table 54.1 Overview of Vattenfall Digital Use Cases Relating to Sect. 54.2.1 (and others)

Category	Initial Situation	Challenges/Goal	Implementation/Results
Communication	Traditional intranet and e-mail; lack of platform for networking	Improve collaboration across hierarchical silos	*ConnectUs* social network was set up in April 2013. Today there are > 18,000 members sharing information in > 2000 groups and projects. Its success was helped by tight integration with the intranet and phonebook
Infrastructure & Operations	Multiple in-house data centers accumulated during a decade of growth by acquisition	Cost reduction and increased flexibility	Adoption of Azure as IaaS platform and focus on SaaS when acquiring new applications or replacing existing applications
Innovations	Since 2012 Vattenfall's German electricity distribution business. *Stromnetz Berlin* publishes open data to stimulate innovative uses and foster the energy revolution or "Energiewende" (see www.netzdaten-berlin.de)	Attract young talents to experiment with the data and develop new applications for the energy of the future	Conducted "Hack Days" in 2013, 2015 and 2017 (see http://energyhack.de/)
IT Services	Videoconference rooms failed to meet the growing requirements for communication between many sites spread across Northern and Central Europe	To support Vattenfall's core value "Cooperation" and a growing number of projects and organizational units setup across multiple (international) sites	Today 10,000 users (about every second employee) have access to desktop videoconferencing. 4000 of them use the system each day. According to the solution provider Polycom the company run the largest installation across Europe. Initial deployment started in 2009 and as usage expanded the company experienced a large variety of incidents, often testing the limits of all components involved. Nowadays the solution is stable and provides many dial-in options ranging from stationary systems in conference rooms, over PCs and notebooks, phones (audio only) to an app running on most smartphones and tablets – even providing interconnections to external videoconferencing systems run by the business partners

Table 54.1 (Continued)

Category	Initial Situation	Challenges/Goal	Implementation/Results
IT Services	Traditional PC workplaces optimized for work from the office, large group of users for videoconferencing	Need to improve support for employees frequently traveling, working from home, collaborating across the organization and with external partners	Digital Workplace based on Office365 (incl. SharePoint, OneDrive and Skype for Business) shall support new ways of working – with anyone, anytime, from anywhere with any device
Customer Service	Customers could not always reach the service team via phone or (e-)mail	Improve customer retention by opening social media channels for communication	In the Netherlands a web care team has been established. Its 10 members respond to customer requests via Facebook and Twitter. >63,000 followers on Facebook and a top 10 ranking among brands on social media (DVJ Insights Social Consumer Monitor 2014)
Apps	Customers mainly interact with utilities when things go wrong	Provide useful information to improve customer satisfaction and understanding for the complex energy system	*Stromnetz Berlin* launched 3 apps: *StromTracker* providing an overview on the customer's energy use, *StromTicker* giving an overview of the electricity supply in Berlin, *Stromwetter* showing when there is a lot of "green" energy in the grid
Sales Channels	Increasing competition from new entrants and other utilities entering Vattenfall's attractive home markets in Berlin and Hamburg	Win new customers on an existing popular market place	Cooperation with Ebay since 2008 used as an additional sales channel (https://www.welt.de/regionales/berlin/ article2483951/Vattenfall-vertreibt-Strom-jetzt-ueber-Ebay. html). Paperless power supply agreement and communication via app ("ENPURE") only
New Business Models	An increasing number of customers want to be more engaged, have more choice and control over how the energy they consume is produced, and seek new ways of interacting. Some home owners have invested in rooftop solar panels. At times these panels produce more electricity than they consume and customers may want an alternative to the feed-in tariff	Engaging customers to help them be more sustainable is an important step in Vattenfall's strategy and in becoming a climate-neutral company by 2050	In June 2016 *Powerpeers* started operation in the Netherlands. *Powerpeers* is a digital marketplace and community where customers can decide from whom they receive their energy and who to supply with their self-generated energy (see www.powerpeers.nl, http://news.vattenfall.com/de/ article/powerpeers-der-interaktive-marktplatz and www. youtube.com/watch?v=hM8sePEoslk)

innovative solutions, particularly at a time during the industry cycle when margins from large-scale generation of electricity were very attractive.

The foundation for the company's current digitization activities was laid shortly after the millennium. About 10 years ago, Vattenfall was one of the first utilities to offer an online product to its customers, based on a portal with self-service contracting and electronic bill presentment. Today the company serves more than one million customers in Germany via this platform; similar solutions are offered in Sweden and in the Netherlands. The original German platform has evolved to a mobile solution that is easily accessible using a smartphone or tablet PC.

Business Exploring Digital Opportunities

Recently, some of the most dynamic businesses, in particular wind generation and all customer-facing units started to experiment with new digital technologies and set up governance boards to guide these developments.

The communications department of the company has set up a Digital Council as a forum for strategic digital questions and development. The members cover different stakeholders from sales, communications, HR and IT, covering all countries. The purpose of the Digital Council is to have a central forum to stay aligned about all larger digital initiatives cross markets, to share knowledge and best practices and discuss common challenges and future needs within the digital area, linked to the overall business goals and strategic direction. The Digital Council is meeting on a monthly basis. All new larger digital initiatives shall be brought to the Digital Council for information. Although it is not a forum for decision-making, the Digital Council can guide and advise.

Positioning Vattenfall IT for Digitization

Following a number of pilots with agile development to support digital business projects Vattenfall IT has recently updated its IT strategy and is currently reorganizing to establish a two-speed IT organization:

Agile IT

Agile IT is intended to be a flexible and agile delivery organization to better respond to the needs of those businesses wanting to explore new and more disruptive ideas while moving fast to beat the competition. Agile IT focuses on digitalisation and flexibility to support Vattenfall in optimizing customer experiences, developing new business models and achieving operational excellence by providing mobile and self-service solutions. Agile IT leverages cloud and big data analytics. Agile IT supports the business in trying out new ideas and technology that may in the future be part of their strategy.

Core IT

Core IT shall meet the high security and stability requirements of businesses such as nuclear and hydro generation as well as staff functions, implementing more incremental changes. Its focus is to deliver and operate stable, reliable and compliant application and infrastructure services in a cost-efficient way.

Besides the CIO Office, which is in charge of overall IT strategy, set-up and communication the new Vattenfall IT organization comprises two additional key elements:

Transformation Office

A Transformation Office manages technology strategies, architecture, and security and secures successful execution of divestments, acquisitions, and group-wide transformations (e. g. consolidation of the various systems in use for Enterprise Resource Planning – (ERP)).

Service Integration

Service Integration manages a portfolio of delivery models and is in charge of performance management and metrics, sourcing, vendor management and governance, service management and project portfolio management.

54.4   Monitoring Success

For the implementation of "two-speed IT" at Vattenfall, stability is a priority. The business will be in the lead of IT transformation and changes are driven by business demand. The IT department aligns its plans and approach with all current major business change projects to avoid or minimize disruptions. The organizational adjustments will be gradual – no big bang! Smaller changes are being executed during 2016 aligned to target picture. The implementation is in tune with the overall pace of Vattenfall's business transformation and risks are actively managed.

Vattenfall IT continues to survey users and business managers to measure their satisfaction and identify and address issues before they grow into problems.

54.5   Conclusion

A traditional corporation in an "old" industry such as Vattenfall in the utilities must balance innovation with the need for stability. While digitization can start with many small projects in different parts, there is a need to establish overarching governance and formulate a strategy.

The IT organization must respond by adapting their approaches, organizational structure, employee skills, culture and sourcing strategy to remain relevant and transform from service provider to value creator. The implementation must be well aligned with the business to minimize disruption, make it possible to learn from pilot projects, and continuous improvement [8].

Driving cultural change is a key factor for successful digitization of a traditional company. This includes engaging in proactive and transparent communication with external stakeholders via social media – instead of relying exclusively on classic public relations and advertising. Employees have been addressed with numerous roadshows and training offerings ranging from traditional courses to short video clips on the intranet. Executive sponsors have contributed to the credibility of these messages.

Development and marketing of new products and services must be as customer-centric as possible, realizing that today's customers can choose and compare a wide array of options to meet their needs. They have enormous transparency, so instead of traditional marketing pushing offerings to consumers, companies must engage in conversations with their (potential) customers, learn about their needs and respond to their feedback to create "pull" for their offerings. The internet and social media provide many platforms to amplify "word of mouth". In response to these developments, it is no longer sufficient to manage clients with the main goal of customer satisfaction – as measured by the Customer Satisfaction Index (CSI). Instead, companies should rather aim to maximize customer engagement – as measured by the Net Promoter Score (NPS) [9].

While promising quicker delivery of tangible results, an agile approach is also demanding a constant high level of engagement from business and IT: When following the traditional "waterfall" approach, project phases last for months, and the activity level heats up towards the end of each phase, with business primarily engaging in sign-off, testing and training, the agile approach requires a high level of engagement to ensure delivery of the agreed product increment at the end of each sprint every two weeks.

Vattenfall's journey towards more sophisticated use of business intelligence has exposed the need for solid master data management as the foundation for generating credible insights from combining data from various sources. IT needs to support this effort by developing and implementing an architecture that allows combining data from systems of record (e. g. SAP ERP), operational systems (e. g. SCADA), systems of engagement (e. g. Facebook and Twitter) and other external sources. A challenge is the shortage of data scientists who are able to make sense of these new opportunities.

By sharing the above use cases and best practices, the authors wish to support other organizations in their effort to make best use of their IT services.

References

1. "www.voice-ev.org/sites/default/files/VOICE_Handout_2016.pdf," 2016. [Online]. [Accessed 20 October 2016].
2. "www.vattenfall.com," [Online]. [Accessed 20 October 2016].
3. M. Böhm, "IT-Compliance als Triebkraft von Leistungssteigerung und Wertbeitrag der IT," *HMD-Praxis der Wirtschaftsinformatik, Issue 263,* pp. 15–29.
4. S. Helmke und M. Uebel, Managementorientiertes IT-Controlling und IT-Governance, Wiesbaden: Springer Fachmedien, 2016.

5. A. Wiedenhofer, "Flexibilitätspotentiale heben – IT-Wertbeitrag steigern," in *HMD-Praxis der Wirtschaftsinformatik, Issue 289*, 2013, pp. 107–116.
6. M. Skilton, Building the Digital Enterprise, Palgrave Macmillan, 2015.
7. W. Van Grembergen, From IT Governance to Enterprise Governance of IT: A Journey for Creating Business Value Out of IT, IFIP, 2010.
8. M. Nilles und E. Senger, "Nachhaltiges IT-Management im Konzern – von den Unternehmenszielen zur Leistungserbringung in der IT," *HMD-Praxis der Wirtschaftsinformatik, Issue 284,* pp. 86–96.
9. P. Samulat, Methode für Messungen und Messgrößen zur Darstellung des "Ex-post" Wertbeitrages von IT-Projekten, Wiesbaden: Springer Fachmedien, 2015.

Further Reading
10. R. Kohli und V. Grover, "Business Value of IT: An Essay on Expanding Research Directories to Keep up with the Times," *Journal of the Association for Information Systems, Vol 9, Issue 2,* pp. 23–39, January 2008.
11. J. vom Brocke und T. Schmiedel, BPM-Driving Innovation in a Digital World, Springer, 2015.

Don't Lose Control, Stay up to Date: Automated Runtime Quality Engineering

Thomas Gabor, Marie Kiermeier, and Lenz Belzner

Abstract

Modern industrial settings require great flexibility of systems. For example, in automated factories, smart cities or smart grids, systems are exposed to highly variable and dynamic environments: Not all events can be modeled at design time, system components may fail to operate as desired at runtime, and stakeholder requirements may change at high frequency. In order to handle these challenges, systems have to expose highly flexible behavior. Due to the complexity of application domains, deterministic specification and validation of system behavior and quality is no more feasible. Instead, new approaches for building flexible systems yield probabilistic behavior at runtime. While this defeats the purpose of design time testing and quality assessment, it is indeed possible to shift the standard design time engineering activities towards runtime. This enables monitoring and validating system behavior at runtime, incorporating information not available a priori and using it to keep the dynamic system under control at runtime.

T. Gabor (✉) · M. Kiermeier · L. Belzner
Ludwig-Maximilians-Universität München
Munich, Germany
e-mail: thomas.gabor@ifi.lmu.de

M. Kiermeier
e-mail: marie.kiermeier@ifi.lmu.de

L. Belzner
e-mail: belzner@ifi.lmu.de

© Springer-Verlag GmbH Germany 2018
C. Linnhoff-Popien et al. (eds.), *Digital Marketplaces Unleashed*,
https://doi.org/10.1007/978-3-662-49275-8_55

55.1 Introduction

Modern business requirements are highly volatile. Smart factories are considered to realize production lines able to reach lot size one. This enables highly flexible adjustment to customer requirements and needs. Financial markets react to available information within moments. Electricity demand is changing at minimal rates, with high variance, while production capabilities in the smart grid are depending on weather conditions, and thus also constantly changing. Modern industrial systems have to cope with these settings, both effectively and safely.

The raise of digitization in terms of sensory information and infrastructure for data aggregation and distribution has put massive amounts of valuable data at the fingertips of system designers. However, the complexity and amount of available information in combination with ever-changing situations and requirements heavily impacts the effectiveness of classical approaches to designing and operating systems. Identifying currently relevant value in massive amounts of data is no longer feasible at design time.

To this end, software has to analyze and transform runtime data into decisions about system configurations, reorganization and adaptation. This gives rise to a number of questions:

- How can data analysis be performed effectively, given the sheer amount of available data?
- How can analysis be performed accounting for current business and customer requirements?
- How to transform analysis into system decisions?

It has been shown that autonomous systems endowed with the capability to learn and self-organize can provide a promising approach to tackling the increasing complexity of software engineering [1]. However, increasing flexibility of systems severely impacts classical mechanisms of quality assurance. This challenge yields additional questions to be answered.

- How to ensure performance, if runtime conditions are not exactly known when designing the system?
- How to assure that a system meets its qualitative requirements, even though it is allowed to reconfigure itself according to situations that only arise at runtime?
- How to test a system reorganizing itself at runtime?

In this Chapter, we want to sketch potential approaches to answering these questions. We will discuss how systems can be made "smarter" by enabling them to know about their ultimate goals and to learn how to fulfill them best. This will lead us to the important question how self-learning processes can be always kept in check and how we can engineer them in our best interest.

55.2   Getting Value from Your Runtime Data

In this Section, we outline an approach to enable software driven systems to transform data becoming available at runtime into decisions about configuration and reorganization that increase or maintain the potential to satisfy requirements and remain concordant with a given specification.

55.2.1   Shape the Future to Your Needs

One of the keys to effectively transforming available runtime data into valuable decisions is to provide a system with means to evaluate future trends and developments. The central idea is to build a predictive model (i. e. a simulation) of application domain dynamics, both from expert knowledge and from data available at system design time. See [2] and [3], e. g., for recent research directions on the matter of transforming available data into applicable predictive models.

Once an accurate model is available, it can be fed with data gathered at runtime in order to estimate future trends and consequences of system configuration and reconfiguration. Consider a smart factory that is able to reposition its current production machines. A model can be used to evaluate the consequences of different configuration and reorganization decisions, e. g., in terms of time to production, but also in terms of energy cost or any other metric of interest.

While the ability to drive decisions based on reflection about future consequences enables flexible system reaction to a variety of production requirements not known a priori, it poses a big challenge for quality assurance. We argue that many of the non-functional requirement assessment activities can be pushed into system runtime, by also exploiting the model and evaluating consequences of system decisions. The difference is only in the metric of interest evaluated when simulating: For example, when a smart factory decides to reorganize its machines to meet current production requirements, one can at the same time assess not only time to production or energy cost, but also whether performance or safety requirements will be met.

55.2.2   Today's Decisions Drive Tomorrow's Opportunities

In many cases, the choices a system performs at a given moment have consequences for the choices it is able to make in the future. Imagine an autonomous car: Acceleration now yields higher speed in the future, and stopping or steering a fast car is different from doing the same for a slow one. A smart factory that reorganizes its production machines in order to produce items of type A as efficiently as possible may take a long time to reorganize for production of type B items. It is therefore crucial to use available models to evaluate *sequences* of system decisions. In the example, given a model about potential future requests, this would allow the factory system to identify valuable trade-off configurations that enable good performance for type A items, while maintaining flexibility to change to production for items of type B.

Typically, as the model about requests is based on incomplete information (e. g., some recent patterns in orderings), it would be given in a probabilistic form to capture the designers' uncertainty about the ordering dynamics. See [4] for a scientific discussion of incomplete information, uncertainty and probability. See [5] for a discussion of the relation of model-free and model-based decision making, and [6] for a recent survey of sequential decision making under multiple objectives.

While sequential planning of system decisions is straightforward on a concept level, this approach yields exponential growth of problem space with larger planning horizons (i. e., number of sequential decisions considered). However, we require our systems to make their decisions in time: Decisions have to be made before their estimated evaluation becomes invalidated due to environmental changes and events. For example, consider a smart factory system trying to find an optimal trade-off configuration for type A/B items (see above), given a particular new ordering situation requiring preference of type A performance, given some probability that in the future type B items will be preferred again. Then, if the preference for type B occurs while the system still optimizes for the previous (now old) requirement, all effort was useless.

We therefore approach system reconfiguration in an *online* way: Decision making mechanisms are to be designed in order to constantly be able to produce (nearly) optimal (i. e., good enough) results, given all currently available information and resources (such as computation time until decision). If decision mechanisms are well designed, they are (a) able to exploit available information and resources effectively and (b) always able to return the decision currently being estimated to be optimal.

55.2.3 Better Good Now than Getting Better Forever

In order to allow for such resource-sensitive decision making, we resort to sampling approaches. These estimate decision quality by sampling potential consequences from the model instead of taking into account all potential ones. This ensures scalability of the approach, and often some quality of the estimate can be computed as well (i. e., a confidence in the decision mechanism's current result).

While it would be possible to sample the space of potential reconfigurations with respect to an uninformed heuristic (e. g., uniformly random or by grid search), it is more effective to use information generated from sampling the model to drive further simulations. For instance, if a smart factory decision mechanism has found some generally promising direction of reconfiguration, it should distribute available computational resources accordingly. Consider the system has found (by previous sampling) that moving machine X close to machine Y is producing many high quality samples. Then, it should use this configuration as a starting point for further reorganization refinement (e. g., po-

Fig. 55.1 Two feedback loops of a simulation-based adaptive system

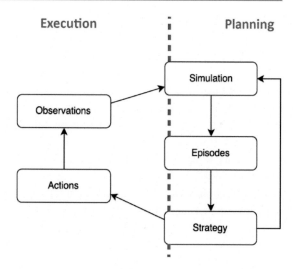

sitioning machine Z). However, the system should not stop to investigate completely different, potentially even more promising configurations. In the literature, this dilemma is known as the exploration-exploitation trade-off (c.f. [7]), and there exist numerous sample-based approaches to tackle that trade-off, which can be readily used for application in modern systems such as a smart factory.

Fig. 55.1 illustrates the idea schematically: The system incorporates two feedback loops. The first feedback loop describes the systems interaction with the environment in an online manner, based on the current estimate of an optimal strategy. It is depicted on the left. The second feedback loop is of higher frequency than the left one, and captures the influence of previous sampling results on the sampling strategy. It is shown on the right.

An important challenge to be further explored are the issues of analysis, scalability, transparency and quality assurance of systems that continuously drive their decisions based on statistical estimates and runtime data. In the following two Sections, we will discuss our approaches and ideas in this direction.

55.3   Get to Know Your Software: Non-Functional Requirements for Adaptive Systems

In the previous Section, we discussed how to shift some activities traditionally placed in the design time of the software development process towards runtime. We showed how planning can be used to make a software product adhere to specified functional requirements during runtime. However, software development is also concerned with non-functional requirements (NFRs), i. e., properties like performance, scalability or robustness, the fulfillment of which can be just as crucial to many software applications.

55.3.1 NFR Assessment

In the traditional software development process, non-functional requirements are assessed on a per-domain basis by respective experts. For example, for a web shop application, performance can be defined as the average time-to-respond to requests on the web shop's site or the maximum load of users the web shop can serve at the same time. For factory automation software, performance might be defined as the throughput of parts that can be achieved or as the maximum time it takes to employ a desired change of production in the factory setup. Even in these quickly sketched examples it becomes clear that there often is an intricate trade-off between multiple non-functional requirements: A factory may be able to improve its reaction time to changes by keeping a relatively large amount of equipment in a state of stand-by; but this decision may in turn diminish the throughput the factory is able to provide when no change is required at all.

Thus, even though non-functional properties are often sufficiently general in their definition so that they apply to a wide array of systems built for various different functional purposes, the exact measurements of interest need to be suitably engineered to match the problem at hand [8]. To this aim, the product owner (or whoever is responsible for the requirement specification in the employed development process) typically defines a series of use cases related to non-functional properties. These could read like this:

- "When 50 or less users are putting an order into the web shop at the same time, the maximum response time for the server to any of these users must be at most 500 milliseconds." (Performance)
- "When orders to the smart factory have not changed for more than one hour, the throughput should be at least 100 items per hour." (Performance)
- "When a machine in the smart factory crashes, it should take at most 15 min for the factory to reconfigure so that the faulty machine is compensated for." (Robustness)

As the number of specific use cases increases, it becomes increasingly probable that there exist situations where conflicts between different requirements may arise. A prioritization of the defined use cases is thus an intrinsic part of a specification of non-functional requirements.

In today's software, these kinds of engineering decisions are made by experienced developers with detailed knowledge of the working domain of the software and the likeliness of various environmental events and thereby resulting adaptations. In future software applications, like industry 4.0 setups, e. g., decisions of similar magnitude may be imposed onto some online adaptation mechanism: As intelligent software may deem it necessary to re-organize a smart factory's configuration to respect a change in functional requirements, the importance and meaning of several non-functional requirements defined for the previous system configuration may change significantly. As a consequence, the process of NFR engineering, i. e., ensuring the fulfillment of non-functional requirements, needs to be performed at runtime or–more specifically–any time autonomous adaptation may occur.

55.3.2   Building Models for NFRs

This argument presupposes a strong form of adaptation which may among other things introduce structural changes to the system and may be based on goal changes completely unpredicted at design time. For simpler systems, which can only make very limited decisions, i. e., adapt in few dimensions statically specified at design time, it is often possible to prove NFR properties statically at design time by simply iterating over all possible system configurations that may occur. In this case, NFR engineering can also be performed quite similarly to how it is executed for classical, non-adaptive systems. However, for modern applications like industry 4.0 settings, checking against all possible configurations a system may adopt during its runtime is not feasible.

Nonetheless, any small change in a system's configuration may have a detrimental impact on non-functional properties. Thus, for any configuration in the decision space of the autonomous software and for every NFR of interest for the system under test, we can get a different point of measurement when assessing to what degree a specific NFR is fulfilled for a given configuration of the system. When performing autonomous adaptation in the system under test, we thus need to consider that every small adaptive change can also cause our NFR measurements to yield different values. The resulting relation between system changes and consequential degree of NFR fulfillment is also called the *NFR landscape* of a given system.

Most non-functional properties are hard to predict analytically without actually running the software. The availability of a powerful simulation tool is thus of central importance to be able to test and measure non-functional properties without threatening the effectiveness of the real system at work. Fortunately, the need for high-accuracy simulations of industrial hardware has been recognized in various areas of engineering and adequately comprehensive simulations are (while still being subject of current research) being made available to system builders [9, 10]. Still, which configurations to simulate is yet another decision to be made automatically at runtime if the whole process of NFR engineering is to be executed online.

The main focus point of automated NFR engineering can thus be described as discovering the most relevant use cases to test the system's current behavior against. The term "most relevant" in this scenario is a bit tricky to define adequately, though. Simply speaking, we are mostly interested in all extreme cases, i. e., use cases where non-functional properties are fulfilled to the least extent and those use cases which yield the best result with respect to non-functional properties; but we also want to achieve a relatively good coverage of all possible cases, i. e., we also want to look for exemplary cases which encompass a lot of different scenarios. For the first part, assessing NFRs is then not unlike any standard optimization problem and can be tackled using the same techniques such as meta-heuristic search [11] employing, e. g., evolutionary algorithms [12]. For the second part, we need to adequately estimate which regions of the search space of test cases might be of more interest than others but then search them in balanced manner so that the search process does *not* converge towards just a few regions (or even only one single region) of interest. It is thus important to decide the value of various test cases not only based on how bad the system under test handles them but also with respect to how many other test cases with similar outcomes there are, and how different their setup is from other test cases that may have already been found when producing a test suite. Certainly, coming up with a proper metric that respects all of these aspects is one of the key steps towards more automated NFR engineering that is suitable for autonomous systems.

In any case, more resources spent on NFR evaluation are likely to improve the results of automated NFR engineering as the process of automated NFR engineering as described above can be likened to a probabilistic search algorithm on the NFR landscape. However, computation time is in most cases a very limited resource and especially so when we need to (re-)evaluate NFRs online while continuing the system's normal operations. It is thus beneficial to guide the search through the NFR landscape towards regions that are more likely to become relevant with respect to the system's actions and their planned outcomes, respectively. To do so requires a tight integration of online planning and NFR tests and checks with NFR engineering into a system's online adaptation cycle [10, 13, 14]. However, it allows the developers to continuously monitor and update the degree of fulfillment for NFRs in an ever-changing system.

55.4   Quality Assurance in Smart Factories

The vision of a smart factory is to have a production plant which organizes its production processes on its own. In doing so, the production processes are automatically adapted to current production orders, resource availability or other changing requirements. For example, in case of a breakdown of a machine the system re-organizes itself automatically in such a way that the work-pieces are redirected to another machine, and the production does not have to be stopped. Another use case is, that the system adapts its production dynamically to the current production orders. This means, that after recognizing that the demand for washing machines, e. g., has increased significantly, the system stops producing dish washers and re-organizes itself so that washing machines can be produced. In contrast to classic manufacturing factories, the system makes this decision autonomously without any human interaction.

This "smartness" is made possible by the fact that the process flow for the production of a work-piece is not explicitly fixed in advance. Instead, a kind of "recipe" is given to the system, which just lists the necessary steps, but not the explicit machines or stations where the single actions have to take place at. The system then decides at runtime how to put these "recipes" into practice. The advantage of this approach is that—for these decisions—the system can take the current situation into account (e. g., current production orders or current resource availability), and can thus optimize the process flow with respect to these matters.

In other words, the way of producing a workpiece is not anymore limited to explicitly predefined process flows. Actually, there are not even limitations regarding the production of certain workpieces as long as the corresponding "recipe" can be put to practice using the system's components.

One example where the "smartness" of a factory really can increase efficiency is the so-called lot size one production. In lot size one productions every workpiece is produced just once, i. e., the desired properties of no two workpieces are exactly the same. Using the aforementioned "recipe"-based approach, this means that the system just receives a list of the necessary steps for each workpiece. Based on these, the system defines autonomously—without human interaction—the explicit work flow. Since this planning phase takes place at runtime, the resulting process can be optimized with respect to the current requirements.

However, regarding the task of quality assurance in such systems, this new paradigm also poses new challenges. Especially the fact that, in theory, every possible way through the production plant using any combination of machines or components can be put to practice, is challenging. Depending on the complexity of the system and the number of the system's components, the number of possible work flows increases exponentially. Obviously, beyond a certain number, not all of them can be tested in advance. Thus, the classical approach to test at design time to assure the quality at runtime does not work anymore. To assure the quality anyway, new methods have to be applied at runtime, which on one hand detect misbehavior immediately and on the other hand provide information about possible root causes. Based on this information, the system can be analyzed, potential weak points can be detected, and so the quality be assured.

In the next section, we list concrete challenges and corresponding requirements which have to be taken into account when developing such new quality assurance methods for smart factories.

55.4.1   Challenges

Basically, there are three main challenges when developing quality assurance methods for smart factories: Volume of data, distribution of data, and volume of possible process flows.

Volume of Data   Essential for all the "smart" decisions of the system is that the system knows as much as possible about the current state of the system, its nearby environment, the current tasks and optimization requirements. Thus, the first key challenge is to handle all this information. Although the problem is not to transmit and save the mass of data, the real challenge is to extract the relevant information. In addition, since most of the data is provided just-in-time by sensors which monitor the relevant units of the system, there is also the requirement of real-time processing of the incoming data.

As a consequence, quality assurance methods in smart factories have to be able to process incoming data streams in real-time. Otherwise, important information cannot be extracted and is not available for the evaluation of the system's behavior.

Distribution of Data As already mentioned, most of the data which is used in smart factories is provided by sensors which are applied to relevant units in the system. They are, depending on the spatial dimensions of the production plant, more or less widely spread. To communicate their measurements anyway, they are connected (via WLAN, e. g.) and form a network where messages can be exchanged. However, in order to avoid unnecessary communication overhead in the network, as many data processing tasks as possible should be worked on in a distributed manner. This means that not all relevant information is first sent to one central unit, which then processes all data. Instead, at least partial results are pre-calculated by singular sensors or small sensor groups, and then put together to the end result.

Regarding quality assurance methods for smart factories, this ability to work in a distributed manner is the second requirement which can be derived by the fact that smart factories are sensor networks.

Volume of Possible Process Flows Since the production in a smart factory is not anymore limited to explicitly predefined process flows, the third key challenge is to handle the volume of possible process flows. Especially with regard to quality assurance, this is the most critical aspect. In contrast to classic quality assurance procedures in smart factories, it is no longer possible to test all work flows in advance. To assure the quality anyway suitable methods have to evaluate the behavior of the system at runtime. In addition, these methods should provide further information which can help to detect the root cause for misbehavior of the system. Based on this analysis, countermeasures can be taken to avoid future faults, and thus assure the quality.

To evaluate the behavior of the system at runtime, it is essential to know of all allowed process flows. Since these can be very numerous, suitable compressing methods are needed to handle the volume of possible process flows. The idea of such compressing methods is that all possible work-flows are covered while not all have to be stored explicitly. Thus, when developing quality assurance methods for smart factories, managing to construct such compressed representations of possible work flows is the third challenge.

55.4.2 A Summary on Quality Assurance in Smart Factories

Smart factories are the next generation of manufacturing. Key feature of this new paradigm is that the process flows are not predefined in advance. Instead, the system decides autonomously depending on the current state and requirements at runtime how to put the given "recipe" into practice. However, this approach poses new challenges for quality assurance. As a consequence the quality assurance procedure has to be shifted into runtime.

Table 55.1 Challenges and resulting requirements for quality assurance methods in Smart Factories

Challenges	Resulting Requirements
Volume of Data	Real-Time
Network Structure	Distributed
Volume of Possible Process Flows	Compressing

Accordingly, in this Section we listed three main challenges and resulting requirements which have to be considered when developing such quality assurance methods which can be applied at runtime: first, the methods have to process the incoming data streams in real-time; second, it should be possible that the processing tasks can be worked on in a distributed manner; third, to handle the volume of possible process flows, suitable compressing techniques are required, which build an adequate representation of all possible process flows.

A summary of the aforementioned challenges and resulting requirements for quality assurance methods in smart factories can be seen in Table 55.1.

55.5   Conclusion & Outlook

In this Chapter, we discussed potential and challenges of systems with the ability to autonomously decide about their configuration and behavior. To this end, efficient transformation of available runtime data into evaluation of alternatives is of key importance. However, this new behavioral freedom yields new challenges for system analysis, scalability, transparency and quality assurance. We propose to move classic design time quality assurance activities such as non-functional requirement engineering and system testing into runtime in order to enable coping with highly volatile system environments and requirements.

Autonomous systems are built in order to react to changes in the requirements on a much smaller time scale than is typically necessary for humans to be involved. This feature alone enables new possibilities for products and services like, e. g., "lot size one" production or coordinating production processes with the current market value of required goods. This is enabled by human experts defining relatively abstract goals for autonomous systems to strive after instead of engineering the complex process in-detail. When the embraced observation, control and safety techniques prove to be working for these kinds of scenarios, one can think of entrusting autonomous systems with increasingly more broadly defined tasks and thus transferring growing amounts of business logic into the system's requirements specification. Eventually, system autonomy typical for industry 4.0 may then be a feature that does not only affect production lines but also the way management decisions are made or what is even considered a management decision in the first place.

Key challenges for further research in this direction are (1) increasing accuracy of predictive models built from data, (2) enable model scalability by adaptive (e. g., requirement-sensitive) abstraction in feature space and time scales, and (3) establishing methods yielding statistical guarantees for systems that act under adaptive abstraction and concept drift in their application domains.

References

1. Barry Francis Porter and Roberto Rodrigues Filho. Losing control: the case for emergent software systems using autonomous assembly, perception and learning. 2016 IEEE 10th International Conference on Self-Adaptive and Self-Organizing Systems (SASO).
2. Sebastian Thrun and Lorien Pratt. Learning to learn. Springer Science & Business Media, 2012.
3. Max Kuhn and Kjell Johnson. Applied predictive modeling. Springer, 2013.
4. Edwin T Jaynes. Probability theory: The logic of science. Cambridge university press, 2003.
5. Samuel J Gershman, Arthur B Markman, and A Ross Otto. Retrospective revaluation in sequential decision making: A tale of two systems. Journal of Experimental Psychology: General, 143(1):182, 2014.
6. Diederik Marijn Roijers, Peter Vamplew, Shimon Whiteson, and Richard Dazeley. A survey of multi-objective sequential decision-making. Journal of Artificial Intelligence Research, 2013.
7. Thomas T Hills, Peter M Todd, David Lazer, A David Redish, Iain D Couzin, Cognitive Search Research Group, et al. Exploration versus exploitation in space, mind, and society. Trends in cognitive sciences, 19(1):46–54, 2015.
8. Norha M Villegas, Hausi A Müller, Gabriel Tamura, Laurence Duchien, and Rubby Casallas. A framework for evaluating quality-driven self-adaptive software systems. In Proceedings of the 6th international symposium on Software engineering for adaptive and self-managing systems, pages 80–89. ACM, 2011.
9. Edward H Glaessgen and David Stargel. The digital twin paradigm for future nasa and us air force vehicles. In 53rd Struct. Dyn. Mater. Conf. Special Session: Digital Twin, Honolulu, HI, US, pages 1–14, 2012.
10. Thomas Gabor, Lenz Belzner, Marie Kiermeier, Michael Till Beck, and Alexander Neitz. A simulation-based architecture for smart cyber-physical systems. In Workshop Models at Runtime, Proceedings of ICAC 2016, 2016. to be published.
11. Mark Harman and Bryan F Jones. Search-based software engineering. Information and software Technology, 43(14):833–839, 2001.
12. Donald Berndt, J Fisher, L Johnson, J Pinglikar, and Alison Watkins. Breeding software test cases with genetic algorithms. In System Sciences, 2003. Proceedings of the 36th Annual Hawaii In- ternational Conference on, pages 10–pp. IEEE, 2003.
13. Steven Carl Bankes. Robustness, adaptivity, and resiliency analysis. In AAAI fall symposium: complex adaptive systems, volume 10, page 03, 2010.
14. Tomáš Bureš, Vojtěch Hork, Michal Kit, Lukáš Marek, and Petr Tuma. Towards performance-aware engineering of autonomic component ensembles. In International Symposium On Leveraging Applications of Formal Methods, Verification and Validation, pages 131–146. Springer, 2014.

Part XIII
Big Data and Analytics

Preface: Big Data and Analytics

56

Rolf Schumann

56.1 Why Are We Talking About a Data Revolution? What Is Actually Meant by the Notion of "Big Data" and "Analytics"?

In the last 20 years, the amount of data in existence has risen 100-fold. However, this data surge is not unique in history – one similarly rapid increase has occurred before, between the years 1450 and 1500. The volume of data in the world doubled during this period thanks to the advent of Gutenberg's printing press, which meant a revolution in society at the time. Today, the worldwide data volume is doubling every 18 months. However, what is often not considered in this context is this: while in the year 2000 almost three-quarters of all data were still in analog form, for example on paper, less than 15 years later this figure is less than 1%. A previously analog world has gone digital, which changes everything.

Although data is becoming ever more important in our lives, it has not yet been possible to establish a widespread understanding of the change our society is undergoing. If you cannot yet imagine the actual meaning behind terms such as "big data" or the "Internet of Things," you are not alone.

What accounts for the new quality of big data? There is no single, universally accepted definition of big data. But there is an approach cited most often in journalism and science when we talk about the topic, and which will certainly help you get to grips with it.

Extract from the published book "Update – Why the data revolution affects us all" (Rolf Schumann, Prof. Dr. Michael Steinbrecher, 2015, Campus Verlag. ISBN 978-3-593-50332-5).

R. Schumann (✉)
SAP SE
Walldorf, Germany
e-mail: rolf.schumann@sap.com

© Springer-Verlag GmbH Germany 2018
C. Linnhoff-Popien et al. (eds.), *Digital Marketplaces Unleashed*,
https://doi.org/10.1007/978-3-662-49275-8_56

56.2 Definition of Big Data and Analytics

This approach is based on the four Vs: volume, velocity, variety and veracity (see Fig. 56.1). We've already established that big data is large – after all, the name does hint at it. However, big data is also fast, varied and can sometimes even contain vague data. And this is supposed to trigger a revolution that turns our lives on their head? Exactly.

The velocity in particular has engendered a real spirit of optimism in business. Companies can monitor which traffic light could soon malfunction, which parcel is currently where, and which pipe needs to be replaced in real time – and react immediately. But it doesn't just present opportunities for businesses – it will change your day-to-day life too. In a networked home, you can observe while on vacation how high the room temperature is or in which room a conversation is currently taking place. Many things become possible. The question you will ask yourself again and again is: How do I want to live?

What is special about the third V, variety? We used to gather data for ONE specific purpose. Once we had used the data to find out what we wanted, we perhaps saved it somewhere, but it was then generally useless. However, in the world of big data it remains valuable. Because it is precisely this linking of seemingly non-related data that makes big data so exciting.

The fourth V is for veracity. Even inaccurate, vague data can be useful in the age of the data revolution. Although it sounds unspectacular, in combination with the other three Vs it has far-reaching consequences.

Many constituent parts of big data already existed as individual elements. There has always been data, and computers have also long been with us. However, it is not, as one may assume from the term BIG data, the data VOLUME alone that is changing the world. It is all four elements together, with all of their interactions: volume, velocity, variety and

Fig. 56.1 The four Vs of big data

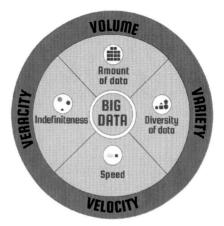

veracity. It is a cocktail consisting of these four elements that is intoxicating so many. A cocktail that releases energy and imagination.

Four Vs are simply not enough for some, so further Vs are sometimes added, for example the value of the data. But as we do not wish to further complicate the definition, we will stay with the original four Vs.

56.3   The Technical and Economic View of Big Data and Analytics

The data cocktail has created a new situation in a structural sense, too. We all know that the array of possibilities for transferring data have accelerated our lives. The days of the stagecoach that would carry our hand-written letters will not come back. We no longer have to wait days for an answer. With the advent of e-mail, an exchange is possible in seconds – a far-reaching change that has long since become part of day-to-day life in our society.

From the perspective of companies, however, being able to process large projects and complex data quickly was until recently anything but normal. The latest technological developments enable data to be processed at up to 3000 times the speed at a comparable cost. How does this technological leap affect us? In order to deepen our understanding of this, we will perform a little thought experiment. Imagine a flight from San Francisco to Frankfurt, Germany. Today, such a flight usually takes between nine and eleven hours. However, if one applied the latest advance in information technology to the aviation industry, this flight could take only 20 s.

You read it right – 20 s! This is reminiscent of the vision of "beaming" that has for decades appeared utopian and fascinating in equal measure, and not just to Star Trek fans. Would you still see this as a "proper" flight? Surely it would no longer be the same. Exactly this is the point. The idea of something being technically impossible and therefore not worth pursuing further has become obsolete on many levels.

In connection with our topic, this means that progress will significantly change the way in which we handle and live with data and information. After all, the latest technologies allow these enormous quantities of data, originating from completely different information, to be processed efficiently and in full.

These changes open up previously undreamed-of possibilities. Interactions at different interfaces are changing – on the one hand between people, but also between people and objects, i. e., devices and machines. You still frequently see yourself as being in control. You have to read operating manuals and know how to make the device do what you expect it to. However, an entirely new user experience is emerging.

Because of the rapid pace of change in our globalized world, the sheer number of changes in the complexity of how companies, markets and people are networked far exceeds anything we could have ever imagined before. The latest technology makes it possible to respond to every piece of information in real time and using cognitive intelligence. Many large corporations have recognized this development or even driven it forward themselves. It offers them great opportunities while at the same time raising new questions for society.

If we apply these new technical achievements and knowledge to the theoretical plane journey mentioned above, you will already have an idea of what the possible effects might be. These technologies fundamentally change existing business processes and business models, while also enabling completely new business ideas that were previously unimaginable. Just think what a flight from San Francisco to Frankfurt in 20 s would mean. An airline would not simply market them as "faster" flights, as that wouldn't come close to the quantum leap in air travel they were offering. Imagine how the whole process would change! Would a classic catering service really be profitable for a journey time of 20 s? How many booking classes such as Economy, Economy Plus, Business and First Class would generally be needed? If a flight only took 20 s in the future, you would have to ask yourself what the product actually is if passengers spent 30 min waiting for their luggage or going through security. All of these questions immediately arise if you are suddenly able to perform business processes in real time while using enormous amounts of data. In other words, we have to question existing processes, find out what possibilities real-time processing offers us and moreover generate completely new ideas.

From a corporate perspective, big data is producing new business models that unleash optimism and euphoria. But, to continue with our example, who still needs flight attendants on a flight that only lasts 20 s? Do we even need pilots? What will happen to the catering companies that previously supplied the airlines? Or, returning to your own life: Do you actually like the further acceleration of our lives? Wasn't such a long-haul flight also an opportunity to break the flow of work and watch the films you missed over the previous weeks? And even if the person sitting next to you takes up more space than you might like, haven't we all at some point enjoyed an interesting conversation on board a flight?

Many publications examine the opportunities big data and analytics presents to businesses in the finest detail. New business models are drawn up, new paths for innovations illustrated. It's certainly important to understand the logic and the new philosophy of companies and industry, and we will have another look at this topic in the following four papers in this chapter.

Unlocking the Doors of Frankfurt Airport's Digital Marketplace: How Fraport's Smart Data Lab Manages to Create Value from Data and to Change the Airport's Way of Thinking

Katharina Schüller and Christian Wrobel

Abstract

In March 2015, Fraport AG in Frankfurt carried out an experimental Smart Data Lab (SDL). For the first time, experts from a variety of departments worked together in a laboratory situation. They defined four concrete problems to be solved with analytics, using a huge collection of data from different sources within the company.

The effective communication of problems and results helped promote the acceptance of the lab's data based recommendations. Analytics and the use of huge amounts of real-time data which were integrated into the IT systems for the first time, allowed for the correction of some established decision rules. Most of all, not only the problems defined above were solved and the business processes behind were improved, but also several new data-based business ideas with cross-departmental impact were generated.

Results from the Smart Data Lab were widely noticed and accepted by Fraport's executive board, which in turn has decided to make SDL a permanent institution: The second round of Smart Data Lab was completed in April 2016.

K. Schüller (✉)
STAT-UP Statistical Consulting & Data Science GmbH
Munich, Germany
e-mail: schueller@stat-up.de

C. Wrobel
Fraport AG
Frankfurt on the Main, Germany
e-mail: c.wrobel@fraport.de

© Springer-Verlag GmbH Germany 2018
C. Linnhoff-Popien et al. (eds.), *Digital Marketplaces Unleashed*,
https://doi.org/10.1007/978-3-662-49275-8_57

57.1 Background: Transformation of Airports

57.1.1 from Product-Centric to Customer-Centric Perspective

Airports around the world are confronted with the challenge to transform themselves from infrastructure managers to service providers in order to compete successfully in the global market. To a great extent, this transformation is driven by digitalization. While so far technology was mostly used to support business processes and thereby enable airports to realize their business models effectively, digital transformation means that new business models are developed around the technology itself. From a European perspective, the major airports in Europe, Middle East and North Africa are directly affected by that challenge since they are the key hubs for transferring intercontinental passengers around the globe. In general, for most enterprises digital transformation means a big change in an organizational and cultural way which directly affects all employees and the nature of their thinking and collaboration. The main objective of this effort is to establish new products and services which help airports to set themselves apart from competitors and gain market shares.

Fraport has given itself a new corporate mission statement: "Gute Reise! We take care." This mission statement reflects the transformation process in particular and switches the strategic focus from the "Airport Manager's" perspective to the customers' perspective. In the past, an airport's strategic focus was about providing and maintaining runways, buildings and processes for handling aircraft operations of freight and passenger flights – the so-called product-centric perspective. Today passengers and visitors are strongly moving into the attention of an airport's business interest. However, running a successful airport business from a customer-centric perspective requires much more than providing a smooth handling of aircraft operations. As well, if not even more, it requires the provision of a positive and stress-free experience for all people around the airport. This involves for example attention on entertainment, information services, process optimization, simplification of travelling, shopping experience and assistance.

As most of us certainly know, travelling by plane involves both positive and unpleasant situations. While the planning process of the new trip is often connected with pleasant anticipation, the mood often turns into tension – at the latest when the journey finally starts. This tension sometimes results in heavy stress especially if queuing at check-in is backed up, if security screening takes very long or if problems with luggage occur. A pleasant journey seems hardly imaginable at that point and the desire to go shopping or to use other services just evaporates. Those situations need to be avoided to guarantee the most comfortable trip and to persuade passengers to use Frankfurt Airport again in the future.

57.1.2   Unlocking the Digital Marketplace with a Smart Data Lab

Digitalization supports the fulfilment of those requirements by providing data about passengers, visitors, shops, transactions, flights, freight and so on – almost anything could be tracked digitally and the data generated could be used to generate knowledge and value. However, many stakeholders are involved. To create value from data, data must be harvested by reduction and abstraction ("How can we track meaningful data?"), cleaned and linked through processing and organization ("How can we generate information from data?"), analyzed, interpreted ("How can we gain knowledge from information?") and applied ("How should we act, based on that knowledge?"). Data "form the base or bedrock of a knowledge pyramid" [1].

In the age of digitalization, data seem to be ubiquitous and endless. However, data are both under- and overvalued. They are undervalued because data-generating systems provide endless amounts of bits and bytes that are neither linked nor organized and therefore cannot be turned into power. Then again, they are overvalued as the whole world gets excited about "the power of data". In a narrow sense, a digital marketplace needs to be established between data owners from different departments as many of them are not used to sharing their data. In a wider sense, that marketplace would include every single stakeholder: merchants, airlines, suppliers, public authorities like customs and the police and, most important, passengers.

Major hub airports are under considerable economic strain because of two main reasons. The first one results from the growth of Low-Cost-Airlines and thus from a significant change in price structure for legacy Airlines like Lufthansa or Air France. The second reason results from massive capacity expansions of Middle East airports like Dubai, Abu Dhabi or Istanbul which cause noticeable shifts on market shares regarding transfer passengers. For example, the route from New York to Singapore can nowadays be operated using different stopovers. Finally, the decision about which stopover will be chosen is made based on the price and experience of former trips. Since the majority of passengers at Frankfurt Airport are transfer passengers and Lufthansa operates most of the flights, Fraport is greatly affected. Recently, additional reasons like changes in the geopolitical situation and fear of terrorism restrain passengers from travelling via Frankfurt Airport have come up.

In order to compete on price and quality with Middle East airports, Fraport has to optimize their processes permanently and react fast on changing requirements. Therefore, Fraport coined a new instrument to identify potential improvements and possibilities for optimization based on data analysis – the Smart Data Lab. The term "Smart Data Lab" is widely used to characterize a type of innovation lab that uses data as resources and develops new business ideas from that data, s. Fig. 57.1.

In reality, many Smart Data Labs rather create algorithms that are more or less useful to be applied in business, which sooner or later affects the acceptance of the labs. We claim that a Smart Data Lab can and should be viewed as something much more fundamental. A Smart Data Lab provides the key to open the digital marketplace. Focusing on concrete

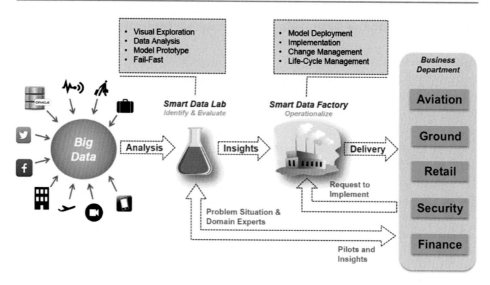

Fig. 57.1 Smart Data Lab as the first step in the transformation process

problems, with a clear factual, temporal and also spatial concentration, the lab itself could function as a hub, connecting not only data, but also experts and ideas. The major task is not a technical one. It is a political one. It is the task to persuade stakeholders to share and trade their data in a digital marketplace in order to create more value for everyone involved and to make that value clearly visible.

In our opinion one of the characteristics of Smart Data Lab is the "non-sugarcoated truth" of data and data analytics. Possible optimization of processes, (labor) changes or any improvements resulting from a Smart Data Lab may unsettle or upset the affected department and/or the management. This requires undoubtedly that the Smart Data Lab has to prove that any of its results is derived from analytics of data only and is not biased by human retention, defense or justification of current practice. *It's not about blaming someone* or someone's processes – it's about optimization and getting new insights.

57.2 Data Structures at Airports

The main system of an airport is the Airport Operational Database (= AODB). It consolidates all relevant data for flight operations from different sources. In this context, the AODB operates as an integrator of all relevant information as well as a delivery hub to provide that information to all stakeholder. Data are coming from different sources like sensors, business process applications, radar sources, airlines, public authorities, ground handlers or freight forwarders. The main business object is a flight, uniquely identifiable by airline, trip number, arrival/departure indicator and its scheduled date. With approximately 1400 flights per day that looks like a rather small amount of data on the main business object. But considering that each flight has over 5000 attributes and gets updated over a thousand times during its lifecycle, a significant volume of (at least in part) real-time and heterogeneous data needs to be stored and managed reliably. Data describing the airport core processes will still reside in a low terabyte range and not in petabyte dimensions.

Those core business relevant data can roughly be classified in the following categories listed in Table 57.1.

The data consist to a great extent of timestamps and numeric information and are stored in a complex data model composed of more than 450 tables. Managing and providing this information for reporting and free data analysis requires very experienced data managers who have deep expert knowledge of the business and the ability to match this to the technical data model. For all data analysis projects, the data manager is an essential resource and a key factor for the success of the project.

Since most of the data are structured and stored in a relational format, the size of this information is comparably small in contrast to other industries. Rather than handling big volumes of data, the main effort for airports is to manage the variety of sources and therefore the complexity of data integration and the velocity of incoming streaming data for real-time data analysis and decision making.

Besides flight relating data, other business departments like human resources, finance, project management or real estate management also possess a lot of interesting data. However, those data are stored separately. For years, data has enjoyed special observance from controlling and reporting since they are mostly based on standard applications and standard business procedures. Free data analysis and data exploration wasn't on the spotlight so far but the linkage of both data platforms will be the next big thing to address.

Table 57.1 Categories of and examples for business relevant data at airports

Category	Examples
General flight data	Airline, aircraft, gate, airport, runway
Passenger data	Total on board, transit, transfer, reduced mobility
Flight operation data	Arrival and departure time, deicing, taxi time
Baggage data	Dangerous goods, palettes, animal transportation
Freight data	Coordinates overall activities
Passenger handling	Security, check-in, boarding, border control
Ground handling services	On/off-loading, passenger transportation via bus, baggage transportation, freight transportation, supply and fueling, aircraft push-back, special orders

57.3 Airport Analytics Now and Then

Data is the new oil of the 21th century. This slogan and similar ones fuel the expectations of data analysis to help companies master their challenges and easily solve all their problems. It has to be proven in the future whether this approach really works out for all potential scenarios, but as of today there are some good examples demonstrating the possibilities of capturing insights and finding the solution for business problems inside a company's raw data. However, high expectations and the urge to engage in the field of data analytics was occasionally rather harmful than helpful. Since the top management became aware of the idea that data might be an asset, it has often ended up in doing things for the sake of doing things and significant but haphazard investments in analytics related facilities and services, like hardware/infrastructure, software/tools and consultancy.

Data analysis is not new at all. In the past, data analysis relied on sophisticated statistical methods to extract even the tiniest drop of information from scarce data. Now data is abundant and analytics faces very different problems, like how to link huge and heterogeneous amounts of data and how to separate signals from pure noise. Companies not typically receptive for this topic now slowly start to change their organizations and build novel structures concerning both IT and human resources, often after they have experienced costly failures when first dealing with data and analytics in the way described above.

Fraport therefore created the Smart Data Lab and established it within the entire organization. Some of the expectations towards the lab focused on its more direct results, as for example the hope for discovery of unknown correlations that would lift the potential for quality improvement, cost reduction or profit increase. Data was supposed to generate clear and objective decision bases. Furthermore, expectations also stretched out to more indirect effects. The networking of employees with high logistical and mathematical skills would hopefully promote an innovation culture, reduce silo mentality and support a non-hierarchical development of human resources.

Before we describe two of the projects the Smart Data Lab worked on, which we will do in the next chapter, we will characterize the concept and implementation in short. The Smart Data Lab is primarily supposed to be an agile and innovative laboratory environment which would operate independently from existing hierarchical structures and allow experimental exploration and free trials of new ideas based on data analysis. From the beginning, failure was not only an option but was seen as an opportunity to learn and do better (fail-fast mentality). Interdisciplinary teams with cross-qualifications perform data-driven solution finding in an independent work unit that can be mandated by all departments and subsidiaries. Most important, the basic rule is that of a guard room free of restrictions.

All departments of Fraport can use the Smart Data Lab if they submit a precise problem statement and provide skilled employees. The latter is very useful to foster commitment and acceptance of the lab's work by the departments. It also makes clear that the lab institution and its services are extremely valuable, if not to say precious, because whoever wants to benefit from it needs to contribute. Last, but not least, skill and knowledge transfer throughout the whole company are guaranteed.

Questions submitted can be of strategic, tactical or operational nature. An example for a strategic problem was the question of how the positioning of flights at the gates affects retail revenues and which contractual conditions result from this insight, concerning future negotiation with airlines. A tactical problem mostly encompasses the improvement of equipment and staff planning and an example for operational situations is the prediction of more accurate arrival times during flight approach which could help optimize ground handling processes.

The Smart Data Lab is conducted once a year and involves five important phases – selection of relevant questions, clarifying the problem situation, analysis phase, presentation of results and transition into production. We present these phases in the following subsections.

57.3.1   Selection of Problem Statements

Every business department has the chance to submit a problem or research question to the Smart Data Lab. At first stage a small team from the Smart Data Lab consisting of employees from corporate development and IT department verify the relevance and feasibility of execution. Finally, the executive board selects four questions out of the list which guarantees the compliance and commitment according to corporate priorities and strategic objectives.

Now that the Smart Data Lab is well established, there is usually a wide range of problems and research questions to choose from. The business departments and the executive board have been convinced that using predictive analytics will help them make smarter, earlier decisions that address a wide range of business challenges. This is usually not the case when the lab is initiated for the first time. It may be hard to persuade a department to be the first to submit a problem, mostly for political reasons. A department needs to be persuaded that at least some of their biggest business challenges might be susceptible to a predictive approach and that it is worth a try. "This persuasion task is probably more difficult than any technological issues that might come up [2]."

57.3.2   Clarifying the Problem Situation

In multiple workshops with the Smart Data Lab team and a group of qualified employees the problem is discussed in detail and is rendered more precisely. Typically, people from the relevant business department start to explain the procedure of the business process including exceptions and standard activities. At that point it is very helpful for the entire team to take some time and observe the process in reality or visit control centers and planning offices to sharpen the comprehension for the problem.

Besides a good notion of the problem itself it is also very useful to understand the motivation and possible benefit of solving the issue. The goal of this phase is to achieve a fine grasp for all team members and to determine the expectations from the business department. It has turned out to be helpful trying to define possible solutions classified as "gold, silver and bronze". This classification reveals the basic minimum requirements determined for a bronze solution and the more advanced, but nice-to-have features covered in the gold solution. Since time for analyzing the problem is strictly limited, the classification provides a useful orientation for the team during the next phase.

57.3.3 Data Analysis Phase

In the data analysis phase the Smart Data Lab is called together for four weeks in total. During that time, it is very important that all members are completely released from daily business so they can focus on working in the lab. This is inevitable as those four weeks typically are the most intense and time consuming phase of all phases during a lab cycle.

Up to 15 members work self-organized using agile methods like Kanban in a collaborative manner. The members are assigned to one primary problem but are willing to work on other issues as well if help is needed. The members are marked with the following special skills described in Table 57.2.

The Smart Data Lab serves as a guard room during that phase in order to protect the members and the insights collected from outside influences. It also guarantees the idea of a free and experimental working ethic where it is possible to fail without fearing any consequences. All members get unlimited access to all company data and are willing to use any available tool they feel comfortable with. In this way, a maximum of efficiency and effectiveness is achieved.

It should be mentioned that it takes substantial time and effort to reach that status of a "neutral place" within the company. During the first lab phase we experienced some intense discussions with department managers who feared that the lab might uncover fail-

Table 57.2 Roles and associated skills in the Smart Data Lab

Role	Skill profile
Data scientist	Comprehensive knowledge about data mining, statistics, data engineering and advanced computing
Business analyst	Visual data exploration skills and statistical knowledge
Data expert	Knows where to find the information tracking and describing a business situation within the data model, i. e. related variables and their meanings, codes, documentation issues, etc.
Business expert	Represents the business department, knowledge about background, business demands and existing decision rules
Project manager	Coordinates overall activities

ures in their past and current decision practice. It is often ignored that changing decision processes from experience- and command-driven to data-driven decision making would potentially attack hierarchical structures. We cannot emphasize enough the importance of communication, political work and sensitivity, as a Smart Data Lab, if it should function as intended, would initiate a change process for the organization as a whole which requires professional change management.

Change, however, is also necessary in terms of skill profiles of the analysts, especially when the focus of analytics turns from description to prediction or even prescription [3]. Descriptive analytics seeks to answer questions like: what and when did something happen? (Almost) no understanding of the underlying process or data is needed and particularly, time frames are irrelevant for the analysis. On the next stage, diagnostic analytics, one looks for explanations: why did it happen. To avoid the confusion of correlation with causation, the data-generating business process needs to be understood. When it comes to the next stage, predictive analytics, it is often necessary to transform data structures significantly, e. g. from a transactional data set to a data set consisting of customer signatures and from an ex-post to an ex-ante perspective [4]. Time plays an important role when it comes to questions like: what is likely to happen next? It can become a difficult and time-consuming task to re-build the necessary historical views, requiring professional skills in data management. Finally, prescriptive analytics in the last stage supports decisions: how can we make things happen? A model of the business process, its single components and their interactions is needed in order to optimize it. Therefore, skills in operations research and optimization techniques, e. g. numerical methods, are crucial.

At the end of the data analysis phase the results can be of different nature. This can be a prototype of a product for predicting long term staff planning or new insights about the analyzed business process. And sometimes it is even the realization that that the data quality or data coverage is insufficient to get reliable results.

57.3.4   Presentation of the Results

After the data analysis phase has ended, the results collected by then are firstly presented to the business department and afterwards to the executive board. The business departments have to assess the potential of the solution by calculating a business case and verifying the practicability of deploying the solution in daily business. According to the outcome of this evaluation the Smart Data Lab results are considered to be enhanced to an operationally mature product.

57.3.5   Transition into Production

The Smart Data Lab plays an important role in the procedure of problem solving steps, but it is only the first step. If a result is considered to be used in production the responsibility is handed over to the Smart Data Factory in order to create stable and reliable products running in productive environment. The Smart Data Factory has the responsibility to implement the product using standard components and procedures and to maintain and manage the life cycle of that analytical product. The most important tasks for the Smart Data Factory are the completion of model implementation, the management of the realization project and the change management initiated by the lab's results. Also, the factory is supposed to maintain and support the product, to monitor and retrain the model, to further develop the product and, not to forget, to train and coach the users.

The integration of analytical components into a productive application requires more than classical application maintenance and support like keeping up a system and running and guaranteeing a certain performance. The use of models means to ensure high quality of model generated information and to deliver the right information at the right time to the right people. Therefore, it is necessary to monitor and recalibrate models or to re-engineer them immediately if basic assumptions have changed. Most of the products are used in high critical production environments like operational control centers or security offices. The requirements regarding quality and availability are accordingly high.

57.4 Results from Smart Data Lab

57.4.1 Retail-Oriented Positioning of Flights

A big share of the profit in airport business is realized in the segment of retail and properties. Airports mostly act as concessionaire and not as shop owner. In that way, they earn money based on revenue participation and store rent with high margin and low cost. At Frankfurt Airport, the shopping range is significantly different within the terminals. Product offering, premium brands availability and shop presentation can vary considerably. The offering ranges from fashion & accessory over cosmetic and electronic devices to luxury goods like valuable watches or exquisite liquor. As manifold as the offering is presented, so are the preferences and needs of the customers. At an airport like Frankfurt, up to 200,000 passengers are moving through the terminal infrastructure passing shops and marketplaces constantly. At the end the purchase trigger depends on various factors like personality traits, the route to the gate, shops passed on this way, waiting and walking time or travel occasion. These are just a few examples of potential influencing variables explaining shopping behavior at an airport, s. Fig. 57.2: Variables and their relationships in the positioning model.

The positioning of a flight directly affects some of these variables. The amount and type of shops available close to the departure gate is one important factor directly affected. For transferring passengers, the positioning of arrival and departure flights results in routing and thereby in time needed for walking through the terminal and processing time for passing required check points. Frankfurt Airport guarantees a minimum connecting time

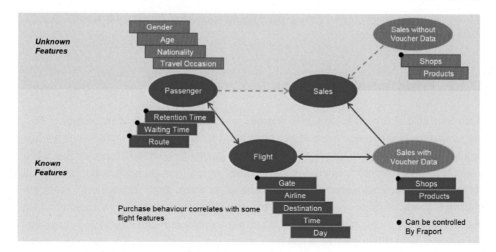

Fig. 57.2 Variables and their relationships in the positioning model

of 45 min from any gate-to-gate location. During the flight planning phase this objective is currently one of the highest priorities for positioning.

The task of the Smart Data Lab was to identify important variables and the strength of their influence on retail revenues and purchase probability by combining all available data and processing them with data analytics techniques. It is important to know which variables can be controlled by Fraport and how to adjust them to maximize retail revenues without running into other operational problems. For the first time the correlation of high waiting times, transfer distances or nationalities regarding retail revenues could be expressed in a multivariate model helping to understand their influences.

An analytical challenge was the substitution of known effects which was necessary for different reasons. Some of the passenger characteristics cannot be tracked for reasons of data privacy, e. g. their nationality. We used destination instead but found that data about the nationality itself, theoretically available from existing data sources, would lead to more accurate predictions. So, there are ongoing discussions on how that information could be gathered without violating privacy. Other characteristics like spending capacity or the motivation for traveling simply are not available on a customer level. An organizational challenge was the overcoming of existing decision rules that turned out to be myths. It was hard work to explain the difference between correlation and causation, including the issue of spurious or partial correlation, and the difference between a multivariate prescriptive model and descriptive, bivariate analysis. That challenge required excellent communication skills including an idea of political structures among the organization.

Two very important applications can be derived from the results generated out of the Smart Data Lab. First, the insights can be used for future negotiations with airlines about positioning scenarios or the exclusive and prioritized use of terminal areas. Second, current flight planning process in agreement with existing arrangement can be optimized to achieve some quick-wins on revenue lift without impairing superior objectives like the guaranteed transfer time.

57.4.2 Prediction of Arrival Time

Each time an aircraft arrives at a gate, various activities are kicked off immediately. Passengers jump off their seats impatient to grab their belongings and leave the aircraft while ground handlers open the airlock to unload baggage and freight containers are just a few examples of what might happen directly after the aircraft has stopped at the gate. What seems to be an ideal situation where ground handlers arrive just in time ready to start aircraft operations, is quite challenging in reality. There are two extreme situations which describe how the problem the Smart Data Lab was confronted with effects daily business. On the one hand this would be a situation where the aircraft arrives at the gate without all required equipment and staff available yet. On the other hand, it would be a situation where ground handling resources are bounded on position waiting for the aircraft to come to rest. While the first problem results in an inconvenience for passengers with missed connection flights and malus payments due to failing service level agreements, the second one implies high cost because of resources occupied while waiting for operation to start. The task of the Smart Data Lab was to improve the prediction of an arrival flight currently approaching the Frankfurt Airport in order to optimize dispatching of resources and thus reduce waiting time for both the passengers and ground handlers.

The final model combined different components: a model for the airspace movements, a ground movement model, a model for the usage of runways (especially dealing with swing-over probabilities) and a model for wheeling time. Not only the construction and parametrization of the different models was a challenge, but so was their combination and the interaction of parameters, including restrictions. An organizational challenge occurred as well. Data that were so far not included in managing the business process turned out to be extremely valuable in predicting arrival times. It also turned out that innovative operating figures invented by the Smart Data Lab would significantly improve the prediction. That means, it could become necessary to change the whole process, involving more than one department.

By combining data from radar, weather and flight operations, the Smart Data Lab has implemented a prototype of a prediction model which would reduce waiting times up to 60% and would contribute to improve the quality of service for passengers and airlines and to reduce the cost for ground handlers caused by idle capacity. Since the solution worked out by the Smart Data Lab affects a broad range of stakeholders including ground handlers, airlines, federal authorities and shippers, it is considered to be a mission with critical components essential for smooth operations in daily business.

57.5   Summary and Outlook

One of the key lessons learned was that problem solving with big data and analytics needs a lot more than expert knowledge in analytics and big data. The task of persuading other departments that analytics would be inevitable to make smarter decisions and would turn Frankfurt Airport into a digital-driven marketplace, turned out to be more difficult than any technological issues that came up. The incorporation of interdisciplinary practical expertise into nearly every single phase of the analytics process was crucial, in order to correctly interpret the results and to identify pitfalls which would have led to severely misleading conclusions.

The change process so far has only started. New business models discussed are co-operative Smart Data Labs with partners like Lufthansa, Deutsche Bahn etc. in order to create novel, integrative passenger services. Fraport also thinks of partner data models or even open data strategies, involving as many stakeholders as possible, not only as data providers, but also as users of the data and as developers of new applications. Finally, analytics-as-a-service driven by customer needs might lead to the development of smart applications. We observe a huge cultural transformation of the whole organization, turning Fraport into a digital marketplace both regarding the inner core of the company and its interactions with other parties.

References

1. R. Kitchin, The Data Revolution : big data, open data, data infrastructures & their consequences, London: Sage, 2014.
2. S. Goldsmith und S. Crawford, The Responsive City : engaging communities through data-smart governance, San Francisco: Wiley, 2014.
3. R. Sharda, D. Delen und E. Turban, Business Intelligence and Analytics : Systems for Decision Support, Essex: Pearson Education Limited, 2014.
4. G. S. Linoff und M. J. A. Berry, Data Mining Techniques for Marketing, Sales and Customer Relationship Management, Indianapolis: Wiley, 2011.

The Digitization Dilemma of Europe's Non-Profit Organizations: Software as a Service to the Rescue!

58

Florian Fuchs, Michael Liebmann, and Frank Thelen

Abstract

Europe's 5.5 million non-profit organizations (NPOs) with their 250 million members and volunteers are an integral part of European society. They include local clubs (e. g. sports, social, environmental), governing bodies (national/regional associations) and professional associations as well as educational institutions.

Radical societal and technological change is putting strong pressure on them to modernize and digitize. At the same time they suffer from an innovation dilemma.

We argue that the Software as a Service (SaaS) model offers them the only path to overcome these challenges. It will transform the pressure to digitize from a challenge into an opportunity and unfold both a strong business opportunity and an enormous social return for the society.

58.1 Introduction

Europe boasts more than 5.5 million non-profit organizations (NPOs) with 250 million members and volunteers. Examples are local clubs (e. g. sports, social, environmental),

F. Fuchs (✉) · M. Liebmann
doo GmbH
Munich, Germany
e-mail: florian.fuchs@doo.net

M. Liebmann
e-mail: michael.liebmann@doo.net

F. Thelen
e42 GmbH
Bonn, Germany
e-mail: frank@e42.com

© Springer-Verlag GmbH Germany 2018
C. Linnhoff-Popien et al. (eds.), *Digital Marketplaces Unleashed*,
https://doi.org/10.1007/978-3-662-49275-8_58

651

governing bodies (national/regional associations) and professional associations as well as educational institutions. The European Union (EU) has for many years emphasized the "social and economic cohesion" promoted by non-profit organizations (NPOs) and their "considerable economic contribution" [1]. It clearly recognizes both the challenges faced by NPOs and the potential of cloud computing for business model transformation.

However, the EU's recommendations for the "professionalization" and "moderniza-tion" of NPOs and educational enterprises are far from being met. According to the Commission "the main challenge for this sector are [...] the changes in the way peo-ple volunteer", and "growing tension as volunteers are confronted with increasingly de-manding tasks that require specific competences and skills". The Commission therefore recommends that the "professionalization" of non-profits and "the specific need of various groups (elderly, young people) must be better taken into account" [2].

On the other hand, the EU pushes the Digital Agenda for Europe and emphasizes the opportunities of cloud computing and the need to "enhance interoperability" and "strengthen online trust and security" in Software as a Service offerings in the cloud [3]. It works towards establishing one Digital Single Market in order to unlock the scale nec-essary for cloud computing to reach its full potential in Europe.

In this chapter we describe the specific challenges, which NPOs face and share in terms of digitization. We explain why NPOs are particularly threatened to be left behind and argue that the Software as a Service (SaaS) model of software delivery represents the only path to survival. To underpin our conclusion we compare SaaS adoption in other industries and estimate the social impact of a SaaS offering for NPOs on Europe's society.

58.2 Europe's Non-Profit Organizations Struggle with Digitization

Europe's NPOs are being left-behind by digitization: In spite of generating >160B € in revenues each year, the vast majority of Europe's 5.5 million NPOs are still using man-ual, 'archaic' processes for communication, interaction, administration and payments [4]. Member interactions mostly happen offline and are un-automated, unscalable and typi-cally very local. Even very large associations on national level still work with fax and offline processes. Even they are missing out on being role models for their smaller and more local affiliates. In a time of rapid societal change, this implies specific drawbacks.

58.2.1 Need to Digitize

Firstly, they have limited access to young people. Today's students face increasingly demanding curricula and employers expect higher flexibility and mobility from young professionals. This means that young people simply have less time for community and extracurricular activities. Furthermore, the "digitally native" generation tends to avoid tra-ditional interaction (post, fax, phone, checks ...).

Secondly, 85% of NPOs face difficulties staffing leadership positions [5]. As such, many NPOs are characterized by aging leadership, typically with less IT knowhow.

Lastly, increasing regulation and cost pressure increase workload and create frustration within NPOs – particularly as they heavily rely on manual processes.

To overcome these challenges, NPOs – just like any other enterprise – have to start taking advantage of digital technologies and automate manual procedures. At the same time, they must also increase member engagement through greater online and mobile interaction. However, this digital transformation is significantly more complex for NPOs than for profit-driven businesses, because of their inherent innovation dilemma and lack of scale.

58.2.2   Digitization Dilemma

The innovation dilemma in NPOs means that they face much greater difficulties adapting to the digital transformation than other business areas. As demonstrated in Fig. 58.1, lack of budget means that buying software from a typical systems provider far exceeds the budgets available to NPOs. Furthermore, with largely unpaid staff, lack of IT know-how prevents NPOs from choosing the best IT partners and managing implementation projects. Finally, leadership characterized by outdated admin procedures and unawareness of cloud services means that, more generally, NPOs have low innovative capacity.

This unfolds a vicious cycle: NPOs with lower innovative capacity drift further away from attracting new and young members. Yet, without youth engagement, there is limited chance to increase innovative capacity. As a result, the digital landscape within NPOs ranges from purely paper-based processes to a patchwork of half-integrated solutions. Indeed, for NPOs that are using some SaaS applications, a second dimension to the dilemma

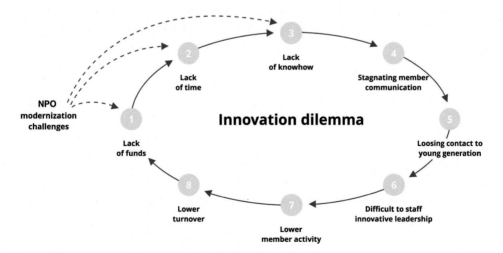

Fig. 58.1 Vicious cycle of innovation dilemma in NPOs

emerges – with NPOs struggling to manage multiple, stand-alone applications that have to be used separately and have different policies for using (or misusing) their data.

58.3   Characteristics of Software as a Service

Fostered by the proliferation of cloud computing, Software as a Service (SaaS) has become a popular licensing and delivery model for software:

> [Software as a Service is] software that's developed and hosted by the SaaS vendor and which the end user customer accesses over the Internet. Unlike traditional packaged applications that users install on their computers or servers, the SaaS vendor owns the software and runs it on computers in its data center. The customer does not own the software but effectively rents it, usually for a monthly fee [6].

Such a delivery model for software carries multiple benefits [7]:

Quick access to innovation SaaS enables vendors to manage updates themselves. As a result, customers have the benefit of always working with the latest version and vendors can innovate faster because they have to maintain only one version.

Fewer upfront costs SaaS is provided as a ready-to-use service. So customers do not have to purchase hardware or fund an IT project upfront in order to get started.

Fast deployment Being a ready-to-use service, SaaS enables customers to start using it immediately. Through easy-to-use user interfaces SaaS vendors will make sure that none or only very little training is required.

Lower Total Cost of Ownership (TCO) SaaS vendors handle software and hardware maintenance as part of their offering so customers do not have to budget for additional maintenance cost. Since vendors enjoy economies of scale, they can distribute cost across all their customers and therefore usually demand much lower prices.

Greater processing efficiencies SaaS fosters specialization so SaaS vendors are dedicating all their resources to carrying out the desired task and therefore have should have a very efficient solutions. On the other hand SaaS customers are able to focus their resources on their core competencies instead.

Early insights into best practices and benchmarks SaaS vendors with a critical mass of customers gain valuable insights in best practices and benchmarks of the targeted industry. This data is usually unique and not available elsewhere. It enables SaaS vendors to improve their service offering further and to educate their customers, thus benefiting all of them.

Easier integration with standard tools SaaS vendors want to address a broad audience. So they make sure that their solutions can be integrated with existing software and systems out-of-the-box.

Less risk Taken together all the characteristics above result in a very low risk level for adopting a SaaS solution. It is cheap, quick and easy to test-drive before deciding to adopt it and come with only little commitments while using it.

In summary, SaaS offers significantly less development, operational and maintenance cost (as it is shared across all customers) with specialized knowhow and central focus at vendor level to crack the most complex workflow requirements. What is more, offering tools in the form of web plugins can radically simplify integration into a NPO's existing website.

Empirically the typical cost reduction potential through SaaS averages at 30% across industries when compared with traditional software cost [8]. Taking into account process cost savings from less manual labor, savings are even more significant: survey results from the NPO sector estimate annual cost savings of 50–70% besides a strong engagement uplift of members upon mobile and online interaction [9].

58.4   Software as a Service is a Game-Changer for the Digitization of Non-Profit Organizations

Contrasting the benefits of SaaS with the needs of Europe's NPO, s. Table 58.1, shows that SaaS offers a way out of the innovation dilemma.

However, the applicability of the SaaS model to NPO's depends on the existence of shared requirements among this target group so that economies of scale can be achieved.

58.4.1   Non-Profit Organizations Share Common Demands

Based on user feedback of existing doo [10] customers (over 4000 customer interviews within 10 months) and existing research in NPO operations [9] the process requirements of NPOs on software have been identified. In addition a specifically designed survey investigating NPOs' IT needs was conducted in March 2015 by doo and the University of

Table 58.1 NPO's innovation dilemma vs. characteristics of SaaS

Dilemma of NPOs	Characteristics of SaaS
Lack of budget	Fewer upfront cost, lower total cost
Lack of time	Fast deployment, greater processing efficiencies
Lack of know how	Quick access to innovation, insights into best practices and benchmarks, less risk

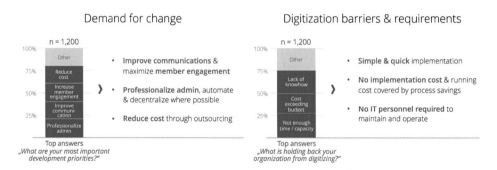

Fig. 58.2 Excerpt of survey results. (Source: University of Freiburg; N = 176)

Freiburg [11]. It was completed by over 176 European NPOs of different sizes. The results were strongly consistent across all types of NPOs, s. Fig. 58.2, with a clear modernization demand and struggle to overcome adoption obstacles. The results indicated that reducing costs, increasing member engagement, improving communications and professionalizing admin were the main needs.

What is more, strong time requirements, high cost and lack of knowhow are constantly stated as the main digitization barriers. Over 90% of respondents identified cloud and SaaS technology as viable option to help overcome modernization barriers, but experienced difficulties identifying and selecting the best software tools for their activity and were worried about data security.

58.4.2 Digitization of Member Interactions

The analysis mentioned above found that NPOs will particularly benefit from digitizing typical member interactions because these have the highest potential for fostering member engagement and lowering process handling cost. Member interactions can be categorized as follows:

Improve member communication The majority of interactions with members are via multiple 'offline' communication channels (phone, fax and mail). Newsletters are sometimes sent by email, but non-integrated and without state-of-the-art tracking capabilities. Thus, valuable information such as readership or interactive feedback gets lost. In clubs and associations where information and education play a major role, it is particularly vital to know which offering reaches and engages their members.

Facilitate member activities and engagement All NPOs offer some kind of events or activities to their members. This requires the registration of participants, gathering of participant data and sometimes collection of ticket prices. Today's members expect user-friendly, mobile registrations with online payment, while most NPOs are still stuck at offline methods thus frustrating members and hindering engagement.

Empower members through self-service In most organizations, member admin is a central issue that requires on-site manual labor. Empowering members to do most of their admin themselves through a web or mobile application significantly reduces manual effort and enables new services for further increasing member engagement (feedback/voting tools, data sharing and privacy preferences, etc.)

This list allows to identify three functional modules, which need to be covered by a SaaS offering for NPOs:

Community Communication Distribution of news and other content as well as the promotion of activities and events to the community. The required feature set includes email newslettering, email and social marketing campaigns as well as tracking and collection of feedback.

Activity Management Handling activities, registrations, payment/invoicing, participants and accounting usually demand huge manual effort. Integration should be light-weight, e. g. through web plugins, so that entire activity calendars can easily be integrated in existing websites and taken online and mobile. NPOs have very different feature requirements that typical booking tools cannot fulfil, thus specialized feature sets are required.

Member Self-Service Empowering community members to update their master data such as personal details, manage payments and update or cancel registrations or bookings.

Offering these three module in one integrated platform benefits each of them in return:

Community communication allows to promote activities and benefits from up-to-date member data collected from registration processes and member self-services.

Activity management makes use of community communication to distribute information about activities and profits from member self-services, which empower members to manage their registrations themselves.

Member self-service empowers members to control their communication preferences themselves and manage their activity registrations and payments.

In summary, a SaaS offering which covers these three modules would enable NPOs to break out of the innovation dilemma and to leverage digitization in order to increase member engagement and significantly lower admin cost.

58.5   Discussion

Why SaaS has benefited many other industries before and is addressing the NPOs sector only now can be explained by the S-curve of Software as a Service adoption. The impact it will have on society as a whole will be much greater still.

58.5.1   S-Curve of Software as a Service Adoption

NPOs are not a market traditionally associated with significant growth, as the number of entities, members, and budget size will not noticeably change over the coming years. However, the NPO market is experiencing stronger and stronger pressure to shift budgets towards modernization and digitization, and particularly towards SaaS solutions. Across all industries, SaaS is experiencing growth of 15–20% p. a.

While for-profit enterprises are noticeably more advanced in SaaS-adoption, NPOs are – as previously demonstrated – strongly behind. This can be simply illustrated using the S-curve model typically used to demonstrate innovation adoption, s. Fig. 58.3. For-profit enterprises are the fastest adopters of SaaS solutions. Larger companies are following, while typical SMEs are gaining traction. NPOs on the other hand are still in an early stage. This typically indicates that extreme growth is to be expected in the coming years.

This growth potential is also demonstrated by existing research: in a survey of 176 NPOs, 90% of respondents indicated that SaaS and cloud services will become increasingly important for their organization in the near future [11].

58.5.2   Social Impact

NPOs will benefit from adopting a SaaS platform in three main areas: (1) increased member engagement, (2) increased admin efficiency and (3) admin cost reduction.

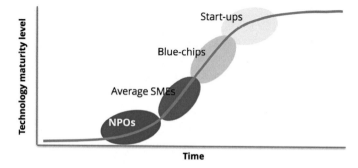

Fig. 58.3 S-curve scheme for SaaS adoption. (Source: doo)

To achieve the three benefits mentioned above, NPOs typically face a significant step-up in IT/platform cost (which creates a high adoption risk). One of the huge advantages of SaaS, particularly with a pay-per-use business model, is the ability to offer and integrate feature richness at significantly lower cost, effort and complexity compared with customized on-premise solutions (that require long implementation, costly development and expensive maintenance contracts).

As shown in Fig. 58.4 (column 1), the average European NPO has an annual budget of 29,100 €, of which ~ 25% is spent on administration (activity registration, communication, payments, etc.). As shown in column 2, around 60% of this admin cost bracket is dedicated to manual labor and 40% to IT and systems cost (this means an average IT budget of 2900 €, smaller clubs spend usually much less and larger associations significantly more).

NPOs that modernize and automate their member interactions and admin (column 3), typically get rid of 75% of their process cost (from 4500 to 1100 € on average). However, adapting an IT system requires significant investment. Based on a total-cost-of-ownership (including maintenance and upgrades) customized/on-premise systems can cost more than they save. This is one of the main drivers of the innovation dilemma in NPOs. Very large NPOs are willing to pay the price, as member engagement and admin professionalization are more important than cost reduction. However, the majority of NPOs are unable to increase IT spending.

A SaaS cost scheme and pay-per-use revenue model turns things around (column 4): now the aforementioned benefits are available in one integrated platform, while even reducing IT cost (from 2900 to 2100 € on average). The key here: smaller NPOs pay only relative to their usage. Thus, all kinds of NPOs can make full use of a SaaS offering – unlike the offering of typical in-house software providers that bill by the hour!

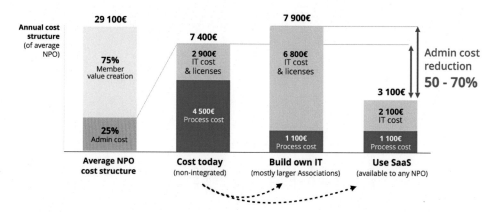

Fig. 58.4 SaaS cost advantage compared to today and on-premise solution. (Source: University of Freiburg)

Benefit	Method	Lever	NPO impact p.a. in €		Rational
			per NPO	Base 2020	
Admin cost reduction	Side-by-side cost comparison	Process cost reduction (i.e. more automation)	3 500	185M	>80% of manual processes in NPOs are member-related and highly repeatable (avg. NPO member admin cost 4 500€ p.a., saving ~75%)
		IT cost reduction (i.e. no licese, maintenance or development cost)	800	42M	Avg. IT spend ~2 900€, SaaS platform cost -30% based on interviews/ studies (note: reduction vs. on-premise solutions significantly higher)
Increase in admin efficiency	Social return	Freed-up member/user time (due to less manual interactions)	1 960	104M	Saving 18mins per month per member, 45 members per entity with avg. salary of 12 EUR/h (i.e. 44 EUR per member per year)
		Attracting higher leadership qualification with same budget	1 000	53M	Measured as 10% increase in annual salary, without additional payout (applied 10K annual salary to reflect voluntary/paid mix)
Increase in member engagement	Social return	Increasing activity/offering usage (i.e. member activity)	1 940	103M	~10% incr. in activity usage, quantified as +10% gross value add for activities (avg. revenue per NPO is 29K €, thereof 2/3 activty offering)
		Increasing offering effectiveness (i.e. improve in content relevance)	485	26M	~5% incr. of educational effects, quantified as +5% membership value add (avg. revenue per NPO is 29K €, thereof 1/3 memberships)
		Total	9 685	513M	

Fig. 58.5 Social return of a SaaS offering for NPOs. (Source: University of Freiburg)

NPOs main modernization goals are increasing member engagement and professionalizing administration. Since NPOs are not profit-driven per-se, but have community- or network-oriented goals, it is not possible to calculate direct economic effects from these benefits. We can, however, calculate the social return, allowing us to capture and quantify community-oriented and social effects.

When professionalizing admin, we essentially liberate members to dedicate more time to supporting member value creation (e. g. in sports: training and coaching). The annual social return of more member free time is estimated at 1960 € per NPO (see Fig. 58.5). Additionally, more professional admin processes help to attract leadership with more time-consuming daytime jobs but higher qualification and management skills, with an effect of additional social return of 1000 € per NPO.

Increasing member engagement happens on two levels (quantity and quality): (1) increasing member sign-ups for activities and other offerings. Significantly eased registration/interaction and more astute communication will lift the overall engagement level by at least 10%, corresponding with 1940 € per NPO per year. (2) Increasing the effectiveness of the offering as NPOs gain better visibility of what their members actually demand and consume adds another 485 € per NPO.

The total impact of a SaaS offering for NPOs is 9865 € per NPO per year, considering direct economic effects and social return combined (see Fig. 58.5). Comparing the average NPO 21,700 € spend on member value-add, such a SaaS offering will be able to increase this value-add by 45%. The mere social return of the a SaaS platform 2020, serving more than 50,000 NPOs thus reaches a combined value of more than 513 million €. This is just for 50,000 NPOs out of the 5.5 million in the EU.

58.6   Conclusion

Europe's 5.5 million non-profit organizations (NPOs) with their 250 million members and volunteers are an integral part of European society. However, they are left-behind by digitization and caught in the vicious cycle of an innovation dilemma: Due to lack of funds, time and know how they are stuck with outdated technology and struggle with keeping up leadership motivation and member engagement, which prevents them from escaping this downward spiral.

Cloud computing has led to the emergence of Software as a Service (SaaS) as a delivery model for software. It transfers the task of developing, maintaining and running a software from the customer to the vendor and thus significantly reduces the risk for the customer. For the vendor it creates massive economies of scale, which enables them pass on cost savings to their customers of 50–70% per year.

For NPOs and their need to digitize their member interactions SaaS therefore offers an escape route from the innovation dilemma: It allows them to use high-quality software instantly, with no upfront cost and little running cost. Based on our requirements analysis a SaaS offering for NPOs needs to provide workflows for community communication, activity management and member self-services.

Compared to other industries, NPOs will be late adopters of SaaS. However, it will not only have a business impact but also an impact on society. The social impact of a SaaS offering for NPOs was estimated as 9865 € per NPO per year increasing this value-add by 45%. The mere social return of a SaaS platform which serves 50,000 NPOs thus reaches a combined value of more than 513 million € by 2020.

References

1. European Committee of the Regions, The contribution of volunteering to Economic and Social Cohesion, 2008.
2. European Commission, Erasmus Plus Programme Guide, 2015.
3. "Digital Agenda for Europe," [Online]. Available: https://ec.europa.eu/digital-agenda/en/digital-single-market. [Accessed 02 08 2016].
4. J. &. L.-C. A. Ariza-Montes, ICT Management in Non-Profit Organisations, Business Science Reference, 2014.
5. E. Priller, Associations on the border, Social Science Center Berlin, 2013.
6. M. Levinson, "Software as a Service (SaaS) – Definition and Solutions, cio.com," 2007. [Online]. Available: http://www.cio.com/article/2439006/web-services/software-as-a-service--saas--definition-and-solutions.html. [Accessed 02 08 2016].
7. H. Cheang, "The Arguments for Software-as-a-Service (SaaS)," cimpl.com, 2014. [Online]. Available: http://blog.cimpl.com/bid/205831/The-Arguments-for-Software-as-a-Service-SaaS. [Accessed 02 08 2016].
8. Z. Diamadi, A. Dubey, D. Pleasance und A. Vora, Wining in the SMB Cloud: Charting a path to success, McKinsey & Company, Tech, Media and Telecom, 2011.
9. D. Neumann, M. Liebmann und F. Thelen, Digitization on the Non-profit Sector – Overcoming the Innovation Dilemma, Freiburg: University of Freiburg – Public and Non-profit Management – Concept-Paper-Series, 2015.
10. doo, "doo – Smart Online Event Management & Marketing Software," doo.net, 2016. [Online]. Available: https://doo.net. [Accessed 02 08 2016].
11. D. Neumann und M. Liebmann, Cloud Software – Chance or Risk for Small Non-Profit Institutions?, Freiburg: University of Freiburg – Public and Non-profit Management, 2015.

Consumer Journey Analytics in the Context of Data Privacy and Ethics

Andreas Braun and Gemma Garriga

Abstract

By *Big Data Analytics* we understand new technologies and methods that go beyond how data and analytics was previously handled. On the data side, extremely large data sets can be stored and processed, even real-time, and at reasonable cost. On the analytical side, methods are no longer limited to hard-coded (business) rules or statistics, but leverage Artificial Intelligence (AI) and particularly Machine Learning (ML). In this paper we argue that Big Data's quickest business wins and first tangible impact is in the domain of customer/consumer analytics, summarized as *Digital Consumer Journey Analytics*. Such journeys are constructed from people's movement and navigational patterns in both the virtual and physical world; while individual data points are at first not very expressive, the picture created by continuous collection of ubiquitous data and their history, allows to unveil almost any identity profile. Under this increasingly digital environment, staying in the relevant set of consumers is of utmost importance for businesses. Big Data Analytics can support by, e. g., driving product and service design and customer experience improvements. However, there are increasing limitations to the possibilities of Big Data Analytics in consumer businesses, in particular Data Privacy and Data Ethics. Businesses have to deal with a growing appetite of legislation and prudential regulation, e. g., the EU GDPR. The challenge is to make data-driven offerings trusted in the digital age. In this paper we will illustrate the journey in an

A. Braun (✉)
Allianz SE
Munich, Germany
e-mail: andreas.braun1@allianz.com

G. Garriga
INRIA Research Center
Rocquencourt, France
e-mail: gemma.garriga@inria.fr

© Springer-Verlag GmbH Germany 2018
C. Linnhoff-Popien et al. (eds.), *Digital Marketplaces Unleashed*,
https://doi.org/10.1007/978-3-662-49275-8_59

insurance business to grow successful Big Data Use Cases in Consumer Analytics and discuss Privacy by Design (PbD) and Private Enhancing Technologies (PET) as means to build trusted data-driven products and services.

59.1 Introduction

Big Data Analytics plays a key role in transforming traditional businesses to digital ones. While many typical applications of Big Data are relatively well understood and uncritical—typically all analytics on non-person related data and information—both the biggest immediate business impact as well as challenge comes with person related data (or personally identifiable information, PII). These threats to companies now become even more tangible as we are approaching the implementation of the General Data Protection Regulation/Act (GDPR/A) in Europe. In this paper, we focus on challenges implementing data protection, privacy, and ethics by the example of consumer analytics and digital consumer decision journeys more specifically. We argue that respecting privacy under the regime of the GDPR requires trusted technical means and measures, such as Privacy by Design (PbD) and Privacy Enhancing Technology (PET) frameworks.

The *consumer decision journey* [1–3] refers to the life cycle of a consumer from the moment of first contact to the ultimate purchase (see Fig. 59.1); this cycle includes also end-to-end user experience, starting from an initial trigger, via several touch points, to a purchasing decision, continue using the product or service, and finally being an advocate. The consumer decision journey is structured in loops, representing consideration, enjoyment, and loyalty (different authors may use other terms). The model of a consumer journey appreciates the fact that todays' consumers have many options, and many of them may get into the picture during the evaluation phase, hence creating a far more dynamic and agile process than traditional funnels.

Fig. 59.1 The life cycle in a consumer decision journey

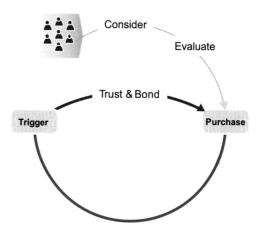

In fact, the graph of a journey tells the overall story across multiple touch points in various channels. The big change in the digital world are especially the speed and vastly increasing turnaround times, the dynamic set of options, and the number of external influencers, such as product ratings, social media, etc. As today most touch points are digital (social media, page and ad impressions, TV (return channel), product ratings, search topics, ...), the data representation of the digital consumer journey abounds.

Big Data and analytics capabilities have been in turn developed to analyze digital journeys and to understand and influence consumer journeys in real-time. Potential questions are translated into hypothesis applied in analytics, such as e. g., *Consumer profile*—by which category can a distinct consumer be described? *interest*—what is the specific consumer interest? *Next best product*—what is she most likely to buy next? *Cross- and upsell*—what other product or services can be offered? *Trends in consumer interest and behavior*—how is consumer interest changing and how to adapt to stay relevant? How can a brand innovate based on trends in consumer behavior?

59.1.1   Big Data Enabled Digital Consumer Analytics

Big Data infrastructures and analytics are the technology enablers that can ingest and process large semi- and unstructured data needed to build models and predict propensity behavior. For example, when ingesting large digital consumer journey data sets, these are represented by heterogeneous set of digital traces such as web logs, cookies from different devices and pages, tracking pixels, sensor data, online surveys, discussions and online blogs, emails and others. With data engineering we merge and match all the various collected data sources to build knowledge representation from the sources. Machine Learning (ML) models can then utilize these representations indifferent ways: e. g. by learning behaviors from known historical data, by modeling higher level abstractions with complex structures, like non-linear transformations, by finding complex patterns to explain and model a given phenomenon. Learned models can be used in real-time to predict propensities (i. e., to convert, to churn, to cross and up-sell, next best action etc.).

Hence, Big Data Analytics actively shapes the decision journeys of consumers by allowing businesses to continuously optimize processes, understand the needs of consumers and stay in control. Consumer journeys have become central to the customer's experience and as important as the products itself. As in an ever faster digital game, customers switch digital services and products at the tip of a finger, user experience will be the key differentiator. In the Experience Economy [4], each product or service will need to strive for constant user 'sensations' in contrast to focusing company's internal needs.[1]

---

[1] Extending on the "Experience Economy", we believe that eventually the biggest impact of big data analytics lies beyond customer analytics. However, customer analytics and journeys are used here to explain to the current state and conflicts with data privacy topics.

59.1.2 A Broader Notion of Digital Marketing

As competition and the speed of decisions making—for or against a product—ever increases, today's challenge for businesses is to *stay in the relevant set of brands of consumers*. This broadens the borders of sales and expands the notion of marketing. We believe that marketing will become programmatic blending into real-time and online algorithms to go beyond recommending the next best product and eventually compiling product bundles and creating services on-the-fly tailored for one single customer and beyond 'one-size fits all' (*the segment of one*).

Although understanding digital journeys is key to stay relevant, we argue that promoting journey innovation and customer experience is the next step. Businesses can use Big Data Analytics to understand and promote new digital business models for example. This implies going to phases of continuous prototyping and gathering data of how new services, features and totally new ideas are received by users. The analysis of the consumer and customer reactions tells the story of how these new business ideas can develop into bigger contexts and markets.

59.1.3 From Analytical Veracity, Data Privacy and Ethics to Trust in the Digital Age

Big Data is a technology-driven game changer with impact on but not limited to traditional IT, analytics, marketing, and privacy. We now realize and get a firm grasp on the positive influencers, e. g., how horizontal-scaling systems change IT, how ML takes analytics to the next level, and how digital consumer journeys broaden the notion and role of marketing, while marketing in turn boosts user experience. In contrast, we just start to understand the challenges. Big Data can and is used to unveil personally identifiable information (or PII) and identities in supposed anonymized information. For instance, mobile movement patterns and trajectories can be used to identify almost all individuals in a country, even though all source data is anonymized [5]. People are increasingly tracked, profiled, and analyzed in social media, web, while using mobile phones, or connected cars.

The following discussion is based on our experiences in conceiving, building, and anchoring a Big Data Analytics competence center in a very large multi-national organization. We will illustrate our approach to focus on Big Data-driven marketing, consumer analytics, and experience to deliver value fast. Most importantly, we describe how the privacy by design framework (general frameworks presented in [6, 7]) can help to ensure privacy and how we can address data ethics to deliver trust in the digital age.

59.2   Staying in the Relevant Set of Consumers

In today's digital business world, consumers are empowered to compare and benchmark. The traditional linear sales funnel [1, 8]—starting with an initial set of options and working towards a decision—is not valid anymore. Consumers arrived at an interactive and iterative process. This brings fail fast and trial and error to the purchasing process and the digital consumer journey as such became *agile*[2]. The combination of Big Data technology and advanced analytics helps businesses to enter and remain in the relevant set of their customers. This means that all internal processes are supported in an automated way to streamline the different journey steps.

Artificial Intelligence (AI) and Machine Learning (ML) play an important role to help businesses staying in the relevant set of consumers. ML is a discipline in AI and refers to technology and algorithms that can learn and make predictions based on large data sets, including historical events. For example, deep learning, is inspired by advancements in neurosciences where algorithms learn abstract representations from data by using multiple processing layers with complex structures. Deep learning is nowadays applied successfully e. g., in image and speech recognition. Another relevant example of ML is online learning, where algorithms adapt predictive models on the fly as data is being continuously processed. Notable examples can be found in online advertisement and customer journey classification.

The ML approach in Big Data Analytics is different from, and overcomes the limitations of, rule engines or statistics. Patterns and features learned can be enormously complex and go way beyond human limitations of cognitive perception. ML models can be designed to be dynamically, interactive, and online, which means that they can be self-improving 'on-the-fly'. ML today further allows for very fast and real-time application in digital consumer journeys. Using ML and predictive analytics in general is not a new topic for digital businesses and brands that digitize their interactions with customers. Within the context of Big Data and the analysis of Digital Consumer Journeys, ML goes one step beyond by boosting prediction power and supporting the optimization and automatization of processes within the journey decision.

Examples of successful digital customer journey/analytics use cases developed within the insurance business are e. g.:

- Customer retention and improved customer experience. We build models to understand and segment consumers and prospect customers. With advanced data engineering, we blend data from all collected data sources—either based on past interactions, transactional systems, product usage, Web logs and internal cookies—and build ML models that will accurately predict the propensity of a customer to churn based on the stored digital traces. Beyond that, we also build complementary models that can identify the

---

[2] *Agile development* is a paradigm in software engineering that embraces lightweight processes, quick iterations, prototyping/trial and error, and subsequent improvement iteration (Beck).

"pain points" that most likely will turn customers unsatisfied with the experience of our brand. For that, we collect also NPS (Net Promoter Score, [9]) data and correlate it to the current observed effects on churning customers. Our models can subsequently be used to monitor those issues and target the most efficient repair. Repairing the experience of a customer goes in hand by offering a better service and a better deal, for example for specific customer segments. In this sense, ML models will then predict what is the next best action for a customer in order to retain her and continue being in the relevant set. All these models are streamlined in real-time systems that support re-contacting the customer with the next best action.

- Proactive personalization. We use information about users navigating on the Allianz websites—e. g. based on past interactions if we detect that the user is a customer, on past navigation patterns and external data sources—in order to dynamically customize the experience of a user on our website. Our models predict the most probable interest of the user at a given point in time and therefore, Web pages and applications can be rearranged accordingly. The required analytic models for proactive understanding of the customer needs, help to personalize and optimize next steps of a consumer journey. For example, for good value customers we can take the action to personalize with the best-value offer; e. g. if a frequent traveler customer comes to the Allianz website, we can personalize content in order to help the customer understand the most useful dynamic upgrades of her travel insurance.

- Consumer quote conversion and best discount accommodation. We identify consumers with high potential and interest to become future customers of Allianz. Based on the digital traces of previously submitted quotes of a given insurance product, we build models that predict the best moment to approach the consumer and the best possible discount to funnel the buying decision. We also integrate these models into real-time processes linked to call centers or agencies within Allianz. For example, for a user that is detected to have submitted several quote requests for a car insurance with different parameters online, we can predict the best time to approach her with the right offer that suits better her car insurance needs.

- Cross- and Up-selling bundled products to fit the new customer needs. We build predictive models to understand what might be the needs of our customers in order to provide a simplified bundled set of insurance products into one. Our models predict the propensity to buy a new product in the Allianz portfolio (cross-sell) or to upgrade the current product that the customer owns (up-sell). This task is easily combined in real-time with the proactive personalization discussed in the use case above. Indeed, by understanding better the customer needs, we can optimize the best price for upgrades and bundled cross-selling products such that the customer obtains better coverage for the best suited price. For example, for a customer with a house insurance product that has been navigating on the Allianz website in search of legal insurance, we can automatically personalize content in order to offer a bundle of the two products with best legal service included in the household.

- Real-time monitoring to adapt to current consumer trends. We track customers across different channels and blend data from multiple sources—e. g. from past interactions, transactional systems, Web logs and external data—in order to have single view of what customers are doing and what happens as a result. We create comprehensive views of the digital costumer journey in the form of dynamic clusters and segmentations that can be easily visualized by business experts. Every cluster is explained for the business analyst, e. g. the segment of young family consumer that own a small car and are likely to change to a more spacious car in the near future. Our monitoring application provides dynamic segmentation models and interfaces with Market Management departments, who can then monitor in real-time trends and address concerns such as conversion of quotes, retention or optimizing parameters of products.
- Fraud prevention and fast-paying of "white" claims. We provide a flexible approach for claim fraud detection, prevention and claim management within Allianz. This is also part of the experience in the experience phase of a customer journey, as customers would like to engage with companies that keep fraud processes under control so to avoid overloads in premiums and get back money paid for claims fast. Internal and external data sources are blended to explore networks of involved parties and compute fraud indicators associated to claims. Predictive models can then predict the propensity of fraudulent behavior in a network and within a set of filed claims. These models are combined with an ensemble of predictions at the level of filed documents, history of claims and geo-location of incidents. Complementary, with the same data we also build models that decide when claims are not fraudulent and therefore can be paid quickly and fast-tracked. Fraud analytics is also considered important to improve the user perception, as while on the one side it is important to keep the portfolio clean of fraudsters to protect the candid policy holders, it also improves their user experience as they are paid faster.

In all the above described use cases, a critical issue is to continually do A/B testing to compare alternative versions of the decision process (e. g. a Group A would follow the journey as planned by a predictive model and a Group B would be the control group that would simply follow the regular traditional approach without much influence). Continuously testing, evaluation, and adaption in a rigorous scientific way helps to identify what works better and how internal processes need to be adapted to improve even further.

59.3   The Era of New Digital Business Models

The value of chain of digital business models is fully embedded in digital processes. Interface with other processes or entities are digital, e. g., even human interactions occur on smart phones, within apps etc. Further, a digital business model does not copy a legacy model 1:1, but focusses on what is done best in the digital world and may not fully cover or copy the traditional end-to-end process. Digital business models are based on auctions, peer-to-peer, or crowd-sourcing, for instance. We use external and internal data to expand the digital journey and pursue innovative business models for our customers and prospect customers. Ultimately, the goal is to rethink the insurance business and identify sources of value in any new way that matters to customers.

Focusing on specific digital journeys for car insurance for example, innovation could be to go beyond motor insurance products fixed to one specific car. Telematics-based motor insurance products do not quite fit the digital aspiration as they mainly extend the traditional model by adding more fine-grained data to the underwriting process (driver specific data, such as age, residence, was always included in premium calculation). Further, they lack aspects of the experience phase.

The next phase would be, in our view, a digital mobility service. This new product would cover any type of movement of a customer (e. g. with own car, bike, walking, taxi, shared car, bus, etc.), with insurance coverage applied seamlessly and transparently (e. g., automatically at any time, or for a desired period of time, at the click of a button in an app, etc.). The advantage for the customer is that a mobility insurance can be adapted to the usage of any transportation means where she would like to be protected. The new customer would be sharing critical information (such as spatial data) just for the time the insurance is required. Big Data analytics would create models of adaptive risk prediction to estimate the best price for the current trajectory of the customer at a limited time span.

More interestingly, peer-to-peer services between costumers can be added in order to create a network to complement any sort of digital mobility journey. This can be used to share information on predicted dangerous routes, traffic conditions, or free parking lots which might also be shared or handed over between participants in the network. Other data-driven insurance models can evolve around crowd insurance, where a group of comparable customers are pooled so that they jointly cover their risks backed by pre-paid premiums. If paid claims fall below of the pooled amount, then insurance becomes cheaper for the whole pool of customers. If claims exceed the pre-paid premiums, coverage is limited to the available amount (back pay or re-insurance could also be applied). This approach also leverages a fully digital business model, hence significantly reducing operational cost. The choice of pooled customers as well as their likelihood to be accepted for the crowd framework, would be controlled once more by advanced predictive models that can predict individual risk and the effect on the whole pool.

Ultimately, the move from selling insurance products to managing risk-preventing and social enhancing customer journeys requires continuous testing and evaluation in a controlled environment. New business ideas can be now easily tested given the new data-driven approach. Data helps understanding what works and what can be done better to continuously add value, improve, and refine journey innovation of customers.

Data-driven businesses can only deliver value when data is shared and is made available. Hence, next generation Data Ecosystems support data sharing and data consumption/use without the need for data ownership. Data ecosystems refer to a highly heterogeneous data environment, where users generate data from any connected devices, from cars to smartphones and toasters. Usually, each device initially only sees its individual and isolated context, hence is relatively blind and dumb. Data and information from various devices and potentially across corporate platforms should be shared with the underlying ecosystem. The ecosystem can open up data for a certain purpose or service at a certain point in time or timeframe (based on security/privacy rules, see Privacy by Design). The data ecosystem becomes the engine and brain behind digital devices, providing them with contextual information and predictive services.

These possibilities in fact raise however very important issues of data protection, trust, and data ethics, such as e. g., who owns the data in a data ecosystem? How can data be shared ensuring data protection? How can businesses prove acceptable use of data to their customers, and how can customers be in control? In the next section we will approach this issue and argue for technology-driven framework and Privacy by Design specifically.

59.4   Data Protection, Trust, and Data Ethics

As data and analytics become increasingly business relevant, governments, agencies, and public companies increasingly accumulate massive amounts of person-related data and information. The nature of Big Data, however, is to store data beforehand for later use, not initially knowing what that would be. As such, from a consumer perspective, immense knowledge about people is aggregated, potentially with negative impact. The GDPR accounts for this by putting a bundle of regulations around the acquisition, storage, and use of personally relatable data—along with substantial fines. In turn, companies may pile up the next asbestos if end-to-end data processes are not fully compliant and controlled. Hence, data privacy and ethics beyond IT security will tremendously grow in importance as leveraging data on the one side will deliver significant competitive advantage and eventually better products and services, on the other hand puts an immediate risk on companies if they do not comply with future laws.

Data protection basically comprises security plus privacy. Security is a rather technical IT[3]-related topic, focusing mainly on protecting physical, infrastructural, and software-related topics, such as confidentiality (information is protected from unauthorized views), integrity (data is not changed or removed without rights), availability (services and data are available when needed), and non-repudiation (proved traceability of data-related transactions, ACID-guaranteed) (see e. g., [10]). Security is a legal requirement and obligation. (Data) privacy, in contrast, is closely related to analytics and not IT. Focus areas are typically principles/guidelines: transparency, freedom of choice, consent, personal identifiable information (PII), data economy (data minimalism), prior stated purpose, necessity, direct inquiry, and appropriation. Privacy is a legal right, often a constitutional right.

---

[3] We define IT as infrastructure, hardware, and basic software, such as operating systems; we exclude higher-level layers, such as business applications, data, and analytics.

Data ethics is far less tangible and considers even philosophical questions, such as "who is the owner of the data?" vs. "will there be data ownership at all[4]"?—the human being creating the data or the supplier of the technical device recording it? What are the ethical limits of analytics and potential actions triggered? How can data be shared and leveraged while respecting individual's rights? Data ethics still is more in the grey area of feelings, opinions, and right treatment. That is also why people are willing to open up much more data for a company if they receive a useful service in return. Also, the potential (use, value, damage) of data given away by consumers is usually opaque and perceived very differently by individuals.

The European Union (EU) rightly treats Big Data and privacy as topic on their own and discusses a data protection regulation since the first legislative proposal of the Commission in 2012. Data anonymity (or the concept of personal identifiable information, PII) is no longer sufficient given the new Big Data possibilities. By enriching and blending previously anonymous data with external or historical data personal information can be eventually reconstructed easily [5]. Moreover, extremely rich information, such as personal profiles (socio-economic, psychological, political etc.) can be created, leaving individuals unaware of this analytical process happening in the background—plus, given the issue of analytical veracity, results can easily be wrong or misleading. For example, credit risk ratings based on Facebook profiles and likes have been proven to be inaccurate [11].

Hence, data protection, privacy, and ethics are important for any organization that runs a business built on trust. Frameworks such as Privacy by Design [6] are a must. In our perspective the major principles of a Privacy by Design for data-driven services should consider the following.

- Data sharing with the authorization of the owner of the data, for specific time frame and for specific purpose. In a world of data ecosystems, the creator of the data should be also considered to be the owner of the data. Only the owner decides with which business to share the data and purpose should be always clear. For example, in the insurance business, a customer could be sharing her movement data stored on her smartphone for the last few weeks in order to get an instantaneous quote to insure a trip in a shared car for the next few hours. Sharing of the data should be then consented and limited to a specific time frame.
- Data owner consent and data limits. Businesses should have a clear and unambiguous consent from owners to data usage. Use of data should be limited to the purpose of the request; for example, for providing a quote on traveling insurance, data from health records would not be considered as necessary.

---

[4] Another way to see this is to remove the notion of ownership from data, focusing the discussion around *data controllers* and *data processors*.

- Not using data against customers in hindsight. Data should be used for the only purpose established between the owner and the business at the moment of applying data services.
- Confidentiality. Data shared by an owner to a business should remain confidential and not be shared with third parties, unless in agreement with the owner.
- Necessity and proportionality. Business should only store and process data that is necessary to fulfil its services and deliver data-driven products.

Implementing Privacy by Design principles requires the technical enablers to ensure the above principles. For example, sensitive data may be kept on a user device, in an encrypted form where the user holds the key; or data may be distributed across business entities where the user is the only one who can re-compile the data through personal keys. The goal is to create the enabler to give control to the user, while still sensitive data resides somewhere in the business systems. In this respect, privacy engineering, e. g. [12], appears as an emerging discipline aiming at providing tools and techniques such that the engineered systems have good levels of privacy. Machine Learning research develops strongly on the area of "differential privacy" [13]. Intuitively, it requires that the mechanism outputting information about an underlying dataset is robust to any random noise change of one sample, thus protecting privacy.

Beyond the technical capabilities for protecting data privacy, the notion of data ethics should be grounded in business processes and organizations. Having clear privacy policies and enabling user consent via Privacy by Design/PET frameworks gives users control over their data and enable transparency that builds the needed bond of trust.

59.5   Summary and Conclusion

In this paper, we discuss the challenges of digitalization for traditional businesses. We argue that the ability to improve the customer experience and innovate by using the model of digital customer journeys is the most tangible immediate change to leverage the "big data" era. Big Data Analytics already leverages the tools to improve, fine-tune, and automatize customer experience. Companies can therefore continue staying in the relevant set of consumers by delivering value, customer-centric offerings, and creating positive impact on the life of people.

Going beyond that, new digital business models around Big Data ecosystems can excel with the help of advanced analytics. The ecosystem can technically open up data for a certain purposes or services and Machine Learning is there to understand the consumer needs based on data. The data ecosystem becomes the engine and brain behind digital devices, providing them with contextual information and predictive services. In this context, privacy and ethics is of outmost importance—for consumers but also for companies themselves. Privacy by Design and Privacy Enhancing Technologies require technical enablers to ensure basic privacy principles which should be implemented on a case-by-case basis.

Privacy by Design principles should be implemented in any digital product/service and data ecosystem. This is an engineering topic to ensure that analytics can continue working on data for the best purpose of the consumer, but only under the consumer control.

References

1. D. C. Edelman, "Branding in the digital age," *Harvard business review,* pp. 62–69, 2010.
2. D. Elzinga, S. Mulder and O. Vetvik, "The consumer decision journey," *McKinsey Quarterly,* June 2009.
3. D. Edelman and M. Singer, "The new consumer decision journey," *McKinsey Quarterly,* September 2015.
4. B. J. Pine II and J. H. Gilmore, "Welcome to the experience economy," *Harvard Business Review,* July-August 1998.
5. Y.-A. de Montjoye, C. Hidalgo, M. Verleysen and V. Blondel, "Unique in the Crowd: The privacy bounds of human mobility," *Scientific reports,* 2013.
6. P. Schaar, "Privacy by design," *Identity in the Information Society,* pp. 267–274, 2010.
7. A. Cavoukian and J. Jonas, "Privacy by design in the age of big data," Information and Privacy Commissioner of Ontario, Ontario, Canada, 2012.
8. E. K. Strong, The psychology of selling and advertising, McGraw-Hill book Company, 1925.
9. F. F. Reichheld, "The one number you need to grow," *Harvard business review ,* pp. 46–55, 2003.
10. D. Chen and H. Zhao, "Data Security and Privacy Protection Issues in Cloud Computing," in *Computer Science and Electronics Engineering (ICCSEE),* 2012.
11. Knowledge@Wharton, "The 'Social' Credit Score: Separating the Data from the Noise," 5 June 2013. [Online].
12. S. Shapiro, N. Washington, J. Miller, J. Snyder and J. McEwen, "Privacy Engineering Framework," MITRE Privacy Community of Practice.
13. C. Dwork, "Differential privacy," in *Encyclopedia of Cryptography and Security,* Springer US, 2011, pp. 338–340.

Further Reading
14. G. Coulouris, J. Dollimore and T. Kindberg, Distributed Systems – Concepts and Design, Amsterdam: Addison-Wesley Longman, 2005.
15. K. e. a. Beck, "Manifesto for agile software development," http://www.agilemanifesto.org/.

On the Need of Opening the Big Data Landscape to Everyone: Challenges and New Trends

60

Rubén Salado-Cid, Aurora Ramírez, and José Raúl Romero

Abstract

The great variety and intrinsic complexity of current Big Data technologies hampers the development of analytic processes for large data sets in domains where their business experts are not required to have specialized knowledge in computing, such as data mining, parallel computing, machine learning or software development. New approaches are therefore necessary to simplify, promote and open to everyone the establishment of these technologies in those sectors like health, economy, market analysis, etc., where such a data processing is highly demanded but it still needs to be outsourced. In this context, workflows are conceptually closer to the business expert, and a well-known mechanism to represent a sequence of domain-specific activities that enable the automation of data processes, independently of the infrastructure requirements. In this chapter, we discuss the current challenges to be faced in the widespread adoption of workflow-based Big Data processes. Further, existing workflow management tools are analyzed, as well as the new trends for the development of custom solutions in multiple domains.

R. Salado-Cid (✉) · A. Ramírez · J. R. Romero
University of Córdoba
Córdoba, Spain
e-mail: rsalado@uco.es

A. Ramírez
e-mail: aramirez@uco.es

J. R. Romero
e-mail: jrromero@uco.es

© Springer-Verlag GmbH Germany 2018
C. Linnhoff-Popien et al. (eds.), *Digital Marketplaces Unleashed*,
https://doi.org/10.1007/978-3-662-49275-8_60

60.1 Introduction

Many organizations around the world are massively generating and analyzing large amounts of data, but they still look for better approaches to get significant insight with the aim of achieving a leading position in the marketplace. According to a survey on information technologies (IT) and business leaders conducted by Gartner in 2015 [1], up to 75% of companies will be investing in Big Data over the next two years. Similarly, a recent report presented by Accenture [2] lays out that high-performing companies are incorporating analytics to support decision-making and decision processes. In this industrial scenario, important players in the global market agree that Big Data solutions are a competitive addition to companies as a key basis to increase productivity and innovation.

To meet the great demand for Big Data applications in the industry, a large number of technologies and techniques has emerged in the last few years, composing a wide and heterogeneous Big Data landscape. Annually, FirstMark Capital publishes an overview [3] of the most important Big Data technologies classified into different categories like infrastructure, analytics and applications. All these technologies make possible the development of Big Data solutions in a wide range of application domains, such as healthcare, manufacturing or marketing, where the analysis of large amounts of data is essential to discover relevant knowledge.

Nevertheless, technologies within the Big Data stack usually have a steep learning curve due to the required knowledge in diverse areas of the computing field like data mining, machine learning, software engineering or distributed computing [4], among others. Therefore, Big Data seems to be more commonly adopted in those domains whose companies can hire experts in knowledge discovery. Other times, developments need to be outsourced. Thus, companies in those sectors where data processing is highly demanded require suitable mechanisms and tools to facilitate, open and promote the adoption of Big Data analysis.

In this context, workflow technology brings a framework to conduct data analysis processes closer to the business expert, who has the domain-specific knowledge but probably not the necessary computing skills. A *workflow* [5] is a high-level mechanism to automate and describe processes as a set of activities that collaborate to produce a desired outcome. In general, workflows allow business experts to provide the definition of domain-specific actions for their data analysis processes without specifying infrastructure requirements. The workflow automation is delegated to a workflow management system (WfMS) [6], which manages and efficiently executes the corresponding actions using all the available computational resources in the environment. Thus, business experts only need to focus on the representation of the domain-specific specification, without requiring computational skills that are not related with their own application domains.

This chapter analyzes the need of both opening the Big Data ecosystem to a wider range of professionals and considering the challenges that this involves. With this aim, different application domains are discussed to learn more about which approaches are currently the most commonly deployed. The required computing knowledge to create custom applications hampers the adoption of Big Data in multiple domains where the use of workflows is presented as a suitable solution. Here, workflow technology helps business experts to simplify the specification of domain-specific data analysis processes, since WfMS allow their automatic execution and facilitate the integration of data processing technologies like Apache Hadoop. KNIME, RapidMiner or Taverna are some of the most relevant workflow systems. However, there are still open issues concerning their extensibility and applicability to a broader range of domains.

The rest of the chapter is organized as follows. Sect. 60.2 discusses about the Big Data landscape and its current application to diverse business domains. In Sect. 60.3, workflows are presented as a high-level mechanism for defining, representing and automating data analysis processes. The basic terminology and operability are explained, as well as a simple running example. Next, Sect. 60.4 depicts the open issues on developing specialized Big Data applications, and discusses current trends and novel solutions. Finally, conclusions are outlined in Sect. 60.5.

60.2   The Big Data Landscape

The challenges brought by Big Data have led to the development of innovative techniques and software tools in order to meet the new requirements imposed by data intensive applications [7]. The Big Data landscape is described as a technological stack where a broad range of tools are built on top of one another. This stack can be broken down into three main categories: infrastructure, analytics and applications. All the different, heterogeneous tools comprised in these groups constitute the Big Data ecosystem.

Firstly, infrastructure tools provide low-level access to computing resources like storage systems, network services, security tools or data manipulation techniques as technological pillars to support Big Data processing. Apache Hadoop [8] can be currently said to be the *de facto* standard processing system at this level, being used as a core component for most of the other existing Big Data technologies. Apache Hadoop enables the distributed processing of large data sets across clusters of servers and it is composed of the following main elements: the Hadoop distributed file system (HDFS), the MapReduce framework and the resource management platform YARN. Additionally, a great variety of components have been added on top of Apache Hadoop for different purposes, such as Apache Pig[1] for analyzing large data sets; Apache Spark[2] for large-scale data processing; Apache Hive[3] for reading, writing and managing large data sets stored in a distributed storage using SQL; Apache HBase[4] for real-time read-write access to data store; or Cloudera Impala[5] for massive parallel processing of stored data.

---

[1] Apache Pig. https://pig.apache.org.
[2] Apache Spark. http://spark.apache.org.
[3] Apache Hive. https://hive.apache.org.
[4] Apache HBase. https://hbase.apache.org.
[5] Cloudera Impala. https://cloudera.com/products/apache-hadoop/impala.html.

Secondly, analytics tools make use of infrastructure systems to facilitate the rapid development of applications in an easy way. Many different platforms and services have emerged in this analytical layer to provide machine learning functionalities like Microsoft Azure[6], real-time processing capabilities (e. g., AWS[7]) or artificial intelligence techniques (e. g., IBM Watson[8]), among others.

Finally, on top of the stack, tools in the application layer provide specific ready-to-use solutions that support business experts to carry out the tasks in their respective domains, such as healthcare, government or manufacturing. A more detailed description of these specific solutions is presented in the following paragraphs. Notice that the large variety of potential applications facing diverse requirements has led to the development of countless Big Data solutions.

60.2.1 Healthcare

Healthcare information systems are gaining relevant attention due to the massive amount of managed information in different disciplines and forms: electronic health records systems, personal health records, mobile healthcare monitors or genetic sequencing are only a few examples. The use of IT and analytical tools is turning the whole healthcare process into a more efficient, less expensive data-driven healthcare process [9].

After the successful application of different knowledge discovery techniques, the emergence of Big Data allows managing and analyzing a great variety and amount of data that was impossible to handle, to date. The improvement of diagnosis and treatments of severe diseases, the discovery of side effects of certain drugs and compounds, the detection of potential relevant information, or the reduction of costs [10] are just some benefits that are significantly helping patients and healthcare staff, and supporting medical research. In this context, Apache Hadoop and its application ecosystem is being used for the development of specialized solutions [11, 12]. Moreover, the paradigm of cloud computing makes more powerful the Big Data solutions in healthcare [13]. For instance, IBM Watson Health[9] is a cloud healthcare analytics service used to discover new medical insights from a large number of users considering a real-time activity.

60.2.2 Government

Governments are favoring the massive digitalization of data [14] and the application of open government approaches [15] in order to improve public services. The U.S. govern-

---

[6] Microsoft Azure Machine Learning. https://azure.microsoft.com/en-us/services/machine-learning.
[7] Amazon Web Services. https://aws.amazon.com.
[8] IBM Watson. http://www.ibm.com/watson.
[9] IBM Watson Health. http://www.ibm.com/watson/health.

ment is one of the main promoters of the open government data to encourage innovation and scientific discovery [16].

In this context, Big Data analytics support public bodies in extracting and discovering meaningful information that serves to improve basic citizen services, reduce unemployment rates, prevent cybersecurity threats or control traffic peaks [17]. As already discussed in [18], governments are becoming aware of its importance and investing large sums. For instance, the U.S. government performs real-time analysis of high-volume streaming data, whereas the European Union plans to deliver sustainable economic and social benefits to EU citizens as part of a Big Data strategy to leverage public data hosted in data centers. Similarly, the U.K. government implemented Big Data programs to deal with multi-disciplinary challenges like facing the effects of climate change or analyzing international stability and security.

Apache Hadoop is also the main option for supporting Big Data in this field. Since it requires highly specialized skills, there are a number of platforms built on top of this framework like IBM InfoSphere[10] or IBM BigData[11] that are preferably selected by some governments in order to make easier the management of their data and analysis processes.

60.2.3   Manufacturing

Recently, Big Data has led to new paradigms in the field of manufacturing with the aim of improving the approaches based on traditional data warehouses and business intelligence tools [19]. An example is smart manufacturing, also known as predictive manufacturing, which takes advantage of Big Data to integrate data collections, perform data analytics and decision making in order to improve the performance of existing manufacturing systems. Similarly, cloud manufacturing adopts the cloud computing paradigm to deliver manufacturing services in order to access distributed resources and improve the performance of the product lifecycle to reduce costs.

In [20], Oracle explains how Apache Hadoop can be used to improve the manufacturing performance. Some components built on this framework, like Flume or Oracle Data Loader, are used to efficiently manage large amounts of data and migrate them between Oracle databases and Hadoop environments.

60.2.4   Other Application Domains

Many other different areas are gradually adopting Big Data solutions [21] in order to deal with the new challenges that business experts are facing. To mention some examples, banking makes use of Big Data stack to cover some challenges like tick analysis,

---

[10] IBM InfoSphere. https://www-01.ibm.com/software/data/infosphere.
[11] IBM BigData. https://www-01.ibm.com/software/data/bigdata.

card fraud detection, trade visibility or IT operation analytics. In communications, media and entertainment need to collect and analyze data in order to extract valuable information, leverage social media content or discover patterns of audience usage. Insurance companies make use of Big Data to improve their overall performance by optimizing their pricing accuracy, their customers' relationships or preventing loss, among other issues. Educational institutions analyze large-scale educational data to predict the student's performance and dropout rates, as well as to audit the learning progress. Additionally, other areas where Big Data approaches are being implemented include transporting [22], sports [23], astronomy [24], telecom [25], among others.

As shown above, Big Data is being used in very diverse domains. However, the technologies to be deployed, from Hadoop and its application ecosystem to other custom solutions, would require experts with highly specialized skills in different computing areas. Opening the Big Data landscape not only to IT professionals but also to business experts becomes a priority to enable the deployment and appropriate use of new applications, what necessarily entails simplifying the entire development process and making it accessible to all the stakeholders.

60.3 Workflows for Big Data Processing

Workflows provide a high-level mechanism to define, represent, manage and automate all the specific activities and resources involved along the data analysis processes, while hiding low-level infrastructure requirements. They make easier to fill the cognitive gap between the inherent complexity of Big Data applications and the expertise of the business experts, who can focus on modeling the specific sequence of tasks to be accomplished (*what*), instead of focusing on how it would be executed or the resources arranged (*how*).

60.3.1 Terminology and Operation

A workflow was originally defined by the Workflow Management Coalition [5] as "*the automation of a business process, in whole or part, during which documents, information or tasks are passed from one participant to another for action, according to a set of procedural rules*". Nevertheless, the workflow technology has been also adopted into areas with data-centric requirements, what makes necessary to develop a more comprehensive definition. Thus, a workflow could be considered as the automation of a sequence of domain-specific actions and their dependencies, which collaborate to reach a particular goal, making use of all resources available in the environment.

A workflow is usually expressed in terms of a workflow language, which provides a set of concepts, connections and semantic rules to closely represent and annotate the problem domain. In this way, business experts are able to understand, validate and develop custom solutions, independently of any infrastructure requirement. In fact, a workflow is often depicted as a graph that contains the different activities to be performed, representing how data flow and their mutual dependencies. The representation of any domain-specific resource or the specific type of activity is properly integrated into the workflow notation, where execution and computation details are hidden.

60.3.2   Workflow Management Systems

A WfMS can be mainly divided into two core, interconnected components: workbench and engine. The former element is the environment where users interact and can define their workflows by composing domain-specific actions and the required resources, e. g., data sets, images or any file. It usually provides a graphical user interface that allows visually creating workflows by operating a number of pluggable blocks that represent domain-specific actions. Connections stand for both data and temporal dependencies. Additionally, the workbench can include assistance capabilities, modeling templates, real-time validation and execution control. The scheduling of resources and execution of workflows is then performed by the engine. Restrictions like the availability of computational resources, data formats, security issues, interoperability, parallel and distributed computing, or performance are handled in this layer with the aim of improving the computational power and reducing the execution time.

There is currently a variety of WfMS working on different application domains. Each tool usually has its own set of capabilities, which hampers their mutual interoperability and increases the training time. A brief comparison of the best-known systems is presented next, focusing on their capability to provide Big Data Solutions. Table 60.1. shows some technical differences among these WfMS.

A first proposal is KNIME Analytic Platform [26], an open WfMS for data-driven solutions and analytics. It provides a large set of algorithms for data loading, processing, transformation, analysis and visualization, and has been successfully applied to banking, manufacturing and life science informatics, among other domains. Big Data processing

Table 60.1 Summary of technical features of WfMS

	KNIME	RapidMiner	Xplenty	Taverna
Main scope	Data mining and analytics	Predictive analysis	Data integration	Data processing
Supported languages	Java	R and Python	None	Java
Platform	Desktop and Web	Desktop and Web	Web	Desktop
IT skills required	Yes	Yes	No	Yes
Extensibility	Yes	Yes	No	Yes
Big Data integration	Yes	Yes	Yes	No

requires installing some add-ons like the Performance Extension, which exploits the computational power of Hadoop and Spark.

RapidMiner Studio [27] is a WfMS mostly focused on machine learning, data mining and predictive analytics. It provides an extensive catalog of algorithms for data analysis that can be upgraded by the supporting developer community, requiring some skills in R or Python. RapidMiner has been applied by data scientists and experts in business intelligence to very diverse domains like predictive maintenance, marketing, supply chains or politics. Further, RapidMiner Radoop extends its core functionality in order to design and perform predictive analysis on Hadoop, using Hive, MapReduce, Spark or Pig. It is precisely under the Hadoop technology where Xplenty[12] primarily operates. Xplenty is a workflow-based solution specifically devoted to data integration, an important phase to enhance value of data extracted from heterogeneous sources. It allows creating processes that are directly run on a cloud-deployed Hadoop environment. Xplenty provides the end user with a fixed set of actions to manipulate large volumes of data.

Finally, Taverna [28] is a WfMS mostly directed to scientists with some programming skills, being capable of integrating external code to build their solutions in form of remote services or pieces of Java code. Thus, Taverna allows modeling and executing scientific workflows in diverse domains like bioinformatics, cheminformatics, medicine, astronomy or social science. It also offers several custom editions in order to promote its use in these domains by non-IT experts, such as Taverna for astronomy, bioinformatics, biodiversity or digital preservation.

60.3.3   Illustrative Example

A simple workflow in the field of healthcare, extracted from [29], is presented below in order to illustrate how different phases of the data processing can be modeled by sequencing domain-specific actions, independently of how large the data are (see Fig. 60.1). The workflow is focused on detecting outliers, i. e. the identification of claims with an unusual high cost for a specific disease. After acquiring data, they are preprocessed and then those claim records, whose cost deviates from the average value of the group they belong to, are identified and visualized.

Notice that each of the three phases composing this workflow (data acquisition, data preparation and data analysis) is made up of one action or a limited group of actions, where the outputs of one task serve as inputs for the next action(s) in the sequence, in such a way that the data flow of the workflow is properly defined.

In this example, the *Inpatient Claims* action specifies how the data set including claim records is inserted into the system. These data may need to be transformed before operating the rest of tasks for human comprehension. Therefore, the task *Preprocess Labels* discretizes age values so that "55" would be replaced by the category "Under 65". Ad-

---

[12] Xplenty. https://www.xplenty.com.

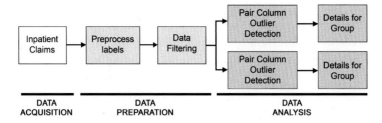

Fig. 60.1 Workflow for outlier detection in medical claims

ditionally, irrelevant information for the operation or the subsequence decision-making process is discarded by *Data Filtering*, subject to restrictions like the minimum number of days in the hospital. Then, two branches of the flow are created in order to simultaneously detect outliers of claims having unusual high costs. More specifically, the upper branch considers a single category of the data set, e. g., certain disease, as represented by the *Single Column Outlier Detection* action. Similarly, in the lower branch *Pair Column Outlier Detection* applies two criteria, such as giving a certain disease and the duration of stay, in order to detect the outliers. In both cases, the process *Details for Group* displays relevant information about the obtained outcomes. Notice that this parallel processing is performed transparently to the business expert, who just deals with the representation of the different branches.

60.4   Open Issues and New Trends

There is a large gap between current technologies in Big Data and companies from a great diversity of business domains that would require incorporating these tools into their value chain. It is mainly due to the difficulties entailed in facing the challenges presented by having multi-domain, business-wide solutions, or the need to hire experts to build and manage them outside the core business. Besides, this is in accordance to investment costs and deployment time constraints. Even though workflow technology pretends to become an interesting alternative to allow companies to model and execute their own business-specific data analysis, there are still some open issues that require further discussion.

Firstly, the wide adoption of custom workflow-based Big Data solutions requires the adaptation of WfMS to domain-specific data analysis processes. As a way to mitigate development costs, some WfMS already provide a number of different configurable components to be reused in a variety of business domains. However, this configuration process is still limited to similar application domains with similar requirements, implying a lot of development effort and technological skills. More abstract, intuitive and ready-to-use workflow tools on their own specific domains rather than generic and complex WfMS are demanded by business experts.

Additionally, notice that running Big Data workflows is an extremely demanding task in terms of resource requirements. The infrastructure required to efficiently execute data-intensive procedures demands new approaches to lower operating and maintenance costs. Cloud computing seems a suitable solution here for executing workflows according to an on-demand model, avoiding infrastructure facilities, management costs and technicians. Nevertheless, this approach involves considering that WfMS should provide cost-aware mechanisms to schedule the optimal workflow execution according to a well-planned, but restricted, use of resources like computation power or data transfer rates.

Designing a workflow is a manual, time-consuming and error-prone task. Notice that in many contexts, it is hardly possible to represent and configure a correct domain-specific data processing and to decide on appropriate analytical methods without deep knowledge about these methods. As previously mentioned, workflows should be represented using an user-friendly notation, meaning that business experts would be able to easily achieve the necessary skills to model their data requirements. Even further, such a representation should be formally defined in terms of a well-defined language at a high level of abstraction, offering new opportunities for automating the development of data analysis processes and increasing the flexibility, portability, easiness to learn and interoperability of the resulting workflows. Additionally, combining well-defined workflows with semantic technologies might enrich their specification with domain-specific properties, enabling the inline validation of workflows or the discovery of the aforementioned ready-to-use components.

New trends are focusing on separately addressing these issues. In this context, WorkGenesis[13] is a novel framework to simplify the creation of new custom WfMS, which enables the definition and execution of business-specific data analysis processes. WorkGenesis uses MDE (model-driven engineering) and highly decoupled components to automatically generate custom WfMS by reusing pieces of knowledge from different workflow definitions, as well as software components and the declaration of previous data types and processes. It provides a set of domain-agnostic configurable software elements that can be selected, adapted and reused within the specific business domains. The resulting WfMS provides ready-to-use actions and resources, fully adapted to each business expert's particular interests, who only needs to focus on the specification instead of the technical development.

WorkGenesis is divided into three layers: (1) a meta-tool for the automatic generation of domain-specific WfMS from domain-independent components and resources; (2) a customizable workbench to draw and assemble workflows including those components, previously configured by the meta-tool; and (3) a flexible, portable and extensible workflow engine, responsible for deploying the data analysis processes and resources into different computational models, e. g., from a local parallel execution to a distributed grid-based platform like Apache Hadoop. As a result, WorkGenesis facilitates the creation of solutions for specific business domains by reusing knowledge assets (e. g. predefined

---

[13] WorkGenesis. http://www.workgenesis.com.

nested workflows or imported processes), saving development costs and reducing the time to market.

60.5   Concluding Remarks

Big Data is causing a paradigm shift in industry, where increasingly often large amounts of data are produced in or retrieved from heterogeneous data sources. In fact, it is expected that 75% of companies will invest in these technologies within the next two years. Actually, Big Data solutions have already being successfully applied to domains like health, manufacturing, governance, education, banking and others. Nevertheless, the excessive product offer, associated cost and complexity of current technologies, platforms and tools may hamper its business-wide adoption, making it dependent on the investment options of each specific sector.

This chapter has discussed about the difficulties found to generalize the use of Big Data solutions to business experts. However, workflows have already proved to be applicable to and cost-efficient in diverse domains as a way to bring these experts closer to how they usually specify and represent their own application domains. Workflows allow defining the specific sequence of actions to be performed during the data analysis process. Apart from providing a visual notation, WfMS can manage the efficient execution of each workflow, transparently to the business expert. However, there is still a number of open issues to address, such as the lack of standard solutions for data-intensive applications like Big Data or the need of highly specialized teams for undertaking new developments, among others. WorkGenesis has been introduced as a novel solution to overcome these shortcomings by automatically generating custom WfMS and reducing the time to market.

References

1. R. van der Meulen and V. Woods, "Gartner survey shows more than 75 percent of companies are investing or planning to invest in Big Data in the next two years," Gartner, 2015. [Online]. Available: http://www.gartner.com/newsroom/id/3130817.
2. D. Simchi-Levi, J. Gadewadikar, B. McCarthy and L. LaFiandra, "Winning with analytics," Accenture, 2015.
3. M. Turck, "Is Big Data still a thing? (The 2016 Big Data landscape)," FirstMark Capital, 2016. [Online]. Available: http://mattturck.com/2016/02/01/big-data-landscape.
4. D. Loshin, "Achieving organizational alignment for Big Data analytics," in *Big Data Analytics*, Morgan Kaufmann, 2013, pp. 21–28.
5. Workflow Management Coalition, "Terminology & Glossary," 1999.
6. J. Yu and R. Buyya, "A taxonomy of workflow management systems for grid computing," *Journal of Grid Computing,* vol. 3, no. 3, pp. 171–200, 2006.
7. R. Frye and M. McKenney, Information granularity, big data, and computational intelligence, Springer, 2015.
8. T. White, Hadoop: The definitive guide, O'Reilly Media, 2015.

9. IBM Software, "Data-driven healthcare organizations use big data analytics for big gains," 2013.
10. B. Kayyali, D. Knott and S. Van Kuiken, "The 'big data' revolution in healthcare: Accelerating value and innovation," McKinsey & Company, 2013.
11. D. Adamson, "Big Data in healthcare made simple: Where it stands today and where it's going," [Online]. Available: https://www.healthcatalyst.com/big-data-in-healthcare-made-simple. [Accessed 10 08 2016].
12. W. Liu, Q. Li, Y. Cai, Y. Li and X. Li, "A prototype of healthcare big data processing system based on Spark," in *8th International Conference on Biomedical Engineering and Informatics*, 2015.
13. S. Rallapalli, R. R. Gondkar and U. P. K. Ketavarapu, "Impact of processing and analyzing healthcare Big Data on cloud computing environment by implementing Hadoop cluster," *Procedia Computer Science,* vol. 85, pp. 16–22, 2016.
14. L. Skiftenes Flak, W. Dertz, A. Jansen, J. Krogstie, I. Spjelkavik and S. Ølnes, "What is the value of eGovernment – and how can we actually realize it?," *Transforming Government: People, Process and Policy,* vol. 3, no. 3, pp. 220–226, 2009.
15. E. Kalampokis, E. Tambouris and K. Tarabanis, "A classification scheme for open government data: Towards linking decentralised data," *International Journal of Web Engineering and Technology,* vol. 6, no. 3, pp. 266–285, 2011.
16. The White House, "Transparency and Open Government. Memorandum for the heads of executive departments and agencies," 2009. [Online]. Available: https://www.whitehouse.gov/sites/default/files/omb/assets/memoranda_fy2009/m09-12.pdf.
17. V. Vijayakumar, V. Neelanarayanan, J. Archenaa and E. A. Mary Anita, "Big Data, cloud and computing challenges A survey of Big Data analytics in healthcare and government," *Procedia Computer Science,* vol. 50, pp. 408–413, 2015.
18. G.-H. Kim, S. Trimi and J.-H. Chung, "Big-data applications in the government sector," *Communications of the ACM,* vol. 57, no. 3, pp. 78–85, 2014.
19. B. Esmaeilian, S. Behdad and B. Wang, "The evolution and future of manufacturing: A review," *Journal of Manufacturing Systems,* vol. 39, pp. 79–100, 2016.
20. Oracle Enterprise Architecture, "Improving manufacturing performance with Big Data. Architect's guide and reference architecture introduction," 2015.
21. M. Gaitho, "How applications of Big Data drive industries," 2015. [Online]. Available: http://www.simplilearn.com/big-data-applications-in-industries-article.
22. C.-S. Neumann, "Big data versus big congestion: Using information to improve transport," McKinsey & Company, 2015.
23. B. Marr, "Big Data: The winning formula in sports," *Forbes,* 2015.
24. Y. Zhang and Y. Zhao, "Astronomy in the Big Data Era," *Data Science Journal,* vol. 14, 2015.
25. Deloitte, "Opportunities in telecom sector: Arising from Big Data," 2015.
26. M. R. Berthold, N. Cebron, F. Dill, T. R. Gabriel, T. Kötter, T. Meinl, P. Ohl, C. Sieb, K. Thiel and B. Wiswedel, "KNIME: The Konstanz Information Miner," in *Studies in Classification, Data Analysis, and Knowledge Organization*, Springer, 2007.
27. M. Hofmann and R. Klinkenberg, RapidMiner: Data mining use cases and business analytics applications, Chapman & Hall/CRC, 2013.
28. K. Wolstencroft, R. Haines, D. Fellows, A. Williams, D. Withers, S. Owen, S. Soiland-Reyes, I. Dunlop, A. Nenadic, P. Fisher, J. Bhagat, K. Belhajjame and F. Bacall, "The Taverna workflow suite: Designing and executing workflows of web services on the desktop, web or in the cloud," *Nucleic Acids Research,* vol. 41, no. W1, pp. W557–W561, 2013.
29. KNIME, "Outlier detection in medical claims," [Online]. Available: https://www.knime.org/knime-applications/outlier-detection-in-medical-claims. [Accessed 15 08 2016].

Further Reading

30. D. C. Schmidt, "Guest editor's introduction: Model-driven engineering," *Computer,* vol. 39, pp. 25–31, 2006.

Part XIV
Cloud Technologies

Preface: the "Cloud Way" to Digital Transformation and New Business Models

61

Sabine Bendiek

Tomorrow, traffic will be safer, more sustainable and more efficient. Autonomous vehicles will move around without direct driver input to transport people and goods, on demand, from door to door using the most efficient routes. They will interact with other transport systems, offering seamless end-to-end journey connectivity and producing convenient and affordable mobility to everybody.

Tomorrow, healthcare will be more reliable, more individual and more preventive. The access to a massive amount of digitized data combined with analytics and artificial intelligence will enable researchers as well as physicians to develop more specific measures and more personalized treatments – enhancing medical care on a large scale.

Tomorrow, manufacturing will be smarter, more agile and more resilient. Connectivity and the internet of things will allow companies to react faster and more directly to customers' needs, producing and delivering better products at lower costs – creating better value for businesses and consumers all over the world.

Tomorrow, work will be more flexible, more mobile and more productive. New technologies will enable virtual teams to collaborate without boundaries and to seamlessly share knowledge and ideas – enhancing freedom of thinking and creativity.

Similar changes will soon occur in many other areas and profoundly affect our lives. Enabling that transformation are intelligent systems that help us gain insight and take action from large amounts of data – based on the power of cloud computing (see Fig. 61.1).

S. Bendiek (✉)
Microsoft Deutschland GmbH
München Schwabing, Germany
e-mail: sabine.bendiek@microsoft.com

© Springer-Verlag GmbH Germany 2018
C. Linnhoff-Popien et al. (eds.), *Digital Marketplaces Unleashed*,
https://doi.org/10.1007/978-3-662-49275-8_61

Identify the right opportunities to drive your digital transformation

Fig. 61.1 Identify the right opportunities to drive your digital transformation

61.1 Democratizing Companies and Markets

Cloud computing enables ubiquitous, on-demand access to computing power – databases, servers, storage networking, software, analytics and more – at low costs and high speed over the internet. It relies on the sharing of resources to achieve coherence and economy of scale over a network. It allows companies and organizations to get their applications running faster, to adjust resources and thus becoming more flexible, and to focus on their core business instead of infrastructure. Cloud computing offers high computing performance, scalability and availability. In the cloud even vast amounts of computing resources can be provisioned within minutes. The cloud enables small companies to benefit of similar technological means as large multinationals, providing them with new competitive advantages and thus democratizing markets. Cloud computing facilitates the access to data and services by offering full device and location independence, as users can connect anytime and anywhere and work on the same data simultaneously. In the cloud, knowledge becomes transparent and accessible to everybody – it can no longer be exploited as an instrument of power or misused to mark hierarchical differences – thus democratizing companies from the inside.

61.2 Creating Disruptive Business Models

Cloud computing marks a big shift from the way we used to think about IT – and while some organizations only just start to understand to what extent it will change our world, others have already fully realized the power of the cloud. They have set up new business models that deeply transform consumer behavior and expectations within a very short time. These new businesses based on the power of cloud computing typically act like platforms bringing together producers and consumers in high-value exchanges. Their chief assets are information and interactions – perfectly matched in the cloud they create amazing value:

- Facebook, the biggest news-machine in the world, does not produce any content.
- Uber the largest taxi-service, owns no cars.
- AirBnB, the prevalent lodging-provider, operates no hotels.
- Alibaba, the most valued retailer, has no warehouses.

These are the most prominent but by far not the only examples for the disruptive power of cloud computing. In January 2016 VentureBeat counted 229 so called unicorns – start-up companies valued at over $1 billion. The largest include platform companies like Uber and Airbnb, Palantir, Snapchat, Pinterest, Dropbox or Spotify – all of them operating a business model directly based on cloud computing.

61.3 Becoming a Digital Business Starts with Cloud Services

Cloud computing technology and a flexible consumption-based price structure associated with off-premises hybrid, private, or public cloud compute models have created the ability to deliver new offerings to market, which were simply not achievable in the past.

But cloud technologies not only allow the creation of new and highly disruptive business models, they also enable the transformation of existing businesses. By implementing a strategy to capitalize on the cloud, companies can stop just running business and start making it thrive.

Becoming a digital business starts with cloud services and cloud solutions gain rapidly in importance on corporate management agendas. According to a joint study by BITKOM and KPMG, the attitude of German companies towards cloud computing has improved significantly in recent years. Today 54% of all German enterprises use cloud computing solutions while an additional 18% are planning or considering their introduction in the coming years.[1] Smaller businesses that were hesitating in the past are now massively catching up (see Fig. 61.2).

Assessing the overall cloud computing market, the Experton Group forecasts growth rates in the high double-digit percentage range for the year ahead. For instance, in 2016 growth is forecast at 35% leading to an overall market value of nearly EUR 12 billion.

While security concerns are still the major obstacle to the proliferation of the cloud in Germany, new offerings designed to meet the special needs of German customers will further foster the demand for cloud solutions in the near future (see Fig. 61.3).

---

[1] https://www.bitkom.org/Presse/Anhaenge-an-PIs/2016/Mai/Bitkom-KPMG-Charts-PK-Cloud-Monitor-12-05-2016.pdf.

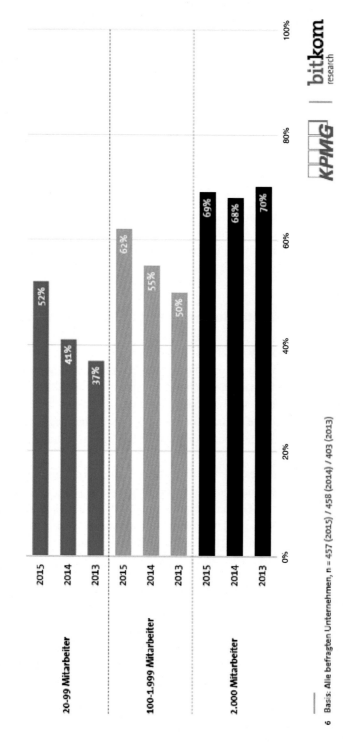

Fig. 61.2 Application of Cloud-Computing

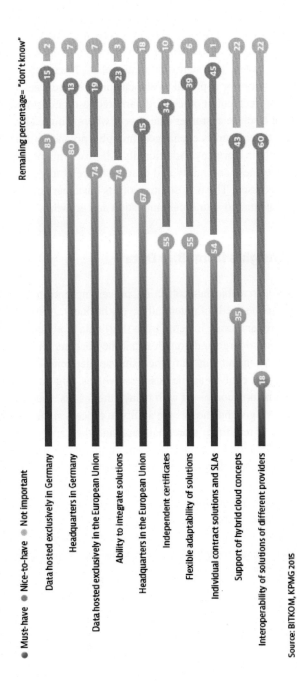

Fig. 61.3 Requirements of Cloud Computing Customers in Germany

61.4   Offering Customers More Flexibility and Choice

As for German customers it is a major requirement that their data is hosted exclusively in Germany, several cloud providers have started to open new datacenters in Germany. Microsoft is the first public cloud company to deploy a data access model where a German Data Trustee controls access to customer data in accordance with German law. Operations or other tasks that require access to customer data or infrastructure will be performed or supervised by the Data Trustee, T-Systems International. As Microsoft does not have access to customer data without prior approval by the customer or the Data Trustee, it is unable to respond if a law enforcement or other third party request for customer data occurs. The Data Trustee will not disclose customer data except where required by German law. Data between the German datacenters is exchanged through a private network to guarantee that data resides exclusively in Germany. Additionally, Microsoft maintains redundant sites in Germany to ensure business continuity and customers are at any time able to view how and where data is processed. The new solution offers customers increased flexibility and choice and has the potential to spur local innovation and growth.

61.5   Drawing Insights from (Big) Data

Cloud computing offers scalable data collection, processing, and analysis capabilities flexible enough to adapt to the needs of potentially every business. Above all, the power of the cloud to harness, store, and draw insights from (big) data is a game changer. Big data – a collection of datasets so large and complex that they become difficult to process using on-premises database management and processing applications – needs a flexible, scalable compute model that evolves as the business evolves. Big data has to be contextual and, through its very nature, combined with many other assets, sources, and datasets.

Only cloud solutions give businesses the ability to process significant amounts of data, whether it's latent or in real time; store that data; and then apply rules and structure to it for consumption. The cloud also enables even more data to be unlocked by enabling businesses to pull data in from different sources and across different line-of-business assets and devices.

When using cloud-based solutions for storage and analysis, companies can combine data from multiple sources without worrying about capacity constraints or the significant costs that might result from building out on-premises infrastructure and automate—through filters, rules, triggers, or other means—the intelligent processing of that data.

61.6 Responding More Quickly to Competition and Changing Market Conditions

In the cloud companies can unlock new value by making the best use of both existing and new data sources. Deep mining of data from disparate sources creates new insights and even predicts future outcomes. Analyzing data that has been acquired over a long period of time is helpful to find patterns and correlations to uncover trends that offer new insights about how products are used or how customers behave under certain conditions. With machine learning capabilities from the cloud, companies can apply historical data to a new problem by creating a model and using it to successfully predict future behavior or trends. Data insights from the cloud help to respond more quickly to competition, supply chain changes, customer demand, and changing market conditions.

The Experton Group expects the German big data market to grow from EUR 1.4 billion in 2015 to almost EUR 3.8 billion in 2020. At present, big data technology in Germany is largely driven by the internet, e-commerce, and advertising sectors. However, thanks to its competitiveness and export orientation, the German economy is expected to quickly adapt to the needs for optimized production, logistics, and sales process to become an international "big data champion," according to BITKOM[2].

61.7 Connecting Things to People and to Services

Cloud computing not only helps to run business more efficiently by simplifying and automating operations and processes with data and intelligence. It also has the power to create new customer experiences and to support the invention of new product offerings and business models. Last but not least cloud computing is also about engaging and empowering employees by enhancing collaboration and supporting new mobile workstyles.

To take full advantage of all these possibilities, bringing data into the cloud is not enough. We need to build systems of intelligence around customers, employees, operations, products and business models. Today, leading companies are exploring the correlation of connecting things to people and to services, creating a new form of intelligence synergy.

61.8 Starting with Small Changes for Big Impact

That might sound complex. But it is a long-term process that can start with simple steps, marking small changes for big impact. In the beginning it is important to focus on the areas

---

[2] https://www.gtai.de/GTAI/Content/EN/Invest/_SharedDocs/Downloads/GTAI/Fact-sheets/Business-services-ict/fact-sheet-software-industry-en.pdf?v=3.

of business that provide quick return. Digital transformation should start with identifying the one process, product line, or location that might matter the most, for example:

- Connecting robots on the factory floor with back-end systems to create a production line with more continuous uptime.
- Sharing diagnostic images from a CT-scan machine in near real time with radiologists at another medical facility and the family doctor to improve patient care.
- Connecting one handheld device to the inventory system to get real-time customer service on the sales floor.
- Comparing results from different store locations to identify the most successful services and roll them out nationwide.
- Connecting point-of-sale scanners on a retail floor to warehouse systems and analytics software at headquarters to increase efficiency in inventory.
- Adding expiration dates to the data set for pharmacy inventory to save substantial amounts of money in wasted medications.

61.9 Creating a More Prosperous Economical World

In the middle of the next Industrial Revolution, companies need to ensure that they stay relevant in their unique competitive markets. They need to be able to engage with their customers in new ways to drive loyalty and growth, and use digital insights to engage with them more personally. They need to empower their employees to be more effective across all aspects of their jobs, they need to optimize their operations to drive efficiency and they need to enable new products and business models.

The proliferation of the cloud and connected systems and devices allows industries to be more open to collaborate and to share practices and information from production to delivery of a product or a service. With the advent of machine learning and new intelligence tools with enterprise security on the end point, these budding ecosystems are ready to become more intelligent than ever, thus promoting greater margins for all players and in general, creating a prosperous economical world with accelerating GDP.

Data Virtualization: a Standardized Front Door to Company-Wide Data Opens the Way for (Digital) Business Success

62

Christian Kurze, Michael Schopp, and Paul Moxon

Abstract

Marc Andreessen famously said that software was "eating the world," and today, this rings particularly true, as many companies, if not most, are transforming into software-oriented companies. All major industries are going digital and are shifting their emphasis from hardware to software, from product to service, and from process to data and analytics. However, today's digitization initiatives face a number of problems. Complex IT landscapes have been built during the last 10 to 20 years, and although the architectures are in place and fulfill their current purposes they result in data silos from which data cannot easily be accessed, combined, or used for new (digital) initiatives. This chapter, supported by several real-world examples, describes how data virtualization provides access to complete, company-wide information across multiple data silos in an economically and technologically feasible way. Data virtualization helps to deliver quality data on time, while also offering enterprise features like security and auditing. Moreover, data virtualization enables companies to combine the best aspects of different technologies to build a solid, flexible, and maintainable data architecture for today and the future.

C. Kurze (✉) · M. Schopp · P. Moxon
Denodo Technologies
Munich, Germany
e-mail: ckurze@denodo.com

M. Schopp
e-mail: mschopp@denodo.com

P. Moxon
e-mail: pmoxon@denodo.com

© Springer-Verlag GmbH Germany 2018
C. Linnhoff-Popien et al. (eds.), *Digital Marketplaces Unleashed*,
https://doi.org/10.1007/978-3-662-49275-8_62

62.1 The Need to Go Digital

In recent years, power has shifted from the companies to the customer. With a few clicks, customers can check competing offers and easily switch from one vendor to another. The customer, in short, is king, and expects to be treated like one. Today, to attract and retain customers, businesses need to transform from being product-centric to being customer-centric, and strive for business continuity in all processes. Such a transformation is not easy, despite the fact that the world's information, much of which is made up of customer and machine data, is doubling every 1.5 years, and is expected to double every day by 2050. Buckminster Fuller has first stated this exponential growth in his book "Critical Path" back in 1982 [1] and proves to be right nowadays with the advent of Big Data and the Internet of Things (IoT).

Such a transformation requires businesses to be able to quickly access massive databases of customer data and immediately respond to customers' needs, even when their needs change in a few minutes, such as after a purchase or a similar compelling event. Such a transformation also requires an optimized supply chain and a completely reimagined value chain. It also requires an open dialog between management, business departments, and IT about streamlined integration across business functions, with an increased focus on project outcomes, better decision-making, efficient operations, and an orientation towards developing new products and services that meet changing customer needs.

The biggest impediment to digital transformation continues to be massive quantities of heterogeneous data, since it is located in separate silos, requiring costly, time-consuming integration, or multiple, manual steps to process a simple query across the entire data set. Nearly all initiatives driven by digitization require rapid data integration in one form or another, including the deployment of new APIs, big data and/or cloud sources, mobile solutions, SaaS offerings, and interfaces with the Internet of Things.

The model of the monolithic enterprise data warehouse (or data mega store) fades away, and data heterogeneity has come to be accepted as the new normal. Hadoop, Cloud, NoSQL and other new sources appeared rapidly during the last years. This new world of distributed and diverse data needed by many apps and users is real, and it will not go away. Such a world demands that businesses develop a fast data strategy; otherwise, businesses will simply not be able to leverage the wealth of data that is already in their hands. As Forrester [2] says, "Business stakeholders at the executive and line-of-business level need data faster to keep up with customers, competitors, and partners." Well-known numbers underpin the need for timely data availability: Fixing a product after delivery costs 10 to 30 times more than during its construction or production process. Retaining an annoyed customer may cost $100 in discounts, agent calls, and process costs, whereas fixing the problem earlier could cost as little as $5.

Data virtualization enables the use of agile, real-time, self-service data technologies that deliver data to business users in real or near-real time, to effect faster outcomes.

62.2   Modern Strategies and Architectures

Many companies begin their transformation by building data labs and analytics, and establishing data science teams within the business departments. But the biggest challenge is how to provide these teams with all the data while still maintaining compliance.

Data silos, as we mentioned above, hinder the flexible access and shared usage of data across the organization. Ideally, all analytics, reports, processes, and applications (web, mobile, desktop) should see exactly the same customer, product, and partner data.

To meet this ideal, a variety of vendors proposes technology solutions and architectures. Gartner categorizes them into three integration and semantic layer alternatives [3]:

1. *Applications and business intelligence tools as the data integration or semantic layer*: This approach delegates data integration to end-user tools and applications, but results in a duplication of effort, since it is necessary to perform integration multiple times in different tools, so changes in the back-end would require reengineering on the front-end. In addition, the primary focus of end-user tools is not to function as integration middleware, but as user-friendly applications.

2. *Enterprise data warehouses as the data integration or semantic layer*: In this scenario, infrastructure vendors provide access to data not stored in the data warehouse in a pure query federation mode, often coupled with the traditional replication of data into the data warehouse. The data warehouse, as the integration and semantic layer, remains the "center of the data universe." Although this approach appears attractive to organizations that are already heavily invested in enterprise data warehouses, it does not address the big picture. What happens when there are more than one enterprise data warehouses (often based on different technologies)? Not all data can be replicated into, or accessed via, the data warehouse, and project and storage costs would increase.

3. *Data virtualization as the data integration or semantic layer*: Moving data integration and the semantic layer into an independent data virtualization platform leverages the native capabilities of such an abstraction layer to access data across multiple heterogeneous data sources. Recommended by Gartner, this approach provides business-oriented models for the underlying data via a logical-to-physical mapping. Moreover, the virtual layer enforces common, consistent security and governance policies. Advanced data virtualization solutions provide – in addition to the commonly accepted relational access to data – native support for complex data structures commonly found in recent big data technologies, which are effective for providing timely data to any data consumers.

We argue that an optimal fast data strategy is built around data virtualization, since it establishes an intelligent abstraction layer above the heterogeneous sources, which acts as a unified data access layer across the entire enterprise. Data virtualization makes it possible to combine any kind of data, such as big data and streams from the IoT, with existing data assets like customers and products.

62.2.1   How Can Data Virtualization Transform a Business?

Let us take a closer look at the transformation to customer-centricity, effected by leveraging data virtualization.

To support cross- and up-sell initiatives, sales teams need complete, updated information about the customer as well as related information about products, channels, and warranties. Marketing, support, and executive teams all need access to the same information for their different purposes.

The typical IT architecture presents a challenge, since it is often the result of more than 20 years of development and, as we mentioned above, is often characterized by siloed data stored across many disparate systems. In these architectures, each department accesses different systems in different, manual ways and IT responds with multiple point-to-point data integrations and even more data silos for each application. As a result, business users do not get answers in time to complete their business. As Forrester [2] says, "data bottlenecks create business bottlenecks."

In the past 10 to 15 years, data warehouses have provided the solution to this problem. But recently, NoSQL, big data, and cloud technologies have challenged the data warehouse approach. In contrast with these technologies, data warehousing is too expensive, or it simply takes too much time to replicate data within the enterprise. Also, legal restrictions forbid businesses to physically store data in certain cases, though they are allowed to use the data in different combinations. However, these new technologies do not immediately solve the heterogeneity problem; they may be able to store data in any format, but a user can only access or query across data in a format that their individual application can accept.

Data virtualization eases these challenges by providing a data abstraction layer which has access to all data sources – either internal or external data, on-premise or in the cloud, structured, semi- or unstructured. As shown in Fig. 62.1, the data abstraction layer acts as a single virtual repository that integrates any data in real time or near real time from disparate data sources, whether internal or external, into coherent data services that support business transactions, analytics, predictive analytics, and other workloads and patterns [2].

Data is published to various data consumers in multiple protocols, made available for querying, searching, and browsing in request/reply or event-driven mode. More importantly, a robust data abstraction layer provides an enterprise-ready security and governance framework, which enables the secure delivery of data [4]. Data virtualization provides governed self-service for all human and machine users of data, both inside and outside of the company. With such a broad access layer, special focus has to be put on performance and scalability – horizontally and vertically – in order to ensure Service Level Agreements for data. Current software solutions offer robust answers to the questions. Furthermore, with the help of the flexible, advanced role-based access and authorization mechanisms, data isolation for privacy and legal reasons is possible and can be audited with built-in mechanisms. Common data exchange based on files or shadow IT solutions by-pass such capabilities completely.

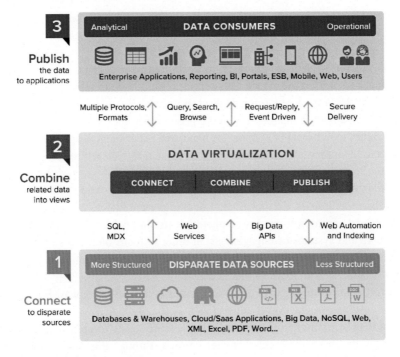

Fig. 62.1 Data Virtualization Architecture

The strategic value of data virtualization, as the standardized front door to company-wide data, is fourfold:

1. Unifying a diverse universe of data assets and helping to enforce data policies, focusing on data governance, discovery, unified modeling, security, and data auditing.
2. Maintaining efficiency in data operations with an eye towards reducing costs and shielding users from complexity, minimizing data replication, and encouraging data reusability and collaboration.
3. Enabling business agility with initiatives like enterprise data marketplaces, which focus on agile lines of business and enabling these lines to quickly launch new products, get closer to the customer, and offer data visibility and rapid data provisioning.
4. Innovating through big data and by adding new sources for enterprise use.

62.2.2 How Do Companies Transform?

Transforming a company cannot happen overnight. In addition to legacy systems and siloed data and applications, companies also often have to struggle with political and legal barriers. Usually, there is a management decision about the expected business outcomes, which should be followed by a digital initiative.

It is critical for the data virtualization architecture to enable full transparency between business and IT to encourage fluent communication between both teams. In addition, it must provide the flexibility to enable business departments to take full responsibility for new digital outcomes while enabling IT to keep control over data asset management, which includes security, governance, self-service, cloud-first strategies, API-based integration, and the delivery of new (digital) services.

In undergoing a transformation, many enterprises experience a conflict between stability and efficiency (traditional IT) on the one hand, and experimental, agile IT on the other, which is focused on time-to-market and app evolution, and is therefore more aligned with the business. Some describe this as a conflict between systems of record (like Enterprise Resource Planning, Customer Relationship Management, etc.) and systems of engagement (like data warehouses, data lakes, etc.). It is important to note that apps, reports, and humans need data from both modes of operation (traditional and experimental, or systems-of-record and systems-of-engagement) in order to focus on the customer and value creation networks. Because data virtualization can provide access to any source, it enables companies to address both modes simultaneously.

A transformation of this nature could be executed in the following way: First, complete a matrix of customer interaction channels (such as social media, website, point of sales) and critical decision points in the buying process (early stage to up-sell and cross-sell), and determine the most important customer journeys through this matrix. For example, a customer might see a viral video on YouTube about a particular product or offering. Later on, he visits the website and performs more research on the product. If he then visits a point-of-sale, he might make a purchase or his decision to make a purpose can be – at least – influenced. Alternatively, a customer might go to a garage for service and end up purchasing a new car. By recognizing and mapping out the customer interaction channels and critical decision points in the buying process, the next-best-action is clear. For example, when providing a courtesy car to a customer whose car is being serviced, should the dealer provide a larger model of the same brand (e. g. an upgraded SUV) because the customer has reached the age when she might be thinking about starting a family and, hence, might be interested in a larger vehicle? In doing so, the dealer can instill the idea of buying a new vehicle that matches the customer's life circumstances, but also (and most importantly, from the dealer's perspective) buying within the same brand.

Second, the enterprise architecture team needs to design the architecture that would best support these (and future) customer journeys. The design should reflect a combination of application and data assessment that would result in capabilities supported by specific systems and data stores. The team develops clear guidelines concerning the best use of tools and vendors, and these guidelines act as blueprints for individual projects. The architecture is constantly evaluated based on its ability to deliver the defined customer journeys. As soon as the use cases are fulfilled, the architecture matures.

In the third stage, build services: functional services (e. g. open purchase order), data services (e. g. master data), and combined services (which execute functions and read or modify data). As always, the service creation follows the modeled customer journeys.

62.3   Use Cases: Data Virtualization Driving Digital Innovation

In this section, we describe five common usage patterns of data virtualization, illustrated by real-world examples.

62.3.1   Governed Self-Service: Business Intelligence & Analytics

Agile business intelligence embraces approaches like logical data warehouses, virtual data marts, (governed) self-service, and operational business intelligence and analytics. All of these approaches rely on one or more data warehouses that are unified by data virtualization, which provides a logical data access layer to the disparate sources. Compared to a physical data warehouse, and the cost of maintaining multiple ETL (extract, transform and load) processes, such a solution can cost as much as 80% less.

One of the largest CAD software vendors leveraged data virtualization to switch from using a perpetual license model to using a subscription-based model, without disrupting BI and other business users. From a technical perspective, they built up an 800+ terabyte cloud-based data lake and combined this data with on-premise customer and financial data. Data consumers are not only reports and dashboards, but also operational and cloud-based applications. The company leveraged data virtualization because of four main benefits:

- **Availability:** Channeling end-user access through a single governance point simplifies administration.
- **Usability:** The logical data warehouse provides a single (virtual) repository, simplifying end-user access and enhancing BI.
- **Integrity:** Only the published views in the logical data warehouse are publically available. Along with data ownership, this guarantees the quality and proper licensing of the entire data set.
- **Security:** The logical access layer provides a single point for authentication, authorization, audit trail creation, and monitoring, for all enterprise-class operations.

With the new architecture in place, projects that might have required five weeks of skilled programmer time (focusing on ETL and web services development) and four weeks of testing, can now be completed in two weeks, using just one data virtualization developer and two testers. The company could also forego the need for additional hardware and software, as well as the need to maintain a heavy maintenance schedule over multiple years.

62.3.2   Big Data and Cloud Integration

Integrating big data implementations with cloud sources in real time comes into play for a wide variety of modernization initiatives, including advanced analytics, data warehouse offloading, the liberalization of big data and the cloud, SaaS integration, and hybrid analytics. The benefits of such initiatives derive from combining big data with enterprise data in real time, providing insights for informed business decisions. For example, wearables, smart home appliances, and industrial sensors often leverage up-to-date Hadoop technologies. Combining this real-time streaming data with existing enterprise data – some companies call it "small" data – for the larger context, provides real insight and value for digital businesses. The key is to make multiple data sets appear as a single data set, without replicating all data into a single repository. Even on top of a single data lake, the standardized and business-user friendly access layer has proven to be valuable.

Let us consider the example of a heavy equipment manufacturer. The company's sensor data is captured and stored in a Hadoop cluster, but this data alone does not provide value to the company. It is the combination of this data with the parts inventory, the historical maintenance data, and the internal and external dealer data that enables the company to effectively train its predictive models, which predict potential failures. These models provide value to the company in two ways: end-users gain productivity by reducing unplanned downtime, and "pays the company back" with increased loyalty. The company increases revenue from the improved sale of service and parts, while at the same time reducing the costs of parts failure. In addition, by integrating the full supply chain of spare parts, the company benefits from the "network effect": On a regular basis, the right parts are at the customer's site when needed, along with a service technician with the skills to install them.

62.3.3 Broad Data Usage: Data as a Service

Data virtualization provides a way to provision data beyond the traditional methods based on SQL (Structured Query Language). Data virtualization establishes a data API and therefore serves as a single layer for all data services, published in multiple formats, such as RESTful or SOAP web services. This capability accelerates the agile development of applications by providing a unified data services layer, logical data abstraction, and linked data services. Developers no longer need to hunt down data, which can save thousands of developer hours.

Drillinginfo is a company that not only provides industry-leading oil and gas intelligence, tools and services, but also provides the most widely adopted software platform in the oil and gas industry. With the help of data virtualization, Drillinginfo reduced its new-product launch time from two weeks to less than a day. In addition, the company's data API is made public to consumers so as to automate real-time data provisioning. Some of the dashboards are made public on the company's website: https://diindex.drillinginfo.com/.

In the reinsurance industry, large players leverage data virtualization for 360° views of customers, contracts, deals, and risks, and these views are accessible company-wide, via RESTful web services that follow the OData standard. This data virtualization layer enables end-users to navigate through the data without a deep knowledge about the underlying schemas and the ways in which heterogeneous data sets are connected. Portals, and applications that serve internal data consumers and self-service customer portals, also access the standardized layer.

62.3.4   Operational Excellence: Single-View Applications

Data virtualization enables applications to provide a single, authoritative view across myriad disparate data sets. A single view of the customer enables call centers and portals to improve responsiveness and accelerate upselling opportunities; a single view of the product yields streamlined catalog services; a single view of the inventory speeds reconciliation efforts; and vertical-specific views enable self-service search, discovery, and exploration functionality. Combined with linked data services, navigation through business-oriented entities is a core capability that provides considerable power to business departments.

Jazztel leveraged data virtualization to enable an application to provide unified views of the customer across more than 30 data sources, including systems for provisioning, invoicing, CRM, incidents, and ERP. These views are consumed by the contact and call center, as well as the client extranet. Internal reporting draws on the same virtual entities. Client call times were reduced by 10% while solving 90% of the problems during the first call; customer retention has doubled, and the back office workload has been reduced by more than 50%.

62.3.5   Modernization, Mergers and Acquisitions, Divestments

Many businesses struggle to provide value-added services to their customers because of legacy systems that are hard to integrate. Data virtualization not only offers abstraction capabilities that ease this burden by integrating the data without replicating it, but also ameliorates mergers and acquisitions as well as divestments. It provides consumers with access to the data, regardless of the disposition of the relevant sources.

The story of AAA demonstrates the importance of decoupling data consumers from data sources in large corporate transformations. Regulatory forces mandated that AAA separated its non-profit automobile club from the profitable insurance business. Unfortunately, the organization operated highly interconnected systems and a single data center. To ease the burden of the physical migration, the whole application landscape was decoupled, via data virtualization, in horizontal and vertical layers. This step not only led to faster compliance with the regulations, but it also opened up time for the physical system migration. Also, during the migration phase, the new data center was able to communicate with the old data center in a controlled way through the virtual layer; even complex applications were changed step-by-step without interfering with the physical system migration. AAA called the initiative "changing the wheels at 70 miles per hour".

In modernization initiatives and other corporate transformations, data virtualization can minimize the number of point-to-point connections, ease access to the data, provide view spanning across multiple systems and therefore reduces the necessary efforts and increases the potential for IT to create new strategic value.

Data virtualization can also ease the migration of whole architectures, or parts of it, into the cloud. Think of IoT cloud offerings; they are easy to set up, but they still need to integrate into the company's data backbone.

62.4 Summary

Digital transformation is becoming the new status quo. Uber and Airbnb, now household names, are also familiar examples of traditional businesses being disrupted by software based businesses. But also consider the fintech and insurtech industries. All kinds of new technologies are disrupting traditional on-premise models in automotive, retail, and other industries. 3D printing disrupts typical production and retail processes; the IoT and wearables are about to disrupt even more sectors, e. g. manufacturing, pharma, and life-sciences.

To stay ahead of these developments and transform into real, data-driven enterprises, IT and business teams need to work closely together, with IT holding responsibility for information management and provisioning, and business teams being responsible for an-alytics and acting on outcomes. Fact-based decision making needs to be incorporated into all processes, which requires the appropriate technologies. The key asset is data, supported and protected by effective information management.

The IT infrastructures of most companies have been in development for more than 20 years and are challenged by all the new technologies that have emerged in the last five years. Many data silos still exist, and to leverage data for digital business outcomes, com-panies need fast data strategies for delivering data at the speed of business. This chapter outlined an approach that uses data virtualization as a data integration layer, providing data consumers with instantaneous, unified views of the data across myriad, disparate sources. The data virtualization layer enables governed self-service across the whole enterprise, with access to the data for all groups in the enterprise, fully aligned with security and access policies.

The five use cases that we presented illustrate shifts from traditional to digital business models. As seen in these examples, data virtualization creates a path for process optimiza-tion, big data integration, and cloud analytics. Data virtualization also paves the way for enhancements to the data warehouse, business intelligence modernization, and the overall transformation of IT architectures, all while maintaining regulatory compliance.

With this kind of power, companies are able to respond immediately to customers' changing needs and have the capacity to disrupt traditional limitations across the entire business lifecycle. Manufacturers, for example, might be able to design a sports shoe, a fashion accessory, or a car body, using just a laptop, and bring the products to market in just a few days. With the power of data virtualization, companies are limited only by their imaginations.

References

1. R. Fuller Buckminster, Critical Path, 2nd Edition ed., New York: Griffin, 1982.
2. Forrester Research, "Create A Road Map For A Real-Time, Agile, Self-Service Data Platform," 2015.
3. Gartner Research, "The Big Data Warehouse Deal: The Future of Data Management Solution for Analytics," 2016.
4. R. van der Lans, Data Virtualization for Business Intelligence Systems, Watham: Morgan Kaufmann, 2012.

The Cloud Native Stack: Building Cloud Applications as Google Does

63

Josef Adersberger and Johannes Siedersleben

Abstract

Cloud giants like Google, Twitter or Netflix have released their core cloud technologies open source. The cloud pioneers' knowledge how to plan, build and run cloud applications are now accessible for free. Everyone can develop applications as scalable, as efficient and as resilient as Google's. This is called *GIFEE* (Google Infrastructure for Everyone Else), or more descriptively *Cloud Native Stack*. This stack is composed of cloud technologies open-sourced by cloud giants like *Kubernetes* from Google, *Mesos* from Twitter and the *Netflix OSS*. In this paper we describe the anatomy of the cloud native stack, map available technologies onto it and help decide when to move towards cloud native applications, gauging luring benefits and looming risks.

63.1 Cloud Native Disruption

The term *Digitalization* disguises the world's perplexity about the immense success and the hegemony of digital age companies – notably the *GAFA* gang (Google, Apple, Facebook, Amazon) which are often called *disruptors* for having disrupted classical industries such as retail, banking and travel. Other areas like insurances, logistics and mobility will be affected before long. The digital disruptors not only have had bright business ideas and good strategies to grow and monetize but have been clever at vastly improving non-

J. Adersberger (✉) · J. Siedersleben
QAware GmbH
Munich, Germany
e-mail: josef.adersberger@qaware.de

J. Siedersleben
e-mail: johannes.siedersleben@qaware.de

© Springer-Verlag GmbH Germany 2018
C. Linnhoff-Popien et al. (eds.), *Digital Marketplaces Unleashed*,
https://doi.org/10.1007/978-3-662-49275-8_63

functional properties such as *hyperscale*, *continuous feature delivery* and *antifragility*, all of them unknown until recently.

Hyperscalability[1] is the ability to scale up and down in real time as data or traffic vary, even if this happens at exponential rates. Opportunity costs are reduced through high utilization and pay-as-you-go resource consumption. Hyperscale systems scale inductively: adding or removing a single resource to N resources present requires a constant effort independent of N. Examples for hyperscale systems are Facebook and Apple: Facebook scaled from 1200 Harvard students in 2004[2] to 100 million users in 2008 and has reached two billion users across the globe in 2016[3]. Apple has rolled out Siri, a highly computing-intensive service, on tens of thousands of nodes, adopted by hundreds of millions of users.

Continuous feature delivery [1] is all about continuously delivering new features to the customer. Starting from a minimum viable product (MVP), the system is steadily being enhanced by small, quick steps. This can be seen as another form of inductive scaling in terms of features rather than in data or traffic. New features are developed by independent teams with little synchronization involved. This requires a suitable software architecture and highly automated post-development tasks such as acceptance test, deployment and all kinds of standard operations procedures. Continuous feature delivery presupposes agile development; it is incompatible with whatever looks remotely like a waterfall. Look at Walmart: Back in 2012 they were deploying a new version every two months – way too slow when competing with Amazon. Today, in 2016, they manage over 1000 deployments per day, directly triggered by their development teams[4].

Antifragility is one of the ultimate aims of software engineering. This term, coined by [2], conveys the idea of systems not only coping with the fact that *everything fails all the time[5]* but handling failures gracefully and emerging invigorated from mishaps. Hardware fails, software is buggy. When failure is not an option, we need resilient systems, processes and organizations. Leanness is an important ingredient of antifragility: what isn't there cannot fail. You are done when there is nothing left to remove. Systems with no accidental complexity left and essential complexity boxed are easily hardened. Twitter used to be notorious for its *fail whale[6]*, a last resort error message presented to end-users in case of serious production problems. In 2007 Twitter was down for no less than 6 days, in 2008 it crashed during Steve Jobs' keynote at MacWorld. But Twitter has been able to harden

---

[1] http://whatis.techtarget.com/definition/hyperscale-computing (retrieved 10/18/2016).
[2] https://www.theguardian.com/technology/2007/jul/25/media.newmedia (retrieved 08/25/2016).
[3] http://www.statista.com/statistics/264810/number-of-monthly-active-facebook-users-worldwide (retrieved 08/25/2016).
[4] http://oneops.com.
[5] Werner Vogels, CTO Amazon.
[6] http://business.time.com/2013/11/06/how-twitter-slayed-the-fail-whale.

their technology successfully: the fail whale has been gone since 2013 with uptime next to 100%.

The GAFAs and other digital disruptors have gathered top engineering talents to commoditize the technology necessary for hyperscale, antifragile systems and enabling continuous feature delivery. They did the heavy lifting and then released much of their achievements as open source projects to the world. These projects enable everyone to develop systems like the GAFA's. This is called GIFEE (Google Infrastructure for Everyone Else), or more descriptively Cloud Native Stack because of the technology targeted at cloud computing applications. Systems running on top of the Cloud Native Stack are called Cloud Native Applications, and the whole thing (stack and applications) is called Cloud Native Computing.

Cloud Native Computing leverages disruptive digital solutions but requires deep changes in organization, methodology and technology. Organizational and methodological changes raise acceptance barriers to be overcome gradually by means of pilot projects and small teams exploring the new approach. Let the change grow only if you know what you are doing. Technological change is risky indeed because the available technology is at least partly immature, the knowhow is restricted to few experts and the complexity of Cloud Native Applications is inherently higher than that of conventional ones. So, it is again advisable to start with proofs of concept, small pilot projects and to further move on to suitable building blocks, using well-tried technology taming the essential complexity of Cloud Native Applications.

Our view is that of a friendly but critical observer: we describe the cloud native world out there, its features, advantages, the costs and risks. The cloud native world has emerged over the last few years, with no a priori roadmap. We, normal mortals not hired by GAFA, woke up one day and saw a cloud that had arrived. Now, let's make the best of it, which means: Cloud Native technology enables applications no one would have thought few years ago, billions of users, terabytes of data can now be handled, at least by some types of applications. Cloud Native technology opens the door to a new world. On the other hand, it might or might not be useful for applications meeting standard requirements. This paper contains some hints as to how much Cloud Native Technology standard application need, but it would be foolish to expect any definite answer beyond the obvious *It depends*.

63.1.1   Organisational Change

The organisational change amounts to rotating the IT by 90 degrees (Fig. 63.1), replacing a sequential pattern with a parallel one. Referring to Gardner's bimodal IT[7], the cloud native development paradigm is mode 2. In mode 1, IT is organised along the waterfall process: artefacts go all the way from design and architecture via development and test into production causing new features being delivered in stages say three times per year which

---

[7] http://www.gartner.com/it-glossary/bimodal (retrieved 10/18/2016).

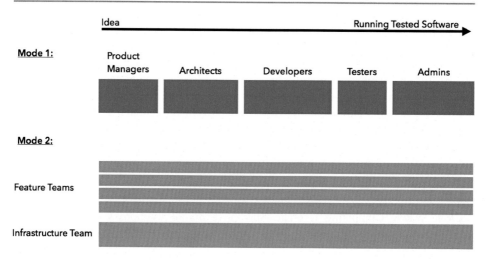

Fig. 63.1 Mode 1 vs. Mode 2 Organization

doesn't correspond exactly to the idea of continuous delivery. Mode 2 requires therefore a parallel organisation instead: several teams work in parallel, largely independently and with little interaction. The infrastructure team manages whatever the feature teams need: professionally run platforms, cross-sectional tasks, and the build pipeline. Several feature teams create and run each a disjoint set of features. Boundaries between single systems and system landscapes vanish, making room for something new: a vast set of features we call the *feature lake*, gradually ousting conventional systems.

63.1.2 Methodological Change

Cloud Native Applications are incompatible with conventional, waterfall-like methods with at best two or three deliveries per year. They heavily rely on two premises:

- A *software architecture* suitable as a basis for non-functional requirements, the most important being flexibility and extendibility.
- A *feature driven development process*, enabling many feature teams working in parallel, and based on *emergent design*.

Software architecture is about decomposing systems into cohesive and loosely coupled units, the components and their required and provided interfaces. Components drive how teams are organized: each team is responsible for one or more components. Interfaces drive the interaction of components as well as that of teams. Design decisions present themselves at two levels: *Macro decisions* affect many teams and are taken by a suitable architectural authority. *Micro decisions* affect one team only and are locally dealt with.

All decisions are deferred as long as possible; uncertainty is part of the game, rather than an undesirable state to be evacuated quickly. This organisation has been chosen by many teams and, for the time being, seems to be the best one at hand.

63.1.3   Technological Change

A lot of new technology is available, waiting to be apprehended and tamed. It is important to understand the basic concepts and the anatomy of a cloud native stack and cloud native applications. There are two fundamental technological concepts: *Ops Components* and *Data Centres as a Computer*. In what follows we describe the facts, the tools available, their features and how they interact, very much like a biologist would describe a particular species: we explain the animal as it has developed very quickly during the last five years or so. It is the result of the accumulated but largely unsynchronized efforts of many clever minds at the GAFAs.

Ops Components
They are called Microservices, Nanoservices [3, 4], self-contained systems[8] or twelve-factor apps[9], but essentially they're all based on the same concept: *Ops Components*. Ops Components transfer the idea of component-based software into the realm of operations. Ops Components feature interfaces such as:

- *Lifecycle interface* for start, restart and termination (e. g. Docker container).
- *Remote interface* exposing the component's functionality (often as a REST interface).
- *Diagnosis interface* providing access for tools monitoring metrics, traces, and logs (e. g. *collectd* and *logstash* agents).

An Ops Component is many things at the same time, namely:

- *A testing unit.* It can be tested in isolation, with other Ops Components mocked away or fully integrated.
- *A release unit.* It can be released stand-alone.
- *A deployment unit.* It can be deployed stand-alone.
- *A runtime unit.* It can be started and terminated independently. It has a lifecycle of its own.
- *A scaling unit.* Ops Components live as arbitrarily many parallel instances being added and removed on demand.
- *A transport unit.* It can be moved around across nodes.

---

[8] http://scs-architecture.org.
[9] https://12factor.net.

An Ops Component does not run in vacuum. It requires other Ops Components it depends on as well as some special infrastructure like service discovery, API gateway or configuration & coordination server. More about this infrastructure as part of the cloud native stack in Sect. 63.2.3.

Data Centre as a Computer

The idea of a *Data Centre as a Computer* has been introduced by [3]. It can be thought of as an operation system for clusters of up to tens of thousands of nodes rather than for a single one, abstracting away the essential complexity of distributed computing. This is also called a *Cluster Operating System* [5]. It manages many Ops Components on a cluster, performs standard procedures like deployment, scaling, or rollback, and provides drivers for cluster resources such as processors, storage, network or memory. A cluster scheduler distributes Ops Components on suitable nodes, optimising utilisation; a cluster orchestrator is in charge of keeping all Ops Components up and running. Sect. 63.2.3 contains more details.

Cluster resources are treated as cattle rather than pets, a metaphor invented by Bill Baker (Microsoft): pets have got individual names and are pampered till death, cattle is identified by numbers, made use of and killed when time is up. Cluster operating system can also be useful for mode 1 applications which benefit from automated operations, improved utilisation and availability.

63.2 Applied Cloud Native Computing

In this section we outline how cloud native computing can be applied: what design principles count and how Ops Components can be derived from Dev Components. We then describe the anatomy of the cloud native stack, containing the ops component infrastructure on top of a cluster operating system, and finally report on available open source technology.

63.2.1 Design Principles

When designing cloud native applications on a cloud native stack the following design principles apply:

Design for Performance Be performant in terms of responsiveness (provide feedback as fast as possible), concurrency (parallelize tasks as much as possible) and efficiency (consume as little resources as possible).

Design for Automation Automate stereotyped tasks. All processes are cast into code: building, testing, shipping, deployment, running and monitoring.

Design for Resiliency Tolerate failures by compensating errors and healing root causes.

Design for Elasticity Scale dynamically and fast. Detect automatically the need to scale, see to adding or removing instances within seconds and without tampering components running in parallel.

Design for Delivery Focus on short round trip times from coding to production, automate the delivery process and have components loosely coupled.

Design for Diagnosibility Provide a cluster-wide way to collect, store and analyse the plethora of diagnosis data such as metrics, logs and traces. Focus on lowering the *MTTR* (Mean Time to Repair).

These principles apply for any cloud application because the intended non-functional properties are exactly what cloud computing is about: if performance or elasticity is no issue, why bother building a cloud application? Depending on the requirements, other principles may enter the stage, such as *design for security*. Anyway, with these design principles in mind we are prepared to discuss how cloud native applications can be designed.

63.2.2 From Dev Components to Ops Components

Software components or *Dev Components* are units of software design and development. It is well known how to design and implement them using methods like domain-driven design [6] or component-based software development. They are often represented as separate build projects with well-defined dependencies. Dev Components remain what they have always been, unaffected by whatever new technology. They are rocks on which we stand. The question is how to cut well-known Dev Components into as yet largely unexplored Ops Components.

Fig. 63.2 shows different levels of either type (Dev and Ops), which makes us ask at which level Ops Components are to be carved out. The *monolith approach* crams the whole system into one big Ops Component, whereas transforming each and every application service into a single Ops Component leads to as many nanoservices. Microservices represent a compromise, with application services suitably grouped into Ops Components. Rigid rules such as "microservices must not exceed 1000 lines of code" (or not fall below, for that matter) are not helpful. Instead we present some arguments for small-grained Ops Components, followed by others in favour of large-grained ones. Please note that we are discussing Ops Components as opposed to Dev Components, which are, as we have shown, largely invariant as Ops Components are fused or split.

Fig. 63.2 Levels for cutting out Ops Components

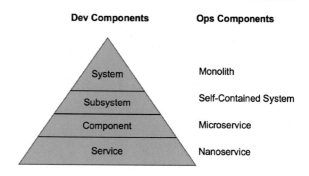

Why should Ops Components be small?

Scaling Small Ops Components scale easily by multiplication. This saves resources.

High availability As a rule of thumb with obvious limitations one can say that small components do less harm when crashing than large ones. Small components is a useful prerequisite for resilience and high availability. If one ops component crashes only this one gets unavailable but the system has a chance to survive.

Dependency management With ops-components reflecting more or less 1:1 the Dev Components dependencies can be managed better. Dependencies are explicit because cross-component dependencies are always remote. No accidental in-code dependency can occur and dependencies and interfaces are always explicit. A further benefit is that component interfaces are more in focus as they're remote interfaces and have to be exposed and described explicitly.

Testability Each Ops Component can be run and tested in isolation, surrounded by mocks or in partial or full integration. Start-up times and round trips are reduced, leading to higher productivity.

Parallel development Each ops-component can be assigned to a single team. Teams can work in parallel, following different release cycles. Suitable interfaces decouple Ops Components as well as teams. Teams would agree on interface definitions, provide mocks early and manage interface changes or incompatibilities, thus minimising mutual dependencies.

Independent deployment Each team is free to release and deploy their Ops Components whenever they feel like as long as all deliverables are thoroughly tested and all interface contracts fulfilled, thus reducing time to market.

And why should Ops Components be large?

Reduced complexity Few Ops Components are easier to handle than tens, hundreds or thousands of them.

No distribution debt Every software distribution creates a *distribution debt*: cross-component calls are more complex and have a higher latency than local ones; cross-component refactoring gets more complicated. A monolith has no distribution debt.

Improved diagnosability Failures within a monolith are confined to the context of that single process. So it is easy to analyse the logs, metrics and traces and correlate them to user actions. In a heavily distributed system it is a challenge to correlate all logs, metrics and traces across all nodes involved.

Improved scalability Scaling a monolith is easy: just clone it. But with many Ops Components working in parallel it's hard to figure out what component to scale when performance deteriorates. This is particularly true in the frequent case of non-linear distributed execution traces.

Easy integration Integration of monoliths is well-understood: a continuous integration system takes all the code, compiles it, tests it and thereby figures out how well-integrated the current code baseline is.

Reduced resource consumption Each Ops Component produces overhead: memory required for a virtual machine (like the JVM), disk space required for libraries. A monolith produces overhead exactly once per instance. Systems with lots of different Ops Components induce overhead for each and every instance.

And now? It depends.

The following opinionated approach is proven in practice: Start with a monolith and leave it at that if it is good enough. Decompose it whenever the demand arises [4]. This is called the *Monolith First* approach. If a monolithic Ops Component doesn't work satisfactorily, examine every Dev Component and decide if it is worth deriving a separate Ops Component or if it can be clustered into a single one, forming a unit of runtime, scaling, release and deployment. Ops Component should not be larger than a team of three up to five engineers can handle. Do not cut down to the nanoservice level unless you know exactly what you are doing. At nanoservices level, each Dev Component is divided into several Ops Components, thus dissolving its logical boundaries.

To summarise we would like to stress that all desirable software properties discussed above are achieved at two levels:

1. A good software architecture is paramount, regardless of how Ops Components are cut.

2. Suitably designed Ops Components at the level of subsystems or components make sure that the potential of a given architecture is fully exploited.

How to Handle State?

The cloud community regretfully mostly ignores the issue of state handling across Ops Components. State handling is paramount for performance and robustness. Within a distributed system handling shared states between different Ops Components or even different instances of the same Ops Component is hard. As partition tolerance is a must-have for distributed applications you can only decide between consistency and availability (with eventual consistency) according to the CAP theorem [7]. You can use state synchronization mechanisms based on gossip protocols if you want availability or based on consensus protocols if consistency is required.

How to Handle Transactions?

Conventional distributed transaction handling mechanisms like two phase commit are not partition tolerant and thus unsuitable for clusters. Distributed technical transactions are nowadays considered bad architecture style anyway. The best practice for distributed transactions has been the same for long, regardless of mode 1 or 2: Have technical transactions confined to single components and provide business-specific undo workflows as distributed rollbacks.

How to Communicate with Other Components?

Ops Components communicate over remote interfaces. Asynchronous communication is the preferred way as it improves responsiveness. For synchronous communication the REST protocol prevails; more efficient binary protocols like gRPC are available. Asynchronous communication works on REST as well as on gRPC. Synchronous calls may be performed asynchronously on the client side. Messaging protocols like AMQP, JMS or Kafka are asynchronous by concept, thus suitable for async-only communication.

How to Provide a User Interface?

There are multiple ways how to tackle user interfaces of cloud native applications:

1. A standalone user interface is provided by each Ops Component; all of them are linked together with hyperlinks. This is the so-called self-contained system approach.
2. A standalone user interface is provided by a particular UI Ops Component.
3. A user interface frame is provided by a UI Ops Component which integrates partial UIs from other Ops Components.

The suitable approach depends on how modular the UI should be. If it is completely modular (1) or (3) should be chosen. If the UI is rather integrative then (2) might be the best option.

63.2.3   The Anatomy of a Cloud Native Stack

The Ops Components need a stack to run upon. This stack is called the cloud native stack. Its anatomy converges to what is show in (Fig. 63.3), with many new technologies continuously emerging. As described in Sect. 63.1.3, there is basically a cluster operating system (*COS*) to execute applications on a cluster and a platform atop of the COS providing all required infrastructure for cloud native applications (*Cloud Native Application Platform*).

The *Cluster Resource Manager* represents the bottom of the COS. It provides a uniform interface for allocating and releasing cluster resources (computing, networking, storage, memory). To unify resources regardless of their provenience (IaaS cloud, virtualized ore bare metal resources) the cluster resource manager uses overlay techniques like operating system virtualization for computing resources, software-defined networks for networking, distributed file systems for storage and in-memory data grids for memory. The analogy of a cluster resource manager on a single node is the driver subsystem of an operating system.

The *Cluster Scheduler's* task is to execute Ops Components packaged in a container. The Cluster Scheduler uses the cluster resource manager to acquire and allocate resources, applies a scheduling algorithm to determine where and when to execute containers and finally monitors the container execution throughout the container lifespan. Scheduling is a multi-objective optimization e. g. aiming at high utilization, high throughput, short make

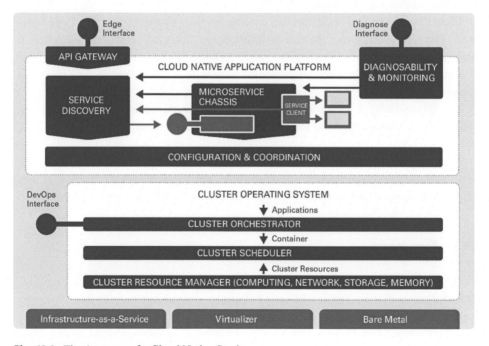

Fig. 63.3 The Anatomy of a Cloud Native Stack

span and fairness [5, 8, 9]. The analogy of a cluster scheduler on a single node operating system is the process scheduler.

The *Cluster Orchestrator* runs an application on a cluster. It uses the cluster scheduler to execute and monitor all application containers (Ops Components) and automates a lot of standard operations procedures such as application deployment, rollback, scaling and configuration changes (*DevOps Interface*). Complex deployment scenarios like canary releases and green-blue deployments are usually supported as well. The cluster orchestrator also detects and handles failures by performing rollbacks or by re-scheduling to other resources. The analogy of a cluster orchestrator on a single node operating system is the init-daemon. Examples for a COS are Kubernetes, DC/OS, and Docker Datacenter.

The Cloud Native Application Platform provides several infrastructure components for implementing cloud native applications on top. Its features include:

The *Microservice Chassis* (syn. Microservice Fabric, Microservice Container) is a container for microservices or Ops Components in general which handles the microservice lifecycle and exposes its interfaces. Examples are Spring Boot and JEE micro containers like Wildfly Swarm or KumuluzEE.

The *Service Client* calls other Ops Components. It performs service lookups, client-side load balancing and failure handling using the circuit breaker pattern. An example is Netflix Feign with Ribbon and Hystrix.

The *Service Discovery* is used by Ops Components to register their own services and lookup others. It may also perform service health checks. Examples are Consul or Eureka as well as a DNS provided by the COS like Mesos-DNS.

The *API Gateway* (syn. Edge Server) exposes services to the outer world (Edge Interface). The API gateway uses the service discovery to lookup the appropriate services. It performs actions like authentication and authorization, load shedding, load balancing, rate limiting and request validation. Examples are Traefik, Zuul, marathon-lb, or Kubernetes Ingress.

The *diagnosibility & Monitoring Service* provides for cluster-wide collecting, storing and analysing metrics, logs and traces. Examples are Prometheus, ZipKin, and the ELK stack.

The *Configuration & Coordination Service* stores consistently cluster-wide configuration states and coordinates services such as locks, messages and leader election. It uses consensus protocols such as Raft or Paxos. Examples are Zookeeper, etcd, or Consul.

63.3 Summary

The cloud native stack allows everyone to build applications that hyperscale, are antifragile and allow continuous feature delivery. It abstracts away the complexity of a cluster by making it look like one single, huge machine. Applications are operated as one or many Ops Components. Ops Components transfer the idea of component-based software into the realm of operations and are stand-alone units of testing, releasing, deploying, scaling and transporting software.

Building applications like Google does is not only about technology – organizational and methodological changes are required as well. The benefits are clear: improved scalability in terms of traffic, data and features. The risks arise from barriers to change within an organization, less than mature technology, additional complexity and the lack of widespread know-how. But all of them can be mitigated by starting small: if you don't know what you are doing, don't do it on a large scale.

References

1. J. Humble and D. Farley, Continuous Delivery: Reliable Software Releases Through Build, Test, and Deployment Automation, Addison Wesley, 2010.
2. N. N. Taleb, Antifragile. Things that Gain from Disorder, Penguin Books, 2012.
3. L. Barroso, J. Clidaras and U. Hölzle, The Datacenter as a Computer: An Introduction to the Design of Warehouse-Scale Machines., Morgan and Claypool Publishers, 2009.
4. M. Fowler, "www.martinfowler.com," June 2015. [Online]. Available: http://martinfowler.com/bliki/MonolithFirst.html. [Accessed 25 08 2016].
5. B. Hindman, "Mesos: a platform for fine-grained resource sharing in the data center," 2011.
6. E. Evans, Domain-Driven Design. Tackling Complexity in the Heart of Software., Addison-Wesley, 2003.
7. N. L. S. Gilbert, "Brewer's conjecture and the feasibility of consistent, available, partition-tolerant web services," 2002.
8. M. Schwarzkopf, A. Konwinski, M. Abd-El-Malek and J. Wilkes, "Omega: flexible, scalable schedulers for large compute clusters," in *SIGOPS European Conference on Computer Systems (EuroSys)*, Prague, 2013.
9. A. Verma, L. Pedrosa, M. Korupolu, D. Oppenheimer, E. Tune and J. Wilkes, "Large-scale cluster management at Google with Borg," in *Proceedings of the European Conference on Computer Systems (EuroSys)*, Bordeaux, 2015.

Further Reading
10. S. Newman, Building Microservices, O'Reilly, 2015.

The Forecast Is Cloud – Aspects of Cloud Computing in the Broadcast Industry

Klaus Illgner-Fehns, Rainer Schäfer, Madeleine Keltsch, Peter Altendorf, Gordana Polanec-Kutija, and Aylin Vogl

Abstract

Cloud computing is one of the latest trends in information technology enabling the creation, organization and distribution of media content in a networked world. Media assets and media processing are no longer handled on local infrastructure, but can be outsourced and operated remotely and geographically distributed in public, private or hybrid clouds. While cloud-based applications such as e-mail communication, storage and streaming services are already established in everyday life, cloud computing is now gaining increasing relevance in the broadcast and media industry despite its specific requirements and challenges.

The article analyses aspects of cloud computing from different angles while paying specific attention to media and broadcast; from an IT and infrastructure perspective, from a user's perspective comprising creative and technical media professionals, from

K. Illgner-Fehns (✉) · R. Schäfer · M. Keltsch · P. Altendorf · G. Polanec-Kutija · A. Vogl
Institut für Rundfunktechnik
Munich, Germany
e-mail: klaus.illgner@irt.de

R. Schäfer
e-mail: rainer.schaefer@irt.de

M. Keltsch
e-mail: madeleine.keltsch@irt.de

P. Altendorf
e-mail: peter.altendorf@irt.de

G. Polanec-Kutija
e-mail: gordana.polanec@irt.de

A. Vogl
e-mail: aylin.vogl@irt.de

© Springer-Verlag GmbH Germany 2018
C. Linnhoff-Popien et al. (eds.), *Digital Marketplaces Unleashed*,
https://doi.org/10.1007/978-3-662-49275-8_64

the perspective of media distribution to end users, as well as from a legal perspective with respect to security and privacy.

Based on that the authors come to the conclusion that major challenges for applying cloud technologies in media productions are already being addressed, amongst them activities by providers who react on legal requirements (especially for the European and German market), or technical initiatives that enable low-latency and synchronous audio and video transport across large IT networks. Major challenges remain the general availability of high speed data networks all over the country, a certain risk of a vendor lock-in as well as changes within company organizations and personal skills of employees. Users on the other hand are primarily interested in a service rather than the underlying technology. So they are often already using clouds – knowingly or unknowingly – for a long time, and are therefore expected to adopt such services quickly. For on-demand distribution cloud computing can be regarded as established as it is already used at a large scale.

In summary, cloud computing is expected to be ready for an evolutionary introduction, e. g. via "production islands" in traditional houses, for green-field deployments of media plants in a larger scale, especially for certain production workflows, e. g. file-based production. Nevertheless, technologies for more complex low-latency live processing are also being developed and are expected to enter the market over the next years.

64.1   Introduction

While cloud-based applications such as e-mail, file sharing and streaming services are already established in everyday life, cloud solutions for the professional broadcast and media production only slowly prevail. Perhaps this is more a matter of perception due to the complexity and opacity of the term "cloud computing", which – depending on who you are talking to – can have very different meanings. This is the same for the term "broadcast", where the extent to which elements of the value chain are associated with broadcasting varies from market to market. Important to note is that "broadcast production" includes a very broad range of genres, from news to features, to fiction, sports, and shows. Besides all technical and operational aspects cloud computing has a substantial economic impact as it changes the business models and the market players.

64.2   Today's Common Understanding of "Cloud" Is IT-Centric

64.2.1   Setting Cloud in a Structural Perspective

Today the cloud is omnipresent and the terms cloud or cloud computing are used for a multitude of different developments and solutions. It seems to be "in vogue" to offer some kind of cloud service and everybody wants to have a piece of the cake. Among experts, however, the definition from the National Institute of Standards and Technology (NIST) of the United States of America has become the established standard (see Fig. 64.1). The German Federal Office for Information Security (BSI) relies on the cloud computing definition by NIST as well, which states:

> Cloud computing is a model for enabling ubiquitous, convenient, on- demand network access to a shared pool of configurable computing resources (e. g., networks, servers, storage, applications, and services) that can be rapidly provisioned and released with minimal management effort or service provider interaction. This cloud model is composed of five essential characteristics, three service models, and four deployment models [1].

According to NIST and BSI cloud computing is also defined by the following five characteristics [2]:

(1) On-demand self-service – Automatic provision of resources/services by the user
(2) Broad network access – Availability of resources/services via the Internet/network
(3) Resource pooling – Provider resources are (virtually) pooled to serve multiple consumers
(4) Rapid elasticity – Resources can be rapidly and elastically provisioned
(5) Measured services – Use of resources can be measured and monitored

Cloud computing, therefore, also includes a comprehensive control and management authority (orchestration layer) to achieve the stated automatic scalability and resource pooling. This, above all, is what distinguishes it from simple virtualization or even outsourcing solutions.

Cloud computing distinguishes three service models: Infrastructure (IaaS), Platform (PaaS) and Software as a Service (SaaS) (see Fig. 64.2). While IaaS only comprises the

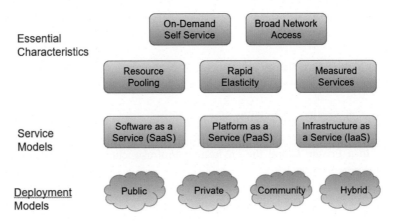

Fig. 64.1 Cloud computing model according to NIST

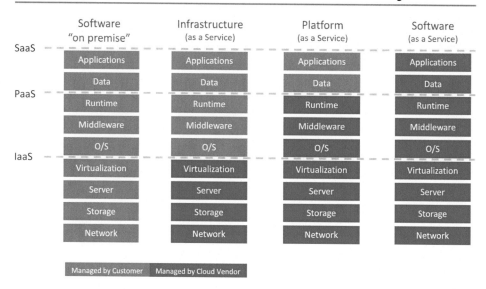

Fig. 64.2 Cloud service models

provision of IT resources such as compute power and storage space, PaaS provides a complete development environment with the appropriate tools like frameworks and libraries. Finally, SaaS provides even more abstraction as it comprises the provisioning of applications and services. The actual infrastructure remains hidden to the user. A typical example of an IaaS is "Amazon Web Services" with its services "EC2" for compute power or "S3" for storage space. For PaaS, "Heroku" is a well-known provider. However, today almost everything is offered "as a service" SaaS from a vast number of providers. One well-known SaaS provider is Google with its products "Gmail", "Drive", "Hangouts", "Docs", etc. or Adobe's "Creative Cloud". There are the so-called full service providers that offer services across all three layers such as e. g. Microsoft. With their Azure platform they offer infrastructure, platform and software services depending on the client's requirements. In the Azure-Cloud an extensive set of services for professional media processing is being offered already.

Along with the differentiation by services, cloud computing can also be distinguished by deployment. Four models have been established:

(1) Public: In a Public Cloud the environment/infrastructure is hosted and managed by an external service provider.
(2) Private: In a Private Cloud the environment/infrastructure is managed and hosted within the organization.
(3) Community: In a Community Cloud the (private) infrastructure is shared exclusively within a specific group of consumers or organizations.

(4) Hybrid: In a Hybrid Cloud the infrastructure is a mixture of both private and public cloud – for example, the use of a public cloud as a failover for load peaks.

Cloud computing poses new challenges to IT but also promises great opportunities. Those vary from industry to industry. From a media and broadcasting perspective the attractiveness of cloud computing is certainly the elasticity/scalability of computing resources. Media production can be extremely demanding, which requires to build very powerful processing resources, where the full utilization over time is difficult to achieve. Cloud bursting, for example, offsets load peaks by dynamically adjusting the cloud service to the (IT) requirements by requesting additional cloud services when the demand for computing capacity exceeds the booked capacities. This is in particular interesting in a hybrid cloud approach, where the broadcaster operates its own IT for basic services and adds extra resources dynamically on demand and only pays for them when they are used.

From a management perspective on-demand self-services simplify workflows, while still an overall orchestration layer allows control. However, media production and distribution is very sensitive to data security. While Netflix moved its media processing into the Amazon Cloud ("public cloud"), other media companies are much more reluctant and prefer private or hybrid cloud solutions.

64.2.2 Getting Services into Cloud

When a cloud should be used, the question is: How to get applications into the cloud? When porting a media application into a cloud a couple of aspects turned out to be relevant:

- The operational requirements for the application. Elements belonging here are for example
  - Scalability and reliability
  - Multi user operations
  - Data security (very important for media). Content must not be visible/accessible for any other application or even other instances of the same application. Any transfer or storage of media content must be protected.
  - Processing and response times
  - Network connectivity for upload and download (Media files, in particular in production can be very large, from several gigabytes to terabytes)
  - Cost models of the target platform
  - Business model for offering the application, if the application is to be offered to others as well
- Software architecture to achieve the operational requirements
  - General approach: IaaS or PaaS or SaaS
  - Identification of cloud-specific adaptations, e. g. need to use specific services/APIs of the chosen cloud-platform (e. g. databases).

– Which functionality exists already on the cloud platform either as intrinsic service or by third parties and could be used?
– Which software technologies are supported?
– Performance of virtual machines and supported frameworks with the VM
– Concepts for authentication, authorization and accounting
– Support for user interfaces/WEB UI

It is important to note that the answer to all these considerations can substantially vary from cloud platform to cloud platform. For instance, the database concepts supported vary, which may require to update the application concept. For big data acquisition and processing the cloud platform may come with different services, e. g. for handling the massive IO-traffic and storing the data, impacting the overall application design.

Moving services into a cloud requires quite some conceptual effort. Besides technical considerations business considerations are important. Placing an application in the cloud incurs permanent operational cost, which vary depending on the application design. Furthermore, depending on the concept (X)aaS, additional operational effort, e. g. to configure the runtime environment, is required.

Hence, the barrier to move an application or even a complete business from one provider to another is high and costly. The question of cloud interoperability and migrating services between cloud providers remains open so far.

64.2.3 Operating Services and Business Considerations

Scalability is a key benefit of cloud computing. The own IT-Infrastructure needs not be designed for peak usage, as the cloud provides the resources when needed. This changes the business paradigm as resources are paid only if needed. From a financial perspective cloud computing has substantial impact on investment planning and general accounting as costs shift from capital expenditure (CAPEX) to operational expenditure (OPEX). Whether the use of a cloud is really more cost-effective, depends on the individual business model of the cloud provider (billing per GB, CPU, storage, download/upload volume, PUT/GET, etc.) and the particular application.

Cloud Computing not only changes business models but also enables very flexible business models. The various parameters like computation resources, storage, network bandwidth, execution time, execution location, and many more build an N-dimensional optimization space. Currently, in the media space there is a focus to charge besides for computational resources for download volume. Optimal utilization of the IT-resources of the cloud infrastructure is certainly key. Today Internet companies dominate the field (Google, Amazon, Microsoft). Obviously the capability to scale at the one side and at the same time the capability to optimize the resource utilization over time can be achieved better the larger the cloud computing infrastructure is.

Note, that so far the analysis predominantly applies for a public cloud as in case of a private cloud the infrastructure is operated company internal which requires CAPEX and most likely does not provide the same level of scalability as a large public cloud. From a media perspective the operational benefit of a private cloud is in particular the ability to protect data and maintain confidentiality. Whether an in-house solution is at the end more secure in operational practice, has to be critically examined. Some media professionals prefer to rely on a big public cloud with the argument, that the cloud provider has a very high business interest to optimally protect the data of its clients which he can do economically more efficient than in a small private cloud.

Cloud platforms offer another interesting business perspective. Cloud computing simplifies also deployment and sales of third party applications. It is not only the global availability and easy access as with any other Internet service, but depending on the cloud platform the application can quite easily be connected to other cloud services and applications. When it comes to media production, or likewise in on-demand media distribution, a broad range of functionality is needed which typically maps to a set of cloud applications. An orchestration unit connects the applications to establish the workflow needed. The arrangement depends obviously on the applications available on the cloud platform.

In the media domain exist lots of small companies providing services and also producing content. The investment budget available is typically small, or even too small to purchase expensive tools and IT-equipment. Cloud computing has the potential to enable small, creative companies to efficiently produce content and provide services around media production.

Finally, it is advisable to precisely examine the contractual details before using a cloud service. The use of a public cloud service always entails a certain dependency on the cloud (service) provider by relinquishing control over one's own data and applications to an external authority. For this reason, the appropriate service level agreements (SLAs) are to be precisely defined beforehand, e. g. agreements on data protection and service availability or the liability in case of non-compliance. An availability of 99.9% still means a possible downtime of several hours per year. For a critical broadcast service this probably constitutes an intolerable amount of (down-)time. Before stepping into the cloud, it is essential to know the workflows, applications and services and their requirements to determine what availability (99.9...%) is tolerable at any given time and how much data has to be transferred and processed.

64.2.4   Challenges for Media

Cloud computing poses several challenges on media production and distribution.

Files in media production can be large, very large (> 1 TByte). For fluent operation an excellent network connectivity both in terms of capacity and reliability is key. If the connection is malfunctioning or completely down, the cloud service is directly affected. In the worst case you cannot use it at all. In media this can be mission critical.

Reliability is generally a key factor in media and in particular for broadcasting. It must not happen that broadcast services are down because cloud services are not available. Broadcasters in particular used to have elaborate redundancy concepts to ensure service continuation even in harsh situations. While at least global cloud services certainly are able to offer comparable reliability levels, it needs to be seen which cost advantage can be realized. There is the example of a radio station some years ago operating its service out of a cloud and being down for several hours.

Media companies have a substantial concern in terms of data security, not only for media assets but also to protect information sources. Especially there is high sensitivity in terms of privacy. This is still the main reason for companies hesitating to move to the cloud. Either one relies on the security concept of the cloud provider or in case of a private could has to take care of all necessary elements like identity management, access control, monitoring, emergency management, maintenance/patch management as well as privacy and legal concerns.

Overall, cloud computing offers operational flexibility and potential cost savings, but also poses specific challenges for media production and distribution, including broadcasting. In order to leverage these benefits, a careful analysis of the field of application and operational implications is required.

64.3 The Cloud from a User Perspective

64.3.1 Media Production

Media production in general – and especially news production – is mainly driven by the needs of journalists who have a strong demand to "work from everywhere", to "work with whatever helps to complete the story" from own tablets and personal devices, to "investigate everywhere and everything", including data journalism that applies big data techniques to data available in the cloud, and to "stay connected and to collaborate everywhere". The research project "Broadcasting 2025" [3] investigating the needs for cross media production revealed that journalists consider the unavailability of countrywide broadband access and the restrictions to use personal devices as the major pitfalls of flexible and effective media acquisition and production, whereas they are increasingly less concerned about the production tools itself and their technical features.

Nevertheless, whole workflows have to be considered in order to guarantee a quick throughput in media production and especially in news. The technical staff thus has to have an intrinsic interest to satisfy the flexible needs of the journalist users, whilst maintaining fast overall workflows and adequate monitoring of the overall technical structure. As a consequence, the traditionally monolithic broadcast infrastructure is more and more split up into functional elements – often implemented as service oriented architecture (SOA) or as a series of so-called "microservices" – that can quickly be orchestrated for changing needs in varying workflows. Such an approach also fosters splitting of broadcast systems into application layers and underlying infrastructure which in turn maps quite well onto cloud architectures. Single services can even be called from another cloud in a hybrid architecture and can be booked on demand. In consequence, such a modular cloud based approach supports [4]

(1) fast adaptation to new production challenges,
(2) quick changes of workflows,
(3) increased flexibility for changing and short time demands.

Since clouds "per se" are pure IT solutions, they seem to be limited to application areas that do not require a special A/V infrastructure like SDI cables or crossbars at first glance. For file-based production, these special functions, except for a small part of the ingest and playout, have already become unnecessary. Solutions are also in sight for the professional live production requiring very low latencies over IT networks: in the form of the IP-based SMPTE 2022 standards and (still) proprietary solutions building on it [5], as layer II-based solutions via AVB [6], although these solutions place higher demands on the network and therefore seem less appropriate for the use in public clouds for now, or AES67 for audio signals. The IP-based acquisition via mobile radio networks and satellite is already established, however with noticeable but moderate latencies. Certainly with the introduction of these systems there will be challenges to master, but it is already apparent today that live productions can do without special cables and infrastructures in the medium term. So another obstacle could be overcome on the path towards moving the signal transmission and processing into a purely IT-based infrastructure and thus principally into clouds, as well.

Of course, different genres of media have different requirements in production and thus show a different likelihood to be processed in clouds:

(1) News require extremely fast operations for cross-media, are sometimes live but mainly rely on "near live" file based production workflows. Editing may be decentralized, but should have access to a common content management system. Cloud solutions are already in use e. g. for planning, material acquisition, and editing.
(2) Fictional and feature productions have less strict requirements in quick end-to-end processing and rapid planning decisions, but require much more elaborated post-processing tools and completely make use of file based workflows. Remote access during editing helps to speed up editorial decisions and approvals and thus to save money. Movie productions are heavily relying on cloud infrastructures.
(3) Live productions (e. g. sports and some shows) are still a major challenge for pure cloud architectures due to the extremely hard requirements with respect to low latencies, A/V synchronism, and the fact that IT networks do not provide a simple means for carrying synchronized low latency audio/video. It is unclear to what extent existing cloud infrastructures already do or will fulfil any new requirements from the standards that are being developed.

Nevertheless, there is already a variety of web-based and also cloud based tools available in professional media production. Web-based applications have been increasingly observed in various areas over the past few years. Starting with rather classic client-server concepts such as web frontends for a client-independent access to central production systems and dedicated clients for mobile access "from the outside", they now range from hybrid approaches to completely cloud-based solutions, e. g. externally hosted systems for entire live productions, from contribution to distribution via streaming on the Internet.

Vendors of established broadcast production systems mainly focus on expanded client-server concepts to make their products accessible via the Internet e. g. to ENG (Electronic news gathering) crews or regional and foreign studios in distant locations. The Annova Systems GmbH, for example, offers the modules "AnyPlace" and "MobileApp" to allow access to its well-established newsroom system "Open Media", which is running on internal servers at various broadcasters. Similarly, "Media Composer Cloud" expands Avid's "Interplay" production environment with collaborative workflows that enable the exchange and processing of essences and projects via the Internet – also with lower bandwidths thanks to proxy videos. And by modern streaming technologies, "QTube Edit" by Snell Advanced Media (SAM) and Adobe's "Anywhere" even allow for frame-accurate editing of video projects with a full and familiar range of editing tools on a central server without the need to download AV essences [7].

In contrast to these solutions that are partly promoted with the marketing buzzword "cloud" but do not always represent "real" cloud applications (at most, they can be assigned to the private cloud category), several sometimes new vendors offer "real" cloud services for media production. These services either cover fundamental functions of the media production, such as encoding, transcoding or quality control, or provide more comprehensive cloud-based solutions that are built on top of such fundamental functional services.

Examples of the former are "QCloud" by Tektronix, "Vidcheck OnDemand" by Vidcheck and the "MXF Analyser Cloud Service" by IRT for quality control, or "Zencoder" by Brightcove and "Vantage Cloud" by Telestream for transcoding services. Cloud services for transcoding and quality control sometimes completely rely on cloud-based workflows (e. g. QCloud processes media content in Amazon "EC2" instances and stores it in the Amazon cloud ("S3")) but can also be realized as a hybrid scenario. These services are typically integrated by an API and use a pay-per-use billing model.

An example for solutions built on top of fundamental cloud services is "Pageflow", a production and publication platform for multimedia content developed in collaboration with German public-service broadcaster Westdeutscher Rundfunk (WDR). It also uses Amazon's "S3" cloud storage to store its media content (audio, video, pictures). From there the content is transferred to Brightcove's "Zencoder" cloud service where it is transcoded for various end devices (e. g. different formats, codecs, resolutions). "Pageflow" can be used as an entirely cloud-hosted service at various tariffs or – thanks to its open source code – can be installed on your own servers for a hybrid cloud scenario. Another example of such solutions is Cube-Tec's "MXF Legalizer" a tool that – in addition to quality control – repairs files in the cloud that are detected as damaged.

Established manufacturers like Imagine Communications are also moving to the cloud. They offer products that are purely cloud-based like CloudXtream, an end-to-end solution for media content distribution and monetization which comprises (even) live video, video on demand (VOD), cloud DVR (cDVR), dynamic ad insertion (DAI), packaging, encoding, transcoding, storage management, and cloud orchestration. Services that already exist as a product/appliance and are now offered as a cloud service like Versio, a channel playout, or SelenioFlex for live encoding. All tools are offered as services on the Microsoft Azure cloud.

Two other providers of SaaS solutions for the media industry that rely on "Amazon Web Services" as the underlying cloud platform are Reelway with their product of the same name and Sony with the product "Ci". Both solutions offer CMS (Content Management System) or MAM functionality (Media Asset Management) for media content stored in the cloud. "Reelway" offers various MAM functions such as cataloguing and the organization of and search for media assets. In addition, it offers a rough cut editor, the possibility to export editing decision lists (EDLs) and other features. Sony's "Ci" on the other hand provides a number of functions for collaborative work in the acquisition domain along with the storage and organization of the clips. By the means specially developed camera adapters, proxies can be directly uploaded into the cloud from the filming location via wireless networks and then can be annotated, exchanged and edited (rough cut) with the help of the Ci applications.

"ioGates" regards itself as a MAM addition that aims to simplify complicated conversion and ftp-based transfers by storing and processing the media content in the cloud. The focus lies on workflows in the TV service productions segment where it is necessary to coordinate or optimize processes across several service providers. The BMBF-funded project "dwerft – linked film and tv services", of which IRT is a partner, is doing research in this field. One of the project's goals is the development of an extensible knowledge representation (ontology) that shall improve the lossless exchange of information (metadata) between different media production applications and services.

"Make.TV" [8] is a live video cloud solution that provides users with a cloud-based live video production toolset. With this set of tools, consisting of "Acquire", "Selector", "Manager" and "Playout", the user works in a shared environment to acquire, manage and distribute (near) live or recorded videos on the Internet, fully realized in the public cloud (see Fig. 64.3). For acquisition, different acquisition devices (smart phones and tablets using the "Streamtag App", PCs, but also professional cameras with downstream and external encoders) can be used to stream signals into the live video cloud. Inside the live video cloud, these signals can be acquired, monitored, and routed by the "Aquire" tool. For organizing, selecting, monitoring, and routing of live video feeds, "Selector" provides the user with a video router inside the cloud. Management tasks like browse, filter, trim, and download of video feeds or the function to receive alerts or transfer video feeds to MAM/PAM systems and ingest recorded video feeds are provided by the "Manager" tool. For distribution, the "Playout" tool provides the user with a playout inside the cloud to schedule 24/7 live streams and distribute content simultaneously on multiple platforms,

e. g. live via the internet to the end customer, transferred to your own production infrastructure or directly to a CDN. Simultaneously, input signals or the final production can be archived in a simple CMS in the cloud. The different tools are controlled via a browser-based application on a tablet or PC using the proxy streams transcoded live in the cloud. In addition, signal paths for the communication via intercom or a chat between the production participants and red light signals (tally) are available. Of course, the produced signal can also be fed into existing production systems via a decoder gateway. Therefore, the critical signal paths for maximum quality of the final product are the source signals to the mixer in the cloud and, of course, the distribution to the signal destination. Note, however, that "live" is not equivalent to "low latency".

Other examples of providers with a similar concept are companies like VJU iTV Development GmbH with their product Streemfire, Media IT Profy with his product Broadcast.me or SintecMedia with his product CloudOnAir.

Last but not least, with the "Media Services" or "Media Tools", Microsoft, Amazon and Google provide a range of different cloud services via their marketplaces that can be useful for broadcasters. While these are mainly SaaS offerings in the case of Google (e. g. research and verification with "Google Search", visualizations with "Google Maps" and "Google Earth", publication with "Google+" and live streaming with "YouTube" etc.), Microsoft with its cloud-platform "Azure" offers services for editing and preparation of content (live ingest, live encoding, upload, encoding, conversion, live streaming etc.). Azure also allows you to develop your own cloud-based applications according to the broadcasters' requirements – even across several layers, for example as a hybrid solution. Such platforms can support broadcasters and media companies in creating custom SaaS applications according to their needs.

Furthermore, SaaS services for file synchronization and sharing that are not especially targeting the media industry are becoming increasingly popular also in media production. Thanks to "Dropbox" and others these services have conquered the market in a very short time and have become part and parcel of everyday life and also gained tremendous importance for broadcasting. Especially for journalists and editors who travel a lot and need access to their data anytime and anywhere, such a service enormously facilitates work. Data can be synchronized between different devices, shared with others, and it enables collaborative work on documents etc. However, recent data-related scandals (cf. the iCloud hack in 2014) increase doubt about the security and reliability of such a solution since the data is usually kept on the (cloud) provider's servers and thus elude direct control by the user. These and other questions about security and data protection still seem to be unclear and therefore require special attention, especially when it comes to the usage in broadcasting and journalism. At the same time companies like Uniscon invent systems particularly providing a very high security of the data stored in the cloud.

Products available on the market today already demonstrate that sections of the professional media production can be implemented through Internet- or cloud-based applications. This is especially the case for applications/services that do not have special hardware requirements and require no or only minimal installation of special software adjusted to

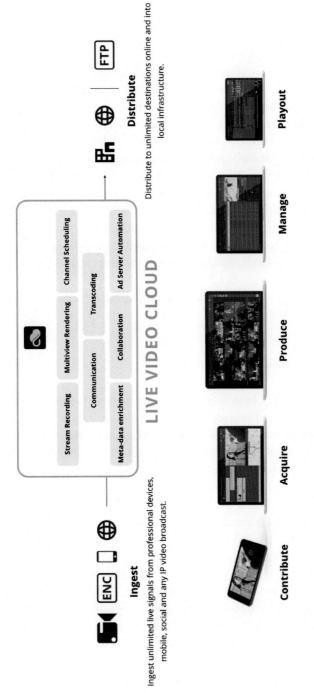

Fig. 64.3 Make.TV Overview. (© http://www.make.tv)

clients. The handling of the tools is also usually designed in a way that the applications can be used without extensive training. Often, however, compromises (still) have to be made, especially with regard to quality and stability. In the short to medium term, cloud services – especially if used via public networks – do not yet represent a full replacement of current production infrastructures and at best serve as a supplement in appropriate use cases. On the other hand, many of today's solutions demonstrate that in the long term more of these tools will be used in the production since they, above all, meet the creative needs and are thus increasingly requested by the editorial departments.

Business and integration models are still to be confirmed. Many solutions are offered as a complete cloud solution with no or rather simple programming interfaces, e. g. for upload and download. They can be used quite easily as an extension to an existing broadcasting infrastructure. Connecting single modular media services from e. g. Azure, Amazon AWS, or Google and orchestrating them for an effective production workflow is, however, a much more complex integration task that requires in depth knowledge and a clear vision how the final infrastructure of a media house should look like, including any metadata. Cloud based services typically charge for CPU usage, CPU up-time, and the amount of data download rather than data upload. It is obvious that costs in a self-orchestrated infrastructure are more complex to predict. Moreover, the cost modell for cloud services drives the design of applications and workflows. Thus, may be today's charging models undergo substantial changes in the future.

64.3.2 Media Distribution

Cloud services have already been very successfully deployed in the field of media distribution. In fact, some cloud providers started to build up infrastructures for their own business in media distribution and only later decided to offer parts of that infrastructure to the public for more general use. At first, those services focused on the transport of data, but in the meantime such services can consist of several cloud-based services. The range extends from processing of video and audio (encoding and/or transcoding) to data storage and distribution via different streaming technologies all the way to monitoring and troubleshooting. So called content delivery networks (CDN) were created to deliver data reliably, safely and fast to the end user. By optimized transport algorithms (consisting of server management, routing, caching) the different kinds of data (video/audio, email, web pages etc.) are routed through several networks to the end user.

Today, CDN services are essential for many content providers (e. g. VoD providers but also providers of linear programs) to handle the huge amount of requests from their users. YouTube for example has more than a billion users worldwide. That corresponds to almost one-third of all Internet users. Every day YouTube clips with a total duration of several hundred million hours are played and billions of views are generated [9]. In Germany major sports events like soccer championships or the Olympic games regularly result in peak loads which the German public broadcasters have to handle. And the trend points still upwards, comparing the European soccer championship 2016 with the World soccer championship in 2014, twice as much traffic was streamed.

In the field of video streaming, cloud encoding and transcoding has increasingly become popular. Apart from professional hardware encoders more and more cloud encoding services are used. Whereas hardware based encoders need to be purchased, maintained and placed somewhere, the corresponding cloud-service are easily accessible anywhere and anytime and offer a pay-per use billing model. The better scalability of a process chain and the close link to CDNs are very positive effects, as well.

Today content providers have to make their content available in many different formats due to the constantly changing and versatile end user devices as well as the varying access to the content (e. g. smart TV, smart phone, laptop). Therefore, the streams have to be provided in various formats. VoD (Video On Demand) or live streams via e. g. HDS, HLS, MPEG-DASH, HbbTV in SD, HD or even UHD are just a few requirements the providers have to meet to remain competitive. The need for more scalability and large data volumes causes more and more content providers to step into the cloud.

As more and more parts of the distribution workflow are shifted to the cloud it is essential for content providers to regain a certain degree of control over their streaming services; not least to guarantee the best possible service for the end user (cf. QoS – Quality of Service). Comprehensive monitoring from encoding to the end user is the only option to identify errors or problems and to react as quickly as possible. Some high end products are even a step ahead. They are able to respond nearly in real time and if necessary take measures to prevent or improve the situation at the end user side.

Such business models are already pursued by several companies, with Conviva and Akamai as the main players. However, they do not necessarily meet all the requirements of e. g. the German public broadcasters. Therefore, IRT together with "Das Erste" developed a QoS monitoring plugin (ARGOS) [10] which suits the broadcasters needs as well as data protection regulations.

64.4   The Viewer and the Cloud

Of course the viewers and consumers have been using the cloud for a long time – consciously, or probably unconsciously – in the form of social networks; services such as "Dropbox", "Google Drive", "OneDrive", "Amazon Cloud Drive"; Google, Apple and Microsoft accounts for fixed or mobile devices; online video recorders and video stores or vendor-specific accounts for smart TVs. Technically skilled users operate their own home NAS servers or streaming servers and make them available "on the go". There is a fundamental need to have "one's own" photos, video clips or TV content available anywhere and anytime. An increasing number of end devices include cloud-based software solutions along with the hardware – from photo cameras to video editing to heating, lighting and TV control via home automation in the cloud. "User-generated content" is distributed on virtual channels via "YouTube" and is marketed in a highly profitable way. Video and audio consumption over CDNs has been widely established. In those cases, the main task of the cloud is to accept and store data, to transcode to various representations and to deliver data as a non-interrupted stream.

However, cloud offerings start to reach clearly beyond such scenarios, especially when user or device identifications – or in general user data – become an integral part of the service: The "Second Screen Framework" of IRT and T-Systems developed for the ARD.Mediathek und "rbbtext" [11] establishes a virtual connection between smart TVs and mobile devices as a 2nd screen irrespective of the manufacturer. The ADAMS project [12] has developed cloud based mechanisms to continue media consumption across various devices while the user is moving through his home or within a city. CE manufacturers are starting to interconnect their media devices with household appliances in smart homes – in fact, these household devices themselves are more and more becoming media devices. Data exchange is usually handled through a public cloud operated by manufacturers, telecom companies and others.

There are various business models: sometimes cloud usage is free for the life-time of the device which has been bought and which connects into the cloud and in some cases the user has to pay a regular fee. Models where the costs become dependent on the usage and amount of data are not yet common, but may emerge with services that require more intense data exchange.

In all cases, the service integrity, data security and privacy is a significant risk. Data transfers and logins to the cloud can be subject to hacking attacks. For many services, the user even accepts that the cloud operator analyses the users' data and his behavior as a basis for further business, i. e. the user "pays with his data". However, experience tells us that viewers are willing to sacrifice personal data and take on risks in exchange for comfort and convenience. It is precisely this convenience and comfort at a comparably low cost coupled with interesting performance features that the consumer is already used to and that professional (media) applications will be measured against in the future, because A/V acquisition, storage, processing and distribution in high quality have long ceased being a distinguishing feature of large media companies and can be principally acquired from the cloud via a mouse click by everybody.

64.5 The Cloud from a Legal and Privacy Perspective

64.5.1 The Legal Background

(Public) cloud computing and protection of personal data are two subjects that have triggered many discussions recently. Especially the Snowden revelations and the latest spectacular court decisions stirred up the controversy (cf. United States of America vs. Microsoft Corporation). The issue behind is that cloud computing does not care about national borders. On the one hand the cloud logic implies that the location of data processing is not guaranteed in advance. On the other hand, traditionally the jurisdiction is bound to the location were the data processing takes place. Thus, up to now it was common practice for globally operating cloud providers that the location of the corporate headquarters determined the jurisdiction and not the location of the data center itself. This was particularly important with regard to subcontractor structures. The latest court ruling in the so called "Microsoft Ireland" case between the Microsoft Cooperation and United States of America started to change that practice. The case began in 2013 when a warrant was issued by a New York court requesting Microsoft to hand over emails and private information associated with a certain account hosted in a Microsoft data center in Dublin. After Microsoft lost the first trial in 2014, on July 14, 2016 the U.S. Court of Appeals for the 2nd Circuit ruled that Microsoft is not required to comply with the warrant. The ruling is seen as a victory for the whole industry and as a landmark decision. During the trial Microsoft got a lot of support from the industry (Amazon, Apple), the media (CNN, Washington Post) and even from the Irish and European government. Now it remains to be seen what impact and consequences this ruling will have on the jurisdiction and in practice regarding global cloud computing services.

Despite the ruling in the Microsoft Ireland case and its possible consequences many German companies prefer a cloud solution hosted and registered in Germany. Some cloud services providers acknowledge the particular requirements for protecting personal data. Microsoft for example responded to this demands with the "Microsoft Cloud Deutschland", as part of the Azure-Cloud. As its data centers are situated in Germany (Frankfurt & Magdeburg), data will be stored and processed in Germany only according to German law. The data centers are not managed by Microsoft itself, instead T-Systems acts as a data trustee, monitors all access on the customer data and ensures its legality while Microsoft has no access to the data or even the data centers. However, this impacts the achievable scalability/elasticity of cloud services and will certainly have an impact on pricing.

Cloud providers headquartered in Germany are subject to the Federal Data Protection Act (Bundesdatenschutzgesetzt, BDSG) when processing personal data. The Data Protection Act states that the cloud provider only performs contracted data processing. Responsible for personal data and its protection is still the client/cloud user (§11 BDSG). And he has the right and obligation to ensure that the cloud provider complies with the German data protection rules. A certification of the data center according to e. g. ISO/IEC 27001 already covers a considerable part of the legal requirements.

An EU-wide regulation for data protection is the Data Protection Directive of the European Union[1]. It describes the minimum standards for data protection that have to be ensured in all EU member states. Personal data may be forwarded to third party states from EU member states only if they have a data protection standard comparable with the EU legislation. As the Data Protection Directive is in force since 1995 it is outdated today and will be replaced by the General Data Protection Regulation (GDPR) (Regulation (EU) 2016/679) which was published on 4 May 2016 and shall apply from 25 May 2018. With

---

[1] Officially called: Directive 95/46/EC on the protection of individuals with regard to the processing of personal data and on the free movement of such data.

the GDPR the Commission intends to strengthen and harmonize the data protection laws for individuals across the European Union (EU). The primary objectives of the GDPR are to give citizens more control over and easier access to their personal data and to unify the regulation within the EU to facilitate international business. The regulation applies if the data processor or the data subject is based in the EU but it also applies (unlike Directive 95/46/EC) to an organization based outside the EU that processes personal data of EU residents. That means that the future EU data protection laws will also apply to cloud providers like Amazon and Google. Also the GDPR strengthens the so called "right to be forgotten" which refers to the right to have one's data deleted or not further disseminated after a fixed period of time [13].

For international business and data transfers the Safe Harbor Privacy Principles were the most important agreements. They were signed between the European Union and the United States to enable the legal transatlantic movement to and storage of personal data in the United States. US companies storing personal data of EU citizens would self-certify that they adhere to 7 principles and therefore comply with the data protection requirements of the EU. However, Safe Harbor came under much criticism because it could be bypassed by the US Patriot Act which allowed U.S. intelligence to gain access to the stored data of U.S. companies (via court order). So on October 24, 2015 the Safe Harbor Privacy Principles were overturned by the European Court of Justice. This resulted in new talks between the European Commission and the US authorities to develop "a renewed and sound framework for transatlantic data flows" [14] – the birth of the EU-US Privacy Shield. The Privacy Shield is a framework for the transatlantic exchange of personal data for commercial purposes between the European Union and the United States. It aims to protect "the fundamental rights of individuals where their data is transferred to the United States and ensure legal certainty for businesses" [15]. This new arrangement imposes strong obligations on U.S. companies to monitor and enforce the protection of personal data of EU citizens. The Privacy Shield includes written commitments and assurance by the U.S. that any access by public authorities to personal data transferred under the new arrangement on national security grounds will be subject to clear conditions, limitations and oversight, preventing generalized access [15].

Apart from the Safe Harbor Privacy Principles the USA PATRIOT Act has also been suspended. The provisions expired on June 1, 2015 and since then have been replaced by the USA FREEDOM Act (H.R. 2048, Pub.L. 114–23) which restored in a modified form several provisions of the Patriot Act. Its supporters claim that the Freedom Act imposes new limits on the bulk collection of telecommunication data on U.S. citizens by American intelligence agencies like the National Security Agency (NSA). But critics argue that the Freedom Act actually has produced only very marginal gains for privacy and that the mass surveillance program continues (e. g. the collection of call records) just under slightly changed circumstances.

When it comes to media law there are no regulations dealing with cloud computing directly. But of course existing media laws also apply to the usage of cloud (services). Copyright laws, personal rights, license agreements and film rights, which can come with strict requirements on security and access protection, must be observed in the cloud as well.

64.5.2   Implications on Broadcasters and Media Companies

The legal framework addresses personal data and data associated with the personality of individuals. The consequences may not be always immediately obvious. For instance, there is the notion that an IP-address used by an individual to communicate with a server is regarded "personal data". Also logging into a cloud service for maintenance and configuration creates "personal data".

The legal framework on personal data substantially affects the media domain as e. g. all on-demand services and personalization include processing of personal data. For on-demand services (e. g. VoD) cloud services are commonly used. Also (big) data analytics relevant for personalization maps well to cloud services. With the usage varying significantly over the day the load either for transcoding, data IO, data base access etc. varies sharply over the day as well. Thus the scalability of the cloud is a huge advantage.

While in the former example personal data is stored and processed, personal data is being created as well when using cloud services in the context of media production. Think of a non-linear editing tool in the cloud. Each time the cutter uses the tool, this usage and the information who is using it establishes personal data as well, which requires protection according to the legal framework.

In media there is another source of "personal data". The protection level of sensitive information about investigative research or data that may require identity protection of sources or informants must even be higher than for personal data. As a potential access of cloud systems by government authorities or criminals cannot be ruled out, it is advisable not to use in particular public cloud systems.

For media prior to using a public cloud (service) it needs to be evaluated and precisely defined what personal data shall and is permitted to be stored there. Also a data classification by required level of protection should be conducted. But note that the legal framework for protecting personal data applies also to any in-house processing, e. g. in a private cloud.

The legal framework poses particular requirements on personal data. But the media file itself requires a high level of protection as well. For media companies and broadcasters theft or loss of their media assets is the main concern when thinking about cloud usage. There have been some incidents recently that made headlines e. g. the iCloud hack in 2014 where celebrity photos were stolen. But as the hack of Sony pictures in 2014 shows you can also suffer from a cyber-attack in your own data center. The cloud does not have to be less secure than your own data center. In fact public clouds are highly secure. Most of them meet various different international and industry-specific compliance standards (like ISO 27001, HIPAA or SOC 1 and 2) and are audited by third-parties regularly. Most company data centers cannot by far compete with that. So sometimes it is more a question of perceived security and trust. But it may be true that the risk of secret access by governments or intelligence services to your data may be higher in the public cloud.

Generally, for media data that is moved into the cloud encryption and keeping encryption and key management in one's own hands should be the key principal. This is probably the only way to guarantee an end-to-end encryption and to safely store your data in the cloud.

64.6   Conclusions

The cloud has already arrived in broadcast operations and among viewers – as a private cloud in one's own data center with virtualized servers, as a service of a central service provider for several production sites in a secure corporate network, or indeed in the form of services in a public cloud. Cloud is common for OTT linear and on-demand media distribution. The functions range from IaaS to SaaS – with SaaS being especially relevant in the private area, but also for complete solutions addressing the professional media market. Deployments in media houses that build in IaaS or PaaS, or those who build on single services and orchestrate these modules as part of an own (cloud based) integration work, are much less frequent, since they require deep technical planning knowledge and maintenance efforts by the media house itself.

Creative user focus on a comfortable availability of functionalities required for investigation, search, media acquisition, finishing and distribution of media, regardless whether this can be achieved by using clouds or by more traditional concepts. The comfort using services on smartphones and so on sets the expectation bar also for professional usage.

Business models still need to prove their sustainability or even to be developed. However, the chance for quick deployments, a high degree of scalability and the potential of a very high utilization of resources in public clouds of major vendors strengthen confidence that clouds will have their established position in media houses. In particular for (public) broadcasters the shift from CAPEX to OPEX is important to note.

The performance and wide availability of high bandwidth network connections to public clouds will play a key role for acceptance. However, bandwidth demands also highly depend on the genre of media production or the application, with decreasing requirements from live production, file based "near live" (news) or offline feature production, down to supporting functions like search and planning.

In principle, clouds bear a certain risk for security and privacy, but some cloud vendors have already reacted on new European legislation initiatives and offer solutions fitting specific national legislation requirements. Moreover, the level of security reached in a cloud has always to be compared with the level of security that can in practice be achieved in private solutions.

Clouds, however, do not necessarily replace traditional broadcast technology but expand it with new possibilities and thus will open new workflow opportunities. The flexibility of cloud based applications will certainly impact today's workflows. Technologies for carrying live audio and video in "studio quality" across larger IP networks into the cloud further extend application ranges, but still need further development and validation. The task is to take the opportunity to also "think in clouds conceptually", to perceive the associated new and very flexible solutions and to implement the appropriate applications based on the individual needs regarding security and privacy, process reliability, maintainability, effort to minimize the risk of cloud vendor lock-in, personnel structure and training expenditure. Cloud-based concepts definitely offer opportunities for broadcast – and good knowledge of all aspects helps to avoid risks and to implement tailor-made solutions.

References

1. National Institute of Standards and Technology, "The NIST Definition of Cloud Computing," NIST, Gaithersburg, 2011.
2. Federal Office for Information Security (BSI), "Security Recommendations for Cloud Computing Providers," BSI, Bonn, 2012.
3. M. Verhovnik, "www.irt.de," [Online]. Available: https://www.irt.de/fileadmin/media/downloads/veranstaltungen/2016/Trimedialitaet-Praesentation1_IRT-Kolloquium.pdf. [Accessed 06 September 2016].
4. R. Schäfer, "Medienfabrik 4.0", IRT Jahresbericht 2015, pp. 8–10, [Online]. Available: http://www.irt.de/webarchiv/showdoc.php?z=ODExNCMxMDA2MDE3I3BkZg==. [Accessed 07 September 2016].
5. C. Pfeifer, "IP-netzwerke für die Live-Produktion," *FKT*, pp. 500–504, 2014.
6. M. Schneider und P. Schut, "IEEE 802.1 AVB: Video über Ethernet in Produktionssystemen," *FKT*, pp. 527–?, 2013.
7. K. W. Rößel, "Vernetzte Produktionsabläufe – 'Anywhere' für Video," *FKT*, pp. 631–635, 2014.
8. "www.make.tv," [Online]. Available: www.make.tv. [Accessed 29 08 2016].
9. "YouTube Statistik," [Online]. Available: https://www.youtube.com/yt/press/de/statistics.html. [Accessed 01 09 2016].
10. S. Siepe, "www.fktg.org," [Online]. Available: https://www.fktg.org/argos-datenschutzkonforme-qualitaetsueberpruefung-von-streaming-angeboten. [Accessed 06 September 2016].
11. C. Ziegler, "Second screen for HbbTV — Automatic application launch and app-to-app communication enabling novel TV programme related second-screen scenarios," *2013 IEEE Third International Conference on Consumer Electronics Berlin (ICCE-Berlin), Berlin,* pp. pp. 1–5, 2013.
12. M. Stiller, "www.irt.de," [Online]. Available: http://www.irt.de/webarchiv/showdoc.php?z=NjY2OCMxMDA1MjE3I3BkZg==. [Accessed 07 September 2016].
13. European Commission, "European Commission – Fact Sheet, Questions and Answers – Data protection reform," [Online]. Available: http://europa.eu/rapid/press-release_MEMO-15-6385_en.htm. [Accessed 29 08 2016].
14. European Commission, "European Commission – Speech – [Check Against Delivery], Commissioner Jourová's remarks on Safe Harbour EU Court of Justice judgement before the Committee on Civil Liberties, Justice and Home Affairs (Libe)," [Online]. Available: http://europa.eu/rapid/press-release_SPEECH-15-5916_de.htm. [Accessed 29 08 2016].
15. European Commission, "European Commission – Fact Sheet, EU-U.S. Privacy Shield: Frequently Asked Questions," [Online]. Available: http://europa.eu/rapid/press-release_MEMO-16-2462_en.htm. [Accessed 29 08 2016].

Data & IT Security, a Challenge for the Cloud Computing Trend

65

Ralf Rieken

Abstract

The most important and greatest global challenge in cloud computing is to be able to fulfill data privacy and compliance demands and ensure IT security. In its 2012 published study "On the Security of Cloud Storage Services", the Fraunhofer Institute for Secure Information Technology (SIT) mentions three potential security vulnerabilities it detected: Access by unauthorized third parties during data transfer, interception of the database itself, and possible abuse through the actual cloud service provider. Security experts consider the former two loopholes as closed, if

1. correct SSL/TLS encryption protects the data during transfer, and
2. cryptographic procedures secure the stored data.

Present paper elucidates how basic Sealed Cloud technology covers the third security risk, in which the service provider has access to clear text data in processing servers.

65.1   Introduction

Experian, the world's leading information services group, has released a "Data Breach Industry Forecast 2016" report that substantiates the following: the most important and greatest global challenge in cloud computing is to be able to fulfill data privacy and compliance demands and ensure IT security. In order for businesses to be able to rise to this

R. Rieken (✉)
Uniscon GmbH
Munich, Germany
e-mail: ralf.rieken@uniscon.de

challenge, economies need clear data protection and compliance laws that keep up with technical developments, as well as technology with which to actually be able to enforce those demands [1].

The various online communications forms, e-mail, file sharing, and messaging, on the one hand, increase productivity and efficiency. On the other hand, however, their use is also risky, raising technology security concerns. After all, vulnerable business internal and external communication security can grant unauthorized parties access to servers and unencrypted data. A major security loophole consists in the fact that providers of clouds that process data can access unencrypted data through their application servers. A further security issue consists in the fact that even metadata, that is encrypted end-to-end in a cloud, may still be analyzed and accessed and, hence, misappropriated for profiling very easily.

65.2   Data Security & Compliance Requirements for Businesses

Private enterprises or public authorities, that process personal or personally identifiable data of customers or other third parties, are subject to data privacy law and respective (European, federal, state, etc.) data protection acts. EU directives, international and business internal conventions and agreements, and established practices provide further regulation. As a result, both private enterprises and public authorities are subject to a wide variety of statutory obligations, which, if not met, can lead to high fines and substantial liability claims [2].

Business external online communication, for example, poses one of the greatest risks: Employees often deem encryption measures inconvenient, which is why documents are frequently sent in unencrypted form. Even if information is encrypted, data centers can still process it merely in unencrypted form.

Consequently, when data is processed within a cloud, in both internal and external data centers, it remains accessible, especially when cloud provider staff can or must access it, e. g. for typical administration purposes. In the past, since data breaches in conventional systems customarily postulated multiple-party cooperation, organizational measures sufficed for the protection of personal and personally identifiable data, data that was subject to professional and official secrecy, classified data, and confidential matters in general. However, since a high degree of networking and miniaturization have found their way into almost all data processing systems, today, one individual misappropriating data is often all it takes, to do great damage. The high-profile case around whistleblower Edward Snowden substantiates this perfectly.

For this reason, the technology and market research firm Forrester Research provocatively calls the security model that has become necessary owing to said trend, the "Zero Trust Security Model" [3]. Forrester excoriates that conventional security models divide their world into "trustworthy inner" and "untrustworthy external" areas, thus focusing too much on perimeter security, which relies on a combination of organizational and "human"

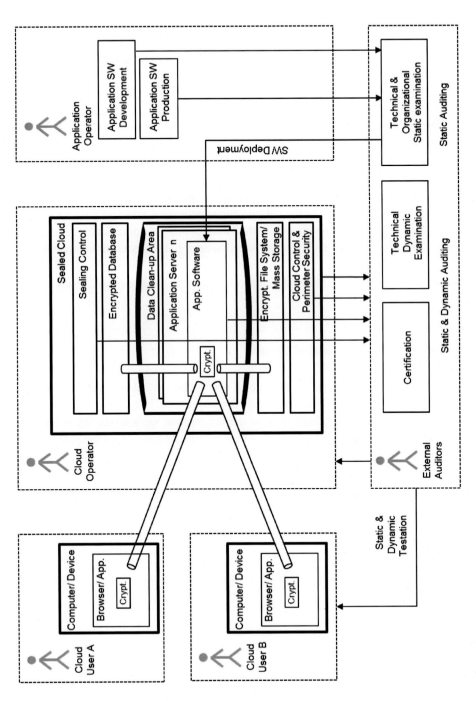

Fig. 65.1 Sealed Cloud System Overview

measures, to protect their infrastructures, applications, and data against external attacks, while neglecting security against potential internal attacks. In equal measure as per novel information security model presented herein, protection along the first line of defense should be warranted internally and externally via technical measures only.

The following chapter illustrates the basic principles of the Sealed Cloud safety concept (see Fig. 65.1). It elucidates how named approach protects content and metadata alike, without compromising service availability or any of its features [4].

65.3 The Technology's Basic Concept

The root idea of the Sealed Cloud technology consists in the combination of performance and convenience of a conventional web service, on the one hand, and essential, compliant information security, on the other. "Performance" postulates that the networks' access capability may be exploited efficiently and operations performed effectively on communication content. In contrast, "compliant security" implies that a set of technical measures effectively and verifiably exclude all unauthorized access, both to content and metadata alike. Organizational measures against internal and external spying along the first line of defense, in particular, become redundant, thus excluding the "human" risk factor altogether.

65.3.1 Secure Access to Sealed Cloud

The device is connected to Sealed Cloud via SSL encryption, so that no special software need to be installed. In order to ensure imperative, compliant security, the system merely admits strong ciphers, i.e. long keys with no implementation weaknesses. As opposed to conventional web servers, the system also bars all private keys on server side, thus ensuring "perfect forward secrecy" [5].

65.3.2 Protection Against Data Access During Processing

In addition to encryption, named technology also hermetically "seals" the system, so that infrastructure providers and service provider staff have no way of accessing user data during processing whatsoever. The following components constitute said sealing technology:

a) Data Center Segmentation
   The data center is subdivided into multiple segments, which can each operate independently of one another. This ensures redundant connectivity of operations, even during data clean-up, as described below.

b) Technical Entry & Access Control, Alarm System

The application servers are located in the data clean-up area in special mechanically sealed units ("cages"), whose access is controlled via electromechanical locks. Electronic server interfaces not needed for the application's operation are deactivated or provided with filters, in order to prevent any unauthorized access to server content, including that of administrators or maintenance staff. A further feature pertaining to the servers engaged in this area, is that no persistent memory is used that could record application data. Both the mechanical cage components and the servers are secured against manipulation by a multitude of sensors. This ensures that any access attempt whatsoever, be it on a physical level, be it on a logical one, immediately triggers an alarm that instantly deletes all the data on the respective servers.

c) Data Clean-Up

Said alarm instantly triggers data clean-up. In doing so, user sessions on the affected servers are automatically routed to non-affected segments, and all data on the affected segment is deleted. What's more, deletion is additionally ensured by sufficient (10-second) automatic power supply disconnection to the servers.

d) Integrity Checks

Before a server begins to operate after data clean-up, the entire hardware and software are subject to an integrity check. This postulates individual production and signing of software for each respective server. In other words, should a maintenance worker try to install components during maintenance that have not been cleared or attempt to manipulate the hardware, the integrity check prevents reintegration of that affected server.

65.3.3   No Decryption Keys in the Database

"Sealing" comprehends special key distribution, in which the service provider disposes of no key with which to decrypt a database's protocols or a file system's files. In practice, this means that the keys to a database's protocols consist of hash chains of user names and passwords. The instant a hash value is ascertained, the user name and password are rejected. At the end of a session, the determined hash value is also deleted. The latter two procedures constitute crucial focal points of independent auditors' inspection and certification protocols.

65.3.4   Additional Metadata Security Measures

In order to prevent metadata information from being deducted from external data traffic observation, the system communicates traffic-volume dependently and in a pseudo-random, deferred, i. e. time-delayed manner. The volume of transmitted data is scaled to the standard next in size [6]. This prevents deduction of metadata per size correlation. After all, even if cloud data is encrypted end-to-end, "confidential content may still be disclosed indirectly via metadata", states attorney-at-law Steffen Kroschwald, Research Associate of provet, the Constitutional Technology Design Project Group at the University of Kassel [7]. Since linked metadata reveals a great deal of information, parties obliged to professional and official secrecy, in particular, e. g., must do all that is possible to ensure maximum data security.

65.4 Alternative: Homomorphous Encryption

Combining homomorphous encryption [7] with a mix network would ensure high data security. This is a promising scientific approach. In practice, the customary approach with currently available technology entails both technical and economic difficulties. Homomorphic encryption does, indeed, enable further processing of already encrypted data, without said data having to be decrypted prior to processing. However, this encryption option incurs exponentially increasing costs compared to conventional data processing and will most likely continue to do so for quite a long time.

In contrast, the mix network does not transfer information directly from the sender to the recipient but rather via multiple intermediate stations (mixes). This technological combination allows the data's origin to be concealed yet does not protect the metadata (connection data) effectively. The pseudonyms (aliases) communicating with each other, i. e. who communicates with whom, remains visible. As a result, pseudonyms are easy to uncover.

65.5 Application as Basic Technology

Sealed Cloud was developed by Uniscon GmbH and refined, as a basic technology for wide application in manufacturing and trade, in a consortium with AISEC (Fraunhofer Institute for Applied and Integrated Security) and SecureNet within the framework of the German Federal Ministry for Economic Affairs and Energy's Trusted Cloud program. Today, the interfaces at hand may be adapted to the most diverse applications and services imaginable. Hence, since Sealed Cloud's maximum security may be integrated into companies' individual solutions, the technology also ensures businesses a competitive edge on the global market. This is corroborated, among others, by a variety of international corporations and German global players applying the technology.

The technology allows small and medium-sized enterprises to use the secure infrastructure in two ways: On the one hand, applications can be added directly to the platform and implement the basic principles of Sealed Cloud themselves. At the same time, applications can use the generic features of the existing communication service iDGARD via said interfaces and integrate the service directly into existing business procedures.

65.5.1   iDGARD Web Service for Collaboration & File Exchange

By virtue of Sealed Cloud's maximum security, iDGARD service enables safe document and message exchange both business internally and externally. And that to such a high degree, that, in March 2016, iDGARD was one of the first services ever to be certified pursuant to the Federal Ministry for Economic Affairs and Energy's Trusted Cloud Data Protection Profile (TCDP). iDGARD was certified maximum-security Class 3 protection, which allows even parties subject to professional and official secrecy obligations, to process personal and personally identifiable data via public cloud.

Since iDGARD is a cloud offer, applying the service requires no special or added software. All a user needs is a web browser and a mobile device app. This leads to the following application scenarios, which meet the data privacy and compliance demands of any business fully:

- Confidential file exchange with staff, customers, and partners; i. e., safe file transfer
- Team workspace, project and data rooms for business internal and external collaboration
- Mobile access to business documents
- Chats via any mobile device
- Scheduling & resource planning

Secure business internal and external communication is possible, because the entire key management remains indiscernible to the user yet well protected within Sealed Cloud. For this reason, it is not necessary for an external dialogue partner to dispose of an own iDGARD license, if a member of an organization wishes to communicate with him or her. Instead, the license owner simply grants that party a Guest License. To do so, he or she simply creates a Privacy Box, i. e. a common project workspace, by entering the recipient's name, e-mail address and mobile number. What's more, Privacy Boxes may be upgraded to Data Rooms. In the latter, all activity is recorded in an auditable journal. Further features include anti-forwarding measures, such as watermarks, view-only options, etc.

Considering the facts and figures that exist to date, as to how quickly the service for secure collaboration is written off, allows the technology's financial benefits to be assessed also for other applications: If a business wishes to establish an infrastructure with which to communicate with external parties, it has to expect costs for merely installing a secure system; Not to mention further expenses for system operation and management, maintenance and repair, and its actual campaign against cybercrime. When using the cloud service iDGARD, businesses are spared the cost of installation. What's more, this carries the benefit that the business uses the service in line with demand (pay per use). From project experience, a cloud based collaboration service is already amortized within one to two months. Likewise, commensurate financial benefits may also be calculated for all Sealed Cloud based applications.

65.5.2   A File Sharing Solution on the Sealed Cloud Platform

Group Business Software (GBS) is a provider of solutions and services for the IBM and Microsoft Collaboration Platforms. One of its applications is iQ.Suite Watchdog FileSafe [8], which enables confidential and compliant e-mail file transfer per Sealed Cloud interface: When an e-mail attachment is sent, it is automatically sourced out to a maximum-security cloud area, where it is substituted by an e-mail link. The recipient receives this link with a one-time, non-recurring password. He or she can then log on to the protected cloud and access the respective data.

65.5.3   Compliant Big Data Analysis

A further feature, Sealed Freeze, enables data privacy compliant memory of big data applications. In conjunction with the rapid expansion of big data applications, secure data memory is, indeed, still dealt with less than data preservation; yet big data bears much greater risks in terms of data abuse. Basically, big data is based on the collection of tremendous amounts of data for the mere purpose of analysis.

The Sealed Freeze concept ensures adequate protection of big data against access, by technically enforcing rules specified ex ante, in which, for example, the parties granted access, the duration of data storage, and rules pertaining to the deletion of data are defined prior to use. Sealed Freeze technology is already implemented by iDGARD and widely applied by global players.

65.5.4   Data Protection & Compliance

Under the Regulation 2016/679 of the European Parliament and of the Council of 27th April 2016, no disclosure of any confidential data by unauthorized parties should be feasible whatsoever. Almost always, not only content but also metadata constitutes a professional secret. Parties obliged to professional or official secrecy are not free to tacitly accept or acquiesce to possible disclosure of such data from conventional business internal and external communication. In contrast, an application based on Sealed Cloud technology, such as iDGARD, enables parties obliged to professional secrecy to communicate online internally and externally in compliance with data privacy law.

The latter even ensures requisite data confiscation protection. This is merely possible by virtue of Uniscon's Sealed Cloud technology, which has already been patented in leading countries worldwide[1].

---

[1] EP: 2389641, et al.

65.6 Conclusion

Since today's IT market is largely dominated by American service providers, German IT solutions are often regarded with suspicion. At the same time, the US attitude is frequently considered lax, when it comes to data privacy. The past few months have substantiated this assumption: owing to Snowden's disclosures and the public's increased awareness of US authorities' stance as to foreign clients' data privacy. Trust in German quality, in data protection, in particular, now plays an increasingly important role. With Sealed Cloud, German and European users are provided a platform that complies with their security needs. As a result, they are now able to reap the economic benefits of cloud computing also for business essential applications ignored to date and, hence, reduce costs significantly.

This greatly redounds to German providers' advantage, who are given a competitive edge with this technology. After all, German cloud providers not only enjoy greater trust than American ones. Today, such a consumer confidence fostering technical solution is also a blessing in the competitive market worldwide. This applies to IT providers, hosting firms, and system integrators alike.

The Author

Ralf Rieken has two decades experience in the network infrastructure and IT industry in Germany and the USA. At Siemens, he played a leading role in the development of value-added services for telecommunications networks. In the United States, he served as Vice President of Software Development at Optisphere Networks and, until 2007, as CEO of Fujitsu Siemens Computers in Silicon Valley. Back in Germany, he managed IT Data Center Consulting at Fujitsu Technology Solutions in Munich. In 2009, he founded the IT company Uniscon with Dr. Hubert Jäger and Arnold Monitzer.

References

1. Experian, "Third Annual 2016 Data Breach Industry Forecast," Experian, 2016. [Online]. Available: http://www.experian.com/data-breach/2015-data-breach-industry-forecast.html. [Accessed 18 5 2016].
2. S. Kroschwald und M. Wicker, Kanzleien und Praxen in der Cloud – Strafbarkeit nach §203 StGB, 2012, pp. 758–764.
3. Forrester, "No More Chewy Centers, Introducing The Zero Trust Model Of Information Security," [Online]. Available: http://solutions.forrester.com/zero-trust-model?intcmp=mkt:blg:sr:ts-airwatch&scid=701a00000025sCn. [Accessed 20 6 2016].
4. H. Jaeger und e. al., "A Novel Set of Measures against Insider Attacks – Sealed Cloud," in *Proceedings of Open Identity Summit 2013, Lecutre Notes in Informatics*, Bd. 223, 2013.
5. J. Schmidt, "Zukunftssicher verschlüsseln mit Perfect Forward Secrecy," Heise, [Online]. Available: http://www.heise.de/security/artikel/Zukunftssicher-Verschluesseln-mit-Perfect-Forward-Secrecy-1923800.html. [Accessed 11 9 2014].

6. H. Jaeger und E. Ernst, "Telekommunikation, bei der nicht nur Inhalte, sondern auch Metadaten geschützt sind," in *D-A-CH Security 2014 – Bestandsaufnahme, Konzepte, Anwendungen, Perspektiven, Ferven*, 2014, pp. 191–202.
7. S. Kroschwald, "Informationelle Selbstbestimung in der Cloud. Datenschutzrechtliche Bewertung und Gestaltung des Cloud Computings aus dem Blickwinkel des Mittelstandes," *DuD Fachbeiträge*, 2016.
8. B. Hayes, "Alice and Bob in Cipherspace," American Scientist, 09/10 2012. [Online]. Available: http://www.americanscientist.org/issues/pub/2012/5/alice-and-bob-in-cipherspace. [Accessed 16 7 2016].

Further Reading

9. M. Borgmann, T. Hahn, M. Herfert, T. Kunz, M. Richter, U. Viebeg und S. Vow, "On the Security of Cloud Storage Services," Fraunhofer SIT, 2012. [Online]. Available: https://www.sit.fraunhofer.de/fileadmin/dokumente/studien_und_technical_reports/Cloud-Storage-Security_a4.pdf. [Accessed 23 9 2016].
10. TCDP, "Trusted Cloud Datenschutzprofil Version 1.0, ed. Pilotprojekt Datenschutzzertifizierung für Cloud-Dienste," [Online]. Available: http://www.tcdp.de/data/pdf/TCDP-1-0.pdf. [Accessed 24 9 2016].
11. Donar Messe, "iQ.Suite Watchdog FileSafe," 2014. [Online]. Available: http://donar.messe.de/exhibitor/cebit/2014/W327921/iq-suite-watchdog-filesafe-ger-286785.pdf. [Accessed 11 9 2014].

Part XV
Internet of Things

Preface: Internet of Things

66

Goodarz Mahbobi

I am very happy and thankful to live in today's world – with all the technological innovation and the transformation of society, factories etc. The rapidly changing technological environment can be compared to the generational transition: from my birth until the age of five, there was barely any technical revolution or rather not a visible one. At least it was certainly not comparable to the revolution of mobile development during the first five years of the life of my daughter from 2003 until 2008.

If we want to predict the business world of tomorrow, we have to observe the purchase behavior of our children: they walk into a store, have a look at the products, compare the prices on the spot by using their smartphones and order the product online if the price is more favorable. I have not taught my children to do so. However I can see them applying this particular behavior almost daily. It is exactly how we sometimes save money. The same applies to the communication of the future. Today our children ask us why we are using old-fashioned mediums like e-mails in our company; messengers such as WhatsApp or the likes seem to be far less complicated . . . !

Not only the purchase behavior of the next generation is changing, the whole society is. Therefore especially retailers must prepare themselves. New technologies are changing our lifestyle. The basis for this change is formed by the internet of things (or in abbreviated form "IoT").

In my point of view, the entire technical revolution of IoT is based on four main pillars *Mobile Technology, Big Data, Cloud Computing* and *Collaboration* (see Fig. 66.1). Those four pillars are framed by three additional components *network and ICT infrastructure, IT know-how* as well as *development of new business models*. I will comment on each component in more detail hereinafter:

G. Mahbobi (✉)
axxessio GmbH
Bonn, Germany
e-mail: mahbobi@axxessio.com

© Springer-Verlag GmbH Germany 2018
C. Linnhoff-Popien et al. (eds.), *Digital Marketplaces Unleashed*,
https://doi.org/10.1007/978-3-662-49275-8_66

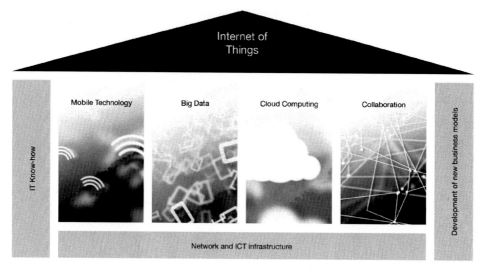

Fig. 66.1 Internet of Things

- *Mobile Technology*

  The entire way of communication has been completely changed by the widespread introduction of smartphones. Put in global terms, today even more IP-based devices are in use compared to an everyday item like toothbrushes. This is an upward trend. I would even go as far as to say that, for example, in the near future all employees of a factory will only able to perform their daily activities by the use of mobile devices. Other industries will also have to deal with mobile technology, if they want to keep up with the current trends. In short: "no app – no business".

- *Big Data*

  This term refers to the collection and analysis of data as well as the recognition of patterns within that set of data, as far as I understand it. New insights will be gained and future events can be predicted by the use of big data.

- *Cloud Computing*

  In the near term, the cloud will replace personal computers. In the United States of America, more than 67% of users make use of cloud services and benefit from the ability to store data externally. Moreover users are able to access and run their data from any physical place in the world. The trend "data everywhere" will further increase since cloud services are scalable and more cost-effective compared to local storage devices.

- *Collaboration*

  As previously described, the purchasing behavior is changing. Known processes in procurement and sales have to be reassessed. Based on those findings, we have to learn and adapt ourselves to the new generation. This phenomenon applies to all other areas: the current IT approach will change radically as well and consequently also the cooperation between people, processes, data and mobile.

- *Network and ICT infrastructure*

  The above mentioned trends are only viable and functional as long as we have an intelligent, fast and reliable global network at our disposal. Another essential factor to be considered is the security of that network. The amount of sensitive data that is sent over the internet will dramatically increase. Precisely for this purpose, the provision of a secure infrastructure is essential.

- *IT Know-how*

  Anyone who wants keep up with current challenges needs qualified employees. In large organizations, the management has to be sensitized at first. Afterwards, the skills of all employees have to be further developed within the company. However, the focus is no longer just on employees. Rather the entire IT know-how of the upcoming generation has to be enhanced. It is imperative to enhance the syllabi and training schedules and to continuously train teachers, so that they train and encourage the employees of tomorrow.

- *Development of new business models*

  The development of new business models is the result of all abovementioned components. Only those who understand and purposefully implement the concept are able to develop new business models on medium and long term. This is how one can maintain and expand its competitive advantage.

IoT is the basis for all future concepts; this includes buzzwords like smart factory or smart city. The entire transformation of the industry will be based on, not only existing but also secure, internet of things platforms. The fact that standards need to be defined is self-explanatory.

The technical revolution is accompanied by a shift of emotions, which must not be neglected. It is our duty to prepare today's society. The next generation however, the generation of our kids, is already "digital savvy" and requires no special preparation, they need a lot more education in handling of technologies.

We experience the emotional change very differently through our society. 20 years ago, it was unthinkable to entrust credit card details to a stranger. In modern days, all payment details are stored at companies such as PayPal or credit card institutions. In China people even make all payments on WeChat, a Chinese Facebook/WhatsApp equivalent. What we call modern technology now, will be a given in the future.

IoT is not only altering the work environment, but it also affects our way of live. And we are just at the beginning of a fundamental transformation.

Cloud Technologies – May 'Fog Computing' Help out the Traditional Cloud and Pave the Way to 5G Networks

67

Robert Iberl and Rolf Schillinger

Abstract

Innovation is at the heart of today's ever changing IT infrastructures. Core technologies of the Internet Age periodically are refined through sizeable innovations. Currently, two of these core technologies are undergoing a major reshape, with Cloud Computing being extended to cover computing nodes that do not reside within carefully designed data centers, and mobile networks which are currently moving towards their fifth generation termed "5G". This chapter describes these advancements by introducing the Fog Computing paradigm and its very specific requirements as well as potential 5G architectures that are able to handle these requirements.

67.1 Introduction

In the 2015 Gartner Hype Cycle [1], the Internet of Things (IoT) is assessed as being on top of the Peak of Inflated Expectations. This usually means that the hype surrounding IoT technologies will gradually subside while at the same time real world applications of IoT technologies will be seen more and more frequently. In order to fully tap the potential of these new IoT applications, however, a solid foundation for processing, transferring,

R. Iberl (✉)
Bayerische Forschungsallianz GmbH
Munich, Germany
e-mail: iberl@bayfor.org

R. Schillinger
Fachhochschule Würzburg Schweinfurt
Würzburg, Germany
e-mail: rolf.schillinger@fhws.de

© Springer-Verlag GmbH Germany 2018
C. Linnhoff-Popien et al. (eds.), *Digital Marketplaces Unleashed*,
https://doi.org/10.1007/978-3-662-49275-8_67

763

and analyzing is imperative. Fog Computing and 5G networks are potential technologies to help exploit the full potential of IoT.

Fog Computing is a relatively new concept, coined in the years 2013 and 2014 and originating mainly in the IT industry, not the research community. In short, Fog Computing describes the increasing permeability of Cloud Computing technologies across provider and consumer boundaries. Traditionally, the popular approach to Cloud Computing is to regionally centralize the computing power in large data centers whose architectures strictly adhere to Cloud Provider boundaries. As a result, these infrastructure architectures guarantee lower operational costs and stronger application security. The obvious need for redundancy and resilience is fulfilled through industry standard provisions within the Cloud provider's sites (e. g. redundant SANs, highly available virtualization infrastructures) and by providing the possibility for other data centers within the Cloud provider's own network to take over parts of the workload in case of a catastrophic failure to one of the sites. This approach is very common these days and scales to millions of users of a single service without a problem.

Millions of users and sharply defined services are not the reality in an Internet of Things (IoT) setting, however. In the IoT, user figures are in the billion range and applications in the IoT are of a very diverse nature. The sheer amount of input data that will be received from globally distributed sources makes such central data processing structures less than ideally suited for these tasks.

Another defining factor of the IoT is its "always-on" approach that requires secure, reliable and performant network connections everywhere on earth. 5G networks can be designed to allow for such a connection for the billions of devices projected to join the IoT in the next years.

In this chapter, the relation between Fog Computing and 5G networks will be analyzed by first defining Fog Computing requirements on mobile networks and relating some current 5G network architecture proposals to these requirements.

67.2 Fog Computing

According to Stojmenovic et al., Fog Computing "extends Cloud Computing and services to the edge of the network" [2]. A typical and frequently described use case for Fog Computing is the processing of the vast amount of data originating in the Internet of Things (IoT), with billions of sensors and mobile and stationary computing devices with varying performance profiles and a wide range of capabilities. Each of these devices is a potential Fog infrastructure node taking part in the execution of Fog services. Thus, actual computing workloads with an attached set of data and respective inputs and outputs are distributed and executed across these (arbitrary) nodes.

In general, the distinction between Fog Computing services and traditional Cloud Computing services is not clear cut. An often cited distinction between the two concepts is just the "location" of the computing process itself. While the physical location of each running process is always known to at least the service provider's backend systems, a strictly and unambiguously defined cutoff point for the distinction between Cloud and Fog cannot be defined. The further this process is moved toward the end user, the more likely the resulting construct is termed Fog Computing [2, 3], however.

Distributing workloads in this fashion has a number of palpable benefits. A very frequently mentioned advantage is the Data Locality [2, 3], describing the obvious proximity of the data sources to the data processors. This is an essential property for systems processing data on IoT scales, as today's Big Data systems do not require access to the raw data material in order to arrive at meaningful results. Careful extraction, filtering, and aggregation at the closest available nodes is an excellent countermeasure to data privacy and data security problems associated with transmitting IoT sensor data across the globe while at the same time limiting the consumed bandwidth.

Lowered latency is another benefit frequently attributed to Fog architectures [2, 4]. It is important to note, however, that the described latency is not the latency of a user-facing application but rather the latency with which data sources and data processors communicate. Low latency is essential for many applications in the IoT that do the above mentioned filtering and aggregation of data before sending it off to upstream data processing components in Cloud Computing centers.

A further defining benefit of the Fog paradigm is its support for Mobility [5]. Many IoT scenarios like Vehicle Ad-Hoc Networks (VANETs) require that the data processor constantly and reliably receives data from sources travelling at potentially high velocities [6]. Having data processors executing on potentially any node on the edge of the network renders this possible since the data processor can move alongside its linked data source by being migrated to suitable nodes within the data sources' vicinity.

Up until now, the research community as well as key industry players advocating the Fog allocated it the role of an IoT enabler but do not expand Fog Computing into a larger context. There is, however, the possibility to further extend Fog Computing concepts by simply relaxing the requirement that the Fog nodes at the network edge must be under control of either a single or of multiple but collaborating organizations. In such a – so far mostly hypothetical – scenario, the Fog would be extended to encompass locally available computing resources regardless of their respective operators, choosing the computing node solely on properties like its location or its current utilization.

Considering this definition of the Fog, a future 5G network architecture needs to support the following functionalities in order to be a suitable platform for this type of Cloud evolution:

- Location Awareness – to permit data locality, the underlying network needs to provide location awareness functionality to its application layer.
- Quality of Service – to sustain reliable latency during connections, the network has to support QoS provisions and needs to be able to automatically broker suitable connection parameters.

- Mobility framework – to fully provide Mobility as postulated above, the network needs to combine Location Awareness, Quality of Service, and an intelligent protocol suite to form a Mobility framework.
- Security – Fog Computing has the potential to allow execution of arbitrary workloads on arbitrary nodes without a central instance that could reliable certify the security of both, the workload and the nodes. Therefore, the network has to provide basic and advanced security services in order to alleviate the security problems attached to this paradigm.

67.3 Mobile Networks in the Context of Fog Computing

In the mid-seventies first steps towards cellular networks had been undertaken. While the first generation of cellular networks was purely analogue, a major step towards fully digital networks followed already with the advent of 2G networks. These networks, also known as GSM, were rolled out all over the world in 1992 and paved the way to groundbreaking inventions like roaming or data transfer over cellular links. Thus, GSM was the standard for the years to come.

Mobile data transfers gradually became more demanding; this is why the Universal Mobile Telecommunications System (UMTS) became the core network architecture around the turn of the millennium. By combining aspects of the 2G network with new technology and protocols, the data delivery rate was significantly increased. In addition to being more secure than its predecessor, 3G telecommunication networks, by relying on bandwidth and location services, enabled the design of applications not previously available to mobile phone users. Today, most of the networks rolled-out LTE technology, a so-called 4G network. They are based on the International Mobile Telecommunications-Advanced (IMT-Advanced) standard. The core of these networks is purely IP based and consequently voice calls are carried via Voice-over-IP (VoIP). Moreover, 100 Mbps must be delivered as data speed, and multiple network types must be supported. Thus, going from 4G to Wi-Fi and vice-versa is a feature which is only hampered through network providers' efforts. 5G networks are currently in the planning phase and will see widespread deployment within the next 4–5 years. The overall success of 5G networks is dependent on the development of a secure and robust environment that provides users with a safe, fast, and reliable connectivity and underpins the future generation of applications and services. 5G is not only a merger of fixed and mobile networks, it will also take into account sectors that are especially data-intensive (e. g. automotive). 5G networks additionally appear to be the ideal underlying platform for smart services on the IoT since they facilitate the necessary mobility of intelligent data processing to arbitrary network locations while allowing to maintain the availability of smart gateways, also known as intelligent access solutions and their communication paths to the Cloud also considering Fog computing.

67.3.1   5G Network Stack

The socio-technical evolution in the last few decades has been significantly driven by the evolution of mobile communications and has contributed to the economic and social development of both developed and developing countries. Mobile communication has become closely integrated in the daily life of the whole society. It is expected that the socio-technical trends and the evolution of mobile communications systems will remain tightly coupled together and will form a foundation for society in 2020 and beyond.

In the future, however, it is foreseeable that new demands, such as larger traffic volume, rapidly increasing number of devices with diverse service requirements, pursuit of better quality of user experience (QoE), and better affordability by further decreasing costs, will require an increasing number of innovative solutions. It is up to the 5G network designers to take all these demands into account during the current specification phase.

It is required to consider framework guidelines for IMT's 2020 (5G) capabilities targeting 2020 and beyond, as well as to assess spectrum implications, technological and applications trends, potential traffic growth and new users. As one example, ultra-low latency may be achieved on control and data planes by considerable enhancement and new technical solutions concerning both network architecture aspects and radio interface [7].

As already mentioned, 5G is not only a merger of fixed and mobile networks, it will also take into account sectors that are especially data-intensive (e. g. automotive). Fig. 67.1 depicts the different industry approaches and considers new to develop radio link connections to cope with machine to machine communications (e. g. Industry 4.0). In the end, the *Future IMT* (International Mobile Telecommunications) will be ready for enhanced mobile broadband.

An example for the EU's vision of 5G networks was initiated under EU Commissioner OETTINGER's initiative: high level discussions and collaboration between TELCO association and the ACEA (European Automobile Manufacturers' Association) lead to the consideration of Connected Advanced Driver Assistant Systems and automated vehicles in 5G networks. Major features within this vision include: [8]

- High-density platooning, communicating convoy: Chains of multiple vehicles travelling on highways at distances below 5 m and at speeds of up to 100 km/h.
- See-Through – Sharing sensor data of one vehicle to other vehicles: Data sharing of essential sensors of a single vehicle are shared with all other vehicles nearby
- Tele-operated driving, remotely controlled vehicle: Driving tasks performed remotely by a human driver who is located outside the vehicle
- Map update for highly automated driving: High definition (HD) map information for roads and corresponding infrastructure

Other application cases in Industry 4.0 and in the IoT in general exhibit very similar characteristics.

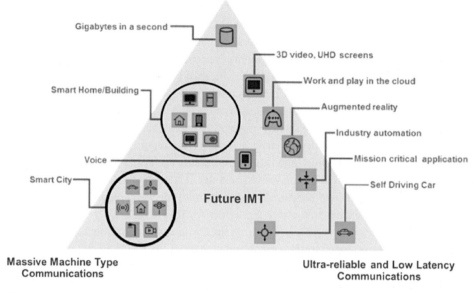

Fig. 67.1 Source: Recommendation ITU-R M.2083, https://www.itu.int/rec/R-REC-M.2083-0-201509-I/en (09/2015)

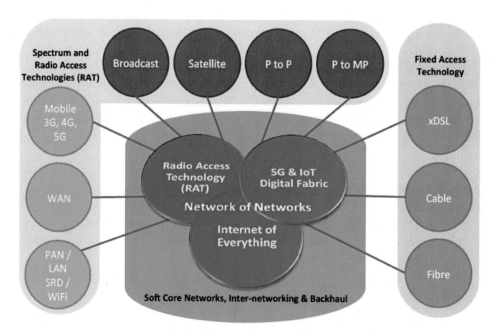

Fig. 67.2 Stuart Revell, University of Surrey

Anticipating the widespread 5G deployment, we envision that many functional entities will merge into one big network (Fig. 67.2).

This converged network will follow certain market drivers and use cases, which are Competiveness, Internet of Things, Safety & Security and Video with very high throughput. Thus, coverage, capacity or efficient spectrum utilization is a key driver. On the other hand, the to be expected massive growth in IoT applications will influence strategies for critical infrastructure, smart cities or automotive applications. Not to forget the safety and security topics like finance/payments, public safety or cyber security through design or massive bandwidth needs for Virtual & Augmented reality, higher resolution, Broadcast or video on demand.

All these market drivers and use cases have been identified and developed over the last years to e. g. cope with industrial process automation or remote surgery.

67.3.2 Fog Computing and 5G

In addition to the distinctive organizational characteristics of Fog Computing examined above, the Fog has some very distinct technical characteristics. Fog Computing nodes are distributed at the network edges and geographically available in much larger numbers than traditional Cloud nodes. The main data centers are typically away from the Fog Computing Nodes (FCN). FCNs can cope with mobility of devices, thus a kind of handover between different Fog nodes is mandatory. It is comparable to the handover process in cellular phone networks, thus no information will be lost. In addition, advanced services can be offered that may only be required in the IoT context (e. g. translation between IP and non-IP transport) [9]

In Fig. 67.3, the technical characteristics of the Fog and Cloud Computing paradigms are compared.

	Fog Computing	Cloud Computing
Target User	Mobile users	General Internet users.
Service Type	Limited localized information services related to specific deployment locations	Global information collected from worldwide
Hardware	Limited storage, compute power and wireless interface	Ample and scalable storage space and compute power
Distance to Users	In the physical proximity and communicate through single-hop wireless connection	Faraway from users and communicate through IP networks
Working Environment	Outdoor (streets, parklands, *etc.*) or indoor (restaurants, shopping malls, *etc.*)	Warehouse-size building with air conditioning systems
Deployment	Centralized or distributed in reginal areas by local business (local telecommunication vendor, shopping mall retailer, *etc.*)	Centralized and maintained by Amazon, Google, *etc.*

Fig. 67.3 T H. Luan et. al. "Fog Computing: Focusing on Mobile Users at the Edge"

By reaching out to the *network edges*, storage, control and configuration of the Fog resources will be performed there as well. The concept to adaptively implement F-RANs at the edge devices means closer to the end users. However, the main advantage has to be seen in the Radio Network of 5G, which means pooling of Radio Resources, the user equipment (cell phone) itself gets smarter and control tasks can be processed on the cell phone.

While talking about Fog Computing with immediate effect Mobile Edge Computing (MEC) will be perceived either. Despite the fact that there are some similarities in network scenarios, there are also some differences [10]. The differences are single-tenant versus multi-tenant, point of processing data and the way to approach connectivity, e. g. combining functions of connectivity versus operating independently.

To overcome shortcomings like real-time response or long-thin connection between Cloud and mobile applications, Fog Computing has recently emerged as a more practical solution to enable the smooth convergence between Cloud and mobile for content delivery and real-time data processing [2]. The idea of Fog Computing is placing a light-weight Cloud-like facility at the proximity of mobile users (cf. Sect. 67.2); the Fog therefore can serve mobile users with a direct short-fat connection as compared to the long-thin mobile Cloud connection. More importantly, as deployed at localized sites, Fog Computing can provide customized and engaged location-aware services which are more desirable to mobile users [11].

67.3.3   Emerging Network Architectures

There are different network architectures under evaluation for 5G and proposed by the major infrastructure providers. For instance, a big infrastructure provider (NOKIA) sees its future network architecture (Fig. 67.4) to entail the full use of open source software technologies, industry compliance and greater cooperation with IT players. At the same time, standardization bodies and organizations such as 3GPP and ETSI will continue to help define the best standard for 5G, assuring interoperability with regard to the air interface and associated software and mobility control architecture.

Crucially, because it is not possible to foresee all future uses, applications and business models, the network needs to be flexible and scalable to cope with the unknown [12]. Following the basic requirements laid out in Sect. 67.2 can only be considered as a minimalist starting point in this regard.

A different infrastructure provider (Ericsson) follows the principle of slicing.

Network slicing allows networks to be logically separated, with each slice providing customized connectivity, and all slices running on the same, shared infrastructure. This is a much more flexible solution than a single physical network providing a maximum level of connectivity. As illustrated in Fig. 67.5, network slicing supports, for example, business expansion due to the fact that it lowers the risks associated with introducing and running

Fundamental transformation in overall network architecture

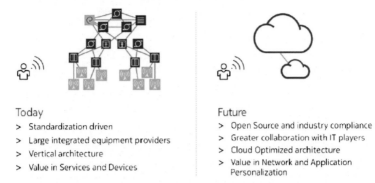

Today
> Standardization driven
> Large integrated equipment providers
> Vertical architecture
> Value in Services and Devices

Future
> Open Source and industry compliance
> Greater collaboration with IT players
> Cloud Optimized architecture
> Value in Network and Application Personalization

Fig. 67.4 Nokia: The network architecture for the 5G era will adapt new paradigms

new services—the isolated nature of slices protects existing services running on the same physical infrastructure from any impact.

Evolved virtualization, network programmability, and 5G use cases will change everything about network design, from planning and construction through deployment. Network functions will no longer be located according to traditional vertical groupings in single network nodes, but will instead be distributed to provide connectivity where it is needed.

To support the wide range of performance requirements demanded by new business opportunities, multiple access technologies, a wide variety of services, and lots of new device types, the 5G core will be highly flexible [13].

Both of these architectures, however, are not specifically geared towards Fog Computing. The Fog can be incorporated with the emerging networking technologies with

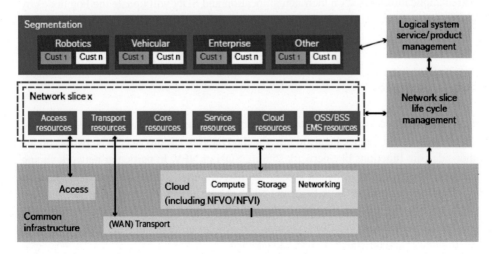

Fig. 67.5 Ericsson: Network slicing supports business expansion

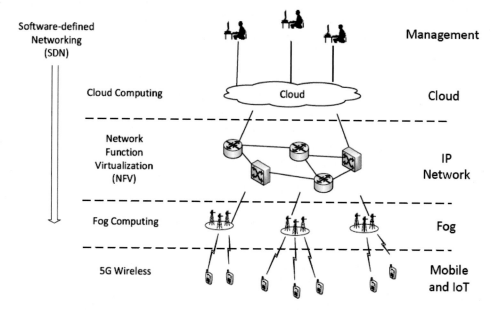

Fig. 67.6 T H. Luan, Fog computing in emerging technologies

a layered architecture as shown in Fig. 67.6 and described below. Network Slicing is generally tied to Virtualization, however layered architecture to physical separation.

Three main functions can be distinguished, namely 5G technologies, network function virtualization (NFV) and software-defined networking (SDN). The focus is on localization and the already available access networks can be adapted to serve also Fog nodes resp. layers. Virtualization with regards to Fog computing will enable mobile users to get desired applications based on their actual location and SDN will update the Fog nodes by using the Cloud on a global network view. Thus, the entire network can be managed using a SDN approach [11].

67.4 Conclusion

In general, we elaborated on the previous pages on different topics with regards to 5G and Fog computing. On the one hand side we touched the Ran (Radio Access Network) on the other side core functions like network slicing, SDN or NFV. In particular network slicing is predestined for fast and efficient access for different industrial applications and seamless broadband for consumers. With SDN and NFV, network slicing is extremely flexible from core to access. The concept to adaptively implement F-RANs at the edge devices means closer to the end users. SDN for control is a kind of centralization while the F-RAN has a distributed characteristic, based on edge devices.

An important key asset of Fog Computing is information on *Localization*. The network and user information are collected from the mobile edge networks used locally and shared to other service providers, to enrich the set of services based on the location of a mobile user. As compared to Cloud, Fog Computing can provide enhanced *Service Quality (QoS)* with much increased data rate and reduced service latency and response time. Moreover, by downloading through local connections without going through the backbone network, the users can benefit from the reduced bandwidth cost. Thus, real-time applications and communication is already now possible due to latency in the range of 1 millisecond as demonstrated by German Telecom (5G:haus) in Barcelona at the Mobile World Congress in 2016. To grant full *Mobility*, the network needs to combine Location Awareness, Quality of Service, and an intelligent protocol suite to a Mobility framework. Currently, a couple of different approaches are under consideration by the standardization groups. One of them is the DMM (Distributed Mobility Management), which has to support functions like minimizing packet loss during cell changes, maintaining the same IP address assigned to a user across different cells and minimizing impact to the user experience (e. g. minimization of interruption time). And eventually, *Security,* therefore the network has to provide basic and advanced security services in order to alleviate the security problems. Although Fog Computing is defined as the extension of the Cloud Computing paradigm, its distinctive characteristics in the location sensitivity, wireless connectivity, and geographical accessibility create new security issues [14]. There is still work to be done to elaborate in more depth this complicated topic.

Fog server store, compute and communicate hardware resources, which leads to three-dimensional service-oriented resource allocations. Moreover, with the three-tier Mobile-Fog-Cloud architecture and rich potential applications in both mobile networking and IoT, Fog Computing also opens broad research issues on network management, traffic engineering, big data and novel service delivery. Together, data virtualization and fog computing help bring intelligence and analytical capabilities to the data, which opens a wide range of business opportunities, e. g. driverless car or smart logistics. Therefore, we envision a bright future of Fog Computing [11] and we will have to further elaborate whether Fog Computing together with Mobile Edge Computing (MEC) forms the perfect tandem.

References

1. "Gartner's 2015 Hype Cycle," 2015.
2. I. Stojmenovic, S. Wen, X. Huang und H. Luan, "An overview of Fog computing and its security issues," in *Concurrency and Computation: Practice and Experience*, 2015.
3. L. Vaquero und L. Rodero-Merino, "Finding your Way in the Fog: Towards a Comprehensive Definition of Fog Computing," HP Laboratories, 2014.
4. F. Bonomi, R. Milito, J. Zhu und S. Addepalli, "Fog Computing and Its Role in the Internet of Things," Cisco Systems, 2012.

5. N. Truong, G. Lee und Y. Ghamri-Doudane, "Software Defined Networking-based Vehicular Adhoc Network with Fog Computing," in *IFIP/IEEE IM 2015 Workshop: 7th International Workshop on Management of the Future Internet(ManFI)*, 2015.

6. M. Yannuzzi, R. Milito, R. Serral-Gracià, D. Montero und M. Nemirovsky, "Key ingredients in an IoT recipe: Fog Computing, Cloud Computing, and more Fog Computing.," in *2014 IEEE 19th International Workshop on Computer aAided Modeling and Design of Communication Links and Networks (CAMAD)*, 2014, pp. 325–329.

7. "Recommendation ITU-R M.2083-0: IMT Vision - Framework and overall objectives of the future development of IMT for 2020 and beyond," ITU-R Radio communication Sector of ITU M Series Mobile, radio determination, amateur and related satellite services, 2015.

8. C. Rousseau, "The 5G HUDDLE 2016," Groupe Renault, 2016.

9. E. Borcoci, "Fog-computing versus SDN/NFV and Cloud computing in 5G," DataSys Conference, 2016.

10. M. T. Beck, M. Werner, S. Feld, and T. Schimper, "Mobile Edge Computing: A taxonomy," in 6th International Conference on Advances in Future Internet (AFIN 2014), 2014.

11. T. H. Luan, L. Gao, Z. Li, X. Y. und L. Sun, "Fog computing: Focussing on mobile users at the edge," in *arXiv preprint arXiv:1502.01815*, 2015.

12. "Network architecture for the 5G era," Nokia: Future Works, 2015.

13. L. F. e. al, "Ericsson Technology Review," Ericsson, 2016.

14. Y. Wang, T. Uehrara und R. Sasaki, "Fog Computing: Issues and Challenges in Security and Forensics," in *3 : Computer Software and Applications Conference (COMPSAC)*, IEEE 39th Annual, 2015, pp. 53–59.

Further Reading

15. M. Firdhous, O. Ghazali und S. Hassan, "Fog Computing: Will it be the Future of Cloud Computing?," in *The Society of Digital Information and Wireless Communications (SDIWC)*, Proceedings of the Thrid International Conference on Informatics & Applications (ICIA2014), 2014.

16. "Gartner Says 6.4 Billion Connected "Things" Will Be in Use 2016, Up From 2015," 2015.

A Generic Model for Coordinating the Individual Energy Demand of Electric Vehicles: Optimizing the Coordination Problem Between Electric Vehicles and Charging Points with the Implementation of a Genetic Algorithm

68

Malte Zuch, Arne Koschel, and Andreas Hausotter

Abstract

Modern vehicles contain several sensors for recognizing their direct environment. Their computational capabilities get enhanced continuously by including more calculation power, more memory storage capacity, and better communication technologies into the vehicles. Especially electric vehicles can offer those new technologies and are able to share data concerning the current state of charge of their batteries and their current positions. Such data can be used to coordinate and support electric vehicles during their search for unoccupied charging points. Therefore, a generic model will be described to handle those data in a uniform manner. Based on this standardized data representation, a genetic algorithm will be applied to optimize the coordination between electric vehicles and charging points.

68.1 Introduction

The market of electric vehicles is globally growing. Just for Germany [1, p. 10] the German government expects one million electric (and plug in hybrid) vehicles for the year 2020 in Germany. Worldwide, the market will grow to about 20 million electric vehicles by 2020 [2, p. 9]. Modern vehicles embed several sensors and communication technologies

M. Zuch (✉) · A. Koschel · A. Hausotter
University of Applied Sciences and Arts in Hanover
Hanover, Germany
e-mail: malte.zuch@hs-hannover.de

A. Koschel
e-mail: arne.koschel@hs-hannover.de

A. Hausotter
e-mail: andreas.hausotter@hs-hannover.de

© Springer-Verlag GmbH Germany 2018
C. Linnhoff-Popien et al. (eds.), *Digital Marketplaces Unleashed*,
https://doi.org/10.1007/978-3-662-49275-8_68

and are able to share data. So finally, even vehicles become digitalized. Their digitalization offers the possibility to add even more value to the product "electric vehicle". The direct integration of advanced services into vehicles, like collaborative traffic management services, will lead to a new experience of mobility. This is provided by sharing information amongst the vehicles. Especially the growing market of electric vehicles will lead to new "e-mobility data scenarios". Electric vehicles have to be recharged frequently with electric power. This could be done at home or at public charging points.

Depending on the vehicle's actual location, the driver will look for unoccupied charging points in the near environment. If a large number of drivers of electric vehicles will look up on their own for unoccupied charging points, this will lead to mutual blocking between the drivers. To reduce the risk of driving to occupied charging points, a collaborative coordination system is required, which is able to handle individual charging requests and consider individual constraints. Therefore, a generic approach of handling such demands will be introduced and a genetic algorithm will be applied exemplary to optimize the general coordination problem between vehicles and charging points to reduce overall waiting times.

But especially for Germany, the current generation of vehicles is still restricted concerning their digitalization. The possibilities to integrate additional digital services with or into such vehicles, for example, real-time information services about charging points including prices or utilization, are still limited.

The vehicle manufacturers are still restricting the board systems of the vehicles. Only some board systems have already integrated such charging point finding services. But those services are still limited by the manufacturer. They are not showing the whole market data with all charging points to the drivers and the resulting limited information is often out of date.

So today, drivers of vehicles have to use smartphone apps to integrate additional services, which are based on data with a better quality. These restrictions are motivating to investigate the benefit of collaborative coordination systems within this work.

For the near future, there is a noticeable trend within the automotive industry to become more open, concerning the integration of additional third party digital services like such a collaborative coordination system. Most of the leading companies of the automotive industry have already announced to integrate standardized platforms, known and established from the smartphone market.

The car manufacturer Daimler will integrate the Apple Carplay platform into their vehicles [3]. Volkswagen, Audi, and BMW are offering the possibility to integrate both leading platforms, Apple Carplay and Android Auto, into their vehicles [4–6].

Summing up, more vehicles will become digitalized. This ongoing digitalization offers options to share and receive data while driving. So more vehicles will be able to share their positions and the state of charge of their batteries. Such data can be optimized in a collaborative manner.

Today, drivers of electric vehicles simply do not have collaborative information about other drivers and do not know where other drivers could probably charge. This missing information amongst the drivers will lead to mutual blocking at already occupied charging points and will cause avoidable waiting times. Utilizing a collaborative coordination service could reduce waiting times to a significant degree.

Within this work, such a collaborative coordination service will be presented. It will be compared to the default charging behavior of nowadays typical drivers, who are always driving to the nearest charging point in range. This behavior serves as general benchmark scenario, which will be compared with the scenario of a collaborative coordination. The latter is based on a genetic algorithm and uses the (now) shared information of the electric vehicles (position and state of charge). With this additional information, the genetic algorithm is utilized to recommend better charging points to the drivers with less occupation and waiting times. This optimization should lead to an improved situation of charging for all drivers, which is more efficient than the benchmark scenario.

The next section presents the related work concerning this topic. Afterwards, the approach of the data model is explained, followed by the discussion of the general coordination problem and the approach to solve this problem with a genetic algorithm. The results of the genetic algorithm will be presented and discussed followed by a final conclusion.

68.2   Prior and Related Work

In prior work, the general architecture of a charging point information system as well as initial data partitioning methods have been described [7, p. 5]. The discussion about the potential risk of volatile loads in traffic coordination system during rush hour motivated to follow a matrix based calculation approach within this work. This approach allows to divide and distribute the data over several systems to compute the data in parallel.

A coordination approach for plug-in electric vehicles during their search for parking spaces and the resulting effect on smart grids is presented in [8, pp. 9, 10]. The resulting effect was considered within a simulation. It shows that there is a potential to stabilize smart grids by coordinating the energy demand of electric vehicles. Another work has also shown that loads in smart grids and general waiting times at charging points could be reduced up to 50% with the approach of "swarm intelligence (SI)" [9, pp. 9, 21]. Also the pricing of charging points could be adapted to gain efficiency within electro mobile coordination scenarios [10, pp. 88, 89].

A dynamic pricing model for charging points shows the effects of adapting to different behaviors of drivers [11, p. 2]. Drivers of electric vehicles were separated into two groups, cooperative and selfish drivers with respect to dynamic prices of charging points. The coordination of those groups increased the profit of charging points by about 18% and has shown further potential of coordination systems [11, p. 2]. Another approach for PHEV-vehicles (plug in hybrid electric vehicle) shows how to save 10% of energy and extend the driving range by a coordination system with route optimization [12, pp. 41, 42].

Within long range scenarios, a further coordination approach for electric vehicles has been described including a route assistance system [13, p. 139]. The point of view of data partitioning is based on a static perimeter around the different charging points. Electric vehicles within this perimeter are considered as standard partition. Building of dynamic partitions is not considered, because the primary focus of this work is the dynamic rerouting over several charging points for long range routes. So, the mentioned related work focuses more on specific scenarios. None of this work attempts to describe a general approach with genetic algorithms, various and flexible preferences of the drivers and their individual behavior while searching for charging points and motivates to offer such a (basic) model within this work.

In general, the whole market of communicating vehicles will produce a continuous data stream while asking a charging point information service for unoccupied charging points. Referring to those continuous data streams, a related "parallel complex event processing" model has been explained and realized a speedup factor by $14 \times$ in [14, pp. 196, 200]. Such a model could also be used to support the handling of data within scenarios for the coordination of electric vehicles in parallel. Coordination approaches for electric vehicles could be seen as services, which support the drivers in finding (unoccupied) charging points. Those services can benefit from a uniform and generic representation and optimization of data within electro mobility traffic scenarios, which is part of this work.

Therefore, the next section explains a general model to handle the data of electric vehicles in such a uniform and generic way in dependency of the actual states of charge and positions of the vehicles. This data model will be used to describe the general coordination problem. A genetic algorithm will be applied to optimize the coordination problem to recommend better vehicle-charge-point-assignments to the drivers.

68.3 The General Data Model of the Coordination Problem

Electro mobility traffic scenarios are influenced by some elementary parameters. The number of electric vehicles and charging points, their locations, the state of charge and the average energy consumption of the vehicles:

Number of electric vehicles:	$m \in \mathbb{N}$
Number of charging points:	$n \in \mathbb{N}$
State of charge in (kWh):	$\vec{soc} = [soc_1, \ldots, soc_m]$
Energy consumption of vehicles (kWh/km):	$\vec{con} = [con_1, \ldots, con_m]$
Latitude of vehicles:	$\vec{xv} = [xv_1, \ldots, xv_m]$
Longitude of vehicles:	$\vec{yv} = [yv_1, \ldots, yv_m]$
Latitude of charging points:	$\vec{xc} = [xc_1, \ldots, xc_n]$
Longitude of charging points:	$\vec{yc} = [yc_1, \ldots, yc_n]$

The input parameters will be handled by matrices. Handling the data with matrices allows the representation of several vehicles and charging points in a uniform way. This uniform representation of data with matrices offers the possibility to divide the general vehicle coordination problem in sub-matrices/partitions. So the general coordination problem of all vehicles over all cities could be separated with this matrix approach in sub-matrices for single cities. Those sub-matrices/partitions could be distributed over several computers to solve the general vehicle coordination problem in parallel for the individual cities. For example, solving the problem for New York and Moscow together makes no sense. The Atlantic Ocean prevents that electric vehicles in New York could build up a situation of competition with electric vehicles from Moscow during their search for unoccupied charging points. Dividing the problem for far away cities seems reasonable. But nearby cities will still interact with each other. So dividing the problem has to be done carefully and results in a tradeoff between gaining calculation speed and potentially cutting of additional information. Especially a matrix design offers the possibility to divide the problem easily. To solve this coordination problem, a general model is applied to process those input parameters within three steps. The first step prepares the latitude and longitude data for building matrices. The second step calculates with these matrices the distances between all vehicles and charging points. The third step summarizes the data in context of the actual states of charge of the electric vehicles and their remaining driving ranges. The resulting matrix includes the information, which charging points could be reached by which vehicles.

This matrix is then utilized to optimize the vehicle coordination with a genetic algorithm. The matrix approach offers the possibility to integrate even more information for supporting such charging point coordination systems. For example, additional matrices with information of the prices of charging points or the behavior of the drivers and their individual preferences concerning energy prices and required charging power could be added. Those additional matrices could be integrated easily by overlaying the existing ones (explained in Sect. 68.3.2). This could achieve an even more accurate individual coordination of the vehicles. In the following, each of the aforementioned three steps is described in more detail.

68.3.1   Step 1 – Preparing the Data in Matrix Form

The one-dimensional latitude and longitude vectors $\vec{xv}, \vec{yv}, \vec{xc}$ and $\vec{yc}$ will be expanded into two-dimensional $m \times n$ matrices to calculate all possible combinations of distances at once. Therefore, the vehicle matrix is aligned vertically and the charging point matrix horizontally (s. Fig. 68.1).

The different horizontal and vertical alignment of the elements inside the matrices is necessary for the calculation of distances in step 2. By overlaying the horizontal and vertical aligned matrices, all combinations of distances between vehicles and charging points may be calculated at once (s. Fig. 68.2).

With this design, even very large matrices might be divided and distributed easily over several computers to calculate huge amount of data quickly in parallel. Beside of the data preparation of the latitude and longitude vectors, a similar preparation is required for

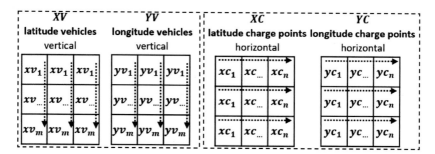

Fig. 68.1 Preparation the data in matrix form

the vectors of the state of charge ($\overrightarrow{\text{soc}}$) and the individual energy consumption ($\overrightarrow{\text{con}}$) of the electric vehicles. The actual state of charge of the batteries and the average energy consumption is leading to a limited driving range for all m electric vehicles:

$$r_i = \frac{\text{soc}_i}{\text{con}_i} \quad \text{for all} \quad i = [1, \ldots, m] \tag{68.1}$$

All elements r_i for all m vehicles will also be arranged into a $m \times n$ matrix by the following scheme for all n charging points:

$$R = \begin{bmatrix} r_1 & \cdots & r_1 \\ \vdots & \ddots & \vdots \\ r_m & \cdots & r_m \end{bmatrix}_{m \times n} \tag{68.2}$$

This matrix R specifies the maximal driving range of all electric vehicles. It has the same dimensions as the aforementioned latitude and longitude matrices. The equality of

$$D_{i,j} = \sqrt{\left(XV_{i,j} - XC_{i,j}\right)^2 + \left(YV_{i,j} - YC_{i,j}\right)^2} \text{ with all } i = [1, \ldots, m] \text{ and } j = [1, \ldots, n]$$

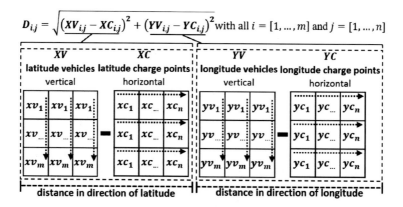

Fig. 68.2 Calculation of the distances between all electric vehicles and charging points

dimensions allows an efficient calculation between the distance matrix D and the maximal driving range matrix R, explained in the next sections.

68.3.2   Step 2 – Calculating the Distance Matrix

With the data preparation in step 1, all possible distance combinations between all vehicles and charging points can be calculated at once with the single $m \times n$ matrix D (s. Fig. 68.2).

This distance matrix D will be processed with the matrix of the maximal driving ranges R in the next section to identify the situation of competition and blocking amongst the vehicles, while they are searching for unoccupied charging points.

68.3.3   Step 3 – Identifying the Potential of Blocking Amongst Vehicles

The logical comparison between the matrices D and R from the previous sections will lead to the binary selection matrix Z. This matrix marks all possible combinations of vehicles and charging points, reachable with the actual state of charge of their batteries. Those combinations are building up the situation of competition and can cause blocking amongst the vehicles:

$$Z_{i,j} = \begin{cases} 1 & \text{if} \quad R_{i,j} \geq D_{i,j} \\ 0 & \text{if} \quad R_{i,j} < D_{i,j} \end{cases} \quad \text{for all} \quad \begin{aligned} i &= [1,\ldots,m] \\ j &= [1,\ldots,n] \end{aligned} \tag{68.3}$$

This competition matrix Z offers two main options to extract information. The extraction of row vectors contains the information which charging points are in range by a considered vehicle (row). The extraction of column vectors contains the information which vehicles are potentially demanding a considered charging point (column). Especially the extraction by column in combination with the distance matrix D could be used to identify possible situations of competition. If more than one driver is looking for the same charging point (column), only the driver with the shortest distance to the charging point will actually be able to charge right away, while all other drivers will be blocked by this firstly arriving vehicle (s. Fig. 68.3).

The example in Fig. 68.3 shows a traffic situation with two vehicles F2 and F4 with a low state of charge and two vehicles F1 and F3 with a high state of charge. So, vehicle F1 and F3 have the option two choose between more than one charging point. Vehicle F2 and F4 have no choice concerning their low state of charge and have to charge at one particular charging point. If the vehicles won't use a collaborative coordination service and if they would just drive to the nearest charging points in range, there would be a high risk of blocking between each other.

For this simple scenario, the calculated competition matrix Z is shown in Fig. 68.3 and includes all possible sets of competition. This matrix Z and the distance matrix D are the

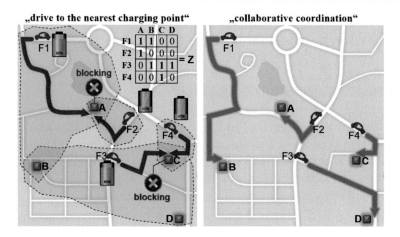

Fig. 68.3 Example of an electro mobile traffic situation of competition amongst vehicles

basic inputs for the coordination problem and will be used to optimize the coordination within the next section.

68.4 Optimizing the Coordination Problem

The general coordination problem was defined with the competition matrix Z and the distance matrix D in the last section. If drivers of electric vehicles are just driving to the nearest charging point in range, this could cause mutual blocking amongst the vehicles on arrival at the charging points.

Alternatively, they could use a collaborative coordination service. Concerning their individual driving ranges, they could be guided by such a collaborative coordination service to alternative charging points in their individual range. This could minimize the blocking of other vehicles, which have less charging options reasoned by their low state of charge. This information is integrated in the competition matrix Z, which already includes the alternative charging options (rows) of the vehicles. The goal is to recommend optimized "vehicle-to-charge-point-assignments" to provide a better situation of charging for all drivers. These optimized recommendations of charging points are represented by the binary configuration matrix X. Within this matrix, the value "1" marks recommended charging points (columns) for the vehicles (rows). The specific configuration of this matrix will be optimized with a genetic algorithm to improve the situation of charging for all drivers:

$$X = \begin{bmatrix} x_{1,1} & \cdots & x_{1,n} \\ \vdots & \ddots & \vdots \\ x_{m,1} & \cdots & x_{m,n} \end{bmatrix} \quad \text{with} \quad x_{i,j} \in \{0, 1\} \text{ and } \sum_{j=1}^{n} = 1 \quad \text{for all} \quad \begin{matrix} i = 1 \ldots m \\ j = 1 \ldots n \end{matrix}$$

m: amount of vehicles

n: amount of charging points

(68.4)

The constraints for the optimization are defined by:

- Every vehicle gets a recommended charging point with the matrix X.
- Only one single vehicle can charge at a charging point at the same time.
- Usually there are less charging points than vehicles in the market. Because of the last two constraints, every driver/vehicle will get at least one optimized recommended charging option. So they could get the recommendation to charge at the same charging point, because there are not enough charging points for all vehicles in the market. Out of those vehicles, only the vehicle with the shortest distance (matrix D) will realize the charging option. Others will have to wait.
- The optimization aims to reduce overall waiting times for all vehicles by recommending better charging points with an improved configuration of the matrix X, considering the maximal driving ranges of the individual vehicles, their states of charge and current positions.

The general coordination problem provokes an exponential complexity of combinations. To solve the problem fast during real-time traffic conditions, a heuristic approach was chosen. Within the mentioned constraints, the genetic algorithm will search for a configuration X which should lead to an improved situation of charging for all drivers with less waiting times and blocking between the vehicles on arrival at the charging points. The results are shown in the next section.

68.5   Results of the Optimization

To evaluate the optimization, vehicles and charging points were initialized with random positions. The capacity of the batteries of the vehicles was set to 20 kWh and the average consumption was 15.3 kWh / 100 km. This default configuration represents common vehicles with a typical driving range of about 130 km under real driving conditions. Fully charged vehicles are not looking for charging points and totally depleted vehicle are technically not able to reach any charging point.

So the initial state of charge was initialized randomly between 10 and 50% of the maximal capacity of their batteries to generate directly a representative situation of competition for the simulation with no totally charged or depleted vehicles. Vehicles are (currently) driving by air-line distance directly to the charging points. The implementation of real street data will follow in 2017 by using OpenStreetMap [15] and the traffic simulation framework MATsim [16].

This article focusses on the general optimization of the coordination problem and how a genetic algorithm could be used for this optimization. An optimized configuration X will lead to less blocking between vehicles and will allow to deliver a higher amount of energy from the charging points to the requesting vehicles. So the indicator for measuring the performance of the optimized "vehicle-to-charge-point assignment" is based on the delivered amount of energy per time to the vehicles.

The results of the genetic algorithm [17] are compared with the default scenario. The delivered amount of energy in the default scenario defines the basic benchmark with 100%. In the default scenario, vehicles are only driving to the next charging point in range without using additional information and without any further optimization. Applying the genetic algorithm leads to the following results (see Table 68.1).

The configuration of the genetic algorithm is based on standard values with a population size of 50 individuals and a selection of 5% of the best individuals per generation. The genetic crossover function is defined with 80%. The stopping criteria is 1% over 50 generations. So if 50 generations will not generate an individual which is at least 1% better than the last known best one, the genetic algorithm will stop. The general situation of competition amongst the vehicles is influenced by the availability of charging points in relation to the amount of requesting vehicles. A situation of low competition is defined with a sufficient amount of charging points with 50% of the number of vehicles, shown with line 3, 6 and 9 in Table 68.1. The genetic algorithm is able to gain on average a +59% improvement in such situations with a low competition compared to the default situation without any optimization. A situation with a high competition is generated with a low amount of charging points with only 10% of the number of vehicles. This is shown with line 1, 4 and 7 in Table 68.1. The genetic algorithm is still able to gain on average a +39% improvement in such situations with a high competition. The average performance of the genetic algorithm over all nine simulated scenarios results in an improvement of +48.7% compared

Table 68.1 Results of the optimization with the genetic algorithm

	Amount vehicles	Amount charging points	Performance "default situation" (in %)	Performance "genetic algorithm" (in %)
1	100	10	100	143.6
2	100	25	100	152.5
3	100	50	100	165.2
4	200	20	100	141.8
5	200	50	100	140.7
6	200	100	100	162.9
7	300	30	100	131.3
8	300	75	100	151.2
9	300	150	100	149.2

to the default scenario where drivers will only drive to the nearest charging point in range without using additional information or optimized coordination. The implemented genetic algorithm took about 294 generations per simulation to find an optimum within 13 s with common hardware of the year 2016 (4×3.5 GHz CPU, 8 GB RAM).

68.6   Conclusion and Future Work

Electric vehicles have to find unoccupied charging points and require long charging times. To reduce the blocking between vehicles at charging points, an optimization model is needed. The presented matrix model shows a solution for aggregating data in traffic scenarios with electric vehicles. Actual positions and states of charge of vehicles are combined with the locations of charging points in a uniform way. A matrix model was designed to be expandable by additional matrices. For example, individual preferences of drivers like preferred energy prices of charging points or preferences of a desired arrival time at specific charging points could be integrated easily with additional matrices. The integration of those additional matrices should lead to a more accurate and personal coordination of electric vehicles and is part of future work and could be used in related traffic management systems.

Within this work, the matrix model has been applied to describe the general situation of competition between electric vehicles with the mentioned matrix Z. To optimize the coordination problem for electric vehicles in search for charging points, a genetic algorithm was utilized for several situations of competition.

It has been shown that a genetic algorithm could be a suitable approach to optimize the general coordination problem. If every driver will cooperate and adapt to those recommended alternative charging options, there is a huge potential. The optimization could lead to an average performance of about $+48.7\%$ of served energy to the electric vehicles, compared to the default driving scenario, where drivers are only driving to the nearest charging point in range without optimization.

Under real driving conditions, this potential of optimization would be less, because not every driver will cooperate and adapt to those recommended and optimized alternative charging points. The effect of those uncooperative drivers will be examined in future work.

References

1. Bundesregierung, "Regierungsprogramm Elektromobilität," 01 05 2011. [Online]. Available: https://www.bmbf.de/files/programm_elektromobilitaet.pdf. [Accessed 11 01 2016].
2. Clean Energy Ministerial, "Global EV Outlook," OECD/IEA, OECD/IEA, Paris, France, 2013.
3. Daimler AG, "Premiere: Apple "CarPlay" in der neuen C-Klasse: Mercedes-Benz bleibt Trendsetter bei Smartphone-Integration," Stuttgart, Germany, 2014.
4. Volkswagen AG, "VOLKSWAGEN CAR-NET - APPS UND DIENSTE IM ÜBERBLICK," Wolfsburg, Germany, 2015.

5. Audi AG, "Audi connect & Mobilität," Ingolstadt, Germany, 2015.
6. BMW AG, "Rede Harald Krüger, Vorsitzender des Vorstands der BMW AG," Munich, Germany, 2015.
7. M. Zuch, "Effizienz im elektromobilen Massenmarkt," Lecture Notes in Informatics, Gesellschaft für Informatik, Cottbus, 2015.
8. Muhammad Ismail, Ehab F. El-Saadany, Weihua Zhuang, Mostafa F. Shaaban, Real-Time PEV Charging-Discharging Coordination in Smart Distribution Systems, Waterloo, Canada: IEEE Transactions on Smart Grid (Volume: 5 , Issue: 4), 2014.
9. Rutger Claes, Stijn Vandael, Niels Leemput, Tom Holvoet, Geert Deconinck, Kristof Coninx, Anticipatory Coordination of Electric Vehicle Allocation to Fast Charging Infrastructure, Leuven, Belgium: EnergyVille, Department of Electrical Engineering, 2014.
10. R. Waraich, Agent-based simulation of electric vehicles: design and implementation of a framework, Zürich, Switzerland: ETH-Zürich, 2013.
11. Y. Han, Y. Chen, F. Han and K. J. Ray Liu, "An optimal dynamic pricing and schedule approach in V2G," IEEE, Maryland, USA, 2012.
12. V. Larsson, Route Optimized Energy Management of Plug-in Hybrid Electric Vehicles, Göteborg, Sweden: Department of Signals and Systems - Chalmers University of Technology, 2014.
13. M. N. Mariyasagayam and Y. Kobayashi, "Electric Vehicle Route Assistance Using Forecast on Charging Station," in *ENERGY 2013, The Third International Conference on Smart Grids, Green Communications and IT Energy-aware Technologies*, Lisbon, Portugal, 2013.
14. M. Hirzel, "Partition and Compose: Parallel Complex Event Processing," DEBS '12 Proceedings of the 6th ACM International Conference on Distributed Event-Based Systems, New York, USA, 2012.
15. openstreetmap.de, "OpenStreetMap - Deutschland," 11 10 2016. [Online]. Available: www.openstreetmap.de. [Accessed 11 10 2016].
16. Technische Universität Berlin, Swiss Federal Institute of Technology Zurich, Senozon AG, "The Multi-Agent Transport Simulation," 11 10 2016. [Online]. Available: http://matsim.org. [Accessed 11 10 2016].
17. The MathWorks GmbH, "How the Genetic Algorithm Works," 20 08 2016. [Online]. Available: https://de.mathworks.com/help/gads/how-the-genetic-algorithm-works.html. [Accessed 20 08 2016].

Matteo Cagnazzo, Patrick Wegner, and Norbert Pohlmann

Abstract

Communication has changed dramatically in recent years due to the dawn of new ICT technologies and the need of people to communicate in real time. This paper will introduce a little communication theory as a background, compare current technologies and finally introduce a smart, efficient and secure communication platform. It will furthermore address further improvements to the new platform.

69.1 Communication Means Sharing Information

Nowadays information has an unprecedented importance. It has never been easier to share information with other entities. An information is based on characters that are connected via a syntax and grammar to form data. Setting this data into context is information. "Sharing information" creates knowledge and to share information one must communicate. There must be a sender and a receiver who communicate. It surrounds our everyday life more than ever, especially at work. Communication can reach different degrees of efficiency and organized in various ways. Efficiency can be determined by individual skills of participants as well as differences in the established communication structure and culture [1].

M. Cagnazzo (✉) · P. Wegner · N. Pohlmann
Institute for Internet-Security
Gelsenkirchen, Germany
e-mail: cagnazzo@internet-sicherheit.de

P. Wegner
e-mail: wegner@internet-sicherheit.de

N. Pohlmann
e-mail: pohlmann@internet-sicherheit.de

© Springer-Verlag GmbH Germany 2018
C. Linnhoff-Popien et al. (eds.), *Digital Marketplaces Unleashed*,
https://doi.org/10.1007/978-3-662-49275-8_69

Communication can be ranked in terms of relevance. Should this information be accessible by everyone or just a special group of people? Or is there one specified recipient for one specific information. Depending on this classification and the criticality of the transferred information a secured and trustworthy environment may be needed. Technologically speaking this means to establish a trust and security level through end to end encryption or at least transport layer encryption to secure the transmission. Adding such security measures will result in a complex system which can create a trustworthy connectedness of the participating entities.

Corporate communication includes every communication process no matter if it is in- or outbound. This includes the sharing of information between employees as well as communication of the corporation to employees. Through communication an organization gains knowledge and if this knowledge is managed properly an organization can draw strategic decisions from it which gives them competitive advantages. That is why communication is such an integral part of modern businesses [2].

69.2 Digital Communication in Organization Nowadays

Through installed telecommunication systems e. g. mail client, social business network or telephone organizations connect their employees so that they can communicate. Nowadays there is a focus on e-mails through which most of the communication inside of organizations happens, no matter how big or small. Worldwide the number of in- and outbound mails is 116 billion with an upward trend. On average this means that every employee deals with 123 mails per day [3]. The time that is expended daily to answer those mails is not negligible. If every mail is processed for just one minute, an employee is occupied for two hours on average. If it's an executive this number increases and they are spending most of their time at work with communication.

Optimization of such communication habits are already on the rise. Especially mailing is being questioned because of the excessive amount of mails being exchanged on a daily basis and therefore not being too efficient. Even though the decade old system works and is being used by a majority of people it is not capable of dealing with today's technologies.

Mailing is nowadays characterized by formalities formulated personally but they are not meant personal. Repeating salutation and farewell patterns, empty phrases, and disclaimers are generating a significant overhead. The information of a mail can be one sentence but due to the overhead the mail becomes long and extensive. If this mail becomes part of a collaborative exchange because of a document that a group of people is working on it results in poorly structured, swelling and never ending discussions. This offers a possibility to break with norms and structure communication more efficient, smart and modern.

Apart from this way of transmitting information mailing is not capable of dealing with today's security requirements and it is comparatively unsafe to write a mail. It is easy to manipulate whole messages or forge the address of sender or receiver [4, 5].

There are possibilities to protect against such frauds for example end-to-end encryption with "Pretty Good Privacy, PGP" but they are not usable out of the box [6]. Due to the complexity and not usability by non-professionals such solutions to the trust and security problems are not popular. There are ways to secure the transport layer e. g. STARTLS so that the user can be sure no one eavesdrops on their communication but it does not offer security on the different nodes through which a mail is routed [7]. The harm done by digital attacks against companies is estimated at $400 billion a year [8]. This clarifies the need for a suitable secure communication solution. There has to be an exchange of technology which offers new ways to share critical information in businesses.

69.3 New and Efficient Communication Approaches

New and modern approaches help to optimize the communication behavior in organizations and establish a culture of efficient communication. A robust foundation is necessary which is depicted by a modern, forward looking and secure architecture. An efficient, smart and secure communication tool is not a trivial task but it is a very complex challenge not just from a technological point of view. One of the main challenges is to offer the user new and efficient ways of sharing information which are intuitively and easily usable and on the other hand offer a reasonably high security level. Based on these more complex scenarios are implementable e. g. depicting business processes to digitize them and transform businesses.

69.3.1 Transforming Old into New

A first step towards an efficient and modern communication technique is already available but the idea behind it is not new. Instant messaging is existent for more than 40 years and gained popularity in the mid 1990's [9]. Programs like ICQ and AOL messenger were the most prominent tools available. They enabled real time communication from sender to receiver no matter how many miles apart [10, 11].

Favored by the increasing popularity of smart phones and social networks instant messaging gained a lot of traction in the past years. The most popular messenger nowadays is WhatsApp with one billion users [12] and over 30 billion exchanged messages a day [13]. Our everyday communication is moving from asynchronous towards a synchronous real time exchange of information.

These change in behavior is especially remarkable for adolescents for who instant messaging becomes an inherent part of their life [14].

Analyzing behavior there is huge increase of pictorial representations (e. g. with emoji's) of expressing feelings instead of describing them textual. Whole phrases can be reduced e. g. "see you" is shortened to "cu". The transmitted information is the same but "cu" saves 66% of the characters. Especially greeting and farewell phrases are shortened and common phrases like "for your information" – fyi.

There is more to the change in behavior than just the shortening of phrases. The "hashtag" for example is a modern element which gained popularity through micro blogging services. Buzzwords in a message are "hashtagged" (e. g. "#hashtag") and therefore these words become searchable, because they are now tagged. With this tagging language now becomes searchable and this offers new possibilities and dimensions in communication. In a closed system certain messages are easy to find and can be brought in context with other topics and can be categorized and the whole message gets a defined context. Furthermore, it is possible to analyze the relation of hashtags and key performance indicators e. g. "Done with the module #milestone" by the frequency of the hashtag and weighting of it.

The current boom of new techniques and possibilities in communication paired with new mechanics need to be transferred into the business sector right now because those modern and efficient approaches are mapping the needs of corporations to digitize themselves. One question to ask is which requirements should a platform meet to digitalize a business in a holistic way.

69.4   Efficient Business Tools and Security

Meanwhile, there are some systems which are concerned with the transfer of the in Sect. 69.3 introduced approaches from the private to the business environment. However, these systems focus mostly on a particular topic. For example, they enable effective communication through the implementation of instant messaging concepts or focus on other specific features, such as document management. Dedicated social networks for internal communication in organizations take an additional step by focusing on relationships between employees. The security subject is treated individually by all available solutions, so that a different number of security features may be included, both from the perspective of the user as well as at technical level.

Instant messaging slowly but surely finds its way into business communication. The popular cloud-based collaboration tool Slack shows this development by its steadily growing number of up to three million daily active users [15]. Slack offers possibilities to communicate with employees in the same organization through different types of channels. Direct messages can be easily exchanged between two persons. In contrast, open channels provide space for group discussions, such as special topics or projects.

The first positive effects can already be observed in using this service. The number of internally sent emails has been reduced by up to 48.5% [16]. Furthermore, an increase in productivity as well as a reduction of necessary meetings can be determined, which additionally confirms the concept and emphasizes the use of new modern, efficient and smart tools in business communication.

Table 69.1 Overview of leading apps in private and business sector

Product	WhatsApp	Dropbox	Slack
Sector	Private	Both	Business
Focused on	Messaging	Document Management	Messaging
Business compliance	No	No	License depending
End-to-end encryption	Yes	No	No
Encryption of data in transit?	Yes	Yes	Yes
Encryption of data at rest?	Yes	Yes	Yes
Provider has access to user data?	Maybe	Yes	Yes
Provider use data for itself?	Yes	Yes	Yes
Users must trust provider?	Yes	Yes	Yes

When reviewing the security practices of that service, it can be seen that the concept does not include all possibilities to protect the customer's data. While all traffic in transit goes over an encrypted connection, so no one can eavesdrop on it and customer data is encrypted at rest by the service provider on their servers, using the latest recommended secure cipher suites, there is no end-to-end encryption included [17]. Therefore, customers still hand over their data to a third party by sending it to the provider's servers. This approach is followed by several solutions in the business environment. WhatsApp is also a popular instant messaging service which is also establishing end to end encryption but they offer no compliance to business systems so that processes can be integrated. It is solely focused on being a product for customers and not for businesses (s. Table 69.1).

69.5   Quvert – Smart. Efficient. Secure.

Quvert is a modern and innovative communication tool and enables fast, reliable, usable and secure business communication. It is tailored for daily internal corporate communication with the primary goal to increase the effectiveness without sacrificing security, privacy and usability. These points were considered from the beginning of the planning phase and form parts of the foundation of the platform.

Quvert is chat-based and includes all now well-known advantages of instant messaging, such as sending text messages in real time, exchanging different types of media or using hashtags and similar techniques. However, Quvert does not stop here. In addition to introducing new approaches for transferring information between employees, like the concept for the exchange of internal company knowledge, Quvert also integrates business processes.

The foundation of Quvert is a secure, distributed and reliable server based on XMPP and Erlang with various database-schemes (e. g. Postgres or CouchDB) available to ensure up to 99.99999% service uptime. The mobile and desktop applications have a composed user interface and are easily usable by non-professionals. They also provide security in terms that user input can be concealed and all messages are encrypted on transport and application layer before they are being transmitted to the server. The encryption scheme is the Signal protocol that has already proven that it is capable of securing connections efficiently also in asynchronous transportations by using ratchets [18]. The whole platform is designed by the following principles:

1. Business by design: Inclusion of business processes into a communication Platform
2. Compliance by design: Data autonomy and legally watertight archiving
3. Security by design: Usable and economic security from the start of development
4. Privacy by design: Privacy is dealt with during the development process to preserve it
5. Usability by design: Easy and usable for users, low training periods

Quvert has no access to user data and does not use it to generate personalized advertisements or feedback. Furthermore, no data is transmitted to third parties and companies can use an on premise server to be sure they do not share any sensible data with the service and everything is kept in house. To be compliant Quvert offers Handshakes where users can define business relevant topics to be archived. If users do not send a specified handshake the server acts as a zero knowledge server. If the handshake is activated the server stores the message in an encrypted database which is only decryptable via four eyes principle to offer legally watertight agreements (s. Fig. 69.1). One side effect of this is that business irrelevant communication is not stored by the service and therefore usage of disk space can be reduced.

Quvert has a module called Quvert.Knowledge which uses anonymized data to get an overview of the knowledge available in the company and what kind of profile a new

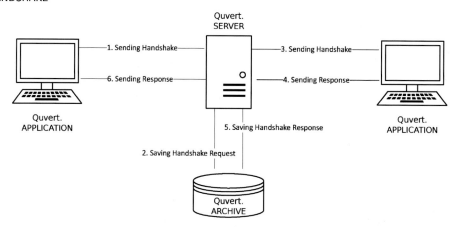

Fig. 69.1 Handshake flow

employee should have to grant an increase in knowledge available in the organization. This is especially vital in times of demographic change where staff grows older and leaves the company and therefore their knowledge is gone and on the other hand less young people are joining the company [19].

69.6   Summary

To create an usable, secure and efficient communication tool is not a trivial task. In terms of security for the platform there has to be a solution to post quantum cryptography and how to modify the Signal protocol to gain the highest possible security. Table 69.2 shows Quvert in comparison to a few of other business communication tools on the market.

Furthermore, it is essential to verify the functionalities offered by Quvert to get to know how the platform is accepted by users. Therefore, testers have been acquired but at the time of writing this paper no results could be drawn from the feedback and this is to be analyzed in the future. There will also be penetration testing in the near future to evaluate possible threat vectors for the platform and to prevent data leakage.

Current research is in the field of Internet of Things to connect Smart Objects to the platform and offer interactive and configurable control panels based on the transmitted certificate attributes by Smart Objects [20].

All in all Quvert shows a promising approach towards a smart, efficient and secure communication platform that is usable on all current operating systems, whether they are mobile or stationary. It also adds real value to currently used communication systems by offering an integrated lightweight yet highly utilizable knowledge management and one can conduct legally watertight agreements. In the near future the connection to the Internet of Things will also serve as a unique identifier for the platform.

Table 69.2 Quvert in comparison

Product	WhatsApp	Dropbox	Slack	Quvert
Sector	Private	Both	Business	Business
Focused on	Messaging	Document Management	Messaging	Business processes
Business compliance	No	No	License depending	Yes
End-to-end encryption	Yes	No	No	Yes
Encryption of data in transit?	Yes	Yes	Yes	Yes
Encryption of data at rest?	Yes	Yes	Yes	Yes
Provider has access to user data?	Maybe	Yes	Yes	No
Provider use data for itself?	Yes	Yes	Yes	No
Users must trust provider?	Yes	Yes	Yes	No

References

1. D. Leonard-Barton, "Wellsprings of knowledge: Building and sustaining the sources of innovation," *University of Illinois at Urbana-Champaign's Academy for Entrepreneurial Leadership Historical Research Reference in Entrepreneurship,* 1995.
2. R. e. a. Thorpe, "Using knowledge within small and medium-sized firms: A systematic review of the evidence," *International Journal of Management Reviews,* pp. 257–281, 2005.
3. The Radicati Group, Inc., "Email Statistics Report, 2015–2019," Palo Alto, CA, USA, 2015.
4. M. E. J. Newman, S. Forrest und J. Balthrop, "Email networks and the spread of computer viruses," *Phys. Rev. E,* p. 4, 09 2002.
5. Z. Durumeric, D. Adrian, A. Mirian, J. Kasten, E. Bursztein, N. Lidzborski, K. Thomas, V. Eranti, M. Bailey und J. A. Halderman, "Neither snow nor rain nor mitm … : An empirical analysis of email delivery security," *Proceedings of the 2015 ACM Conference on Internet Measurement Conference,* pp. 27–39, 2015.
6. P. Zimmermann, "Phil Zimmermann – Why I Wrote PGP," 06 1991. [Online]. Available: https://www.philzimmermann.com/EN/essays/WhyIWrotePGP.html. [Accessed 17 08 2016].
7. P. Hoffman, "Smtp service extension for secure SMTP over TLS," 1998.
8. S. Gandel, "Lloyd's CEO: Cyber attacks cost companies $400 billion every year," Fortune, 23 01 2015. [Online]. Available: http://fortune.com/2015/01/23/cyber-attack-insurance-lloyds/. [Accessed 21 10 2016].
9. T. Van Vleck, "The History of Electronic Mail," 01 02 2001. [Online]. Available: http://www.multicians.org/thvv/mail-history.html. [Accessed 19 08 2016].
10. ICQ LLC, "ICQ," 1998–2016. [Online]. Available: https://icq.com/. [Accessed 19 08 2016].
11. AOL Inc., "AIM," 2016. [Online]. Available: https://www.aim.com/. [Accessed 19 08 2016].
12. WhatsApp Inc., "WhatsApp Blog," 01 02 2016. [Online]. Available: https://blog.whatsapp.com/616/Eine-Milliarde. [Accessed 31 08 2016].
13. E. Kim, "WhatsApp's Insane Growth Continues: 100 Million New Users in 4 Months," Business Insider INDIA, 07 01 2015. [Online]. Available: http://www.businessinsider.in/WhatsApps-Insane-Growth-Continues-100-Million-New-Users-in-4-Months/articleshow/45786867.cms. [Accessed 31 08 2016].
14. J. B. Graham, "Impacts of Text Messaging on Adolescents' Communication Skills: School Social Workers' Perceptions," 2013.
15. Slack Technologies, "A little update about a lot of people using Slack," 25 05 2016. [Online]. Available: https://slackhq.com/a-little-update-about-a-lot-of-people-using-slack-f16c5b331647. [Accessed 26 08 2016].
16. Slack Technologies, "How can Slack help my team?," [Online]. Available: https://slack.com/results. [Accessed 26 08 2016].
17. Slack Technologies, "Slack Policies," 01 12 2015. [Online]. Available: https://slack.com/security-practices. [Accessed 30 08 2016].
18. T. Frosch und C. e. a. Mainka, "Horst Görtz Institut for IT-Security, Ruhr University Bochum," 2014. [Online]. Available: eprint.iacr.org/2014/904.pdf. [Accessed 31 08 2016].
19. J. Poterba, "Economic Implications of Demographic Change," *Business Economics,* Bd. 51, Nr. 1, pp. 3–7, 2016.
20. M. Cagnazzo, M. Hertlein und N. Pohlmann, "An Usable Applicationan for Authentication, Communication and Access Management in the Internet Of Things," *Communications in Computer and Information Science,* 2016.

City as a Service and City On-Demand – New concepts for intelligent urban development

Georg Klassen and Martin Buske

Abstract

Urban growth in developing and developed countries is changing our lives, and causing explosive growth of data generation in an interconnected world. Moreover, billions of new relationships between all parts of our environment will be created. Policy makers will face high complexity and will have to handle these challenges under fast changing and highly dynamic circumstances. Nowadays, a city can be represented as a "living body" with networks as the nervous system, administrative authorities as the brain, transportation systems as the circulatory system, and further stakeholders as organs. Socio-technical aspects of a Smart City should be cultivated and treated in the most efficient way for a better city development. Rationalization in all areas of urban life is a main driver of smartness. Investigation of the quality of life in cities is a kind of rational consideration of prevalent living conditions. Relationships between quality of life, residents' needs and available services are important for resident-centered design of a Smart City. City On-Demand is a new approach that is characterized by reliable and user friendly Smart Services that probably do not exist before request and occur in real-time upon receipt of the request. Citizens' lives will be improved through an efficient use of customized services. For deeper understanding, the authors describe the status quo of leading Smart Cities – Barcelona, Amsterdam Hamburg and New York. This article introduces the most important definitions related to a Smart

G. Klassen (✉)
Rohde & Schwarz GmbH & Co. KG
Munich, Germany
e-mail: georg.klassen@rohde-schwarz.com

M. Buske
Buske Consulting GmbH
Sankt Augustin, Germany
e-mail: mbuske@buske-consulting.de

© Springer-Verlag GmbH Germany 2018
C. Linnhoff-Popien et al. (eds.), *Digital Marketplaces Unleashed*,
https://doi.org/10.1007/978-3-662-49275-8_70

City, explains a new approach of 'City as a Service' and 'City On-Demand' concepts and provides an outlook 2025 for autonomously driving cars, e-health and citizen services.

70.1 Main Definitions and Concepts

The urbanization process all over the world impacts all areas of life. Cities account for a major share of global economic output [1]. The United Nations predict that by 2050 about 64% of the developing world and 86% of the developed world will be urbanized [2]. More and more cities can be considered as Digital Cities because of extensive use of information and communication technology (ICT). During the last several years, the focus has been moving from the technology perspective to the smartness of a city. ICT remains very important. Its efficient use, resulting in smart services, play a very important role in a city's development. There are various definitions of Smart City and the concept of Smart City is very broad and evolving. The implementation of this concept depends on specifics of a city, such as its story, brand, values, policies, objectives and socio-technological constraints. According to the EU, the definition of a Smart City is "a city seeking to address public issues via ICT-based solutions on the basis of a multi-stakeholder, municipally based partnership" [3]. The main goal of a Smart City is to improve the quality of life (QOL) by developing and offering ICT-based services that meet residents' needs and boost efficiency of services [4]. Technology focused definitions of the Smart City are not treated further in this article.

Fig. 70.1 shows a QOL perspective on of a Smart City and mentions the most important relationships between QOL, residents' needs and available services. In this context, need is the goal, service is the method and QOL is the indicator of target achievement.

A Smart City is one example of a complex ecosystem with numerous digital touch points between citizens, businesses, authorities and other service providers, powering

Fig. 70.1 Magic triangle of a Smart City from the QOL perspective

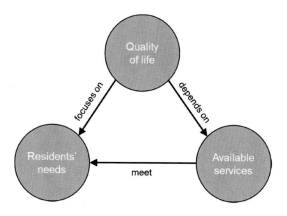

exponential growth in global data generation. Rationalization as a main aspect of urbanization in all areas of citizens' lives can, and should, be driven by these data.

Quantification of quality of life has become an important indicator for many cities. Its calculation by Mercer is well-known [5]. The cities are evaluated by several factors grouped in 10 categories: 1) Political and social environment; 2) Economic environment; 3) Socio-cultural environment; 4) Medical and health considerations; 5) Schools and education; 6) Public services and transportation; 7) Recreation; 8) Consumer goods; 9) Housing; 10) Natural environment.

Six dimensions of smartness defined by the EU operate in similar categories as shown in Table 70.1. This overlap roughly shows the link between quality of life and smartness of a city.

Furthermore, definitions of "City as a Service" and "City On-Demand" are being introduced to allow a new view of the Smart City and six dimensions of smartness.

The term "City as a Service" is relatively new. The main point is that cities are starting to apply service design to improve certain urban practices. Holistic approaches are being applied to different areas, such as management of public spaces, demand-based parking, resident-centered living concepts etc [6].

Table 70.1 Six dimensions of smartness and categories of QOL. (In dependence on European Parliament [3]; Mercer LLC [5])

Dimension/Area of QOL	Definition
Smart Economy/Areas of 'Economic environment', 'Consumer goods'	E-business and e-commerce using ICT-enabled manufacturing and service delivery as well as ICT-enabled innovation, creation of new services and new business models
Smart Mobility/Area of 'Public services and transportation'	ICT-enabled transportation system including public transport, such as buses, trams, subways, cars, trains, cyclists as well as pedestrians using these modes of transport and businesses using them for their logistic needs
Smart Environment/Areas of 'Natural environment', 'Housing', 'Medical and health considerations'	ICT-supported energy solutions, ICT-enabled smart grids, pollution monitoring, green urban planning and buildings, smart waste management and water resource systems, efficient street lighting and other services
Smart People/Area of 'Schools and education'	People that possess various skills, enable them to use ICT-based services and to work in such an environment, create new products and services and foster innovation
Smart Living/Areas of 'Social-cultural environment', 'Recreation'	Healthy and safe living, behavior and consumption habits of people that integrating ICT-supported services and products into their everyday life
Smart Governance/Area of 'Political and social environment'	City governance characterized by a high level of interaction with involvement of citizens, businesses, institutions and further stakeholders, enabling objective and transparent e-government

The existing studies on 'User-centric service composition' should help to understand this approach: "A potential benefit of service composition is that it allows new services to be created rapidly, as a combination of existing basic services, instead of being developed from scratch ... Dynamic orchestration of service composition activities enables true user-centric service delivery" [7, 8].

Since no clear definition of "City as a Service" has been found, the following working definition is used in this article:

> *City as a Service* is a service-oriented approach to urban development that considers the city as a service platform where different service providers (the city itself, further authorities, institutions, businesses as well as residents) can offer their services and interact in the most efficient way.

"City On-Demand" is a new approach. No definition has been found, that we could use for our needs. Therefore, we propose the following working definition:

> *City On-Demand* means Smart Cities, which already operate the City as a Service model AND allow the creation of new services in real-time that probably did not exist before the request.

At this new meta-level, existing services are considered to be resources for newly-created ones. Residents' needs, habits, and behavior, as well as availability and quality of resources and further constraints, are considered to fulfill all requirements in the most efficient way real-time. For example, a citizen has a need – "recreation over the weekend". When expressing this need to his personal digital butler a new service is created considering all information mentioned above with the goal of the best recreation value within the given period. In turn, this new service uses other services and data as resources. Resources used in the new service can be with costs or free of charge:

- health data from his smartwatch
- his/her favorite sports and meals and other leisure preferences
- his/her preferred social contacts (e. g. from his Facebook or Twitter account or personal phonebook)
- weather forecast
- details on events and what's happening in the city over the weekend
- traffic situation
- information about current use of public places etc.

An important requirement for enabling City On-Demand is the city's smartness at different socio-technological levels – not only within the six dimensions of smartness defined above, but between these dimensions, too. The rationale is: the smarter particular parts of the whole are, the smarter the whole can be. This can only be achieved by stronger networking and interoperability between all relevant elements of a Smart City. That should take place along all dimensions of a Smart City as exemplary shown for enterprise [9] or government interoperability [10].

Please permit us to explain, using the following example. The working definition of Smart Mobility (s. Table 70.1) requires smart transportation systems that consist, among others, of smart components, such as autonomously driving cars and intelligent traffic lights. The working definitions of Smart People and Smart Living (s. Table 70.1) require e-skills and the ability to integrate ICT-supported services and products into everyday life. An interconnection between these three dimensions of smartness – smart mobility, smart people and smart living – can be shown as follows.

Autonomously driving cars need to have a well implemented collision detection for accident-free traffic. This requires smart infrastructure, consisting of static and dynamic interactive elements. The interaction between cars and intelligent infrastructure will improve collision detection and reduce crashes [11, 12]. For this purpose, various types of data need to be exchanged – exact position, movement direction, speed, size, status of traffic lights, speed limitation, street signs etc.

External traffic participants (pedestrians, cyclists), as smart people, have to possess skills to integrate relevant devices into their everyday life. In particular, they should be willing to buy (consumption aspect) and to wear clothes (lifestyle and behavior aspects) equipped with sensors that interact with autonomously driving cars and other traffic participants and elements.

Therefore, the car does not have to be able to determine all necessary parameters itself, but it must be able to interact and to rely on data it gets from its environment. This new relationship between Smart Mobility, Smart People, and Smart Living improves quality of life by reducing crashes, but means a higher complexity of each part and of the whole.

70.2 Examples

There are several Digital City and Smart City initiatives, which were founded during the last 10 years. Based on a study by the European Union there are already 240 cities or 51% of all cities in EU-28 with more than 100,000 residents, which have implemented or proposed Smart Cities. There are Smart Cities in all European countries, but they are unevenly distributed. Smart City characteristics are Governance, Economy, Mobility, Environment, People, and Living [3]. All initiatives with one or more projects in European Smart Cities cover at least one of those characteristics.

First, we will look at a few examples from Europe and also one international example to better understand the development of the existing Smart Cities today. The highest absolute number of Smart Cities in Europe are in the UK, Spain and Italy. Italy, Austria, Denmark, Norway, Sweden, Estonia and Slovenia have the highest share of Smart Cities.

Overall, Smart Cities are still at an early stage of development. The stage of development or the maturity level of a Smart City depends primarily on whether only one strategy or policy exists or initiatives have already been successfully launched and are available to the public or are implemented. Smart Environment and Smart Mobility have the largest share of the initiatives in a number of cities. Hamburg, Helsinki, Barcelona and Amsterdam were best ranked in assessing both the Smart City characteristics and performance. All Smart City initiatives share the vision of transforming the city into a place with a better quality of life.

Since a Smart City consists not only of components, but also people, it is also important to secure the participation of citizens and relevant stakeholders. The structure of knowledge management with access to relevant data, open standards and data privacy as well as data security is another success factor. The best-ranked cities above fulfill most of these success factors.

70.2.1 Barcelona

The City of Barcelona, Spain ranked as number one Smart City globally [13] and has a wide range of Smart City initiatives [14].

With its Open Data initiative, the Barcelona City Council provides public data, so that a range of individuals and entities can easily access and reuse the data. This resulted in the creation of new companies, services and products, which has increased the city's social and economic value and improved individuals' lives.

With the Telecare service, Barcelona supports 70,000 elderly people 24 h a day 365 days per year. It offers appropriate response to users' requests for assistance and takes preventative actions by maintaining frequent contact with individuals to prevent unsafe situations, isolation or loneliness. In this way, the domestic care service helps to improve the quality of life and independence of people who are elderly, disabled, or dependent on others, and those who live or spend many hours alone at home.

There are also more common initiatives, such as the Barcelona Wi-Fi, which offers the largest free-access, public Wi-Fi network in Spain and one of the most advanced in Europe.

After starting Smart City initiatives in pilot projects Barcelona began to launch city-wide services. Today a large number of Smart City initiatives are available as part of the Smart City strategy, for example control of lighting zones, smart parking or e-governance.

Barcelona seems to be on a good way to offer connected services that help to achieve a City as a Service status by following a data-driven approach but it requires a greater involvement of enterprise-oriented initiatives [15].

70.2.2 Amsterdam

In Amsterdam, the Netherlands, several Smart City initiatives have been launched to achieve the goal of being part of the international top of sustainable cities in 2040 [16].

The Utrechtsestraat Climate Street is one of these initiatives with the aim of realizing CO_2 reduction and environmental saving [17]. The Utrechtsestraat Climate street is to become the first living sustainable showroom in the world to determine which technologies, cooperative agreements and approaches are the most successful to make the city's (shopping) streets more sustainable on a large scale. At a later stage, this concept is planned to be rolled out to the rest of the Netherlands.

As part of the Ship-to-Grid project in Amsterdam IBM and Cisco partnered with Dutch utility companies to provide energy management systems and smart meters to about 500 households [18]. Via utility-side data management and analysis, the households themselves and the city as a whole are able to optimize their energy consumption and reduce waste. It is also possible to predict peaks and coordinate energy generation and consumption in a more sustainable way.

A similar environment-focused initiative is the ITO Tower Project [19]. In this project intelligent technology collects, monitors and analyzes the building's programing and utility data to identify energy consumption inefficiencies and lower the building's carbon footprint.

The Health Lab initiative is linked to the people and their living characteristics [20]. Health Lab focuses on increased care efficiency resulting in greater end-user independence. This initiative is intended to support and stimulate Digital Health developments in the Amsterdam metropolitan area. Innovation in care needs the cooperation of many different organizations especially in order to produce technologies, service the market, educate on use new technologies and adapt them.

The focus of Amsterdam lays on environment-oriented initiatives. More mobility and economy-oriented initiatives and connecting those services via extending and connecting the open data hub would help to achieve the status of a City as a Service [21].

70.2.3   Hamburg

For its Smart City strategy the City of Hamburg focused on environment, people and economy [22]. With its rapidly growing urban population, the Hamburg government recognizes the need to answer the questions about mobility, public infrastructure, service, energy consumption, emissions and quality of life. Therefore, the Smart City, as a connected and intelligent city, is the ideal strategic solution to improve the quality of life. The city aims to achieve this goal through intelligent, innovative infrastructures, which help to make mobility more efficient, to conserve resources and reduce negative environmental impacts. Sensors and information technologies thereby will continue to gain importance in the future.

The harbor is the heart of Hamburg's economy. The government does not want to build unlimited roads, railways and waterways. Therefore, the Port of Hamburg is planned to be developed into a smartPORT in the coming years to increase the efficiency of the existing lines, and thus the quality of its services [23].

In addition, an intelligent infrastructure in Hamburg should be established which includes, among other things, an intelligent control of traffic signals. Traffic lights recognize how many people wait and traffic signals switch accordingly, while sensors in streetlights measure the outside light so that they only light up when it is really dark.

Another initiative is the virtual citizens' stand. Pressing a button in a small kiosk at malls or libraries allows citizens to make video calls to an administrative assistant via Internet. The kiosk is equipped with a small desk with a monitor showing a touch tablet to display documents and allow inputs or video presentations. In addition, citizens can immediately print forms via the connected printer [24].

Hamburg just started its way to become a City as a Service. The currently available services and initiatives are not well connected and some areas are not well represented. For example Hamburgs Open data service is more a content search engine than a data hub [25].

70.2.4 New York

For the City of New York, USA a Smart City means an equitable city. To guide connected devices and Internet of Things (IoT) implementation, serve as the coordinating entity for new technologies across all city agencies and foster collaboration with academia and the private sector are important tasks to better the lives of all New Yorkers [26].

Especially data and analytics are the main pillars for New York's Smart City strategy. Real-time information enables a more responsive government and better data generates cost savings and increased impact. Additionally, enhanced analytics allow for increased equity in the delivery of services while sensors and digital tools allow for more efficient use of city infrastructure and resources.

One concrete example is the Community Air Survey, which uses approximately 100 monitors installed throughout NYC to study how pollutants from traffic, buildings and other sources impact air quality in different neighborhoods. This includes monitoring fine particles, nitrogen oxides, elemental carbon, sulfur dioxide, and ozone, which can cause health problems. This project focusses on people, environment and living characteristics.

The same characteristics are important in the Vision Zero View project [27], which has the goal to eliminate deaths and serious injury from traffic crashes. Vision Zero View displays the location of every traffic fatality and serious injury within the last 5 years in an innovative presentation of data relating to crashes, serious injuries, deaths, safety improvement projects and public outreach efforts.

Other projects, such as MyNYCHA, establish new services via smartphone applications [28]. The MyNYCHA mobile application from the New York City housing authority allows public housing residents to manage maintenance service requests, view alerts and outages related to their developments and view their scheduled inspections via smartphones and tablets. This empowers residents to create service requests 24/7 and reduces the need for individual calls.

Table 70.2 Smart City Initiatives in selected cities and mapping to Dimensions

City	Initiative	Dimensions
Barcelona	Open Data Initiative	Smart People, Smart Living, Smart Environment, Smart Governance
Barcelona	Telecare	Smart Living, Smart People
Barcelona	Barcelona Wi-Fi	Smart Living, Smart Economy, Smart Mobility
Amsterdam	Climate Street	Smart Environment, Smart Economy, Smart Living
Amsterdam	Ship-to-Grid	Smart Environment, Smart People, Smart Living
Amsterdam	ITO-Tower	Smart Environment, Smart Economy
Amsterdam	Health Lab	Smart People, Smart Living
Hamburg	smartPORT	Smart Mobility, Smart Economy
Hamburg	Infrastructure	Smart Mobility, Smart Environment
Hamburg	Virtual Citizen Kiosk	Smart Governance, Smart People, Smart Living
New York	Community Air Survey	Smart Environment, Smart People, Smart Living
New York	Vision Zero View	Smart Mobility, Smart People, Smart Living
New York	MyNYCHA	Smart Governance, Smart Living, Smart People

It seems like New York is on a very good way to achieve the City of a Service status. Services are already interconnected in some areas. There's a huge volume of underlying data to combine services via New York open data hub which helps to create more integrated services covering multi dimensions in near future [29].

Table 70.2 represents the cities and initiatives considered in this article. It also shows to what dimensions these initiatives are assigned.

70.3   Conclusion and Outlook

In the current stage of development of Smart Cities, the relevant actors – municipalities, educational institutions, businesses and citizens – already work together on specific projects. It can also be seen that many Smart City initiatives that initially merely had a pilot project in a narrowly defined temporal and spatial context, launched these later on in the urban area for the entire population or companies and thus develop real lasting effect. In many cases, multiple characteristics of smartness – Governance, Economy, Mobility, Environment, People, and Living – are considered in the projects. Thus, the involvement of different actors and characteristics lead to overarching project approaches with far-reaching implications and effects for each Smart City.

However, there are no recognizable approaches which proactively create added value for citizens through predictive analysis of data streams, appropriate anticipatory generating and offering services in real-time. Especially due to the high dynamics of change and the short-term occurrence of events, city councils, businesses, and above all citizens responding precisely would be of great value and a decisive advantage. Here, the current developments in technology and in the processing, analysis, and use of data are very helpful.

If one dares an outlook, by 2025 autonomous driving will have changed the cityscape of Smart Cities decisively in several forms. Through the interplay of city infrastructure (sensors and traffic control), not only the public transport optimally takes place, but the transport of goods and the delivery logistics can be significantly optimized. Therefore, optimum usage of vehicle types (taxi, bus, tram, subway, etc.) is possible based on the foreseeable traffic at any time of day and for any type of event. Urban delivery traffic can be shifted to low-traffic times through intelligent traffic control. Shipping and storage processes by autonomous vehicles with fully automated warehouses, in conjunction with accurate calculation of consumption make this possible. Through all available data streams from retail stores and private households, goods consumption needs of the population can be updated daily to help to predict reorders. Transit times within cities can be calculated to the minute, since all vehicles in city traffic and transportation systems are networked. Thus, waiting times and accident risks are significantly reduced.

The health sector is significantly enhanced, as fewer office visits for patients arise because of targeted and accurate diagnoses. This is made possible by fitness trackers that provide the health information of residents in an encapsulated networked system and allow direct exchange of this data and possible disease symptoms with the network of physicians and hospital system in case of negative warning signals. In addition, time and costs for the individual and the community can be reduced, since the automatic guidance to best available doctor or hospital reduces multiple trips and waiting time loss.

Citizen services, which previously represented only a digital complement to the traditional system of forms and manual interaction with government officials will become fully digital. Chatbot systems that permit voice dialog between citizens and "digital" government employees simplify procedures and reduce the time and costs of bureaucracy. Citizens Service solution as an intelligent government butler with 24 h availability to serve citizens in their individual situation, with context-based support, whether the questions on tax payment or short-term event parking thirty minutes before the event takes place.

Feedback and interaction approaches for citizens' interaction with administration authorities are also simplified by the augmented reality solutions implemented by then – similar to today's popular game, Pokémon Go [30]. Citizens can report defects or make suggestions in real-time and on-site. Incentive systems can play an important role for the use of these solutions to increase and thus to pass a large number of improvement proposals. Similar to WeChat [31] the cooperation of social networks with local businesses greatly enhances the Smart City services and simplifies cooperation with citizens. An important success factor is the quick and easy start of direct communication between service providers and clients as well as monitoring service implementation and evaluation afterwards.

The authors recommend to pursue City as a Service approach to increase efficiency as well as to adopt City On-Demand idea to focus on residents' needs for a better quality of life. Besides this, they also recommend to implement an agile approach of testing and launching new innovative concepts and solutions from other regions. That helps to stay on track with the fast changing technology and product development nowadays. New networks of Smart City experts should be created for a better knowledge and experience exchange – besides the established conferences and awards. This would help to achieve a faster adoption from citizens and local enterprises and finally achieve a highly connected City as a Service.

On the other hand, stakeholders of a Smart City should be aware of risks that concern areas of privacy, security and safety. Misuse of personal information, loss of control over connected environment, service failures due to hacker attacks such as Distributed Denial of Service would decline the Quality of Life. The implementation of a Smart City should consider and prevent these risks.

Acknowledgements
Further enablers of this article were the phenomena of a Smart City itself, or of a smart country. The authors thank Digitale Stadt München e. V [32]. for the access to the relevant network; BITKOM e. V [33]. for deeper insights into status quo of worldwide Smart City initiatives; Rohde & Schwarz GmbH & Co. KG [34] for deeper technological insights into the topic of Internet of Things; WorkRepublic [35] for the highly efficient working environment with an open-space ideology for a better interdisciplinary exchange of experience and knowledge [36].

References

1. C. Etezadzadeh, Smart City – Future City?, Wiesbaden: Springer Fachmedien, 2016.
2. United Nations, "World Urbanization Prospects: The 2014 Revision," United Nations, Department of Economic and Social Affairs, Population Division, 2014.
3. European Parliament, "Mapping Smart Cities in the EU," European Union, Policy Department A: Economic and Scientific Policy, 2014.
4. Wikipedia, "Smart City," [Online]. Available: https://en.wikipedia.org/wiki/Smart_city. [Accessed 20 08 2016].
5. Mercer LLC, "2016 Quality of Living Rankings," [Online]. Available: https://www.imercer.com/content/mobility/quality-of-living-city-rankings.html. [Accessed 28 08 2016].
6. Y. Korobeynikov and M. Belyaev, "City as a Service: How to Design a New Urban Experience," Aventica, 03 10 2015. [Online]. Available: http://de.slideshare.net/sdnetwork/city-as-a-service-how-to-design-a-new-urban-experience-yegor-korobeynikov-mikhail-belyaev-aventica. [Accessed 25 08 2016].
7. E. M. Goncalves da Silva, User-centric service composition – towards personalised service composition and delivery, Enschede, The Netherlands: University of Twente, 2011.
8. E. M. Goncalves da Silva, L. Ferreira Pires and M. van Sinderen, "A-DynamiCoS: A Flexible Framework for User-centric Service Composition," in *IEEE 16th International Enterprise Distributed Object Computing Conference*, Beijing, 2012.
9. D. Chen, Framework for Enterprise Interoperability, Talence, France: Université Bordeaux, 2009.

10. Government of the UK, "e-Government Interoperability Framework," Office of the e-Envoy, London, 2004.

11. M. Bertoncello and D. Wee, "Ten ways autonomous driving could redefine the automotive world," McKinsey&Company, 06 2015. [Online]. Available: http://www.mckinsey.com/industries/automotive-and-assembly/our-insights/ten-ways-autonomous-driving-could-redefine-the-automotive-world. [Accessed 22 08 2016].

12. Startup-Buzz, "nuTonomy Announces Partnership with Singapore's Land Transport Authority to Begin Trials of an Autonomous Mobility-on-Demand Transportation Service," 01 08 2016. [Online]. Available: http://www.startup-buzz.com/6416-2/. [Accessed 16 10 2016].

13. Juniper Research, "Barcelona Named 'Global Smart City – 2015'," 17 02 2015. [Online]. Available: http://www.juniperresearch.com/press/press-releases/barcelona-named-global-smart-city-2015. [Accessed 19 08 2016].

14. City of Barcelona, [Online]. Available: http://smartcity.bcn.cat/en. [Accessed 25 08 2016].

15. L. Laursen, "Barcelona's Smart City Ecosystem," MIT Technology Review, 18 11 2014. [Online]. Available: https://www.technologyreview.com/s/532511/barcelonas-smart-city-ecosystem/. [Accessed 22 10 2016].

16. City of Amsterdam, "Amsterdam," [Online]. Available: https://amsterdamsmartcity.com. [Accessed 23 08 2016].

17. City of Amsterdam, "Amsterdam," [Online]. Available: https://amsterdamsmartcity.com/projects/climate-street. [Accessed 23 08 2016].

18. Greentech Media, Inc., "IBM, Cisco Partner on Amsterdam Smart Grid Project," [Online]. Available: http://www.greentechmedia.com/green-light/post/ibm-cisco-partner-on-amsterdam-smart-grid-project. [Accessed 23 08 2016].

19. BusinessWire, "Accenture to Help City of Amsterdam Become European Union's First 'Intelligent' City," [Online]. Available: http://www.businesswire.com/news/home/20090607005030/en/Accenture-City-Amsterdam-European-Union%E2%80%99s-%E2%80%98Intelligent%E2%80%99-City. [Accessed 23 08 2016].

20. E. Mendès, "Health Lab – Amsterdam SMART CITY PROJECT," [Online]. Available: https://challenges.openideo.com/challenge/mayo-clinic/inspiration/health-lab-amsterdam-smart-city-project-. [Accessed 24 08 2016].

21. City of Amsterdam, "Gemeente Amsterdam," 22 10 2016. [Online]. Available: https://data.amsterdam.nl/publisher. [Accessed 22 10 2016].

22. City of Hamburg, "City of Hamburg," [Online]. Available: http://www.hamburg.de/smart-city/. [Accessed 24 08 2016].

23. Management Circle AG, "Technischer und sozialer Fortschritt in der Smart City Hamburg," [Online]. Available: http://www.management-circle.de/blog/smart-city-hamburg/. [Accessed 24 08 2016].

24. F. Wegener, "SmartCity – die Zukunft der digitalen Stadt: Leistungsfähiger, kundenfreundlicher und preiswerter?," [Online]. Available: http://www.gruene-gladbeck.de/?p=1229. [Accessed 23 08 2016].

25. City of Hamburg, "Transparenzportal Hamburg," 22 10 2016. [Online]. Available: http://transparenz.hamburg.de/open-data. [Accessed 22 10 2016].

26. City of New York, "Innovative Projects – Smart City," [Online]. Available: https://www1.nyc.gov/site/forward/innovations/projects.page. [Accessed 23 08 2016].

27. City of New York, "NYC – Vision Zero," [Online]. Available: http://www.nyc.gov/html/visionzero/pages/home/home.shtml. [Accessed 24 08 2016].

28. City of New York, "NYC – About NYCHA," [Online]. Available: http://www1.nyc.gov/site/nycha/about/about-nycha.page. [Accessed 20 08 2016].

29. City of New York, "NYC OpenData," [Online]. Available: https://nycopendata.socrata.com/. [Accessed 22 10 2016].

30. Niantic, Inc., "Pokémon GO," [Online]. Available: http://www.pokemongo.com/de-de/. [Accessed 28 08 2016].

31. Tencent Inc., [Online]. Available: http://www.wechat.com/. [Accessed 28 08 2016].

32. Digitale Stadt München e. V., "Digitale Stadt München e. V.," [Online]. Available: http:// digitalestadtmuenchen.de/. [Accessed 28 08 2016].

33. BITKOM e. V., "BITKOM," [Online]. Available: https://www.bitkom.org/. [Accessed 28 08 2016].

34. Rohde & Schwarz GmbH & Co. KG, "Rohde & Schwarz," [Online]. Available: http://rohde-schwarz.com/. [Accessed 28 08 2016].

35. pro.work GmbH, "WorkRepublic," [Online]. Available: https://www.workrepublic.de/. [Accessed 28 08 2016].

36. ISO/IEC JTC 1 Information technology, "Smart cities – Preliminary Report 2014," ISO, Geneva, Switzerland, 2015.

Personal Applications in the Internet of Things Through Visual End-User Programming 71

Yannis Valsamakis and Anthony Savidis

Abstract

The Internet of Things is based on ecosystems of networked devices, referred to as smart objects, effectively enabling the blending of physical things with digital artifacts in an unprecedented way. In principle, endless automations may be introduced in the context of daily life exploring the numerous opportunities offered by the deployment and utilization of such smart objects. However, in practice the demands for such automations are highly personalized and fluid effectively minimizing the chances for building commercially successful general-purpose applications. In this context our vision is to empower end-users with the appropriate tools enabling to easily and quickly craft, test and modify the automations they need. In this chapter we initially discuss a few possible future scenarios for automations relying on smart objects. Then, we elaborate on the visual tools we currently develop, followed by a brief case study using the tools. Finally, the potential of publishing such automations in typical digital markets is considered.

Y. Valsamakis (✉)
Foundation for Research and Technology Hellas (FORTH)
Crete, Greece
e-mail: jvalsam@ics.forth.gr

A. Savidis
University of Crete
Crete, Greece
e-mail: as@ics.forth.gr

© Springer-Verlag GmbH Germany 2018
C. Linnhoff-Popien et al. (eds.), *Digital Marketplaces Unleashed*,
https://doi.org/10.1007/978-3-662-49275-8_71

71.1 Introduction

The presence of personal smart devices like smart phones and smart watches in the market has increased exponentially in the last decade. At the same time, a novel paradigm called Internet of Things (IoT) has appeared, referring to the vision of connecting physical things featuring sensors, tags (e. g. RFID tags), software and connectivity capabilities, to the network. IoT concept is the pervasive deployment of a variety of network connected smart objects around us, including physical things, smart devices, applications, etc. in the environment.

In this context, people's daily lives could benefit from using smart objects, as they can offer an environment of automations for everyday activities. However, in practice, the demands for such automations are highly personalized and fluid, resulting in a respective digital market that is either inexistent or marginal. Consequently, in order to fully benefit from the capabilities of this environment, individuals should be able to interact with smart objects, potentially managing, parameterizing and even programming applications involving them. The latter is not an easy task as it implies end-users who directly manipulate smart objects in a developer perspective, ranging from parameterizing and linking together, to actually programming the control and coordination of a set of smart objects. While such tasks are typically handled by experienced developers as they require programming skills, the research domain of End-User Programming (EUP) focuses on enabling end-users with virtually no programming background performing moderate and even comprehensive programming tasks.

Several approaches have been developed in the domain of EUP. The most popular approach is the *Spreadsheets* which are widely applied by individuals and businesses (e. g. grading by teachers, spreadsheets for accountants etc.). *Scripting Languages* is another technique which, in the context of EUP enables the extension and adaptation of existing applications by end-users. Scripts are the most powerful EUP tools, however they present end-users with considerable learning cost and they are prone to errors. Another approach which is based on scripting languages is the *Natural Languages* phrases interpretation. While the latter sounds promising for programming purposes, existing approaches seem to have problems and restrictions in use; that's why they are applied only in research and not in industry. The aforementioned approaches are based on text-based environments and it seems that they aren't the best choice for portable EUP applications for smart objects. However, there is another approach called *Visual Programming* which is based on graphic artifacts that have been mapped to the correspondent high level functionalities according to each *Visual Programming Language* (VPL). The most popular category of such artifacts for the VPLs are based on *jigsaws* which first appeared in *Scratch* [1]. Another approach of VPLs is *flow diagrams;* for example *Microsoft VPL* [2] is based on flow diagrams for building robotics applications.

In our work, we develop a portable touch-based visual end-user programming environment for personal applications, running on typical smart phones and tablets, where end-users may discover smart objects in their own surroundings and compose custom applications reflecting their own needs. Similar to our approach is HomeKit [3] which is a framework for communicating and controlling connected accessories in user's home. Also, the graphical control logic editor oBeliX [4] is a proof of concept tool for IoTSyS [5], an integrated middleware of IoT.

The rest of this chapter is organized as follows; In Sect. 71.2, existing smart objects in people's daily life are described. In Sect. 71.3, we discuss potential scenarios that end-users may develop. In Sect. 71.4 our approach in visual programming for smart object applications is described. Then, we present a case study developing the scenario described in Sect. 71.3.2. We continue by discussing the potential of digital markets for smart object applications. Finally, we briefly discuss the visual programming requirements of end-users in the context of IoT.

71.2 Smart Objects in Daily Life

The main building blocks of the IoT are smart objects. The concept of the IoT started in early 2000's with the RFID tags, and network connectivity of physical things. Furthermore, there are numerous smart devices available on the market which are already used in the context of IoT. In particular, devices which are commonly used in daily life have been evolved to smart connected devices by offering extra services and automations (e. g. tracking information, remote control, exchanging data with other smart objects etc.). The refrigerator is a representative example of a device used on a daily basis. Its main function is to maintain and store food items and fresh produce. But as a smart object, apart from the above functions, it will also be able to do other more complex functions such as identifying, enumerating, and holding important information about the food items it contains. Smart refrigerator notifies users when a food item is close to expire or if it has already expired. Furthermore, the refrigerator is able to display through an embedded screen, recipes based on the food items that are currently stored. Moreover, the users can remotely view what is stored in their refrigerator.

In addition, apart from the physical connected things and the smart devices, there is a huge number of applications online and day by day this exponentially increases. These applications could be used in the world of IoT and could be considered as smart objects which are connected online and are able to communicate through web-services. Such applications could be available via digital marketplaces. Examples of applications could be weather forecast, a clock, a chronometer etc. Furthermore, examples of such applications that could be interoperated with the smart refrigerator are a nutrition calendar and online shopping. Using these smart objects, the user will be able to program a weekly meal plan based on which the refrigerator could automatically place online orders in authorized food shops.

Taking into account the aforementioned about the smart objects which are available in people's daily life, people may like to have custom automations based on their needs. In the next section, we discuss such example applications.

71.3   Scenarios

Using existing smart objects, we discuss potential scenarios which could be developed by end-users based on the visual end-user environment we develop. However, the scenarios discussed below are just indicative, since by offering end-user programming features and due to the fact that there is a huge variety of smart objects available, the possibilities are endless.

71.3.1   Remote Hospitality

Many times people would like to be at home (or office) when their doorbell rings but instead they happen to be somewhere else. This happens either when there is a meeting for which they couldn't be there on time or in case of a surprise visit. Before the existence of IoT concept, visitors could only call the potential hosts in order to communicate with them. Thanks to IoT, people are able to use smart doorbells which are supported by appropriate software applications. The latter notify users when the doorbell rings and help them communicate with the person who rang it. On the one hand, smart doorbell software provides support for all possible services of the device, on the other hand, it is impossible to provide support for other smart objects that users would like to use with the smart doorbell. For example, end-users may like to have an application which uses home smart objects in order to host visitors remotely until they go back at home as depicted in Fig. 71.1. The smart door gives access to the visitors, while the smart lights turn on or

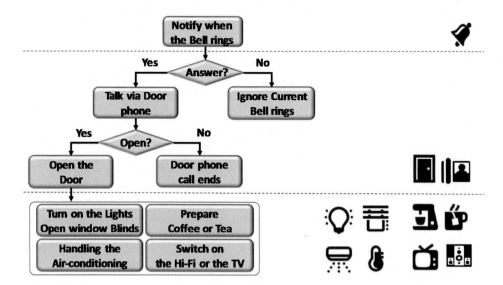

Fig. 71.1 The flow of Remote Hospitality Application and the involved smart objects

window blinds open depending on the time of the day. Furthermore, the home temperature can be regulated using the air conditioning system and the thermometer. Then, the smart Hi-Fi or TV could take on the visitors' entertainment. In addition, drinks can be prepared by the smart coffee machine or the smart kettle.

Someone would wonder why we have to create a new application using smart objects and not use all the provided applications from our smart objects. The answer is twofold. Firstly, users would like to have custom automations without having to use each of the applications of the smart objects. In addition, running applications for each smart object would be impossible in case of using several smart objects for one task something which would be a common scenario in the concept of the IoT which is based on the pervasive deployment of smart objects around the world. Secondly, there are several cases that smart objects are based on the events and data of other smart objects. A representative example of such application is discussed on the next section describing morning automations.

71.3.2 Morning Automations

One of the most difficult times of the day for people is waking up and their morning habitual tasks. There are several things that people have to do when they wake up such as, have a bath, prepare their breakfast, be informed about the news and their messages, prepare for their work, leave home for work etc. Using the existing smart objects, several processes could be automated and users would gain some more minutes of sleep, find their home temperature regulated, not forget to be informed about the news, leave home without worrying if they forgot to lock the windows or turn off lights, electric devices etc. All these automations can be accomplished when related events are triggered as depicted on the Fig. 71.2.

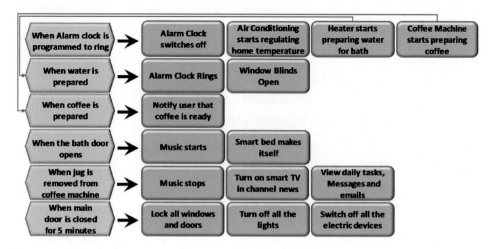

Fig. 71.2 Morning Automations triggered by environment events

The first event of application is based on the time that the alarm clock is programmed to ring. When the event is fired, the alarm clock is switched off before it rings, then the air conditioning regulates the home temperature, while heater starts preparing water for a morning bath and the coffee machine prepares the first coffee of the day. Then, when water for the bath is ready, the alarm clock rings and the window blinds open. Also, when coffee is prepared, the coffee machine notifies the user. Afterwards, when the user opens the bath door, the smart Hi-Fi automatically starts playing music and the smart bed makes itself. Afterwards, when the user starts serving coffee (once she has finished with her bath) music stops and it is time to catch up with the news and view the daily tasks she has to do, messages or email she has received. Finally, when leaving home for work, smart objects take on the home safety by locking all windows, window blinds and outdoors which are still open, switching off not used electric devices such as the air conditioning, the TV etc. turning off the lights and activating the alarm system.

71.3.3 Self-Caring Home

Continuing the previous scenario of morning automations, end-users could design automations for tasks which are required by their home such as cleaning, gardening, shopping etc. using appropriate smart objects. However, these are mainly calendar based tasks of the home that are executed repeatedly either with the specific frequency or not. The events defined for the application of home self-care automations are categorized on three categories home cleaning, shopping goods and care for the garden as depicted in Fig. 71.3.

The first task is programmed to be executed every day, when home is empty the windows open for half an hour for airing purposes. Then, windows close and the vacuum starts sweeping the house and then the house is mopped by the smart mop. In addition, when washing machine is full, it checks that it will not rain for the next 3 days and starts

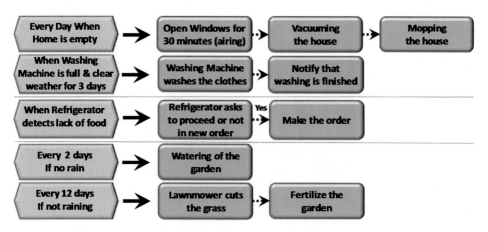

Fig. 71.3 Home care automations triggered by smart objects and calendar events

washing. When it finishes, the washing machine sends the respective notification. Also, the refrigerator checks for the availability of goods based on the nutrition calendar and in case something is missing it makes an order of goods. Additionally, tasks for care of the garden are defined as seen in the last part of Fig. 71.3. The first task cares for the watering of the garden by checking if the garden needs watering every two days and completes the task after checking that it will not rain for the next day. The second task cares for the fertilization and mowing of the garden by repeating the process every 12 days. In addition, before it starts the process, it checks that it won't rain for the next two hours.

71.4 Visual Programming

71.4.1 Discovery of Proximate Smart Objects

The first task end-users have to do for their development process is to discover and register the smart objects which will participate in their applications. Furthermore, as discussed previously in the context of IoT, there are numerous proximate smart objects available in people's surroundings. Hence, the management of the smart objects through the visual end-user programming platform is necessary. The smart objects may be positioned in different locations where people operate such as the home, the workplace, the gym etc. and smart objects' position may change (e. g. smart watch). Based on this fact, our approach in order to facilitate the smart objects organization, is to be able to define virtual environments in which the smart objects could be placed during the registration of the platform by selecting the respective environment. Furthermore, inner environments can be defined in each environment (e. g. Home, Home/Living room, Home/Bedroom, Home/Garden).

In addition, during the registration of the smart objects, the end-user is able to insert respective icons improving the visualization of smart objects. An example of environments and smart objects is represented in the left of Fig. 71.4, using an example of two defined environments the home and the office where smart objects have been placed. Also, the registration of a light smart object in the home environment is presented on the right screen of Fig. 71.4. Moreover, end-users are able to hide functionalities that may not like to use in their development process.

Furthermore, using the concept of environments, the end-user can have a quick wide view of the smart objects' information in each environment and can more easily focus in the smart objects of a specific environment in order to develop automations for this environment. The latter is common practice, and it doesn't restrict the end-users from developing custom automations which include smart objects from more than one environments. An example of such automations could be a "back to home" application using smart objects exist both in the office and at home environments. Moreover, the development process does not require that the smart objects should be connected thanks to the registration of the smart objects in the platform which has generated and maintained the smart object specifications.

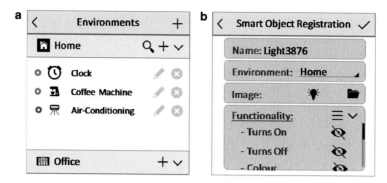

Fig. 71.4 View of defined environments of smart objects (**a**). Registration process of a light smart object (**b**)

71.4.2 Visual Programming of Smart Objects

Using the VPL of IoT, the end-users main task will be the handling of smart objects that will be involved in their applications. Each of the smart objects provides different functionalities which have to be published via a well-defined API in the context of IoT. Based on this, our system builds the smart object data to a JavaScript object from which the respective visual programming elements are generated and revealed to the visual programming environment.

Using as example the air-conditioning, total kind of smart object functionalities are depicted in Fig. 71.5 by presenting the mapping of the source code in JavaScript and the visual code of our visual programming language. There are four main categories identified for the smart object functionalities which are based on their I/O. In particular, there are functionalities without I/O such as the action "*turnOn*" of the *air-condition* which is depicted in Fig. 71.5. The visual element of our VPL is the blue box which consists of the respective smart object icon and the inner white box includes the selected functionality. By clicking the white box area, the end-user can view total functionalities of the air-condition and change the selection. The mapping of the generated source code of this element is the statement "`AirCondition.turnOn();`". Furthermore, there are functionalities with input or output which are visually represented in Fig. 71.5. Based on the types of the input arguments and the output when white boxes are clicked, the visual programming editor gives only the valid possible variables, values etc. in order to facilitate the end-users by limiting or eliminating their errors. Finally, the last category of smart object functionalities based on I/O includes both input and output elements.

Moreover, another category of smart object functionality is based on the responses which are triggered asynchronously and one or more actions could be defined for execution when it responds. The air-condition supports an asynchronous response "*onChangeTemperature*" as depicted in Fig. 71.5. The source code actions which will be executed in case of the response corresponds to a callback function in JavaScript while

Text Program	Visual Program
`AirCondition.turnOn();`	Turns on
`AirCondition.setTemperature(26);`	Set Temperature▾ 26

`AirCondition.onChangeTemperature(`
`function () {`
`    AirCondition.turnOn();`
`    . . .`
`});`
	When temperature changes
	Turns on
	■■■

`var temperature =` `    AirCondition.getTemperature();`	temperature = Temperature▾

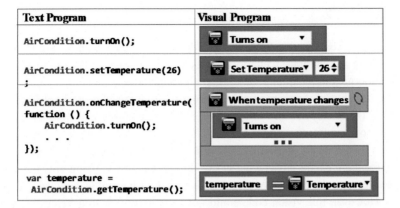

Fig. 71.5 Air-Conditioning object functionality (*left*), Use of the object and mapping to the visual programming language (*right*)

this maps to a block of statements which are the respective statements of the callback function body as shown.

Furthermore, the main context of the applications in the IoT is focused on the ecosystem of smart objects that exchange data and interact in an automatic or semi-automatic way based on events. As result, the design of events has to be one of the main concepts of the VPL for smart objects. Such events are the aforementioned asynchronous responses; however, these events are not adequate to define total events of applications in the context of IoT efficiently. Firstly, there are smart objects which partially support or not support functionality of asynchronous responses. In this case, the VPL has to support these events by defining such events and core takes on the functionality by using polling which checks the concerned value with appropriate frequency. Moreover, end-user would like to define event actions when combined data of more than one smart objects values change state. In addition, there is the need to define calendar events like the presented in the scenario of self-caring home. These events are separated in three different types based on the times to be executed. First category is the non-repeatable events which are executed once (e. g. on Tuesday smart garden fertilizes the grass). Second category is the finite number of times that events will be executed (e. g. On Tuesday, Friday smart garden sprays the plants suffer from a disease). The last category is the periodic execution of events (e. g. Every 2 days the grass is watered). Also, in case of IoT there are events which could be connected or disconnected to the application system by other events and vice versa. In the following case study, some of the VPL event elements have been used as shown in Fig. 71.7.

71.5 Case Study

Using the visual programming tools we develop, we have carried out a case study based on the morning automations scenario described in Sect. 71.3.2. The smart objects are included in morning automations are shown in Table 71.1.

The functionality of these smart objects are visually mapped respectively with the air conditioning as depicted in Fig. 71.5. For the development of this application, the end-user has to develop six different events. The first four events could just use the events which is supported by the smart objects as shown in Table 71.1 and the visual code has to be developed for these events as depicted in Fig. 71.6 respectively. Using only the provided smart object events, the respective visual code for the fifth event is depicted in Fig. 71.7 (top, left). However, this visual code could not be an easy task to develop for everyone

Table 71.1 Morning Automations Smart Objects and their functionalities

Smart Object	Functionality	Events
Alarm Clock	Switches on/off Start/Stop rings Is switched on Sets alarm time	When rings
Heater	Prepares water Is water prepared	When water is prepared
Coffee Machine	Prepares Coffee Rest Coffee Cups Is coffee jug out	When coffee is prepared When coffee jug is out
Air Conditioning	Turns on/off Is turned on Sets/Gets temperature Environment temperature	When temperature changes
Window Blinds	Opens/Closes Is open	–
Bed	Makes it self	When process is completed
Door	Opens/Closes Is open Lock	When opens When closes
Hi-Fi	Plays/Stops music Music list	–
TV	Starts/Stops Switch on/off Channel list	–
Light	Turns on/off Is turned on	–
Plug	Switches on/off Is switched on	When switches on When switches off

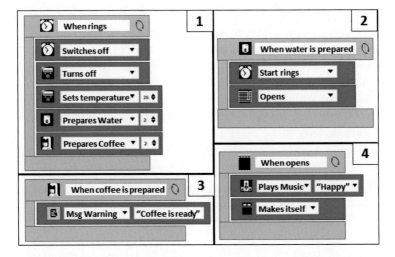

Fig. 71.6 EUP of the first correspondent four events of the morning automations depicted in Fig. 71.2 using our visual programming tools

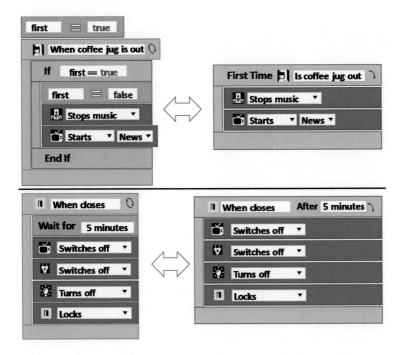

Fig. 71.7 EUP of two last events depicted in Fig. 71.2: using events of SOs (*left*); using visual expressions of our VPL (*right*)

because of the basic programming skills it needs. In this context, as it is aforementioned in Sect. 71.4.2 we have designed appropriate visual code expressions making programming the events more user-friendly. The respective visual code for the development of the fifth event using such visual expressions is depicted in Fig. 71.7 (top, right). Moreover, we have developed the last defined event from Fig. 71.2 using asynchronous functionality "*onDoorClose*" which is supported by the main door, by adding an extra visual statement of wait 5 min and then executing the rest defined visual statements of the event as shown in Fig. 71.7 (bottom, left). So by using the visual expressions we have defined, the end-user programming of this event could be developed as shown in Fig. 71.7 (bottom, right) alternatively.

71.6   Marketing Personal Applications

The development of smart object applications will be created by end-users, could be helped in its growth by the potential of publishing such applications to digital market-places as custom software products. In this context, end-users could share their applications, re-use other end-users' applications and be inspired by them.

Digital marketplaces have been recently used for the mobile applications (e. g. iPhone App Store, Google Play) giving the consumers access to a vast number of mobile applications and also enabling individuals to reach a mass audience for their applications. These digital marketplaces have created a long tail of mobile applications, helping in the growth and maturity of the respective markets. In fact, we are developing all visual tools and respective runtimes to execute on existing mobile operating systems, so that the resulting end-user applications can be directly published on existing application stores. Effectively, the latter opens a new digital marketplace, that of the personal smart automations in the context of the IoT.

71.7   Discussion and Conclusion

The plethora of applications which can be applied in the context of IoT shows that a wide audience would like to use visual programming platforms in order to develop automations for their necessities. Furthermore, the audience requirements for such a platform will differ. The majority of people would like to develop pure automations. However, there are end-users who would like to develop more complicated applications. This has as a result that the visual programming tools for smart objects have to provide different programming levels based on the requirements (e. g. pure adjustments of smart objects imply the corresponding convenience and directness) and the experience of end-users. There are approaches which provide more than one skill level based on the experience of the end-user such as *TouchDevelop* [6] and Tynker [7]. Furthermore, *TouchDevelop* provides templates with different kind of programs, so the end-users choose the most appropriate for their development process to avoid starting programming from scratch. Both of the aforementioned approaches and generally total visual end-user approaches are focusing on learning programming and most of them are specialized for children. However, end-user programming for smart objects is aimed at a huge range of people with different background knowledge, wide range of ages and level of experience in the context of the smart objects, programming etc. This results that the visual end-user programming platform for smart objects has to provide differ EUP paradigms to be able to match with different background knowledge and in parallel cover the total requirements of the potential end-users. In addition, taking into account that the IoT era is in its infancy, there are new necessities which will arise in the future. That means that the VPLs designed for IoT have to be flexible with appropriate mechanisms for adding new features for the smart objects either from the developers of the VPL or from end-users. There are related approaches which support new expressions and features to the VPLs such as *Scratch* and *Blockly* [8].

This chapter presents our vision of personal applications in the IoT through Visual Programming by presenting scenarios which end-users may develop using end-user programming features. Furthermore, we describe our approach and then we present a case study using our tools. Finally, we discuss the potential of a new digital marketplace of the personal automations in the context of the IoT.

References

1. M. Resnick, Maloney, A. J. Monroy-Hernández, N. Rusk, E. Eastmond, M. A. Brennan K., E. Rosenbaum, J. Silver, S. B. und Y. Kafai, Scratch: Programming for all, Commun, 2009.
2. "Microsoft VPL," August 2016. [Online]. Available: https://msdn.microsoft.com/en-us/library/bb483088.aspx.
3. "HomeKit developed by Apple," August 2016. [Online]. Available: http://www.apple.com/ios/homekit/.
4. M. H. E. Jung, W. Kastner und A. Jara, "Short paper: A scripting-free control logic editor for the Internet of Things," *Internet of Things (WF-IoT), IEEE World Forum, Seoul*, pp. 193–194, 2014.
5. "IoTSyS – Internet of Things integration middleware," August 2016. [Online]. Available: http://www.iue.tuwien.ac.at/cse/index.php/projects/120-iotsys-internet-of-things-integration-middleware.html.
6. N. Tillmann, M. Moskal, J. Halleux, M. Fahndrich und S. Burckhardt, "TouchDevelop: app development on mobile devices," in *In Proceedings of the ACM SIGSOFT 20th International Symposium on the Foundations of Software Engineering (FSE '12)*, New York, NY, USA, ACM, 2012.
7. "Tynker," August 2016. [Online]. Available: https://www.tynker.com/.
8. Blockly, August 2016. [Online]. Available: https://developers.google.com/blockly/.

Part XVI
Global Challenges – Local Solutions

Preface: Global Meets Local

Daniel Hartert

When people explain what "Digital" really means, they typically mention large global brands like Facebook, Amazon, Google or Twitter as the example. Certainly, these assets combine a lot of market power, customers, and innovation, and their sheer size is already a competitive advantage. Following these leading firms in their respective categories, many other companies have joined their ecosystems and benefit from the associated value. However, like in the traditional non-digital world, next to global brands the world provides a lot of space for local brands, niche players and startups.

New digital business models are making use of platforms that provide value to diverse participants, and this applies globally as well as locally. Global trends, such as the partial convergence of the automotive, car rental, transport and tourism industries into what we now call simply "mobility", are affecting local markets and national systems. The way how we get from A to B is changing, based on a combination of factors that are all contributing: generation Y being less keen to own a car, traditional traffic systems being overloaded or over-polluted, car sharing business models being well accepted, train and flight operators attempting to offer better end-to-end solutions, and new taxi services being based on convenient booking platforms.

Digital is often being characterized to be associated with a principle business model where value is driven by a combination of product + service + experience. "Product" in this equation is often the hook for traditional industries to get into digital business, i.e. enriching existing product categories with additional services for better experience and therefore loyalty by the customer.

In the western world, but also increasingly in developing countries, a significant percentage of physical consumer goods is owned and marketed by global brands. For tele-

D. Hartert (✉)
Bayer AG
Leverkusen, Germany
e-mail: daniel.hartert@bayer.com

vision, audio/video products, computers, smartphones and cars, there is almost no local product available anymore. Consumer Packaged Goods (CPG) often still carry local brands, but are increasingly owned by global conglomerates. As a consequence, the digital strategies linked to such product categories are mostly defined on a global corporate level, with little influence or variation by individual countries. Brand owners strive to protect the power of their brands globally, and therefore even prescribe the associated digital marketing plans on local levels. As a consequence, product related digital business models, product-embedded digital extensions such as connectivity to social platforms, as well as related Apps are mostly designed and deployed on a global level.

However, when digital business models are based on "service + experience", omitting a product to be involved, then there exists a very significant degree of local business development, creativity and variation: local social platforms, transportation, tourism, banking and insurance, real estate, labor and temporary work, energy providers, common interest platforms, e-Government solutions – the list is long and associated platforms are growing fast.

Two fundamental challenges of our world – Food and Health – are facing industry-wise their own set of challenges. Due to regulated environments, they also carry different characteristics when it comes to globalization and localization as outlined above. For the remainder of this article, I will focus on Digital Farming in the context of global Food Supply.

One of the most pressing challenges of the 21st century is the need to secure future food and water supply for a rapidly growing global population – estimated to reach 9.7 billion by 2050. It is a challenge that must also address associated issues such as global warming and environmental protection.

The need for fast growing food supply is not only driven by demographics, but even more by the fact that the world population is becoming wealthier and therefore increases its meat consumption. As a result, overall calories intake is estimated to grow by more than 50 % in the period from 1999 to 2030. Taking into account that available farmland continues to slightly shrink over the next decades (from a peak of appr. 1.5 billion hectares in the early 2000's), it becomes very clear that the food supply challenge requires innovative solutions that will not only change associated industries, but very likely also the profession of farming.

Between 1970 and the year 2000, farming was able to consistently increase its yield for major crops by an annual percentage of about 3 %. That's an impressive number, but unfortunately Moore's law does not apply to farming processes. The current growth rate is a mere 1 % – which is by far not sufficient to feed the world by 2050.

But growth and yield are not only dependent on available farmland. Water resources, new kinds of pests as well as more resistant pests, and new weather situations incurring with the ongoing climate changes all influence our crops as well. While traditional methods of breeding improve the quality and resilience of crops and farm animals, the deployment and utilization of modern technologies to generate a higher degree of precision and efficiency in agricultural management practices is detrimental. With such new technologies, farmers will experience a fundamental shift of their focus areas and a related necessary upskilling, while at the same time new ecosystems will change the landscape of traditional value chains.

The bad news is there is no silver bullet. But the good news is that within the digital farming framework, there are many new ways to address the challenge and to deliver tangible improvements. At the core of any such new approaches is data. Better local weather prognosis, hourly available spread of pests and diseases, sensors delivering soil and plant data, GPS systems enabling to analyze crops within a resolution of a square foot, predictive analytics connecting different data sources to deliver better prognosis and recommendations – the combination of new technologies can deliver a very powerful set of tools helping the farmer to further increase quality and yield at reasonable levels of effort.

Based on available satellite imaging, fields can be scanned and analyzed for spots of drought or certain diseases. Intelligent algorithms interpret the raw images, determine amongst other factors the bio mass growth, and calculate specific dosage of substances to be sprayed by the farmer in the field. The related data can be provided in standard formats to be read on the go by the tractor, allowing to only spray where necessary.

Applying such digital technologies will not only lead to a more convenience for the farmer's job, but has the potential to fundamentally change the agro business model. Instead of selling large volumes of product which is being sprayed across entire fields today, agrochemical companies might switch to outcome based business models, by which they offer the farmer a weed-free or disease free-field.

Applying the digital farming business models on a local level comes with a set of diverse challenges. While it makes economically sense for large fields as you find them in the US or in Brazil, the many very small farms in countries like India are less suitable to benefit. However, because of the small size of their fields, satellite images have no advantage over local ground inspection anyway. The creativity in these countries has already led in the early phases of Digital to local solutions that provide a better fit. For example, running heavy supply chain solutions with thousands of local dealers in remote areas is not possible. But having local service agents who visit local dealers on a daily level by motorbike works well. They quickly scan barcode slips of sold products with a smartphone App, transmitting the related data to the corporate sales offices.

The latter example is also pointing at another potential local roadblock: underdeveloped digital infrastructure in remote areas. Being economically driven, Telecom providers are focusing on areas with maximum subscription potential when building out new broadband and mobile infrastructure. Big cities have highest priorities, and often investment priorities are leading to replacing the latest xG technology in the cities before even bringing the last generation to remote areas. A balanced deployment of broadband infrastructure across high and low population areas is the basis for equal opportunities in the digital economy. Governments must ensure that the local coverage is further increasing, also to prevent further rural exodus and urbanization.

When infrastructure conditions are met, Digital Farming will certainly contribute to achieve a higher yield of crop on the same size of land. At the same time, it has the potential for less usage of chemicals. The combination of continued R&D for superior crop protection solutions and more resistant seeds, with digital solutions, should help to compensate the decreasing availability of arable land and adverse effects on climate changes. In that context, Digital is of significant importance to overcome the global food challenge.

Based on the example of Digital Farming, the characteristics of global brands and their digital implementation into local environments, and the four articles in this Section "Global Challenges", we can conclude that any of the major global challenges will require a variety of answers and solutions on a local level. Even with "Digital" and a borderless Internet, the way you approach local markets will remain a key success factor for any business.

Energy Is Essential, but Utilities? Digitalization: What Does It Mean for the Energy Sector?

73

Ines Varela

Abstract

Digitalization changes customer behavior, consumer needs, business models, competition, and markets or at least will have a very high impact on all sectors. But digitalization offers as well opportunities for optimized processes, new digital products and services, and new data-driven business models.

Considering the energy sector the existing business models are not sustainable any more. This industry stands at the tipping point of multiple disruptive changes. The increased ratio of renewable and decentral energy generation leads to an increased volatile, distributed (Distributed energy consists of a range of smaller-scale and modular devices in-cluding storage devices designed to provide energy in locations close to consumers [1].) energy production. The time of energy as a commodity is over. Customers want to be engaged and expect providers to care about their individual values and needs. New market players intrude the energy market, and the Information and Communication Technologies (ICT), the Internet of Things (IoT) and digital technologies create the basis for these new players to get into the energy market and/or to network together cross border. ICT/IoT will play a central role in the transition of the energy sector.

I. Varela (✉)
Stadtwerke Düsseldorf AG
Düsseldorf, Germany
e-mail: ivarela@swd-ag.de

© Springer-Verlag GmbH Germany 2018
C. Linnhoff-Popien et al. (eds.), *Digital Marketplaces Unleashed*,
https://doi.org/10.1007/978-3-662-49275-8_73

829

73.1 Energy Sector in Transition

The traditional utility companies face dramatic economically losses. The liberalization of the energy market, changed regulatory frameworks, the increase of renewable and decentral energy generation disrupted the energy branch already. Now, with the liberalization of the metering point operations the utility industry transformation is in full swing. New and more advanced technological opportunities affect not only the generation, transmission, distribution, storage and trading, but as well the consumption of energy. Consumer needs and behavior change. Costumers consume less, save more and produce more energy themselves. Additionally, the increase of digitalization and new market participants further unleash the energy market.

73.2 Digitalization as a Game Changer

Due to *Huawei* digital economy is growing at 10% a year – more than triple the rate of overall worldwide economic growth, and *Huawei* estimates, that by 2025 the number of connected devices will reach 100 billion [2]. The industrial Internet of Things is supposed to reach US$150 billion by 2020 [3].

Digitalization has made its way into nearly all industries, creating new products and services, new production processes, and new ways of collaborating with customers and other market participants. Digitalization can change every sector more or less, and slower or faster. Digital disruption has a profound impact on the role that Information & Communication Technology (ICT) plays in almost every enterprise. And, ICT and the Internet of Things (IoT) play a central role in the energy sector transition. But considering the energy branch *Deloitte* expect the sector to be on a long fuse but the impact will be a big bang [4].

73.3 Technology Disrupting Branches

New or improved technologies like sensor based M2M[1] Communication, mobile devices and IoT offer better connectivity and data transmission. Big data analytics, In Memory Technologies, hadoop, or new databank technologies like SAP HANA (High Performance Analytic Appliance) and Cloud Services offer the possibility to manage and to analyze huge quantities of data on the fly. Distributed ledger technologies like Blockchain tech-

---

[1] Machine-to-machine (M2M) communications is used for automated data transmission and measurement between mechanical or electronic devices. The key components of an M2M system are: Field-deployed wireless devices with embedded sensors or RFID-Wireless communication networks with complementary wireline access includes, but is not limited to cellular communication, Wi-Fi, ZigBee, WiMAX, wireless LAN (WLAN), generic DSL (xDSL) and fiber to the x (FTTx) [5]. A smart meter is such a M2M device.

nologies, cognitive technologies/artificial intelligence or augmented reality help to bridge the digital world and the physical world to create new systems. Just to name some.

So, ICT is no longer just a supporting service but shaping strategies and business models. ICT creates value by increasing productivity and delivering a better customer experience. And, ICT and IoT will play a key role in developing a future energy system and help to realize the Internet of Energy in which all components are intelligent, electronical interconnected. Complicated, complex networks of interlinked applications, interfaces and databases communicating with internal and external systems will increase. In a smart energy world all components are connected to match dynamically supply and demand, providing volatile energy integration, real-time grid planning and operations, incl. predictive maintenance and real-time distributed energy management. Smart meter and smart grids will play a key role in this smart energy system.

73.3.1 Smart Meter

The "Energy Act" (EnWG) passed in 2011 created the framework for the implementation of intelligent metering systems[2]. And recently the German "Act of the digitization of the energy transition" ("Gesetz zur Digitalisierung der Energiewende")[3] just came into force. Starting in 2017, large-scale consumers and generators of electricity will be equipped with intelligent metering systems. As of 2020, these systems will be rolled out to private households using more than 6000 kWh of electricity per year.

The introduction of intelligent metering systems involves detailed consumption of data. This data plays a central role in integrating renewable and decentral energy sources. Smart measurement systems will assist in the "smart grid" by measuring the electricity fed and the power consumption. Furthermore, equipment whose power consumption can be controlled and timed, such as night storage systems and electric vehicles, can be charged at automatically optimized times. Meter can be read remotely. Also it will record voltage failures and provide information for the grid operations by automatically balancing grid loads and using grid capacity more efficiently [7]. And, it gives transparency in the energy consumption. Consumers will benefit from having their own power consumption visible and they can be offered flexible "customized" tariffs.

The massive growing number of sensors, embedded systems and connected devices as well as the increasing horizontal and vertical networking of the value chain results in

---

[2] Currently German household consumers mainly use electromechanical electricity meters (Ferraris meters). These traditional meters only provide very limited information and no electronic data transfer. In comparison intelligent measuring systems consist of a digital meter and a communication unit, the smart meter gateway, which allows the integration of the smart meter into a smart grid.

[3] The "Digitisation of the Energy Turnaround Act" ("Gesetz zur Digitalisierung der Energiewende") contains a framework for the electricity sector to become digital. The central part of the Act is the "Smart Meters Operation Act" ("Messstellenbetriebsgesetz"), that deals mainly with the installation and operation of intelligent metering systems [6].

a massive continuous data flow. With the implementation of intelligent metering systems, the data volume and data processing will increase tremendous. In 2011 the Federal Network Agency (Bundesnetzagentur or BNetzA)[4] already mentioned in their frameworks "smart grid" and "smart markets", that they suppose, that data management will become essential due to the fact that nearly all business models will be based on metered data [9]. And, according to *IBM* smart meters are expected to produce more than 150 quadrillion bytes of data per year worldwide by 2020 [10][5].

Smart meters used with the right analytic systems are the enablers of an interconnected energy system – where demand and supply can be balanced in much more intelligent ways. The data from meters is useful not just for the energy consumer, but especially for the suppliers and the National grid operator.

73.3.2 Smart Grids

Nowadays the electricity system is characterized by an increase in renewable and decentralized generation that leads to an increased volatile energy production. But volatile generation needs flexibility in generation, transmission & distribution, storage and consumption. The question is how to integrate renewable energy, and how to manage the increase of decentralized energy supply? To ensure system reliability and resiliency electricity generation and consumption need to be kept in balance. Generation and consumption have to be connected efficiently and intelligently. Therefore, grids have to become smart to be able to manage an increased number of distributed and variable sources of power generation. They need to balance the fluctuating power generated with renewable energy and the actual consumption. They will become open, flexible, interconnected and interactive with integrated grid controls and new distribution grid management. Smart Grids are becoming an essential component of the energy system [11].

The digitalization of the energy grid will play a key role in the transition of the energy system. Electronical networks and energy grids will be created with complete new structures and functionalities. They will be connected, integrated and partially sharing same infrastructure. Previously standalone operational production systems/distributed control systems will be connected with the commercial IT systems and will be integrated into the corporate infrastructure of a utility company, and with the internet. ICT based smart grids will be mandatory for the realization of the Internet of Energy.

With so much digitalization going on in the sector, cybersecurity becomes more and more important. Therefore, a key requirement for the recently issued German "Metering

---

[4] The Federal Network Agency is the German regulatory office for electricity, gas, telecommunications, mail and railway markets. It is a federal government agency of the German Federal Ministry of Economics and Technology [8].

[5] The information is based on an internal presentation on Opus, screened for utilities during a recent event. With Opus IBM wants to build a system that optimally plan and orchestrate energy systems of the future by using its expertise in analytics, big data and the Internet of Things.

Point Operating Act" ("Messstellenbetriebsgesetz") is to ensure a very high level of data protection and data security. Additionally, as operator of critical infrastructures German utilities are obliged to implement a special and very high level of IT Security and data protection due to the recently issued "Act of IT Security" ("IT-Sicherheitsgesetz"). The act contains principals for sector-specific data protection, and is to require the compulsory use of protection profiles and technical guidelines, and data access for the safe use of smart meters to ensure data protection, data security and interoperability [12].

73.3.3 IP Based Utility Networks

With the increased digitalization of the energy world, cybersecurity is becoming more and more important. Secure connectivity for smart meters and the smart grid is becoming essential. Therefore, it should be considered to build an own private communication infrastructure for the utility branch with a non-public, own radio frequency network. This will be a real game-changing for utilities. An own radio frequency networks allows utilities to ensure their critical data transfer and offer the utility the possibility to secure their critical grid applications, and to be prepared for the future development of the distribution grid. Smart meter and additionally other intelligent wireless devices could be migrated to support the smart grid management. Additional to the energy grid the utility would operate an IP based network, where all information and data would come together in a private network. In this case the boundary to other markets like the telecommunication market would be unleashed.

73.4 Digital Sales Business Models

Smart meters in connection with smart grids help to increase productivity and are the base for new customer centered business models. The customer could become the epicenter of a utility. This customer centered approach is new to utilities with their former centralized generation structure and their technical driven attitude.

73.4.1 Digital Living Solutions for B2C-Customers

In the past, utilities were monopolies that didn't interact closely with their end customer. But today it is not enough to provide people with reliable power anymore. Costumers demand tech-enabled products and services. The younger customers want more of their energy to come from renewable sources, and they want digital applications to have more information about their consumption. They conduct online research before buying, expect omnichannel communication, and they want to be social media connected to their utility [13].

And, people are interested in connected living solutions. The automated home solutions market, including assisted living components like health and security applications is expected to reach worldwide USD 121.73 billion by 2022 [14]. But currently it is still a problem of technical compatibility and inter-operability of the different digitally connected and controlled devices. And the question is, if smart home is a new, profitable business model for a utility. Non-utility players like *Miele, Bosch, Samsung, Apple* and *Google* already entered the connected home market, acting faster and more cost efficient. Probably it might be more successful for the utility in partnering with those industries.

On top, ICT/IoT offer the utility the possibility to analyze huge amount of real-time structured and unstructured data, and to use big data analytics to track the journey of the customers. By using data analytics of intelligent measuring systems to get more information about the consumer innovative, personalized pricing models can be offered. Additionally, behavior patterns can be analyzed in combination with socioeconomic data to get information about cross- and upselling sales potentials.

73.4.2   Digital Service Provider for B2B-Customers

Utilities are still large, centrally driven supply companies, but consumers prefer more and more to produce their own energy. A concept to fulfill customer wishes could be a digital based business model to take care of the complete energy management of decentral produced (preferable regenerative) energy of industrial companies or real estate management companies. The utility could become the digital service provider by offering remotely managed smart energy supply concepts, that includes smart energy storages and flexible demand side management by software-based steering the energy flows. Utilities might be shifted from huge, central driven production companies to distributed and bi-directional energy providers and managers.

The question here is as well, if the utility company is the first to be addressed for this digital-based service or if the company is more interested, if it is at least in cooperation with other technical supporting and building firms.

73.4.3   Digital Infrastructure Provider for the Public Sector

By 2050, 70% of the world's population will live in cities [15]. As such, finding new methods of supporting municipal authorities is becoming increasingly important. *Gartner* predicted, that in 2016 there will be 1.6 billion connected things used in smart cities, with 314 million connected things installed by utilities, and it will double in the next two years [16]. Smart cities have digital technologies embedded across all city functions providing an intelligent, energy- and traffic optimized infrastructure.

The utility could become the smart infrastructure provider for such a sustainable, energy-optimized, safe smart city/municipality providing via a smart, private and secure communication infrastructure smart lighting, sensor-based, intelligent Waste Management, smart intermodal transport solutions and ICT/IoT based intelligent energy and water systems. Just to name some options.

The technologies for energy intelligent and traffic optimized cities exist. Companies like *Cisco, IBM, Microsoft* or *Siemens* invest billions in smart city technologies. The challenge will be the cooperation and networking of the central utility company with the municipal authorities and global acting industrial technology firms.

73.4.4   Platform Provider for Energy Market Places

Imaging 2020 and the largest utility company in the world will not own any assets (no grid and no generation assets). This is the vision of *Zarko*, distinguished Analyst at Gartner [17]. And he is not alone. The economist *Jeremy Rifkin* believes that a decentralized network of alternative energy sources will replace the existing vertically integrated energy industry. It will be made up of "prosumers"[6] generating their own power and networking together through a smart grid that routes power to where it is needed. In the long run, energy will be available at zero marginal cost [18].

In *Harvard Business Review* you can read that the technology most likely to change the next decade of business is not the social web, big data, the cloud, robotics, or even artificial intelligence. It's the blockchain technology[7] [21]. The peer to peer architecture allows a distributed network of computers to reach consensus without the need for a central authority [22]. A blockchain enables anyone to directly and securely make a transaction between two people or companies, without having to go through any third parties. The blockchain technology might be the base for decentral transaction and energy supply systems, where "prosumers" act without a central utility company [21].

And this is already reality: In New York 10 households exchange between each other their self-produced solar energy. Blockchain-based microgrids[8] enable them to exchange and to sell and buy their self-produced energy between each other without any participation of the central utility company, regulator or any authority, that monitors or controls the transaction [24]. The digital distribution platform creates an open energy market which brings together those who generate energy with those who consume it. It requires a network operator who manages and ensures the reliability of the energy grid, and a sharing

---

[6] A "prosumer" produces and consumes energy.

[7] A blockchain is a type of distributed ledger, comprised of unchangeable, digitally recorded data in packages called blocks. These digitally recorded "blocks" of data is stored in a linear chain and each "block" contains data, a timestamp and a link to a previous block. The blocks of cryptographically hashed data drawn upon the previous-block in the chain, ensuring all data in the overall "blockchain" has not been tampered with and remains unchanged. It is a peer to peer platform using blockchain ledger to report transactions (e. g. bitcoin transaction) [19, 20].

[8] Microgrids are localized grids that can disconnect from the traditional grid to operate autonomously [23].

energy economy platform operator who brings the participants together and calculates the costs.

It might be still more a conceptual framework for the energy blockchain and there might be a lot of issues to clarify like regulatory and security aspects, the responsibility of a blackout and technical subjects like how to integrate the micro grid into the existing grid and how to coordinate the micro grids with the rest of the system. But technical there are no barriers and this new concept of energy market fulfills the consumer wishes of independency, autonomy and supports the sharing economy and might lead in the long run to a zero margin economy.

73.5   Outlook

Digitalization is opening the door to new market players to intrude the energy sector. Competition is becoming tougher and new players are entering the market. But digitalization also offers the energy branch the option to improve processes, new ways to reach and to interact with the customers, to change how they partner and who they partner, and it offers the possibility in generating new business opportunities by creating new products and services as well as new business models. And, digitalization unleashes the boundaries to other sectors. New marketplaces and market forms as well as new platform based business models in cooperation with different other market players will emerge everywhere.

ICT and IoT will play a significant key role in an unleashed energy world and will be a central success factor for an efficient new energy supply system. With the further digitalization, cybersecurity will become more and more important. So, an own, private communication network for utilities should seriously be taken into consideration. The technical challenge is to bring the different requirements of the electric and electronic world together but it also needs a culture change and digital capabilities of human being. Utilities have to re-invent themselves using the opportunities digitalization offer, if they want to continue to play a central role in the market.

References

1. energy.gov, 2016. [Online]. Available: http://energy.gov/oe/technology-development/smart-grid/distributed-energy. [Accessed 1 August 2016].
2. Huawei Technologies Co., Ltd., "Global Connectivity Index 2016 Whitepaper," 2016. [Online]. Available: http://www.huawei.com/minisite/gci/en/. [Accessed 12 August 2016].
3. marketsandmarkets, "MarketsandMarkets," January 2016. [Online]. Available: http://www.marketsandmarkets.com/Market-Reports/industrial-internet-of-things-market-129733727.html. [Accessed 30 August 2016].
4. Deloitte GmbH and Heads!Executive Consultancy, "Deloitte," April 2015. [Online]. Available: https://www2.deloitte.com/content/dam/Deloitte/at/Documents/strategy/ueberlebensstrategie-digital-leadership_final.pdf. [Accessed 02 August 2016].

5. Gartner, 2016. [Online]. Available: http://www.gartner.com/it-glossary/machine-to-machine-m2m-communications. [Accessed 22 07 2016].
6. "Germanenergyblog," 19 April 2016. [Online]. Available: http://www.germanenergyblog.de/?p=19634. [Accessed 31 August 30].
7. BMWI, "BMWI-Eneriegwende," July 2016. [Online]. Available: http://www.bmwi-energiewende.de/EWD/Redaktion/EN/Newsletter/2016/13/Meldung/topthema.html; jsessionid=59EABE1F5599AEDB66C1D3A1CF4B7224. [Accessed 12 August 2016].
8. Wikipedia, "Wikipedia," [Online]. Available: https://en.wikipedia.org/wiki/Federal_Network_Agency. [Accessed 8 August 2016].
9. Bundesnetzagentur, "'Smart Grid' und 'Smart Market'. Eckpunktepapier der Bundesnetzagentur zu den Aspekten des sich verändernden Energieversorgungssystems," Bundesnetzagentur, Bonn, 2011.
10. IBM, 2016. [Online]. Available: http://www.research.ibm.com/client-programs/seri/. [Accessed 21 July 2016].
11. Federal Ministry for Economic Affairs and Energy www.bmwi.de , 2016. [Online]. Available: http://bmwi.de/EN/Topics/Energy/Grids-and-grid-expansion/smart-grids.html. [Accessed 12 August 2016].
12. Federal Ministry for Economic Affairs and Energy www.BMWI.de, 2016. [Online]. Available: http://www.bmwi.de/EN/Topics/Energy/Grids-and-grid-expansion/digitisation-energy-transition.html. [Accessed 29 August 2016].
13. Accenture, 13 July 2016. [Online]. Available: https://newsroom.accenture.com/news/millennials-strong-interest-in-new-products-and-services-will-drive-the-most-future-value-for-energy-utilities-but-they-are-much-more-demanding-consumers-finds-research-from-accenture.htm. [Accessed 10 August 2016].
14. marketsandmarkets.com, "MarketsandMarkets," May 2016. [Online]. Available: http://www.marketsandmarkets.com. [Accessed 29 July 2016].
15. Population Reference Bureau, "Population Reference Bureau," 2016. [Online]. Available: http://www.prb.org/Publications/Lesson-Plans/HumanPopulation/Urbanization.aspx. [Accessed 01 August 2016].
16. Gartner, "Gartner Newsroom," 7 December 2015. [Online]. Available: http://www.gartner.com/newsroom/id/3175418. [Accessed 27 July 2016].
17. G. Zeiss, "geospatial.blogs," 11 February 2016. [Online]. Available: http://geospatial.blogs.com/geospatial/2016/02/distributech2016-by-2020-largest-power-utility-will-not-own-generation-or-network-assets.html. [Accessed 27 July 2016].
18. J. Rifkin, "The Zero Marginal Cost Society," Talks at Google, 15 April 2014. [Online]. Available: https://www.youtube.com/watch?v=5-iDUcETjvo. [Accessed 8 August 2016].
19. Blockchaintechnologies, "Blockchaintechnologies," 2016. [Online]. Available: http://www.blockchaintechnologies.com/blockchain-definition#sthash.l6iOrK1p.dpuf. [Accessed 02 August 2016].
20. Techopedia, "techopedia," 2016. [Online]. Available: https://www.techopedia.com/definition/30246/blockchain. [Accessed 2016 August 02].
21. D. Tapscott and T. Alex, "Harvard Business Review," 2016. [Online]. Available: https://hbr.org/2016/05/the-impact-of-the-blockchain-goes-beyond-financial-services. [Accessed 02 August 2016].
22. ValueWalk, "ValueWalk," 31 July 2016. [Online]. Available: http://www.valuewalk.com/2016/07/blockchain-ethereum-vs-bitcoin/. [Accessed 02 August 2016].
23. energy.gov, "energy.gov," [Online]. Available: http://energy.gov/oe/services/technology-development/smart-grid/role-microgrids-helping-advance-nation-s-energy-system. [Accessed 01 August 2016].

24. A. Rutkin, "New Scientist," 2016. [Online]. Available: https://www.newscientist.com/article/2079334-blockchain-based-microgrid-gives-power-to-consumers-in-new-york/. [Accessed 14 July 2016].

Harnessing the Digital Marketplace in India: Revolutionary Growth, Challenges and Opportunities

74

L. L. Ramachandran, M. P. Sebastian, and R. Radhakrishna Pillai

Abstract

Digital marketplaces are disrupting the established traditional marketplace models and transforming the economy and societies in India, by providing a platform for innovations. This disruption impacts drastically the way Indians' shop, bank, work, book their holidays, and even hailing a cab. India's unique demographic dividend with 50% of the 1.2 billion population less than 25 years, rising middle class income, and the mobile and internet growth are fueling the highest e-commerce growth rate in the world. This paper analyses the revolutionary growth of digital marketplace in India based on the four key pillars of digital marketplace, namely payment landscape, logistics, mobile/internet infrastructure and business and revenue model, and illustrates how these pillars are undergoing innovations and transformations. The paper also analyzes the key challenges to digital marketplace growth and illustrates how various organizations have made use of the unique opportunities provided by India, with appropriate examples. Entry of major players such as Alibaba and Rakuten are expected to make the online marketplace more competitive and propel India to enter into the third wave of *Digital Marketplace 3.0* – the golden era of Digital Marketplace in India. The inno-

L. L. Ramachandran (✉)
BPCL
Kochi, India
e-mail: ramachandranll@bharatpetroleum.in

M. P. Sebastian · R. R. Pillai
IIM Kozhikode
Kerala, India
e-mail: sebasmp@iimk.ac.in

R. R. Pillai
e-mail: krishna@iimk.ac.in

© Springer-Verlag GmbH Germany 2018
C. Linnhoff-Popien et al. (eds.), *Digital Marketplaces Unleashed*,
https://doi.org/10.1007/978-3-662-49275-8_74

vative practices, processes and models adopted by the various firms analyzed in this paper could serve as a template for digital marketplace evolution in emerging markets.

74.1 Digital Marketplaces in India: An Overview

74.1.1 Introduction

India is at a tipping point on the digital market place growth. There is a lot of interest and positive forecast about the digital marketplace growth in India. All the stakeholders like online retail companies, financial institutions, public, government, logistics companies, banks, payment companies, mobile and internet service providers have a positive outlook on the rapid growth of this sector. India's unique demographic dividend with 50% of the 1.3 billion population less than 25 years, rising middle class income, the mobile and internet growth are fueling the highest e-commerce growth rate in the world.

As given in Table 74.1, India has become the highest in digital online retailing growth worldwide and is predicted to retain the leadership position in the coming years [1].

Morgan Stanley predicts that India's online retail market will reach USD 102 billion by 2020 and will have a CAGR growth of 66% from 2013 to 2020 [2]. In spite of having the highest growth rate in the world, the ratio of percent of online retail sales to total retail sales in India, as given in Table 74.2, is very less compared to other countries in the world [1]. The online retail in China was only 1% of the total retail market in 2008, but it rose to 8.4 in 2013 [1]. One of the reasons for this was doubling of internet penetration during this period. The inflection point in China was in the year 2010–11 when Smartphone overtook Personal Computers. During that 2–3 year period Chinese online market grew from USD 70 billion to USD 300 billion [2]. In India the Smartphone is overtaking personal computers and the Indian internet users are leapfrogging to mobiles. With high internet penetration, especially mobile internet and Smartphone penetration, we see a tipping point of digital marketplace in India from 2014.

India has online demographic advantage for the growth of digital economy. As of May 2016, 50% of India's 1.3 billion populations are below the age of 25 years, median age

Table 74.1 Online retailing growth in India (in percentage). (Source: eMarketer [1])

Country	2014	2015	2016	2017	2018	2019
India	133.8	129.5	75.8	60.3	40.1	23.9
China	48.6	42.1	35.6	32.6	29.8	25.8
USA	14.4	14.2	13	12.2	11.6	11
Russia	23.5	22.7	19.3	17.4	15	14.7
Germany	15	12	11.5	10.9	8	6
Worldwide	26.3	25.1	22.7	21.9	20.7	18.7

Table 74.2 Retail e-commerce sale as a percentage of total retail sales. (Source: eMarketer [1])

Country	2014	2015	2016	2017	2018	2019
India	0.8	1.7	2.6	3.6	4.4	4.8
China	12.4	15.9	19.6	23.8	28.6	33.6
USA	6.4	7.1	7.8	8.4	9.1	9.8
Worldwide	6.3	7.4	8.6	9.9	11.4	12.8

is 27 and 65% of population is below the age group of 35 years. The younger citizens are digital savvy, use mobile phones and internet, and hence are potential online shoppers who can drive the online retail growth.

74.1.2 The Key Market Players in India

The e-commerce eco system in India consists of online travel and ticketing, online retail, online marketplace, online deals and online portals. The top two segments are online travel and ticketing (about 70%) followed by online retail [3]. Some of the leading local players in India include Flipkart, Snapdeal, Paytm, Olacabs, Zomato and Bigbasket. International players like Amazon, eBay and Uber also have their presence. Even though Amazon wants to make India its second largest market after US, they have only 12% of the market share and lags behind Flipkart (45%) and Snapdeal (26%) [4]. These three companies are the top three players in the horizontal market in terms of sales in Gross Merchandise Value (GMV) and volume of social conversation [4]. The Chinese online marketplace behemoth Alibaba has plans to enter the Indian marketplace [5]. Rakuten, the Japan's largest marketplace operator, may also follow its Chinese peer [6]. In the Indian horizontal market, it is a high volume low margin game. All the above key players have reported only losses and are yet to make profit.

In the vertical space many specific niche vertical players like Jabong, Lenskart, Pepperfry, Urban ladder and Bigbasket are also growing [7, 8]. The vertical marketplace companies are focusing on products in specific areas. Fashion segment is one of the fastest growing verticals. Jabong and Myntra are the two leading players in the fashion segment and they together cater to three fourth of the fashion market. The next leading verticals are furniture and grocery. In the furniture marketplace, Urban ladder and Pepperfry are the leaders while in grocery, Bigbasket and Aaram shop are the leaders. With many vertical players, the India's online marketplace is growing more as a democratic market like Europe, unlike China where the market is dominated by a few big players.

Many innovative methods are being adopted by the digital marketplace players to drive their growth in India. These include convenient payment models like cash on delivery, customer friendly policies like easy returns, which drive the sales growth. With the growth of smart phone users, *app* only sales models are gaining edge over web models. As the customers in India are highly price conscious, new concepts such as invite-only discounts, loyalty programs and special discounts, and cash back offers are also popular. Similarly, people celebrate many festivals across India and used to shop during these seasons [9, 10]. The special online discount sales during these periods, also drives the growth. As the market is crowded and the competition is intense, multiple models are adopted by these companies [11]. All the players adopt many innovative business models and processes to sustain the hyper competition in the digital marketplace in India.

74.2 Challenges and Opportunities

Even though India is predicted to have the largest growth rate in the coming years companies are faced with many challenges. Some of the key challenges faced by these companies in future growth include internet and technology infrastructure, business models, hyper competition, customer retention, logistics, electronic payment system, legislation, taxation structure and valuation.

74.2.1 Internet and Technology Infrastructure

India has 462 million internet users as of July 2016, which is the second largest internet user base in the world [12]. But as shown in Table 74.3, the percentage of population using the internet is less compared to the other BRIC countries and developed nations.

As per the United Nations UNCTAD Report, the online buyers' share in India as a percentage of internet users is only 27% compared to 55.7% in China [13]. The reasons include limited broad band and mobile bandwidth availability and also the quality of service. As per Akmai 2016 Q1 report shown in Table 74.4, the average broadband connection speed in India is less compared to many other nations [14].

India has one of the highest mobile internet users. More than 50% of the internet users are mobile users. As per Akamai Q1 2016 shown in Table 74.5, the average mobile internet bandwidth is also low compared to other developed countries and China [14]. In addition of low average speed, there are congestion and connectivity issues. High speed internet

Table 74.3 Worldwide Internet user base. (Source: Interstat [43])

Country	Users million	% of population
India	462	34.8
China	721	52.2
USA	286	88.5
UK	60	92.6
Japan	115	91.1
Russia	102	71.3
Brazil	139	66.4

Table 74.4 Average Broadband connection speed. (Source: Akamai [14])

Country	Avg. MBPS	Peak MBPS	% Above 4 MBPS	% Above 10 MBPS
India	3.5	25.5	23	4.8
China	4.3	31.0	44	2.1
South Korea	29	103.6	97	84
USA	15.3	67.8	86	57

in mobile and broadband has become the need of the hour for providing good customer experience and growth of digital market place ecosystem in India.

With 462 million internet users as of July 2016, the Indian government and telecommunication companies are setting up robust digital infrastructure to promote adoption of mobile internet. Many telecom operators are investing in 3G, 4G and 5G networks. Mobile internet user base is expected to grow to 314 million with a CAGR of 28% from 2013 to 2018 [15]. India has also become the third largest smart phone market in the world. The number of Smartphone users is projected to reach 369 million by 2017 [15]. The price of smart phones is also coming down and the 3G handsets are available for prices as low as USD 40.

The key technologies that build and drive the e-commerce platforms are mobile technologies and applications (Apps), internet infrastructure, cloud computing, search engine optimization and analytics. The market place companies are offering their interface through mobile and website. As more users are accessing internet through mobile app interface is more popular. Hence most of the companies are getting leveraged in app economy and hence have given focus to app mode, rather than website model. Many experiments and innovations are being tried out by the companies in identifying the best interface model. Myntra, India's largest fashion portal found that 90% of the traffic and 70% of company's business was through app [16]. And they shut down their website/portal and went to app only mode. They became app only market place and started driving app only strategy. They were the first not only in India but also globally to adopt app only mode. But they had to roll back and re-launch their desktop version later [17]. Myntra claims that rationale behind the roll back was from women consumers who have a preference for browsing and shopping in multiple platforms. Cloud computing, Analytics and

Table 74.5 Average mobile internet connection speed. (Source: Akamai [14])

Country	Avg. MBPS	Peak MBPS
India	3.2	20.9
China	6.5	29.3
USA	5.1	19.8
South Korea	13.0	73.8

Search engine optimization are also equally important areas which are of great significance for the growth of digital marketplace companies.

74.2.2 Business Models

The e-commerce in India operates with the established models like B2B, B2C, C2C, aggregator and hybrid. The B2C segments include online travel, online retail, online classified, online health, online entertainment, online education, financial services and digital download. In the B2C marketplace there are horizontal and vertical players. The horizontal players sell many vertical products and dominate the market. The vertical players in India operate in specific vertical such as grocery, fashion, furniture and many other specific products. Flipkart, Amazon and Snapdeal dominate the market and they adopt a managed market place model.

As the market is crowded and the competition is intense, multiple models are adopted by these companies. The business models adopted by the global leaders include inventory, pure marketplace, managed marketplace, hybrid plus and hybrid. The advantage of a managed market place model is that they are less capital intensive, do not hold any inventory, and just provide the platform. In India, due to regulatory restrictions, Amazon operates a managed market place model though Amazon in the US operates a hybrid plus model [11]. Alibaba, the world's largest e-commerce company and dubbed by Economist magazine as the world's biggest bazaar, adopts a different strategy in China. They operate two market places Tmall and Taobao. Tmall is a B2C managed market place and is an open platform for merchants to run their own stores. Taobao is a C2C pure market place. They are also planning to enter in Indian online market place with managed market place model. In India Flipkart started with an inventory model moved to hybrid and today they are operating a managed market place model. Myntra, the fashion retailer, was following a hybrid model till 2014. They were selling premium brands through inventory and local brands through marketplace model. After their acquisition by Flipkart they also follow managed marketplace model. To survive in the market, all Indian companies also take advantage of revenue models like transaction fee model and advertising revenue models.

74.2.3 Hyper Competition and Customer Retention

In India the customers are highly price conscious and hence discounts, price war and promotional sales are rampant. This makes online market place a hyper competitive market place [9, 18]. Even though the customer base is increasing, retaining customers in a real challenge as customers switch platforms based on discounts or negative experiences. As there are many players doing the same business, same way and same price, there is no switching cost. Hyper competition and mega discounts results in customer acquisition and retention costly for these companies. With heavy price discounts, aggressive pricing strategy and free home delivery, the hyper competition impacts the profitability and sustainability of the companies. In developed countries customers switch between brands and in India customer switching happens based on price and discounts. This makes customer retention challenging in a hypercompetitive Indian market place.

74.2.4 Logistics

Logistics is a key enabler for the growth of digital market place. It is also emerging as a key differentiator in terms of customer delivery, customer experience and differentiation. Today most of the e-commerce companies operate mostly in metros and Tier I cities (population 0.1 million and above). Some key challenges in logistics include shortening of delivery time, ensuring consistency and improving the predictability. Here 90% of goods ordered move through air which increases the delivery cost. The cities are traffic logged and streets are not numbered sequentially.

The marketplace companies are spreading their reach from metros to Tier 2 (population between 50,000 and 99,999) and Tier 3 (population between 20,000 and 49,999) cities and rural areas due to emergence of low cost smart phone and internet penetration. But the poor last mile connectivity is a key bottleneck for a time bound delivery. In small towns and villages there is lack of organized physical addresses. The other major challenges specific to India are Cash-on-Delivery as a preferred option and consumer expects returns of goods as a seamless and convenient process. This calls for a good reverse logistics. The fragmented logistics and poor physical infrastructure causes delivery delays and errors. The above logistics factors make logistics cost in India expensive as 10 per cent of the GMV of the product against 3–10% for most companies in China. In many BRIC countries, consumers have cited free delivery as one of the factors influencing digital market place.

As per KPMG the logistics sector pertaining to e-commerce companies in India is valued in 2014 at USD 0.2 billion with a potential growth of CAGR 48% growth and expected to reach USD 2.2 billion by 2020 [19]. The leading logistic providers in India like Blue Dart, Fedex and DTDC have specifically added e-commerce solutions to their offering. The Flipkart's logistic company EKart handles about 85% of Flipkart's logistics. Flipkart is in the process to monetize the logistics investments and build data for e-commerce which can bring additional revenues and reduce the cash burn [20]. Flipkart's logistics arm Ekart is starting a customer facing courier service which will be competing with traditional logistics companies like such as Gati and Blue Dart. Ekart thus wants to be most transformative supply chain provider in India. For this Flipkart has also acquired a major stake in mapping company called MapMyIndia. The company has a mapping platform called Flip which will enable customers to mark the pickup point using pins.

India Post which is the postal department of India is also playing a leading role. India Posts have 460,000 employees across 155,000 post office and handling 6 billion mails annually to take care of goods to customers including rural areas [21]. In the past two years about 400 e-commerce companies, including Flip kart and Amazon, have tied up with India Post for delivery of goods. Due to the e-commerce growth, Indian Post hopes to slash its USD 800 million annual deficit and improve profitability at its rural post offices. India post, world's largest postal system is in a process to become world's leading e-commerce delivery platform [22].

74.2.5 Payment

Cash on Delivery (CoD) is the most preferred and popular option of payment for Indian digital marketplace transactions and 60% of sales happens through CoD. This is in contrast of 50% in China and 69% in Russia [2]. Manual cash collection and deposit is tedious, risky and expensive. They also elongate the working capital cycle and bring higher administration and handling costs. Many logistic companies charge 3% for the service and may also hold the money for few days. Forty one percent of India's population are unbanked and coverage is low compared to BRIC economy [2]. Due to lack of high bandwidth, poor connectivity and inefficiencies in payment gateways, high failures in online payment transactions are also common. Concerns around security of online transactions, low usage of debit and credit cards and payment gateway failures have limited the use of electronic payments which is a big challenge for digital marketplace growth.

Rising mobile and internet penetration, evolving payment technologies, entry of new players in the payment ecosystem and the initiatives of Government of India and the Central bank – Reserve Bank of India, the payment landscape is undergoing a big change in India. One of the payment modes which is getting wider acceptance is mobile wallets. These wallets are issued by mostly by leading banks in India or companies having a tie up with banks. Two such products issued by the top two banks are State Bank of India's SBI buddy and ICICI Banks' Pockets.

India is a cash dependent economy. The amount of cash in circulation is 12% of GDP [23]. India has the largest unbanked population of 41% compared to 36% in China and 12% in USA. Many schemes are initiated for electronic payments. One such scheme to bank the unbanked is Pradhan Mantri Jandhan Yogna (Prime Ministers people money scheme) which is India's national mission program for financial inclusion. The scheme is to provide bank account for the unbanked. Under the program, 220 million accounts are opened as of August 2016. The second initiative is Rupay card which is a domestic card facilitating electronic payments at all banks and financial system with low cost of transaction. This is targeted for consumers in rural India who do not have access to banking and financial services. Another major initiative is the Universal Payment Interface (UPI) by the National Payment Corporation of India NPCI [24]. The UPI makes transaction through various modes such as debit cards, credit cards, digital wallets, net banking and prepaid cards. UPI is also expected to propel instant payment via mobile, web and other applications. It supports economic growth and also meets the goal of financial inclusion.

74.2.6   Regulations – Taxations and Legislations

Taxation is an important aspect for the marketplace companies. The tax rate is different for the different states in India. With Goods and Service Tax (GST) implementation there will be uniformity in the taxation. Similarly there are some caps on the FDI in investments in this sector. FDI is allowed 100% for managed market place model and is not permitted for Inventory model. But many reforms are happening to support the companies in this space.

74.2.7   Financing and Valuations

The digital marketplace companies are not only disrupting the traditional marketplaces but also setting new benchmarks in valuations. In the year 2015, the poster boy of India's online retail, Flikart's valuation was USD 16 billion and this exceeded the individual market capitalization of over 99% of 5500 listed companies in India's Bombay Stock Exchange [25]. In the year 2015, six unicorns of India were valued more than USD 1 billion plus. But Flipkart continued to post losses, even after several years of continuous operation. Most of the capital was used to acquire customer through heavy discounting like cash back, discounts, bonus, rewards and free shipping. The capitals were also used for acquisitions/consolidations, improving logistics, scaling the business, technology infrastructure, advertising and recruiting talents.

Morgan Stanley has recently downgraded the valuations of the Flipkart. They have also downgraded the valuation price to USD 11 billion in February 2016 and to USD9.3 billion in May 2016 [26]. Morgan Stanley also wrote down the valuation of many unicorns of India. Investors who accepted cash burn during initial growth phase find it hard to justify now. This has made companies to focus from GMV to profitability. Making the economics right and evolving sustainable market place business model will be challenge for the future.

74.3   Key Emerging Trends

Many trends are evolving in the digital marketplace growth in India. Some of the key trends transforming the digital marketplace growth include traditional retailers going online, supplier development, online to offline model, customer loyalty programs and vernacular language implementations.

74.3.1 Traditional Retailers Going Online

As per KPMG, the retail industry in India is USD 534 billion in 2013–14 and is expected to reach USD948 billion in 2018–19 [27]. The top 5 leading retailers in the organized sector are owned by the leading business houses of India which include Future Group, Tata Group, Reliance, Godrej and ITC. Seeing the growth in the online retail in India, these traditional retailers are also venturing into the online space. There are four business models adopted by the retailers. In the first model, retailers are entering into online business through existing online players. Future group for their Shopper Stop retail has tied up with existing market place player Snapdeal for their online store. In the second model retailers are hosting an online platform themselves. Reliance Retail, one of the largest modern retailers, joined the fashion e-commerce race by launching an online store ajio.com. This is the second initiative after reliancefreshdirect.com, a grocery delivery platform. The third model is followed by some companies who enter into the online space by acquiring online marketplace startups. Titan industries, part of Tata group and a leading company in watches, optical and branded jewelry, had a tied-up initially with the traditional online market place companies. Recently they acquired an online market place start up Caratlane for its online jewelry business [28]. The fourth and the important trend is Omni channel model.

Retailers are adding click factor and turning their traditional stores brick and mortar into 'bricks and clicks' store and offering them 'click and collect' service [29]. The retail store becomes in store and pick up points. Reliance, one of the biggest business houses in India has launched a project called Reliance Jio which connects pan India with digital services [30]. Reliance Jio promises to usher a digital revolution in India by providing end to end digital solution including mobile, broadband for business, institution and household including rural India. Reliance also has the huge offline retail presence. They plan integration of advanced technology infrastructure built by Jio and physical retail to create a differentiated Omni channel and Omni commerce model to the retail business in India [31]. The Tata group with market cap of USD 134 billion and having 7.8% of market cap in India leading Bombay Stock Exchange also has a large retail presence. They have entered into e-commerce space through launch of their online market place CLiQ. This market place is first of its kind phygital (Physical + digital) an online marketplace that will blend online and in store shopping experience. Tata CliQ will follow a curated market place model. Unlike an online marketplace where sellers are free to sell any product, Tata CliQ will carefully choose the product making it exclusive [32]. They also plan to have an asset light marketplace model where a product brought through online are delivered from retail outlet which cuts down the overheads on warehousing and logistics.

Meanwhile the reverse trend is also happening. Some of the pure online market place players are also building physical stores. Myntra, one of the leading online fashion market place, is planning to open its first physical store. The leading vertical players in eye wear like Lenskart and furniture market place player Pepperfry have already opened physical stores and have started to see significant contributions to their revenue and profit from their physical stores [33]. All these trends are going to revolutionize the online retailing models in India.

74.3.2 Supplier Development

Snapdeal, one of the leading players in India says that they are a technology company connecting the dots between demand and supply in India [34]. In a managed market place model one of the biggest challenge is to bring more merchants/sellers in to the market place platform. None of the leading players formally disclose the number of suppliers. As per company's website information sources in August 2016, Flipkart has 85,000, Snapdeal has 0.3 million and Paytm has 0.11 million suppliers. All the companies are in the process of supplier development. Amazon ran a program called Amazon Chai Cart where Amazon deployed three wheeled mobile kart to various parts of India, served tea, water, lemon juice to small business owner and taught them how to sell online. In four months Amazon's team travelled 15,280 kilometers, 31 cities, served 37,200 cups of tea in journey to a large market and engaged 10,000 sellers [35]. Amazon also launched Amazon Tatkal which enables small business to get online in less than 60 min.

One of the major groups in the sellers segment in India is Micro, Small and Medium Enterprise (MSME) and Small and Medium Enterprise (SME). They are backbone of Indian economy and engine of growth, economic development and job creation. In the year 2014 SME sector contributed 45% of India's industrial output, 40% of total exports and 17% of GDP. SME in India add over 1.3 million jobs per year. Government of India initiatives like Make in India, Digital India, Skill India are programs for improving their growth. The vision is to boost SME contribution to India's GDP to 20–25% by 2025 [36] by facilitating growth of SME in country and to enable them to participate in the growth of digital marketplace. The digital marketplace will act as a catalyst to SME with increased revenues and margins, improved market reach, access to new markets, less marketing cost and customer acquisition. China which is the largest e-commerce market in the world has a great role played by SMEs. In china the SME's contribute 60% to GDP and 75% to urban employment [37]. China acts as a good lesson and example to India in this regard. India's largest bank, State Bank of India, has partnered with Snapdeal to offer loans to SME. The bank uses data analytics gathered by Snapdeal to assess sellers credit worthiness instead of standard documents like balance sheet and P&L [38]. SME's would be a major contributor for the growth of digital market place in India in the coming years.

74.3.3 Online to Offline

Another innovative model which is the next big thing in the online market place is online to offline (O2O) model, estimated to be one of the fastest growing models. Typically in this O2O model a consumer using a website or mostly apps will book a service online and make purchase offline at a restaurant, cab or a gas station. AirBnB and Uber operate on app based O2O model. There are three key aspects to this model [39]. One is that the deals here are hyper local, real-time and the prices can fluctuate really quickly. Secondly, it usually involves a 'perishable services' like restaurants, movie tickets or a similar product or services. Finally, the deals are offered online and the actual transaction takes place offline. Mobile payment will also get a boost with O2O model. According to HSBC Chinese O2O market is more than USD 150 billion with just 4% penetration. Alibaba sees this as a growing and attractive model in China [40]. In India, Paytm is trying to replicate the Chinese parent Alibaba's strategy. When other players like Flipkart and Amazon are building their warehouse capacities, Paytm has added none and adopting the O2O model and this strategy differentiates them. Another pioneer in this model in India is Little. The O2O model would be a key model in Indian online market place.

74.3.4 Price and Loyalty Programs

In the early stages of e-commerce in India, the major challenge of market place players like Flipkart was making customers switch to online. This was done by offering heavy discounts. With the growth of e-commerce the customer retention and loyalty has become a big challenge. In a recent survey by PWC reveals that along with good price, trust in the brand is also equally important aspect. Recently Amazon has launched its Prime service in India an offering that has helped it to build customer loyalty. The subscriber gets thirty minute early access to daily deals in app and website and faster delivery [41]. Flipkart is now set to replace its existing loyalty program namely Flipkart First with a new version called F-Assured to take Amazon's Prime [42]. The F-Assured comes with improved service and stricter quality checks a better return policy and next day free delivery service. These loyalty services could be big game changers for the Indian digital market place.

74.3.5 Vernacular Languages

India has 88% non English speaking population and Hindi is the largest conversed language. Officially there 22 languages in India. In rural area 64% of the users browse the content in their regional languages which will enhance the user experience of app and website. As of June 2015, the local language internet users are 127 million in the total users of 269 million growing by 47% year after year as per survey conducted by IAMAI. With increasing users, many online marketing places have started displaying the product information in local languages. Snapdeal was the first online market place to launch regional language versions. Vernacular language in website and apps will be the game changer for digital marketplace in the coming years.

74.4   The Outlook

The first wave of *Digital Marketplace 1.0* started in India with very limited companies, few travel aggregators and online classified websites. The market place players in India adopted the hybrid model (inventory + market place) or Inventory model, adopted by Amazon in the US. The challenge during this wave was to bring the users to the habit of online buying and building the ecosystem for an online market place, which was done by offering heavy discounts and promotional sales. In the second wave *Digital Market-place 2.0,* the leading players like Flipkart, Snapdeal and other companies migrated to a purely managed marketplace model. This was because of the success of marketplace model in China and the customer, market, income level and the distribution in India were more similar to China. There were also regulatory restrictions in India.

Today India is at an inflexion point of online market place growth. With the Smartphone penetration, mobile internet and online demographic advantage, India has the highest on-line retailing growth rate in the world. Indian economy is also showing a good sign of GDP growth of 7.5% in the year 2015–16. The four key pillars of e-commerce, namely payment landscape, logistics, mobile/internet infrastructure and business and revenue model, are undergoing innovations and transformations. In addition to transform retailing, the digi-tal marketplace companies in India are also facilitating the MSME sector by financing, technology and training. The developments and transformations will also bring the next generation of internet users (rural based, mobile centric, local language focused) online. With this, the digital marketplace growth in India is also predicted to reach USD 100 billion by 2020. Entry of more multinational online retailers will make the online mar-ketplace more competitive. These factors will propel India to enter into the third wave of *Digital Marketplace 3.0* which will be the golden era of Digital Marketplace in India.

74.5   Conclusion

In this paper, we have analyzed the revolutionary growth of the digital marketplace in India. The key market players in India, their unique challenges and opportunities are also analyzed. The digital market place infrastructure in India is analyzed in comparison with other emerging and developed market places. The issues related to hyper competition and customer retention, logistics, payment, financing, valuation and regulations are also discussed. The key emerging trends such as retailers going online, supplier development, loyalty programs and support for vernacular language are also presented. The innovative practices, processes and models presented in this paper can serve as a template for digital marketplace evolution in the emerging markets.

References

1. eMarketer, "Worldwide Retail eCommerce sales : Emarketer's updated estimates and forecast," eMarketer Inc, New York , USA, 2014.
2. P. Gupta, A. Agrawal, C. Ahya, R. Desai, J. Garner, V. Hjort und M. Pradhan, "The Next India Internet – Opening New oppurtunities," Morgan Stanley Research, 2015.
3. Price water House Coopers (PwC), "e Commerce In India accelerating growth, page 5," Price water House Coopers (PwC), India, 2015.
4. R. Maheshwari, "'Etail gaints like Snapdeal, Amazon lose market share in 2015; small etailers emerge as real winners'," *The Economic Times* , 26 February 2016.
5. D. Marshal, "Alibaba Starts building team for India foray," *The Times of India-Tech,* 7 June 2016.
6. S. A. Rasul Bailay, "Japan's Rakuten opens office in Bangalore; poaches mid-level managers from Flipkart, Amazon," *The Economic Times,* 11 April 2016.
7. Deloitte Assocham, "Future of e Commerce : Uncovering Innovation," Deloitte Assocham, India, 2016.
8. Deloitte and Confederation of Indian Industry , "e-Commerce in India: A Game changer for the economy," Deloitte and CII, India, 2016.
9. S. V. Mihir Dalal, "Flipkart, Snapdeal, Amazon start discount war," *Live mint,* 13 October 2015.
10. S. Alagh, "How Amazon, Snapdeal, Flipkart performed during festive season," *The Financial Times,* 10 November 2015.
11. S. Varadan, "Deciphering the right ecommerce model for India – Blog," INFOSYS Technologies, 2015 January 2015. [Online]. Available: http://www.infosysblogs.com/retail-cpg/2015/01/Deciphering%20the%20right%20ecommerce%20model%20for%20India.html.   [Accessed 21 November 2016].
12. "Internet Live Stats," 2016. [Online]. Available: http://www.internetlivestats.com/internet-users/india/. [Accessed 31 08 2016].
13. "UNCTD B2C e-Commerce Index 2016," United Nations Conference on Trade and development, 2016.
14. Akamai, "Akamai's [State of internet] Q1 2016 report," 2016. [Online]. Available: https://www.akamai.com/uk/en/multimedia/documents/state-of-the-internet/akamai-state-of-the-internet-report-q1-2016.pdf. [Accessed 30 08 2016].
15. KPMG, "India on the Go: Mobile Internet Vision 2017," 2015.
16. R. Basuah, "Ranaditya Basuah, 2016, Why India's leading Fashion e-tailor abandoned its app-only strategy," *Knowledge@Wharton.,* 24 /july 2016.
17. A. Peermohamed, "Myntra's app-only dream is dead; to relaunch desktop website on June 1," *Business Standard,* 04 May 2016.
18. R. Saighal, "India's e-Commerce wars: a consumer perspective," *Livemint,* 15 April 2016.
19. "Fulfilled! India's ecommerce retail logistics growth story," KPMG-CII, 2015.
20. A. Peermohamed, "Flipkart's Courier seeks to monetize logistics investments build data for e-Commerce," *Business Standard,* 20 May 2016.
21. Alwar, "India Post rides e-Commerce wave as villagers turn online shoppers," *The Hindu Business Line,* 21 February 2016.
22. S. Rai, "e-Commerce Resuscitates Moribund India Post, World's Largest Postal System," *Forbes India,* 3 November 2015.
23. M. Shetty, "India's love for cash costs – $3.5 bn a year," *The Times of India,* 14 January 2015.
24. S. Asthana, "All you need to know about UPI, the Unified Payment Interface," *Business Standard,* 12 April 2016.

25. P. S. Reeba Zachariah, "Startup challenges lists cos valuation; At $16 bn Flipkart beat IOC, Tata Motors," *The Economic Times,* 8 September 2015.

26. FE Bureau, "Morgan Stanley pegs Flipkart below $10 bn," *The Financial Express,* 28 May 2016.

27. KPMG, "Indian retail: The next growth story," 2015.

28. Press Trust of India, "Titan to acquire 62 percent stake in Carat Lane for Rs.357.24 crore," *The Economic Times,* 14 July 2016.

29. ET Bureau, "Retailers add click factor to make bricks-and-mortar tick," *The Economic Times,* 3 August 2016.

30. Reliance Industries Ltd, "Annual Report," 2015.

31. V. Jain, "Reliance Retail bets big on multichannel initiatives," *ETRetail,* 5 August 2016.

32. Tata group, "E-Commerce to get #Phygital with TataCLIQ.com," 27 May 2016. [Online]. Available: www.tata.com/media/releasesinside/tatacliq-phygital-certified-authentic-merchandise-everybody-loves. [Accessed 16 August 2016].

33. M. Chanchani, "Etailer like LensKart, Pepperfry scaling up physical presence to close in on brick and mortar stores," *The Economic Times,* 28 June 2016.

34. "Snapdeal: Connecting the Dots between Demand and Supply in India," 2014.

35. Amazon, "Annual report," 2015.

36. V. Chadha, "The journey to a large market," *The Hindu Business Line,* 7 April 2016.

37. KPMG-Snapdeal, "Impact of e-Commerce on SMEs in India," 2015.

38. Press Trust of India, "SBI partners Snapdeal to offer loans to e-Commerce sellers," *The Hindu Business Line,* 15 January 2016.

39. V. Babu, "Online to Offline: Rise of O2O Commerce," *Business Today Magazine,* 24 April 2016.

40. Trefis Team, "Why is Alibaba strengthening its O2O (online to offline) presence," *Forbes,* 31 December 2015.

41. A. Peermohamed, "Amazon starts faster delivery via Prime," *Business Standard,* 27 July 2016.

42. M. C. Aditi Shrivastava, "Flipkart to launch F-Assured; promises improved delivery service," *The Economic Times,* 19 July 2016.

43. Interstat, "Internet Users by Country (2016)," 2016. [Online]. Available: http://www.internetlivestats.com/internet-users-by-country/. [Zugriff am 30 08 2016].

Further Reading

44. R. Z. &. P. Sinha, "Startup Challenges lists cos valuation; at $16 bn Flipkart beat IOC, Tata Motors," *Economic Times,* 8 September 2015.

45. G. Sachs, "India Internet: Unlocking the potential of a billion digital users," 4 May 2015. [Online].

46. D.-C. o. I. Industry(CII), "e-Commerce in India: A Game changer for the economy," Deloitte, India, 2016.

47. D. A. India, "Future of e Commerce : Uncovering Innovation," 2016.

48. P. Gupta, A. agrawal, C. aya, r. Desai, J. Garner, V. Hjort und M. Pradhan, "The Next India Internet – Opening New oppurtunities," Morgan Stanley Research, 2015.

49. 2. Digbijay Marshal, "Alibaba Starts building team for India foray," *The Times of India Tech,* 7 June 2016.

50. G. Coulouris, J. Dollimore and T. Kindberg, Distributed Systems – Concepts and Design, Amsterdam: Addison-Wesley Longman, 2005.

51. M. Ahmed, "Is Omni-channel Strategy the way forward for Retailers?," *BW CIO world,* 5 October 2015.

52. Wikipedia, [Online]. Available: http://de.wikipedia.org/wiki/Remote_Method_Invocation. [Accessed 26 05 2011].

53. " Worldwide retail e-Commerce Sales: eMarketer's updated estimated and forecast through 2019," eMarketer, 2014.

Digital Revolution, High-Speed Democracy and the Brave New Working World: Learnings from an Austrian Public Online Consultation Process

Peter Reichl and Andreas Kovar

Abstract

In the summer of 2015, the president of the Austrian Federal Council has initiated a parliamentary initiative on "Digital Change and Politics", in order to systematically investigate the political and legislative changes considered to be necessary for an optimal use of the Digital Revolution. Based on a comprehensive public online consultation process, the resulting Green Book discusses the impact of digitization to the working world, quality of life, society, politics and especially the future form of democracy. In this chapter, we reflect outcomes from and experiences with this deliberative process, focusing on economic policy, labour law and the development of future digital marketplaces. While our original material mainly reflects an Austrian point of view, the resulting conclusions are valid on a rather general level, and allow interesting insight into the fundamental challenges of digitization from the perspectives of a huge variety of related stakeholders. At the same time, we discuss opportunities and limitations of the process itself, and thus deliver an authentic description of first steps towards an Internet-based future high-speed democracy which may lead to rather disruptive forms of political debates and decision-making processes.

P. Reichl (✉)
University of Vienna
Vienna, Austria
e-mail: peter.reichl@univie.ac.at

A. Kovar
Kovar & Partners GmbH
Vienna, Austria
e-mail: andreas.kovar@publicaffairs.cc

© Springer-Verlag GmbH Germany 2018
C. Linnhoff-Popien et al. (eds.), *Digital Marketplaces Unleashed*,
https://doi.org/10.1007/978-3-662-49275-8_75

75.1 Introduction

While the rise of the World Wide Web and the evolution of the Internet into a global information infrastructure have started merely two decades ago, already now the rapidly increasing level of digitization has led to a new economy of immaterial products and services. With the advent of the Internet of Things (IoT), an entirely new industry with novel value chains and networks as well as new forms of logistics is about to be created. There is a broad consensus that this digital revolution will have fundamental impact on the future society, especially with respect to the future working world [1], and therefore has to become a central topic in the political discussion, while, at the same time, it will provide also the new tools, mechanisms and platforms for leading the discussion itself.

Recognizing the urgency and complexity of the topic, in July 2015 the Austrian Federal Council has started a parliamentary initiative which has led to compiling a state of the art report exploring the consequences of digitization on tomorrow's working environments, quality of life, society, politics and democracy. This so-called "Green Book" [2] provides a comprehensive overview on potential legal and political changes which are required for Austria to be in a position which allows to make use of the presumed huge opportunities of the digital revolution, and has become subject of a parliamentary enquiry ("Enquete") held at the Federal Council in Vienna on Nov 18, 2015.

Of course, the idea of using Internet-based online tools and platforms for such a process is not really new, and in fact it has been realized already on many occasions, different levels and/or contexts. Nevertheless, this specific Austrian initiative is considered remarkable in terms of its political innovativeness: while the deliberative process has been performed bottom up as usual, in this case it has complemented with a (top down) parliamentary decision making process. Hence, eventually, the crowd-sourcing participation process has been tied directly to formal parliamentarian proceedings, which have been concluded by a binding legislative resolution. The Austrian government is now forced to consider and use the ideas collected, developed and discussed in the public participation process as a starting point for the upcoming Austrian digital agenda. Moreover, from a broader political perspective, the Federal Council, which – as second chamber of the parliament – often is considered acting in the shadow of the national council and the national government, with this initiative has managed to step forward towards an independently operating dialog-orientated parliamentarian platform, a development which is fully in line with the results of another parliamentary Enquete Commission held in spring 2015 which has been focusing on the question of how to further strengthen democracy in general.

Especially in times of decreasing voter participation and increasing disenchantment with politics, more and more people are interested to actively shape the political debate outside of elections and traditional parties. Many of today's citizens wish to contribute to political discussion and are interested in following transparently the process of decision-making. As a vivid democracy today includes the cooperation of elements of representation, direct democracy and public deliberation, the digital change may create new supra-regional models of participation and corresponding fora for citizens which lead to a participative and dialog-oriented form of democracy. This occasion, i. e. allowing for the first time larger parts of our society to directly take part in democratic deliberation and decision processes constitutes a huge and unique opportunity for democratic systems, and hence serves as a guiding motivation for the supporters of the initiative "Digital Change and Politics", first and foremost the president of the Federal Council.

Hence, based on the acting president's initiative, a public brainstorming has been started, with the primary question about which actions of legislation bodies were considered to be able to cope with and make optimal use of the ongoing digital transformation. Using an online participation platform [3], more than 200 statements, 100 comments and more than 1000 votes were posted within a period of eight weeks. In addition to this online research, a small number of expert meetings have been conducted as well. This input has then been compiled into a draft version of the Green book which has been published online. All participants of the discussion then had again the opportunity to provide feedback or further remarks. The finalized document has eventually been handed over to the president of the Federal Council and forwarded to the parliamentary inquiry – a one day event where a broad range of experts and representatives of the Parliament, Federal Government and State Governments as well as interest groups met to exchange publicly their opinions, before eventually the Federal Council took a formal decision, first in a committee meeting, then in the plenary. Further details are described in [4]. Note that, while in this chapter we mainly focus on economic policy, labour law and the development of future digital marketplaces, the Green Book covers also further consequences from the digital revolution for a broad range of topics, including data protection issues, copyright and liability law, consumer protection, transportation and tourism politics as well as the economics of electricity.

75.2   Learnings from the Consultation Process

Summarizing the key outcomes from this deliberative process, one of the most important questions has concerned the presumed need of action for the legislation. Note that, when this question has been asked, the political level (regional, national and/or European) was not specified. Participants replied describing their expectations on the impact of digitization to the working world, quality of life, and future society. Further contributions were focusing on both economic changes and the development of future digital marketplaces, as well as expected consequences for politics and future democracy, with transformation being a challenge for policy making (both governments and legislation).

The answers of the consultation show that the vast majority of political fields and parliamentarian committees are challenged to provide political solutions for a new legal framework and regulations for the transformed markets and upcoming innovations. For instance, more than 60% of the Austrian parliamentarian committees are called to negotiate reforms, where most of this challenges need coordinated actions of two or more ministers. The demand focuses on infrastructure and technology politics, science and education, internal and economic affairs, justice, tax law and treasury, to name the most important issues, while all government departments are in charge of digital transformation.

While developing appropriate political solutions, political decision-makers are facing a problem: the dynamics and very high speed of the changes make it difficult for many people, for organizations and also for political institutions to keep pace [4]. Legislation has to implement their reforms in an evidence-based way and quickly – typically, adaptations should happen within months or only few years in the worst case. While this does not sounds very progressive, note that current legislation often takes many years to be prepared, negotiated and implemented. Moreover, current best practice requires legislation to first watch ongoing changes before starting legal actions. In a period of fast transformations, like the age of digitization, this way of reacting is too slow to benefit from the offered opportunities. As a consequence, politics needs to develop new procedures: an evidence-based high-speed decision-making process is requested, in order to allow legislation to use try and error, tests and reviews in brief periods.

In general, this deliberative process has been new for the Austria Federal Council, and thus the experiences are rather diverse. On the one hand side, it has clearly exhibited the valuable potential opportunities of the Federal Council with organizing deliberative processes for the sake of shaping public opinion and preparing legislation in an early stage. Besides the obligations as representative of the federal interests and the competences in EU politics, this is a new encouraging narrative and political role for the Federal Council. The secondary position of the second chamber of the Austrian Parliament, the bridging function between the national and the federal political level, and the more flexible internal regulations of the Federal Council are of clear advantage in this respect. From this point of view, the process has been a real success, especially as it has been concluded effectively with a unanimous resolution to the Austrian federal government which is now in process of implementation. At the same time the project has demonstrated also the current limitations, including the need of experience of both the organizational team and (far more) the potential participants, and last but not least the need of development of efficient and intuitive technical tools, applications and platforms for realizing such public consultations, fulfilling the following key requirements:

- *Easy and intuitive access for all sections of the population*: proposing own ideas and placing discussion contribution should not be hindered by complicated technical mechanisms (for instance registration or authentication) or a non-intuitive user interface.
- *Creating interest and motivation for participating in political discussions*: In this context, a key role could be played by a clear feedback mechanism which allows users to follow transparently their ideas/contributions and how they eventually have affected the discussion process and its final outcome.
- *Efficient integration into political decision processes*: The compulsory outcome of a serious political discussion has to be a political result. Hence, specific account has to be taken of the requirements of decision-makers, in order to enable a broad consideration of discussion results for instance within parliamentary processes.

- *Enhanced moderation capabilities*: Very often, political discussion benefits from clear overall structures as well as guidance by a moderator who needs specific support for an efficient performance of his/her duties and responsibilities, based on the fact that the aim of public deliberation is less on creating new insight but mainly on sorting out and developing novel solution options.
- *Transparent documentation*: In this context, it is also highly important to develop and implement an elaborate concept for transparent documentation that allows organizing content and resulting knowledge in a manageable way. While this may pose specific scalability challenges due to the sheer amount of user input to be expected during public deliberation processes, integrating crowd intelligence approaches might become especially valuable here.
- *Increased integration and usage of social networking channels*: Today, social networks like Facebook or Twitter have developed into an important space for conducting political discussions, hence it is imperative to integrate these channels into future online deliberation platforms.
- *Usability on mobile platforms*: Online consultation and deliberation also has to take the strongly increasing mobile usage of the Internet into account, for instance by providing a suitable adapted and simplified platform version with reduced functionality for mobile user equipment.
- *Interface between digital and analogue discussions*: Also in the foreseeable future, discussions between persons that are physically present will stay essential for the political discourse, hence it is of fundamental importance to find efficient ways of integrating this transition between the analogue and digital world into future participation platforms.
- *Security and privacy aspects*: The fundamental user requirements in terms of security and privacy will play a key role with respect to the acceptance of such online platforms, together with its usability and universal accessibility.

Based on these requirements, a proof of concept has been carried out by University of Vienna and Kovar & Partners, and subsequently a participatory application for the deliberative development of documents has been developed within the *pnyxnet* project [6].

75.3   Working World and Digital Marketplaces of the Future

While the question of how the digital change will affect the future working world still is heavily debated, leading to a broad range of varying opinions, there is a consensus at least in one respect: none of the discussion participants has assumed that the number of jobs will increase. This is in line with [6] arguing that around half of the current jobs will be at least affected, if not destroyed, by the digital change. However, if it comes to legislative requirements for future market places and the job market, all proposed concepts for using this change as an opportunity for economic growth and as a job machine pretty much resemble classic recommendations for strengthening the business location and labour market: education, research, free markets without laissez-faire, as well as legal and planning security.

For instance, one line of suggestions has strongly focused on deregulating the free movement of workers (e. g. by reforming the Employment of Aliens Act), in order to create a vibrant international scene where especially young people feel comfortable. More generally, the reduction of traditional labour types and its shift towards new models, observed already now for instance in creative industries and leading e. g. to an increased ratio of free lancers fighting for contracts on global platforms, working without clearly specified working times and in legally unclear situations, will render traditional legal frameworks as well as current social security systems no longer applicable for larger parts of the working population.

This trend is further supported by upcoming forms of "shared economies", like Airbnb or Uber, which tend to be not always fully compatible with existing legal and taxation frameworks. The same is valid for the increasing number of crowd workers, one person enterprises and digital peons who make their living out of short-term limited working contracts. For all of them, social security turns out to become a key challenge: on the one hand side, traditional revenue streams of social security systems do no longer comply with the new payment flows (for instance, it turns out to be very difficult to integrate contributions for social security into contract negotiation platforms which only target hourly wages), while increasing parts of these groups lack of an adequate social security at all. Therefore, reforming the social systems and adapting them to the new forms of employment is considered an urgent political task.

On the other hand, in order to deal with such new business models, it must at least be ensured that there is a "level playing field" between established and new service providers. Staying with inefficient ways of production only because incumbents are protected by partly outdated regulations does not help much, however it is also not sufficient to leave the field only to regulation which could ward off or prevent new services. Instead, it would be beneficial to use this situation as a starting point for carefully checking the existing legal framework and make it a future-proof one.

The impact of digital change on the individual work-life balance is much less clear. While the borderline between professional and private life is about to disappear, this new flexibility in many cases can be experienced as very helpful in this context, but also the opposite may easily be the case. The increase of mobile work creates a new reality way beyond a traditional 9-to-5 mentality and will require experimenting with novel solutions and finding a consensus about viable models without regulating the extent and direction of these new structures from the very beginning.

The prospect of much less labour to be distributed among the population also may have positive aspects and, according to [6], simply might lead to people concentrating on other types of occupation (usually even more agreeable ones) if the request for their former work is diminished. However, this will of course require distributing the "digital dividend", which originates from the increase of productivity, equally among all members of the society, while the increasing polarization of earnings and possessions rather points into the opposite direction and creates considerable fears. Here again, the need for a new decision culture becomes apparent, for instance in the currently starting debate about an unconditional basic income for everybody, to be paid independently of the actual working situation. In this context, an important element will be the possibility of experimenting with various different options in order to create a sufficient data base for evidence-based decisions. Similarly, the legislation bodies, especially the parliament, will need new decision models, which should be based much more than previously on hearings, online consultation and direct communication with experts already in early stages of the legislation process. The resulting deliberative democracy will at the same time increase the motivation and attraction for public initiatives which are directly linked with formal decisions. It is interesting to note that – at least in the case of Austria – this would not even require fundamental changes in the parliamentary rules of procedure and could be easily carried out within the existing legislative structures and frameworks.

Another topic discussed in detail by the participants of the deliberation process has concerned current and future taxation laws. In this context, four main issues have been raised:

- *Taxation-based distortion of market competition*: While it should not be underestimated to which extent the current taxation framework, for instance due to accounting and IT requirements, prevents enterprises which offer online services from fully exploiting the potential of digitization, on the other hand also stationary trading faces severe disadvantages. For instance, it is currently very difficult, if not impossible, to ensure that Value-Added Tax (VAT) for digital goods, which are paid by the consumer, are correctly attributed to the fiscal budget of the country where the value has been eventually created.

- *Increasing tax avoidance*: The rapidly increasing internationalization also leads to severe problems with income taxes and corporation taxes. As far as Europe is concerned, so far neither the European Council nor the European Commission have succeeded in avoiding a critical taxation competition. At least the recent proposals for a digital European market aim at a more transparent taxation.

- *Fiscal situation of start-up enterprises*: While start-up enterprises strongly profit from simplified rules for instance with respect to trading with end customers, at the same time their fiscal situation is often a bit unclear. This applies as well the financing of start-ups.

- *Impact on national budget*: The question of how to finance the national budget if tax revenue from labour will further decrease is a crucial one, with very different scenarios to be discussed, as it is hard to predict which types of work will eventually be lost, and which will be created, due to effects of the digitization. The current expectation that mainly jobs with manual activity might be affected while jobs requiring a high level of education and training are considered to be safe also on a long-term perspective may be wrong: for instance, software might easily start replacing highly trained accounting and controlling staff, while robots could increase productivity in a way that certain industry jobs might even return to Europe or Northern America. Under these circumstances, it is pretty much unclear how to finance our current social market economy in the future and how resilient our current systems are indeed. However, this only increases the urgency of political decisions, and governments are well advised to try to open new degrees of freedom early enough, in order to avoid being completely carried away by the speed of upcoming changes.

For decades, the question of how the future of our society should look like had a rather simple answer: it was supposed to be a smooth evolution of the present situation. This is no longer the case with the Digital Revolution. Instead, we will be facing a phase of massive change of existing structures, which is already announced by the immense investments into new technologies and their effects on productivity, labour market and income distribution which we observe today. Hence, this requires an active, open and goal-oriented discussion about how our society will be able to cope with the upcoming disruptive structures – a discussion which in addition has to be led on an international level.

75.4 Summary and Outlook

The Digital Revolution is about to leading to a change whose economic and social importance can hardly be underestimated. The impact of the upheavals lying ahead can without any doubt be compared to the industrialization or the age of enlightenment. Especially the parallels between the digital transformation and the industrial revolution are evident. Then and now, the driving factors were new fundamental technologies and resulting technical changes. Today, new applications are essential for the social and political evolution, because they are used to advance organizational changes in economy as well as in the entire social fabric. This structural change will go far beyond technical changes, and the digital transformation is of significant impact to society and politics. Therefore, it has become a social and political issue, just like new philosophies, political movements, social insurances, universal and equal suffrage and emancipation were the answers to the industrialized society (and, after all, the industrialization has led in the 19th and 20th century to new political orders, the disappearance of five empires and the development of welfare states).

Hence, from our point of view, the key consequences of this dramatic evolution may be summarized as follows. Note that, while our conclusions are based on the outcomes of the participation process triggered by the Austrian parliament as sketched above, we are fully convinced that they are similarly valid also for all other countries with a comparable democratic system.

- *E-participation as an opportunity for evidence-based decisions*: If politics is facing the requirement of dynamic changes, decision making can be supported by new technical solutions. The possibilities in direct communication between experts, citizens and decision maker can enable deliberative democracy in a new quality. Thus, diverse knowledge can be introduced in the formation of opinion in a much earlier stage and with a wide participation. As the project has shown, consultation procedures, performed under the existing parliamentarian rules of procedure, can provide a valid basis for decisions within a few weeks. The only thing required in these deliberative processes are a developed self-image and an adapted behaviour of the Members of Parliament. In the interest of open legislation that brings better and more accepted political decisions, new pre-legislative process must be developed. Project reports, green papers, stronger scientific support and consultation procedure may allow interested citizens and the MPs a substantial participation in the development of policies and bring about better policy decisions.

- *Political culture and practice*: Until now, a culture of e-participation has not been properly developed in Europe. As much as the Internet may facilitate the participation, it is not an amplifier for political interest and political participation itself. Facing the new opportunities, the existing digital divide must be acknowledged and be taken care of. Economic, social and technological factors are relevant for the individual opportunities. Therefore low-threshold offers must be provided. During the consultation, also creating a common federal standard for e-participation has been proposed. The discussion on e-voting will gain weight in a digitized society, despite of the still unresolved security concerns.

- *Adaptability as an essential locational policy factor*: The consultation has also clearly demonstrated that the challenge now is to create scope for innovation and entrepreneurship. Existing conditions must be checked, and regulatory tasks have to be put on the legislative agenda. Regions that are able to involve expert knowledge will have a competitive advantage, and this knowledge is often very easily available. However, the transfer into the political sphere is the critical factor. Moreover, policy requires also new forms of strategic early warnings.

- *Changes in the politics and media labour market*: Publishers, journalists, think tanks, public affairs managers and political consultants are concerned with new tasks. The changed political markets will bring new demands. Also increasing is the need for guidance, information and community management. A revolution in political life would create new jobs. This "revolution" would lead to new political actors and create new types of organization. In this way, new competitors would occur for the classical parties, political media, pressure groups and existing think tanks.

- *The parliament as deliberative centre of politics*: The present project has demonstrated interesting opportunities for the Austrian Federal Council with respect to strengthening the dialog oriented (deliberative) democracy in Austria. Following this path may lead to a general new orientation of this second chamber of the parliament, thus creating a novel, clear and more self-confident image of this legislative institution. As a result, it would become a driving force for organizing public participation and deliberation activities, which at the same time would significantly strengthen both parliamentarianism and representative democracy in this country.

Summarizing, the digital revolution offers indeed significant opportunities on the way to new forms of high-speed democracy. As the history of the industrial revolution has taught us, however, it typically takes quite some time for technological advances and breakthroughs to lead to innovative applications and subsequent changes in society and politics. Hence, the phase of dynamic disruptions due to the Digital Revolution may still lie ahead of us.

Acknowlegements

The authors would like to thank all participants of the initiative "Digitaler Wandel und Politik" for helpful discussions, and especially Gottfried Kneifel and Bettina Fernsebner-Kokert for their valuable input.

References

1. J. Rifkin, The End of Work, Putnam Publishing Group, 1995.
2. A. Kovar, H. Leo und F.-K. B., "Grünbuch Digitaler Wandel und Politik," November 2015. [Online]. Available: www.besserentscheiden.at. [last access 15 September 2016].
3. [Online]. Available: www.besserentscheiden.at. [last access 2016 September 2016].
4. P. Reichl, A. Kovar, G. Kneifel, G. Jacoby, P. Gfaeller und S. Berck, "Towards High-Speed Democracy: Lessons from the Austrian 'Digital Change and Politics' Initiative," *Proceedings CeDEM'16, Krems, Austria,* May 2016.
5. [Online]. Available: www.pnyxnet.com. [last access June 20, 2017].
6. C. B. Frey und M. Osborne, "The Future of Employment: How Susceptible are Jobs to Computerisation?," *Oxford University Programme on the Impacts of Future Technology,* September 2013.

Build It and It Will Disrupt: a National Broadband Platform to Fuel New Zealand's Digital Economy

Fernando Beltrán

Abstract

The fibre-to-the-home, high-speed broadband network in New Zealand known as the Ultra-Fast Broadband (UFB) network is already changing the landscape of the telecommunications market in the country. The future New Zealand broadband ecosystem is being shaped by decisions that impact both the structure of the market and the supply-side of the ecosystem. UFB embodies the infrastructure of New Zealand's digital platform. It is not only a high-speed broadband network; it is also conceived as an open-access platform whereby any service provider can and will provide services. Opting for an open-access, high speed broadband platform New Zealand is effectively instigating major changes in the structure of the market, which in turn are expected to deliver profound changes in the range of services and the way they are delivered to consumers. This chapter presents the New Zealand case as an example of the scope and impact of digital disruption with major changes in infrastructure ownership and market structure and competition encouraged by UFB's open-access architecture and regulation. The main argument is that both the technical characteristics of the broadband network and major policy and regulatory decisions must necessarily shape the potential for digital markets creation, transformation, and growth.

76.1 Introduction

The transformation of the market place in many sectors of New Zealand's economy is fuelled by the deployment and adoption of faster, more reliable and robust broadband net-

F. Beltrán (✉)
University of Auckland Business School
Auckland, New Zealand
e-mail: f.beltran@auckland.ac.nz

© Springer-Verlag GmbH Germany 2018
C. Linnhoff-Popien et al. (eds.), *Digital Marketplaces Unleashed*,
https://doi.org/10.1007/978-3-662-49275-8_76

works. Access to high-speed communications networks by consumers and businesses is seen as a critical factor of success, if not survival. But the road to improved communications infrastructure demands high levels of investment. Telecommunications companies must upgrade, replace or deploy new technologies, which usually render the existing facilities obsolete.

Telecommunications networks capacity encounters a bottleneck in the access to endusers. Current technologies, such as Digital Subscriber Line (DSL), that use the telephone network lines to provide access to broadband services deliver a range of speeds to support broadband services. However the increasing demand for capacity from new services or the evolution of established services, render the DSL technology insufficient for such purposes. This situation is further exacerbated by the fact that in households and business users' devices rely on multiple access to broadband wireless, such as Wi-Fi, but usually on one single connection to the Internet. In order to keep up with the demand for access data rate fibre-to-the-home (FTTH) technology is viewed as a solid replacement of copperbased broadband technology, while being highly reliable.

Fibre, as an enabler of end-user access to the network has proved superior to copper and has been in the market for some time yet its adoption has been slow. In countries such as New Zealand and Australia governments have acknowledged that the transformation of the telecommunications network from copper-based technologies to fibre will not happen if only private investment is expected. Therefore, those governments have stepped in to provide much needed funds and managerial oversight on nation-wide projects that accelerate fibre-based access networks deployment and adoption.

New Zealand started a transformation of its telecommunications networks and markets by investing public funds in a high-speed, fibre-based broadband network, expected to reach 80% of households and almost every business in the country. The FTTH, broadband network deployment in New Zealand is a reliable, high-speed telecommunications infrastructure regarded as a precursor to the creation of an entrepreneurial digital ecosystem that will most certainly fuel the creation of digital marketplaces. Not only is such modern communications infrastructure enabling businesses to turn technological features such as speed, reliability and cost into factors that must positively affect their business case, but also, and most importantly, the techno-economic decisions made about its ownership and operation are facilitating strategic business factors that should contribute to business competitiveness on a global scale.

The premise of this chapter is that infrastructure is the facilitator of digital markets. In the 1990's with the widespread adoption of personal computers and the availability of modem devices operating over the telephone lines, the Internet transitioned from labs and university facilities to the general public. Soon it was realised that the open architecture of TCP/IP would facilitate the creation of software applications that would create a direct link between a provider of goods and products and the consumers without the intervention of either the infrastructure's owner or intermediaries. Fast forward to today's conditions and as markets develop and transactions are completed on websites and portals, the need for more reliable, faster networks are an imperative. Such new networks, as pointed out, require large investments. When a government decides to invest in the country's telecommunications infrastructure, policy, financial, legal and business decisions have to be strongly aligned in order to achieve an optimal return. If a broadband platform enables easy, sustained and effective operation of digital platforms which, in turn, facilitate the efficient establishment and growth of markets, it can then be argued that general public broadband policy, and technical and regulatory mandates are reaching their goals.

New Zealand's national broadband network seems to have been conceived on a "build-it-and-they-will-join" approach. Although the public debates revolved around the need for higher speed and more reliable access for consumers, in the end, political willingness mixed with hopes for the best played an important role in the decision-making process. Build-it-and-they-will-join is slowly solidifying; policy initiatives affecting the network architecture and regulatory measurements recently introduced are helping consumers feel reassured about their decisions to leave their copper connections behind and adopt the new fibre-based access connections. With that in sight this chapter argues that the old adage is changing. As high expectations for productivity and growth have been placed on the new broadband ecosystem, a feeling of "build-it-and-it-will-disrupt" seems to be taking hold of the sector which has unfolded in three stages: (1) an ambitious infrastructure upgrade accompanied by major policy changes and ensuing transitional regulations; (2) a steady uptake of fibre and the creation of a remarkable number of service retailers on the fibre; and (3) an emergent broadband platform that stimulates the creation of digital platforms for entrepreneurs and innovators. This chapter will describe and analyse those three stages.

76.2   Broadband FTTH: Enabler of Digital Markets

The worryingly low New Zealand Internet speed and broadband quality-of-service ranking positions in 2008 led the contending political parties to propose changes to the telecommunications infrastructure. Aiming for an ambitious infrastructure upgrade of the access network via FTTH, in 2009 the newly elected National government announced it would spend close to NZD $1.6 billion in broadband expansion by means of a programme to deploy FTTH in the urban areas complemented with an initiative for upgrades and access improvements in rural areas. The former is known as the Ultrafast Broadband (UFB) project and the latter is the Rural Broadband Initiative (RBI). Funded through two investment models agreed with four partners, the UFB network is a based on a public-private-partnership model of investment, a contract between a government and a private investor that seeks an alignment of the partners' objectives as it shifts a substantial amount of risk onto the private partner.

In 2011 the UFB project promised New Zealand that, by 2019, 75% of households – a figure revised up to 80% in 2015 – and most businesses would be enjoying high-speed broadband by means of optical fibre access. Crown Fibre Holdings (CFH), a government-owned company, was created to search for private investment and manage the project, providing the government with an executive body that oversees the construction. The search ended with a bidding process that saw four companies win shares of the available funds in 2011. The companies, known as Local Fibre Companies or LFCs, were to deploy fibre in four mutually exclusive geographical regions. Shortly after, Telecom and Vodafone won respective bids to become CFH's partners in the RBI.

A 'recycling shares' model was signed with three LFCs. Under such PPP model funds are used to build the fibre passing the premises, also known as dark fibre; when a customer decides to subscribe to the UFB network, the partner builds the "drop" into the customer's premises [1]. At this point the customer has already made a decision as to which of the many Retail Service Provider (RSP) to subscribe to, which in fact starts a subscription-based retail commercial relation. Unlike LFCs, RSPs are allowed to deal directly with the end-users. Once the subscription is started, the RSP is ensured of a revenue stream from such customer, which in turns creates a flow of funds to the LFC. Such funds are then used by the LFC to buy shares in the government-funded part of the UFB network. Depending on the subscription turnover by new customers, the recycled funds will allow that the ownership of the network gradually shifts from CFH to the private investing partner.

Participation in the UFB project brought the split of the former incumbent, Telecom NZ. As the company sought to bid for a share of the project the Government conditioned any bidder's participation to only companies not operating the wholesale and the retail sectors. In other words, only non-vertically integrated firms would be able to become partners in the fibre deployment initiative. Following such decision Telecom NZ demerged into two completely separate companies, Chorus, owner the old copper network and looking forward to own UFB fibre assets, and Telecom Retail retaining the switched network, the wireless network and the national backhaul (transport) network. Telecom Retail was later rebranded as Spark. The contract signed with Chorus differs from the contract signed the other LFCs: the Crown invests directly in Chorus with Chorus bearing the risk associated with the uncertain demand uptake. The investment amounts to a zero interest loan and in return Chorus has to comply with specific coverage and uptake goals.

The RBI's goal is to bring rural New Zealand to a higher development of broadband capacity. RBI's strategy lies on deploying a mixed wired and wireless infrastructure. On one hand DSL connections using latest Long Term Evolution (LTE) standard, are being upgraded. On the other, a nationwide cellular telephony tower expansion program has been completed [2].

In UFB areas consumers and business can choose their provider among a substantially high number of RSPs; LFCs can only provide wholesale services to such RSPs and are forbidden from direct deals with end-users. As of mid-2016 about 68% of the build-up (about 100,000 connections) in UFB areas had been completed, with over 240,000 users connected to UFB services [2]. In average 425 homes have been "passed" every day since construction began; a home passed by fibre is a household enabled to get hooked onto the street fibre backbone if only its owner decides so. In 2014 the average cost for a premise passed was about NZD $2134 (USD $1810) [3] and the cost of connecting a premise was about NZD $1233 (USD $1050) [3].

A significant number of small cities and towns are already fully covered by passing fibre. In contrast, the two largest urban areas, Auckland and Wellington, lag behind with completion rates among the lowest in the country.

An early assessment of the effectiveness of the UFB deployment [4] suggests that the contractual form signed by the government with the three small LFCs (also known as the funds-recycling scheme) is providing a higher incentive for fast deployment than the contractual arrangement with the incumbent (a combination of the investment model with technology replacement).

76.3 Open Access: Facilitating Innovation

Infrastructure and connectivity are not the only goals devised by the government-supported broadband initiatives in New Zealand. LFCs are de-facto monopolies but their networks must be open to any RSP willing to provide end-user services in their coverage areas. The policy upon which such operational scheme rests is called open-access. In the context of a government-funded, high-speed broadband network deployment this section explains open-access and discusses it economic implications.

As of mid-2016, the total number of RSP in New Zealand had almost reached 100 across the country with a customer being able to choose among 10 to 25 different RSPs, depending on her geographical location. This is in stark contrast to the pre-UFB time when an average consumer would not have more than 4 or 5 different copper-based internet service providers to choose from in major urban centres but even less in small towns. Thus, along with the healthy steady uptake of fibre, open-access is providing the creation of a remarkable number of service retailers on the fibre.

In 2007 open-access was mandated on Chorus (formerly Telecom) copper network, resulting in the introduction of choice for consumers. Such open-access is a dual regulatory tool that includes Unbundled Bitstream Access (UBA) and Unbundled Copper Local Loop (UCLL); both allow the promotion of entry by new Internet access providers. Over the last decade benefits to consumers have accrued from the market structure that emerged from UBA and UCLL and their regulated access prices imposed on the network provider.

76.3.1 Open Access and a Infrastructure Platform

Even though there is no definitive, agreed definition for open access [4], in general terms, and in the context of modern telecommunications access network, open access is a wholesale agreement by which access is granted – enforced or voluntary – to operators seeking and needing to use broadband facilities, which commonly belong to a dominant carrier. The main rationale for regulators to apply open access is that usually access facilities cannot be economically replicated. Open-access is a mode of facilitating non-facilities based competition. It can be provided on a profit or non-for-profit basis. When the facilities are owned by a private agent, voluntarily providing open-access is quite rare.

Open access is usually associated with fixed-access networks which provide broadband services. It is used to designate mandated wholesale access to different layers, and even on different technologies. Using the hierarchical layer model of a modern telecommunications network – inspired by the OSI layer model, OECD (2013) distinguishes open access on the three lower layers as follows:

On the physical layer open access means being able to use conduits and facilities that allow the access seeker to install own equipment. It also means local loop unbundling, on DSL lines, and dark fibre leasing, on fibre optics networks. On the network layer it means access to bistream, using the packet-based delivery of digital information.

What the tiered description of open access above implies is a variety of technical implementations and a relatively wide scope for differentiated services. Fig. 76.1 is a schematic representation of the open-access concept when applied to a FTTH network, such as New Zealand's UFB. In the model depicted in the figure LFCs are both Physical Infrastructure and Network providers, whereas RSPs are the Service providers.

Currently any RSP seeking to provide end-user services purchases wholesale services from the LFC; the service is based on bitstream open access, over which a number of end-user services can be implemented. They all depend on variations on upload/download data rate combination. Residential users can get up to 100 Mbps download. Negotiated contracts between CFH and each LFC include provisions for access to lower layers after 2020, which will include unbundling of fibre access. The ongoing discussion in New Zealand is explained in Sect. 76.4.

Fig. 76.1 Functional layered structure of a fibre-based network

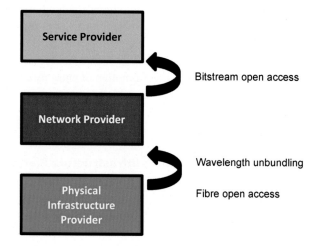

76.3.2   Open Access and a Two-Sided Market

The combination of technological characteristics of the network and policy and regulatory conditions render the UFB an open-access network. The service delivery model and the market conditions that follow turn the UFB into a platform. In economics the term "two-sided" platform has been used to designate markets whereby two sides exchange services and/or goods, with the platform facilitating the matching. As explained in [5] the UFB network can be regarded as a platform that facilitates the interaction in two markets: the access market and the content market. Access is provided by the platform to end-users and RSPs; in turn, RSPs themselves can turn into platforms for delivery of contents. The latter is the one market structure likely to grow and transform the digital marketplaces.

The two markets economic characteristics are explained as follows (see [5] for further details):

- Access market: the access market operates on the access platform where end-users pay no fees to join and RSPs must pay regulated wholesale charges according to the demand they face.
- Content market: the content market is a multi-platform competitive market whereby RSPs compete to attract content providers and other service providers, on one side, in order to attract consumers on the other.

The most important characteristic that a two-sided platform model reveals is the existence of cross-networks effects. A conventional FTTH investment approach by an incumbent not only would have been lengthy but it also would have been amounted to connection charges on consumers, a typical instance of a one-sided, telecommunication access market. Instead UFB's platform model, with expectations created around the possibility that end-users can now meet a substantially attractive number of RSPs, adopted a price model, limited to the first nine years after the deployment started, at zero connection fee. Thus, the welfare-promoting role of such CFH's decision, alongside an unexpected raise in the price of wholesale copper services by the Commerce Commission, have resulted – so far – in a healthy uptake of the fibre.

On the content market, a RSP is a multi-product firm that serves end-users (residential and business), allowing them access to contents and other services. Some RSPs may simply enable Internet access for end-users; some may start their own content offers; yet some may regard their position as a platform mediating two sides: content providers and end-users. Such RSPs will try to exploit cross-networks effects that emerge as content providers meet end-users, mediating the conditions and ability to monetize the mutual attractiveness between the two sides. If enough RSPs contend for customers on the basis of operating as platforms, engaging in inter-platform competition may translate into higher consumer benefits than those that other, single-sided operator RSPs can offer. In this environment product differentiation and economies of scale will also play an important role in any RSP's build-up of market share.

76.3.3 Digital Platforms

A broadband platform endowed with an open-access policy may encourage the creation of digital platforms. Digital platforms are changing business models in many markets; they are basically two-sided markets that seek to leverage the availability of information to provide products and services in a way that maximises the efficiency of matching the two sides.

Ingenious ideas brought to fruition have developed as digital platforms that bring together consumers and producers, two sides that find mutual attraction. Many examples of digital platforms exist which have been created to operate on the Internet. They do not depend on a particular access technology to thrive as abundant cases demonstrate it. However, innovative ideas that exploit the strengths of a broadband platform such as the UFB, namely, ultra-high speed, reliability and open-access, will be better positioned to use the digital platform model to succeed. For certain RSPs, platforms or not, if their business case entail product visualization, simulated user experience, high-resolution graphics, or virtual reality the technical characteristics provided by the technological platform most definitely provide them with the necessary inputs; such businesses cannot thrive on DSL connections.

Compared with their single-sided counterparts, platforms have shown to shorten the time to reach critical mass and, the most successful, produce very attractive returns on investment. Positive cross-network effects fuel the platform's growth as both sides find the presence of more agents on the other side ever more attractive, therefore creating a positive reinforcement cycle. Such platforms have reversed the 'old economy' pathway to growth and higher returns from supply economies of scale – and monopoly protection in some cases, to an environment where demand economies of scale prevail [6]. A seller in a market where supply economies of scale prevail needs to focus on exploiting its declining average production cost in order to use price as a strategic factor. In contrast, platforms whereby demand economies of scale may abound use technological improvements on the demand side to their advantage. For instance, in addition to efficiencies in social networks and demand aggregation [6] point at app development as technological improvement that impacts the demand side.

In the new digital landscape one of the most exciting prospects appears to be what [6] state about strategy and innovation. To a platform, strategy is no longer about controlling internal resources but managing external elements and finding adequate conditions for community creation and engagement. Then innovation can happen because of the presence of community participants throughout the platform.

76.4 Policy Issues in the Transition from Copper to Fibre

New Zealand's UFB network is already providing high-speed connections to consumers. Its customer base is growing and so are the new players, RSPs, which have arrived to the market. Their business propositions will compete in the market and, as argued above, some will turn the technical conditions and regulatory factors to efficient use as digital platforms.

Providing business stability and reducing uncertainty to fibre investors is crucial if New Zealanders are expected to benefit from their access to the UFB network and the markets that, operating on the broadband platform, will deliver products and services. In their first stage, UFB wholesale service prices (fixed until 2020) are regulated following a negotiation between CFH and its partners. The tariff structure includes several end-user upload/download services at different combinations of data rates with price slightly increasing or slightly decreasing until 2020 depending on the service. Fixing the prices clearly ameliorates risk to RSPs as they know the cost they face on the inputs needed for standard and premium, home or business fibre connections for the remainder of the decade.

In late 2015 the New Zealand's Ministry of Business, Innovation and Employment (MBIE) launched a review of the 2001 Telecommunications Act – the Review [7] – with a consultation process that has inquired about the best regulatory approach to the provision of access services on the existing copper network and the growing fibre-based broadband deployment. The review reiterates the need for strong competition in all markets and/or regulation that supports it. In invoking the need for a regulatory regime the review acknowledges that its operation has created a visible degree of uncertainty and warns about the risk posed by regulation that only pertains and is applied to a particular industry. In accordance with current developments around the UFB network the Review insists that consumers should be able to get high-quality fixed and mobile broadband connectivity at competitive prices; operators and other players should be able to innovate and compete; and the network should be "reliable, secure and resilient" [7].

As is usually discussed in many regulatory reforms across the world minimisation of regulatory uncertainty becomes also a factor to an efficient, innovation-friendly regulatory framework. In New Zealand, for a number of years the current transition will occupy the attention of the Commerce Commission. In the meantime, as long as consumers still use the copper network and Chorus still operates the public switched telephone network convergence and the need for consistent regulation will be the key issues to be addressed to minimise the uncertainty.

Previous sections argued that UFB as a broadband platform is first and foremost a disruption of the telecommunications infrastructure. As the UFB consolidates a broadband ecosystem whereby competition in the provision of services is expected to flourish, major changes will start to occur to the telecommunications markets. However, the current regulatory framework is not capable to promote the goals sought by the broadband policy, neither is it a good fit to the challenges posed by the new techno-economic structure of the renewed telecommunications infrastructure and the fibre-based broadband services to be provided. In what follows two major issues of concern to future regulatory approach affecting the broadband ecosystem are discussed: consistent regulation and the potential unbundling of fibre.

76.4.1   Economic Efficiency and Consistent Regulation

The Review prescribes that the access price regime needs to be based on "a holistic view of the interdependencies between UFB and copper networks" [7]. Pricing of access services refers not only to access to the copper network-based services but to the wider range of access modes enabled by the UFB network. In New Zealand the construction and operation of the UFB network sets the field for an important regulatory distinction that will remain for the foreseeable future. Any upgrade or change to current regulations will need to deal with the growing presence of fibre-based access services while still having to deal with copper access services.

The Review needs to seriously address the interplay between economic efficiency and regulation to ensure the welfare of consumers and producers. However, from a regulatory perspective and even with high competition, regulation not always promotes competition to protect long-term interests of end-users. A recent decision by the Commerce Commission on the price of access exemplifies the latter point.

In 2015 the Commerce Commission released its final decision setting the wholesale prices the copper incumbent, Chorus, would be able to charge to retailers for using its local copper lines, including the wholesale broadband services UCLL and UBA. The decision was the outcome of a lengthy and thorough review process that involved a dispute between Chorus and the Commission resulting in hurdles on the ability of copper to compete in the home broadband market. The key issue faced by the Commission in setting the prices of the UCLL and the UBA services was to provide right incentives to the industry, that is, network providers and RSPs, to accelerate the migration to UFB.

The new copper prices, used as the reference pricing point for selling UBA and ULLA to retailers, may be incidentally aligning with the desire that the fibre is promptly adopted as the preferred mode for consumers to access broadband services. Nevertheless the way the UFB deployment is being carried out does not require customers of the copper network to switch anytime soon, neither does it provide a financial fund to purchase copper lines and convert them to fibre. This situation reaffirms the need for consistent regulation, able to incentivise players to follow preferred policy goals.

76.4.2   Unbundling in the Fibre Era

One contentious point for the future of the UFB refers to the mandate that post 2019 LFCs will be required to unbundle their network by providing "dark fibre" services, which – already possible on a point-to-point connection basis – will need to be provided on a point-to-multipoint way. As shown in Fig. 76.1 access provided on a bitstream mode enables RSPs to reach end users; the diversity and scope of such services are superior to what copper can offer. The latter questions the need to provide unbundling at a lower layer, the physical infrastructure. The Government supports its determination to have dark fibre on the opportunities that would open to RSPs to introduce innovative services; however, it is not yet clear how the interplay between the robustness that the network infrastructure offers and the rising importance of wavelength unbundling will unfold. Those developments will determine the need for fibre unbundling at the physical layer.

LFCs may be particularly doubtful of the incentives to innovation that unbundling at the physical layer may bring to the market because in the new broadband ecosystem structure, innovation and service differentiation are expected to mainly be driven by competition. Thus, an interesting tension between unbundling and competition seems to be emerging. While the copper-based environment unbundling led to competition, in the fibre environment competition has been introduced by decisions made about the network architecture and functionality. LFCs consider that their physical infrastructure/network layer monopolistic presence is threatened by any proposal that seek to further open the network on such layers. Any regulatory insight into this situation will have to address questions about the social gains in efficiency of physical layer unbundling.

The issue is perhaps more important than the simplified view of a potential threat to a monopolistic network provider. It is about the best pathway to innovation. On one hand is the role of the RSP as a single-side market; Layer 1 unbundling would effectively provide a RSP with a more flexible vehicle to reach end-users and an input to modify and improve the LFC's wholesale service catalogue upon which retail services are built. On the other hand it is the RSP's role as a truly digital platform. As previously discussed, as a service provider a retailer is able to turn its market role from being one link in a conventional supply chain to becoming a digital platform its strategy is less reliant on managing internal resources, such as seeking unbundled Layer 1 services, and more dependent on creating and sustaining a thriving community. Managing the virtuous circle that positive cross-network effects may generate becomes the platform's main challenge.

76.5 Conclusion

This chapter postulates that New Zealand's Ultra-Fast Broadband network deployment under construction during the second decade of the 21st century, with its technical and regulatory decisions made thus far, offers the right kind of telecommunications infrastructure that will best ease up the road to efficient digital markets.

As a platform, fibre uptake has benefitted from policy decisions on the consumer side; in particular, government investment pays for a fibre connection at zero cost to any consumer (the household side) at any time during the first 10 years. The other side, the retailer side, has seen the arrival of close to 100 retail service providers nationwide that have started businesses on the UFB.

Policy and regulation are proving to be factors that shape the UFB broadband ecosystem; in the transition from copper to fibre in New Zealand, regulation will play a fundamental role in accelerating the opportunities for entrepreneurs to develop their fibre-based services and the consumers to benefit from competition on the content market, that is, the market developed by retailers.

The platform model cannot only be observed on the UFB as retailers meet consumers (seeking access to fibre); it is a model that could be followed by leading retailers willing to exploit the synergies between content providers and consumers eager for content. As much as the most successful model of digital disruption is seen in the creation and development of digital platforms that have overturned conventional markets and created communities around them, new players in New Zealand's digital ecosystem too could also realise the untapped potential that a technologically superior infrastructure offers and leverage it with innovative services that fully demand and use its most prominent features such as high speed, reliability and open access. Regulatory changes will have to be carefully introduced so that the nascent ecosystem is able to deliver quality, low prices and innovation.

Acknowledgements
the author wants to acknowledge partial funding from the University of Auckland Business School Dean's AP fund.

References

1. F. Beltrán, "Ultra-Fast Business; Rewiring New Zealnad Economy," Auckland, University of Auckland Business Review, 2014, pp. 26–35.
2. MBIE, "Broadband Deployment Update Q2-2016," 06 2016. [Online]. Available: http://www.mbie.govt.nz/info-services/sectors-industries/technology-communications/fast-broadband/documents-image-library/june-2016-quarterly-broadband-deployment-update.pdf. [Accessed 15 08 2016].
3. M. Gregory, "How much do FTTP NBN connections really cost?," 18 09 2015. [Online]. Available: http://www.businessspectator.com.au/article/2015/9/18/technology/how-much-do-fttp-nbn-connections-really-cost. [Accessed 20 04 2016].
4. OECD, Broadband Network and Open Access. OECD Digital Economy Papers, 2013, 2013.
5. F. Beltrán, Using the economics of platforms to understand the broadband-based market formation in the New Zealand Ultra-Fast Broadband Network, 36 Hrsg., Bd. 9, Telecommunications Policy, 2012, pp. 724–735.
6. G. Parker, S. P. Choudary and M. Van Alstyne, Platform Revolution: How Networked Markets Are Transforming the Economy and How to Make Them Work for You, W. W. Norton & Company. Kindle Edition, 2016.
7. MBIE, "Review of the Telecommunications Act 2001," 2001. [Online]. Available: http://www.mbie.govt.nz/info-services/sectors-industries/technology-communications/communications/regulating-the-telecommunications-sector/review-of-the-telecommunications-act-2001. [Accessed 15 08 2016].

Further Reading
8. M. Van der Wee, "The Efficiency and Effectiveness of a Mixed Public-Private Broadband Deployment: The Case of New Zealand's Ultra-Fast Broadband Deployment," 2016. [Online]. Available: http://ssrn.com/abstract=2732829 or http://dx.doi.org/10.2139/ssrn.2732829 [Accessed at 15 02 2016]. [Accessed 15 02 2016].

Part XVII
Active Cyber Defense

Securing the Opportunities of the Digitized Economy

Yuval Diskin

Abstract

The three of us have accumulated lots of experience in IT, Cyber Security and in protecting the critical infrastructure of the State of Israel, which is one of the world's most attacked states by cyber criminals or by certain states.

In 2012, we founded our Cyber Security consulting firm called D.A.T, offering high-level technological surveys of software and hardware systems to check their immunity against remote cyber-attacks.

Our objective was to better understand the challenges and threats of the interconnectivity on the digital economy through working in different sectors: Telecommunications, Finance and Insurance, Industry (production/assembly lines) and Energy.

Four and a half years later, after we carried out complex projects in various sectors, I can say that the revolution of the digital world and the digitized economy, which is accelerating every day, is an enormous economic and social opportunity, but it is also folding inside dramatic and even strategic challenges.

Based on the knowledge, know-how and the insights we gained, we teamed with Volkswagen in September 2016. Together we founded a new company to develop Cyber Security systems and to provide Cyber Security services for Internet-connected cars and self-driving vehicles. The new company, CyMotive Technologies Ltd., will be 40 % owned by the VW group and 60 % by me and my two colleagues.

We identified the following main insights of how to secure the opportunities of the digitized economy.

Y. Diskin (✉)
Cymotive Technologies Ltd.
Herzlia, Germany
e-mail: yuval.diskin@cymotive.com

© Springer-Verlag GmbH Germany 2018
C. Linnhoff-Popien et al. (eds.), *Digital Marketplaces Unleashed*,
https://doi.org/10.1007/978-3-662-49275-8_77

77.1 Strategic Partnering

Cyber Security is no longer only a technology challenge. The Cyber Security industry, which today is led by very talented technology experts, is suffering from a lack of Dynamic Defense strategies. These strategies exist only partially in some states in the government level, and are lacking in different industries and in the private sector. For this to happen, governments should encourage Cyber Security experts and strategists from the government and security systems, to migrate to the private sector and at the same time, to find ways to civilize some of the technologies used by the governments. Another good step would be to partner up with companies accountable for critical national infrastructure such as aerospace and defense. Both ways would establish a relationship that may be able to take actions against adversaries.

77.2 Intelligence Is Key

Dynamic Defense should become the new Cyber Security approach as soon as possible. This means that we need a comprehensive dynamic approach which involves both, External and Internal Intelligence. For a company it is crucial to maintain up-to-date intelligence by getting information about Cyber Security threats from own records, but also from third parties. Those external sources are fundamental as experts can give greater insight of the current state-of-the-art, have prepared threat profiles, and reveal attack vectors, i. e. specific strategic paths hackers take to get inside a network. The wide variety of contextual information helps a company to get a deeper understanding of the threat and the potential approach an attacker is going to pursue together with corresponding countermeasures.

New knowledge about the behavior of an attacker should be extracted following the intelligence cycle in order to enable faster decision making. By defining the weak spots of their company's network and estimating the technical capabilities of an attacker, a Cyber Security team can acquire knowledge about a known adversary's typical tactics, techniques, and procedures (TTPs). After setting up sophisticated threat profiles, suitable approaches should be integrated into the system and upgraded over time, including both, an increase of internal sensors for monitoring and external resources. In order to make active defense be able to process the high amount of data emerging from log files and user records, a dramatic increase in automation is needed.

77.3 Always Awake Security Brain

Thus, cutting edge technology solutions and products are needed including a future generation of SIEM and SOC: AASB ("Always Awake Security Brain") involving Artificial Intelligence and Machine Learning capabilities will enable real time security decision-making for fast and effective responses to new threats. Internal hunting teams are often used to actively search for and manage cyber-attackers. Finding them is a hard task, as hackers have the advantage of first move and a wide array of tools and techniques to hide their entry and activities. For that matter, Cyber Security operators need to identify and analyze internal use patterns, access logs and scan applications to detect anomalies. In order to understand what constitutes to abnormal behavior, profiles of "normal" user behavior are created manually and refined using machine learning. It is crucial to perform vulnerability analysis for detecting the most dangerous intrusion strategies. Once found, strategies revolve around handling the intruder. While the reflexive approach suggests to expel the threat as fast as possible, a detected intruder can be analyzed for valuable information regarding his arsenal of tools, and of course his actions. A wise decision is typically to waste the attacker's time by setting up honey pots, tar pits, and deceptive sand boxes.

77.4 Improved Research and Development

Aside all these we will always need best practices and professional governmental regulation of high Cyber Security standards for all sectors and industries. One of the first things that should be regulated in the era of Internet-of-Things, is the deep integration of Cyber Security experts in the research and development processes of software and hardware products. Companies need to be aware that conventional passive defense mechanisms, such as firewalls and intrusion detection systems, are by far not enough to compensate the broad bandwidth of attacks they might face against adversaries. Therefore, already in the very early conception stage of software and hardware, active measures need to be respected that aim at monitoring an attacker's behavior. This will eventually help reducing slow response times to intruders and zero day exploits.

77.5 The Diversity of Threats

Cyber Security solutions and products should be developed not only for the **Known-Known Threats**, but also for the **Unknown-Known Threats** and even for the **Unknown-Unknown Threats**. This approach already exists in the field of counter-terrorism and should be adopted to the field of Cyber Security.

Most companies traditionally focus on threats from external actors, and therefore orienting the defense system against outer threats. However, insiders, especially personnel of the own company, are generally trusted while having access to valuable data. Because access privileges are often not managed appropriately, insiders are susceptible against methods such as social engineering which no intrusion detection system may prevent. It is unavoidable to implement a data loss protection (DLP) and change the mind-set of internals to protect against internal threats.

Such insider threats may be subdivided into three categories. An errant insider might be unaware of current security protocols and may accidentally compromise important information of the network by forwarding an email with high confidentiality. Hijacked insiders are the most common type of breaches and involve stolen credentials, i. e. via key loggers, for example. Malevolent insiders, that is internals that compromise the network at will, mostly do so because of bribery or coercion. This depicts a great risk and can often be spotted with strict DLP rules. A chain of trust and structured concepts for access privilege need to be employed to keep up with those type of threats.

77.6 Conclusion

The digitized economy is developing very fast but Cyber Security is still far behind. The strategic challenges and threats folded in these tremendous opportunities are already here. The faster we move to the next generation of Cyber Security the more it will enable us to enjoy the fruits of the digitized economy and to live in a more secured world.

Black Market Value of Patient Data

78

Christina Czeschik

Abstract

Personal health data is a coveted resource for a variety of interested parties. One of these is agents operating in illegal markets, comparable to the black markets on which stolen credit card data and other unlawfully obtained information are sold. Since the safety of personal health data is not only dependent on the quality of safety measures adopted by health care entities but also on the motivation and resources of potential attackers, the question of the value of personal health data on the black market is a highly critical one and not an easy one to answer. Illegal actors can extract profits from patient data in a variety of ways, the best documented of which are direct sale and extortion of ransom. Prices attained in these transactions can help to estimate the financial value of patient data on the black market in the US – where instances of health care data breaches have been most frequent and well documented – and in Germany.

78.1 Valuing Personal (Health) Data

Like every kind of personal data[1], personal health data is inherently valuable. However, different stakeholders will value a set of health data in very different ways, some of which are:

---

[1] According to the OECD Privacy Guidelines: "any information relating to an identified or identifiable individual" [1].

C. Czeschik (✉)
Serapion Beratung & Fachredaktion
Essen, Germany
e-mail: czeschik@serapion.de

© Springer-Verlag GmbH Germany 2018
C. Linnhoff-Popien et al. (eds.), *Digital Marketplaces Unleashed*,
https://doi.org/10.1007/978-3-662-49275-8_78

- Health care providers require patient records and other kinds of patient data as the basis of professional diagnostic and therapeutic decision-making.
- For insurance companies, personal health data facilitates prediction of health risks of insured and not-yet-insured individuals, thus allowing them to adapt premiums or forego contracts altogether.
- Universities, research organizations and pharma companies require patient data, to develop and test new diagnostic and therapeutic means, such as novel drugs.
- Consumer-oriented companies covet personal health information to optimize their product marketing, e. g., in the fields of wearable technologies or nutritional supplements.
- For the patient, finally, the value of personal health data lies of course in the potential improvement of health that can be achieved when it is used by health professionals – but even more than the above-mentioned parties, the patient is also concerned with keeping private information private.

Thus, one could say that while it is valuable for health care providers and companies in the private sector to *have* an individual's personal health data, its value for patients lies both in having and in *not sharing* it – at least not involuntarily.

The OECD Report "Exploring the Economics of Personal Data" [1] has examined more formally the problem of attributing value to personal data. Here, methods of assigning a monetary value to personal data are divided into two broad classes: (1) those based on *individuals'* valuation and (2) those based on *market* valuation.

If individuals' valuation is to be the main aspect, the following measures may serve as a basis:

- Surveys and economic experiments
  (i. e., monetary value of personal data as reported by probands in surveys and economic experiments)
- Individual willingness to pay to protect data
  (i. e., monetary amount individuals are willing to pay to keep their data private)

When considering market valuation, possible measures are:

- Market capitalization, revenues or net income per data record
  (i. e., a company's market capitalization, revenues or income divided by number of personal data records used by the company)
- Market prices for data
  (i. e., price for data record in data broker market)
- Cost of a data breach
  (i. e., cost incurred by a company or individual to recover from a data breach)
- Data prices in illegal markets

According to the OECD, the latter may even be a more accurate measure of the value of data sets than other suggested measures because illegal data may represent a rival good, i. e., a good in which the value decreases as more customers gain access to it. Hence, an illegal market's market-clearing price may be closer to the good's full market price. One of the disadvantages of valuing personal data by illegal market prices is, of course, the lack of market transparency. Also, prices tend to fluctuate with momentary ups and downs in supply and demand [2].

Data prices in illegal markets have been well-investigated for years with regard to data sets that lend themselves more easily to financial exploitation than personal health data, such as credit card data [3]. The mere fact that personal health data as well is sold and bought in illegal markets, however, is shifting into focus only recently, with the increasing digitalization of processes and patient information in hospitals and practices [4] and the advent of ever more sophisticated (and surprisingly unsophisticated) malicious attacks on health care providers' IT systems [5].

Hence, the black market price of personal health data is relevant not only from a theoretical standpoint – as one of several measures to assess the monetary value of personal health data – but also and maybe more importantly to answer the question regarding what kind of profit attackers and data thieves targeting the health care system expect to gain from their activities. However, before tackling this issue, the next section of this chapter will discuss whether or not patient data are actually at risk for theft and misuse.

78.2   Data Theft in Health Care

The Ponemon Institute's Fifth Annual Benchmark Study on Privacy & Security of Healthcare Data [6], which included 90 health care organizations in the US and 88 business associates of health care organizations, states that 2015 was the first year in which criminal attacks were the most frequent cause of data breaches in health care. Compared to 2010 results, criminal attacks had increased by 125% and constituted 45% of data breach causes, replacing lost or stolen devices (43%) as number one on the list. Experts suggest that the health care sector replaced the financial sector as top target for cyber attackers, not only because of the inherently valuable data but also because its information security defenses are inferior in comparison [7, 8].

Another study by the Ponemon Institute [9] showed that, averaged over a variety of industries, the cost per capita per data breach is highest in Germany (for 2012), with 199 USD compared to an average cost of 136 USD. At the same time, averaged for each industry individually, the cost of a data breach is highest in the health care sector, with 233 USD. Every breach of health care data is even more costly than a breach of financial data, which is second on the list with average costs of 215 USD per capita. Although data for the German health care market have not been reported separately, the aggregated data suggest that data breaches in the German health care sector might be the most costly among all important sectors in the industrialized countries. This, of course, pertains to the costs of recovery of a data breach, including "incident handling, victim notification, credit monitoring and projected lost opportunities" [10]; it cannot be concluded from these figures that German health care data will obtain the highest prices on the black market.

While Ponemon's data was collected by querying health care providers and business associates, the SANS Institute, a privately funded organization that offers training and research in the field of information security, surveyed the Norse threat intelligence infrastructure, a network of sensors and so-called honeypots[2], to monitor malicious events and traffic on the Internet [10]. Thus, sources of suspicious traffic were identified and filtered for health care related organizations, meaning that these organizations were most likely infected by malware and hence partaking in attacks against honeypots and other online entities. In this sample, captured over the course of 12 months in 2012 and 2013, malicious traffic from 275 compromised US-based health care entities was recorded; 72% of the traffic had its source in direct health care providers, e. g., hospitals, clinics and private offices. Among devices and software most often compromised were:

- VPN applications and devices (33% of malicious traffic)
- Radiology imaging, videoconferencing and teleconsultation software (17%)
- Firewalls (16%)
- Internet-facing databases with personal health data, including a large call center website (12%)
- Routers (7%)

Thus, ironically, the very systems and devices employed to keep an organization's network safe were the main infection sites for malware.

Regarding individual data breach incidents, the US health care industry was hit hard, especially in 2015:

- By using malware to gain access to an employee's login information, intruders obtained "up to 80 million records that included Social Security numbers, birthdays, addresses, email and employment information and income data for customers and employees, including its own chief executive" [11] from the for-profit health insurance company Anthem, Inc. Analysts pointed out the lack of encryption in the compromised database [11].
- The non-profit health insurance company Premera Blue Cross experienced a data breach exposing contact information, medical information, bank account numbers and social security numbers. It is estimated that data of around 11 million individuals were affected [7].
- The non-profit health insurance company Excellus Blue Cross Blue Shield lost "personal information for as many as 10 million individuals, including name, date of birth, Social Security number, mailing address, telephone number, member identification

---

[2] A honeypot in a network that is set up with the purpose to attract attackers and study their behavior and techniques.

number, financial account information, and claims information" [12] in another data
breach.

- Up to 4.5 million patient files were compromised in the UCLA Health System, a hospital and primary care network. The part of the network that was compromised "contained names, dates of birth, Social Security numbers, Medicare and health plan identification numbers as well as some medical information such as patient diagnoses and procedures" [13]. Again, a lack of encryption was criticized in the aftermath of the incident [13].

In Germany, patient data has been the target of insider and outsider attacks as well,
albeit on a smaller scale:

- In 2013, an IT administrator copied data, including medical, from doctors' offices and pharmacies. He was employed by a medical data center performing data processing for these entities [14].
- Backup tapes with data of approximately 200,000 to 300,000 patients were (physically) stolen from Klinikum Mittelbaden in 2012 [15].
- Intruders stole endoscopy equipment from a hospital in Bad Berleburg, including digital patient data stored on these devices [16, 17].

As the last two instances show, compromise of health care data is not restricted to
network-related events. During the consolidation of the German health care landscape,
many small hospitals were decommissioned, and often the funds necessary to store patient
records were lacking. Local media reported several breaches in the states of Northrhine-
Westphalia and Lower Saxony in which intruders gained access to poorly secured archives
in the otherwise vacant premises of former hospitals [18]. While the legal situation regarding patient files of doctors' offices seems to be resolving, no conclusive legislation exists
regarding patient files in defunct hospitals [19]. However, patient data online can of course
be compromised on a far larger scale – with as much as several million records exposed
in a single breach [20] – and with much less risk of discovery by authorities.

A special kind of online attack on patient data is executed with the help of so-called
cryptotrojans. Several varieties of this kind of malware, also known as ransomware, have
been circulating on the Internet for years but gained special notoriety with a wave of hospital computer system infections in 2016 in Germany, the USA, Canada and New Zealand
[21–24]. Malware of this kind invades computer systems as email attachments and proceeds to encrypt all data it can reach on the system. The user is then prompted to pay
a ransom (usually in the anonymous bitcoin currency) to buy the decryption key and regain access to the encrypted data [22]. However, while attackers have supposedly been
"honest" in many cases, not all ransom payments have led to recovery of the data [24].

As a survey of international online media shows, countries such as France and Spain are
worried about online piracy of health data as well [25–27]. In Spain, no major incidents
have been reported so far [25], which observers attribute to the insurance system, which

does not incentivize medical identity theft (which, however, did not protect Germany from health data breach incidents). Regarding the situation in France, a L'Obs (formerly Le Nouvel Observateur) report hypothesizes that it is merely due to a lack of transparency in the French (as opposed to US and German) health care system that no major data breaches have been made public [27]. As the article points out, France's 1000 hospitals employ only around 50 cybersecurity experts in total.

In summary, there is no lack of opportunity for malicious intruders to gain access to patient data, and as the saying goes, "opportunity makes the thief".

78.3   Black Market Value of Patient Data

Computer security analysts of the FBI's Cyber Security Division estimated in 2014 that one individual's health care record is worth 50 USD on the black market [12, 28]. Don Jackson of cybercrime protection company PhishLabs estimated that health care credentials are worth around 10 USD per record, based on his analysis of dark web transactions [8] – still 10 to 20 times more than, for instance, credit card data. Katherine Keefe of cyber liability insurer Beazley again estimates a black market price of 40 to 50 USD per health care record [11].

Recently, news of the largest known transaction of patient data on the black market surfaced in online media. A hacker who called himself "thedarkoverlord" offered three separate databases of patient data (including medical data) on the black market website TheRealDeal (which is accessible by anonymous Tor networking only). In total, these contained 655,000 records. On the day after, he followed up with another database, containing 9.3 million records. Approached by data security journalists, thedarkoverlord revealed that he had gained access to the first three databases through user names and passwords that were stored without any encryption on misconfigured networks. The fourth attack was made possible by a vulnerability in Windows' Remote Desktop Protocol [29].

The attacker stated that he had first attempted to extort money from the victims, who, however, had been unwilling to pay to avoid publicity, leading thedarkoverlord to offer the results of his heist on a public market. For the first three databases, he set prices of 100,000 USD to 395,000 USD (based on bitcoin rates at the end of June), and the fourth and largest one was supposed to be sold at 500,000 USD (converted) [29, 31].

He did not divulge how much ransom he had asked from the exposed health care organizations, except for one from which he attempted to charge 160,000 USD. However, in each case, the ransom was below 1 million USD, as reported by the attacker himself [29].

Based on these offers, health care data may sometimes fall under a "bulk discount" on the black market, if an especially large volume of data is acquired by the attacker. Another factor may have contributed to the low figure of 0.05 USD per patient record in these last incidents: in an attempt to validate information that was voluntarily provided by the attacker for this purpose (see Fig. 78.1 for an anonymized example), an anonymous

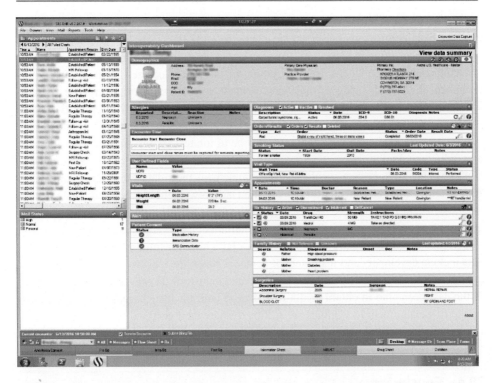

Fig. 78.1 Anonymized sample of health care data offered by thedarkoverlord on TheRealDeal marketplace, as reported by DeepDotWeb. (https://www.deepdotweb.com [30])

information security blogger ascertained that the data was indeed real. However, in some instances in this sample it was several years old [31].

In documented cases of ransomware infections in hospitals and clinics with the "Locky" trojan, ransoms of around 300 USD or 200 € were demanded [32, 33]. However, in targeted attacks, sums of up to 3.6 million USD were reported [34].

In summary, estimated market prices for selling and buying health care data as well as response to extortion range between 0.05 USD and 50 USD per record.

Buyers most likely show interest in these records because they facilitate both medical and other identity thefts. Medical identity theft is especially worthwhile in health care systems without compulsory health insurance, the most well-known example being the US health care system. It enables non-insured persons to obtain health care and may also serve as a source for obtaining prescription drugs, which can then be sold on the black market as well [25]. As the FBI states, health care data can be used "to file fraudulent insurance claims, obtain prescription medication, and advance identity theft. Theft of electronic health records (EHR) is also more difficult to detect, taking almost twice as long as normal identity theft" [28]. Offering stolen data to the compromised organizations themselves to extort a ransom, on the other hand, may be the natural first step for fencers of stolen data before going public on the black market [29].

Still, there are other modes of profit extraction. In 2008, the *Los Angeles Times* reported that employees of the UCLA Health System unauthorized accessed medical records of prominent individuals, such as musicians Britney Spears and Michael Jackson, actress Farrah Fawcett and Maria Shriver (John F. Kennedy's niece, formerly married to Arnold Schwarzenegger) [35, 36]. However, no figures of actual payments were made public.

In theory, stolen health care data may also be of interest for private insurance companies, who commonly rely on information supplied by their clients to calculate premiums. Unfiltered health care data would at least supplement their data in an interesting way. As one anonymous commenter on the website Darkdotweb glibly remarked: "As a health insurance agent I would love to buy your medical records. My company would give me a large raise and a company car" [37]. This is, admittedly, pure supposition at the moment, as no cases of this kind have been reported so far. Other potential buyers of health care data include developers and marketers of personal health devices, wearables and the like, as well as R&D departments of health care related industries. However, these parties have in the past been able to obtain health care data in bulk for their purposes because a surprisingly great number individuals are willing to share their personal data in exchange for free services and social media opportunities [38].

78.4 Conclusion

Owing to the nature of the question regarding selling and buying prices of data on the black market is difficult to obtain in a reliable way. Moreover, most available data is specific to the US market – a characteristic that is not limited to the black market but applies to the overall problem of valuing personal data [1]. Since medical data for the purpose of medical identity theft is a less coveted resource in countries such as Germany with almost complete health insurance coverage of the population, US figures may be exaggerated in comparison to the German market. However, other modes of profit extraction are applicable in Germany and other countries as well as in the US:

- demands of ransom, including both ransomware and individual extortion of hospitals and other entities,
- selling data for purposes of financial and other identity theft, since bank account and other personal data are often part of breached records,
- selling data to other interested parties such as the media, and supposedly, other private enterprises.

Hence, patient data are valuable assets that, according to industry analysts, are not nearly sufficiently protected in the majority of health care organizations globally [5, 11, 12, 21, 25–27, 29, 31, 37]. More sophisticated countermeasures are therefore needed to prevent large-scale data breaches, and data security and privacy belong among the top items on the list of priorities of health care officials.

References

1. OECD, "Exploring the Economics of Personal Data," in *OECD Digital Economy Papers*, 2013.
2. D. Walker, "Research examines cost of stolen data, underground services'," SC Magazine, 11 12 2014. [Online]. Available: http://www.scmagazine.com/news/prices-have-dropped-for-stolen-data-on-the-black-market/article/387945/. [Accessed 13 07 2016].
3. T. Zeller, "Black Market in Stolen Credit Card Data Thrives on Internet," *The New York Times,* 2005.
4. H. Krügel-Brand, "Digitale Transformation: Zukunftsfragen," Aerzteblatt, [Online]. Available: http://www.aerzteblatt.de/archiv/175605. [Accessed 13 07 2016].
5. N. Yaraghi, Hackers, phishers, and disappearing thumb drives: Lessons learned from major health cara data breaches, 2016.
6. Ponemon Institute, Fith Annual Benchmark Dtudy on Privacy & Security of Healthcare Data, 2015.
7. D. Bowman, Why health insurers are an enticing hack target [Q&A], Fierce Healthcare, 2015.
8. C. Humer und J. Finkle, Your medical record is worth more to hackers than your credit card, Reuters, 2014.
9. P. Institute, 2013 Cost of Data Breach Study: Global Analysis, 2013.
10. B. Filkins, Health Care Cyberthreat Report, SANS Institute, 2014.
11. R. Abelson und M. Goldstein, Anthem Hacking Points to Security Vulnerability of Health Care Industry, The New York Times, 2015.
12. F. Rashid, "Why hackers want your health care data most of all," InfoWorld, 14 09 2015. [Online]. Available: http://www.infoworld.com/article/2983634/security/why-hackers-want-your-health-care-data-breaches-most-of-all.html. [Accessed 08 07 2016].
13. C. Terhune, UCLA Health System data breach affects 4.5 million patients, 2015.
14. ÄrzteZeitung, "Illegale Ausspähaktion: Massenhaft Patientendaten gestohlen," 29 11 2013. [Online]. Available: http://www.aerztezeitung.de/praxis_wirtschaft/recht/article/850930/illegale-ausspaehaktion-massenhaft-patientendaten-gestohlen.html. [Accessed 31 07 2016].
15. Klinikum Mittelbaden, Datenschutz, Mittelbaden: Klinikum Mittelbaden, 2012.
16. WDR – Westfalen-Lippe-Nachrichten, "Bei Diebstahl auch Patientendaten verschwunden," 31 05 2016. [Online]. Available: http://www1.wdr.de/nachrichten/westfalen-lippe/patientendaten-verschwunden-diebstahl-medizinische-geraete-berleburg-100.html. [Accessed 31 07 2016].
17. E. Demtröder, "Medizingeräte-Diebstahl: Helios spekuliert nicht über Motiv," WAZ, [Online]. Available: http://www.derwesten.de/staedte/nachrichten-aus-bad-berleburg-bad-laasphe-und-erndtebrueck/medizingeraete-diebstahl-helios-spekuliert-nicht-ueber-motiv-aimp-id11842565.html. [Accessed 31 07 2016].
18. D. Seher, "Diebe stehlen tausende Patientenakten aus Klinik-Kellern," WAZ, 08 02 2015. [Online]. Available: http://www.derwesten.de/politik/diebe-stehlen-tausende-patientenakten-aus-klinik-kellern-id10932347.html. [Accessed 28 07 2016].
19. H. Krüger-Brand, Archivierung von Patientenunterlagen: Arzt muss weg – Patientenakten weg?, Deutsches Ärzteblatt.
20. DeepDotWeb, New Breach: Healthcare Insurer Database of 9.3 M Records Being Sold, Deep Dot Web, 2016.

21. W. Ashford, "Ransomware makes up a quarter (and rising) of UK cyber attacks, finds research," ComputerWeekly, 28 04 2016. [Online]. Available: http://www.computerweekly.com/news/ 450294545/Ransomware-makes-up-a-quarter-and-rising-of-UK-cyber-attacks-finds-research. [Accessed 01 08 2016].

22. D. Borchers, "Ransomware-Virus legt Krankenhaus lahm," heise online, 02 12 2016. [Online]. Available: http://www.heise.de/newsticker/meldung/Ransomware-Virus-legt-Krankenhaus-lahm-3100418.html. . [Accessed 01 08 2016].

23. S. Gallagher, "Two more healthcare networks caught up in outbreak of hospital ransomware," Ars Technica, 29 03 2016. [Online]. Available: http://arstechnica.com/security/2016/03/two-more-healthcare-networks-caught-up-in-outbreak-of-hospital-ransomware/. [Accessed 01 08 2016].

24. M. Smith, "Kansas Heart Hospital hit with ransomware; attackers demand two ransoms," Network World, 22 05 2016. [Online]. Available: http://www.networkworld.com/article/ 3073495/security/kansas-heart-hospital-hit-with-ransomware-paid-but-attackers-demanded-2nd-ransom.html. . [Accessed 01 08 2016].

25. C. Sánchez, "La seguridad en los hospitales españoles: tu salud y tus datos, ¿en peligro?," eldiario.es, 09 09 2015. [Online]. Available: http://wwweldiario.es/hojaderouter/seguridad/ hospitales-sanidad-seguridat_informatica-ciberataques-datos-privacidad_0_427657312.html. [Accessed 01 08 2016].

26. J. Carballo, "Les données de santé attirent les hackers," Le Figaro, 13 02 2015. [Online]. Available: http://sante.lefigaro.fr/actualite/2015/02/13/23393-donnees-sante-attirent-hackers. [Accessed 01 08 2016].

27. N. Devillier, "Piratage de données médicakes; la France n'est pas prête," Rue89, 05 04 2016. [Online]. Available: http://rue89.nouvelobs.com/2016/04/05/piratage-donnees-medicales-france-nest-prete-263632. [Accessed 01 08 2016].

28. FBI Cyber Division, Health Care Systems and Medical Devices at Risk for Increased Cyber Intrusion for Financial Gain, FBI Cyber Division, 2014.

29. D. Dissent, "655,000 patient records for sale on the dark net after hacking victims refuse extortion demands," The Daily Dot, 27 01 2016. [Online]. Available: http://www.dailydot.com/ layer8/655000-patient-records-dark-net/. [Accessed 03 08 2016].

30. DeepDotWeb, New Breach: 655000 Healthcare Records (Patients) Being Sold, Deep Dot Web, 2016.

31. D. Dissent, Lording it over the healthcare sector: health insurer database with 9.3 M entries up for sale, Office of Inadequate Security, 2016.

32. H. Gierow, "Security: Ransomware-Bosse verdienen 90.000 US-Dollar pro Jahr," golem.de, 06 03 2016. [Online]. Available: http://www.golem.de/news/security-ransomware-bosse-verdienen-90-000-us-dollar-pro-jahr-1606-121292.html. [Accessed 04 08 2016].

33. J. Breithut, "Trojaner 'Locky': Erpresser-Software infiziert 17.000 deutsche Rechner an einem Tag," SPIEGEL ONLINE, 19 02 2016. [Online]. Available: http://www.spiegel.de/netzwelt/ gadgets/locky-17000-windows-rechner-in-deutschland-taeglich-infiziert-a-1078318.html. [Accessed 04 08 2016].

34. S. Gallagher, "Patients diverted to other hospitals after ransomware locks down key software," Ars Technica, 17 02 2016. [Online]. Available: http://arstechnica.com/security/2016/02/ la-hospital-latest-victim-of-targeted-crypto-ransomware-attack/. [Accessed 04 08 2016].

35. A. Blankstein, Eyes on celebrity records multiply, Los Angeles Times, 2008.

36. M. Neil, "Celebrity Medical Files Breached at UCLA," ABA Journal, 04 07 2008. [Online]. Available: http://www.abajournal.com/news/article/celebrity_medical_files_breached_at_ucla/. [Accessed 31 07 2016].

37. A. Guerrilla, Tor's Co-Creator: Your Medical Revords Have Bullseyes On Them, Deep Dot Web, 2016.
38. D. Nield, "Google Fit vs. Apple Health: Who's Winning the Race?," Read-Write, 24 03 2015. [Online]. Available: http://readwrite.com/2015/03/24/google-fit-vs-apple-health/. [Accessed 03 08 2016].

Christian Schläger, André Ebert, Andy Mattausch, and Michael Beck

Abstract

The term "Cyber Sovereignty" has been tossed around panels (See for example the International Cybersecurity Conference 2016 in Munich, Panel: Digital Sovereignty – the Right Concept for Securing Europe's Industry?), newspaper articles, and blogs for quite some time. However, a practical solution to reach a state of sovereignty in the field of implementing fitting and trustworthy cyber tools and products in one's company is still missing. We have come to the conclusion that the idea of cyber sovereignty – undoubtedly charming and worthwhile – cannot be pursued with the usual military and national approach but must be addressed using a community of users and experts. Combining the concepts of digital user communities and cyber sovereignty led several German DAX companies to found the Deutsche Cyber Sicherheitsorganisation (German Cyber Security Organization) – DCSO in 2015 where the authors implemented the idea of a "Product Evaluation and Integration" Service (PEI). This PEI Service enables the founding members and DCSO customers to execute cyber sovereignty through testing,

C. Schläger (✉)
Giesecke & Devrient GmbH
Munich, Germany
e-mail: christian.schlaeger@gi-de.com

A. Ebert · A. Mattausch · M. Beck
Ludwig-Maximilians-Universität München
Munich, Germany
e-mail: andre.ebert@ifi.lmu.de

A. Mattausch
e-mail: andy.mattausch@campus.lmu.de

M. Beck
e-mail: michael.beck@ifi.lmu.de

© Springer-Verlag GmbH Germany 2018
C. Linnhoff-Popien et al. (eds.), *Digital Marketplaces Unleashed*,
https://doi.org/10.1007/978-3-662-49275-8_79

evaluating, and prototyping state of the art and future cyber security products, services, and vendors.

This article will elaborate on the main idea behind the foundation of the DCSO and go into detail of how valuable the PEI service has become for the security measures of German DAX companies. It will give concrete examples of the implementation and encourages similar initiatives for other problems like cyber security.

79.1 Motivation and Problem Formulation

Today, Cyber Security and Cyber Risk are on every CIO's agenda. As cyber risks threaten to destroy every CIO's project or program, a company's new business venture, the partaking in Industry 4.0 value chains, and digitalization strategy, they have made their way from being a purely CISO/ISO subject to the highest board levels. In fact, there is hardly a CFO or CEO who doesn't want to be constantly informed about their company's cyber risk footprint. Information Security risks (including IT security, data privacy, and Cyber risks) make up at least 20% of a global player's top ten Op-Risks overall[1] and it is expected to grow.

The need to defend oneself against Cyber Threats is apparent. The question remains how best and most effectively. Historically (if by "Cyber" this term can be used at all), IT security (meaning security focusing on technical measures and tools, i. e. software) drew from lessons learned in the military and defense area. This led to approaches fueled by the idea that only national products and services could be used to defend oneself against the outside world. We subsume these initiatives under the term "Cyber Sovereignty". The question of national cyber sovereignty is discussed frequently on panels, summits, and conferences, e. g. on the Munich Security Conference MSC on a panel discussion at the 2. International Cyber Security Conference 2016. National vendors emerge claiming to be 100% trustworthy as they develop and produce only in a national market[2].

The number, the complexity, and the heterogeneity of cyber adversaries (including individuals, organizations, networks, and technologies) cannot be defeated by one nation or one community alone but needs to rely on the full potential of tools, software, services, organizations, knowledge, and people available to the modern company and its management. Attackers organize their skills and develop their technological arsenal globally – so why would an approach limited to national borders be more effective or efficient?

If national thinking can't be the answer to Cyber risks – what can? In our view, Cyber Sovereignty must be based on knowledge, not on national boundaries. This knowledge in the increasingly complex world of cyber products and services must be created jointly and independently, and must be easily available from a trusted source.

---

[1] Spot check of 4 major DAX companies in 2015 (financial, health care, automotive, and chemical industries).
[2] See e. g. "IT Security made in Germany" initiative from 2012.

With the founding of the DCSO (Germany Cyber Security Organization – Deutsche Cyber Sicherheits-Organisation[3]) four major DAX companies have founded a managed security service company that will provide best-of-breed services to the German industry and its value chain. A study from 2015, conducted among the founding members' information security staff, showed that among the needed services "Proof of Concept Testing for Security Products" ranked top. Security professionals in all companies searched for a way to evaluate tools, products, and services in the area of information security or with considerable impact on information security. The DCSO team lead by security professionals from Allianz and researchers from the Ludwig Maximilian University Munich (LMU) developed a concept of evaluation that aims at giving its customers back Cyber Sovereignty. Besides evaluation products and services, the concept also generates knowledge about the right integration and usage of a product or service. We call this DCSO product "Product Evaluation and Integration" in short PEI.

Key principles of this PEI service are objectivity and independence, usable and customer focused results, completeness and timeliness, quality and transparency.

Customers have access to three distinct but connected sub-services:

1. a cyber-landscape ranking and classifying over 800 security products and services (or products and services with considerable impact on security)
2. a database of test results from the detailed evaluation of products and services – each done in a PoC (Proof of Concept)
3. an implementation guidance from our testers and administrators on tested products and services as a knowledge base when applying the product/the service

Basis for the testing is the foundation of a virtual enterprise, the so called "DCSO Blue Print SE". This virtual company comprises the common core of the DCSO founding members and its advisory board. This company is "headed" by the PEI team and uses every security product or service in its own infrastructure.

To get usable and customer focused results that allow for a comparison of products and services, the DCSO Blue Print SE has comparable tools, software products, network designs and, very importantly, IT and security processes where a security product must show its value in connection with other tools and software and in well-defined processes.

The evaluation of a product or service with the help of the DCSO Blue Print SE as well as with defined test procedures regarding the trustworthiness of the vendor, product functionalities, security testing (i.e. penetration testing), and the feedback from the DCSO community allow for a knowledgeable assessment of a product regardless of its national origin. Using the PEI service and its database, local and national companies can execute their Cyber Sovereignty in choosing deliberately and knowingly from a catalogue of products which promises the best merit to their security.

---

[3] DCSO – www.dcso.de – established by Allianz SE, BASF SE, Bayer AG and Volkswagen AG in November 2015.

The capability to obtain such knowledge and decision making skills must be delegated to an objective and trustworthy entity. They cannot be generated alone in one company anymore as the number of PoCs, assessments, and evaluations outgrows the potential of any single IT Security department.

79.2 General Idea

79.2.1 Founding of DCSO

In early 2015, the CIOs of four major DAX companies decided to cooperate in depth in the area of cyber security and operational cyber security services. Their idea was supported by the German Ministry of the Interior. The general idea of "making Germany more secure" and building a service company "business for business" (b4b) was in line with several other initiatives from various players in the DAX community like the foundation of the CSSA (Cyber Security Sharing and Analytics association[4]) or the Digital Society Institute at the ESMT[5].

Founders' security experts were tasked with setting up the new company as a start-up-like business in Berlin and Munich focusing on building a service portfolio, adding value to existing security tools and processes. Besides the founding companies and the German Ministry of the Interior 25 DAX/MDAX companies and institutions are organized in an advisory board to steer the young company and develop its service portfolio further.

79.2.2 Community Approach – the General Idea to Gain Sovereignty

One corner stone of the DCSO is the greater idea of forming a user community to support each other in tackling a problem too big for one single player. This idea was already successfully implemented at CSSA.

The basic concept behind the traditional definition of sovereignty bases on the same idea: one community (i. e. a nation and its government) defines a trusted space in which solutions can be found that are not shared with adversaries. However, in the cyber world national boundaries have lost their meaning just as they already had in the business world for multinational companies. The new concept that is needed is based on the community approach. Cyber security fulfills all the needed criteria for forming a community among business players:

---

[4] CSSA: founded in November 2014 by seven major German companies as an alliance for jointly facing cyber security challenges in a proactive, fast and effective manner as an association (Cyber Security Sharing and Analytics e. V.) in Berlin.
[5] ESMT Berlin was founded in 2015 by leading global companies and institutions to support society on its secure way in the digital era.

1. The problem is agnostic to their business, meaning all companies irrelevant of their industry face the same problem
2. The solution doesn't hold potential for a strategic business advantage, meaning that the implementation of effective cyber defenses doesn't directly lead to a competitive advantage but the lack thereof poses an immense risk
3. Players are heterogeneous enough to profit from sharing experiences and knowledge, meaning that among the DAX/MDAX companies security teams have specialized in different areas due to the lack of resources
4. The market has so far not developed a suitable or comparable solution that would be an alternative to forming a community

The other advantage of true sovereignty in a certain field lies in the trustworthiness of the solution. It is reckoned that within one's chain of development and production one controls all relevant steps and thus the trustworthiness of the final solution. In cyber security and more generally in IT the pursuit of such sovereignty is extremely hard to realize. Interconnections, dependencies and R&D investments are too complex or high to enable one single nation to master all aspects alone. Nevertheless, cyber security depends on trustworthy components.

The solution to this challenge can also be found in the community approach. The setup of the PEI service at DCSO relies on intensive testing and evaluation of products to minimize the so-called "bad apple" problem of integrating an unsecure security solution in one's security architecture. Furthermore, the testing concentrates among other things on the trust aspect of the provider. Various information sources and numerous experiences and references can be combined to form a holistic picture of the service provider or manufacturer.

As the community consists of users and experts in the field of business security architectures sharing knowledge, experiences, and also text scenarios and test bed installations security products and services can be rated and evaluated according to their potential for integration. The potential for integration is defined by the PEI team as a product's or service's ability to integrate itself seamlessly in a commonly accepted blue print architecture. The idea behind this KPI is the reasoning that a product might be perfect on its own to solve a given problem but cannot deliver this value in combination with existing systems like SIEM, LogFile Repositories, IDS, firewalls, and especially existing processes (manual, semi-automatic and automatic). For a CISO or a SOC Manager this capability cannot be underestimated. Our experiences show that a CISO would rather opt for the 2nd best product if well integrated than for the best single product on the market.

The PEI cyber security community's USP lies mainly in the evaluation of integration. It is an essential piece of information about a security product or service.

Coming back to the general idea of founding a cyber security service provider from the industry for the industry and generating cyber security sovereignty, the PEI service and the closed community of user companies and their knowledge is currently the best implementation known to the authors and the DCSO community. The successful combination of a service provider approach with the strength of the digital community approach in a closed environment gives its members cyber security sovereignty through knowledge sharing and closed group testing rather than using traditional national concepts.

79.3 Product Evaluation and Integration (PEI) as a Service

This section shortly describes the features and unique selling points of the PEI service. To this end, first, a general overview of the project idea and its core components is given. Subsequently, the particular sub-services of the PEI service are discussed in a more technical way.

79.3.1 The PEI Services – a General Overview

The key idea of the PEI service is to provide a comprehensive and novel service for deeply investigating and analyzing IT security products, including both hardware and software solutions. Furthermore, the PEI service provides tools and the competence to identify suitable products fitting the current needs of its customers. The following three components are seen as the key drivers of the PEI service:

1. The PEI Landscape of Security Products
   The PEI Service maintains a comprehensive database of available IT security products. This enables customers to easily identify up-to-date products for protecting their systems and services against security threads.
2. The PEI Testbed
   The PEI team hosts various servers for simulating a corporate network infrastructure. The PEI testbed enables system administrators to quickly provide the setup for testing several security products in real world scenarios.
3. The PEI Production Line
   This is the core of the PEI service: The PEI production line defines several modules for analyzing and testing security products with respect to various objectives. Most of the tests are performed after the product has been successfully integrated into the PEI testbed. For example, scalability of the product is tested; to this end, load tests are being performed in order to analyze whether the product is applicable in mid- to large-scale environments.

   In the following, these components are discussed more in depth.

79.3.2   The PEI Landscape of Security Products

The PEI service aims to provide a comprehensive and up-to-date database of security products. Products are classified and categorized in accordance to their intended purpose. Companies and users can benefit from this database by easily accessing information about how they can protect their networks against recent security threads. The PEI landscape provides the tools for monitoring the market of security solutions and guides the user to novel and/or alternative products for specific purposes. For example, a company/user observing recent attacking attempts, can refer to the landscape to quickly identify suitable products for protecting against these threats.

For this purpose, first, a unique taxonomy was developed and proposed by the PEI team allowing to clearly classify several security products into various categories. Subsequently, the categories are merged with the possible threats which they will prevent.

This taxonomy is based on technical guidelines presented by the BSI[6] (the German Federal Office for Information Security) and others.

79.3.3   The PEI Testbed

The PEI testbed is a cloud-based network infrastructure (private cloud) that enables testers to quickly install security products. The testbed simulates a company network with all the services that are commonly installed in those environments (e. g. several client systems, e-mail services, databases, etc.). Testers can quickly integrate new products and perform several tests, e. g. functional testing, load testing, and penetration testing. Also, the compatibility of the product to other components of the testbed can be analyzed.

79.3.4   The PEI Production Line

In general, multiple IT security products can be investigated and analyzed simultaneously. For this to work, each product is placed on a virtual "production line" and runs through various "production steps". As, in general, multiple products need to be investigated, several production lines are installed and run in parallel.

This is depicted in Fig. 79.1: Here, a production line is shown (denoted as "Production Line 1"). This production line provides several modules (e. g. the virtual "production steps"). Each module requires some input (e. g., information, results from another module, technical prerequisites etc.) and provides some technical or non-technical output (e. g. analysis results, documentation, measurement results, etc.). Each module of a production line can be initiated as soon as the required input is available. This enables the PEI team

---

[6] As a basis for the taxonomy various technical guidelines of the BSI such as BSI TR-03108 or BSI TR-03103 were used.

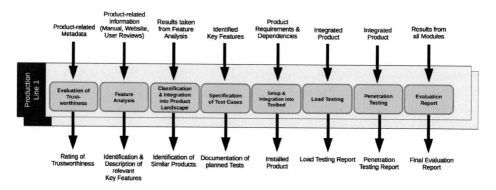

Fig. 79.1 Product Evaluation and Integration – Production Line

to not only parallelize progress by working simultaneously on multiple, *independent* production lines; beyond this, work distribution is optimized by enabling the team to work efficiently on several modules that are part of the *same* production line.

In the following, the particular modules of a production line are discussed, including their respective dependencies/requirements and the provided outcome. It might be noteworthy to mention that, despite of the fact that most production lines of the PEI service look very similar to the production line depicted here, some product-related adaptations and extensions might be beneficial to the analysis of some products.

In general, the modules of a production line are as follows:

1. Evaluation of trustworthiness
   To this end, the credibility of its origin (i. e. the vendor of the product or the organization behind the product) is evaluated and rated based on internal criteria. Furthermore, the trustworthiness of the product itself is evaluated. This is done by deeply analyzing the background of the product, screening security databases for known open issues and previous vulnerabilities that appeared in the past. Also, the responsiveness of the vendor is considered as an important factor; it is measured how fast and how extensive the vendor reacted in order to cope with open issues in the past.
2. Feature Analysis
   In this step, relevant product features are identified and selected. In particular, vendor-provided information is considered as an input for this module
3. Classification and Integration into Product Landscape
   The previously selected features are weighted based on their importance and the product is integrated into the product landscape. Therefore, the product features are classified with respect to various categories of the landscape.
4. Specification of Test Cases
   In this step, (technical) test cases are being defined as a pre-requirement for further, technical analysis of the product. Despite the fact that this module discusses rather

technical details of the PEI evaluation service, this does indeed involve some important management decisions: This module defines both the breadth and depth of all subsequent tests that will be performed for the respective product.

As part of this module, prerequisites are identified that are needed in order to perform further testing, including, but not limited to the following:

- Which features of the product should be tested, to what depth, and how?
- How should load testing be performed? Which parts of the products should be analyzed with respect to various load settings?
- What should be the focus of the penetration testing to be performed?

5. Setup and Integration into the testbed

   In this step, the product to be tested is integrated into the PEI testbed installation. The product is linked to several other services of the testbed, e. g. for installing an antivirus product, e-mail messaging servers are configured accordingly in such a way that all incoming/outgoing e-mails are inspected before delivery.

   The output of this module is twofold: first, it provides the installation of the product itself, which is a prerequisite for the load testing and penetration testing steps. Second, expert knowledge is derived from the installation process itself. Any difficulties that come with the integration of the product itself are documented, and all the odds and ends that need to be considered by the system administrator are mentioned.

6. Load Testing

   This is a highly technical module: here, the product is tested with respect to different load settings, i. e., various load patterns are simulated inside the testbed installation and the performance of the product is examined. During these tests, CPU and memory usage are constantly being monitored in order to derive evidence whether the product is able to cope with various load settings.

7. Penetration Testing

   This module analyzes certain security aspects of the product. Here, several penetration testing steps are being performed. Depending on the characteristics of the product, various standards are being considered by the PEI team (as an example, the recommendations of the OWASP Application Security Verification Standard are built into several test cases).

8. Evaluation Report

   This is the overall outcome of all test modules of a production line. All findings and insights made during the testing period are collected, scored, and documented.

In the foregoing section the three key components of the PEI Service were presented. It focused on the details of the PEI Landscape product taxonomy, the technical aspects of the PEI testbed and the different steps of the PEI product evaluation.

79.4 Conclusion, Portability, and Outlook

Indeed, cyber sovereignty is something desired by CISOs, SOC Managers and CIOs alike. The advisory board of DCSO has selected the PEI service to be among the top three services to be developed primarily.

The presented PEI service shows a way to profit from the idea of sovereignty in the cyber world without the limitations of national boundaries. To achieve sovereignty by knowledge, the national concept is abandoned in favor of a closed community group of users building a service that leverages the power of modern testing facilities with the combined knowledge and references of major business players and their expert teams.

The PEI service is available not only to DAX/MDAX companies or members of the DCSO advisory board but is made available in general to industrial users. To best share the efforts in costs for this service, the service is offered as a subscription.

The presented concept of community building for problems too big for a single player can be transferred to other areas as well. It is important to respect the needed prerequisites as stated in Sect. 79.1 and to facilitate the usability by a service company. If needed, this service company must be designed and founded just for that purpose. It is imperative to keep this company/service provider neutral and objective as far as vendors and security providers are concerned.

Coming back to the problem of finding suitable and effective security products and services, the PEI service does not only have the position of a testing service. In contrast to, e. g., state owned testing services the PEI service has the obligation to steer providers and give feedback to producers. Problems found in a product or service must be eradicated. Missing components must be named and roughly defined in order to give providers a chance to build better products and services to ensure the ongoing security of its customers, i. e. the community.

In addition to that the PEI service will play the role of a facilitator and promoter of new ideas and technology companies. It lies in the interest of the community to give new players a chance and foster start-up companies to develop new ideas against attacks and vulnerabilities. Only through the constant evolution of security products and services can the race against attackers be followed.

Acknowledgements
The authors like to thank Dr. Ralf Schneider (CIO of Allianz) and Rainer Göttmann (CEO of metafinanz) for giving us the opportunity of working in this great project. Furthermore, we like to thank Mrs. Nina Schläger for the tedious proof-reading work of our article.

Further Reading

1. Open Web Application Security Project: Application Security Verification Standard 3.0, h. O. (kein Datum).

Smart Authentication, Identification and Digital Signatures as Foundation for the Next Generation of Eco Systems

Markus Hertlein, Pascal Manaras, and Norbert Pohlmann

Abstract

Nowadays the daily live relies on digital identities, mainly in the context of the Internet. These identities are used for opening a bank account, for online shopping, to access company resources in the business environment and in many more situations. Therefor it is necessary to have strong identification and authentication of the identities owner and to create legally binding electronic signatures. Today password- and TAN-based authentication is still the most prevalent form of authentication. But with new requirements emerging from new scenarios like the Internet-of-Things (IoT) password-based authentication mechanisms become outdated. A new approach for identification, authentication and electronic signature creation is the use of the user's smartphone, equipped with cryptographic material in combination with protocol-based authentication instead of transmission of secrets. Furthermore this setup enables the use of one system in different scenarios and ECO-Systems. Interoperability and federation with existing authentication and identification systems is the key for a wide spread acceptance by service providers. From the users point of view the use of its own smartphone is more comfortable than handling passwords and usernames. That leads to a high level of acceptance by potential users. The idea is to provide an adaptive multifactor authen-

M. Hertlein (✉) · P. Manaras
XignSys GmbH
Gelsenkirchen, Germany
e-mail: hertlein@xignsys.com

P. Manaras
e-mail: manaras@xignsys.com

N. Pohlmann
Institute for Internet-Security
Gelsenkirchen, Germany
e-mail: pohlmann@internet-sicherheit.de

tication that can be used flexibly in many different use cases from business or IoT-platforms to the use in the urban environment of smart-cities. For an easy integration and a high degree of usability different entry points for authentication and electronic signature creation are used. As example for a modern and smart identification, authentication and electronic signature system the XignQR system [1] will be described in the following chapters.

80.1 Introduction

20 years ago only a few people would have thought, that the rise of the Internet would affect our lifestyles in such a fundamental way, as it's the case today. The handling of transactions, the opening of a bank account and even shopping are only the beginning of internet-based applications. As a whole, all provided services gain sensibility in the face of its users' data, which is a part of their digital identities and thus needs to be stored in a secure manner. The access to and the use of a digital identity need to be restricted to the user, which it represents. To check if a user is the user he claims to be and if he is allowed to use a certain digital identity, different service providers use different forms of user authentication. On one hand this authentication chaos leads to many different trust levels of the provided digital identities. On the other hand the user has to manage all these different authentication forms (s. Fig. 80.1). The effect is that the usability and the security of the system are limited.

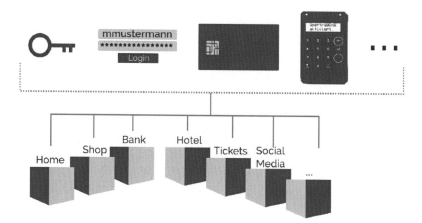

Fig. 80.1 Overview of the different authentication forms

80.1.1 Trust Is Everything

Passwords & The Hack of TV Monde

The most prevalent form of authentication is the combination of an username and a corresponding password. This form is considered as insecure and longwinded [2]. To counteract these problems, XignSys developed a concept for a modern authentication and digital signature system called XignQR, that doesn't rely on passwords, but on strong cryptography. Relying on a challenge response mechanism and backed by a PKI [3], XignQR eliminates the need for passwords completely. As passwords are the most prevalent form of authentication today, they have to be very secure, to prevent fraud or identity theft. Secure passwords have certain properties, such as a minimal length or special characters that must be contained, that add to the complexity of the use of passwords. As a result the password will be written down or stored in an insecure manner by most users.

The consequences of handling passwords that way were demonstrated by the hack of TV Monde a French TV broadcaster. The passwords needed for authentication were written down on piece of paper that was visible during a live news broadcast and were subsequently exploited by hackers.

Validity of Data

Since more and more commercial Internet services emerge, a service provider needs to have confidence in the data that is provided by its users. Therefore he must ensure that the data provided is valid, to prevent identity fraud and to protect its business. In this context XignQR offers two very trustworthy identification mechanisms that rely on the new German identity card. Besides being able to electronically read the information stored on the id card, XignQR supports a new mechanism called VideoIdent, with which the user is identified via a video chat application while presenting the id card and certain built in security features.

Several service providers depend on the personal data of users in order to deliver their services accordingly. Besides that, most users are registered with more than one of them (e. g. EBay and Amazon). That means, that their data is spread over all services they registered with. With XignQR the spread of personal user data can be reduced.

The whole system is designed to store and deliver information of different kinds in many different formats. Relying on standard technologies and protocols, the system can be integrated into a variety of services. Using the XignQR system the user has total control over the flow of his personal data, as he can also prevent the transmission of his data to the service provider.

80.1.2 Achieving Trust in the User's Identity

Besides user identification, authentication is a main task for using a digital identity. The XignQR system uses the user's personalized smartphone as a personal authentication device (PAD) and a QR Code for the identification of a service provider (e. g. Website, Terminal, Shop System, . . .). The authentication process can be described as: 1. Scan QR Code 2. Check the required and optional attributes 3. Confirm the process.

Due to the use of the QR Code, the XignQR System can be used everywhere a QR Code can be displayed or printed. Using smartphone as PAD results in to two main benefits: On one hand a personal digital identity could be used in a variety of use cases beginning from the login at webpages at home or at work to the authentication at terminals in urban areas. On the other hand it is possible to provide a very secure solution that is still easy to use.

Strong Adaptive Multi-Factor-Authentication

XignQR introduces a smart mechanism for authentication – called adaptive multi-factor authentication (A-MFA) – that makes use of the user's and the service provider's preferences. The authentication factor can be dynamically negotiated during the authentication process. It is possible that a login into a website can be done by scanning the QR Code without any further interaction, only exposing a unique user-pseudonym for that service. But if a user wants to unlock a car-sharing vehicle, he can be forced to enter a PIN or to use a biometric factor or even a combination of several factors.

Authentication as a Service

Add to that, the infrastructure of the XignQR system cannot only be used to authenticate users, but also to authenticate any system against another. That means XignQR can also be applied in the context of the Internet of Things and Industry 4.0.

80.1.3 Affected Markets

National borders do not limit today's markets. Trading has developed to a globally interacting eco system. As part of the digital transformation the EU released the eIDAS regulation [4]. The eIDAS regulation enables the digitalization of all paper-based processes for national and international trading. XignQR relying on digital signatures and smartphone based A-MFA in combination with eIDAS, enables usable mobile digital signatures for legally signing documents, transaction, bills and other data in the cloud. That leads to a completely new set of use cases, simplifying our private and business lives.

80.2 Concepts

This chapter focuses on some of the core concepts of the XignQR system, which enables the development of new markets, such as mobile shopping but also secures existing markets such as Online-Banking, Online-Shopping and authentication in general. The main idea behind XignQR is the separation from the user data that is necessary to fulfill a service, the identification of the service and the authentication process itself. The general

Fig. 80.2 Concept of the components interaction

idea is to have a QR Code to dynamically a service, the users personalized smartphone to authenticate the user and the trusted third party as trust anchor s. Fig. 80.2.

80.2.1 Requirements

A modern and secure authentication system, must fulfill several requirements to be widely accepted. Since acceptance is a requirement for the use of the system itself, we'll list the most important requirements:

- High Level of Security and low complexity
- Balance between security and usability
- Simple integration in existing systems
- Interoperability, flexibility and maintainability
- Protection of data and data thrift
- No additional hardware requirement (such as card readers)
- Transparency and informational self-determination
- Simple to manage

XignQR addresses these requirements through the use existing technologies. The wide spread of smart devices and the XignApp, as a part of the XignQR system, enables the use of the QR code as an entry point for authentication and thus the elimination of passwords in lots of different scenarios.

80.2.2 Registration & Identification

Digital identities build the foundation of authentication in the digital world. These identities are generated when the user registers with a service provider and consists of parts of the users real identity. Since the validity of data is essential to the service provider, the collection of data in a trustworthy manner is crucial. The trustworthy collection of data can be referred to as identification and is one of the most important features provided by the XignQR system. XignQR supports four Levels of identification, the trust levels. Each level distinguishes itself from the others by the trustworthiness of the collected data.

Level 1 – Not Verified
The user types in his personal data manually. The data has no trust anchor and is not verified. As a trusted third party does not verify the data, Level 1 is the lowest trust level supported by XignQR.

Level 2 – E-Mail Verification
The user verifies his identity via e-mail. During registration the user has to provide his e-mail address to which the system sends an e-mail containing a special link. Following this link verifies the possession of the provided address and thus the identity of the user. Since the only verified data is the e-mail address itself, this level is suitable for authentication at blogs or social networks, but not at e-business websites.

Level 3 – VideoIdent
The user proves his identity via video chat. A trained staff member that is connected to the user through the video chat application checks the user's identity. The German Federal Financial Supervisory Authority (BaFin) approved this form identification in 2014 and today several businesses emerged, providing or using such mechanism to identify their users at registration. The identification via VideoIdent is used especially in Germany, since on one hand the eID-functionality of the new German ID card, which enables the id card's ability to be electronically read, is not activated in most of the issued cards. On the other hand many service providers do not support eID as the required security infrastructure is very expensive. The use of VideoIdent only results in level 3 trust because the person checking the identity of the user can make a mistake at some point, which results in accepting false data or manipulated id cards.

Level 4 – eID
The user proves his identity via the eID-functionality of his id card. Since the data read from the card is sovereign information and the process of collecting the data cannot be prone to human error, it is very trustworthy [5]. Registration via the ID card results in the highest trust level supported by the system, because the design of the ID card guarantees confidence in the data read. At this point we have to add, that the security of and the con-

fidence in the data is achieved through a trade-off in usability, because every workstation must have a NFC card reader and an eID-client installed.

The data that is collected during the registration and identification process is converted into a distinct ID, the so-called derived identity. The derived identity can be represented in different formats, one of which is a representation as a digital certificate, which is used by XignQR. The digital certificate (i. e. the derived identity) is installed on the user's device during the personalization process and is subsequently used to authenticate against the system.

Personalization

The personalization process takes place right after the registration is completed. It consists of several stages involving the generation of digital certificates by a Public Key Infrastructure (PKI), binding the certificates and cryptographic keys to the device and storing necessary information in the system and on the device.

80.2.3   Strong Adaptive Multi-Factor-Authentication (A-MFA)

Authentication is achieved through interaction of all components of XignQR. This way XignQR offers strong and usable MFA providing several features such as pseudonymity to prevent tracking of users across multiple domains or services.

New Factors for Multi-Factor-Authentication

Additionally to the known factors possession, knowledge and inherence, XignQR realizes new combinations of factors. Through the cryptographically bound hardware token (XignSC) a new scheme called multiple possession is introduced by which the requirement for input of a PIN is eliminated. Authentication via PIN and VideoIdent can be requested for access management in high security environments or for critical processes. During authentication the user must then present his ID card and type in his PIN to accomplish the process.

Multi-Layered Security

Since the system counts on smart devices as a personal authentication device, the sensors of the device can add to the security of the authentication process. In general the information used, is called contextual information and consists of GPS data, network information and data of other sensors such as the gyroscope or the acceleration sensor. The information is processed and analyzed by the system to increase the trust in the authentication process. The processed information can be used to detect fraudulent behavior and forms the base for the request of additional authentication factors during authentication.

Choose the Required Authentication Factors

The user can choose the authentication factors, which are required for the use of the Xign-App. For non-critical applications he can for example forgo the use of PIN and is thus able to use the XignApp without further interaction. That means the user can set its own personal security level. While this might be beneficial for the user, the security of a service provider can also be jeopardized through this mechanism. As a result the use of the right authentication factors depends on both parties, the user and service provider. If a user's personal security level is too low, the service provider is able to enforce a certain security level for the authentication.

Smartphone as a Secure Display

While using password based authentication mechanisms the user has no insurance that the display shows correct data. XignQR provides a secure display using the smartphone and the XignApp. The XignApp shows information about the service provider. Additionally the user can choose which personal information is transferred to the service provider. If the authentication takes place in the process of carrying out a transaction, the XignApp also shows the transaction data, which will be processed by the server. s. Fig. 80.3. The user can verify the validity of the shown data. Any tampering can thus be recognized and the void transaction can be cancelled.

Fig. 80.3 XignAPP with data
to be verified before signing.
Example payment transaction

80.2.4   Beyond Authentication

For the process of digitalization it is necessary to have trusted and legally bound processes. The foundation for legal digital processes is electronic signatures. As mentioned the European Union has released the eIDAS regulation. The eIDAS regulation allows two new kinds of electronic signatures. The first on one is the creation of electronic seals. Electronic seals are signatures bound to legal instead of natural persons. The second innovation is the possibility to create legal electronic signatures in the cloud, the Remote Qualified Electronic Signatures (rQES).

Remote Qualified Electronic Signatures With rQES the user has the possibility to digitally sign contracts and documents and to checkout shopping carts of online shops while on the go. Due to that fact many new use cases are emerging. The creation of legal electronic signatures needs a very high level of trust and confidence. Therefor strong identification and authentication is mandatory. XignQR with its smartphone-based A-MFA offers an authentication form that allows creation of rQES. Furthermore the QR code initiated authentication process matches the flexibility and usability that is necessary to reach many users and service providers.

For the user and for the service provider the sequence for creating a rQES is very similar to the authentication process. The service provider sends the data that should be signed to the XignQR signing service and receives a QR code. The user scans the QR code with his XignAPP. To be able to validate the data, the XignApp displays the corresponding information to the user before signing. s. Fig. 80.3. If the user accepts the data and initiates the signing process the strong authentication process will be started. On success the data will be signed on the server-side and transmitted to the service. For the user the whole process is as easy as the authentication process.

80.3   The Use Cases

This section focuses on the use cases that are covered by the XignQR system. The use cases are categorized and distinguished by different sectors.

80.3.1   Governance

Over the years governments started offering certain governmental services to their citizens to relieve the corresponding agencies of their workload, which in turn means a reduction of costs. The provided services range from the reservation of license plates to the notification of a change of one's residential address. To fulfill their services these institutions have to identify the user. Since in Germany the majority of citizens refused to activate the eID functionality of their id cards only a few citizens are able to use the governmental services, because the agencies don't support any other authentication mechanism.

With XignQR agencies are able to provide services all users alike, as the data collected in level 3 and 4 is sovereign and thus trusted.

80.3.2 Enterprise

In an enterprise there are lots of tasks that require authentication. Employees must authenticate to gain physical access to the premises of their workplace, typically realized via a smartcard-based employee ID cards. The employee then has to log into his workstation using his password and username, which were generated by the IT department of their employer.

Besides recovering lost and replacing stolen passwords, the IT department also has to enforce change of these regularly which adds to the complexity of IT management. The larger the enterprise the larger complexity dealing with passwords. Since XignQR can be delivered as on-premise solution, these complexities can be dealt with easily, because XignQR does not rely on passwords, but on a Public Key Infrastructure. Lost or stolen credentials can be revoked and replaced easily with a single click.

Alongside authentication, signatures also play a major role in larger enterprises. There are contracts, transactions or vacation requests that have to be authorized by a superior. Problems occur if one or more superiors are not available, due to illness or external meetings.

These problems are conquered using XignQR. Relying on asymmetric cryptography the concept of digital signatures is used throughout the whole XignQR system. Using the smartphone enables superiors to easily sign, which has to be signed. Additionally the amount of paper used, can also be drastically reduced, hence enabling digital transformation.

80.3.3 Financial Sector

In the financial sector every single process needs a high level of confidence. Starting from the access to the online banking portal over stock trading to all kinds of direct trading from B2C, C2C, and B2B.

In particular the security level and the usability level can vary in a very broad range in the financial sector. One the one-side there are high-value transactions that have to be confirmed by more than one person and must strictly bound to a user and on the other-side there are low-value transaction, where the user wants the transaction to happen seamlessly.

XignQR with its ability to manage the level of trust between security and usability, is able to answer this challenge.

For example, a transaction that transfers a high value could be secured with the combination of three factors. Therefor the signature will only be created if the user is in possession of the XignAPP, knows the corresponding PIN and a face-recognition algorithm has verified the user's identity by the use of the smartphone camera.

A low value transaction could be signed using the XignAPP in combination with a PIN omitting the confirmation display.

80.3.4   xCommerce

Commerce and shopping use cases are depending on transaction and user attraction. In the online environment a shop must be very easy to use. In the best case the user is able to purchase products without the need of long registration processes. If the user has to authenticate itself against the shop, the authentication failure rate must be as small as possible. If that criteria are not matched the shop will miss spontaneous purchases.

XignQR enables an online shop owner to focus on its products, instead of the user-management processes. A XignQR user can fill his shopping cart and start the direct checkout by scanning the displayed QR Code. The items of the shopping cart will be concatenated with the users personal data and will be signed using the user's personal cryptographic material. The shop owner is now able to invoice. With XignQR e- and mCommerce and retail trade can be easily connected. The QR Code cannot only be generated dynamically. A static QR code can be used to identify items instead of service providers. An example in which retail trading and online commerce get in touch is the window shopping scenario. s. Fig. 80.4.

Fig. 80.4 QR Codes as bridge between retail trading and online commerce

80.3.5   Online – X

Most users will use XignQR for their daily online life that consists of logging into blogs, social networks or other platforms, that don't need much of user information. Most sites operate on a single verified information, i. e. the email address. Though these sites pose little to no harm to the user if credentials are lost or stolen (financial loss or endangerment of personal health), no one wants attackers to harm one's online reputation. XignQR helps service providers such as blogs, platforms or other websites to prevent the taking over of accounts by attackers. XignQR is designed to be easily integrated into websites via several protocols SAML or OpenID Connect and facilitates the protection of user accounts.

80.3.6   Internet of Things and Industry 4.0

It is predicted that until 2020 there will be up to 30 billion devices [6] connected to the Internet. To ensure a minimum level of security every device has to be authenticated to be able to automatically access data and resources. Beside the authentication of the device to a network and other devices, the authentication by a user against IoT devices will be one of the most authentication scenarios in the near future. Because of the amount of authentications it will be necessary that the authentication process is easy, fast and secure.

Since IoT connects the real and digital world IT security and thereby strong authentication becomes an important part to ensure safety.

The DDOS attacks with the "Mirai botnet" [7] in October 2016 shows, that the use of password-based authentication is insufficient.

To solve the IoT password problem the devices can be equipped with digital certificates and digital attribute certificates. With that combination the IoT devices can be connected to the XignQR infrastructure. The devices are now able to authenticate them self against other devices connected to the XignQR infrastructure in the same way a user will authenticate its self by using the smartphone. The authentication process is completely the same, only the smartphone is replaces by the IoT device. The entry point for the devices authentication can be a QR Code, like it is in the users authentication process, but also other authentication trigger can be included, for example an alert of an temperature sensor.

The identification of a device with a QR Code or NFC trigger helps to gain maximum flexibility. If a user wants to interact with an IoT device, it can use XignQR to authenticate itself in the same way the user authenticates itself against a website. On the one hand XignQR implements a high level of security by the substitution of the insecure password based authentication, for example the mentioned "Mirai Botnet" attack could not be realized with the use of XignQR. And on the other hand a user can easily interact with the IoT devices [8], also in an environment where the implementation of keyboards or other hardware is expensive or no possible, for example in the urban environment of "smart cities".

The digitalization of the production industry leads to many different and complex scenarios. It starts with the connection of different departments within a company and ends with the interconnection of production machines and the automation of production and business processes, based on decisions invoked by a machine signal. Therefor it is inalienable that process and data is authenticated.

But even the existing problems in the industry environment can be solved with XignQR. For example a massive problem is the access to production machines for maintaining.

Today the physical access to production machines is still done with a mechanical key and lock. To access the terminal at a production machine a strong password up to twenty and more characters is needed.

This combination is highly insecure and needs a lot of administration. For example, a maintenance worker needs to get the key to gain physical access and the strong password. The passwords are usually written down, because nobody is able to remember these types of passwords. Sometimes the passwords are directly noted at the terminal of the production machine.

The use of strong and flexible certificate based authentication is a solution the addresses all the mentioned problems.

Using XignQR improves the user experience for the administration and for the maintenance worker. An administrator can grant physical access for a defined timeframe to an explicit user or user group. And at the terminal there is no need for passwords, thereby no passwords can be written down at the terminal. Since the system can be remotely managed, also authorization processes can be implemented due to the substitution of the password.

80.4   The Authentication Process

The Fig. 80.5 shows the process of authentication with XignQR. Authentication is achieved through the interaction of the three main components of the system, the Xign Manager, the XignApp on the user's smartphone and the service provider. The Xign Manager builds the core of the system. It mediates between the XignApp and the service provider to authenticate users. Users are authenticated using the Xign App, while the Xign Manager delivers QR codes, authentication events and user information to the service provider, who then grants or denies access to his services on behalf of the received information. An authentication is initiated by the service provider that sends an authentication request to the Xign Manager. The Xign Manager responds with a QR code that has to be displayed to the user. The user scans the QR code using his Xign App to authenticate against the Xign Manager leveraging a cryptographic challenge-response-mechanism. The result of the challenge-response scheme is transferred back to the service provider afterwards. The result message contains the status of the corresponding authentication process and a token that is used to request the user information from the Xign Manager.

Fig. 80.5 Authentication
process

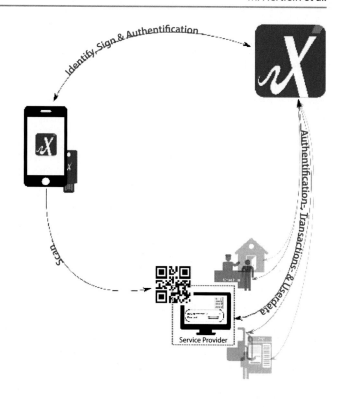

References

1. M. Hertlein, P. Manaras und N. Pohlmann, "Bring Your Own Devide For Authentication (BYOD4A)," in *In Proceedings of the ISSE 2015 – Securing Electronic Business Processes – Highlights of the Information Security Solutions Europe 20151 Conference*, Wiesbaden, Springer Vieweg Verlag, 2015.
2. C. Okyle, "Password Statistics: The Bad, the Worse and the Ugly (Infographic)," [Online]. Available: http://www.entrepreneur.com/article/246902 [Accessed 17 August 2016].
3. S. Goswami, S. Misra und M. Mukesh, "A replay attack resilient system for PKI based authentication in challenge-response mode for online application," *3rd International Conference on Eco-friendly Computation and Communication Systems*, 2014.
4. E. Union, "REGULATION (EU) No 910/2014 OF THE EUROPEAN PARLIAMENT AND OF THE COUNCIL," [Online]. Available: http://eur-lex.europa.eu/legal-content/EN/HTML/?uri=CELEX:32014R0910 [Accessed 17 August 2016].
5. M. Schröder und M. Morgner, "eID mit abgeleiteten Idenititäten," in *DuD Datenschutz und Datensicherheit 8-2013*, Heidelberg, Springer, 2006.
6. H. Bauer, M. Patel und J. Veira, "The Internet of Things: Sizing up the opportunity," [Online]. Available: http://www.mckinsey.com/industries/high-tech/our-insights/the-internet-of-things-sizing-up-the-opportunity. [Accessed 28 October 2016].
7. S. Cobb, "10 things to know about the October 21 IoT DDos attacks," [Online]. Available: http://www.welivesecurity.com/2016/10/24/10-things-know-october-21-iot-ddos-attacks/. [Accessed 28 October 2016].

8. M. Cagnazzo, M. Hertlein und N. Pohlmann, "Information and Software Technologies: An Usable Application of Authentication, Communication and Access Management in the Internet of Things," in *22nd International Conference, ICIST 2016*, Druskininkai, Lithuania, Springer International Publishing, 2016, pp. 722–731.

Implications of Vulnerable Internet Infrastructure

Haya Shulman

Abstract

As awareness for Internet attacks gains traction, multiple proposals for defences are put forth. The proposals include, among others, secure access and communication to services, such as web, email and instant messaging. Do these efforts suffice to guarantee a secure Internet for clients and services? To answer this question we review the state of the Internet infrastructure security and show that it is still largely vulnerable to attacks. Although defences exist, they mostly are deployed incorrectly or not deployed at all, hence not offering security benefits. We report on our studies of vulnerabilities and obstacles towards adoption of security mechanisms. We show how insecurity of Internet infrastructure foils security of defences for applications and provide example attacks against common systems.

81.1 Introduction

The last decade was marked with revelations on cyber espionage, monitoring and censorship by governments, devastating Denial of Service (DoS) and malware attacks launched by terror or military organizations, credentials and identity theft, robbery of sensitive and private information by cyber criminals, and more. The attacks target individuals, enterprises, governments, critical and civil infrastructures.

The surge of cyber attacks resulted in increased awareness to the need to protect the clients and services. As a result, during the last decade multiple defences were put forth for securing the communication between clients and services, most notably with the use

H. Shulman (✉)
Fraunhofer Institute for Secure Information Technology SIT
Darmstadt, Germany
e-mail: haya.shulman@sit.fraunhofer.de

© Springer-Verlag GmbH Germany 2018
C. Linnhoff-Popien et al. (eds.), *Digital Marketplaces Unleashed*,
https://doi.org/10.1007/978-3-662-49275-8_81

of SSL/TLS [RFC5246] for email, web servers and instant messaging. Indeed, a recent study (by heise.de) reported that encrypted traffic in the Internet reached 50%.

Intuitively it seems that protecting the communication to services should suffice to prevent attacks against clients. In particular, if the communication, say between a user and its bank, is encrypted and authenticated, then the attacker should not be able to snoop on the exchanged messages, nor modify them. In this chapter we consider the following question: *How effective are defences for clients and services in the current Internet?*

We answer this question in two steps. First, we review the security of the Internet's fundamental building blocks, focusing on the inter-domain routing with Border Gateway Protocol (BGP) [RFC1105], naming with Domain Name System (DNS) [RFC1035], and Small Office/Home Office routers [RFC3022]. As we report, not only do these critical systems have a long history of attacks, but they are also still susceptible to attacks on a daily basis. Many attacks are detected too late after a significant damage is inflicted, while a large number of others are not identified at all. Although defences exist, they mostly are not deployed. Worse, we show that deployed countermeasures are often not effective since many deployments of security are incorrect, leading to illusion of security.

Then, in the second step, we review a number of widely used security mechanisms, including password recovery on popular websites, anti-spam defences and encryption with SSL/TLS. We show that vulnerabilities in fundamental systems of the Internet render defences for clients and services exposed to attacks.

Our analysis and conclusions apply also to other fundamental Internet systems, such as Network Time Protocol (NTP), Internet telephony, cloud platforms and others.

Organization

In Sect. 81.2 we present selected Internet Infrastructure systems, discuss their vulnerabilities and attacks against them, and provide our measurements on the state of adoption of security mechanisms. In Sect. 81.3 we list popular defences and show that they can be foiled given the insecurity of Internet foundations. We conclude in Sect. 81.4.

81.2 Fundamental Internet Infrastructure Systems

In this Section we review Domain Name System (DNS), Border Gateway Protocol (BGP) and SOHO routers. BGP computes the path that the packets should take between communicating parties in the Internet, DNS provides an address of the destination while SOHO routers protect the networks of clients and enterprises.

DNS and BGP were not designed with security in mind, and both have experienced a long history of attacks. To mitigate the problems, security mechanisms were designed and standardized for both of them more than two decades ago. However, most of the networks and systems are still running the basic protocols without the security protection. Hence they are susceptible to frequent attacks. Even when security mechanisms are deployed, this is often done incorrectly, not offering any security benefits. The same applies to SOHO routers: although vulnerabilities are long known, many networks are vulnerable to attacks which allow attackers to take over the routers and networks. In this section we review the vulnerabilities, provide example attacks and report on our measurement evaluations showing that defences are mostly not deployed or deployed incorrectly.

81.2.1 Domain Name System (DNS)

Domain Name System (DNS), [RFC1034, RFC1035], plays a key role in the Internet: it translates domain names to IP addresses and provides a platform for distribution of security mechanisms, such as digital certificates [RFC6698], anti-spam defences [RFC7208]. For instance, when clients access websites the first step is a request to a DNS resolver asking to lookup an IP address for the desired domain name, say www.amazon.com. Using the IP address, the client can then access the service.

The correctness and availability of DNS are critical to the security and stability of the Internet. However, its significance also made it a target of attacks, most notably, DNS cache poisoning, [1–5].

DNS Cache Poisoning
In the course of a DNS cache poisoning attack the attacker provides spoofed values in DNS responses. In order for responses to be accepted by the victim, the attacker needs to match several fields, which are checked by the recipient's DNS software. These fields include the port from which the request was sent and a DNS transaction identifier (TXID). As a result, the victims are redirected to incorrect and attacker controlled hosts. DNS cache poisoning attack is initiated when a client sends a DNS request to the DNS server asking to look up a desired domain. If the attacker responds of a real DNS server instead, and the client accepts the response with malicious DNS records, it will have the IP address for an incorrect (malicious) machine, instead of a real one. If the client uses the malicious values it received from the attacker it is exposed to credentials theft, malware distribution, censorship and more. For instance, the attackers can utilize DNS cache poisoning to hijack emails to victim email servers in order to steal victims' credentials to sensitive services, such as ebay.com or amazon.com, by using their password recovery procedures. As we show in Sect. 81.3.1, the attackers can then hijack the victims' credentials that are sent by these services, since the credentials are sent to the incorrect email IP address provided by the attacker in poisoned DNS records.

DNS cache poisoning attacks are known to be practiced by governments, e. g., China for censorship, [6], USA with the *QUANTUMDNS* program [7] (see Fig. 81.1), as well as by cyber criminals. Research works also performed measurements of spoofed DNS responses in the Internet [8–11].

Fig. 81.1 QUANTUMDNS
program

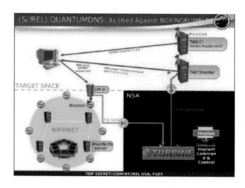

Defences Against Cache Poisoning

DNS cache poisoning is detrimental for the security and stability of the clients and services, yet cache poisoning attacks are often practiced by governments and cyber criminals. Due to the threat that cache poisoning attacks pose, multiple defences were proposed and standardized. Non cryptographic defences recommend randomizing values in the existing fields, such as in UDP and DNS headers, to make it difficult for the attacker to create a response with correct values. The most common defence is source port randomization and others, see [RFC5452]. Source port randomization makes the attack more difficult, since the attacker has to guess the port value in its malicious responses, so that it matches the value selected by the DNS resolver in its DNS request. Since the port is 16 bits long, the attacker can try multiple variations until a correct one is hit. In order to check how many systems adopted source port randomization we performed a large scale evaluation of port randomization in DNS resolvers in the Internet and found that 1% send DNS requests using static (fixed) source port and 17% use predictable ports, e. g., sequentially incrementing. These systems are trivially exposed to DNS cache poisoning attacks. In recent works [12, 13] we showed that some randomization algorithms, recommended and standardized in [RFC6056] are insecure. Hence also systems supporting these algorithms can be attacked.

Cryptographic defence with DNSSEC [RFC4033–RFC4035] recommends using digital signatures in order to authenticate the records in DNS responses. The receiver can then verify that the signatures over the records are correct. The security is guaranteed since only the domain owner is in possession of the secret signing key that produced the signatures. The attacker does not have the key and hence cannot generate signatures instead of the domain owner.

Although proposed in 1997, DNSSEC still is not widely deployed. One of the factors impeding deployment is the requirement for significant changes to the DNS infrastructure as well as to DNS protocol. In particular, the DNS server should serve signed records in DNS responses, which should then be validated on the client side by the DNS resolvers. The resolvers should accept and cache only the records with correct signatures. Unfortunately, studies show that less than 3% of DNS resolvers validate DNSSEC signatures

[14]. Furthermore, our recent measurement evaluation [15] of Top Level Domains (TLDs) and 1 M-top ranked domains on www.alexa.com (Second Level Domains (SLDs)), shows that 90% of *TLDs* and only a meagre fraction of 1.66% of the domains on Alexa list are signed. Since the users are typically interested in accessing domains on second level such as google.com, protecting the SLDs with DNSSEC is very important. Although very few domains are signed, our experimental evaluation shows that most of those are still not well protected. The problems are manifested in generation and deployment of crypto-graphic material. The first issue is related to validating keys. Specifically, in 0.89% TLDs and 19.46% Alexa domains it is not possible to establish validity of DNSSEC keys and as a result, the signed records in these domains cannot be validated. Another issue is related to the usage of short (insecure) keys. We measured the key sizes in use by the different variations of RSA algorithms. The results, plotted in Fig. 81.2, indicate that a large frac-tion of domains use short DNSSEC keys. In particular, almost 1.4 M keys are below 1024 bits and 10 K keys are 512 bits long [16]. showed that factoring 512 bit keys on a cloud is a practical task, hence these domains are exposed to DNS cache poisoning attacks.

We also found vulnerability in cryptographic material among the signed domains, which allows to subvert the security of the DNSSEC signatures, hence exposing the af-fected domains to attacks. The vulnerabilities are introduced by the registrars and DNS hosting providers which deploy DNSSEC incorrectly. The vulnerabilities are found in do-mains of popular and large registrars such as Network Solutions and GoDaddy.

The measurement results indicate that the majority of signed domains do not gain se-curity benefits by adopting cryptographic defences. Incorrect adoption of cryptographic protection generates an illusion of security causing the domain owners to believe that their clients are protected hence do not deploy additional measures to guarantee security.

We recently developed and set up an automated tool, [15], to measure and report progress in DNSSEC adoption and to evaluate misconfigurations and incorrect adoptions that lead to insecurity, https://dnssec.cad.sit.fraunhofer.de. Our online service allows to check which domains are vulnerable, and to obtain statistics for the status of domains overall.

Fig. 81.2 RSA keys' sizes

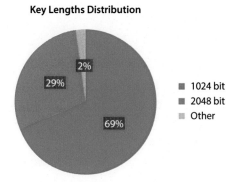

Key Lengths Distribution

81.2.2 Border Gateway Protocol (BGP)

The Border Gateway Protocol (BGP) computes routes between the tens of thousands of smaller networks, called Autonomous Systems (ASes), which make up the Internet. ASes range from large ISPs and content providers to small businesses and universities. In essence, BGP computes the routes that packets should take between a source and any destination in the Internet.

BGP Prefix Hijacks

BGP does not have any security integrated into it, hence is vulnerable to traffic hijacks whereby an attacking AS is able to divert traffic through an incorrect route, which typically includes attacker controlled links. This is done by advertising a prefix which the attacking AS does not own. This allows attackers to attract traffic not destined to them, and exposes the traffic to eavesdropping, censorship, distribution of malware and more. Indeed, BGP has a history of devastating attacks and configuration errors. Consequently, nation states and corporations are in constant danger from attacks that utilize BGP's insecurity to disconnect ASes from the Internet and to launch highly effective man-in-the-middle attacks.

Prefix hijacks are effective and easy to launch, with the extra benefit of a plausible excuse: benign configuration errors [17]. Every year there are thousands of prefix hijacks, some due to misconfigurations, while others are attacks [18–20], and many others go under the radar [21]. See for instance a recent hijacking event (Fig. 81.3) which allowed attackers to eavesdrop on traffic over a long period of time without being detected.

In this attack, the traffic was exchanged between end points in Mexico and the US. The traffic was hijacked by an attacker ISP in Eastern Europe. To avoid detection, the attackers

Fig. 81.3 Traffic hijacking event illustrated by Renesys

were rerouting the traffic back to the destination. This allowed the attack to go undetected for over half a year.

BGP Security

Today's agenda for securing BGP routing relies on Route-origin validation (ROV) [RFC6483, RFC6811] via the Resource Public Key Infrastructure (RPKI) [RFC6480], to protect against prefix hijacks.

RPKI deployment is still very limited and, as a result, prefix and subprefix hijacking remain highly successful. Indeed, to the present date only about 6% of IP prefixes in BGP tables are certified [22].

RPKI certificates bind an IP-prefix with the number and public key of its origin AS, i. e., the AS that "owns" that prefix. The prefix owner can then use its RPKI private key to sign a Route Origin Authorization (ROA) specifying which ASes are allowed to advertise in BGP that IP prefix (or its subprefixes). BGP routers can then utilize the information in that ROA to do route-origin validation (ROV), i. e., reject BGP announcements specifying unauthorized origin ASes for that prefix.

In a recent work we found that only a small number of ASes apply ROV [23]. Worse, a large fraction of signed prefixes are misconfigured [24, 25], further demotivating the adoption of ROV. Fig. 81.4 presents the results of measurement of the status of ROAs available in the January 2016 RPKI database, and the corresponding BGP announcements observed in Route Views, from [23]. The results include mismatches between ROAs and BGP announcements and show that a significant number (about 9%) of invalid BGP announcements, emitted by over 700 organizations, are misconfigured. A few of these may be actual prefix or subprefix hijacking attacks. Yet, the majority is surely a result of configuration errors. ROV performing BGP router would drop all of these announcements,

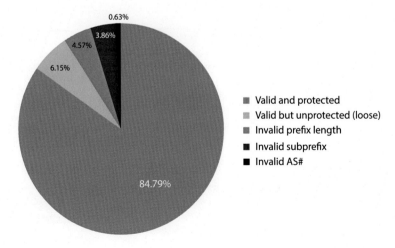

Fig. 81.4 Status of ROAs

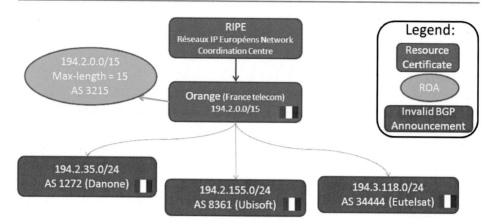

Fig. 81.5 Misconfigured ROA by Orange. (Cohen et al. [23])

thereby refusing to route a significant amount of legitimate traffic, causing loss of revenue and complaints from customers. To illustrate the problems we refer to two real life examples of incorrectly issued ROAs, for more details see [23]. The first example in Fig. 81.5 illustrates Orange (previously France Telecom), a large French ISP, which issued a ROA for the 194.2.0.0/15 prefix with origin AS 3215. Orange has several customers.

For example, Danone announces the (sub)prefix 194.2.35.0/24 with origin AS 1272. Most of these customers, including Danone and two more in the figure, did not issue a ROA. Hence, the BGP announcements made by these customers are invalid according to RPKI and any ROV performing AS will discard all paths to these companies. In the second example, Fig. 81.6, Swisscom, a large Swiss ISP, issued a ROA for the prefix 81.62.0.0/15, with origin AS 3303. Swisscom also advertises several BGP announcements, for this pre-

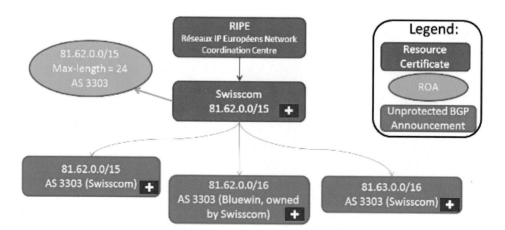

Fig. 81.6 Misconfigured ROA by Swisscom. (Cohen et al. [23])

fix and for subprefixes, e. g. 81.63.0.0/16. However, the ROA is generated incorrectly, allowing an attacker to launch prefix hijacks. For example, to hijack all traffic to the prefix 81.63.0.0/16, the attacker can send BGP announcements with AS-path 666-3303-81.63.0.0/17 and with AS-path 666-3303-81.63.128.0/17 (where 666 is a malicious AS).

81.2.3 Small Office/Home Office (SOHO) Routers

A Small Office/Home Office (SOHO) router is a network device that connects computer networks by relaying packets between internal and external interfaces. SOHO routers often also perform a Network Address Translation (NAT) [RFC2663] functionality, run services such as DHCP [RFC2131], DNS [RFC1035], and are responsible for the connection and configuration of end devices to the Internet. All communication between the end hosts on the local networks and the Internet services (e. g. web, email, video conferencing) traverses the SOHO router. SOHO routers typically provide web interfaces for convenient and easy configurations of the network, devices and the router itself. Connection to the administrative interface provides information about the network, the connected devices, the traffic and more.

SOHO Routers Security

The security of SOHO routers is critical for the privacy and stability of the clients and services in the Internet – yet the attacks against SOHO routers are widespread. During the last two decades multiple vulnerabilities were reported [5, 9] in popular SOHO routers, e. g., BT home routers, Linksys, D-link. The vulnerabilities include buffer overflows, traditional web attacks (e. g., XSS and CSRF), Denial of Service (DoS) attacks and authentication bypass attacks. For instance, a recent vulnerability in ARRIS SURFboard router utilizing CSRF enabled attackers to disrupt Internet connections of SOHO networks [7]. The attacks against SOHO routers along with the multiple vulnerabilities published in CVEs raised awareness to the importance of protecting network devices, and patches were issued.

There is a range of protective strategies both enterprises and individuals can employ to improve SOHO router security. We report on results of our Internet scale evaluation of SOHO routers security, focusing on a specific set of vulnerabilities called **authentication bypass**; details follow. Such vulnerabilities allow attackers to perform privileged operations in firmware without being granted the valid credentials of an authorized user. Authentication bypass vulnerabilities can be caused in a number of ways, and result in attackers successfully connecting to the administrative configuration interface. The vulnerabilities that can be exploited to connect to administrative interface of a SOHO router include: insecure connection whereby the credentials are sent in clear text and hence can be inspected by a Man-in-the-Middle (MitM) attacker, a vulnerability in the authentication procedure allowing the attacker to obtain the credentials by exploiting a vulnerability in software or firmware, e. g., buffer overflow, a vulnerability in web interface, e. g., SQL

Country	1. Open Devices	2. Error 401	3. Internet Camera	4. SOHO Router	5. UNKNOWN
Brazil	3.43%	9.80%	0.88%	94.53%	4.60%
Egypt	8.55%	33.02%	1.63%	97.98%	0.39%
Estonia	9.66%	6.48%	10.42%	57.64%	31.94%
Germany	6.06%	3.97%	13.57%	71.63%	14.80%
Israel	54.30%	7.19%	0.61%	98.97%	0.42%
Kenya	4.21%	11.41%	0.00%	89.29%	10.71%
Ukraine	15.76%	8.76%	0.75%	97.34%	1.92%
US	10.58%	2.36%	5.78%	91.05%	3.16%
Poland	7.10%	6.07%	14.01%	82.28%	3.71%

Fig. 81.7 Fraction of open devices per country

injection or CSRF, implementation mistakes whereby the credentials are hardcoded into the webpage, or sent in response to the connecting client, or simply using the default credentials configured by the router vendors or the firmware of an Internet Service Provider (ISP), without changing them.

We list the fraction of open routers per country in Fig. 81.7. More than 6.2 Mio. of SOHO routers use port 80 for communication to the configuration interface.

Using the REALM that the routers return, recover the router vendor, and check the default credentials used by that vendor, selected open routers are listed in Fig. 81.8.

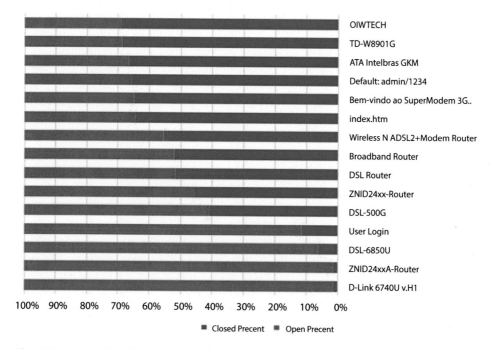

Fig. 81.8 Selected REALMs returned by open SOHO routers

Fig. 81.9 Top popular default
credentials

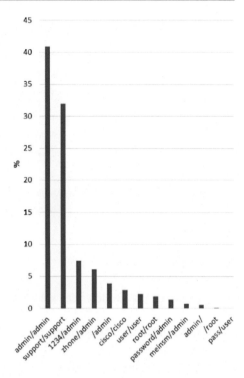

Finally, our study shows that a large fraction of SOHO routers are using default credentials. These credentials can be looked up on routers' vendors websites. We list the most
common passwords in Fig. 81.9.

Configuring secure credentials is critical for security, and especially security of SOHO
networks. Unfortunately, home users often lack the required expertise or understanding
to change default passwords. On the other hand, in many countries we tested the Internet
Service Providers (ISPs) prefer not to take responsibility for their clients, and hence refuse
to distribute patches to mitigate the problems. Indeed, aligned with our results in Fig. 81.7,
in countries with large fraction of open devices the ISPs do not add "security" to the
services that they provide, and do not support procedures for distribution of patches to
clients to change the default network credentials.

The only way to resolve this unfortunate situation is to create policies and legislation
that would enforce the ISPs to add "security" to the services that they provide to home
networks.

81.3   Vulnerable Internet Infrastructure Foils Application Defences

In this section we provide a few selected security services and explain how they can be
foiled when run over insecure Internet Infrastructure.

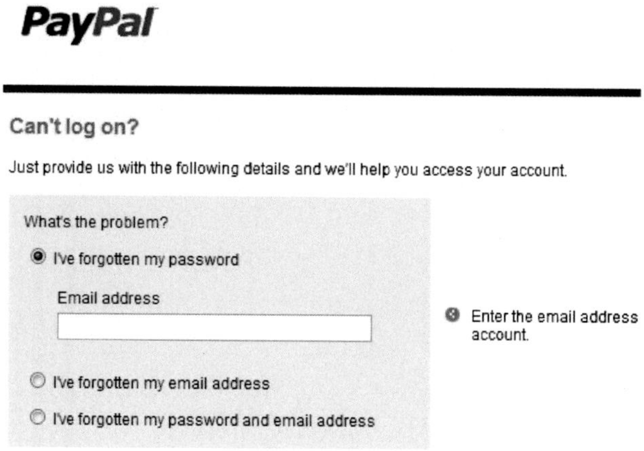

Fig. 81.10 Password recovery
on the Paypal website

PayPal

Can't log on?

Just provide us with the following details and we'll help you access your account.

What's the problem?

◉ I've forgotten my password

Email address

⊗ Enter the email address
account.

○ I've forgotten my email address

○ I've forgotten my password and email address

81.3.1 Password Recovery

Password recovery is a widely used mechanism to enable users to recover their credentials
if they are lost or forgotten. Password recovery is supported by banks, financial services,
online shops and more. For example, see Fig. 81.10 for a password recovery print screen
of paypal.

The user enters his email address, and the password or a link allowing to reset the
password is sent to the provided email address.

An attacker that can poison the DNS server on paypal's network, say injecting a mapping saying that Alice is at IP address 6.6.6.6 (which in fact is the attacker's controlled
machine) will cause the email server on paypal's network to send Alice's credentials for
paypal to an attacker. To do this the attacker will enter the email address of Alice into the
password recovery box: alice@email.com. As a result, the attacker can intercept all the
communication between paypal and Alice.

81.3.2 Web Certificates

Web certificates are needed to enable clients to verify the identity of servers to which
they connect. Web certificates contain the keys which can be used to establish a secure
connection with SSL/TLS to the target server, as well as the identity of the server. For
instance, when connecting to a bank www.commerzbank.de, the client needs to verify
that the machine the connection is established to is indeed that of a bank, and not of an
attacker. When the web server of Commerzbank provides a certificate binding its identity
to secret keys, the client can use it to establish a secure connection to the server. Web
sites that do not use SSL/TLS expose clients to attacks, since the communication to those
sites can be inspected and modified, e. g., causing the client to download a malware or to
expose its private information, such as credit card number, to an attacker.

The generation of a certificate requires checking that the entity requesting a certificate is the owner of the domain. For instance, that the entity requesting a certificate for Commerzbank.de is indeed the owner of domain Commerzbank.de. Otherwise the attacker would be able to issue certificate for Commerzbank.de and impersonate the website of Commerzbank, stealing clients' credentials. The verification of the identity during certificate generation procedure is (typically) done by sending an email to the server in a domain for which the certificate was requested. If the attacker controls routing (via prefix hijacking) it can receive all the communication including the email verifying the identity for the certificate. Similarly, if the attacker poisons the DNS entry, the email will be sent to an attacker controlled host.

81.3.3   Anti-Spam Defences

Spam is a huge problem in the Internet, causing detrimental financial losses and exposing to attacks, such as malware distribution and credentials theft by luring users to malicious websites.

Anti-spam defences allow email servers to verify that an email arrives from authentic sources, and not from spammers, by checking that the sender of the email is real and not spoofed. For instance, if the "from" header of an email message contains someone@commerzbank.de, the email was sent by someone from Commerzbank and not by a spammer, tricking the client into accepting the email as authentic.

Spam can be used to steal credentials, money, and even for distribution of malware.

Most popular defences for sender authentication are DNS based. The idea is that a real sender creates a record and places in its DNS server, that says which email servers is allowed to send email on behalf of its domain. For instance, Commerzbank can place a record saying that only an email server mail.commerzbank.de at IP address 1.2.3.4 is allowed to send an email on behalf of Commerzbank. All the email servers supporting anti-spam will request this record from Commerzbank before accepting the email as authentic. An attacker sending an email from machine at IP 6.6.6.6 impersonating Commerzbank will not be able to trick the email servers to accept its emails, since its email is sent from an IP address that was not authorized by Commerzbank.de.

However, attacks against the DNS infrastructure or prefix hijacking attacks can enable attackers to circumvent the defences and to distribute SPAM. Indeed, attackers often perform DNS cache poisoning as well as BGP prefix hijacking to distribute spam bypassing anti-spam defences.

81.4   Conclusions

In this work we reviewed selected fundamental building blocks in the Internet which are critical for security of clients and services. Our experimental evaluation shows that, although frequent attacks and although defences exist, these building blocks are still unprotected. We show that there are challenges and obstacles towards adoption of the defences that need to be addressed both with respect to misconfigurations and vulnerable deployments as well as with respect to the lack of motivation to adopt security. Deploying security at Internet foundations is critical, in particular, we show that when the fundamental building blocks of the Internet are vulnerable, security of clients and services can be circumvented. This also applies to security mechanisms, which also depend on secure Internet infrastructure.

References

1. J. Stewart, DNS cache poisoning, the next generation, 2003.
2. D. Kaminsky, "It's the End of the Cache As We Know It," *Black Hat conference,* 08 2008.
3. A. Herzberg und H. Shulman, "Security of patched DNS," *Computer Security – ESORICS 2012 – 17th European Symposium on Research in Computer Security, Pisa, Italy,* 10–12 09 2012.
4. A. Herzberg und H. Shulman, "Vulnerable delegation of DNS resolution," *ESORICS 2013 – 18th European Symposium on Research in Computer Security, Egham, UK,* 9–13 09 2013.
5. A. Herzberg und H. Shulman, "Fragmentation Considered Poisonous: or onedomain-to-rule-them-all.org," *IEEE CNS 2013. The Conference on Communications and Network Security, Washington, D.C.,US,* 2013.
6. D. Anderson, Splinternet behind the great firewall of china, 11 Hrsg., Bd. 10, 2012.
7. M. Hu, Taxonomy of the snowden disclosures, Bd. 72, Wash & Lee L. Rev., 2015, pp. 1679–1989.
8. P. Levis, "The collateral damage of internet censorship by DNS injection," *ACM SIGCOMM Computer Communication Review,* Nr. 3, 2012.
9. K. Schomp, T. Callahan, M. Rabinovich und M. Allman, "Assessing DNS vulnerability to record injection," in *Passive and Active Measurement*, Springer, 2014, pp. 214–223.
10. M. Wander, C. Boelmann, L. Schwittmann und T. Weis, Measurement of globally visible DNS injection, Bd. 2, IEEE, 2014.
11. A. Borgwart, S. Boukoros, H. Shulman, C. van Rooyen und M. Waidner, "Detection and forensics of domains hijacking".*2015 IEEE Global Communications Conference (GLOBECOM).*
12. H. Shulman und M. Waidner, "Fragmentation Considered Leaking: Port Inference for DNS Poisoning," *Applied Cryptography and Network Security (ACNS), Lausanne, Switzerland,* 2014.
13. A. Herzberg und H. Shulman, "Socket Overloading for Fun and Cache Poisoning," *ACM Annual Computer Security Applications Conference (ACM ACSAC), New Orleans, Louisiana, US,* 12 2013.
14. W. Lian, E. Rescorla, H. Shacham und S. Savage, "Measuring the Practical Impact of DNSSEC Deployment," *Proceedings of USENIX Security,* 2013.
15. T. Dai, H. Shulman und M. Waidner, "Measuring DNSSEC Pitfalls in Signed Domains," *International Conference on Cryptology and Network Security,* 2015.
16. L. Valenta, S. Cohney, A. Liao, J. Fried, S. Bodduluri und N. Heniger, Factoring as a service.
17. BGPMon, BGP Routing Incidents in 2014, 2015.
18. renesys.com, "The New Threat: Targeted Internet Traffic Misdirection," 11 2013. [Online]. Available: http://www.renesys.com/2013/11/mitm-internet-hijacking/.

19. A. Toonk, BGP Hijack Incident by Syrian Telecommunications Establishment, BGPMon Blog, 2015.
20. A. Toonk, "Hijack Event Today by Indosat," [Online]. Available: http://www.bgpmon.net/ hijack-event-today-by-indosat/.
21. P.-A. Vervier, O. Thonnard und M. Dacier, "Mind Your Blocks: On the Sealthiness of Malicious BGO Hijacks," NDSS – The Internet Society, 2015. [Online]. Available: http://www. internetsociety.org/events/ndss-symposium-2015.
22. NIST, "NIST RPKI Monitor," 2015. [Online]. Available: http://rpki-monitor.antd.nist.gov/.
23. A. Cohen, Y. Gilad, A. Herzberg, M. Schapira und H. Shulman, Are We There Yet? On RPKI's Deployment and Security, NDSS, 2017.
24. Cisco, BGP Origin AS Validation, Cisco IOS guide, 2013.
25. S. Goldberg, Why is it Taking so Long to Secure Internet Routing?, 10 Hrsg., Bd. 57, Commun. ACM, 2014, pp. 56–63.

Further Reading
26. A. Pastor, BT Home Flub: Pwnin the BT Home Hub, 2007.
27. Embedded Device Hacking. Reverse Engineering a D-Link Backdoor, 2013.
28. D. Longenecker, SURFboard modem unauthenticated reboot aw, ARRIS (Motorola), 2016.